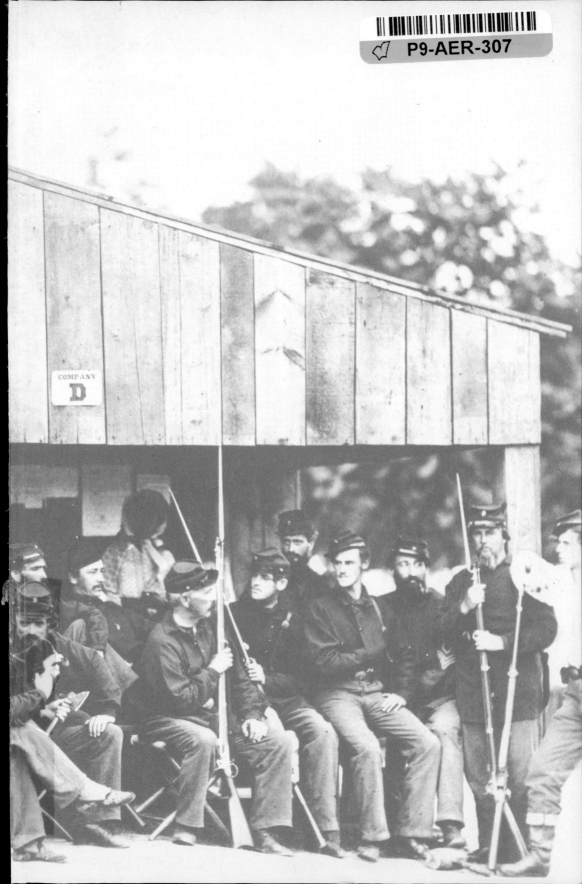

THE LIFE OF JOHNNY REB

THE LIFE OF BILLY YANK

THE LIFE OF JOHNNY REB
The Common Soldier of the Confederacy

THE LIFE OF BILLY YANK
The Common Soldier of the Union

BELL I. WILEY

Essential Classics of the Civil War
Book-of-the-Month Club
New York

JOHNNY REB

Thomas Taylor, Private, Company K, 8th Louisiana Regiment. He served under Stonewall Jackson, was wounded at Sharpsburg and taken prisoner.

THE LIFE OF JOHNNY REB

The Common Soldier of the Confederacy

To
M. F.

TABLE OF CONTENTS

LIST OF ILLUSTRATIONS

"Then call us Rebels, if you will,
We glory in the name,
For bending under unjust laws,
And swearing faith to an unjust cause,
We count as greater shame."
—Richmond *Daily Dispatch*, May 12, 1862

PREFACE

THE common soldier of the Confederacy has for a long time borne the title of Johnny Reb. The name seems to have originated from the practice of Yankees who called out, "Hello, Johnny" or "Howdy, Reb" to opponents across the picket line. Gray-clads liked the sobriquet, and accustomed as they were to appropriation of Federal food, clothing and guns, they saw no reason to spurn a catchy name because it was used first by their opponents. So they adopted the term in both its separate and combined forms. Descendants might be irked by the connotation of rebellion, but not the original Johnny. He not only considered himself a rebel but he gloried in the name.

Only a few years after Appomattox one of Lee's veterans remarked that future historians "would hardly stop to tell how the hungry private fried his bacon, baked his biscuit, smoked his pipe" and performed the various other details of camp life. This Reb's prophecy has been fulfilled to an impressive but regrettable extent. For in the flood of history and near-history published during the past half-century, the doings of common soldiers have usually served as a hazily sketched backdrop for dramas featuring campaigns and leaders. The present work is an attempt to give the man of the ranks, who after all *was* the army, something of his rightful measure of consideration.

Since the writer's dominant aim has been to present soldier life as it really was, and not as a thing of tradition, he has based his narrative chiefly on primary sources. The most extensively used records were wartime letters and diaries. These interesting and fascinatingly human documents were found by the thousands in public depositories and in private possession. The most vivid and the most significant information was frequently obtained from the barely decipherable missives of rustic privates.

Mary Frances Wiley, my wife, contributed so vitally to the research and writing as to deserve a co-author's rating, and it is only her firm refusal that prevents this recognition. In gathering material for this study we were impressed anew with the efficiency and courtesy of Southern archivists and librarians, and to them we owe a heavy debt of gratitude. Fellow historians and their wives who entertained and assisted us all along the route of research added greatly to our well-being and enjoyment. Laymen far and wide, and in such numbers as to preclude individual mention, generously gave us untrammeled access to family papers. Professor J. G. de Roulhac Hamilton of the University of North Carolina and Mr. W. B. Phillips of the University of North Carolina Press read the manuscript and made helpful suggestions. Richard D. Steuart, editor of the Baltimore *News-Post*, read chapter XV and from a wealth of knowledge acquired as an arms collector set me right on a number of statements about Confederate guns.

The writer makes grateful acknowledgment for financial assistance received from the Julius Rosenwald Fund and the Social Science Research Council. Without these subsidies the research for this book would not have been possible.

BELL IRVIN WILEY

University, Mississippi.
5 January, 1943

CHAPTER I

OFF TO THE WAR

The man who was to be Johnny Reb was "rarin' for a fight" in the spring of 1861. "So impatient did I become for starting," wrote a young enthusiast from Arkansas, "that I felt like ten thousand pins were pricking me in every part of the body, and started off a week in advance of my brothers." [1]

Countless other men throughout the South showed a similar eagerness to be off to the war. They were urged on by many different motives. Some were incited to arms by a deep-seated hatred of the North which had been accumulating from the time of their earliest recollections. Antipathy aroused by Northern opposition to admitting Missouri as a slave state had been increased by recurrent threats to levy a "tribute" on the agricultural South in the form of a high protective tariff; further aggravation had come from the attempt of Northern congressmen to bar Southerners from the fruits of the Mexican War by closing western territory to slavery. And in the fifties the Negro question came to be the highest provocation of all.

Most Southerners were convinced that Northerners were utterly unreasonable in their attitude toward the "peculiar institution," and in support of this opinion they advanced these charges: The Yankees refused to live up to the Federal law requiring the return of fugitive slaves; they closed their eyes to the beneficent aspects of slavery; they made heroes of such fantasies as Uncle Tom, and chose to look upon Christian slaveholders as Simon Legrees; they tolerated monsters like William Lloyd Garrison; they contributed money and support to John Brown, whose avowed purpose was the wholesale murder of Southern women and children, and when he was legally executed for his crimes they crowned his vile head with martyrdom. Yankees, moreover, were considered a race of hypocrites: While they were vilifying Southerners for enslaving blacks, they were keeping millions of white factory workers in a condition far worse than slavery; while denouncing Southern wickedness, they were advocating free love and all sorts of radical *isms.* All in all, Yankee society was a godless and grasping thing.

15

So long as Northern Democrats worked with Southerners to hold the more radical elements in check, there was hope that the South might secure something like her just due under the Union. But in the late fifties there was wide defection among Northern Democrats on the slavery issue, and a rise to political power of the Republican Party, made up of elements deemed hostile to Southern institutions. At the head of this new party was Abraham Lincoln, a man regarded by many Southerners as the epitome of unreason and vulgarity. The election of Lincoln to the presidency seemed to spell the doom of Southern security under the Union: States' rights would be trampled under foot; tariff rates would increase beyond endurance; slavery would be restricted to the narrowest limits that fanatical abolitionists could impose, or done away with altogether. Non-slaveholding whites of the South were told by their favorite editors and politicians that emancipation would be followed by measures to enforce social equality of the races, and the specter of their women being jostled on the street by "big black niggers" was too fearful for contemplation.

There were of course many moderates in the South, including some of the most influential planters, who wanted to give the Lincoln government a trial, even after South Carolina seceded. Not that they doubted the right of secession. The question was rather one of expediency. But Fort Sumter and Lincoln's call for volunteers took the ground from under these middle-of-the-roaders. The issue now was whether to fight with or against secessionists, and this left no choice for most Southerners.

Hatred for the North received a tremendous boost from the prevailing agitation in favor of secession. The fire-eating element, made up largely of country editors, preachers, lawyers, and politicians-on-the-make, was the most vocal and eloquent. Recrimination and name-calling in private conversation, in public meeting, in editorial columns, from professor's desk and country pulpit, produced a tide of emotion in the early months of 1861 that reached all sections and all classes. Its effect is illustrated by the fulmination of an overseer on a plantation forty miles below New Orleans. On June 13, 1861, he wrote in his journal:

"This day is set a part By presedent Jefferson Davis for fasting & praying owing to the Deplorable condishion ower Southern country is In My Prayer Sincerely to God is that Every Black Republican in the Hole combined whorl Either man woman o chile that is opposed to negro slavery as it existed in the Souther confederacy shal be trubled with pestilents & calamitys of all Kinds & Dragout the Balance of there existence in misray & Degradation with scarsely food & rayment enughf to keep sole & Body togeather and O God I pray the to Direct a bullet or a bayonet to pirce the Hart of every northern soldier that invades southern Soile & after the Body has Rendered up its Traterish Sole gave it a trators reward a Birth In the Lake of Fires & Brimstone my honest convicksion is that Every man wome & chile that has gave aide to the abolishionist are fit Subjects for Hell I all so ask the to aide the Sothern Confedercy in maintaining Ower rites & establishing the confederate Government Believing in this case the prares from the wicked will prevailith much Amen." [2]

Whether or not the scribbler of this entry went to war is not known, but the spirit that provoked his hostile utterance contributed greatly to the wave of volunteering which swept over the South during the first year of conflict.

It would be misleading, however, to give the impression that all who took up arms in 1861 were moved by hatred of Yankees, or that all who expressed hostility felt any considerable depth of antipathy. Later events proved the contrary. The dominant urge of many volunteers was the desire for adventure. War, with its offering of travel to far places, of intimate association with large numbers of other men, of the glory and excitement of battle, was an alluring prospect to farmers who in peace spent long lonely hours between plow handles, to mechanics who worked day in and day out at cluttered benches, to storekeepers who through endless months measured jeans cloth or weighed sowbelly, to teachers who labored year after year with indifferent success to drill the rudiments of knowledge into unwilling heads, and to sons of planters who dallied with the classics in halls of learning.

Long before Virginia seceded restless boys at the state university and at Washington College raised the Confederate flag on their respective campuses.[3] At the University of Mississippi a company was recruited on the campus, and the faculty advanced the date of examinations so that students could be off to the war.[4] The Centenary College faculty assembled on October 7, 1861, for the purpose of opening the fall session, but "there being no college students and few preparatory students," the dispensers of learning had to go home. Opposite the minutes of this futile session in the faculty record book the secretary splashed in bold script diagonally across the page this entry: "*Students have all gone to war. College suspended: and God help the right.*" [5]

The University of Alabama continued to operate, but with reduced enrollment and increased emphasis on military training. That this compromise by no means alleviated the eagerness of young men for the battlefield, however, is indicated by the letter of a student to his father early in 1862:

"I have delayed answering your letter in order that I might reflect on its contents. I have done so and come to the conclusion that if I do not participate in this war it will be the source of the deepest regret and disappointment in life. Like a bird of evil omen it will follow me and mar all my undertakings. . . . I believe I know the value of an education . . . but the time has come when even this can be neglected. . . . Shall I sit ignobly here and suffer [others] to fight my battles for me. . . . I rejoice that there is scarcely one of our name in all the South but who are engaged in some capacity in this glorious cause; and, moreover, I hope and pray you will not allow it to be said that there was even one, capable of bearing arms, not on the list of his country's defenders." [6]

There was also a large group of those who volunteered not from any great enthusiasm, but simply because enlistment was the prevailing vogue. Scions of leading families rode about the country organizing companies for their command, thus adding the weight of social position to that of patriotism. Community belles offered their smiles and praise to men who joined the ranks of "our brave soldiers," but turned with the coolest disdain from those who were reluctant to come forward in defense of Southern womanhood. In some communities young men who hesitated to volunteer received packages containing petticoats, or were seized by boisterous mobs and thrown into ponds.[7] Thousands of persons indifferent to enlistment, and many who were downright opposed to it, were swept into the ranks in 1861 by the force of articulate popular pressure.

Henry M. Stanley, famous after the war as the searcher for Livingstone in Africa, is a case in point. Of English birth and only recently established in this country, he was temporarily living in Arkansas at the outbreak of war. He volunteered simply to follow the example of his acquaintances, and to avoid social ostracism. After fighting bravely at Shiloh he was captured. When offered release from prison in return for Federal service, he joined the Yankees and fought for some time against his erstwhile comrades. And he evidently suffered no qualms of conscience for his turncoating.[8]

Men so indifferent as Stanley, however, formed only a small minority of the Confederate volunteers. And even those, once they had "joined up," shared in most cases the prevailing desire to come to blows with the Yankees, and that quickly. Almost everyone seemed to think that the war would be decided by a battle or two in Virginia or Kentucky; it was necessary, therefore, to get to the fight with dispatch or run the risk of not making it at all.

But most of these recruits were to endure a long siege of waiting before they thrilled to the excitement of conflict. Filling up the companies took time—and there was an interval, sometimes long and sometimes short, before they could be mustered in by the Confederate Government. Sometimes there was an intermediate step of being accepted into state service.

In the meantime the companies had been looking for arms, clothing and other equipment. State and Confederate authorities soon exhausted their supplies, and volunteer units had to scramble for themselves. But during the high tide of patriotism of 1861 there was no lack of will and effort to provide all necessities.

Women volunteered to make uniforms, and even bullets. Wealthy men gave money for the complete equipment of entire companies. Society leaders raised funds by putting on fairs and amateur plays. Blacksmiths repaired ancient muskets and contrived deadly looking knives and sabers from farm implements and scrap steel. Local leatherworkers fashioned saddles, harness and bridles. But all this caused a delay that was hard to bear.

Meanwhile the recruits were learning how to drill. In some instances militia units already in existence furnished a nucleus for the volunteer groups, and in these outfits the exercises were apt to be well done. But in other cases the initial efforts were exceedingly awkward—and this maladroitness often persisted unduly because of the lackadaisical attitude of the men, and because of the inefficiency and ignorance of self-appointed officers. But on the whole, thanks largely to the popularity of military education among the upper classes, the volunteers made fair progress in acquiring the rudiments of drill.

At some convenient stage in their organization companies and regiments elected officers. This was a privilege jealously cherished by the volunteers, and much ado was made of its exercise. In many cases the office of captain was more or less automatically voted to the person who had been most active in raising the company; to some extent this was true also in the choice of colonels. Rivalry was generally keen enough to produce considerable electioneering. A Georgia private encamped in North Carolina expressed his view of these high-pressure methods:

"Our election has not yet come off, and to one who like myself is not a candidate it is a time replete with feelings of disgust and contempt. The candidates of course are interested and busy. I could start out here now and eat myself dead on 'election cake,' be hugged into a perfect 'sqush' by most particular, eternal, disinterested, affectionate friends. A man is perfectly bewildered by the intensity of the affection that is lavished upon him. I never dreamed before that I was half as popular, fine looking, and talented as I found out I am during the past few days." [9]

As might be expected, such elections often resulted in ill feeling. Candidates disgruntled by defeat sought transfers or discharges. Privates who backed losers sometimes expressed their disappointment in emphatic terms, as is evidenced by a Mississippian's statement that the "'Madison Guards' rebelled and disbanded on account of the election of regimental officers," and "the 'Brown Rebels' were put in their place." [10] Elections were repeated at the expiration of the original term for which the unit was pledged to serve.

The names of some of the volunteer companies reflected their patriotism and the terror which they sought to inspire. The following are characteristic:

Tallapoosa Thrashers; Baker Fire Eaters; Southern Avengers; Amite Defenders; Butler's Revengers; Bartow Yankee Killers; Chickasaw Desperadoes; Dixie Heroes; Clayton Yellow Jackets; Hornet's Nest Riflemen; Lexington Wild Cats; Green Rough and Readys; Raccoon Roughs; Barbour Yankee Hunters; Southern Rejectors of Old Abe; Cherokee Lincoln Killers; Yankee Terrors; and South Florida Bull Dogs.

A few titles had an occupational flavor, as for instance Coosa Farmers, Cumberland Plough Boys, and Cow Hunters. Chivalry was not forgotten in such captions as Ladies' Guards, Pocahontas Rescues, and Ladies' Dragoons. An Alabama cavalry group called itself the Burr Tailed Regiment, and a mounted aggregation from Tennessee had the title of Bell's Babies.[11]

As the time ripened for Johnny Reb to take his departure for the seat of war, he was a part of a ceremony that was staged with such flourish as to thrill the hearts of the homefolk if not his own. This was the flag presentation—and files of newspapers for 1861 indicate that the exercises were almost identical throughout the length and breadth of Dixie. Speeches of presentation and response were as stereotyped and platitudinous as the high-school valedictories of later years.

A battle flag was considered indispensable to organization. So when a company or battalion was being formed, some woman, frequently one having or hoping to have a heart interest in one of the volunteers, began the making of a banner. In due time the work was completed, the speeches memorized, and a time appointed for the presentation. This might be at a dress parade, a banquet, a religious assembly, or a mass meeting called especially for the ceremony. After being duly assembled the volunteers listened to the flowery tribute of some beauteous, behooped patriot, kept eyes fixed as an officer stepped up to receive the banner, and then gave respectful hearing to the grandiloquent response of their captain.

Among the innumerable companies that received flags from fair hands in 1861 were the DeSoto Rifles of Louisiana. A reporter of the New Orleans *Daily Crescent* recorded the presentation ceremony which took place in late April, 1861. Miss Idelea Collens offered the colors with "appropriate remarks," including the following:

"Receive then, from your mothers and sisters, from those whose affections greet you, these colors woven by our feeble but reliant hands; and when this bright flag shall float before you on the battlefield, let it not only inspire you with the brave and patriotic ambition of a soldier aspiring to his own and his country's honor and glory, but also may it be a sign that cherished ones appeal to you to save them from a fanatical and heartless foe." [12]

The color-sergeant, who advanced with his corporals to receive the flag, rose to the occasion with an impressive response:

"Ladies, with high-beating hearts and pulses throbbing with emotion, we receive from your hands this beautiful flag, the proud emblem of our young republic. . . . To those who may return from the field of battle bearing this flag in triumph, though perhaps tattered and torn, this incident will always prove a cheering recollection and to him whose fate it may be to die a soldier's death, this moment brought before his fading view will recall your kind and sympathetic words, he will . . . bless you as his spirit takes its aerial flight. . . . May the God of battles look down upon us as we register a soldier's vow that no stain shall ever be found upon thy sacred folds, save the blood of those who attack thee or those who fall in thy defence. Comrades you have heard the pledge, may it ever guide and guard you on the tented field . . . or in the smoke, glare, and din of battle, amidst carnage and death, there let its bright folds inspire you with new strength, nerve your arms and steel your hearts to deeds of strength and valor." [13]

Even more flowery were the remarks of a Georgia captain who in response to the presentation of a banner to the Mercer Guards by a Miss Collier in May 1861 said: "Those tri-colors are emblematical of your rosy lips, fair cheeks, and your blue eyes; in future when we look up at those glorious stars which borrow a lustre from your bright eye, and whose radiance will guide us to victory and fame, we will fondly remember the loved ones at home." [14]

Occasionally a presentation ceremony would be marred by a flaw in the proceedings. When some ladies of Fayetteville, North Carolina, presented a flag which they had made to the Forty-third North Carolina Regiment, not one of them could be found who was willing to make the speech. As a consequence, they invited a local male who enjoyed some reputation for eloquence to speak on their behalf. The proxy must have been a bit nervous, for before the ceremony he imbibed too heavily of liquor. As he rose to perform his part of the program his unsteadiness was obvious. He managed to get through with his speech in a halting manner, but then as if utterly oblivious of that which had gone before, he said most of it a second time. After this he sat down and cried. It is not hard to imagine the mortification of the women and the amusement of the soldiers.[15]

Speechmaking over, the hour finally came when Johnny Reb was to take leave of his home community. Let New Orleans furnish the setting for the departure, and let the troops be the Battalion of Washington Artillery. Members of this organization are men of wealth and high standing in the community. The time is late May, 1861. Soldiers of the battalion are gathered at the depot waiting to board the train. They have listened to a patriotic and admonitory sermon by the Reverend B. M. Palmer. A large company of relatives and friends is present to bid them farewell and to load them down with parting gifts.

Writing a few years after Appomattox, one of them recalled: "That certainly is the only time we can remember when citizens walked along the lines offering their pocketbooks to men whom they did not know; that fair women bestowed their floral offerings and kisses ungrudgingly and with equal favor among all classes of friends and suitors; when the distinctions of society, wealth, and station were forgotten, and each departing soldier was equally honored as a hero." [16]

The day is an exceedingly hot one, the discomfort increased by the surging crowds, and two soldiers die from sunstroke before the train is boarded. At length the partings are finished, and the three hundred men composing the battalion begin the long and uncertain train ride to Virginia.

As the coaches roll along the men partake generously of the delicacies with which they have been loaded. Some achieve merriment after long pulls at their heavily charged flasks. But fatigue eventually triumphs, and the volunteers settle into such fitful slumber as circumstances will allow.

The next morning the train stops near a stream of running water. The volunteers pile out to relieve their thirst and to bathe, taking combs, soap, towels, and other articles that a year hence will be regarded as luxuries and excess baggage. When travel is resumed packs of cards appear, and for many poker becomes the order of the day.

At almost every station crowds wave, and shout godspeed. At Iuka, Mississippi, the battalion gets out for a reception and feast. (Early in the war companies of soldiers traveling in the South could get a free meal in any city or town by giving prior notice of their arrival.) At Huntsville, Alabama, there is another stop for a reception and a brief round of dancing. At various intermediate stations bolder and more agile members of the group take advantage of the slowing down of the coaches to jump off and steal, with such ease as hardly to incur guilt, kisses from pretty lassies who adorn the right of way.

Eventually they reach Richmond, and as they march down the streets of the capital city to patriotic tunes played by a brass band brought from Louisiana, their resplendent uniforms—made, allegedly, by New Orleans' best tailors at a cost of $20,000—their lustrous array of sabers, and their other fine accouterments afford a spectacle that dazzles the eyes of Richmond's citizens. Little wonder that President Davis remarks, when the battalion reports to him, that no organization ever presented a braver appearance. And that their valor was not limited to their appearance was shortly to be proved by the baptism of fire at Manassas and to be vouchsafed by a record of distinction unmarred during four years of conflict.[17]

Other organizations of volunteers had experiences similar to the Washington Artillery, but few moved to the seat of war in such luxurious state. Captain B. F. Benton's company, recruited in the environs of San Augustine, Texas, had to make the first stages of their journey to Richmond on foot. After a flag ceremony they left San Augustine on September 12, 1861. The first day they marched two miles, camped, and "proceeded to prepare Super which was rather an Awkard thing for new beginners." [18] The second day they marched three miles. At the beginning of the third day they were drawn up in line of battle tó hear a patriotic address by a veteran of the Texas and Mexican Wars. When this function ended, they "Set out on the line of March in Earnest for Richmond, Va., with Collors flying, Fife and drum Sounding the never to be forgot Tune The Girl I Left behind Me." [19] The subsequent march of 120 miles to Alexandria produced sore feet and other discomforts, but the volunteers joked and bantered all along the way. At Alexandria they boarded a ferryboat—the captain was too impatient to wait for a steamboat—and proceeded jauntily down the Red River. The troops amused themselves en route by shooting alligators which were sighted frequently along the banks of the stream. Presently they were transferred to a steamboat which took them to New Orleans, whence they boarded a train for Richmond, arriving there in early October.[20]

Another Texas company, a cavalry outfit called the W. P. Lane Rangers, moved in the opposite direction from most of the volunteers. Their course was westward for service on the frontier. On April 19, 1861, they assembled at Marshall for the election of officers. This took up most of the day, and by night many of the "Rangers" and the citizens as well were considerably affected by the tippling that had accompanied the day's festivities. But the Reverend Mr. Dunlap proceeded to preach a farewell sermon, according to schedule. The next day, after being lauded and feasted, they set off toward Austin.

Like most troops departing for service in 1861, they were overloaded with equipment. W. W. Heartsill, one of these Rangers, who in the seventies printed his reminiscences at odd times on his own hand press, gave the following enumeration of his "cargo": "Myself, saddle, bridle, saddle-blanket, curry comb, horse brush, coffee pot, tin cup, 20 lbs. ham, 200 biscuit, 5 lbs. ground coffee, 5 lbs. sugar, one large pound cake presented to me by Mrs. C. E. Talley, 6 shirts, 6 prs. socks, 3 prs. drawers, 2 prs. pants, 2 jackets, 1 pr. heavy mud boots, one Colt's revolver, one small dirk, four blankets, sixty feet of rope with a twelve inch iron pin attached . . . and divers and sundry little mementoes from friends." And he added that he was no exception in the matter of equipment.[21] Little wonder that the Rangers began to shed accouterments in the early stages of their march!

A bugler tooted occasionally to keep the troopers on the right road, a precaution all the more necessary because of saloons visited along the route, and the barrel of beer that was sent to them by the citizens of Marshall. At Springfield they were greeted with the firing of anvils. Their arrival at the Texas capital was celebrated with a banquet tendered by the Austin Light Infantry. In San Antonio the Rangers went on a big spree, only four out of a total of about one hundred and two showing up at camp in the evening. Before they left San Antonio for Camp Woods, 200 miles to the west, they were sworn into Confederate service and equipped with uniform arms.[22]

Going to war in 1861, whether to west Texas, northern Virginia, western Kentucky, the seaboard of the Carolinas, or the Gulf coast of Florida and Alabama, was a rollicking experience for the men of the South. Their ardor could not be repressed by the speeches that invariably accompanied the gift of articles ranging from flags to frying pans, and to "a wagon load of bandages to be worn next to the skin in case of the fatigue and sickness to which all young men are exposed upon setting out to and encountering the roughness and exposure of military life." [23] After all, the speeches might soon be forgotten and useless gifts could be discarded when train or boat had placed a polite interval between donor and receiver. Along the way there were pretty girls to be kissed, and Unionists like "old Brownlow" and Andy Johnson to be hissed, or perhaps shot, if they would but show themselves.[24]

For many volunteers the train ride itself was a novel experience. When they rode in boxcars, the occupants often used the butts of their guns to knock holes in the sides for ventilation and sight-seeing, and as they rode along yelling and singing, with their heads sticking out of the openings, they reminded onlookers of chickens in a poultry wagon. The practice of climbing atop the coaches, though forbidden by officers, resulted in the injury and death of a regrettably large number. Doubtless the liquor which flowed so freely among war-bound troops contributed in some part to the general recklessness and unsteadiness.[25] But the prospect of exciting times made tolerable all the discomfort and risk of the journey.

Youngsters left behind found their lot almost unbearable. Sadly and enviously they bade more fortunate friends adieu. When J. E. Hall, en route from Montgomery to Virginia in May 1861, passed through Auburn, Alabama, a number of schoolmates whom he had recently abandoned for the allurements of army life boarded his train. "They were all so glad to see me," he wrote his sister, "I thought they would kill me. I could not shake their hands fast enough. . . . When the cars started Henry Harris and some others . . . said they couldn't leave me and went on to Opelika with me and there got off, all but H. Harris. He said he still must go farther and went to West Point [Georgia] with me." [26]

An Alabama recruit, after getting settled in camp near Memphis, wrote home about the awesome sights in the "citty" and urged his brother to come on up and bring a shotgun with him.[27] To this and countless other country boys, the travel following upon enlistment opened up a wonderful new world. And great was the awe inspired by the novelty of their experiences.

The reaction of J. B. Lance, a Tar Heel rustic who in 1861 joined the Twenty-fifth North Carolina Regiment, was probably quite typical. He left his native Buncombe County, in the North Carolina mountains, for Charleston and Beaufort on the South Carolina coast. Not long after his arrival he wrote his father back in North Carolina:

"Father I have Saw a rite Smart of the world Sence I left home But I have not Saw any place like Buncomb and henderson yet." [28]

Johnny Reb joined the army to fight, and he was not disposed to tolerate any interference with this purpose. The experience of a company of Mississippians who got only within earshot of the first battle at Manassas illustrates this temper. Four days after the battle, W. G. Evans, a sergeant of the company, wrote to his sister in Aberdeen:

"Sunday a scene was enacted here long to be remembered. . . . Our Company, much to our regret, were not participants in the action. . . . A railroad collision on Saturday evening detained us. The conductor was court martialed and shot, charged with bribery by court and intentionally producing the collision so as to prevent reenforcements. . . . We first heard the cannonading when about 18 miles distant. Imagine our impatience on a freight train going only 6 miles to the hour." [29]

But these volunteers, like most of the others, were to discover that much preparation must come between the "joining up" and the shooting. Drilling three or four times a day was serious and unromantic business, the more so when these exercises were done under the scorching rays of the summer sun. Chopping down trees lost little of its odium by being dignified with the name of "policing." [30] Marching to new locations, preparing food, washing clothes, fighting lice and cleaning camp were duties that bore little resemblance to Johnny Reb's conception of soldiering. But of all camp and field duties standing guard was rated the most noxious and the most senseless. Why walk up and down a beat, or keep on the alert with gun in hand when there wasn't a Yankee in two hundred miles? Officers must lie awake nights thinking up meaningless duties for privates!

At first the volunteers were inclined to regard routine tasks jauntily— and at times this attitude was encouraged by the attitude of officers, who realized as well as the men that they held their positions in virtue of the good will of their charges. Under these circumstances it is not surprising that soldiers of '61 frequently left camp without the formality of a pass, went to sleep when assigned to guard post, omitted drill when the ground was wet, and balked at the performance of other non-fighting duties.[31]

Orderly Sergeant A. L. P. Vairin, of the Second Regiment of Mississippi Volunteers, throws significant light on the frame of mind of the man who was destined to bear the brunt of the Confederacy's cause on scores of battlefields, by a note in his diary, dated May 1, 1861: "Made my first detail . . . for guard duty to which most men objected because they said they did not enlist to do guard duty but to fight the Yankees—all fun and frolic." [32]

But this attitude could not persist. Under the supervision of "old-timers" like Joseph Johnston, Robert E. Lee, Braxton Bragg, and Thomas Jackson, complaisant officers were gradually weeded out and West Point ideas of discipline were adopted in the Southern armies. Before the campaigns of 1862 Johnny Reb was for the most part a changed man. He had shed most of his surplus equipment, and, of much greater importance, he had abandoned the idea that military life was "all fun and frolic."

In short, the volunteer had become a soldier.

CHAPTER II

THE BAPTISM OF FIRE

SOLDIERS of all times have been eager for their first trial at arms, but Confederate volunteers who rushed so impetuously to war in 1861 seem to have been exceptionally zealous to come to blows with the enemy. Most of them had to wait until 1862 for this to be realized, but in the meantime they never ceased longing.

"Often at the still hour of midnight," wrote one who was stationed near a border stream during the war's first winter, "I wish the next day will be the 'cross over,' and we will meet the 'grand army' on fair ground." [1]

The accidental firing of a shot or two on the picket line would cause a precipitate, unordered lining up for battle of men still in process of dressing. Even those who had been confined to their cots for days with sickness would join the rush to arms; and when a messenger would announce another false alarm, all would go back to their tents "looking as downcast as if they had lost a purse laden with gold." [2]

When finally the day of battle arrived and the order to advance was given, so great was the urge to meet the foe that it was almost impossible for officers to prevent troops in the rear from marching through lines in front.[3] But before the ordeal of fire was begun, a halt was called to permit officers of artillery to complete disposition of their units, and to give opportunity for full contact of supporting ranks. These adjustments required perhaps an hour or two.

What are the thoughts and feelings of these Rebs who stand on the threshold of their first battle? Fear? Yes, of a sort. Most of them have in months past expressed contempt for Yankees and made positive statements as to the licking which they would administer at first opportunity to the "vandals" who dared to invade the South. Now that the zero hour has come, will they be able to match word with deed? Can they stand up under the actuality of combat—the sharp whistle of Minié balls, the hideous screeching of shells, the thunderous roar of cannon? Or will they, seized by an uncontrollable panic, play the quaking coward? Anxiety over ability "to stand the gaff" probably was greater in initial conflicts than was concern for life and limb. "I may run," wrote a Reb in anticipation of his first fight, "but if I do I wish that some of our own men would shoot me down." [4]

Some who were philosophically inclined pondered over the fact that now for the first time in their lives they were going to attempt to destroy their fellow beings. A few abhorred the folly and wickedness of the impending destruction. Many thought fondly of homefolk—wives, sweethearts, parents, children, sisters, brothers—and hoped earnestly to be spared to them through the approaching conflict. Christians gave themselves to spiritual meditation and silent prayer; sinners, in some instances, sought emergency benefits of Providence by temporary renouncement of their evil ways.

The dominant sensation, however, was that of extreme nervousness; this rather than fear. Some sought to conceal or escape their keyed-up condition by joking or by casual conversation, but with little success. Perspiration dotted the brow, a dull emptiness seized the stomach, and breathing became difficult. The craving for movement, for action, was so great as to seem intolerable.[5]

What a tremendous relief, then, when finally came the order to charge or to fire. After the first volley or so the initial tension would abate to a remarkable degree, and some who had been the most nervous were now surprised to find themselves able to load and to discharge their weapons with what seemed complete indifference to the pandemonium raging about them.

The metamorphosis was well described by one who was at First Manassas. "With your first shot you become a new man," he said. "Personal safety is your least concern. Fear has no existence in your bosom. Hesitation gives way to an uncontrollable desire to rush into the thickest of the fight. The dead and dying around you, if they receive a passing thought, only serve to stimulate you to revenge. You become cool and deliberate, and watch the effect of bullets, the showers of bursting shells, the passage of cannon balls as they rake their murderous channels through your ranks . . . with a feeling so callous . . . that your soul seems dead to every sympathizing and selfish thought." [6]

Attitudes and impressions brought out by the baptism of fire varied considerably with different individuals. Not all felt their tension supplanted by a sense of calm and indifference. Some skulked and ran, though these constituted a decided minority. Others were keenly sensi-

tive to the injury and death of friends. A few continued to think of
home and loved ones throughout the fight.

"This was my first battle," wrote S. G. Pryor to his wife after an engagement in the fall of 1861. "It was a pretty severe anniciation [ini-
tiation] the test was severe but thank god I had the nerve to stand
it. . . . Time rolls off very fast in time of battle when wee had been
in . . . 3½ hours it appeared to me that it hadent been two . . . I
have been told that at such a time that men did not care for anything
but it is different with me I thought of more things in a short space
of time than ever I did before a man to go out with the expectation of
being shot every minute he has but a short time to think a heap in the
thought of you and those dear little ones hurt me worse than anything
else." [7]

The calm which new soldiers professed to experience was to a great
extent an illusion. They were cool only in comparison with the excessive
agitation which they felt before the battle. Unconscious excitement
lingered throughout the fight, manifesting itself in such phenomena as
savage yelling, throwing away of canteens, haversacks and bayonets,
and improper use of guns. More than one Reb forgot to bite off the
end of the paper that encased bullet and powder before he placed the
charge in his musket. As a result the spark did not set off the powder
when the trigger was pulled. But Johnny, with utter unwareness of the
failure of his piece to fire, continued to ram in charge upon charge,
with intermittent though quite futile aiming and trigger pulling, until
the barrel refused to receive further ammunition. [8]

Many Rebs who were able to load and discharge their guns properly were singularly ineffective in their first fights when it came to
drawing a bead on the Yankees. One who was lying in a fence corner
during an early skirmish, taking careful aim at every fire, had to shoot
about five times before he attracted sufficient notice to provoke a
reply. [9]

Granted that a considerable amount of wild shooting is inevitable in
any battle, evidence points strongly to the conclusion that marksmanship at Manassas, Shiloh and other fights involving for the most part inexperienced soldiers was notoriously bad. "I recollect their first volley,"
wrote George Baylor of a Virginia regiment at Bull Run, "and how
unfavorably it affected me. It was apparently made with guns raised
at an angle of forty-five degrees, and I was fully assured that their
bullets would not hit the Yankees, unless they were nearer heaven
than they were generally located by our people." [10]

Photo by U. S. Army Signal Corps

CONFEDERATE WORKS IN FRONT OF ATLANTA

Photograph from Barnard's Photographic Views of Sherman's Campaign.

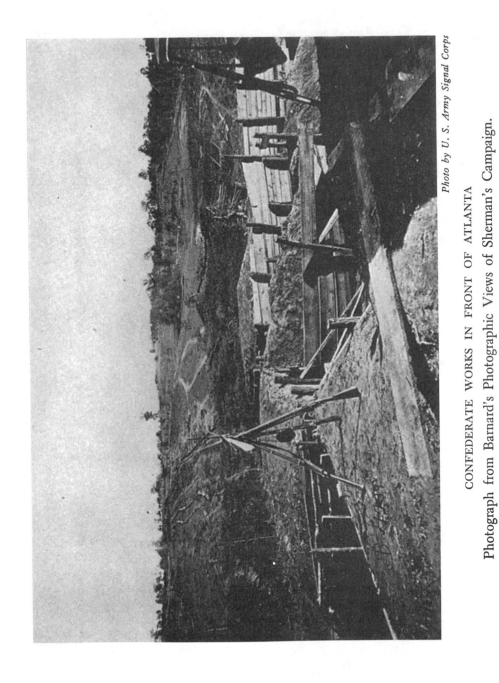

CONFEDERATE WORKS IN FRONT OF ATLANTA

Photograph from Barnard's Photographic Views of Sherman's Campaign.

Such ineffectiveness was not wholly without benefit, however, as the excitement and disorganization attendant upon early battles sometimes resulted in troops firing upon their comrades. During the Peninsula campaign of 1862, a Mississippi regiment, mistaking two Georgia regiments for Yankees, fired upon them. The Georgians, naturally assuming that their assailants were enemies, returned the fire immediately without waiting for a command. The only damage done by the Georgians, according to the report of one of them, was the killing of their own major's horse! [11]

A general characteristic of Rebs fighting their first battles was the informality with which they conducted themselves on the field. When Private A. N. Erskine became tired in a charge at Gaines's Mill he "halted in an apple orchard to blow," while his regiment went on over a hill. At First Manassas troops suffering from hunger and thirst "would stop in the middle of the fight and pick blackberries, loading, firing, and eating by turns." In this conflict also "most of the Southerners would rush forward, aim and discharge their pieces, and then retire behind trees and bushes and there reload, and again advance."

First Manassas, like Shiloh, had more the character of a conglomeration of small engagements, featuring individual combat, than of a single co-ordinated enterprise. It was almost exceptional for a man to find himself at the day's end with his own regiment. Not infrequently a soldier fought with several different outfits in the course of twelve hours of battle, taking time off at intervals for rest and sustenance. An officer who commanded a company at Bull Run turned, after leading a valorous charge at twilight, to thank his men for their gallant day's work; the group receiving his compliment was "composed of three of his own men, two 'Tiger Rifles,' a Washington artilleryman, three dismounted cavalry of the 'Legion,' a doctor, a quartermaster's clerk, and the Rev. Chaplain!" [12]

Soldiers participating in their first engagements frequently had curious and humorous experiences. A South Carolina sharpshooter was annoyed to hear the Reb in his immediate front cry out to the cannon balls flying overhead, "Howl, ye dogs of war." [13] Another Reb, seeing the large balls ricocheting across a wheat field, remarked that they were hopping along like rabbits. [14] Private W. A. Fletcher reported the most surprising experience of all. "I with a number of others," he said, "were sufferers from camp diarrhea, as it was called, and up to that time we had found no cure—so, entering the battle, I had quite a great fear that something disgraceful might happen and it was somewhat uppermost in my mind; but to my surprise the excitement or something else, had effected a cure. I inquired of some of the others and they reported a cure." [15]

In the wake of his baptism of fire Johnny Reb experienced a deep and persistent depression. His complete exhaustion, coupled with the incessant groaning and piteous wailing of the wounded, pierced his unhardened soul to the quick. The sight of dead bodies, many of them mutilated beyond recognition, overwhelmed him with horror and made the thought of continuing war utterly repulsive. His sensitiveness to the scene of carnage was often so great as to keep him from smiling or even talking for several days, and to make his nights fearful with recurrent nightmares of the ghastliness of combat.[16]

For most of the participants this introduction to the horror of war was by far the most terrible experience of their lives. They naturally were anxious to communicate their doings and impressions to those who meant most to them. So, as soon after the battle as possible, they "took pen in hand" to address wives, parents and sweethearts. For some the experience of letter writing was almost as novel as that of fighting. And the letters that went out from camp on the day after a battle gave vivid expression to the sharpness of reaction to the baptism of fire.

After the battle of Gaines's Mill, June 27, 1862, a Texan wrote to his wife:

"Yesterday evening we (the Texas Brigade) was in one of the hardest fought battles ever known . . . I dont think the Regt (4th Tex) could muster this morning over 150 or 200 men & there were 530 yesterday went into the engagement. . . . I got some of the men from the 5th Regt to go and look up our wounded. . . . I never had a clear conception of the horrors of war untill that night and the [next] morning. On going round on that battlefield with a candle searching for my friends I could hear on all sides the dreadful groans of the wounded and their heart piercing cries for water and assistance. Friends and foes all togather. . . . Oh the awful scene witnessed on the battle field. May I never see any more such in life. . . . I am satisfied not to make another such charge. For I hope dear Ann that this big battle will have some influence in terminating this war. I assure you I am heartily sick of soldiering." [17]

A like reaction was expressed by a Georgian:

"I felt quite small in that fight the other day when the musket balls and cannon balls was flying around me as thick as hail and by best friends falling on both sides dead and mortally wounded Oh Dear it is impossible for me to express my feelings when the fight was over & I saw what was done the tears came then free oh that I never could behold such a sight again to think of it among civilized people killing one another like beasts one would think that the supreme ruler would put a stop to it but wee sinned as a nation and must suffer in the fleash as well as spiritually those things wee cant account for." [18]

Thomas Warrick, who was evidently a member of that under-privileged group of Southerners known for lack of more accurate designation as "poor white," laboriously recounted to his Alabama wife his impressions of the Battle of Murfreesboro:

"Martha . . . I can inform you that I have Seen the Monkey Show at last and I dont Waunt to see it no more I am satsfide with Ware Martha I Cant tell you how many ded men I did see . . . thay ware piled up one one another all over the Battel feel the Battel was a Six days Battel and I was in all off it . . . I did not go all over the Battel feeld I Jest was one one Winge of the Battel feeld But I can tell you that there Was a meney a ded man where I was men Was shot Evey fashinton that you mite Call for Som had there hedes shot of and som ther armes and leges Won was sot in too in the midel I can tell you that I am tirde of Ware I am satsfide if the Ballence is that is one thing Shore I dont waunt to see that site no more I can inform you that West Brown was shot one the head he Was sent off to the horspitel . . . he was not herte very Bad he was struck with a pease of a Bum" [19]

Another Alabamian, his handwriting barely decipherable and his spelling marked by an unusual degree of originality, expressed a strikingly similar disillusionment following his introduction to the fighting at Chickamauga:

"We have had avery hard fite a bout ten miles from Chat ta nooga on Chick a mog ga creak in gor ga . . . i com out safe but it is all i can say i have all ways crave to fite a lit [tle] gust to no what it is to go in to a bat tle but i got the chance to tri my hand at last anough to sad isfi me i never wan to go in to an nother fite any more sister i wan to come home worse than i eaver did be fore but when times gits better i will tri to come home thare has ben agrate meney soldiers runing a way late ly but i dont want to go that way if i can get home any other way." [20]

An unidentified soldier who participated in the Shiloh fight utilized a sheet of stationery that he picked up near an abandoned Federal tent to tell his wife of that engagement:

"April 17 April the 17 run Yank or die Yankey paper
    Yankey paper Corinth Miss April 17
Dear Wife: i take the opitunity to rite you a few lines to let you now i am well at this time and i hope these few lines may come to hand and find you enjoying the same blesson. . . . we was in a battle on the 6 and 7 day of April we got one cild two woned the captin was woned slitly in the arm i come out saft i was . . . sceard at first i tell you it is not . . . [what it] was cract up to be i was glad to git out of it shore as you bonn i was not in the regiment i was in the tenth miss regt i saw plenty of yankeys out ther i thout every minet was the las the ball whisle around me worse than ever bees was when they swarm but i am saft yet this it some them paper i got in there camps i got a par shoes i . . . [got an] over coat it is caintuckey geans and a larg nife five pound two foot in the blaid well i could a got eney thing i wanted if i coulda toated it." [21]

The reaction of these five soldiers is typical: sensitiveness to bloodshed, revulsion from carnage, and a yearning to be done with the horror of war. But with the passing of time, for the most part spent in active campaigning, the specter of the first conflict lost its sharpness of horror. The second and third battles were faced with greater composure and were followed by less acute reaction. Soldiers who nervously dodged screaming missiles at Shiloh cheered each other onward at Perryville, rendering superfluous the forward command of officers, disdaining with a few exceptions to seek any sort of shelter. "The men stood right straight up on the open field," wrote one who was in the Perryville fight, "loaded and fired, charged and fell back as deliberately as if on drill." [22] This is perhaps an overstatement of the case, but there can be no doubt of the hardening influence of continued experience under fire.

By the time of the Atlanta campaign it was not uncommon to see a Reb walking around in a hail of bullets with the apparent unconcern of a man taking a relaxing stroll in the cool of the day; and during the siege of Petersburg a veteran whose bacon frying was disturbed by a Minié which scattered his fire took no further notice of the interruption than to pull the coals back together and remark: "Plague take them fellows! I 'spect they'll spile my grease yet before they stop their foolishness." [23]

A certain amount of philosophizing contributed to the soldier's increasing indifference to danger. He consoled himself by the time-worn maxim that comparatively few die in battle, and the conviction that he would be among the lucky majority who were destined to survive. "If killed in battle," wrote J. E. Hall during the Wilderness campaign, "what more glorious death would you wish me die?" His next statement, however, belied his aspiration to immediate immortal renown: "But I do not expect to be killed," he said. "All men that go into fights are not killed. Why should I not be one to escape." [24] Another fatalistic philosophy of comfort heard frequently as the long roll sounded was, "When a fellow's time comes, down he goes. Every bullet has its billet." [25]

Not only did the seasoning of experience bring steadiness under fire, but it also inured the men to scenes of suffering and bloodshed. Soldiers were mystified by the hardening process which they underwent. "I saw the body [of a man killed the previous day] this morning," wrote Private Henry Graves, "and a horrible sight it was. Such sights do not affect me as they once did. I can not describe the change nor do I know when it took place, yet I know that there is a change for I look on the carcass of a man now with pretty much such feeling as I would do were it a horse or hog." [26]

Many troops were as appalled by their growing insensitiveness to human suffering and death, as they were surprised by their increasing indifference to danger. John T. Sibley wrote from Vicksburg in March 1863 that he was expecting a fight soon but the time of its coming gave him no concern whatever. Recently, he said, a shell had taken away the arm of a man standing near him, but no one seemed to manifest the slightest fear, though the bombardment continued with unabated fury. "I am astonished at my own indifference," he added, "as I never pretended to be brave; it distresses me at times when I am cool and capable of reflection to think how indifferent we become in the hour of battle when our fellow men fall around us by scores. . . . My God what kind of a people will we be?" [27]

Countless others who experienced a similar change were too thoroughly hardened to give the ultimate consequences a thought.

CHAPTER III

BESETTING SINS

SOLDIER life is notoriously conducive to degeneration of some standards of morality. This has been true since organized warfare came into being. To those of us whose own kinfolk were wearers of the gray the thought comes easily and pleasantly that the Confederate Army offers a striking exception to the rule. But this conception is as mistaken as it is pleasant. Granting an impressive susceptibility to religious impulse, as witness periodic outbreaks of great revivals among the fighting men, objective study of soldiers' letters and diaries makes inescapable the conclusion that all the evils usually associated with barrack and camp life flourished in the Confederate Army.

The Old South was orthodox, Calvinist, evangelical. It took the Bible with great literalness, rigidly ranked an infringement of any one of the Ten Commandments as sin, and spread the designation over borderline cases. The mores might often be in opposition to the religious conceptions, but there was no confusion in the conceptions.

The most pervasive of the "sins" which beset Johnny Reb was gambling. General Lee issued an order in November of 1862 in which he announced that he was "pained to learn that the vice of gambling exists, and is becoming common in this army." [1] If Lee was just then discovering this propensity of his troops he was far behind time, for that evil had flourished in the Army of Northern Virginia, as elsewhere, long before he assumed command. Soldiers from Louisiana, Tennessee, Mississippi, Texas, and other sections of the South gambled extensively as they rode to war in 1861, and when they landed in Richmond they found innumerable games of chance already in progress among their Virginia comrades. In spite of the prohibitions of Lee and his fellow generals, and in disregard of the warnings of chaplains, the vice gained as the war went on. In February 1864 a soldier wrote: "A young man cannot guard himself too closely in camp . . . where to be considered an accomplished gentleman it is necessary to be a scientific and successful gambler." [2]

Pious soldiers in all Southern armies were appalled at the prevalence of gambling. G. W. Roberts of Mississippi was one of the many who chafed at his enforced association with the evil. But his messmates, who were evidently chronic gamblers, gave him little heed. "I have ask them to quit playing cards in our tent or about our tent," he wrote. "It does not become any man to entrude upon me like they do. If they wish to play cards let them Build a house off to themselves then they could play to their own satisfaction." Roberts resolved to deal patiently with the sinners and prayed God for grace to win them from their evil ways. But his efforts were unsuccessful. Gambling continued to flourish under his tent roof, provoking finally the observation, "There is men in this encampment that does not care for anyone." [3]

Another Mississippian, apprehensive of the effects on a younger brother, unburdened himself in a letter of advice. "I hope that after you join the army you will not forget the virtuous resolutions that have directed you so far in life," he wrote in December 1863. "The temptations that will beset you will be very great. . . . of all the evil practices that abound in Camp, gambling is the most pernicious and fraught with the most direful consequences." [4]

The commonest form of gambling was card playing—poker, twenty-one, euchre and keno. Cards—some of them decorated with likenesses of Jefferson Davis and of high-ranking generals—were stocked by sutlers, but as the war progressed they became increasingly difficult to procure.[5] In some instances new decks were obtained from Yankee prisoners, and from the haversacks of the dead, both Rebel and Federal. But in 1864 and 1865 cards dealt around Confederate campfires generally were as ragged and battleworn as the uniforms of the players.

Faro and chuck-a-luck, banking games played respectively with cards and with dice, were also common devices for gambling. There was a notorious gamblers' den near Fredericksburg known as "Devil's Half-Acre," where soldiers ran chuck-a-luck boards for weeks during the winter of 1862-1863, and this despite repeated efforts of officers to break up the nuisance. "Crap shooting," while not without its devotees, was not nearly so popular among Rebs as among their grandchildren.

Raffling, in some form or other, was also popular. "You never heard of so much gambling as is carried on here," wrote a soldier from Yorktown in December 1861; "raffling of any and everything—watches, gold pins, coats, and blankets. You can hear on every side someone saying, 'Do you want to take a chance for a watch?' or something else." A year later one of Bragg's command wrote from Murfreesboro: "There is a panfel [painful] spell of Rafalin here at this time But I dont take no hand in non of it Some makes money at it But some Dus Loose all That they have got." But this soldier admitted having had his fling at the evil, with what he seemed to regard as great cost. "I lost one half of a Dollar," he said, "and that Broke me from sucking Eggs that is one thing s[h]ore." [6]

In cavalry outfits the laying of wagers on horse races had a considerable vogue. Stakes in some of these affairs reached proportions that would have made the fifty-cent raffling loser dizzy. Wrote A. E. Rentfrow from Fort Chadbourne, Texas, in 1862:

"I have bin Horse racesing since I left home. I have Lost one hundred dollars an have got arace to be run on Saturday next I have got dick [his horse] bet on the race and if I loose him I will loose aheap more on the day of the race. I am going to win or loose something." [7]

The racing of horses for bets, even while on duty, became so notorious in the Texas Frontier Regiment that Colonel McCord was constrained to issue the following order on June 17, 1863:

"All officers belonging to the Texas Frontier Regiment . . . are hereby required to prohibit gaiming by horse racing . . . whenever the same in any company or detachment shall become a nuisance to the service. If any member of the Regiment should so far lose sight of the interest and reputation of the service as to be caught horse racing or gaiming while on duty . . . the same shall be punished by court martial or otherwise." [8]

Lacking race horses, cards, dice, or other facilities, chance-loving Rebs would readily find a way to diminish or increase their holdings. Those quartered along rivers sometimes fitted tiny boats with paper sails and raced them for wagers. Even the vermin that infested the camp were pitted against each other in trials of speed. The louse races were staged on pieces of canvas or on other small objects. One soldier, who boasted a champion speedster, insisted on having each of the competitors placed on a plate, the winner being the louse that first vacated its dish. After this promoter had won a great deal of his comrades' money, it was found that the consistent success of his louse was due to his heating the plate before each contest.

Even more remarkable than these races were the louse fights. The omnipresence of the pests and their ever-readiness to attack Rebs probably suggested setting them against each other for stakes. A canteen side, having a circle marked off with charcoal, made a convenient arena. Contestants placed in the circle would, soldiers claimed, go at each other savagely, until one—and sometimes both—was *hors de combat*. "It was nothing unusual," according to a veteran, "to see a dozen groups of men so engaged, eagerly witnessing one of these encounters." [9]

Stakes of gambling contests were adapted to the circumstances of the gamesters. Money was, of course, the most desirable prize, but cash was notoriously scarce among Confederates. Consequently cards were drawn and dice were cast for a great variety of items such as pocket knives, jewelry, clothing and even rations. A Louisiana veteran recalled a card game late in the war in which the stake was a stolen chicken. [10]

Several factors influenced the amount of gambling. Payday always provided a powerful fillip. Many gambled then who at other times were not attracted by dice or cards. If the paymaster's tent happened to be a mile or so from camp, some would lose six months' wages before they got back to their quarters. [11] Long periods of inactivity, as while men were in winter quarters, also led to gaming as a relief from the intolerable boredom. Holidays, particularly Christmas, were usually marked by an increase of the sport. Among factors tending to diminish gambling were religious activities of officers and chaplains. The great revival movements among troops were always accompanied by an abatement of betting in all its forms. An officer of respected piety such as Stonewall Jackson might by influence and example prevent to some degree open and flagrant gambling, but there were indications that Jackson's chief accomplishment in this connection was driving the betting under cover. [12] Issuance of general orders prohibiting gambling was extremely ineffective. In fact, during flush periods all deterrents failed and gamblers waxed bold.

"Yesterday was Sunday," wrote Ruffin Thomson right after a visit of the paymaster, "and I sat at my fire and saw the preachers holding forth about thirty steps off, and between them and me were two games of poker, where each one was trying to fill his pockets at the expense of his neighbor. Chuck-a-luck and faro banks are running night and day, with eager and excited crowds standing around with their hands full of money. Open gambling has been prohibited, but that amounts to nothing." [13]

The immediate prospect of battle brought fear of death and the punishment of an angry God to the hearts of many gamblers. The result was a temporary renunciation of the instruments of sin. The road to the battlefield was commonly littered with playing cards and dice. For a brief season during and after the battle cards would be as conspicuously missing as Bibles were everywhere to be seen.[14] But there was one gambler who went into a conflict without throwing away a deck of cards that he was carrying loose in his pocket. During the battle a bullet struck this pocket, was deflected by the cards, and so the soldier's life was saved. By strange coincidence a comrade next in line, who was carrying a Bible, had his pocket struck also. The Bible failed to turn the bullet and this man was killed instantly.[15] Such an incident must have confused sinners and driven religious expositors to that portion of the sacred word which reads: "How unsearchable are his judgments, and his ways past finding out." [16]

An evil hardly less prevalent than gambling in the Confederate Army was excessive drinking. This showed itself early in the war, and during the long period of inactivity that followed First Manassas it increased. According to a chaplain, "Drunkenness became so common as to scarcely excite remark, and many who were temperate . . . at home fell into the delusion that drinking was excusable, if not necessary, in the army." [17]

Commanding generals were appalled at the prevalence of the vice. In December 1861 Braxton Bragg issued an order prohibiting the sale of liquor within five miles of Pensacola. His accompanying statement throws significant light on the deleterious effects of tippling: "The evils resulting from the sale of intoxicating liquors in Pensacola have become intolerable. More than half the labor of the courts-martial result from it—demoralization, disease, and death often prove it. . . . Our only military executions have been caused by it. We have lost more valuable lives at the hands of whiskey sellers than by the balls of our enemies." [18]

Impressed by General Bragg's action on the Gulf, the War Department issued a general order early in 1862 entreating commanders of all grades to suppress drunkenness by every means in their power. "It is the cause of nearly every evil from which we suffer," the order stated; "the largest portion of our sickness and mortality results from it; our guard houses are filled by it." [19]

Some improvements doubtless resulted from the policy adopted at that time by Richmond authorities of keeping encampments away from cities as much as possible, but even so, drunkenness continued to an alarming extent throughout the war. Prohibitive orders were issued periodically from the capital and from headquarters of the various armies, but these lost their effectiveness in many instances because of the poor example of lieutenants, captains, colonels and even generals. A Southern editor charged that "a large number of the officers of our Southern Army are both profane and hard drinkers, where they are not drunkards." [20]

In spite of a decided decline in the distilling of spirits after 1862, soldiers continued to obtain and to consume alcoholic beverages in amazing quantities. Sources and methods of procuring them were devious. Troops who were stationed near cities—and it was impossible entirely to avoid establishing camps in urban localities—were always able, by sundry stratagems, to get to town in large numbers. Here those who had the price and who were not too critical as to quality were able, almost without exception, to obtain liquor in sufficient doses to make them gloriously tight—and Rebs were as accustomed to the term as are we—or to furnish swift oblivion. Newspapers of Richmond, New Orleans and other urban centers testify repeatedly and convincingly to the fact that drunken soldiers were a common sight on the streets.

Complained the Richmond *Examiner* of June 9, 1862: "Whiskey —the sale of this popular but vitiating and deleterious beverage is lamentably on the increase in the alleys and purlieus of Richmond. Upwards of a dozen drunken soldiers were knocked down in the streets and robbed Saturday night." Earlier in the year this paper had observed: "One has to go into the streets of the city [at night] and see hundreds of good looking young men wearing the uniform of their country's service, embruted by liquor, converted into bar room vagabonds." [21]

When cities were not within reach, some Rebs were able to satisfy their thirst by visits to the country. And in many cases whiskey was obtainable in camp. Sutlers and camp followers sold it on the sly; soldiers representing bootleggers, or dispensing on their own account stocks sent by homefolk, sold it by the drink or by the bottle; and peddlers from city or countryside sold it under the guise of legitimate wares.[22]

A correspondent wrote from camp near Dalton, Georgia:

"A stranger would be smitten with the great number of mysterious men seen walking around with canteens by their sides and tin thimbles in their hands retailing pestilence at the rate of two dollars a jigger." [23]

During periods of unusual exposure to dampness, or of excessive hardship, whiskey was included in the regular ration issued to soldiers. The amount was small but by bargaining with teetotaler comrades some were able to accumulate sufficient rations to make them merry if not dead drunk.

"A soldier will get whiskey at any risk—if anywhere in the neighborhood," wrote a lieutenant who was having trouble with his men on this score.[24] One group of Rebs noticing a pile of liquor barrels in front of a store put on a "circus" to detract the shopkeeper's attention; after the performers passed on the merchant discovered to his amazement that a full barrel had been replaced by an empty one.

And the ruses devised for "flanking" the officers were ingenious. These same soldiers took to camp a barrel of whiskey, which they had secured by some other trick, and buried it above a spring to which they were accustomed to go for water. They were thus, to the utter dismay of their officers, enabled to keep themselves continually in a state of buoyancy.[25]

Members of a Mississippi company smuggled a half-gallon of liquor into camp in a hollowed-out watermelon, cached it beneath the floor of their tent, and tapped it with a long straw. When one of them wanted a drink he lay flat on the floor and sucked the straw. His comrades stood by to cut him off after his Adam's apple registered his ration of two swallows.[26]

But the most daring stratagem of all was attributed to an Irishman of the Second Tennessee Volunteers. The colonel of this outfit while walking through camp one day saw Pat elevate his gun and take a long pull at the muzzle. He called out:

"Pat, what have you got in your gun?"

Came back the answer, "Colonel, I was looking in the barrel of my gun to see whether she was clean."

And after the unwary officer walked on the Irishman completed draining his gun barrel of the whiskey thus smuggled in from a near-by town.[27]

Naturally some of the contraband liquor was vile. The frequently used epithet "mean" was a gross understatement for some of the bootleg concoctions described by the Richmond *Enquirer* in an article headed "The Whiskey Erysipelas." According to this account, the scarcity of spirits in Virginia in 1863 produced "as arrant a race of rogues as ever breathed. They doctor whiskey. They make whiskey out of apple brandy, and French brandy out of whiskey, all sorts of brandies

and wines out of ingenious concoctions of all three. The whiskey—
that is to say the most of it—is not composed of but about thirty per
cent of genuine alcohol, and the rest is made up with water, vitriol,
and coloring matter. An old and mellow taste is secured by adding the
raw flesh of wild game, or young veal, or lamb . . . [and] soaking for
three or four weeks." [28] Little wonder that Rebs referred to contraband liquor as "bust-head," "pop-skull," "old red eye," "spill skull,"
and "rifle knock-knee."

Certainly these and other bootleg products obtained by soldiers were
not lacking in potency. Violent and strange were the doings of some
who applied themselves too long to the bottle. Hotels in Savannah,
Georgia, and Grand Junction, Tennessee, were torn up by rioting
inebriates; officers were attacked or insulted on numerous occasions by
drunken privates; and one berserk Reb was moved to damn "the whole
Southern Confederacy." Private John Brown of the Seventh South
Carolina Cavalry rode up to a civilian's house and asked for a refilling of
his whiskey bottle; when refused he drew his pistol, spurred his horse, and
rode on into the house. John Anderson of the Texas Rangers went to
town one day to have some teeth pulled; in the afternoon he returned
minus his molars but full of liquor. As he approached the camp he
began to shoot his pistol and to yell with such energy that the captain,
thinking he was being attacked in force by hostile Indians, called out his
men and rode full tilt to meet the enemy. During the Battle of Lees-
burg a Confederate staff officer was so befuddled by whiskey that he
mistook a group of Yankees for Southerners, rode up to them and ordered them to charge a group of gray-clads whom he thought to be Federals. The men receiving the order, thinking that the aide was one of
their own officers, obeyed, and in the resulting attack quite a number of
them were killed.[29]

Another evil of far-reaching proportions among Confederate soldiers
was that of theft and destruction of private property. One of the
earliest examples of this was the stealing of rails for campfires by
volunteers and their servants. As time went on the practice spread,
and in the spring of 1862 it had become so prevalent that President
Davis was constrained to take notice of it, as the following note from
the Secretary of War to General Joseph E. Johnston indicates: "I am
instructed by the President," wrote Randolph, "to call your attention
to the habit in which many of the regiments have fallen of burning the
fences near their encampments and bivouacs, and I must request that
you will issue orders requiring . . . Army Regulations to be executed.

... Unless the destruction of fences can be arrested it will materially lessen the crop ... and impair the power of the Government to subsist the Army." [30] General orders enjoining the practice were issued by Johnston and by commanders óf other armies from time to time, but with little result. By the spring of 1865 a rail fence in an area occupied for any considerable length of time by a Rebel army was rarely to be seen.

The theft of hogs and poultry was another form of plundering which showed up early in the war. And this evil, like rail burning, increased as the conflict went on. This was due in part to the diminishing quantity and quality of army rations. A hog that made the mistake of wandering near a camp at any time during the war had small chance of survival. Soldiers of all units of the army enjoyed a story, always applied to one of their particular outfit for the sake of realism, illustrating the weakness of Rebs for stray pigs. Details varied somewhat, but the gist of the incident was this:

One day a soldier came to camp with a bulky object concealed under his coat. On being asked by an officer what he was carrying, he immediately responded, "It's a pig."

When the officer inquired if he was aware of rules against such practices as shooting hogs, he responded, "Yes, sir, I know it's against the rules, but I killed the pig in self-defense."

"How was that?" asked the officer.

"Well," responded the culprit, "I was coming up to camp when I heard something roaring, and looking that way, I saw a pig coming out of a hole in the ground, and just before it got to me, I fired, and the pig ،was killed."

Whereupon, as the story goes, the officer smilingly appropriated the meat for his own use.[31]

A great many soldiers undoubtedly accepted the tenet that the country for which they were fighting owed them sustenance, and when meat was not forthcoming from regular sources they saw little if any wrong in taking it from the. noncombatants. This point of view is suggested by one Reb's statement to his brother that "the Government tries to feed us Texains on Poor Beef, but there is too Dam many hogs here for that, these Arkansaw hoosiers ask from 25 to 30 cents a pound for there pork, but the Boys generally get it a little cheaper than that I reckon you understand how they get it." [32]

Another Texan expressed pride in his ability to get food by informal means. "We dont get much to eat here," he wrote. "Sometimes we

. . . get it by the slide of hand and that is not very hard for me to do, for I can steel the buttons of[f] an old negroes coat when he is wide awake so you can see that I can get along pretty well for [a] new beginner but I think David Lane can beat me at it and pretty bad." [33]

Gardens, orchards and watermelon fields were often visited by Confederate soldiers in search of additions to their rations. Smokehouses and beehives were likewise plundered. "I now have some idea of the devastating effects of an army marching through a Country," wrote a Reb to his wife June 2, 1862, from a camp near Baldwyn, Mississippi; "our Soldiers act outrageously, not with standing the strict orders and their sure cxccution in reference to the destruction of private property. Our soldiers have not left a fat hog, chicken, Turkey, goose, duck, or eggs or onions bchind." [34]

Theft and plunder were most common in areas where nearness of the Yankees or prospect of attack had caused withdrawal of part of the civilian populace or a reduction of policing. Thus an exposed section of Virginia was robbed to such an extent in the autumn of 1861 as to elicit a stinging rebuke to offending soldiers by General Magruder. Columbia, Tennessee, witnessed a siege of pillaging of both public and private property the day following Federal evacuation in November 1864. The vicinity of Tupelo, Mississippi, experienced such a wave of depredation at the hands of soldiers of the Army of Tennessee in January 1865 that Hood talked of issuing an order for the summary shooting of soldiers who were found killing livestock.[35]

The cavalry seems to have been more addicted to the evil of pillaging than the infantry. This was probably due to the greater mobility of this branch of the service; contact with the commissariat was hard to maintain when on roving missions, and there was greater opportunity of stealing with impunity. Commissary officers in the field were authorized to impress necessary commodities under certain conditions. This encouraged plunder-bent privates and subalterns to pose as duly qualified officers with manufactured orders, for the purpose of making illegal appropriations for their own use.

The outfits that were the most notorious for theft and destruction were those more or less independently operating units known as partisan rangers or independent scouts. A great many of these companies, raised under state or Confederate authorization—and holding a status so uncertain as to be a continual source of argument among commanders of armies, the War Department and state governors—operated in areas near Federal lines. They undoubtedly attracted more than their share of undesirable characters, and the detached, irresponsible nature of their service subjected them to especial temptation to plunder. Complaints of villainies suffered at their hands poured into Richmond from western Virginia, eastern Tennessee, Missouri, Kentucky, North Carolina, Mississippi and western Louisiana.

While it is true that much of the pillaging attributed to cavalrymen was done by unauthorized groups of guerrillas posing as soldiers, it must be admitted in the light of abundant and reliable evidence that accredited scouts and partisan rangers were guilty of plenty of plundering. In 1863 Secretary of War Seddon expressed the conviction that the policy of authorizing such outfits had proved to be a mistake, and that their license and irregularities had frequently "excited more odium and done more damage with friends than enemies." Governor Z. B. Vance, though frequently given to overstatement when corresponding with Richmond authorities, expressed an opinion widely held among civilians and soldiers alike when he wrote Seddon in December 1863:

"If God Almighty had yet in store another plague worse than all others which he intended to have let loose on the Egyptians in case Pharaoh still hardened his heart, I am sure it must have been a regiment or so of half-armed, half-disciplined Confederate Cavalry." [36]

Both infantry and cavalry were guilty to a regrettable extent of robbing fellow soldiers of clothing, knives, watches, blankets and other personal belongings. "They steal for practice," complained one Reb of his comrades. Another gave his opinion that "the men in this Regiment are the most scientific stealers I ever saw, they can steal anything and hardly ever be found out." A third said that "petty stealing has . . . developed into a perfect epidemic in our brigade." A South Carolinian boldly stated in 1863 that a soldier had to steal to live, and that he thought no more of taking another Reb's cup, spoon, or plate than he did of shooting a Yankee.[37]

Perhaps the form of pilfering that ranked lowest in Rebel esteem was that of plundering dead comrades, but there were some who were mean enough not only to take their money and watches, but also the clothing from their bodies.[38] Ransacking of deceased Federals was regarded with less disapproval and was therefore woefully common, though a distinction was made by some between dead and dying Yanks. Jim Randall was observed after a fight sitting near a Union officer. When asked what he was doing he replied: "Am waiting for this fellow to die, so I can get his watch and ring." But just at this moment another Reb of less delicate conscience came up and took the articles, much to Randall's chagrin and disappointment.[39] However, instances of despoiling dead Yankee soldiers are less frequently reported than of robbing live Southern civilians.

The number of pillagers in the Confederate Army was always large. And despite repeated interdictions by Lee, Bragg, Longstreet, Polk and other commanding generals, remonstrances of Richmond authorities, and the meting out of severe punishments by courts-martial and other military tribunals, plunder and theft increased with the declining fortunes of the Confederacy. So great were the proportions attained by the evil that soldiers wrote home that a visitation of Rebels was hardly less disastrous than that of Yankees. A Georgian thus sized up the situation for his wife:

"I have but little or no fears that the Yanks will ever git down to whare you are, but I think that you will be pesterde by our own soldiers . . . strowling about . . . and stealing your chickens, etc. I had almost as leave have the Yanks around my hous as our own men, except they will not insult ladies." [40]

Descendants of Confederate soldiers have derived great satisfaction from the conduct of the men in gray during their invasion of Pennsylvania in 1863. The order of General Lee requiring strict respect for private property is frequently offered as evidence in proof of their exemplary behavior. But observations made during the campaign by some of the soldiers themselves indicate considerable discrepancy between Lee's pronouncement and the troops' obedience.

A private wrote his homefolk of sharing in the destruction of a wheat field that was ready for harvesting, and of taunting the protesting owners with reminders of similar havoc wrought by Federals who invaded the South.[41]

A surgeon noted in his diary while at Chambersburg that "hogs, sheep, and Poultries stand a poor chance about here for their lives," and added significantly, "We are living on the 'fat of the land'." [42]

A Virginia captain wrote to his wife:

"We . . . today marched into Pennsylvania. . . . The men . . . made many threats of vengeance before coming here. . . . We are sitting by a fine rail fire. It seems to do the men good to burn Yankee rails as they have not left a fence in our part of the country. . . . In spite of orders, they step out at night and help themselves to milk, butter, poultry, and vegetables." [43]

Another Virginia officer told his family that Southern soldiers "took everything" from farms along the line of march to Harrisburg. "They even stripped their houses," he said, "though it was against orders. . . . I was made sorry at times for some who looked so inosent and so much alarmed." [44]

It would be misleading to infer from these testimonials that the Gettysburg campaign was nearly so destructive as Sherman's march through Georgia; but it is equally erroneous to assume that Confederates who plundered comrades and fellow citizens were transformed into gentlemen by crossing the Mason and Dixon Line.

Another besetting sin of Confederate soldiers was swearing. Many Rebs who successfully withstood other camp influences fell victim to the practice of "cussing." Private Adrian Carruth of Mississippi affords a good instance of a soldier whose one slip from consistent and triumphant righteousness was the utterance of an occasional oath. With great seriousness he addressed his sister on the subject of his patent weakness. "I think if we could have Brother Stovall here," he wrote in August 1863, "we could get up a considerable meeting—and I am sure one was never needed more than at this place and time. You can have no conception of the wickedness that is carried on here in the Army by Swearing and gambling, the latter of which I am as clear as the new born babe. I have never bet a cent on any thing since I entered the service, but must confess . . . with Shamefacedness that I am guilty to some extent of the former, though it is quite seldom that I make use of profane language; and think every day of my life that I will quit it." [45]

Private Carruth, who was religiously inclined, placed himself with a small group when he said that his use of profanity was rare. Those who swore frequently constituted a much larger class. "You have no idea how demoralizing camp life is," wrote a Mississippi Reb to his wife. "Oaths, blasphemies, imprecations, obscenity, are hourly heard ringing in your ears until your mind is almost filled with them." [46]

Certainly there was no lack of provocation to swearing. Long marches, rain, mud, putrid beef, weevil-infested beans, inefficient commissaries, shoddy clothing, strutting subalterns, body lice, and objectionable comrades caused no end of irritation, not to mention the greater provocation of Yanks who flanked instead of fighting, who made war on wives and children, and who stooped to such meanness as throwing elongated shells called "lamp posts" in Rebel bivouacs at Shiloh to disturb sleep after the Yanks had been driven off the field.[47]

The case of Robert M. Gill affords a particularly interesting example. When Gill went to the war he was inclined toward religious skepticism, hence his propensity for swearing gave him no great bother. But his wife, a devout woman concerned about the welfare of her husband's soul, urged him continually in her letters to curb his wickedness and to become a Christian. And Gill, impressed by her entreaty and by the uncertainty of a soldier's life, tried diligently to make amends. He finally was able to reduce his evil ways to the one offense of swearing; and he could prevail over this sin except when he was engaged in active combat. In the pitch and excitement of battle all his previously made resolutions were reduced to emptiness, and irrepressible oaths poured forth from his lips. Afterward he would write contritely to his wife and renew his pledges; but these would not survive the next fight.[48]

There were some Rebs who held their cussing within fairly decent bounds; a few even substituted such niceties as "dad burn," "doggone," and "I'll be dad shame"; but these constituted an insignificant minority.

Irate or drunken Johnnies occasionally made the sad mistake of swearing at officers on duty. In such instances they were haled before a court-martial. In the trial that followed the exact phrasing of offensive utterances was made a part of the court records. Search of these records gives convincing evidence that the stock of profane language which Johnny Reb could call to his command was not a whit inferior in robustness and variety to that in use today.

Two specific instances will suffice for illustration. A general court-martial sitting at Savannah, Georgia, found Private George Bedell of the Columbus Artillery guilty of calling his commanding officer "a damned son of a bitch, a damned tyrant, a damned puppy, a damned rascal," and of "using other disrespectful and contemptuous language." And another court sentenced Private Spencer Carlton of the Joe Thompson Artillery to a ball-and-chain assignment for saying to his captain: "I want to go home; my furlough has been signed, and you must let me go; but by God! I intend to go tonight if I have to wade up to my neck in mud, blood, or sh-t." [49]

Allied to the sin of profanity was indulgence in obscene expression and anecdote, and there are indications that this had a wide prevalency in Southern armies. A Mississippian whose background was conducive to broadmindedness remarked shortly after he entered the army, "I had no idea of the filth and vulgarity of men in camp until I tried this little experiment." [50] Another Mississippian expressed even greater revulsion at the licentiousness that he encountered. "You have no idea," he wrote his wife, "how I loath a soldier's life. The more I see of it, the more I hate . . . the low flung camp jest, the disgusting, nauseating obscenity universally indulged in by soldiers." On another occasion he said, "I abhor [such society] from my inmost soul—one unceasing tide of blasphemy & wickedness, coarseness and obscenity. . . . Is it possible that God will bless a people as wicked as our soldiers? I fear not." [51]

Allowance should be made for this soldier's maladaptation to army life and for his extreme religiousness, but even so, there was much support for his observations. In more than one instance Rebs who were advised of intended visits of their wives in camp wrote regretfully, but with obvious alarm, advising that they had better not come on account of the coarse and vulgar language to which they would unavoidably be exposed. [52]

Sabbath-breaking was an evil which caused no end of grief to chaplains and others who were interested in the religious well-being of the soldiers. Confederate generals encouraged Sabbath observance as much as possible by ordering cessation on Sundays of drill and all other military activities that could be suspended without danger to Confederate arms; but the conditions of camp life were such as to discourage respect of the fourth commandment. Fatigue from marching, boredom and general indifference to things spiritual caused many soldiers to spend the holiday not in Bible reading or attendance upon religious exercises, but rather lolling about, gambling, washing clothes, and playing games.

"If you were to ride up just now," wrote a soldier to his wife in 1862, "You would think it was anything else but the 'holy Sabbath day' here. In the company next to us . . . is a fellow playing the fiddle . . . in an old field near by are several boys playing ball & by looking around doubtless I could find several playing cards." [53] This letter was written from Arkansas on a Sunday of October 1862, but it might have come from almost any camp during any period of the Confederacy.

The evil of illicit sexual indulgence, though admittedly common to every large army that history has known, is scantily treated in Confederate records. The difficulty of obtaining information on this point is attributable to several factors. One is the veil of reticence which enshrouded the whole subject of sex in generations past—though strange is the inconsistency of a society which utterly barred mention of sex in polite conversation, and yet permitted column-length advertisements of venereal remedies on front pages of the daily paper, as well as elaboration in police columns of obscene details of bawdy-house raids. Admitting the inconsistency, there can be no doubt of the effectiveness of the taboo enforced by delicacy—so effective, indeed, that a soldier could not address his wife on the prescribed subject except with the most obvious embarrassment, as witness the following:

"We have a good spring of water and the health of our Regt. is good except some disease that I feel a delicacy in spelling them out to you as you are a female person but however I reckon you cant blush at little things these times. It is the POCKS and CLAP. The cases of this complaint is numerous, especially among the officers, and by the by Co. A has got one officer toillin with the pock and one private with the clap. I now drop the subject as I have no interest [idea] it will interest you to be reading about that." [54]

Another reason for scarcity of material on this point is the touchiness of the war generation and its immediate descendants as to the reputation of Confederate soldiers. The author has questioned several veterans about the irregularities of their comrades, but with meager results; one octogenarian, obviously nettled at the inquiry, testily responded, "Confederate soldiers were too much gentlemen to stoop to such things."

The jealous regard for the good name of comrades and of kinsmen has no doubt led to many instances of suppression of letters and other items that treat of soldier incontinence. But the present generation of descendants is more inclined toward the viewpoint that Johnny Reb can be presented in his various aspects, the bad as well as the good, and still be appreciated. Those who take this attitude have been of great help to historians by turning over to them uncensored diaries and correspondence with the privilege of unrestricted use. From occasional references in letters and journals of the soldiers, from court-martial proceedings, from scattered regimental sick lists, and from police reports in newspapers chronicling arrest of disorderly prostitutes and their uniformed guests, a general picture of the seamiest side of army life may be drawn.

There were some instances of prostitution on military premises.

Early in the war the presence of women in camp was not unusual, and that some of these were of the unsavory sort is indicated by a communication that Israel Gibbons, a soldier-reporter serving with Albert Sidney Johnston's army, sent to his paper at New Orleans in the winter of 1861. "It is really curious to observe how well and how strictly the three classes of women in camp keep aloof from each other," he wrote. "The wives and daughters of Colonels, Captains and other officers constitute the first class. The rough cooks and washers who have their husbands along . . . form the second class. The third and last class is happily the smallest; here and there a female of elegant appearance and unexceptionable manners; truly wife-like in their tented seclusion, but lacking that great and only voucher of respectability for females in camp—the marriage tie." [55]

As the war progressed, increasing hardship and roughness eliminated the great majority of respectable women, and tightening discipline got rid of most of the undesirables. Even the domestics associated with the army declined in number. It is not unlikely that an order requiring that "company laundresses who do not actually wash for the men must be discharged," was inspired by affinity of bad women for Rebel camps.[56]

Some lewd women probably continued to make occasional visits to winter encampments throughout the war, the excuse for their coming being the theatricals presented by soldiers. In March 1863 a group of Rebs quartered near Fredericksburg staged an all-male burlesque which featured the complete disrobing of one of the principals. In the audience there were a goodly number of civilians, including some women; of these, one of the soldiers remarked, "they ware dresses [but there is about them] not much of the Lady." [57]

In rare instances virtueless women were able to hoodwink officers and maintain their camp connections. The Richmond *Enquirer* of October 31, 1864, reported an incredible example. "Two females of questionable morality, answering to the names of Mary and Mollie Bell, *alias* Tom Parker and Bob Morgan, arrived in this city on Friday night by the Central train in charge of a guard," wrote the reporter. "They were dressed in Confederate uniforms, and were sent to this city from Southwestern Virginia, where they have been in service during the past two years." The charge against them was "aiding in the demoralization of General Early's veterans." They were committed to a military prison, but it is doubtful if persons possessed of such boldness and ingenuity remained long in close confinement.[58]

But for the most part Rebs were forced to go beyond the limits of camp to find prostitutes, though these hovered as near the army as circumstances would permit. Petersburg, because of its location near the seat of hostilities, was a haven for shady females throughout the war, and some of the young soldiers who patronized them communicated their experiences to boon companions in other localities.

Most of these letters are unprintable, but an excerpt from one of them affords an idea of their general import. "John, about 2 weeks ago there was a woman come from petersburg," wrote a young Tar Heel in the fall of 1863, "and stoped about 200 yards from our camp several of the boys went up and had lots of fun with her. It was about drill time and one of the boys missed drill and they put him on double duty." Others told of the fees charged by Petersburg prostitutes, and of their contamination with venereal diseases.[59]

During the Chattanooga and Atlanta campaigns Dalton, Georgia, was a favorite resort for prostitutes. In the spring of 1864 a staff officer of the Army of Tennessee wrote to the post commander at Dalton:

"Complaints are daily made to me of the number of lewd women in this town, and on the outskirts of the army. They are said to be impregnating this whole command, and the Commissariat has been frequently robbed, with a view of supporting these disreputable characters."

The vice situation became so serious that General Johnston issued an order to have the town and the surrounding country searched, so that all women who were not able to give proof of respectability and the means of an honest livelihood could be sent to points beyond the reach of soldiers. He ordered further that women who returned after being sent off should be confined in the guardhouse on bread and water. Stringent measures were invoked to guarantee faithful compliance with these instructions by provost marshals and train officials. But in view of previous failures of generals commanding this army to cope with prostitution it is doubtful if these restrictive regulations met with any considerable success.[60]

Mobile, New Orleans and other large towns all over the South were bad enough, but Richmond, being the center of government and the focal point of large-scale military activity, became the true mecca of prostitutes. Frequenting saloons, hotels, restaurants, bawdy houses, and walking late in the day on the city's popular promenades, they made known their unsavory characters to troops on leave. One madam had the temerity to open a lewd establishment immediately across the street from a soldier hospital run by the Young Men's Christian Association. Thereafter the manager had occasion to complain to the provost marshal that the recovery of the patients was being deterred by the doings of the prostitutes, who appeared at windows in semi-undress and made gestures calculated to lure convalescents to chambers of vice, and whose efforts were not devoid of success.[61]

A few weeks before the Seven Days' campaign a newspaper reported a large influx of prostitutes of both sexes into the capital, and remarked that "they have been disporting themselves extensively on the sidewalks, and in hacks and open carriages . . . [indulging in] smirks and smiles, winks, and . . . remarks not of a choice kind in a loud voice." [62]

Press comments then and throughout the war indicate that female solicitors had a large patronage among Confederate soldiers. Mayor Mayo, in commenting on this evil in the autumn of 1864, said: "Never was a place more changed than Richmond. Go on the Capital Square any afternoon, and you may see these women promenading up and down the shady walks jostling respectable ladies into the gutters." He observed that during public soirées prostitutes arrayed in flashy finery had been seen leaning upon the arms of Confederate officers.[63]

Previously the growth of vice had so alarmed one lover of decency that in a letter to the papers he advocated horsewhipping the abandoned women. The Enquirer's comment was that nymphs du monde were as invariable and necessary a concomitant of large armies as the vultures and buzzards, and a protest was therefore made against the flogging proposal.[64]

But prostitution was by no means restricted to towns and cities. When large bodies of soldiers camped for a considerable time in a rural area, the vice flourished there as well. Sergeant A. L. P. Vairin entered in his diary on December 27, 1862, near Weldon, North Carolina, the statement that "this section of the country seems to abound in very bad women." [65] Private Orville C. Bumpass wrote to his wife from the piny section of northern Alabama, "The state of the morals is quite as low as the soil, almost all the women are given to whoredom & the ugliest, sallowfaced, shaggy headed, bare footed dirty wretches you ever saw." [66] Concerning a brief sojourn in southwestern Texas a soldier observed, "Some of the boys broke themselves . . . dissipating, running after women &c. I did not however expend a cent in that way." [67]

Captain Thomas J. Key, stationed near the Georgia-Tennessee line, confided to his diary January 2, 1864, that "the war appears to have demoralized everybody," that the girls thereabout were said "to smoke, chew tobacco, and drink whiskey" and that "almost half of the women in the vicinity of the army, married and unmarried, are lost to all virtue." [68]

A few months before, Major W. J. Mims had written to his wife from a camp in eastern Tennessee that two pickets had been lured from their posts of duty by the "arts of designing women" and shot. After the comment, "I hardly think a Union woman could be invested with such personal charms as to woo me successfully for a moment from the post of duty to the treacherous embrace," he makes the following observation as to the general state of morals in this vicinity: "I will state as a matter of history that female virtue if it ever existed in this Country seems now almost a perfect wreck. Prostitutes are thickly crowded through mountain & valley, in hamlet & city." "I suppose," he adds, "[that] the influence of the armies has largely contributed to this state of things, as soldiers do not seem to feel the same restraints away from home, which at home regulated their intercourse with the gentler sex." [69]

The unhappy aftermath of visiting bawdy houses was the outbreak in camp of venereal diseases. The medical data is too sparse to permit any accurate estimate of the prevalence of syphilis and gonorrhea in the Confederate Army. But scattered sick reports in the National Archives for sundry regiments of the Army of Northern Virginia, covering mainly the period from July 1861 to March 1862, afford significant information as to venereal tendencies during the first part of the war.[70]

These reports give only the number of new cases coming to the attention of regimental surgeons each month. In July 1861, 12 regiments representing 5 states and having a mean strength of 11,452 men reported 204 new cases of gonorrhea and 44 new cases of syphilis. The next month 29 regiments from 7 states with a mean strength of 27,042 had 152 additions to the gonorrhea list and 102 new syphilitic patients. In September the figures were: 38 regiments, 33,284 mean strength, 148 new cases of gonorrhea, and 70 of syphilis. In December, 43 regiments from 7 states with 34,865 mean strength had 36 new cases of gonorrhea and 40 of syphilis. In March 1862, 28 regiments from 7 states, 19,942 mean strength, reported 14 new cases of gonorrhea and

10 of syphilis. From April to September there is a hiatus in the reports, and after December they cease altogether. But in one fall month of 1862, 8 regiments from 2 states, with 6,253 mean strength, had 36 new cases of gonorrhea and 10 of syphilis.

These figures became yet more significant when given in terms of 1,000 of mean strength. In July 1861 there were for each 1,000 men, 17.8 new cases of gonorrhea and 3.8 of syphilis; in August, the figures were 5.6 and 3.8 respectively; in September, 4.4 and 2.1; in December, 1.03 and 2.1; in March 1862, .7 and .45; and in a fall month of 1862, 5.7 and 1.6.

It is readily apparent that venereal infection gradually declined from a high rate in July 1861 to a negligible figure in the spring of the following year, and that in the fall of 1862 it was on the increase. Keeping in mind the thinness of data for the summer of 1861 and the fall of 1862, some explanation of this fluctuation may be offered. The large number of new cases appearing in July 1861 may be attributed in part to the concentration in Richmond and vicinity in June and July of large bodies of troops recently arrived from the deep South. Poor discipline, excessive drinking, the festivity incident to going to war, and the lure of a strange city teeming with prostitutes, combined to send large numbers of volunteers to Richmond bawdy houses.

William R. Barksdale, recently arrived in the capital city with a group of Mississippians, wrote on June 11, 1861, that there was a great deal of sickness in his regiment, and that measles and improper sexual indulgence accounted for most of the cases.[71] Regimental sick reports show that the Tenth Alabama Regiment, which arrived in Richmond in the early summer of 1861 and remained there for some time before joining Joseph E. Johnston, had in July (with a mean strength of 1,063 men), 62 new cases of gonorrhea and 6 of syphilis. Other regiments had similar experiences. The Eighteenth Mississippi (mean strength—975) had 25 new cases of gonorrhea in July, and in August the Sixteenth Mississippi (mean strength—972) reported 32 new cases of gonorrhea and 11 of syphilis. The Eighth South Carolina (mean strength—828) in the same month reported 25 new cases of gonorrhea.

The decline in the rate of infection in the autumn and fall must have been due to the tightening of discipline and to the fact that active campaigning took the bulk of the army away from Richmond. Close confinement in winter quarters from December to March probably accounted for the further decline during these months. No data are available for the summer of 1862, but the increased outbreaks in the fall bear striking relation to the assignment of some of the North Carolina regiments to provost duty in Petersburg—a town that was notorious as a resort for camp followers. The Fifty-fifth Tar Heel Regiment, for instance, was transferred from Kinston to Petersburg on October 1, 1862, and remained on guard duty in the latter city throughout the month; and regimental sick reports from that month list, for a mean strength of 420 men, 13 new cases of gonorrhea. The Forty-seventh North Carolina (mean strength—838), likewise engaged, had for the same month 10 new cases of gonorrhea.

A dark picture of the bad effect of city vice districts on army morals and health is presented by an article in the Richmond *Examiner* of December 1862: "If the Mayor of Richmond lacks any incentive to stimulate . . . breaking up the resorts of ill-fame in the city, let him visit the military hospitals, where sick and disabled soldiers are received for treatment, and look upon the human forms lying there, wrecked upon the treacherous shoals of vice and passion which encounters the soldier at the corner of every street, lane, and alley of the city." The correspondent proceeds to quote a lieutenant of artillery stationed near Richmond to the effect that out of a company of forty-five men, thirteen were in the hospital for venereal diseases. "In this way," concludes the writer, "more than by wind and weather—more than by natural causes—is the army depleted, and the efficiency of its soldiers weakened." [72]

The author of this article let his zeal for reform lead him into an overstatement of his case. It is very easy for anyone in discussing evil to fall into the same error. Hence it is necessary in this survey of the sins of Johnny Reb to guard against the impression of a too great prevalency of the vices considered. For every regiment that had a score of new venereal cases breaking out in any given month, there were several that had none; and regiments having only three or four new cases were far more numerous than those having as many as ten. The majority of Confederate soldiers—probably the overwhelming majority—could in reference to fornication say with Private Bumpass, "Uncomtaminated I left home & so I expect to return," and this at war's end.[73] Likewise a decided majority probably were innocent of plunder and theft. Larger numbers certainly took to gambling and swearing, but even so a substantial portion was guiltless of all of these offenses.

With these basic postulates in mind, it may be admitted that the category of evils which the Reverend Mr. Ransom designated as "sins of the camp viz. Sabbath breaking Drunkenness, Stealing, Cardplaying & Profanity" [74] flourished among Confederate soldiers from the beginning, and that with brief interruptions occasioned by religious revivals they increased with the passing of time until they affected such great numbers as to support a soldier's advice to his wife: "dont never come here as long as you can ceep away for you will smell hell here." [75]

CHAPTER IV

IN WINTER QUARTERS

THE chief campaigns of the war were fought in the northern part of the Confederate States. The winters of Virginia, North Carolina, Tennessee, Kentucky, Arkansas, and the northern half of Georgia, Alabama and Mississippi are surprisingly cold and marked by heavy rains and occasional snows. The commanders of neither side were particularly anxious to carry out large-scale movements under such circumstances. Consequently, when the rigors of winter besieged military encampments the prevailing practice was to lay aside offensive weapons and to go into a state of semi-desuetude, known politely as winter quarters.

The move to winter encampments generally took place in late November or early December, but sometimes active fighting kept on much longer. The Fredericksburg campaign of 1862 did not end till mid-December; the bloody battle of Murfreesboro was fought two weeks later, and Hood's Tennessee expedition of 1864-1865 kept troops on the move until January. In such cases the soldiers were known to dub their tardily constructed shelters as "spring quarters." [1] The time for ending hibernation was also variable, but it normally occurred in March or April.

When cold weather set in, the commanding general of an army would try to select—so far as the disposition of the enemy allowed—a good place for his troops to spend the winter. There must be plenty of wood and water, adequate drainage, and the necessary facilities for transportation. In 1864 General Lee tried to get wood in advance for his troops about Richmond, but failed because planters were reluctant to lend the services of their slaves. Likewise a plan of General Joseph E. Johnston to have barracks constructed before the coming of winter in 1861 was defeated by delays and misunderstanding. [2]

Such shelters as were built to keep out the blasts of winter were generally constructed by the soldiers themselves. Some officers compelled their men to erect wooden houses, while others left the whole matter to the discretion and ingenuity of the privates.

59

The prevailing type of shelter was a small hut made of logs, chinked and daubed after the fashion of a pioneer cabin. These houses were thrown up with speed and zest, particularly when officers promised a gallon of whiskey to the Rebs who first completed their shelter. Each project was shared by a group of from four to ten men, usually those composing a mess. First the builders went into a wood or thicket with axes—rarely did they have saws—and chopped down the necessary trees. These were trimmed and cut to the proper length and snaked back to camp. Men in the artillery and cavalry used horses for pulling the logs, but the less fortunate infantrymen had to drag them in with their own muscles.[3] With the logs assembled each group selected a site for its cabin and began the heavy and tedious work of notching and laying the logs. When the walls were about eight feet high, some sort of roof had to be devised. If a frow and a maul could be obtained, and there was sufficient energy left for splitting large timbers, a substantial covering of boards would be put on. But more often a tent cloth would be used. The outside construction was completed with the building of a chimney.[4]

Once the roof was on, openings for doors and windows could be cut at leisure. The laying of a floor could be dispensed with—but there were a surprising number of Rebs who insisted not only on having wood beneath their feet but many conveniences that were not strictly necessary. Some put up partitions so as to have separate rooms for cooking and other purposes. A few built double or triple-decker sleeping bunks. Others added a comic touch by scrawling across their cabin fronts such appellations as "Growlers," "Howlers," "Pilgrims," "Buzzard Roost," "Sans Souci," and "No. 4 Carondolet." [5]

Seats were mostly made of boxes—begged from the commissary or the quartermaster, or sent with provisions from home—logs, ammunition chests and kegs. Tables were rigged up from pieces of board laid across upright barrels or sections of sawed logs. Slight modifications of these contrivances might be optimistically referred to as chairs and desks. The more skilled and fastidious of the soldiers were able to devise furnishings of considerable comfort if not of impressive appearance, an example being the curved-back seats made of flour barrels.[6] Kitchen utensils and tableware varied to an extent beyond description.

But regardless of their appearance and equipment, when the huts were completed they became the pride of their occupants. "We have finished our house," wrote a Texan to his mother from Virginia in January 1862. "It is made [of] pickets chinked and dubbed with a tent fly for a roof. We have the best fire place and chimney in the company. The fire place is made of brick to above the Jam and from there up *mud and sticks.* Our house is about 12 feet square . . . our guns are in racks on the walls; our utensils consist of one skillet a stew kettle a bread pan a frying pan & a large kettle Our *china ware* is, half dozen plates and the same number of forks & spoons (silver of course) our cups are of tin, 4 quart cups and two pint cups. Just above the fire place you will see something which we call a mantle piece and is made by making two holes one in each side of the fire place putting pegs in them and putting plank on them. . . . There are only four of us in this house."

In a letter written five weeks later he said that the return of two messmates from the hospital necessitated the building of a larger cabin; but that "we sold our old house to some of the boys for ten dollars." [7]

A Georgian whose quarters were considerably less pretentious than these was no less boastful. "I hate to leave 'my chimney,'" he wrote his "Dear Molley" from Fredericksburg, early in March, 1863. "You would be surprised to know how comfortable aplace I have to live in a white hous and good fire place and a box, chunk, or the ground which are all used for seats." [8]

There was one drawback to all this comfort. When the call came periodically to take a turn on the picket line, the contrast was so great as to make the duty almost intolerable. But as one Reb observed, "You have to go or march to the guardhouse," and "the latter is no good place to be in now as a fellow has no fire and of course freezes nearly every day during confinement." [9]

Occasionally the threat of a Yankee foray or the whim of some officer would compel a shift of encampments in the dead of winter. Then loud were the lamentations of those who dwelt in huts, and longing the glances cast back toward the cabins as the line of march to unprotected expanses was begun.

Doubtless the uncertainty of tenure contributed to the failure of many soldiers to build any huts at all. Most of those who reneged, however, contrived some other mode of combating the weather.

Much ingenuity was shown in adapting tents for the purpose. A common device was to build a wall of plank, brick, or stone about the sides of the tent, and to erect a fireplace at the end opposite the door. Many of the men, however, from laziness or lack of materials did without the wall and simply provided heating facilities. "The Tensas

Cavalry," wrote Theodore Mandeville, "are in Winter quarters, which means fireplaces to their tents." [10]

Probably the most industrious of the tent dwellers were a group of Louisianians who wintered near Columbus, Kentucky, in 1861-1862. These soldiers dug cellars under their tents and covered them over with boards. The canvas-enclosed upper story was used as a sleeping room, while cooking and eating were done "deep in the earth beneath." [11]

Instead of building chimneys and fireplaces for their tents, some of the soldiers attempted to solve the heating problem by making underground furnaces. This scheme, however, proved less successful than building fires in large perforated kettles suspended from the tent poles.[12] A final remnant of the shiftless or hardy followed the line of least resistance and shivered away the winter months without making any attempt to heat their quarters at all.

There were never enough tents to go round in the Confederate Army, and a considerable number of Rebs, without building materials or canvas, either had to improvise some other form of protection or to suffer intolerably from cold. This led to various forms of "digging in." Soldiers encamped near Columbus, Kentucky, during the first winter of the war devised shelters which they called "gopher holes." Some of these were prepared on an elaborate scale. First a large open-top room was dug in the side of a ravine; then fires were built to dry and harden the sides and bottom. Logs were next laid across the top and covered with a foot or more of earth. At the inner end a big fireplace was dug out, and along the outer, three-tier bunks were constructed. When a mess table and other furnishings were added, the occupants considered themselves quite snug and cozy.[13]

During the last winter of the war soldiers about Richmond spent a great deal of time in dugouts called "bombproofs." Wood was unobtainable, and the chill and dampness of these structures, the restricted space, the rats and the foul air, made them utterly noxious for any long abode. They were consequently abandoned, whenever possible, for small shelters of board or canvas along the edge of the trenches.[14] Of this type of shelter O. T. Hanks said:

"Some build a small pen about Twelve inches high. Cover it over on top with Small split pine poles put leaves & pine straw on them Spread a Blanket over & that is the bed It is now Roofed with Small Tent Cloth Captured from the Enemy . . . We now have a real Snug little Nest for two Fellows." [15]

Troops who lived in huts and in heated tents were fairly comfortable except in very cold weather. At first the respite from drill and marching, the inactivity of the Yankees, and plenty of time for lounging and sleeping brought to the campaign-weary Rebs a delightful sense of coziness. Haircuts and shaves, combs, brushes, mirrors, towels, soap, shoeshines, a "biled" shirt now and then and the privilege of puttering about in a homelike cabin added to the soldiers' satisfaction in their new way of life.[16]

But as weeks lengthened into months most Rebs tired of the inactivity and confinement. Small mannerisms that had once seemed amusing now provoked irritation, jokes and stories no longer entertained, and conversation became dull. Discipline, once accepted as a matter of course, now began to irk and offend. Officers who were followed gladly on the battlefield now became the subject of gossip and criticism. Resentments deepened, tempers quickened, quarreling and fighting increased.

Some relief was found in reading and the other recreations of camp life. Prayer meetings and preaching claimed the interest of those who were religiously inclined, and on several occasions these grew into revivals that played havoc in the ranks of the sinners. A long-continued cold spell sometimes made skating possible—but skates were hard to get, and the sport put a heavy strain on Confederate shoe leather. Sledding was also popular, even when the sleds were makeshift affairs. The building of snow men—snow effigies, as one Reb called them—was also popular from time to time.[17]

But of strictly winter sports snowballing was by far the most pervasive and the most hilarious. Day after day, from the first arrival of a few inches of snow in November or December until the melting of the last particles by the spring sun, soldiers were wont to pelt each other unmercifully with tightly packed snowballs. Even officers were not spared. "I knew that I would have to be snow balled at some time," wrote Colonel C. Irvine Walker from Dalton, Georgia, in 1864, "for the men did not let off any one in the brigade except Gen'l M. So I thought it would be best to go down and take part in the fight and be snow balled. . . . The men made however a regular Pandean frolic of it. All distinctions were levelled and the higher an officer the more snow balling he received." With evident satisfaction the Colonel observed the salutary consequences of his good sportsmanship: "After that I did not have a snow ball thrown at me." [18]

Small-scale and impromptu hurling fests gave way on occasion to affairs planned and executed after the fashion of a bona-fide trial-at-arms. As if unable to satisfy his martial urges by fighting Yankees with guns and sabers in regular season, Johnny Reb now armed himself with snowballs, formed regiments and brigades from his own ranks, dubbed opposing comrades "the enemy," raised a yell, and charged with a realism that quickened the pulse of participants and spectators. And when the contest had been pushed to the victory of one side or the other, there was a further similarity to actual combat in the black eyes, skinned heads, sprained ankles and sometimes more serious wounds of the combatants, as some of them, with more zeal than sportsmanship, would load their pellets with cores of rock or lead. "Prisoners of war" were also brought in for parole or exchange.

And these affairs had their heroes just like scraps with Yankees. T. B. Hampton wrote from Dalton, Georgia, March 24, 1864:

"We had a Great Battle yesterday between the 63rd and 54th Va. Regt. It lasted some 2 or 3 hours. I never saw such a snow balling before some times one would drive the other & then in return the other would charge and drive them. I did not Intend to engage in it but the 54th was like to drive us all out of camp & I let in made a charge & drove them out Kept them out until we quit the Officers of the 54th invited me over after the fight was over to drink with them complimenting me for Bravery they saw I wounded more men than nearly all the rest of the Regt last night I was visited by some of them & complimented at a very high Rate they seemed to think as the Indian thought about Washington that they could not hit me though I was the nearest to them I enjoyed the sport fine but it made me horse [hoarse] on account of our great charges and cheering." [19]

The pandemonium and excitement that characterized large-scale snowball engagements is vividly indicated by a letter of a Georgia private who witnessed several combats in Virginia during the second winter of the war:

"Some times the hole brigade formes, and it looks like the sky and the hole elements was made of snow and a hole had broke right through the middle and it is no rare thing to see a Cpt or a Col with his hat nocked off and covered in snow Gen Longstreet and his agitant took regs the other day and had a fight with snow balls but the Gen charged him and took them prisners." [20]

The diary entry of Lieutenant T. Otis Baker for March 22, 1864,

A TAR HEEL'S SKETCH OF REBEL WINTER QUARTERS

Note the three types of shelter: (1) A tent with chimney: (2) a "barricaded tent—i.e. walls of logs; (3) a log hut. (From John Steele Henderson Papers, University of North Carolina. Henderson belonged to the 10th North Carolina Regiment.)

LOUSE RACE

This drawing was made by Private Harry St. John Dixon in his diary (manuscript, University of North Carolina); it accompanied the entry for June 20, 1864. Dixon served with the 28th Mississippi Cavalry.

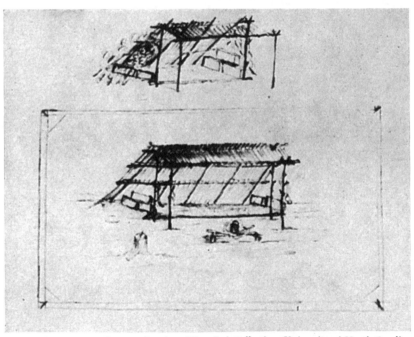

TEMPORARY WINTER QUARTERS, AS SKETCHED BY A SOLDIER

The shed roof consisted of pine limbs. Boxes, in which supplies had been sent from home, were stacked at each end to act as walls. (From George W. F. Harper Papers, University of North Carolina.)

was devoted largely to the account of a snow battle in which the fighting was so realistic and so martial that his account reads like an official report of a genuine encounter with the Yankees:

"About the latter hour 9 A. M. two lines of battle were formed by the 10 & 44 Regts which charged the . . . [camp] of the 41st Miss. On the route [they] were reinforced by a few recruits from the 7th & 9th Miss. The result of the battle was the dispersion of the 41 who for a short time fought stubbornly, the capture of their Colonel and several other officers and the occupation of their Regimental Parade. When we began to retire our adversaries rallied and being joined by our faithless allies of the 7th & 9th they made an attack upon our rear. Three times a halt was made and the attacks repulsed. After crossing the road and the brook which separate the camps of the enemy from our own we made a determined stand. Many unsuccessful attempts were made by the foe to pass the bridge and to cross the stream lower down. Discouraged by their repeated failures they finally withdrew altogether. In the afternoon they again advanced upon our camp in three columns, having previously made an insolent demand for the unconditional surrender of the army of the East, as we were called, allowing us but ten minutes in which to decide. The demand being refused a hot attack was made and after an engagement of a half or three quarters of an hour terminated in their repulse. Their losses were their commdr in chief, their three corps commanders, besides several other officers of rank, and two or three stands of colors." [21]

The roughness and zeal of these battles were amazing. A soldier diarist told of an affair between Louisianians and Georgians in which the combatants, after rallying every man in camp, both black and white, advanced to the edge of a stream and let loose volley after volley of snowballs and ice. The Louisianians eventually prevailed, though not without heavy casualties. According to the diarist, who participated on the side of the Louisianians, "Capt C H Slocomb lost two front teeth—Lieut Challeron a blackeye—Among the Privates of the 5th Co was 5 bloody noses a Blackeye—all of them more or less bruised among the captured property is the flag of the Ga Regiment 8 or 10 caps and Hats 1 frying pan and 4 or 5 pones of corn bread." [22] Another soldier reported that two men were killed in snow fights near Dalton, Georgia.[23]

Occasionally visitors from neighboring towns and countryside witnessed the encounters. The presence of ladies on the side lines in one instance proved a decisive factor in the tide of battle. "We all commenced snow balling," wrote a participant of this engagement, "our battalion & the 3rd Ga. Regt against the 48th and 22nd Ga. Regts. . . . Gen Wright, his wife and daughters & other young ladies came to see the fight. We got whiped but the ladies were the cause the boys all stoped to look at them and the other side fought so our party kept giving back until the others got the general and the girls prisners." [24] That a group of hard-bitten campaigners should be so overpowered by the presence of feminine onlookers that they let victory slip out of their hands is delightfully revealing of Johnny Reb's chivalry.

Another means of abating the tedium of winter quarters was to visit the city, if one were near at hand, or call on the country folk who lived near camp. A Reb who spent the winter of 1864-1865 near Richmond wrote that "we spend the winter pleasantly here. Sometimes we are granted a pass to visit the Citty. If not we run the Blockade, visit the Theaters maybe get on a big Whope [whoopee?] & Paint the thing red." He added that with good luck such a spree might be enjoyed with impunity.[25]

Ordinarily, common soldiers had little opportunity to meet civilians. But camp-weary Rebs usually knew how to make the most of such chances as came their way; and there were some who showed remarkable ingenuity at securing invitations to private homes without prior introduction, especially when there was likelihood of finding there either food or females. Among these was one Charles Moore of Louisiana. Moore was on exceptionally good terms with the officers of his company; he ingratiated himself not only by helping out with clerical work, for which he seems to have had a flair, but also by giving occasional singing and drinking parties in his tent. His standing certainly was not injured by the custom of taking a lieutenant or captain along with him on social excursions through the countryside. Because, perhaps, of that same charm and talent which endeared him to his superiors, he always had large groups of feminine acquaintances in the vicinity of winter quarters. And the frequency of his calls upon the ladies was nothing short of amazing. Excerpts from his diary for a twelve-day period in December 1861 throw interesting light on his social achievements:

"Dec. 18, 1861, Groves's Wharf, Va. Went out Riding with Miss Lettie on Horse Back
Dec. 19, 1861 After dinner Lieut Adams and Miss Lettie went out Riding also Miss Willie and myself

Dec. 21, 1861 Went to Williamsburg on Business . . .
Dec. 22, 1861 Slept at Pussie's [a feminine acquaintance in or near Williamsburg] last night.
Dec. 25, 1861 Went to a party with the Girls on Board the Steamer Curtis Peck. . . .
Dec. 29, 1861 Took a walk over to Jones Farm with Dr. Sowers Company Surgeon. Introduced the Miss Gambols." [26]

The next winter Moore's penchant for visiting and partying was indulged even more frequently. Sometimes he and a few comrades would visit two or three homes on the same day, singing, dancing, and eating with the girls at each place, and it was not unusual for festivities to extend beyond midnight.[27] He lost a leg as the result of a wound at Gettysburg, but his journal contains no word of complaint. As soon as he was able to hobble about he began a social campaign against Richmond, but we have no information as to his success.

Few indeed were the soldiers who had the respite from winter quarters enjoyed by Moore. Snow fights, reading and cards all offered their hours of diversion, but as the days grew longer and warmer, troops grew increasingly weary of their inactivity and seclusion. When the call came for abandonment of cabins and renewal of active campaigning, the response was, with few exceptions, genuinely enthusiastic. Amid the flurried hubbub of decampment Johnny Reb eased the straps binding the blanket roll to his back, shouldered his musket, fell in line, and set his course in the direction of the Yankees.

CHAPTER V

HEROES AND COWARDS

WHILE it may be granted that there were significant changes in the reactions of soldiers as they became accustomed to combat, the fact remains that the experiences and behavior of those taking part in Confederate battles followed the same general pattern. These more or less common characteristics must be described in some detail.

When an encounter with the Yankees was expected certain preliminaries were necessary. One of these was the issue of extra provisions, accompanied by the order to "cook up" from three to five days' rations, so that time would not have to be taken for the preparation of food during the anticipated action. This judicious measure generally fell short of its object because of Johnny Reb's own characteristics: he was always hungry, he had a definite prejudice against baggage, and he was the soul of improvidence. Sometimes the whole of the extra ration would be consumed as it was cooked, and rarely did any part of it last for the full period intended. About the same time that food was dispensed the general in command would address his men for the purpose of firing their spirit and inspiring them to deeds of valor. Soldiers en route to Shiloh, for example, were thus charged by Albert Sidney Johnston:

"I have put you in motion to offer battle to the invaders of your country. With the resolution and disciplined valor becoming men fighting, as you are, for all worth living or dying for, you can but march to a decisive victory over the agrarian mercenaries sent to subjugate and despoil you of your liberties, property, and honor. Remember the precious stake involved; remember the dependence of your mothers, your wives, your sisters, and your children on the result; remember the fair, broad, abounding land, the happy homes, and the ties that would be desolated by your defeat.

"The eyes and the hopes of eight millions of people rest upon you. You are expected to show yourselves worthy of your race and lineage; worthy of the women of the South, whose noble devotion in this war has never been exceeded in any time. With such incentives to brave

68

deeds and with the trust that God is with us, your general will lead you confidently to the combat, assured of success." [1]

Presently each man would be given a supply of ammunition. This was delayed as long as possible, so that the powder would not become dampened through carelessness of the men. If Confederates held the initiative, the issue of ammunition would take place the night before the attack; but if the Rebs were on the defensive, without any definite knowledge of the time of assault, the issue of cartridges had to take place at an earlier stage. The customary allotment to each fighter was from forty to sixty rounds, a round being a ball and enough powder for a single shot.[2]

Prior to their issue lead and powder for each load had, for convenience, been wrapped in a piece of paper with the bullet at one end, the powder behind it, and the other end closed with a twist or a plug to hold the powder in place. This improvised cartridge was cylindrical in shape, somewhat resembling a section of crayon. When Johnny Reb loaded his gun—usually a muzzle loader—he bit off the twisted end so that the powder would be exploded by the spark when the trigger was pulled, dropped the cartridge in the muzzle, rammed in a piece of wadding and waited for the opportunity to draw bead on a Yankee. Surplus rounds were kept in a cartridge box—a leather or metal container that hung from the belt—or in a haversack, or in trouser pockets.

Knapsacks and other baggage not actually needed on the field were supposed to be left in the rear with the quartermaster, but officers always had trouble preventing their men from throwing aside their equipment at random. After Bull Run and Shiloh most soldiers did not have to be cautioned about their canteens, as the acute suffering from thirst experienced in those engagements was a sufficient reminder to carry well-filled water tins into subsequent fights.

The day of battle finally comes. The men are roused from sleep at a very early hour, perhaps two or three o'clock. The well-known call to arms is an extended beat of the snare drum known as the "long roll." After the lines are drawn up officers inspect equipment, giving particular attention to ammunition, to see that all is in readiness.

Then a few words of advice and instruction: Do not shoot until you are within effective musket range of the enemy; fire deliberately, taking care to aim low, and thus avoid the overshooting to which you have been so markedly susceptible in previous battles. If you merely wound a man so much the better, as injured men have to be taken from the field by sound ones; single out a particular adversary for your fire, after the example of your sharpshooting forefathers at Bunker Hill and New Orleans. When possible pick off the enemy's officers, particularly the mounted ones, and his artillery horses. Under all conditions hold your ranks; avoid the natural but costly inclination to huddle together under heavy fire. When ordered to charge, do so at once and move forward rapidly; you are much less apt to be killed while going steadily forward than if you hesitate or retreat; but in case you have to fall back, do so gradually and in order; more men are killed during disorganzied retreat than at any other time; if your objective is a battery, do not be terrorized—artillery is never as deadly as it seems; a rapid forward movement reduces the battery's effectiveness and hastens the end of its power to destroy. Do not pause or turn aside to plunder the dead or to pick up spoils; battles have been lost by indulgence in this temptation. Do not heed the calls for assistance of wounded comrades or stop to take them to the rear; details have been made to care for casualties, and the best way of protecting your wounded friends is to drive the enemy from the field. Straggling under any guise will be severely punished. Cowards will be shot. Do your duty in a manner that becomes the heroic example your regiment has already set on earlier fields of combat.[3]

Orders to march are now given, and to the waving of colors and the stirring rhythm of fife and drum the regiments proceed to their appointed place in the line of battle. As the dawn mist clears away, a scene of intense activity is revealed on all sides. Surgeons are preparing their kits; litter bearers and ambulances are ominously waiting.[4] Arrived at their place in line, the men wait for what seem interminable hours while other units are brought into position. There is some talk while they wait, though less than earlier in the war. Comrades quietly renew mutual pledges to seek out those who are missing at the battle's end— for help if they are wounded and for protection of belongings and notification of homefolk if they are dead. A few men read their testaments, some mutter soft prayers—a devout captain is observed standing with Bible in hand reading aloud to his Mississippians, but this scene is unusual.[5] Here and there a soldier bites off a chew of tobacco and joins a host of comrades whose jaws are already working. Very rarely an officer or a private sneaks a swig of "How Come You So" to bolster his spirit for the ordeal ahead.[6] Everywhere suspense bears down with crushing force, but is indicated largely by silence.

Presently the rattle of musketry is heard in front. Skirmishers must have made contact with enemy pickets. All are alert. A signal gun is fired and the artillery joins in with accumulating fury. At last the command—"Forward!"—and an overpowering urge to make contact with the enemy. Soon lines of blue are discernible. Comrades begin to fall in increasing numbers. Now the shout, lost perhaps in the din of battle—"Charge!"—accompanied by a forward wave of officer's saber and the line leaps forward with the famous "Rebel yell."

This yell itself is an interesting thing. It was heard at First Manassas and was repeated in hundreds of charges throughout the war. It came to be as much a part of a Rebel's fighting equipment as his musket. Once, indeed, more so. Toward the end of an engagement near Richmond in May 1864, General Early rode up to a group of soldiers and said, "Well, men, we must charge them once more and then we'll be through." The response came back, "General, we are all out of ammunition." Early's ready retort was, "Damn it, holler them across." And, according to the narrator, the order was literally executed.[7]

The Confederate yell is hard to describe. An attempt to reproduce it was made a few years ago when Confederate veterans re-enacted battle scenes in Virginia. But this, by the very nature of things, was an inadequate representation. Old voices were too weak and incentive too feeble to create again the true battle cry. As it flourished on the field of combat, the Rebel yell was an unpremeditated, unrestrained and utterly informal "hollering." It had in it a mixture of fright, pent-up nervousness, exultation, hatred and a pinch of pure deviltry. Yelling in attack was not peculiar to Confederates, for Yanks went at Rebels more than once with "furious" shouts on their lips.[8] But the battle cry of Southerners was admittedly different. General "Jube" Early, who well understood the spirit of his soldiers, made a comparison of Federal and Confederate shouting as a sort of aside to his official report of the battle of Fredericksburg. "Lawton's Brigade, without hesitating, at once dashed upon the enemy," he said, "with the cheering peculiar to the Confederate soldier, and which is never mistaken for the studied hurrahs of the Yankees, and drove the column opposed to it down the hill." Though obviously invidious, the general's observation is not wholly inaccurate.[9]

The primary function of the rousing yell was the relief of the shouter. As one Reb observed after a fight in 1864, "I always said if I ever went into a charge, I wouldn't holler! But the very first time I fired off my gun I hollered as loud as I could, and I hollered every breath till we stopped." [10] At first there was no intention of inspiring terror in the enemy, but the practice soon attained such a reputation as a demoralizing agent that men were encouraged by their officers to shout as they assaulted Yankee positions. In the battle of Lovejoy's Station, for instance, Colonel Clark cried out to his Mississippians, "Fire and charge with a yell." [11] Yankees may not have been scared by this Rebel throat-splitting, but they were enough impressed to set down in their official reports that the enemy advanced "yelling like fiends," or other words to the same effect.[12]

Naturally a thing of such informal character as the Rebel yell varied considerably with the time and circumstance. Mississippians had a note quite different from that of Virginians. Rebs attacking Negro troops injected so much hatred into their cry as to modify its tonal qualities. A most interesting variant was that of the trans-Mississippi Indians organized by the Confederacy. Colonel Tandy Walker, commander of the Second Indian Brigade, reporting an action of his troops in Arkansas, said that when the Federals retreated Private Dickson Wallace was the first man to reach their artillery, "and mounting astride one of the guns gave a whoop, which was followed by such a succession of whoops from his comrades as made the woods reverberate for miles around." [13]

But those Rebs who are now charging at the Yankees know that yelling is only a small part of their business. Yankee lines loom larger as the boys in gray surge forward. Now there is a pause for aiming, and the roar of countless muskets, but the individual soldier is hardly conscious of the noise or the kick of his weapon. Rarely does he have time to consider the effectiveness of his shot. He knows that scores of Yankees are falling, and his comrades as well, but he cannot attend to details of slaughter on either side. He drops to his knee, fumblingly bites off and inserts a cartridge, rams it home with a quick thrust of the rod, then rises and dashes forward with his fellows. On they go, these charging Rebs, feeling now that exaltation which comes after the fight gets under way. "There is something grand about it—it is magnificent," said Robert Gill of his experience under fire near Atlanta. "I feel elated as borne along with the tide of battle." [14]

Presently there is an obvious slowing down of the advance, as resistance increases and attacking ranks become thin. Artillery fire comes in such force as to shatter good-sized trees, and men are actually killed by falling limbs.[15] The lines of gray seem literally to bend beneath the weight of canister and grape, and yelling soldiers lean forward while walking as if pushing against the force of a wind.[16] Slaughter becomes so terrible that ditches run with blood.[17] The deafening noise is likened by one Reb to "a large cane brake on fire and a thunder storm with repeated loud thunder claps." The flight of shells (called "lamp posts" and "wash kettles" according to their size and shape) reminds Robert Gill of "frying on a large scale only a little more so"; and Maurice Simons thinks of a partridge flying by, "only we would suppose that the little bird had grown to the size of an Eagle." [18] Some of the men, unable to confront this holocaust, seek the protection of rocks, trees and gullies. Others of stronger nerve close the gaps and push onward.

The overwhelming urge to get quickly to the source of danger brings an end to loading and shooting. With one last spurt the charging troops throw themselves among their adversaries, gouging with bayonets, swinging with clubbed muskets, or even striking with rocks, fence rails and sticks.[19] Presently one side or the other gives way, and the charge is over.

But not the battle. Before the day's fighting is completed there will be several charges, each followed by lulls for reorganization. And perhaps the conflict, as at Gettysburg, will extend to a second and third day, each characterized by repetitions of attack over various portions of the field; or perhaps the main action, as at Fredericksburg, will be defensive, staving off repeated Federal assaults.

Moving to the charge, though by far the most dramatic part of the fighting, actually made up only a small portion of a soldier's experience in battle. There were hours of lying on the ground or of standing in line, perhaps under the heat of a broiling sun, while troops on other parts of the field carried out the tasks assigned them. Then there was endless shifting, to bolster a weak spot here, to cut off an enemy salient there, or to replenish ammunition. These and many other activities, coupled with repeated advances on enemy positions, took a heavy toll of the soldier's strength.

As the day wore on he was increasingly conscious of exhaustion. Though accustomed before the war to long hours of labor on the farm or extended jaunts in pursuit of game, he found fighting the hardest work he had ever done. Fatigue was sharpened by the fact that rest and food had been scarce during the days before the battle. By midafternoon his strength was often so depleted that he could hardly load and fire his gun, if indeed he was able to stand at all.[20] Those who fought at Shiloh may have joined in the postwar criticism of Beauregard for not pushing the battle as Sunday's sun sank in the west, but officers' reports made soon after the fight show that most of the men were so exhausted that further aggression was impossible.[21]

Increasing with the combatant's fatigue came intolerable thirst. Sweating in the grime and dust, he had emptied his canteen early in the day, hoping to refill it from some stream. But rarely was there any such chance. If he were lucky enough to reach a pond he was apt to find it so choked with the dead and wounded as to be unfit for use. But even so, that soldier considered himself lucky who could sweep aside the gory scum and quench his thirst by greedy draughts of the muddy water underneath.[22]

If the battle happened to be in winter, as at Murfreesboro, Fredericksburg, or Nashville, the suffering from thirst was not so intense. But the exposure to cold was hardly less severe. Discomfort was increased by damp weather, scarcity of clothing, and the inability to make fires. At Murfreesboro, for instance, soldiers lay in line of battle for nearly a week under a cold rain without fire.[23]

When the combat extended over several days, as was frequently the case, hunger was added to other discomforts. At Gettysburg Washington Artillerymen became so famished that a captain sent a detail to gather food from the haversacks of Federal dead.[24] Many other hungry soldiers were not so fortunate as to have this opportunity.

The coming of night usually brought a rest from fighting, but not from suffering. The disorganization which characterized Confederate battles often separated the soldier from his regiment.[25] The command of duty, plus a desire to know the lot of his friends, would cause him, tired to the point of prostration though he was, to set out on a tedious search for his fellows. When he found the scattered remnants of his company he would probably discover that some messmate, committed to his care by mutual pledge before the battle, was missing. Then he must make a round of the battlefield and the emergency hospitals, inquiring patiently, calling out the name of his friend, and scanning by candlelight the ghastly faces of dead and wounded. The quest might end in happy discovery, but more likely it would prove futile. At last the weary soldier would fall down on the ground. And in spite of the piteous cries of the wounded he would sink at once into heavy slumber.

The morrow of a battle, whether its duration was for one or several days, was in some respects more trying than the conflict itself. Scenes encountered in the burial of the dead were strange and appalling: there a dead Yankee lying on his back "with a biscuit in his hand and with one mouthful bitten off and that mouthful still between his teeth";

here "the top of a man's Skull Hanging by the Hair to a Limb some
8 or 9 feet from the ground"; yonder another "man Siting behind a
large oak tree his head . . . shot off"; to the right a small, whining dog
curled up in the arms of a dead Yankee, refusing to be coaxed from its
erstwhile master; to the left a lifeless Reb sprawled across the body of
a well-dressed Federal, the gray-clad's hand in the Northerner's pocket—
a gruesome warning to those who are tempted to plunder during battle;
farther on, the field is strewn with nude figures blackened and mutilated by a fire that swept across the dry foliage in the wake of the
fight.[26] One of the burying party working in Federal-traversed territory
is shocked to find that before his arrival "the hogs got a holt of some of
the Yankey dead." [27] In any direction one chances to gaze lie heaps of
disfigured bodies; to a rural-bred Georgian the scene following Fredericksburg suggested "an immense hog pen and them all killed." [28]

After a prolonged summer encounter the task was unusually repulsive. Wrote a soldier who helped in the burial of the Gettysburg dead:

"The sights and smells that assailed us were simply indescribable—
corpses swollen to twice their original size, some of them actually burst
asunder with the pressure of foul gases and vapors. . . . The odors
were nauseating and so deadly that in a short time we all sickened and
were lying with our mouths close to the ground, most of us vomiting
profusely." [29]

While some were burying the dead, others were walking about
picking up spoils. Trinkets of all sorts, such as Yankee letters, diaries,
photographs, and pocket knives are much in demand as souvenirs to be
sent home to relatives. "I am going to send you a trophie that come off
the battle field at Gettysburg," wrote a Reb to his sister. "I got three
pictures out of a dead Yankees knapsack and I am going to send you
one. . . . The pictures are wraped up in a letter from the person whose
image they are. . . . She signed her name A. D. Spears and she lived
in Main somewhere, but I could not make out where she lived." [30]
Occasionally Rebs laughed over the sentimental contents of such letters. Some soldiers profited financially from their plundering of battle-
fields. Following the Franklin engagement of December 1864 George
Athey wrote:

"I got agood knapsack fuol of tricks whitch I sold $4.5 dolars worth
out of it and cepe as mutch as I wanted." [31]

Articles essential to personal comfort were eagerly gathered up. After the Seven Days' Battles a Reb wrote exultantly:

"We have had a glorious victory with its rich Booty A many one of our boys now have a pair of Briches a nice Rubber cloth & a pair of Blankets also a pair or more of Small Tent Cloths." [32]

The avidity with which an impoverished Confederate might pounce upon the riches left in the wake of Federal defeat, as well as the unhappy consequence of overenthusiasm, is evidenced by an entry in a Tennessean's diary following the battle of Seven Pines:

"I awoke quite early yesterday morning, and everything seemed very quiet, I went over the field seeing what I could see. Here were Sutlers' tents, filled with luxuries, oranges, lemons, oysters, pineapples, sardines, in fact, almost everything that I could think of. My first business was to eat just as much as I possibly could, and that was no small amount, for I had been living on hard tack several days. I then picked out a lot of stationery, paper, envelopes, ink, pens and enough to fill one haversack, then I found a lot of puff bosomed linen shirts, and laid in a half dozen together with some white gloves and other little extras enough to fill another haversack. Then I filled another with nuts and candies and still another with cheese. With this load, I wandered around picking up some canteens to carry back to the boys. Then adding to my load such articles as a sword, an overcoat, etc. . . . I quickened my pace and before I had gone twenty steps, the Yankees opened fire . . . and the balls whistled around me in a perfect shower. I had about two hundred yards to go before reaching my regiment, and by the time I reached it, I had thrown away all my plunder." [33]

If the battle ended in defeat, falling back might be so hurried as to leave the dead and wounded in Federal hands. This, added to the increased hardships of retreat and the disappointment of being whipped, caused the soldier's cup to overflow with bitterness.

But whether victorious or not, Johnny Reb began within a remarkably short time to recall and to enjoy the interesting and humorous detail of the combat. Campfire groups must have delighted in teasing Private Joseph Adams about losing his pants when a shell exploded near him at Murfreesboro; and there was doubtless plenty of laughter when M. D. Martin told how a shell cut off his two well-stocked haversacks and scattered hardtack so promiscuously that "several of the boys were struck by the biscuits, and more than one thought he was wounded." [34]

James Mabley could always get a good laugh with his story of the Reb at Chancellorsville who while in the act of drawing a bead on a Yank was distracted by a wild turkey lighting in a tree before him; the Federal was immediately forgotten, and in an instant the crack of this Reb's gun brought the turkey to the ground.[35]

The men of Gilmor's Battalion never tired of asking their colonel after a valley engagement of 1864 "if spades are trumps"; for during this fight a ball went all the way through an unopened deck of cards that he was carrying in his inside coat pocket, stopping only at the last card, the ace of spades.[36]

Almost everyone could tell of a "close shave" when a bullet hit a knapsack, perforated a hat, or spent itself by passing through a bush immediately in front, to fall harmlessly to the ground in plain view. One soldier marveled at hearing through the din of battle the cry of John Childress as he fell: "I am killed, tell Ma and Pa goodbye for me." [37]

Then someone may have mentioned the tragic case of Jud and Cary Smith, Yale-educated brothers from Mississippi. While in the act of lying down under fire, the younger, Cary, putting his hand under his coat found his inner garments covered with blood; and with only the exclamation "What does this mean?" he died. Jud was so overwhelmed with grief that he spent the entire night muttering affectionate words over his brother's corpse. He passed the next day and night in unconsolable solitude. The third day was that of Malvern Hill, and when the first charge took place Jud kept on going after his comrades fell back under the murderous fire, and he was never seen or heard of again. After the father learned of the fate of his two sons he joined Price's army as a private soldier; when his regiment charged at Iuka, he followed the example set by Jud at Malvern Hill, and he likewise was never heard of again.[38]

But there was not much lingering on tragic notes. It was more pleasant to talk of how Jeb Stuart at Second Manassas beguiled the Yankees into exaggerated ideas of Rebel strength by having his men drag brush along the roads to stir up huge clouds of dust; or of how the Yankee General Banks was duped into abandoning several strong positions during his Red River campaign by such Confederate ruses as sending drummers out to beat calls, lighting superfluous campfires, blowing bugles, and "rolling empty wagons over fence rails"; or of how George Cagle, while lying on a ridge at Chickamauga, kept at work four or five muskets gathered from incapacitated comrades, and as Yankee bullets whistled overhead he simulated the activity of an artillery unit, giving such commands as "attention Cagle's Battery, make ready, load, take aim, fire"; of how Sergeant Nabors scared nervous Yankee prisoners who asked him at Atlanta if he were going to kill them by replying, "That's our calculation; we came out for that purpose." [39]

By no means was all of the fighting in the open field. Warring in trenches—Johnny Reb usually called them "ditches"—made its appearance in the spring of 1862 on the Virginia peninsula where Magruder's army was entrenched for a month. At Vicksburg, where Pemberton's troops were under siege for forty-seven days, soldiers spent most of the time in earthworks along the line, or in caves to the rear. During the Atlanta campaign Rebs of the Army of Tennessee saw considerable trench warfare. But by far the longest stretch of this sort of campaigning was done by Lee's troops, who spent the greater part of the war's last year in the ditches around Petersburg.

Occasionally the routine of trench fighting was broken by an assault of one army or the other, but the time was mostly spent in desultory exchanges of artillery and musket fire. The Federals, being the besiegers and having vastly superior resources, did the larger part of the firing. So unlimited, indeed, were their supplies of ammunition that they could make the countryside reverberate with repeated discharges of their heavy cannon.[40]

The defenders of Vicksburg were subjected to heavier fire than any other trench fighters in the war. Back of them lay the Mississippi, dotted with gunboats, and before them were the troops of Grant and Sherman well equipped with artillery. The besieged were deficient in both guns and ammunition. Hemmed in thus by superior forces and equipment, conscious of their inability to give effective retaliation, living on ever dwindling rations, suffering from a shortage of drinking water, and cut off largely from their friends, they were subjected day after day and night after night to a cannonading that was so severe at times as to make heads ache from the concussion.[41] One of the defenders wrote in his diary at the midpoint of siege:

"The fighting is now carried on quite systematically . . . in the morning there seems to be time allowed for breakfast, when all at once the work of destruction is renewed. There is about an hour at noon & about the same at sunset, taking these three intervals out the work goes on just as regularly as . . . on a well regulated farm & the noise is not unlike the clearing up of new ground when much heavy timber is cut down! Add to that the nailing on of shingles by several men & one has a pretty good idea of the noise. It might be supposed that a score of villages had sprung up all round him & that the inhabitants were vieing with each other to see who could be the most industrious." [42]

The caves dug in the hillside were poor protection against the heavy shells that came screeching through the air with varying notes of terror. If one lifted his head ever so little above the earthworks, the crack of a sharpshooter's rifle, followed instantly by a dull thud, would announce the doom of another Reb. A man who was slightly wounded in the trenches stood in considerable danger of being more seriously injured, if not killed outright, as he traversed the open space between battle line and hospital. Life under such conditions became a torturing ordeal, and the situation was not helped by jesting speculation as to the prospective comforts of Johnson's Island, Camp Chase and Camp Douglas.[43]

In the trenches before Atlanta and Petersburg existence was not so perilous nor so gloomy as at Vicksburg. Common to all, however, was the intolerable heat of the summer sun. Some men sought alleviation by building little brush arbors along the trenches. The sultriness of the ditches became so unbearable at night that some of the men resorted to sleeping on the edge—and when the Federal batteries opened they would simply roll over to safety. But immunity from danger in the Atlanta and Petersburg trenches was only comparative. The killing and wounding of men by Federal sharpshooting and artillery fire were of such common occurrence as hardly to elicit notice save by the company to which the casualty belonged.[44]

The number of killed and wounded would have been much greater but for the skill of the men in side-stepping arched shots. "The mortars are thrown up a great height," wrote an Alabamian from Petersburg, "and fall down in the trenches like throwing a ball over a house—we have become very perfect in dodging them and unless they are thrown too thick I think I can always escape them at least at night." He added that the dugouts which they contrived at intervals along the trenches and which they were wont to call bombproofs were not impervious at all to mortar shells, and that "we always prefer to be out in the ditches— where by using strategy and skill we get out of their way." [45] So confident did the troops become of their ability to escape these lobbed shots of the Yankees that they would keep up a derisive yelling throughout a bombardment.[46]

During periods of truce ladies from Petersburg made several visits to the lines, walking down the ditches in their cumbersome hoop skirts to see how bombproofs were made, climbing upon the parapets to get a look at the Yankees, giggling and oh-ing at the strange sights confronting them. Both Federals and Rebs enjoyed these interludes in crinoline but some of the latter could not refrain from mischievously expressing the wish that the Yanks would throw a few shells over to see if the fair visitors would shake with terror or raise the Rebel yell.[47]

But these tantalizing glimpses of Petersburg belles afforded only brief respite from the terrible filth, the smothering heat of summer and the cold of winter, the rain and mud of all seasons, the restricted movement and the countless other deprivations that made trench warfare the most unpleasant aspect of Confederate soldierhood. Open fighting with all its dangers was immeasurably preferable to such existence as this.

But what of valor and of cowardice on the field of battle? There were numerous manifestations of both, though many more of the former than of the latter. Deeds of Rebel bravery, individual and collective, were of such common occurrence as to be quite beyond all estimation. A few definite instances will serve as examples of the glory that lighted up the fields of Manassas, of Shiloh, of Antietam, of Gettysburg, of Spottsylvania—and of countless others.

At Shiloh Private Samuel Evans refused to go to the rear when a ball passed through both cheeks, "but remained and fought for a considerable length of time, cheering on the men and loading and shooting as fast as he could." An officer who saw his men reduced from twenty-eight to twelve as he led them into the ravaging fire at Seven Pines cried out as he fell pierced through the heart, "Boys, I am killed, but you press on." [48] Private Ike Stone was severely wounded at the beginning of the Murfreesboro fight, but he paused only to bind up his injuries, and when his captain was incapacitated Stone took charge of the company and led it valorously through the battle, this despite a second wound. In the thick of this same fight Sergeant Joe Thompson was overwhelmed with the impulse to take a prisoner; leaping ahead of his comrades he overtook the retreating Federal column, seized a Yank and started to the rear with him; but this man having been shot down in his grasp, Thompson ran back to the still-retreating lines, seized a second Federal and brought him away safely. When Private Mattix's left arm was so seriously injured that he could no longer fire his musket, he went to his commanding officer and said, "Colonel, I am too badly wounded to use my gun but can carry the flag; may I?" Before this three standard-bearers had been shot down in succession, but when the requested permission was given him, Mattix seized the staff, stepped boldly in front of the regiment, and carried the colors throughout the remainder of the contest.[49]

In his official report of Second Manassas Major J. D. Waddell, commanding Toombs' Georgians, said that he "carried into the fight over 100 men who were barefoot, many of whom left bloody foot-prints among the thorns and briars through which they rushed, with Spartan courage and really jubilant impetuosity, upon the serried ranks of the foe." Colonel E. C. Cook of the Thirty-second Tennessee Infantry reported after Chickamauga that one of his men, J. W. Ellis, who had marched for six weeks without shoes, "went thus into battle and kept up with his company at all times till wounded." [50]

At Chickamauga Private Mayfield was wounded in the thigh by a Minié ball and at the same time dazed by a shell. Litter bearers picked him up and were carrying him to the rear when he recovered from the shock and sprang to the ground with the remark, "This will not do for me," and rushed back to continue the fight. In this same engagement Private McCann fought gallantly until his ammunition was exhausted; then he picked up cartridge boxes of the dead and wounded and coolly distributed ammunition among his comrades. When the colonel commended his heroic conduct McCann asked that his bravery be cited in the official report of the battle. Shortly afterward he received a mortal wound and as he was borne dying to the rear, he turned smiling to his colonel and reminded him of the promise of honorable mention.[51]

Of all the brave those who were entrusted with the colors had the most consistent record. Almost every official report of regimental commanders mentions the courageous action of standard-bearers. To keep the flag flying was a matter of inestimable pride, and its loss to the enemy was an incalculable disgrace. Consequently men vied with each other for the honor of holding the cherished emblem aloft in the thickest of the fight.[52] The Federals, knowing the close association of morale and colors, and being easily able to single out standard-bearers because of their conspicuousness, were wont to concentrate an unusually heavy fire upon them. Literally thousands of those who aspired to the honor of carrying and guarding the flags paid for the privilege with their lives.

"In my two color companies," reported Colonel Jenkins of the Palmetto Sharpshooters after Seven Pines, "out of 80 men who entered 40 were killed and wounded, and out of 11 in the color guard, 10 were shot down, and my colors pierced by nine balls passed through four hands without touching the ground." At Antietam the First Texas Infantry lost eight standard-bearers in succession, and at Gettysburg, the Twenty-sixth North Carolina lost fourteen.[53] At Antietam also, the flag of the Tenth Georgia—which regiment lost fifty-seven per cent of its men and officers in this one engagement—received forty-six shots. The standard of Lyle's Regiment was torn to tatters at Corinth, and color-bearer Sloan when last seen by his comrades was "going over the breast works waving a piece over his head and shouting for the Southern Confederacy." [54]

Color Sergeant Rice of the Twenty-eighth Tennessee Infantry, downed by a bullet at Murfreesboro, still clung to the flag, holding it aloft as he crawled on his knees until a second shot brought death and delivered him of his trust. On another part of this bloody field Color Sergeant Cameron advanced too far ahead of his comrades and was captured. He tore the flag from its staff, concealed it on his person, carried it to prison with him, escaped, and brought it back to be unfurled anew above its proud followers.[55]

Murfreesboro likewise afforded the setting for perhaps the most extraordinary of all color-bearer feats. While this contest raged at its greatest fury the opposing lines came very near each other in that portion of the field occupied by the Nineteenth Texas Cavalry (dismounted). A Yankee standard carrier stood immediately to the front of the Texas Color Sergeant, A. Sims, waving his flag and urging the blue column forward. Sergeant Sims, construing this as something of a personal insult, rushed forward, planted his own flag staff firmly on the ground with one hand and made a lunge for that of his exhorting adversary with the other. At the moment of contact, both color-bearers, Yankee and Rebel, "fell in the agonies of death waving their banners above their heads until their last expiring moments." The Texas standard was rescued, but not until one who rushed forward to retrieve it had also been shot down.[56]

Confederate authorities sought to stimulate the men by offering medals and badges to those who were cited by officers. Unable to supply these emblems, Congress passed an act in October 1862 providing for the publication of a Roll of Honor after each battle which should include the names of those who had best displayed their courage and devotion. Such lists were read at dress parades, published in newspapers and filed in the adjutant general's office. As a further inducement commissions were offered to those who should distinguish themselves, and special inscriptions were placed on flags of those regiments that captured artillery or gave other proof of unusual achievement. [57] But the most effective incentive was probably that of personal and family pride. This was strikingly evidenced by the remark of a Georgian to his brother after Franklin: "I am proud to say that there was no one between me and the Yankees when I was wounded." [58]

Cowardice under fire, being a less gratifying subject than heroism, has not received much attention from those who have written or talked of the Confederate Army. Of the various sources of information on this obscure point the most fertile are the official reports of battles by commanders of units ranging from regiments to armies. But the most numerous of these reports—those submitted by regimental commanders—are characterized by a reluctance to admit wholesale cowardice because of possible reflections on the conduct of the commanders themselves. This reluctance sometimes resulted in misrepresentation of the rankest sort, as in the following case: After the attack on Battery Wagner, Morris Island, South Carolina, July 18, 1863, Colonel Charles W. Knight, commanding the Thirty-first North Carolina Regiment, said in closing his report, "It is useless to mention any officer or man, when all were acting coolly and bravely." In the body of his report he mentioned being repulsed, but there is absolutely no suggestion of bad conduct on the part of the regiment. But when Knight's superior, General William B. Taliaferro, reported the battle, he said: "The Thirty-first North Carolina could not be induced to occupy their position, and ingloriously deserted the ramparts. . . . I feel it my duty to mention . . . [their] disgraceful conduct." [59]

In the reports of higher ranking officers, who could admit bad conduct of portions of their commands with more impunity than colonels, and in the wartime letters and diaries of the common soldiers, much testimony on the subject may be found. This evidence shows clearly that Confederate soldiers were by no means immune to panic and cowardice.

At First Manassas a few Rebs fled into the woods when shells began to fly. There was disgraceful conduct at the beginning of McClellan's peninsula campaign, when General D. H. Hill wrote that "several thousand soldiers . . . have fled to Richmond under pretext of sickness. They have even thrown away their arms that their flight might not be impeded." At Seven Pines there were a few regiments that "disgracefully left the battle field with their colors." General W. H. C. Whiting in reporting the battle of Gaines's Mill said: "Men were leaving the field in every direction and in great disorder . . . men were skulking from the front in a shameful manner; the woods on our left and rear were full of troops in safe cover from which they never stirred." At Malvern Hill, General Jubal Early encountered "a large number of men retreating from the battle-field," saw "a very deep ditch filled with skulkers," and found a "wood filled with a large number of men retreating in confusion." [60]

Men ran, skulked and straggled by the hundreds at Shiloh. A Tennessee regiment took fright during an advance, ran back on supporting lines crying, "Retreat! Retreat!" and caused great confusion; but they were rallied and set in motion toward the Federal position; again they were overcome with fear, and this time they rushed back so precipitately that they ran over and trampled in the mud the color-bearer of the regiment behind them. A Texas regiment behaved in the some manner; placed in line of battle it began firing, but before the guns had all been discharged, "it broke and fled disgracefully from the field." An officer who attempted to bring back the fugitives and threatened to report them as "a pack of cowards" was told that "they did not care a damn" what they were called, they would not follow him. When General W. J. Hardee tried to rally another demoralized regiment he was fired on by its members. Some of the straggling for which Shiloh was notorious was due to circumstances that exonerate those involved, but there can be no doubt that a large part of those who found various pretexts for leaving the firing line were playing the coward. Said Colonel O. F. Strahl in his official report: "On Monday morning we . . . had a great number of stragglers attached to us. The stragglers demonstrated very clearly this morning that they had strayed from their own regiments because they did not want to fight. My men fought gallantly until the stragglers ran and left them and began firing from the rear over their heads. They were then compelled to fall to the rear. I rallied them several times and . . . finally left out the stragglers." General Beauregard clinched this evidence in his official report: "Some officers, non-commissioned officers, and men abandoned their colors early in the first day to pillage the captured encampments; others retired shamefully from the field on both days while the thunder of cannon and the roar and rattle of musketry told them that their brothers were being slaughtered by the fresh legions of the enemy." [61]

General Bushrod Johnson reported that at Murfreesboro troops on his right became demoralized and "men of different regiments, brigades, divisions, were scattered all over the fields," and that he was almost run over, so precipitate was their flight. Captain Felix Robertson said that he had never seen troops so completely broken as those demoralized at Murfreesboro. "They seemed actuated only by a desire for safety," he added. "I saw the colors of many regiments pass, and though repeated calls were made for men of the different regiments, no attention was paid to them." [62]

At Chancellorsville and Gettysburg the conduct of the soldiers seems to have been exceptionally good. This may have been due in some part to vigorous efforts of General Lee and of the War Department early in 1863 to tighten up the discipline of the Army of Northern Virginia. The fighting before Vicksburg was marred by shameful conduct in the action of May 16, 1863, of which General Pemberton said: "We lost a large amount of artillery. The army was much demoralized; many regiments behaved badly," and Colonel Edward Goodwin reported of a small number of troops immediately in front of him:

"At this time our friends gave way and came rushing to the rear panic-stricken. . . . I brought my regiment to the charge bayonets, but even this could not check them in their flight. The colors of three regiments passed through. . . . We collared them, begged them, and abused them in vain." [63]

The wholesale panic which seized Confederate troops at Missionary Ridge was as notorious as it was mystifying. A soldier who took part in the battle wrote in his diary, "In a few minutes the whole left gave way and a regular run commenced." After a retreat of several hundred yards, this Reb's battalion rallied momentarily, "but it was in such a confused mass that we made but a feeble resistance, when all broke again in a perfect stampede." His conviction was that the troops acted disgracefully, that they "did not half fight." [64]

General Bragg in his official report of the fight said that "a panic which I had never before witnessed seemed to have seized upon officers and men, and each seemed to be struggling for his personal safety, regardless of his duty or his character." He added that "no satisfactory excuse can possibly be given for the shameful conduct of the troops on our left in allowing their line to be penetrated. The position was one which ought to have been held by a line of skirmishers against any assaulting column, and wherever resistance was made the enemy fled in disorder after suffering heavy loss. Those who reached the ridge did so in a condition of exhaustion from the great physical exertion in climbing, which rendered them powerless, and the slightest effort would have destroyed them." What stronger indictment could there be of any soldiery by its general-in-command! [65]

But the woeful tale is not ended. In connection with Early's campaign of 1864 in the Shenandoah Valley occurred some of the most disgraceful running of Confederate history. After an engagement near Winchester on July 23, General Stephen Ramseur wrote his wife:

"My men behaved shamefully— They ran from the enemy. . . . The entire command stampeded. I tried in vain to rally them & even after the Yankees were checked by a few men I posted behind a stone wall, they continued to run all the way to the breastworks at Winchester—& many of them threw away their guns & ran on to Newtown 6 miles beyond. They acted cowardly and I told them so." [66]

On September 19, 1864, during another hard fight near Winchester, a panic of unprecedented proportions struck the ranks of Early's army. Regiment after regiment broke and fled back toward the town. General Bryan Grimes, appalled by the demoralization and fearful that his brigade would succumb to it, threatened "to blow the brains out of the first man who left ranks," and then moved over to confront the fugitives, waving his sword and giving many a Reb the full weight of its flashing blade.[67] But fleeing regiments, increasing now in number, could not be stopped. They poured into the town, out the valley pike, and some continued their disordered course for miles beyond. "The Ladies of Winchester came into the streets and beged them crying bitterly to make a stand for their sakes if not for their own honor," wrote a captain who witnessed the rout; but "the cowards did not have the shame to make a pretense of halting." [68]

A month later at Cedar Creek, plunder combined with cowardice to inflict upon Early's veterans one of the most shameful defeats of the war. In the morning, by brilliant action, the Confederates pounced upon the Federals and drove them from their camps. As the Southern lines advanced large numbers of soldiers and officers turned aside, against positive orders, and began to ransack the rich stores abandoned by the foe. While the victors were absorbed in pillage, the Federals rallied, and in the afternoon they counterattacked. The disorganized Confederates broke first on the left, and then all along the line. Efforts of division commanders and of others who attempted to stay the tide of panic was to no avail, and the field was utterly abandoned.

"It was the hardest day's work I ever engaged in," Grimes said, "trying to rally the men. Took over flags at different times, begging, commanding, entreating the men to rally—would ride up and down the lines, beseeching them by all they held sacred and dear, to stop and fight, but without any success. I don't mean my Brigade only, but all." [69]

Price's Missouri expedition of 1864 was marked by an instance of large-scale panic. When the Federals attacked the Confederate rear on October 25, near Carthage, Missouri, demoralization set it. As Price rode rapidly to the point of danger he "met the divisions of Major-Generals Fagan and Marmaduke retreating in utter and indescribable confusion, many of them having thrown away their arms. They were deaf to all entreaties or commands, and in vain were all efforts to rally them." [70]

While the Atlanta campaign seems to have been remarkably free of demoralization under fire, there were at least two instances involving a considerable number of men. In a skirmish on June 9, 1864, a Texas cavalry unit that had a distinguished record in battle broke upon slight contact with the Federal cavalry, and fled in a manner described as disorderly and shameful by General Ross. Later, in the Battle of Jonesboro, August 31, 1864, an advancing brigade of Confederates halted without orders when it came to the Federal picket line, the men seeking shelter behind piles of rails. They seemed "possessed of some great horror of charging breastworks," reported Colonel Bushrod Jones, "which no power of persuasion or example could dispel." [71]

The last instance of large-scale panic during the war was at Nashville, December 16, 1864. On this occasion the division of General Bate, when assaulted about four o'clock in the afternoon by the Federals, began to fall back in great confusion and disorder. In a few moments the entire Confederate line was broken, and masses of troops fled down the pike toward Franklin. All efforts to rally the troops proved fruitless. General Bate in his official report leaves the impression that the rout, due to extenuating circumstances, cast little if any reproach upon his men. But General Hood, in chief command, was evidently of contrary opinion, as he says that Confederate loss in killed and wounded was small, implying that withdrawal took place without much resistance. He says further that the break came so suddenly that artillery guns could not be brought away. [72] Captain Thomas J. Key says in his diary that "General Bate's division . . . shamefully broke and fled before the Yankees were within 200 yards of them," and that there "then ensued one of the most disgraceful routs" that it had ever been his misfortune to witness.[73]

There were innumerable cases of individual cowardice under fire. When men are assembled in such large numbers, especially when many of them are forced into service, a certain proportion are inevitably worthless as fighters. Some of those who fled wanted earnestly to act bravely, but they had not the power to endure fire unflinchingly. This type is well exemplified by the Reb who covered his face with his hat during the battle of Fredericksburg, and who later, when told that his turn at the rifle pits was imminent, "made a proposition that he would go out from camp and strip" and let his comrades "get switches and whip him as much as they wanted" if they would obtain his release from the impending proximity to Federal fire.[74] A similar case was encountered by Colonel C. Irvine Walker. A man had been reported for cowardly behavior on the field. Walker called him to task and told him that he would be watched closely during the next engagement. When the time came the colonel went over to check his performance as the regiment advanced. "I found him in his place," reported Walker, "his rifle on his shoulder, and holding up in front of him a frying pan." The man was so scared that he sought this meager protection, yet he moved forward with his company and was killed.[75]

Another case of infamy converted to valor was cited by Colonel William Stiles, of the Sixtieth Georgia Infantry. During a charge this officer saw a robust Reb drop out of line and crouch behind a tree; the colonel slipped up and gave him a resounding whack across the back with the flat of his sword, and shouted, "Up there, you coward!"

The skulker, thinking evidently that he was the mortal victim of a Yankee shot, "clasped his hands, and keeled over backwards, devoutly ejaculating, 'Lord, receive my spirit!'"

After momentary bafflement, Stiles kicked the prostrate soldier violently in the ribs, exclaiming simultaneously, "Get up, sir! The Lord wouldn't receive the spirit of such an infernal coward."

The man sprang up with the joyful exclamation, "Ain't I killed? The Lord be praised," grabbed his musket, rejoined his comrades, and henceforth conducted himself with courage.[76]

Other officers had less success. Men who had no shoes were often excused from fighting, and a good many soldiers took advantage of this rule by throwing away their shoes on the eve of conflict. Others left the field under pretext of helping the wounded to the rear, and this in spite of strict orders against removal of casualties by anyone except those specifically detailed for the purpose. Still others feigned sickness or injury. A favorite ruse was to leave one's own regiment during the confusion of battle, and then to evade duty by a pretense of endless and futile searching for the outfit intentionally abandoned.[77]

Infuriated officers would curse these shirkers, beat them with swords and even threaten them with shooting, and on occasion carry out their threats on the spot. Commanders would place file-closers in the rear with instructions to arrest, and in some instances to shoot down, those who refused to do their duty.[78] Courts-martial sentenced great numbers to hard and disgraceful punishments. Private soldiers covered spineless comrades with scorn and ridicule.[79] But these measures were only partially effective.

There can be no doubt that the trying conditions under which Confederate soldiers fought contributed to the bad performance of some on the field of battle. Men often went into combat hungry and remained long under fire with little or nothing to eat. Sometimes, as at Antietam and Gettysburg, they fought after exhausting marches. Many of those who participated in the routs at Chattanooga and at Nashville were without shoes. Often the Confederate artillery protection was inadequate. The superior number of the Federals made Rebel flanks unduly vulnerable, and flank sensitiveness was the cause of more than one panic. Casualties among line officers were unusually heavy, and replacement with capable men was increasingly difficult after 1863.

When all of these factors are considered, it is rather remarkable that defection under fire was not more frequent than it actually was. Those soldiers who played the coward, even granting that the offenders totaled well up in the thousands, were a very small proportion of the Confederate Army. Taken on the whole of his record under fire, the Confederate private was a soldier of such mettle as to claim a high place among the world's fighting men. It may be doubted that anyone else deserves to outrank him.

CHAPTER VI

BAD BEEF AND CORN BREAD

"Next to the Yankeys Comes Rations which most interest a Soldier," wrote Private Jerome Yates from Virginia in January 1864.[1] He erred only in the emphasis. His statement should have been, "Next to rations comes the Yankees," for food was undoubtedly the first concern of Johnny Reb.

During the early part of the war, Confederate authorities optimistically appropriated as their standard for Southern soldiers the official ration prescribed for armies of the United States.[2] And for a while the volunteers in some camps fared bountifully.

"We have better meat hear than you have in St. James," wrote Fred Taber to his sister in September 1861; "we have Ice Water & Coffee three times a day." [3] Several months later a Louisianian stationed in Kentucky boasted of loaf bread from a "Confederate bakery," and "fresh beef all the time"; he concluded with the most obvious satisfaction that he was "in clover." [4]

But this abundance was short-lived, except in camps that were close to food-producing areas. As early as July 1861 many of the troops began to feel the pinch of diminishing rations. A week after First Manassas Beauregard wrote Davis not to send any more men to the Virginia front as "Some regiments are nearly starving." [5] In August Joseph E. Johnston was asking for more bacon, and several weeks later Commissary General Northrop was bemoaning a shortage of sugar.[6] In mid-September one of Johnston's soldiers (who was generally notable for his patience) revealed a continued shortage of food by jotting in his diary on one day that he "flanked" his dinner, on another that he whittled for his supper, and on a third that he had "a Scrummy breakfast." [7] There was apparently an improvement in the quantity of rations before Virginia troops went into winter quarters, but an investigating committee of Congress reported an inadequate supply of vegetables, milk, and molasses in January 1862.[8]

Soldiers of Albert Sidney Johnston's army wintering near Columbus, Kentucky, fared even worse than their Virginia comrades. Lard was issued occasionally as a substitute for bacon; beef was so tough that a Louisiana colonel threatened to requisition a lot of files to prepare the teeth of his men for mastication; and so many shanks and necks were included in the issue that this officer begged the meat contractor "for God's sake not to start throwing in the hoofs and horns." Livestock attached to the camps were said to be so famished that they were chewing away at wagon beds, bridle reins, halters and stumps; one mule was even charged with attempting to devour a horse's tail.[9]

In the spring of 1862 Confederate authorities were forced by dwindling stores to declare a general reduction of the ration authorized at the war's beginning.[10] Generals Lee and Beauregard ordered parts of this ration to be increased, but both were called to task by the War Department; and instead of an increase, there were further curtailments.[11] In January 1863 Commissary General Northrop decreed a reduction of the meat issue, and on the eve of the Chancellorsville campaign Lee informed Seddon that for some time his army had been subsisting on a daily ration of eighteen ounces of flour, four ounces of bacon, and occasional supplies of rice, sugar or molasses.[12] Troops in the West fared somewhat better, but in the autumn of 1863 Northrop ordered a diminution of the bacon issue to one-third of a pound.[13] The year 1864 brought a further decrease of the flour or meal ration to one pound.[14]

Specifications made up in Richmond indicate little except general trends—for there was generally a wide discrepancy between the rations authorized and the issues received by soldiers in the field. Four months before Lee's surrender Northrop admitted that "for over two years he had found it impossible to provide the ration set up by army regulations, and that the issue had been gradually declining." [15] For a real picture of the deprivations experienced, it is necessary to turn to the reports of generals in the field and the immediate testimony of common soldiers.

These indicate that hunger was greater and more frequent during periods of active campaigning than in times of comparative quiet. The first large-scale suffering seems to have occurred in connection with the Fort Donelson incident, where, according to General Buckner, men received no regular issue of rations for several days, and the situation was made worse by the want of cooking facilities.[16]

But the destitution at Donelson was neither so great nor so prolonged as that experienced in the spring campaign in Virginia. Deep mud and poor organization combined to cut off large bodies of Rebs falling back before McClellan. For several weeks rations were scant, being restricted largely to flour and salt meat. The rear guard of this action, composed mainly of D. H. Hill's division, subsisted for three days on dry corn, issued in the shuck and shelled and parched by the men.

"I came nearer starving than I ever did before," wrote one soldier after the long march from Yorktown to Richmond; and another testified:

"I have never conceived of such trials as we have passed through. We were for days together without a morsel of food, excepting occasionally a meal of parched corn. . . . The army was kept on the march day & night and the roads were in some places waist deep in mud. . . . Many of the men became exhausted and some were actually stuck in the mud & had to be pulled out. . . . The men on the march ran through the gardens . . . devouring every particle of vegetables like the army worm leaving nothing at all standing. Whenever a cow or hog were found it was shot down & soon despatched." [17]

During the Seven Days' fighting, as in many other actions where the enemy was forced to retreat, Rebs were able to alleviate their hunger somewhat from Yankee spoils. Even so, many claimed they could get only hard crackers and fat meat, but under the circumstances this seemed as good as chicken pie at any other time.[18]

The Shiloh campaign, especially the falling back after the fight, was accompanied by considerable hardship, but suffering was not nearly so great as that experienced later in 1862 when Bragg moved into Kentucky and when Lee ventured into Maryland. In each of the latter cases, rapid movement, particularly in retreat, made it difficult to maintain a flow of supplies to men on the march. Cooking was so hindered as to be almost impossible. Had it not been for the cornfields and orchards dotting the country traversed by Lee, the suffering of his men would have been much greater.

The day after the awful carnage of Antietam, a Reb wrote to his wife:

"We have got some verry good apples all through this country. . . . I have had plenty of them sense we left Richmond infact we have lived some days on raw baked and rosted apples some times on green corn and some times nothing." [19]

Four days later another participant noted in his diary:

"Our army is . . . almost starved out. Our rations has been Beef and flour since we left Richmond [August 22] and not more than half enough of that many times we had Green Corn and apples issued to us and were glad to get that." [20]

And after the army got back to Culpepper, Virginia, a Tar Heel remarked to his parents: "People says that a man borned of woman and enlisted in Jacksons army is of a few days and short rations and i think it is nearly the same way with Longstreets." [21]

During Bragg's withdrawal from Kentucky an artilleryman wrote:

"Our company drew a young yearling today the first beef we have had for many weeks. We ate it raw, without salt or bread." [22]

The colonel of a South Carolina regiment sharing in this retreat recalled later that he "frequently saw the hungry Confederate gather up the dirt and corn where a horse had been fed, so that when he reached his bivouac he could wash out the dirt and gather the few grains of corn to satisfy in part at least the cravings of hunger. Hard, dry, parched corn . . . was for many days the sole diet for all." [23]

The scantiness of food at Perryville and Antietam was repeated to a large extent in connection with the Chancellorsville-Gettysburg campaign, and the Bragg-Longstreet operations in Tennessee of the fall and winter following. But the nadir of Rebel deprivation was probably reached by soldiers under siege at Vicksburg and Port Hudson. At the beginning of the forty-seven-day period of encompassment Pemberton's army was subsisting on one-third of the meat ration and two-thirds of the meal issue prescribed at Richmond. Field peas were ground and mixed with meal, and later in the siege soldiers were introduced to a copper-colored, elastic sort of concoction made entirely of pulverized peas but optimistically referred to by subsistence officers as bread. Ground rice was also used as a substitute for meal. Eventually, though not until the last days of siege, bread of all sorts was dropped from the ration. Wheat flour was largely reserved for the sick, though after the near-exhaustion of meal, about the middle of June, four-ounce portions were distributed to all for a while. To supplement the dwindling ration half-grown peaches, unripe blackberries, cane roots, tree buds, and even grass and weeds were simmered in a little water and used for food. By June 28 troops were receiving only "one small biscuit and one or two mouthfuls of bacon per day." [24]

Then came mule meat! It is possible that some of the hungry men had previously partaken of the flesh of dogs, of horses and of mules, but if so they had acted on their own responsibility. It was not until July 3 that the butchering of mules was officially ordered. The following is a copy of the historic document issued to brigade commissaries by Pemberton's chief of subsistence:

OFFICE, CHF OF SUBS
Vicksburg, July 3, 1863

MAJOR:

The issue of meat tomorrow will be one half (½) pound of mule to the ration. Please report to me at once the amt you require for your Command so that I may have it prepared

Respectfully
GEO. S. GILLESPIE
Maj. & C. S. [25]

Major Simons, commissary officer of Moore's Brigade, indicated that his requirement was 5,106 pounds, and this amount was issued to him on July 4. Apparently on this, the day of capitulation, and possibly in some portions of the army on the night before, soldiers at Vicksburg ate the first and only bona-fide mule issued to them by Confederate subsistence officers. Rations were drawn on July 5 from Grant's commissariat, and with what zest and envy did famished Rebs attack the abundance of Yankee larders! The five-day portion issued by the Federal officers "appeared to be as much as we have for some time drawn for a month supply," observed Major Simons.[26]

How did the mule meat taste? Soldiers who tried it said it wasn't bad. "The flesh," according to one, "seemed of coarser grain, but more tender than that of the ox, and had a decidedly 'horsey' flavor." Yet he deemed it "sweet" under the circumstances. Another said that it was tolerable, but he did not relish it like the beef pie that he was accustomed to eat.[27] Major Simons must have thought it passable as he ate it for two meals on the day of surrender. His only remark was "a new way to celebrate the fourth of July or rather a new dish!" [28]

The Confederate garrison at Port Hudson, several miles below Vicksburg, did not surrender until July 9. The deprivation experienced there seems to have been greater than that suffered at Vicksburg. One of the besieged stated in his diary that he and his comrades ate "all the beef—all the mules—all the Dogs—and all the Rats" that could be obtained prior to the capitulation.[29]

Soldiers taking part in the Georgia campaigns of 1864 fared better than usual from the standpoint of meat, bread, and rice. The same cannot be said of sugar, as is shown by the entry of March 4 in a Louisianian's diary:

"Drew twelve gobers pease [goober peas, i. e., peanuts] . . . today as ra[t]ions in lieu of four days rations of sugar." [30]

Here, as elsewhere, there was a chronic deficiency of vegetables. Irish potatoes and dry peas were issued now and then, but never in ample quantities. Greens and other fresh vegetables were dispensed on rare occasions by subsistence officers, but as one Reb observed, "when they have to be divided among so many they amount to little." [31] Scurvy and emaciation naturally followed. "Our old Ration of Corn Bread and meat . . . has very nearly worn [me] out," wrote one of Johnston's veterans to his wife in August; he added that his weight had fallen during the summer from 162 to 137 pounds.[32]

In the Shenandoah Valley movements of 1864, General Early's men also were subjected to great deprivation as a result of their rapid shifts of position and the previous ravaging of the country which they traversed. General Bryan Grimes testified that on one march his command had not a particle of bread for forty-eight hours, and very little meat; and that occasionally when General Rodes or Early passed the line, the cry was "bread, bread, bread." [33] A lieutenant wrote that some troops had to eat bacon raw and without bread, and that combined effects of heat, dust, exhaustion and hunger caused a few men to drop dead in the ranks.[34]

Soldiers of the trans-Mississippi Department were, with few exceptions, better fed than those east of the river. From 1862 on there were complaints of the poor quality of beef issued, but rarely of the quantity of meat and meal. Until the latter part of 1862 supplies of these two staples were generally ample.[35]

Late in 1864 great suffering accompanied General Hood's disastrous movement into Tennessee. During the October march from Palmetto, Georgia, to Tuscumbia, Alabama, a private remarked that he and his associates subsisted for three days on parched corn; and Colonel Ellison Capers of the Twenty-fourth South Carolina Infantry reported that in late November his command proceeded northward through rain and mud for two days sustained only by an issue of three biscuits a day to each man.[36]

The final campaigns in the East were marked by the most acute suffering for food. In January 1865 the temporary breakdown of the Piedmont Railroad forced Lee to make a personal appeal to the people of Virginia to supply food for his army. In February he wrote Seddon that his command had been without meat for three days.[87]

The retreat to Appomattox in April, with its failure of supply trains and general demoralization, brought still greater misery. Concerning the period of final operations, a soldier wrote:

"Two days fasting, marching, and fighting was not uncommon; . . . no rations were issued to Cutshaw's battalion of artillery for one entire week, and the men subsisted on the corn intended for the battery horses, raw bacon captured from the enemy, and the water of springs, creeks, and rivers." [38]

And an erstwhile member of Jackson's staff stated, "Once I took some corn from my horse, beat it between stones and tried to swallow it." He, like comrades reduced to similar straits, doubtless found that "chewing the corn was hard work" and that it "made the jaws ache and the gums so sore as to cause almost unendurable pain." [39]

The continually dwindling ration of soldiers from early months of the war till the closing campaigns of 1865 was all the more tragic in view of the fruitfulness of Confederate fields. Rebel armies were in no sense famished because of failure of food production. By voluntary action, by public pressure and by state legislation cotton acreage was sharply curtailed during the war, and much of the land thus diverted was given to the growth of cereals, peas, potatoes and other foodstuffs. Everywhere in the South, except in sections drained by invading or occupying armies and infertile areas peopled largely by less privileged whites, Negro workers grew bountiful crops in every year of the war. Production, with the possible exception of meat, was always more than ample for both civilians and soldiers. The failure, then, was not one of production but of distribution.[40]

Several factors contributed to poor distribution. There was doubtless some corruption on the part of lesser commissary officials, but this was of far less importance than inefficiency.[41] The subsistence department was the worst administered of all Confederate bureaus. L. B. Northrop, the head of this division, was a veritable "sour-puss" who, by his obstinate devotion to red tape, antagonized every general in the field, and who apparently took greater satisfaction in consistency than in delivering food to the army.[42]

A RABBIT IN A CONFEDERATE CAMP

Rabbits were stalked in wood or meadow and killed with rocks and clubs, or hemmed in and caught by hand. Drawing by W. L. Sheppard, one of Lee's soldiers, from *Battles and Leaders of the Civil War.*

GROUP OF CONFEDERATE PRISONERS

(No date, no place)

Another cause of scarcity in the midst of plenty, particularly of meat, was the dearth of salt and of other preservatives. This unhappy condition caused the loss or waste of untold quantities of precious provisions.

But far and away the most serious difficulty was the inadequacy of transportation facilities. The Confederacy's railroad system was never equal to war needs, and after 1862 it began to deteriorate rapidly from inability to replace worn-out rails and rolling stock. From 1863 till the war's end, while armies were struggling along on half-rations, immense quantities of foodstuffs assembled by commissary agents and collectors of the government's tax-in-kind simply rotted at the depots.[43]

Another explanation of deficiency is found in Confederate finance. Commissary officers complained repeatedly of lack of funds. And they had difficulty procuring supplies with the money that was available, because the constant depreciation of Rebel currency made producers hold their crops as long as possible in order to take advantage of ever soaring prices. Then, after resort to impressment of supplies, farmers were reluctant to take provisions to market, lest they be pounced upon en route by ubiquitous government agents.

A further hindrance was the shortage of sacks, kegs, boxes, cans and barrels for the packing of fruits, vegetables, sugar and meat.

Finally, the cutting in two of the Confederacy by Yankee operations along the Mississippi in 1863 did incalculable damage by reducing to a mere trickle the flow of meat, sugar, molasses and other essentials produced west of the river.

Because the government could not deliver to him the abundance produced by his homefolk, Johnny Reb fought the Yankees for four years on rations composed mainly of cornbread and beef. There were, to be sure, admixtures now and then of field peas—which humble plant General Lee was said to have called the Confederacy's best friend —of flour, pork, potatoes, rice, molasses, coffee, sugar and fresh vegetables, though it was for the last that the soldiers always suffered most. But meal and meat were the staple fare. A Texas Reb summed up the food situation with fair accuracy for all when he said of his own experience: "Well Lizer, I will let you know what I livon . . . beef & bread bread an beef upper crust under crust an crum Som Sugar & molasses when that is said all is said." [44]

Since cornbread was the most constant item in the diet, Rebs naturally became exceedingly tired of it—especially since the meal was generally coarse and unsifted. A Mississippian wrote his sister in 1863,

"I want Pa to be certain and buy wheat enough to do us plentifully—for if the war closes and I get to come home I never intend to chew any more cornbread." A Louisianian was even more pointed: "If any person offers me cornbread after this war comes to a close," he observed just before Lee's surrender, "I shall *probably* tell him to—go to hell!" [45]

Unfortunately for Johnny Reb, his rations were poor in quality as well as short in quantity. Flour bread was called everything from "leather" to "ginned cotton." But it was upon beef that the heaviest denunciation fell. In more generous moments, a Reb would refer to his meat simply as "mule." But under provocation he could rise to heights of derogatory eloquence.

"Take it as it comes hare skin and dust and it is so rank that it can hardly be eat," was the appraisal of a Georgian whose language was undoubtedly restrained by ministerial inclinations.[46] "[Our] poor Buck and Grind Stone bread would kill the Devil," mused a Texan.[47] "The beef is so poor it is Sticky and Blue," commented another Reb; "if a quarter was thrown against the wall it would stick." [48] An Alabamian declared that the cows which supplied the meat for his outfit were so emaciated that "it takes two hands to hold up one beef to shoot it." [49] And a Mississippian expressed the conviction that "buzzards would not eat it at any season of the year." [50] With full allowance for the exaggeration of wrath, this beef must have been pretty bad.

Sometimes dissatisfaction with rations went beyond mere grumbling. When a group of Texans received an issue of spoiled beef from their regimental commissary, they took it to brigade headquarters and presented it to the major of subsistence with their compliments; in two instances troops refused to draw their meat ration because of its poor quality.[51] After being deprived of beef for a few days, some Rebs camping near Fredericksburg made a night raid upon the commissary for what they termed a "special requisition," and another meat-hungry outfit of even greater temerity visited the stock pen attached to the headquarters of General Rodes and made off with the milch cow reserved for that officer and his wife.[52]

Several companies of Louisiana troops were provoked to open mutiny by what they construed as a "huge swindle" to deprive them of supplies. According to the report of an observer of this affair, "The sutlers' establishments were the first reached, and were speedily gutted, while the butcher and quartermaster saved themselves by running off." [53]

That more frequent and serious mutinies were not incited by the food situation is a tribute to the adaptability and forbearance of the Confederate soldier.

Johnny Reb's hunger was often forestalled by his own efforts and devices. During the first two years of war food was frequently sent from home. With transportation getting worse this practice declined after the summer of 1863, but even in 1864 the railroads continued to deliver such a quantity of home packages to the army as to reflect on the judgment of shipping officials, who should have given precedence to more vitally needed military stores.

In some cases express companies offered free transportation to provisions for soldiers. An Alabamian serving in Lee's army wrote from Petersburg, October 25, 1864:

"Sister 1 want you to send me a box of proveshens . . . some potatoes and meat and butter and some honey if yo have got it if yo have not got the honey send me some surrup send me some pepper too yo nead not to fear to express them for the ex agence [express agency] . . . has takend mo[r]e responseibility on they sellf they have in shord [insured] all frate that belongs to soldiers in the armmy or boxes to go threw saft they will ship them first if they dont ship eney thing els." [54]

An immense amount of food from home was carried by personal agents, with or without railroad assistance, depending on distance and other factors. In this multitude of neighborhood-army commuters, were troops on furlough, domestic servants, relatives and friends. Soldier relief societies furnished considerable assistance in storing and delivering commodities. Letters written during the war indicate that boxes of foodstuff went from homefolk in Alabama to Tennessee in 1862 and 1863, to Georgia during the Atlanta campaign, and to Virginia during the last year of the war; from western Virginia to Georgia in 1864, and to Johnston's army in North Carolina in March 1865; and from Texas to Arkansas from 1862 to the war's end. Transmission over shorter distances was frequent throughout the conflict.

Foods in greatest demand were vegetables and sweets, and these seem to have constituted the great bulk of packages sent from home. But there was often an inclusion of delicacies not obtainable from other sources. Fried chicken was received with surprising frequency by troops serving around Richmond early in the war, and in one instance 300 live fowls were shipped from Mecklenburg County, Virginia, to soldiers stationed at Jamestown.[55]

Private John Crittenden proposed to send his brother a lot of ammunition in exchange for a mess of squirrels. He also asked his wife to send along a bottle of tomato catsup and a jar of green-pepper pickles.[56]

Private T. B. Hampton was immensely pleased with the "little notions" sent by his wife, including apple butter, sausages, and chestnuts. "The Butter and Honey was also devoured," he said, "with as much ferocity as a wolf would devour a sheep." He requested that on the next occasion she add "more of the buck wheat Bread," or send "a small bunch of flower." [57] But the simpler request of Private George W. Athey for "alofe of lite bread and abig potatoe" was doubtless more typical of the majority of Rebs.[58]

A considerable proportion of the packages sent by rail was lost in transit, and many articles delivered by both express companies and private individuals were in bad shape when they arrived. In acknowledging receipt of supplies soldiers mentioned shattered jars, broken eggs, rancid butter and "strong" meat, and sometimes when a box of provisions escaped all hazards to reach camp in good condition it was spoiled by lying on the shelf until a period of active campaigning was finished.[59]

But after all is said about provisions from home, the fact remains that these items supplemented government issues only to a slight extent. A more productive expedient was the purchase of supplies in camp or its environs from peddlers and producers.

Sutlers made their appearance early in the war. A Mississippian wintering at Manassas observed in December 1861 that "the sutlers kept a great many luxuries which we could buy at reasonable prices." [60] This statement does not correspond with the reputation generally held by camp vendors. A newspaperman attached to Joseph E. Johnston's command said, in 1861, that sutlers made profits of several hundred per cent on their transactions.[61] Excessive charges for ginger cakes, half-moon pies, dried fruit and other stock items was a source of chronic irritation to officers, and sometimes soldiers became so infuriated that they ran the Shylocks out of camp—minus their provisions.[62] But despite their increasing unpopularity, sutlers continued to flock about Rebel camps at payday, and to take a lion's share of wages, until late in the war when paymasters virtually ceased to function.[63]

The most reasonable source from which troops might purchase foodstuffs, and the one patronized most frequently, was the producer himself. Sometimes farmers came to camp with their provisions, and on other occasions soldiers sought out the countrymen. If Rebs had no money, they might trade in kind from their army rations; for instance, some men on picket duty in Tennessee exchanged three pounds of sugar for two gallons of buttermilk.[64] The character of the purchase was determined largely by the soldier's financial state on the one hand and the producer's stock on the other.

To prevent exorbitant charges, General Bragg resorted to the expedient, in 1863, of permitting Rebs to take without payment the produce of citizens who placed excessive prices on items brought to camp.[65] In another instance he forbade soldiers buying anything from civilians near Chattanooga because of the suspicion that Union sympathizers had poisoned the pie offered for sale.[66] In portions of the country long occupied by troops, exhaustion of supplies often made impossible any purchase from civilian sources.

The most successful subsister on the citizenry encountered by this writer was a private in Bragg's army named L. G. Hutton. On the Kentucky campaign of 1862, he bought along the way almost every conceivable item of food, including milk, butter, chickens, eggs, flour, molasses, cider, whortleberries, strawberries, peaches, apples, watermelons, meat and lightbread. Repeatedly he used the excuse of flux or colic, frequently vouched for by surgeon's certificate, either to go ahead of the columns or to lag behind. His alleged ailments also enabled him to unload his accouterments on the wagon or upon some sympathizing and perhaps conniving friend. Utilizing fully the advantage of his comparative freedom, and in utter disregard of the alleged frailty of his digestive system, he surfeited himself on the abundance of Kentucky and Tennessee flocks, fields and orchards. Often he dined at the tables of farm people for a fee of twenty-five or fifty cents, or for nothing. On one occasion, at least, he took some flour to a citizen's house and had it baked into bread. He was apparently unhampered by lack of funds.[67]

But few soldiers were as well equipped financially as Hutton. And where money was lacking other means must be found for supplementing government rations. Troops stationed along streams frequently procured fish by setting out hooks, by seining, and by "grabbling." [68] Rabbits, squirrels, possums and other small game were run down, stalked, or shot. Birds of various sorts were trapped or knocked from their roosts at night with sticks. An Alabamian boasted of a sparrow pie prepared by his mess in 1863.[69]

Soldiers in seacoast areas found variety in oysters and crabs, and a group of Georgians serving in Florida treated themselves to the meat of an alligator. "He tasted a good deal like catfish," according to one who sat in on the feast.[70] Even greater relish was professed by a Texan who helped consume a roasted armadillo. "I . . . found it to be very fine," he wrote his sister, "far superior to any possum meat I ever eat." He added that he and his friends had eaten a number of these little animals, which they referred to as "iron clad possum." [71]

The getting of food by any means other than purchase was known as "foraging." Included under this polite designation were activities as various as the gathering of nuts, berries and pawpaws, the plucking of fruit and vegetables from abandoned orchards and gardens, the solicitation of milk, eggs and other edibles at farmhouse doors—accompanied sometimes by woeful recitations of the sickness of comrades—and clandestine forays on stock pens and chicken roosts. Whether of the innocent or the blamable sort, foraging was a widely used and effective means of replenishing scant larders.

Of all possible ways of getting extra food capture from the Yankees was the most satisfying. During the battle of Shiloh avid rustics from Rebel ranks were wont to lag behind on captured camp sites, spread out blankets marked with Federal symbols, load them with spoils and strike out southward. In the wake of Seven Pines famished gray-clad troops had a field day among the delicacies left by the retreating Yankees. Even richer returns were enjoyed by soldiers who raided Federal depots at the command of Jackson and Stuart. At Gettysburg and elsewhere, the kits of slain enemies were rifled for hardtack and bacon. Men operating with Forrest had to learn to grab a bite on the run when they were riding in hostile country. A youngster participating in a thrust toward Nashville in the fall of 1864 wrote:

"We were now permitted to get something to eat. I ran into a store, got hold of a tin wash pan, drew it full of molasses, got a box of 'good Yankee' crackers, sat down on the ground in a vacant lot, dipped the crackers into the molasses, and ate the best fasting meal I ever had. I had [had] only two crackers since Wednesday and this was Saturday." [72]

Of all the goods obtained from Federals none was more appreciated than coffee. This became scarce in the early months of the war, and at the beginning of 1862 it disappeared from government issues to parts of the army. When notice came in January 1862 to the Washington Light Infantry that coffee rations would have to be suspended, German members of that organization arranged a pageant deemed appropriate for the observance of such a calamity. At night they filed into camp in a torchlight procession, "1st an illumination on one side a coffee pot pierced with an arrow, words 'no more grounds for complaint'. Other side—coffee mill—words 'the last grind'. Pall bearers followed, then priest—companies bearing lights. They marched through the camp, halted; a sort of funeral ceremony was performed, preaching, and singing, in German, and bonfire made and the last grounds burnt." [73]

In July 1862 a Texan suffering from chronic headache bemoaned: "How much I miss the good coffee I used to get at home. I would cheerfully pay one dollar for as much like it as I could drink. . . . We got some ground coffee from the Yanks in the Seven Days fight," he added, but since then, the only way to get it was "to pay two dollars and a half a pound." [74]

Like the folk at home, Johnny Reb concocted all sorts of substitutes for the precious coffee. An amber fluid was optimistically brewed from parched peanuts, potatoes, peas, dried apples, corn, or rye. "Tea" was made of corn bran, ginger and herbs of various sorts. Sassafras tea was drunk in large quantities by privates and generals alike.

Once foodstuff was procured, the problem of cooking had to be considered. And this, in view of the circumstances of army life, was no easy matter. Some of the more fortunate Rebs had Negro cooks, but for the most part, food consumed by privates was prepared by the soldiers themselves. Early in the war military authorities attempted to establish bakeries for each brigade, where bread enough for everybody would be cooked under the supervision of details trained for the purpose. This policy could not be carried out on a large scale, however, because of the difficulties of active campaigning. During periods of siege, as at Vicksburg and Petersburg, cooking was done en masse, and the food carried to men in the trenches. But the general practice was preparation of rations by individuals or small groups.

The most immediate worry of the soldier cook was a shortage of utensils. Rarely did an outfit have anything like enough kettles, pans and skillets. Typical was the plight of a regiment whose colonel complained to his superiors in the fall of 1863:

"I have not a single vessel to cook one morsel of bread my cooking has to be done as we can beg the citizens to do it. . . . For God and the country's sake, make your fair-promising but never-complying quartermaster send me skillets, ovens, pots or anything that will bake bread or fry meat. . . . Send me skillets 225 in number. I cannot fight any more until I get something to cook in." [75]

But Rebs elsewhere, if not in this case, were becoming hardened to a scarcity of utensils. "The boys have made frying pans out of plates and picked up vessels until they ask Bragg no odds," wrote a soldier whose regiment had been deprived of its original equipment by the active campaigning of Chickamauga.[76]

To make up for such deficiencies, the troops contrived various expedients. Skillets, plates and corn graters were made from halves of captured canteens. Hollow stumps and wood pestles were used to convert corn into grits for dodger pones.[77]

The practice of broiling beef over the fire on sharpened sticks was so universally followed as to become standard. Bacon was often cooked the same way, though the necessity of conserving grease for shortening made the use of skillets preferable.

Bread was mixed and kneaded in turtle shells and pumpkin rinds, on oil cloth, shirt-tails, boards, stumps, chips of wood, or any other surface that was available. One Negro cook when given a barrel of flour to prepare under duress knocked off the head, poured in river water and other ingredients as needed, and thus converted the entire contents into dough with rare dispatch.[78] A prevalent mode of cooking flour bread was by wrapping the dough about a ramrod and turning it over the fire until brown. Both cornbread and wheat bread were cooked on a board or some other flat surface, placed in a slanting position near the fire; or the batter might be wrapped in a shuck and buried in hot ashes.

Corn on the cob was likewise roasted in the original husk. Potatoes, sweet and Irish, were baked in their jackets beneath heaps of glowing embers. Given time and a lucky forage, Johnny Reb might indulge in a treat of barbecued lamb, pig, turkey, or beef quarter, prepared with critical finesse over a pit of lazy coals. But empty stomachs and over-active salivary glands protested against such a slow process.

Shortage of utensils and ingredients combined to produce some astonishing dishes. The most frequently mentioned was a concoction known as cush—dubbed "slosh" by one of its less admiring partakers. This dish was born of the greater convenience of cooking small portions of meat together instead of separately; but let a soldier give the recipe: "We take some bacon & fry the grease out, then we cut some cold beef in small pieces & put it in the grease, then pour in water and stew it like hash. Then we crumble corn bread or biscuit in it [some soldiers made mush or paste of flour or meal and added one or both of these at this point instead of crumbs] and stew it again till all the water is out then we have . . . real Confederate cush." He added that he and his comrades on Missionary Ridge considered the preparation to be quite a luxury.[79]

Another combination dish was made of Irish potatoes and green apples, boiled together, mashed, and seasoned with salt, pepper, onions, or garlic.

A third mixture grew out of an emergency retreat from Nashville in late 1864: Soldiers having flour, side meat, Irish potatoes and a stew pot, but nothing in which to bake bread, "boiled some meat and potatoes together until about done, when some one suggested that we have what they called at his home 'drap dumplins,' which was to make batter for flap jacks, and while potatoes and meat were boiling to drop in a spoonful of batter at a time, and we eventually stirred the whole together, ate supper that night, and next morning for breakfast in cutting it out of the camp kettle, we got meat, bread, and potatoes all in the same slice." [80]

During the early days of the war Johnny Reb was a notoriously bad cook. Newspapers attributed a considerable portion of the prevalent sickness to improper preparation of food by volunteers. An investigating committee of Congress reported in January 1862 that while rations were sound and wholesome, "the cooking particularly the bread, rendered it unsuitable for either sick or healthy men." [81]

But with experience the preparation improved, and in late 1862 a Reb was boasting to his wife that "I will be able to learn you something in the art of cooking by the time I get home." [82] Not only did soldiers become adept at preparing staple items of diet, but some also developed proficiency at concocting such specialties as huckleberry pie, plum preserves, molasses custard, grape pie, yeast rolls, roast turkey, and baked 'possum "chained with potatoes."

Taking the good with the bad, Confederate fare could hardly have been relished except by men whose appetites were unduly sharpened by hunger and whose digestive systems were hardened from abuse. And bread made of flour mixed with muddy water, without soda and lard, or army crackers soaked to softness and then fried in bacon grease, or stew made from beef so poor that ribs would come apart when the hide was removed, "strong" from age, and deficient in salt— these must have tried even the war-inured stomachs of Rebs.[83]

Scarcity of tableware came to be universal after a year or two of fighting. For example, a member of an officers' mess in Johnston's army wrote from Georgia in February 1864:

"We have no utensils to eat with. We have but one knife, i.e. case knife, in our mess and no plate nor fork nor spoon." [84]

Sticks, splinters and pocketknives had to suffice for eating implements. And in numberless cases, Rebs sopped molasses from tin cups, or even from hats, and transferred greasy bacon or "cush" from skillet to mouth with no better means than their scrawny fingers. A slab of solid fat pork laid on a piece of hardtack "was passable or luscious as the time was long or short since the last meal." [85]

During the early months of the war a degree of order was maintained in some camps in the serving of meals, and in one formality was carried to an extreme. This was at Camp Beauregard in Louisiana where, according to testimony of a volunteer, "we are marched to our meals in company, stand behind our respective chairs until the command is given 'take seats,' after which a certain time is allowed for eating, when we are commanded to 'rise' and are marched back in regular convict style. We are not allowed to speak to the waiter at all but must ask the orderly who sits at the head of the table for whatever we want." [86] Such punctiliousness was exceptional even at the time, and after the spring of 1862 it must have been without parallel save in a few military academies.

The general rule was for Rebs to prepare and consume their food in messes of from four to eight men, with each taking his turn at cooking, cleaning the skillet belonging to the group or borrowed from another, going after rations, and performing other duties incident to the preparation and serving of food. Messes were usually composed of men who were drawn together by ties of kinship or congeniality. As would be expected, such groups were beset occasionally with drones who shirked duties, avoided contribution of their proportionate share to the mess fund, and consumed more than their share of the food. And woe to that soldier who was not present in full force when the meal was attacked! A Georgian who took time out to read a letter brought to him at lunchtime wrote later to his wife:

"Yours of the 29th was received to day Jest as I commenst eating dinner we had chicken pie made out of bacon and of corse I could not eat enny more untel I read your letter and by the time I got through it was all eat up so I lost my dinnor." [87]

Informality was the prevailing vogue. Uncertainty of food issues led to the practice for a time in Lee's army of the commissary blowing a horn or beating a pan when supplies sufficient to merit distribution came to hand.[88] Food was eaten, not according to a set schedule, but rather when availability, appetite and other circumstances dictated.

"Som times I Git a nuff and Som times I don't," wrote an Alabamian in 1863 from Bragg's army. "We dont have no Regeler way out here of Eatting we Eat just when we git Hungerey." [89]

Occasionally the Yankees would interfere with culinary activities. In one instance during the Atlanta campaign Federal artillery opened on a group of Rebs as they were cooking their noon meal. One of the number was sent to a point of observation to call the shots so that the cooks could lie down after each salvo until the shells passed over.[90]

More than one meal was interrupted by the sounding of the long roll, and hungry men, snatching up hot remnants, fell into line cursing Yankees for their lack of consideration.

When he first went to war Johnny Reb was wont to grumble much about the many bad features of his fare: scantiness, poor quality, lack of variety and slovenly preparation. Toward the end he complained little of anything save quantity. His years of deprivation brought him to the point of view expressed by a Mississippian in the last year of conflict. "If I ever get home to live in peace," he said, "I am going to have plenty to eat that is good and nice." He added that he and his comrades swore that in future cotton would give way to food crops. "I think carriages horses &c nice house & going in style an[d] all [are] good things," he concluded, "but having plenty of good things to eat . . . is . . . worth all the rest." [91] And a Texan sorely tried by the failure of Bragg's commissariat during the Chattanooga campaign said that if he ever got back to his father's house he intended "to take a hundred biscuit and two large hams call it three days rations, then go down on Goat Island and eat it all at ONE MEAL." [92]

CHAPTER VII

FROM FINERY TO TATTERS

THE Confederate private envisioned by Richmond authorities in 1861 was a nattily dressed person.

His coat was a long double-breasted tunic of cadet gray, fronted with two rows of buttons and trimmed at the edges and at collar and cuffs with colors designating the branch of service—infantry in blue, cavalry yellow and artillery red; the collar was the stand-up type, very much like that worn by soldiers of recent times. For fatigue purposes a double-breasted light-gray blouse with turn-down collar might be worn instead of the tunic.

Trousers were of sky blue, cut loose in the leg and of sufficient length to spread well over the shoe.

Overcoats, or "great coats" as they were sometimes called, were of gray flannel, double-breasted and fitted with capes; for the infantry, capes were short, extending only to the elbows, while those of the cavalry extended the full length of the arm.

The headpiece was a cap modeled after the style of the French kepi; the crown was of cloth, colored to designate the branch of the wearer's service. Havelocks, of white duck for summer and of oil cloth for winter, were prescribed.

The cravat was of black leather. Boots were of the Jefferson type. Shirts, socks, and drawers completed the official regalia, but no requirements were published as to the color or material of these lowly items.[1]

These specifications were published in *Army Regulations* year after year without change, and when the *Official Records of the Union and Confederate Armies* were compiled long after the war ended, a section was included which set forth in rich color the uniforms thus prescribed.[2]

But there was considerable difference between the clothing designated and that actually worn by the soldiers. This discrepancy came first from the inability of the Confederate Government to provide uniforms for the men who were called to arms. Captains who wrote in

108

to Montgomery to inquire about equipment for companies in process of organization were informed that "the volunteers shall furnish their own clothes." [3] The reason was obvious: Jeff Davis and company had none in stock, nor were any to be forthcoming until contracts with Southern manufacturers should bear fruit, or purchasing operations in Europe could be completed; and this was to require a long time.

In the meantime volunteer companies did the best they could. Some received issues of clothing from state authorities, though these were faced with problems of supply very much like those of the central government.

A procedure widely followed during the early months of the war was for captains to take funds appropriated by local authorities or donated by philanthropists—who sometimes were the captains themselves—or contributed by the recruits, to purchase cloth from whatever source it might be obtained, and to have the uniforms made up by local tailors or seamstresses. In many cases the volunteers arranged individually for the fabrication of their outfits.

Women of the South responded nobly to the difficulties by organizing sewing clubs and knitting societies. As a general rule the aid rendered by the volunteer seamstresses was both timely and valuable, though there were numerous instances where coats, pants and socks turned out by the ladies indicated considerably more zeal than skill. [4]

The inevitable result of these devious sources and methods of supply was a miscellany that made mockery of the Richmond regulations. This is not to imply that the regalia worn by early volunteers were of poor quality. On the contrary many of the companies were resplendently clothed. Captain Alexander Duncan of the Georgia Hussars, a regiment hailing from Savannah, boasted that $25,000 was spent for that organization's initial outfit. [5]

In not a few instances, regiments went into Confederate service garbed in the flashy suits which they had worn for parade purposes as militia organizations. The Orleans Guard Battalion of New Orleans arrived at Shiloh while the battle was in progress, and went into the thick of the fight wearing blue dress uniforms. Fellow Rebels mistook the newcomers for Yankees and began to shoot at them. When the Guards realized the cause of their plight, they hastily turned their coats inside out so as to present a whitish color instead of blue; and thus they went through the battle. [6]

But blue was just one of many colors worn by soldiers of '61 and '62. The Emerald Guards of Mobile went to Virginia attired in dark green, a color adopted in honor of old Ireland, the land from which most of the members came.[7] Captain Patterson's company of East Tennesseans dressed themselves in suits of yellow to give meaning to their previously adopted designation of "Yellow Jackets." [8] The Granville Rifles of North Carolina sported uniforms featuring black pants and flaming red flannel shirts that must have made easy targets for Yankees considerably removed.[9] Some of the Maryland companies who espoused the cause of the Confederacy were clothed in uniforms of blue and orange.

But most resplendently attired of all were the Louisiana Zouaves, whose trousers were of scarlet cloth, cut in such fashion as to suggest the term "bloomers" to derisive comrades, belted at the waist with large blue sashes and bound at the ankles with gaiters of white; jackets were heavily adorned with varicolored lace; shirts were of blue, cut low to reveal sunburnt throats and hirsute chests; headpieces consisted of fezzes, perched at angles indicating the jauntiness of the wearers.[10]

These flashy regalia contrasted markedly with other types observed in the streets of Richmond in the summer of 1861. Here might be seen a rugged Texan mounted on a high-pommel saddle, attired in homespun gray, peering disinterestedly from beneath the expansive brim of a western hat; there a native of the southern Appalachian area, ambling along in bearskin blouse, nondescript trousers and rawhide leggings. Occasionally one might encounter "the dirty gray and tarnished silver of the muddy-complexioned Carolinian; the dingy butternut of the lank, muscular Georgian, with its green trimming and full skirts; and the Alabamians from the coast nearly all in blue of a cleaner hue and neater cut." [11]

As the war went into the second and third years clothing became simpler and less diverse. Contributing to this change was the increasing ability of the quartermaster general to meet requisitions made upon the government for uniforms. By the end of 1862 Caleb Huse's purchasing operations had yielded substantial returns in trousers and cloth for coats. Contracts with domestic manufacturers were also beginning, after heartbreaking delays, to achieve a partial degree of fulfillment. In recognition of these developments Congress, on October 8, 1862, passed an act which modified the prior policy of allowing cash payments of fifty dollars a year to soldiers who clothed themselves, and announced the intention of the government to provide the uniform prescribed by regulations. The following schedule of allowances, based

SOUTHERN WOMEN MAKING CLOTHES FOR THE SOLDIERS

From a wartime etching by Dr. A. J. Volck of Baltimore, Maryland. Volck made more than a score of etchings of Northern and Southern subjects in 1861-1863. He was eventually captured by Federals and imprisoned at Fort McHenry. Only a few copies of his etchings were ever run off. The plates were then sent to England where they were injured beyond use.

SOLDIER IN HOMESPUN SHIRT

William Decatur Howell in the homespun shirt his mother made him to go to war in. He was a Mississippian and served as private in Forrest's Cavalry.

upon that used in the United States Army prior to the war, was published for the guidance of captains and quartermasters:

	1st year	2nd year	3rd year	Price
Caps, complete	2	1	1	2.00
Cover	1	1	1	.38
Jackets	2	1	1	12.00
Trousers	3	2	2	9.00
Shirts	3	3	3	3.00
Drawers	3	2	2	3.00
Shoes	4	4	4	6.00
Socks	4	4	4	1.00
Leather stock	1			.25
Great coat	1			25.00
Stable frock (mounted men)	1	1	1	2.00
Fatigue overalls (engineers, ordnance) ..	1		1	3.00
Blanket	1			7.50 [12]

Company officers were required to keep a record of clothing dispensed—two general issues a year were contemplated, one of winter uniforms in the fall, and the other of summer outfits in the spring—and soldiers who did not draw the full amount allowed were to be credited on the pay roll with the value of articles due them; on the other hand, those who overdrew their allowances were to be charged in like manner with items received in excess of the quantity authorized.[13]

Nothwithstanding the intention expressed by the act of October 8, 1862, the clothing issued by government quartermasters deviated considerably from *Army Regulations*. Blue trousers, for instance, seem to have been the rare exception rather than the rule. Certainly the impression derived from soldier correspondence is that gray was the standard color for trousers as well as coats, and this impression is corroborated by wartime uniforms on display in various Confederate museums. But the cadet gray of 1861 and 1862 gradually gave way, as the blockade drove the South to an increasing dependence on her own resources, to a yellowish brown resulting from the use of dye made of copperas and walnut hulls. This peculiar tint was dubbed butternut, and so wide was its use for uniforms that Confederate soldiers were rather generally referred to by both Yanks and Southerners as "butternuts." [14]

In a few instances at least, undyed outfits were issued by the government. The Second Texas Regiment was the recipient of such an issue a few days before leaving Corinth for Shiloh. When the men beheld the whitish-looking garments exclamations of the most unorthodox character went up on every hand such as "Well, I'll be damn'!" "Don't them things beat hell?" "Do the generals expect us to be killed and want us to wear our shrouds?" After the battle a Federal prisoner was said to have inquired: "Who were them hell cats that went into battle dressed in their graveclothes?" [15]

Boots soon proved ill adapted to hard marching and were replaced by more practicable and serviceable brogans. Short-waisted, single-breasted jackets took the place of coats so pervasively as to fasten irrevocably on Rebs the name "gray jackets."

Caps and havelocks prescribed by regulations may have been issued in considerable numbers, but hats were the prevailing vogue. Soft hats were preferred not only because they were more comfortable, but also because they gave greater protection from sun and rain; and at night they made "capital pillows." [16] Shapes varied from high-crowned "bee-gums" to low-topped bowlers, but the medium-brimmed slouch was by far the most popular. Not infrequently a Reb of modish bent pinned up the brim on one side of his hat and stuck in a feather.

The "Tiger Rifles" of New Orleans yielded even more to the decorative urge. Every man of the company in 1861 painted a picture or a motto on the band of his hat. Typical slogans were: "Lincoln's Life or a Tiger's Death," "Tiger by Nature," "Tiger during the War," "Tiger on the Leap," "Tiger—Try Me," "Tiger in Search of a Black Republican," "Tiger Bound for the Happy Land," and "Tiger in Search of Abe." [17]

It is doubtful if cravats were dispensed in any considerable numbers. Certainly they were not popular among seasoned soldiers. The attitude toward such nonessentials as ties is typified by a statement made by an Alabamian in a letter to his brother. "I . . . receive . . . the bundle you sent me," he wrote, and "can put everything to advantage except the cravat—If I was to put it on the Boys would laugh at me." [18]

Rebs who drew clothes from the government complained frequently of misfits. Trousers and sleeves were too long or too short, and coats were cut on too skimpy a scale. "We all look like a set of school boys," wrote a Louisianian after an issue of clothes early in the war. [19] Sometimes the ill-fitting garments were sent home to be remodeled by wives or mothers. In other instances, soldiers traded about among their fellows until passable sizes were procured. [20]

The intention implied by the Confederate Government in the law of October 8, 1862, of supplying the major portion of clothing for the army was destined to fall far short of fulfillment. The tightening of the blockade and the shortage of specie prevented the importation after 1863 of large quantities from Europe. The failure of importation was offset to a considerable extent by increased production of Southern factories. But the output of many of these establishments was gobbled up by state authorities, who insisted on outfitting their own soldiers and collecting commutation from the central government.

This would have been well enough if the supplies procured by each of the states beyond the needs of her own troops had been made available to Richmond authorities. But overzealous governors like Vance of North Carolina insisted on holding on to huge surpluses against the possible future needs of their own regiments while less fortunate Rebs suffered from deficiencies. North Carolina had forty textile factories in 1864, half as many as all the other Confederate states combined. She claimed the output of these almost exclusively for her own soldiers, despite the fact that she drew large quantities of wool and other raw materials from sister states.[21]

The most damning commentary on the disastrousness of such a shortsighted—though withal "constitutional" and well-meaning—policy is the fact that while Lee complained repeatedly of the raggedness and barefootedness of his men in the war's last winter, Vance hoarded in North Carolina warehouses "92,000 uniforms, great stores of leather and blankets, and his troops in the field were all comfortably clad." [22] This was State's Rights carried to its most costly extreme.

The combined—or perhaps it would be more accurate to say competing—efforts of Confederate and state authorities were unable to keep the majority of Confederate soldiers supplied with adequate and comfortable clothing. To meet deficiencies various expedients were invoked by Rebs themselves. One of these was to call on the folks at home. Letters to wives and parents, particularly those written during the winter months, were full of requests for garments of various sorts and for blankets.

In response to these importunities wives, mothers, and sweethearts, in co-operation sometimes with groups of slaves, brought forth spinning wheels and looms from outhouse and attic and set up home factories that rivaled the production of the more elaborate establishments of town and city. Jackets, trousers, hats, shirts, drawers, socks and other articles made by individual women and by soldiers' aid societies were packed in boxes and sent to camp on trains, or carried in small bundles by body servants or comrades on furlough.

Many soldiers preferred homemade clothing to that issued by the government, both for comfort and for durability. An Alabamian, who received garments from his wife regularly, wrote in the spring of 1864:

"Bettie I send you a couple of shirts and a pair of drawers. Use them as you please. I had rather wear your make. The reason I drew them was that they are so much cheaper than you can make them. You can use them in making clothes for the children." [23]

Soldiers who were short of clothing frequently borrowed the needed articles from messmates or kinsmen. A striking instance of fraternal assistance is revealed by the letter of a Texan to his sister in 1863.

"Me Joe and Grace all got together yesterday for the first time. Grace was the gladest fellow to see us that ever came a long he . . . is all most naked his Breeches is in strings all he has got fit to ware is a over shirt Joe gave him a par of drass [drawers] & shirt I gave him a par of breeches all I have except what I have on." [24]

When a Reb received fancy additions to his wardrobe from home-folk he was apt to be besieged for loans by socially minded fellows. A Mississippian wrote his mother in the spring of 1864:

"My Hat and boots are the admiration of all the Boys they all want them two of the Boys went out Courting the next day after I got here. I had to loan one my Hat and the other my overshirt." [25]

If a soldier had a little money to spare, he sometimes replenished his wardrobe by purchasing sundry items from comrades who were more amply supplied than himself. Now and then penny-wise Rebs capitalized on the near-nakedness of fellow soldiers by peddling among them at a profit clothing received from homefolk. A Virginian who had just returned from furlough with surplus apparel wrote to his wife:

"I sold my pants, vest, shoes, & drawers for sixtyone dollars so you see I am flush again. . . . You will have to make me more pants and drawers, if you can raise the material make two pair of pants & four pair of drawers & I will have A pair of pants & two pair of drawers for sale in that way will get mine clear . . . if you could make up a good supply of pants vests shirts and drawers, I could be detailed out to come after them."

A postscript was added cautioning her not to "tell any one what good pairs pants will bring in camp if they knew it they would go to peddling in clothes keep dark whether you make any for sale or not." [26] In some portions of the army the practice was followed of selling at auction the clothing of men who died in camp.[27]

A considerable portion of the Rebel clothing deficiency was supplied by the Federals. The cavalry branch of the service, because of its ability to make swift raids into Yankeedom, profited most in this respect. A Mississippian who was not inclined to exaggeration wrote his mother just after Christmas in 1862 that he had recently seen about six thousand cavalrymen pass his post and "every man had a complete Yankee Suit consisting of hats coats pants Jackets and boots." [28]

Infantrymen frequently did well by themselves in the wake of a battle. The writer's great-uncle told of a comrade who lost an arm on the night of the battle of Raymond, Mississippi, attempting to appropriate the uniform of one whom he thought to be a dead Yankee. The practice of reshoeing at the expense ot dead and live Yankees was so common that the remark became trite among troops, "All a Yankee is worth is his shoes." [29]

Following the battle of Shiloh a newspaper correspondent wrote from Corinth that "other results of our victory are also everywhere visible. Unless he knew better, a stranger would mistake our army for first rate Yankees. Fully three-fifths of the men are dressed in Federal hats and overcoats." [30]

The practice of wearing Union uniforms was apt to be disastrous if persisted in during a period of active campaigning. General orders were issued repeatedly enjoining the custom, but seemingly to no greater avail than to have a portion of the forbidden articles laid aside. In many companies the combination of butternut jacket and Yankee pants came to be so prevalent as to be considered in an unofficial way as the standard uniform.[31]

The following general order issued by Forrest in December 1864 indicates one method which was used to make practicable the wearing of captured clothing:

"All men & officers belonging to this command who have blue yankee overcoats & clothing and who do not have them dyed by the 20th Inst *The Coats Especially* will be taken from them. . . . Division Commanders will order an inspection on the date above specified and see that this order is complied with. And in an instance when the Inspectors find the coats have not been dyed, they will be taken from the owners and turned over to the Qr M of The Division." [32]

But despite all the exertions of Confederate and state authorities, of soldiers and their families, and the enforced contributions of the Yankees, frazzled uniforms were much in evidence in Rebel ranks after the first half-year of conflict, and as a general rule raggedness increased as the war progressed. Rare indeed was that veteran who did not have occasion in 1863 and 1864 to inform his homefolk of embarrassing circumstances as to the seat of his britches.

"The 16th section of my uniform pants wore out," wrote one Reb to his wife, and another confided to his sister that he had been compelled to buy a new pair of trousers "as I had a 'flag of truce' hanging from a prominent part of my old 'uns." [33] But it remained for a Texan to sum up the situation in general. "In this army," he wrote from near Atlanta in June 1864, "one hole in the seat of the breeches indicates a captain, two holes a lieutenant, and the seat of the pants all out indicates that the individual is a private." [34]

A great many of the soldiers carried little sewing kits—called housewives—with which to keep their uniforms in repair. The results of rehabilitory measures were as amusing as they were varied.

"John Wilson and myself has been patching the seat of our britches this morning," wrote S. G. Pryor to his wife in the summer of 1861. "John puckered his patch bad but I got mine on finely as good as a heap of women would do that has a house full of children. . . . I can beat anybody that I've seen attempt it yet in camp." [35] "We are getting so we can do anything," boasted a Mississippian of Bragg's army. "Dr. Tankersly had a pair of Drawers that were too small and I had a pair that were too large. So we cut a piece out of mine and spliced his. So we have got a pair of Drawers better for both." [36]

Practice in patching undoubtedly led to improved technique among Rebel seamsters, and some attained such deftness with scissors and needle as to abandon the more prosaic modes of repair for fancy designs. One morning Ben Lambert appeared at roll call displaying on the seat of his britches a large red flannel patch, shaped after the fashion of a heart. This example unloosed a plethora of aesthetic efforts among Lambert's comrades of the Richmond Howitzers, and soon trousers that had a short time before been showing white in the rear were splashed with figures of eagles, horses, cows and cannon. One artist depicted on one hip Cupid holding his bow, and just across on the other, in tribute to the Love God's dead-eye marksmanship, was a heart pierced with an arrow—all done in flaming red cloth.[37] Johnnies would have their fun, at the expense of their woes.

But there were many soldiers who either spurned the use of the needle or else felt unequal to its manipulation. Such men frequently invoked the assistance of women living in the environs of camp or sent tattered garments home for repair. In innumerable instances, however, Rebs took no remedial steps whatever, but simply wore their rags with the splendid indifference of seasoned campaigners.

To this spirit of indifference, indeed, must be attributed much of the raggedness which Confederates suffered. The beginning of almost every march was the occasion of a general discarding of surplus items of clothing, for veteran soldiers made a fetish of traveling light.

The observation of a Georgia captain in early 1863 was widely applicable. "The Company begins to look as ragged as ours ever did," he wrote; "the cause of it is that they have to toat their extra clothing and rather than toat it they wont have it." [38]

The tendency to get rid of extra garments was accentuated during the pressure of battle and of retreat. A Reb who during the withdrawal from the North Carolina coastal area in 1862 had lost everything but the sparse uniform he was wearing wrote significantly to his mother:

"The fight we had the other day has taught me one thing, and that is never to carry anything more with me than I absolutely need and can carry on my back in case of necessity. It will not do to try to play soldier and gentleman at the same time. . . . You must take it rough." [39]

Doubtless it was this philosophy that caused many Rebs to forego without complaint some of the garments ordinarily deemed indispensable by civilized peoples. "I would like to have a pr socks," wrote a Mississippian to his mother in 1862, but "I can dispense with draw[er]s." [40]

A factor contributing markedly to the unhappy state of soldier wardrobes was the infrequency of launderings. Negro body servants and government-paid washerwomen may have been fairly ample for the laundry needs of the army in the early months of the war, but after 1862 most of the common soldiers had to do their own washing.[41] The situation was further complicated by a widespread scarcity of soap, dating from early in the war. In the summer of 1862 a Reb wrote disgustedly to his mother:

"Soap seems to have given out entirely in the Confederacy & consequently it is almost impossible to have any clean clothes. I am with out drawers today both pair of mine being so dirty that I cant stand them." [42]

Cold water, no soap, and dirty clothes was a combination-complaint found in many soldier letters.

But possession of all the facilities for washing would have availed little during periods of active campaigning when men had to spend the daylight hours of week after week marching and fighting. If perchance there was a short respite, the need to rest was usually so strong as to make filth preferable to further exertion. If a Reb did muster the energy to seek out a creek and wash his clothes, he was frequently compelled by lack of a change to loll about unclothed until the laundered articles were dry enough to put on.

When these circumstances are considered, along with the fact that there were always some who were deterred from washings by sheer indolence, it is not surprising frequently to find in wartime correspondence instances of Rebs going for two, three and four weeks without once removing their shirts, trousers or underclothing. And there were cases of considerably longer duration. A Georgian wrote his wife in 1864 that some of his comrades had gone for two months without stripping, and a Texan testified early in 1865 that "something ner half of the command has not changed shirts for 4 or 5 months." [43] An inevitable consequence of practices such as these was a premature rotting of clothing that could ill be spared.

Deficiencies in clothing varied, of course, from time to time and from organization to organization. North Carolina troops seem generally, as a result of the jealous exertions of their governor, to have fared better than those from other portions of the country. Border-state troops probably suffered most of all, on account of inability of their home governments to supplement Confederate issues. An example of the extreme condition to which these orphan regiments might be reduced was the appearance at inspection on a cold November day in 1864 of a group of Missourians dressed in their drawers.[44]

Some articles of clothing were less scarce than others. Of socks, shirts and underclothing the central government seems to have had a fairly ample supply even in the winter of 1864-1865; want of these items must have been largely due, therefore, to failure of transportation or to delinquency of low-ranking quartermasters.[45] Overcoats and blankets were generally hard to get after the first year of war. Of the conflict's last winter a soldier stationed near Petersburg wrote: "I do not remember the issue of a single overcoat, and but a few blankets." [46] An Englishman who visited Lee's army during the Gettysburg campaign observed that many of the soldiers had blankets made of carpet strips, and that these gaily hued coverlets were adapted to use as overcoats in cool or damp weather by the cutting of holes in the middle, through which the men stuck their heads.[47]

When blankets of no sort could be obtained troops frequently resorted to the expedient of shifting the campfire just before bivouacking and lying down on the earth that had thus been warmed.[48] By occasionally adding rails to smoldering coals during the night, and by "scrooching" up close to his messmates, a Reb might fare tolerably well in dry weather. But rain rendered any degree of comfort impossible. The soldier's only recourse then was to huddle up to a tree and cat-nap as best he could between shivers and showers. "Cussing" the Yankees generally accompanied his sufferings, and his thoughts frequently must have been along the lines expressed by Private Bill Cody: "If we do strike them Yankees again," he wrote during a cool spell of late 1864, "they will get wone of the worst whippings they ever had for the most of the boys are mighty anxious to get a lick at them for some blankets." [49]

But the most pervasive and the most keenly felt of all deficiencies was that of shoes. The Rebel army was a walking army. Soldiers who followed Lee, Jackson, Bragg and other Confederate generals on their long and swift thrusts at the enemy won undying fame for themselves and their leaders. But the expenditure of leather entailed by these arduous marches was tremendous and, as circumstances proved, considerably beyond the producing and purchasing capacities of the South.

Shortage of shoes began to trouble generals and government officials before the war was a year old. Not long after First Manassas Joseph E. Johnston informed Quartermaster-General A. C. Myers that his army needed shoes. Myers replied that "we have sent to Europe for shoes, and I have officers travelling over all the Confederate States purchasing shoes, making contracts with farmers for leather, and with manufacturers for making leather into shoes." He expressed apprehension, however, that he would not be able to meet the demands of increasing mobilization.[50] His fears proved to be well founded. Several thousand pairs of the European purchase arrived in due time on Confederate shores. Contracts with Southern factories yielded considerably more. But the approach of cool weather in 1862 found troops in decidedly greater need of shoes than they had been the previous year.

Shortly before Lee began his march into Maryland a newspaper correspondent estimated that forty thousand pairs of shoes were needed by the army.[51] This estimate may have been exaggerated, but there can be no doubt that thousands of Rebs failed to participate in the fighting of September 16-17 because the condition of their feet made it impossible for them to march with their comrades.[52] It may easily have been true that the difference between a victory and a draw for Lee at Antietam was his want of a few thousand pairs of shoes.[53]

In October and early November, 1862, about ten thousand pairs of shoes were issued to the Army of Northern Virginia, but there still remained in Longstreet's Corps a shortage of over six thousand. A South Carolinian stationed at Culpepper wrote his mother on November 20, 1862:

"I thought that I had experienced a rough time of it last winter but that is nothing in comparison to what we have had to endure lately. There are men in my company who have been barefooted the last month, having to march all the way from Winchester to Culpepper (sixty miles) in that situation—cold and frosty mornings at that." [54]

Congress took cognizance of the deplorable state of affairs by authorizing the detail of two thousand men to make shoes.[55] Extraordinary efforts such as this, plus the reduced wear incident to winter quarters, resulted in a general improvement of the situation in the early months of 1863. But the strenuous campaigns of Gettysburg and Chattanooga played havoc with the government's leather supply, and the winter months of 1863-1864 brought a chorus of complaints from all quarters. An Alabamian wrote to his homefolk from camp on the Rapidan:

"The weather is as cold as the world's charity. I counted out on inspection yesterday, thirty-one men in Battle's Brigade who did not have a sign of a shoe on their feet, yet they are compelled to perform as much duty as those who are well-shod." [56]

A Louisianian serving in the Army of Tennessee noted in his diary of January 3, 1864, that about one-half of the men in his company had refused to do duty on account of being barefooted.[57] In some portions of Lee's army, men gathered up hides from commissary butcheries, traded them for leather, and made their own shoes; and the products of their handwork were said to be considerably better than those obtained from government contractors.[58]

In the Army of Tennessee men tried making moccasins from the raw hides, but results were not satisfactory. One Reb said of his experiment, "I made myself a pair & made a nice Job too they fit Splendid But behold after two or three days drying around the fire they were about two inches too Short behind." [59] Another soldier complained that his rawhide sandals "stretch out at the heel . . . the[y] whip me nearly to death they flop up and down they stink very bad and i have to keep a bush in my hand to keep the flies off of them." [60]

During the early months of 1864 good factory-made shoes were at such a premium that a lieutenant of Johnston's army declared, "It is not safe to pull off shoes & go to sleep or one would wake up minus a pair." [61]

The nadir of deprivation of shoes, and of other clothes as well, seems to have been reached by men who accompanied Hood on the Tennessee campaign during the war's last winter. Many of the troops began the northward movement in November with shoes so worthless that, according to a Reb who went along, they would not endure a week's marching. Consequently hundreds were barefooted before they reached Columbia, Tennessee; and in some brigades, one-fourth of the men marched barefooted over frozen roads from Franklin to Nashville through blasts of sleet and snow, leaving behind them smears of blood.[62]

Retrogression after defeat on December 16 was accompanied by perhaps even greater distress. The rapid marching, necessitated by pressure of Yankee pursuers, took an increasing toll of sole leather. To protect their bleeding feet from the frozen ground men contrived shoes not only of rawhide, but of hats and coat sleeves as well. But these Rebs could still sing, and as they dragged themselves along they lifted their voices in an impromptu adaptation to the old tune "The Yellow Rose of Texas":

> "And now I'm going Southward,
>   For my heart is full of woe,
> I'm going back to Georgia
>   To find my 'Uncle Joe.'

You may sing about your dearest maid,
And sing of Rosalie,
But the gallant Hood of Texas
Played hell in Tennessee." [63]

And a remnant did go back, to draw in Mississippi some "sorry" government shoes and in the spring many of them followed "Uncle Joe" Johnston into North Carolina to fight their last battle at Bentonville. By their grim perseverance these veterans of the Army of Tennessee and their comrades of other commands, who marched and fought with ever-dwindling protection from rain and snow through four years of war, achieved for soldiers of the Lost Cause a fame no less lustrous than that won by the heroes of Valley Forge.

CHAPTER VIII

TRIALS OF SOUL

THE South entered the war in the spring of 1861 with high spirit. The people were, with few exceptions, thoroughly convinced of the rightness of their cause—the defense of their homes against tyrannous and godless invaders. They were overwhelmingly confident of success. Men of the South, they thought, accustomed to an active outdoor life, were more robust than factory- and shop-bred Northerners. Southerners were also deemed tougher in temper than Yankees.

Overweening certainty of Rebel superiority was shown in wartime textbooks for the common schools. Johnson's *Elementary Arithmetic*, published in North Carolina, proposed these problems for patriotic youngsters:

"(1) A Confederate soldier captured 8 Yankees each day for 9 successive days; how many did he capture in all? (2) If one Confederate soldier kill 90 Yankees how many Yankees can 10 Confederate soldiers kill? (3) If one Confederate soldier can whip 7 Yankees, how many soldiers can whip 49 Yankees?" [1]

Southerners generally believed that the majority of Northerners were opposed to fighting, and those who were so foolish as to essay conflict with brave secessionists could not stand up under the rigors of battle. The war would doubtless be a short one, but short or long, most of the South's young men wanted to have a part in it—and many of the old ones.

In the flood tide of patriotism which rose during the first months of war there was an irresistible rush to arms. "All Mississippi is in a fever to get to the field, and hail an order to march as the greatest favor you can confer upon them," wrote Governor Pettus to President Davis in May 1861.[2] Everywhere men formed themselves into companies and regiments, with or without authorization, and importunately demanded immediate transfer to camps of instruction, or better still to prospective seats of war. Letters from state officers and from private citizens flooded Richmond authorities asking for induction into Con-

123

federate service, for arms and for assignment to active duty. Secretary of War Walker informed President Davis in July 1861 that applications on file in his office left no doubt "that if arms were only furnished no less than 200,000 additional volunteers for the war would be found in our ranks in less than two months." [3]

Some volunteers were so imbued with ardor that they not only equipped themselves, but also refused to take pay for their army services.[4] The revival-meeting type of zeal which characterized the first days of the Confederacy was further expressed by recruits choosing to sleep in the open when tents were available, and taking over the lowlier duties of army life. In a few instances this ardor ran to fantastic extremes. After one of the early battles a group of prowling Rebs came across a trunk full of United States currency. Such was the rampant state of their patriotism that, according to the recollection of one of them, they "scorned the filthy lucre and consigned it to the flames, only reserving a little as mementoes." [5]

Naturally the first swell of enthusiasm did not continue for long. In fact signs of defection made their appearance while ardor was still at flood stage. These were in connection with the length of service pledged by volunteers. When the war began Richmond authorities accepted troops for a twelve months' period, with equipment to be furnished by the War Department. Shortage of accouterments, combined with maturer consideration, caused Davis and his associates to revise this policy and to equip at Confederate expense only those volunteers who should enlist for three years, or the duration of the war. Twelve-month volunteers would be received, but only on condition that they provide their own equipment.

Announcement of this policy a short time after the fall of Fort Sumter aroused a widespread cry of protest. Some men of moderate means objected on the score that in view of the small compensation of soldiers they could not afford to pledge themselves to so lengthy a service. Non-slaveholders complained that rich men could enlist for the one-year period because of ability to equip themselves, while they, because of their lack of means, were required to enlist for three years or not at all.[6] Thus before a battle was fought, selfishness and class strife were fouling the pure waters of patriotism.

As weeks turned into months enthusiasm for military service gradually dwindled, and long before the passage of the first conscription act of April 1862 the initial flood of volunteering had ebbed to a mere trickle. The first draft law gave new life to volunteering, but it was of a spiritless sort, occasioned primarily by the desire of men subject to conscription to escape the odium attached to forced service. Each subsequent conscription act was followed by a similar reaction. By August 1863 General Daniel Ruggles was constrained to write that "the spirit of volunteering has ceased to exist," and the great bulk of available evidence verifies the approximate correctness of his observation.[7]

After the first enthusiasm had spent its force, not even conscription could bring the South's available man power into military service. The policy of forcing enlistment by law was never more than a meager success. Its chief benefit was to hold in the army at critical times men whose volunteer periods were about to expire, and to stimulate the immediate enlistment of a small portion of civilians subject to draft.

Coercive acts of the Confederate Congress were subjected to sabotage on every hand. State governors insisted on the exemption of local defense troops, and thousands of militiamen of conscription age thus escaped Confederate service. Provincial-minded executives like Georgia's Joe Brown and North Carolina's Zeb Vance went so far as to demand immunity from draft of many petty officials, including justices of the peace, on the claim that they were essential to the discharge of governmental functions. They also encouraged resistance to conscription by declaiming the unconstitutionality of draft laws; and some state justices added their influence by issuing writs of habeas corpus on behalf of those held for their violation. Local physicians handed out certificates of disability with great nonchalance which, until the law was rectified, conscription officers were bound to accept at face value, even when presented by the most robust individuals. In many communities public sentiment was so lethargic or so hostile during the last two years of the war as to defeat all efforts to compel slackers to service. Granted that the policy of conscription was impaired by defects in administrative machinery and personnel, the main cause of its failure must be found in the dwindling morale of the people.[8]

One of the most striking evidences of this was the practice of evading military service by substitution. As early as the fall of 1861 the War Department permitted release from the army of volunteers who presented able-bodied proxies to serve in their stead. The first conscription act sanctioned the practice. A conscriptee, when summoned to a camp of instruction, might take a substitute with him; if the proxy upon examination proved to be of sound body and not subject to military service on his own account, the "principal" was permitted to return home and the substitute accepted in his place. Only one substitution a month was allowed in each company, but this provision was frequently violated.

Objections to substitution were voiced soon after the policy was initiated, and the protest grew with the declining fortunes of the Confederacy. But the practice increased. Newspapers carried bids for the service of proxies, ranging from about $500 in 1862 to several thousand dollars in the latter part of 1863. Occasionally men not liable to conscription, induced by the lucrative hire and by the bounty which Richmond authorities allowed to enrollees, advertised their availability as substitutes.

Transactions were handled with the detached formality incident to regular trade, by banks, factors and merchants; laws of supply and demand eventually led to the setting up of substitute brokerages. Such a business was naturally accompanied by endless fraud and deceit. Men who were hired as substitutes frequently deserted, sometimes to multiply their gains by repeated substitutions under different names. By connivance with examining authorities, persons of unsound bodies were unlawfully accepted as proxies. Under the best conditions men thus inducted into service were not good soldier material. Many were aliens having little interest in the fortunes of the Confederacy. Most of them were mainly concerned with getting as much money and rendering as little service as possible. In a great many cases, by devising fraudulent papers, men who had no substitutes at all remained out of service on the pretext of having engaged them.

Substitution was originally designed to mitigate the apparent harshness of conscription, for it must be remembered that before the Confederacy's first law a general draft had never been resorted to in America. It was thought too that essential talent for home production would find the necessary release from army service. But the policy did not turn out as expected. Granted, as Howell Cobb pointed out, that a considerable number of men who availed themselves of proxies were substantial and patriotic citizens, all too frequently they were of another sort.[9] In numerous cases men who were released from service resorted to speculation and profiteering. Many of them revealed their true character by fleeing to the North when eventually ordered into the army or by procuring for "a consideration" some petty clerkship in the government offices at Richmond.

The presence of able-bodied men at home in large numbers, especially after Vicksburg and Gettysburg, was in itself the source of great dissatisfaction to men in the army and to their families; disgruntlement was particularly strong among the poorer classes who saw additional proof of their growing conviction that this was "a rich man's war and a poor man's fight." After frequent and futile efforts to purge the substitute system of its defects and abuses, Congress early in 1864 took the bull by the horns and abolished it. But even then there were many hangovers in the form of judicial claims of unconstitutionality.[10]

The number of men who purchased exemption from military service by substitution while the system was in force cannot be ascertained because the War Department records are inadequate. In the summer of 1863 General Bragg estimated the total at 150,000, but this outright guess was probably extravagant.[11] Secretary of War Seddon in his report to the President of November 1863 ventured an estimate of "not less certainly, than 50,000."[12] Seddon's figure is probably conservative. However that may be, the spectacle of nearly as many men as constituted Lee's effective force in the Army of Northern Virginia in the fall of 1863 escaping military responsibilities under the guise of purchased proxies—most of whom rendered poor service or none at all—is a shameful reflection on Confederate patriotism.[13]

While the morale of soldiers seems always to have been better than that of civilians, the army experienced a growing defection of spirit as the conflict went on. Expressions of war-weariness began to creep into their letters after Rebs had undergone only a few months of service. By that time it had become apparent that the Yankees were not to be whipped in one campaign, and camp life had lost the glamor of novelty.

Disillusionment sometimes found its first expression in advice to friends and relatives against volunteering. "I still advise you, and as strongly as ever," wrote an Alabamian to his brother in the spring of 1862, "to not come to the war. I tell you you will repent it if you do I do believe. You have no idea of what it is to be a soldier. . . . and be you assure[d] that if I had your chance to stay out of it I would do [so]. I do think that you would do very wrong to come unless they draught you."[14]

In not a few instances the change of tone as to the joys of soldiering was sudden, being influenced by some unhappy experience. Such was the case of Private Joe Shields.

In June 1861 he wrote enthusiastically from Vicksburg, "Dear Pa, we have arrived here all safe the troops are all in a jolly humor. . . . we are all well we had a pleasant time last night we sleep in the cabin on the floor. . . . I am in good spirits we have such a jolly crowd that a fellow cant have the blues."

A few days later he moved on to Memphis, where he and his comrades suffered disappointment in what they construed as inhospitable reception. Shortly after this experience Shields wrote his folk that "the Troops are all displeased at the treatment" and that "some are in favor of quitting & going either home or to Virginia."

He went to Virginia, but this failed to revive his spirit, for he wrote from Lynchburg on July 1, "Dear Pa . . . I hope you will stay at home for you could not stand it it is too hard a life. . . . I would advise all my friends unless they wish to live like negroes to stay at home I know if there is another war this chicken wont be *thar* when they enlist." [15]

But the most thorough case of disillusionment encountered by the writer was that of a young Mississippi aristocrat. In April 1861 this man wrote his sister that he had failed of admittance to the Washington Artillery because of his low stature but was drilling in New Orleans with a group of prospective infantrymen. "I am better-fitted for a soldier than anything else," he exulted. "I believe I am brave and not afraid to meet an enemy. . . . I am anxious to go—for I honestly and candidly believe that one Southern man is a match for any two Northern fanatics. . . . If they conquer us we can[t] be anything but rebellious provinces—And if we conquer them we will make them our slaves. . . . If I live I will hand down the name of Mandeville to posterity and to history—And if I perish it will be said I did so gallantly & not from a shot in the back. . . . When I go it will be to make a name."

He succeeded in getting in service a short time later and was sent to Virginia, where he was exposed to some strenuous marching. In August 1861, less than five months after having professed such enthusiasm for soldiering, he wrote his homefolk: "It is the opinion of the people here that we will be home by the first of October & I hope so for I am heartily tired of this life." [16] He died early in 1863, but whether under such circumstances as to make lustrous the name he bore is not known.

The long months of military quietude that followed First Manassas, with its introduction to the tedium of winter quarters, increased considerably the nostalgia and gloom of Confederate camps.

A Louisianian wrote despondingly to his mother in December 1861:

"As to the War I cannot tell when it will end . . . I wish . . . I was home by my own fireside. . . . I have seen quite enough of A Soldiers life to satisfied me that it is not what it is cracked up to be."

With the arrival of the Yule season his lot became almost insufferable, and in January 1862 he proposed to desert if his folk would but say the word.[17]

A homesick Alabamian wintering near Shelbyville, Tennessee, wrote mournfully to his father:

"My shoes is wering out very fast and my pants is warin out as fast as my Shoes is . . . I have bin troubble very bad lately I am heaire and my mind is wit you at home I wish the waire would stop fur I cant live in any pease attall heaire." [18]

A more comprehensive view of the decline in morale that came after a few months of comparatively inactive service was given by General Will T. Martin. In a letter to his wife, written from Virginia on October 20, 1861, he said:

"I am afraid there will be even worse complaints in the army than now exists. There is plenty already. The first flush of patriotism led many a man to join who now regrets it. . . . The prospect of winter here is making the men very restive and they are beginning to resort to all sorts of means to get home." [19]

Some soldiers seem to have experienced the depths of depression during the first winter, for then they felt homesickness at its worst, and they were not yet toughened to the hardships of war. As they became accustomed to separation from loved ones and more thoroughly inured to the discomforts of army life, they suffered less acutely, and consequently bore subsequent winters in camp with more fortitude than the first.

For most of the Rebs, however, greater depths of gloom were yet to come. Resort to conscription in April 1862 was a severe blow to their morale. Many objected to the policy as unconstitutional; others resented deeply the fact that the law deprived them of the privilege of visiting homefolk at the end of their year of volunteered service; still others found fault with the list of exemptions. Not a few saw in forced service an admission of despair on the part of government authorities.

The reaction of a South Carolinian serving at Yorktown was typical:

"The Conscript Act will do away with all the patriotism we have. Whenever men are forced to fight they take no personal interest in it. . . . My private opinion is that our Confederacy is gone up, or will go soon. . . . A more oppressive law was never enacted in the most uncivilized country or by the worst of despots." [20]

Active campaigns in the spring, summer and fall of 1862 buoyed morale considerably, but going into winter quarters again, with its implication of another season of conflict, led to an unprecedented wave of war weariness. A Texan wrote his sister from Arkansas in late November, 1862, that he had "enough of Yanks." "I would to God," he added, "that I could do my share of fightin and come home though I see no chance for that." But he consoled himself with the observation, "There is one thing Sure the war cant go on always I will either go up the flew or come home before a graitwhile."

Several weeks later this man wrote another member of his family, "Well Leiza I wish I could tell when this custiard [cursed] war will come to an end. I fear the time is so fare off we will be a ruined people."

His brother was even more outspoken: "God speed the day when that time [war's end] shall come," he wrote, "for I am tired of camp life, especially in this country. it is no pleasur to be away from my folks and if this war dont stop before next fall I am coming home you can look for me in twenty days after white frost." [21]

This second winter's wave of despondency overwhelmed some who hitherto had shown great enthusiasm for army life. A case in point is that of E. J. Ellis of Louisiana. On June 9, 1862, Ellis had written to his mother:

"This war has done me good in many ways—It has taught me patence and endurance & 'to labor & wait'. . . . it has learned me to be less particular in a great many things—when I see dirt in my victuals, I take it out and eat on—If I taste it, I swallow & eat on. . . . If my bed is hard & my head not high enough, I content myself with the idea that it might be worse & go to sleep. . . . I think I have seen the dark side of soldiering and although it is tolerably hard, yet there aint any use of calling it intolerable."

In eight months this Reb's consoling philosophy had petered out, and he was singing a very different tune. "The fact is," he said in commenting on a slight but incapacitating injury suffered by a fellow soldier at Murfreesboro, "I would like first rate to get such a wound.

. . . Oh! wouldnt it be nice to get a 30 days leave and go home and be petted like a baby, and get delicacies to eat . . . and then if I ever run for a little office I could limp and complain of the 'old wound.' "

The passage of another month found him still harboring this idea, though the desired wound was increasing in seriousness. If "some friendly bullet" would "hit me just severely enough to send me home for 60 or 90 days," he wrote wistfully, "I would gladly welcome such a bullet and consider the Yankee who fired it as a good kind fellow." [22]

Numerous other Rebs indulged in similar musings, and according to a story circulating persistently through the camps, at least one soldier tried to carry out his wishes by taking a position behind a tree during battle and waving his arms up and down on either side. An officer who asked the gesticulator what he was doing allegedly received the amazing answer, "I'm feeling for a furlough." [23]

While soldier Ellis was pining for a wound, an Alabama comrade was speculating on the war's termination. "If the soldiers were allowed to settle the matter," he wrote in February 1863, "peace would be made in short order," and he expressed the hope that he and his family might eat watermelons together the next summer.[24] But instead of watermelon cuttings on home lawns, the summer of 1863 brought Vicksburg and Gettysburg. And before the year's end Bragg's Chattanooga battles filled the cup of Confederate disaster to overflowing. Many soldiers came now to despair of ultimate success.

A Georgia Reb home on sick furlough wrote to his brother in camp that his leave had already been extended twice, and if it was not renewed a third time he thought he would just stay at home anyhow. "There is no use fighting any longer no how," he said, "for we are done gon up the Spout the Confederacy is done whiped it is useless to deny it any longger." [25]

Another Georgian, serving in the Army of Northern Virginia, wrote his wife a few weeks after Gettysburg that "the men from N. C. held [a] meeting yes[t]erday I believe they will go back into the Union the men from Ga say that if the enemy invade Ga they are going home I dont believe an army will fight much longer. I know that miny will or would say that I am whiped . . . I would say to them if they would com and see and feel what I have they would feel as I do." [26]

A Mississippian who had heard reports of orders to destroy cotton wrote to his wife in December 1863, "As to cotton being burnt, I have but little to say as I think it & Confederate money will be worth nothing to me in a few months as I think our prospects are growing worse daily." [27]

In the spring of 1864 an Alabamian expressed conviction that "we never can whip the North Fer tha hav so meney moer men [th]an we hav got." [28]

No doubt some of those who succumbed to defeatism at this stage of the war were men who had never felt any strong enthusiasm for the struggle. But that troops of consistently good morale were also affected is seen in the case of Charles Moore, a young Louisianian. Moore, who served with the Army of Northern Virginia, was of unusual buoyancy of spirit. His diary fairly exudes cheerfulness and optimism during the first two years of war. A serious wound at Gettysburg, followed by amputation of his leg, evokes not a word of complaint or of pessimism. But on February 26, 1864, he enters in his journal the despairing note "no use of us fighting," and this was his first hint of despondency.[29]

Governmental and military authorities exerted themselves greatly to stay the tide of pessimism which besieged Rebel camps during the war's third winter. President Davis visited the Army of Tennessee and regaled the soldiers with optimistic sentiments. Confederate and state political leaders followed his example by visiting and addressing this and other portions of the Southern fighting force. The system of furloughs was broadened by some commanders. Sham battles were staged on grand and realistic scale to fire enthusiasm for spring campaigns.[30]

Officers high and low used the technique of suggestion and example with great effectiveness to induce en masse re-enlistment of men whose three-year terms were to expire in the spring of 1864. True, the continued service of these men was *required* by a recently enacted conscription law, but the gesture of voluntary action was desired as a fillip to general morale. A favorite device of officers to inspire pledges to further service was the assembling of men for dress parade, addressing them in patriotic vein, moving the flags up a few paces ahead, and then asking all those who were willing to re-enlist for the duration of the war to step up to the colors. When the lead was taken, whether by few or many, the impulse for all to follow suit was usually overwhelming.

Such action was recognized in a manner calculated to arouse the patriotism of other units. For example, on February 3, 1864, Lee promulgated General Order Number 14, in which he said: "The commanding general announces with gratification the reenlistment of the regiments of this army for the war. . . . This action gives new cause

for the gratitude and admiration of their countrymen. . . . It is hoped,"
he added significantly, that "this patriotic movement, commenced in
the Army of Tennessee will be followed by every brigade of the Army
of Northern Virginia, and extend from army to army until the Soldiers
of the South stand in one embattled host determined never to yield."
He then proceeded to name the batteries, regiments and brigades that
had initiated the movement "so honorable to themselves and so pleasing to the country." [31] Congress added the weight of its influence by
voting resolutions of thanks to various organizations as they renewed
their commitments. In the Army of Tennessee, furloughs at the rate
of one to every ten men present for duty were promised to regiments
that re-enlisted.[32]

The response of the soldiers delighted the officers. The enthusiasm
that accompanied the pledging ceremonies was often unrestrained. Instead of promising renewal of service for three years or the duration, a
few regiments of Johnston's army suggested avowal of forty- and fifty-
year periods, while the Twentieth Mississippi Regiment proposed re-
enlistment for ninety-nine years or the war.[33]

There are inklings, however, that the actual enthusiasm did not
keep pace with these outward manifestations. When Georgia regiments
accompanied their commitments to extended service with resolutions
of censure of Governor Brown and the two Stephenses for non-co-
operation with Confederate authorities, Brown retorted that the resolutions "were prepared by the officers before the men were convened,
and that only a small portion of the troops attended the ratifying
meeting, and of those present only a small part voted." [34] This must
be taken with a grain of salt because of the Governor's tendency to
extreme statements under duress.

More convincing is the testimony of a sergeant in the Forty-sixth
Mississippi Regiment, Army of Tennessee. On March 31, 1864, he
wrote in his journal: "On the night of the 25th a meeting of the . . .
men of the regiment was called to consider the subject of reenlisting
for the war. . . . We reenlisted . . . by adopting some very bold resolution of the original fire eating sort (but which I endorse) and were
mustered in for the war." But he added significantly, "I am compelled
to say that it was the immediate prospect of obtaining furloughs that
induced many of the men to reenlist." [35]

There can be no doubt, however, that the various expedients invoked during the winter of 1863-1864 had a good effect on army morale.
Grant's failure to take Richmond during the following summer also

raised the general spirit. But the evacuation of Atlanta, followed by the march of Sherman's hosts through the heart of the Southland and Hood's overwhelming disaster at Nashville, caused so deep a depression in Confederate camps as to set at naught every effort to boost morale.[36]

The increasing despondency is vividly reflected by the tone of letters coming from camp. "The soldiers are badly out of heart," wrote a Georgian from Charleston in January 1865, "for they have been a suffering for nearly four long years and there is no prospect of doing better." [37] An Alabamian in Lee's army who had previously testified to the good spirits of his comrades observed about the same time that "the successful and . . . unopposed march of Sherman through Georgia, and the complete defeat of Hood in Tennessee, have changed the whole aspect of affairs." [38] A soldier of the Army of Tennessee returning from furlough in mid-January was struck by the depression that had overtaken his fellow soldiers. "When it comes to discussing the prosecution of the war," he said, "they are entirely despondent, being fully convinced that the Confederacy is gone." [39]

On February 1, 1865, one of Lee's soldiers wrote that "the men is not a gone [going] to stay in the field any longer for they Say that they have fout longe a nuff and that they will not fight any more." On March 19 another observed, "The campaign is a bout to open here and I think there will bee hard . . . fighting here before they will give up and it is a nuff to put enney boddy out of hart to think that we will fight on when we can see at home and in the armey at this time that we hant done eney thing with the enemy this winter." [40] In view of the demoralization that pervaded the armies during the war's last winter, formal surrender in the spring had somewhat the character of a postlude to defeat.

Several factors, in addition to reversals on the field of battle, contributed to the decline of morale in the Confederate Army. Important among these was the poor quality and meager quantity of the rations. Rebs proved in countless instances that men can march and fight well on empty stomachs, but even so, the long continuing and gradually increasing shortage of food, particularly of meat, was depressing.

"If I ever lose my patriotism, and the 'secesh' spirit dies out," wrote a private to his homefolk in October 1862, "then you may know the 'Commissary' is at fault. Corn meal mixed with water and tough beef three times a day will knock the 'Brave Volunteer' under quicker than Yankee bullets." [41]

This Reb was hitting close to a bull's-eye. In the spring of 1863 some of Bragg's troops refused to drill because of the reduction of their fare to bread made of meal and water. They were put in the guard-house, but one of their officers expressed apprehension that the Federals might ultimately triumph by starvation of the Southern armies.[42]

General Lee worried chronically about the dangerous consequences of empty haversacks. On January 22, 1864, he wrote the Secretary of War that "short rations are having a bad effect upon the men both morally and physically," and that desertions to the enemy were becoming more frequent as a result. A year later he implored an increase of the food issue to the Army of Northern Virginia in order to combat the alarming tide of absenteeism that had set in.[43] But his efforts were of little avail, and defection increased.

Shortage of clothing did its part. The long marches without shoes made straggling inevitable, and exposure of thinly clad men to the rigors of Tennessee and Virginia winters produced a high degree of discontent.

Even more depressing than their own hardship was the knowledge that wives, children and parents at home were deprived of sufficient food and clothing. An Alabamian wrote to his wife in October 1863 that he was going to try to get a furlough, but if he failed in his efforts he intended to come home anyhow, "for I cant Stand to here," he said, "that you and the children are Sufren for Bread." [44] And thousands of Rebs were moved by just such sentiments to set out for home without benefit of either furlough or discharge.

The conviction of soldiers that they and their families were being swindled by speculators, most of whom were thought to be slackers, was another factor working strongly against morale. The high prices that naturally followed inflation of the currency were widely believed to be the result of shady manipulations by heartless profiteers.

A Mississippian in Lee's army fairly boiled with rage when he heard that in his own community draft dodgers were "cramed down in every hole and corner speculateing and extortioning on those who try to live honest." "I believe," he said, "that such things are going on all over the C. S.," and that "impressing officers have pressed that to which they have no right for the intention of speculation." He decried the effect of such wrongdoing on the prospects of victory for, he opined, "the Old Book says that man can not serve both God & Mamon." [45] Doubtless most soldiers had exaggerated ideas about the prevalence of speculation, but whether they were right or not, their belief had a demoralizing effect on their patriotism.

Failure to receive their pay was another blow to the resolution of the men. The payment allowed by law for infantry and artillery privates was eleven dollars a month.[46] Even under normal conditions this was a miserly sum, but with the constant depreciation of money values the amount shrunk in 1864 and 1865 to the merest pittance. Congress failed to adjust wages to meet inflation. In fact no boost in pay was provided at all until June 1864, when the dilatory legislators at Richmond finally voted an increase of seven dollars a month for all non-commissioned officers and privates.[47] Payment was slow, and when it actually came the money was worth only a fraction of its original value. This fact did not escape pay-conscious Rebs. On March 4, 1864, William P. Chambers recorded in his journal:

"Yesterday we were paid up—wages to Jany. 1, 1864 and commutation for clothing for the year ending Oct. 8; 1863. As the 'old issue' of Confederate notes will soon be worthless, it seems the Treasury Department is very anxious to get rid of it—hence the large installment of wages we received." [48]

Letters and diaries of soldiers, as well as official communications of commanding officers, show that it was not unusual for pay to be six months behind, and in some instances troops went for a year without receiving any money from the government. In despair of getting their pay, not a few Rebs set up an informal business among their comrades in order to make enough money to buy tobacco, stationery and other conveniences. Some peddled eggs obtained from sources that probably would not have borne official investigation; others bought and sold fruit and vegetables. Still others had whiskey, food, clothing and other items sent to them from home for vending in camp. In the fall of 1862 such bargaining became so rife in the Army of Northern Virginia that General Lee issued a prohibitive order.[49]

For the most part discontent over delayed payment was expressed in mere grumbling—which according to one general was the soldier's greatest luxury—but in two cases at least it led to insubordination. A regiment of Pemberton's command in South Carolina gave notice in March 1862 that it would not obey an order to move to the support of Albert Sidney Johnston in Tennessee until it was paid; and two Mississippi companies stacked arms in February 1864 when the signal was given for dress parade, and announced that no more duty of any kind would be performed until they received at least a part of the wages due them.[50]

DEAD CONFEDERATE SHARPSHOOTER AT THE DEVIL'S DEN, GETTYSBURG

It is said to be Andrew Hoge, Private, Company E, 4th Virginia Infantry. The identification appears in a note on a copy of this photograph on file in the National Archives Collection of Brady Photographs.

AFTER THE BATTLE

Photograph taken back of rail fence on Hagerstown Pike, September 17, 1862, after the Battle of Antietam.

Dissatisfaction in regard to pay was always widespread, and General Lee in 1865, after investigating the cause of increasing desertion in his army, concluded that "insufficiency of food and non-payment of the troops have more to do with the dissatisfaction . . . than anything else." [51]

The transfer of men to places far from their homes was a common cause of desertion. This was not true early in the war, because it was generally thought that the struggle would be short, and a trip to Virginia or Kentucky was regarded by Louisianians, Texans and others as a sort of holiday excursion. Nor were single men as much affected as those who were married. But after it became apparent that the war was to be long, and that various portions of the South were to be invaded, the thought of being far away from families who were helpless and in danger caused many a Reb to cast longing and uneasy glances toward home.

The question of furloughs also entered into the situation, for leaves seemed harder to get when the distance was great, and even if an absence of forty days was granted poor transportation cut short the stay at home. Then, too, homesickness from natural causes seemed to bear some relation to distance. However sound these latter deductions may be, there can be no doubt that after 1861 men objected strongly to transfers that took them far from home. An order of troop removal from Western Virginia to the vicinity of Richmond in December 1862 provoked wholesale desertion.[52]

A Mississippi regiment that was transferred from its native state to North Georgia in late 1863 made a similar protest. One of its members wrote that "the Ouls caught 45 of our men the night before we started and the next day and night they caught them at every Depot and on the wayside when they run slow I think about 125 of the Regt left us." [53]

But removals of soldiers from west of the Mississippi to points east of the river caused still greater demoralization. The mere rumor of such transfer produced great excitement in a Texas regiment, and the men swore that they would never cross the river. In another Texas group large-scale desertion followed such a report. A soldier of the latter regiment expressed himself thus:

"As for my part I take crossing in mine although it is a bitter pill. I cant believe the present Suffering of the Soldiers will last long this Hell roaring war cant exist long . . . it is rather cool for a man to leave his home exposed to the enemy an[d] go to protect one that is all reddy over run though I cant tell what is best neither do I give a darn blew button." [54]

One reason for the reluctance to grant furloughs to trans-Mississippians was the difficulty of getting them back across the river. A Louisianian said that a colonel of his brigade who was sent across the Mississippi from the Army of Tennessee in 1862 to collect absentees was able to assemble about four hundred men, but that when he started to recross the river with them, all but twenty-five escaped his custody.[55]

Another cause that contributed greatly to the decline of soldier morale was the consolidation of military units. With the dwindling of regiments, brigades and divisions through casualties and absences to small fractions of their full strength in 1863 and 1864, some adjustment had to be found. Recruiting was resorted to, to fill up the ranks, but with slight success. Conscripts and substitutes were frequently scorned by veteran volunteers, and these enrollees dreaded the prospect of being put in with men who would taunt and despise them.[56]

So with the failure to build up skeleton outfits by recruiting, Richmond authorities considered it necessary to combine them. But such a policy ran counter to the pride which old soldiers felt in their organizations, and this pride was too deep-seated to be readily laid aside. A regiment such as the Second Texas Infantry, for instance, jealous of the awe in which it was held by opposing Yankee outfits—as evinced after parole at Vicksburg by the respectful and admiring tone adopted by Federals when they said, "There goes the Second Texas!"—would naturally be unwilling to lose its identity, its battle flags and its hard-won reputation for gallantry on numerous fields of battle, by consolidation late in the war with a miscellany of regiments garnered perhaps from states other than the glorious Lone Star Republic.[57] And when such fusions were pushed down their throats, consequences were apt to be disastrous.

"Our Brigade has been cut up," wrote a Mississippian in 1862, "25 La. 30 Miss & 37 Miss . . . put into other Brigades and Anderson has taken 2 Florida Regts Our Regt is a brag Regt & . . . we are dissatisfied now." [58] Another Mississippian wrote early in 1865, "The boys do not like the consolodating of the companys . . . and . . . some . . . . has run away . . . I do not think [the others] will stay here much longer." [59]

In numerous cases officers testified to the harmful effect on morale of such combinations. "Both officers and men bitterly object," wrote an inspector of Gordon's division in 1864; "strange officers command strange troops," and "old organizations feel that they have lost their identity and are without the chance of perpetuating the distinct and separate history of which they were once so proud." [60]

The dismounting of cavalry outfits aroused even more discontent than the consolidation of infantrymen. Yet the heavy loss of horses through battle casualties, overuse and undernourishment made it necessary sometimes to convert cavalrymen into foot soldiers. The mere proposal of such an action, however, would almost invariably cause a wave of desertion.[61]

The matter of furloughs was a tremendous source of discontent. Any request for leave had to run a long gamut of approvals, and frequently action came only after months of delay. While soldiers waited they naturally chafed. When their requests were finally acted on they were generally refused. This led to a conviction that those in authority were heartless and unreasonable.

Then, there always seemed to be grounds for finding partiality in cases where furloughs were granted, and these were seized upon and magnified by those who were disappointed. Married men complained that single comrades were preferred, and vice versa; poor men were convinced that wealthy men were favored, privates grumbled that officers received a disproportionate share of leaves.

But the greatest dissatisfaction came from the failure of military authorities to grant furloughs which had been promised as rewards for re-enlistment, for procuring recruits and for returning deserters. The answer of those in authority to such complaints was that change in the military situation, increase of desertion, or overstaying of leaves that had been granted made impossible the fulfilment of agreements as made. But to homesick soldiers who after long effort had earned promise of a visit with homefolk, all such excuses seemed utterly invalid. The natural reaction was to "go anyhow," and thousands did.

Mistreatment by officers, fancied or real, in matters other than furloughs was often a factor in demoralization. One Deter Jochum wrote to his mother in 1864:

"The tiranny of officers is as great as can be the numerous desertions which occur at every retreat of ours is mainly caused by the tyranny of officers with their high pay they enjoy themselves no matter how high the prices while the poor soldier suffers." [62]

Sensitiveness to authority was unusually keen among the less literate classes of Rebs. The sharpness of reaction in such cases is vividly illustrated by a Texan's letter to his homefolk:

"We see hard times, and you can guess it is tolerable bad for me as I am Not allowed the chance of a dog I have come to The conclusion that I will stay and tuff it out with Col Young and then he can go to Hell for my part you know that if any one will try to do I can get along with Them but when they get Hell in their Neck I cant do any thing with them and so I don't Try if a man treats me well I will stick up to Him till I die and then see that my spirit helps him when I am gone to my long Home but he has acted the dam dog and I cant tell him so if I do they will put me in the Guard House . . . but I can tell him what I think of him when this war ends and as to go with him I wont do it to save his life . . . I will come [home] when my time is out or die I wont be run over no longer not to please no officers they have acted the rascal with me . . . I am so sick of war that I dont want to heare it any more till old Abes time is out and then let a man say war to me and I will choke him." [63]

Extravagant words, obviously, but there can be no doubt of the depth of his resentment and dissatisfaction, or of numerous parallels among fellow soldiers.

No small portion of the dissatisfaction in the Confederate Army must be attributed to the drabness of camp routine. Most Rebs were country bred, and to men accustomed to the freedom of field and farm an existence regulated in every detail by drum beats and bugle blasts was particularly distasteful.

"Oh how tiresome this camp life to me," wrote a Mississippian, in 1864, "one everlasting monotone, yesterday, today & tomorrow." [64]

Another had written several months previously, "I sometimes get very much vext at . . . [drill] orders and am all must fit to bite my lips. So very much so that I dont think I will ever waunt to hear of one a gain. nor hear the naim of officer dril are [or] Soldier gard or detail eny more after peace is made. Oh how glad I will be when the day comes that We . . . never . . . hear the Tap of a drum a gain which bids us rise and drill." [65]

Still another expostulated, "When this war is over I will whip the man that says 'fall in' to me." [66] The endless chore of guarding, marching, reveille and roll call made doubly sweet the prospects of home.

"If I was Jest free I would Com Back to old Coosy in a hery," wrote a nostalgic Alabamian. "I expect to spend my days in old Coosa if I get Back." [67] But this was only the summer of 1862, and for him and multiplied scores of chafing comrades, months of soul-trying monotony still lay ahead.

Added to military disaster, deprivation of food, clothing and pay, highhandedness of officers, loss of regimental identity, and the intolerable boredom of camp were still other factors tending to demoralize. Some soldiers whose spirit remained strong under all other hardships were revolted by the apparently futile slaughter of the war's last years; others were crushed by the repeated lamentations of their homefolk; still others were broken by the stench and filth of their surroundings; not a few were dispirited by squabbling and inefficiency among commanding officers and governmental authorities; and most depressing of all were the multiplying evidences of greed, selfishness, and ebbing patriotism that permeated army and citizenry alike after the summer campaign of 1863.

Declining morale revealed itself in several ways besides those already noted. One of these was the evading of responsibility by feigning sickness. This subterfuge, referred to as "playing old soldier" by Rebs, made its appearance early in the war.

In June 1861 William R. Barksdale wrote from a camp near Harper's Ferry that "many are reported sick who have little or nothing the matter but only desire to avoid drill. It reminds me of Jake and his chills to see some of these fellows drooping about here trying to look sick." [68] In spite of the efforts of officers and surgeons to put a stop to such shamming, it continued to flourish throughout the war. The prospect of a hard march, of a turn on picket, or of some other unpleasant duty almost invariably produced a swelling of the sick lists.

A less frequent resort to avoid service was the self-infliction of an injury of some sort. One Reb shot himself in the foot, and another in the hand, to escape service. A Louisianian amputated some of his fingers. A South Carolinian secured sick leave by making his arm sore, and extended his sojourn in the infirmary by tampering with the wound. Another South Carolinian managed to keep himself hospitalized for the greater part of the war by aggravating the infection of a toe.[69]

But physical disabling was a serious business. A much more common ruse to evade service was that of getting detailed to some softer assignment than soldiering. "When a person gets a Government contract or agency," wrote Lee to Seddon in 1863, "his first endeavor appears to be to get his friends out of the army in order to help him.

Then there are hundreds who go home on sick furloughs, and while there look out for places to which to be detailed, and forward petitions, stating in strong terms the necessity, &c, inclosing surgeons' certificates showing their competency for that work and no other. . . . There are some regiments reduced almost to insignificance by these details." [70]

After adoption of conscription many would-be slackers sought release from the army by claiming exemption on the basis of age, of election to state office, or of coming under the provision allowing immunity from service for ownership of fifteen or twenty slaves. And in numerous cases, by resort to the writ of habeas corpus, such shirkers were successful in obtaining discharges.[71]

A favorite practice was to secure transfer, by regular means or otherwise, to free-booting cavalry outfits or to state organizations in which duties were comparatively light. The prevalence of this practice is convincingly attested by the frequent complaints of departmental commanders and of other high-ranking officers that leaders of independent scouts, partisan rangers and home guards had recruited large numbers of infantry absentees. Such irregularities were invalidated and denounced repeatedly by Richmond authorities, but return of one of these infantrymen to his regular connection involved difficulties so vast that it was seldom accomplished. And the indications are that literally thousands of demoralized Rebs used these shady attachments to effect their escape from the full service due the Confederate Government.

Another method of dodging duty was abuse of the furlough system. Some soldiers, particularly those of partisan ranger companies, connived with their captains to secure leaves without authority from higher officers. Others purchased furloughs from comrades who had legally received them, for considerations ranging from twenty-five dollars to a horse. Others "bought" recruits—i.e. paid men to enlist in their outfits—so that they might secure the forty-day furlough authorized for each addition to the army. Still others told their parents to write letters to commanding officers telling of woeful conditions at home. And some Rebs went so far as to write their own furloughs, and "got by" with it.

Once arrived at home, they found great temptation to prolong the leave. And in countless instances some means of extension were found. A favorite technique was to get a local doctor to write a note saying that the absentee was ill, attaching a certificate of disability, and to mail this to army headquarters; another device was to overstay the furlough for a few days, then on reaching camp to tell of broken-down transportation, the rising of swollen streams or some other hindering act of man or God. Such events were actually frequent enough to make the stories plausible.

By far the most striking manifestation of sagging morale was the increase in the number of soldiers improperly absent from places of duty. Included among these were: first, men absent without leave, such as convalescents who failed to report for duty as ordered, troops who straggled from the ranks on the march, and those overstaying their furloughs; second, soldiers absent with leave, but not in accord with policies authorized by highest authorities; third, men absent under improperly granted detail; fourth, troops serving with organizations other than those to which they were regularly assigned; and fifth, men who without benefit of disguising techniques deserted to the enemy or to the protecting fastnesses of native mountains, swamps and forests.[72]

Unwarranted absentees, as all those who took leave of their assigned duties without proper authorization may be conveniently called, became a source of concern for Confederate leaders very early in the war. Their number was considerably boosted by the announcement in the spring of 1862 that all soldiers between eighteen and thirty-five years of age whose one-year terms of enlistment were about to expire would be held to continued service by conscription. This forcing of unwilling men to prolonged army connection, and induction after April 1862 of draftees whose spirits were already damaged by exposure to such epithets as slackers and conscripts, further enhanced the lists of improper leave-takers. General Lee was deprived of from one-third to one-half of his effective fighting force on the Antietam campaign by straggling; after his return to Virginia he wrote to Davis that "desertion and straggling . . . were the main causes of . . . retiring from Maryland." [73] Remedial legislation was sought by the President, and state governors were asked to co-operate in bringing shirkers to justice. But these efforts were only temporarily effective.

After the disasters of July 1863 leave-taking waxed greater in volume and boldness. Pemberton's men flocked home in such numbers following their parole at Vicksburg that Davis was forced to forego his desire to hold them together pending exchange, and instead to give the general leave-taking a semblance of validity by granting wholesale furloughs.[74] In the wake of Gettysburg the highways of Virginia were crowded daily with homeward-bound troops, still in possession of full accouterments; and, according to one observer, these men "when halted and asked for their furloughs or their authority to be absent from their commands, . . . just pat their guns defiantly and say 'this is my furlough,' and even enrolling officers turn away as peaceably as possible." [75]

The Assistant Secretary of War estimated at this time that the number of soldiers evading service by devious means, but chiefly by unauthorized absence, reached 50,000 to 100,000.[76]

Once arrived in their home country, these men from the mountains of North Carolina, Georgia, Virginia, Tennessee and Arkansas, from the piny woods of Alabama and Mississippi and from the lowlands of Florida, were wont to organize themselves into armed bands. In this way they were able to defy, with few exceptions, all efforts of Confederate authorities to bring them to justice. Secret societies, with imposing signs and rituals, were also formed for self-protection and for urging the cessation of war; to this latter end connivance with Federals, even to the extent of making friendly signs in battle to avoid being shot, was furthered.[77]

Many of the deserters were consistent Union sympathizers conscripted into the army against their will. Such was the case with a Georgia private who wrote his father in 1863:

"I am this day as strong a Union man as ever walked the soil of Va. I would hate to desert but if I ever get a good chance I will be sure to do it. I never expect to kill a Union man." [78]

Others were persons who, because of extreme youth or of little learning, had never gained a clear idea of what the war was about and consequently had little concern as to its outcome or little conception of the seriousness of desertion. Still others felt that they had to choose between continuing army service and returning home to rescue families from starvation, and they chose the latter. Some were cowards, but there were many whose bravery had been proved on the field of battle.

The defeats and privations of 1864 were accompanied by an alarming increase of unwarranted absenteeism. General Lee wrote apprehensively of the thinning of his ranks in August, and Secretary Seddon observed in September that "desertion is committed almost with impunity." [79] President Davis, according to the Richmond Enquirer of October 6, "emphatically announced the startling fact that two-thirds of the army are absent from the ranks."

The three months preceding Appomattox saw an ever mounting tide of leave-taking. Small groups of men assigned to picket duty slipped away nightly from their posts all along the Virginia front; scores of others took advantage of the cover of darkness to crawl from the trenches. In the retreat from Nashville Hood's troops straggled by the hundreds, never to rejoin their commands. Across the Mississippi 400 of General Price's men deserted in one day of February 1865.[80] Between February 26 and March 8, 779 men deserted from the Army of Northern Virginia, according to a report of General Lee, and from March 15 to 25, 1,094; in one instance an entire brigade deserted en masse.[81]

John S. Preston, Superintendent of the Bureau of Conscription, stated in February 1865 that there were over 100,000 deserters scattered throughout the Confederacy, and compilations from other sources indicate that his estimate is conservative.[82] But, as stated previously, figures for desertion tell only part of the story; unfortunately, due to lack of data covering absence other than desertion, the complete tale cannot be told.

There is significant information, however, in a composite tabulation prepared by the War Department from the last returns sent in by the various armies. This compilation shows a total of 198,494 officers and men absent and only 160,198 present in the armies of the Confederacy on the eve of surrender.[83] The figure for absentees includes of course those excused for wounds, sickness and other legitimate purposes, but even so, it is shamefully large. Interpreted most generously, available evidence is such as to merit the observation that months before Appomattox the Confederacy's doom was plainly written in the ever swelling tide of men who were unpatriotically taking leave of their comrades-in-arms.

But in the midst of all the defection that cursed the Confederacy, and in the face of increasing hardship, there were a large number of Rebs whose spirit remained strong. It is pleasant to turn from the woeful subject of evasion to consideration of those who stood firm at their posts of duty.

Morale seems to have been considerably better among the upper and middle classes than it was among less privileged groups. This better spirit can be attributed not so much to the greater material stake involved as to intangible factors of education, travel, experience and self-confidence. A broad background led to a more wholesome point of view and to greater adaptability. Aristocratic organizations like the Washington Artillery, the Mobile Cadets and the Richmond Blues were able to maintain a consistently higher morale than were the toughest of mountaineer troops.[84] And desertion was noticeably worse among soldiers of lower classes than it was among those of moderate and superior means.[85] But there were, of course, innumerable instances of strongheartedness among the humblest of Rebs.

A patriotic and optimistic attitude on the part of friends and relatives at home was a powerful stimulant to soldier morale. The will to persevere must have been strengthened by a note such as that penned by Mollie Vanderberg to her sweetheart in the army:

"*Dear Henry,*

"I feel more *lonely* and *sad* than I have been in some time—perhaps tis because the last companie have taken off nearly all of the gentlemen I respect in Texas. . . . Oh! that I knew what the termination of this awful conflict would be. Henry I want to see you but dont you come—join for the War if tis forty years if you get killed tis the most honorable death—if you escape *I will rejoice. I love thee still.*" [86]

Likewise, the attitude of a father such as that of C. L. Stephens must have been an effective deterrent to desertion. "I have not tolde you Pa's sentiment about this war," wrote Stephens to his cousin in March 1865. "Some time he is in mighty good spirits and at another time he is out of heart but he does not believe in desertion atall he told me when I was at home [on furlough] that he did not want none of his boys to desert and ly in the woods . . . that he had reather [lose] our wate in gold than for any of us to runaway . . . I had rather die than to runaway myself." [87]

But the morale of many Rebs remained good *in spite of* expressions of gloom on the part of homefolk, as shown by statements of mild censure in letters sent home. "I am sorry . . . the people at home are whipped," wrote a Georgian to his father, in the spring of 1864; "Yes more than whipped. Some are both whipped and defeated. The army lacks a great deal of being whipped." [88] Several months later while dark clouds of defeat were overcasting Confederate skies a Mississippian observed to a fellow soldier, "Citizens seem very gloomy and desponding about our cause but *this* Army still retains its high spirits: *we are all sanguine.*" [89]

Statements of soldiers about the general morale of the army cannot be accepted at face value when addressed to homefolk, because optimistic letters were sometimes merely attempts at lightening depression. But there is considerable significance in the very fact that men in the army must often rouse the lagging spirits of those at home.

The dogged and cheerful performance of duty in the most trying circumstances repeatedly testified to the staunch-heartedness of a portion of the army from beginning to end of the conflict. After the strenuous campaign about Yorktown in the spring of 1862 General J. B. Magruder reported that "from April 4 to May 3 this army served without relief in the trenches. Many companies of artillery were never relieved during this long period. It rained almost incessantly; the trenches were filled with water; the weather was exceedingly cold; no fires could be allowed; the artillery . . . of the enemy played upon our men almost continuously day and night; the army . . . subsisted on flour and salt meat, and that in reduced quantities, and yet no murmurs were heard . . . patriotism made them indifferent to suffering, disease, danger, and death." [90]

After the terrible ordeal of Vicksburg, where men lived for forty-seven days and nights under almost constant shelling, nourished by the scantiest of rations and by maggot-infested water, officers of several units testified to a dauntless spirit. Colonel Ashabel Smith of the Second Texas infantry said that "up to the last moment of siege the men bore with unrepining cheerfulness" the overwhelming hardships which they experienced. "When I think of their buoyant courage under these circumstances," he added, and "the alacrity with which they performed every duty, it appears to me no commendation of those soldiers can be too great."

General F. A. Shoup gave similar testimony of the spirit of his brigade. Concerning the capitulation he said:

"At 10:00 A. M. [July 4] we moved out of our trenches by battalion, stacked arms, and then returned to our old quarters in town. The men were full of indignation [because of the surrender]. . . . I have rarely heard a murmur of complaint. The tone has always been, 'this is pretty hard, but we can stand it.' " [91]

Admitting in these cases, as well as in others, a tendency of officers in official reports to overpraise the conduct of their men, there remains substantial evidence of the highest kind of courage and determination.

Shortly after General Lee had driven Meade back across the Rappahannock in the fall of 1863, he wrote to Secretary Seddon:

"Nothing prevented my continuing in his front but the destitute condition of the men, thousands of whom are barefooted, a great number partially shod, and nearly all without overcoats, blankets, or warm clothing. I think the sublimest sight of the war was the cheerfulness and alacrity exhibited by this army in the pursuit of the enemy under all the trials and privations to which it was exposed." [92]

One reason for this high morale in the face of great want was the inurement of the men to hardship, accompanied by a sort of do-or-die reaction. An Alabama captain noticed this tendency in his company. After the terrible suffering experienced by Longstreet's command in the war's third winter, he wrote to his father:

"If anyone had told me before the war that men could have borne for month after month . . . what we have, I would have thought it all talk. And I recollect when we first came into the service we grumbled at fare that we would now think the greatest luxuries." [93]

Three privates of Lee's army stated the viewpoint of common soldiers hardened to adversity. "I am in good spirits myself," wrote one in December 1863; "whenever I hear of a misfortune instead of its giveing me the blews it prepars me for battle & I feel like striveing to regane that which is lost." A second observed in May 1864, "As for myself, I am getting pretty tired of it, but am not ready yet a while to say Enought. I think I can stand thru three more years yet and I think before that time they [the Yankees] will get Middling tired of it." The third wrote during the latter stages of the Wilderness campaign: "I am been quite sick with fever for the last 4 or 5 days. They want me to go to Richmond but I am determined to see this fight out if it costs me my life." [94]

Even in the midst of all the shirking and defeatism that marked the last year of war there was much disapproval of the widespread defection. "Let a man try to 'play out' now by feigning disability," wrote a participant in the Atlanta campaign, "and he is jeered at and when exposed by the Surgeons he is greeted with shouts of derision." [95] A Louisianian aired his opinion against the seekers of soft appointments. "I have a profound contempt," he wrote, "for all men croakers who are hunting easy places at home to avoid the dangers of the battle field." [96] And, of course, good soldiers everywhere denounced the mounting tide of desertion that encompassed them.

Even in the hour of defeat the spirit of some was unyielding. Scores of Lee's men slipped away from Appomattox to avoid the intolerable humiliation of formal capitulation. And when General Bryan Grimes announced the surrender to his command, one Reb threw away his musket and with upraised hands cried out, "Blow, Gabriel! Blow! My

God, let him blow, I am ready to die." Another grasped his leader by the hand in farewell and sobbed, "Good-by, General; God bless you, we will go home, make three more crops, and try them again." [97]

Most soldiers of good morale were subject to occasional lapses of spirit, but there was one Reb of such consistent and high patriotism as to merit special mention. This man was J. T. Terrell, of Aberdeen, Mississippi. Though of superior background and education, he left military school to enlist as a private in the spring of 1861; and while he undoubtedly could have secured a lieutenancy through his influence, he never held a commission.

His letters fairly overflow with buoyancy from beginning to end of his service. On November 16, 1862, for instance, he wrote his mother:

"A soldier's life never was hard to me I can get along anywhere and under any circumstances. I have been in camp so long that I feel perfectly at home, and if I was anywhere else I . . . would have a natural feeling of not being in my proper place."

To his mother's suggestion after his sojourn in a Northern prison in 1862 that a substitute might be procured for him, he responded:

"I can say I do not want any as I think it is the duty of every man to bear an equal part in this struggle. . . . I think all men that own property to any extent and especially negro property Should take a part in this war as it has a tendency to encourage the poorer classes."

Just after re-enlistment for the duration of the war by his regiment in early 1864, he exulted:

"I tell you we are not by any means subjugated or despondent. There is life in the old land yet."

Two months later while on his way to participate in the defense of Atlanta, he wrote encouragingly to his mother:

"Hold up your hand and behold the Sky as it brightens. Day is fast dawning upon our infant Confederacy."

After the lapse of a few weeks he boasted:

"Our army is buoyant, enthusiastic, and hopeful in feeling. There is no better army anywhere nor is there any that is better officered. You need not fear the result when the Shock comes." [98]

Two and one-half months later "Tom" Terrell was dead—his brain pierced by a sharpshooter's bullet while on picket before Atlanta. After a few days his father at Quincy plantation in Mississippi received a letter from the hands of his soldier son's Negro body servant, Gabriel, telling of the tragedy. The missive, written by one of Tom's comrades on the very day of his death, is an eloquent testimony to unfaltering devotion to duty:

> IN THE DITCHES ATLANTA GA.
> Aug 22 1864

COL. B. M. TERRELL

My Dear Friend It becomes my duty to inform you of the death of your noble and gallant son. . . . Tom was a favorite with the whole regiment and all concur in saying that he was the best soldier in the regiment There can be said more for him than can be said for one in Ten thousand. he has never missed a roll call a drill a tour of duty never been absent a day without leave never reported to a surgeon nor has he ever slept out of camp unless on duty the loss of such men can not be supplied. Tom was strictly moral I never saw him out of humor in my life. . . .

> Very respectfully your friend,
> G. W. PENNINGTON [99]

If this tribute be accurate, Tom Terrell was truly "the good soldier" of the "lost cause."

How tragic for the Confederacy that there were not more like him. In the months that followed his death, the morale of both citizens and troops came to be in ever sharper contrast to the loftiness of spirit exemplified by Terrell, until on the eve of Appomattox evaders and absentees far outnumbered soldiers who were present for duty.

At the time of surrender an Alabama private addressed his captain on the sad fate that had overtaken the Southland. "Who was the cause of it?" he asked. "Skulkers Cowards extortioners and Deserters not the Yankees that makes it woss." [100] And in light of the shirking that surrounded him, this lowly Reb's observation carries an impressive conviction of truth.

CHAPTER IX

BREAKING THE MONOTONY

SOLDIERING can be a very dull job. Granting that "Old Peter" Longstreet, Stonewall Jackson, "Marse Robert" and most of the other generals managed to find an uncommon amount of scrapping for Johnny Reb to do, comparatively little time was occupied in actual fighting. The long hours in camp were wont to bear heavily on the Confederate private, as on soldiers of all armies since the beginning of organized combat. James Hampton Kuykendall, a Reb encamped in Texas, expressed a sentiment well-nigh universal among troops when he wrote in his journal on an autumn day of 1862:

"None can imagine, who has never experienced a soldier's life, the languor of mind—tediousness of time, as we resume—day after day the monotonous duties devolved upon." [1]

But Johnny Reb was, for the most part, a volatile, sociable person; his disposition, plus his innate love of fun, caused him to invent all sorts of escapes from the boredom of camp life. So frequent and varied were diversions, particularly during the first two years of conflict before deprivation and war weariness began to interpose so heavily, that a considerable number of men seemed to find more pleasure than hardship in soldiering. Some, indeed, after four years of campaigning could say convincingly that they enjoyed the war.

Perhaps the favorite recreation of the Confederate Army was music. In camp and on the march Johnny Reb found comfort in the sentimental melodies of the time. During the long wearisome stands on picket, he hummed or whistled softly to himself strains that recalled scenes of home and of childhood—or if his post was along the Chickahominy, the Rappahannock or the Chattahoochee, as it so frequently was, he might derive genuine pleasure from the playing by Yankee bands of "Cheer, Boys, Cheer," "Lorena," "Faded Flowers," and "Who Will Care for Mother Now." [2] But the greatest enjoyment came from informal singing about the campfire. Vocalizing in small groups seems to have been the general thing, but now and then mass singings on

151

such scale as to be called "musical sprees" or "jubilees" were staged. Once in a while song fests acquired additional zest by combination with convivial drinking.[3]

Johnny Reb had at his disposal an exceedingly wide repertoire of songs. Publishing firms, such as Blackmar and Werlein of New Orleans, Schreiner of Macon, and J. W. Randolph of Richmond, ground out a large quantity of sheet music, and Northern publishers sent Rebel tunes through the blockade.[4]

Much of the musical publishing, North and South, consisted of the reissuing of favorites, old and new; but a considerable quantity of fly-by-night trash came forth under the guise of patriotic melodies—items that frequently had more patriotism than melody. To supplement sheet music, Southern presses issued several pocket songbooks containing the words of sentimental and patriotic tunes. Among these brochures were the following: Songs of the South (Richmond, 1863); Stonewall Song Book (Richmond, 1863); Rebel Songster (Richmond, 1864); Army Songster (Richmond, 1864); Jack Morgan Songster (Raleigh, 1864); Songs of Love and Liberty (Raleigh, 1864); Southern Soldiers' Prize Songster (Mobile, 1864); Hopkins New Orleans 5¢ Song Book (New Orleans, 1861); Beauregard Songster (Macon and Savannah, 1864); General Lee Songster (Macon and Savannah, 1864); and Southern Flag Song Book (Mobile, 1864).[5] Letters, diaries and reminiscences of soldiers indicate that the great flood of new songs published during the war made little dent on Rebel ranks. The list of camp favorites was fairly small and it was made up to a large extent of melodies familiar before the war.

"Home, Sweet Home" was probably the most popular of all songs sung by wearers of the gray, but Payne's immortal work was closely pressed for top honors by two lugubrious ballads entitled "Lorena" and "All Quiet Along the Potomac Tonight." "Annie Laurie" and "Juanita" also ranked very high in soldier esteem. Other tender melodies heard frequently about the campfire were "Annie of the Vale," "Sweet Evelina," "Lilly Dale," "The Girl I Left Behind Me," "Bell Brandon," "Her Bright Eyes Haunt Me Still," "Listen to the Mocking Bird," and "Just Before the Battle, Mother."[6] The last-named song, like several others that were popular among Confederates, was borrowed from the Yankees.

An impressive portion of sentimental favorites had doleful themes. But soldiers had at their command also a number of rollicking songs that reflected lightheartedness and optimism. Sometimes as they

Courtesy North Carolina Historical Commission, Raleigh, North Carolina

CAMP THEATRICAL PROGRAMS

Programs for theatricals staged by Confederate prisoners at Johnson's Island.

THOMAS FONDREN McKIE, KILLED AT GETTYSBURG

"You recollect, Mother, we walked out into the garden and you cryed." From Maud Morrow Brown, *The University Greys* (Richmond, 1940). McKie was a private in the University Greys, Company A, 11th Mississippi Regiment. He was a Mississippian.

trudged along through mud and rain their voices rose in unison to a verse that ran:

> So let the wide world wag as it will,
> We'll be gay and happy still.[7]

Another song heard occasionally among gray-clads contained this thrust at the Yankees:

> The Sixteenth Louisiana charged them with a yell,
> Bagged the Bucktail Rangers and sent them all to hell.[8]

Soldiers of Bragg's army liked a saucy tune with this refrain:

> We are sons of old Aunt Dinah,
> And we go where we've amind to
> And we stay where we're inclined to,
> And we dont care a damn cent.[9]

A Tar Heel regiment had a rollicking ditty which paid tribute to the girls back home:

> Ho for the maids of Kenansville
> A Song for Carolina's fair
> We'll sing a stan[za] with right good will
> To beaming eyes & f[l]owing hair
> To rosy cheeks & teeth of pearl
> And drink to each fair girl
> But who shall be the toast, I say,
> Who shall be the toast, Miss K?
> If eyes of azure & bright & beaming
> With angels smiles will set you dreaming
> Then indeed the toast shall be
> A bumper full for lovely Annie—
> If eyes as dark as the gazell's
> Brightly flashing warm your fancy
> Drink to ½ Doz belles
> But G may drink to lovely Nancy
> Too long 'tween drinks will never do
> My boys they're all too good for you
> Stay at your camp attend the drill
> Keep out of scrapes & Kenansville
> Fill up your glasses, hold your jaw,
> A toast to all hip-hip huzzah!
> A glass & cheer for each fair maid
> And a tiger give for our Brigade [10]

Camp repertoires in some portions of the army included indecent and ribald songs, but no documentary record of titles or content was found.[11]

Among patriotic songs "Dixie" was the most popular. Variations and parodies were numerous. One of these, found among the war letters of a Texan, is a sort of running commentary on Yankee leadership and fighting ability:

> I wish I was in the land of cotton
> Simmon seed and sandy bottom—away in Dixie.
> Stonewall Jackson have you any wool
> Yes my master *Baltimore* full.
>
> Burnside Burnside whither dost thou wander
> Up stream down stream like a crazy gander.
> Pope and McDowell fighting for a town
> Up jumped Lee and knocked them both down
> Nelson Bull Nelson fly away home
> Your army is scattered and your cannon all gone.
>
> I tell you what it is and what I am thinking
> Our Jeff Davis can whip old Abe Lincoln
> He whiped on the battle field I'll tell you the reason why
> He always makes the *Yankee* cowards run hog or die.
>
> There was a Yankee general by the name of Banks
> But he couldn't climb over a Stonewall fense.
> Lincoln! oh Lincoln how sad was the day
> When the Southrons did meet us in battle array
> They came in their power their might and their main
> And scattered our legions like sheep on the plain.[12]

Another parody, said to have been sung by the "Bienville Rifles" enroute from Louisiana to Virginia in 1861, bore the title "I wish I was in Richmond":

> I. From home and friends we all must go,
>   To meet a strong but dastard foe.
>   Look away, look away, look away to Richmond town;
>   And ere again those friends we see
>   We vow to die or all be free;
>   Look away, look away, look away to Richmond town;
>
>   . . . .

III. Old Abe they say is monstrous tight,
 And cannot sleep a wink at night.
 Look away, look away, look away to Richmond town;
 But when he comes to Richmond City,
 The way we'll cool him 'tis a pity.
 Look away, look away, look away to Richmond town.

. . . .

V. We'll meet old Abe with armies brave,
 And whip the lying scoundrel knave.
 Look away, look away, look away to Richmond town;
 As he pleads for terms and whiskey,
 We'll give him hell to the tune of Dixie.
 Look away, etc.[13]

Popular also, particularly during the early months of the war, was the "Bonnie Blue Flag," a composition inspired by the single-starred first flag of the Confederacy, and set to the music of an old Hibernian song entitled the "Irish Jaunting Car." The opening verse and chorus suggest the rousing appeal of this song:

We are a band of brothers, and native to the soil,
Fighting for the property we gained by honest toil;
And when our rights were threatened, the cry rose near and far,
Hurrah for the Bonnie Blue Flag, that bears a Single Star!

Hurrah! Hurrah! For Southern Rights Hurrah!
Hurrah! For the Bonnie Blue Flag that bears a Single Star.[14]

"My Maryland," written in 1861, was hardly less popular than "Bonnie Blue Flag." The heart of many a volunteer doubtless was fired with patriotic valor as he sang the memorable lines beginning:

The despot's heel is on thy shore,
 Maryland! My Maryland!
His torch is at thy temple door,
 Maryland! My Maryland!
Avenge the patriotic gore
That flow'd the streets of Baltimore,
And be the battle queen of yore,
 Maryland! My Maryland!

and ending:

I hear the distant thunder-hum,
    Maryland! My Maryland!
The Old Line's bugle, fife, and drum,
    Maryland! My Maryland!
She is not dead, nor deaf, nor dumb—
Huzza! she spurns the Northern scum!
She breathes—she burns! she'll come! she'll come!
    Maryland! My Maryland! [15]

Several regiments had glee clubs which gave occasional programs for the entertainment of officers and men. One of the most famous of these was composed of members of the Fourteenth Tennessee Infantry. This club, organized in 1861 and maintaining an unbroken personnel throughout the war, had some unusually talented singers who not only presented camp concerts, but who also sang occasionally to comrades on the march. June Kimble, the club's violinist, left the following record of a memorable incident that took place as the army was heading northward for the Chancellorsville-Gettysburg campaign:

"The time was about one o'clock A. M. Surgeon Wright, riding at the head of his regiment caught the inspiration of the moment, took his flute from his saddle pockets . . . and electrified his comrades . . . with 'Home Sweet Home' . . . Instantly the other members of the Glee Club gathered around him and in subdued tone joined in the chorus. The effect was indescribable. The sweetness and beauty of it all may never be duplicated in song or scene. Then followed 'Annie Laurie,' 'Swanee River,' 'Massa in the Cold Cold Ground,' 'The Old Kentucky Home,' 'Bonny Blue Flag,' and the climax 'Dixie Land.' " [16]

Instrumental music was another important source of diversion. Regularly organized company and regimental bands provided marching airs for drills and gave occasional night concerts. An Alabama brigade which boasted two or three regimental bands was entertained with "the best kind of martial music every morning and evening." [17] Selections were of great number and variety. Captain D. S. Redding of the Forty-fifth Georgia Regiment records in his diary that on July 3, 1863, he heard the following pieces: "Shells of Ocean, Lone Rock by the Sea, Dixie, Marseilles Hymn, They Told me not to Love Him, Bonny Eloise, Fare thee well Kittie, Irish Emigrant's Lament, Prarie Flower, Leila is Gone, Mocking Bird, Katie Darling, Old Hundred, Do They Miss Me at Home, Grand March Innovation, Gentle Annie, Belle Brandon." [18]

Captain Redding failed to remark on the skill of the musicians to whom he listened, but James J. Kirkpatrick of the Sixteenth Mississippi Volunteers suggested that the band of his regiment was distinguished more by zeal than by ability. On October 30, 1863, he made the following entry in his diary:

"Camp, 2 miles South of the Rappahannock. Drilling as usual. went over to the Band in the evening to hear some vocal and instrumental music. Our band is a great institution. It always keeps its numbers undiminished, and labors with the greatest assiduity at 'tooting'. Their music, however, is never the sweetest nor most harmonious." [19]

Difficulty of procuring instruments, scarcity of cultivated talent, and the stringencies of campaigning prevented the maintenance of high-class bands. European visitors to Southern camps were shocked by the "discordant braying" of some of the musical organizations, and there can be little doubt that the majority were of inferior rating.[20] But even so, their contribution to happiness and morale was considerable.

A South Carolina private who heard several bands play "Pop Goes the Weasel" at the conclusion of a public function in 1861 said: "I have never heard or seen such a time before. The noise of the men was deafening. I felt at the time that I could whip a whole brigade of the enemy myself." [21]

And General Lee, after listening to a brass serenade in 1864, remarked: "I don't believe we can have an army without music." [22]

In addition to regularly organized bands, many military units had informal groups of "artists" whose dominant motive was the entertainment of those who made the music. Such an organization was the minstrel band of Kennedy's Louisiana Battalion. Some of the instruments of this band were difficult to classify. There was a "cross fiddle" made of a drum head "nailed over half a whiskey keg with a rough pine neck, and strings and screws accordin"—but the melody achieved by the minstrels was such as to make them in great demand not only for camp "hoe-downs," but for civilian programs as well.[23]

Instrumental music that Johnny Reb used most frequently, and perhaps enjoyed most thoroughly came not from any organized group at all, but from one or two messmates who had brought highly cherished fiddles and banjos from home and who at night labored away at familiar tunes about the campfire. A good fiddler was a popular personage in any outfit, and a mess that could boast a violin-flute combination or a fiddle-banjo duet was the object of widespread envy. The favorite repertoires included such numbers as "Hell Broke Loose in Georgia," "Billy in the Low Grounds," "Arkansas Traveler," "Money Musk," "The Goose Hangs High," "When I Saw Sweet Nellie Home," "My Old Kentucky Home," "Oh Lord Gals One Friday," and "Dixie." [24]

In their home letters soldiers spoke often and appreciatively of the prowess of informal camp musicians. Edward T. Worthington, of a Mississippi company, wrote to his cousin from camp in Kentucky:

"We have a lively time here . . . every fellow full of life. . . . every night fiddlers are plentiful such as the break down and work out. When we want something nice we borrow the fiddle and go to our tent Will *tries himself* and draws a tent as full as they can stick around in it. . . . I wish . . . you could happen in sometime while Will Mason is playing the violin & see some of our capers." [25]

With fiddlers enjoying such popularity as this, it is not surprising that the price of instruments rose dizzily. An Alabama private, who must have been much better at music than he was at spelling, wrote proudly to his brother in October 1861:

"Tobe I have got the best violent in the Regment Jo Jackson ses it is worth one Hundred dollars." [26]

A favorite exercise of musicians, both vocal and instrumental, was to go about at night serenading fellow soldiers of the encampment and young ladies of the countryside. These were occasions gala enough, but serenadings of popular officers seem to have elicited the maximum of jollity. Private J. E. Thornton wrote enthusiastically to his wife of an affair in Mississippi in which he participated in the fall of 1861:

"We had a great seranad the night after we were Transferred [from state to Confederate service] we all turned our coats rong side out and seranaded all the big officers we allowed to serenade Enterpris last night but General Oferil sent us word that he was sick and he rather we would wait till he got well So the eighth Regiment Seranad us last night it was a pretty sight all the Regiment together with pretty music." [27]

Officers thus complimented were expected to give tangible expression of appreciation. When Captain Thomas J. Key of the Army of

Tennessee was serenaded without prior notice by the band of General Polk's brigade ("composed of one cornet, one bass horn, two violins, two flutes, and one guitar"), a doctor friend came gallantly to his rescue by bringing out a bottle of whiskey, while the captain "refreshed the band by slicing up a loaf of light bread." [28] Few captains could have responded more nobly, even with forewarning.

Next to music, Johnny Reb probably found more frequent and satisfactory diversion in sports than in anything else. When leisure and weather permitted, soldiers turned out in large numbers for baseball. Captain James Hall of the Twenty-fourth Alabama Regiment observed that his men, while Joe Johnston was waiting at Dalton to see what Sherman was going to do, played baseball "just like school boys." The same could have been said of almost any other regiment of the Confederacy. The exercise might be of the modern version, with players running four bases, or it might be two-base townball. The bat might be a board, a section of some farmer's fence rail, or a slightly trimmed hickory limb; the pellet might be nothing better than a yarn-wrapped walnut; but enthusiasm would be so great as to make the camp reverberate with the cheers and taunts of participants, if not of spectators. And the game might become so rough as to necessitate precautionary steps. "Frank Ezell was ruled out," wrote a Texas Ranger in his diary, because "he could throw harder and straighter than any man in the company. He came very near knocking the stuffing out of three or four of the boys, and the boys swore they would not play with him." [29]

Football and cricket are mentioned by a few soldier correspondents, and there is one reference to a game called "hot jackets," in which each participant attacked his opponent with a limber hickory switch.[30] But common exercises were foot racing, wrestling, boxing, leapfrog, hopscotch, quoits, and marbles. Some Rebs played tenpins after a fashion ironically unique, by rolling cannon balls at the pins, or at holes in the ground.[31] Swimming was popular in encampments near the seacoast and streams; and Johnny Reb was not the sort of person who would halt his bathing for cold weather, particularly if the "gray backs" were gnawing in strong force. Water near camp sites was also utilized for fishing, seining and grabbling, though the sporting urge was frequently secondary to that of hunger. Hunting, likewise, was prompted by a double motive, and in many instances mess larders were enriched as a result of successful forays for quail, robins, turkeys, rabbits, squirrels, 'possums and deer. On many quests for game scarcity of ammunition plus greater effectiveness of other methods led to the laying aside of guns. Rabbits were stalked in wood or meadow and killed with rocks and clubs, or hemmed in and caught by hand. Hungry, emaciated Rebs could give almost any sort of edible animal a lively run, and their diaries and letters tell of amazing quarries. "The boys had lots of fun catching squirls clubing & shaking and yeling them out of the trees," wrote a Mississippian in 1862, and a comrade noted in his diary about the same time that "the soldiers of our Brigade chased and caught a Red fox which was quite a myracle." [32] Shortly after the Antietam campaign a Virginian wrote his mother:

"Yesterday a covey of partridges was flushed in the Field where we camped, they grew bewildered & squatted about in the field; three or four were caught. I caught one plump & full grown; yes and eat him too, picking his bones clean." [33]

The most successful hunting-without-arms venture, from the standpoint of quantity of game brought in, is recorded by Private J. H. Puckett. Late one afternoon in February 1863 he and seven comrades slipped off from their camp near Shelbyville, Tennessee, and concealed themselves under a robin roost which had been visited with good results by other soldiers the previous night.

He wrote his wife this account:

"When night came, I could hardly believe my eyes. As far as I could see the heavens were blackened with these little Robins coming in to the Cedar brakes to roost. . . . When sufficiently dark, Book took 2 others and went way around, clum up bushes and whistled so as to let us know where to drive. We lit our torches and went thrashing through the bushes from one tree to another until they would light in the ones where our boys would be stationed and then of all the little chicken hollowing you ever heard, it beats all they come into the tree so fast and thick that they would [light] in our faces, on our heads feet hands and sometimes you can catch them with your mouth . . . [we] caught . . . in all about 50 . . . It took me ½ day to sew up my jeans pants where they bursted climbing through the thick cedar branches . . . but . . . I felt amply repaid when we set down to a big chicken stew made of Robins and they were the fattiest things I ever saw of the feathered tribe." [34]

Cavalrymen found diversion on occasion in staging "ring tournaments." [35] More exciting pastime, however, was gander-pulling. In this sport, horsemen riding at full tilt attempted to catch the head of a live gander that hung by its feet from a point barely within the rider's reach. Gander-pulling, when featured at dress parades, aroused great enthusiasm in both soldiers and civilians.[36]

Card games were another highly favored diversion in Southern camps. Indeed, accuracy would not be much stretched if the scriptural passage were parodied to read, "Wherever two or three Confederate soldiers were gathered together, there would a deck of cards make its appearance in the midst of them." Much of the playing, as has been previously noted, was for stakes, but many hands were held with fun as the sole objective.[37] Sessions were frequently of long duration—one mess habitually spent six hours a day playing cards—and interest of the players ran high.[38] Chess was not without its devotees in Rebel ranks, but it seems never to have gained any considerable popularity.[39] Draughts, or checkers, and a kindred game called "Fox and Geese" were played to a limited extent.[40]

Reading provided a source of recreation for many soldiers, though army routine was not conducive to a great deal of it. During the day, except in winter, there was little time for reading. In winter quarters there was usually ample leisure, but tents or huts were frequently so cold that soldiers sought comfort between blankets. At night fatigue, poor lighting and the activities of restless comrades made reading almost impossible. Also, interesting books and periodicals were hard to obtain. But in spite of these factors, there was a vast amount of reading done in the Rebel Army. Newspapers were the most eagerly sought of available reading materials. Frequent army movements and chronically deficient mail facilities made delivery of papers irregular and uncertain. But when subscribers did receive their journals from Richmond, Atlanta, Memphis, Jackson, or some other city, they read them avidly and then passed them on to a line of impatient comrades until the none-too-substantial pages were literally worn out. Periodicals such as the *Southern Illustrated News, Southern Field and Fireside,* and *De Bow's Review* also had a considerable circulation in the army.[41]

Better-educated and more fortunate soldiers procured and read books in considerable numbers. And there is evidence of good taste in numerous instances. W. M. Barrow, a Louisiana private with some college education, read, while in camp and prison, among other books, Thiers' *French Revolution,* Swift's *Gulliver's Travels,* and Dumas' *Count of Monte Cristo.* The camp reading list of Charles Woodward Hutson, a cultured young South Carolinian, included works of Shakespeare, Milton, Bulwer, Shelley, Scott, Coleridge, Beverly Tucker and

"Bill Arp," along with *Arabian Nights* and the New Testament.[42]
Harry St. John Dixon of Mississippi read *Paradise Lost, David Copper-field*, Baldwin's *Flush Times of Alabama and Mississippi* and Fanny
Fern's *Rose Clark*, but of Harriet Beecher Stowe's masterpiece he
wrote: "[Spent] all day coughing & reading that d——d Yankee lie
Uncle Tom's Cabin."[43] Edward A. Pollard, Cowper, Macaulay and
J. J. Hooper were read by some, but their writings were not so popular
as Hugo's *Les Misérables* and Scott's *Ivanhoe*. The most widely read
of all books was the Bible.

As a rule even novels of indifferent interest and merit were eagerly
read when available. But among some of the more serious-minded and
religiously inclined troops there was a strong prejudice against fiction.
Private H. A. Stephens of Mississippi reflected the attitude of this
group in a letter to his sister:

"If you cant get good books to read do not read any. any composition of fiction falsehoods calculated to excite the mind, to a great
extent should not be read by anyone. . . . when any one gets used to
reading anything very excitable they cant read any other composition
with intrst. . . . I have seen too many brilliant minds of young men
almost ruined, Just in this way, during this war. one of my mess who
had an excelant mind, read Novals a long time. he con clded a short
time ago to study grammar if i would instruct him, & of cors i could
not refuse, but it is the hardest work i ever saw for him to keep his
mind on it he is a gorgian."[44]

Men of Stephens' serious bent of mind constituted a comparatively
small minority of the army. Most Rebs looked at the lighter and
brighter side of life. This tendency expressed itself in many forms of
teasing and horseplay. If a comrade or visitor happened to make an
appearance in some sort of unusual garb, he immediately became the
object of a chorus of gibes.

Favorite greeting for a man with a large new headpiece was "Come
out of that hat! I see your legs," or "Look out, that parrot shell you're
wearing's going to explode," or "Take that camp kettle home, aren't
you ashamed to steal a poor soldier's camp kettle?"[45]

And the donning of a new pair of boots would call for: "Come
up outer them boots; come out; too soon to go into winter quarters; I
know you're in thar; I see your arms sticking out."

A staff officer who rode through camp sporting a long and finely
twisted mustache was apt to receive from behind tents and trees the

irreverent suggestion, "Take them mice out'er your mouth; take em out; no use to say they aint thar, see their tails hangin' out." An unduly luxuriant beard might provoke the invitation, "Come out 'er that bunch of har. I see your ears a workin'." [46]

If some Reb happened to mimic a chicken, a cow, or a donkey the whole camp might break out in a frenzy of cackling, crowing, shooing, braying or bellowing. Let some visitor inquire as to the whereabouts of Company F, and a soldier down the line would yell, "Here's Company F"; others would take up the cry and soon the entire brigade would echo the refrain. When an old soldier on the march greeted a friend with "How are you, Jim?" fellow Rebs were almost certain to follow suit until Jim was overwhelmed with the salutations of a brigade or division.[47] Mischievous Confederates had a slang expression, "Here's your mule," which they bandied about in much the same fashion as American Legionnaires use the phrase "Where's Elmer?" [48]

Soldiers sometimes stole one another's letters, and discovery of a saccharine missive from some indiscreet sweetheart would immediately lead to making public the contents and ribbing the embarrassed or angry owner. A Texas private named J. W. Rabb one day received a poetically endearing letter from his sister Bet. When this note fell into the hands of Rabb's comrades they immediately concluded that Bet was his sweetheart and proceeded to tease him roundly. Rabb's barely decipherable narration of the incident to his sister gives a delicious insight into the bantering, fun-loving character of the Confederate soldier:

"You roat me such a good long letter i like it so much for The boys all thought that it was from my jularky and one little fellow develed me so much about Fly home to thy native home gentle dove he sayed that I looked more like a paterage." [49]

Another Texas private who had trouble with spelling wrote a friend back home about a trick of which he had recently been the victim:

"I mett with an accident yesterday it was my cook day and I was getting souper we had [a] pretty good size yong turky a cooking some develish fellows had been watching me when I put it in the pot well at souper time I went to take it out and put it on the table do you think I found the turky no by God it was nothing but the feather." [50]

Fondness of horseplay manifested itself in such activities as bumping comrades against trees, rolling them in mud, smoking them out of their tents, or loading their firewood with powder.[51] Putting a nervous recruit on picket with an unloaded gun—a fact concealed of course from the recruit—impressing on him the peril and responsibility of his position by telling him to die at his post like a man, and subsequently charging his station with hostile yells to see him run was considered a capital joke.[52] Little wonder is it that pranks innocently conceived sometimes had fatal consequences.[53]

A diversion from which soldiers throughout the South derived enjoyment was the staging of shows and stunts. These dramatic efforts were of great variety. Texas Ranger troops liked to indulge in circus performances.[54] The Richmond Howitzers' "Law Club" held occasional moot court sessions that were said to have been marked by brilliant discussions.[55] Many companies had lone artists who entertained their comrades informally about the campfire. The Kennedy Battalion of New Orleans enjoyed the occult tricks of "A no. 1 slight-of-hand man"; and another outfit boasted a "chin music" performer who for a jigger of whiskey would put his hand to his chin and make with his teeth "a sound like rattling bones, keeping time to his song and pat." [56]

A Texas Ranger told in his diary of an unusually versatile entertainer:

"April 12, 1862 . . . A fellow by the name of Vaughn is amusing the boys just now, he is a perfect curiosity—born in the city of New York, partly raised on the ocean, and having the advantage of general information, and personal observation gave him a decided advantage over us poor back woods fellows that was wonderful, he could sing funny Songs, dance clog, make funny speaches, play tricks, turn somer saults, and other things two numerous to mention." [57]

Frequently the talent of various organizations was combined for the preparation of elaborate minstrel or varieties programs. To these affairs the public was usually invited, and admission was charged for the benefit of wounded soldiers, impoverished civilians, or for some other benevolent purpose. The performances were staged in camp or in the theater of a town near by.[58]

If camp was the place of performances, considerable preparation was necessary to provide properties and accommodations for spectators. A location resembling a natural amphitheater was cleared of brush and rubbish. Seats were sometimes borrowed from a neighboring school or church, but more frequently soldiers had to stand, and visiting ladies were seated on boxes, barrels, planks, or "pinelogs, flattened on one side to prevent their rocking." The stage was usually of rough boards raised two or three feet above the ground, the "footlights" a dozen or so candles, the heating facilities a few log fires built around the edges of the location, and the curtain a tent fly or a blanket.[59] The program was made up of songs and instrumental music, magicians' tricks, clog dances by overly painted "Ethiopians," and ballets by terpsichorean artists whose heavy feet and large frames belied the crinoline that awkwardly draped them. But the inconsistency between dancers and apparel only added to the merriment. Pantomimes, tableaux, dialogues and plays completed the roster of offerings. These might occasionally have serious themes, but usually they were comic.

A program presented by Fenner's Battery at the beginning of the Atlanta campaign featured burlesques of the use of snuff by Georgia females, "the practice of soldiers shooting pigs and chickens, and visiting farm houses with doleful tales of hunger, the honesty of Quartermasters, and the inferior quality of Confederate whiskey." [60] Take-offs on officers were probably the most popular of all dramatic offerings.

A theatrical group from the Stonewall and Louisiana brigades wrote and presented a skit called the "Medical Board," satirizing the surgeons.

The rise of the curtain revealed a group of doctors sitting about a table playing cards and drinking brandy. Presently inquiry is made as to how such good liquor is obtained in these hard times.

The immediate answer is, "Oh, this is some that was sent down from Augusta County for the sick soldiers, but the poor devils can't need it, so we'll drink it."

Then a courier comes in with the message that a badly wounded soldier is outside. "Bring him in! Bring him in!" says the chief surgeon.

After a casual examination, the patient is told that his arms must be amputated. He inquires if he can have a furlough after the operation.

"Oh, no," replies the surgeon, who shortly announces that a leg also must be cut off.

"Then can I have a furlough?" asks the soldier.

"By no means," answers the doctor, "for you can drive an ambulance when you get well."

The surgeons now go in consultation and decide that the wounded man's head must be amputated. "Then I know I can have a furlough," observes the patient.

"No, indeed," says the chief physician. "We are so scarce of men that your body will have to be set up in the breastworks to fool the enemy." [61]

One of the most famous theatrical groups in the entire Confederate Army was that of the Washington Artillery. Variety shows staged by these players during the war's second winter were amazingly elaborate. Programs were printed in Richmond and distributed widely among soldiers and civilians. For the second performance, presented in February 1863 at camp near Fredericksburg, a special train was run from the capital; Lee, detained by business, sent a note of regret but Longstreet and other generals attended in full regalia; common soldiers flocked from all divisions, some coming on foot from points as far removed as twenty miles. Music was furnished by the combined bands of the Twelfth and Sixteenth Mississippi Regiments. The main feature of the show was a burlesque entitled "Pocahontas, or Ye Gentle Savage," and according to one who was present, "the house came down any number of times and the audience appeared delighted. Following the feature there was an after-piece called 'Toodles'. The program was brought to a rousing conclusion by a band rendition of 'Bonnie Blue Flag'." [62]

Theatricals not only afforded great amusement in the preparation and the showing, but also provided topics of conversation and subject matter of letters for days to come. After attending "a kind of Negro Show called the Lone Star Minstrels" in the Pine Bluff Court House by Flournoy's Texans, a member of that regiment wrote to his sister: "Bully for Flournoy's Regiment we are some punkins, Youll Bet." [63]

Occasionally a group of Rebs would break the boresome routine of camp life by having a party or spree. Return of a popular officer provoked one of these celebrations in the Ninth Texas Cavalry in February 1862. The soldiers staged an "uncommon big War Dance," according to a diarist of the regiment, "firing guns by platoons, anvils by the dozen, in fact alarming the whole country—& finally getting after the Dutch Sutler who they seem to think is extortioning in the prices he is charging . . . threaten to hang him . . . and finally taking 50 condemned wagons near by and piling them up all around his shanty literally causing the old fellow to leave in haste next morning." [64]

In another instance, a celebration in a Mississippi regiment had the nature of a command performance, according to Private C. W. Stephens. "Our Col. got drunk last Saterday night," he wrote his sister in October, 1863, "and had the boyes dancing off theare doble dutie he also danced and pated for them he told them that he intended to present our flag a monday and he said if theare was airie man in the Regt that did not intend to foler it he waunted them to be missing the next morning . . . we all a gread to foler it eny wheare." [65]

Sometimes when women were allowed to visit camp in sufficient numbers, bona-fide dances were enjoyed, but these occasions were so rare that dance-loving Rebs were impelled to stage womanless affairs. If bonnets and other articles of feminine attire could be had, they were donned by those soldiers playing the parts of the belles, but usually the boys paired off as they were and performed the convolutions of the waltz, or went through the mazes of the square dance to such tunes as "Gal on the Log," "Rackinsack," and "Leather Breeches." [66] The music was usually provided by a fiddler or two belonging to the participating outfits.

Occasionally there were disturbing religious qualms. "The Capt and myself had a regular concert," wrote a banjo-playing Reb, "winding up in a stag dance, the Capt being a member of the Methodyst church wouldnt play for the dance so the 'Ordinary Sergent' fiddled." [67] But another private who did not dance himself viewed tolerantly the capers of his comrades, on the score that he "like[d] to see the Boys have their fun." [68]

A birthday of a popular comrade would often call forth a celebration. Charles Moore entertained his friends on his birthday. "I invited my companions to assist me in Emptying 3 canteens of 'Oh! be Joyful'," he wrote, "then spent the balance of the evening Singing—until Tattoo then we parted in Good Spirits." [69]

Christmas and New Year almost always brought a round of parties, and when whiskey could be obtained it added to the jollity of the celebration. A Texan wrote to his brother in January 1863 that "we got 3 gallons and a half of whisky with our $140.00 and had a jolly time of it Christmas eve night," but added significantly, "I dont want you to say anything about our *Frollick, to any body.*" [70]

The commissary department sometimes issued whiskey rations on festive days, but the amount was usually so small as to cause complaints of stinginess and favoritism.[71] Officers frequently took note of Christmas by serving whiskey to their men; that this was not always satisfactory is indicated by a soldier's report to his sister that "the General [Reuben] Davis sent up a barrel of whiskey to the camp, but it was such villainous stuff that only the old soakers could stomach it." [72]

Sometimes Rebs went to great pains to obtain whiskey suitable for a Christmas eggnog only to find that there were no eggs available. One soldier thus baffled wrote disgustedly: "If it were in my power I would condemn every old hen on the Rio Grande to six months confinement in close coop for the non-conformance of a most sacred duty." [73]

A regiment in the Army of Tennessee observed the Fourth of July, 1862, with a celebration featuring speeches and a barbecue. A member of the regiment passed off the incongruity of Rebels celebrating a "national holiday" with the remark: "Anniversary of our national independence we still struggling for the same, etc." His continuing observation overlooked another inconsistency: "Rev. Ransom preached . . . we had some good apple brandy to drink—all got lively, etc." [74]

Occasionally some statesman or eminent divine from back home would deliver an address to the soldiers in camp. No doubt such affairs were sometimes attended more from a sense of duty than of diversion, but there were many soldiers who, like Private C. W. Stephens, derived genuine enjoyment from almost any sort of oratory. In a letter to his father from Columbus, Mississippi, in November 1863, Stephens, struggling mightily with his spelling, observed:

"The ornerabel [honorable] C. K. Marshal addrest the peopel last night I listend to him 3 hours and as I was un well I retired I never heard a better speach fall from eny ones lips than that of his he could dive deaper in to the futer and farther back on the past than eny one I ever heard . . . I can hear speaking every night nearly . . . I like to heare the legislature members dispute which I can heare every day." [75]

Not a few Rebs found recreation in meetings of fraternal and benevolent associations. The Masonic order was particularly active among some portions of the army, and its sessions were apparently well attended by soldier members.[76] For still others the monotony was occasionally broken by visits from wives, sweethearts, parents and home acquaintances. When regiments composed of soldiers from the same neighborhood came into convenient proximity, there was an immediate and refreshing exchange of calls. Furloughs home and short visits to cities or to countryside acquaintances, whether obtained by authorization or by "flanking" sentinels, also had their part in the easing of army tedium. But opportunities for visiting and being visited came all too infrequently.

In moments when other resorts failed him Johnny Reb frequently fell back on the age-old diversion of "shooting bull." Topics ranged over an exceedingly broad field. The political situation and the war came in for a full share of attention, although discussion of military matters was frowned on by some groups.[77] If facts failed as topics of conversation, the soldiers could always turn to rumor to keep the conversational ball rolling.

Very early in the conflict the most fantastic tales began to pervade the Confederacy. Robert M. Gill wrote to his wife Bettie from Louisville, Kentucky, on April 29, 1861, in all seriousness, "It is reported by a gentleman here just from Washington City that Abe Lincoln had been drunk for thirty six hours & was still drunk when he left." And throughout the war, rumors of even more extravagant proportions from sources considered wholly reliable were accepted without question by campfire idlers and passed on with enriched detail and growing inaccuracy: General Kirby Smith in possession of Cincinnati; Lincoln and his whole cabinet captured by Jeb Stuart; General Grant killed; General Beauregard accompanied on the march by "a train of Concubines & wagon loads of champagne"; the Confederacy recognized by England and France; peace to be concluded in six weeks.[78]

For the most part these and other fictions were enjoyed, but one private was surfeited to the point of revulsion. "I never heard so many lies told in my life," he wrote to his aunt, "as are told in camp. I have got disgusted and quite [quit] lieing and . . . I find I get along bout as well as usual." [79]

At times the conversation around campfires took a serious turn to such topics as "wheather it is right that we men fight with the same Ardor while the young folks are dancing at home," "the proper mode of raising children," or the probabilities and consequences of McClellan's election to the presidency.[80] Again the talk would treat of such trivialities as who eats the most, or who had most of the blanket last night.[81] Not infrequently some gifted raconteur with a racy imagination would occupy the center of attention with stories of love and adventure. Unfortunately not all would-be storytellers were so accomplished, but it seems that even bores could command an audience in Confederate camps. Listeners had a particular fondness for stories that dealt with the supernatural. A soldier said in the fall of 1861 that he had told again and again the thrillers of Poe, Dumas and others.[82]

A few companies had mascots or pets which were the sources of much diversion. The Troupe Artillery of the Army of Northern Virginia had as mascot a small cur named Robert Lee. The dog lived up to his namesake in individual encounter, but in battle he utterly belied his illustrious name. At Chancellorsville he was observed skulking behind a tree exactly after the fashion of a demoralized man. But his survival gave point to the adage, "He who fights and runs away will live to fight another day."

Stonewall, canine pet of the Richmond Howitzer Battalion, was, in happy contrast to "Bob Lee," the very soul of heroism in battle. And he was idolized by the artillerymen, who would grab him up when orders came to shift position under fire and give him sheltered transportation in a limber chest. During periods of leisure one of the men taught Stonewall to attend roll call and to sit up on his haunches in line. He also made a little pipe for the dog. When the orderly sergeant, before commencing the roll call, would cry "pipes out," his trainer would stoop and transfer the pipe from Stonewall's mouth to his paw and the dog would sit rigidly at attention until roll call was over.[83] A considerable number of individual soldiers had gamecocks as pets.[84]

Another source of recreation was handicraft. Hour after hour the Rebs whiled away in camp and prison by making pipes out of cobs or clay, for themselves and comrades, in contriving rings from shells for wives, children and sweethearts, and in whittling countless gewgaws from pine boards for no one in particular. The urge to make pretty things was, in some cases, impeded only by lack of materials. Thomas Warrick wrote from camp in Shelbyville, Tennessee, to his wife in Alabama:

"Tell Mahaly that I will make her them Rings she Rote to mee to make as soon as I can get Something to make them out of. . . . Tell all of the girls that I will send them one." [85]

A few Rebs sought amusement in drawing, using camp scenes for themes and cartridge boxes for desks.[86] Others relieved the tedium by decorating their tents or equipping them with some of the comforts of home. In 1863 a group of Louisianians went so far as to plant a garden for the benefit of their regiment.[87]

Another unusual diversion was the publication of camp newspapers. Officers and men of John Morgan's command printed, at irregular intervals in 1862 and 1863, a sheet called the *Vidette* which told of battle exploits, announced general orders, and taunted the Yankees.[88] A similar paper, bearing the name *Missouri Army Argus*, was published for a while in 1861 and 1862 by some of Price's followers.[89] More pretentious in both format and content than either of these was a paper called the *Daily Rebel Banner* and printed apparently by members of Bragg's army.[90]

The vicissitudes of campaigning and the lack of facilities prevented the publication of printed papers in the great majority of Rebel camps. But in a few instances soldiers of strong journalistic bent partially overcame these difficulties by writing out or "pen printing" small news sheets. The first of these ventures seems to have been launched by a group of young Alabamians stationed at Fort Barrancas on the Gulf coast. On February 23, 1861, they released volume 1, number 1 of "The Pioneer Banner." Nine weeks later the second issue appeared. There may have been subsequent numbers, but no record of them was found.[91]

While at Camp Hudson on the western frontier during the early months of the war, the W. P. Lane Rangers circulated over twenty issues of "The Camp Hudson Times," and when they moved to Fort Lancaster about the first of February, 1862, they established "The Western Pioneer," which ran for an unknown length of time.[92]

Soldiers stationed at Port Hudson on the lower Mississippi during the war's second winter put out rival papers designated respectively as "The Mule" and "The Wood Chuck." [93] And in Lee's army a sheet called "The Waltonville War-Cry" and another entitled "The Rapid Ann" had brief existences.[94]

These manuscript papers were made up exactly after the fashion of a regular news journal. At the head of the first page the title was inscribed in large, ornate letters, accompanied in some instances by a decorative shield or a motto. The second issue of "The Pioneer Banner" contained a well-executed original drawing of Fort Barrancas by one of the "staff artists." Contents of the sheets were devoted to editorials, camp news and gossip, poetry, jokes, obituaries and advertisements.

"The Pioneer Banner" started out as a trimonthly affair, "for the Young Ladies of the Union Female College," but failing of its original schedule, the second issue was headed by a note announcing publication "semi-occasionally." It is doubtful, in view of the restricted reading-public anticipated by the editors and the exceedingly meticulous care devoted to preparation, that there were later issues of "The Pioneer Banner." But with what absorbing zest must the girls of the academy have read their copies for tidbits about individual doings in camp! And eventually one imagines the issues were treasured in the memory book of one of the most interested readers and cherished in the years that were to elapse before they found a final resting place in historical archives. Papers issued by the other groups were intended for wider circulation; consequently they were duplicated and given comparatively far-reaching distribution. A Lane Ranger said concerning publication of "The Western Pioneer" that first an original of each issue was prepared in complete detail; next, members of the staff made as many copies as they desired; and finally comrades who wanted duplicates to send home were allowed to write them off.[95]

Any cataloguing of kinds of diversion in the Confederate Army would be incomplete without a mention of tobacco. It is doubtful if any single item except food, water, and letters from home was so highly cherished by Johnny Reb as "the delightful weed." References to its scarcity, to its availability, to cost, to its quality and to its soothing powers appear repeatedly in soldiers' correspondence and diaries.

"Nancy what do you do fur tobacco to chew?" inquired a Reb of his wife; "I have to pay two dollars a plug fur what I chew." [96]

Another scribbled to his sister:

"Well Bet I herd you got three plugs of tobacco to go on I am glad to here that old Milan [his home county in Texas] can afford it. last Friday I got three plugs of No. one I cant sleep of nights Since for chewing $1.50 per plug and would not take twice the money for it . . . Tell Mass John that I am all right while my Tobacco lasts." [97]

A third wrote:

"Tell Bettie not to be uneasy about my using tobacco. I shall not chew it, nor hurt myself smoking it. I am convinced that it has been of some benefit to me." [98]

This was certainly a case of understatement. More enthusiastic was the Reb who observed "I . . . got my pipe and I woulddant take a dead negro for it," and another who boasted, "I am as Sassy as a big house Niggar got money and tobacco a plenty for the present." [99]

A note of despair creeps into Sergeant Frank Moss's communication to his sister "Lizer" when he observes:

"Tobacco is only worth $2.50 cts per plug and I have taken my last chew this morning So you may guess I will have a hard tim as I dont use that kind of tobacco." [100]

It is little wonder, in view of the exceedingly important roles played in army life by plug and pipe, that an anticipated cut in tobacco rations prompted more than one general to begin an impatient correspondence with the crotchety commissary general at Richmond; nor is it any wonder that many Rebs, who had resorted to everything from singing to smoking to make army life tolerable, should, on reaching home at war's end, inquire first, after the round of embraces, as to the prospects of the tobacco crop.

CHAPTER X

CONSOLATIONS OF THE SPIRIT

SOUTHERNERS of the nineteenth century were a religious people. Church affiliation was regarded as a badge of respectability; for both private functions and public enterprise the presence of the clergy was sought. The minister was preferred to the magistrate in the marriage ceremony, and community gatherings, whether picnics or political rallies, were usually opened with prayer. Most academies and colleges had daily chapel services which both faculty and students were required to attend. There was sometimes a wide divergence between the preacher's message and the laity's conduct, just as there is today, but religious sanction was demanded by the righteous—always a powerful minority—approved by the lukewarm and accepted by the wicked; all felt better to have had the blessing of the church.

It was only natural, then, that Johnny Reb should be sent away to war with a benediction. A vital part of most of the going-away ceremonies in 1861 and 1862 was a talk and a prayer by a local minister. In the knapsacks of many, if not most volunteers a Bible, donated by a mother or a sweetheart, was tucked away. When the Summit Rifles left their home community in Mississippi, a pretty girl handed each man a pocket Testament that had been bought by the Summit Bible Society.[1] Frequently one of the local ministers went along to look after the company's spiritual welfare.

In spite of these auspicious beginnings, religion did not thrive in camp during the first year or two of conflict. Sunday services were held irregularly and with small attendance. Testaments collected dust from disuse; many were lost or thrown away. In some quarters the faithful few who persisted in their devotions were scorned as weaklings. One soldier reported that a man of his encampment found reading the Bible was apt to be hailed with such remarks as "Hello, parson, you must be scared. I don't think there will be any fighting soon," or "Hello, parson, what time do you expect to start a revival?"[2]

Troops who wintered at Cumberland Gap in 1861-1862 were not sufficiently interested in religious services to provide shelter for them.

174

Concerning the general attitude of these men a chaplain said, "Very few of the commissioned officers were religious. The large proportion of the soldiers were wicked and many were reckless. For more than a year very few manifested any desire to become Christians save the sick or wounded." [3]

Throughout the army many men who at home took an active interest in church affairs lapsed into a state of indifference after a short time in the army. Some of the ministers who accompanied volunteer outfits to camp became so disheartened by the general spiritual desuetude that they despaired of their missions and went home. "Mr. Allen is going to quit the army," a Mississippian wrote in December, 1862; "he says it is an uphill and discouraging business preaching to Soldiers— I think so too—He hears nothing but the worst of language, his ears are greeted hourly with oaths." [4]

Among the factors contributing to the spiritual indifference which distinguished camp life in 1861 and 1862 was the festive spirit with which volunteers went to war. Few of the men realized that the conflict would be long and bloody. There was a widespread inclination to lay aside the inhibitions and conventions to which they had been accustomed in order to enjoy thoroughly the respite from quiet civilian life. By a majority, perhaps, soldiering was regarded as a grand lark and they wanted to derive the greatest possible pleasure from it while it lasted. Most of the soldiers were from the country, and the transition from farm to camp assumed to a large extent the character of a visit of rural youths to a city. They might have been good boys when they left, and they would be good boys after they returned, but in the meantime they wanted to have a fling at gambling, drinking and swearing, and they did not wish to be bothered with preachers.

Once this reaction got under way it was hard to stop. Chaplains were few in number and their efforts were not well organized. No agency existed for the promotion of wholesome recreation. After a while drill and camp routine became dreadfully monotonous. Fleas, lice, short rations, hard marching and ragged clothing taxed patience beyond endurance. For all these woes poker, keno, liquor and profanity appeared to offer the most convenient antidote. Those who wished earnestly for righteousness were often in despair. "I hope when you go to Pray you will think of me," wrote a discouraged Tar Heel in 1862; "I am a pore Harted sinner and never expect to Be no other way as long as I do remain Hear for agrivation is my Brexfus Dinner and supper." [5]

In the meantime church leaders of the South had come to a realization of the army's vast spiritual needs and had instituted movements that eventually were to be of tremendous influence. Among the most important of these was the setting up of agencies for the procurement and distribution of religious literature.

Shortly after the war broke out, Southern affiliates of the American Bible Society severed their connection with the parent institution and initiated the Bible Society of the Confederate States. This organization pledged itself to the publication and circulation of the scriptures among various groups, but principally among soldiers. Few Bibles were printed in the South before the war and the Confederate Bible Society had great difficulty in obtaining Testaments. Most of the Northern societies took the view that scriptures were contraband and stopped making their publications available for Southern distribution. The one great exception to the general rule was the American Bible Society. This organization made several donations of Testaments, including one of 100,000, to groups in the Confederacy active in servicing the army. Another outstanding benefactor was the British and Foreign Bible Society, which made large contributions and extended unlimited credit without interest for the purchase of Testaments.[6]

The various Protestant denominations were active in procuring and publishing Bibles, Testaments and other literature for soldiers. Southern Presbyterians sent M. D. Hoge to Europe to solicit and purchase religious materials. People at home were asked to contribute surplus Bibles for distribution in camp. When soldiers were killed their families were requested to permit the donation to comrades of Testaments belonging to the deceased. Chaplains and interested troops went over battlefields to gather up Bibles left by both friend and foe.[7] These several expedients yielded a large quantity of Bibles but never enough to meet army demands.[8]

In addition to providing Bibles, church organizations published religious periodicals for soldiers. The Evangelical Tract Society, an interdenominational body organized in 1861 at Petersburg, Virginia, which came to have a position in the South analogous to that of the American Tract Society in the North, issued the Army and Navy Messenger. The Presbyterian Board of Publication sponsored a monthly paper called the Soldier's Visitor. Southern Methodists published two semimonthly organs; the Soldier's Paper was issued from Richmond for troops in Virginia and the Carolinas, and the Army and Navy Herald from Macon, Georgia, for commands of the Southwest. Among papers initiated by the Baptists was a sheet published in Atlanta under the name of the *Soldier's Friend*. These and other periodicals designed specifically for camp readers were devoted largely to reading matter calculated to create abhorrence of evils most common to army life, and to inspire soldiers to Christian living.[9] The first issue of the *Army and Navy Herald* affords a good example of the general character and purpose of all. Included among article headings are these: "Come to Jesus," "A Model Boy," "The Whiskey Erysipelas," "Washington's Prayer," "The Scoffer Rebuked," and "The Soldier's Death." In an editorial the sponsors promised "to furnish the reader with such original productions and eclectic Christian literature as will in some humble measure compensate for the absence of books . . . and elevate his conceptions to the comprehension of a purer and more peaceful area . . . than the strifes of the times." [10]

The most numerous and most influential of religious publications issued to soldiers were those which came under the head of tracts. Every major sect, and several interdenominational organizations, issued these pithy leaflets in great quantity. The output of all sources totaled hundreds of millions of pages. The Baptists were particularly zealous in this work. The Virginia Sunday School and Publication Board alone published and distributed over thirty millions of pages of brochures. The Evangelical Tract Society and the South Carolina Tract Society were also exceptionally well represented in this field.[11]

Some of the tracts were reprints of those issued to English soldiers during the Crimean War. A few consisted solely of the Psalms, of the Gospel of St. John and of various other excerpts from the scripture. But the great majority were pointed spiritual essays prepared especially for Confederate soldiers by eminent Southern theologists. The publications were pocket-size and the usual length was four pages, though some contained as many as sixteen and a few ran as high as twenty-four. Some emphasized the importance of conversion; others told how to seek religion; many warned against specific sins; a few gave practical advice as to health of body and of mind; and a great number had as their central theme the danger of procrastination. A favorite technique was the use of personal incident and experience. Washington, Cromwell and various heroes of the Confederacy were cited as examples of Christian fortitude. Military allusions and analogies were frequently employed. The style of writing was usually unctious.

A recurring subject of the tract writers was the evil of cursing. The title of one leaflet was *Profane Swearing*, and of another *Why Do You*

Swear? The latter written by J. N. Andrews of North Carolina argued against profanity on the ground of its futility, its injury to self-respect, and its debasement of the user to the level of liars, murderers, thieves and adulterers. Still another tract captioned *The Silly Fish* charged the swearer with biting at the devil's bare hook on the ground that there was no possible satisfaction to be derived from the sin.

Gambling was another favorite topic. A tract entitled *The Gambler's Balance Sheet* listed the gains of the evil as: lewd and base companions; idleness and dissipation; poverty; and mental anguish. Losses are given as: time; money—"which ought to be sent home to your wife and babies, or to an aged father or a widowed mother"; feeling—"a young man in New York not many years ago played cards on his brother's coffin"; love of truth—the gambler will try to cover up his loss by a falsehood; self-respect; character—"your friends will disown you, your mother will be ashamed of you, your sisters will blush when your name is mentioned"; happiness; and soul. The balance, according to the author, could be nothing but "ETERNAL MISERY."

Drinking was a third target for writers of tracts. One of the most pungent of the brochures on this subject was that headed *Lincoln and Liquor*, written allegedly by a physician. It attempted to show the inconsistency of throwing off the Lincoln yoke and at the same time becoming enslaved to drink. It attributed recent defeats to liquor and predicted blighting drouths in the Confederacy if bountiful crops continued to be used in "distilled damnation." Finally it scorned the argument advanced by some that whiskey prevented disease, protected against cold, or was beneficial to those about to go into battle.

Another tract was devoted to the subject of *Depredations on Private Property*. Several were slanted to capitalize on the soldiers' repeated exposure to death; *Prepare for Battle* was the title of one of these, and *A Word of Warning for the Sick Soldier* that of another.

The hell-fire note was pressed in some; in *Sufferings of the Lost* a thorough roasting over the lake of fire and brimstone was promised in excruciating detail to unrepentant sinners.

The most popular of all the tracts was an eight-page pamphlet called *A Mother's Parting Words to Her Soldier Boy*. This work, by J. B. Jeter, was written in letter form. In the first year of publication about 250,000 copies were issued to soldiers. The style is direct, simple, crisp and unencumbered by the unctious sentimentality that mars many tracts. In the beginning a good tonic for morale is administered: The mother professes to give up her son without reluctance because he goes to support a righteous cause—"The great fundamental principle of the American Revolution that all authority is derived from the consent of the governed"; if she had ten sons she would sacrifice them with equal cheerfulness. In this sacred cause the mother implores her son to be a good soldier, obedient to his superiors and courageous in battle. She admits that the genius and spirit of Christianity are "utterly opposed to war," but says that the scriptures convince that "a just and defensive war" is not incompatible with righteousness. Then follows practical advice as to religion in camp: First, the son is urged to become a Christian lest his soul perish; but the argument is made with restraint and without appeal to fear. Second, he is admonished to keep his Christianity— "guard against drunkenness . . . as you would . . . against henbane" and avoid profanity. Third, the son is assured that piety is not effeminate—"some of the bravest soldiers of the world have been humble Christians; Cromwell, Gardiner, and Havelock . . . were as devout as they were heroic. . . . Washington maintained the claims of Christianity amid the demoralizing influences of the Revolution." Finally there is a benediction and a commitment of the son to the providence of the Almighty.[12]

Distribution of Bibles, tracts and other religious publications was accomplished through special agents called colporteurs, through chaplains and through interested soldiers. Usually the items were donated outright, but occasionally a small sum was required of recipients. A captain in the Twelfth Georgia Regiment testified that his company raised sixty dollars on a single day as a contribution to a regimental fund for religious literature.[13]

Hospitals were favorite resorts of colporteurs and no charge seems to have been made for literature distributed to the sick and wounded. Dearth of reading matter and the genuine interest of some in spiritual instruction made the disseminator of tracts a welcome visitor in camp. J. W. Jones said of his own experience:

"I had a pair of large saddle bags which I used to pack with tracts and religious newspapers, and with Bibles and Testaments. . . . Thus equipped I would sally forth and as I drew near the camp some one would raise the cry, 'Yonder comes the Bible and tract man,' and such crowds would rush out to meet me that frequently I would sit on my horse and distribute my supply before I could even get into the camp. . . . The poor fellows would crowd around and beg for them as earnestly as if they were golden guineas." [14]

Captain Lewis Minor Coleman testified that one of his men who made no pretensions to Christianity read the Psalms and the New Testament through twice during a month's encampment at Strasburg because he had nothing else to read.[15] Ministers sent out to raise funds for colportage had a good store of incidents at hand telling of the conversion of hardened sinners by tracts that came accidentally into their possession. Typical of these was the story of a wounded officer "who was awakened and led to Jesus while in camp by a 'fragment of a religious tract' which he picked up in an adjoining grove." [16]

By the beginning of 1863 distribution of religious literature had reached large proportions. By this time, likewise, efforts of the various churches to supply the army with chaplains and missionaries had attained considerable success. In the spring of 1863 there came the first of the great religious revivals which swept periodically over Confederate encampments.[17] The connection between this spiritual awakening and the high tide of pamphleteering and preaching was unmistakable.

The revivals apparently began in Stonewall Jackson's Corps in the latter part of March. On April 12, 1863, a private wrote from camp in Caroline County, Virginia:

"We are having a glorious time about now . . . we commenced a protracted meeting in this Brigade about four days ago. . . . Gen. Jackson (God Bless him) has given us the privilege to be exempt from Morning's Drill in order that we may attend preaching . . . we have two sermons each day & although we have no church to worship in we all sit around on the ground and listen to the sweet sound of the Gospel." [18]

About the same time another of Lee's soldiers told of the organization of an Army Christian Association that held prayer meetings three times a week, "sometimes in the quarters occupied by a captain—sometimes in the house occupied by a mess of privates—and all unite—without respect to rank or former denominational associations—in the worship of God"; he added that many soldiers had become zealous workers "who were never before connected with any church." [19]

The evacuation of winter quarters followed by the Chancellorsville and Gettysburg campaigns interrupted evangelistic activity. But in the autumn the flames were rekindled and during the winter of 1863-1864 the wave of revivalism reached unprecedented heights not only among troops quartered along the Rapidan, but also in the Army of Tennessee and in other commands throughout the Confederacy.

From a camp near Minden, Louisiana, a soldier wrote:

"A revival of religion has commenced in camps . . . I never saw such a difference in men in my life There is but one man in my knowledge who makes a regular business of swearing. . . . When I first came out in the army we could scarcely hear any thing else but profanity . . . over 250 have been converted since last summer in this divis[ion]." [20]

Another wrote from Bragg's headquarters in North Georgia:

"Thousands have professed Religion and the work is still going on . . . I do not think there is as much wickedness in our Regt as there used to be . . . it resembles more a camp meeting than it used to . . . around the fire you can see Groups of men singing." [21]

From Virginia one of Lee's veterans wrote:

"We have preaching in camp every day . . . & prayer meeting at night . . . I dont think I ever saw more interest taken in a protracted meeting." [22]

As winter came on soldiers built log tabernacles and equipped them with pulpits, seats and lights. In one instance there was apprehension that a theater erected by less pious comrades in the vicinity of their log church would lure away the congregation. But the minister, "Kentucky Andrew Broaddus," proved to be the greater attraction and, according to the report of a chaplain, "in the great revival that followed, the owners of the theatre and some of the actors, professed conversion, the 'plays' were suspended, and Brother Broaddus was invited to hold his services in the theatre as that was a larger and more comfortable building. . . . He readily consented to do so." [23]

Circumstances did not permit the building of tabernacles by all brigades, but the zeal of some worshipers was so great that they were not deterred from religious service by lack of shelter. One chaplain told of preaching to a group of Mississippians for forty minutes in a steady rain; "not a man stirred" and this despite the minister's suggestion that the congregation ought to disperse and seek cover. In another instance an exhorter preached to a large assembly of Virginia troops who stood in several inches of snow for the duration of his sermon; no less than fourteen of the men were barefooted. J. W. Jones testified that he saw shoeless men in attendance many times at services held on snow-covered ground.[24]

Word got around rapidly among civilians in the fall of 1863 concerning the outbreak of revivals in camp. This precipitated a rush to the front of prominent divines who welcomed an opportunity to abandon lukewarm home constitutencies for eager congregations of soldiers. Such preachers as John A. Broadus, J. B. Jeter, J. B. McFerrin, Stephen Elliott, B. M. Palmer, J. C. Stiles, J. N. Waddell and a host of others equally eminent, thrilled to the response accorded their messages by tatterdemalion veterans; and by their presence and influence, as well as by the eloquence of their addresses, these men aided greatly the tide of revivalism.

Among the professions of faith received by outstanding ministers were those of Generals Bragg, Ewell, R. H. Anderson, Rodes, Pender, Paxton and Colonel Lamar.[25] Bishop-General Leonidas Polk in the spring of 1864 baptized Generals Hood, Hardee and Joseph E. Johnston. President Davis also became a communicant during the war. After these additions to the church, personal workers who approached lowly camp sinners were not lacking in examples to cite of lustrous association to be had in paths of righteousness.

The hard fighting about Atlanta and in the Wilderness naturally caused a decline of religious activity in the Confederacy's two principal armies. The abatement of services and the strain of campaigning were accompanied by a large-scale backsliding, though many converts were impelled to constancy by the ever-present prospect of death. In the Trans-Mississippi Department, where military duties were less arduous, revivals continued into the summer of 1864.[26] The winter of 1864-1865 witnessed a renewal of religious interest in the Army of Northern Virginia. About sixty chapels were built along the lines about Petersburg, and J. W. Jones expressed the opinion that revivals among Lee's troops during the last winter of conflict were as general and as powerful as at any prior time.[27] This conclusion may be correct, but it is probably not applicable to other commands. Certainly it was not true of the Army of Tennessee where Hood's disastrous Nashville campaign interfered greatly with the religious program. For the Confederacy as a whole the peak of revivalism was attained in the winter of 1863-1864.

Evangelistic outbreaks in the army seem to have been of a restrained character emotionally. Certainly they were accompanied by much less bombast than some of the revivals in hinterland areas earlier in the century. There were no evidences of such phenomena as "barking" or "jerking"; and very few correspondents mention the ecstatic hollering known as "shouting" so common at "big meetings" before and after the war. Perhaps audiences made up largely of hard-bitten campaigners were less susceptible than civilian congregations to such fervid exercises. Few camp ministers attempted to work up an emotional lather among their hearers. Seekers of religion were rarely brought to a mourners' bench and subjected to long sessions of praying, high-pressure exhorting and beating on the back. The most common procedure was for the declarations of repentance and faith to be made by the simple expedient of walking up to the rostrum and shaking hands with the preacher.

The factors that gave rise to large-scale revivalism among Confederates afford interesting ground for speculation, particularly in view of the fact that Federal armies experienced no such phenomenon. As has been previously indicated, one significant cause for the first series of eruptions in 1863 was the success at that time of efforts of Southern churches to provide the army with tracts and preachers. To a large extent the spiritual awakening was the result of extensive and well-organized denominational propaganda; and in a sense, the revival thus launched persisted for the war's duration, the recurrent waves being but variations of its intensity.

A second cause is to be found in the character of the Southern soldiery. Most wearers of the gray came from communities where the church was fervid, aggressive, and influential, and where revivals were common. True, there was a reaction against religion when men first went to camp, but by the beginning of 1863, this had exhausted itself and the normal susceptibility to evangelism had been restored.

A third and a very important cause lay in the state of mind which pervaded both the army and the citizenry after the second year of conflict. In 1861, 1862 and early 1863, optimism was rampant. Confederate armies were winning great victories and suffering few defeats. These successes, coupled with prospects of European recognition, seemed to assure triumph and independence. The favor of God was sought and acknowledged, but extreme confidence in human endeavor tended to belittle reliance on divinity, or make its expression perfunctory.

The series of setbacks that began with Gettysburg and Vicksburg produced a marked change of attitude. Both civilians and soldiers began to question the invincibility of Southern arms. Churches began to sound the note that military defeats were punishments inflicted by the Almighty as a rebuke to sin and to overweening reliance on the strength of man. The feeling gained wide currency that God would not permit the South to triumph unless and until her people humbled themselves, did genuine penance, and committed themselves to the keeping of providence.[28] This sentiment was particularly strong when the shock of military reversals first came, and it is significant that evangelism reached its peak immediately after Gettysburg and Vicksburg.

A fourth and final factor contributing to revivalism was the increasing prospect of death which confronted soldiers as the war went into its last years. Veterans who saw regiments dwindle in strength from hundreds to handfuls could not escape the realization that their chances of surviving the bloody battles yet to be fought were slim. The urge was strong, therefore, to escape damnation and to gain assurance of eternal peace by getting religion. From this and from other motives vast numbers of Rebs answered the call to salvation. According to a preacher-historian who made an extensive study of army revivals, no less than 150,000 soldiers made professions of faith during the war.[29]

Religious services in the Confederate Army consisted largely of preaching and prayer meetings. The usual time of the former was Sunday morning, but the demands of campaigning and a shortage of chaplains caused frequent changes in the schedule. When the army was on the march all services had to be held at night. In such instances the minister took his place in the open, with his congregation clustered about him on stumps, logs, or on the ground. Illumination was afforded by a flickering campfire or by the moon.

Prayer meetings were more frequent than sermons. They were usually held at night. Scripture reading, hymn singing and prayer usually constituted the bulk of the service. Occasionally there was a brief commentary on some Biblical passage or spiritual topic. These meetings were led by chaplains, missionaries, or visiting ministers when they were available, but in the absence of preachers some layman would be called on to direct the exercises.

Sometimes the meetings were very small and informal, having as their participants the six or eight men composing a mess, or other groups drawn together by convenience and congeniality. During periods of active campaigning chaplains often assembled their flocks very early in the morning for a brief session of prayer and scripture reading prior to the beginning of march. When a battle was immediately impending religious leaders attempted to invoke a benediction on troops before they went into action.

In a number of instances prayer meetings became the objects of enemy fire. Such situations produced a severe strain on religious faith. Robert Stiles told of the opening of Federal batteries on a service held during the Seven Days' campaign. When shells began to fall near by, Stiles peeked about to note the effects on the kneeling men. The simple-hearted worshipers felt that it would be sacrilegious for them either to open their eyes or to get up while prayer was in progress, yet their faith was not so great as to prevent their seeking shelter. Much to the amusement of their spying observer, therefore, they began to crawl about on hands and knees with eyes still closed, groping for trees, stumps, or any other available cover.[30]

During periods of revival, experience meetings were common. At these assemblages Christians would arise, either of their own initiative or on invitation of a leader, and tell of their spiritual experiences. If they were recent converts, their remarks would usually have to do with factors leading to profession of faith and the feeling which ensued as a result of their renunciation of evil. If sinners were present they might be given an opportunity to request the prayers of righteous comrades.

Every season of revival was accompanied by a succession of baptizings. These were usually featured by songs and prayers, but the main ceremony was the administration of the baptismal rites. If the candidates were members of denominations requiring immersion, a stream or lake had to be sought by those in charge of the service.

Sunday schools were also held in many camps. At one time it was reported that every company in Dole's Brigade of Lee's army had a Bible class. Sometimes these gatherings were conducted by a leader on a formal basis, in other instances they consisted simply of a group of worshipers gathering to hear the reading of a Testament by one of their comrades.[31]

Priests were active among troops who came from Catholic communities. When circumstances would permit, services were held each morning in tents used exclusively for religious exercises.

An Englishman who served in the Army of Northern Virginia during the early months of the war said that he frequently saw "General Beauregard and other officers kneeling with scores of privates at the Holy Communion Table." This authority paid particularly high tribute to the work of the Jesuits.[32]

In most services singing played an important role. Some of the tract societies compiled favorite hymns of the various denominations and issued them to the soldiers in pocket-size booklets. Among the most popular of songbooks were these: *The Army Hymn Book*, consisting of 191 selections, issued by the Richmond Presbyterian Committee of Publications; *The Soldier's Hymn Book* published by the South Carolina Tract Society, which in the second edition included 271 songs; and *Hymns for the Camp*, published by an unidentified agency and consisting in the third edition of 151 numbers.[33] Most of the selections were of a purely religious character, but patriotic songs were occasionally included. One booklet of Confederate imprint contained "America," without benefit of title, and for the phrase "Land of the Pilgrim's pride" the publisher substituted "Land of the Southron's pride." Other instances of specific adaptation to Confederate use are indicated by this stanza of a hymn classified under "Praise and Thanksgiving":

"These Southern States at thy command
Rose from dependence and distress;
And stablished by thy mighty hand,
Millions shall join thy name to bless."

and by a verse of a song set to the tune of "God Save the King":

"Our loved Confederacy,
May God remember thee
And warfare stay;
May he lift up his hand
And smite the oppressor's hand
While our true patriots stand
With bravery." [34]

The favorite hymns of camp and field were not those contrived for the moment, but rather the old songs endeared by associations of home and childhood. Ranking particularly high in soldier esteem were such hymns as these: "All Hail the Power of Jesus' Name," "Amazing Grace, How Sweet the Sound," "How Firm a Foundation," "Jesus, Lover of My Soul," "Just As I Am, Without One Plea," "Nearer My God to Thee," "O Happy Day," "On Jordan's Stormy Banks I Stand," "Praise God from Whom All Blessings Flow," "Rock of Ages," "There Is a Fountain Filled with Blood," and "When I Survey the Wondrous Cross." [35]

To promote spiritual fellowship and religious constancy "Christian Associations" were formed in many brigades. In addition to sponsoring services these organizations set up committees to distribute tracts, to organize prayer groups, and to perform various other helpful functions.[36] In some commands soldiers banded themselves together to oppose the use of strong drink. A convert to moderation wrote thus to his home-folk:

"I thank you very kindly for sending me the things . . . The whiskey you may depend will be used moderately as I belong to the Temperance society of whom Gen Braxton Bragg is president." [37]

In most army services, denominationalism was minimized. On one occasion a visiting minister reported: "We had a Presbyterian sermon, introduced by Baptist services, under the direction of a Methodist chaplain, in an Episcopal church." [38] But it was difficult for preachers who were steeped in sectarianism to avoid offending soldiers sensitive to doctrinal differentiation.

"I heard a sermoned the other night," wrote a Mississippi Baptist; "the preacher was a missionary and of corse preached Methodist doctrine but it is not my business to criticisize." [39]

A Reb of unknown affiliation made this guarded thrust at a Christian chaplain: "The Boys are taking fast with the Camelite persuation . . . The preacher talks good sense and if He is right that is certainly an easy way to get to Heaven." [40]

Ministers who exhorted soldiers varied considerably in character and ability. The compensation provided by the government was not enough to attract men of talent. The law of May 31, 1861, authorizing President Davis to appoint and assign such chaplains as he thought necessary, provided a monthly salary of eighty-five dollars, and no allowances were made for food, clothing or other expenses. Two weeks later the stipend was reduced to fifty dollars. In the autumn of 1861 legislation was modified to permit chaplains to draw the same rations as privates. An act of April 19, 1862, raised compensation to eighty dollars and continued the ration allowance. In January 1864 Congress belatedly made provision for chaplains to draw forage for their horses.[41]

Men with families—and preachers were no exception to the rule of the period in the matter of large families—could not begin to provide for them from such meager salaries, and when pay was reduced from the original eighty-five to fifty dollars, many chaplains resigned and returned to their homes.[42] But some managed to get along by frugal living and by supplementing their salaries from other sources.

The life of a chaplain who worked conscientiously at his job was an arduous one. His usual constituency was a regiment, though in some instances a single preacher attempted to serve a brigade. In addition to holding services he attempted to talk individually with Christians to bolster their faith, and with sinners to persuade them to salvation; some kept records on every man under their charge in which they set down data as to home circumstances, church connections, change of religious status and other information pertinent to performance of their duties. Care and consolation of the sick and wounded was an important part of the chaplain's work. He had to write to the families of bedridden soldiers telling of their condition; in case of death, he addressed words of comfort to the bereaved. Illiterate Rebs often asked him to take down halting dictation of home messages. In some instances the camp minister took upon himself the organization and teaching of classes in reading and writing.[43]

The faithful chaplain shared the hardships of his flock. During periods of active campaigning he slept on the ground under the open sky. His fare was the scant ration issued to private soldiers. Some ministers had horses, but there were many who marched shoulder to shoulder with veteran infantrymen. When fighting began the chaplain usually took a position near the ambulances or the field hospital in order to have ready access to the wounded.

Dr. Charles Todd Quintard, of the First Tennessee Regiment, one of the most distinguished of all army ministers, was trained in medicine as well as in theology; when he moved among the wounded he filled the double role of doctor and preacher.[44]

In many instances chaplains thus engaged were exposed to Federal fire. Some, indeed, insisted on taking weapons and joining in the conflict.[45] At Chancellorsville, T. L. Duke, chaplain of the Nineteenth Mississippi Regiment, grabbed a musket, moved to the forefront of the line, and directed the movement of skirmishers.[46]

According to a newspaper report, Parson Brady of Tappan's Regiment, in an action near Columbus, Kentucky, shot a couple of Yankees and slashed the throat of another with his knife. His excitement then became so great that he forgot his ministerial vows and rushed after the retreating foe yelling, "Go to Hell, you damned sons of bitches"; this lapse caused him no end of teasing by the soldiers.[47] Several chaplains were cited in official reports for gallantry under fire, and a few were killed in action.[48]

The chaplain who braved the dangers of battle, whether with or without arms, lifted himself greatly in the esteem of the rank and file. R. H. McKim, who during the war laid aside the musket, took up the prayer book and assumed the chaplaincy of a Virginia cavalry regiment, related the following incident from his own experience. When the regiment moved forward to battle for the first time after he joined it, he took a position in the advancing column. This was a shock to the men and one called out:

"Hello, Parson, are you going with us into battle?"

"Oh, yes," replied McKim good-humoredly, "I'm an old infantry soldier—I don't mind these little cavalry skirmishes."

At this remark, a hard veteran rose in his stirrups, brandished his saber and yelled, "That's right, Paason. You stick to us, and we'll stick to you!"

And from that time, according to McKim, this rough trooper was a faithful friend.[49]

There were some chaplains who lacked learning, and others who lacked zeal; a few were deficient in both. The hardships of camp life eliminated the unconscientious, but in the early months of the war their number was considerable. An Englishman who had firsthand acquaintance with camp life said that a horde of incompetent ministers came to Richmond in the spring and summer of 1861 and were "saddled off on our regiments." These he characterized as "long-jawed, loud-mouthed ranters . . . offensively loquacious upon every topic of life, save men's salvation," and some of them "betrayed alarming proficiency in handling cards at a social game of poker." Such men, he said, "were seldom or never found administering to the sick or dying" and were rarely seen holding services; fortunately for the soldiers their sojourn in camp was comparatively brief.[50]

Native Rebs had occasion now and then to find fault with their spiritual guardians. "We have in our company two parsons," wrote a Mississippian in his diary; "truth forbids that I should say they are eminent or even thoroughly posted upon Biblical questions . . . The progress of religion amongst us is greatly impeded by this embarrassing fact." [51]

A Texan reported after listening to a camp exhorter, "I got enough . . . [preaching] in about 15 minutes to last me during the Campaign —he is a whale all but the oil—he pronounced servile, serveile—parental, parentual—said have came, etc . . . he gave the boys a regular rant." [52]

A Virginian complained that the regimental preacher "spoiled his sermon by whining & gasping it out." [53]

Other soldiers denounced their chaplains on the score of cowardice. "We got into a little row with the 'Yanks' a few days ago," wrote an

Alabamian, "and our parson . . . took to his heels when the shells commenced flying and I have not seen him since." [54]

A Reb who participated in the Atlanta campaign noted that while fighting was in progress the ministers attached to his brigade forsook the troops and went to the rear where they loitered about with cooks and quartermasters. "Surely," he said, "they will meet their reward." [55]

Some of the best and most effective preaching to which soldiers listened was that which came from officers active in the service. Bishop-General Leonidas Polk was able on occasion to exhort the men of his command. General William N. Pendleton, whom the rank and file credited with the exploit at Manassas of drawing a bead on the enemy and remarking, "Lord preserve the soul while I destroy the body," held services rather frequently during winter months. A sergeant who heard him speak in a log tabernacle in December 1864 wrote afterward: "I never listened to more solemn & impressing remarks." [56] General M. P. Lowrey and Captain Lewis Ball of Mississippi also preached to army audiences on numerous occasions. The former was a minister of notable eloquence.[57]

Sermons delivered to camp audiences, whether by chaplains, officers, or visitors, were usually couched in simple terms. Subjects receiving most frequent attention were the necessity of repentance, the uncertainty of life, the consequences of sin, the terrors of hell, the importance of Christian vigilance, the omnipotence of God, and the universality of divine mercy.

The diary of Bartlett Malone, a North Carolinian of Lee's army who faithfully jotted down texts used by camp preachers, reveals a close relation between camp sermons and military vicissitudes. In the spring of 1862 while McClellan's army was being assembled for the march on Richmond, Malone recorded listening to a discourse centering about 2 Kings 6:15-17—"Behold an host compassed the city both with horses and chariots. And his servant said unto him, Alas, my master! how shall we do? And he answered, Fear not: for they that be with us are more than they that be with them. And Elisha prayed . . . and, behold, the mountain was full of horses and chariots of fire round about Elisha." With what assurance must the minister have drawn a parallel between Elisha and the hard-pressed Confederates!

Shortly after the great Southern victory at Fredericksburg in December 1862, Malone heard a sermon on Psalms 126:3—"The Lord hath done great things for us; whereof we are glad." On the eve of the eventful Chancellorsville-Gettysburg campaign of 1863, the Tar Heel was impressed by an exhortation based on Proverbs 18:24—"There is a friend that sticketh closer than a brother." And on the very day of Stonewall Jackson's death a minister consoled Malone and his crushed associates with a message having as its text Romans 8:28—"And we know that all things work together for good to them that love God." [58]

Some officers manifested indifference toward religious activities, and a few openly opposed them. A brigadier general allegedly declared that chaplains were "the scourge of the army" and occasionally a colonel protested that emphasis on fear of divine punishment is detrimental to men in combat.[59] But the great majority of leaders approved of spiritual exercises. President Davis periodically ordered the observance of fast days. Lee and other commanding generals repeatedly enjoined unnecessary interference with Sunday services. The encouragement given by officers to the work of chaplains derived in great part from their own spiritual inclinations. But they undoubtedly attributed to religious influence a salutary effect on the rank and file, particularly in such practical matters as discipline, morale and conduct under fire.[60] If the leaders were correct in this view—and there seems to be no valid ground for challenging it—it is indeed regrettable that backsliding was as common as it was, and that a majority of Confederates made no profession of faith and had no church affiliation.[61]

CHAPTER XI

DEAR FOLKS

A VERY important part of the soldier's life was the exchange of letters with his family and friends at home. One of the first things he did after getting settled in camp was to collect pen, ink and paper and write his loved ones about details of his new existence. And thereafter, until death or war's end, he continued to write of things that he observed and experienced in camp, on the march, under fire and in prison. At the same time, he received missives—though not so often as he sent them—telling of crops, dogs, parties, gossip, health of the family and countless other details of life at home.

Never in the history of the South has there been such a tide of letter writing as that which was raised by the Confederate War, for on no other occasion has so large a proportion of the people been away from home for so long a time. Letters written by soldiers were more apt to be preserved than those received in camp, and these faded missives, now reposing by the thousands in private possession and in public depositories, constitute a valuable and largely neglected source for the South's social history.

It is a significant fact that during the Confederacy a large portion of the middle and lower strata of Southern society became articulate for the first time. Certainly from no other source can so much first-hand information be obtained of the character and thought patterns of that underprivileged part of Southern society often loosely called "poor whites."

Most Rebs enjoyed writing letters. The new world that was unfolded to them by travel to remote places, by association with many different kinds of people, and by contact with the horror of battle, gave them thrills and shocks that demanded expression. This flood tide of reaction found a natural outlet in correspondence with homefolk. The writer's vanity was flattered by his knowledge that the persons addressed had undergone no such experiences themselves.

But writing letters seemed less important than receiving them. Mississippian John Barksdale wrote to his brother in 1862:

192

"I do wish I could say something to provoke a reply. I care not how short it might be or long my say. I would be tempted to 'cuss' a little if that would produce the desired result or would breathe words soft as the memory of buried love if that would effect the object. . . . Leave the all engrossing cotton field for fifteen minutes, and write me at least one letter . . . you will certainly not loose more than the picking of twenty five pounds of staple and that you can have made up some other time; if not I will see that you are paid for it." [1]

Intense eagerness to get mail was almost universal. "Boys who will lie upon their backs with hardly energy enough to turn over," wrote an Alabamian, from Tupelo, "will jump up and hurry to the captains tent to get it." [2]

Another Alabamian, of very poor educational background, scribbled to his wife:

"Martha I waunt you to write often and send me all the nuse for I am one of the Glades[t] fellows that you Ever seen when I git a letter from you you dont no how much good it dus me to here from you."

Several months later he wrote:

"I haint got nary letter from you for somtime when you fail to Rite . . . it ceeps mee uneasy all the time." [3]

Yearning to hear from homefolk was so acute at times as to be pathetic. E. K. Flournoy wrote his wife in the spring of 1863 that he "was almost down with histericks to hear from home." [4]

Wilson Athey complained that he had "bin hear in camps three months and have never received but one letter from papy," and threatened to "take to righting to the girls" to see if they would quench his thirst for news. [5]

"To now be debared the pleasure of writing to you and hearing from those I love would be next to death," wrote William J. Whatley to his wife on one occasion. A week later he observed, after repetition of failure to hear from home, "I feel mightily down when the mail comes in and the other boys gets letters and I dont but it has not been that way often." [6]

The consuming desire to get mail led, in one case at least, to the repentance of a boy who had left home under a cloud of parental disfavor. After a few weeks in camp he wrote to his father:

"Wishing to hear from you I write you this, it being the fourth letter that I have written home and as yet have received only one from those I so dearly love. . . . It looks very hard Father and still I deserve it all and more too—but when you come to reflect that you have seen me for perhaps the last time on earth I feel as though I ought to hear from home at least once a week—but you may be right in this . . . after giving you the trouble and anxiety that I have, but father I ask I beg of you to forget and forgive all, and I promise to do better in the future. The time may come yet when you will be proud of your wild —reckless and disapated Son as I have been called, my mind is made up to be in the front rank if we ever get into a fight and there to make my mark." [7]

Such offense as the father felt must have been abated by this poignant missive, and his parental heart must have swelled with pride when he heard of the subsequent valor of his son in the baptism of fire at Fort Donelson.

The writing materials used by Johnny Reb varied greatly. When he first went to war he was able to procure elaborately ornamented envelopes and sheets. These, especially the envelopes, bore martial and patriotic insignia and poetry.

One of the most elegantly designed envelopes found by the writer was that enclosing a letter written by Ruffin Thomson of the Eighteenth Mississippi Volunteers. The cover, printed specially for Thomson's company, the "Brown Rebels," had on the left end an intricately drawn emblem showing among other things a bale of cotton, a steamboat, a cannon, a fort and a spray of stars. In the center was a flag-draped likeness of "Jeff. Davis, Our First President, Confederate States of America." Across the top of the envelope this verse appeared:

> When the tempest of war o'er shadows our land,
> Its bolts shall ne'er rend freedom's temple asunder,
> For unmoved at its portal, Jeff. Davis shall stand,
> And repulse with his braves the assault of its thunder. [8]

Patriotic verses on envelopes, and occasionally at the top of letterheads were very popular among soldier correspondents in 1861. Themes were varied but all were of an ebullient character. One was a rousing call to conflict:

> Men of the South, arise, arise—
> Hurl back the invading foe,

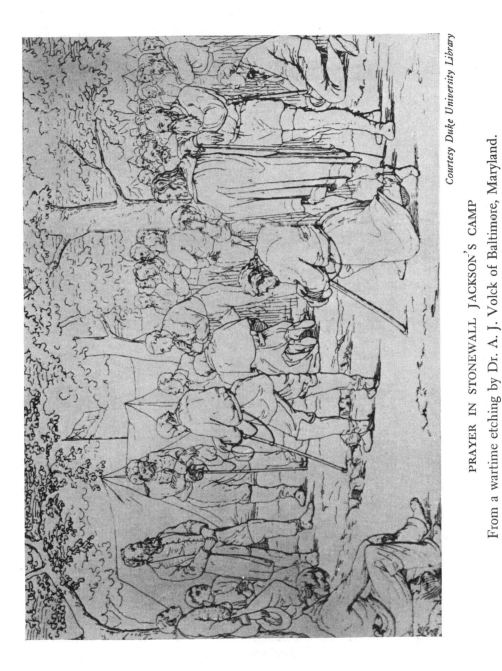

PRAYER IN STONEWALL JACKSON'S CAMP

From a wartime etching by Dr. A. J. Volck of Baltimore, Maryland.

CONFEDERATE COLOR-BEARER MOVING FORWARD IN BATTLE:
UNION SOLDIER'S CONCEPT

Drawing of Chas. W. Reed, soldier artist, Army of the Potomac. From
Chas. W. Reed Papers.

The sunny land must-aye-be free
    Tho' blood of thousands flow:
Shall we who worship only God,
    To a despot bend our knee?
No! No! men of the South arise,
AND SWEAR YOU WILL BE FREE.[9]

An unintended touch of irony was lent to these fire-eating sentiments by the postman's stamp, in bolder letters, of the words "Due 10."

Another exemplified the overweening confidence of the war's early
days:

May those Northern fanatics who abuse their Southern neighbors,
Approach near enough to feel the point of our sabres;
May they come near enough to hear the click of a trigger,
And learn that a white man is better than a nigger.[10]

The oft-repeated themes of Yankee depravity and Southern pride
appeared in this:

To arms! To arms! quick be ready
Think of what the South has been
Onward, onward strong and steady
Drive the vandals to their den
On, and let the watchword be
Country, home, and liberty! [11]

A fourth contained a note of desperate determination:

To arms! to arms! ye Southern braves
    The avenging sword unsheath,
And 'round your heads or o'er your graves,
    Entwine the laurel wreath.[12]

The strongest defiance was reflected in these lines:

Stand firmly by your cannon,
Let ball and grape-shot fly,
And trust in God and Davis
But keep your powder dry.[13]

These poetic efforts were usually accompanied by patriotic pictures
and designs. In addition to the likeness of President Davis, the following were commonly used: the Confederate flag, a firing cannon, musket-
armed infantrymen, a mounted cavalryman.

Sometimes these figures, separately or in combination, were used without accompanying poetry. One design consisted of a Confederate flag floating over a tree; from a limb Abe Lincoln is suspended by his feet, and about his neck an axe and a rail are tied; a Southerner viewing the scene stands on the Stars and Stripes.[14] Another decoration was simply the Confederate flag with the legend, "Remember Bethel, Sumpter, & Manassas, Forti et Fideli nil Difficile." [15]

Stationery of fancy design, while popular for a few months among the first volunteers, was rarely used after 1861. As the war moved into its second and third year, good paper of any sort was increasingly hard to get. In fact, the declining fortunes of the Southern Confederacy may be strikingly traced in the degeneration of the stationery used by ordinary soldiers. By the spring of 1863, and in many instances earlier, Rebs and their homefolk were writing on scraps of wrapping paper and resorting to many other expedients to keep up the flow of correspondence.

In accordance with a prewar custom many letters of the Confederate period were mailed without envelopes, the writing sheet simply being folded, sealed with wax and addressed on the outside. But the greater protection and privacy afforded by covers, and the inconvenience of keeping wax, tended toward a general use of envelopes in the army. In many instances soldiers made covers out of ledger sheets and wrapping paper. Occasionally they reversed an envelope of a letter received and used it for a missive of their own. Numerous covers were of wallpaper, the pattern being folded in. The most unusual container found by the writer was one made from a wallpaper issue of a newspaper. The outside of the wallpaper constituted the outside of the envelope, with the address written across the colored design, while the inside of both wallpaper and envelope was covered with French newsprint.[16]

But writing paper of any sort, in adequate quantities, was always harder to get than envelopes. The growing scarcity of paper, along with increasing inflation, boosted prices to a level almost beyond the reach of an ordinary soldier. Complaints occur repeatedly in the letters themselves. After paying a camp sutler five dollars for a quire of paper and three dollars for a bunch of envelopes, William R. Stillwell wrote to his wife, "How do you think that a soildier can save much money at eleven dollars per month?" [17] In November 1863 Thomas Caffey observed that the cost of a letter totaled fifty cents, and in midsummer of 1864, S. W. Farrow bemoaned, "Unless paper becomes more plentiful I shall have to quit writing it is worth a dollar a sheet." [18]

Johnny Reb had many devices to combat this paper shortage. One practice much in vogue was the inclusion of a request that the letter be passed around among various relatives and friends. A Texas private who worried chronically over the scarcity of writing materials began in late 1862 to reduce the size of his script, and after that time his handwriting, ordinarily difficult to read, was on such small scale as to be almost undecipherable. As an added conservation, he utilized canceled envelopes for writing paper.[19] Thomas Caffey, and doubtless others as well, erased the penciled messages of letters received and used the sheets thus cleared for the writing of answers, but with doubt as to its legibility. [20] Elers Koch instructed his parents, "When you write to me leave some blank paper for me to write back again." [21]

The desire to save paper, while probably not the main reason, doubtless contributed to the practice of writing joint or combination letters. The Moss brothers, Frank and W. M., often shared letters to their homefolk. Their co-operative technique varied. Sometimes Frank would fill the top portion of two sheets, front and back, and leave the lower portion for W. M. Again Frank would begin a letter, and W. M. would finish it. One missive was a multiple affair as to both the senders and addressees: W. M. wrote the first two pages to a sister; then Frank directed the third page to "My Dear Sisters"—there were three or four of them; the fourth page was written by Frank to a brother; and the envelope was addressed by W. M. to one of the girls.[22] The farthest limit of co-operation in this respect was reached by an epistle written seriatim to Bolling Hall of Alabama on September 15, 1863, by his five sons in the Confederate Army.[23] This item is indeed so remarkable as to be unmatched in Confederate letter writing, and perhaps in soldier correspondence of all time.

Envelopes and writing sheets were only a part of the problem confronted by correspondents. Ink became scarce, pale and expensive after the first year of the war. John Crittenden wrote to his wife in 1864:

"Bettie I have not been able to get any ink to write with yet . . . A Sutler here . . . has small Ink Bottles that will hold about three thimbles full. These he asks three dollars for could you fix me up some and send it to me?" [24]

Most Rebel ink users had long since fallen back on their own initiative. The greater portion of the soldier-made ink was derived from polk berries and oak balls. Pens were almost as hard to obtain as ink.

Substitutes for these were found in goose quills, cane quills and various other devices. A Texan scribbled to his sister in December 1864:

"I am writing with a corn Stalk pen when it wont write on one Side I turn over on the other. pen points are worth a dollar a peace Scarce at that." [25]

A great many writers resorted to pencils, but these, too, became expensive and hard to get.

Temporary relief was often unwittingly afforded by the Federals. Every Southern victory was followed by a flood of letters home written on elegant paper decorated with the Stars and Stripes.

After Chancellorsville a Georgian who had been lamenting the costliness and scarcity of stationery exuberantly informed his wife that he had captured from fifty to seventy-five dollars' worth of sheets and envelopes.[26]

And in the wake of the Rebel seizure of Plymouth, North Carolina, in April 1864, a Tar Heel lieutenant addressed his wife:

"I am seated in an old field surrounded by men . . . dividing out their captured spoils. I write to you on Yankee paper, with a gold pen, & Yankee envelope, with Yankee ink smoking Yankee cigar, full of Yankee sugar coffee &c with a Yankee sword, navy repeater & other 'fixins' buckled about me." [27]

When he was able to get his materials together, the letter-bent Reb still faced many difficulties. Writing desks were almost unheard of outside officers' tents and winter quarters. The usual writing platform consisted of a knapsack, a drum head, a canteen, a stump, or a board, and the seat was rarely anything but terra firma. Ordinarily the letter had to be composed in the hubbub of camp. Writing at night was made almost impossible by the scarcity of candles and by fatigue; and in the daytime there were frequent interruptions for drill and other camp duties. Under these circumstances the writing of a letter of any considerable length often extended over a period of several days.

In winter, when leisure afforded ample time for correspondence, extreme cold was a frequent handicap. One Reb wrote that "my hand keeps getting so cold that I have to stop and warm it in my pocket before I can go on"; and another complained that "for three days the weather has been so cold that . . . the ink froze on my pen as I wrote." [28]

A vivid picture of the difficulties which beset the camp correspondent is drawn by J. H. Puckett, in a letter to his wife dated June 27, 1862:

"I am seated in a beautiful grove of 'black Jack' with my back leaning against one, flat in the dust, short pencil, no board, nothing but my knee and finger to keep my paper straight, my face Southward, fires and smoke all about me, boys cooking dinner, crowds in talking distance discussing the great question [the war situation]. . . . You can give a pretty good guess what chance a fellow has to write sense. It is impossible to write a sentence without being disturbed." [29]

If the Yankees had just been firing away, this Reb must have experienced at one sitting practically every annoyance possible; and the Federals must not be forgotten, for more than one soldier interrupted his letter to answer the "long roll" and returned to complete it after the fight was over. Merely desultory shooting might or might not interrupt the writing.

A Tar Heel scribbling away under fire in the Petersburg trenches observed to his mother:

"I need not tell you that I dodge pretty often . . . for you can see that very plainly by the blots in this letter. Just count each blot a dodge and add in a few for I dont dodge for every shot." [30]

Another writing under similar circumstances from Atlanta remarked to his brother:

"The Yankees keep Shooting so I am afraid they will knock over my ink so I will close." [31]

Inability to pay postage often prevented letter writing. According to regulations of the time, payment could be made by the addressee, but this did little good in the many cases where homefolk were as short of money as the soldiers. Many Rebs did take advantage of the custom, however, including those whose families were well off; but the writer generally made some sort of apology for imposing on his correspondent.[32]

A great part of Confederate correspondence, perhaps the most of it, was delivered without benefit of postal facilities. Soldiers going home on furlough or on sick leave were almost invariably loaded down with letters of their comrades. Likewise relatives, clergymen, politicians, servants and other occasional visitors to camp were pressed into service. Soldiers home on furlough sometimes published notice in local papers that they were returning to camp at a certain time, and that they would be glad to take letters of friends and relatives of comrades belonging to their portion of the army. Rebs who sent letters home by comrades on leave frequently suggested in their communications that answers be returned by the same method. Through these informal means the correspondence of soldiers was greatly helped along.

In at least one instance a soldier was detailed by the military authorities for the specific purpose of carrying army mail. Absalom Grimes, a Missourian recently escaped from Federal prison, conceived, in the spring of 1862, the idea of gathering up letters among the friends and relatives of soldiers from the St. Louis area serving with Price's army in Mississippi and taking them across the Yankee lines. Through his daring and ingenuity, and with the assistance of influential friends in St. Louis, Memphis and elsewhere, he was able to establish a fairly regular mail service between troops and their correspondents in Missouri.[33] General Price was so impressed by the salutary effect on morale of Grimes's work that he had him commissioned official mail carrier for his command.[34] Subsequently Grimes made several trips between various Northern points and the Rebel camps with large cargoes of mail. Once he was captured with a carpetsack in his possession containing about three thousand letters addressed to Confederate soldiers and was sentenced to be shot, but with the characteristic boldness that carried him safely through four years of hair-raising adventure, he contrived his escape and resumed his perilous job. His most notable exploit was the establishment, in co-operation with a partner, Robert Louden, of mail service for soldiers under siege at Vicksburg.[35]

A pertinent reason for resort to irregular mail agencies was the notorious undependability of the Confederate Postal Department. As early as December 1861 a Richmond correspondent who had been instructed to post communications so that they would reach a New Orleans editor each Sunday wrote that the thought of such regularity was laughable. "Hang me if we've received a Western mail for the last four days," he remarked, "and the Southern, like the wind in Scripture, cometh and goeth where it listeth, and it listeth very much after the fashion of an awkward attack of ague and fever, the paroxysms of which occur on the second, third, or fourth, or fifth, or some other exceedingly incalculable day." [36]

But with the subsequent deterioration of the always overloaded transportation system, postal facilities continued to degenerate and deliveries became matters of the greatest caprice. Early in October 1863 a Mississippian serving in Virginia received a letter mailed by his wife on September 27. A short time later he received another dated August 10.[37] In April 1863 a Texan soldiering in Mississippi received a note written ten months before by his wife.[38] Many Rebs resorted to the practice of numbering letters by placing the figure 1, 2, 3, 4 and so on at the head of the missives in the order dispatched, so that correspondents might know with what regularity and in what proportion they were being received.

Soldiers chafed exceedingly at the tardiness of mails. "Just think," wrote a Georgian to his father from Petersburg in August 1864, "I have been from home five months and over, and have not received a letter from anyone of you."[39] About the same time, a Mississippian serving in Georgia remarked to his mother: "It is a constant incessant complaint in the army . . . in regard to not receiving any letters from home and their friends and relatives not receiving those they write to them. There is quite a defect somewhere, not to say gross negligence on the part of some one." [40]

Most soldiers, like these, attributed their failure to get mail to the postal authorities. But there were some correspondents who were inclined erroneously to lay the fault at the door of loved ones, who were thought to become delinquent in writing because of dwindling affection or carelessness. In such instances the note of hurt and despondency creeping into home letters was nothing short of poignant.

But in spite of all difficulties of writing and hazards of delivery, many soldiers continued to dispatch letters home with striking regularity until the end of their service. Some husbands wrote their wives once a week, usually on Sunday, regardless of conditions in the army. Others wrote more often, and not a few combined ingenuity with luck to secure the delivery of a large portion of their correspondence.

The writer has in his possession a file of 165 letters written by one Mississippi soldier to his wife from April 14, 1862, to August 28, 1864. These are letters that were delivered and preserved through the years. Doubtless some that the wife received were not saved. This soldier wrote on a rather flexible schedule approximating three letters a week. The average length was about three pages.[41]

The form and style of the letters naturally varied with the cultural background of the correspondents. Missives of well-educated men reflected the elegance and polish for which the letter writing of this period was distinguished. But as such men were exceptional, so were letters that approached excellence of composition. A good part of them were of fair quality in language, spelling and organization, being in general much like average' letters of today except for their formal and euphuistic style. But a larger part were badly written from every standpoint of external form. Because of their prevalence, however, and especially because of their graphic detail, these more humble letters deserve particular attention.

Usually the correspondent opened his letter after the fashion of Private W. J. Honnoll: "My Dear cusin I Seat my Self down one time more to drop you a few lines to let you kno that I am in the best of helth I hope this will find you all enjoying the Same like blessing"; [42] or according to the manner of Private G. W. Athey: "Dear Mother I take my pen in hand to write you a few lines to let you no that I am well as common hoping that these few lines May come safe to hand and find you in Joying the best of helth Mother I have nothing of importants to write to you at the presant." [43]

The introductory phrases "I seat myself" or "I take pen in hand" were widely used. Variations such as "I snatch my pen" and "I quickly draw my pen from its Scabbard" are found occasionally.[44]

One correspondent scribbled confusedly: "it is with pleasure this morning that I take my Seat and pen in hand to drop you a few lines." [45]

Good wishes for the health of the addressee and information about that of the writer were standard practices from which few deviated. Frequently occurring, too, was an apology for the absence of important information. Unless a letter was full of startling items, such as accounts of battles, it was apparently not considered newsworthy. One correspondent remarked: "I dont know that I can say Eny thing that is very Strange at this time." [46] Frequently Rebs who began letters by saying, "I haint got any thing of importance to rite" would proceed to the composition of several pages of material that must have been vitally interesting to the recipient.[47]

Difficulty of expression is shown by the recurrence of such statements as the following: "I have got so much to say But I Cant think of all that I doo waunt to say"; or "I dont know wife that I've got much news to write you—but I shall Keep Scratching a long untill I get Some more of this filled up." [48]

When the end of the letter was reached, the correspondent often closed with the stereotyped pledge, made ominous by the fact of war,

"I remain your Son untel death." [49] Thomas Warrick sometimes resorted to the variant, "I Ever Remain youre Husbin untell Deth when this you see Rem[em]ber me though meney miles a parte We Bee." [50] Another hackneyed phrase of prewar origin had particular point in the circumstances: "My pen is bad, my ink is pale; my love for you shall never fail." [51]

A striking characteristic of many letters is the inclusion of such formal and stilted expressions as "I can inform you that all goes well in camp," or "I am pleased to say to you that I am getting plenty to eat." There was gross inconsistency at times, as illustrated by a Reb who addressed his father as "Honored Sir," and later referred to him in letters to his wife as "the old man." [52]

"John I want you to write to me more plainer than you have bin a writing," complained Private Charles Futch to a brother serving in another portion of the army; he said further that he had recently carried a bundle of John's letters through two regiments and that "they was not a man that could read even the date of the month." [53]

And how fervently does the historian echo the wish that John Futch and thousands of his comrades had written more legibly! The handwriting of most letters was bad, but the spelling was worse. When these deficiencies are combined with haphazard punctuation, promiscuous capitalization, inferior paper and pale ink, the deciphering becomes indeed a task.

Concerning many Rebel letters this writer can repeat today the observation made of one particular missive by a correspondent in 1862: "I had not a like to a maid out half of yourre words theare is some that I hant maid out yet." [54] But modern scholars are drawn to these difficult manuscripts, if for no other reason than that of adventure. For the choicest originalities are often encountered just beyond the veil of apparent undecipherability.

Misspellings of simple words occur repeatedly. A few random samples will indicate tendencies:

accitment	for excitement	cear	for care
afeard	" afraid	ceep	" keep
agetent	" adjutant	cerce	" scarce
ancious	" anxious	Coossey	" Coosa
bin	" been	crawsed	" crossed
boath	" both	cullur	" color
bregad	" brigade	daingeroust	" dangerous
carey	" carry	dus	" does

eyedear	for idea	rickolect	for recollect
forchin	" fortune	ridgement	" regiment
furteege	" fatigue	rote	" wrote
furloe		sadisfide	" satisfied
furlow	" furlough	saft	" safe
garde	" guard	sirtenly	" certainly
horspital		sity	" city
horspittel		snode	" snowed
hospitly	" hospital	sow	" so
orpital		staide	" stayed
hurde	" heard	taulk	" talk
knews		toilse	" toils
noose	" news	tords	" towards
nuse		unbenoing	" unbeknown
medison	" medicine	waulking	" walking
meney	" many	waunt	" want
mity	" mighty	wee	" we
moer	" more	wether	" weather
perperce	" purpose	wod	" would
pestearred	" pestered	wonst	" once
porchun	" portion		

When correspondents attempted to use long and unfamiliar words, they were apt to get unusual results, as shown in the following:

A brim ham lillkern	for Abraham Lincoln
Chic a har mana	" Chickahominy
comodate	" accommodate
coummling	" Cumberland
dyereaer	" diarrhoea
experdission	" expedition
Fluriday	" Florida
horspitibel	" hospitable
mungunry	" Montgomery
physitian	" physician
regislatury	" legislature
rumatis	" rheumatism

The ordinary Reb was nearly always subject to greater defeat by a word like *Chattanooga* than by the Yankees.

Difficulties with spelling caused some writers to combine two words into one, as *ought not* into "ortent," *roasting ear* into "roastinear," *a miracle* into "american," and *Irish potatoes* into "ashpotatoes"; or contrariwise to make two words of one, as "lew tennante" of *lieutenant*, "a nough" of *enough*, "comma sarry" of *commissary*, and "trance fur" of *transfer*.

A common practice was the prefixing of the archaic sign a to verbs, as "you ask how I was agetting along," or "I am agoing to Tennessee." Frequently the article a is combined with the adjective or noun following as "afew," "abig," "afurloe." Letters are sprinkled with other colloquialisms common among rural folk of English antecedents, such as "haint" and "hant" for *have not* or *had not*; "nary" for *none* or *not any*, "ary" for *any* or *either*, "hit" for *it*, "seen" for *saw*, and "fiten" for *fought*.

Occasionally rustic figures of speech were invoked. One Reb remarked that the Yankees were "thicker than lise on a hen and a dam site ornraier"; another said that his comrades were "in fine spirits pitching around like a blind dog in a meet hous"; and a third reported that it was raining "like poring peas on a rawhide." [55]

Poor spelling and writing were due in some measure to haste and carelessness. An Alabamian of fair education observed on one occasion: "I have written this Letter as well as many others I write in great hast Never haveing time to read them over." [56] That many other correspondents did likewise was evidenced by the fact that words spelled correctly at the beginning of letters were sometimes misspelled when repeated near the close.

To indifference and hurry also must be credited much of the repetition and incoherence that characterized soldier correspondence. The Alabamian referred to above said, "I have But Little system in Writing Letters the first thing I think of is the first thing I Write down, up one side of a sheat of paper and down the other"; and his method was by no means unusual. [57]

An interesting by-product of increased practice in letter writing was a marked improvement in quality. By 1864 soldiers who at first had experienced much difficulty in expression and penmanship were showing a noticeable progress in both handwriting and composition. Letters at this time are marked by less circumlocution, by greater ease of style and by increased coherence. But too much confidence caused some correspondents to overstep their abilities, sometimes with ludicrous results. A Tar Heel requested his folk to give kindest regards to all his "concomitants"; and a comrade who had heard rumors of an armistice said in all seriousness: "I hope they will have and [an] army mistress"! [58]

The two letters which follow will illustrate common characteristics of spelling and style. The first was written by a Louisiana soldier early in the war:

"*Dear Wife:* i take the opitunity to write to you to let you now that i am well an i hope these few lines may come safte to hand and find you injoying the same blesson we was sworen in the confedert states for durin the war i dont now when will see you i want to see you verry bad write to me as soon as you get my letter i send my best love to you and mark [a son] cis [kiss] mark for me i stod on gard las nite for the first time we fare tolible well yet we are now on rediness to go to new orleans they are therty five thousand yankes at chip ilant [Ship Island] now we are looking for a call every moment weare in the fiftenth regment tell mother i am well and i wold like to see her verry well tel her to write to me i have seen a great deal here they are fore regments here now . . . write to me as soon as you git my letter Dear wife my ink is pail my pen is bad my love to you shall never fail god bless you. cis mark for me and think of me as little as you can for i will never see no more pleser in this world i sent my likeness to you write to me if you got it or not i must come to a close remain your husband ontell death direct your letters to camp more in the cear of C E Hosea J. M Guess to Elminy Guess Remember me God bless the in cear of C E Hosea" [59]

The second was penned in the last year of conflict by an Alabamian:

"*Diere Sisteer* I Seat my Self this morn to Anter youer kine letteer which cam to han a bout ten Days a go this is the Fierst time I hav had the chance to Write this leave me on[l]y tole well I hoe this Few lins may cum to han An Fine you all well Dear Sisteer you want to no Soph a bout your husban he was well a Few Days go he cum out all Saft So fur I have cum out Saft So Fur but I am march Downn we hav bin run From the Yankey an Fiten them a bout 12 Days I am getin tierd of hit tha like to got me tha Shot a hole throw my Sacel an I had hit on my back but a mis is good as a mile Dear Sisteer I want you to write to me and giv me all the nus you hav got I can Say to you that brother James got woned in the thy Sly Jides darky got kill Stevn lyeman got woned I wod bee glad to see you all I hope this war will brake up Soon we never can whip the north Fer tha hav So meney moer men an we hav got I think we will move on to Atlant be Foer we Stop but I dout [t]hat tha will dow So I will close Fer I cant write I dnt no [whet]her you can read this or not hit is bad dun I will mane your Brother tel Deth write Soon"

"A WIDEMAN" [60]

These examples give point to the comment of a Texas soldier in a letter to his sister, "tell Bob he need not quit writing I can guess at his dutch if I cant read it." [61]

Soldiers who could not write called on acquaintances to take down letters at their dictation. Sometimes company officers performed this favor, but usually the scribes were messmates or relatives. Such service was generally free of charge, but occasionally payment was made in kind by performing camp chores, washing clothes, or half-soling shoes. Secretarial duties in companies where there was much illiteracy were apt to be heavy.

"Some body is nearly always after me to write for them," remarked a North Carolinian; "this makes 8 letters I have wrote . . . I backs [i.e., address] a good meny letters and reads letters to. I read 3 last night." [62]

The spelling and handwriting of some who took dictation were so bad as to suggest cases of the halt leading the maimed. Such a situation is indicated by the following postscript to a Georgian's letter: "Rote by I. T. Hight for I. J. Owen to Anderson Owens & deny Owens." [63]

Now and then an illiterate Reb learned to scribble out his own letters. An interesting case of this kind was revealed in the statement of Private W. W. Brown: "Mother when you wright to me get somebody to wright that can wright a plain hand to read I Cold not read your leter to make sence of it it wrote so bad I have lurned to do my own wrading and writing and it is a grate help to me." [64]

What did ordinary soldiers write about in their letters home? The answer must be everything, for there is hardly an item in the entire range of human activity and interest that does not find some place in their correspondence. Life, death, joy, sorrow, sin, righteousness, fidelity, fornication, comedy and tragedy are all reflected and elaborated in the letters which poured from Rebel encampments. Only a few glimpses of this variegated subject matter can be given here.

A substantial portion of the average letter was devoted to a statement of things that the soldier wanted his correspondent to discuss in later communications. First of all, if he was a father writing to his wife, he wanted to hear about his children: what they talked about, what new accomplishments they had achieved, or new tricks they had learned; whether they were obedient; if they were faithful in the performance of chores; how rapidly they were growing; did they show any increasing resemblance to their mother or father; what smart sayings had they uttered; were they making satisfactory progress at school; and did they recall their dad. One of the greatest apprehensions of fathers was that their young children would forget them.

"I often ask myself whether our little Callie speaks of her 'pa'," wrote Robert Gill to his wife. "Does she remember me? You must not whip her. I have a perfect horror of whipping Children." Later he remarked: "You say Callie is as pretty and Smart as ever, that May can walk and is just as Mama would have her to be. Are you not proud of them? What do you call them in your little talk to them, little Cherubs, or would that be sacraligious? Does Callie say her prayers right now or does She Still Say 'Punny's Soul' or 'Ma's Soul,' as the Case may be?" [65]

"I want to see the children very bad," wrote D. Hunter to his wife; "their is sevril men in the same fix that I am in that [they] hav young babs at home that they never saw." [66] In such cases as that of Hunter— and their number was large—interest in the appearance and doings of infants was unusually keen. A Georgian on receiving notice that he was shortly to become a father wrote teasingly to his spouse, "Molly you need not talk about and other boy war or not war I must have a girl if you go to talking that way I sal not lik it atall it must be a girl and its name must be Virginia [if] it is a boy I will call it Bull Run." [67]

Another Reb who chided his wife good-naturedly for presenting him with a girl instead of a boy received this mischievous retort: "I think you give your boys to some one else. I expect if I knew it you will have several boys scattered about against this war ends." [68] And a North Carolinian who had recently been visited by his wife inquired significantly of her "whether I done eny thing for you when you was out hear." [69]

Occasionally fathers in the army would address portions of their letters to their offspring. An Alabamian concluded a note to his wife thus: "I will say a few words to the Childern Willia I waunt you to Bee a good Boy and minde youre Mother Markus I waunt you and Willia to Bee smarte and make smarte men and all ways tell the Truth and mind what you are told and minde your'e Mother." [70]

Next to his children, the ordinary Reb was interested in hearing about other close relatives, about domestic pets, particularly his dogs, and about crops, especially fruit, vegetables and other edibles that he so longed for.

"How is the Crops?" inquired Jerome Yates of his mother. "You must write me every particular of the Crop how high the cotton and corn is where it is the Largest how fat the plow Horses are How the Cows look How much milk you get How the Hogs look. How looks the Colts . . . How many Chickens you have." [71] The minutiae of home affairs and of community life were of vital concern to the soldier, and he liked for the narration of details to have some verve and humor, as was suggested by a Texan's observation to his sister:

"Your very interesting letter . . . was written in a style that Suits me exactly. I always like something Spiccy, but these dry affairs that are written on the old Sing, Song, style and that are utterly destitute of Spirit never afford me any pleasure to read them I want something funny, something that will make me laugh, haw haw Something that will raise my spirits while sojourning in these low grounds of Sorrow." [72]

But the greater portion of letters received by Confederates fell considerably short of the standards desired by this soldier. Many were written in the sing-song style that he decried, and the frequency of tactlessness in the choice of subject matter was amazing. In cases so frequent as to aggregate thousands, home folk elaborated their own hardship and gloom. They complained of bad crops, of fear of Yankee raids or of havoc already wrought by Federal visitation, of trouble with overseers, of slothfulness and insubordination of slaves, of scarcity of food and clothing, or of apprehension of such scarcity, of the undue prolongation of war, of the hopelessness of victory, of deprivation of the company of their absent sons or spouses, of sickness or the anticipation of it, and of innumerable other woes.

One wife, after apparently exhausting the supply of ordinary complaints, upbraided her soldier husband for fathering the several children already born to her, and while complaining of his absence, expressed dread of his return lest she again be subjected to motherhood. "Was peace established & you at home," she wrote, "You know the horrible nightmare which would always frighten away any little happiness that might occasionally cross my path." [73]

A South Carolinian whose wife allegedly played the harlot with a train of stay-at-homes, including "the preacher," had the scandal's nauseating details revealed to him by neighborhood gossips. [74]

Communications carrying tidings of such unpleasant character as marital infidelity were exceptional, but those reciting other doleful subjects were regrettably prevalent. "You know not how . . . Depressing it is," wrote one Reb who was fortunate in having cheerful correspondents at home, "to get letters that breathe a spirit of Discontent. I tell you sister Scottie that one half of the Desertions from the southern army is caused by the letters they receive from . . . home." [75]

Another Reb, likewise fortunate, told his spouse of a comrade's correspondence: "A friend read me his wife's letters a short time ago. I was tired long before he closed. 'Oh do come home darling—oh for one hour with you—I would come to you if I could etc.' Now isn't that childish? Thank God you have more sense than that." [76]

Childish or not, there can be no doubt that letters of homefolk telling of dwindling larders, citing instances of immunity from arrest of army absentees, and openly urging return to families, played havoc with Confederate morale. [77]

There was apparently no systematic effort at censorship. People at home wrote what they would, and with impunity. [78] Troops were forbidden to disclose army strength, and private letters telling of current military operations were barred, but the ordinary Reb felt these restrictions to an insignificant extent. [79] Control of any sort over correspondence must have been difficult in view of the fact that such a large portion of the letters never got into regular postal channels. So Johnny Reb wrote with comparatively free rein to his homefolk. If he was tired of the war, he did not fear to say so, and in a considerable number of cases he announced to his relatives that he was coming home shortly, by regular means if possible, but he was coming anyhow.

Of the variety of subjects which filled the home letters of soldiers, none elicited such detailed treatment as battles. Rebs whose letters were ordinarily brief would extend themselves to many pages in narrating an experience under fire at Shiloh, Murfreesboro or Gettysburg. And frequently battle accounts would be carried over to a second and a third missive.

Food also occupied a prominent place in correspondence. Repeatedly the soldier told of the quantity of his regular rations, what he was procuring on the side by "foraging" activities, how present rations compared with past issues, what the prospects were for an increase or a diminution of food; how tough the beef was, how he was preparing his meals and who composed his mess. He kept close tab on fruits and vegetables in season at home, and on such epoch-making occasions as hog killing; if he was within convenient distance he sometimes requested that a portion of home abundance be sent to him; if not, he merely gave himself to expressions of wishfulness and regret.

Soldiers of slave-owning families made frequent mention of the servants. A very common postscript was "tell the Negroes howdy," or sometimes "give my respects to the colored members of the family." Occasionally a portion of the letter proper would be addressed to slaves commending them for good behavior, or warning them against failure in their duties during the master's absence. William J. Whattey wrote:

"I want you to tell the negroes, that if they dont go ahead with their work and do right and behave themselves while I am gone that I will certainly call them to an account when I come home; and I may be there before they look for me I am now having a harder time than any of them and if they wont behave themselves and work while I am gone that they need not expect any favors from me, tell Marshal that I will hold him accountable for his bad conduct." [80]

Descriptions of camp and of camp life were always favorite subjects. For instance a Texan wrote to his sister:

"Well lizeer I will tell you what is going on in camps today Jo is out on picket guard I am in the Tent writen on my nap Sack Dan Mayes & A Chatham geting diner A Norton has goan to Alins regment Dutch writin to Miss Mary Giles Glozner is Sick and Dolf waiting on him Jack Martin is ansurin his letter from Al that constitutes our famley A Granger I forgot he is playin marbles I would like to know whare we will be a month from today" [81]

Another Reb told proudly of the comfort he had achieved in bivouac: "We have a great invention for a bed. We put up 4 forks & lay sticks across them upon whitch are placed cane or reeds out of the river bottom and canes are lashed together with the inside of the paw-paw bark when a blanket is spread over these they make a sort of spring bed." And to make sure that the addressee obtained an accurate idea of his device, he made a rough sketch of it at the bottom of the page.[82]

Tidbits of camp gossip were frequently passed on, as well as asides on the conduct of men from the home neighborhood: this soldier under arrest, that one thieving, and this one guilty of deserting to the enemy while on sentry post. Such derogatory reports sometimes elicited disclaimers or explanations from those accused.

"I heard that Some boddy wrote to Coffeeville that all the boys here was a playing poker," remarked T. J. Newberry to his father. "I am in hops that you dont believe that I have come to that as much as you have cautioned me about it." [83]

Another Reb under censure of homefolk wrote to his wife: "You spoke in yours that William had written home that Crittenden Joe Batts and myself was all tight. . . . Wee had bought a bot of whiskey about that time, the first that I'd had for two months before and haven't seen any since I did not think that any of us felt that wee had drank so much I suppose he had nothing else to write." [84]

A third soldier who was being slandered by community gossips exclaimed disgustedly to his spouse: "The people . . . that . . . speakes slack about me may kiss my——— . . . Mollie excuse my vulgar language if you please." [85]

Unmarried Rebs were greatly interested in the doings of girls of their home neighborhood and their letters contain frequent inquiries about them: who was courting whom, what marriages had taken place, were the girls as beautiful as formerly, and were parties as well attended as before the war. Indirect messages of love-starved campaigners to sprightly maidens were numerous and varied: tell them that they all must not marry, as soldiers want some to be left for courting on their return home, or tell Miss So-and-So to be true to me and not marry a slacker. But of all such communications that of a rough and ready Louisianian was the most pungent: "What has become of Halda and Laura?" he inquired of a friend; "have you seen them and what did they have to say when you see them again give them my love—not best respects now but love by God." [86]

The ordinary soldier shied away from the subject of death in his correspondence, out of consideration for his anxious loved ones at home, and for the sake of his own morale. But occasionally he was forced to write a note of sympathy to the wife or parents of some comrade killed in battle. In such letters the bereaved family was informed in as great detail as possible of the circumstances of the casualty: at what time the deceased fell, where he was situated when he was struck, who saw him fall, whether he lingered or died instantly, what his last words were, and what disposition was made of his body and his personal effects. The letter usually closed with a eulogy of the man's character and bravery, and with expressions of condolence. In not a few cases, these messages were written by a brother of the fallen soldier who was serving with him at the time of his death. Such letters represent the height of sadness in soldier correspondence. Their tone and character is indicated by the following communication written the day after Antietam to a bereaved wife in Texas:

My dear afflicted Sister
It gives me intensest pain to tell you of death of my dear brother, your devoted husband Andrew. Oh: how desolate is my sad heart at the loss of that brother twice indeared by the hardships and perils we have passed through togather. But if my heart is so sad, what must yours be my sister, deprived of a husband and a friend. I cannot comfort you, but can only commend you to the tender mercies of our Heavenly Father who hath said he doth not willingly afflict. He hath said he will be a Father to the fatherless, a husband to the widow. I pray him to have mercy on you and your little children. Our dear one suffered no pain in death for he was shot through the temples. He was killed on yesterday morning in the fight at Sharpsburg [also known as Antietam]. Of the conflict being undesided, his body has not yet been recovered, but Maj. George has promised to attend to his interment. I am too badly wounded to return to look after him. having been shot through the left arm and twice, slightly in the side. I cannot write more now, but will do so in a few days. My heart is too sad. To God I commend you my dear sister, Your sorrowing brother,

A. M. ERSKINE [87]

Johnny Reb was, with few exceptions, a sentimental person and this side of his nature often asserted itself in his correspondence. Thoughts of home and loved ones might inspire such an outburst as this:

"How pleasant are home and its associations. My Dear 'old log hut' how sweet are the memories that cluster around my heart at thy mention! how near to me Seem thy delapidated Strength, Even the Kitchen with its puncheon floor, the Cistern with oaken iron bound bucket, the ricketty old gail, and corn crib with cracks unstopped, Even old Becca's strained unmolodius tunes would be music to me. Then, how much dearer to me would be the playful laugh of Callie in her childish glee, the sweet & innocent smile of May, and the ever pleasant smile of Welcome Bettie!" [88]

Again tenderer emotions would seek expression in verse. Often this was nothing more than adaptation of trite jingle. One Reb complimented his wife with these lines:

> "The Rose is red
> The Grass is green
> The days is past
> That we have seen!" [89]

Another sent these surprisingly intimate stanzas to his spouse:

> "The rose is red
> The vilet is blue
> Shogar is sweet
> And so are you
>
> "The sea is deap
> And in your armes
> I long to sleep
> A heap Nancy" [90]

A third addressed his father:

> "The night was cool
> The day is hot
> Our parting hours
> Is not for got" [91]

A few soldiers composed original verses for their wives. The meter was usually unconventional, figures of speech were often strained and spelling poor, but even so, some revealed a genuine poetic feeling. A lowly Georgian wrote a poem captioned "Evening Moonlight" which had for its inspiration the familiar theme of home:

> 1 "this world is verry lonely now
>   Sens Im so fare from home
>   I have not a frind with me to bow
>   before my fathers throne
> 2 long and lonely have bin the days
>   Sens I have Seen my wife
>   the moon is dark it hath rays
>   and not much pleasure is my life
> 3 I am setting now in the broad moonlight
>   and thinking of the past
>   that awful and that solumn knight
>   you held me to your bosom fast

4 Our little boy was fast asleep
  I though he would not miss
  and while I stood by his bed to weep
  upon his cheek I plased a Kiss

5 I am going now wheer Iv often gon
  to appear before the throne
  and pray the father oh how long
  Before I shal see my home

6 the Lord has bin very good to me
  in all the conflicks past
  he has promised that a frind hed be
  and gide me safe to the last

7 Mollie you have my hart and life
  and if on the battle feeald I die
  you are my darling and my wife
  my only request is to by your side to lye" [92]

The poet also explains the circumstances of composition:

"Molly thar were several other verses but having to write it by moonlight and with a pensil I can not read them this morning I hav composed meny such sens I hav bin from home and as I walked my post at knight this will show you that not withstanding my long absens from home and has seen so much murder I still have the same tender feelings that I evar had." [93]

Another Reb, an Alabamian, sent a poem of exceptional tenderness to his wife:

"I'll think [of] thee when far-far away
  And dwell with rapture on yore name
  Oh! you for whom I write whoose harte can melt
  At the Soft thriling voice of love.

"In pleasant dreames or Sorrows hours
  In crowed hills or lonely bowers
  The pleasure of my mind Shall be
  Forever to remember thee.

"Aadress and compliment by vision
  Make love and court by intuistion
  Tis ore this Scene my me[m]ory wakes
  And final broods with miser care

"Though fortune may frown me and frends forsake me
May banich me far from the presece of thee
Though wherever I roam and whatever is my lot
You will not you can not be for got

"May yore thought ever be of love
May your footsteps ever be a love sors
May your smiles ever be Smiles of love
May your tears ever be tears of Joy.
                    Forget me not

"When that quenly orb of night
Throws back her veail of Ether blue
And fads in beauty and in light
I will gase on it and think of you

"No dearest I'll forget thee not
Tis traced too clearly on that brow
To think that thou will be forgot
Whilest memory clings to naught below

"Oh who the exquisit delight can tell
Or who can painte the charm unspeakable
Two Souls with one thought
Two hearts with one beat." [94]

When the transcription of this verse had been completed, the correspondent took his pen and painstakingly drew an elaborate though crude design of a leafy vine around the tops of the two pages, the pattern being different for each page. In each upper corner of the second page he sketched a figure resembling a potted plant. Hard-bitten, unlearned and backwoodsy though this soldier was, his character was rich with gentleness, and his spirit responded to beauty.

And like him were countless others who wore the gray. They were regrettably crude in speech, inept in writing, tatterdemalion in dress and rustic in background. On the march they were incalculably tough, and under fire they were a host of yelling savages. But their haphazard appearance, their rough ways, and their bloodthirsty demeanor on fields of battle belied their deeper selves. Basically and fundamentally they were, for the most part, men of warm affection, and susceptible to the tenderest of emotions.

CHAPTER XII

KICKING OVER THE TRACES

THE day was August 1, 1861. The scene, Camp Louisiana, headquarters of the battalion of Washington Artillery on the northern Virginia front. As the hour of ten o'clock approached, Private Napier Bartlett sat grimly in the tented hall of justice awaiting the convening of the special court-martial ordered the day before for his trial.

Presently the members of the court filed in. Private Bartlett recognized them immediately as officers of the first three companies of his battalion, namely, Captain W. B. Miller of his own Third Company who had been designated as the president of the court, Lieutenant C. C. Lewis of the Second Company, and Lieutenant J. B. Whittington of the Third Company. Lieutenant Whittington had been designated as judge advocate for the trial.

The accused did not have to wait long for proceedings to get under way. First Captain Miller read the order of the major requiring assembly of the tribunal. Then Judge Advocate Whittington swore in the other members of the court, and he, in turn, was sworn in by President Miller. Thereupon, the judge advocate, who acted in a role corresponding generally to that of prosecuting attorney in civil proceedings, read aloud the following charge against the accused.

"Charge—conduct to the prejudice of good order and military discipline. Specification—in this that he the said Bartlett of the 3rd. Co. B. W. A. being encamped on or about the 27th July 1861 near Centreville, Va. in the vicinity of the enemy, and he the said Private Napier Bartlett . . . being regularly posted as a sentinel did wilfully and deliberately lie down on his post and was found asleep. All this in camp near Centreville, Va. on or about the 27th of July 1861

"John J. Garnett, Lieut. C.S.A. Comdg Section W. A.
"Witnesses: Lieut. John J. Garnett
Corporal William Fellows Jr."

When he had finished reading the charge, the judge advocate faced the prisoner who had been led to the bar and said, "Private Bartlett, you have heard the charge preferred against you, how say you—guilty or not guilty?" To which the accused, or his counsel, responded "not guilty."

Then Lieutenant Garnett was called to the witness stand by the judge advocate, sworn in and asked to tell what he knew of the charges against the prisoner.

Garnett said that he had been awakened about midnight of July 27 by the corporal of the guard who told him that a sentinel was asleep at his post. He arose and went with the corporal to a fence beyond the camp where he found Private Bartlett fast asleep. He shook the accused violently and said, "Bartlett, what are you doing?" or "What do you mean?" Bartlett replied that the corporal had given him permission to sit down at his post. Under cross-examination Garnett admitted that Bartlett may have said that the corporal told him to sit down.

The prosecution then swore in William Fellows who testified that he was corporal of the guard on the night of July 27, and that in accordance with instructions from Lieutenant Garnett he had assigned Bartlett to sentry post. A short time later he found the accused asleep. He then aroused Garnett and pointed out to him the condition of the accused. He testified further that at the time he posted the sentinels Bartlett had asked if he might sit down. He had responded, "Yes, but you must not go to sleep." Cross-examined as to Bartlett's condition when found, the witness said that the accused was "leaning against the fence asleep."

The defense then swore in Private Adams as witness. Adams testified that he heard Bartlett make some complaint to Corporal Fellows at the time he was posted on guard, but that he didn't recall its nature. Another defense witness said that he and Bartlett had been absent without leave during the night of the twenty-seventh, returning to camp about 11:15. During their walk of about six miles, to avoid the sentries, Bartlett had complained of a sore leg and had been forced on two occasions to stop for rest. When they returned to camp they were informed that they must immediately go on guard as punishment for their absence. He stated further that he heard Bartlett say to the corporal of the guard that he did not believe himself able to stand sentry on account of his leg.

The accused "made his statement and defence," either directly or through counsel, to which the prosecution responded. The court then found the accused guilty and imposed the following sentence: "That he be condemned to police his company's quarters every day for thirty days and . . . be debarred the privilege of leaving camp under any consideration for the same period of time."

There being no further business, the court adjourned. Subsequently the proceedings were written up, signed by Captain Miller and forwarded to the battalion commander for approval.[1]

The body that tried Private Bartlett was known as a special court-martial to distinguish it from a judicial organ of wider authority known as a general court-martial. Special courts-martial, consisting of three officers, were limited in jurisdiction to non-capital offenses of privates and subalterns. They were appointable by commanding officers of corps, regiments, barracks, forts, garrisons and other lesser posts of military service. They could not inflict a fine exceeding one month's pay, nor a period of hard labor or imprisonment exceeding thirty-one days.

The jurisdiction of general courts-martial included all persons and offenses subject to military law, including sutlers, drivers and all others receiving pay from the army. They were composed of from five to thirteen officers, preferably of rank higher than that of persons on trial. They were appointable by generals in the field, and by any other officers in charge of separate departments. A few weeks before Lee's surrender the authority to summon courts-martial was extended to include generals in command of state reserves.

The findings and sentences of both types of courts-martial were subject to the review of the officer by whose command the trials were ordered. Authority to review carried with it the power to execute sentence, to mitigate punishment, or to pardon. A simple majority was sufficient for conviction, save in capital offenses where concurrence of two-thirds of the court was required.[2]

Sentence in the case of Private Bartlett was strikingly out of proportion to the gravity of his offense. Mere confinement to camp and policing of company quarters for thirty days of a man found guilty of one of the most serious charges known to military practice, that of sleeping at post of duty in the presence of the enemy, was nothing short of preposterous. Under published regulations he might have been given the death penalty. Private Bartlett gave effective illustration of the evil consequences of easy sentences. For within six months of his first offense it became necessary to hale him again before court-martial, on the charges of feloniously taking away one of the government horses and remaining absent without leave for an entire night.[3]

But the leniency shown to Bartlett was apparently not out of harmony with early practices of Confederate courts-martial. Judicial sessions held at Corinth subsequent to Shiloh treated the offense of desertion with such lightness as to draw from Beauregard the following rebuke: "In those cases in which the charge of desertion has been established by the testimony . . . the sentence of the court is wholly inadequate to so grave an offense. In future the General Commanding will not approve of such trivial punishment." [4]

This tendency toward overleniency was perhaps a factor contributing to supplementation of the court-martial system in the fall of 1862; but the change came mainly from considerations growing out of the Antietam campaign. The jurisdiction of courts-martial did not cover adequately, except where martial law was proclaimed, offenses committed by stragglers beyond the boundaries of military encampments. Such cases were supposed to be tried by civil courts.[5] But in a borderland area, such as that traversed by Lee on the Maryland campaign, civil tribunals were apt to be so disorganized by removal of population and by other circumstances attendant on invasion, that their effectiveness was greatly hampered. Consequently crimes could be committed by roving soldiers with comparative impunity. Then, in the purely military realm, courts-martial were not adapted to conditions of active campaign, such as the Antietam movement. Time could not be taken out in the midst of operations for the convening of the court. And afterward witnesses might be either dead or so scattered as to make trials inconvenient and costly to the service. Delay incident to assembling and hearings, followed by review of findings by commanding officers, impeded the swiftness of action that was necessary to preserve discipline. In particular the wholesale straggling that marked the Maryland campaign presented a situation demanding immediate action that was impossible under the existing system.[6]

These considerations moved Lee in September 1862 to request remedial action of Davis. The president addressed the congress on the subject, and on October 9, 1862, a law was approved providing for the creation of special military courts. According to this law a court composed of three judges having colonel's rank and one judge advocate with captain's rating was assigned to each army corps. These courts were given extensive authority including the power to summon civilian witnesses. Their jurisdiction included that exercised by courts-martial and, in addition, offenses defined as crime by civil laws, but it did not apply to officers ranking higher than colonel. The new system was not intended to eliminate the function of courts-martial, but subsequent policy tended toward lessening of the latter's jurisdiction.[7]

Inauguration of the new judicial system appeared to produce salutary results. Secretary of War Seddon in 1863 expressed the conviction that the military courts had, by expediting court action, improved both discipline and morale. But the growing magnitude in 1864 of the related evils of straggling and desertion indicate a failure to achieve the ends for which Lee and others had hoped. James Phelan, one of the court members functioning in Mississippi, wrote a letter to President Davis on October 2, 1864, criticizing severely the exercise of pardoning power by corps commanders as allowed under the law creating the court system. When he assumed his judicial capacity, he said, he determined to create a wholesome respect for the new courts by dispensing emphatic justice to first offenders. But he soon found that it was very difficult to convict a soldier who had social position and influential friends. Two such soldiers arraigned before him, who by exertions of able counsel barely escaped conviction of desertion, were found guilty of absence without leave. Acquaintances set up a tremendous agitation for their pardon by the corps commander and "in a few days they were both parading the streets with their friends." In the meanwhile, some men of lesser social position, convicted at the same time, had not been favored by the interposition of wealthy and influential connections and were serving their sentences. Such discrimination, according to Phelan, was "a shame in the eyes of justice," and led to "the most hostile and unhappy spirit among the poor men of the army." Phelan's position and reputation were such as to give considerable weight to his statements.[8]

Rebs who were called before dispensers of army justice, whether courts-martial or special military tribunals, were charged with a great variety of offenses. A rather common cause of arrest was fighting. Most officers attempted to ignore minor altercations between their men, but occasionally contentions were of such a nature as to require official action.

Such was the case involving Privates Koss and Ryan of the Washington Artillery. Koss left his sentry post to warm himself at a fire surrounded by several comrades. Someone mentioned a previous disagreement between Ryan and Koss, whereupon the former spoke up and asked the latter if he wished to settle the matter then and there. Koss replied that he fought only with gentlemen, whereupon Ryan pitched into him.

The row took place near the officers' quarters, and Lieutenant Hawes, officer of the day, ran out to quell the disturbance. In restoring order Hawes struck Koss over the head with a saber and called the fighters "damned sons of bitches." Koss submitted written charges of cruel and unbecoming treatment against the officer, and the latter countered with action against Koss for fighting.

The regimental court-martial, convened to consider the case, found that Hawes used "strong language," but did not feel it necessary to administer any sentence. Koss was adjudged guilty of fighting and ordered to be privately reprimanded by the commanding officer of the battalion, but lest the major speak too harshly the court recommended the prisoner to his mercy.[9] No blood was spilled in this encounter, and had it not been for the conspicuousness of place and the submission of charges against a superior by Koss, it is doubtful if court proceedings would have been invoked. As one Reb correctly observed, the usual mode of discipline in cases where the "boys fall out and pass a few licks" was confinement in the guardhouse on the simple order of a commissioned officer.[10]

The offense for which Private Bartlett was convicted, that of sleeping while on post of duty, claimed the attention of courts with considerable frequency. And punishment varied greatly. Private C. A. Everett of the Washington Artillery, who was found asleep on picket in Virginia three weeks before First Manassas, drew a sentence of three days' close confinement in the guardhouse with bread-and-water ration. In passing sentence the court noted as extenuating considerations the facts that the accused had, prior to trial, been confined the full period allowed by regulations, namely eight days, and had shown "penitence for consciousness of the grievousness of the offense"; but the most amazing explanation of judicial clemency was the court's recognition of the circumstance "that on the night and time stated in the charge the accused had been induced to partake of an extraordinary quantity of liquor to which he was not accustomed." [11] The suggestion of this court would seem to be that men when confronted with a turn of sentry duty should take a heavy dram, compose themselves comfortably, and go to sleep, and if caught, to make demonstrations of abject contrition. A court-martial sitting at Macon, Georgia, in August 1862 handed down, in several cases of sleeping at sentry post, the extremely light sentence of forty-eight hours of double guard duty with public reprimand by a commissioned officer.[12]

Fortunately for Confederate discipline other judiciaries treated the offense more seriously. In 1862 a trans-Mississippi court-martial imposed a sentence of hard labor, with an eighteen-pound ball attached

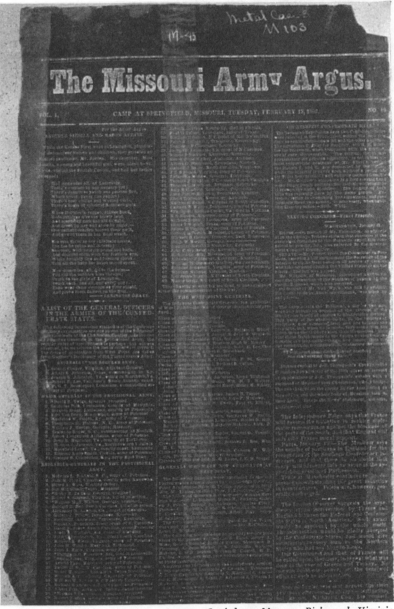

Courtesy Confederate Museum, Richmond, Virginia

THE MISSOURI ARMY ARGUS

Camp newspaper issued for and by soldiers of General Sterling Price's Command.

Courtesy *Military Records Division, Alabama Department of Archives and History, Montgomery, Alabama*

THE PIONEER BANNER

Front page of manuscript newspaper issued by soldiers in camp.

to the leg for the remainder of the war, and then dishonorable discharge.[13] Courts of Lee's army during the last six months of the war meted out such punishments as these: solitary confinement for fourteen days with bread and water diet; six months at hard labor; three months' imprisonment in the guardhouse with ball and chain; in three cases the death sentence was imposed, but interposition of Lee and the Secretary of War forestalled execution. The writer found no instance of a soldier being shot for sleeping at his post.[14]

For drunkenness while guarding prisoners at Tullahoma, Tennessee, in January 1863 Private Henry Jones was required to stand on the head of a barrel with a whiskey bottle hanging from his neck two hours each day for a month, and while not thus engaged to do hard labor.[15] But as a general rule cases of excessive drinking seem to have been disposed of informally without resort to court proceedings. In innumerable instances, however, intoxication was a contributing factor to some offense that did merit the consideration of judicial agencies. For instance, Sergeants Jules Freret and Gustave Aime, who made the mistake of demanding a drink of their captain and then proceeding to cut the ropes of his tent when refused, were given court-martial sentence of reduction of rank, fifteen turns of guard duty, and thirty days' confinement to camp.[16]

Theft and pillaging were, as previously noted, offenses of unusual prevalence, and punishments for them were of great diversity. A Texas private who stole a shirt from a comrade was sentenced to be placarded with the word "thief," mounted face backward on a mule with his feet tied under the animal's belly and paraded before his brigade to the accompaniment of discordant music of drums and bugles.[17] An Alabamian who helped himself to a citizen's honey was required to forfeit a month's pay, and during four hours of each day for ten days to stand on a conspicuously placed barrel wearing a board marked "bee hive."[18] One of Hood's soldiers who stole a saddle on the Tennessee campaign was made to march before his comrades with a large placard pinned on his breast and a saddle tied to his back.[19] Other thieves were given ball-and-chain assignments for periods of one to six months, or imprisoned with forfeiture of pay for varying lengths of time; in rare instances they were suspended by their thumbs for an hour or two with feet barely touching the ground.[20]

The punishment prescribed most frequently of all for pilfering was the barrel shirt. This consisted of an ordinary barrel, with openings at the end and on the sides for head and arms, slipped down over the shoulders and labeled usually with such descriptions of the crime as "stealing from a sick soldier," "robbing a comrade," or simply "thief." Culprits thus attired were made to march before their comrades at dress parade on successive days, sometimes to the tune of the "Rogues March," or "Yankee Doodle," played by regimental bands.[21]

Misbehavior before the enemy was another offense that came rather frequently to the attention of judiciaries. Military regulations authorized the death penalty for cowards but this was rarely invoked. In some instances courts-martial let offenders off with such light punishment as forfeiture of pay for two or three months plus the carrying of rails at dress parade for a few successive days. But the usual penalties were more severe. A Floridian who showed the white feather under duress was required to do hard labor for six months with a ball and chain attached to his ankle, and for the first week of each of the six months he was to be put on a bread-and-water diet. A craven Virginian was sentenced to hard labor for twelve months, with ball and chain, wearing on his back a placard inscribed "coward," and at the end of the year he was to be branded on the left cheek with the letter "C"—said letter to be one inch long—and then to be dishonorably discharged from the service. And for a South Carolinian who failed to stand the gaff of battle, this punishment was ordered: "To be publicly branded in the palm of the left hand with the letter 'C', one and one half inches in length; to have one-half of his head shaved; to be marched in front of his regiment at Dress Parade with a placard fastened to his back upon which shall be inscribed in legible words, 'I am a coward'; and to forfeit six months pay." [22]

It was apparently for cowardice also that one of the severest of all sentences encountered by the writer was handed down. The dictum of the court in this case was:

"He shall be marched bare-headed in a barrel shirt at the point of a bayonet in front of his Regiment on six successive dress parades. He shall be kept bucked and gagged [bucking consisted of setting the culprit down, tying his hands together, slipping them over his knees, and then running a stick through the space beneath the knees and over the arms; gagging was achieved by tying a stick or bayonet in the mouth] at all times when not on the march eight hours each day for 30 days, unless in the opinion of his commanding officer & surgeon, his life shall be so much endangered as to require respite, in which case, he may (for such time only as may be necessary to preserve life) be temporarily relieved of this kind of punishment by being tied to a tree or post in a standing position or be put to hard labor for a like time and purpose. He shall then at the end of his thirty days have a respite of seven days, and at the end of the 7 days shall again undergo the above punishment for a 2nd period of 30 days." [23]

Sentences for absence without leave varied more than for other infractions because of such diverse circumstances as the length of time the accused was away, whether he returned voluntarily and whether he left during a period of active compaign. Punishments decreed in 1862 by courts-martial of the Army of the Mississippi included: two months' confinement in the guardhouse for absences approximating two weeks where the accused returned of their own accord; and thirty days' assignment to stable cleaning, forfeiture of four months' pay, and ten days' wearing of ball and chain (twelve-pound ball, six-foot chain) for a four day excursion to Memphis.[24]

A soldier detected in Natchitoches without a pass received in 1863 the unusual sentence of marking time on the head of a barrel two hours each day for five days.[25] In 1864 absentees for indeterminate periods from Lee's army suffered the following penalties: "head shaved, sit on a pole, ball and chain"; "head shaved, ball and chain, carry a billet of wood"; "forfeit two months pay, bread and water diet"; "marched once before the Regt wearing a barrel shirt with a placard inscribed 'absence without leave' "; "to cut and pack wood three months for his regiment, to stand on a block &c 15 days with a placard on his back labelled 'absence without leave' "; and at least two men who took French leave got off with a mere reprimand.[26] Several members of the Fifty-ninth Alabama Regiment, who in 1864 helped themselves to furloughs, were made to carry rails on their shoulders four hours a day for sixty consecutive days.[27]

Desertion seems to have demanded the attention of courts and general courts-martial more frequently than any other offense.[28] As has been previously intimated there was a widespread tendency early in the war to deal overleniently with this crime. In 1862 courts-martial of the Army of Tennessee let off some men found guilty of desertion with head-shaving, forfeiture of pay and a month's imprisonment with ball and chain.[29] And recurrently during the conflict there were noticeable softenings of punishments. Twice in 1863 Beauregard rebuked courts-martial for meting out light penalties to deserters; one court sentenced five offenders to periods at hard labor with ball and chain of from fifteen to thirty-two days, and a sixth, adjudged guilty of deserting in front of the enemy, was subjected only to four hours of hard labor a day for two months.[30]

Courts of Lee's army continued to hand down some easy sentences in the face of multiplied desertion. In the fall of 1864, for instance, one offender was sentenced to thirty days of hard labor with forfeiture of pay; another to deprivation of six months' wages; and a third to carrying a fence rail for sixty days and forfeiture of a year's pay.[31]

Throughout the conflict judiciaries showed the greatest reluctance to impose the death sentence. In 245 cases of conviction for desertion during the last six months of the war by courts belonging mainly to the Army of Northern Virginia, the extreme penalty was prescribed in only 70 instances. And 31 of these 70 sentences were invalidated by President Davis' general amnesty of February 1865.[32]

Commanding generals, with a few exceptions, were subject to squeamishness when it came to approving the shooting of deserters; and in a number of instances the Secretary of War interposed after sentences had been approved by Lee.[33] Sometimes executions were forestalled at the last minute with storybook flourishes of drama, as witness the entry in a Mississippian's diary:

"June 12, 1863, we were ordered out to our drill grounds this morning to witness the execution of a deserter from the Nineteenth Tennessee Regiment. As the poor fellow was seated upon his coffin, and everything ready for the command to fire, an officer rode up in great haste with a pardon. I was truly glad, but must say some of the boys were disappointed." [34]

Suggestion of the casualness with which desertion was regarded in some quarters is afforded by a letter written by a member of the Twentieth Mississippi Regiment to his father in January 1863:

"About noon today . . . was ordered to procede to Capt Hedden's Hdqrs . . . and there take charge of Six deserters and conduct them to . . . Hd Qr't's of General Tilghman. . . . After the General had given the men a little Fatherly advice—ordered me to march them back to Capt Hedden with orders for Capt H— to still keep them under arrest but to make them do camp duty." [35]

Evidence is not conclusive that this was the extent of their punishment, but such is strongly intimated; if the men were to be shot or dealt with in some other severe manner, why the fatherly advice? The impression of leniency is further supported by the statement of a

Mississippi district judge in 1864 that he knew many men "now in desertion for the fourth, fifth, and sixth times" who had "never been punished." [36]

In the great majority of desertion cases judiciaries invoked sentences lying between the two extremes of death and long-term imprisonment on the one hand and such trifles as carrying rails on the other. Before the passage of an interdicting law in April 1863, whipping was a common punishment.[37] Branding, usually with a red-hot iron, but occasionally with indelible ink, was also a frequently prescribed penalty; the marking was placed on the hip, in the hand, or on the cheek. Frequently whipping and branding were combined with other inflictions.

Private L. A. Childers, for instance, was sentenced "to be publickly flogged with fifty lashes on his bare back, to have the left side of his head shaved, and to be branded on the left hip with the letter 'D', which letter shall be four inches long and three inches broad . . . to wear a ball and chain . . . for six months, and at the end of that time to be dishonorably discharged." [38] Private S. B. Seymour received a similar sentence, with the exception that the ball-and-chain assignment was to run throughout the war, and that the whipping (39 lashes) was to be repeated at three-month intervals for the same period. Private C. H. Allbright of the "Montgomery True Blues" was to be branded, to have his head shaved, to receive ten licks with a paddle, and then to be drummed out of the service to the tune of the "Rogues' March." [39]

In the case of a Texas deserter the court specified, in addition to ball and chain, this interesting detail of punishment:

"He is likewise to ride astride a wooden horse for fifteen days two hours and a half each day, the riding to be done every day in the week except Saturdays and Sundays, the horse to be six feet high, the pole upon which he is to sit to be six inches in diameter . . . he to go through this exercise from two o'clock P.M. until half past four P.M." [40]

When the death penalty was administered to deserters, commanding officers usually staged executions in a manner planned to impress the soldiery. Usually the brigade or division to which the condemned men belonged were marched to the scene of execution and arranged in a hollow square so as to afford all a clear view of the proceedings. Frequently those destined to face the firing squad were required to ride through the encampment, and sometimes through an adjacent town, sitting on their coffins. Arrived at the designated place they were blindfolded and made to sit or stand on coffins, or tied to stakes, or compelled to kneel by open graves. Then amid the awful hush, a detail composed of perhaps twenty-four men was ordered to a position a few paces in front of the condemned. Only half of the guns were loaded, but no man among the executioners knew whether or not his was a blank charge. At the signal "Fire!" the ominous quiet was broken with the roar of muskets and the culprits sank in crumpled heaps to the ground.

A note of unintended horror was sometimes added to these occasions by factors of nervousness and chance. A case in point was an execution that took place in Bragg's army in late 1862. When the firing squad of twenty men, stationed twelve paces from the culprit, discharged its volley, little damage was done. Four men held in reserve against just such a contingency were then ordered to step up and shoot. The prisoner was still not killed. Finally all twenty-four executioners reloaded their pieces and administered the *coup de grâce*.[41]

Home letters of Rebs offer abundant proof that seeing the execution of comrades made a profound impression. And had the death penalty been applied with greater consistency, desertion would doubtless have been checked. The reaction of soldiers to the spectacle of deserter-comrades riddled by firing squads is well illustrated by Private Thomas Warrick of Alabama. On December 19, 1862, he wrote from Bragg's army:

"I saw a site today that made me feel mity Bad I saw a man shot for deserting there was twenty fore Guns shot at him thay shot him all to pease . . . he went home and thay Brote him Back and then he went home again and so they shot him for that Martha it was one site that I did hate to see it But I could not helpe my self I had to do Jest as thay sed for me to doo."

In August 1863 Bragg published Davis' order giving amnesty to all absentees who would within twenty days return of their own accord to posts of duty. Warrick and his comrades probably interpreted this as an indication that in future deserters would be treated with clemency. However that may be, when word came to the Alabamian in October that his family was suffering for food he wrote immediately to his wife that he would try to get a furlough, but that if he failed he would "com home Eny how." He was unsuccessful in his efforts to get leave, but in the weeks that followed he was compelled to witness further executions. To what extent these stringencies influenced him cannot be determined, but his change of tune in reference to taking leave is in interesting parallel to increasing harshness dealt out to deserters. In June 1864 he wrote his folks from Georgia: "I would be glad to see you all now but I recon that I have bin home my last time till this war closes." And he had.[42]

A great number of soldiers appeared before military tribunals on the charge of insubordinate and disrespectful conduct toward officers. Much of the trouble between privates and their superiors could be attributed to undue sensitiveness on the part of the former, and their lack of understanding of military usage. Too frequently men in the ranks were inclined to regard orders as personal affronts when they were issued in the brusque authoritative tone of superior officers. Such seems to have been the reaction of Private Charles Brown of the Washington Artillery whom Lieutenant Roper ordered to procure a missing halter just as camp was about to be moved from Richmond, in June 1861. Instead of obeying promptly the private dawdled away muttering. After a while Lieutenant Roper received word that Brown wanted to see him. When he approached the disgruntled private the latter spoke up in protest against his alleged mistreatment, saying that he wanted the officer to understand that he, Brown, was as much a gentleman as Roper or anyone else and that he was not to be ordered about in any such manner. The lieutenant repeated his order, and when Brown hesitated to comply Roper lifted his saber to enforce obedience. At the same time the private drew a sword that he was carrying. Roper then cursed Brown and struck him with the flat of his saber. The private endeavored to return the blow and then galloped away. Roper gave pursuit, overtook Brown and enforced compliance with his order at the point of his pistol. A court-martial imposed a sentence requiring that Brown have his name erased from the battalion roll, that his uniform be shorn of all distinguishing marks, and that in the presence of his comrades he be drummed out of camp.[43]

For a similar offense, that of resisting and drawing a saber on a commissioned officer, another Private Brown, belonging to the Second Texas Infantry, was sentenced in the spring of 1862 to hard labor for the duration of the war and then dishonorably discharged. But the same court-martial ordered only a public reprimand to a soldier "for severely kicking Sergeant Daniel"; still another who was found guilty of addressing violent and insulting language at his major, and then attempting to hit him, was let off with three months of hard labor. In sharpest and most incomprehensible contrast with other penalties imposed by this body was the death sentence given Private James R. Maxwell for resisting and striking the sergeant of the guard and two sentinels who took him in custody.[44]

The comparative impunity with which privates could address nasty remarks to superiors reflects discredit on the general state of Confederate discipline. A rampant Reb who, when accosted by a corporal on guard duty in downtown Galveston, called him "a damned son-of-a-bitch" received a milk-and-water sentence before his company by way of rebuke from the captain.[45] A Texas artilleryman who pleaded guilty to the charge of inviting his sergeant to kiss his backside was ordered merely to ask the aggrieved officer's pardon in the presence of his company commandant.[46]

One Private Neighbors who, when ordered to be bucked by his lieutenant for disobeying an order, said to that officer, "No one but a damned coward would have a soldier bucked; if you will pull off your insignia of rank I will whip you on the spot," had his ball-and-chain sentence remitted by Beauregard on the score of prior orderliness.[47]

Private James Sweeny who ran amuck with higher authority at Abbeville, Mississippi, striking his sergeant and designating him as a son-of-a-bitch, and telling an interposing lieutenant to "tie him up and go to hell," "kiss his ———," and so forth, drew the severer penalty of forfeiture of pay, confinement at hard labor with ball and chain for three months, and then a head shaving and drumming out of the service.[48]

Resistance and disrespect to officers evoked some unusual sentences. A Mississippian found guilty of insubordination was required to march before the guardhouse three alternate hours of each day for one month, bearing a weight of thirty pounds in a knapsack tied on his back, and during the hours intervening to be held in confinement.[49] A Louisianian who abused those in authority over him while in a state of intoxication had to wear a molasses barrel several times a day for thirty consecutive days.[50] And an artilleryman who violated the canons of respectfulness was ordered, in addition to wearing ball and chain, "to stand toeing a mark for 2 hours a day for the first ten days . . . without resting or changing his position."[51]

In addition to these common offenses there were a number of infractions that came occasionally to the attention of military tribunals. Among these were self-mutilation to escape service, selling whiskey, making seditious remarks, holding correspondence with the enemy, exciting or participating in mutiny, quitting post of duty without authorization, selling equipment, forging passes, breaking guard and refusing to perform some unpleasant task such as policing camp, standing guard, or doing fatigue duty. Penalties handed down for these breaches of discipline were varied, but they consisted mainly of types previously noted.

For offenses as a whole, the most common punishments prescribed by courts and courts-martial were these: (1) Confinement to the guardhouse (sometimes nothing more than a tent, a brush arbor or a circumscribed space which Rebs called a "bull pen"); (2) ball and chain—the ball weighing from six to thirty-two pounds and being attached to the prisoner's leg by a chain ranging in length from two to six feet; (3) wearing a barrel shirt, labeled usually with a description of the infraction; (4) hard labor; (5) carrying a weight, usually a rail or a stick of wood; (6) doing extra guard duty; (7) public reprimand by a superior officer; (8) bread-and-water diet; (9) stoppage of pay; (10) standing or marking time on a barrel, placarded with a description of his offense; (11) confinement in the stocks; and (12) branding.

Military judiciaries supplemented these common penalties with an impressive array of original and exceptional punishments. One offender was required to stand on the head of a barrel two hours a day for a week reading aloud from the articles of war; another had to wear for two months "a twelve-pound iron collar with three prongs round his neck"; a third was chained to a block for thirty days; a fourth was strapped astride a cannon barrel for sixteen hours; a fifth was bound to the wheel of a gun carriage; a sixth was forced to walk about with a log on his shoulder and with a bag of sand tied to each of his legs; a seventh was mounted on a rail, three empty bottles tied to his feet, placarded with the inscription "Ten cents a Glass," and drummed about the camp; an eighth was put to "filling a hollow sack with sand" two hours each day for a month; a ninth was marched in front of the guardhouse with a jug in one hand and a bed tick in another one-half an hour a day for two weeks; and a cavalryman was sentenced to walk from San Antonio to Austin, Texas—a distance of about eighty miles—in three days.[52]

War articles forbade a man being held to confinement longer than eight days without trial. Sometimes prisoners were held for the fullness of this limit before courts-martial were convened. But again cases were tried with the greatest dispatch. On the march a drumhead session might convene at night, try an offender and order his execution on the spot.[53]

An intoxicated Reb riding a boat en route to Portsmouth in June 1861 insulted and tore the dress of a passenger. He was seized by his comrades, placed under arrest just as soon as the vessel docked, and tried within a few hours. The next morning a placard reading, "A coward, but brave enough to insult a woman" was placed on his back, and fellow soldiers drummed him at bayonets' ends through Portsmouth and beyond while an accompanying band played the tune of "Yankee Doodle." [54]

Many trivial offenses committed by Rebs, and some serious ones as well, were handled by commissioned officers without resort to courts-martial or to other military tribunals. Assignment to extra guard duty was the penalty most commonly invoked by those in authority for minor aberrations. Rebs were wont to refer to this punishment as being "put on the roots." A diarist of the Texas Rangers cited an incident illustrating application of this corrective medium:

"March 23, 1862—Today we received news of a big fight in New Mexico, and Arkansas—Victories for the Confederacy, several of the boys were so overjoyed with the news, that they turned their horses loose, and got put on the roots for it, which came very near causing a small riot in camp." [55]

But Major General Hindman of Johnston's army frowned on this type of penalty. "Putting men on extra guard duty," he announced in February 1864, "as a punishment is prohibited. Standing guard is the most honorable duty of a soldier, except fighting, and must not be degraded." [56] Hindman's attitude, however, was exceptional.

Another penalty frequently imposed by company and regimental commanders for slight infractions was that of digging stumps. The number and the character of excavations varied with the gravity of offense and the temper of commanding authorities.

Captain C. R. Hanleiter of Thompson's Artillery, stationed near Savannah for an extended period, was one who favored this mode of punishment. His diary records that on December 8, 1861, he put three men "to grubbing for getting drunk"; and on April 1, 1862, he entered this statement: "Private Holmes having overstayed his leave of absence yesterday was required to extract a couple of pine Stumps—which he did quite scientifically." In the case of a man whom he apprehended under the influence of liquor, Hanleiter applied the unusual punishment of tying the victim with his back to a tree for several hours. He ordered other inebriates and fisticuff offenders to be confined in bombproof dugouts. [57]

"'Tis the flag of the free,"
"We'll ever defend it."

Courtesy Southern Historical Collection, University of North Carolina

LETTER WRITTEN ON "CAPTURED" STATIONERY

Letter written by Private Richard W. Waldrop, Company F, 21st Virginia Regiment. Note crossing out of flag and poetry. This is a sample of an educated soldier's writing. Manuscript, University of North Carolina.

A SOLDIER'S LETTER

A typical "poor white" letter written from a Confederate camp.

Early in the war officers had considerable difficulty in curbing reckless firing of guns.[58] The prevalence of this evil was due in part to the anxiety of volunteers to test their weapons when the long roll sounded, and also to the general excitement that prevailed as men fell in for their first encounters. Results were sometimes fatal. General Cheatham invoked the penalty of marking time from midnight to dawn in an effort to restrain nervous trigger fingers in his command.[59]

To a considerable extent this offense was due to the excessive jauntiness with which volunteers regarded camp routine. Summons to drill in the early months of war was apt to evoke hurrahing, brandishing of weapons, backslapping, ogling, and various other manifestations of horseplay. "General Whiting made some sharp remarks to our boys," observed a member of the Second Mississippi Regiment in 1862, "for hollowing & yelling when called into line he charged it to the new recruits and wants it stoped and no mistake as it is useless & unmilitary." [60]

Other forms of punishment applied by commanding officers included cleaning of camps, bucking, hanging by the thumbs, confinement to guard tents, and riding the wooden horse.[61]

A penalty resorted to by those in authority over the Twenty-seventh Mississippi Infantry deserves special mention for its uniqueness. The sight of swine was the source of great temptation to members of this regiment as to most other Rebs. When a hog was "captured," time and lack of facilities would not permit scalding and scraping according to the usual practice, but instead the victim had to be skinned. A piece of skinned pork came generally to be regarded as a telltale of pillage. When officers of this regiment nabbed pig thieves they took pieces of the skin, cut holes in them, slipped them over the heads of offenders, and required that the "hog-skin cravats" be worn all day in front of the provost guard.[62]

Occasionally the privates took justice in their own hands. A case in point was that involving soldiers stationed near Bowling Green during the war's first winter. One day a civilian came to camp on business. Some Rebs who engaged him in conversation were irked by the strong Union tone of his sentiments. "So without more ado they put him astride of a rail and ducked him in a neighboring pond." [63]

In 1864 members of a Virginia company became so disgusted with the misdeeds of a pestilential comrade that they voted unanimously to get rid of him. He was taken out of bounds, given thirty-nine lashes by a specially appointed executioner, and ordered never to show himself again in camp on pain of even worse treatment.[64]

In a third instance a Texas cavalryman apprehended in the act of rape was, even while officers were taking counsel as to his disposition, removed from the guardhouse by his comrades, hanged, buried, and his effects distributed among the most needy of the company.

In another case the wrath of this same outfit vented itself on an officer. A diarist-observer gave the following account of this incident: "Agt. B— . . . had been thrown out of office & Dud M Jones of Co. I substituted . . . B— was accused of abolitionism and Bigamy, the latter being pretty strongly proven upon him, the boys en masse took him out & hung him & gave his outfit to a poor boy a member of the same Co." [65]

It should be noted in explanation of the extraordinary severity of these last two instances that the period was early in the war, when military usages were not yet established, and in a location where ideas of frontier justice had not been abandoned.

The fact that military courts were overloaded, together with the difficulty of convening courts-martial, tended to place undue disciplinary responsibility on officers commanding companies, regiments and brigades. In the spring of 1864 Brigadier General L. S. Ross wrote to his superior complaining bitterly of inability to secure the co-operation of courts of any sort to check misconduct in his command. Some of the offenders he said had been in arrest for more than a year without trial, and others who had been tried had escaped the full measure of punishment because the courts had failed to publish their findings. "I have arrested and released . . . these men and officers," he added, "and returned them to duty so often without trial that military law has become obsolete." He concluded with the statement that "my command, influence, or authority over them does not depend on their respect for or fear of military law or authority, but simply their love for me as an individual." [66]

General Ross's situation was to some extent exceptional as to failure of judiciaries, in view of the fact that he was stationed in a peripheral area where court functions were more difficult than usual. But his observation as to control being determined by the personal influence which he had over his command applied in large measure throughout the Confederate Army. To a much larger extent than in most military organizations Rebel discipline was an individual matter between an officer and his men. This fact was noted by an inspector of Lee's army in the fall of 1864. In his report he pointed out that there was the greatest diversity of order and authority among the different brigades. One would be characterized by clean weapons, punctual response to signals and efficient performance of drill maneuvers, while another of the same division would be utterly shiftless and deranged. "The brigade," he said, "reflects the character and qualifications of its commander." "Indeed," he added, "the brigadier makes the brigade." [67] And this principle was prevalent on down the line of commands.

The factor of personal equation was at once the secret of the Rebel Army's brilliant achievement and the source of its greatest weakness. Given brave, efficient and respect-inspiring leaders from lieutenants to brigadiers—men who knew how to take into consideration individual pride and at the same time exercise a firm authority—Southern soldiers were insurpassable; but the same troops, when commanded by slovenly disciplinarians, were apt to straggle, pillage, evade drill, neglect equipment and skulk. Rebs might fight even under shabby officers, but too frequently such officers had lost the lion's share of their commands by straggling, overstaying leaves, sham sickness and other evidences of poor discipline before fighting began. In this connection the observation that Confederates were the best of fighters and the worst of soldiers is most significant.

What did ordinary Rebs think of their officers? The close relation between discipline and attitude toward those in authority merits consideration of this question. That there were innumerable soldiers who thoroughly disliked their superiors is indisputable. In letters to their folk they frequently aired their animosity. "Our Gen Reub Davis goes by the name of 'Henry of Navarre' among the boys," wrote a Mississippian, "from the long white plume he wears in his hat. . . . He is a vain, stuck-up illiterate ass, and I dont believe there is a man in the regiment who would willingly go into battle with him." [68]

The objection stated by this soldier to General Davis was one of the main causes of unpopularity. Rebs could rarely look with favor upon an officer whom they deemed guilty of "putting on airs." An Irish member of a Louisiana regiment, on beholding a lieutenant walking about in a resplendent uniform, gave vivid expression to an impression held by the majority of soldiers toward ostentatious officers when he remarked, "Oh Mike, look at that new lefttenant! Don't he think he is purtty wid the new chicken guts (narrow gold lace, insignia of rank) on his arms. Look at his strut." [69]

Another cause of dislike of officers was the belief that they were unduly severe or highhanded. When Colonel Lowry of Mississippi placed some men under arrest for falling out of line to get water while on the march, their comrades began calling him *Corporal* Lowry, and thereafter, until stern measures were invoked, every passage of the general through this portion of the line would elicit a chorus of shouts such as "Here comes the corporal!" and "Make way for Corporal Lowry!" much to the officer's embarrassment.[70] When commanders seemed to bear down on them too heavily, other privates were apt to complain to their homefolk that they were being treated like Negroes.

Resentment of easier circumstances enjoyed by officers was a fertile source of antagonism. "It is only the ones that wear grey coats and Brass Buttons . . . [who] are living better and wear better clothes than they did before the war," a Texan wrote peevishly to his wife in April 1864. "I do not blame them for keeping the war up as long as possible," he added, for "most of them are in no danger, they are always in the rear." [71]

Another Texan complained: "All of our commissioned officers are now absent. If one of them has the *Belly Ache* for a day or two he is posted off to the hospital. While the poor private who has all of the burden to bear, has to stay and tough it out." [72] A third Reb was angered by the belief that officers received their pay while privates had to wait endless months for theirs.[73] Still another couched his disgruntlement at the softer lots of provost guards and commissaries by dubbing them "bombproofs." [74]

Private T. W. Hall fulminated against officerdom in general. "Who is it that has the hardships to under go?" he wrote, "it is the privates." And "who is it that has bacon to eat, Sugar to put in their coffee and all luxuries of this kind?" he added, "the officers." [75]

Even the more intelligent men were susceptible to resentment of discrimination. "The only objection (or at least the greatest one I have) to the life I am now living," observed an Alabamian of unusually good background, "is the restrictions placed on the privates, when the officers can go to town at option, stay as long as they please, and get gloriously drunk in and out of camp when it suits them to do so. If I live through this campaign I for one am done 'sojering.' " [76]

Although there were many foreigners in the Rebel Army, prejudice against officers on the score of non-nativity was sometimes a factor in their unpopularity.[77] It might have been expected that the example of Davis in making Judah Benjamin his highest cabinet official and his closest confidant would have lessened anti-Semitism among soldiers, but such was evidently not the case. When a Texas regiment sent to Richmond in 1861 was transferred to Confederate service, the first colonel appointed by the War Department was a Jew. As the new officer rode up to take charge the displeased Rebs began to make comments in voices raised sufficiently for him to hear. "What?" said one. "What is it? Is it a man, a fish, or a bird?" "Of course it is a man," said another, "don't you see his legs?" The colonel withstood for a day the overt opposition confronting him on every hand, but when he waked next morning to find his horse shorn of tail he gave up his assignment as a hopeless one, and without a word he rode back to the city never to be heard of again by the regiment.[78]

The knowledge or belief that officers caroused, or yielded to the lure of high living, caused revulsion on the part of some men. A Louisianian noted in his diary in 1863 that a new brigadier had been appointed but that the officer was not very well liked. "From what I can learn," observed the diarist, "[he] is better able to command a bottle of whiskey than anything else." [79]

Sometimes intoxication of officers on duty worked a distinct hardship on Rebs, as when a Mississippi colonel abused his command on the march and another forced the men to accelerate their double-duty paces.[80] But again the results were opposite, as witness a comment of Private Jerome Yates: "Capt Davis . . . [is] two good when he is tight he lets us do as we please but when he gets sober he makes up for it." [81]

Inability of officers to perform in a creditable manner the duties of their positions was a cause of much dislike. "He is a man of but little Military capacity," wrote an Alabamian of a newly appointed colonel in the fall of 1861, "consequently a great many of the [company officers] . . . are resigning . . . we poor privates have to stick it out. . . . I dont want to be lead into Battle by an ignoramus, Col. Henry is fit for nothing higher than the cultivation of corn." [82]

Even greater contempt was voiced by a Floridian who said of his regimental leaders: "Our major is a fine man, the rest are not fit to tote guts to a Bear." [83]

The circumstance which caused officers to be held in lowest esteem by their men was any show of cowardice under fire. During the Atlanta campaign there were some instances of bad conduct on the part of company commanders, and these did not escape notice of Rebs. "The boys crack many a joke on some of the officers," wrote an Alabamian. "They were so scared that they went so far as to get their men to refuse to go back [to a charge]. They were afraid to refuse themselves for fear that they would be cashiered." [84]

A second lieutenant became panicky when assigned to a picket post at which a man had recently been killed. Several privates sent to deepen the trench where he was located were unable to get him out of the ditch long enough to permit execution of their assignment. "The boys plagued him a great deal about it," according to a member of the company, but "he had not a word to say." [85]

A most amusing and yet pathetic case of derision for a cowardly officer was an affair growing out of the battle of Secessionville in June 1862. The officer involved was one Lieutenant Doyle, who prior to his show of cowardice had aroused considerable antipathy by undue severity and highhandedness. "He puts on a great many airs . . . when . . . Drilling his company," related an observer. "With his hand grasp around the hilt of his sword and the blade parallel with the ground he would command them to left wheal, with all the cautionary remarks such as steady; steady; on the pivot come round like a gate now hepp. hepp and so on." When word spread about the camp after Secessionville that Doyle had taken to his heels under fire, the men gathered up kettles and other camp utensils and stacked them before the guardhouse. This miscellaneous heap they dubbed "Fort Doyle." Erection of this fort inspired a camp bard to write some verses commemorating the incident, and these when circulated elicited untold amusement. The poem was:

Latest From The War;
The last Fight at Secessionville!

We went to Secessionville a disturbance to quell
Where the Yankees were storming our batteries, in fact raising hell
The boys all pitched in as all who are brave
Not one of them flinching not one of them caved

Except one—Mr. Doyal who stopped when he saw
Shot falling so fast—for want of sand in [h]is craw
He turned on his pivot—swung around like a gate
And made strides from the field from six feet to eight

He left in a hurry, and we all really suppose
His time is the fastest on record—yet nobody knows
He went to the Surgeon and struck for a job
To act as assistant, or be placed in a squad

The Surgeon was busy, and made no reply
So Doyal left the line another place to try
He left swift footed, and we saw him no more
Untill the day was far spent, and the battle was oer

When he again turned on his pivot, swung around like a gate
Walked into supper—sat down and ate
So in honor of him, we've erected Fort Doyal
Costing large sums of money—besides great toil
    A gun shall be fired at the raising of each sun
    In honor of Doyal, who at Secessionville run

Now listen to me, take the advice of a friend
Be true to the country, you've taken arms to defend,
Let your motto be onward and go straight ahead
Though you march through blood and crawl oer the dead

So on ward it is dont flinch "nary" time
Glory, honor, and victory, shall surely be thine
Be kind to the boys, and treat them all well
Or they'll blow up the Fort—and send you to hell
                  —Patriotic [86]

In happy contrast to leaders whose incapacity drew the scorn of ordinary soldiers was that very large group of officers who were able to command the complete respect of their men. Above all, men in the ranks appreciated willingness of superiors to share peril and hardship. When Captain E. J. Ellis of the Sixteenth Louisiana was moved by ill health in 1863 to write out his resignation, his company raised such a protest that he decided to stay on. His own comment on this reaction, given in the spirit of gratefulness rather than boasting, explains the unwillingness of his followers to part with him:

"We have toiled and suffered together, and together have faced the tempest of battle, they have divided their rations with me when they had not enough for themselves and the last drink of water from my canteen was freely and frequently given to them when I knew that many, weary, weary, miles of hot and dusty roads lay between me and the next water." [87]

Soldiers liked, too, ability of officers to blend severity with leniency, seriousness with humor, and willingness to close their eyes on occasion when circumstances required the setting aside of usual regulations.

They must have adored General C. Irvine Walker for his ineptness at distinguishing between scalded and skinned pork when rations were scant.[88] And the stories circulating through the armies of oversight, on the part of various generals, of incidents that deserved sharp rebuke testify to appreciation of this quality.

For instance there was a tale of General Wigfall finding a soldier on guard taking things with undue ease.

"What are you doing here, my man?" asked the general.

"Nothin' much," replied the man, "jes' kinder takin' care of this hyar stuff."

"Do you know who I am, sir?" asked the general.

"Wall, now 'pears like I know your face, but I cant jes' call your name—who is you?"

"I'm General Wigfall," said the officer irritatedly.

Without getting up or giving any other sign of being impressed the sentry extended his hand and said, "General, I'm pleased to meet you —my name's Jones"—and all this with impunity, according to the yarn.[89]

Another story concerned General Cheatham. He allegedly caught Private Jim Heath up an apple tree, on Bragg's Kentucky campaign. Heath was, in soldier parlance, "mortally scared to death" when he saw the general ride up under his perch. But Cheatham's address was, "Young man, drop me down a few of those fine apples."

"Yes, sir, and thank you too," said the private, with astonished relief.[90]

A third incident had to do with Stonewall Jackson. A Reb, beholding a figure slouched down on a horse, swaying precariously in the saddle as the general was wont to do when catching a nap on the march, cried out, "Hello, I say old fellow, where the devil did you get your licker?" As Stonewall, roused from his lethargy, looked up, a light of amazed recognition flickered over the soldier's countenance. "Good God! it's old Jack!" he exclaimed as he jumped a fence and headed for cover. When informed by the staff as to the cause of the Reb's discomfiture, Jackson, according to the story, only laughed.[91]

Soldiers also appreciated reluctance to shed blood, such as that manifested by Johnston before Atlanta. The writer has yet to find an unfavorable remark from a man in the ranks about this officer's Fabian generalship, while compliments are frequently found. Indications are that Hood, whom one soldier called a "butcher," assumed command in the face of an opposition so great as to cause serious apprehension. A Mississippi lieutenant wrote his wife on July 18, 1864:

"Hood is the most unpopular Genl in the army & some of the troops are swearing they will not fight under him. Brig Genls Cols & company officers have been called together to forestall anything like an outbreak Maj Genls & Brig & all regret that Johnston is gone, Johnston has made himself very dear to the soldiers." [92]

Simplicity and friendliness were also factors ingratiating officers with their men. Jackson, though a stern disciplinarian, was loved for his haphazard dress and his unpretentious conduct. This characteristic reaction to democratic conduct came from a Louisianian·

"General Steward often comes around to see how things are going. He was around yesterday by himself, no long train of beardles staff officers with their dazzling uniforms and [would-be] defiant looks attending him. he put me very much in mind of some old farmer, rideing around hunting up some stray cattle and couldnt find them. He is . . . very attentive to any request a private may make of him. . . . While other Generals headquarters are surrounded with Guards he has but one guard that is to guard his stables he is very popular with his command." [93]

Opinion of privates was of course an undependable criterion of a general's real capacity. The same is true to a considerable, but lesser, extent of other officers. In particular, adverse remarks from the ranks as to conduct of lieutenants, captains, and colonels were frequently without just foundation. In some cases these can be attributed to a universal tendency of subordinates to grumble; and in others they were due to false ideas of individual rights and to misconceptions of military usages.

But with due allowance for these considerations, there can be no doubt that much of the dissatisfaction with those in command expressed by ordinary Rebs was due to real incapacity of the officers themselves. The practice of electing company and regimental leaders and even subalterns, which prevailed during the first years of the war and persisted to some extent till near the end, frequently hampered selection of men best qualified for command; and officers once commissioned had an unhappy way of hanging on to their positions long after their incompetency had been proved.[94]

Resort in 1862 to a policy of examination for competency was effective, but in November 1863 the Secretary of War still found grounds to denounce election as giving "undue regard to popularity" and contributing to "a spirit of electioneering subversive of subordination and discipline." [95]

Reports of inspections made at various times of different portions of the army complain of laxity of officers in calling rolls, making reports, publishing and enforcing general orders, and attending to other important phases of camp routine; there is repeated reference also to the lack of sufficient distinction between officers and privates.[96]

Brigadier General John W. Frazier stated in an official report that men of the Fifty-fifth Georgia, which he "regarded as the best regiment for discipline and efficiency" of his command, did in 1863 "ride their colonel on a rail, which he [the colonel] never resented, but on promise to them of better behavior was allowed to resume his command." [97] And a Tar Heel private wrote in 1862 concerning his captain, "He put . . . [me] in the gard house one time & he got drunk agoin from Wilmington to Golesboro on the train & we put him in the Sh-t House So we are even." [98] What amazing commentaries on Rebel discipline!

There can be no doubt that the general state of discipline was notoriously bad in the early months of the war. There was altogether too much individualism. The editor of the Richmond *Enquirer* sized up the situation aptly when he said:

"Men in the army and out of the army thought for a long time the usual laws of discipline inapplicable to them. Were they not all gentlemen? And what gentleman would do a mean thing, steal a horse or plunder a chicken coop? Were they not all intelligent beyond other troops of the world? And what man in his senses would eat up the rations dealt out for five days in one or throw away his blanket because it was heavy? Were they not all brave and bold? And what brave man would linger behind on the march or turn his back to the enemy in battle. It was thought enough at first to operate upon the men by appeals to their zeal, their patriotism, and honor." [99]

This policy proved its error in countless instances and ways. Soldiers at Fort Jackson mutinied after passage of the Federal fleet up the river to New Orleans.[100] Troops of the Sixth Texas Cavalry refused to submit to Colonel Wharton's authority when he was assigned to command them.[101] A Virginia company balked at the use of muskets on the ground that enlistment had been for a "rifle company." [102]

Adjustment to military life, curbing of the evil of election, and other influences led to a noticeable improvement of discipline during the third and fourth years of war. Exceptions to this rule were detached cavalry units whose lack of order was ever notorious. But even after volunteers had become soldiers Rebel discipline fell to a level far below that anticipated by army regulations and thought essential to first-class performance in the field. The Inspector General of the Army of Northern Virginia reported in September 1864: "There is not that spirit of respect for and obedience to general orders which should pervade a military organization." As one evidence of general laxity he offered the item of straggling. "If the orders governing this subject were rigorously enforced," he said, "thousands of muskets would be heard in every fight that are now never fired." [103]

With this report in mind, and recalling the panics which had recently victimized Early's veterans in the Shenandoah Valley, Lee himself in February 1865 issued a circular pleading for the cultivation of discipline. Too much dependence, he said, had been placed on the soldiers' innate merit as individuals, and not enough consideration given to molding them into effective units. "Many opportunities have been lost and hundreds of valuable lives have been uselessly sacrificed," he added, "for want of a strict observance of discipline." [104] But his admonitions had scant opportunity to be carried out. For even as he spoke the shadow of Appomattox was descending on his army.

CHAPTER XIII

THE DEADLIEST FOE

ON AUGUST 9, 1862, an unsophisticated Tar Heel private stationed near Petersburg, Virginia, "took pen in hand" to address his homefolk. "T. G. Freman is Ded and they is Several mor that is Dangerous with the feever," he wrote; "they hev Been 11 Died with the fever in Co A since we left kinston and 2 died that was wounded so you now See that these Big Battles is not as Bad as the fever." [1]

Exactly one week earlier a well-educated Louisiana officer had written his brother from camp near Tupelo, "Look at our company—21 have died of disease, 18 have become so unhealthy as to be discharged, and only four have been killed in battle." [2] These two soldiers, one from the Army of Northern Virginia and the other from the Army of Tennessee, had each in his own limited sphere come face to face with an all-pervasive truth. The most destructive enemies of Confederates were not the Yankees but the invisible organisms which filled the camps with sickness.

Disease did not wait long to strike; and its initial onslaughts were the most devastating. During the first months of service it was not uncommon for half the men of a regiment to be incapacitated at one time by sickness, and frequently the ratio was higher.

In April 1862 Captain Alfred Bell reported that six out of every seven men of the Thirty-ninth North Carolina Regiment were ill. For this distressing situation Captain Bell blamed Lincoln, and he was firmly convinced that the Northern President "ought to be burnt in a hell ten thousand times hotter than fier." [3] Immunization and seasoning lessened the prevalence of sickness, but throughout the conflict disease continued to incapacitate a large number. Joseph Jones, one of the foremost authorities on Confederate medicine, estimated that on an average each Southern soldier was ill or wounded six times during the war, and that there were five times as many cases of sickness as of injury. He estimated further that for every soldier who died as a result of battle there were three who perished from disease. [4]

Various factors contributed to the excess of sickness which beset

Rebel encampments. Prominent among these was the character of men taken into the army. In the flush period of volunteering that followed Fort Sumter almost anyone who could stand on two feet was permitted to enlist. Henry M. Stanley of the Sixth Arkansas Regiment said concerning his induction, "We were not subjected to the indignity of being stripped and examined . . . but were accepted into the military service upon our own assurance of being in fit condition." [5] And what man under three score years was there in 1861 who did not consider himself able to do all the fighting necessary to whip the "craven Yankees"!

The indiscriminate policy of recruiting naturally brought into the army thousands of volunteers who were utterly unequal, because of age or frailty, to the hardships of campaigning. As a consequence many not only fell victim to disease themselves, but also, by the close association incident to camp life, communicated their maladies to hardier fellows.

Not until the fall of 1862, apparently, did Richmond authorities institute a program of physical examination for recruits. Even then there was not ample provision for eliminating the unfit. Examining officers were instructed to follow the general rule that a person who was equal to the active work of ordinary civil life was able to perform the duties of a soldier, and such defects as partial deafness, reducible hernia, muscular rheumatism, blindness in one eye, and loss of a couple of fingers were not to be considered as valid grounds for exemption.[6]

These regulations were of a decided benefit, but even so, great numbers continued to be inducted who were ill-adapted to the exposure, the deprivation, and the strenuous activities of life in the field.

Particularly susceptible to illness were the older men forced into the army by the conscription act of 1864. A surgeon who was put in charge of a regiment made up largely of enlistees under that law wrote in April 1864 that there "was more sickness in this regiment than in all the balance of the division." "It is a great pity that it was ever brought here," he said. "There are in it a great many old men of wealth and position at home who will die here. . . . Such men are entirely worthless here but would be very valuable at home." [7]

Of all the lessons taught by the Civil War, one of the most impressive was the fact that men of forty or over cannot be transplanted from the settled ways of civilian life to the strain and exposure of camp without exacting a heavy toll in sickness and death.

Most of the men who wore the gray were from the country, and this helps explain much of the sickness which plagued the Confederates. The country boys were tough, but they had not been immunized to the diseases common to children of towns and cities. Consequently they were besieged with these illnesses when they went to the army, while their city comrades of softer constitutions enjoyed comparatively good health. Pertinent also was the fact that townsmen knew better how to take care of themselves than the rustics did. Concerning some of the unsophisticates of the Alabama and Georgia hinterland, a North Carolinian wrote:

"They are like little children never away from home before, can't take care of themselves, and need someone to force them to wash themselves and put on clean clothing, when they start out to march they load themselves with more baggage than two men should carry. These are the men which for the most part compose our sick and fill up our Hospitals." [8]

Urban men also adapted themselves psychologically to the vicissitudes of army life more readily than those from the country, and this was a considerable item in physical well-being. From beginning to end of the war, the companies that were noted for the smallest sick rolls were crack outfits, made up of "gay youths of the cities," such as the Washington Artillery, the Richmond Blues, and the Mobile Cadets.[9]

Another factor which contributed to disease was exposure to rain and cold. Poets have delighted to dwell upon the tented field of Confederate days, but canopies were rarely to be found outside the imagination of the verse makers. During the terrible downpours in Virginia of March and April 1862, the great majority of Johnston's forces marched without raincoats and slept on the muddy ground without benefit of shelter; as a result hospitals were teeming with patients on the eve of Seven Pines.[10]

Later in the war oilcloths and tent-flies, both obtained largely from the Yankees, were in greater evidence, but even so, the soldier who had such protection was always the exception rather than the rule.

So habituated did Rebs become to mud and rain that some of them adopted a modified terminology, in which "dry" meant "not absolutely wet" and "perfectly dry" meant "somewhat damp, but not soaked through." [11] The huts built for winter quarters afforded some protection, but often winter quarters were postponed until January. In the meantime scarcity of clothing and lack of blankets combined with low temperatures and cold rains to inflict indescribable misery on the soldiers.

"It is really pitiable to see our boys at night sitting around their fires, nodding and almost asleep," wrote an officer on New Year's Day, 1864. "The ground is too cold for them to lie down on, and their one blanket is not warm enough for them to cover with. This is soldiering, this is." [12]

Suffering was often enhanced by inability to procure wood enough to keep the fires going. Shivering victims might draw some consolation from stories of Valley Forge, but philosophizing was of little effect in impeding the tides of sickness which always followed such periods of exposure.[13]

Much of the bad health must be attributed to an inadequate diet. Very seldom was there enough of vegetables in camp rations. During the greater part of the year fruit was unobtainable, and the day of "juices" had not arrived. When the soldiers did occasionally obtain apples and peaches, frequently they made no discrimination between the ripe and the green, and proceeded to gorge themselves. Rebs liked to brag about their culinary abilities, but the truth was that food prepared by troops was generally not of the most wholesome sort. A standard practice early in the war was to make flour up into slapjacks, and to fry these in a sea of bacon grease. Some regiments lived for month after month on a diet composed almost exclusively of fritters and fat meat.[14] Naturally the consequences were disastrous to digestive systems and to general health. "Much of the sickness our volunteers have suffered under," editorialized the Charleston Courier in 1862, "has been caused by half-done victuals—partially boiled rice and tough-baked bread." [15]

On many occasions impure water played havoc with army health. Troops stationed at Corinth depended in large measure for their water supply on shallow holes which they dug about the camps. Often these were placed so close to refuse deposits as to make contamination inevitable.[16] A newspaper correspondent reported that the water "smells so offensively that the men have to hold their noses while drinking it." [17]

In view of these circumstances it is not surprising to find that as many Confederates perished from disease during the seven weeks' encampment at Corinth in April and May 1862 as fell in the bloody fight at Shiloh.[18] These soldiers at Corinth were probably more careless about the sources from which they obtained water than Rebs generally were, but in all sections of the army and at all periods of the war the practice of drinking from rivers, creeks, badly situated springs and even from puddles was prevalent.

Another explanation of the numerous epidemics is to be found in the filth of many encampments. Ignorance, the overindulgence of elected officers, and the carelessness to which army life readily lends itself combined to defeat the earnest efforts of higher authorities to enforce sanitation. Latrines, or sinks as they were called by soldiers, were often placed too close to tents and bivouacs, and regardless of their location, there was a prevalent indisposition of Rebs to use them. Perhaps this was to be expected of a soldiery that came largely from a rural society in which men were accustomed to relieve themselves at whatever times and places the exigencies of nature overtook them. "Sinks not used," recurs with damning frequency on inspection reports, and in seacoast areas, the notation "beach used for sinks" is sometimes found.[19]

But the most extreme commentary on the nonchalance of toilet practices is that appearing in the diary of a Virginia private: "Dec. 3, 1863. . . . On rolling up my bed this morning I found I had been lying in—I wont say what—something though that didn't smell like milk and peaches." [20]

When soldiers were compelled to spend long periods in trenches, as at Vicksburg in 1863 and at Petersburg in 1864-1865, they were prone to litter the works with beef bones, melon rinds, fruit peelings, and other scraps.[21]

The scarcity of soap and the difficulty of bathing often added the factor of bodily filth. On January 19, 1865, Lee wrote the Secretary of War, "There is great suffering in the Army for want of soap. The neglect of personal cleanliness has occasioned cutaneous diseases to a great extent in many commands." [22] Even when soap and water were available there were always some soldiers who preferred personal filth to the exertion required for cleanliness.[23]

Swarms of pests worked in close co-operation with untidiness to communicate disease. Flies were a special nuisance. "When we open our eyes in the morning," wrote a Louisianian from Virginia in June 1861, "we find the canvas roofs and walls of our tents black with them. . . . It needs no morning reveille then to rouse the soldier from his slumbers. The tickling sensations about the ears, eyes, mouth, nose, etc., caused by the microscopic feet and inquisitive suckers of an army numerous as the sands of the sea shore will awaken a regiment of men

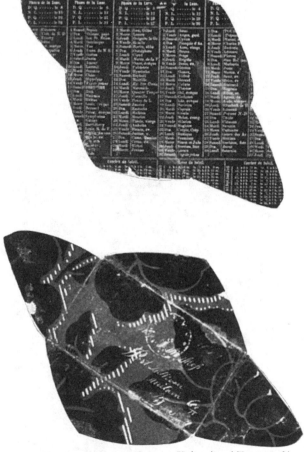

HOMEMADE ENVELOPE

Homemade envelope used by a Texas soldier, Frank Moss. Outside of envelope is wall paper, inside is French newsprint. The soldier made the envelope from a Louisiana French newspaper printed on wallpaper. From Barmore-Moss-Colclough-Rentfrow Papers, University of Texas Archives.

DECORATED ENVELOPE

Photostat of envelope for letter of Ruffin Thomson to his father of Terry, Mississippi, from Kingsville, South Carolina, November 15, 1861. From Ruffin Thomson Letters, manuscripts in possession of Miss Brenda Thomson, Jackson, Mississippi.

from innocent sleep to wide-awake profanity more promptly than the near beat of the alarming drum." [24]

Another Reb complained, "I get vexed at them and commence killing them, but as I believe forty come to every one's funeral I have given it up as a bad job." [25] Seemingly the only recourse was to swearing, but this did nothing to abate disease.

Even more noxious than flies were the mosquitoes that invaded Confederate camps from April to October. These pests, which in soldier parlance became "gallinippers," were declared by some Rebs to be more annoying than Yankee bullets. Naturally tall tales sprang up as to their size and achievements. One Johnny swore that his attackers were of a "preponderous size—almost able to shoulder a musket." [26]

Another a Tennessean serving in the Mississippi lowlands—drew a comparison between those of his native state and those of his present acquaintance. "The Mississippi river fellow is far larger, has a longer and sharper bill," he observed, "and though he sings the same tune, he sings it with far great ferocity"; and whereas the Tennessee pests could muster only squads, those of Mississippi moved in regiments.[27]

Almost invariably comments on attacks by mosquitoes were followed in a few weeks by letters telling of epidemics of chills and fever. But people of Civil War times knew not the connection between the one and the other. Malaria was still attributed to the miasmas or poisonous vapors which rose from the swamps.

In some seasons and localities soldiers complained of the buffalo gnat, a pest described by one as a mischievous creature that "dives into the ear, nose, or anywhere on or under the skin and shylock like calls for blood." [28] "Blow-flies" and "chiggers" also came in for their share of denunciation. Fleas were even more of a nuisance. "I think there are 50 on my person at this time," wrote an Alabamian to his wife, "but you know they never did trouble me." Cryptically he added, "May I have thought of you often while mashing fleas; if you were here you could have your own sport." [29]

A Mississippian recently returned from furlough complained in 1862 of being singled out for special attack by fleas. "They hav most Eate me up since I came Back her," he said. "I was fresh to them so they pitched in." [30]

Another Reb testified that "they collect in companies at knight fall for the purpos of carrying us off . . . though like the Yankeys they are repulsed by desperate efforts & great patience." [31]

A more imaginative comrade declared:

"A great alarm was heard in the upper part of the regiment; hastening to the spot I enquired what was the matter. A man was asleep in his tent and a couple of fleas had taken holt on him and carried him half way to the river intending drownding [him] while asleep for he had sworn vengeance against them." [32]

But the tales of woe inspired by flies, mosquitoes and fleas were insignificant in comparison to those provoked by lice. Lice know no restrictions of time, place, or even of rank.

"There is not a man in the army, officer or private that does not have from a Battalion to a Brigade of Body lice on him," wrote an Alabamian in 1863. "I could soon get rid of them," he added, "but there is always some filthy man in camps that perpetuats the race." [33]

Both body lice, which roamed over the anatomy at large, and crab lice, which confined their attacks to hirsute areas, are mentioned—but the former, being the more numerous, came in for a lion's share of comment. They were dubbed with a great variety of grimly jocular names, such as "graybacks," "rebels," "zouaves," "tigers," and "Bragg's body-guard."

Military terms extended also to methods of extermination. Killing lice was referred to as "fighting under the black flag"; throwing away an infested shirt was spoken of as "giving the vermin a parole," and evading them by turning a garment wrong side out was called "executing a flank movement." [34]

When first infested with lice soldiers commonly experienced a feeling of disgrace; some even threw away their clothes. But as the curse became universal, shame gradually subsided. During periods of rest a few Rebs might always be discerned picking away at their shirts; others sought swifter riddance by singeing their clothes over campfires, a process that reminded one Johnny whose suit was "well stocked with big fat fellows" of popping corn. But respite once achieved was only temporary. Most veterans arrived at a state of splendid unconcern. One indeed claimed that he got to the point where he could not sleep soundly unless he had a few graybacks gnawing on him.[35]

Naturally there were many fantastic stories circulated about these unwelcome creatures. Several Rebs testified to catching lice with the letters C. S. (Confederate States) inscribed on their backs; one asserted that he saw a grayback adorned with the insignia I. W. (In for the War).[36] Another claimed: "I pulled off a Shirt last night and threw it down; this morning I saw it moveing first one way and then another;

I thought at first that there was a rat under it, but upon inspection found it was the lice racing about hunting for a Soldier." [37]

An Alabama rustic whose wife had suggested bringing two children to visit the camp wrote with a degree of seriousness advising against the proposal. "If you was here the Boddy lice would eat up Booth of the children in one knight in spite of all we could doo; you dont hav any idea what sort of a animal they are." [38]

But to Private Shield of the Virginia Light Artillery must be credited the most striking comment on record. One night as he prepared to retire he assumed a prayerful pose and recited:

> "Now I lay me down to sleep,
> While gray-backs oe'r my body creep;
> If I should die before I wake,
> I pray the Lord their jaws to break." [39]

Wonderful indeed was this ability of Rebs to make light of their woes. But unfortunately a sense of humor was neither a preventive nor a cure for the disease which followed in the wake of exposure, hunger, filth and pests.

Of the many illnesses which harassed Confederates, the first to attack in epidemic proportions was usually the measles. This disease was commonest among regiments composed of rural recruits. During the summer of 1861 one out of every seven of the men serving in Northern Virginia had measles, and total cases for three months exceeded 8,000.[40] In one camp of 10,000 recruits, 4,000 men were stricken.[41] So disruptive to the military program did this ailment become that the policy was adopted of withholding new troops from active duty until they were "put through the measles." [42]

Comparatively few men died from measles alone, but the mortality from subsequent complications was heavy. The tendency of patients to get up too soon was widespread, and the results were sometimes tragic.

Soldier correspondence of 1861 is full of such statements as this: "We have some 5 or 6 that is very sick ones in our company. . . . They all had the measles, & were getting well & they turn out to drill too soon after it and they all have relapsed. . . . Piercy and . . . Evans . . . died . . . both were hollering and dying at the same time." [43]

Shortly after the Seven Days' campaign, one of Lee's soldiers wrote his wife: "I have had good health since I left home with the exception of my bowels being disordered. But," he added, "it is a very rare thing to find a man in this army who has not got the diorreah." [44] This Reb was not exaggerating. Dysentery and diarrhea were the most prevalent of all camp diseases.

During the first nine months of the war the Confederate Army of the Potomac, the average mean strength of which was less than 50,000 men, reported 36,572 cases of these maladies. On the basis of figures compiled by Joseph Jones for forces east of the Mississippi, it appears that diarrhea and dysentery constituted no less than one-fourth of all the cases reported in 1861 and 1862.

At the Chimbarazo Hospital in Richmond, one of the Confederacy's largest military infirmaries, 10,503 cases of diarrhea and dysentery were treated during the war; this number represented one-sixth of all admissions for sickness; one out of every ten of the diarrhea and dysentery patients died.[45]

On the whole these maladies were less frequently fatal than some of the others, but allowance should be made for the fact that diarrhea by its weakening effects left the patient susceptible to diseases of a more serious character. Joseph Jones made the significant observation that while the deadlier ailments diminished as the war went on, chronic diarrhea and dysentery progressively increased, and that "more soldiers were permanently disabled and lost to the service from these diseases than from the disability following accidents of battle." [46]

Doctor Jones's statement gives point to a story told of an ordinary Reb. Near the end of the conflict this soldier, ragged, footsore and dysenteric, spied a Yankee cavalryman who seemed perfect in health and dress. "Oh my, oh my! you look like you wuz sich a happy man!" said the Southerner. "You got on sich a nice new-niform, you got sich nice boots on, you ridin' sich a nice hoss, an' you look like yer bowels wuz so reglar." [47]

Several factors, but mainly those of diet and exhaustion, made diarrhea and dysentery not only more prevalent but also much more often fatal among Confederates than among Yankees.[48]

Malaria was also a very common disease in Southern camps. Estimates of prevalency, elusive enough for all diseases on account of the fragmentary nature of health records, are particularly difficult in connection with malaria because of the widespread tendency of soldiers not to report mild cases.

The cause of the malady was not known, and many Rebs followed a practice that they had learned at home of simply knocking along as best they could without seeking medical treatment. If they were able to appear at roll call and carry on routine duties without interruption, as many were, no official cognizance was taken of their illness. [49] From such reported cases as exist, however, some general impressions may be derived.

In 1861 and 1862 malarial fever apparently constituted about one-seventh of all the cases of sickness reported by armies east of the Mississippi. During the first ten months of 1862 the Virginia Valley command, with an average mean strength of 15,582 men, had 3,885 cases of malaria. Soldiers serving in lowland areas fared much worse. The Department of South Carolina, Georgia and Florida, which had an average mean strength of 25,723 men, reported 41,539 cases of malarial fever from January 1862 to July 1863. And during the same period the force around Mobile which averaged 6,752 men had 13,688 cases. In all areas, malaria was much more prevalent during the summer than at other seasons. Fatalities from this malady were comparatively rare. [50]

Less frequent than malaria but far more fatal was typhoid. This ailment was said to have caused one-fourth of all the deaths from disease in the Southern armies. [51] Typhoid made its appearance very early in the war, and by August 1861 it had attained epidemic proportions among troops in Virginia. Large numbers continued to be stricken in the Confederate Army of the Potomac until December 1861 when a decline set in that lasted till May 1862. In June another outbreak occurred which lasted till September. In both instances the epidemics came in the wake of large-scale inductions of troops, most of whom came from rural areas.

Figures upon which to base estimates for the last two years of the war are not available. In all probability, additions to the army in consequence of the conscription law of 1864 caused a temporary increase of typhoid cases, but not to the extent of earlier outbreaks.

Joseph Jones made the statement several years after Appomattox that "typhoid fever progressively diminished during the progress of the war, and disappeared almost entirely from the veteran armies," and evidence drawn from Federal experience tends to prove his statement. [52]

Smallpox was apparently unknown in the Confederate Army during the first year of the war. The disease seems to have made its initial appearance in the Army of Northern Virginia, shortly after the Antietam campaign. This led to the belief that germs were brought from beyond the Potomac, perhaps on captured Yankee clothing, by soldiers participating in the Maryland movement. The theory gained credence from the fact that several hundred cases of smallpox had been previously reported in the Federal Army of the Potomac.[53]

Whatever its origin, the outbreak of this disease caused great alarm throughout the Confederacy. Figures as to the prevalence of smallpox are meager, but indications are that the epidemic which broke out in October 1862 in Virginia reached its peak in the early months of 1863. Several thousand cases were treated in the general hospitals of Lee's army in 1862 and 1863, and the rate of mortality was high.[54]

Vigorous measures were adopted by medical authorities to combat the spread of smallpox. Patients were isolated and a system of quarantine was instituted. Furthermore vaccinations were ordered throughout the army. In order to obtain an adequate supply of virus, surgeons were detailed to vaccinate healthy children who would pledge the donation of resulting scabs to army use. Experiments were also made for the procurement of virus from cows. In many cases soldiers were so thoroughly frightened that they did not wait for the doctors to act, but taking scabs from the arms of their fellows, they proceeded to vaccinate one another with pocketknives. The self-appointed inoculators were inclined to use the lancet rather generously because of a prevalent belief that the bigger the sore the greater the degree of protection. Within a short time after the flurry of vaccinations some of the sores presented a peculiarly loathsome appearance and refused to heal. These infections eventually became so widespread and aggravated as to impair seriously the strength of the army. At the time of the battle of Chancellorsville, 5,000 men were reported unfit for duty on this account. From these untoward circumstances there arose a great controversy over the causes of "spurious vaccination." The belief prevailed among soldiers that the phenomenon had a syphilitic origin, and this idea gained support from one Reb's admission that he had been vaccinated while on furlough by an accommodating inmate of an Augusta bawdyhouse. Most doctors discredited the theory of widespread venereal contamination, and while the argument was never completely settled, medical opinion generally attributed the infections to insanitary methods of vaccination, improper care of scars and lowered resistance in the persons inoculated.[55]

Pneumonia was very prevalent in Southern armies. Joseph Jones estimated on the basis of incomplete figures gathered during the war that for a nineteen-month period in 1862-1863, over 17 per cent of the Confederate forces were stricken by this disease. He found that soldiers in the Army of Tennessee were much more susceptible to the malady than those serving in Virginia, and that troops of the Department of South Carolina, Georgia and Florida were affected only to a slight degree. As a general rule, "Pneumonia prevailed to the greatest extent in the more elevated and northern regions of the Southern Confederacy, and in the armies which were subjected to the severest labors, privations, and exposures." The disease increased during the winter months and diminished in summer. During the period studied by Jones, approximately one out of every six cases proved fatal.[56]

Bronchitis, catarrh, scurvy, erysipelas and pulmonary tuberculosis patients were numerous at various times. In 1861 mumps was occasionally reported. Scarlet fever was rare.[57] Soldier correspondence contained references now and then to jaundice, which was erroneously regarded as a disease rather than as a symptom. In telling of jaundice Rebs often had trouble with spelling, but rarely with expression. "Henry has got the yellow Janders," wrote one; "he is as yellow as a orange and the white of his Eyes is yellow and he is yellow all over." [58] This certainly must have been a case of the obstructive type.

A malady that was rare, but which because of its peculiarity elicited much comment, was "night blindness" or "gravel." When soldiers whose vision in daytime was good first began to complain of inability to see at night, and started walking around holding on to comrades like blind men, doctors were inclined to think that they were shamming. But subsequent investigation proved that the disability was genuine. Connection with scurvy was noted in some instances, thus suggesting what apparently was the true cause of most cases, namely, dietary deficiencies coupled with undue exposure and exhaustion.[59]

Another ailment that gave doctors great concern because of the ease with which it could be feigned was rheumatism; but there can be no doubt that bona-fide afflictions ran far into the thousands.[60]

Syphilis and gonorrhea, though not widely prevalent, existed to some extent in most regiments. Venereal diseases usually increased when troops were stationed near cities, and when furloughs were increased.[61] Other occasional maladies mentioned by soldiers were delirium tremens, sore eyes, sore mouth, dropsy, toothache, and stomach-ache.

A skin disease called "camp itch," or simply the itch, was the cause of much complaint. This ailment was ordinarily of a trivial character, but complications arising from overzealous scratching sometimes were serious. Concerning itch Surgeon L. Guild wrote: "It is not Scabies but Lichen, and of so inveterate and obstinate a character in its chronic stage as to baffle all treatment whilst the patient remains in camp. Very many of these cases are therefore sent to General Hospital." [62] In view of such persistency, one is not surprised to find that one bedeviled Reb attributed his scratching to "the mange." [63]

Treatments for the various ills which beset the army were of the greatest variety. Contributing to this diversity was the tendency of soldiers to doctor themselves. Almost every recruit brought to camp a list of "sure remedies" gleaned from local tradition and experience; these were exchanged freely with cures of equal certainty contributed by comrades from other parts of the country. Editors and pamphleteers added their suggestions, and from this conglomerate of ideas Johnny Reb attempted to frame his prescriptions. For diarrhea and malaria a favorite treatment was hot tea made from the bark of such trees as slippery elm, sweet gum, willow and dogwood. A drink made of spice wood was administered to those suffering with measles. One Reb whose brother was stricken with cramp colic reported his experiments:

"I first gave him 2 doses of morphine, then a dose of my pills. He got no better. I then gave him a large drink of whisky & put a mustard poultice on his stomache. After which he got better & [is] now perfectly easy." [64]

Patients afflicted with chills were drenched with bitters and sundry solutions, the chief ingredient of which was rum, brandy or whiskey. In fact, alcoholic beverages were widely regarded as panaceas, whether taken straight or mixed. Mustard plasters were popular for chest and bronchial infections. One soldier who despaired of cure by his doctor sought haven in a private home where, according to his testimony, he "prety well burnt the pleurasy out of . . . [his] side with pepper and Number six and hot bricks." [65] Many Rebs wore flannel bands about their waist to fend off ill effects of exposure to dampness and cold.[66]

A sample of the advice received from pamphleteers is found in H. W. R. Jackson's brochure entitled *Historical Register and Confederates' Assistant to National Independence*:

"An Item Worth Noticing— . . . To guard against many diseases . . . volunteers should put a small quantity of tar—say a large spoonful —into their canteens. It has often been recommended as a preventative of chills and fever, measles &c. . . . After a day or two it detracts nothing from the taste of the water. . . .

"A good cure for a cold is to drink as much molasses and water (cold) on going to bed as one can swallow. Wrap up warm and rub off with a wet cloth in the morning. Another cure is to drink about a pint of tea made of roasted or baked apples . . . on going to bed, not forgetting the morning ablution. . . .

"Infallible Cure For Toothache—Take equal quantities of alum and common salt, pulverize and mix. Apply to the hollow tooth on a wet piece of cotton.

"A Good Cure For Cough—Vinegar and salt mixed together. A teaspoonful several times a day. . . .

"Remedy Against Fleas— . . . Fresh leaves of pennyroyal sewed in a bag, and laid in the bed will have the desired effect. In the absence of pennyroyal take green peach leaves.

"To Cure The Itch— . . . Take white elder flower ointment and flour of sulphur, each two ounces; oil of peppermint half a drachm. Mix and rub the body all over with it before a good fire for three nights before going to bed.

"Let your beard grow so as to protect the throat and lungs. . . . Keep your entire person clean. This prevents fevers and bowel complaints." [67]

Treatments administered by doctors were almost as diverse as those gathered by soldiers from tradition and almanacs, and in many instances they were almost as archaic. American medical practice was at that time in a state of transition from old to new methods, and confusion was inevitable. In the Confederacy the situation was complicated further by the blockade. Substitutes and variants had to be found for many of the usual medicines and treatments. Surgeon General Samuel P. Moore and his associates, many of whom were exceptionally able men, worked diligently to make the required adjustments. Dr. Francis P. Porcher was put to the task of preparing a treatise on the medical properties of the South's indigenous plants, and the results of his work published in 1863 under the title *Resources of Southern Fields and Forests* made available a storehouse of useful information.[68] But effective substitutes could not be obtained for some of the most essential medicines. And despite dramatic ventures in running Federal lines by patriotic women who concealed the precious medicines in their clothing, importations fell far short of army needs. To an increasing extent as the war progressed physicians depended on their own ideas and resources.

Treatments applied by doctors in diarrheal cases were particularly complicated. This was due partly to shortage of medicines but principally to confusion as to the cause of the illness and the inability to distinguish between dysentery and diarrhea. One Reb who went to the regimental physician "suffering violently with flux" was given some pills of calomel, quinine and opium. "I took them to my quarters," the patient said afterward, "threw them into the street, and . . . by dieting myself . . . [got well]." [69] Another soldier who had been plagued with diarrhea for some time was dosed with a miscellany of tartaric acid water, quinine, morphine and blue mass.[70]

In general, treatments for bowel complaints fell into two main categories: one stressed the use of astringents and the other advocated purgatives. Revealing insight into prevailing technique and procedure was given by a doctor who had ministered to Lee's men. "Early in the morning we had sick call," he said. "Diagnosis was rapidly made, usually by intuition, and treatment was with such drugs as we chanced to have in the knapsack. . . . On the march my own practice was . . . reduced to the lowest terms. In one pocket of my trousers I had a ball of blue mass, in another a ball of opium. All complainants were asked the same question, 'How are your bowels?' If they were open, I administered a plug of opium, if they were shut, I gave a plug of blue mass." [71] It is no wonder, in the light of such methods, that some Rebs called their doctors "damn quacks" and threw their medicine away.[72]

Scarcity of opium eventually forced army physicians to resort to substitutes that could be found near at hand. Blackberry, willow and sweet gum were used for intestinal astringents. Blue mass seems to have been available in fairly large quantities throughout the war, but in isolated instances of scarcity, vegetable cathartics of various sorts were readily obtainable.[73] Surgeons knew that scurvy was due to dietary deficiencies and in portions of the army affected or threatened by this disease, details of soldiers were sent into wood and field to gather wild onion, garlic, mustard, sassafras, pokeweed, artichoke, pepper grass, dandelion and other edible herbs. Vinegar was also used as an antiscorbutic.[74]

Pneumonia was a great puzzle to Confederate physicians. On the theory that this disease was an "inflammation," many doctors resorted to bleeding. "Blagg was very sick," wrote a Virginian of a comrade suffering from pneumonia; "Byrd brought a Doctor down yesterday and he cupped him Severely & it relieved the Stitching in his Side immediately." [75] But death rather than improvement followed bleeding in such a vast number of cases that physicians generally abandoned cupping "in favor of a sustaining treatment of liquor, opium, and quinine." If drugs were not available, patients were given herbal preparations of various sorts along with local applications of time-honored mustard plasters.[76]

While the connection between mosquitoes and malaria was not known in Civil War days, experience taught that smoke smudges, dry camp sites and other expedients which gave relief from the former tended also to lessen the latter. Quinine was the generally recognized remedy for malaria, but as this was an imported drug it became increasingly scarce during the period of the Confederacy. Among the various substitutes brought into use were tonics made from the bark of dogwood, tulip tree (generally called poplar) and willow, with whiskey as the preferred agent. Surgeon General Moore recommended mixing the ingredients according to the following formula: "Dogwood bark, 30 parts; poplar bark, 30 parts; willow bark, 40 parts, whiskey 45 degrees strength. Two pounds of the mixed bark to one gallon of whiskey. Macerate 14 days—dose . . . one ounce 3 times a day." Local application of turpentine was also used as an alternative treatment for malaria. According to Moore, experimentation proved this latter remedy "amply sufficient to interrupt the morbific chain of successive paroxysms—one application only being required in the majority of cases."

Early in the war quinine was widely used as a prophylactic, but its scarcity, coupled with a practice popular among soldiers of selling the drug instead of using it, eventually caused the substitution for this purpose of a tonic of native barks and whiskey.[77]

Itch was widely treated with internal dosages of a poke-root solution, and with external applications of an ointment composed largely of the same substance. Poke was also used in the doctoring of rheumatism, neuralgia and syphilis. One physician reported excellent results in treating gonorrhea with injections of ink ball; he also claimed that it could be cured by administering a combined dose of silk-weed tonic and pills made of pine rosin and blue vitriol.[78] For measles no satisfactory remedy seems to have been found, but in this, as in most other instances of uncertainty, doctors fell back on whiskey.

One of the greatest difficulties of the medical department was maintaining an adequate supply of alcoholic beverages. Ordinary Rebs thought the scarcity due to the insatiable thirst of army doctors. A skit in a camp joke book ran as follows:

> What is the first duty of a surgeon?
> Under the names of drugs and medicines to purchase a full
>   supply of good liquors.

What is the second duty?

To cause all private cellars to be searched, and all the good
    brandies found there to be confiscated, lest the owners
    should smuggle them to the soldier, give them away and
    make the whole army drunk.

What is the third duty?

To see that he and his assistant drink up all of said liquors.[79]

The suspicions of the rank and file were not without foundation.
William H. Taylor admits in his memoirs that he and his fellow surgeons were accustomed to go on a spree the night following each
receipt of spirits and that they succeeded usually in "drinking up every
drop . . . before morning." [80]

Correspondence of high medical authorities indicates a considerable
leakage in the liquor dispensation and reveals the dismissal of at least
one surgeon "for appropriation to his own use of stimulants intended
for the sick." [81]

But impropriety of physicians was only a minor factor in the prevalent deficiency. The chief cause lay in the interference by state
authorities with distillation for Confederate use. Fears of grain shortage
and concern for states' rights were major reasons for this, but belief
that government contracts were used as a shield for manufacture on
private account was also a consideration. The Virginia Legislature
prescribed severe penalties for the fulfillment of any liquor contract
with Confederate authorities. Only by erecting its own distilleries was
the government able to obtain enough alcohol to meet a portion of its
most pressing needs.[82]

Lack of essential medicines, archaic methods of the doctors, laxity
of camp discipline and ignorance of the soldiery were the cause of an
untold amount of disease and suffering. But these constitute only a
part of the picture. Defective organization of medical personnel, incomplete transportation arrangements, and inadequate hospital facilities
also played an important role in multiplying the miseries of the sick.

These latter factors were especially important in the first part of the
war. Then it was that disease struck most heavily and that the country
was least prepared to care for the patients. The people were not lacking in willingness to provide for the sick, as witness the efforts of individual women and of volunteer relief societies.[83] The trouble was
rather in the enormity of the problem and in the lack of co-ordinated
enterprise. Both the citizenry and the army had to grow up to a realiza-

tion of the meaning of war in terms of disease, and to the ability to care for those who became ill.

Richmond papers and army medical records give a vivid insight into the great suffering experienced by the sick of Virginia commands in 1861 and 1862. In August 1861 it was reported that ailing troops were being transported in railroad cars previously used for hauling horses, and from which the manure and other filth had not been removed. Two months later the press told of several hundred sick soldiers being unloaded at Manassas. Rain was pouring down, but no provision had been made for their reception. After a long exposure to wet and cold, with no covering but their thin woolen blankets, the miserable Rebs were piled into cars, without receiving nourishment of any sort, and sent on to Richmond. At the capital there was no one to meet them, and they had either to lie helplessly at the depot until hospital authorities could give them attention, or to totter uncertainly about the streets in search of aid.[84]

It was not always easy for an ailing soldier to find hospitality. A Mississippian who in December 1861 rescued a suffering comrade from the sidewalks of Richmond, took him to a hotel where he offered to pay his room fee; he received a curt refusal from the landlord.[85] Later in the war various volunteer agencies established "Waysides" or "soldiers' homes" for the care of such cases as this, but some of these were denounced as humbugs by those who sought their shelter.[86]

Often the soldiers themselves, or their officers, were responsible for the neglect which they experienced. Surgeon General Moore complained repeatedly that large groups of ill men were sent from camps without prior notification to authorities who were to receive them, that those dispatched frequently exceeded the number reported, that sick cars were overloaded, and that officers ordered men removed from the army to the city who were so sick that they were on arrival "in almost a moribund state."[87]

The publicity given in late 1861 to shortcomings in the handling of the sick caused the War Department to institute an improved system which gave particular attention to transportation. But in early May 1862 a Richmond editor reported that a large number of ailing troops lay for hours on the sidewalk waiting for hospitalization.[88]

Later in the war, with the decline of the rate of illness and the expansion of facilities, such instances became rare. After 1862 hospital resources throughout the Confederacy seem to have been fairly ample for the care of the sick except in short periods following great battles when accommodations were unduly taxed.

In the camps sick soldiers continued to suffer from lack of attention throughout the conflict. There were never enough doctors and nurses. And the indifference bred by war caused troops to become neglectful of one another. It was not uncommon for ill men to lie for hours in their tents or in vacant houses without food or water.

"I did not believe men could be so selfish and indifferent as they have been in our regiment," wrote a Georgia captain on one occasion; "two thirds of them would not wait on the sick if they were not made to do it they would let them lie and suffer." [89]

The hopelessness of proper care and the high percentage of mortality caused most Rebs to contemplate illness with incalculable dread. The pervasive sentiment was well expressed by one who wrote from camp: "It scares a man to death to get sick down here." [90]

In most respects soldiers who were seriously wounded fared worse than those who were ill. The machinery for disposing of battle casualties was fairly simple. When a conflict was imminent, buildings or tents near the scene of contemplated action were designated as field hospitals and marked with flags. A small squad of men, preferably convalescents and others not in best fighting trim, was detailed from each company to remove the wounded to the field infirmaries. Each man so detailed was equipped with a knapsack containing dressings, stimulants and tourniquets; when fighting commenced, assistant surgeons, accompanied by the details, moved forward to dispose of the wounded. Assistant surgeons supervised the administration of first aid and told litter bearers which cases required removal to field hospitals. Regimental surgeons remained at the field infirmaries of their respective brigades to attend to the wounded as they were brought in. They operated immediately on the most urgent cases and directed removal in ambulances—which were simply canvas-covered wagons—of those that were to be transferred to interior hospitals.[91] Patients thus removed were sent first to receiving hospitals; from there they were distributed as soon as possible to the general hospitals located in most cities.

Early in the war the custom prevailed of permitting convalescents to go home as soon as they were able to travel, but consequent relapses from hemorrhages and from improper care, plus increasing reluctance of those on furlough to return to camp, caused an abatement of this practice after 1863.

The system which Confederate authorities set up for the care of the wounded was basically sound, but numerous factors hindered its operation. In the first place commanding generals sometimes failed to inform hard-pressed medical officers of contemplated campaigns in sufficient time to allow for adequate preparations. Lee's medical director complained on one occasion to Surgeon General Moore: "The movements of the army cannot be anticipated by me for the General Commanding never discloses any of his plans to those around him . . . every thing is done hurriedly and mysteriously." [92] Even when ample notice was given and advance preparation carefully made, medical authorities, because of limitations of personnel and essential facilities, were utterly unable to provide prompt and adequate care for the thousands of men who were wounded in every major encounter.

This was particularly true of the Confederacy's first great fights. At Shiloh many wounded lay in the mud of the battlefield all night under a cold pelting rain, without attention of any sort, even though infirmary corps moved about as rapidly as possible and doctors labored to the point of collapse. The falling back of the army necessitated a hurried removal, and shivering, moaning men were loaded into wagons, many of which were not equipped with springs, and hauled more than twenty miles over "the roughest and ruttiest roads in the Southern Confederacy" to Corinth. Here hotels, school buildings, churches and private homes were converted into hospitals, but all these did not provide enough shelter.

For days after the battle groaning men might be seen lying about the depot waiting transportation to improvised infirmaries at Memphis, Holly Springs and Oxford. Doctors came from far and near and made their contributions to the pile of amputated limbs that accumulated in the yard of Corinth's Tishomingo Hotel. Women came too, eager to render what assistance they could. One of them wrote in her diary:

"The foul air from this mass of human beings at first made me giddy and sick, but I soon got over it. We have to walk and when we give the men anything kneel in blood and water; but we think nothing of it." [93]

Less than two months after Shiloh the Seven Days' campaign around Richmond produced a tide of casualties such as the Confederacy had not seen before. Citizens of the capital and of Petersburg took omnibuses and private carriages to the battlefields and piled the injured into stores, tobacco warehouses, factories, residences and tents. But even these extraordinary measures fell short of the need. A newspaper appeal, dated three days after fighting ceased, stated that "hundreds and even thousands of . . . soldiers are lying wounded upon the battlefield waiting in extreme agony for some pitying hands to remove them to a place of refuge from the tortures which they endure." The gruesome results of this neglect were vividly suggested by an article on the treatment of flyblow. Other newspaper notices urged citizens to bring ice and food to the hospitals, to tear up old cotton clothes for bandages, and to volunteer their services as nurses and cooks. Not until more than two weeks after the last of the series of battles was the situation brought under control. In the meantime hundreds, if not thousands, of brave men whom timely attention could have saved had endured unspeakable tortures of hunger, thirst and pain, and had finally died.[94]

Even greater suffering was endured by some of those who a year later marched with Lee into Pennsylvania and fell wounded at Gettysburg. The hasty retreat after the third day's repulse permitted little attention to the wounded. Those who were able to travel, and many who were not, were crowded into rickety wagons and started on the long and rough journey southward. A vivid picture of the tragedy which ensued was given by a high-ranking officer who participated in the retreat:

"For four hours I hurried forward on my way to the front of the wagon train and in all that time I was never out of hearing of the groans and cries of the wounded and dying. Scarcely one in a hundred had received adequate surgical aid. . . . Many . . . had been without food for thirty-six hours. Their torn and bloody clothing, matted and hardened, was rasping the tender, inflamed, and still oozing wounds. Very few of the wagons had even a layer of straw in them, and all were without springs. The road was rough and rocky. . . . From nearly every wagon . . . came such cries and shrieks as these

" 'Oh God! why can't I die?'

" 'My God, will no one have mercy and kill me?'

" 'Stop! oh! For God's sake, stop just for one minute; take me out and leave me to die on the roadside.' . . .

"No heed could be given to any of their appeals. . . . On! on! We must move on. . . . During this one night I realized more of the horrors of war than I had in all the two preceding years." [95]

When abandonment of positions came immediately after the battle as at Gettysburg, Antietam and Shiloh, the greater portion of surgery had to be postponed until the patients arrived at base hospitals in the interior. But under ordinary circumstances, most of the amputations and other emergency operations were performed at field infirmaries. These makeshift quarters, often situated in depressions bordering the scene of action, afforded only the crudest of facilities. Here amid the groans and screams of waiting patients, regimental surgeons wielded scalpels and saws for hour after hour on suffering creatures whose only anesthetic was frequently a drink of whiskey and sometimes not even that.

Surgeon Spencer Welch wrote on one occasion to his wife:

"I then went back to the field infirmary where I saw large numbers of wounded lying on the ground as thick as a drove of hogs in a lot . . . those shot in the bowels were crying for water. Jake Fellers had his arm amputated without chloroform. I held the artery and Dr. Huot cut it off by candle light. We continued to operate until late at night. . . . I was very tired and slept on the ground." [96]

E. D. Patterson, a private who was twice wounded at Frayser's Farm, committed to his diary such a vivid account of his experiences as to merit particular notice. "The first ball that struck me was so close that the musket's breath was hot on my face," he wrote while convalescing, "and I fell forward across my gun, my left arm useless falling under me. . . . I did not at the moment feel any pain, only a numbness all over the body. I felt as if someone had given me an awful jar, and fell as limber as a drunken man. I could not even tell where I was hit." As Patterson was contemplating dazedly the effects of his shoulder injury, he was struck again, this time in the thigh, by a ball that fairly lifted him from the ground. He bled profusely but did not lose consciousness. Through the remainder of the day and on into the night he lay in an open field. He had little hope of seeing the dawn of another day. "I thought of more things in one hour than I could write down in a year," he said. "I thought of a home far away. . . . I wondered if my fate would ever be known to them. I had a horror of dying alone. . . . I was afraid that none of my regiment would ever find me, and that with the unknown dead who lay scattered around me I would be buried in one common ground. . . . The thought was terrible. How I longed for day. Just that some one might see me die." He prayed, but with little faith, because of the realization that the supplication was prompted solely by the emergency. "The loss of so much blood had made me cold," he continued. "I shook until I almost feared that I would shake in pieces. . . . My limbs were as cold as ice and still I wanted water." A young Federal heard his cries for drink and came and ministered to him through the remainder of the night.

The next morning the ground on which he lay was repossessed by Confederates, and he was found by a cousin who was surgeon of a Georgia regiment. The doctor poured a couple of drinks of brandy down him, took him to a near-by house, and operated on his leg. Patterson requested chloroform, but the surgeon thought an anesthetic inadvisable. "I watched him while he laid open the flesh," the patient said, "and it reminded me of cutting fat pork, it cut so smooth and nice, and it hurt." Later Patterson was taken to a private home near Richmond where, after a second operation, he fully recovered.[97]

The permanent and semipermanent hospitals in the interior were of course better equipped than the field infirmaries. The best-administered institutions were usually the general hospitals of the larger towns. Richmond had more of these than any other city of the Confederacy. An effort was made in the capital to house the patients of each state in a separate establishment, and many of the hospitals bore the name of the state from which its inmates came.

One of the most famous and efficient infirmaries in Richmond was that of Sally L. Tompkins. This lady established a hospital on her initiative after First Manassas, and when later the government assumed control of all institutions ministering to soldiers, President Davis was reluctant to give up Miss Tompkins' services. To avoid the irregularity of having a person without title in an official position, he made her a captain and thus gave her the distinction of being the only woman ever to receive a regular commission from the Confederate Government.[98]

At various times of emergency, medical authorities were compelled to call on colleges and churches for use of their buildings. The University of Virginia, the University of Mississippi and the female seminaries at Lynchburg and at Corinth were among the educational institutions that provided facilities for the wounded. In these instances, and in most others, college and church officials contributed the needed shelter without hesitation. But occasionally there was opposition. A Virginia doctor wrote his superiors on one occasion that he had converted three Harrisonburg churches into hospitals, "but not without meeting . . . obstinate remonstrance bordering on physical resistance." [99]

After a Conference with Washington College authorities at Lexington, another doctor reported:

"There is not the slightest propect of obtaining the consent of the Trustees. . . . The salary of the most of the professors will be suspended if the exercises of the college are closed. Several of these professors are family connexions of the trustees who will most certainly protect their interests." [100]

Many soldiers looked with abhorrence on all hospitals, and there can be no doubt that they were justified. Operations were often rendered excruciatingly painful because of the scarcity of opiates and the dullness of scalpels. Some excellent sets of surgical implements were imported and others were captured, but there was never enough of these to go around; those manufactured in the Confederacy were characterized by Lee's medical director as "entirely useless." [101]

Post-operational care was inadequate. In Richmond, where conditions probably were better than average, the supervisor of hospitals reported on one occasion that 131 medical officers, many of whom were occupied with executive duties, were charged with attending 10,200 patients—a proportion of 1 to 70.[102] Inmates of hospitals complained repeatedly of an insufficiency of nourishment, and reports of medical officers leave little doubt that fare in some institutions was notoriously poor. Clothing and bed covering were frequently inadequate and sanitary conditions often left much to be desired.[103] At the Newsom Hospital in Chattanooga soldiers were given clean garments for the duration of their treatment, but on dismissal they were required to wear the filthy attire which they wore when admitted.[104]

"I beleave the Doctors kills more than they cour," wrote an Alabama private in 1862; "Doctors haint Got half Sence." And a Georgian expressed the opinion that army surgeons were the "most unworthy of all the human famaly." [105] These particular Rebs may have had no other foundation for their statements than the tendency of soldiers—well or sick—to grouse. But with full allowance for prejudices and overstatement, the conclusion remains inescapable that much of the suffering endured by the wounded was due to poor physicians. Examinations required of candidates for surgical appointments were sometimes no more than farces. One doctor said that his examining committee was composed of five members of whom one owed his position to the favor of kinsmen, another had failed to pass the course at the University of Virginia, and a third was very drunk.[106]

The practice of appointing surgeons with the understanding that they were to stand examination at a later time led to endless procrastination on the part of some who were of doubtful abilities. The category of doctors known as "contract physicians," who in times of emergency were called on for a considerable portion of army practice, apparently had to take no examination at all; these were, as a rule, utterly undeserving of professional status.[107] Many of the regular appointees of 1861 were young and inexperienced, a circumstance deriving largely from the fact that few of the established practitioners sought army positions.[108]

It would be erroneous to infer that the Confederate surgical corps was made up wholly of "culls," novices and quacks. The high-ranking officials were as a rule men of unusual talent and attainment; many of the regimental surgeons, and some of the assistant-surgeons, discharged their duties ably and conscientiously insofar as the nature of available supplies would permit.

The better class of surgeons, whatever their rank, were unusually resourceful. Of this type, a prominent medical director said:

"I have seen him search field and forest for plants and flowers . . . [that he] could use. The pliant bark of a tree made for him a good tourniquet; the juice of the green persimmon a styptic; a knitting-needle with its point sharply bent, a tenaculum, and a pen-knife in his hand, a scalpel and bistoury. I have seen him break off one prong of a common table fork, bend the point of the other prong and with it elevate the bone in depressed fracture of the skull and save life. Long before he knew the use of the porcelain-tipped probe for finding bullets, I have seen him use a piece of soft pine wood and bring it out of the wound marked by the leaden ball." [109]

Confederate surgeons, good and bad, were handicapped greatly by the undeveloped state of medical science which characterized their period. They believed that suppuration, or "laudable pus," was an essential feature with the healing process. They probed with ungloved fingers; they deterred recovery by tampering with wounds; they worked in soiled uniforms; they used bloodstained bandages; and they were only partially conscious of the importance of clean instruments. It is not surprising in view of these and other shortcomings that gangrene played havoc with their patients.[110]

The majority of surgeons seem to have been men of sympathy and of kindness. Sergeant William P. Chambers recorded in his diary an instance typical of many. When a doctor named Britts approached Chambers to operate he said: "You were soldier enough to get shot I reckon you are soldier enough to have the ball cut out." Chambers remarked that he had no choice in the matter of receiving the wound, and that he supposed the bullet must be extracted. Britts fumbled about uncertainly and said, "Chambers, I don't like to cut there," but presently he seemed to pull himself together, and with the advice "turn your head away, I don't want you to look at me," he began his unpleasant task. The first stroke of the knife struck the missile. When this proved to be only a part of the bullet Britts swore profusely. Not until after a considerable amount of probing, painful to the patient and grievous to the surgeon, was the remnant brought to the surface.[111]

Mortality from wounds, even from those in arms and legs, was woefully high.[112] Patients who recovered often experienced painful setbacks and distressing complications. Indeed no phase of Confederate history is so dark and tragic as that which reveals the incomprehensible torture endured by the sick and the wounded. And if glory be measured by suffering, the South's greatest heroes are not those who died at the cannons' mouth on Cemetery Ridge, or in any of the other gallant charges made by soldiers in gray, but rather those who, sorely wounded or desperately ill, lived to experience the unspeakable agony of hospitalization.

CHAPTER XIV

THE GENTLER SENTIMENTS

"I BELIEVE the biggest half of our Study here is about Something to eat and the other part is about wives and sweethearts," wrote a lonely Reb from camp in December 1862.[1]

His statement was not exaggerated, for woman was of tremendous moment in the life of the ordinary soldier. The reassurance of her smile and the fondness of her farewell warmed his departure from home, and the song which timed his step as he headed for the front was "The Girl I Left Behind Me." Memories of his sweetheart at home were with him ever after. He carried her portrait close to his heart, and the wreaths of smoke that curled from the campfire at night had an uncanny habit of shaping themselves into her elusive image. When exhaustion transported him to the realm of dreams he luxuriated in her fancied presence, and he resented the blatant morning call that took her away. As he prepared for battle his thoughts were mainly of her— it was for her that he must brave the roar and the carnage, for her that the enemy must be driven beyond Southern borders and independence achieved.

More romantically disposed Rebs saw the war as a composite of individual combats, with each soldier playing the knight for his particular lady. One wore a sprig of palmetto in his hat as a lover's token; others called their guns by their sweethearts' names.[2] Even the thoroughfares of camp were given such feminine designations as "Maiden Lane." [3]

Married Rebs thought of peace largely in terms of reunion with wives, and single men counted strongly on the resumption of courtship which should lead shortly to matrimony. "Kiss all . . . [the girls] for me," wrote an unattached soldier in 1862, "and tell them I shall be back some of these days and not one of them shall go uncourted." [4]

Another sent this message: "Tell . . . Miss Mollie when I come home if she wants to Marrie me all she has to do is to say so"; and a third said, "I am tired of camp life and thank God all Mighty if I live

270

through this war I will be stoped roving I intend to come home and marry Miss Lizzie Kemp." [5]

Thought of womankind was poor substitute for the reality. And as month after month passed with scarcely a glimpse of a woman, the craving for feminine association became well-nigh intolerable. "I have not seen a gal in so long a time that I would not know what to do with myself if I were to meet up with one," wrote a disconsolate Virginian, "though I recon I would learn before I left her. . . . I would be glad to [see] one more gal before the Yankees kill me." [6] Another wrote: "I havent hug a girl for so long I am out of practice." [7]

Some soldiers sought relief for their insatiable yearning by making long and reminiscent entries in their diaries.[8] Others took to verse. Of the latter class was an unsophisticated Tar Heel named William Malone in whose journal these poetic squibs were found:

"You are a charming little dandy
Sweeter than the sweetest candy

"Candy is sweet
It is very dear
But not half so sweet
As you my dear

"All I like of being a whale
Is a water Spout and a tail." [9]

The arrival at headquarters of an officer's wife—or even a comely washerwoman—would set a whole camp to gawking. Henry Kyd Douglas told of a visit to the army of the beauteous Hettie Cary shortly after her marriage to General Pegram. As Douglas escorted this lady from the parade ground after a review, an enraptured Reb was almost knocked down by her horse. When she began to apologize the awestruck veteran lifted his shabby hat and said, "Never mind, Miss. You might have rid all over me, indeed you might." [10]

When soldiers on the march encountered a group of girls there was invariably a painful straining of necks, and if the gentle creatures were so thoughtful as to present pails of water, an overpowering thirst was sure to play havoc with the ranks. As the men waited their turn at the dipper they would ply the girls with questions, just for the sound of a feminine voice, and devour them with glances. A young soldier who was thus refreshed wrote the next day to his sister:

"One of them was a perfect wayside lily. . . . I could not help taking off my hat & bowing low to her as the bugle call forward was heard. I dont know her name & shall never see her again, but I am indebted to her for much more than a cup of water."[11]

Random observations in letters and diaries afford interesting insight into the qualities which Rebs esteemed in women. Femininity was regarded as the supreme attribute. Robustness was definitely objectionable, and big feet were almost disqualifying—"They are all too tremendous," complained one soldier of Kentucky girls, and another said disgustedly of backwoods Arkansas women who visited camp: "I have not seen one that would wear less than a number eight pair of shoes." [12]

Beauty was likewise an important consideration, though most soldiers had little use for the vacuous, inane type of beauty. Affectionate disposition and accomplishment in aesthetics were held very desirable. A Tennessean's description of a girl with whom he had been smitten reflects vividly the cardinal points of emphasis:

"She is a regular beauty, sings like an angel, dances like a sylph, talks like an authoress and . . . the English language is inadequate to express how much she does love. . . . Life has been but one dream of her since first I beheld her. The other night she came to the dance gaudy with nature's ornaments. She wore no jewels. Every gem she might have worn would but have hid a charm. Nature has completed for her a toilet which art can never rival. She seems to move in a halo of glory. She has a dowery of pearls but they are in her mouth . . . she . . . possesses a mind enriched with the gems of intellect, and a conversation brilliant with thought, repartee, and wit. She is indeed an angel on earth and no doubt will be an angel in heaven." [13]

Some soldiers revealed a distinct interest in the economic status of prospective brides. Private W. C. McClellan boasted of having found a "shore nuff Sweetheart" who was "worth $50 thousand dollers, a lady a fine sence and education" who lived "in a fine house surrounded by a fine plantation and innumerable slaves and hates the Yankees very much." [14]

Another Reb who aspired to the affection of a wealthy girl was not so fortunate as McClellan. In dejection he wrote to his sister that he had been "thrust through the little end of the horn with such violence as to almost cause contusion." In a fashion characteristic of jilted suitors he joined the ranks of woman haters, though not without a parting shot at the cause of his misery. His valedictory, written in verse, was as follows:

"Depth of mercy, can there be
Mercy yet reserved for me
And I could say to that same woman
Of all the etts
I love Brunets
Therefore you I adore
But of all the Etts
I hate coquets
Therefore you I abhor" [15]

Men who wore the gray had an eye for shapeliness, and some were confessedly overwhelmed by voluptuousness.[16] But the great majority considered modesty an indispensable attribute. Rebs classed as forwardness the opening of conversation by girls to whom they had not been properly introduced.[17] There was one who took exception to the conduct of an officer's wife on the ground that she was "a perfect fidget." [18] Another had his faith in feminine virtue terribly jarred by a woman presenting him this conundrum: "If a Tumble Bug can role an ounce ball up a hill perpendicular how much can he sholder on a levell?" [19]

Amorous dalliance was deemed very *gauche*—one correspondent observed with disgust that he had "yet to find a lady about Fredericksburg that will not let a man kiss and hug them"—but formal betrothal was considered to sanction osculation. "I would have nothing to do with a young lady that would not kiss me . . . after we are engaged," remarked an Alabamian; "kissing is the truest [indication] of love, nothing more so, [not] even tears," he said, but before engagement "it is illegal." [20]

Other forms of conduct held in disrepute were noted by a South Carolinian who was quartered for a while with a private citizen having two daughters. The girls were pretty, he said, but "decidedly fast; the younger about 16, speaks of giving the dogs h-ll & slaps our faces when we *kiss* her; this same 'gal' climbs the trees for peaches, rides to mill on a horse bare back & not with both legs on the same side but one on each—astraddle." [21]

The "ideal girl" as envisoned by Johnny Reb was fairly well typified by a Petersburg belle, whom an adoring suitor described thus:

"She combines more attractions than any other I have seen—the crown of them all too, exceeding womanliness—as distinct from weak insipidity as manliness from bluster. . . . A person of middle size, formed like Hebe, and straight as poplar, graceful as willow, colour which comes and goes, skin clear white, hair black & abundant, always graceful however tossed, voice whose tones ripple soft but clear, and large eyes whose color varies as you look, but are finally seen to be steel gray—A face whose irregularity precludes the term beauty, but whose character makes insignificant a score of acknowledged beauties—Her eyes are . . . flood gates of light and they index the mind clear & quick." [22]

As a general rule soldiers had little opportunity for courtship. Cavalrymen, because of greater mobility and more flexible discipline, were able to get about to see the girls more than footsoldiers. But even the latter contrived occasionally to further their emotional interests. Rebs who received furloughs usually devoted a substantial part of their vacations to seeing the girls of their acquaintance, but Lee and other generals were woefully penurious with leaves. During periods of military inactivity women sometimes attended camp dances and parties, but such affairs were rare and restricted largely to officers.

Circumstances generally forced the ordinary soldiers to seek satisfactory social outlets by visits in the countryside. Many social excursions were accomplished under the guise of foraging for the supplementation of meager army rations, but once at large the provision hunters concerned themselves as much with needs of the heart as of the stomach, and while they were making inquiry as to the farmer's meat supply they were taking a firsthand inventory of his daughters. Not infrequently they succeeded in winning an invitation to dine; this was, of course, seized upon with alacrity, though maybe with a show of hesitation for politeness' sake. After the meal, singing was in order, with one of the girls pumping out tearful tunes at the melodeon. Then came a bit of talk about generalities, accompanied, if suitors were bold and parents had considerately excused themselves, by holding of hands and other mild forms of flirtation. In due time haversacks would be replenished and the foragers would take their leave, but not without seeking permission to make further calls.

Nocturnal absences from camp were rarely allowed, but resourceful soldiers were able to keep up their outside social connections by forging passes and by "flanking" guards. Occasionally a group of Rebs would favor their feminine friends with serenades. As acquaintances developed, parties would be arranged, and soldiers and girls would enjoy dancing and games. Frequently these casual associations ripened with remarkable swiftness into ardent romances.

The technique of Rebel suitors reflects the varied character of the Southern soldiery. Some attempted to enhance their prestige among the ladies by thinly veiled references to the old wound received at Bull Run. A few would boast openly of gallant actions in sundry battles. One pseudo-hero, who regaled wide-eyed listeners with glowing accounts of how he recognized and coolly bowed to acquaintances in enemy ranks amid a flood of bullets at Manassas, had the misfortune to be accused by other suitors of ingloriously absenting himself from the field before the engagement. When his disillusioned admirers subsequently questioned him on the point, he resorted to the explanation frequently used by cowards that the report of his absence was due to the fact that he got lost from his own regiment and fought with another; he also announced a wrathful determination to challenge his accusers.[23]

Suitors often made pretenses of great wealth and high social standing. One Reb of ordinary background had the girls all addressing him by the title of doctor.[24] Others talked of large cotton or sugar plantations, of fine carriages and of innumerable slaves. A Tar Heel private, who boasted of winning fifteen Virginia sweethearts by such exaggerations, wrote thus of his technique:

"They thout I was a saint I told thim som sweete lies and they Believed it all for they love a North Carolinian. I will tell you how I talk a round them After I got acquainted with them I would tell them I got a letter from home stating that five of my negros had runaway and ten of Pappies But I wold say I recond he did not mind it for he had plenty more left and then they would lean to me like a sore eyd kitten to a Basin of Milk." [25]

Rivalry was naturally strong where men were so numerous and women so few. Usually the competition was good-natured and aboveboard. There was some complaint among privates about officers monopolizing the field of courtship, but this they blamed on the girls as much as on the bombproofs. "The picnic was an exclusive affair," bemoaned a Virginian in 1863, "& I having neither Stars, bars, nor braid was not counted worthy to mingle in the very select company. . . . The ladies of this county are said to be addicted to Star-gazing & nothing of less brilliancy attracts their attention. What is a miserable private fit for? A man had as well be a dog." [26]

In rare instances underhand tactics were used by hard-pressed suitors. The meanest and the most effective of these stratagems was to charge a flourishing rival with having a wife and children at home.[27]

Timid Rebs were given to much indirectness in their approach. A delicious description is given in a letter of a girl who, with some feminine acquaintances, made a trip in 1863 chaperoned by an elderly male relative:

"Every stage, every bar, and boat were croudied with Soldiers, and they would talk and wrun on with us and would say . . . [to each other] 'That old man has got a heep prettie Daughters; lest go and talk to them. I know he wantes to get shet of some of them.' . . . there were some of the uglest ones that you ever saw . . . some very prettie soldiers too." [28]

Rebs frequently invoked the services of intermediaries to inquire into their standing with sweethearts. Some indeed were disposed to carry on all phases of the courtship by proxy. A good example of this is afforded by a private who wrote a juvenile kinsman:

"You kiss Soo for me and tell Soo to kiss you for me and by manageing the thing that way I will get two kisses, and tell Feb if he possible can steal me a kiss from Miss Bettie and after he kisses her tell her it was for me I would be very glad, indeed, I would." [29]

Occasionally suitors would slyly instruct *agents d'amour* to tell home sweethearts of their social triumphs while absent and to warn them of a loss of standing unless they showed more devotion.[30]

The methods of some love-smitten Rebs were so indirect and their advances so halting that the war must have ended while their courtships were still in the most immature stages. Private G. W. Roberts of Mississippi was among these slow-moving suitors. While stationed at a parole camp near Demopolis, Alabama, in the spring of 1864, Roberts made the acquaintance of an overseer named Smith, whom he visited repeatedly. The soldier had a noticeable faculty for making an appearance just before mealtime, but his long stays afterward were due mainly to the presence in the family of an eligible daughter.

After a number of such calls Roberts mustered sufficient courage to write Miss Smith a letter asking for the privilege of corresponding with her. There was certainly no reason for resorting to the mails other than the Reb's timidity, for the girl lived within walking distance of camp and the writer had frequent access to her home. But when she received the formal missive her reaction was not one of amusement at Roberts's bashfulness, but rather one of displeasure at his forwardness.

She answered as follows:

"May 19, '64 Sir—although it is the highest complement that can be paid our sex to receive offers calculated to leave a lasting acquaintance I must complain of its precipitate characters of your address to one, who till last March was a total stranger to you, without wishing to say anything harsh, I must confess that I do not feel any motive to entertain so hasty a proposal and have felt bound to lay your letter before my parents as I could not think of concealing from them any correspondence of such a Des[c]ription. Trusting that you will see this in its proper light, eagerly awaiting your Reply — D ——" [81]

The butternut Galahad took the cue of the letter's last sentence and responded promptly:

"May 19, 1864, Demopolis, Ala.:
"Miss D.S.: your letter Reach me safe this morning about 10 oclock which was notice with the highest esteem; By one who has made but a short acquaintance with thee. It was well peruse by the one who is writing to you now. I hope it will be received with pleasure. You stated in your letter that we had but a short acquaintance with Each other. I know that we have but a short acquaintance & that you are perfectly Right in laying my letter before your parents. I am willing as long as I communicate with you by letter for you to do so If I am not mistaken I ask you if I could write to you when I return to camps I have but one request to ask of you can I correspond with you or not. Hoping this will not concur any Dissatisfaction . . . only your highist Respect. G. W. ROBERTS." [82]

Unfortunately there are no later records on this affair, but it is difficult to believe that it ever reached a point where marriage could be plainly mentioned.

There were many gay youngsters in the army who were much more adept at courting than was Roberts. Some had sweethearts on every hill surrounding camp, and a few extras scattered in the valleys.

Harry St. John Dixon, a Mississippi cavalryman who entered the service shortly after leaving the University of Virginia, was among wooers of exceptional prowess. While at Pulaski, Tennessee, in 1863 he listed on a leaf of his diary "the girls I know here" as follows:

> "Miss Emma Rose
> " Celest Rose
> " Amanda Kenery *le belle*
> " Manella Mosely
> " Ida Caldwell
> " Ala Petaway
> " Eugenia McCord
> &c."

This tabulation was postscribed with the comment: "O-o-o-o-o-how I lub you gals!!!—You sweet little criters." [33] Dixon had one romance after another of youthful fire and brevity. His journal, covering four years of war, is, in fact, little more than a cataloging of his *affaires du coeur*. At intervals he chided himself for his susceptibility to feminine wiles, as for example when he wrote: "I wish I was not such a fool about women. They have so much influence with me—it is so easy for them to gain the mastery over me." Then there were times when impetuosity combined with maidenly charm to produce temporary demoralization and a stricken conscience. Such an instance he recorded once in his diary:

"Jan 2, 1864 . . . attended a 'storm' [dance] at Miss Cuny's last evening . . . Took the 'little humming bird'—the little thing was chattering & smelling camphor all evening—Waltzed with Miss Annie Cozart till my right arm ached. What makes men so impure? Why cannot he have the manhood to resist temptation?—Her little bosom rested pantingly upon mine need I confess that I squeezed a little—just a little bit—soft, convulsive! And something else—our knees—*Diable!*"

On yet another occasion he wrote: "I see a pretty ripe, plump pair of lips—wish to kiss them—eminently natural!—Why not?" Dixon's flirtations kept him in emotional hot water a great deal of the time. He loved one whom he called his "pet" supremely, but in a weak moment he pledged undying affection to another.[34]

Even more of a social lion than Dixon was Private Joseph J. Cowand of the Thirty-second North Carolina Infantry. This gallant claimed to be engaged to six girls at one and the same time, and he declared his intention of adding a half dozen more to his list of betrothed.[35]

Many soldiers who played at Cupid's game were losers rather than winners. Sweethearts at home were stolen by militiamen, exempts and others who had the advantage of proximity. Camp romances cooled rapidly when fortunes of war transferred suitors to distant areas; and abandoned maidens quickly recruited new beaux to take the place of those removed. Victims of such emotional caprices reacted in various ways. Some poured out their woe to sympathetic relatives and friends; others took to cards and liquor; and still others addressed reproachful missives to those whose affections had paled. One disappointed Reb who chose verse as the medium of venting his spleen wrote thus:

"Miss—I'm raving I'm furious, I'm mad,
I'm Jealous, uneasy, disheartened and sad
I received information perhaps through the papers
Of your tricks and maneuvers, your pranks and your capers
You know when you left here I bid you beware
Of the fellows, Lieutenants and Captains up there
For you know that you promised that mine you'd be
That evening beneath the old Mulbery tree
When the moon in mid-heaven was shining so bright
And your dark eyes were radiant with love's mellow light
Then happy was I and how perfectly blessed
As your beautiful form to my bosom I prest
But my pleasure so full is now faded and yellow
For I hear that you're loving another young fellow
And if what people tell me so often is true
The courting is carried on chiefly by you
And if you deny it, I'd like much to know
Why so often to visit Miss Mary you go
And why when you meet him your eyes are so bright
With every expression of rhapturous delight
And even your voice ever changes its tone
As soft and as sweet as the turtle dove's moan
And then I'm told the opinion you harbour
The Lieutenant is the nicest young fellow in Barbour
But nice as he is if ever I meet him
As sure as his Bales, I'm going to beat him
But I'm not going to speak of the thing any further
Lest my passions should drive me to some bloody murder
But I'll give you my dear in the close of this letter
Some advice which may suit in the absence of better
For they tell me he's surely engaged to another
And if this is the fact (and I've no reason to doubt it)

Remember the Lamp and the Moth that was hovering about it
For in flying around him there's nothing to gain
But you might accidentally get burnt for your pains
"Yours in good will
"JOHN BUNKAM" [36]

Doubtless much of the heartbreak experienced by soldier suitors was due to overzealous wooing. During the last years of the war many Rebs became obsessed with the idea of getting married. Several factors contributed to this. One was the fear that attractive and eligible women would all marry civilians before the conflict ended. The matrimonial flurries that swept over the South in 1863 and 1864 afforded a real basis for this apprehension. Another consideration was the specter of becoming so old and so worn by military service as to become undesirable as husbands. A third factor was the feeling of uncertainty and insecurity engendered by war.[37]

Repeated exposure to danger resulted in a philosophy that said: Get what you can of life and of love today, for tomorrow you may fall in battle; partake, therefore, of married love while you can; if you die, you will have had at least a brief knowledge of this happiness, and if you live you will have a companion for years to come.

This reasoning, encouraged as it was by the granting of furloughs to prospective grooms, caused many a sudden marriage.

"I never heard of so Much Marring in My life," wrote a Virginia soldier to his parents in December 1863; "Chet Walker just got afurlough This morning of 10 days to go home to get Married. . . . I am a great Mind to start courting Myself . . . to get me afurlough." [38]

In cases where officers refused to grant leaves without tangible proof of forthcoming marriage, Rebs sometimes secured written commitments from their brides-to-be. One such statement, addressed to an Alabamian, was as follows:

"If you come home, I'll marey you any time you come home. Love has pierced me with his never erring dart, I yield to you my hart most willingly in wedlock. I with you would gladly jine, and know fer [you] that I never shall repine." [39]

A few who took war brides were not legally entitled to them. "Lit Dooley was married last weak to a Miss Bailey," wrote a Reb from camp in 1864; "he has a wife at home." [40] A Richmond paper found occasion in 1863 to warn local readers that soldiers who had wives and children in the deep South were escorting Virginia girls to the altar. An instance was cited of a recent case of bigamy involving a young lieutenant. This man had on the same day written a long and affectionate letter to his wife in Louisiana, and another of even greater endearment to his bride of a few weeks who lived near camp. By accident he put the letter of each in the envelope addressed to the other, and thus exposed his perfidy to both.[41]

At least one Reb who entered marital lists during the war did so unintentionally. Following an engagement with the Federals this soldier got drunk on captured whiskey. While in a state of inebriation he managed to strike up an acquaintance with a woman and before he recovered his sensibilities he swore to take her as his wife. In a subsequent explanation of the episode to his sister, he said that the bride was utterly unknown to him and that "w[h]en I woke the next mo[r]ning I was sick at my Stomake [because of] what I have don." He said further that he left her immediately and with the determination never to see her again, for "It wase knot lawfuel in the way it wase done." [42]

Most soldier suitors were compelled by circumstances to do a considerable part of their courting by correspondence. Their love letters were so strained by the stilted formality of the period as to be hardly worthy of the name. A Reb addressing his betrothed would tell of the weather, of the state of his comrades' health, of politics, of the probable course of the war, and of innumerable other trivialities of camp life, but very little of his love. The few allusions he did make to sentiment were frequently couched in such high-flown terms as to be without any resemblance to real-life romance.

Soldiers who wrote for the first time to feminine acquaintances filled their letters with apologies for presumption in opening correspondence. Some continued their apologies in subsequent missives. Attempts at discretion and dignity were sometimes so overdone as to become ludicrous.

The effort to use phraseology that was beyond the reach of the writer's orthography, if not of his vocabulary, produced similar results. One Reb began his letter: "Mutch Esteamed Miss I [s]natch my pen with acricy [alacrity?] to drop you a few lines." After wandering about uncertainly over varied topics he said: "I hope him who does all things well may Guide these few lines Saftly to your handes and may it find you and family all well." He then made the stock observation that he had nothing interesting to write. At the very end he approached a subject close to his heart, but his courage was not equal to a direct statement. "I suppose the youngsters is a marying as fast as tha come home," he said; "I think this is a vary good time to make a Selection, but not to perchous. I always like to hear of Some one doing well If I cant." [43]

Attempts to impart an idea of affection without making an overt commitment sometimes led to strange phrases. A Virginian wrote to his sweetheart that "I had rather see you than to see my Granfather or enny boddy else." [44]

Many letters were overladen with wild and incoherent platitudes. This type is well exemplified by the following excerpt from a missive addressed by a Mississippian to his fiancée:

"I can bare the Storms of the wintery Blast for thy sake oh Miss S.J.H be thou ever Bless as Butiful as thou art and idol to my throbbing hart oh had I the mind of the poet So that I could penetrate the verry depts of my hart but I can but express my Simple thoughts I am hear but my heart is Theire, we are in four miles of the yankees . . . could we not enjoy ourselves better if was at home with the girles . . . vainley I alas thou woulds soothe the pangs I feel, fond love betrayed what hopes I can poses Death alone my greaf may heal then farewell for ever more welth I have none they Farthers care thearefore I love one on Earth that I adore my only wealth is the love I bare then farewell perhaps for ever more never forsake me I Still will faithfull be Still on thy hand every bliss I will imploy Hence duty calls me they first my only love farewell perhaps for ever more but my hopes if far different I think will again meet if nothing happens more then I expect one thought from you would cheer my dropping mind I have more in my hart then ten thousand toungs can express if I had wings of and Eagle to the I would fly me thinks I can hear in my midnight drams thy Soft and gentle voice but alas when I awake I am in a Soldier tent I have nothing of importance to write you at this time but I will write soon and let you know all that happens . . ." [45]

Poetic utterance was a favorite resort for suitors who were hard put for appropriate expression. The ability to compose or to quote rhymes was considered a mark of good taste and of cultural distinction. Furthermore poetry was sufficiently ambiguous to permit whatever interpretation the recipient wished to give it. A suitor who was doubtful of his standing and uncertain of the propriety of affectionate address could, through the medium of verse, put out feelers without great fear of giving offense.

Sometimes the poetic phrases were written into the body of the letter without using verse form. One Reb wrote to his sweetheart:

"I'd mourn the hops that leave if thy smile had left me too I'd weep when friends deceived me if *thou wert like them untrue* The bee through many a garden roves and hums his lay of courtship ore but when he finds the flower he loves he settles there and hums no more." [46]

One of the most frequent and interesting users of the poetic technique was a timid Alabamian named Cribbs, who had a sweetheart as reserved as himself. Their bashfulness was indeed so great that the realization of mutual affection almost escaped them. He began writing to her early in the war that he had a sweetheart at home. Subsequently he described the object of his affections in considerable detail. At the same time she was telling him that she had a beau in the army, and that she would not marry until that particular soldier came home from the war. During the second year of conflict Cribbs finally got the idea across that his addressee was the sweetheart to whom he had been referring all along. But not until 1864 was he able to conclude definitely that the beau about whom she talked was none other than himself. The romance gathered considerable momentum with this discovery, but no records are available as to its outcome.

It was while Cribbs's identity as the beau of his sweetheart's correspondence was still in doubt that he wrote most of the poetry. In November 1862 he addressed these lines to his beloved:

> "You do not know the many snares
> Laid in this World for Thee
> All lovingly I bid thee give
> Thy sweet self unto me
>
> "Then give to me love's magic seals
> That all earth's joys eclipse
> And close to mine in fondness press
> Thy dewey coral lips."

In March 1863 he wrote:

> "My love to you I cant unfold
> It is like some lovly Ring of Gold
> It is pure and have no end
> So is my love to you Friend."

Two months later he resorted, for some unknown reason, to a crude code for communication of his poetic effusions. One verse appears thus in his cryptic medium:

> "Why sh456d 3 b65sh t4 488. 3. 64v2
> T3s 64v2 that 9563 th2 9267s 1 b4v2
> Why sh456d 3 b65sh t4 sly t4 166
> T3s 64v2 that h46ds 7y h219t 28 th9166"

which decoded reads:

> "Why should I blush to onn I love
> Tis love that ruls the relms above
> Why should I blush to say to all
> Tis love that holds my heart enthrall" [47]

Trite rhymes were much in vogue among less cultured correspondents. One of these ran thus:

> "green is the vine
> and read is the rose
> how I love you
> nobody noes."

Other examples are afforded by the following extract from a letter addressed by an uneducated woman to a soldier:

"i feel like a lonesome dove that has lost thair mate the rose is red an the villets blue an hant give me narry present that is purty like you as round as a ring has no end so is my love to you my friend when i am asleep i am dreaming bout you an when i am awake i take no rest ever mournin—my pen is bad my ink is pale my love for you shall never fale i want you to write to me i must come to a close so god bless your buttons—." [48]

Illiterate Rebs sometimes carried on correspondence with sweethearts through amanuenses. Private W. C. McClellan wrote love letters for several comrades in Company F of the Fourth Alabama Regiment. He also read to the suitors the answers which the letters received. McClellan must have been much in demand as a composer and scribe for according to his own statement he succeeded in getting three men engaged in the space of one month. [49] Unfortunately he left no record of his magic formula.

Courtship, whether conducted in person, by proxy, or by correspondence, was a factor of incalculable importance in army life. It had particular bearing on morale. The assurance of a sweetheart's confidence and affection had a buoying influence on a soldier's spirit. It tended to particularize the war and to give him a tangible and individual stake in its outcome. The association in the soldier's mind of women and of purity was a considerable factor in inspiring both single and married men to standards of wholesome conduct. There were, of course, many instances of opposite tendencies resulting from contact with a low type of woman, but all in all the influence of womankind over those thousands who wore the gray was ennobling as well as inspiriting.

CHAPTER XV

MUZZLE-LOADERS AND MAKESHIFTS

"WE CAN whip the Yankees with popguns," a Southern orator boasted in 1860. This was, of course, nothing more than platform exuberance, based on the theory that the North would not fight to preserve the Union.[1] But Fort Sumter and Lincoln's call for volunteers gave the lie to peaceable separation. And as the South prepared feverishly to resist Federal coercion it became strikingly apparent how little better than popguns were the weapons that she had.

Of shoulder arms, which must necessarily be the backbone of equipment in a shooting war, there were only about 150,000 in the whole Confederacy that were fit for use. About 20,000 of these were rifles. The others were smoothbore muskets, a considerable portion of which had been converted from the old Revolutionary flintlock type to percussion models. Both rifles and muskets were muzzle-loaders.[2]

Confederate and state authorities made heroic efforts to supplement this meager supply of guns. Before the outbreak of hostilities North Carolina, Mississippi and other states sent representatives to the North to purchase arms, and after the Confederate Government was organized, Montgomery authorities dispatched Raphael Semmes to New York for the same purpose. These missions resulted in gratifying contracts, but Federal officials clamped down on shipments before many deliveries could be made. Early in April 1861 Caleb Huse was ordered to Europe to buy equipment for the Confederacy. Eventually he succeeded in purchasing large quantities of guns, but shipments were slow in getting under way. Not until the fall of 1861 were there any deliveries to Southern shores.

When Josiah Gorgas was appointed chief of Confederate ordnance in the spring of 1861, he undertook immediately to promote the domestic manufacture of arms. One of the greatest handicaps was the lack of machinery, for such arsenals as existed in the South prior to the war were devoted almost wholly to storage. The seizure of Harper's Ferry by Virginia troops a few days after Fort Sumter's fall gave to the South a substantial amount of equipment for the fabrication of rifles and

286

rifled muskets. A part of this was sent to Richmond and the remainder to Fayetteville, North Carolina. From the captured machinery a monthly output of 5,000 arms should have been realized, but various hindrances, particularly the inadequacy of skilled workmen, prevented the manufacture of more than about 2,000 rifles during any thirty-day period of the war. It was not until September 1861 that any production was realized from these factories.[3]

In the meantime both state and Confederate authorities had entered into contracts with numerous small-scale domestic manufacturers, many of whom had, before the war, been engaged in the fabrication of sporting arms.

McElwaine and Company of Holly Springs, Mississippi, is said to have been the first firm to receive an arms-making contract from the Richmond government. This establishment, known before the war as the Marshall County Manufacturing Company, was encouraged by the Mississippi Legislature in July 1861 to begin making guns of a type used in the Mexican War, a .54-caliber arm commonly designated as the Mississippi rifle. The next month the firm contracted to make 30,000 of these guns for the Confederacy.

Cook and Brother of New Orleans undertook the manufacture of Enfield model rifles for Gorgas, but fulfillment of contracts was delayed by forced removal to Athens, Georgia, before New Orleans was captured in April 1862.

The Shakanoosa Arms Manufacturing Company was organized at Dickson, Alabama, in 1861 to make Mississippi rifles for the state of Alabama. Its output, never very large, was hindered considerably by repeated removals before Federal invasion.

The S. C. Robinson Arms Manufacturing Company of Richmond made several thousand carbines for the Confederacy. Other firms that manufactured small arms for the Confederate or state governments were located in Tallahassee, Florida, and Montgomery, Alabama; Greensboro, Jamestown and Asheville, North Carolina; Columbus, Milledgeville and Macon, Georgia; and Tyler, Texas.[4]

Returns from both domestic manufacture and from foreign purchase were negligible during the war's first year. The original stock-on-hand of 150,000 guns was virtually exhausted before the battle of Bull Run. And still volunteers clamored to be taken into active service. "From Mississippi I could get 20,000 men," wrote President Davis to Joseph E. Johnston, July 13, 1861, "who impatiently wait for notice that they can be armed. In Georgia numerous tenders are made to serve for any time at any place, and to these and other offers, I am still constrained to answer, 'I have not arms to supply you.' " [5]

If the Confederacy had been able to place serviceable weapons in the hands of these multiplied thousands of men who hoped so earnestly for an opportunity to come to blows with the Yankees, First Manassas might well have resulted in an overwhelming movement on Washington instead of in a stalemate.

On the day following the fight there squads of men were sent to the battlefield to gather up guns and other equipment left by the Federals. Back at home, state governments begged the citizens to send or bring their shotguns, rifles and muskets to the county seats. Volunteers were urged to come armed to points of muster. The Tennessee Legislature went so far as to authorize Governor Harris to seize all private weapons for military use. Returns from these measures were disappointing. People living in remote areas were unwilling to part with their chief means of protection against brigands and beasts.

Competing activities of local and Confederate arms collectors raised the issue of states' rights. Governor Clark of North Carolina was provoked to publish a notice saying that Confederate agents "have no lawful authority to seize your private arms, and you will be protected in preserving the means of self-defense." [6] Jealousy of local authorities was a serious deterrent to the armament program throughout the South in 1861, and as conflict between central and state authorities sharpened in the years that followed, the obstacle increased. [7]

Most of the guns collected in the months following First Manassas were sent to state or Confederate armories for remodeling. Small-caliber squirrel rifles were bored out to accommodate regular-size musket balls; ancient flintlocks were adapted to the use of percussion caps; elongated barrels of pioneer "shooting irons" were sawed off in the interest of greater wieldiness; and in some cases bayonets were attached.

But the clamor for arms was abated little if any by these efforts. A projected offensive on the Virginia front in the fall of 1861 had to be called off because of inability to provide weapons for the necessary reenforcements. [8] About the same time Albert Sidney Johnston, commander of the Western Department, was reduced to the sad strait of requisitioning additional flints for the firing of the obsolete muskets carried by many of his troops. Across the Mississippi, almost half of Price's force was armed with shotguns, fowling pieces and flintlocks.

At the battle of Mill Springs, Kentucky, January 19, 1862, the Confederates were hampered by the fact that rain made unusable the flintlock rifles with which many of the regiments were outfitted. Some of the Tennesseans, after several futile attempts to fire their dampened pieces, were seen to break them in exasperation over a near-by rail fence.[9]

Many of the defenders of Fort Henry were armed with shotguns and old sporting rifles; the Tenth Tennessee, described as "the best-equipped regiment of the command," had to depend on "Tower of London" muskets which had been carried by militia in the war of 1812.[10] Shotguns were taken into the action at Shiloh by a considerable number of troops. Some of the regiments engaged at Murfreesboro, December 31, 1862, had half of their men armed with smoothbore muskets. And not until the battle of Franklin, November 1864, was the Tenth South Carolina Regiment able to procure guns of uniform caliber.[11]

The Army of Northern Virginia fared better as to arms after 1861 than the western commands. This may have been due in some measure to favoritism of Richmond authorities, but it was primarily because the Virginia troops had greater access to that richest of all Confederate armories, the camps of the Federals. General Lee reported the capture of 35,000 stands of small arms as a result of the Seven Days' fighting, June 26-July 1, 1862. At Second Manassas 20,000 more were taken, at Harper's Ferry 11,000, and at Fredericksburg 9,000.[12] No figures are available for arms captured at Antietam and Shiloh, but these must have exceeded 15,000. On the Kentucky and Tennessee campaigns of August-December 1862 the Army of Tennessee took 27,500 muskets and rifles.[13] This brought the total of small arms captured in major engagements of 1862 to a figure well over 100,000.

At the beginning of 1863 the South found herself for the first time in possession of a surplus of shoulder arms. Chancellorsville netted an additional 20,000 pieces and Chickamauga 15,000, but losses sustained at Vicksburg, Gettysburg and Chattanooga, plus depletion from breakage and wear, wiped out the favorable balance; and from the beginning of 1864 till near the end of the war there were repeated complaints of deficiencies from all parts of the Confederacy.[14] The Trans-Mississippi Department seems to have experienced particular deprivation. In May 1863 General Magruder estimated his need at 40,000 small arms, and in December 1864 he expressed fear of inability to open the spring campaign unless the government could find a means of supplying his urgent requests for matériel.[15]

Throughout the war, shoulder arms carried by Rebs were characterized by the greatest miscellany of type and effectiveness. The gun in widest use during the first year of conflict was the .69-caliber smooth-bore musket. This weapon was loaded either with a single round ball or with "buck and ball," that is three buckshot behind a regular-size ball. At close range the musket was formidable, but a Yank more than 100 yards away was comparatively safe. Repeatedly Federals, on ascertaining that their opponents were armed with this type of gun, exposed themselves and taunted the Rebs for the ineffectiveness of their fire. Muzzle-loading shotguns charged with buckshot were said to have rendered good service in closeup fighting at Donelson, but their exceedingly short range caused them to be discarded by all except the cavalry as soon as other arms could be procured.

The .54-caliber Mississippi rifle was a great favorite among early volunteers, and it had considerable use throughout the war. In 1861 some of the companies who went from the deep South to Richmond in the expectation of being armed with this type of weapon mutinied when told that they would have to accept smoothbores.[16] Such confidence in the Mississippi rifle was not without foundation, for in ordinary circumstances of distance and load it was a dependable arm. Hardly less effective were the .58-caliber Springfield and Harper's Ferry rifled muskets, a considerable number of which were in use during the early part of the war.

In the second year of conflict shotguns, smoothbores and flintlocks were largely abandoned for more modern types obtained from the Federals or from Europe. In innumerable instances the soldiers themselves made the substitution on the battlefield, a practice that caused no end of worry and difficulty on the part of those charged with the dispensing of ammunition. For the guns "borrowed" from Yankees were frequently of different caliber from those discarded, thus rendering unusable the bullets brought up from Confederate ordnance wagons. But Johnnies often solved the problem by appropriating the necessary cartridges from dead and wounded foes.

Another gun which had considerable use was the Austrian rifle. But it was despised because of its unwieldiness and ineffectiveness. A Reb who had the misfortune to draw one of these weapons remarked that the Europeans for whom it had been devised "must be hard, large-fisted fellows, used to playing with a pair of fifty-sixes," for he continued, "it is certainly the most ungainly rifle mortal ever used, being furnished with a heavy oak stock, and trappings of iron and brass, sufficient to decorate a howitzer."[17] When a soldier got ready to fire one of these monstrosities, he was apt to take a tight grip, brace himself for the shock, draw an uncertain bead, shut his eyes and pull the trigger.[18]

Even worse than the Austrian models were the Belgian rifles, which Confederates used in limited numbers. These were of such fragile structure as to be easily broken; the bore was uneven and the barrels of some were crooked. Yankee soldiers who had to use these shabby guns referred to them contemptuously as "pumpkin slingers." [19] Other types shipped to the South from Europe included the .70-caliber British musket and the Brunswick rifle. No report is available as to the reaction of Rebs to these weapons, but they were probably of an inferior quality.[20]

After 1862 the shoulder arms used by Confederate infantrymen differed little from those carried by the men in blue. The most common types in both armies were the .577-caliber long Enfield rifle musket of English manufacture, and the American-made Springfield rifle musket of caliber .58. Despite the slight discrepancy in the bore of these two guns, the practice prevailed widely of using the same cartridges for both. No doubt much of the clogging of which officers complained in official reports of battles was due to the loading of Enfields with ammunition made for Springfields.[21] The long Enfield rifle musket, over 100,000 of which were purchased abroad by Huse, was about the same size and weight as the Springfield rifle musket. It was perhaps the most popular gun in Confederate service and one of the most effective.[22]

Probably the most accurate of the muzzle-loading weapons were the Whitworth rifles. These excellent guns were used largely by sharpshooters. When equipped with telescopic sights, as they sometimes were, and placed in the hands of expert marksmen concealed in crags, trees and abandoned dwellings, the Whitworths were used with deadly effect on targets far removed.[23]

Comparatively few breech-loading small arms were used by Southerners. But of these the oldest was the Hall rifle invented in 1811. Basic defects of structure rendered this an unsatisfactory gun, and its use was very limited. The Morse rifle, patented in 1856, was manufactured in the Confederacy, and some muskets were converted by the inventor into breech-loaders; but these guns were impracticable because of the difficulty of procuring the special cartridges which they required. A Richmond firm undertook the production of a carbine designed after the fashion of the famous Sharps, but looseness at the breech caused these arms to spit fire into the eyes of their users, and they had to be discarded.[24]

Among cavalrymen the breech-loading Maynard rifles were held in high esteem because of their accuracy and range. But only a limited number of these could be obtained by Confederates. In the latter part of the war some Spencer and Henry repeating carbines were captured by Rebel horsemen, but these deadly guns—which, according to one gray-clad wag, contained so many charges that they could be loaded on Sunday and fired all week—like most of the improved types developed in the North, were of little use because of the difficulty of obtaining metal cartridges.[25]

Throughout the war Southern cavalrymen used extensively the short Enfield rifle. This was a dependable gun, but, like all muzzle-loaders, cumbersome to load, even when the ramrod was attached on a swivel hinge for convenience of horsemen. Until the very end the short double-barrel shotgun, loaded from the muzzle with buckshot, constituted one of the principal arms of the mounted service.

Rare was that colonel in either cavalry or infantry who had enough guns of any one type with which to arm his men. In the infantry a standard practice was to give the best weapons to flank companies because of the importance of their position, and to issue less desirable ones to those in the center. In some regiments there were several degrees of gradation. Colonel Walker of the Tenth South Carolina distributed his arms thus: Company A was equipped with Enfield rifles, Company B with Mississippi rifles, Company E with Harper's Ferry rifled muskets, and the others with smoothbore guns.[26]

The standard projectile for most Confederate rifles was the Minie type bullet. This missile, popularly but incorrectly called a ball, was a leaden cone devised by Captain C. E. Minié of France. Its distinctive feature was a hollow base—plugged sometimes with wood or iron—which expanded at fire so as to fit snugly into the riflings of the barrel. This not only gave greater force to propulsion but also increased the bullet's rotary action. Smoothbore muskets were loaded usually with round balls. A Confederate invention proposed to substitute for the ball an elongated projectile with a pointed lead nose and a base of wood or papier-mâché; the forward position of the center of gravity was calculated to cause the missile in flight to rotate on its axis like an arrow and thus to increase accuracy. But skepticism and red tape in the War Department seem to have prevented extensive trial of the new device.[27]

Courtesy Military Records Division, Alabama Department of Archives and History, Montgomery, Alabama

SOLDIER'S POETRY

Poetry written from Confederate camp by a poor white to his wife.

A SOLDIER'S LETTER

Cartridges for rifles and muskets were usually made up in munitions plants, but early in the war soldiers in the field often had to fashion their own. One Reb gave the following description of the technique used in his company:

"We take a stick 4 or 5 inches long the Size of the Caliber of the Gun, Wrap around a piece of paper which we have prepared. A little of the paper Sticks over the end of the Stick & is tied with String the Stick is withdrawn the Bulit or Shot as the case may be inserted then a wad & next the Charge of Powder Accurately measured then the paper is nicely twisted to Keep the powder from leaking out." [28]

In a few instances soldiers made their own bullets from bulk lead in crude molds of wood or iron. A group of Missouri volunteers used sewing thimbles for molds. "While, the lead was hot," one of them wrote, "a sharp-pointed stick had been thrust into it. This gave the bullet the form of a minie ball which just fitted our guns and we could shoot through a boxcar three hundred yards away." [29] Expedients such as this became unnecessary after the first year of the war.

Most of the guns when issued to the soldiers were equipped with bayonets. These were of two principal kinds, the sword bayonet and the angular one. The former was a straight implement, used principally on cavalry arms; it was equipped with a handle to facilitate use as a detached weapon. The latter, designed primarily for infantry, was usually triangular in shape; it was fixed to the gun barrel by means of a socket which slipped over the muzzle.

Some of the early volunteers had their bayonets made by local blacksmiths from saws, butcher knives and files. But most of the supply was obtained by foreign purchase, by capture, and by government contract with domestic arms manufacturers.

Johnny Reb did not take readily to the use of the bayonet. It interfered with the loading of his gun. As he rammed home the charge in the excitement of battle it was very apt to prick or bruise his hand. He complained, with only half jest, that he could rarely get close enough to a "Blue-belly" to stick him. And when close quarters were achieved, most Rebs seemed instinctively to prefer grabbing their gun by the barrel and swinging the butt at Yankee heads to the gouging technique prescribed by the manual of arms. Certainly the inclination to regard bayonets as unnecessary equipment was so universal as to make it impossible for officers to maintain anything like an adequate supply of them.[30]

Almost as indispensable as a rifle, in the eyes of men who rushed to the colors in 1861, was a pistol of some sort. The pervasiveness of this attitude is indicated by the great number of pistols appearing in photographs of early volunteers. The size of these weapons ranged from delicate little instruments no larger than a pocketknife to awesome pieces having barrels almost as long as carbines. A few months' soldiering sufficed, as a rule, to convince the ordinary infantryman that a rifle was the only kind of gun he needed. Consequently pistols were rarely carried after 1862 by any except officers. But this was not true of cavalrymen, among whom pistols were popular throughout the war.

There was an even greater diversity of pistols than of muskets and rifles. Calibers ranged from .36 to .60, and firing capacity from one to nine shots. Some were muzzle-loaders and a few may have been flintlocks. Many were imported, more were manufactured domestically, and still more were obtained from the North by purchase and capture.

Probably the most popular and the most extensively used of all was the Colt's "six-shooter" revolver. The .44-caliber model of this gun had, in spite of its massiveness, gained a good reputation among Southerners who participated in the Mexican War. In 1861 agents were sent North to contract for large quantities of these and of the newer .36-caliber models. The manufacturers seemed not averse to supplying Southern needs, but Federal authorities prevented shipments of more than half of the number ordered. During the course of the war Rigdon and Smith of Georgia and other Southern manufacturers attempted with a fair degree of success to make revolvers after the fashion of Colt's. The total production of all types of Confederate Colts was small.

Revolvers obtained by capture, in addition to the Colt, included weapons made by Remington, Savage, Whitney, Beal, Joslyn and Starr. From England several brands of five-shooters were procured; among them were products bearing the stamps of Adams, Bentley, Kerr and Tranter, most of which were .44 caliber. Of the various types imported from France the most interesting was the Le Mat or "grape shot" revolver, invented by a New Orleans physician. In 1861 Dr. Le Mat signed a contract for delivery of 5,000 of these guns, to the Confederate Government. When he found that the necessary machinery could not be secured, he boarded the Trent with Mason and Slidell, proceeded to France, and set up his factory. The Le Mat was a nine-shot revolver with two barrels. It had a cylinder with chambers for eight .44-caliber bullets. The lower barrel fired a .60-caliber shot charge. Beauregard, Stuart and other Southern generals carried this type of pistol.[31]

Another weapon which the volunteer of 1861 frequently displayed when he visited the photographer—the usual term of the sixties was "daguerrian artist"—was a "Bowie" knife.[32] A favorite pose showed this ferocious-looking implement jabbed beneath the belt on one side and a pistol on the other. A variation depicted the soldier grasping the knife's handle. Whatever the position, the expression on the face was generally one of grimness if not of vengeance. If Northern appeasers had been given access to Southern photograph galleries of early 1861, they might have obtained convincing support for their argument to let erring Southerners secede in peace.

These pictures are not misleading. Long daggerlike knives were a prevailing fad among the Confederacy's first soldiers. A close observer of doings in Richmond said of the regiments who came to the capital from all parts of the Confederacy in the summer of 1861: "Every man you met, mounted or footman, carried in his belt the broad, straight, double-edged bowie knife." [33] And the Richmond *Enquirer* of September 27, 1861, noted that each man of an Alabama company was equipped with a two-and-one-half-pound knife having a blade nineteen inches long. Some of the models had serrated edges designed for tearing Yankee flesh. Others had curved blades and were made on such a generous scale as to suggest scythes to awe-stricken observers. These outlandish weapons may have proved of some benefit in culinary operations, but they seem to have had little use in battle.[34] As the volunteer became a veteran he sloughed off the Bowie knife along with other excess baggage.

Another unorthodox arm that received serious consideration in high places was the pike or lance. In the spring of 1862, when the Confederacy was facing her most serious shortage of guns, Stonewall Jackson wrote the governor of Virginia that soldiers on the field "must under Divine blessing, rely upon the bayonet, when firearms cannot be furnished." He suggested that companies of recruits be organized, equipped with long steel-tipped pikes and sent against the foe. General Lee indorsed the idea and requested that 1,000 pikes be forwarded to Jackson as soon as practicable.[35] A short time later Lee wrote General Humphrey Marshall that pikes were in production, and offered to honor his requisitions for this type of arm.[36]

Confederate victories in the summer and fall yielded such a rich harvest of arms as to render unnecessary the issuance of the emergency weapons; and army leaders seem to have dropped permanently the idea of using them. But not Governor Brown of Georgia. He was so thoroughly imbued with the vision of hordes of Southerners gouging their way to victory that he ordered the manufacture of thousands of pikes for the troops of his state. Variations of the weapon were developed, such as the addition of a hook with which to grasp and cut bridle reins from the hands of cavalrymen; deprived thus of the control of their mounts, the hapless riders would be easy victims of the pikemen's thrusts. Someone raised the question as to what the horsemen would be doing in the meantime; no answer was forthcoming, but the governor's enthusiasm lost none of its bloom. Some inventive genius carried the idea well nigh to its ultimate absurdity by designing a springed contraption by which the blade of the lance might be drawn back within the staff; when a victim came close the pull of a trigger would release the spring, and the blade would dart forth to transfix him. As far as can be ascertained, neither the simple version of this implement nor any of its variations ever came close enough to a Yankee to be put to a test, but relics in various museums, appropriately labeled "Joe Brown Pikes," bid fair to perpetuate eternally the memory of their fervid protagonist.[37]

Ordinary Rebs who belonged to the infantry did not carry swords, as these ornaments were reserved to the use of officers. But the saber was an accepted part of any cavalryman's equipment. During the early days of the war, state and Confederate authorities had great difficulty in supplying this type of weapon because of the lack of domestic manufacturing facilities. Caleb Huse shipped several thousand sabers from Europe in 1861 and 1862, and large quantities were obtained by capture and purchase from the North. After 1862, however, Southern firms were able to furnish most of the requisitions.[38]

The largest sword factory in the South was apparently that of Haiman and Brother of Columbus, Georgia. Clanton's cavalry regiment was armed throughout with sabers made by this firm. A Columbia, South Carolina, establishment turned out an excellent product fashioned after the North's regulation saber. Another Columbia manufacturer made for some of Hampton's cavalry "long, straight double edged swords, very serviceable and crusader-like with cross hilts." At Nashville a farm-implements concern reversed the Biblical command and turned plowshares into swords; the brass guards of these high-class weapons bore the appropriate markings "C.S.A." and "Nashville Plow Works." [39]

Other manufacturers were less successful in their efforts to provide serviceable weapons. Swords turned out by Froelich and Estvan, of

Wilmington, for the state of North Carolina were said to have been worthless.[40] Cavalry officers complained repeatedly that sabers furnished to their men were of such poor quality that they were thrown away. In this connection, however, it should be noted that there was a widespread indisposition on the part of Rebel horsemen to carry swords of any sort. They chose rather to depend on carbines and pistols, and many doubtless felt more at ease with shotguns than with all other weapons.[41]

The problem of supplying short arms and swords, great though it was during most of the war, was not so formidable as that of providing artillery. The taking over of various coastal forts in the early months of 1861 yielded a considerable number of heavy siege guns, but in none of the arsenals inherited by the Confederacy were there any batteries of light artillery. The only field guns in Southern possession when the war began belonged either to militia companies, such as the Richmond Howitzers and the Washington Artillery, or to the various states. Many of the latter were smoothbore iron guns of a vintage antedating the War of 1812.[42] And from the very beginning, state governors were inclined to hold the pieces in their respective arsenals with an embarrassing tenacity.

Most of the forty-seven artillery pieces in Confederate possession at First Manassas were old six-pounder smoothbores. All, save the four carried into action by the Washington Artillery, belonged to the state of Virginia. Twenty-eight cannon, mostly of rifled bore, were captured by Confederates in this battle.[43]

During the months that followed First Manassas President Davis and his associates made Gargantuan efforts to supply the South's artillery needs. As in the case of small arms, three principal sources were utilized, namely, European purchase, domestic manufacture and capture from the Federals.

Caleb Huse succeeded in making contracts for large quantities of guns in England, deliveries of which began in 1862. During the first two years of the war, Huse's purchases totaled 129 pieces, nearly half of which were bronze six-pounder smoothbores. Other imported types included Blakely rifles of 2.10, 4.5, and 8-inch calibers, Whitworth rifles of various sizes, 8-inch Armstrong rifles, small-caliber bronze howitzers, and twelve-pounder steel rifled cannon. Most of these were muzzle-loading models, though a considerable number of the smaller rifles were charged from the breech. The most widely heralded of all the importations were two enormous Blakely guns bought for £10,000 in 1863 for the defense of Charleston. These titans weighed twenty-three tons each, used a forty to fifty-pound charge of powder, and fired a round shot weighing about five hundred pounds. They were loaded at the breech by means of a screw plug. One of them brought untold grief to the hearts of its purchasers by cracking at first trial. But the damage proved reparable and both cannon were placed in service, though with charges so reduced as to lessen considerably the maximum range.[44]

A delightful story went the rounds of Rebel camps in the latter part of the war about a North Carolinian who was captured at Antietam. As he was being marched to the rear he noticed a number of Yankee fieldpieces. He paused and began to read aloud the marking "U.S." on each gun.

"Well, what now, Johnny Reb?" one of his captors asked good-naturedly.

"I say mister—you-all has got as many of these U.S. guns as we 'uns has," replied the Tar Heel.[45]

The story was not without point. In the halcyon days of 1862 and early 1863, scores of Federal cannon took up forced residence in the Confederacy. Following the Seven Days' fighting Lee reported capture of fifty-two pieces of artillery, and Bragg took eighty-one on his Kentucky-Tennessee campaign. Further accessions at Second Manassas, Harper's Ferry and elsewhere brought the total of artillery prizes for the year 1862 to a figure exceeding 250.[46] There were also substantial captures at Chancellorsville and Chickamauga, but these were counterbalanced by losses at Vicksburg and Chattanooga. After 1863 the South had to look principally to her own resources for the strengthening of the "long arm."

Domestic artillery production was slow getting under way. At the outset of the war there was only one plant in the South capable of turning out large cannon; this was the Tredegar Iron Works of Richmond. The situation as to light artillery was not much better. But Josiah Gorgas and his associates tackled the problem with characteristic vim. Contracts were arranged with a great number of foundries, including Noble Brothers of Rome, Georgia, Leeds and Company of New Orleans, T. M. Brennan of Nashville, and the Columbus Iron Works of Columbus, Georgia. In addition the government developed its own works at Augusta and at Selma. In order to secure the necessary iron, steps were taken to stimulate mining activities in Virginia, North Carolina, Tennessee, Georgia and Alabama. Copper-producing facilities in Eastern Tennessee were expanded, and in Georgia an order was issued for the seizure of copper stills. Public appeals were made all over the South for candlesticks, hearth irons and other items of brass. General Beauregard, inclined toward the dramatic, in March 1862 issued a call for bells belonging to churches and plantations. Braxton Bragg deemed this step sensational and unnecessary, but Richmond authorities and the country at large indorsed the action of the hero of Sumter and Manassas, and bells of all sorts and sizes came pouring into Southern depots for conversion into weapons of war.[47]

All of these efforts eventually yielded results which, in the light of limited resources, shortage of skilled labor, inadequacy of transportation and interference of state governors, were nothing short of remarkable. In the year ending September 30, 1863, the Ordnance Bureau issued 677 fieldpieces, and the Richmond arsenal alone distributed during the period from July 1, 1861, to January 1, 1865, 341 large siege guns, 1,306 pieces of field artillery, and large quantities of caissons, gun carriages, ammunition, friction primers, fuses and other accessories; most of the artillery issued was made at the Tredegar Iron Works. Considerable ingenuity was displayed by ordnance authorities in using substitutes for scarce materials and in developing new techniques of manufacture. Toward the end of the war the Tredegar Works succeeded in making a twelve-inch gun by the water-cooled hollow casting procedure, a method that produced a weapon of great strength and of unusually smooth bore.[48]

But by no means all of the artillery produced in the South was of good quality. Some of the early products were so poor, indeed, as to invoke the utter scorn of generals in the field.

D. H. Hill wrote the Secretary of War repeatedly from the Yorktown defenses complaining of the inaccuracy, short range and fragile construction of the guns of his command. "There must be something very rotten in the Ordnance Department," he blurted on April 24, 1862. "It is a Yankee concern throughout, and I have long been afraid that there was foul play there. Our shells burst at the mouth of the gun or do not burst at all. The metal of which the new guns are made is of the most flimsy and brittle character, and the casting is very bad." [49]

The frequency with which guns burst when exposed to the strain of repeated firing was enough to test faith in the loyalty of their makers. Many of those issued in 1862, and some that were turned out late in the war, were more dangerous to friend than to foe. At Fredericksburg a large Parrott gun exploded in such close proximity to Generals Lee and Longstreet that they seemed to be spared only by the interposition of providence.[50] An additional danger came from the instability of gun carriages. General Magruder wrote from Yorktown that some of his cannon would "dismount themselves after a few fires." [51]

Complaints were also registered against Southern-made guns on the ground of defective boring. This weakness sometimes resulted in woefully inaccurate performance. An artillery sergeant of the Army of Tennessee recorded in his diary on August 6, 1863:

"We are testing our guns today. The target was placed at 1,000 yards; we fired seven shots, not one of which struck the target. As we have splendid gunners, Col. Polk had the rifle guns condemned." [52]

There was a gradual improvement in the quality of domestic-made artillery during the third and fourth years of the war. But new difficulties arose in the form of the dwindling of the horse supply and the scarcity of accessory equipment. At no time after 1861 was this branch of the service able to compete on anything like equal terms with that of the Federals except in personnel.[53]

From beginning to end the Confederates used many different types and sizes of artillery. The biggest guns were the coast and river Columbiads and Blakely's of calibers ranging from thirteen inches on down to eight. But cannon of this size were too cumbersome for field purposes. Gettysburg affords a good example of the artillery in most general use in land engagements. Of the 244 pieces taken into Pennsylvania, 103 were three-inch rifles, 107 were twelve-pounder Napoleons, thirty were twelve-pounder howitzers, and four were small-caliber Whitworth rifles.[54]

Other rifled pieces which had wide use in the Confederacy were the ten-pounder iron Parrott (caliber 2.90 inches), the twenty-pounder iron Parrott (caliber 3.67 inches), the thirty-pounder iron Parrott (caliber 4.20 inches), and the bronze mountain rifle (caliber 2.25 inches). The Parrott guns' distinctive feature was a thick wrought-iron band shrunk around the breech to prevent them from bursting. The scheme was originally devised by Colonel R. P. Parrott of the United States forces, but after the outbreak of war John M. Brooke, designer of the Merrimac, perfected a similar technique for the Confederacy.[55] The mountain rifles were so called because they were of a construction sufficiently light to be carried on horseback over precipitous terrain. For the most part, however, they were transported on light carriages.

With the introduction of trench warfare on a large scale in 1864, the use of short "dumpy" pieces, called mortars, became extensive. These were set at a pronounced elevation so as to lob shells over into the opposing earthworks. In a few instances regular-size guns were adapted to this function by tilting back the mounting for greater elevation and lightening the charge.

Perhaps the most interesting of all the pieces used by Confederate artillerymen was a crude type of machine gun. In fact it is claimed that the first machine gun ever used in battle was the Williams repeating cannon taken into action at Seven Pines. This gun had a four-foot barrel and shot one-pound projectiles. Its firing mechanism was very much like that of a Colt's revolver, except that the cylinder was turned by a crank. Ammunition was fed from a hopper placed above the chamber. Newspaper reports of testings of this gun claimed that it shot eighteen to twenty balls a minute and that it was accurate for a range of a thousand yards. Several other types of automatic cannon were mentioned by the Confederate press, but details are too scant to permit an adequate idea of their appearance and function. Another interesting gun of the Confederate period was a double-barreled cannon.[56]

But far and away the most popular of the Confederate fieldpieces were the twelve-pounder Napoleons. These guns which, in the latter part of the war came to have such wide use as to constitute the backbone of the light artillery, were smoothbore muzzle-loaders of caliber 4.62 inches. Shortly after Fort Sumter, Colonel Andrews of Baltimore went to the Pikesville Armory near that city and copied drawings of the recently tested Napoleons. Immediately thereafter he took the plans to Virginia and persuaded Governor Letcher to order the manufacture of some of these guns on state account. A few were completed in time for use at First Manassas. In the months following, scores of Napoleons were cast for the Confederacy by Tredegar and other domestic establishments. At first they were made solely of bronze, but after brass became scarce an iron model, strengthened at the breech with a jacket, was put into production. Both domestic and imported Napoleons were well suited to Confederate needs because of simplicity of operation, ease of transportation and accuracy at medium ranges.[57]

Grouping of guns into batteries varied considerably with time and circumstances. Early in the war the six-gun arrangement was the most common, four of the pieces being smoothbore six-pounders and two being twelve-pounder howitzers. As three-inch rifles became available they were substituted for the six-pounder cannon. In the last year of the war many batteries were made up wholly of Napoleon guns. The six-gun grouping was modified also, batteries ranging in size from two to eight guns, until late in the war when four guns became the standard. Six-horse teams were usually needed for the handling of the larger fieldpieces. One of the most effective of field units was the horse artillery. Used in conjunction with regular cavalry, the horse artillery was indeed the forerunner of modern "panzer" outfits.[58]

Missiles fired from artillery pieces varied greatly with the type of gun and the purpose of fire. It has been estimated that about seventy different types of projectiles were in use at one period of the Confederacy. If the principal objective was the battering down of a fort, solid shot was used, and in the Confederacy the most common form of solid shot was the iron "cannon ball." For field purposes, where the primary aim was the destruction of men, a bursting charge was preferred. But Confederates used spherical shot to a considerable extent in smoothbore fieldpieces.[59]

Bursting projectiles were of two main kinds: in one, fragmentation was produced at the mouth of the cannon by the explosion which hurled the missile forth; in the other, the shot remained intact until a time fuse or a percussion fuse set off an inner charge. Projectiles of the first kind, while restricted to short ranges, included two of the deadliest agencies known to the Civil War period, namely, canister and grape.

Canister consisted of a large group of small balls inclosed in a cylindrical tin cover, or "can," plugged at the ends with discs of iron or of wood. When thrown from the mouths of advantageously placed cannon, as at Fredericksburg, they rained death upon the advancing foe.

Grapeshot were composed of a group of iron balls, usually about two inches in diameter, but frequently smaller, held together by a series of round discs transfixed with a bolt. These clustered charges were used with terrible effectiveness at ranges extending to several hundred yards. If canister, grape, or other orthodox charges were not at hand, Rebel operators of smoothbore guns did not hesitate to load their pieces with trace chains and other available miscellanies.

Among the exploding type of missiles conical shells were the most common. Shrapnel were also used; these were shaped like shells, but the walls were thinner and the interiors were packed with small balls which scattered like birdshot when the projectiles burst in flight. Some of the spherical shot were loaded like shrapnel and functioned in the same manner. Confederate shells were frequently fitted at the base with bands or sabots of lead or of soft iron to make possible a snug following of the cannons' rifling. Some of the hideous screeching that filled the air during battle and caused such widespread comment on the part of both sides was produced by the ragged edges of the leaden jackets. Colonel J. W. Mallet, one of the most outstanding of the South's ordnance officers, invented a shell with a cavity fashioned so as to assure fragmentation into a definite number of pieces when explosion occurred.[60]

Explosion on contact with the target was obtained by the use of percussion fuses. When the purpose was best served by causing the shell to burst while in flight or after it landed, time fuses were applied. The period of delay was controlled by the length of the fuse. Neither type was very satisfactory. The time fuse often failed of ignition when fired from the piece; or if it was ignited the spark was frequently extinguished by flight through the air or by the shock of landing. The triggers and fulminates which were supposed to set off percussion fuses were similarly disarranged. Such undependability brought constant complaint from officers in the field. In October 1861 Magruder wrote Gorgas from Yorktown that about half the shells fired by his command exploded at the guns' muzzle; and an artillery chief, reporting on the performance of his batteries at Chancellorsville, estimated on the basis of careful observation that only one out of every fifteen of the shells that were fired exploded at all. "I was compelled to watch closely the effect of all the projectiles," he said, "as if we were using entirely solid shot." [61]

The lamentable ineffectiveness of Southern artillery in the first years of the war was due in considerable measure to the poor quality of powder used in fuses, primers, shells and cannon. When the Confederacy was organized there was in all the South's arsenals no more than 60,000 pounds of serviceable powder. Agents were rushed to the North to buy up all that was available, and deliveries were being made in large quantities when Fort Sumter was attacked. Thereafter importations from the North ceased. Blockade runners brought in large shipments from Europe in 1862 and 1863, but to a great extent the Confederacy was compelled to depend upon her own production.[62]

Eventually ample quantities of a high-class explosive were obtained, but the intervening period of experimentation and development was filled with anxiety and error. Scarcity of powder in the fall of 1861 compelled those in charge of defenses at New Bern, North Carolina, to fill shells with sand and use them as solid shot. The commander of the batteries along the Potomac during the war's first winter said:

"The ammunition found in the magazine for the large guns was very indifferent. The powder was a mixture of blasting with rifle powder. Sometimes the Armstrong gun at the same elevation would not throw a shell more than halfway across the river; then again far over the river."

A similar situation was reported by the commander of defenses below New Orleans in the spring of 1862, after his unsuccessful attempt to turn back the Yankee gunboats:

"Generally our shots fell short for lack of elevation and in consequence of the inferiority of our powder. Even our nearest gun, a 10-inch sea-coast mortar, would not reach his boats with the heaviest charges." [63]

Fortunately for the South, President Davis was able to secure for the supervision of powder manufacturing G. W. Rains, a West Point graduate and a man of unusual ability. Colonel Rains's first efforts were devoted to the stimulation of the few small powder mills which existed in the South when war broke out. He then proceeded to develop niter mining in Tennessee, Georgia, Alabama, Arkansas and Texas. At New Orleans he was able to obtain several hundred tons of sulphur that had been imported originally for a sugar factory.[64] He constructed a saltpeter refinery at Nashville which attained a daily production of 3,000 pounds. The principal government establishment, however, was located at Augusta, Georgia. Through a stroke of good luck, Colonel Rains came into possession of a booklet by an Englishman describing the processes and machinery employed at the British Gunpowder Factory at Waltham Abbey. From the information thus obtained Rains and a few talented associates designed with remarkable ingenuity both the Augusta plant and the machinery installed therein. Through subsequent experimentation various short-cuts and improvements in the manufacture of explosives were developed. During its three years of operation the Augusta plant produced 2,750,000 pounds of powder. The cost of manufacture was a little over a third the price paid for powder brought in by blockade runners, and the quality of the domestic product was as good as the finest output of the English mills.[65]

The procurement of sufficient quantities of niter was the source of great concern to ordnance authorities. To supplement the supply obtained from limestone caves in various parts of the country, the earth in cellars and under outhouses was dug up and leached. Niter beds were established in large numbers near cities and towns. These beds were composed of a variety of vegetable and offal substances and when worked for a period of two or three years, yielded several ounces of niter to the cubic foot.[66]

One of the items utilized in the production of niter was human urine. Jonathan Haralson, Agent of the Nitre and Mining Bureau at Selma, Alabama, ran a notice in the newspaper requesting the women of the town to save all the "chamber-lye" accumulating around their premises so that it might be collected in barrels sent around by the Bureau. This advertisement allegedly inspired a local wag named Wetmore to write some naughty verses chiding Haralson for ungallantry, which in turn elicited a poetic defense from the accused. The poetic exchange was supposed to have been printed in broadside form and circulated among the soldiers in the Petersburg trenches, much to their merriment. Be that as it may, there are innumerable copies of the poems in circulation among descendants of those who wore the gray, but unfortunately the content is not of a publishable character.[67]

There was apparently no time during the last two years of the war when the available supply of powder was not equal to the needs of the armies. In April 1865 the Augusta plant had on hand a stock of 70,000 pounds.[68] This progress from nothing to abundance, which Gorgas, Rains and their associates were able to accomplish in the face of formidable difficulties, was one of the most admirable achievements of the Confederacy.

While guns and ammunition were of first importance in a soldier's equipment, there were certain accessory items which were hardly less dispensable. Among these was a container of some sort for drinking water. Tin canteens, fitted with a strap to hang over the shoulder, were ordinarily employed for this purpose, but in 1861 these were hard to get. As a consequence many of the early volunteers quenched their thirst from clay jugs, from straw or leather-covered bottles, and from homemade contraptions fashioned of cedar or cypress.

The most common type of wooden vessel was constructed like a barrel. It was about eight inches in diameter and about two and one-half inches thick. The mouth was plugged with a cork or twig. The owner's name, company and regiment were sometimes carved on the side. Metal canteens were of a variety of shapes and sizes. Probably the greater portion of those carried by Rebs came from their opponents. The standard type of Federal canteen was of tin and resembled two small dinner plates stuck together, only the bulge was greater. Many of them had cloth covers to keep out the heat. Other models were in shape and size very much like the wooden containers previously described. A few were smaller, bearing close resemblance to the medium-sized fruit and vegetable cans seen on grocery shelves today, though somewhat shorter, and equipped with nozzles.[69]

The hard school of experience, such as that conducted by Jackson in the Valley, Bragg in Kentucky, Early in Maryland, and Hood in Tennessee, caused some soldiers to discard canteens as needless encumbrances and to rely solely on the tin cup which, when not in use as a mess pot, dangled conveniently from the belt. On the march or even on the battlefield an ingenious veteran could usually find an opportunity to seek out some branch or spring from which to fill his cup. If not—well, a good soldier could shift his saliva and push on doggedly till the scurry of comrades up ahead gave promise of better luck.

Knapsacks were another item with which enlistees of 1861 and early 1862 equipped themselves. These satchels were designed for carrying not only surplus socks, drawers and shirts, but also such sundries as writing paper, toilet articles, chewing tobacco and cherished miniatures of folk at home. Some were of leather, but the great majority were made of heavy cloth, treated in some cases with enamel or rubber for sturdiness and weatherproofing. Knapsacks were usually fastened on the soldiers' backs by means of straps. Many of the homemade products resembled very much the cloth satchels in which rural school children of today carry their books.

Knapsacks had comparatively little use among Rebs after the first year of the war. Deprivation and inclination combined to reduce extras, whether drawers or daguerreotypes, to the barest minimum. The prevailing practice among veterans was to wrap essential oddities of wardrobe and toilet in a blanket, tie the ends together, cover with an oilcloth captured from the Yankees, and drape this wheel-like traveling bag from left shoulder to right hip.[70]

Rebs carried their rations in kits which quartermasters listed as haversacks, but which camp parlance dubbed with a variety of designations ranging from war bags to mess boxes. Some were made of leather and others of metal, but canvas seems to have been the material in widest use. In shape and structure many of the food bags differed little from knapsacks. As a rule soldiers who discarded the latter carried some of their "little conveniences" in haversacks along with bread and bacon. Of course there were always a considerable number of Rebs who insisted on getting along without either haversack or knapsack.

Included in the impedimenta of most Rebs were two other important items: the cartridge box and the cap box. The former was a rectangular container made of leather of a size sufficient to accommodate at least forty rounds of paper cartridges. The latter was a small square-shaped pouch in which percussion caps were carried. Both types of boxes were commonly attached to the belt. The cartridge container, because of its size and awkwardness, was irksome to many soldiers, and a pervasive practice was to transfer the contents to the pocket, throw the box away, and report it as "lost." [71]

From beginning to end of the war the average Reb went through a combined hardening and shedding process. And the veteran who emerged in the spring of 1865 was as far removed from the volunteer of '61 in accouterments as he was in sinew. One Reb wrote:

"Reduced to the minimum, the private soldier consisted of one man, one hat, one jacket, one shirt, one pair of pants, one pair of drawers, one pair of shoes, and one pair of socks. His baggage was one blanket, one rubber blanket, and one haversack." [72]

His weapon, if he was a walking soldier, was one gun, more than likely a muzzle-loader, sans bayonet. He was the ultima persona of the rule laid down in May 1862 by General "Dick" Ewell to those who were to follow him in the campaign against Banks:

"The road to glory cannot be followed with much baggage." [73]

CHAPTER XVI

BLUE BELLIES AND BELOVED ENEMIES

IT WAS a hot July day in 1862. A Confederate soldier of twenty-three years sat beneath a tree on a hill near Richmond guarding a group of Yankees captured during the recent Seven Days' fighting. Ordinarily this Reb—whose name must remain in the realm of the unknown because of the incompleteness of his records—was a buoyant, zestful character, but on this particular day he was morose and inconsolable. He had just read a list of the casualties of Mechanicsville, Gaines's Mill, Frayser's Farm, and Malvern Hill. Included among the dead were a number of boys with whom he had frolicked during days of peace. But now they were gone.

As he mused over the loss of his comrades this young soldier laid aside his gun, drew from his pocket the small leather-bound diary that his sweetheart had given him when he left for camp, and began to write:

"July 10, 1862 . . . May God avenge us of our infernal enemies—and if I ever forgive them it is more than I Expect. 'Forgive your Enemies' is the Divine precept—a hard one to obey—How can one forgive such enemies as we are contending against? Despoiling us of our property, driving us from our homes & friends and slaying our best citizens on the field are hard crimes to forgive—At any rate let me have a chance to retaliate & *then* I can forgive with a better grace. I hope to see many such epithets as this:

> 'The Yankee host with blood-stained hands
> Came Southward to divide our lands
> This narrow & contracted spot
> Is all this Yankee scoundrel got'

So May it be." [1]

Most soldiers in the Rebel Army had feelings toward the Yankees very much like those expressed by this unidentified Virginian. There were some who excelled him in the pungency with which they recorded their antipathy. "I hope that we may slay them like wheat before the sythe," wrote a North Carolinian to his homefolk; "I certainly love to live to hate the base usurping vandals, if it is a Sin to hate them, then I am guilty of the unpardonable one." [2]

A Mississippi private who had heard that his homefolk were being despoiled by the invaders blurted out, "I intend to fight them as long as I live and after this war stops. . . . I intend to kill Every one that crosses my path." [3]

Not a few Rebs got so worked up over Yankee meanness that they swore to perpetuate hatred of the foe in generations to come. Typical of this group was the Georgian who wrote his wife in the spring of 1862:

"Teach my children to hate them with that bitter hatred that will never permit them to meet under any circumstances without seeking to destroy each other. I know the breach is now wide & deep between us & the Yankees let it widen & deepen until all Yankees or no Yankees are to live in the South." [4]

Hatred of Southern soldiers for those of the North was due to a variety of reasons. In their letters and diaries very few of the rank and file mention violation of states' rights as a cause of their antipathy. While most of them had heard small-fry politicians denounce the Lincoln government on this score, it is doubtful whether many of them either understood or cared about the Constitutional issues at stake. The threat to slavery was resented rather widely, not so much as an unwarranted deprivation of property rights, but as a wedge for "nigger equality."

Common soldiers hated the men in blue primarily because they thought them to be an unsavory sort of people who came from a low and vulgar background. It is amazing how many Rebs commented on the crudity and obscenity of letters found on the battlefields addressed to Union soldiers. One Confederate who read a number of letters found in the Atlanta area in 1864 wrote to his wife, "I would send you a sample of them, but I am ashamed they are so vulgar. . . . I do not believe God will ever suffer us to be subjugated by such a motly crew of infidels." [5]

Another Reb confided to his wife that he had seen a great many letters written by wives of soldiers in Sherman's army, and that they were full of such profane expressions as "d—n liar—damed theaf &c." and that "one who wrote a soft & affectionate letter told her husband that some 'bad talk' about her could not be helped." [6] Other Johnnies, with striking unawareness of their own orthographic and grammatical shortcomings, made fun of the Yankees' inability to write and to spell.

The conviction was rather prevalent in Southern ranks that Federal soldiers made a fetish of money. One Reb cited an instance of this quality which he accepted as being typical:

"One of our boys, in conversation with one of the wounded prisoners who had both eyes shot entirely out, remarked to him that his wound must be very painful. The Yankee replied: 'I don't mind the pain so much, sir, but I wouldn't have both of my eyes shot out for twenty-five dollars.'" [7]

The Federals were also thought to be a bunch of thieves, having little regard for the rights of private property, particularly if that property happened to belong to Southerners. The robbery and despoliation that accompanied Union invasion was, indeed, one of the greatest of all causes of hatred. A Mississippi soldier whose home had been visited by raiders wrote to his mother as his regiment headed Northward on the Gettysburg campaign:

"I can fight so much Harder since I have got a gruge against them it is my Honest wish that my Rifle may Draw tears from many a Northern Mother and Sighs from Many a Father before this thing is over." [8]

Rebs liked to point out the superior regard of their own army for civilian rights. Whenever they invaded the Northern or border country, they were amused at the fear of brigandage manifested by the inhabitants along the way. "Poor fools," remarked a soldier marching with Bragg through Kentucky in 1862, "the Yankees treated them so badly, they thought we would do the same. They soon found out that there is a great difference. The Yankee army is filled up with the scum of creation and ours with the best blood of the grand old Southland." [9]

This Reb's observation gives a clue to an impression that was widely prevalent in the Southern ranks, and accepted by them as a partial explanation of the low character of Union soldiery; namely, that the majority of the Federals were recruited from the lowbred immigrant class which swelled the population of the East and the Midwest. It was pointed out repeatedly in home letters that prisoners encountered by the correspondents could not speak the English language. There can be no doubt that a particularly strong prejudice against foreigners in the South increased hatred of the Yankee soldiery. The comment of a sergeant of Bragg's army is typical of a general attitude. "Quite a number of Northern bums, called U.S. soldiers passed our camps," he wrote; "most of them were imported from Germany." [10]

Another cause for hating the Federals was found in the conviction that they were tricky and deceitful. This was applied more to the native breed than to foreigners—a wartime variant of the ancient concept that New England peddlers foisted wooden nutmegs on unwary Southern purchasers. Rebs cited numerous instances of Yankees using flags of truce for reconnoitering purposes; and of crying out "we are friends" during battle to stop opposing fire or to gain safe entrance into Confederate positions. Early in the war a few metal breastplates were found on the bodies of captured or slain Federals, and the belief was current in Southern ranks that they were worn by many members of the opposing army.[11] Both the public press and private correspondence denounced these protective devices as emblems of Yankee trickiness. A similar view was taken of a contraption found in the trenches before Atlanta with which Yankee soldiers, by the use of mirrors, were able to take pot shots at the Rebels without showing their heads above the parapets.[12]

Some Rebs carried their resentment of Yankee "slickness" to humorous extremes. An Alabamian, for instance, was provoked to write his brother:

"I desire above all things on earth to drive a Bayonet to the heart's Blood of some of the Hell bound invaders of the North. They resort to every mean trick that can be conceived of to Whip us, such as hoisting our colors, concentrating there froces upon us where we are weakist." [13]

The concept of heartlessness or brutality swelled considerably the hatred springing up in the hearts of the soldiers of the South. Atrocity stories circulating through the camps told of the bayoneting and shooting of Rebels after they were captured; of helpless Confederate wounded having throats slashed and tongues cut out; of gray-clads shot in the act of ministering to suffering Federals lying between the lines; of Yankees using poisoned bullets; and of the denuding and abuse by Northerners of defenseless Southern women in areas of invasion.[14]

Warriors of all ages have been quick to resent affronts to women. The South, with its chivalric traditions, was unusually touchy on this score. It was this oversensitiveness that caused the Northern general

B. F. Butler to be so thoroughly despised. For his alleged thievery the General was derided as "Spoon" Butler, but it was his notorious Order No. 28, in which he threatened to regard as harlots some New Orleans ladies who were "acting up" under his rule, that gave him the sobriquet of "Beast."

Rebel leaders promptly utilized the propaganda value of Butler's order. Beauregard made it the subject of a general order to his troops, pointing up its provisions as an indication of the sort of warfare that the North was waging; and not without results.

"Have you seen Butler's proclamation?" wrote one of his soldiers a short time later; "Don't it make you Shudder? Can such a people rule over us. Forbid it almighty God!" [15] Another Confederate, whose anger was uncontainable, resorted to an acrostic:

> "I sing the Chieftain, whom from Boston's shore,
> S ome Yankee Captain to our city bore
> B rutal and vulgar, a coward and knave,—
> F amed for no action, noble or brave,
>
> "B eastly by instinct, a tyrant and sot,
> U gly and venemous—on mankind a blot—
> T hief, liar, and scoundrel, in highest degree,
> L et Yankeedom boast of such heroes as thee!
> E very woman and child will for ages to come
> R emember thee, monster—thou vilest of scum!" [16]

Hatred for Sherman, Sheridan and other generals was hardly less than that for Butler. Lincoln was likewise regarded as low and brutish, so much so in fact that even intelligent soldiers regarded his demise as a blessing, as witness the entry of April 19, 1865, in the diary of Private R. W. Waldrop: "Everything in mourning today for old Abe who ought to have been killed four years ago." [17] The attitude of the man in the ranks toward those of the North, both high and low, was aptly if not accurately summed up by the Virginian who wrote his mother that "the Yankee horde have forgotten the laws of war & have not natural honour and chivalry enough to suggest them on the conduct they enforce. . . . They are like ferocious monkeys which I believe the Spanish proverb makes the most cruel, wicked, and capricious of tyrants." [18]

Another factor which contributed much to Johnny Reb's loathing of the Yankees was the conviction that the men in blue were lacking in courage. This belief had a powerful hold on Southerners before hostilities began; it gained wider currency after the battle of Bull Run, and continued to flourish till the end of the war. Occasionally a soldier's letter or an officer's report of a battle conceded gallantry to the foe. After Missionary Ridge, for instance, Lieutenant James Hall wrote to his father that the scaling of the heights by the Federals "was a sublime spectacle and I could not withhold my admiration." [19]

In similar vein wrote Captain B. E. Stiles after an encounter on the Virginia front in 1862. "It is all stuff saying that the Yankees are cowards," he concluded.[20] "They fought as boldly as men ever fought and they fight well every time I'v been in front of them," was the testimony of still another officer after Second Manassas.[21] But complimentary expressions such as these are amazing for their rarity.

Derogatory sentiments on the other hand were often recorded. "I saw a house full of Yankee prisoners," wrote a Texan in 1861; "they were large hardy looking men, but as you know they lack the courage." [22]

A short time later an Alabamian boasted to his brother, "We whip them everytime We meet, no matter how great their Numbers, or how few ours. The infernal Scoundrels cant stand the Bayonet—they Scamper like a herd of cattle." [23] A year and a half later this Reb held his antagonists in the same low esteem. "I hope it wont be long," he wrote then, "untill fighting Jo Hooker will be able to advance . . . with his army of white livers and give us a chance to enrich some of the poor land of old Virginia with their corrupt Bodyes." But, on second thought he retracted the statement attributing fertilizing qualities to Federal remains, recalling that a farmer whose property included a portion of the Manassas battlefield had told him that "one Yankee body will kill an acre of land whereas a Southerner's bones will enrich it for all time to come." [24]

Sometimes when Johnnies felt constrained to concede particularly desperate fighting on the part of the Federals, they offered in explanation of the valor their conviction that the bravery had been imbibed. Men of intelligence on more than one occasion recorded with all seriousness such statements as "Grant had made his men drunk," or, "Those Federals whom we capture are all drunk, and they tell us all are made so to get them to advance." [25]

It might logically be expected that Confederates would have taken note of the improved fighting quality of their opponents as experience molded men of the Union ranks into seasoned veterans—experience that brought them to the point where they could pin their names to their backs in order to facilitate identification of their bodies, and charge to certain death as Grant's troops did at Cold Harbor. But this was not the case. Evidently prior conceptions could not give way, and if letters and diaries are an accurate indication of attitudes, the overwhelming majority of Confederates remained firm to the end in the conviction that the majority of Yankees were lacking in the stuff that it takes to make good soldiers.

The opinion of Private W. C. McClellan of the Ninth Alabama Regiment was as representative as it was vivid: "Poor deviles," he wrote in 1863, "you have got no sand in your craw. . . . You d—n cowardly Scoundrels [you can't] face the music you blue bellys." [26]

And Private McClellan stood ready to back up in a personal way the contempt he expressed. For in a previous communication of disparaging tone he inserted this sentence: "Some Yankee may get hold of this letter before it gets to its destination [The Federals were moving about in the area of his home]; if so all I have to say is I can whip the hind legs off him before he can say God with his mouth open." [27]

Antipathy toward ordinary Yankees was deep and pervasive, but it was mild in comparison with the hatred which most Rebs felt for Negroes who wore the blue. All in all some 200,000 Negroes were taken into Federal ranks during the war. These colored soldiers did not get to do their full share of fighting, but they did figure prominently in a few engagements, including Port Hudson, Fort Pillow, Brice's Cross Roads and the Crater.[28] The mere thought of a Negro in uniform was enough to arouse the ire of the average Reb; he was wont to see in the arming of the blacks the fruition of oft-repeated Yankee efforts to incite slave insurrections and to establish racial equality. Anticipation of conflict with former slaves brought savage delight to his soul. And when white and black met on field of battle the results were terrible.

Negroes were taken prisoners in several engagements, but if the wishes of the private soldiers who fought them had prevailed, no quarter would have been granted. Most of the Rebs felt as the Mississippian who wrote his mother: "I hope I may never see a Negro Soldier," he said, "or I cannot be . . . a Christian Soldier." [29]

On more than one occasion Negro troops were slain after they were captured.[30] Following the Crater affair a Reb wrote his homefolk that all the colored prisoners "would have ben killed had it not been for gen Mahone who beg our men to Spare them." One of his comrades

killed several, he continued; Mahone "told him for God's sake stop."
The man replied, "Well gen let me kill one more," whereupon, according to the correspondent, "he deliberately took out his pocket knife and cut one's Throat." [31]

But the War of Secession was not all hatred. Many Rebs whose anger flashed to white heat in battle, became indulgent and generous toward the foe when fighting subsided. Others felt little or no hate for the men in blue, even while they were pinning writhing bodies to the earth with their bayonets. To these latter, fighting Yankees was regarded more or less in the light of a regular chore—disagreeable, indeed, but unavoidable.

The war of the sixties has been called a "polite war," and in a sense the designation is apt. The conflict followed generally the pattern of a series of battles. Men of the opposing armies when not actually engaged in a shooting fray were wont to observe niceties that in twentieth-century warfare would be regarded as absurd. And even during combat there were occasional exchanges of courtesy. The conduct of the war in its entirety had something of the flavor of a medieval tournament.

The chivalric concept manifested itself at the very outset of the war. When Beauregard's aides were conferring with Major Robert Anderson in April 1861 on the eve of Sumter's bombardment, one of the Union officers complained jokingly to A. R. Chisolm that the garrison's supply of cigars was woefully short. The Rebel officers said nothing, but when they returned to the Fort for further conference a short time later they brought to the Yankee garrison not only a generous supply of cigars but several cases of claret as well. Before the night was over, these same Rebs gave the order to the batteries to open fire on the Fort—an order calculated to reduce the bastion to utter ruin.[32]

This Fort Sumter incident was but the precursor of thousands of acts of mutual kindness. In many instances the motive was sympathy for an unfortunate antagonist. A Rebel cavalry company while on a scouting expedition in the fall of 1861 surprised a group of Yanks and took several prisoners, including a lieutenant in his late 'teens. The leader of the Confederates wrote his wife the next day that he could have killed "the handsome little fellow," but that he had not the heart to shoot him when he saw his beardless face. So he pulled his youthful prize up behind and as they rode along they "got to be quite good friends." When this officer overtook his company he found to his surprise that the other prisoners had likewise captivated their captors, for "every rascally Yankee was mounted and my men on foot." And thus they proceeded to camp.[33]

During the second battle of Bull Run in 1862, W. F. Jenkins, a seventeen-year-old private of the Twelfth Georgia Regiment, was severely wounded. At nightfall two of his comrades came to take him to the field hospital. As they struggled along through the darkness, they were halted with the query, "Who are you?"

"We are two men of the Twelfth Georgia, carrying a wounded comrade to the hospital," they replied.

"Don't you know you are in the Union lines?" asked the sentry.

"No," answered one of the Rebs.

"You are. Go to your right," said the Federal.

"Man, you've got a heart in you," said the second Reb as the little party turned to the right and headed for the Confederate lines.[34]

In other instances Federals were the recipients of kindnesses. At Vicksburg, at Fredericksburg and at Cold Harbor, Yankee wounded who cried piteously for water as they lay between the lines were given succor by Rebs who dared to run a gantlet of fire to fulfill errands of mercy. During the engagement at Kenesaw Mountain in June 1864 a copse which sheltered some wounded Federals caught fire, threatening the helpless soldiers who lay there. Colonel W. H. Martin, of the First Arkansas Regiment, immediately jumped to the parapet, waved his handkerchief and cried out to the enemy, "We won't fire a gun until you get them away." Shooting on both sides ceased instantly, and the wounded men were removed from danger. At the end of the brief truce a Federal major gave his own fine pistols to Colonel Martin in appreciation of the humane action.[35]

In the wake of many battles the wounded of both sides had their sufferings mitigated by the tender offices of their antagonists. Parched lips were refreshed by pulls from enemy canteens; positions were made more comfortable by the contriving of pillows from overcoats or blankets; piercing pains of shattered thighs were dulled by administrations of copious draughts of brandy. Farewell messages to the folk at home were penned by fingers that a few hours before had wielded hostile weapons; and sincere prayers were offered for the soul's salvation of enemies who lay on the verge of death.

Often the friendly relations between Yanks and Rebs derived solely from convenience. On the night following the battle of Jonesboro, Georgia, in 1864, the armies were in such close proximity that the blue and the gray floundering about in the darkness garnered firewood from

HANDMADE POSTCARD

On the back is a delightful note, in poetic form, chiding the lady for her flirtation. The card is made in color, evidently by a soldier.

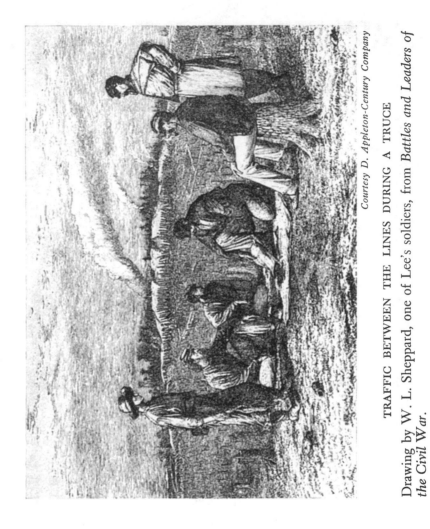

Courtesy D. Appleton-Century Company

TRAFFIC BETWEEN THE LINES DURING A TRUCE

Drawing by W. L. Sheppard, one of Lee's soldiers, from *Battles and Leaders of the Civil War*.

the same rail fence, and knelt to drink on opposite sides of the same narrow stream; the men were conscious that the proceedings were unorthodox, but they said nothing of it.[36]

In Virginia in 1862, and in Mississippi the next year, informal truces were called to give soldiers opportunity to pick the luscious blackberries ripening on the no man's land that lay between the lines.[37]

Occasionally the spirit of mutual helpfulness was carried to amusing extremes. During the Georgia campaign of 1864 Rebel soldiers on picket, lacking digging implements to make rifle pits, were forced to beg spades of Yankee vedettes opposite them; and the Yanks were graciously accommodating.[38] This politeness had a parallel on the Virginia front, but with the men in gray filling the role of lenders.[39]

An instance of *noblessee oblige* more striking than these, however, grew out of the fight at Munfordville, Kentucky, in the fall of 1862. After this engagement Colonel Wilder of the Federals proposed a truce for the burying of the dead. General Chalmers of the Confederates immediately acceded, but to his dismay he found that his men were not equipped for the digging of graves. After brief deliberation he decided to call on the Yanks for assistance. Colonel Wilder very considerately lent spades for the burial of the Rebels.[40]

The spirit of friendliness that sprinkled Yankee-Rebel relations had no more eloquent expression than the musical fetes in which the two armies occasionally participated. Sometimes Federal bands played for the Rebels, as at Fredericksburg during the war's second winter when a crack group of Union musicians posted on the Northern bank of the Rappahannock staged a concert unique in the annals of war. The program began with a medley of Northern airs—patriotic tunes and war songs. This was well enough for the listeners in blue, but not to the complete liking of that part of the audience stationed on the Southern bank.

"Now give us some of ours," shouted Confederates across the river.

Without hesitation the band swung into the tunes of "Dixie," "My Maryland" and the "Bonnie Blue Flag." This brought forth a lusty and prolonged cheer from the Southerners. Finally the music swelled into the tender strains of "Home, Sweet Home," and the countryside reverberated with the cheers of thousands of men on both sides of the stream.[41]

At other times bands of the opposing armies participated in unpremeditated joint concerts. At Murfreesboro, for instance, on the night before the great battle, a Federal band began just before tattoo to play "Yankee Doodle," "Hail Columbia" and other tunes popular in Northern camps. After a little while the Union musicians yielded to the Rebel band which played a group of Southern favorites. These voluntary exchanges had continued for some time when one of the bands struck up "Home, Sweet Home." Immediately the other band joined in, and in a few moments the tune was picked up by a multitude of voices of both camps. For the brief period that the countryside reverberated with the notes of Payne's cherished song the animosities of war were lost in nostalgic reveries, and the fading away of the final notes found tears on the cheeks of scores of veterans who on the morrow were to walk unflinchingly into the maelstrom of battle.[42]

The element of competition was occasionally introduced into these informal concerts. A Confederate band would run through a tune. Then a Federal band would attempt to give a better rendition of the same piece. In these contests—forerunners of present-day "battles of bands"—the Yankees usually came off with the honors.[43]

In the absence of bands the joint fetes often took vocal form. Men on opposite sides of rivers bordering the Confederacy on several occasions united in the singing of "Home, Sweet Home." When in less mellow mood, their efforts were inclined to greater levity. In January 1863, for instance, Lieutenant W. J. Kincheloe of the Forty-ninth Virginia regiment wrote to his father: "We are on one side of the Rappahannock, the Enemy on the other. . . . Our boys will sing a Southern song, the Yankees will reply by singing the same tune to Yankee words." [44] The lieutenant's observation is substantiated by the fact that several Civil War songs had both Yankee and Rebel versions.

One co-operative venture on the Rapidan was of a religious character. Private Goodwin of a Southern regiment, following the example of many of his fellow soldiers, "got religion" during the war, and a group of about fifty of his comrades escorted him down to the river's edge to be baptized. The procession attracted the attention of the Federals, and a considerable number of them came ambling down to the opposite bank to view the proceedings. Presently the Confederates launched into the hymn, "There is a Fountain Filled with Blood." This was a tune familiar to soldiers of both armies, and many of the Yanks joined in the song. Private Goodwin was duly dipped to the satisfaction of all.[45]

This religious collaboration had an unhappy counterpart in interarmy gambling and drinking. There was a little island out in the middle of the Rappahannock where soldiers from both banks were wont to meet now and then to drown their woes in a draught of liquor.[46] Gaming between pickets, and between other troops, was rather frequent. A Rebel officer making an unexpected tour of inspection one night on the Petersburg lines was shocked to find a considerable stretch of the trenches devoid of men. On close inquiry he discovered that the absentees were, by previous arrangement, in the Federal ditches playing cards.[47]

Joint swimming parties were sometimes indulged in by troops stationed along rivers.[48] These were apt to be accompanied by a great deal of "ducking" and banter. In fact, in whatever circumstances Rebs and Yanks came into proximity, there was usually not a little of "smart talk" or "jawing."

The boys in blue would sometimes shout across a Virginia river to inquire how "old Jeff" was getting along. The Rebs would retort by inviting the Yanks to come to Richmond and see, reminding them of several previous unsuccessful efforts to reach the Confederate capital. At Vicksburg the Federals would yell out, "Haven't you Johnnies got a new general—General Starvation?" The men inside the works would come back with the queries, "Have you Yanks all got nigger wives yet? How do you like them?" Before Atlanta the Federals would cry out from their trenches, "What is Confederate money worth?" or "How much do you ask for your slaves?" From the Rebel ditches would come the taunt, "What niggers command your brigade?" or "Have the niggers improved the Yankee breed any?" [49]

A Yank who placed himself in a vulnerable position by shouting to a bedraggled Reb, "Hant you got no better clothes than those?" received the pungent answer from Private Tom Martin: "You are a set of damned fools—do you suppose we put on our good clothes to go out to kill damned dogs?" [50]

On yet another occasion a Federal holding confab with an antagonist between the picket lines said sentimentally, "Why can't this war stop? I love you like a brother." The Reb's reply, in the words of a comrade, was: "You can say more for me than I can say for you for I haven't a dambed bit of love for you." [51]

Good-natured raillery might be provoked by the most unexpected occurrences. One morning early in 1865 a large hawk came flying along over the lines before Petersburg. Soldiers from both sides immediately forgot their potshooting at each other and opened fire on the bird. It became bewildered by the cross fusillade and lit in a tall poplar tree halfway between the trenches. When finally it was shot down, both

Yanks and Rebs let out a tremendous whoop, each side claiming the honors of marksmanship and demanding possession of the prize.[52]

By far the most common form of fraternizing was the exchange of small articles of various sorts by men of the opposing camps. Throughout the war, in all portions of the armies, traffic flourished, and this despite the efforts of superior officers to put a stop to it. The usual method of procedure was for the men to meet at some intermediate point between the lines and there to swap tobacco for coffee, peanuts for pocketknives, pipes for stationery, and Southern for Northern newspapers. A Mississippian wrote his sister in 1864 from Petersburg, "We read each other's Papers in 15 minutes after the News Boys bring them from the Office." [53]

These barter sessions were frequently the occasion of mutual cussing of "bombproof" generals, of grousing over troubles—which were very much the same in both armies—of talk about home affairs, of display, with polite comment, of daguerreotypes of sweethearts, and of expression of hope for a speedy end to the war. Now and then the parley would end with a generous snort of "tanglefoot," drawn perforce from the Yankee canteen. In more than one instance the participants in these get-togethers were members of the same family—brothers, or father and son, drawn to different allegiance by the fortunes of war.[54]

Serious-minded Rebs were sometimes conscience-stricken as a result of these interminglings. A Mississippian who wrote his family of "our boys and the Yankees mixing up and talking together on friendly terms," remarked apologetically, "I threw an old dirty Yank a piece of Tobacco and He threw me a little sack of Coffee—I did not have any chat for them." [55]

A Tar Heel who had trafficked recently with the Feds confided to his father:

"I tell you the Yankees assembled around me like a parcel of buserdes [buzzards] would around a lot of dead horses I chatted [with] them about ½ hour and left I tell you I dident feel rite no way." [56]

Rebs and Yanks separated by narrow rivers developed an ingenious device for carrying on trade. Little boats, some two or three feet long, were made of bark or of scrap lumber, fitted with sails, loaded with coffee, tobacco and papers, and the sails set in such fashion as to carry the craft to the opposite shore. The recipients of the cargo on the other side would in turn load the vessel with items of exchange and head it back to the port of origin.[57] A soldier in Lee's army records the fact that on pleasant days during the spring of 1862 the waters of the Rappahannock near Fredericksburg "were fairly dotted with the fairy fleet." [58]

During the war's last winter, pickets facing each other along the lines before Petersburg, when denied the privilege of trade and communication, resorted to the expedient of tying small articles and messages to grapeshot or shell fragments and tossing them over to the rifle pits of their opponents. In this way they "flanked" the interdiction laid down by superiors.[59]

Now and then a couple of Rebs would go over and spend the night in the Yankee camps, returning just before daylight. In such instances the Yanks might give expression to their good will by filling the haversacks of the parting visitors with coffee and other delicacies rarely seen by men in gray.[60] Rebs likewise played host on occasion. A Delaware lieutenant who made a "hollering" acquaintance with a group of Confederates on picket was invited by them to a party behind the Southern lines. The Rebs called for their guest in a boat, outfitted him with civilian clothing, escorted him to the dance, introduced him to the country girls as a new recruit, and before dawn deposited him safely back on the Federal side of the river.[61]

It would be easy to exaggerate the significance of the fraternizing that dotted the Confederate war. Hatred and fighting far outweighed friendliness and intermingling. But the latter always existed in such proportions as to worry high officers. The fact that the men on both sides spoke for the most part the same language, plus the fact that many had mutual acquaintances or relatives, tended to draw them together. This, coupled with curiosity, war-weariness in both camps, failure to comprehend clearly the issues of the conflict, and the desire to trade, made it increasingly difficult to maintain a definite line of demarcation between the two camps. In the last months of the war, as defeat became more and more apparent, Rebs who went out to swap or to parley with the Yankees failed in increasing numbers to return to their side of the lines.

This inescapable urge of blue and gray to intermingle and to exchange niceties suggests that—grim war though it was—the internecine struggle of the sixties was not only in some aspect a chivalric war but that it was in many respects a crazy and a needless war as well. There is some point, at least, to the observation made by a Reb after a conference on a log with a Yankee vedette. "We talked the matter over," he said, "and could have settled the war in thirty minutes had it been left to us." [62]

CHAPTER XVII

WHAT MANNER OF MEN

THE men who marched under the Stars and Bars were impressively diverse in character. The full range of their variation can never be known, however, because one of the most fruitful sources of information—the original muster and descriptive rolls—is so incomplete. For some companies such rolls were not even prepared; for many, only a part of the required data was given; and for hundreds of others the records were lost or destroyed. But from rolls that are extant, from comments of travelers, from court-martial proceedings, memoirs, diaries and personal letters, a general idea of the South's soldiery may be obtained.

Scattered through the camps of the Confederacy were men of widely varied birth and race. The great majority of the rank and file were Southern-born, of course, but the non-native element was large enough to figure prominently in the general pattern. A considerable proportion came from the country north of Mason and Dixon's line. A random sampling of 42 descriptive rolls covering 21 regiments from six Confederate states yields the names of 86 privates born in eleven northern states.[1] Of these, 37 were natives of New York, 10 of Illinois, 9 of Pennsylvania, 7 each of Indiana, Massachusetts and Ohio, and the rest came from Connecticut, Maine, New Jersey, Vermont and Michigan. An estimate of the total number of Yankee-born men who served the cause of the South could be no more than a guess, but the figure must have run into the thousands.

The foreign-born element in Southern ranks was also large enough to demand attention. A number of companies were made up entirely of foreigners, and several regiments were composed largely of this class.[2] In some Louisiana camps orders on the drill ground were given in French to polyglot organizations containing Irish as well as Latins; and one of the most amazing incidents of the war was the objection raised by a lusty son of Erin to a dictum requiring officers to give their commands in English instead of in French—"I don't know what Oi'll do," he said to his lieutenant. "You want us to drill in English and the devil a wurd I know but French." [3]

Early in the war, Georgia rustics listened with openmouthed awe to Colonel Polignac drill his French-speaking battalion at the Richmond fairgrounds. "That-thur furriner he calls out er lot er gibberish," said one onlooker, "and thum-thur Dagoes jes maneuvers-up like Hell-beatin'-tan-bark! Jes like he wus talkin' sense!" On more than one occasion when Federals and Confederates bivouacked on adjacent sites, Germans of the opposing camps united to sing in their native tongue songs dear to the Fatherland. [4]

Louisiana, whose population in 1860 was more than one-tenth foreign, contributed more non-natives to the Southern cause than any other state. Some regiments recruited from New Orleans were made up largely of Irishmen, others of Germans, and still others combined these two groups with a miscellany from every part of the globe. Company I of the Tenth Louisiana—which Professor Lonn calls "the Cosmopolitan Regiment"—was composed of men from no less than fifteen countries; and in the First Louisiana Regiment thirty-seven nationalities were represented. [5]

Texas was next in the number of foreigners supplied for Confederate service. Several infantry and cavalry companies from Comal, Gillespie, Fayette and Colorado Counties were German. Some of the Texas Germans were notoriously unsympathetic toward the Southern cause, but many served faithfully and gallantly. From the Lone Star State likewise came companies made up largely of Irish, Mexicans and Poles. And here, as in Louisiana, many of the organizations were composed of a mixture of nationalities. [6]

Alabama had a number of companies consisting almost wholly of foreigners. Company I of the Eighth Alabama Regiment, known as the "Emerald Guards," listed 104 men (from a total of 109) who named Ireland as their birthplace. The uniform in which this company went to war was dark green, and the banner showed on one side the Confederate colors with Washington in the center, and on the other a harp enwreathed with shamrock and flashing the inscription "Erin-go-Bragh." Another Alabama company known as the "Scotch Guards" was composed largely of Scotchmen. Still others, principally those from Mobile, had large representations of Frenchmen and Germans. [7]

Virginia and South Carolina contributed many foreign-born soldiers to the Confederacy, most of whom were Germans and Irishmen from Richmond, Charleston and other large towns. In Tennessee, Memphis and Nashville each furnished several companies of foreigners. In fact there was no Southern state that did not count among its enrollees for Confederate service foreigners ranging in number from several hundred up into the thousands. Even North Carolina, which boasted the highest percentage of native population, had several companies composed almost exclusively of Germans or of Irishmen or of mixed nationalities.[8]

Most of the foreigners who fought for the South were infantrymen, though there were considerable numbers in all branches of the service. Of the various nationalities represented, the Irish were most numerous. Frequently they were rough, quarrelsome, plunderous and impervious to discipline, but for the most part they were blessed with a redeeming good humor. They adapted themselves well to the hardships of camp life, and they enjoyed an excellent reputation as fighters. Next to the Irish in number were the Germans. Their love for music enlivened the atmosphere of many encampments, and when convinced of the rightness of the Confederate cause, as they doubtless were in a majority of cases, they acquitted themselves creditably on the firing line. The British, the French, the Poles, the Canadians, the Dutch, the Austrians and the many other nationalities represented in Southern ranks all made their distinctive contributions to the Lost Cause. The total number of foreigners enrolled in the Confederate Army unfortunately must remain unknown, but there can be no doubt that the figure ran well up into the tens of thousands.[9] To this host of immigrants who wore the gray, particularly to those thousands who yielded up their lives in the service, the South owes an incalculable debt of gratitude and honor.

Another of the diverse groups in the Confederate Army was the Indian. Shortly after the formation of the Secession Government Albert Pike was sent to the trans-Mississippi country to make treaties with the various tribes residing in the red man's territory. The emissary's efforts, notably successful, prepared the way for actual recruiting. In November 1861 the Department of Indian Territory was established with Pike as commanding officer. It was Pike's intention to use Indian soldiers largely for defense of their home area, but his plan was overruled by other considerations.

When General Van Dorn began his campaign for the relief of Missouri in early 1862, four regiments and two battalions had been formed from among the trans-Mississippi red men and half-breeds. Later a fifth regiment and several battalions were created. In the latter part of 1864 the Indian troops were organized into three brigades. These were: The First Brigade, composed of Cherokees, Chickasaws and Osages, commanded by Chief Stand Watie, a valiant officer of whom General S. B. Maxey said, "I wish I had as much energy in some of my white commanders as he displays"; the Second Brigade, made up of Choctaws, led by Tandy Walker; and the Third Brigade, of Creeks and Seminoles, headed by D. N. McIntosh.[10]

A few Indians were scattered among white regiments serving east of the Mississippi. The Sixty-ninth North Carolina, recruited from the mountain district of East Tennessee and western North Carolina in 1862, had two Indian companies made up largely of Cherokees. Most of the commissioned officers were white men, but there was one lieutenant named John Astoo-ga Sto-ga, a warrior of imposing physique and good education. One of the Indian companies had a sharp encounter with Federals at Baptist Gap in the latter part of 1862. The red men were victorious, but Sto-ga was killed. His followers scalped several of the fallen Yankees.[11]

The first engagement in which trans-Mississippi Indians participated was the affair at Wilson's Creek in the autumn of 1861. The number of red men involved was small, and their chief contribution seems to have been the rousing war whoop which they had taught to their paleface comrades. In a charge led by Colonel Greer, the savage shriek, issuing from both Choctaws and Texans, blended with the Rebel yell to create surprise, if not alarm, in Union ranks.[12]

The only major encounter in which western Indians took part on a large scale was the Battle of Pea Ridge in early March 1862. As the vanguard of Pike's command came up to join Van Dorn on the eve of this fight, the red men presented a picturesque spectacle. Speaking primarily of the Cherokees, a member of the First Missouri Brigade said:

"They came trotting by our camp on their little Indian ponies, yelling forth their wild whoop. . . . Their faces were painted, and their long straight hair, tied in a queue, hung down behind. Their dress was chiefly in the Indian costume—buckskin hunting-shirts, dyed of almost every color, leggings, and moccasins of the same material, with little bells, rattles, ear-rings, and similar paraphernalia. Many of them were bareheaded and about half carried only bows and arrows, tomahawks, and war-clubs. . . . They were . . . straight, active, and sinewy in their persons and movements—fine looking specimens of the red man." [13]

But the performance of those who took part in the battle revealed patent deficiencies. The discipline of most units was unworthy of the name. General Pike permitted some, in deference to native character and inclination, to go into action with bows, arrows and hatchets. Those who had guns were little better off, on account of the inferiority of the weapons which the government had issued to them. Some who essayed forward movements were demoralized by Federal artillery, which they called Yankee wagon-guns. Their best work was accomplished under cover of trees; some, indeed, climbed up among the branches to fight.

Colonel Watie's half-breeds rendered helpful service as scouts, but the most notable episode of Indian fighting was the capture by a group of Texans and Cherokees of a Union battery. The red men in high elation took one of the pieces, surrounded it with brush and applied the torch; as the flames leaped up they danced about the conflagration and filled the air with savage yells. But the festivity was brought to a premature and tragic end. The gun was loaded, and when it became hot it went off with a resounding explosion, killing and wounding some and thoroughly frightening the rest. In the wake of the battle a few of the Indians reverted to the primitive practice of mutilating the dead. This act was condemned by the great majority, however, and by both native and white leaders.[14]

Following the Battle of Pea Ridge, activities of the red men were limited largely to raiding and scouting. In September 1862 a force led by D. H. Cooper engaged a group of Federal Indians commanded by William A. Phillips. The Confederates were victorious, but both sides acquitted themselves with credit.

The following July another clash came at Honey Springs. The Confederate regiments of Indians were led respectively by Stand Watie, Tandy Walker and D. N. McIntosh. Fighting was stubborn at first, but early in the action red men on the Southern side discovered that their powder was worthless and began to throw their guns away. Demoralization thus begun spread to the other troops and the result was defeat for the Confederates. In the Camden, Arkansas, campaign of 1864, Choctaws commanded by Tandy Walker rendered minor but valiant service.[15]

The Cherokees and Seminoles were never unanimous in their support of the South, and as Confederates suffered reverses large numbers went over to the Federals. The Cherokees were particularly susceptible to discouragement and defection. On two occasions groups belonging to the command of Colonel John Drew abandoned Confederate ranks under duress and went over to the Yankees en masse; the opinion was widely prevalent in the South that John Ross, principal chief of this nation, conspired with the Yankees for his capture. But many of the Cherokees remained loyal to the Confederacy throughout the war, and their troops were among the best of the Indian fighters. The Choctaws and the Chickasaws were overwhelmingly faithful to the Southern cause.[16]

The Indian soldiers of the Confederacy were victims of shabby treatment by their white superiors. General Pike strove assiduously to secure a square deal for them, but he was far removed from Richmond, and opposed by leaders like Van Dorn, Hindman and Holmes, who were concerned primarily with the protection of white areas and who apparently cared little for the welfare of the red men. Pay, food, clothing and weapons intended for the Indians were diverted by these commanders to other troops. Corruption and fraud were rife in the filling of contracts, and in other phases of government service. A general reorganization of late 1864 resulted in some improvement, but the change came too late to be of much benefit.

Treatment of the Indians was, indeed, one of the darkest and most regrettable episodes of Confederate history. While the contribution of the red man to the Southern cause was admittedly insignificant and marked by large-scale defection, it appears, nevertheless, that on the whole he rendered a better measure of service and honor to the Great Father at Richmond than was accorded to him in return.[17]

The visitor to Southern camps in the first year of the war might expect always to encounter a large number of Negroes. These, to be sure, were not soldiers, but their relation to the fighting force was so vital and so intimate as to merit consideration as a part of the army. Conspicuous among the Negroes attached to military personnel were the body servants. When members of slaveholding families enlisted in 1861 it was quite common for them to take along black members of the household to serve them in camp. Some of the wealthier volunteers had more than one servant, but the usual practice was for a single slave to minister to his own master or to a mess of from four to eight men; in the latter case all members "chipped in" to bear the cost of his maintenance. Non-slaveholders sometimes hired Negroes to act as body servants. The duties of these Negroes consisted mainly of cooking, washing, and of cleaning quarters. Those attached to cavalry companies were required to look after their masters' horses. Many became adept at foraging—a term frequently used in the army to dignify the practice known among civilians as stealing—to supplement the usual leanness of rations issued by commissaries.[18]

During battles the body servant usually remained in the rear out of reach of Federal shells. But a few became so thoroughly imbued with the martial spirit as to grab up muskets during battle and take pot shots at the enemy. There are several instances on record of servants thus engaged killing and capturing Federals. On at least one occasion Confederate domestics made prisoners of Negroes serving Yankee officers. When fighting abated, the colored aide usually loaded himself with canteens and haversacks and went in search of his master. If the latter was wounded, the servant carried him to shelter and sought medical assistance; if he was killed, the domestic made arrangements for his burial or escorted the body home. The relation between master and body servant was usually marked by genuine affection. Frequently intimate association extended back to childhood days. When Confederate masters were ill, they were nursed by their black companions, and when the latter were stricken, they sometimes were attended by their owners with the tenderest solicitude. There were some instances of unfaithfulness and of cruel treatment, but the circumstances of the soldier-servant relationship made these much less frequent in the army than on the plantation.

The life of the body servant was generally not a hard one. He seldom lacked for food, and he usually recouped his wardrobe in the wake of each battle from Yankee sources. He had opportunities to earn money by doing odd jobs for his master's comrades, and the stake thus acquired could be increased or diminished by sessions with fellow servants at dice or cards. Occasional visits home for provisions made it possible for him to play the hero among less fortunate inmates of the slave quarters. In camp his ready laugh—whether inspired by genuine amusement or by a keen sense of appropriateness—was a valuable stimulant to soldier morale, as was his proficiency with song and guitar.[19]

It was with real regret, therefore, that most private soldiers dispensed with the service of their colored associates during the second and third years of conflict. But the increasing scarcity of provisions in the army and the greater need of their labor by civilians made it necessary for the Negroes to be sent home. Those who remained in camp after 1863 were largely the servants of commissioned officers or were employed by the government as musicians, cooks, nurses, hostlers and wagon-drivers.[20]

The largest group of Negroes connected with military affairs were those employed for the construction of fortifications. Early in the war great numbers were hired to throw up works in seacoast and river areas and in other strategic portions of the Confederacy. The intrenchments used in resisting McClellan's peninsula movement were largely the work of Virginia slaves. At first planters responded generously to government calls for laborers, but in the second year of the war impressment sometimes had to be used, and in 1864 levies became the general rule. In February 1864 a Confederate law was passed authorizing the Secretary of War to conscript 20,000 Negroes for military labor. This was only partially due to dwindling patriotism of slaveowners, as many planters felt that their Negroes were neglected and abused while in government employ. The controversy between state and national authorities as to the constitutionality of impressment also colored the picture. Opposition to compulsion eventually reached such proportions as to hinder greatly the program of defense.

Planters who objected to the use of slaves for government work were not without grounds for their attitude. The labor was unduly strenuous. In marshy areas and in rainy weather Negroes suffered from exposure and from disease. Food was often inadequate and poorly prepared. Medical attention was frequently deficient. Supervising authorities were sometimes delinquent in releasing laborers at the end of their period of service. All in all the lot of those who toiled on fortifications was a hard one, and "the 'pressin agent" who was sent around to collect the required workers was dreaded by masters and slaves alike.[21]

Negroes served as soldiers in both the Revolution and the War of 1812, and when the Confederacy was created there was a disposition in some quarters to take free men of color into Southern armies. A regiment was organized in New Orleans, but it was not accepted for Confederate service. In 1863 a proposal to arm slaves was launched by the press, but after a brief discussion the subject was dropped. In January 1864 General Patrick Cleburne revived the question by advocating to a group of fellow officers the enlistment of a large force of slaves and offering them freedom as a reward for faithful service. When Cleburne's action came to the notice of President Davis he ordered suppression of the whole matter. But as the gloom of defeat settled down over the South, sentiment favoring the enlistment of Negroes increased. In November 1864 Davis intimated a willingness to consider a limited use of blacks in the ranks. Finally in March 1865 Congress passed a law authorizing the President to call for as many as 300,000 slaves to serve as soldiers. No assurance of freedom was given. In the month that followed a few companies were organized. Colored recruits attired in resplendent uniforms paraded the streets of Richmond only to be splattered with mud thrown by contemptuous white urchins.[22] The ironic spectacle of Negroes fighting for the cause of Southern independence and the perpetuation of their own bondage was prevented from materializing by Lee's capitulation. Slaves rendered tremendously valuable service to the South by their labor on farms, in factories and on fortifications. There were many Confederate leaders who thought they would also give faithful assistance on the field of battle. But the alacrity with which the great majority seized freedom when it was brought to their reach by Federals gives rise to serious doubt of their fighting long for the Confederacy on any condition save that of general emancipation.[23]

Soldiers who marched in Rebel ranks belonged to a wide variety of occupations and professions. This is brought out by examination of the company rolls. One hundred and seven of these representing 7 states, 28 regiments and 9,000 private soldiers, well distributed as to locality, revealed over 100 occupational classifications. Over half of the enlistees —5,600 out of 9,000—listed themselves as farmers.[24] Other well-represented groups in the order of their numerical strength were: students, 474; laborers, 472; clerks, 321; mechanics, 318; carpenters, 222; merchants, 138; and blacksmiths, 116. Other vocations having fifty or more representatives were: sailors, 88; doctors, 75; painters, 69; teachers, 68; shoemakers, 57; and lawyers, 51. Among lesser groups there were 48 overseers, 39 printers, 36 masons, 35 tailors, 31 millers, 31 engineers, 23 coopers, and 21 bakers. Listed also were apothecaries, artists, barbers, bookkeepers, butchers, carriage makers, colliers, cooks, dancing masters, dentists, distillers, drummers, fishermen, horse traders, jewelers, manufacturers, ministers, musicians, patternmakers, peddlers, photographers, planters, publishers, sheriffs, stage drivers, tanners, weavers and wheelwrights. Surprises are occasionally encountered in the list. One recruit is put down as a convict, another as a gambler, a third as a rogue, a fourth as a speculator, and several as gentlemen.

The ages of those who wore the gray were no less diverse than their vocations. Descriptive rolls usually gave the ages of recruits at the time of their induction, and a sample taken from these records, consisting of 11,000 infantry privates most of whom enlisted in 1861-1862, and representing 11 states, 94 regiments, and 141 companies, revealed a personnel varying from mere boys to old men.[25] One recruit on the list was a lad of 13, 3 were 14 years of age, 31 were 15, 200 were 16, and 366 were 17. Boys under 18 years constituted approximately one-twentieth of the 11,000 cases examined. With the 18-year-olds the figure jumped sharply to 971, the highest of all the age groups, and within the limits of 18-25 over one-third of the total cases were included. A decline set in with 23-year-olds, but each age was well represented on through the 20's, and the number of cases included within the 18-29 range was approximately four-fifths of the total. Men in their 30's comprised approximately one-sixth of the aggregate and those in the 40's, one-twenty-fifth. Eighty-six of the 11,000 fell in the 50-59 group, 12 were 60-69, 1 was 70, and the oldest was 73.

The distribution suggested by this sample is applicable primarily to the first year and a half of conflict. The second conscription act may have increased the relative strength in the army population of the 36-45 age group, but the ratio of men above 45 and of boys below 18 was probably higher in 1861 and early 1862 than at any other time. The tidal wave of enthusiasm that swept hundreds of old and young into the ranks at the war's beginning lost its force with the passing of time, and many of extreme ages, beset with debility and with camp-weariness, returned to their homes after a year of service. The conscription law of February 1864 comprehended 17-year-olds and men from 46-50, but these were to be employed only as a reserve force. The great majority of additions to the army after 1862 came from the 18-45 group, through upward extension of the conscription age and revocation of exemptions, substitutions and details.[26] There is apparently little foundation for the charge made by Grant late in the war that the Confederacy was robbing the cradle and the grave to sustain its forces. The overwhelming bulk of the Southern Army from beginning to end appears to have been made up of persons ranging in age from 18 to 35.

Some of the oldsters of the Confederate Army rendered distinguished service. Private George Taylor of the Sixtieth Virginia Infantry, whose three-score years earned for him the sobriquet of father of the regiment, was cited for gallantry at Frayser's Farm. A Mississippian of advanced age named John Thompson, who enlisted as a private when the war began, fought so valorously at Belmont and at Shiloh as to win a commission. After his death at Chickamauga General Patton Anderson paid him high tribute in an official report as a man and as a soldier.[27] But in all probability most men of fifty years or more who had to march in the ranks were more of a burden than a benefit to the cause which they so patriotically espoused. Exposure, inadequate nourishment, and the strain of campaigning combined with ripe age to acquaint them better with hospital and wagon train than with the field of action. The fate of elderly Rebs is well exemplified by the case of a private, E. Pollard, of the Fifth North Carolina Regiment. This soldier, whose seventy-three years entitle him perhaps to the distinction of being the oldest man regularly enlisted in Confederate service, was taken into the army as a substitute in July 1862. In September 1862 a surgeon who examined him reported that he had been unfit for duty three-fourths of the time since his enlistment. Shortly thereafter he was given a discharge for being "incapable of performing the duties of a soldier on account of Rheumatism and old age." [28]

The boy soldiers made a good record. There were a number of instances of teen-age Rebs receiving mention for bravery in official reports and orders. Following an engagement in early May 1862, General Beauregard said in a general order:

"The Commander of the Forces desires to call the especial attention of the Army to the behavior of Private John Mather Sloan of the 9th Texas Vols., a lad of only 13 years of age who having lost a leg in the affair . . . near Farmington exclaimed 'I have but one regret I shall not soon be able to get at the enemy.'"

The general stated his intention at some future time of publicly decorating the hero with a badge of merit. If this occasion materialized, how the heart of Private Sloan must have thrilled to be thus honored by the "Grand Creole." [29]

At Shiloh fifteen-year-old John Roberts was frequently in advance of his company, according to the subsequent report of his commanding officer, "was knocked down twice by spent balls," "had his gun shattered to pieces," and "throughout the whole action . . . displayed the coolness and courage of a veteran." [30]

During an engagement before Atlanta in July 1864, Eddie Evans, a mere boy of the Twenty-fourth Mississippi, asked for the privilege of carrying the colors, and he afterward "bore them with such conspicuous coolness and gallantry," according to the statement of his colonel, "as to elicit the admiration of all. At one time he took his stand in advance of the line without any protection in an open field, distant from the enemy's line not more than fifty yards, waving his colors defiantly and called upon his comrades to rally to the flag." [31]

Some of the youngsters seen about Southern campfires were buglers and drummer boys who had regularly enlisted. Others were unattached waifs adopted by the troops as mascots.[32] A most interesting group having semiofficial capacity were the drillmasters borrowed temporarily from the cadet corps of Southern military schools to assist in the instruction of raw recruits. Most of these boys were quite young but they called out their orders with impressive manliness.

A North Carolina historian, writing of the Hillsboro Military Academy contingent, said:

"It was certainly a novel sight to see the little cadets from thirteen years old and upwards, each tramping his squad of grown and sometimes grizzled men, over the parade ground and to witness the grim seriousness with which the future veterans took their military subjection to their juniors in years." [33]

The work of these youthful instructors and of their co-workers from the Virginia Military Institute and from a number of other campuses was invaluable.[34]

Naturally boys who came into such close contact with army life were fired with a burning desire to smell the smoke of battle. After brief and trying sessions with their studies most of them realized their ambitions. A few of the strongest-willed contrived means of entering immediately into active service. Among these was Charlie Jackson of Memphis, Tennessee, who served as drillmaster for a company raised by his father. When the troops departed for Shiloh, Charlie would not be left behind, and against his parents' entreaties he took an undersized musket made specially for his use, and went with his erstwhile pupils into battle. He served gallantly until near the end of the first day's fighting when a mortal wound brought an end to his career as a soldier.[35]

Under a program sanctioned by government authorities late in the war, students of various Southern institutions were organized into companies and held for reserve purposes.[36] The crowning achievement of college boys on the field of battle was that of Virginia Military Institute cadets in the affair at New Market, May 15, 1864. When General Breckenridge engaged the Federal forces led by Sigel, his command consisted in part of a battalion of over two hundred boys from the Virginia college under one of their professors. As the fight progressed the cadets marched steadily forward under heavy fire to a position beyond the town. There they were called on to join with a Virginia regiment to take a battery that was inflicting serious damage on the Rebel lines. In the advance that ensued the college youths, because of their greater endurance and ardor, outdistanced their veteran comrades, and as a consequence they had to stand in a rain of bullets until the older men could come up for the final dash. But they held their formation and when the order came to charge at double quick they rushed gallantly forward. The guns were soon captured, and when a cadet mounted one of the captured pieces and waved the Institute flag there was a wild yell of triumph. In this notable victory at New Market, the boys won for themselves and their school an undying glory, but at great cost. When the casualties of battle were counted, it was found that the toll of dead and wounded included fifty-four cadets, eight of whom were killed.[37]

Considerable argument has been exchanged as to the age and identity of the most youthful person to serve as a full-fledged Confederate soldier. In 1901 a Floridian wrote the editor of the *Confederate Veteran* stating that when he surrendered in April 1865 he lacked one month of being fifteen years old, and that his service dated back to 1861. If this man's claim be true, he would appear to have undisputed title to the distinction of being the youngest Rebel.[38]

Occasionally, but very rarely, a woman was to be found in Confederate ranks posing, of course, as a man. The motive of some who laid aside skirts for uniforms was immoral, but in other cases the action was prompted by desire to be associated with their husbands. Such was the case with Malinda Blalock, of the Twenty-sixth North Carolina Regiment. When James Moore, recruiting for Company F of this organization, proposed to enlist Keith Blalock, the husband swore not to enroll unless his wife was allowed to join the army with him. Moore agreed to take them and to keep in confidence the identity of Malinda. The latter enlisted under the name of Sam Blalock. For two months she drilled and did all the other duties of an ordinary soldier. Her disguise was not revealed until Keith Blalock was given a discharge for physical unfitness; Malinda then informed Colonel Vance of her true status and was sent home with her husband.[39]

A story so remarkable as to create a doubt of its authenticity is that of one Madame Loreta Velasquez as told by herself. Born in Cuba in 1842 of Spanish parentage, she was sent to New Orleans to complete her education. After some months in school devoted, it seems, more to dreaming of exploits of Jeanne d'Arc and other adventurous characters than to serious study, she eloped with a young United States Army officer. When secession came she persuaded her husband to cast his lot with the South. She also confided to him her own determination to join the army. He tried desperately to dissuade her, but when he had departed for camp she donned a uniform, after fitting herself with a wire frame so shaped as to give her figure a masculine appearance, glued on a false mustache, adopted the title of Lieutenant Harry T. Buford, and set out for Arkansas where she recruited a company of volunteers. As an officer unattached, she took part in the battles of Bull Run, Ball's Bluff and Fort Donelson. At intervals she resumed feminine garb and worked as a spy. In the spring of 1862, after fleeing from New Orleans authorities who had discovered her sex, she enlisted in the Twenty-first Louisiana Regiment. She fought in the battle of Shiloh and was wounded while helping to bury the dead of that engagement. This misfortune revealed her disguise a second time. But afterward she frequently posed as a man, and for the remainder of the war she was engaged in spying and plotting. If Madame Velasquez's account be true, her career was indeed a phenomenal one; if it be false, she deserves high rating as a fictionist.[40]

The variation in education and culture which characterized army personnel has already been noted to some extent in other connections. Here and there among the rank and file were to be found men well versed in the classics and in other branches of learning. Robert Stiles told of a comrade who kept a diary in modern Greek.[41] Other reliable sources reveal instances of private soldiers poring over Latin readers and Greek grammars, or reading the writings of the literary masters.[42] A South Carolinian wrote his mother that he had been reading Macaulay's history but that he had been unable to get to the fifth volume. "I wish to survive this war," he said, "if only to have that pleasure." [43]

The number of well-educated privates scattered through the ranks was larger in 1861 than at any later time because, as a general rule, unusual abilities won promotion in a fairly short time, and recruits of this type were not frequently available as replacements. But in certain choice organizations made up largely of men of means and culture this was not the case.

The First Company of Rockbridge Artillery had on its roll four masters of arts, twenty graduates of Washington College, forty or more students of this institution and of the University of Virginia, and many more who had attended other colleges. Company E of the Eleventh Virginia was composed, for the most part, of boys from Lynchburg College, and its first captain was one of their professors. The First Maryland Infantry, Hampton's Legion, the First Virginia, the Third

Alabama, Company F of the Twenty-first Virginia, the Richmond Howitzer Battalion, the Oglethorpe Light Infantry of Savannah, the Washington Artillery and several other volunteer organizations also had a large
proportion of well-bred and educated men.[44]

Cavalry and artillery units seem to have held special attraction for
scions of first families. In instances where large numbers of exceptional
men belonged to the same company, only a few could hope to win
commissions within the organization, and many frowned upon the idea
of leaving their congenial associates to seek offices elsewhere. In other
words the opinion prevailed in these select circles that it was better to
be a private in the Richmond Howitzer Battalion or in Hampton's
Legion than a lieutenant in most other groups. This sentiment, coupled
with the difficulty of getting transfers, explains to a considerable extent
the continued presence in the ranks throughout the war of many men of
good education and of high social standing.

But the number of these men, like other pleasanter concepts of
Southern history, has been exaggerated. The error may be attributed in
part to writers of the moonlight-and-magnolia school who saw in the
old South a society richly endowed with wealthy landowners who devoted their leisure to the classics. But a more immediate basis for the
misconception is to be found perhaps in the greater articulateness of
the men composing the choice companies. As a general rule the most
interesting and the most widely read of regimental histories and personal memoirs were written by members of the Rockbridge Artillery,
of the Richmond Howitzers, and of other exceptional organizations.
These books naturally emphasized the cultural and social attainment
of the authors' particular groups.[45] There was a tendency for readers
to infer that the companies thus described were representative of the
army as a whole. Veterans of more ordinary groups either remained
silent or wrote volumes of less charm and of a more limited circulation.
The result was distortion in favor of the select few.

At the opposite end of the scale were the illiterate, and their number was considerable. When Company A of the Eleventh North Carolina Infantry was mustered into service 27 men of the 100 enrolled had
to make their marks when called on to sign the descriptive roll. In
another Tar Heel company 36 out of 72 privates signed with an X; in
a third, 30 out of 80, in a fourth 54 out of 100; and the average for 14
companies of thirteen different regiments was 40 out of 100. The ratio
of illiteracy in these units was undoubtedly higher than in the general
run of Confederate organizations, but the great majority of companies

Courtesy Confederate Museum, Richmond, Virginia

A BOY SOLDIER

Randolph Fairfax, killed at the battle of Fredericksburg, December 13, 1862. He enlisted in August 1861 at eighteen as a private in the famous Rockbridge Artillery. The picture was probably taken shortly after his enlistment.

BOY SOLDIERS OF THE CONFEDERACY

John Kennedy (left), Company A, 3rd Tennessee Regiment, and Enoch Hancock, Company A, 3rd Tennessee Regiment. The picture was taken early in the war when they were seventeen.

throughout the army had anywhere from one to a score of members who could not write their names.

Soldier correspondence and other firsthand evidence indicates that most of the Rebel rank and file lay between the two educational extremes. They were neither learned nor illiterate, though it must be admitted that those who were barely literate were much more numerous than those of fair education. Their schooling, like their culture, reflected in a general way the yeoman society to which most of them belonged.[46]

The thought patterns of common soldiers were interesting and varied. Prejudices were numerous and strong. Antipathies of the poor toward the rich and of the well-born toward the underprivileged were not so much in evidence as other aversions, but caste consciousness was present to a limited extent, and class friction occasionally provided the spark for disturbances in camp. Yeomen resented the special status enjoyed by planters under the fifteen and twenty-Negro law. A North Carolinian wrote his wife in the fall of 1864 that she might expect him home soon because "all of the gentel men has got out of it [the war] and i don't intend to put my Life betwen them and their propty." [47]

A Texas private attempted to incite his comrades to desert in September 1863 by saying publicly to them, "It makes me mad to hear poor men that have nothing and are living in small huts, and on other peoples' land, hold up for the South." [48] The feeling that soldiers who owned slaves received better treatment by company officers than that accorded the poor caused another Texan to raise such a row as to receive a severe court-martial sentence for mutiny.[49]

Sensitiveness to class seems to have been voiced more frequently by the rich than by the poor. George Cary Eggleston recalled an instance in a Virginia company where a young private of superior social standing forced a public apology from a lieutenant of ordinary background who had dared to put him on double duty for missing roll call. A Georgian refused in 1861 to obey an order on the ground that the officer issuing the command was no gentleman. Corporal John Hutchins on being called to task for a minor infraction said to his superior, "God damn you, I own niggers up the country," and when private John Shanks was ordered from the drill field to the guardhouse for inebriation he blurted out to his captain, "I will not do it. I was a gentleman before I joined your damned company and by God you want to make a damned slave of me." [50]

A Mississippian who was invited by a colonel to dine at his mess was enraged when he found out that the officers had already eaten and that he was expected to share a second meal with a clerk. The aggrieved soldier wrote later to his wife that he told the colonel's aide "that I considered myself a gentleman, treated every body gentlemanly & demanded the Same of every body & that I eat at Nobodys Second table, not even Gen'l Beauregard." Eggleston testified that he personally knew of "numberless cases in which privates . . . declined dinner and other invitations from officers who had presumed upon their shoulder straps in asking the company of their social superiors." [51]

The aversion of aristocratic privates to plebeian officers sometimes extended to men of high rank. A case in point is that of a young Mississippi gentleman whom the fortunes of war in 1864 placed under the authority of Nathan B. Forrest. The chagrined grandee wrote in his diary:

"The dog's dead: finally we are under N. Bedford Forrest . . . [a circumstance that] I have dreaded since the death of the noble Van Dorn. . . . 'The Wizzard' now commands us . . . and I must express my distaste to being commanded by a man having no pretension to gentility—a negro trader, gambler,—an ambitious man, careless of the lives of his men so long as preferment be en prospectu. Forrest may be & no doubt is, the best Cav officer in the West, but I object to a tyrannical, hotheaded vulgarian's commanding me."

Subsequent entries in this soldier's journal indicate no abatement of his antipathy to his commoner general.[52]

The more frequent manifestations of class prejudice on the part of aristocrats were not due solely to greater touchiness on the subject; another factor was the greater impunity with which they could express their sentiment. An Englishman who served in the Confederate Army told of an officer—unpopular because of his assumption of airs—slapping a soldier with a sword during drill. The recipient of the blow threw down his rifle, stepped from the ranks and stabbed the officer to death with his Bowie knife. The company "looked on and applauded; the culprit quietly wiped his knife, resumed his place in the ranks, and dress parade proceeded as if nothing had happened!" Incidents such as this were reckoned as affairs of honor, according to the Englishman, and courts-martial took no cognizance of them.[53] This statement is probably exaggerated, but it derives partial substantiation, at least, from the complaint of a prominent military judge to President Davis that "to convict a soldier of any offense, who has social position, friends, and influence is but a mockery of form." [54]

Flare-ups of prejudice were less frequent as the war progressed. The tightening of discipline required increasing submissiveness of insubordinate aristocrats; common exposure of rich and poor to the dangers of battle and the hardships of camp enhanced mutual respect, and in some cases produced intimate friendships between men of social extremes. A glimpse of the metamorphosis is afforded by the statement of a Low Country youth who served in Hampton's Legion:

"It would have seemed strange to me once in my ignorance of the world to have found literary taste among mechanics and tradesmen; and yet I have found instances in my own company . . . of admirable taste and large reading." [55]

Prejudice of rural troops toward those from the city was evidenced by the bandying of such sobriquets as "parlor soldiers" and "kid glove boys." [56] Metropolitan dandies retorted by ridiculing farm youths for their rusticity. Provincialism likewise found expression in the nicknames applied by soldiers of one state to those of another. Virginians were called the "Buttermilk Brigade"; South Carolinians, "Sand Lappers"; Alabamians, "Yellow Hammers"; Georgians "Goober Grabbers"; and Louisianians, "Tigers."

Local attachment was so strong that Confederate authorities were forced to keep troops of the same state brigaded together, even when military expediency called for their separation. Concession to particularism was carried to the extreme of providing separate hospitals for the sick and wounded of each state. Difficulties between soldiers of different localities were frequent. Mississippians who were put in the same brigade with Florida troops for the Perryville fight accused their unwelcome associates of shooting at them instead of at the Yankees; when subsequently this hybrid organization passed a Mississippi division on parade, men of the latter yelled out the greeting, "Come on out of that Brigade—we won't fire on you." [57]

Troops of the various states were very jealous of their reputation in battle, and woe to that officer or newspaper representative who seemed in his report to favor Tennesseans at the expense of Texans or to give less than a full measure of glory to each of the units composing the Confederacy.[58] One of the factors which caused so much opposition to consolidation of skeleton regiments was dread of the loss of state identity.[59]

The tendency was widespread for soldiers composing one army to disparage those of another. Rebs who followed Bragg and Joe Johnston referred to those of Lee's command as "Jeff Davis pets"; and they attributed victories on the Virginia front to the fact that Yankees in that locality did not fight so hard as those opposed to Western commands. Lee's men in turn berated the fighting qualities of the Army of Tennessee.[60] Shortly after Pemberton's capitulation an Alabamian serving with Lee wrote in disgust of "the imbecility of officers and the cowardice of our men at Vixburg." The surrender of that city was, in his opinion, "the most disgraceful affair in the history of our country," and his chief consolation was that he was not involved in the shame. "If I live to be a hundred year's old," he said, "I shall always be proud to know that I once belonged to the Army of N. Va." [61]

After Chancellorsville another of Lee's soldiers wrote to his father in North Alabama:

"Tell old Bragg for God's sake not to let the Yanks whip him as he usually does when this army gaines a victory . . . If the armys of the West were worth a goober we could soon have piece on our own terms." [62]

When Longstreet was sent to the assistance of Bragg late in 1863, the troops composing his command took a condescending attitude toward their comrades of the Chattanooga encampment. One of Longstreet's men began to pine for his Virginia connection shortly after his arrival in the West, but he professed himself "willing to help Bragg out of the mud before we go." After the battle of Chickamauga another railed out against Bragg's troops for their failure to back up the Eastern units. "Had we some of the Va army to have supported us," he said, "There would have been no trouble; these Western troops dont know how to fight Yankees." [63]

One of the aversions most frequently expressed was that of infantrymen for cavalrymen. The term "buttermilk cavalry" had almost universal use among walking Rebs as a derogatory sobriquet. The connotation was apparently twofold: softness and thievery—foot soldiers envisaged equestrians lolling about on their mounts begging or stealing buttermilk and other delicacies while they themselves toiled along for endless miles on half rations. An Alabamian expressed a widespread sentiment when he said that every cavalryman ought to have a board tied on his back and the word "thief" written thereon so that good people might be on guard against their depredations. But this branch of the service was more usually condemned for uselessness and cowardice.[64] Whenever a cavalry unit rode by a group of infantrymen, the latter would almost invariably turn loose a flood of invective and derision.[65] One hard-bitten marcher said that the mounted service steered so clear of dangerous combat as practically to constitute a life insurance company.[66]

After one of Early's Valley disasters in the fall of 1864, another infantryman expostulated:

"Our cavalry lost all their artillery . . . I do wish that the Yankees would capture all the Cavalry. . . . They never will fight So I think it is useless to have them in the Army Eating rations." [67]

General Longstreet was alleged to have made the statement following Chickamauga that it was on this battlefield that he first saw a dead Rebel with spurs on.[68] But there was frequently a note of envy in disparagements such as these. The dream of countless footsore infantrymen as they trudged along through the mud stooping beneath the weight of equipment, their impoverished "innards" murmuring protest at every step, was a transfer to the cavalry and the sweet life that would thus be achieved—relief from the grime, sweat and the pain of walking, abundant opportunity to forage, periodic visits home for new horses, pretty girls far and wide brought within easy reach, and virtual certainty of arriving at the nether end of the war in safety and in soundness.

Such was the cavalry as the ordinary Reb envisioned it. And if he had a younger brother at home yearning for the army, he forgot his aspersions and wrote to his parents:

"Tell Him . . . to Join the cavalry . . . if He can not get into the Commisary or Quartermasters Department to never Join as a private . . . but by all means to Join the Cavalry—and bear in mind that a private in The Infantry is the worse place he can possibly be put into in this war—so if he wants to have a good time Join the Cavalry." [69]

And hundreds if not thousands of Rebs made their dreams come true by deserting the infantry and enlisting with Forrest, with Wirt Adams, and with other mounted leaders.[70]

Antipathy of cavalry toward infantry was inconsiderable, though the former did apply to the latter the uncomplimentary term of "web feet," and there was some resentment of the scorn which the foot soldiers expressed for their conduct as fighters. As a general rule, however, equestrians shrugged their shoulders good-naturedly at revilings and congratulated themselves on their good fortune at being able to do their campaigning on horseback. Typical of many was the attitude expressed by a Lone Star cavalryman who wrote when he heard of the commissioning of an infantry acquaintance: "I wood rather be corporal in company F of the Texas Rangers than to be first Lieu in a flat foot company." [71]

There was a pervasive feeling among volunteers that conscripts were second-rate soldiers, and manifestations of this attitude tended undoubtedly to injure the service. When recruits were inducted under the draft legislation they were already in a bad frame of mind because of the stigma attached to compulsion; the scornful glances and the contemptuous remarks which greeted them in camp were ill-adapted to the making of fighters. [72]

Many conscripts, particularly those brought in by the laws of 1862, were good soldier material, and had they been accorded a wholesome reception by volunteers, the majority of them might have fitted congenially and usefully into the military organization. Some developed into first-class troops in spite of the antipathy which encompassed them. After Fredericksburg General James H. Lane reported that conscripts recently added to his brigade conducted themselves creditably, and General A. P. Hill made the significant observation that in this affair they showed an earnest desire to win the respect of their veteran comrades. Major John Harris who commanded a Tennessee brigade at Murfreesboro paid high tribute to the performance of conscripts who served under him in that battle. [73]

But the great majority of testimony, both of officers and of privates, bristled with such uncomplimentary epithets as cowards, skulkers, shammers, useless and worthless. One colonel declared that he would rather have his regiment reduced to a battalion and his rank to that of a major than to replenish his organization with men forced into service. [74] There was undoubtedly a factual justification for much of the criticism, but few veterans realized that their own unfriendliness contributed markedly to the unhappy situation of which they complained.

The contempt for conscripts was mild in comparison to that provoked by militia and reserves. Kate Cumming told of hearing a soldier mimicking "Joe Brown's Pets," as Georgia militiamen were called, from the top of a boxcar in Marietta. This Reb told piteously of his treatment; how he had been in the service for two whole weeks and as yet had not received a furlough; and how he and other brave reservists were nobly defending the rear of Bragg's army.[75]

An Alabamian reported that when a militia unit was assigned to guard duty in the vicinity of the camp, soldiers of his regiment would go out, take away the guards' guns and compel them to sit for long periods on logs.[76] As for fighting, few full-fledged Rebs expected that of "Bob-tail militia." "They had just as well stay . . . [home]," wrote one of Joe Johnston's veterans in 1864; "they aint worth a low country cow tick." [77] And when one of Lee's men heard that state troops had participated in the defense of Petersburg late in the war he exclaimed: "The militia fought! Long be it remembered." [78]

Another object of great contempt was the staff officer. When Rebs saw young aides dashing about in fine uniforms carrying messages and performing other duties with airs bespeaking a sense of unusual importance, they were annoyed. The feeling that such officers used family influence to get soft positions caused them to be designated by some as yellow sheep-killing dogs, which term was soon shortened to "yaller dogs." When one of these officers rode by, Rebs would begin whistling and whooping as if they were calling hounds.[79] As Hood's army was falling back from Nashville after severe fighting in December 1864, a staff officer who came up ostentatiously to a mud-splattered infantryman and ordered him to halt and face the foe received the significant reply: "You go to hell. I've been there." [80]

In the canine category also were placed those ordinary soldiers who because of pretended ailments hung back with the wagon train on the march or during battle. The epithet applied to these shammers was wagon-dogs, and when Terry's Texas Rangers rode by them they raised a song, written allegedly by a cavalryman; it ran like this:

> Come all you wagon dogs, rejoice—
> I will sing you a song,
> If you'll join in the chorus—bow wow wow;
> When we go to leave this world,
> We will go above with sheets unfurled—
> bow wow wow.[81]

Court-martial proceedings indicate that prejudices of nationality sometimes figured in disturbances among enlisted men. Private Henry Brandes of Hampton's Legion received a prison sentence for calling a sentinel an "Irish son of a bitch," and another South Carolinian was punished for denouncing a corporal of the guard as a "blind Dutch son of a bitch." [82] Mississippi regiments stationed at Iuka early in the war were opposed to the induction of Irish levee-builders into their organizations, and when officers forced acceptance of the foreign recruits a free-for-all fight ensued.[83]

Certain random types that appeared in Rebel ranks require special notice. Almost every regiment had a braggart who regaled his comrades at every opportunity with tales of his magnificent doings from early childhood down to the present. His accounts were sometimes listened to because of lack of other diversion, but again he would be taunted into silence. Closely akin to the boaster was the self-seeker—the man who in private life had perhaps made a splash as a petty politician, and who in the army became hell-bent for promotion. This type, too, was the butt of many scornful remarks. The dandy was also in evidence. He sported foppishly cut coats and fancy boots, combed his long hair back over his ears, pinned up one side of his hat, donned a feather and imagined himself a cavalier.

Occasionally there was a snob, such as a youngster from Natchez who refused to join one company because it was composed of commoners, and who, when he finally joined another, looked down his nose at most of his associates. "We are two distinct parties," he said on one occasion, "the Aristocrats and the democrats," and he professed nothing but disdain for the latter. He took offense at his colonel for "putting on airs," ceased saluting him, and swore to call him to task after the war for failure to proffer the recognition due one of his high social standing. His attitude was identical with that of another snob who wrote:

"It is galling for a gentleman to be absolutely and entirely subject to the orders of men who in private life were so far his inferiors, & who when they met him felt rather like taking off their hats to him than giving him law & gospel." [84]

Now and then a brute was found whose soul was so hardened as to make him seemingly impervious to ordinary human emotions. Such a character was a Tennessean who sang in battle from sheer joy of slaughtering, and who would yell out with utmost indifference, "Good-by, Jim," or "Good-by, Sam" as comrades fell one by one at his side; likewise the Louisianian who ran his bayonet through a pig on the march, tossed the gun across his shoulder as if nothing had happened, and bore the squealing animal aloft while it died a slow and painful death.[85]

Another type was the arch-plunderer, a good example of which was Sam Nunnally of the Twenty-first Virginia. Periodically Sam would disappear from camp for interims varying from one to three days. At the end of these absences he would return as mysteriously as he had vanished, but invariably with a plausible excuse and a load of spoils. He was particularly adept at playing wounded after a fight to rifle the pockets of the dead. After one night of such lurid activity he came sneaking into camp with three watches, several knives, some money and various other articles. On another occasion, a foraging excursion among the living yielded not only a large supply of food and other provisions, but a horse for transporting the thief and his prizes.[86]

Almost every regiment had a prankster who was quick to make fun at the expense of the unwary. If a hirsute comrade wished to borrow a razor, he would refuse him positively, but at the same time he would slyly offer his tonsorial services. If the proffer was accepted, the self-appointed barber would shave one half the customer's face with great care, then pocket his razor and take to flight in a roar of laughter.[87] Usually there was a greenhorn for every such mischief-maker—the mentality of a few Rebs ran so low, indeed, as to require their discharge from the service—and the lot of these dullards was as cruel as it was amusing.[88] One such creature was honored with sham election to the post of fifth lieutenant. After the balloting he inquired with all seriousness into the nature of his duties. His electors professed ignorance on the score, and sent him to the lieutenant. This officer, sensing the hoax immediately, replied without hesitation: "His duties are to carry water and catch fleas out of the soldiers' beds." The unsophisticate proceeded to conform in good faith to these instructions until someone convinced him that the whole thing was a joke.[89]

In another instance a recruit of very short stature was brought into camp. Some of his comrades, adjudging him too small to carry a musket, assumed the role of doctors, stripped him, tapped his chest, went through various other motions of a medical examination, and wrote out with charcoal on a scrap of newspaper a certificate of physical disability. The examinee, according to instructions, presented this to his colonel, who laughed and forwarded the case to the brigade surgeon. As a consequence of the joke the recruit received a long furlough.[90]

Eccentrics of various sorts were scattered among the rank and file. An old country gentleman who enlisted in the Twenty-first Virginia took an umbrella to camp, and in sun or rain, on the march and in the field, he insisted on seeking shelter beneath this canopy. His comrades jibed him freely, but to no avail; the parasol remained a constant companion for the duration of his service.[91]

Some of the troops who hailed from the West were very rough in appearance. A Louisianian who in 1863 watched a group of 400 Texans ride by his plantation reported that they bore no resemblance to soldiers. "If the Confederacy has no better soldiers than those we are in A bad roe for stumps," he said; "they looke more like Baboons mounted on gotes than anything else." [92]

Rough-looking likewise were the Mississippi flatboatmen and wharf hands from the waterfronts of Memphis, New Orleans, Mobile and other cities of the Confederacy.[93] Among these, as well as among other groups of formidable mien, there were many individuals whose chief crudities were those of external appearance. But it cannot be denied that the Southern Army had its share of rogues and desperadoes. In Mississippi, Governor Pettus pardoned a number of convicts on condition that they would join the army.[94] From among Federals in Southern military prisons several companies of troops were recruited, and these "galvanized Yankees," as they were called, were generally a tough lot.[95] But cutthroats, robbers and knaves were by no means found only among those who came from behind prison walls. Inspection reports and court-martial proceedings cite numerous instances of brigandage and criminality among recruits drawn from the country at large. Some of the irregular cavalry units operating in border districts appear to have been composed largely of thugs.

Another type encountered with regrettable frequency was the loafer. Rebs of this species imposed on their messmates by seeking the lighter duties of cooking, bringing water and cutting wood. They evaded the hardships of campaigning by malingering. When the order came to march they would rush to the surgeon with some complaint calculated to secure assignment to "Company Q," as the sick list was called, so that they might ride the wagon train and be near the food supply. Some of them succeeded in being sent to infirmaries, and loafers once thus ensconced developed one chronic malady after another—though never quite sick enough to miss a meal—until their attachment to the hospital became more or less permanent. Those who thus evaded duty bore the opprobrious designation of "hospital rats," but they were so degenerate as to be utterly beyond shame.[96]

In happy contrast to these faithless wretches were a group who because of their selflessness and their exceptional devotion to duty were worthy to be called patriots. They consistently bore the hardships of camp without complaint; they insisted on taking their place in line of battle even when they were unwell and when their feet were without the protection of shoes; they were always present at roll call; they refused to seek promotion, and they manifested a cheerful spirit in defeat as well as in victory.

But all these were exceptional types. The average Rebel private belonged to no special category. He was in most respects an ordinary person. He came from a middle-class rural society, made up largely of non-slaveholders, and he exemplified both the defects and the virtues of that background. He was lacking in polish, in perspective and in tolerance, but he was respectable, sturdy and independent.

He was comparatively young, and more than likely unmarried. He went to war with a lightheartedness born of detachment and of faith in a swift victory. His morale wavered with the realization that the conflict was to be long and hard. He was nostalgic and war-weary. He felt the blighting hand of sickness, and it was then that his spirit sank to its lowest ebb. His craving for diversion caused him to turn to gambling and he indulged himself now and then in a bit of swearing. But his tendency to give way to such irregularities was likely to be curbed by his deep-seated conventionality or by religious revivals.

He complained of the shortcomings of officers, the scantiness of clothing, the inadequacy of rations, the multiplicity of pests and numerous other trials that beset him, but there was little depth to his complaints, and his cheerfulness outweighed his dejection. Adaptability and good-nature, in fact, were among his most characteristic qualities. He was a gregarious creature, and his attachment to close associates was genuine.

He had a streak of individuality and of irresponsibility that made him a trial to officers during periods of inactivity. But on the battlefield he rose to supreme heights of soldierhood. He was not immune to panic, nor even to cowardice, but few if any soldiers have had more than he of élan, of determination, of perseverance, and of the sheer courage which it takes to stand in the face of withering fire.

He was far from perfect, but his achievement against great odds in scores of desperate battles through four years of war is an irrefutable evidence of his prowess and an eternal monument to his greatness as a fighting man.

NOTES AND ACKNOWLEDGMENTS

ACKNOWLEDGMENTS

The author wishes to express appreciation to the following persons and firms for permission to reprint material as indicated:

D. Appleton-Century Company, New York, *Battles and Leaders of the Civil War*

Bobbs-Merrill Company, Indianapolis, *The Story of the Confederacy*, by Robert Selph Henry

Dietz Publishing Company, Richmond, Virginia, *Ham Chamberlayne— Virginian*, C. G. Chamberlayne, Editor

E. P. Dutton and Company, New York, *Scraps of Paper*, Marietta M. Andrews, Editor

Longmans, Green and Company, New York, *A Soldiers' Recollections*, by Randolph McKim

University of North Carolina Press, Chapel Hill, North Carolina, "The Diary of William Bartlett Malone," by W. W. Pierson (in vol. 16 of James Sprunt Historical *Publications*)

Yale University Press, New Haven, Connecticut, *Absolam Grimes, Confederate Mail Runner*, M. M. Quaife, Editor

Robert Laurence, New York, *Catalog of the George Walcott Collection of Used Civil War Patriotic Covers*, Robert Laurence, Compiler

Albert Shaw, Jr., New York, *Photographic History of the Civil War*, F. T. Miller, Editor

NOTES

Chapter I

OFF TO THE WAR

[1]Frank P. Peak, "A Southern Soldier's Views on the Civil War, 1860-1862," manuscript in private possession.

[2]Magnolia Plantation Record Book, manuscript, Southern Historical Collection, University of North Carolina. All U. N. C. manuscripts cited hereinafter are from this collection. I am indebted to the late U. B. Phillips for my first knowledge of the item quoted. Intersectional recrimination of the forties, fifties, and early sixties is brilliantly treated in Avery O. Craven's *The Coming of the Civil War*, (New York, 1942).

[3]A. T. Barclay, "The Liberty Hall Volunteers from Lexington to Manassas," *Washington and Lee Historical Papers*, No. 6 (Lynchburg, 1904), 124-127. P. A. Bruce, *History of the University of Virginia* (New York, 1921), III, 256-340.

[4]Diary of Duncan McCollum, entries for April and May 1861, manuscript in private possession.

[5]Arthur M. Shaw, Jr., *Centenary College Goes to War* (Shreveport, Louisiana, 1940), 6-7.

[6]J. B. Mitchell to his father, Feb. 23, 1862, typescript in Military Records Division of Alabama Department of Archives and History, Montgomery, Alabama.

[7]Dorothy Stanley, ed., *Autobiography of Henry M. Stanley* (New York, 1909), 165-166.

[8]*Ibid.*, 140-220.

[9]Henry Graves to his mother, from camp near Wilmington, N. C., May 7, 1862, typescript, Georgia Archives.

[10]Ruffin Thomson to his father, Jan. 10, 1861, manuscript in private possession.

[11]Index of Local Organizations, manuscript, War Records Division, National Archives.

[12]New Orleans *Daily Crescent*, April 29, 1861.

[13]*Ibid.*

[14]*Ibid.*, May 20, 1861.

[15]George Whitaker Wills to his sister, Sept. 10, 1861, manuscript, University of North Carolina.

[16][Napier Bartlett], *A Soldier's Story of the War, Including the*

Marches and Battles of the Washington Artillery (New Orleans, 1874), 16.

[17]*Ibid.*, 18 ff.

[18]O. T. Hanks, "Account of Civil War Experiences," 3, manuscript photostat, University of Texas.

[19]*Ibid.*, 3-4.

[20]*Ibid.*, 7 ff.

[21]W. W. Heartsill, *Fourteen Hundred and 91 Days in the Confederate Army* (Marshall, Texas, 1876), 4-5.

[22]*Ibid.*, 6 ff.

[23]The bandages were presented to the Second Company of Orleans Cadets by a committee of ladies from New Orleans. New Orleans *Daily Crescent*, May 9, 1861.

[24]Diary of A. L. P. Vairin, entries of May 5-9, 1861, manuscript, Mississippi. Archives; Thomas Caffey to his sister, May 7, 1861, "War Letters of Thomas Caffey," Montgomery *Advertiser*, March 28, 1909; Diary of James J. Kirkpatrick, 1861-1864, 4, manuscript, University of Texas.

[25]*Ibid.*; *Battle-Fields of the South* (London, 1863), I, 13-14; James J. Hall to his children, June 11, 1861, manuscript, University of North Carolina; *Official Records of the Union and Confederate Armies* (Washington, D. C., 1880-1901) ser. 1, LI, pt. 2, 114 (to be cited hereinafter as O. R.). Drinking seems to have been more universally indulged in while soldiers were en route to war than at any other time; for sample comments on this point, see: Charleston *Daily Courier*, August 24, 1861; Samuel E. Mays, compiler, *Genealogical Notes on the Family of Mays and Reminiscences of the War Between the States* (Plant City, Fla., 1927), 30-32; J. W. Reid, *History of the Fourth Regiment of South Carolina Volunteers* (Greenville, S. C., 1892), 11.

[26]J. E. Hall to his sister, May 31, 1861, manuscript, among Bolling Hall Papers in Manuscripts Division of Alabama Department of Archives and History.

[27]H. Browning to his sister and brother, Aug. 28, 1861, typescript among Crittenden Papers, University of Texas.

[28]J. B. Lance to his father, Nov. 10, 1861, manuscript, Louisiana State University.

[29]W. G. Evans to his brother "Faulk," July 25, 1861, manuscript, Evans Memorial Library, Aberdeen, Mississippi.

[30]Frank P. Peak, *op. cit.*

[31]Journal of W. R. Howell, entries of May 12, 13, 1861, manuscript, University of Texas.

[32]Manuscript, Mississippi Archives.

Chapter II

THE BAPTISM OF FIRE

[1]G. L. Robertson to his mother, Jan. 19, 1862, Robertson Letters, manuscript photostat, University of Texas.

[2]J. E. Hall to his father, July 1, 1861, manuscript, Alabama Archives.

[3]O. R., series 1, X, part 1, 465.

[4]G. L. Robertson to his mother, Jan. 19, 1862.

[5]Diary of E. D. Patterson, entry of May 6, 1862, typescript in private possession.

[6]New Orleans Daily Crescent, August 5, 1861, quoting Charleston Courier.

[7]S. G. Pryor to his wife, Oct. 5, 15, 1861, typescripts, Georgia Archives. Pryor was a lieutenant.

[8]William G. Stevenson, Thirteen Months in the Rebel Army (New York, 1864), 70-71. Of muskets collected after Gettysburg, 12,000 contained two charges, 6,000 had from two to ten unfired cartridges, and one was loaded with 23 charges rammed down one on top of the other. F. A. Shannon, Organization and Administration of the Union Army (Cleveland, 1928), I, 137.

[9]Robert M. Gill to his wife, May 21, 1862, manuscript in author's possession.

[10]George Baylor, Bull Run to Bull Run (Richmond, 1900), 21. A Mississippi captain wrote in 1864: "I have seen whole regiments and brigades deliver their fire when I was sure that they did not even wound a single man." Richmond Daily Dispatch, April 12, 1864.

[11]John L. G. Wood to his father, July 4, 1862, typescript in Georgia Archives.

[12]A. N. Erskine to his wife, June 28, 1862, manuscript, University of Texas; New Orleans Daily Crescent, Aug. 5, 1861, quoting Charleston Courier; T. C. DeLeon, Four Years in Rebel Capitals (Mobile, 1890), 130-131.

[13]Marcus D. Herring, "War Experiences," typescript in private possession.

[14]O. T. Hanks, "Account of Civil War Experiences," 33, manuscript photostat, University of Texas.

[15]W. A. Fletcher, Rebel Private Front and Rear (Beaumont, Texas, 1908), 20.

[16]John C. Jenkins to his aunt, Feb. 14, 1862, manuscript, Louisiana State University; S. G. Pryor to his wife, Oct. 4, 1861, typescript, Georgia Archives.

[17]A. N. Erskine to his wife, June 28, 1862.

[18]S. G. Pryor to his wife, May 18, 1862.

[19]Thomas Warrick to his wife, Jan. 11, 1863, manuscript, Alabama Archives.

[20]W. C. Athey to his sister, Sept. 29, 1863, manuscript, Alabama Archives.

[21]Manuscript, Confederate Memorial Hall, New Orleans.

[22]E. J. Ellis to his mother, Oct. 21, 1862, manuscript, Louisiana State University; O. R., series 1, XVI, part 1, 1117.

[23]Robert M. Gill to his wife, Aug. 16, 1864; J. W. Jones, Christ in Camp (Atlanta, 1904), 259.

[24]J. E. Hall to his sister, May 29, 1864.

[25]Diary of E. D. Patterson, entry of April 4, 1862.

[26]Henry Graves to his father, June 16, 1862, typescript, Georgia Archives.

[27]John T. Sibley to E. P. Ellis, March 10, 1863, manuscript, Louisiana State University.

Chapter III

BESETTING SINS

[1]O. R., series 1, XIX, part 2, 722.

[2]G. L. Robertson to his mother, Feb. 12, 1864, Robertson Letters, manuscript photostats, University of Texas.

[3]Diary of G. W. Roberts, entries of May 12, 27, 1864, manuscript, Mississippi Archives.

[4]T. C. Holliday to his brother, Dec. 13, 1863, manuscript in private possession.

[5]There are various samples of Confederate playing cards in the Confederate Museum at Richmond, and in the Keith M. Read Collection at Emory University. All Emory University items cited hereinafter are from the Keith M. Read Collection.

[6]Richmond Daily Dispatch, Jan. 5, 1863; R. E. Yerbey to his mother, Dec. 18, 1861, typescript, Georgia Archives; Thomas Warrick to his wife, Dec. 24, 1862, manuscript, Alabama Archives.

[7]A. E. Rentfrow to his sister, Feb. 11, 1862, manuscript, University of Texas.

[8]Manuscript among James Buckner Barry Papers, University of Texas.

[9]Theodore Gerrish and John S. Hutchinson, The Blue and the Gray (Bangor, Maine, 1884), 441; Richmond Daily Dispatch, Nov. 13, 1861; Sam R. Watkins, Company Aytch, Maury Grays, First Tennessee Regi-

ment (Chattanooga, 1900), 46; Diary of Harry St. John Dixon, entry of June 16, 1864, manuscript, University of North Carolina.

[10][Napier Bartlett], *op. cit.*, 24.

[11]W. J. Worsham, *The Old Nineteenth Tennessee Regiment, C.S.A.* (Knoxville, 1902), 62, 185; John C. West, *A Texan in Search of a Fight* (Waco, Texas, 1901), 103-104.

[12]Henry Kyd Douglas, *I Rode with Stonewall* (Chapel Hill, North Carolina, 1940), 197.

[13]Ruffin Thomson to his mother, Dec. 1, 1862, manuscript in private possession.

[14]Samuel Hankins, *Simple Story of a Soldier* (Nashville, no date), 11-13.

[15]Theodore Gerrish and John S. Hutchinson, *op. cit.*, 305.

[16]Romans 11:33.

[17]Jones, *op. cit.*, 267, 268.

[18]Clipping from newspaper scrapbook in Alabama Archives.

[19]O. R., series 4, I, 834-835.

[20]Jones, *op. cit.*, 268. Bragg wrote President Davis on Dec. 1, 1863: "The warfare has been carried on successfully, and the fruits are bitter. You must make other changes here, or our success is hopeless. Breckinridge was totally unfit for any duty from the 23d to the 27th—during all our trials—from drunkenness. The same cause prevented our complete triumph at Murfreesborough. I can bear to be sacrificed myself, but not to see my country and my friends ruined by the vices of a few profligate men who happen to have an undue popularity. General Hardee will assure you that Cheatham is equally dangerous." O. R., series 1, LII, part 2, 745. A similar intimation is contained in correspondent "Sallust's" communication of Dec. 2, 1863, to the Richmond *Dispatch* (issue of Dec. 11). "You will be surprised and mortified to learn," he wrote, "that this army is not free from the vice of intemperance. I refer to the painful subject here merely to warn those officers who are guilty of this abominable offense that, if I forbear for the present to publish their names, it is only to give them an opportunity to reform their habits, and do their duty. If they persist in their criminal courses no power on earth shall prevent their exposure, if life be vouchsafed to me and you will print my letters."

[21]Quoted in New Orleans *Daily Crescent*, Feb. 7, 1862.

[22]Diary of A. L. P. Vairin, entries of Nov. 27-30, 1862, manuscript. Mississippi Archives; Diary of Robert E. Jones, entry of Nov. 8, 1863, typescript in private possession; O. R., series 1, XLV, part 1, 1259, report of Capt. Wm. A. Reid, to Col. E. J. Harvie, Inspector General, Army of Tennessee, Nov. 29, 1864; Henry Bryan to Gen. L. McLaws, March 28, 1861 [1862], manuscript, Heartman Collection; John Crit-

tenden to his wife, Feb. 13, 1864, typescript, University of Texas; C. W. Stephens to his father Jan. 21, 1864, manuscript in private possession.

[23]Mobile *Daily Advertiser & Register*, Feb. 4, 1864, quoting Augusta *Chronicle and Sentinel.*

[24]John Brynam to Thomas Morris, March 22, 1862, manuscript, Louisiana State University.

[25]New Orleans *Daily Crescent*, Sept. 26, 1861, correspondence of Israel Gibbons.

[26]*Confederate Veteran*, V (1897), 276.

[27]Stevenson, op. cit., 46-47.

[28]Quoted by the *Army and Navy Herald*, Oct. 15, 1863.

[29]Anonymous diary of a Louisiana soldier, entry of Oct. 3, 1862, manuscript in Heartman Collection; New Orleans *Daily Picayune*, Aug. 7, 1861; diary of D. P. Hopkins, entry of April 12, 1862, typescript, University of Texas; *Daily Richmond Enquirer*, Sept. 17, 1864; Eppa Hunton, *Autobiography* (Richmond, Va., 1933), 55-56.

[30]O. R., series 1, XI, part 3, 526.

[31]See letter of Marcus D. Herring to editor of Jackson (Mississippi) *Clarion Ledger*, [undated but evidently May 1927], in scrapbook of Marcus D. Herring. This item is in private possession.

[32]V. S. Rabb to his brother, Jan. 4, 1863, manuscript photostat, University of Texas.

[33]Robert Fore to James Reding, Jan. 2, 1863, manuscript, University of Texas.

[34]Letter of Robert M. Gill, manuscript in author's possession.

[35]O. R., series 1, XLV, part 1, 1255; part 2, 783; LI, part 2, 222, General Order No. 57; Richmond *Daily Dispatch*, Feb. 8, 1865.

[36]O. R., series 1, XXXI, part 3, 622; XXXII, part 2, 622-623; XXXIV, part 2, 942-943; XLIV, 412; XLV, part 2, 688-689, 798-799; XLIX, part 1, 1010-1011; part 2, 1124-1125; and series 4, II, 289, 1061; III, 763.

[37]William W. Christian to Carrie Harmon, April 27, 1861, manuscript, Duke University; Frank Richardson to his sister, Dec. 6, 1861, manuscript, University of North Carolina; Edwin Tillinghast to his sister, Aug. 24, 1863, manuscript, Emory University; J. P. Cannon, *Inside of Rebeldom* (Washington, D. C., 1900), 163.

[38]Diary of W. S. Rinaldi, entry of June 1, 1862; O. R., series 1, XX, part 1, 726.

[39]Baylor, op. cit., 179.

[40]William R. Stillwell to his wife, July 8, 1864, manuscript, Georgia Archives.

[41]W. C. McClellan to his sister, July 9, 1863, manuscript in private possession.

[42]Diary of J. B. Clifton, entry of June 28, 1863, typescript, North Carolina Historical Commission.

[43]William N. Berkeley to his wife, June 27, 28, 1863, manuscript, University of Virginia.

[44]Thomas F. Boatwright to his wife, July 9, 1863, manuscript, University of North Carolina.

[45]Adrian Carruth to his sister, Aug. 4, 1863, manuscript in private possession. There were, of course, a great number of instances of soldiers eschewing profanity because of religious conversion, and for other reasons. H. A. Stephens wrote his sister Nov. 22, 1863, "I have quit cursing and taken up smokeing. I find that it is of benefit to me or I would not do it. tell Ma I will quit it when the war is over." Manuscript in private possession

[46]Confidential letter dated May 2, 1863, typescript in private possession; the chaplain of a Tennessee regiment wrote in 1864 that he had heard more cursing in twenty-four hours in the army than he had heard in all his prior life. "The air, indeed, is so filled with profanity," he said, "that it seems to swear without a tongue." Joseph Cross, *Camp and Field* (Macon, 1864), Book I.

[47]Brig. Gen. William Nelson, Commanding Fourth Division U.S. Troops, in his official report of Shiloh said: "The men lay upon their arms. Lieutenant Gwin, of the Navy, commanding the gunboats in the river, sent to me and asked how he could be of service. I requested that he would throw an 8-inch shell into the camp of the enemy every ten minutes during the night, and thus prevent their sleeping, which he did very scientifically, and, according to the report of the prisoners, to their infinite annoyance." O. R., series 1, X, part 1, 324.

[48]See Robert M. Gill to his wife, June 10, 14, and July 25, 1864. Gill was a lieutenant at the time these letters were written.

[49]General Orders, Department of South Carolina, Georgia, and Florida, Confederate Archives, chapter II, volume 42, p. 57 and volume 43, pp. 137-138, manuscript, National Archives.

[50]William R. Barksdale to his brother, June 11, 1861, manuscript in private possession; Harry St. John Dixon of the 28th Mississippi Cavalry wrote in his diary March 21, 1864; "Oh! if I could see the little girl this morning instead of . . . listening . . . to boisterous laughter over obscene brutal jokes." Manuscript, University of North Carolina.

[51]Orville C. Bumpass to his wife, Sept. 18, 1864, and March 2, 1865, manuscripts, Evans Memorial Library.

[52]For example, see J. M. Jordan to his wife, Dec. 17, 1863, typescript, Georgia Archives.

[53]E. P. Becton to his wife, Oct. 26, 1862, manuscript photostat, University of Texas.

[54]J. M. Jordan to his wife, Feb. 8, 1864.

[55]New Orleans *Daily Crescent,* Jan. 8, 1862.

[56]General Order, dated Sept. 1, 1862, Headquarters of Heavy Artillery, Vicksburg, Mississippi, document in Heartman Collection. Army Regulations permitted each company to have four laundresses, but required that they furnish certificates of good character. J. W. Randolph, editor, *Confederate States Army Regulations, 1863* (Richmond, 1863), 12, 77.

[57]W. C. McClellan to his sister, March 16, 1863, manuscript in private possession.

[58]S. A. Boston of a Virginia regiment wrote to his sister June 24, 1861, concerning the "Louisiana Tigers": "A woman dressed in the same uniform [striped male attire] is one of their Lieutenants & two other girls act as markers. Of course they are women of no standing." Manuscript in private possession. Colonel Arthur Fremantle said that a nice-looking woman was pointed out to him on the train between Chattanooga and Atlanta in June 1863, who had fought as a private soldier at Perryville and Murfreesboro. "Several men in my car had served with her," he added, "and they said she had been turned out a short time since for her bad and immoral conduct. They told me that her sex was notorious to all the regiment, but no notice had been taken of it as long as she conducted herself properly." Arthur J. Fremantle, *Three Months in the Southern States* (London, 1863), 173.

[59]Manuscripts from confidential sources.

[60]Army of Tennessee, Letters, Orders, and Indorsements, Confederate Archives, chapter II, volume 15½, pp. 142-143, manuscript, National Archives.

[61]Richmond *Daily Dispatch,* May 6, 1862.

[62]*Ibid.,* May 18, 1862.

[63]Daily Richmond *Enquirer,* Aug. 22, 1864.

[64]Richmond *Enquirer,* Nov. 6, 1863 (semiweekly edition).

[65]Manuscript, Mississippi Archives.

[66]Letter of Oct. 22, 1864, manuscript, Evans Memorial Library.

[67]George M. Deckerd to "Rehum," manuscript photostat among Reding Papers, University of Texas.

[68]Wirt A. Cate, editor, *Two Soldiers* (Chapel Hill, 1938), 20-21.

[69]Letter of June 6, 1863, typescript in possession of Prof. Glover Moore, Mississippi State College.

[70]These reports covering sixty-two regiments are filed with Confederate Regimental Records in the War Records Division of the National Archives.

[71]Letter of June 11, 1861, manuscript in private possession.

[72]Daily Richmond *Examiner,* Dec. 5, 1862.

[73]Letter to his wife, Oct. 22, 1864, manuscript, Evans Memorial Library.

[74]Diary of L. G. Hutton, entry of Nov. 9, 1862, manuscript, University of Texas.

[75]Undated letter of J. M. Guess, manuscript in Miscellaneous Collection, Confederate Memorial Hall, New Orleans.

Chapter IV

IN WINTER QUARTERS

[1]New Orleans *Daily Crescent*, Feb. 14, 1862.

[2]O. R., series 1, V, 941-942, 951, 1014; XLII, part 2, 1261.

[3]Cavalrymen rarely built huts, as the nature of their duties required frequent moving about even in winter, and their greater mobility made it possible for them to disperse themselves to such an extent as to procure accommodations from civilians. Gen. Will T. Martin wrote to his sister Jan. 31, 1863, from Morristown, Tenn.: "The infantry is all in winter quarters. The cavalry in our army never goes into winter quarters." Typescript in private possession.

[4]G. L. Robertson to his mother, Jan. 4, 1862, manuscript photostat, University of Texas. In some instances the hut's walls were built by driving timbers into the ground after the fashion of a stockade. George Whitaker Wills to his sister, Nov. 19, 1862, manuscript, University of North Carolina.

[5]William M. Owen, *In Camp and Battle With the Washington Artillery* (Boston, 1885), 68-69.

[6]Montgomery *Daily Mail*, Feb. 17, 1863.

[7]G. L. Robertson to his mother, Jan. 4, Feb. 12, 1862.

[8]William R. Stillwell to his wife, March 7, 1863, manuscript, Georgia Archives.

[9]Thomas Caffey to his sister, Dec. 19, 1861, in "War Letters of Thomas Caffey," Montgomery *Advertiser*, April 9, 1909; diary of James J. Kirkpatrick, entry of Dec. 18, 1861, manuscript, University of Texas.

[10]Theodore Mandeville to his sister, Jan. 3, 1862, manuscript, Louisiana State University.

[11]New Orleans *Daily Crescent*, Dec. 11, 1861, correspondence of I[srael] G[ibbons].

[12]Peak, *op. cit.*; Theodore Mandeville to his sister, Jan. 3, 1862.

[13]New Orleans *Daily Crescent*, Dec. 11, 1861, correspondence of I[srael] G[ibbons].

[14]J. E. Hall to his brother, Bolling Hall, Jan. 28, 1865, manuscript, Alabama Archives.

[15]Hanks, *op. cit.*, 120.

[16]Carlton McCarthy, *Detailed Minutiae of Soldier Life in the Army of Northern Virginia 1861-1865* (Richmond, 1882), 87, 89.

[17]Diary of James J. Kirkpatrick, entries of Feb. 19, March 23, 1864; G. L. Robertson to his sister, Jan. 15, 1862, manuscript photostat, University of Texas.

[18]C. Irvine Walker to Ada Sinclair, April 15, 1864, typescript, University of Texas.

[19]T. B. Hampton to his wife, March 24, 1864, typescript, University of Texas.

[20]William R. Stillwell to his wife, Feb. 17, 1863.

[21]Diary of T. Otis Baker, entry of March 22, 1864, manuscript, Mississippi Archives.

[22]Journal of E. Mussence, entry of March 31, [1863?], manuscript fragment among Washington Artillery Papers, Confederate Memorial Hall, New Orleans.

[23]O. L. Barnett to his family, April 4, 1864, manuscript, Emory University.

[24]Grant D. Carter to his sister, March 24, 1864, typescript, Georgia Archives.

[25]Hanks, *op. cit.*, 120-121.

[26]Diary of Charles Moore, manuscript, Confederate Memorial Hall, New Orleans.

[27]*Ibid.*, entries of Feb. 28-April 28, 1863.

Chapter V

HEROES AND COWARDS

[1] O. R., series 1, X, part 2, 389.

[2]Forty rounds was evidently the capacity of an ordinary cartridge box. After the battle of Gettysburg the War Department sent out a circular to army and departmental commanders enjoining the practice, except on special order of the general commanding, of issuing on the eve of battle twenty rounds of ammunition, "over and above the capacity of the cartridge boxes." O. R., series 1, XXVII, part 3, 1091.

[3]This summary of pre-battle instructions is derived from various sources. For examples, see O. R., series 1, X, part 2, 325-326, 535, and XI, part 3, 410-411. State pride was sometimes appealed to in these addresses. George Whitaker Wills to his sister, June 28, 1862, manuscript, University of North Carolina. General T. C. Hindman sought on one occasion to invoke hatred of the enemy as a pre-battle conditioner: "Remember that the enemy you engage has no feeling of mercy," he

said. "His ranks are made up of Pin Indians, Free Negroes, Southern Tories, Kansas Jayhawkers, and hired Dutch cutthroats. These bloody ruffians have invaded your country, stolen and destroyed your property, murdered your neighbors, outraged your women, driven your children from their homes, and defiled the graves of your kindred." Broadside, dated Dec. 4, 1862, Emory University.

[4]T. W. Montfort wrote to his wife from Ft. Pulaski, April 5, 1862: "There is something sad and melancholy in the preparation for Battle. To see so many healthy men prepareing for the worst by disposing of their property by will—to see the surgeon sharping his instruments & whetting his saw . . . men engaged in carding up & prepareing lint to stop the flow of human blood." Typescript, Georgia Archives.

[5]Journal of William P. Chambers, entry of May 18, 1864, Mississippi Historical Society *Publications*, Centenary Series, V, 321. This source will be cited hereinafter as P.M.H.S.

[6]Robert M. Gill wrote to his wife from line of battle in Georgia, June 23, 1864: "I saw a canteen upon which a heavy run was made during and after the charge—I still like whisky but I do not want any when going into action for I am or at least was drunk enough yesterday without drinking a drop." Manuscript in author's possession.

[7]J. H. Belo, *Memoirs* (Boston, 1904), 40.

[8]For example, see O. R., series 1, XXX, part 2, 237.

[9]O. R., series 1, XXI, 664. A Virginia veteran attributed the greater resonance of the Southern battle cry to the rural background of most Confederates. In isolated areas, he said, hallooing was a necessary means of communication, while in the cities and towns from which a substantial portion of Yankees came, there was hardly ever an occasion for shouting. In comparing the sounds of the two yells, he said that the Federal cheer was a repeated "hoo-ray," with prolonged emphasis on the second syllable, while the Confederate cry was a series of "woh-who—eys" with a heavy subsiding accent on the blended "who" and "ey," the effect being a sort of "whee." J. Harvey Dew, "The Yankee and Rebel Yells," *Century Magazine*, XLIII (1892), 953-955. Other veterans referred to the Yankee shout as a practiced "hurrah," or a concerted "hip, hip, huzza, huzza, huzza," and to the Rebel Yell as a "yai, yai, yi, yai, yi," but nearly all stress the individual informal quality of the latter. W. H. Morgan, *Personal Reminiscences of the War of 1861-1865* (Lynchburg, 1911), 70; A. P. Ford, *Life in the Confederate Army* (New York, 1905), 58. Douglas Freeman told the writer in an interview that the Confederate cheer was a battle-field adaptation of the fox hunter's cry, which cry the Richmond *News Leader* designated in the Aug. 17, 1936, issue as a wild "y-yo yo-wo-wo." The writer leans toward the theory that the "who-ey" version was the one most commonly used.

[10]Journal of William P. Chambers, entry of Aug. 4, 1864, *P.M.H.S.*, Centenary Series, V, 332.

[11]*O. R.*, series 1, XXXVIII, part 3, 922.

[12]For example, see *ibid.*, series 1, XXXIV, part 1, 752.

[13]*Ibid.*, series 1, XXXIV, part 1, 849.

[14]Robert M. Gill to his wife, July 28, 1864.

[15]*O. R.*, series 1, X, part 1, 583; XXXVI, part 1, 1093-1094.

[16]Morgan, *op. cit.*, 200; E. D. Patterson, in his diary entry of June 28, 1862, says that at Gaines's Mill when he and his comrade went over a ridge they encountered such heavy fire "that the whole brigade literally *staggered* backward several paces as though pushed back by a tornado." Typescript in private possession.

[17]*O. R.*, series 1, XXXVI, part 1, 1093-1094, General Samuel McGowan's report of the "Bloody Angle" phase of Spottsylvania Court House; McGowan says further that a 22-inch oak tree was cut down by the heavy musket fire, injuring several soldiers when it fell. *Ibid.*

[18]John L. G. Wood to his aunt, May 10, 1863, typescript, Georgia Archives; Robert M. Gill to his wife, Oct. 6, 1863; diary of Maurice K. Simons, entry of May 31, 1863, manuscript photostat, University of Texas.

[19]*O. R.*, series 1, XXX, part 2, 305, Gen. T. C. Hindman's official report of Chickamauga; XXXIX, part 1, 821, Maj. E. H. Hampton's report of Allatoona; XXXI, part 2, 726, 750-757, Gen. John C. Brown's and Gen. P. R. Cleburne's reports of Lookout Mountain; XXVII, part 2, 486-487, Maj. Samuel Tate to Gov. Z. B. Vance, July 8, 1863, concerning Gettysburg; A. C. Redwood, "Jackson's Foot Cavalry at the Second Bull Run," *Battles and Leaders of the Civil War* (New York, 1887-1888), II, 535-536; Walter Clark, editor, *North Carolina Regiments, 1861-1865* (Raleigh and Goldsboro, 1901), II, 376.

[20]*O. R.*, series 1, XXXVIII, part 3, 689.

[21]For condition of troops before and during the Shiloh fight see *O. R.*, series 1, X, part 1, 454, 464, 498, 499, 522, 547, 569-570, 586; and XVII, part 2, 641.

[22]A young Georgian, writing of his experience at Manassas, said, "As we were retiring I stopped to take a mouthful of mud—scarcely could it be called water—my mouth was awfully hot and dry." New Orleans *Daily Crescent*, Aug. 8, 1861.

[23]Thomas Warrick to his wife, Jan. 11-13, 1863, manuscript, Alabama Archives.

[24][Bartlett], *op. cit.*, 192-193.

[25]For instances of scattering of regiments under fire, see *O. R.*, series 1, X, part 1, 467, 584; XXV, part 1, 984-985; LI, part 2, 199. Also John Crittenden to J. S. Bryant, Jan. 29, 1863, typescript, University of Texas; and J. E. Hall to his father, June 3, 1862, manuscript, Alabama Archives.

[26]Heartsill, *op. cit.*, 159; Hanks, *op. cit.*, 29, manuscript photostat, University of Texas; Henry L. Graves to his aunt, Aug. 7, 1862, typescript, Georgia Archives; G. A. Hanson, *Minor Incidents of the Late War* (Bartow, Florida, 1887), 36; *O. R.*, series 1, XXX, part 2, 418.

[27]J. W. Rabb to his mother, Jan. 14, 1863, manuscript photostat, University of Texas.

[28]John L. G. Wood to his wife, Dec. 18, 1862, typescript, Georgia Archives.

[29]Robert Stiles, *Four Years Under Marse Robert* (New York, 1903), 219-220.

[30]Harmon Martin to his sister, Aug. 25, 1863, typescript, Georgia Archives.

[31]George W. Athey to his sister, (no date, but Dec., 1864), manuscript, Alabama Archives.

[32]Hanks, *op. cit.*, 35.

[33]Diary of E. D. Patterson, entry of June 2, 1862.

[34]*O. R.*, series 1, XX, part 1, 957; M. D. Martin to his parents, May 8, 1863, typescript in private possession.

[35]James Mabley to his sister, May 16, 1863, manuscript, Emory University.

[36]Harry Gilmor, *Four Years in the Saddle* (New York, 1866), 141.

[37]Diary of E. D. Patterson, entry of Aug. 31, 1863.

[38]Stiles, *op. cit.*, 116-117.

[39]*O. R.*, series 1, XII, part 2, 736; W. W. Heartsill, *op. cit.*, 159; Robert M. Gill to his wife, July 25, 1864.

[40]Diary of Maurice K. Simons, various entries, May 17-July 3, 1863.

[41]*Ibid.* River water next to the east bank became contaminated with maggots from the great number of dead animals thrown in, and cisterns were either polluted or exhausted. *O. R.*, series 1, XXIV, part 2, 392.

[42]Diary of Maurice K. Simons, entry of June 13, 1863.

[43]*Ibid.*, entries of May 27, 31, 1863.

[44]Diary of James J. Kirkpatrick, entry of Aug. 5, 1864; Robert M. Gill to his wife, July 9, Aug. 16, 1864; Bolling Hall to his sister, Laura, Sept. 20, 1864, manuscript, Alabama Archives.

[45]Crenshaw Hall to his father, Oct. 16, 1864, manuscript, Alabama Archives.

[46]Crenshaw Hall to Laura Hall, Feb. 20, 1865. A Virginia officer charged with building a redoubt on the Petersburg line kept a man posted to call out the Yankee shots. At each flash of their guns he would call out "down" and the men would fall flat in the trench. The Federals got on to the trick and resorted to the device of setting off a blaze of powder to deceive the Rebs, and then giving them the real load as they rose up from their shelter. C. G. Chamberlayne, editor, *Ham Chamberlayne—Virginian* (Richmond, 1932), 267-268.

[47]J. E. Hall to Laura Hall, Oct. 15, 1864, Feb. 8, 1865; Crenshaw Hall to Laura Hall, Feb. 20, 1865.

[48]O. R., series 1, X, part 1, 589; XI, part 1, 950.

[49]Ibid., XX, part 1, 730, 747, 867.

[50]Ibid., XII, part 2, 593; XXX, part 2, 379.

[51]Ibid., XXX, part 2, 190, 379-380.

[52]Ibid., XXV, part 1, 1003.

[53]Ibid., XI, part 1, 950; XIX, part 1, 933; Clark, op. cit., II, 350-354.

[54]Ibid., XVII, part 1, 400; XIX, part 1, 875.

[55]Ibid., XX, part 1, 719, 852.

[56]Ibid., 931.

[57]Ibid., X, part 2, 528; XI, part 2, 992-993; XX, part 2, 494; Robert Ames Jarman, "History of Co. K, 27th Mississippi Infantry," 10, typescript in private possession.

[58]James A. McCord to his brother, Dec. 3, 1864, manuscript photostat in private possession.

[59]O. R., series 1, XXVIII, part 1, 418-419, 524.

[60]Mays, op. cit., 36; O. R., series 1, XI, part 2, 563, 612; part 3, 506, 571.

[61]O. R., series 1, X, part 1, 391, 432, 571-572, 576-577. For other evidences of reprehensible conduct under fire at Shiloh see ibid., 401, 501, 507, 546, 570, 589.

[62]Ibid., XX, part 1, 761, 879.

[63]Ibid., XXIV, part 2, 88.

[64]Anonymous diary of a Louisiana soldier, entry of Nov. 25, 1863, manuscript, Confederate Memorial Hall, New Orleans.

[65]O. R., series 1, XXXI, part 2, 665-666; see also Bate's General Order of Nov. 28, 1863, ibid., 744. News correspondent "Sallust" wrote from a point near the battlefield at midnight of November 25: "The Confederates have sustained today the most ignominious defeat of the whole war—a defeat for which there is but little excuse or palliation. For the first time during our struggle for national independence, our defeat is chargeable to the troops themselves and not to the blunder or incompetency of their leaders. It is difficult for one to realize how a defeat so complete could have occurred on ground so favorable." Richmond Daily Disptach, Dec. 4, 1863.

[66]Stephen Ramseur to his wife, July 23, Aug. 3, 1864, manuscript, University of North Carolina.

[67]Pulaski Cowper, compiler, Extracts of Letters of Maj. Gen. Bryan Grimes (Raleigh, 1883), 69-70.

[68]G. P. Ring to "My own Darling," Sept. 21, 1864, manuscript, Confederate Memorial Hall, New Orleans. General Grimes also mentions the pleading of the women. Cowper, op. cit., p. 70.

[69]Cowper, op. cit., 77-78; O. R., series 1, XLIII, part 1, 598-600; R.

W. Waldrop to his father, Oct. 21, 1864, manuscript, University of North Carolina.

[70]*O. R.*, series 1, XLI, part 1, 637, official report of General Price.

[71]*Ibid.*, XXXVIII, part 3, 835; part 4, 766-767.

[72]*Ibid.*, XLV, part 1, 660, 747, 749, 750.

[73]Cate, *op. cit.*, 169.

[74]Fletcher, *op. cit.*, 84.

[75]C. Irvine Walker to Ada Sinclair, July 28, 1864, typescript, University of Texas.

[76]Stiles, *op. cit.*, 135.

[77]*O. R.*, series 1, XXX, part 2, 183-184; part 4, 715.

[78]*Ibid.*, LI, part 1, 273; William R. Stillwell to his wife, May 2-3, 1863, manuscript, Georgia Archives; Thomas Caffey to his sister, Feb. 16, 1863, "War Letters of Thomas Caffey," Montgomery *Advertiser*, April 25, 1909.

[79]For example, see Fletcher, *op. cit.*, 84.

Chapter VI

BAD BEEF AND CORN BREAD

[1]Jerome Yates to "T. O. D.," Jan. 18, 1864, manuscript, Heartman Collection.

[2]*O. R.*, series 1, X, part 2, 571. The prescribed ration, taken from the 1857 U. S. Army Regulations, was: "Three-fourths of a pound of pork or bacon, or one and a fourth pounds of fresh or salt beef; eighteen ounces of bread or flour, or twelve ounces of hard bread, or one and a fourth pounds of corn bread, or one and a fourth pounds of corn meal; and at the rate, to one hundred rations, of eight quarts of peas or beans, or in lieu thereof, ten pounds of rice; six pounds coffee; twelve pounds sugar; four quarts of vinegar . . . and two quarts of salt." J. W. Randolph, editor, *Confederate States Army Regulations*, 1861 (Richmond, 1861), article 42, paragraph 1069, p. 140.

[3]Fred R. Taber to Lillie Trust, Sept. 12, 1861, manuscript, Louisiana State University.

[4]Theodore Mandeville to Rebecca Mandeville, Dec. 29, 1861, manuscript, Louisiana State University.

[5]*O. R.*, series 1, LII, part 2, 204. It was about this time also that Beauregard wrote Davis, "The want of food & transportation has made us lose all the fruits of our victory." Quoted in Beauregard to Davis, Aug. 10, 1861, manuscript, Duke University.

[6]*O. R.*, series 4, I, 872.

[7]Diary of Charles Moore, entries of Sept. 14, 17, 18, 1861, manuscript, Confederate Memorial Hall, New Orleans.

[8]O. R., series 4, I, 887-889.

[9]New Orleans Daily Crescent, Jan. 23, 1862, correspondence of I[srael] G[ibbons], quartermaster, Kennedy's Battalion.

[10]O. R., series 1, XIX, part 2, 716.

[11]Ibid., series 1, X, part 2, 530-531, 571; XIX, part 2, 716; XXI, 1016; Order Book for Crescent Regiment, manuscript, Confederate Memorial Hall.

[12]O. R., XXI, 1110-1111; XXV, part 2, 687-688; Confederate States Army Regulations, 1863, article 42.

[13]O. R., series 1, XXIV, part 3, 1055-1056.

[14]Ibid., series 4, III, 930-932.

[15]Ibid.

[16]Ibid., series 1, VII, 334.

[17]John A. Johnson to Ella Arnold, May 18, 1862, typescript in private possession; C. C. Blacknall to his wife, May 18, 1862, manuscript, North Carolina Historical Commission; O. R., series 1, XI, part 1, 408-409, 605-606; Ruffin Thomson to his father, May 24, 1862, manuscript in private possession.

[18]Grant D. Carter to his mother, July 4, 1862, typescript, Georgia Archives.

[19]William R. Stillwell to his wife, Sept. 18, 1862, manuscript, Georgia Archives.

[20]Diary of T. J. Ford, entry of Sept. 22, 1862, manuscript, Heartman Collection.

[21]Joseph Singleton to his parents, Nov. 11, 1862, manuscript, Richard D. White Collection, North Carolina Historical Commission. The parodied allusion to hardness of service with Jackson went the rounds of the army in devious forms. A full and popular version was this: "Man that is born of a woman, and enlisteth in Jackson's army, is of few days and short rations. He cometh forth at reveille, is present also at retreat, and retireth apparently at taps. When, lo! he striketh a bee-line for the nearest hen-roost, from which he taketh sundry chickens, and stealthily returneth to his camp. He then maketh a savory dish, therewith he feasteth himself and a chosen friend. But the Captain sleepeth, and knoweth not that his men are feasting." Royall W. Figg, Where Men Only Dare to Go: Story of a Boy Company (Richmond, 1885), 64.

[22]Diary of George W. Jones, entry of Oct. 20, 1862, typescript in private possession.

[23]Postwar addition by C. Irvine Walker to a letter that he wrote to his bethrothed, Ada Sinclair, Sept. 30, 1862, typescript, University of Texas.

[24]Journal of William P. Chambers, *P. M. H. S.*, Centenary Series, V, 279-280; Ephraim Anderson, *Memoirs* (St. Louis, 1868), 337-338; *O. R.*, series 1, XXIV, part 2, 392; part 3, 983.

[25]Diary of Major Maurice K. Simons, entry of July 3, 1863, manuscript photostat, University of Texas.

[26]*Ibid.*, entries of June 3-July 5, 1863; *O. R.*, series 1, XXIV, part 1, 278-279; Winchester Hall, *The Twenty-sixth Louisiana Infantry* (no place, 1890?), 89-90; E. L. Drake, editor, *Annals of the Army of Tennessee*, I (1878), 106.

[27]Journal of William P. Chambers, *P. M. H. S.*, Centenary Series, V, 279-280; J. W. Westbrook, "Reminiscences," 5-6, typescript, University of Texas.

[28]Diary of Maurice K. Simons, entry of July 4. While the soldiers were eating mule meat, there were 38,241 pounds of bacon and 427 pounds of salt pork stored away in commissary depots; this had been held in reserve for use in the event of a movement to break the siege. *O. R.*, series 1, XXIV, part 3, 987.

[29]Diary of R. L. McClung, 29, typescript, University of Texas. The portion of this document prior to November 1863 is in reminiscent rather than diary form. An officer who escaped from Port Hudson while capitulation was being arranged testified immediately afterward: "About the 29th or 30th of June, the garrison's supply of meat gave out, when General Gardner ordered the mules to be butchered, after ascertaining that the men were willing to eat them. . . . The men received their unusual rations cheerfully. . . . Many of them, as if in mockery of famine, caught rats and ate them, declaring that they were better than squirrel." Richmond *Daily Dispatch*, July 23, 1863, quoting Mobile *Advertiser*. D. P. Smith in his *History of Company K, First Alabama Regiment* (Prattsville, Alabama, 1885), 76-77, testifies to the use of both mule and rat meat at Port Hudson.

[30]Anonymous diary of a Louisiana soldier, manuscript, Confederate Memorial Hall.

[31]John Crittenden to his wife, June 28, 1864, typescript, University of Texas.

[32]T. B. Hampton to his wife, Aug. 10, 1864, typescript, University of Texas.

[33]Cowper, *op. cit.*, 58.

[34]Stuart Noblin, "Leonidas Lafayette Polk" (Ph.D. thesis in progress, University of North Carolina), chapter 3.

[35]See Moss-Barmore-Colclough-Rentfrow correspondence, 1862-1864, and diary of M. W. Barber, manuscripts, University of Texas; also *O. R.*, series 1, XLI, part 4, 1071-1073.

[36]Thomas Warrick to his wife, Nov. 13, 1863, manuscript, Alabama Archives; *O. R.*, series 1, XLV, part 1, 736.

[37]O. R., series 1, XLVI, part 1, 382; part 2, 1074-1075.

[38]McCarthy, op. cit., 57.

[39]Ibid., 128; Douglas, op. cit., 331.

[40]B. I. Wiley, Southern Negroes 1861-1865 (New Haven, 1938), 44-62.

[41]William Watson, Life in the Confederate Army (London, 1887), 164-166.

[42]Douglas S. Freeman, R. E. Lee (New York, 1934), II, 494-495.

[43]Wiley, op. cit., 48; Charles W. Ramsdell, "The Confederate Government and the Railroads," American Historical Review, XXII (1917), 809-810.

[44]Frank Moss to his sister, Oct. 7, 1862, manuscript, University of Texas.

[45]Adrian Carruth to his sister, June 5, 1863, manuscript in private possession; Johnny C. Murray to "Sig," March 28, 1865, manuscript, Confederate Memorial Hall.

[46]William R. Stillwell to his wife, May 13, 1863.

[47]Frank Moss to his sister, Dec. 7, 1864.

[48]Hanks, op. cit., 81, manuscript photostat, University of Texas.

[49]P. L. Dodgen to his wife, May 17, 1863, typescript, Georgia Archives.

[50]Adrian Carruth to his sister, March 4, 1863.

[51]W. M. Moss to "Mrs. R.," Dec. 28, 1863, manuscript, University of Texas; C. W. Stephens to his father, Jan. 5, 1864, manuscript in private possession; T. B. Hampton to his wife, Jan. 1, 1863.

[52]William R. Stillwell to his wife, March 4, 1863; Thomas Caffey to "Mary," Jan. 15, 1864, "War Letters of Thomas Caffey," Montgomery Advertiser, May 9, 1909.

[53]E. J. Ellis to his father, Oct. 12, 1861, manuscript, Louisiana State University.

[54]W. C. Athey to his sister, manuscript, Alabama Archives.

[55]William H. Phillips to his parents, Aug. 3, 1861, manuscript, Duke University.

[56]John Crittenden to his wife, May 3, 1863, and March 31, 1864.

[57]T. B. Hampton to his wife, March 14, 1865.

[58]George W. Athey to his wife, Nov. 11, 1863, manuscript, Alabama Archives.

[59]T. B. Hampton to his wife, May 29, 1864.

[60]Diary of James J. Kirkpatrick, entry of Dec. 18, 1861, manuscript, University of Texas.

[61]Richmond Daily Dispatch, Dec. 21, 1861.

[62]Ephraim Anderson, op. cit., 213-214.

[63]Diary of James J. Kirkpatrick, entries of Nov. 1, Dec. 24, 1863. Confederate Army Regulations of 1862 prohibited sutlers selling on

credit to enlisted men to an amount exceeding one-third of monthly wages without written permission of post commandants; and with such permission the amount of credit was not to exceed one-half the wages. *Confederate States Army Regulations, 1862* (Richmond, 1862), article 204.

[64]John Crittenden to his mother, Feb. 16, 1863.

[65]John Crittenden to his wife, May 3, 1863.

[66]P. L. Dodgen to his wife, July 20, 1862.

[67]Diary of L. G. Hutton, various entries for period from April to October, 1862, typescript, University of Texas.

[68]Grabbling is a term applied to the practice of probing with the hands for fish under banks, roots and rocks.

[69]Thomas Caffey to his sister, March 24, 1863.

[70]J. M. Jordan to his wife, March 21, 1864, typescript, Georgia Archives.

[71]G. L. Robertson to his sister, Jan. 15, 1864, manuscript photostat, University of Texas.

[72]Maud Morrow Brown, editor, "Reminiscences of the War of the Confederacy by R. O. B. Morrow," manuscript in possession of the editor.

[73]Samuel Saltus to his sister, Jan. 13, 1862, manuscript, Heartman Collection.

[74]A. N. Erskine to his wife, July 20, 1862, manuscript, University of Texas.

[75]O. R., series 1, XXX, part 2, 789.

[76]J. H. Puckett to his wife, Oct. 16, 1863.

[77]The canteens were easily halved by the insertion and setting off of a small charge of powder. Albert T. Goodloe, *Some Rebel Relics from the Seat of War* (Nashville, 1893), 41. Some "canteen plates" are on exhibit in the Confederate Museum at Richmond. Graters were made by driving numerous nail holes in canteen sides. J. F. Coghill to "Dear Mit," Oct. 18, 1862, manuscript, Duke University.

[78]A. C. Redwood, "The Cook in the Confederate Army," *Scribner's Monthly*, XVIII (1879), 560-568.

[79]James A. Hall to his sister, Oct. 22, 1863, manuscript, Alabama Archives. For other descriptions of ingredients and processes, see Heartsill, *op. cit.*, 186; and McCarthy, *op. cit.*, 59.

[80]Jarman, *op. cit.*, 28-29.

[81]O. R., series 4, I, 889.

[82]William M. Whatley to his wife, Oct. 21, 1862, manuscript photostat, University of Texas.

[83]John Crittenden to his wife, Nov. 3, 1864; McCarthy, *op. cit.*, 65; J. E. Hall to his father, April 11, 1864, manuscript, Alabama Archives.

[84]T. B. Hampton to his wife, Feb. 21, 1864.

[85]McCarthy, op. cit., 65; diary of J. Stanley Newman, entry of July 26, 1861, manuscript, Confederate Museum; James C. Nisbet, *Four Years on the Firing Line* (Chattanooga, 1914), 255.

[86]J. B. Mitchell to his father, Sept. 9, 1861, typescript, Alabama Archives.

[87]William R. Stillwell to his wife, April 1, 1863.

[88]Jerome Yates to "T. O. D.," Jan. 18, 1864; Charles W. Hutson to his mother, March 4, 1862, manuscript, University of North Carolina.

[89]Thomas Warrick to his wife, April 2, 1863, manuscript, Alabama Archives.

[90]C. Irvine Walker to Ada Sinclair, July 23, 1864.

[91]Robert M. Gill to his wife, Aug. 28, 1864, manuscript in author's possession.

[92]Heartsill, op. cit., 164.

Chapter VII

FROM FINERY TO TATTERS

[1]O. R., series 4, I, 369-373; *Confederate States Army Regulations*, 1862, article 47. The 1861 *Army Regulations* did not contain provisions concerning uniform and dress; this was due probably to the tardiness of the War Department in releasing data on this subject.

[2]See *Atlas to Accompany Official Records of the Union and Confederate Armies* (Washington, D. C., 1891-1895), plate 72.

[3]O. R., series 1, LI, part 2, 15.

[4]*Ibid.*, IV, 479; New Orleans *Daily Crescent*, May 4, 1861; F. B. Simkins and J. W. Patton, *The Women of the Confederacy* (Richmond, 1936), 18 ff; "War Reminiscences of Anne Pelham Finlay," typescript, Greenville, Mississippi, Public Library.

[5]Randolph H. McKim, "Glimpses of the Confederate Army," F. T. Miller, editor, *Photographic History of the Civil War* (New York, 1911), VIII, 109.

[6]Stanley Horn, *The Army of Tennessee* (Indianapolis, 1941), 140-141.

[7]Kate Cumming, *A Journal of Hospital Life in the Confederate Army of Tennessee* (Louisville and New Orleans, 1866), 37.

[8]H. M. Doak, "Reminiscences," 13, typescript, Tennessee State Library.

[9]Oscar W. Blacknall, editor, "Papers of C. C. Blacknall," introduction, typescript, North Carolina Historical Commission.

[10]DeLeon, op. cit., 71-72.

[11]*Ibid.*, 96-97.

[12]*O. R.*, series 4, II, 382-383.

[13]*Ibid.*, 229-230; III, 1039-1040.

[14]*Southern Historical Society Papers*, XXXI (1903) 246; E. P. Thompson, *History of the Orphan Brigade* (Louisville, 1898), 203; Miller, *op. cit.*, VIII, 120.

[15]*Confederate Veteran*, XII (1904), 116. The issue of white uniforms to some conscript outfits caused stigma to be attached to their wear by volunteers. Members of the Twenty-sixth Louisiana had to be threatened with severe punishment before they would don the undyed regalia. Hall, *op. cit.*, 59-60.

[16]McCarthy, *op. cit.*, 20-21; "Simpson War Reminiscences," manuscript, Tennessee State Library. William R. Stillwell wrote to his wife from camp in Virginia April 30, 1864: "I have not got my hat yet I need it very bad most burnt up with the sun face blistered I dont think I will ever ware another cap while I live." Manuscript, Georgia Archives.

[17]New Orleans *Daily Crescent*, May 29, 1861.

[18]W. C. McClellan to Robert McClellan, August —?, 1861.

[19]Theodore Mandeville to his sister, Aug. 27, 1861.

[20]John E. Hall to his father, Oct. 14, 1861, manuscript, Alabama Archives.

[21]*O. R.*, series 4, III, 691-692, 1039-1040.

[22]F. L. Owsley, *States Rights in the Confederacy* (Chicago, 1925), 126.

[23]John Crittenden to his wife, March 24, 1864.

[24]Frank Moss to his sister, Oct. 28, 1863, manuscript, University of Texas.

[25]Jerome Yates to his mother, April 2, 1864, manuscript, Heartman Collection.

[26]William H. Routt to his wife, March 13, 1863, manuscript, Confederate Museum, Richmond.

[27]E. P. Becton to his wife, Dec. 14, 1862, typescript, University of Texas.

[28]J. T. Terrell to his mother, Dec. 29, 1862, manuscript in private possession.

[29]Charleston *Daily Courier*, Sept. 3, 1862.

[30]Richmond *Daily Dispatch*, April 24, 1862.

[31]DeLeon, *op. cit.*, 185.

[32]Manuscript among L. M. Nutt Papers, University of North Carolina.

[33]J. H. Puckett to his wife, April 15, 1863; Thomas Caffey to his sister, Feb. 16, 1863.

[34]Sebron Sneed to his wife, June 7, 1864, manuscript, University of Texas.

[35]Letter of August 6, 1861.

[36]Diary of H. S. Archer, entry of Nov. 9, 1863, manuscript microfilm, Vanderbilt University.

[37]William M. Dame, *From the Rapidan to Richmond* (Baltimore, 1920), 36-37.

[38]S. G. Pryor to his wife, Feb. 4, 1863.

[39]James A. Graham to his mother, March 9, 1862, manuscript, University of North Carolina.

[40]Andrew M. Chandler to his mother, Aug. 31, 1862, manuscript photostat in possession of Mrs. Ella Mae Chandler, West Point, Mississippi.

[41]Wiley, op. cit., 134.

[42]R. W. Waldrop to his mother, Aug. 27, 1862, manuscript, University of North Carolina.

[43]J. M. Jordan to his wife, June 27, 1864, typescript, Georgia Archives; T. B. Hampton to his wife, Feb. 3, 1865, typescript, University of Texas.

[44]Maj. Henry C. Semple to his wife, Nov. 3, 1864, manuscript, University of North Carolina. Soldiers of the Army of Tennessee thought that partiality in clothing issues was shown by Richmond authorities to troops of Lee's command.

[45]O. R., series 1, XLII, part 3, 1268-1269; series 4, III, 1039-1040; Lee to A. P. Hill, Jan. 20, 1865, manuscript, Confederate Museum.

[46]J. F. J. Caldwell, *History of Gregg's and McGowan's Brigade* (Philadelphia, 1866), 196-197.

[47]Fitzgerald Ross, *A Visit to the Cities and Camps of the Confederate States* (London, 1865), p. 31.

[48]General Order No. 47, issued by Longstreet, Nov. 7, 1862, manuscript among Washington Artillery Papers, Confederate Memorial Hall New Orleans.

[49]William H. Cody to his sister, Oct. 18, 1864, in E. C. Burnett, editor, "Letters of Barnett Hardeman Cody and Others," *Georgia Historical Quarterly*, XXIII (1939), 379.

[50]O. R., series 1, V, 785.

[51]Charleston *Daily Courier*, Sept. 3, 1862.

[52]O. R., series 1, XIX, part 2, 590-591.

[53]The Richmond *Daily Dispatch* of October 9, 1862, carried a pungent editorial on the subject of clothing for Lee's army. In reference to the Antietam campaign the editor said: "Posterity will scarcely believe that the wonderful campaign which has just ended with its terrible marches and desperate battles, was made by men, one-fourth of whom were entirely barefooted, and one-half of whom were as ragged as scarecrows. . . . We cease to wonder at the number of stragglers, when we

hear how many among them were shoeless, with stone bruises on their feet."

[54]Richard Lewis, *Camp Life of a Confederate Boy* (Charleston, 1883), 35.

[55]O. R., series 4, II, 204.

[56]Thomas Caffey to his mother, Nov. 12, 1863. Generals in command were evidently forced to require duty of barefooted men to prevent would-be shirkers from throwing away their shoes to avoid drilling and fighting. See O. R., series 1, XXX, part 4, 715.

[57]Anonymous manuscript in Confederate Memorial Hall, New Orleans.

[58]Richmond *Enquirer*, April 12, 1864. General Lee complained of the poor quality of some of the shoes issued by government quartermasters during the winter of 1863-1864. O. R., series 1, XXXIII, 1131-1132.

[59]Hanks, op. cit., 78.

[60]John H. Hancock to his parents, Nov. 11, 1862, manuscript among Richard D. White Papers, North Carolina Historical Commission.

[61]Robert M. Gill to his wife, July 30, 1864.

[62]O. R., series 1, XLV, part 1, 735-736, 747.

[63]Robert Selph Henry, *The Story of the Confederacy* (Indianapolis, 1931), 434.

Chapter VIII

TRIALS OF SOUL

[1]L. M. Johnson, *An Elementary Arithmetic Designed for Beginners* (Raleigh, 1864), 34, 38, 44.

[2]O. R., series 4, I, 277.

[3]*Ibid.*, 497.

[4]*Ibid.*, 380.

[5]Undated but postwar letter of J. M. Montgomery to Victor Montgomery, manuscript in private possession.

[6]O. R., series 4, I, 352-353, 380.

[7]*Ibid.*, series 1, XXIV, part 3, 1053-1054.

[8]This summary of conscription is based primarily on data from the fourth series of the *Official Records of the Union and Confederate Armies*. Extensive and scholarly treatments of the subject are to be found in A. B. Moore, *Conscription and Conflict in the Confederacy* (New York, 1924), and Owsley, op. cit. A thorough survey of judicial aspects of the question is available in William M. Robinson, Jr., *Justice in Grey* (Cambridge, 1940).

[9]O. R., series 4, III, 48-49.

[10]This account of substitution is drawn principally from series four of the *Official Records*, from Professor Moore's excellent chapter on the subject in his *Conscription and Conflict in the Confederacy*, and from J. B. Jones, *A Rebel War Clerk's Diary* (Philadelphia, 1866). William M. Robinson, Jr., has helpful comments on judicial harangues over substitution in his *Justice in Grey*.

[11]*O. R.*, series 4, II, 696.

[12]*Ibid.*, 997.

[13]Exception should be made of some men, not subject to military service, who engaged substitutes as a gesture of patriotism. The number of such cases, however, was so small as to be of insignificant proportion to the aggregate of proxies. See *O. R.*, series 4, III, 12, General Order No. 3, Adjutant General's Office. Men and officers reported as "present for duty" in Lee's army in April 1863 aggregated 64,799. *Ibid.*, II, 530.

[14]Joseph A. E. Boyd to "De" Boyd, April 12, 1862, manuscript, Alabama Archives.

[15]Joe Shields to his father, June 10, 14, and July 1, 1861, manuscript, Louisiana State University.

[16]Theodore Mandeville to Rebecca Mandeville, April 22, Aug. 17, 1861, manuscript, Louisiana State University.

[17]Fred R. Taber to his homefolk, Dec. 13, 25, and Jan. 11, 1862, manuscripts, Louisiana State University.

[18]George W. Athey to his father, Jan. 18, 1862, manuscript, Alabama Archives.

[19]Will T. Martin to his wife, Oct. 20, 1861, typescript in private possession.

[20]Reid, *op. cit.*, 76.

[21]Frank Moss to "Lou" Moss, Nov. 27, 1862, and to Mrs. A. E. Rentfrow, Feb. 14, 1863; W. M. Moss to Mrs. A. E. Rentfrow, Jan. 31, 1863, manuscripts, University of Texas.

[22]E. J. Ellis to his mother, June 9, 1862, Feb. 15 and March 18, 1863, manuscript, Louisiana State University.

[23]This version is from a letter of John H. Munford to his cousin Sallie, Oct. 24, 1862, manuscript, Duke University.

[24]John Crittenden to his wife, Feb. 20, 1863, typescript, University of Texas.

[25]John R. Hopper to his brother, Sept. 9, 1863, manuscript, Heartman Collection.

[26]William R. Stillwell to his wife, Aug. 13, 1863, manuscript, Georgia Archives.

[27]Orville C. Bumpass to his wife, Dec. 1, 1863, manuscript, Evans Memorial Library.

[28]A. Wideman to his sister, Mrs. Thomas Warrick, May 19, 1864, manuscript, Alabama Archives.

[29]Diary of Charles Moore, manuscript, Confederate Memorial Hall.

[30]"I witnessed the other day a fight between the divisions composing Hardee's Corps. It was the grandest affair I ever witnessed. . . . One part presented the Confederate States Army and one the Yankees army. The Yankees made the attack. They marched up with banners flying to the tune of Yankee Doodle. As soon as the Confederates charged them they fled apparently in the . . . wildest confusion. Five rounds to the man was expended. The battle lasted about three hours. Nearly the whole of Hood's corps witnessed it." John R. Crittenden to his brother, April 9, 1864.

[31]O. R., series 1, XXXIII, 1144-1145; see also ibid., XXXII, part 2, 571-582.

[32]Ibid., XXXII, part 2, 582, 665, et passim.

[33]J. T. Terrell to his mother, March 12, 1864, manuscript in private possession.

[34]O. R., series 4, III, 374.

[35]P. M. H. S. Centenary Series, V, 311-312.

[36]There were some who took a pessimistic view of the situation even after Grant's setbacks in the Wilderness. On June 13, 1864, Sgt. William H. Phillips wrote his parents: "We hav bin in the habit of Driving away Every army of the North that has ever come close to Richmond But I am afraid that old Grant is rather too much for us this time he cant [can] outnumber Genl Lee so fare I think it will be hard to get him away this time, if Grant would Keep fighting of us we soon get him so weak that we could Drive him away but he has stoped and fortified himself and is waiting for us to fight him." Manuscript Duke University. General Stephen D. Lee noted a deleterious effect of the unsuccessful defense of Atlanta on fighting qualities. "The majority of the officers and men were so impressed with the idea of their inability to carry even temporary breastworks," he wrote, "that when orders were given for attack, and there was a probability of encountering works . . . they did not generally move to the attack with that spirit which nearly always assures success." O. R., series 1, XXXIX, part 1, 810.

[37]J. J. Hardy to his cousin, Jan. 24, 1865, typescript, Georgia Archives.

[38]Thomas Caffey to his sister, Jan. 15, 1865, "War Letters of Thomas Caffey," Montgomery Advertiser, May 16, 1909.

[39]P. M. H. S. Centenary Series, V, 356.

[40]James H. Baker to his father, Feb. 1, 1865, manuscript, Duke University; Daniel Albright to his homefolk, March 19, 1865, manuscript, Duke University. Baker was a captain.

[41]Robert W. Banks to his homefolk, Oct. 22, 1862, typescript in private possession.

[42]Crenshaw Hall to his father, May 27, 1863, manuscript, Alabama Archives.

[43]O. R., series 1, XXXIII, 1114; XLVI, part 2, 1143.

[44]Thomas Warrick to his wife, Oct. 26, 1863, manuscript, Alabama Archives. Private Andrew J. Patrick of the 37th Mississippi Regiment wrote his wife, Oct. 26, 1862: "I would not mind living hard if I node you was not suffering but you are there and I am here and cant tend to you." On November 2, 1862, he wrote further on the subject: "I am uneasy about you and the children getting something to eat . . . there is alredy a heap of men gone home and a heap says if their familys gets to suffering that they will go if they have to suffer [punishment]." Typescripts in private possession.

[45]H. A. Stephens to his sister, Jan 1, 1864, manuscript in private possession; T. B. Barron of the Fiftieth Virginia Regiment wrote to his parents, Aug. 8, 1863: "It is truly hard for the soldier to content himself in the field . . . when he sees his government give the speculator the advantage of him & his family *speculation* will cause *desertion* & *desertion* will be our ruin." Manuscript, Confederate Museum.

[46]For scale of pay prescribed by Congress by an act of March 6, 1861, see O. R., series 4, I, 130.

[47]O. R., series 4, III, 492. The Georgia Legislature petitioned Congress for an increase to $20 per month of the pay of privates in April 1863, but to no avail. *Ibid.*, II, 485.

[48]P. M. H. S. Centenary Series, V, 308.

[49]O. R., series 1, XIX, part 2, 722.

[50]*Ibid.*, VI, 408; P. M. H. S. Centenary Series, V, 298.

[51]O. R., series 1, XLVI, part 2, 1143.

[52]T. B. Hampton to his wife, Dec. 15, 1862, typescript, University of Texas.

[53]C. W. Stephens to his father, Nov. 6 [26], 1863.

[54]Frank Moss to his sister, Aug. 16, 1864; V. S. Rabb to his mother, Aug. 22, 1864, manuscripts, University of Texas.

[55]Anonymous diary of a Louisiana soldier, entry of Dec. 18, 1863, manuscript, Heartman Collection.

[56]O. R., series 4, III, 48-49.

[57]*Ibid.*, series 1, XXIV, part 2, 393-394. For detail of reaction of officers and men to such a proposal, see petition of Johnson's brigade in *ibid.*, series 1, XLII, part 2, 1264-1265.

[58]Robert M. Gill to his wife, Aug. 22 and Nov. 27, 1862, manuscripts in author's possession.

[59]C. W. Stephens to his sister, March 5, 1865.

[60]O. R., series 1, XLIII, part 1, 609-610, report of Major Moore, and indorsement of Assistant Adjutant and Inspector General Peyton; see also *ibid.*, XXXII, part 2, 778-779.

[61]*Ibid.*, series 1, XLI, part 4, 1112-1113.

[62]Deter Jochum to his homefolk, Jan. 30, 1864, manuscript, Confederate Memorial Hall.

[63]W. M. Moss to his sisters, Dec. 28, 1863, manuscript, University of Texas.

[64]Orville C. Bumpass to his wife, Oct. 22, 1864.

[65]C. W. Stephens to his sister, Jan. 30, 1864.

[66]Robert M. Gill to his wife, June 9, 1862.

[67]Thomas Warrick to his wife, June 15, 1862.

[68]William R. Barksdale to his brother, June 11, 1861, manuscript in private possession.

[69]Richmond *Enquirer*, Nov. 3, 1863; Correspondence of Medical Director of General Hospitals in Virginia, 1864-1865, Confederate Archives, chapter VI, volume 365, p. 214, manuscript, National Archives; General Orders and Circulars, Department of South Carolina, Georgia and Florida, *ibid.*, chapter II, volume 43, p. 329-330; diary of C. M. Horton, entry of July 7, 1863, manuscript, Confederate Memorial Hall. Henry C. Semple to his wife, Dec. 19, 1862, manuscript, University of North Carolina; Alfred W. Bell to his wife, Sept. 17, 1864, manuscript, Duke University.

[70]O. R., series 1, XXV, part 2, 639.

[71]Robinson, *op. cit.*, 252-254; O. R., series 4, II, 465; III, 68-69.

[72]Confederate authorities attempted on occasion to differentiate between deserters and other unwarranted absentees, and historians have been constrained in some instances to follow their example. But the line of demarcation is so thinly drawn and so variable as to be largely arbitrary. At what point, for example, did a man who overstayed his furlough, or a convalescent who failed to report for duty, become a deserter? And in what category was the infantryman to be placed who, without ample authority, secured transfer to a cavalry company? The purpose of this study is better served by classifying as unwarranted absentees deserters and all other soldiers who absented themselves by irregular devices from the service to which they were assigned.

[73]O. R., series 1, XIX, part 2, 597, 605, 622; Philip Slaughter, *Sketch of the Life of Randolph Fairfax* (Richmond, 1864), 33, quoting a letter of Fairfax from Bunker Hill, Va., Oct. 3, 1862; Richmond *Daily Dispatch*, Sept. 26, 1862, Jan. 14, 1864; Freeman, *op. cit.*, II, 411-412. A factor contributing to straggling was, as Freeman points out, the exhausted and shoeless condition of many of the troops.

[74]O. R., series 1, XXIV, part 3, 1007, 1010, 1018.

[75]*Ibid.*, series 4, II, 721.

[76]*Ibid.*, 674; an editorial in the Richmond *Daily Dispatch* of Jan. 11, 1864, said: "Nearly half our military force is scattered over the country, and if returned to its proper position not another man would be needed

in the field." Three days later the *Dispatch* editor reverted to the subject of straggling with this inquiry: "Where was the balance of the 110,000 men on Bragg's muster roll when he fought the battle of Chickamauga with less than 40,000? . . . Where are the stragglers and deserters who swarm in the mountains and infest the lower country like locusts?"

[77]*O. R.*, series 4, III, 397-398, 802-803; series 1, XXXII, part 3, 681-682; XXXIX, part 2, 588-589; Ella Lonn, *Desertion During the Civil War* (New York, 1928), 62-105; Georgia Lee Tatum, *Disloyalty in the Confederacy* (Chapel Hill, 1934), 24 ff.

[78]J. M. Jordan to his father, Feb. 14, 1863, typescript, Georgia Archives.

[79]*O. R.*, series 1, XLII, part 2, 1175-1176; series 4, III, 689-690. The Richmond *Daily Dispatch* of Jan. 26, 1865, quoted a correspondent of the Atlanta *Appeal:* "If one-half of the men of the Confederacy capable of bearing arms would cease to shirk their duty . . . and . . . come to the front we could expel the invaders from our soil within six weeks."

[80]Lonn, *op. cit.*, 23.

[81]*Ibid.*; *O. R.*, series 1, XLVI, part 2, 1265, 1293.

[82] *O. R.*, series 1, LI, part 2, 1065; Lonn, *op. cit.*, 30.

[83]*O. R.*, series 4, III, 1182. Returns are for varying dates, ranging from Dec. 31, 1864, to April 17, 1865, for different armies of the Confederacy.

[84]DeLeon, *op. cit.*, 142.

[85]Lonn, *op. cit.*, 123.

[86]Mollie Vandenberg to C. H. Clark, March 11, 1862, manuscript in private possession.

[87]C. L. Stephens to E. A. Stephens, March 5, 1865, manuscript in private possession.

[88]James L. G. Wood to his father, March 31, 1864, typescript, Georgia Archives.

[89]J. Joe Evans to John Holliday, Jan. 7, 1865, manuscript in private possession.

[90]*O. R.*, series 1, XI, part 1, 408-409.

[91]*Ibid.*, XXIV, part 2, 392-393, 410.

[92]*Ibid.*, XXIX, part 1, 408.

[93]Bolling Hall to his father, April 15, 1864, manuscript, Alabama Archives.

[94]H. A. Stephens to his sister, Dec. 6, 1863; Jerome Yates to his friend, "T.O.D.," May 4, 1864; E. G. Higgason to his mother, Oct. 29, 1864, manuscript in private possession.

[95]Robert M. Gill to his wife, April 16, 1864.

[96]Joseph Renwick to his wife, April 14, 1865, manuscript, Louisiana State University.

[97]Cowper, *op. cit.*, 122-123.

[98]J. T. Terrell to his parents, Nov. 16, 1862, March 12, May 2, June 6, 1864.

[99]Manuscript in private possession.

[100]J. M. J. Tolly to James R. Hall, April 22, 1865, manuscript, Alabama Archives.

Chapter IX

BREAKING THE MONOTONY

[1]Journal of James Hampton Kuykendall, entry of Aug. 27. 1862, typescript, University of Texas.

[2]William M. Worthington to his sister, July 15, 1864, manuscript in private possession; diary of A. L. P. Vairin, entry of July 6, 1862, manuscript, Mississippi Archives.

[3]Diary of Charles Moore, Jr., entries of Sept. 24, 1861, and Feb. 27, 1862, manuscript, Confederate Memorial Hall; New Orleans *Daily Crescent*, May 8, 1861.

[4]Duke University, the University of Virginia and the Confederate Museum each has large collections of Confederate sheet music.

[5]Most of these items may be found in the Confederate Museum. Others were examined in collections at Emory University and the Library of Congress. Several more songbooks are listed by Richard B. Harwell in *Confederate Belles-Lettres* (Hattiesburg, Miss., 1941), but these were not seen by the writer. A veteran of the Tenth Virginia Regiment wrote: "We kept song books with us and passed much of our leisure time singing. I carried my book even through prison and brought it home with me." James Huffman, *Up and Downs of a Confederate Soldier* (New York, 1940), 68.

[6]Popularity of these songs was established by references in soldier correspondence and diaries and by recurrence in pocket songbooks. All of the melodies listed were mentioned in letters or diaries.

[7]Randolph McKim, "Glimpses of the Confederate Army," Miller, *op. cit.*, VIII, 122.

[8]*Fort Lafayette Life, 1863-1864*, in *Extracts from the Right Flanker* (London, 1865), 10.

[9]Walter A. Clark, *Under the Stars and Bars* (Augusta, Ga., 1900), 79.

[10]Manuscript among W. J. Clarke Papers, University of North Carolina.

[11]Harry St. John Dixon of the Twenty-eighth Mississippi Volunteers wrote in his diary on Jan. 14, 1863, "a soldier's usual occupation has whiled away my time, listening to vulgar songs, yarns . . . smok-

ing, and reading." Manuscript, University of North Carolina. Edmund C. Burnett of the Carnegie Institution repeated to the writer a stanza of an obscene song sung by a Rebel prisoner, but the words are unprintable.

[12]Manuscript among G. L. Robertson Letters, University of Texas.

[13]New Orleans *Daily Crescent*, July 9, 1861. For other parodies on "Dixie," see W. L. Fagan, editor, *Southern War Songs* (New York, 1890), 7, 36 and 238.

[14]Original sheet music as published by A. E. Blackmar & Brother, New Orleans, 1861, Duke Sheet Music Collection. An ex-Confederate recalled hearing Harry McCarthy, stage songster who wrote the words and who did much to popularize the song, "often . . . sing it when thousands of people went wild with excitement." H. M. Wharton, editor, *War Songs and Poems of the Southern Confederacy, 1861-1865* (Philadelphia, 1904), 23.

[15]For full text see original sheet music as published by Blackmar and Brother, Augusta, 1862, Duke Collection. In the Blackmar edition "touch" is used instead of "torch." This is evidently a printer's error. The song lost caste with Maryland's failure to give wholehearted support to the Confederacy; as one soldier expressed it, "About the third year of the war . . . we began to think Maryland had 'breathed and burned' long enough and ought to 'come.'" Southern Historical Society *Papers*, I (1876), 80.

[16]June Kimble, "The 14th Tenn. Glee Club," typescript, Confederate Museum. For reference to another glee club see James Peter Williams to his aunt, March 16, 1865, manuscript, University of Virginia.

[17]James T. Searcy to his sister, Stella, from Corinth, Miss., May 5, 1862, manuscript, Alabama Archives.

[18]Diary of D. S. Redding, entry of July 3, 1863, typescript, Georgia Archives.

[19]Diary of James J. Kirkpatrick, entry of Oct. 30, 1863, manuscript, University of Texas.

[20]Fremantle, *op. cit.*, 71-72; *Battle-Fields of the South*, II, 101-103.

[21]Reid, *op. cit.*, 60.

[22]Clark, *North Carolina Regiments*, II, 397-400.

[23]New Orleans *Daily Crescent*, Dec. 21, 1861, and Jan. 8, 1862, correspondence of I[srael] G[ibbons].

[24]Robert E. Park, *The Twelfth Alabama Infantry* (Richmond, 1906), 101; Edward McMorries, *Historical Sketch of the First Alabama Volunteers* (Montgomery, 1904), 52.

[25]Edward T. Worthington to Amanda Worthington, Oct. 4, 28, 1861, manuscript in private possession.

[26]James N. Thrower to his brother, Oct. 27, 1861, manuscript, Alabama Archives.

[27]Letter of Oct. 20, 1861, manuscript in private possession.

[28]Cate, op. cit., 30.

[29]James A. Hall to Joe Hall, April 18, 1864, manuscript, Alabama Archives; diary of D. P. Hopkins, entry of March 15, 1862, typescript, University of Texas.

[30]New Orleans Daily Crescent, Oct. 29, 1861; Alfred Chisholm to his mother, April 11, 1863, manuscript, University of North Carolina; J. F. Sale to his aunt, Sept. 3, 1863, manuscript, Virginia State Library.

[31]Diary of James J. Kirkpatrick, entry of Jan. 3, 1863; Samuel Saltus to his sister, March 12, 1862, manuscript, Heartman Collection.

[32]Diary of A. L. P. Vairin, entry of April 19, 1862; diary of T. J. Ford, entry of Oct. 23, 1862, manuscript, Heartman Collection.

[33]Chamberlayne, op. cit., 130. Chamberlayne told also of the fox-catching episode.

[34]J. H. Puckett to his wife, Feb. 10, 1863, manuscript, University of Texas.

[35]In these affairs speeding riders attempted to snatch with lances hoops suspended from tall uprights. For vivid description of a large-scale contest see Joseph C. Robert, "A Ring Tournament in 1864," Journal of Mississippi History, III (1941), 293-296.

[36]J. W. Ward to his sister, May 27, 1863, manuscript, Heartman Collection; T. J. Newberry to his father, June 8, 1862, manuscript in author's possession.

[37]W. H. Neblett to his wife, April 28, 1863, manuscript, University of Texas.

[38]Ibid.

[39]Robert M. Gill to his mother, Oct. 16, 1862, manuscript in author's possession.

[40]Walter Keeble to his wife, Feb. 2, 1862, manuscript, University of Texas; diary of L. G. Hutton, entry of Feb. 5, 1862, manuscript, University of Texas.

[41]Fred R. Taber to his homefolk, Oct. 19, 1861, manuscript, Louisiana State University; J. T. Terrell to his parents, various dates, 1862-1863, manuscripts in private possession.

[42]W. H. Stephenson and Edwin A. Davis, editors, "The Civil War Diary of Willie Micajah Barrow," Louisiana Historical Quarterly, XVII (1934), 436-451, 712-731; various letters of Hutson for 1861-1862, manuscripts, University of North Carolina.

[43]Diary of Harry St. John Dixon, entry of May 19, 1862, et passim, manuscripts, University of North Carolina.

[44]H. A. Stephens to his sister, Jan. 31, 1864, manuscript in private possession.

[45]George W. F. Harper to his wife, April 5, 1864, manuscript, University of North Carolina; Robert M. Gill to his wife, July 13, 1862; [Bartlett], op. cit., 54.

[46]"Personne" [F. G. DeFontaine], Marginalia; or Gleanings from an Army Notebook (Columbia, S.C., 1864), 108.

[47]Journal of B. L. Ridley, undated entry (April, 1865), Confederate Veteran, III (1893), 134.

[48]Horn, op. cit., 469. A. L. P. Vairin gives this explanation of the origin of "Here's your mule" in his diary: "The first I heard of it was this—some man in the neighbourhood had lost an old gray mule and was . . . enquiring for it among the Regiments—Co. B. had straw in their tents to sleep on. . . . Among them Tom Nance . . . his hair was very thin on his head and his ears seemed all the larger for it— Under the general excitement of the day he laid down in his tent to sleep—some lively fellows roving about . . . happened to look in Tom's tent and being struck with his appearance called out for the mule man —Here's your mule others came to see and repeated the saying . . . and fun and yeling being the order of the day the words soon reechoed alover the camp and those adjoining and became a by word everywhere." Undated entry, but evidently late 1861. A song of Confederate origin gives a version differing in detail from Vairin's; see Fagan, op. cit., 319-320.

[49]Manuscript photostat, no date, no place, University of Texas.

[50]Robert Fore to "Mr. Readon," Jan. 2, 1863, manuscript among Reding Papers, University of Texas.

[51]Journal of E. Mussence, undated entry [Jan. 1863?], manuscript (fragment) among Washington Artillery Papers, Confederate Memorial Hall; diary of T. J. Ford, entry of Dec. 28, 1862.

[52]G. L. Robertson to his mother, June 25, 1864, manuscript, University of Texas.

[53]John Crittenden to his mother, March 25, 1864, manuscript, University of Texas.

[54]Diary of D. P. Hopkins, entry of April 1, 1862.

[55]Stiles, op. cit., 49.

[56]New Orleans Daily Crescent, Oct. 29, 1861; Confederate Veteran, V (1895), 134.

[57]Diary of D. P. Hopkins, entry of April 12, 1862.

[58]"McLaws Minstrels a company composed of young men from Barksdale's Brigade . . . have been playing 3 times a week for the last month to large audiences." Diary of William H. Hill, Thirteenth Mississippi Regiment, entry of Feb. 27, 1863, manuscript, Mississippi Archives. In some instances log theaters were built in camp for winter entertainments.

[59]New Orleans Daily Crescent, Oct. 29, 1861; Montgomery Daily

Mail, March 29, 1863, quoting "Personne" of Charleston *Courier;* Mobile *Daily Advertiser and Register,* March 30, 1864.

[60]Mobile *Daily Advertiser and Register,* March 30, 1864.

[61]J. O. Casler, *Four Years in the Stonewall Brigade* (Guthrie, Okla., 1893), 307-309.

[62]Owen, *op. cit.,* 205-206. This program was repeated the next winter. Diary of Charles R. Walden, Oct. 22, 1863, typescript, Georgia Archives.

[63]V. S. Rabb to his sister, March 18, 1863.

[64]Diary of G. L. Griscom, undated entry [about Feb. 10, 1863], manuscript, University of Texas.

[65]C. W. Stephens to his sister, Oct. 14, 1863, manuscript in private possession.

[66]New Orleans *Daily Crescent,* Oct. 1, 19, 1861; [Bartlett], *op. cit.,* 67-68. In the fall of 1861 some South Carolina Rebs bought lumber and erected a hall for the holding of regular dances. The first dance held in the new edifice ended in a free-for-all fight. Milton S. Walker to his mother, Sept. 13, 1861, manuscript, Duke University.

[67]Diary of D. P. Hopkins, entry of April 14, 1862.

[68]S. W. Farrow to his wife, Jan. 18, 1864, manuscript, University of Texas.

[69]Diary of Charles Moore, Jr., entry of Sept. 24, 1861.

[70]V. S. Rabb to his brother, Jan. 4, 1863, manuscript photostat, University of Texas.

[71]Anonymous diary of a Louisiana soldier, entry of Dec. 25, 1863, manuscript, Confederate Memorial Hall.

[72]Letter of Theodore Mandeville, Dec. 29, 1861, manuscript, Louisiana State University.

[73]Journal of James H. Kuykendall, entry of Dec. 25, 1862.

[74]Diary of L. G. Hutton, entry of July 3-4, 1862.

[75]Stephens failed to date this letter.

[76]See for instance diary of William H. Hill, various entries of April and July, 1863; also letter of William J. Whatley to his wife, Dec. 25, 1862, manuscript, photostat, University of Texas.

[77]New Orleans *Daily Crescent,* Oct. 19, 1861.

[78]Robert M. Gill to his wife, April 29, 1861, June 3, 12, and Sept. 13, 1862, July 9, 1863; V. S. Rabb to his mother, July 9, 1864.

[79]Charles H. Clark to Mrs. Mary Johnston, Aug. 7, 1861, manuscript in private possession; J. B. Mitchell wrote his mother, July 23, 1862: "Notwithstanding the great number of sick in our regiment they seem to be generally content and cheerful. They amuse themselves by circulating all sorts of improbable stories and telegraphic dispatches. The latest news detailed to me by one of Capt Slaughter's men is that

Africa has recognized the Southern Confederacy." Typescript in Alabama Archives.

[80]Jerome Yates to his mother, April 20, 1864, manuscript, Heartman Collection; Stephenson and Davis, op. cit., 445; diary of M. W. Barber, entry of Sept. 23, 1864, typescript, University of Texas.

[81]James T. Searcy to his sister, Dec. 16, 1862, manuscript, Alabama Archives.

[82]New Orleans *Daily Crescent*, Oct. 19, 1861.

[83]Stiles, op. cit., 170-171. The Fourth North Carolina Infantry Regiment had a fine St. Bernard dog taken during the Seven Days' campaign while guarding the corpse of a Yankee colonel. Cowper, op. cit., 17-18.

[84]*Battle-Fields of the South*, I, 161-162; John H. Worsham, *One of Jackson's Foot Cavalry* (New York, 1912), 75; Watkins, op. cit., 59.

[85]Thomas Warrick to his wife, May 18, 1863.

[86]William Decatur Howell to his mother, May 11, 1864, manuscript in possession of Maud Morrow Brown, University, Mississippi.

[87]Mobile *Daily Advertiser and Register*, March 20, 1863.

[88]Winifred Gregory, editor, *Union List of Newspapers* (New York, 1937), 655; Basil W. Duke, *Morgan's Cavalry* (New York, 1906), 154-206; Mrs. Irby Morgan, *How It Was: Four Years Among the Rebels* (Nashville, 1892), 79, 187-204; Cecil Fletcher Holland, *Morgan and His Raiders* (New York, 1942), 139 ff., 151, 156-157.

[89]Gregory, op. cit., 344. The writer examined a copy of this paper in the Confederate Museum. Other issues are in the Library of Congress, the Missouri Historical Society, and the Minnesota Historical Society.

[90]The writer has been able to locate only one copy of one issue of this paper. This is in the Tennessee State Library. Contents of another issue are summarized in the *Confederate Veteran*, IV (1896), 344.

[91]The first two issues of "The Pioneer Banner" are in a scrapbook in the Military Records Division of the Alabama Department of Archives and History. The author is indebted to Mr. Peter Brannon, efficient Division Director, for permission to make photostats of this item.

[92]For a reproduction of the contents of sample issues of these items see Heartsill, op. cit., 56 ff.

[93]McMorries, op. cit., 51.

[94]Owen, op. cit., 73-74; Henry, op. cit., 300-301.

[95]Heartsill, op. cit., 86.

[96]Jonas A. Bradshaw to his wife, April 11, 1863, manuscript, Duke University.

[97]Frank Moss to his sisters, Lou and Bet, Nov. 27, 1862, manuscript, University of Texas.

98John Crittenden to his father, Dec. 20, 1863.

99Thomas Warrick to his wife, May 18, 1863; William R. Stillwell to his wife, Nov. 10, 1862.

100Frank Moss to his sister Lou, Aug. 29, 1862.

Chapter X

CONSOLATIONS OF THE SPIRIT

1New Orleans *Daily Crescent*, May 23, 1861.

2Hankins, op. cit., 11-13.

3J. W. Jones, op. cit., 564.

4 Robert M. Gill to his wife, Dec. 23, 1862, manuscript in author's possession.

5Joseph J. Cowand to his cousin, Dec. 1, 1862, manuscript, Duke University.

6Bible Convention of the Confederate States of America, *Proceedings* (Augusta, Ga., 1862), 1-15; J. W. Jones, op. cit., 148-151.

7William R. Stillwell, a lay-preacher who served as courier in the Fifty-third Georgia Regiment, wrote his wife May 10, 1863, that he had obtained, as a result of the Chancellorsville fight, numerous "him books" and "testaments by the holdsale [wholesale]." He probably distributed these items among fellow soldiers. Manuscript, Georgia Archives.

8J. W. Jones, op. cit., 148-151.

9*Ibid.*, 158-161. W. W. Bennett, *A Narrative of the Great Revival Which Prevailed in the Southern Armies* (Philadelphia, 1877), 74-76.

10This issue, dated Oct. 15, 1863, is among the Van David Papers, University of Texas.

11Richmond *Daily Dispatch*, July 5, 1862; Jones, op. cit., 156-161.

12This summary is based on a study of a large collection of tracts at the University of North Carolina and smaller lots at Emory University and at Louisiana State University. *A Mother's Parting Words to Her Soldier Boy* (no place, no date) is in the Keith M. Read Collection at Emory University. In this collection also there is a list of 103 brochures published by the South Carolina Tract Society.

13S. G. Pryor to his wife, April 26, 1863, typescript, University of Texas.

14J. W. Jones, op. cit., 155.

15Richmond *Enquirer*, April 15, 1862.

16J. W. Jones, op. cit., 194.

17Some revivals were reported in Virginia camps in the winter of

1861-1862, but these were on a comparatively small scale. New Orleans *Daily Crescent* (quoting Charleston *Courier*), Feb. 3, 1862.

[18]R. B. Hudgens to his uncle, manuscript among Thomas F. Boatwright Papers, University of North Carolina.

[19]Montgomery *Daily Mail*, April 10, 1863.

[20]W. S. Douglass to his sister, Dec. 20, 1863, manuscript, University of Texas.

[21]Robert Edward Hill to his sister, June 21, 1863, manuscript, University of Texas.

[22]F. W. Thompson to his sister, Aug. 14, 1863.

[23]J. W. Jones, *op. cit.*, 262.

[24]*Ibid.*, 248-249.

[25]*Ibid.*, 42.

[26]*Ibid.*, 552-553.

[27]*Ibid.*, 353.

[28]Calvin H. Wiley, *Scriptural Views of National Trials* (Greensboro, N.C., 1863), 187 ff.

[29]J. W. Jones, *op. cit.*, 390.

[30]Stiles, *op. cit.*, 114.

[31]J. W. Jones, *op. cit.*, 357.

[32]*Battle-Fields of the South*, I, 280. For reference to a Catholic service in Bragg's army see Henry C. Semple to his wife, March 15, 1863, manuscript, University of North Carolina.

[33]These three booklets are in the Keith M. Read Collection at Emory University.

[34]*Soldier's Hymn Book* (Charleston, 1863), 198, 202, 233.

[35]The popularity of these songs is established by references to them in soldier correspondence and diaries and by their recurrence in camp hymn books.

[36]Thomas F. Boatwright to his wife, Sept. 9, 1863, manuscript, University of North Carolina; Mobile *Advertiser and Register*, Oct. 1, 1863.

[37]Isaac Alexander to his mother and sister, June 27, 1862, typescript, University of North Carolina.

[38]J. W. Jones, *op. cit.*, 223.

[39]H. A. Stephens to his sister, Oct. 5, 1863, manuscript in private possession.

[40]Jerome Yates to his sister, May 4, 1864, manuscript, Heartman Collection.

[41]Matthews, *Statutes at Large of the Confederate Government* (Richmond, 1862-1864), Provisional Government, Second Session, chapters 1 and 22, Third Session, chapter 69; Permanent Government, First Congress, First Session, chapter 56, Fourth Session, chapter 13.

[42]Richmond *Daily Dispatch*, Nov. 21, 1861. The contributor of this article protested against the reduction on the ground of discrimination. By a law of Congress, he said, chaplains were ranked as first

lieutenants, and the pay prescribed for officers of that grade was ninety dollars a month.

[43]J. W. Jones, op. cit., 226-230, 363; R. H. McKim, A Soldier's Recollections (New York, 1910), 219-221.

[44]Arthur H. Noll, editor, Dr. Quintard, Chaplain, C.S.A. (Sewanee, Tenn., 1905), pp. 4 ff; Charles Todd Quintard to George C. Harris, Nov. 5, 1861, manuscript, Tennessee State Library.

[45]J. W. Jones, op. cit., 522.

[46]O. R., series 1, XXV, part 1, 873.

[47]Typescript of scrapbook of Miss Alphine Sterrett, Alabama Archives; the clipping is dated Nov. 9, 1861.

[48]O. R., series 1, XXV, part 1, 873; XXXIV, part 1, 620; XXXVIII, part 3, 845, 933

[49]McKim, op. cit., 219-221.

[50]Battle-Fields of the South, I, 278-279.

[51]Journal of James H. Kuykendall, entry of Dec. 14, 1862, typescript, University of Texas.

[52]E. P. Becton to his wife, Aug. 12, 1862, manuscript photostat, University of Texas.

[53]R. W. Waldrop to his mother, April 6, 1862, manuscript, University of North Carolina.

[54]Thomas Caffey to his sister, Nov. 19, 1863, in Montgomery Advertiser, May 9, 1909.

[55]John Crittenden to his wife, July 15, 1864.

[56]William R. Stillwell to his wife, May 28, 1863; J. P. Williams to his sister, Dec. 9, 1864, manuscript, University of Virginia.

[57]Diary of H. S. Archer, entry of April 12, 1863, et passim, manuscript microfilm, Vanderbilt University.

[58]W. W. Pierson, editor, "Diary of Bartlett Yancey Malone," James Sprunt Historical Publications, XVI (1917-1919), 18, 27, 32, 33.

[59]J. W. Jones, op. cit., 226-230.

[60]O. R., series 1, II, 954; J. W. Jones, op. cit., 240, 252, 537; G. C. Eggleston, A Rebel's Recollections (New York, 1878), 240-241.

[61]J. W. Jones, op. cit., 390.

Chapter XI

DEAR FOLKS

[1]John Barksdale to his brother, June 12, 1862, manuscript in private possession.

[2]John Crittenden to his wife, June 28, 1862, typescript, University of Texas.

[3]Thomas Warrick to his wife, Feb. 12, June 23, 1863, manuscript, Alabama Archives.

[4]E. K. Flournoy to his wife, March 21, 1863, manuscript, Alabama Archives.

[5]Wilson Athey to his cousin, June 16, 1862, manuscript, Alabama Archives.

[6]William J. Whatley to his wife, Nov. 2, 9, 1863, manuscript photostats, University of Texas.

[7]C. E. Taylor to his father, July 14, 1861, Sept. 28, 1862, manuscripts, Heartman Collection.

[8]This envelope contained a letter written by Thomson to his father, Nov. 5, 1861, from Kingsville, S. C., manuscript in private possession.

[9]Filed with letter of John N. Shealy to his wife, July 17, 1862, manuscript, Louisiana State University.

[10]Robert Laurence, Catalog of the George Walcott Collection of Used Civil War Patriotic Covers (New York, 1934), 248.

[11]On envelope of J. M. Brown's letter to his mother, Aug. 31, 1864, typescript, Georgia Archives.

[12]On letterhead used by Crenshaw Hall in a note to his father, June 26, 1861, manuscript, Alabama Archives.

[13]At head of sheet in letter of Thomas Mandeville to Ellwyn Mandeville, Aug. 31, 1861, manuscript, Louisiana State University.

[14]Laurence, op. cit., 258.

[15]On envelope used by J. M. Robertson, found among Robertson Papers, manuscript photostats, University of Texas.

[16]This item is filed with Moss-Barmore-Colclough-Rentfrow Papers, University of Texas.

[17]William R. Stillwell to his wife, April 11, 1863, manuscript, Georgia Archives.

[18]Letter of Nov. 19, 1683, "War Letters of Thomas Caffey," Montgomery Advertiser, May 9, 1909; S. W. Farrow to his wife, June 2, 1864, manuscript, University of Texas.

[19]William J. Whatley to his wife, Nov. 2, 9, 1862.

[20]Montgomery Advertiser, May 9, 1909.

[21]Elers Koch to his parents, April 20, 1863, manuscript, Louisiana State University.

[22]Manuscript dated March 11-12, 1863, University of Texas.

[23]Manuscript among Bolling Hall Papers, Alabama Archives.

[24]John Crittenden to his wife, July 15, 1864.

[25]Frank Moss to Mrs. A. E. Rentfrow, Dec. 6, 1864, manuscript, University of Texas.

[26]William R. Stillwell to his wife, May 10, 1863.

[27]Stuart Noblin, "Leonidas Lafayette Polk" (Ph.D. thesis in progress, University of North Carolina), chapter 3.

[28]Bolling Hall, Jr., to his father, Nov. 19, 1861; Will T. Martin to his sister, Jan. 31, 1863, typescript in private possession.

[29]J. H. Puckett to his wife, June 27, 1862, manuscript, University of Texas.

[30]Captain James A. Graham to his mother, Sept. 13, 1864, manuscript, University of North Carolina.

[31]Z. J. Armistead to his brother, May 31, 1864, typescript, Georgia Archives.

[32]Only fifteen out of sixty letters written by W. C. McClellan were prepaid. T. J. Newberry in a letter to his father of Feb. 20, 1863 said: "I dont put Stamps on my letters [because] they Say they will go better without them." Manuscript in author's possession. The Confederate postal rate was raised from five to ten cents (per half ounce) on April 19, 1862. Matthews, *Statutes at Large of the Permanent Government*, First Session, chapter 45.

[33]M. M. Quaife, editor, *Absalom Grimes, Confederate Mail Runner* (New Haven, 1926), 49 ff.

[34]*Ibid.*, 65.

[35]For the engrossing details of these feats, see Quaife, *op. cit.*, 113 ff. Subsequent publication in St. Louis newspapers of the captured letters must have produced considerable embarrassment among Confederate sympathizers. See Missouri *Democrat*, Sept. 8, 10, 1862, and Missouri *Republican*, Sept. 7, 8, 9, 1862.

[36]New Orleans *Daily Crescent*, Dec. 4, 1861.

[37]Robert M. Gill to his wife, Oct. 6, 1863, manuscript in author's possession.

[38]Diary of Maurice K. Simons, entry of April 24, 1863, manuscript photostat, University of Texas.

[39]James L. G. Wood to his father, Aug. 5, 1864, manuscript, Georgia Archives.

[40]J. T. Terrell to his mother, July 9, 1864, manuscript in private possession.

[41]Letters of Robert M. Gill to his wife; Gill was mortally wounded near Atlanta, Aug. 31, 1864.

[42]W. J. Honnoll to his cousin, Aug. 27, 1863, manuscript, Emory University.

[43]G. W. Athey to his mother, Nov. 11, 1863.

[44]J. F. Coghill to "Dear Mit," April 10, March 28, 1862, manuscripts, Duke University.

[45]W. C. Simmons to his cousin, Feb. 12, 1862, manuscript, Emory University.

[46]Thomas Warrick to Ab Widman, Feb. 12, 1863, manuscript, Alabama Archives.

[47]W. J. Honnoll to his wife, Aug. 27, 1863.

[48]Thomas Warrick to his wife, Oct. 6, 1862, and Jan. 11, 12, 1863.

[49]W. B. Lance to his father, Aug. 18, 1863, manuscript, Louisiana State University.

[50]Thomas Warrick to his wife, April 8, 1863.

[51]For a misquotation of this rhyme, see undated letter of J. M. Guess to his wife, from Camp Moore, La., manuscript, Confederate Memorial Hall.

[52]Letter of Thomas Warrick to his father, Sept. 10, 1862, and those of various subsequent dates to his wife.

[53]Charles Futch to John Futch, Oct. 16, 1861, manuscript, North Carolina Historical Commission.

[54]Thomas Warrick to Martha Ann Warrick, April 30, 1862.

[55]Spencer G. Welch, *A Confederate Surgeon's Letters to his Wife* (New York, 1911), 121; John Rogers to his brother, June 24, 1861, manuscript, Emory University; J. L. Anderson to his mother, Jan. 21, 1862, manuscript, Emory University.

[56]W. C. McClellan to his sister, Aug. 31, 1861.

[57]W. C. McClellan to his brother, Oct. 6, 1861.

[58]J. F. Coghill to his brother, Oct. 6, 1864, and James K. Wilkerson to his sister, Aug. 29, 1864, manuscripts, Duke University.

[59]Undated letter of J. M. Guess to his wife.

[60]Manuscript dated May 19, 1864, Alabama Archives.

[61]Frank Moss to his sister, March 21, 1863.

[62]James K. Wilkerson to his father, June 3, 1862; S. W. Farrow wrote his wife July 19, 1863: "If I had a good place to write on I would soon be a good pensman, as I write ten letters for other men to where I write one for myself. Sometimes I write five or six a day for the Boys." Manuscript, University of Texas.

[63]Letter of Aug. 2, 1863, manuscript, Georgia Archives.

[64]W. W. Brown to his mother, June 4, 1862, manuscript, Duke University.

[65]Robert M. Gill to his wife, June 15 and Nov. 30, 1862.

[66]D. Hunter to his wife, June 9, 1862, manuscript among Miscellaneous Civil War Letters, University of Texas.

[67]William R. Stillwell to his wife, Nov. 30, 1862; the child proved to be a girl and was apparently named Virginia.

[68]Mrs. Alfred W. Bell to her husband, Sept. 5, 1862, manuscript, Duke University. Bell had previously teased his wife about flirtation with "fancy girls'" in the environs of camp.

[69]John H. Hartman to his wife, Feb. 6, 1864, manuscript, Duke University.

[70]Thomas Warrick to his wife, Jan. 11, 1863.

[71]Jerome Yates to his mother, Jan. 11, 1864, manuscript, Heartman Collection.

[72]V. S. Rabb to his sister, July 2, 1864, manuscript photostat, University of Texas.

[73]Manuscript dated Aug. 13, 1863, location and correspondents restricted to confidence.

[74]Confidential manuscript dated Dec. 1, 1863.

[75]Robert E. Hill to Mary Scott Hill, April 29, 1864, manuscript, University of Texas.

[76]E. P. Becton to his wife, Oct. 16, 1862, manuscript, University of Texas.

[77]See O. R., series 1, XXIII, part 2, 951; XXV, part 2, 746; LI, part 2, 712.

[78]Occasionally letters from homefolk containing disloyal sentiments fell into the hands of military officers and were passed on to higher authorities, but apparently no action was taken to prevent delivery of other such mail in camp. Ibid., series 1, XXIII, part 2, 951.

[79]Ibid., series 4, III, 642.

[80]William J. Whatley to his wife, Oct. 12, 1862.

[81]Frank Moss to his sister, Nov. 27, 1862.

[82]William Decatur Howell to his mother, June 26, 1864, manuscript in possession of Maud Morrow Brown, University, Mississippi.

[83]T. J. Newberry to his father, April 18, 1863.

[84]Capt. S. G. Pryor to his wife, Feb. 20, 1863, typescript, Georgia Archives.

[85]Lt. John B. Evans to his wife, June 6, 1864, manuscript, Duke University.

[86]Erastus Higgins to James Reding, April 25, 1865, manuscript, University of Texas.

[87]Copy of letter filed with A. N. Erskine Papers, manuscript, University of Texas.

[88]Robert M. Gill to his wife, June 14, 1862.

[89]R. G. Hutson to his wife, Feb. 17, 1862, manuscript, Duke University.

[90]Jonas A. Bradshaw to his wife, Jan. 26, 1862, manuscript, Duke University.

[91]B. L. Mobley to his father, Nov. 3, 1861, manuscript, Emory University.

[92]Undated item, but evidently October 1863, found among William R. Stillwell Papers. Stillwell wrote the poem while serving with the Army of Tennessee near Chattanooga.

[93]Ibid.

[94]Manuscript among Thomas Warrick Letters.

Chapter XII

KICKING OVER THE TRACES

[1]A manuscript copy of the proceedings is filed with Washington Artillery Papers in Confederate Memorial Hall, New Orleans. This collection will be cited hereinafter as W. A. Papers.

[2]Robinson, op. cit., 362-365.

[3]Regimental court-martial proceedings, manuscript, Confederate Memorial Hall.

[4]General Order Book of the Army of the Mississippi, Jan. 6-Aug. 24, 1862, manuscript, Confederate Memorial Hall.

[5]In the spring of 1862, however, General Beauregard approved a sentence of hanging for murder handed down by a general court-martial in the case of one Dan Whritson, even though such a sentence was beyond authority conferred by war regulations. His reason for setting aside established rules was that the crime was committed in Kentucky, "where ordinary resort to a civil court for his punishment was impossible." Ibid.

[6]O. R., series 1, XIX, part 2, 597-598.

[7]Robinson, op. cit., 367-369.

[8]O. R., series 4, II, 288, 1003; III, 709.

[9]Miscellaneous court-martial proceedings, W. A. Papers.

[10]William J. Whatley to his wife, Nov. 18, 1862, manuscript, University of Texas.

[11]Miscellaneous court-martial proceedings, W. A. Papers.

[12]General Order No. 55, 1862, Headquarters Department of South Carolina, Georgia, and Florida, p. 2, pamphlet, National Archives. Pemberton, the departmental commander, ordered remittance of the sentences on the ground that they were absurdly light. Ibid., 10.

[13]Miscellaneous court-martial proceedings, W. A. Papers.

[14]Court-Martial Records, Confederate Archives, chapter I, volumes 194-201, manuscripts, National Archives. The cases cited are from volume 198, pp. 384-498. The eight volumes consist mainly of sentences imposed by general courts-martial and military courts, though portions of volumes 197 and 198 give the offense as well as the sentence; in many instances the offense can be ascertained from the nature of the penalty. The records extend over the entire period of the war and include both eastern and western commands, though the Army of Northern Virginia is better represented than other departments. Total cases listed run well up into the thousands. A portion of volume 199 is devoted to indorsements of and correspondence concerning courts-martial. Hereafter in this chapter these records will be cited as C. M. Records.

[15]Records of the First Kentucky Brigade, Confederate Archives, chapter II, volume, 308, p. 333.

[16]Miscellaneous court-martial proceedings, W. A. Papers.

[17]General Order No. 26, 1863, Headquarters Trans-Mississippi Department, in bound volume of printed separates, Confederate Archives, chapter II, volume 74, p. 223.

[18]C. M. Records, chapter I, volume 194, p. 152.

[19]*Ibid.*, volume 198, p. 443.

[20]Lewis R. Tomlinson to his grandfather, Oct. 1, 1864, manuscript among miscellaneous Civil War Letters, Duke University.

[21]C. M. Records, chapter I, volume 194, p. 214, and volume 197, p. 120; General Order No. 197, 1863, Headquarters District of Texas, New Mexico, and Arizona, in Confederate Archives, chapter II, volume 114, p. 103; General Order No. 11, 1863, Headquarters Army of the West, *ibid.*, volume 211, pp. 35-36. Sometimes offenders thus punished were dishonorably discharged from the army at the completion of their sentence.

[22]C. M. Records, chapter I, volume 194, p. 13; volume 195, p. 61; and volume 198, pp. 390, 421, 435. In the case of the South Carolinian, General Lee remitted the branding.

[23]*Ibid.*, volume 195, p. 341.

[24]General Order Book, Army of the Mississippi, Jan. 6-Aug. 24, 1862.

[25]General Order Book Crescent Regiment, Sept. 1862-Sept. 1863, manuscript, Confederate Memorial Hall.

[26]C. M. Records, chapter I, volume 197, pp. 131, 137; volume 198, pp. 383, 385, 393.

[27]Crenshaw Hall to his father, March 21, 1864, manuscript, Alabama Archives.

[28]Of 913 cases, covering roughly the last six months of the war, for which both offenses and sentences are recorded in the Confederate Archives, 372 are for desertion. Other offenses in the order of their frequency are: absence without leave, 177; conduct prejudicial to good order and military discipline, 99; misbehavior before the enemy, 44; disobedience of orders, 40; neglect of duty, 34; theft and robbery, 20; mutiny and exciting mutiny, 19; insubordination and disrespect to superiors, 16; drunkenness, 12; sleeping at post of duty, 11; quitting guard and otherwise deserting post of duty, 10; breaking guard, 6; self-mutilation, 3; straggling, 3; selling clothes, 2; miscellaneous, 45. These cases were largely from the Army of Northern Virginia. They were about evenly distributed between military courts and general courts-martial. C. M. Records, chapter I, volume 198, pp. 382-512.

[29]O. R., series 1, XXIII, part 2, 954-955; XLVI, part 2, 1230.

[30]General orders and circulars, Department of South Carolina, Georgia, and Florida, July 19, 1862-May 28, 1863, Confederate Archives,

chapter II, volume 43, pp. 289, 408. Rather than permit the setting of a precedent for such trifling punishment, Beauregard remitted the sentences.

[31]C. M. Records, chapter I, volume 198, pp. 384-402.

[32]Ibid., 382-512. Sixty-seven of the culprits were to be shot and three to be hanged. Further evidence of lenient tendencies on the part of these courts and courts-martial is evidenced by the fact that in 112 cases (in addition to the 245) where prisoners were charged with desertion, the tribunals substituted the charge of absence without leave.

[33]Ibid.; O. R., series 1, XXIX, part 2, 806-807.

[34]Diary of George W. Jones, typescript in private possession. One prisoner thus spared by a last-minute reprieve deserted the next night and successfully evaded capture for the remainder of the war. W. J. Worsham, op. cit., 77.

[35]C. E. Taylor to his father, Jan. 17, 1863, manuscript, Heartman Collection.

[36]O. R., series 1, XXXII, part 3, 626.

[37]An insight into flogging technique is afforded by the following report in the Richmond Dispatch, October 6, 1862, of the punishment of a deserter named Owen Maguire: "A stout dragoon from Captain Wrenn's Company volunteered to perform the duty. Maguire was tied up to a tree by the hands and feet and received the punishment with much wiggling and twisting. It seemed to be awful; it was honestly laid on with a double leather strap, broad and long. When let down he looked quite exhausted." Private J. F. Coghill of North Carolina wrote his father March 29, 1863, that two soldiers had recently died as a result of floggings. Manuscript, Duke University.

[38]C. M. Records, chapter I, volume 194, p. 55.

[39]Ibid., volume 195, pp. 73, 87.

[40]General Order No. 22, 1863, Headquarters Trans-Mississippi Department, Confederate Archives, chapter II, volume 74, p. 229. Riding the wooden horse was used occasionally for offenses other than desertion.

[41]John Crittenden to his wife, Dec. 20, 1862, typescript, University of Texas.

[42]Thomas Warrick to his wife, April 11, June 11, Dec. 19, 1862, Oct. 26, 1863, and June 11, 1864, manuscripts, Alabama Archives.

[43]Miscellaneous court-martial proceedings, W. A. Papers.

[44]General Order No. 24, 1862, Headquarters Department of Texas, pamphlet among O. M. Roberts Papers. The writer found several instances of death being prescribed for violence against superior officers, but such sentences were amazingly rare, and some of them were set aside by higher authority.

[45]Ibid.

[46]General Order No. 6, 1861, Headquarters Department of Texas, pamphlet among O. M. Roberts Papers. The offender in this instance was a corporal.

[47]Confederate Archives, chapter II, volume 41, pp. 20-21.

[48]General Order Book, Army of the Mississippi, Jan. 6-Aug. 24, 1862.

[49]General Order No. 87, 1863, Headquarters Department of Northern Virginia, pamphlet among C. S. Venable Papers, University of Texas.

[50]General Order Book, Crescent Regiment, Sept. 1862-Sept. 1863.

[51]General Order No. 26, 1863, Headquarters Trans-Mississippi Department, Confederate Archives, chapter II, volume 74, p. 223.

[52]C. M. Records, chapter I, volume 194, pp. 96, 210; volume 195, pp. 338, 445; volume 198, p. 403. Noll, op. cit., 13. Welch, op. cit., 45. Joseph Hergesheimer, Swords and Roses (New York, 1929), 308. Sentence in the last mentioned case—that of the march from San Antonio to Austin—was remitted by the departmental commander. General Order No. 8, 1864, Headquarters Department of Texas, New Mexico, and Arizona, Confederate Archives, chapter II, volume 113, pp. 34-35.

[53]Robinson, op. cit., 365.

[54]New Orleans Daily Crescent, June 25, 1861.

[55]Diary of D. P. Hopkins, typescript, University of Texas.

[56]O. R., series 1, XXXII, part 2, 654.

[57]Diary of C. R. Hanleiter, manuscript, Atlanta Historical Society, entries of Dec. 8, 1861, April 2, 1862, and July 25, 1863.

[58]In his official report of Shiloh, Bragg complained of the ill effects of random shooting by troops en route from Corinth to the scene of battle; firing by volleys and single shots, he said, was kept up "all night and until 7 A.M. next morning April 5, by the undisciplined troops of our front, in violation of positive orders, under such circumstances little or no rest could be obtained by our men." O. R., series 1, X, part 1. 464.

[59]James A. Hall to his father, Jan. 17, 1862, manuscript, Alabama Archives.

[60]Diary of A. L. P. Vairin, entry of April 19, 1862, manuscript, Mississippi Archives. Walter K. Wendell made this entry in his diary while stationed near Fredericksburg, June 16, 1861: "Sentinels gave several false alarms last night. Picket guard fired at and killed 1 dog dead , . . . He was made this morning to carry ye dead dog in his arms around the encampment double quick." Typescript, Tennessee State Library.

[61]General Hindman in 1863 tabooed the wooden horse and "other methods of punishment having the character of torture." O. R., series 1, XXXI, part 3, 881.

[62]Robert A. Jarman, op. cit., 25, typescript in possession of Maud Morrow Brown, University, Mississippi.

[63]Peak, op. cit., manuscript in private possession.

[64]Record Book of Company I, First Virginia Regiment, entry of Sept. 18, 1864, manuscript, Confederate Museum.

[65]Diary of G. L. Griscom, entries of Oct. 31 and Nov. 13, 1861, manuscript, University of Texas.

[66]O. R., series 1, XXXII, part 3, 877.

[67]Ibid., XLII, part 2, 1276-1277.

[68]Theodore Mandeville to his sister, Dec. 29, 1861, Jan. 3, 1862, manuscripts, Louisiana State University.

[69]John McGrath, "In a Louisiana Regiment," Southern Historical Society Papers, XXXI (1903), 104.

[70]William Decatur Howell to his mother, June 2, 3, 4, 1864, manuscript in possession of Maud Morrow Brown, University, Mississippi.

[71]Letter of S. W. Farrow, April 19, 1864, manuscript, University of Texas.

[72]John Crittenden to his wife, April 23, 1863, typescript, University of Texas.

[73]William S. Whatley to his wife, Dec. 4, 1862, manuscript photostat, University of Texas.

[74]Diary of James J. Kirkpatrick, entry of Aug. 13, 1863, manuscript, University of Texas.

[75]T. W. Hall to his sister, Jan. 28, 1862, manuscript, Alabama Archives.

[76]Thomas Caffey to his sister, June 26, 1861, "War Letters of Thomas Caffey," Montgomery Advertiser, March 28, 1909.

[77]Heros von Borcke, Patrick Cleburne and other foreigners were quite popular with their men, but most non-native officers, including Cleburne, had greater difficulty securing promotion than did Southern-born men. Ella Lonn, Foreigners in the Confederacy (Chapel Hill, 1940), 132 ff.

[78]Nicholas A. Davis, The Campaign from Texas to Maryland with the Battle of Fredericksburg (Richmond, 1863), 18-19.

[79]Anonymous diary of a Louisiana soldier, entry of Oct. 25, 1863, manuscript, Confederate Memorial Hall.

[80]Diary of William H. Hill, entry of Aug. 10, 1861, manuscript, Mississippi Archives; C. W. Stephens to his sister, Oct. 14, 1863, manuscript in private possession.

[81]Jerome Yates to his mother, Aug. 20, 1861, manuscript, Heartman Collection.

[82]W. C. McClellan to his brother Bob, Nov. 9, 1861, manuscript in private possession.

[83]Captain James Hays to his wife, Jan. 20, 1863, typescript, Georgia Archives.

[84]John Crittenden to his wife, May 31, 1864, typescript, University of Texas.

[85]John Crittenden to his father, July 12, 1864.

[86]Anonymous diary of a Louisiana soldier, entry of Aug. 5, 1862, manuscript, Heartman Collection.

[87]Letter of March 18, 1863, manuscript, Louisiana State University.

[88]Note on letter of General Walker to his wife, Nov. 28, 1864, typescript, University of Texas.

[89]Randolph H. McKim, "Glimpses of the Confederate Army," Miller, op. cit., VIII, 129.

[90]Diary of George W. Jones, entry of Sept. 18, 1862.

[91]Douglas, op. cit., 115-116.

[92]Robert M. Gill to his wife, manuscript in author's possession.

[93]Anonymous diary of a Louisiana Soldier, entry of April 8, 1861.

[94]W. A. Rorer, an officer of intelligence and good standing, wrote to his wife, Nov. 12, 1863: "The officers of our regiment made an effort to get rid of our colonel on account of drunkenness and incompetence, all wanted him disposed of, there was no difficulty in proving everything, yet he got out on a legal quibble. Our army here is cursed with incompetent and drunken officers, yet there is no way to get rid of them." On March 31, 1864, while functioning as president of a court-martial, he observed: "I am weary of it, there is folly, mismanagement and meanness everywhere in the army. With good management we could have the finest army in the world. I have no heart to punish men for disobeying the orders of fools, still it must be done." Manuscripts among W. M. Willcox Papers, Duke University.

[95]O. R., series 1, XLVI, part 2, 1249; series 4, II, 205-206, 1001.

[96]Ibid., series 1, XLVII, part 2, 1149-1152; report to William H. Boggs of inspection of Wharton's Cavalry Corps, Jan. 30, 1865, manuscript among L. M. Nutt Papers, University of North Carolina.

[97]O. R., series 1, XXX, part 2, 611-612.

[98]A. L. Harrington to his brother, June 13, 1864, manuscript, Duke University. A general court-martial, sitting at Charleston in early 1863, found that a Georgia captain gambled on one occasion with his soldiers while a tentful of enlisted men looked on, and that in another instance he permitted a private to say to him with impunity: "You are a damned rogue and a thief, and if you will take off your stripes I will give you a damned licking." Confederate Archives, chapter II, volume 43, pp. 491-493.

[99]Daily Richmond Enquirer, Nov. 4, 1864.

[100]O. R., series 1, VI, 531.

[101]Ibid., XXXII, part 3, 877-879.

[102]*Ibid.*, LI, part 2, 111.

[103]*Ibid.*, XLII, part 2, 1276-1277.

[104]*Ibid.*, XLVI, part 2, 1247-1248. On January 20, 1865, Lee wrote A. P. Hill concerning inspection reports of the latter's corps: "The superior officers, except the Brigadier in McRae's Brigade, visit and inspect the troops very seldom. There is also a general deficiency in the instruction of men and officers in drill and tactics . . . . Public animals are not well treated or fed." He intimated further that deficiencies in equipment and clothing were due in part to negligence of officers. Manuscript, Confederate Museum.

Chapter XIII

THE DEADLIEST FOE

[1]J. W. Love to his family, manuscript, Duke University.

[2]E. J. Ellis to Stephen Ellis, manuscript, Louisiana State University.

[3]Alfred Bell to his wife, April 25, 1862, manuscript, Duke University.

[4]*Southern Historical Society Papers*, XX (1892), 115; Surgeon General of the United States Army, *Medical and Surgical History of the War of the Rebellion* (Washington, D. C., 1870-1888), Medical History, III, 1. Hereinafter the abbreviation Surgeon General will be used for the author of this work. There is apparently a discrepancy between Jones's estimate of the ratio of deaths from disease to those from casualties in battle as given in the Southern Historical Society *Papers* and as cited in the *Medical and Surgical History*. The writer accepted the figure given by the *Medical and Surgical History* because of the alleged examination and approval of that figure by Confederate Adjutant General S. Cooper.

[5]Stanley, *op. cit.*, 169.

[6]Matthews, *Statutes at Large of the Confederate Congress*, Permanent Government, Session II, Chapter 41; O. R., series 4, II, 408-409; General Order No. 58, Adjutant and Inspector General's Office, August 14, 1862, Confederate Archives, chapter I, volume 4, manuscript, National Archives.

[7]A. E. McGarity to his wife, April 21, 1864, typescript in possession of E. C. Burnett, Washington, D. C.

[8]Frank Richardson to his mother, October 8, 1862, manuscript, University of North Carolina.

[9]DeLeon, *op. cit.*, 142; McGrath, *op. cit.*, 112.

[10]O. R., series 1, XI, part 3, p. 454.

[11]C. Irvine Walker to Ada Sinclair, Nov. 10, 1864, typescript, University of Texas.

[12]Diary of Arthur M. Hyatt, manuscript, Louisiana State University.

[13]*O. R.*, series 1, XLI, part 4, 1003.

[14]*Battle-Fields of the South*, II, 112-113.

[15]Charleston *Daily Courier*, April 10, 1862.

[16]C. Irvine Walker to Ada Sinclair, May 19, 1862.

[17]*O. R.*, series 1, X, part 1, 776.

[18]Southern Historical Society *Papers*, XX (1892), 130.

[19]*O. R.*, series 1, XXVIII, part 2, 589-590, 598-600.

[20]Diary of Richard W. Waldrop, manuscript, University of North Carolina.

[21]*O. R.*, series 1, XLII, part 2, 1273.

[22]*Ibid.*, series 1, XLVI, part 2, 1099-1100.

[23]J. M. Jordan to his wife, June 27, 1864, typescript, Georgia Archives.

[24]New Orleans *Daily Crescent*, June 11, 1861.

[25]H. A. Tutwiler to "Nettie," June 25, 1862, manuscript among McCorvey Papers, University of North Carolina.

[26]Montgomery *Daily Mail*, April 17, 1863.

[27]D. M. Key to his wife, April 30, 1863, manuscript, University of North Carolina.

[28]*Ibid.*

[29]J. H. Puckett to his wife, March 7, 1862, manuscript, University of Texas.

[30]J. E. Thornton to his wife, March 5, 1862, manuscript in private possession.

[31]E. T. Clark to Mary Johnston, Aug. 10, 1861, manuscript in private possession.

[32]Ben Robertson to his sister, Feb. 2, 1862, manuscript photostat, University of Texas.

[33]W. C. McClellan to his sister, Jan. 12, 1863, manuscript in private possession.

[34]Diary of William E. Bradley, entry of April 25, 1865, manuscript in private possession.

[35]W. C. McClellan to his sister Jan. 12, 1863; J. H. Puckett to his wife, March 23, 1863; Fletcher, *op. cit.*, 22.

[36]Hanks, *op. cit.*, 81; Cate, *op. cit.*, 31.

[37]W. C. McClellan to his sister, April 22, 1863.

[38]Thomas Warrick to Martha Warrick, March 22, 1863, manuscript, Alabama Archives.

[39]Gerrish and Hutchinson, *op. cit.*, 180.

[40]Surgeon General, *op. cit.*, III, 649.

[41]W. B. Blanton, *Medicine in Virginia in the Nineteenth Century* (Richmond, 1933), 296.

[42]O. R., series 1, VI, 817.

[43]William H. Phillips to his mother, Aug. 13, 1861, manuscript, Duke University.

[44]A. N. Erskine to his wife, July 27, 1862, manuscript, University of Texas.

[45]Surgeon General, op. cit., II, 26-30.

[46]Blanton, op. cit., 296-297.

[47]Marietta M. Andrews, editor, *Scraps of Paper* (New York, 1929), 88.

[48]Surgeon General, op. cit., II, 26-32.

[49]*Ibid.*, III, 106.

[50]*Ibid.*, 102-108.

[51]Blanton, op. cit., 292.

[52]Surgeon General, op. cit., III, 31, 205, 207. Conclusions concerning typhoid are difficult to draw because of the confusion of nomenclature. The term "continued fevers" is used in the *Medical and Surgical History of the War of the Rebellion* to designate typhoid, typhus and "common continued fevers." The meaning of the last-named classification is not clear, but apparently it was used to designate chicken pox, scarlet fever and various diseases resembling typhoid, which could not be clearly recognized as such. Among Confederates "camp fever" seems to have had divers connotations, though in some instances the term was used synonymously with typhoid. Joseph Jones, *Medical and Surgical Memoirs* (New Orleans, 1876-1890), I, 669. Professor George Worthington Adams in a splendid article entitled "Confederate Medicine" says: "There was considerable argument as to whether the 'camp fever' which bedeviled the army was typhoid or some vague newcomer. The disputants could arrive at no definite decision, but the modern student is inclined to suspect that the paratyphoids, then unknown, made the variant cases whose presence confused the doctors." *Journal of Southern History*, VI (1940), 162.

[53]Surgeon General, op. cit., III, 627-628. An argument was carried on with some vehemence, but with no settlement, between W. A. Carrington and L. Guild as to whether or not the disease was introduced into the army from Virginia hospitals or into the hospitals from the army. See Letter Book of the Medical Director of the Army of Northern Virginia, June 28, 1862-Aug. 29, 1862, Confederate Archives, chapter VI, volume 641, pp. 22, 70, 71, manuscript, National Archives; this source will be cited hereinafter as Guild, Letter Book.

[54]Surgeon General, op. cit., III, 627-628.

[55]*Ibid.*, 638-648. Guild, Letter Book, volume 641, 83-84. Inspection Reports and Letters Sent, Office of the Medical Director of Hospitals

in Virginia, Confederate Archives, chapter VI, volume 416, pp. 65-67 (to be cited hereinafter as Carrington, Inspection Reports), manuscript, National Archives. Correspondence of the Confederate Surgeon General's Office, Confederate Archives, chapter VI, volume 739, pp. 193, 250, 362, 523, 529 (to be cited hereinafter as Moore, Correspondence), manuscript, National Archives.

[56]Jones, *Medical and Surgical Memoirs*, I, 650-666. Jones and other wartime authorities do not mention influenza, but a present-day medical historian says: "During the Civil War a type of endemic pneumonia was described corresponding to our understanding of influenzal pneumonia." Blanton, *op. cit.*, p. 248.

[57]Courtney R. Hall, "Confederate Medicine," *Medical Life*, XLII (1935), 479-480; Surgeon General, *op. cit.*, III, 31.

[58]Thomas Warrick to his wife, June 15, 1862. Another Reb wrote, "Ben Parker has the yellow Ganders." J. E. Thornton to his wife, March 5, 1862.

[59]Surgeon General, *op. cit.*, III, 707-708; B. E. Yerbey to his father, Jan. 31, 1862, typescript, Georgia Archives.

[60]In 1861 and 1862, according to Joseph Jones, 29, 334 cases of rheumatism were reported. Surgeon General, *op. cit.*, III, 31.

[61]See *supra*, chapter 3.

[62]Guild, Letter Book, volume 642, p. 13; *Confederate States Medical and Surgical Journal*, March, 1864.

[63]Walter Keeble to his wife, May 3, 1863, manuscript, University of Texas.

[64]Thomas S. Taylor to his wife, Oct. 4, 1861, manuscript, Alabama Archives.

[65]J. W. Rabb to his sister, Dec. 5, 1861, manuscript, University of Texas.

[66]Charles W. Hutson to his mother, July 6, 1861, typescript, University of North Carolina.

[67]Jackson's pamphlet was published by the Augusta (Georgia) *Constitutionalist* in 1862. The extracts quoted are from pages 21-34.

[68]Published in 1863 by West and Johnson of Richmond.

[69]Ruffin Thomson to his father, April 21, 1862, typescript in private possession.

[70]Robert M. Gill to his wife, Oct. 23, 1863, manuscript in author's possession.

[71]William H. Taylor, *De Quibus* (Richmond, 1908), 316.

[72]Theodore Mandeville to his sister, Aug. 24, 1861, manuscript, Louisiana State University.

[73]Moore, Correspondence, volume 739, p. 290, and volume 740, pp. 105-113.

[74]O. R., series 4, II, 467.

[75]J. M. Kiracofe to his wife, March 20, 1864, manuscript, Duke University.

[76]Adams, op. cit., 159-160; David Thompson to his sister, March 19, 1863, manuscript, University of North Carolina.

[77]Moore, Correspondence, volume 739, pp. 290, 537; volume 740, p. 679; volume 741, pp. 185, 352.

[78]Adams, op. cit., 159.

[79]The Camp Follower (Augusta, Ga., 1864), 45.

[80]William H. Taylor, op. cit., 320.

[81]Carrington, Inspection Reports, volume 364, p. 214; volume 416, p. 118. Moore, Correspondence, volume 741, p. 326.

[82]Moore, Correspondence, volumes 739-741 passim; O. R., series 1, XLVI, part 2, 1217; series 4, III, 875-879, 1074. The difficulty of procuring barrels was also a factor in the liquor shortage.

[83]Simkins and Patton, op. cit., 82 ff.

[84]Richmond Daily Dispatch, Oct. 22, 1861; Moore Correspondence, volume 739, 5.

[85]Harry St. John Dixon to his mother, Dec. 1, 1861, manuscript, University of North Carolina.

[86]An army correspondent wrote from Selma, Alabama, Dec. 15, 1864: "The so called 'soldiers homes' or 'Waysides' in most cases are the greatest humbugs of the war. The officials, as in the hospitals, are gorged with the good things which unsophisticated mankind sends there, believing it for the soldiers, and the poor soldier is cheated and humbugged in a most extravagant manner." He said further that Negro servants at these places charged $1.00 for shoe shines. Montgomery Daily Mail, Dec. 28, 1864.

[87]Moore, Correspondence, volume 739, pp. 66, 137, 139.

[88]Richmond Daily Dispatch, May 6, 1862.

[89]B. E. Stiles to his mother, April 4, 1862, manuscript, University of North Carolina.

[90]William H. Phillips to his father, Oct. 14, 1861.

[91]Richmond Daily Dispatch, June 3, 1862; O. R., series 1, X, part 2, 326, 533; XI, part 3, 616.

[92]Guild, Letter Book, volume 641, pp. 36-37.

[93]Cumming, op. cit., 13-17; Richmond Daily Dispatch, April 24, 1862.

[94]Richmond Daily Dispatch, July 1-25, 1862.

[95]John W. Imboden, "The Confederate Retreat from Gettysburg," Battles and Leaders of the Civil War, III, 424.

[96]Welch, op. cit., 26-27.

[97]Diary of Edmund Dewitt Patterson, entries of Aug. 30, 31, 1862, typescript in private possession.

[98]Simkins and Patton, op. cit., 86.

[99]Moore, Correspondence, volume 741, p. 353.

[100]Carrington, Inspection Reports, volume 416, p. 61.

[101]Guild, Letter Book, volume 641, p. 121.

[102]Carrington, Inspection Reports, volume 416, p. 109.

[103]Ibid., 110, and volume 364, p. 356; Cumming, op. cit., 46.

[104]Cumming, op. cit., 63.

[105]John A. Hall to A. M. Morrow, May 3, 1862, manuscript, Emory University; William R. Stillwell to his wife, Oct. 10, 1862, manuscript, Georgia Archives.

[106]Blanton, op. cit., 275.

[107]Carrington, Inspection Reports, volume 416, p. 109.

[108]O. R., series 4, I, 889.

[109]Southern Historical Society Papers, XVII (1889), 7-8.

[110]Adams, op. cit., 164-165.

[111]P.M.H.S., Centenary Series, V, 345-346.

[112]Courtney Hall, op. cit., 473.

Chapter XIV

THE GENTLER SENTIMENTS

[1]William J. Whatley to his wife, Dec. 4, 1862, manuscript photostat, University of Texas.

[2]Dubose Eggleston to Annie Rouhlac, June 9, 1861, manuscript, University of North Carolina; John L. Quince to his sister, Feb. 26, 1865, manuscript, University of North Carolina.

[3]Lieut. William E. Quince to his mother, no place, but 1861, manuscript, University of North Carolina.

[4]John H. Barksdale to his brother, June 12, 1862, manuscript in private possession.

[5]W. C. McClellan to his brother, Aug. 7, 1861, manuscript in private possession; W. M. Moss to his sisters, Nov. 5, 1862, manuscript, University of Texas.

[6]William H. Phillips to his cousin, June 29, 1861, manuscript, Duke University.

[7]Lucius Haney to his sister, March 21, 1863, manuscript, Duke University.

[8]Diary of Albert Moses Luria, entry of Sept. 21, 1863, typescript, University of North Carolina.

[9]Pierson, op. cit., 10-11.

[10]Douglas, op. cit., 326.

[11]Chamberlayne, op. cit., 79.

[12]Theodore Mandeville to his sister, Jan. 3, 1862, manuscript, Louisiana State University; Ben Robertson to his sister, Sept. 7, 1862, manuscript, University of Texas.

[13]Ethelred Crozier to his sister, Jan. 19, 1864, typescript, Tennessee State Library.

[14]Letter to his sister, Dec. 25, 1861.

[15]W. M. Edmonds to his sister, Feb. 10, 1862, manuscript, Emory University.

[16]Diary of C. R. Hanleiter, entry of June 22, 1862, manuscript, Atlanta Historical Society; diary of Harry St. John Dixon, entry of Jan. 2, 1864, manuscript, University of North Carolina.

[17]Ben Robertson to his sister, Sept. 7, 1862.

[18]Diary of D. S. Redding, entry of Sept. 29, 1863, typescript, Georgia Archives.

[19]H. A. Stephens to his sister, Nov. 22, 1863, manuscript in private possession.

[20]W. C. McClellan to his sister, Jan. 3, 1863; John D. Williams to his cousin, Sept. 28, 1863, typescript, Tennessee State Library.

[21]Edwin Tillinghast to his sister, Aug. 24, 1863, manuscript, Emory University.

[22]John H. Chamberlayne to his mother, Dec. 7, 1864, in Chamberlayne, op. cit., 295-296. Chamberlayne was well educated and a captain. His eloquence was considerably greater than that of the average private, but his estimate of women was as representative of common soldiers as of officers.

[23]B. E. Stiles to his mother, Aug. 31, 1861, manuscript, University of North Carolina.

[24]A. B. Simmons to Annie Roulhac, Sept. 21, 1861, manuscript, University of North Carolina.

[25]Joseph J. Cowand to Winaford Cowand, Dec. 29, 1862, manuscript, Duke University.

[26]Diary of Richard W. Waldrop, entry of August 29, 1863, manuscript, University of North Carolina.

[27]Ephraim Anderson, Memoirs, 265.

[28]Carrie Aycock to Mary Stephens, Oct. 12, 1863, manuscript in private possession.

[29]William H. Phillips to his cousin, Sept. 21, 1861, manuscript, Duke University.

[30]J. W. Ward to his sister, May 27, 1863, manuscript, Heartman Collection.

[31]Diary of G. W. Roberts, entry of May 19, 1864, manuscript, Mississippi Archives. Roberts copied both the letter and his answer in his journal.

[32]Ibid.

[33]Entry of April 27, 1863, manuscript, University of North Carolina.

[34]Diary of Harry St. John Dixon, entries of Jan. 2, Jan. 9, Jan. 11, 1864, and June 26, 1865.

[35]Joseph J. Cowand to his cousin, Dec. 29, 1862.

[36]Manuscript among Comer Papers, University of North Carolina. John Bunkam is evidently a pseudonym for either Wallace Comer or C. L. Comer, both of whom were soldiers.

[37]Ethelred Crozier to his sister, Jan. 19, 1864; C. W. Stephens to his sister, April 13, 1864; C. E. Taylor to his sister, Jan. 29, 1864, manuscript, Heartman Collection.

[38]William H. Phillips to his parents, Dec. 20, 1863.

[39]Quoted in a letter of James T. Searcy to his sister, March 15, 1864, manuscript, Alabama Archives.

[40]Letter dated Feb. 21, 1864, and signed "Abe," manuscript among J. A. Clement Papers, University of North Carolina.

[41]Richmond *Daily Dispatch*, March 21, 1863.

[42]W. R. Hutson to his sister, Dec. 2, 1862, manuscript, Duke University.

[43]William Moss to Cinderilla C. Honnoll, Jan. 23, 1864, manuscript, Emory University.

[44]Ben C. Richardson to "Miss Nola," March 20, 1862, manuscript, Virginia State Library.

[45]John N. Dale to Sarah Jane Honnoll, April 5, 1862, manuscript, Emory University.

[46]Daniel Kern to "Dear Friend," Aug. 10, 1862, manuscript among George W. Frank Letters, Duke University.

[47]Henry C. Cribbs to Ann Honnoll, Nov. 9, 1862, March 26, 1863, and May 19, 1863, manuscripts, Emory University.

[48]This extract was quoted in a letter from James A. Hall to Hines Hall, May 31, 1862. The dashes are probably for deletions. Manuscript, Alabama Archives.

[49]W. C. McClellan to his brother, Jan. 25, 1862.

Chapter XV

MUZZLE-LOADERS AND MAKESHIFTS

[1]W. L. Fleming, *Civil War and Reconstruction in Alabama* (New York, 1905), 19.

[2]Josiah Gorgas, "Notes on the Ordnance Department of the Confederate Government," Southern Historical Society *Papers*, XII (1884), 68.

[3]Huse sent over a number of English mechanics to work in Southern arms factories. But when they arrived in Wilmington it was discovered that they had been promised pay in gold. This the ordnance authorities could not afford, but a compromise of one-half gold and one-half Confederate money was proposed. The Englishmen would not accede to the proposition and had to be sent home. "Of all obstinate animals I have ever come in contact with," said Gorgas later, "those English workmen were the most unreasonable." Late in the war many ordnance employees were taken into the army. In October 1864 Gorgas reported: "While two years ago it was difficult to get machinery, we now have a surplus and cannot get workmen to run it. . . . Workmen will not fight and work both." *Ibid.*, XII, 84; II, 60.

[4]Richard D. Steuart, "How Johnny Got His Gun," *Confederate Veteran*, XXXII (1924), 167-168. From this and from other excellent articles on Confederate ordnance by Steuart in the *Confederate Veteran* the writer has drawn freely for the preparation of this chapter.

[5]O. R., series 1, II, 976.

[6]Steuart, *op. cit.*, 167.

[7]Owsley, *op. cit.*, 5 ff.

[8]O. R., series 1, V, 829-830, 886, 896.

[9]W. J. Worsham, *op. cit.*, 22.

[10]Horn, *op. cit.*, 23, 58, 69, 82.

[11]Postscript (added after the war) to letter of C. Irvine Walker to Ada Sinclair, Jan. 15, 1863, typescript, University of Texas.

[12]O. R., series 1, XI, part 2, 498; XII, part 2, 558; XIX, part 1, 141; and XXI, 555.

[13]*Ibid.*, XVI, part 1, 1097.

[14]*Ibid.*, XXV, part 1, 819; XXX, part 2, 23; XXIX, part 2, 628; XXXI, part 3, 874; XXXII, part 2, 604, 697. The dwindling of manpower through desertion and absence without leave in the early months of 1865 gave Lee an excess of weapons. *Ibid.*, XLVI, part 2, 1245-1246.

[15]*Ibid.*, XXVI, part 2, 24; XLI, part 4, 1113.

[16]*Ibid.*, LI, part 2, 111.

[17]*Battle-Fields of the South*, II, 107.

[18]Shannon, *op. cit.*, I, 124.

[19]*Ibid.*, 125.

[20]One reason for the shipment of so many inferior guns to America was the fact that leading European nations had adopted improved types before the outbreak of the Civil War and therefore had huge surpluses of antiquated models on hand. The importunities of American buyers, particularly of Northerners, gave these countries a welcomed opportunity to get rid of their outmoded weapons. According to the Count of Paris, "The refuse of all Europe passed into the hands of the American volunteers." *Ibid.*, 118-119.

[21]O. R., series 1, XXX, part 2, 82-83, 202, 314. After Chickamauga an ordnance officer reported: "This brigade is mostly armed with Enfield rifles, using ammunition calibers nos. .57 and .58; . . . caliber No. .57 was loose and never choked the guns, while the No. .58, after the first few rounds, was found too large, and frequently choking the guns to that extent that they could not be forced down, thereby creating some uneasiness among the men using that number of ammunition." Ibid., 277.

[22]Steuart, op. cit., 169.

[23]A few Kerr rifles were imported from England for Confederate sharpshooters, ibid. The high esteem in which sharpshooters held their choice pieces is reflected in the fact that an Alabamian referred to his long range gun as a "Yankee-killer." "Bolly" Hall to Bolling Hall, Sr., July 18, 1863, manuscript, Alabama Archives.

[24]Steuart, op. cit., 168.

[25]The Confederates devised a machine for making metallic cartridges of the type used in Spencer rifles but the war closed before it could be put into operation. Ibid., 169. Another repeating gun having very limited use among Confederates was the Colt's revolving rifle, the loading mechanism of which was the same as the famous Colt's six-shooter. George W. Elkins to his sister, May 25, 1862, manuscript in private possession.

[26]C. Irvine Walker, Rolls and Historical Sketch of the Tenth South Carolina Volunteers (Charleston, South Carolina, 1881), 74.

[27]Miller, op. cit., V, 168.

[28]Hanks, op. cit., 15-16, manuscript photostat, University of Texas.

[29]Quaife, op. cit., 21.

[30]Fremantle, op. cit., 157; McCarthy, op. cit., 27; Robert E. Lee to A. P. Hill, Jan. 20, 1865, manuscript, Confederate Museum.

[31]Steuart, "A Pair of Navy Sixes," Confederate Veteran, XXXIII (1925), 92-94.

[32]The long knives carried by soldiers were generally called Bowie knives, "although few of them would have been recognized by the hero of the Alamo" for whom they were named. Steuart, "Confederate Swords," Confederate Veteran, XXXIV (1926), 13.

[33]DeLeon, op. cit., 97.

[34]After First Manassas it was rumored that the Louisiana Tigers threw away their guns and rushed at the Yankees yelling and brandishing their knives; this and similar stories enhanced the popularity of this type of weapon. Confederate Veteran, XXXIV (1926), 14.

[35]O. R., series 1, XII, part 3, 842, 845.

[36]Ibid., X, part 2, 374.

[37]L. L. Knight, Georgia Landmarks, Memorials, and Legends (Atlanta, 1913), II, 656; Gorgas, op. cit., 74.

[38]Richmond *Enquirer*, Nov. 24, 1864.

[39]Steuart, "Confederate Swords," *Confederate Veteran*, XXXIV, 12-13.

[40]*Ibid.*, 12.

[41]*O. R.*, series 1, X, part 2, 334.

[42]Steuart, "The Long Arm of the Confederacy," *Confederate Veteran*, XXXV (1927), 250-251.

[43]*Ibid.*, 251. Jennings C. Wise, *The Long Arm of Lee* (Lynchburg, 1915), I, 71.

[44]*Ibid.*; Gorgas, *op. cit.*, 94.

[45]Douglas, *op. cit.*, 172.

[46]*O. R.*, series 1, XI, part 2, 498; XII, part 2, 558; XVI, part 1, 1094, 1097; XIX, part 1, 141.

[47]Gorgas, *op. cit.*, 68 ff; *Confederate Veteran*, XXXV (1927), 251-253. For Bragg's reaction to Beauregard's proclamation see his letter to Mrs. Bragg of March 20, 1862, manuscript, Duke University.

[48]Gorgas, *op. cit.*, 81, 94.

[49]*O. R.*, series 1, XI, part 3, 461.

[50]*Ibid.*, XXI, 566.

[51]*Ibid.*, LI, part 2, 307. Much of the difficulty with mountings could be attributed, of course, to the fact that guns of the Civil War period had no spring recoil facilities.

[52]Diary of George W. Jones, typescript in private possession.

[53]Stiles, *op. cit.*, 52; Wise, *op. cit.*, II, 572 ff.

[54]Wise, *op. cit.*, II, 571; Wise says that the Whitworths were six-inch caliber, but Steuart, from a study of ammunition found on the battlefield, concludes that the caliber was not over three inches. *Confederate Veteran*, XXXV (1927), 253.

[55]*Confederate Veteran*, XXXV (1927), 252-253. The Brooke gun had a unique feature in the utilization of the so-called air space to lessen the initial tension of the explosive gases.

[56]Steuart, "First in the Art of War," *Confederate Veteran*, XXXV (1927), 333-334. A battery of six Williams guns was in use in the Confederate Army of the West in 1862, but these had to be discarded because of trouble with the breech lock caused by expansion after repeated firing. Wise thinks it probable that the inventor of the famous Gatling machine gun developed in the North got his idea from the Williams model. Wise, *op. cit.*, I, 32-33. Jackson attempted the use of a mule battery of mountain rifles at Port Republic, but the experiment failed on account of the action of the mules under fire, these animals rolling over on the ground to rid themselves of the guns. This afforded much amusement to infantrymen who with a show of seriousness would inquire of exasperated artillerymen whether the mules or the guns were intended to go off first. *Ibid.*, 174-175.

[57]Gorgas, op. cit., 93. Steuart, "The Long Arm of the Confederacy," Confederate Veteran, XXXV (1927), 252.

[58]Wise, op. cit., I, 110-111; II, 911-918. At the beginning of the war the personnel of a battery of light artillery consisted of 1 captain, 2 first lieutenants, 2 second lieutenants, 1 sergeant-major or first sergeant, 1 quartermaster-sergeant, 6 sergeants, 12 corporals, 2 buglers, 1 guidon, 2 artifers and from 64 to 125 privates. Ibid., I, 110-111. For "panzer" uses of horse artillery see ibid., I, 166 ff.

[59]Miller, op. cit., V, 176-178.

[60]Ibid., 190. The wrought-iron sabot shell was invented by Dr. Reed of Alabama before the war and perfected during the Confederacy. This invention was of vital importance in that it assured the practicability of rifled artillery. Wise, op. cit., I, 47, 67.

[61]O. R., series 1, IV, 674-675; XXV, part 1, 881.

[62]Gorgas, op. cit., 68-69; O. R., series 4, II, 382-383.

[63]O. R., series 1, IV, 664; VI, 525; Samuel French, Two Wars (Nashville, 1901), 143.

[64]A. P. Van Gelder and Hugo Schlatter, History of the Explosives Industry in America (New York, 1927), 107-109.

[65]Ibid., 111-113.

[66]Fleming, op. cit., 153.

[67]The writer is much indebted to Honorable Francis G. Caffey, formerly of Alabama but now Judge of the United States District Court, Foley Square, New York City, for information about the saltpeter poems. Judge Caffey was related to Haralson and talked with him about the poetry.

[68]Van Gelder and Schlatter, op. cit., 113.

[69]This description of canteens is based largely on types observed in various museums of the South. All of the models discussed may be found in the Confederate Museum at Richmond. One particularly interesting water container in this collection is a doughnut-shaped affair made of brown porcelain. It was carried in the Revolution by Private James Ward, and in the Confederate War by his grandson, Lt. R. A. Ward of the Twenty-second Virginia Battalion.

[70]Josiah Gorgas to Jefferson Davis, Feb. 8, 1878, manuscript, Heartman Collection.

[71]Cap boxes and cartridge boxes are on display in most Confederate museums. The scarcity of leather compelled the use of fabric to some extent in the making of these items. Gorgas, op. cit., 74.

[72]McCarthy, op. cit., 26.

[73]O. R., series 1, XII, part 3, 890.

Chapter XVI

BLUE BELLIES AND BELOVED ENEMIES

[1]Manuscript in possession of Mrs. G. R. Maloney, Richmond, Virginia.

[2]H. C. Kendrick to his homefolk, no date, but early 1863, manuscript, University of North Carolina.

[3]John Wesley Tucker to his father, Feb. 3, 1863, manuscript in possession of Mrs. J. H. Lide, Corinth, Mississippi.

[4]T. W. Montfort to his wife, March 18, 1862, typescript, Georgia Archives.

[5]John Crittenden to his wife, May 29, 1864, typescript, University of Texas.

[6]Robert M. Gill to his wife, July 25, 1864, manuscript in author's possession. Andrew J. Neal made this notation on a Yankee letter that he sent home after the Chickamauga fight: "This is the only respectable letter I have seen of thousands. They are all full of the grossest and vulgarest language." Typescript, Georgia Archives.

[7]Diary of William S. White, entry of June 27, 1862, in *Contributions to a History of the Richmond Howitzer Battalion* (Richmond, 1883), pamphlet no. 2, p. 119.

[8]Jerome Yates to his mother, June 17, 1863, manuscript, Heartman Collection.

[9]Diary of George W. Jones, entry of Sept. 10, 1862, typescript in private possession.

[10]*Ibid.*, entry of May 23, 1863.

[11]Richmond *Daily Dispatch*, April 24, May 10, May 12, 1862.

[12]O. R., series 1, XXXVIII, part 3, 716.

[13]W. C. McClellan to Robert McClellan, Jan. 25, 1862, manuscript in private possession.

[14]O. R., series 1, XII, part 2, 202-203; XX, part 1, 880; and LI, part 2, 329; Robert M. Gill to his wife, Oct. 9, 1862, Aug. 7, 1864.

[15]Robert M. Gill to his wife, May 24, 1862.

[16]Manuscript, Heartman Collection.

[17]Diary of R. W. Waldrop, manuscript, University of North Carolina.

[18]A. C. Haskell to his mother, May 4, 1861, manuscript, University of North Carolina.

[19]Letter of Dec. 2, 1863, manuscript, Alabama Archives.

[20]Letter to his mother, April 19, 1862, manuscript, University of North Carolina.

[21]S. G. Pryor to his wife, Sept. 2, 1862, typescript, Georgia Archives.

[22]G. L. Robertson to his father, Sept. 14, 1861, manuscript photostat, University of Texas.

[23]W. C. McClellan to Robert McClellan, Nov. 9, 1861.

[24]W. C. McClellan to his sister, April 2, 1863.

[25]Colonel Laurence Keitt to his wife, May 31, 1864, manuscript, Duke University; J. Joe Evans to his brother, May 11, 1864, manuscript in private possession.

[26]Letter to his sister, June 11, 1863.

[27]*Ibid.*, to his father, Feb. 27, 1862.

[28]Bell Irvin Wiley, *op. cit.*, 310 ff.

[29]Jerome Yates to his mother, Aug. 10, [1864?].

[30]Jerome Yates to his sister, Aug. 3, 1864; Thomas Roulhac to his mother, March 13, 1864, manuscript, University of North Carolina; J. M. Jordan to his wife, Feb. 21, 1864, manuscript, Georgia Archives.

[31]W. C. McClellan to Robert McClellan, Aug. 15, 1864.

[32]*Battles and Leaders of the Civil War*, I, 82.

[33]Will T. Martin to his wife, Nov. 19, 1861, typescript in private possession.

[34]Clipping from *Confederate Veteran* (no date) in U.D.C. Collection, Georgia Archives.

[35]Horn, *op. cit.*, 336.

[36]W. J. Worsham, *op. cit.*, 132.

[37]Frank Smith, "The Polite War," *Coronet*, III (1937), 44; J. O. Casler, *op. cit.*, 134.

[38]W. J. Worsham, *op. cit.*, 132.

[39]Clark, *North Carolina Regiments*, III, 357.

[40]*O. R.*, series 1, XVI, part 1, 977-978.

[41]Freeman, *op. cit.*, II, 496.

[42]Horn, *op. cit.*, 199.

[43]Mays, *op. cit.*, 46-47.

[44]W. J. Kincheloe to his father, Jan. 12, 1863, manuscript among John W. Daniel Papers, University of Virginia.

[45]*Confederate Veteran*, XXV (1914), 471.

[46]Diary of E. D. Patterson, entry of Jan. 20, 1863, typescript in private possession.

[47]Miller, *op. cit.*, VIII, 136.

[48]Richmond *Daily Dispatch*, July 23, 1864.

[49]W. C. McClellan to Robert McClellan, April 13, 1862; diary of Maurice K. Simons, entry of May 25, 1863, manuscript, University of Texas; A. J. Neal to his father, May 15, 1864.

[50]Diary of R. W. Locke, entry of Nov. 19, 1862, manuscript, Mississippi Archives.

[51]H. A. Stephens to Amelia Stephens, Oct. 5, 1863, manuscript in private possession.

[52]James Elliott, *The Southern Soldier Boy* (Raleigh, 1907), 46.

[53]Jerome Yates to his sister, July 19, 1864.

[54]Frank Smith, *op. cit.*, 44-46; Thomas F. Boatwright to his wife, Sept. 27, 1863, manuscript, University of North Carolina; Diary of James J. Kirkpatrick, entries of July 4, 10, 1864, manuscript, University of Texas; Sam Houston Hynds to his mother, Sept. 28, 1861, typescript, Tennessee State Library; Journal of William Chambers, entry of May 25, 1863, *P.M.H.S.*, Centenary Series, V, 272-273; Anderson, *op. cit.*, 333-334.

[55]Jerome Yates to his mother, Jan. 11, 1864.

[56]C. N. Mason to his father, Dec. 9, 1862, manuscript, North Carolina Historical Commission.

[57]Thomas Caffey to his sister, March 24, 1863; James Dinkins, *Personal Recollections and Experiences in the Confederate Army* (Cincinnati, 1897), 66; Ruffin Thomson to his father, Feb. 26, 1863.

[58]Stiles, *op. cit.*, 157.

[59]Richmond *Daily Dispatch*, Sept. 6, 1864.

[60]Diary of D. Griffin Gunn, entry of May 10, 1863, manuscript, Confederate Museum, Austin, Texas; D. E. Johnston, *The Story of a Confederate Boy* (Portland, Ore., 1914), p. 276.

[61]Frank Smith, *op. cit.*, 46.

[62]*Confederate Veteran*, XXIV (1916), 91.

Chapter XVII

WHAT MANNER OF MEN

[1]The Southern states represented by these rolls were Alabama, Arkansas, Louisiana, Mississippi, Georgia and Texas. The rolls referred to here and in subsequent connections are largely from the files of the War Records Division of the National Archives, though some are from collections in archives of Southern states and in private depositories.

[2]Ella Lonn, *Foreigners in the Confederacy*, 93-131, 200-240. Professor Lonn's scholarly work, to which I am much indebted, is based primarily on descriptive rolls.

[3]Southern Historical Society Papers, XXXI (1903), 105-106.

[4]Lonn, *Foreigners in the Confederacy*, 121, 213-214.

[5]*Ibid.*, 109, 210.

[6]*Ibid.*, 124-128.

[7]*Ibid.*, 96-101.

[8]*Ibid.*, 116-123.

[9]*Ibid.*, 220.

[10]Annie Heloise Abel, *The American Indian as Participant in the American Civil War* (Cleveland, 1919), 25, 155, 326-330; Robinson, op. cit., 352.

[11]Clark, *North Carolina Regiments*, II, 729-730.

[12]S. B. Barron, *The Lone Star Defenders* (New York, 1908), p. 33.

[13]Anderson, op. cit., 159-160.

[14]*Ibid.*, 174; Abel, op. cit., 26-34; *Battles and Leaders of the Civil War*, I, 335-336.

[15]Abel, op. cit., 194-195, 288-289, 326-327; Robinson, op. cit., 351-352. At the Battle of Honey Hill the Confederate force consisted of Texans as well as Indians.

[16]Robinson, op. cit., 351-352.

[17]Abel, op. cit., 150, 268, 333, 337-351.

[18]Bell Irvin Wiley, op. cit., 134-138.

[19]*Ibid.*, 136-144.

[20]*Ibid.*, 110-113, 134.

[21]*Ibid.*, 114-133.

[22]*Ibid.*, 146-160.

[23]There were innumerable examples of faithfulness under duress, and of rejections of freedom when offered. But instances of loyalty in invaded areas were restricted largely to old Negroes, and to house servants whose attachment to masters had been strengthened by intimate association, and who, because of their favored position, had much to lose by emancipation. Field hands, who constituted the great majority of servants, generally abandoned their masters when the coming of the Federals guaranteed immunity from punishment. *Ibid.*, 3-23, 63-84.

[24]Only 11 of the 9,000 were listed as planters. It is likely, therefore, that compilers of rolls did not always distinguish between small and large agricultural operatives, and that some planters are included among those classed as farmers.

[25]Cavalry companies were not included because of the meager descriptive rolls for this branch of the service.

[26]Moore, op. cit., 141 ff. On Oct. 18, 1864, Private William H. Routt wrote to his wife from near Petersburg: "There are a great many new men coming in & they are mostly young men who have managed to keep out until now." Manuscript, Confederate Museum.

[27]*O. R.*, series 1, XI, part 2, 851-852, XXX, part 2, 319-320.

[28]Descriptive Roll, Co. D, Fifth North Carolina Regiment; Descriptive Book, Fifth North Carolina Regiment; and Personal File of E. Pollard. All of these items are in the National Archives. The doctor who filled out Pollard's certificate of disability put his age down as sixty-two, but the Descriptive Roll and the Descriptive Book give the age as seventy-three. These latter should be more reliable than the former. William M. Dame of the Richmond Howitzer Battalion testified that

he knew personally of six men over sixty years of age who served in the ranks throughout the war. Dame, *op. cit.*, 2-3.

[29]Records of the First Kentucky Brigade, Confederate Archives, chapter II, volume 305, p. 35, manuscript, National Archives.

[30]*O. R.*, series 1, X, part 1, 589.

[31]*Ibid.*, XXXVIII, part 3, 803.

[32]*Confederate Veteran*, II, (1894), 12-13.

[33]Clark, *North Carolina Regiments*, V, 637-638. One of the thirteen-year-old Hillsboro boys named William Cain was rated as the best drillmaster in Confederate service by the lieutenant colonel of the Twenty-fifth North Carolina Regiment. Written statement of H. C. Dearing, dated November 13, 1861, manuscript in John L. Bailey Collection, University of North Carolina. Originally drillmasters were engaged under informal arrangements by the states. In 1862 Congress authorized the President to employ them for pay at rates to be fixed by the Secretary of War. Matthews, *Statutes at Large of the Permanent Government*, First Session, chapter 46.

[34]Freeman, *op. cit.*, I, 493-494.

[35]*Richmond Daily Dispatch*, May 6, 1862.

[36]*O. R.*, series 1, XLI, part 4, 1041-1042.

[37]*Battles and Leaders of the Civil War*, IV, 483-485. The cadets engaged numbered 260, 35 of whom composed a battery section. The entire corps participated save about 30 left behind to guard the college buildings. Philip Alexander Bruce, *Brave Deeds of Confederate Soldiers* (Philadelphia, 1916), 260.

[38]*Confederate Veteran*, IX (1901), 352.

[39]Clark, North Carolina Regiments, II, 330-331.

[40]C. J. Worthington, editor, *Madame Loreta Janeta Velasquez (otherwise known as Lt. Harry T. Buford), The Woman in Battle* (Hartford, 1876), 43 ff.

[41]Stiles, *op. cit.*, 49.

[42]Henry L. Graves to his mother, Oct. 3, 1862, typescript, Georgia Archives; Stephenson and Davis, *op. cit.*, 436-451, 712-730.

[43]Charles W. Hutson to his mother, July 13, 1861, typescript, University of North Carolina.

[44]E. A. Moore, *The Story of a Cannoneer under Stonewall Jackson* (New York, 1907), 311; W. H. Morgan, *op. cit.*, 39; Dame, *op. cit.*, *passim*; McKim, *op. cit.*, 51-55; Stiles, *op. cit.*, 49 ff; S. H. Baldy to his mother, May 31, 1861, manuscript, Emory University; R. W. Waldrop to his father, July 23, 1861, manuscript, University of North Carolina.

[45]E. A. Moore, *op. cit.*; Dame, *op. cit.*; McKim, *op. cit.*; Stiles, *op. cit.*; McCarthy, *op. cit.*

[46]For enlightening information as to the prevalency and character of yeomen in the ante-bellum rural population see Blanche Henry

Clark, *The Tennessee Yeoman, 1840-1860* (Nashville, 1942), Herbert Weaver, "Agricultural Population of Mississippi" (unpublished dissertation, 1941), and other studies of middle-class Southern farmers sponsored by Prof. Frank L. Owsley at Vanderbilt University; also Frank L. and Harriet C. Owsley, "The Economic Basis of Society in the Late Ante-Bellum South," *Journal of Southern History*, VI (1940), 25-45.

⁴⁷Wade H. Hubbard to his wife, Oct. 16, 1864, manuscript, Duke University.

⁴⁸General orders, District of Texas, New Mexico and Arizona, December 1862-December 1863. Confederate Archives, chapter II, volume 114, p. 61.

⁴⁹*Ibid.*, 89.

⁵⁰Eggleston, *op. cit.*, 35-36; General Orders, Department of South Carolina, Georgia, and Florida, Confederate Archives, chapter II, volume 40, p. 298-299; volume 43, p. 341-349; General and Special Orders, Division of Virginia Volunteers, *ibid.*, chapter VIII, volume 239, p. 68-69.

⁵¹Robert M. Gill to Bettie Gill, June 10, 1862; manuscript in author's possession; Eggleston, *op. cit.*, 36.

⁵²Diary of Harry St. John Dixon, entries of Nov. 18, Dec. 23, 1864, manuscript, University of North Carolina.

⁵³*Battle-fields of the South*, I, 17-19.

⁵⁴*O. R.*, series 4, III, 709.

⁵⁵Charles W. Hutson to his family, Sept. 14, 1862.

⁵⁶R. W. Waldrop to his father, July 23, 1861, manuscript, University of North Carolina.

⁵⁷Robert M. Gill to his wife, Aug. 22, and Nov. 27, 1862.

⁵⁸Eleanor D. Pace, editor, "The Diary and Letters of William P. Rogers, 1846-1862," *Southwestern Historical Quarterly*, XXXII (1929), 293-295; New Orleans *Daily Crescent*, Jan. 14, 1862.

⁵⁹See *supra*, chapter 8.

⁶⁰Peter McDavid to his sister, Oct. 7, 1863, manuscript, Duke University; Dubose Eggleston to Annie Rouhlac, Sept. 27, 1863, manuscript, University of North Carolina.

⁶¹Unidentified soldier of Eleventh Alabama Regiment (signature torn off) to Miss Annie Rouhlac, Aug. 7, 1863, manuscript, University of North Carolina.

⁶²W. C. McClellan to his father, May 15, 19, 1863.

⁶³Peter McDavid to his sister, Oct. 7, 1863; Dubose Eggleston to Annie Rouhlac, Sept. 27, 1863.

⁶⁴James A. Hall to Joe Hall, April 18, 1864, manuscript, Alabama Archives.

⁶⁵Henry Slade of Longstreet's Corps wrote to his brother, July 26, 1863: "The cavalry is about *played out* in this Army. They are hollered

at and made the laughing stock of the whole Army." Manuscript, Duke University.

[66]Robert M. Gill to his wife, Feb. 2, 1864.

[67]Samuel P. Collier to his parents, Oct. 11, 1864, manuscript, North Carolina Historical Commission.

[68]J. P. Strange, Notes on Operations of Freeman's Battalion, dated Sept. 15, 1866, manuscript among L. M. Nutt Papers, University of North Carolina.

[69]Jerome Yates to his mother, Jan. —?, 1863, manuscript, Heartman Collection.

[70]In June 1864, Colonel George Brent wrote after an inspection that 654 deserters were borne on the rolls of the Forrest's command, O. R., series 1, XXXIX, part 2, 642. For other instances of desertion of infantry to join the cavalry see ibid., XXXII, part 2, 604, 622-623.

[71]J. W. Rabb to his mother, June 29, 1862, manuscript, University of Texas.

[72]Eggleston, op. cit., 49-51; O. R., series 1, XVIII, 772.

[73]O. R., series 1, XX, part 1, 741; XXI, 647-648, 656.

[74]Pace, op. cit., 294; Caldwell, op. cit., 124; Eggleston, op. cit., 49-51; DeLeon, op. cit., 185; John Crittenden to his wife, April 13, 1863; David Thompson to his sister, Jan. 19, 1863, manuscript among Frank Nash Papers, University of North Carolina.

[75]Cumming, op. cit., 104.

[76]John Crittenden to his wife, no date, no place.

[77]C. M. Hardy to his sister, Sept. 18, 1864, typescript, Georgia Archives.

[78]Diary of James J. Kirkpatrick, entry of June 10, 1864, manuscript, University of Texas.

[79]Watkins, op. cit., 39.

[80]William J. McMurray, History of the Twentieth Tennessee Regiment (Nashville, 1904), 349-350.

[81]Fletcher, op. cit., 99-100.

[82]General Orders, Department of South Carolina, Georgia and Florida, Confederate Archives, chapter II, volume 42, p. 94; volume 43, p. 508.

[83]Reminiscences of J. M. Montgomery, manuscript in possession of Mrs. B. B. Payne, Greenville, Mississippi.

[84]Theodore Mandeville to various members of his family, April 15, Aug. 31, 1861, and March 17, 1862, manuscripts, Louisiana State University; diary of Harry St. John Dixon, entry of May 18, 1863.

[85]Reminiscences of John N. Johnson, 103, typescript, Tennessee State Library; Lewis, op. cit., 11-13.

[86]Casler, op. cit., 294-295, 316.

[87]Southern Historical Society Papers, I (1876), 81.

[88]For instances of discharge for mental deficiency see Court-Martial Record, Confederate Archives, chapter I, volumes 194-200 *passim*.

[89]Johnston, *op. cit.*, 34-35.

[90]Charles T. Loehr, *History of the Old First Virginia* (Richmond, 1884), 31.

[91]John H. Worsham, *op. cit.*, 75-76.

[92]Robert A. Newell to Sarah Newell, March 1863, manuscript, Louisiana State University.

[93]Richmond *Daily Dispatch*, April 29, 1862.

[94]Robinson, *op. cit.*, 97. Pettus sent twenty-five of the toughest criminals to an Alabama penitentiary.

[95]Journal of William P. Chambers, *P.M.H.S.*, Centenary Series, V, 350; McMurray, *op. cit.*, 148; U. R. Brooks, editor, *Stories of the Confederacy* (Columbia, S. C., 1912), 313-322.

[96]Mobile *Advertiser and Register*, Sept. 11, 1862; Robert M. Gill to his wife, July 4, 1862; Gerrish and Hutchinson, *op. cit.*, 130; O. R., series 1, XLII, part 1, 903.

BIBLIOGRAPHY

BIBLIOGRAPHICAL NOTE

The tremendous volume of material on the Confederate soldier entirely precludes the possibility of listing all items consulted in the preparation of this study. It is to be hoped that the following brief comment on various types of sources will be of some help to those who are interested. Full data on all specifically cited items may be found in the footnotes; for the reader's convenience location of each manuscript is given the first time it is cited in every chapter.

MANUSCRIPTS

The most interesting and the most informative of manuscript sources are the letters of private soldiers. These are to be found in amazingly large quantities in both public depositories and private possession. The largest public collections are those at the University of Texas, Duke University and the University of North Carolina. Of smaller collections those belonging to the Military Records Division of the Alabama Department of Archives and History, the Tennessee State Library, Louisiana State University, the Georgia Department of Archives and History, and Emory University are the best. The Georgia Archives collection consists largely of typed copies of letters gathered by local chapters of the United Daughters of the Confederacy, and transcription seems to have been accurately done. Certainly there are no evidences of correction of spelling and grammar that one encounters occasionally in copies that have been made by squeamish descendants. Most of the letters in the Tennessee State Library are typescripts made by Works Progress Administration employees. Correspondence of commissioned officers was read in large quantity, but as a rule it was less frank, less revealing and less vivid than that of common soldiers.

Comparatively few of the rank and file kept diaries for any considerable length of time, and such journals as are extant throw considerably less light on soldier life than do letters. But there are a few of exceptional merit. The journal of Harry St. John Dixon (1861-1865) acquired recently by the University of North Carolina affords an intimate picture of the details of camp life as experienced by a young aristocrat from Mississippi. A very interesting diary kept by an unidentified Louisianian suffered the misfortune of division, and now part one (May 25, 1861-Oct. 18, 1863) is in the Heartman Collection (sold recently by Charles F. Heartman to the University of Texas) and part two (Oct. 18, 1863-May 7, 1864) is in the Confederate Memorial Hall of New Orleans. The diary of Charles Moore (1861-1865) in Confederate Memorial Hall gives a spicy account of courting, of foraging and of fighting in Lee's army. A microfilm copy at Vanderbilt University of H. S. Archer's diary (1862-1864) affords an enlightening view of a soldier-preacher's vicissitudes. The Mississippi Department of Archives and History has three excellent journals. That of William H. Hill (1861-1863) tells of the experiences of a private or subaltern of the Thirteenth Mississippi Regiment; the diary of G. W. Roberts (April 27-June 26, 1864) is a brief but unusually human account of life in an Alabama parole camp; the narrative of A. L. P. Vairin (1861-1864) is an orderly sergeant's impressions of service in the Army of Tennessee. An exceptionally moving portrayal of personal reactions and experiences in battle is given in the privately owned diary of E. D. Patterson (1861-1865).

Other pertinent manuscripts consist largely of muster and descriptive rolls, general orders, official correspondence, regimental sick reports, and court-martial proceedings. The National Archives has by far the richest collection of these materials, but Southern state depositories have many items not to be found in Washington. Exceedingly rare official records of various sorts turn up now and then in the personal papers of Confederate generals. The writer was pleasantly surprised at the extensiveness and the richness of the medical and court-martial records stored in the National Archives; these sources apparently have had little use by Civil War historians.

PRINTED CORRESPONDENCE AND DIARIES

As a general rule the best of letter-diary material remains unpublished, and most of that which has appeared in print has an officer's slant. The letters of John Hampden Chamberlayne, edited by C. G. Chamberlayne under the title of Ham Chamberlayne—Virginian (Richmond, 1932), are exceedingly well written and interesting; the correspondent held a commission during most of the war, but he makes detailed and significant comments on the doings of his men. Extracts of Letters of Major-General Bryan Grimes to his Wife (Raleigh, 1883), edited by Pulaski Cowper, is a frank account of a North Carolinian who served in the Valley campaign. J. W. Reid's History of the Fourth Regiment of South Carolina Volunteers (Greenville, S. C., 1892), consisting largely of the letters of a private soldier to his family, appears to be an authentic reproduction of wartime correspondence. The same cannot be said of J. B. Polley's A Soldier's Letters to Charming Nellie (New York, 1908); these letters doubtless have a substantial basis of fact, but they savor more of reminiscences than of contemporary correspondence.

Of printed diaries one of the best is that of a Tar Heel rustic named Bartlett Yancey Malone, edited by William Whatley Pierson for the James Sprunt Historical *Publications*, XVI (1917-1919). A well-educated Louisianian's experiences are interestingly recounted in "The Civil War Diary of Willie Micajah Barrow," edited by Edwin A. Davis and Wendell H. Stephenson in the *Louisiana Historical Quarterly*, XVII (1934). John C. West's *A Texan in Search of a Fight* (Waco, Texas, 1901) consists of the diary and letters of a private of Hood's Brigade.

PRINTED REMINISCENCES

Personal memoirs have been published in profusion but these must be used with great care on account of the caprices of recollection, particularly its tendency to minimize weaknesses and to magnify virtues. I have attempted to follow the policy of rejecting all reminiscent items which did not square with records of a more substantial character. J. O. Casler's *Four Years in the Stonewall Brigade* (Guthrie, Oklahoma, 1893) is a very interesting and unusual account, but the author occasionally lets his desire to tell a good story overshadow accuracy. The same may be said of Sam R. Watkins' "Co Aytch," *Maury Grays, First Tennessee Regiment, or a Side Show of the Big Show* (Chattanooga, 1900), of James Dinkins' *Personal Recollections and Experiences in the Confederate Army* (Cincinnati, 1897), and of Harry Gilmor's *Four Years in the Saddle* (New York, 1866). David E. Johnston's *The Story of a Confederate Boy* (Portland, Oregon, 1914) is impaired by excessive sentimentality. Noble C. Williams' *Echoes from the Battlefield* is surcharged with romanticism; likewise are Lamar Fontaine's *My Life and My Letters* (New York, 1908), Isaac Hermann's *Memoirs of a Veteran* (Atlanta, 1911), and William G. Stevenson's *Thirteen Months in the Rebel Army* (New York, 1864).

Marcus B. Toney's *Privations of a Private* (Nashville, 1907) is a substantial narrative based in part on a war diary. Comparatively reliable also are W. A. Fletcher's *Rebel Private Front and Rear* (Beaumont, Texas, 1908), A. P. Ford's *Life in the Confederate Army* (N. Y., 1905), Frank Mixson's *Reminiscences of a Private* (Columbia, S. C., 1910), and Edwin A. Moore's *The Story of a Cannoneer under Stonewall Jackson* (N. Y., 1907). John Allan Wyeth's *With Sabre and Scalpel* (New York, 1914) presents an engaging picture of a very young soldier. Eppa Hunton's *Autobiography* (Richmond, 1933) is the work of an officer, but it contains realistic and significant information about ordinary soldiers.

Carlton McCarthy's *Detailed Minutiae of Soldier Life in the Army of Northern Virginia* (Richmond, 1882) is the most interesting and the most informative of all memoirs written by privates; its charm is enhanced considerably by the deliciously human illustrations of Lieutenant William L. Sheppard. But the reader must keep in mind always that McCarthy, because of his connection with the Richmond Howitzer Battalion, an exceptional organization from standpoints of education, culture, and morale, acquired a somewhat roseate view of the Confederate Army. Among other fascinating books that have a similar distortion are Robert Stiles's *Four Years Under Marse Robert* (N. Y., 1903), George Cary Eggleston's *A Rebel's Recollections* (N. Y., 1887), Randolph H. McKim's *A Soldier's Recollections* (N. Y., 1910), and William M. Dame's *From the Rapidan to Richmond and the Spottsylvania Campaign* (Baltimore, 1920).

REGIMENTAL HISTORIES

Histories of companies, regiments and brigades vary greatly in quality and in character. The most complete list is that contained in *Bibliography of State Participation in the Civil War, 1861-1866*, published in 1913 by the United States War Department. Frequently these accounts consist of little more than a summary of printed official reports, but some that are based on more extensive research tell much of soldier life. Maud Morrow Brown, *The University Greys* (Richmond, 1940), is an illuminating and interesting study of an organization that had its origin on the campus of the University of Mississippi. J. F. J. Caldwell's *History of Gregg's or McGowan's Brigade of South Carolinians* (Philadelphia, 1866) is, in view of its publication date, surprisingly objective. Daniel P. Smith's *Company K First Alabama Regiment* (Prattsville, Alabama, 1885) is an excellent and brief study, unmarred by the rhapsodic tone which characterizes many company histories. Robert Emory Park's *Sketch of the Twelfth Alabama Infantry* (Richmond, 1906) is devoted in part to a war diary kept by the author. Edward Young McMorries' *Historical Sketch of the First Alabama Volunteers* (Montgomery, 1904) and Lewellyn Shaver's *History of the Sixtieth Alabama Regiment* (Montgomery, 1867) are exceptionally sound. William J. McMurray's *History of the Twentieth Tennessee Regiment* (Nashville, 1904) is generally reliable though at times overly fervid. William Miller Owen's *In Camp and Battle with the Washington Artillery* (Boston, 1885) derives unusual merit from the fact that the author kept a detailed diary. Winchester Hall's *The Story of the Twenty-Sixth Louisiana Infantry* (no place, 1890?) has the earmarks of accuracy. C. Irvine Walker's *Rolls and Historical Sketch of the Tenth Regiment South Carolina Volunteers* (Charleston, 1881) had the benefit of examination and correction by several of the author's comrades before it went to press. William V. Izlar's *Sketch of the War Record of the Edisto Rifles* (Columbia, S. C., 1914) is a substantial work. John Berrien Lindsley, editor of *The Military Annals of Tennessee* (Nashville, 1886), and Walter Clark, editor of *Histories of the Several Regiments and Battalions from North Carolina in the Great War, 1861-1865* (Raleigh and Goldsboro, 1901) have given valuable information, but unevenness resulting from varied authorship requires extreme caution in using them.

NEWSPAPERS AND PERIODICALS

Newspapers were useful to this study chiefly for editorial com ments on general army conditions and occasional reports of special military correspondents. Local news columns throw considerable light on the unorthodox doings of Rebs on furlough. Good newspaper collections may be found at the University of Texas, Louisiana State University, the Alabama Department of Archives and History, the Charleston Library Society, the University of North Carolina, Duke University, the Confederate Museum, and the Virginia State Library. Of periodicals, the state historical journals deserve special mention for publication in recent years of significant diaries and letters. The Lightfoot, Cody, and McGarity correspondence edited recently for the *Georgia Historical Quarterly* by Edmund C. Burnett is of paramount interest and value. The *Confederate Veteran* (Nashville, 1893-1932) combines masses of irrelevancy with a wealth of useful information; Richard D. Steuart's seven articles on matériel (volumes XXXII-XXXV) are of exceptional value. The *Southern Historical Society Papers* (Richmond, 1876-) may also be searched with profit by the discriminating historian. Of less value are *Our Living and Our Dead* (Raleigh, 1874-1876), *The Land We Love* (Charlotte, 1866-1869) and the *Southern Bivouac* (Louisville, 1882-1887).

PICTURES

The National Archives and the United States War Department have enormous collections of Civil War photographs taken for the most part by the famous Matthew C. Brady. These photographs are mainly of Northern subjects, but Brady and his associates succeeded in making a surprising number of Rebel pictures. The National Archives collection contains, in addition to a few photographs made by Southerners, a considerable number of Confederate Army scenes sketched by Allan C. Redwood and others. Originals of the William L. Sheppard drawings for McCarthy's *Detailed Minutiae of Soldier*

Life are in the Virginia State Library. The Confederate Museum has, in addition to several splendid color sketches by Sheppard, some very interesting daguerreotypes of individual soldiers.

Of printed collections, F. T. Miller's *Photographic History of the Civil War* (New York, 1911) is the best, but it contains comparatively few Confederate items. *Battles and Leaders of the Civil War* (New York, 1887-1888) has some attractive sketches by the accomplished artists Redwood and Sheppard. Many photographs of individual Rebs are reproduced in Walter Clark's and J. B. Lindsley's previously mentioned studies of North Carolina and Tennessee troops, and in the *Confederate Veteran*.

OFFICIAL DOCUMENTS

The 128 volumes of *Official Records of the Union and Confederate Armies* (Washington, 1880-1901) contain a vast amount of data relating to the life of the common soldier but the infinite labor of culling these cumbersome books can be appreciated only by those who have had the experience. Indispensable information on Confederate medical history is to be found in the *Medical and Surgical History of the War of the Rebellion* (Washington, 1870-1888) particularly in part three of the medical volume. *Statutes at Large of the Confederate Congress* (Richmond, 1862-1864), edited by J. M. Matthews, supplemented by *Laws and Joint Resolutions of the Last Session* (Durham, N. C., 1941) edited by Charles W. Ramsdell, are essential for the tracing of military legislation. *Confederate Army Regulations* (Richmond, 1861-1864) have much relevant material. Another amazingly rich source consists of *General Orders* issued periodically by the adjutant general's office in Richmond and by commanders in the field. Many of the departmental orders are scattered among personal papers and miscellaneous collections.

INDEX

A BILLY YANK AND HIS COLORED AIDE

The soldier is a private of the Second Rhode Island Infantry Volunteers

THE LIFE OF BILLY YANK

The Common Soldier of the Union

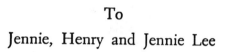

To
Jennie, Henry and Jennie Lee

ACKNOWLEDGMENTS

The author wishes to express appreciation to the following persons and firms for permission to reprint material as indicated:

Louisiana State University Press, Baton Rouge, *With Sherman to the Sea: The Journal of Theodore F. Upson*, edited by Oscar O. Winther.

University of California Press and Harold A. Small, Berkeley, *The Road to Richmond: The Civil War Memoirs of Major Abner R. Small*, edited by Harold A. Small.

Yale University Press, New Haven, John William De Forest, *A Volunteer's Adventures: A Union Captain's Record of the Civil War*, edited by James H. Croushore.

Abraham Lincoln Association, Springfield, Illinois, Bell I. Wiley, "Boys in Blue," *Abraham Lincoln Quarterly*, December 1951.

American Association for State and Local History, Sturbridge, Massachusetts, Bell I. Wiley, "Men in Blue," *American Heritage*, winter 1952.

Association for the Study of Negro Life and History, Incorporated, Washington, D. C., Bell I. Wiley, "Billy Yank and the Black Folk," *Journal of Negro History*, January 1951.

John D. Barnhart, Bloomington, Indiana, letters of "Prock" and other articles in the *Indiana Magazine of History*.

State Historical Society of Iowa, various articles in the *Iowa Journal of History and Politics*.

Virginia Quarterly Review, Bell I. Wiley, "Billy Yank Down South," autumn 1950.

Wisconsin Historical Society, "A Badger Boy in Blue: The Letters of Chauncey H. Cooke," in the *Wisconsin Magazine of History*, Volumes IV and V.

TABLE OF CONTENTS

LIST OF ILLUSTRATIONS

PREFACE

My IMMEDIATE reason for undertaking this book was to get acquainted with the foes of Johnny Reb. I wanted to know what sort of men they were, what caused them to fight, how they reacted to combat, what they thought about the land and people of Dixie, how well they stood up under the strain of prolonged conflict, what they thought of their leaders, and how they compared with their opposites in gray. All of this, and more, I wanted to learn and write down in a companion volume to *The Life of Johnny Reb*.

A remoter aim was to pursue further an inveterate interest in the humble folk, the little people, who have always comprised the bulk of our population, but who for that very reason, and for being relatively inarticulate, have appeared only hazily on the pages of history.

The Civil War affords an unusually good opportunity for the study of the plain people, for during that conflict unprecedentedly large numbers of them were away from home. Absence from loved ones caused lowly folk who rarely took pen in hand during times of peace to write frequent and informative letters and to keep diaries, and thus to reveal themselves in rare fullness. More than that, their war experience caused them to be written about to an unusual extent, in newspapers, court-martial proceedings, hospital records and official reports. The Civil War, coming as it did when the picture-making art was attaining a practical basis, also resulted in producing the first large-scale photographing of America's humbler citizens.

True, larger numbers of this class were to be taken from home in the world wars of our generation, but by that time censorship and other restrictions, which for all practical purposes were nonexistent during the Civil War, had made letters and diaries less meaningful as social documents.

My main concern in this study, as in *The Life of Johnny Reb*, has been social rather than military. To put it another way: I have been trying to write social history of men in arms.

In choosing the title for the present work I am not on as firm historical ground as in that of the earlier volume. The term Johnny Reb had considerable usage during the conflict; so did the designation Yank.

13

But the name Billy Yank seems to have been a postwar creation. I have
adopted it for euphony and balance and in so doing I have followed the
example of one of Lee's veterans, Alexander Hunter, who in 1905 published his Confederate memoirs under the title *Johnny Reb and Billy
Yank*.

Many types of material have been used but the basic source has been
the undoctored writings of the soldiers themselves, especially the manuscript letters. In quest of these fascinatingly human documents I traveled
twenty-three thousand miles and visited twenty-four states. In addition,
material was borrowed in microfilm, photostat or typescript from several
depositories not visited, including the Huntington Library, the Western
Historical Manuscripts Collection of the University of Missouri, Luther
College Library, Washington and Jefferson College, the New York State
Historical Association at Cooperstown and the Nebraska Historical Society.

During these travels I became indebted to many people. Custodians
of manuscripts kept extra hours to expedite research and in some cases
obligingly lent keys so that I might work at odd times. Historians along
the way extended courtesies far beyond the call of duty. Numerous private collectors and descendants of Union soldiers generously placed their
treasured holdings at my disposal. These and others assisted immeasurably by their active interest and friendly encouragement. Limitations
of space preclude individual mention of those whose kindness I received.
I can only state that their help is deeply appreciated and that without it
this book could hardly have been written.

I cannot refrain from making specific acknowledgment of the great
value to this project of the inventories and guides prepared under the
auspices of the Historical Records Survey of the Works Progress Administration. Use of these aids made possible a detailed planning of the
research itinerary and saved many precious hours.

I am indebted for indispensable financial assistance to the Rocke-
feller Foundation, whose directors awarded me a Post-War Fellowship;
the Social Science Research Council for two grants-in-aid; Louisiana
State University; Emory University; and the Carnegie Foundation for
the Advancement of Teaching.

The experience of looking at "the war" from the Northern point of
view and through the eyes of the men who wore the blue has been enormously interesting and stimulating to one who was nurtured in Confederate tradition and whose focus has been on the Southern side. In
the initial stage of research I was fearful that my long attachment to

Johnny Reb would prevent my treating his foe with the sympathy that he deserved and fair historical treatment required. But this anxiety was short-lived. For as I came to know the Northern soldier through his diaries and letters, I came to respect him, and as the acquaintance ripened I developed a genuine affection for him. I mean to pay him a high compliment when I state that he was no less admirable than the man he fought. Indeed, the two were so much alike that the task of giving this book a flavor and character distinct from *The Life of Johnny Reb* has at times been a difficult one.

Emory University, Georgia   BELL IRVIN WILEY
5 January, 1952

CHAPTER I

SOUTHWARD HO!

THE South's attack on Fort Sumter fell like a thunderclap on the country north of Dixie. True, there had been talk of war, especially since the secession of the cotton states and the organization of the Southern Confederacy, but the agitators, consisting mainly of politicians, journalists, preachers and reformers, many of whom were on the make, were relatively few. A substantial portion of the population still hoped for a peaceful solution of the sectional crisis even after Jeff Davis set up his rival government.[1]

Fort Sumter changed all this. The flag had been affronted. Men wearing the American uniform had been forced by hostile fire to surrender a Federal fort and march out in acknowledged defeat. And with that humiliating incident peaceable secession lost all respectability. The die was cast.

Lincoln's request for troops was in a sense an anticlimax. The roar of cannon at Charleston, like the crash of bombs eighty years later at Pearl Harbor, was the country's call to arms.

During most of the war the raising of troops was a slow and painful process. But in the weeks following Fort Sumter the opposite was true. From Lake Superior to the Ohio, from Maine to Minnesota, and even from far-off California men rushed to arms with camp-meeting fervor. "Everybody eagerly asks everybody else if he's going to enlist," wrote a Detroit reporter on April 19, and the same might have been said of almost any other town or city in the North.[2]

The tremendous surge of patriotism manifested itself in various ways. In Bangor, Maine, schoolgirls pounced on a boy who came among them wearing a palmetto flag and destroyed the despised emblem. At Pembroke, Maine, a lawyer of alleged Southern sympathies was threatened with a ducking in a river, and at Dexter, Maine, a group of volunteers "rode a Mr. Augustus Brown . . . on a rail for . . . saying that he hoped every one of them would be shot."[3] Elsewhere Southern sympathizers, real or imagined, were pelted with rotten eggs or otherwise put

17

in their places. And if traitors could not be found, patriots full of excitement and liquor often fell to fighting among themselves.[4]

Epidemics of "Star-Spangled Fever" struck many communities. The Detroit *Free Press* noted on April 18:

The Star-Spangled Banner rages most furiously. The old inspiring national anthem is played by the bands, whistled by the juveniles, sung in the theatres . . . sentimentally lisped at every piano by patriotic young ladies, ground out on church organs . . . hammered on tin pans by small boys, and we had almost said barked by the dogs. The banner itself . . . floats proudly and beautifully in every direction . . . from the roofs of houses . . . from all public places. . . . Omnibus men decorate their vehicles and horses.

Little wonder that the same article announced: "The supply of bunting is rapidly becoming scarce." [5]

Preachers catching the spirit of the hour, and perhaps not unmindful of the drawing power of martial themes on sinners as well as saints, proclaimed the gospel of patriotism from the pulpit. In Bath, Maine, the Episcopal rector was the first to enlist, and in Madison, Wisconsin, on the Sunday after Lincoln's call for troops the Reverend William Brisbane of the Baptist church, a recent volunteer in a local company, preached his farewell sermon in his shiny new uniform.[6]

The women were the most spirited of patriots. Usually their activities consisted of displaying flags, singing martial songs, raising funds and making clothing for the volunteers. But occasionally they chose more aggressive roles. The ladies of Skowhegan, Maine, for example, on a Saturday afternoon in April rolled out the village artillery piece and treated their neighbors to "a salute of thirty-four guns." [7]

For males the order of the day was volunteering, and the fever extended to all ages and classes. At Shenango, Pennsylvania, the young boys organized a "company," elected a thirteen-year-old captain and held weekly drills in the schoolyard to the accompaniment of a dinner-bucket drum corps.[8] And in Belfast, Maine, thirty-odd veterans of the War of 1812 responded to Lincoln's initial call by forming themselves into a company and tendering their services to the state.[9]

Nowhere was the war spirit more rampant than in the classrooms. At Bowdoin College the students on hearing of Sumter's fall rang the chapel bell, displayed the national colors, defiantly waved a skull-and-crossbones banner and shortly began daily drills on the campus.[10] In Oxford, Ohio, Ozra J. Dodds, a senior in the college, rose in the chapel and proposed organization of a University Rifle Company. Within a few minutes 160 students and local boys signed up for service in what was to become Company B, Twentieth Ohio Volunteers. Girls of the neighboring female college, not to be outdone, set themselves to making red shirts, flannel underclothing and a flag for the volunteers.[11]

From the University of Wisconsin a student wrote his parents on April 20: "Madison is in a great state of military excitement. The fever has penetrated the University walls. Seven of the boys have enlisted in the Governor's Guards." Four days later he reported the dismissal of his geometry class "to see the soldiers off." At the University of Michigan five companies were organized within a fortnight of Sumter's surrender.[12]

The war fever was rampant at Oberlin College where the quick formation of a company among the boys was matched by the organization of a "Florence Nightingale Association" by the girls. Effects of martial activities on the academic program were vividly revealed by a student who wrote on April 20 to his brother: "War! and volunteers are the only topics of conversation or thought. The lessons today have been a mere form. I cannot study. I cannot sleep, I cannot work, and I dont know as I can write." [13]

In most cases college authorities seem to have admonished their students against hasty enlistment. One faculty, with a view to satisfying the martial urge of their charges without forfeiting their presence in the classroom, hired a drillmaster to conduct military exercises on the campus.[14] But in a few instances college authorities took the lead in the patriotic movement. President Burgess of Eureka College in Illinois became the first captain of a company made up largely of his students, and President Hovey of the Illinois State Normal College took command of the Thirty-third Illinois Infantry, the roster of which included so many faculty and students that it came to be known as the "Normal Regiment." [15] President Hovey eventually became a general.[16]

The action of the colleges was not without parallel among lower-ranking institutions. The lone teacher in a log school near Wayzata, Minnesota, a boy not yet twenty years old, responded to the Fort Sumter crisis by immediately suspending operations, though the regular closing time was only a week away, and taking about half of his "grown" students to Fort Snelling to enlist.[17]

The war spirit reached far beyond the halls of learning. Jacob Dodson, a colored man employed in the United States Senate, offered to the Federal authorities 300 free Negroes for defense of the nation's capital. And a few days later the Secretary of War received from far-off

Minnesota a message stating that Chief Pug-o-na-ke-shick, or Hole-in-the-Day, of the Chippewa Nation, "deeply impressed with the sentiments of patriotism, and grateful for the aid and protection extended to him and his people . . . desires . . . to tender . . . the services of himself and 100 [or more] . . . of his headmen and braves to aid in defending the Government and its institutions against the enemies of the country." [18]

The problem of responsible authorities during this flood tide of patriotism was not to obtain men but to hold volunteers to manageable numbers. Governor Dennison of Ohio, of whom Lincoln on April 15 requested thirteen regiments, wrote a week later that "owing to an unavoidable confusion in the first hurry and enthusiasm of . . . our people," a much larger force had already mobilized. Indeed, he added, "without seriously repressing the ardor of the people, I can hardly stop short of twenty regiments." [19] What a pity that the government did not accept and constitute as a national reserve this horde of men who in the spring of 1861 so eagerly sought service! More than a million recruits could have been had without difficulty then. But within a year volunteering had slowed down to a trickle and before Second Manassas, despite all sorts of inducements in the form of bounties, authorities had to resort to threats of draft in order to meet the President's modest calls for troops.[20]

The first men who went to war usually entered the service as members of militia companies. These organizations were for the most part military only in name, their peacetime activities rarely going beyond holiday parades and ceremonial functions. Of later recruits, some were inducted into Regular Army units and others went as conscripts or substitutes. But the overwhelming majority of those who wore the blue entered the army as members of volunteer regiments formed under state auspices and mustered into Federal service for periods ranging from three months to three years.

Going-away experiences of the volunteer organizations were very much the same throughout the country, and except for a decline in enthusiasm the pattern did not greatly change with the passing of time.

The lead in forming units was usually taken by men who aspired to be officers. Often governors promised colonelcies to prominent citizens who would raise regiments, and the prospective colonels in turn offered captaincies to friends on condition that they recruit the minimum number required for a company. In some cases the impetus came from the other direction, with would-be officers signing up men and then using the lists as claims for commissions.

Those attempting to organize units, whatever their authority, solicited recruits by personal appeal, broadsides and advertisements in newspapers. After bounties became the vogue, these were given prominent place in all promotional activities. Sometimes commission-bent recruiters supplemented authorized bounties with financial inducements of their own, though this practice on occasion resulted in men playing one promoter against another to force up the bid.[21]

Mass meetings were a standard feature of recruiting efforts. Here leading citizens joined prospective officers in regaling audiences with oratorical outbursts full of allusions to country and flag and breathing defiance at slaveholders and traitors. Between speeches, brass bands played patriotic airs. If veterans of former wars were available they were featured as speakers or as adornments for the platform. The total effect of these influences was sometimes tremendous, especially in the early days of the war, so that when the cry "Who will come up and sign the roll?" was given at the end, men rushed to the front like seekers at a backwoods revival, each vying with the other to be first on the list.[22]

Once a nucleus was signed up, the recruits were put to the task of bringing in others. At speakings, picnics and other public gatherings volunteers were given special recognition. The girls helped recruiting efforts mightily by showing a preference for those who responded quickly to the country's call. A timid young Hoosier, delightfully surprised at the attention received from a local belle after volunteering, wrote in his journal: "If a fellow wants to go with a girl now he had better enlist. The girls sing 'I am Bound to be a Soldier's Wife or Die an Old Maid.' "[23]

An effective means of adding members was demonstrated by the Eighth Kentucky Regiment, which in the process of recruitment made the rounds of the community picnics. Here, as one of the veterans recalled, "we hoisted our flag, headed by our three amateur musicians, playing their one and only tune, 'Sally is the gal for me.' As each recruit fell into the moving line, loud cheers rent the air."[24]

The filling up of units was accompanied by steps for provision of clothing and equipment. From necessity and inclination commanders looked to state and local sources for initial outfitting. Some of the governors were able to provide their units with handsome and durable suits of uniform pattern, color and material. But many of the early organizations had to go to war in their gaudy militia regalia. Heavy reliance for initial needs was placed on women's sewing groups and while the results sometimes were gratifying, in many cases the handiwork indicated more zeal than skill.[25]

In consequence of these various expedients Federal encampments of 1861 and even later were marked by the greatest diversity of clothing. Almost every conceivable color and shade was represented. Materials ranged from broadcloth to satinette, and styles from the outlandish fezzes and bloomers of the Zouaves to "stiff and old-fashioned" suits of ancient militia organizations. In some regiments each company had a distinctive uniform.[26]

Soldier letters and diaries indicate that gray was a favorite color among early volunteer units. Indeed, in the first months of the war gray seems to have been almost as popular in Northern as in Southern camps. This circumstance led to unfortunate results on more than one battle-field. At First Manassas the gray-clad soldiers of the Second Wisconsin were said to have been mistaken for Confederates and fired on by their comrades, and at Cheat Mountain a similar circumstance caused Ohio troops to shoot at soldiers of the Thirteenth Indiana, killing and wounding several of them.[27] At Wilson's Creek early in 1862 Louisiana and Arkansas troops were allowed to maneuver within musket range of Sigel's command because the opposing troops wore the same color.[28] Three days before Shiloh, Grant reported that some of his men were "still in the gray uniform," owing to their reluctance to swap the good-quality gray garments for the shoddy blue dispensed by the quartermasters.[29] Not until the summer of 1862 could the term boys in blue be applied accurately to the Union forces, and deviations were to be found occasionally until the close of the war.

The story of equipment was about the same as that of clothing. Shifting in large measure for themselves in the early days, commanders armed their men with a miscellany ranging from modern Sharps rifles to obsolete muskets hardly less dangerous to the wielder than to the target. Ignorance of the volunteers combined with the generosity of local donors to weight the soldiers down with such extras as dueling pistols, drinking tubes, havelocks, nightcaps, bulletproof vests and vicious-appearing daggers.[30]

Sometimes failure of authorities to provide necessary clothing and equipment forced the disbandment of volunteer organizations. Several three-month Massachusetts regiments were discharged in August 1861

after vainly waiting eight weeks for arms. Some of the members registered their protest by sending a box of wooden muskets to the governor.
And one of them had his say on the clothing situation by covering a
gaping hole in his trousers with a shingle on which was inscribed "The
Last Shift of a Soldier." [31]

Recruits were supposed to be checked for physical fitness, but apparently among early volunteers this provision was sometimes overlooked.[32]
And in many cases where it was observed the examination was a farce.
Private Charles Barker of Massachusetts wrote in November 1861 that
the examining surgeon felt his collarbones and said, "You have pretty
good health don't you?" When Barker replied affirmatively the doctor
remarked, "You look as though you did." After inquiring if the recruit
had fits or piles the examiner marked him able for service.[33]

Leander Stillwell of Illinois gave the following account of his examination:

The surgeon, at that time, was a fat, jolly old doctor by the name of
Leonidas Clemmons. I was about scared to death when the Captain
presented me to him, and requested him to examine me. I reckon the
good old doctor saw I was frightened, and he began laughing heartily
and saying some kind things about my general appearance. He requested
me to stand up straight, then gave me two or three little sort of "love
taps" on the chest, turned me round, ran his hands over my shoulders,
back, and limbs, laughing and talking all the time, then whirled me to
the front, and rendered judgment on me as follows: "Ah, Capt. Reddish!
I only wish you had a hundred such fine boys as this one! He's all right,
and good for the service." [34]

But the crowning commentary on the ineffectiveness of the examining
system is the number of women who, passing for males, succeeded in
entering the volunteer ranks.[35]

Little wonder that Frederick Law Olmsted after a fifteen-month investigation of recruiting conditions in the army reported to Lincoln in
July 1862: "The careless and superficial medical inspection of recruits
made at least 25 per cent of the volunteer army raised last year not
only utterly useless, but a positive incumbrance and embarrassment." [36]
Subsequently detailed examining procedures were prescribed by the medical department, but these were in large measure nullified by failure to
provide anything like an adequate staff of examiners.[37]

Not the least important of organizational activities was the selection
of an appropriate name for the volunteer company. Among early choices

were to be found such inspiring designations as "Union Clinchers," the "Oxford Bears," the "Douglas Guards," the "Cass Light Infantry," the "Huron Rangers" and the "Detroit Invincibles." [38]

At some point in the process of organization the volunteers moved to camp. Usually the initial encampment was a temporary one located in the home community, but occasionally the regimented life was begun at points of rendezvous or camps of instruction farther removed, though normally not so far away as to prevent exchange of visits with the home-folk. Indeed, some of the volunteers loaded wives and children on company wagons and took them along to camp, though a short stay among the soldiers usually sufficed to demonstrate the impracticability of this procedure.[39]

Among initial activities of camp was the designation of commissioned and noncommissioned officers. Election of captains and lieutenants by the men and of colonels and majors by company officers was common practice, with governors issuing commissions to those so selected. But frequently, if not usually, the voting was a mere formality, it being a foregone conclusion that persons responsible for recruiting the units, or previously approved by the governor, would become the officers. That highhanded tactics were not unknown is evidenced by an Illinois soldier's notation in his diary: "In the evening Col. Cumming meets us in our barracks and tells us that Adj. Gen. Fuller insisted on hurrying up our regimental organization—*that he (Col. C.) not knowing of any objection on our part (?) (!) had our acting officers . . . mustered into the U. S. Service . . .* that an election was only a matter of *form* (!) then put it to us by *word of mouth*, whether or not we would sustain him, and no one *daring* to object, he was sustained—This is called an election! What a farce!" [40]

Freedom of choice was allowed most often for lieutenancies, and the filling of these lowly positions, which some of the men referred to disparagingly as "pumpkin rinds" (suggested by the appearance of the shoulder straps), might be accompanied by lively electioneering on the part of the candidates.[41] It was not uncommon for defeated aspirants to quit the service.

Elections, whether free or rigged, were often followed by speechmaking, feasting and drinking, with successful candidates serving as hosts to both officers and men.[42]

Induction into Federal service, preceded in some cases by muster in as state troops, was another incident of early camp life. The Federal ceremony, conducted by a Regular Army officer, was an impressive one.

After being formed by company the men and officers were inspected individually and collectively, following which they were required to take the oath of allegiance as prescribed in the tenth article of war. Then came the reading of the articles of war, a long and tedious exercise which regulations required to be repeated twice each year.[43] Sometimes reading of the articles preceded the swearing in, but the inadvisability of this procedure was indicated by an Iowa volunteer who wrote in his diary in June 1861: "The fact that nearly all violations . . . called for the death penalty or some other severe punishment so depressed a number of the boys that six of them hurriedly made their exit and were not thereafter heard of in connection with the company." [44]

The parting words of many mothers to their soldier sons were "Send me your picture." And during their first weeks in uniform countless soldiers visited the "daguerrean artists" who set up shop in camp or in near-by towns.[45] Many Yanks had never before confronted a photographer, and this no doubt accounts for the stiffness which characterized the "likenesses" or "shadows" sent back to the homefolk.

No one could consider himself a soldier until he learned to march and use his weapons. Hence instruction in the drill and the manual of arms as laid down by Winfield Scott, William J. Hardee or Silas Casey was an important part of initial activities. Since volunteer officers usually were chosen for popularity or political prestige rather than military accomplishment, guidance in rudimentary training frequently had to be sought from other sources. Fortunately most units had in their ranks veterans of the Mexican War or immigrants with European service who could act as drillmasters. The aid rendered by foreigners, schooled in the excellent systems of Prussia, France, Switzerland and other Western European countries, in training the Union forces was tremendous, and their service in this connection deserves far more recognition than it has received.

One of the greatest obstacles to training was the lack of system and direction. The present generation, accustomed as it is to an elaborate hierarchy of schools and a profusion of literature covering in detail all phases of training, has difficulty in appreciating the vastly different situation prevailing in Civil War times. Officer-training schools worthy of the name did not exist. Leaders had to learn their duties on the job from poorly written and skimpy manuals. Many regiments set up their own schools for officers and noncommissioned officers, but these, owing to lack of guidance and experienced personnel, often hobbled along in the fashion of the blind leading the blind. The manuals outlined fundamentals for the school of the soldier and for company, battalion and brigade, but uniform progressive-training programs prepared in higher headquarters, with time allotments for the various subjects and stages, were unknown. The same could be said of charts, models, slides and other streamlined training aids which did so much to simplify and vivify instruction in World War II.

The training problem might have been eased had the Regular Army been distributed among volunteer organizations as cadremen or instructors, but the War Department elected to keep regular organizations intact for use as a steadying or saving leaven in battle. Occasionally West Point cadets and Regular Army sergeants were used, apparently on a loan basis, for instructional purposes.

For the most part early volunteer organizations had to work out their own salvation, though some higher commanders, notably McClellan, and some lesser ones, with Sherman affording a good example, gave effective guidance to subordinate units.

A few of the volunteer organizations had the benefit of systematic preparation in their home states. In Michigan, Fort Wayne, near Detroit, was designated in June 1861 as a camp of instruction for the Fifth, Sixth and Seventh Regiments. Officers and noncommissioned officers were sent to this camp in advance of the privates. Here in skeleton groups, after being instructed by the most accomplished drill sergeants chosen from among their number, the leaders took turns commanding one another. Thus by the time the fillers arrived the instructors had acquired both a knowledge of fundamentals and a degree of self-confidence.[46]

But such well-conceived procedure was highly exceptional. As a general rule, officers and men started out together in equal ignorance and blundered along with inadequate equipment through varying periods of training. The results were pitiful. Infantrymen trying to execute the order to charge bayonet stuck one another, and cavalrymen drilling with sabers frightened their horses into running away.[47] Typical conditions among early volunteer units were described by a Pennsylvania soldier in the summer of 1861: "Col. Roberts has showed himself to be ignorant of the most simple company movements. There is a total lack of system about our regiment. . . . Nothing is attended to at the proper time, nobody looks ahead to the morrow, and business heads to direct are wanting. . . . We can only be justly called a mob & one not fit to face the enemy."[48]

One of the most grievous deficiencies of early training—and it persisted to an amazing extent throughout the war—was the lack of target practice. A few regiments did have systematic instruction in musketry and one commander even had enough imagination to set up replicas of Jeff Davis for his men to shoot at, but references to marksmanship exercises are notable chiefly for their absence.[49]

In some instances training was not only poor but woefully abbreviated. Of a unit organized as late as August 1862 a soldier wrote: "Within three weeks from the day this regiment was mustered into service, and before it had ever had what could properly be called a battalion drill, it was in the battle of Antietam." [50]

Activities on the drill grounds were accompanied by indoctrination in less formal aspects of camp life. Individuals of like habits and tastes soon discovered one another and formed messes, the members of which ate together and took turns in preparing meals. Often they occupied the same quarters and some even adopted nicknames. Private James Snell and his twelve associates in Company A, Eighty-second Illinois Regiment, called themselves the "Hyena Mess," with individual designations as follows:

Soldier	Nickname	Position
Snell	Elephant	President
Murray	Bulldog Clipper	Correspondent
Ellis	Greyhound	Grand Scribbler
Barnes	Rhinoceros	Reporter (Shorthand)
Leslie	Piss-ant	Artist
Murphy	Spaniel	Fry-master
Harrington	Jackal	Historian
Kutcher	Weasel	Absent, in his hole, asleep
Lane	Buffalo	Inspector-General
Swanson	Tiger	Scout & Foragemaster
Simpson	Monkey	Acrobat & Tumbler
Sanderson	Fox	Chesterfield gent.
Miller (cook)	Chicken	Caterer General [51]

Individual reactions to the new way of life were generally favorable. "I and the rest of the boys are in fine spirits . . . feeling like larks," wrote a New Yorker shortly after enlistment, while an Illinois youth reported: "I never enjoyed anything in the world as I do this life." [52] Youngsters, especially those from the country, were more enthusiastic than older men. Rural boys were thrilled by the new sights, the teeming crowds and the constant activity, and most of them found camp conditions no more uncomfortable and military duties no more onerous than those known at home. Some were startled by the abundance of material things which army life afforded. An Iowa farmer recently inducted wrote his homefolk that "I have got the best suit of clothes that I [ever] had in my life"—a statement often heard among rural recruits—and a little later he added, "I was perfectly surprised to find such good accommodations." [53] This rustic, like thousands of his kind, found in soldiering a thoroughly agreeable life.

At the other extreme were men who utterly detested the army. A few objected to the lack of privacy, some to the rampant ungodliness, others to the discipline and still others to the deprivation and hardship. "The way we have been treated is enough to make a preacher swear almost," wrote Private O. W. Norton from a camp in Pennsylvania. "We are cheated in our rations about half the time. Our clothes are all dropping off from us." [54] Another Yank of five weeks' service featured by long marches complained: "If there is anything peculiarly attractive in marching from 10 to 20 miles a day under a scorching sun with a good mule load, and sinking up to one's knees in the 'Sacred Soil' at each Step, my mind is not of a sufficiently poeticle nature to apreciate it." [55] So strong was aversion to the new order in some instances, owing to the combined influences of poor leadership, discomfort and homesickness, that units almost disintegrated before their officers could get them accepted into Federal service. In such cases a hard rain at a critical juncture would probably have spelled the difference between going south or going home.

But a majority of soldiers were neither exuberant nor mournful in their initial reactions. And whatever their first attitudes, the passing of time tended to bring all to the common denominator of good-natured conformity—though not without the chronic growling that has ever characterized the American soldier.

At some time during the course of their early training, officers and men put on their best appearance and manners for the flag presentation. The colors were often the handiwork of local women, and the donor almost invariably was one of the feminine patriots. The presentation ceremony was frequently the occasion of a vast assembly of relatives and friends.

When the Fourth Michigan received its colors at Adrian on June 21, 1861, special trains brought in hundreds of citizens from the surrounding country. At 2:30 in the afternoon the regiment in full uniform and "with such equipment as it had" formed in a hollow square on the local parade ground. Presently a carriage brought to the platform within the enclosure Mrs. Josephine Wilcox, accompanied by three maids of honor and the regimental color sergeant. Following the unfurling of the flag, made by the ladies of Adrian, Mrs. Wilcox addressed the soldiers:

When you follow this standard in your line of march or on the field of battle, and you see it waving in lines of beauty and gleams of brightness, remember the trust we have placed in your hands. We will follow you in our hearts with our hopes and our prayers. You are the sons of brave men, who under this banner achieved the glorious victory of our national independence. . . . We are the daughters of the brave women of '76. . . . Our trial has come, our spirits waken and we feel the blood of heroes stirring in our veins. The eyes of the world are placed upon our republican institutions. . . . Sustain this banner for the love you bear to woman, for under no standard in the wide world is woman so blessed as are Columbia's daughters. . . . You are to go forth to the conflict to strike for . . . our noble Constitution, for freedom of speech, for freedom of thought, for God and the right.

Then Mrs. Wilcox soared to her climax:

The eagle of American liberty from her mountain eyrie has at intervals during the past few years given us faint warnings of danger. Now she swoops down on spreading pinions with unmistakable notes of alarm; her cries have reached the ears of freemen, and brave men rush to arms. She has perched on this banner which we now give to your keeping. Let your trust be in the God of battles to defend it.

Colonel Woodbury, responding for the regiment, promised that the trust reposed in him and his men would not be abused; that the flag would "never be given up to traitors" or disgraced, but would be defended by himself and his associates with their lives and its luster increased by deeds of valor. The colonel's stirring pledge was endorsed by prolonged cheering of the men.

After other speeches by prominent citizens the soldiers treated the crowd to a series of battalion and regimental maneuvers.[56]

At Detroit the Ninth Michigan's colonel, W. W. Duffield, received the regimental colors from the hand of his father, the eminent minister, George Duffield, who made a long speech closing with the words: "Human government . . . is the ordinance of God. . . . Rebellion therefore against a lawful government, lawfully administered, is rebellion against God." The son in receiving the emblem remarked: "We wish no conquest. We desire no subjugation. . . . Our swords are drawn for the Union and our watchword shall be 'the Union, now and forever, one and inseparable.' " [57]

These scenes and these sentiments were repeated with only slight variation throughout the length and breadth of the land as the volunteers were mobilized for the mission before them. "The University Recruits" of Upper Iowa University were presented colors made by the girls of that institution. In appreciation of this service the boys permitted the girls to choose the color sergeant. At the balloting held in the reception room of the Ladies' Hall, Henry J. Grannis was elected standard-bearer. As it turned out the girls chose the regimental color-bearer, for when the university boys became Company C of the Twelfth Iowa, Grannis was elevated to that position.[58]

Not all the ceremonies were marked by the eloquence or beauty which characterized those described above. One of the less pretentious affairs was described by a Massachusetts lieutenant who participated in it:

This eve we were presented with a flag by the ladies of this town. A very homely young lady (though she was the best looking one in town) made a speach which she learned (at least she thought so, but I did not for she went through with [it] about as smooth as one might come down a rocky hill in the dark). Col. Gordon then answered it. Three cheers were then proposed for him which sounded a good deal as old bad Fali [the lieutenant's cat] did when her tail was stepped on. The officers of the regiment then gave the ladies three cheers which made them turn pale. The band play[ed], we took the [flag] . . . and went home.[59]

After varying periods of training in home areas came the trip to a camp near the scene of hostilities. The general direction of the "seat of war," as the fighting zone was usually called, for most units was southward—to the environs of Washington for Eastern regiments and to Missouri, Kentucky or Tennessee for Western organizations. But there was considerable deviation from this general pattern, with Western troops making the long journey to Maryland or Virginia and Eastern units going to Tennessee or Kentucky.

The southward move was usually preceded by rumors and false starts. During the final days before departure many Yanks received furloughs to bid their families good-by. The home farewells were solemn occasions often marked by tears of mothers or wives and painful silence on the part of male members of the household.

Public leave-taking of the unit, when finally the day of departure came, presented a different appearance. At the depot or wharf, speeches,

DIGGING IN

Drawing by Charles W. Reed

MOURNFUL ONES AT SICK CALL
Drawing by Charles W. Reed

music, bouquets and farewell gifts were the order of the day. The first troops to leave Madison, Wisconsin, in April 1861 were addressed at the depot "by Judge Vilas & Gov. Randall & the Star Spangled Banner was sung by Miss Susan Devin, actress. . . . Norcross & Ball of the Univ. boys stood it well, but Miller Wyse & Smith were much affected." [60]

In August 1861 the citizens of Kalamazoo gave the Sixth Michigan Regiment a tremendous send-off. The long train consisting of five baggage cars, twenty-two first-class passenger coaches and "the magnificent directors' car" was pulled by the railroad company's two crack engines, the "Ranger" and the "Stag Hound." The lead locomotive was elaborately decorated with banners "and a neatly executed head ornament consisting of two clasped hands supporting a shield, the whole being surmounted with a circular piece on which was painted 'death to traitors.'" The directors' car was occupied by the officers while the men rode the coaches. The railroad's favorite conductor was in charge of the train, and the superintendent went along to see that everyone was made comfortable.[61]

Incidents of departure ranged from the ridiculous to the sublime. When the Second Massachusetts entrained at Boston a mother said earnestly to the commander, "We look to you, Col. Gordon, to bring all of these young men back in safety to their homes." [62] A few hours' delay in the departure of the Sixth Massachusetts was utilized by one of the members for arranging a last-minute marriage. Accompanied by his lieutenant this soldier went to the city hall for the license, engaged the services of a clergyman and set out for the home of his lady love. And there, according to the lieutenant, "At the Early morning hour while all were moved to tears the marriage rite was performed." The ceremony was completed in time for the groom to leave with the regiment at nine o'clock.[63]

Once the train or ship was under way, the soldiers' spirits took an upward turn. Joking, pranking and general merriment became the order of the day. In many instances the festive bent was helped along by drinking. A New York volunteer wrote his mother on arrival in Virginia: "After we got out of their hearing the boys acted as if they had forgoten their mothers and . . . wives, that they had just . . . left . . . with tears in their eyesNot but a few minutes before the band boys handed wround the whisky bottle among themselves . . . one of the members of the band got drunk." [64] Another New Yorker who made the southward trip by boat in 1863 wrote: "Whiskey was freely used. . . . I 'piled in' down in the hole with a man half tight, while those that were wholly so made merry until a late hour . . . poor liquor was sold for a dollar a pint." [65] Now and then a volunteer made bold and unsteady by liquor would fall from the top of the cars or tumble overboard with fatal consequences. On rare occasions some sot would go berserk. A Connecticut sergeant en route to Annapolis recorded such an instance: "During the night a man on board was taken with the tremens and of all the Horrid noises and actions I ever saw . . . it took five strong men to hold him." [66]

If drink was not provided by friends at the parting or if the initial supply needed replenishing, soldiers now and then made raids on taverns along the way. A Pennsylvania regiment bound for Baltimore stole a keg of beer at "little York" and took it aboard their train. Here one of the soldiers beat the head in with the butt of his musket, but with disappointing results. "The beer shot up into the air 15 feet like a fountain & fell foaming on everything & person . . . very little of the beer was left." [67]

It is not meant to imply that southward movements were liquor orgies or that drinking was universal. Many soldiers deplored the conviviality and some took refuge in spiritual contemplation. But the number of these who resorted to the Bible seems less than those who sought the bottle.

The festive mood of the war-bound volunteers frequently found expression in song. Some regiments moved south to the strains of "The Star-Spangled Banner," while others tauntingly blended their voices in "Dixie." The 116th Pennsylvania sang "Johnny Is Gone for a Soldier" as their train rattled southward, while Germans of the Ninth Ohio made the coaches ring with their native "Morgenroth." [68] After Lincoln's call of July 1862 for 300,000 troops, departing volunteers began to sing,

> We are coming Father Abraham
> Three hundred thousand more.[69]

But the favorite going-away song for the war as a whole was the soul-stirring "John Brown's Body." [70]

Some units needed all assistance that song or stimulants would afford to alleviate the discomfort and hardship of travel. Few volunteers journeying by train enjoyed the luxuries provided for the Sixth Michigan as already described. In a far greater number of instances, accommodations consisted of boxcars equipped with backless benches of rough plank and inadequately, if at all, provided with heat, ventilation, food, water and sanitary facilities. Inferior tracks and poor roadbeds made for rough riding. Breakdowns were commonplace and wrecks frequent. Soldiers often cleared the stuffy atmosphere of the crowded cars by "smashing a good allowance of holes through the sides and ends." [71] On reaching their destination officers and men were sometimes so exhausted that they threw themselves on the station platform and slept for several hours.[72]

Soldiers traveling by river boat seem to have been relatively comfortable, but those who made long journeys by coastal craft were often subjected to extreme hardship because of crowded quarters, inadequate provisioning and rough seas. A soldier borne by steamer from Portland, Maine, to Fort Monroe with "men packed in a nasty hold so close that they could scarcely lie down . . . a part of them a drunken boisterious pack" compared his experience with that of slaves transported from Africa as human cattle.[73] And another whose route was from New York to Annapolis wrote: "We were huddled together more like a lot of pigs than human beings. . . . I was compelled to sleep on the floor. . . . Our rations we could hardly force down. In fact, most of it was rotten or nearly so. The water was very dirty. Yet we were glad to get enough of it." [74]

To some expeditions hurricanes and seasickness brought peril and misery. "It bloud up a storm and knocked us about," a Pennsylvanian wrote after landing in South Carolina, "and made some of the boys very sick and ye gods what a time some was praying and some was swaring and others wanted to be throd overboard." [75]

Some of those who made the long voyage from the East in Butler's Louisiana invasion of 1862 seem to have suffered most. One of the ships, the *Mississippi*, ran aground near Port Royal in sight of Rebel guns, forcing the dumping of many provisions and requiring a whole company to pump day and night to keep the vessel afloat.[76] Deprivation, sickness, gloom and death marked the cruise of the transport *North America*. The letter-diary of a Maine officer on board gave the following account:

Feb. 8th [1862] Saild. . . . Quite a number crazy drunk. . . . 300 men sea sick.
Feb. 12th. We have at least 300 men on board more than the ship can decently accommodate in the morning the air & filth between decks is enough to sicken a dog.
Feb. 15th. Making no progress. Uncomfortable hot could not sleep last night. . . . We have plenty of provisions but the arrangements for cooking are insufficient & the men complain bitterly for want of 'Grub'

. . . today we find that we are short of water & commenced dealing it out by the pint. . . .

Feb. 16th. . . . The man that died [of diphtheria] was buried in the Sea. . . .

Feb. 24th. . . . We feel anxious about our provisions & water—dirt & disease the men between decks are getting lousey. O horrid I imagine they are on me every day.

Feb. 26th. . . . Another man died of lung fever. . . .

Feb. 28th. . . . it is a hard place for a sick man between deck when 900 are crowded in—dirty, lousey, bad air it is a wonder how they live. . . .

March 4. . . . The squall struck us with terrible force. . . . No one could walk or stand without holding on with both hands. . . . Night came upon us without any abatement. . . .

March 6th. Another man died yesterday. . . . We are all getting heartily tired of the voyage.

March 8th. Made . . . [Ship] Island this morning. . . . We rent the air with cheers.[77]

A Vermont corporal on board the *Wallace*, another ship in the Butler expedition, revealed similar experiences in his journal:

March 12th. Sick myself. O dear, sick enough: sea-sick and sick of the sea. Wish I was home sugaring off for Aunt Elvira, or some of the girls. Wind due South and . . . hot as harvest.

March 13th. Dead calm, and all hands dead sick. . . .

March 18th. . . . A sad sight this evening;—a poor old father burying his son at sea. . . . The body was wrapped in a blanket, with iron slugs tied to the feet and slid over the side on a plank.

April 5th. Made Ship Island, after having sailed four weeks with almost nothing to eat, and much of the time with only a half pint of water per day. . . . Much of the time we had a little hard bread and salt, two or three times, boiled potatoes and salt, sometimes a little meat with our "white oak chips" [hardtack]. . . .[78]

Volunteers who traveled southward by land or river early in the war had their journey lightened by enthusiastic attentions of people along the way. For many the trip was a series of ovations, marked by speeches, music, feasting, handshaking and kissing. Members of the First Vermont, as they proceeded from Bradford to New York in May 1861, at Bellows Falls were "met by the citizens. The [town] Band and the Fire Company . . . escorted [us] through the streets . . . to partake of refreshments prepared by the ladies." At other villages cannon were fired and at Troy, New York, the townsmen fed the soldiers at the depot and the officers at a hotel.[79] A soldier of the Second Michigan wrote of his trip from Detroit to Washington in June 1861: "We was treated as good as a company could bee at every station their was a crowd to cheer us and at about every other one they had something for us to eat. We got kisses from the girls at a good many plaises and we returned the same to them." At Baltimore, where the Sixth Massachusetts had been attacked by a mob in April, he reported "a little fus with the rebles" during which one of his comrades was hit with a stone, but the soldier shot his assailant "ded on the spot," after which the regiment moved on to its destination.[80]

None of the early organizations was sent southward more enthusiastically than the First Minnesota, concerning whose river-land journey a supernumerary wrote:

After leaving Has[tings] we landed at Red Wing, Lake City, Wabashan and Winona, at which places great scenes were Enacted. . . . The good steamer Northern Bell kept us upon the *Father of Waters* until Eleven O'clock that night. We were transferred to a train of cars immediately and started for Chicago. . . . All along the road through Wis., Ill., Ind., Ohio, Penn., Md, we were cheered from almost every home. The boys tired themselves more yelling than from any thing they had to perform. In Pitts. we were treated to a supply of warm coffee. . . . At every station we found old men and women ready to greet us . . . and in one instance an old lady, grey headed and trembling sat in her door as we passed and blessed us in words & actions so fervently that she resembled a spiritual medium passing through her gyrations.[81]

Many soldiers from both West and East passed through Philadelphia, and most of them who stopped in the City of Brotherly Love seem to have enjoyed the hospitality of the Cooper's Shop, the Civil War's most famous volunteer way station, where within a year 87,518 transient soldiers were fed and refreshed.[82] The dining room, sleeping quarters and other facilities were operated on a twenty-four-hour basis, and apparently no man in uniform was turned away. Soldier letters and diaries paid the highest tribute to the fare and the treatment.

Other way stations maintained a high order of hospitality throughout the war, but the same could not be said of the citizenry as a whole. For as the conflict extended from months to years and the moving of soldiers from the hinterland to the front became a common occurrence, the enthusiasm of the people subsided and patriotic endeavor lost its sharp edge. The changed situation is vividly reflected in a Hoosier's description of his experience in Cincinnati while en route to war in September 1863:

We slept a little that night in the depot. Next morning . . . [we] had no breakfast as our haversacks were empty. About 7 o'clock we were marched to the principal part of the city . . . where we sat down in the street to wait for further orders. After waiting awhile some of the kind and benevolent Buckeyes were so generous as to pass each one of us an advertisement of a patent medicine. it was a noble present to hungry Hoosiers but poorly appreciated. In the course of time another very *savory dish* was served up to us in the shape of an advertisement telling us where we could make splendid bargains by buying rich military goods at high costly prices. . . . After a while some patriotic citizen made us each a present of Gen Logan's famous speech. Not long after American Messengers Tracts, Soldier Hymn Books &c &c were passed around. . . . About 1 o'clock we partook of bread, half boiled ham—coffee and an onion. . . . After our meal was finished we stood around in the market house until the rain was over when we marched to the ferry crossed over to Covington, Ky.[83]

But in the early period going to war was a tremendous picnic. The battlefield if given a thought seemed remote, and lack of martial experience made its horrors incomprehensible.[84] Hence, most Yanks gave themselves to enjoyment of the movement. Country boys, many of them having their first trips, marveled at the mysteries of trains and boats and gawked at the sights along the way. At the first opportunity they took pen in hand to tell the homefolk of the wonders of nature and the miracles of man. Struggling mightily with spelling and grammar, an Ohio rustic recently arrived in Maryland wrote to a friend:

Frank since I seen you last I hav seen the elephant. We started from urbana [Ohio] at three oclok p m . . . we run that night and the next day till ten oClock am We got to bellair on the bank of the ohio river then the thing was to get rit over again We got over and in the Cars . . . we past within 4 mils of Whelling virginia. we past through some of the damdes plases ever saw by mortel eyes. We run under som of the god dames hills it was dark as the low regeons of hell We past through one tunel too miles long . . . as we was passing from tunelton to New Crick the cars run onto a stone that would weigh 500 lbs it was put on the track by rebels it was just whair the track runs close to the river if the engen had not bin so hevy we would hav all went to hell in a pile or some other seaport. We went in to Camp four days after we left urbana.[85]

A Wisconsin boy wrote his parents on completion of the first stint of his trip:

We came in the cars to Madison from La Crosse. It was a new experience for me, I was wide awake the whole day. I was afraid we were off the track every time we crossed a switch or came to a river. At the towns the girls swarmed on the platforms to ask the boys for their pictures and to kiss the best looking ones. A young Frenchman . . . small and quick, got the most kisses. He was so short the boys held him by the legs so he could reach down out the windows to kiss the girls. Many times some old fellows held the girls up so she could be reached. It was fun anyway.[86]

Many Yanks compared what they saw with what they left behind and the new usually came off second best. "Since I left Nineveh everything has been new," wrote a provincial New Yorker, "but I must say deliver me from citty life." [87] Even Washington, to which countless Yanks eventually found their way to roam public buildings and gape at the great, proved disappointing to some. A New Englander who stopped off in the capital en route to Virginia in September 1861 noted in his diary:

We strolled from one end of the city to the other . . . we went into the Capital and in the picture galery. . . . Then ascending the stairs to the top of the building . . . had a fine view of Washington and the neighborhood, but I was struck with the mean appearance of the city of Washington with the exception of the Government Buildings there is not a building in the whole city which can be called a good one in comparison with the Stores and dwelling houses of Boston.[88]

Arrived at their southern destinations, the volunteers—now usually a part of large organizations containing a sprinkling of Regular Army officers—got down to the business of preparing for war.

At this point it is appropriate to raise the question of motives. Why did the men in blue go to war? For what were they fighting? Immediate impulses were varied. As already intimated the prevailing excitement, the lure of far places and the desire for change were dominant factors in the enlistment of many. Countless men joined up because of the example of friends and associates. A young Vermonter tied to his home by the illness of a parent revealed the force of the martial tug: "I was glad . . . to here that you had Enlisted," he wrote to a friend in June 1861. "Oh how I wish i could go I can't hardly controll myself I here the solgers druming round. If you get your eye on old Jef Davis make a cathole threw him. I am agoing to join a training Company that they are a getting up here so that I can realise a little of the fun that solgers have." [89]

The economic motive influenced many. At first thought it seems preposterous that thirteen dollars a month, the pay of infantry privates during most of the war, should be an attraction. But the first months of the war were marked by depression, and unemployment recurred periodically until 1863. Too, bounties early became a part of the recruiting system and these were steadily increased until early in 1864 a soldier was able to write: "I receive for reenlisting nearly . . . Eight hundred dolars which I shall devote to straightening things at home." [90]

If soldier pay was low, so were wages in general, and army employment had a certainty and permanence rarely found in field or factory. Duplicated frequently throughout the land was the situation of a Pennsylvanian who wrote to his wife in November 1861: "It is no use for you to fret or cry about me for you know if i could have got work i wood not have left you or the children." [91]

Financial inducement seems to have been especially cogent among the immigrants, about two million of whom had flocked to the North in the 1850s. Poverty, difficulties of employment, prior acquaintance with military life and a strong desire to acquire property combined with other influences to drive thousands of them into the army. A good case in point is that of William O. Wettleson, a Wisconsin Norwegian who wrote to his parents shortly after enlisting: "It seemed as if I were compelled to go in order to get out of debt and to buy Heddejord [a farm, apparently] which is Ingeborg's dearest wish." [92]

After resort to conscription the urge to avoid the stigma of forced service plus the desire to obtain certain privileges allowed only to volunteers, such as bounties and choice of unit, caused thousands to enlist. A leading Civil War historian, referring specifically to Ohio, characterizes the desire to avoid the draft as "the great spur to enlistment." [93]

Combination of a sense of duty and a fear of compulsion in inducing enlistment is well illustrated in the instance of a Vermonter who wrote in his diary on August 18, 1862: "Made application for membership in the 'Rutland Light Guard.' . . . God knows that the country needs men and I regard it as the duty of every able bodied man who can possibly do so to enlist at once—the sooner the better, and it is better by far to enlist voluntarily than to be dragged into the army a conscript. Nothing to me would appear more degrading." [94]

Love of country and hatred of those who seemed bent on destroying its institutions impelled many to enlist, though often patriotism was indistinguishably blended with practical urges. Sometimes idealistic sentiments were vaguely comprehended if at all, though their utterance by orators undoubtedly helped to stimulate emotions favorable to volunteering. A Detroit journalist wrote of encountering at a mass meeting in 1861 "a mild-looking blue-eyed little man [who] told us . . . that he was going to 'have his rights and stick to the constitution.'" The same reporter said of other recruits, "[They] expect to have a fight with somebody, but they dont exactly know who or what for." [95]

But some gave serious thought to their reasons for going to war and revealed considerable appreciation of the issues involved. Among these was Philip Smith, an immigrant member of the Eighth Missouri Regiment, who on July 22, 1861, wrote in his diary:

> As I lay in my bed this morning I got to thinking. . . . I have left home and a good situation . . . and have grasped the weapon of death for the purpose of doing my part in defending and upholding the integrity, laws and the preservation of my adopted country from a band of contemptible traitors who would if they can accomplish their hellish designs, destroy the best and noblest government on earth, merely for the purpose of benefiting themselves on the slave question.[96]

Similar sentiments were expressed by Samuel Storrow, a Harvard student who against his parents' wishes enlisted as a corporal in the Fortyfourth Massachusetts in the fall of 1862. In a letter to his father Storrow justified his action thus:

> I went to Cambridge and resumed my studies with what zeal I could. During that week we heard that the rebel forces were pushing forward and Northward. . . . I assure you, my dear father, I know of nothing in the course of my life which has caused me such deep and serious thought as this trying crisis in the history of our nation. What is the worth of this man's life or of that man's education if this great and glorious fabric of our Union . . . is to be shattered to pieces by traitorous hands. . . . If our country and our nationality is to perish, better that we should all perish with it.[97]

Hence, original impulses of individuals ranged from material considerations and a mere craving for excitement to profound idealism and hatred of traitors. It seems clear, however, that the great bulk of volunteers responded to mixed motives, none of which was deeply felt.

The same was generally true of the more permanent or basic influences. One searches most letters and diaries in vain for soldiers' comment on why they were in the war or for what they were fighting. While the men in blue were not so irreverent toward high-sounding appeals to patriotic sentiments as were their khaki-clad descendants in World War II, yet American soldiers of the 1860s appear to have been about as little concerned with ideological issues as were those of the 1940s.[98] For Billy Yank, as for his great-grandsons, the primary interests were physical comfort, food, drink, girls, furloughs, mail and gambling, in about that order, and ultimate objectives sooner or later simmered down to finishing an unpleasant though necessary job as soon as possible and getting home.

Of soldiers who did indicate personal commitment to broad issues, a few professed to be fighting for such concepts as law, liberty, freedom and righteousness. The phrase "fighting to maintain the best government on earth" was found in a number of letters. An Iowan who declared it his aim to "fight for my country so long as I can shoulder my musket" specified his objectives as "free Speach, free press and free Governments in General." [99]

Some fought to free the slaves, but a polling of the rank and file through their letters and diaries indicates that those whose primary object was the liberation of the Negroes comprised only a small part of the fighting forces. It seems doubtful that one soldier in ten at any time during the conflict had any real interest in emancipation per se. A considerable number originally indifferent or favorable to slavery eventually accepted emancipation as a necessary war measure, but in most cases their support appeared lukewarm. Even after the Emancipation Proclamation zealous advocates of the Negro's freedom were exceptional.[100]

The hordes of young men whom the historian James Ford Rhodes represents as roused to Republicanism and emancipation by *Uncle Tom's Cabin* seem either to have stayed home or to have lost the sharpness of their enthusiasm before joining the army.[101] Yanks who in their war letters and diaries revealed even a knowledge of Mrs. Stowe's hero were rare.

Among the minority whose mainspring was freedom was Chauncey H. Cooke. When Cooke, a mere boy, left home with the Twenty-fifth Wisconsin in November 1862 he was told by his father: "Be true to your country, my boy, and be true to the flag, but before your country or the flag be true to the slave." Cooke, like many other abolitionists, saw in Frémont's removal after the premature emancipation order a threat to the cause of freedom. In January 1863 he wrote: "I am awful sorry that Fremont was set down on by Lincoln. . . . I have no heart in this war if the slaves cannot be free. . . . I am disappointed in Lincoln." [102]

His first contact with Negroes in Kentucky two months later elicited the comment: "The slaves, contrabands we call them, are flocking into Columbus by the hundred. . . . I never saw a bunch of them together but I could pick out an Uncle Tom, a Quimbo, a Sambo, a Chloe an Eliza or any other character in *Uncle Tom's Cabin*." [103]

As the regiment continued its southward course, the Negro's relation to the war was frequently discussed and Cooke often found himself on the defensive. After the fall of Vicksburg he wrote from Mississippi: "I tell the boys right to their face I am in the war for the freedom of the slave. When they talk about the saving of the Union I tell them that it is Dutch to me. I am for helping the slaves if the Union goes to smash. Most of the boys have their laugh at me for helping the 'Niggers.'" [104]

This youngster was from the Midwest whence came many others strongly imbued with antislavery principles. The cause of freedom was especially strong among Scandinavians and other immigrant groups noted for their individualism and democracy. "Is it not unnatural and inhuman," wrote a Norwegian after a close-up view of slavery in Maryland, "that in a family where there are twenty siblings of about the same color of skin, the father keeps fifteen as slaves; whereas the five are pampered dolls of fashion?" [105]

The antislavery urge was also strong among some of the native New Englanders. "Slavery must die," wrote a Vermont corporal from Louisiana, "and if the South insists on being buried in the same grave I shall see in it nothing but the retributive hand of God." [106] A Maine soldier viewed the North's failure in arms early in the war as divine punishment for acquiescing in slavery. "We well deserve it," he wrote in October 1862; "god punished Phario for keeping the children of israel in bondage and why should we go unpunished for we have committed a like sin." [107]

Massachusetts soldiers had a reputation for abolitionism which made them targets of many a jibe about the campfire. But one of the most intense enemies of slavery encountered among diarists and correspondents was Urich N. Parmelee of Connecticut who went out from Yale in 1861 as a private "to free the slave." Like other abolitionists he chafed enormously at the failure of the government to avow emancipation as an object of the war, writing bitterly to his mother before Antietam, "You cannot expect me . . . much longer to remain with this army as it is. If it does not change *soon*, either in its principles or its actions I trust in God that I shall have the moral courage to desert it." [108]

When the Emancipation Proclamation was issued Parmelee was doubtful of its execution, but as the reality of a change in the direction of the war toward freedom dawned upon him he became enthusiastic. "I do not intend to shirk now there is really something to fight for," he wrote on March 29, 1863. "I mean *Freedom.* . . . I do not expect any great success at present, but so long as I am convinced that we are on the right side I trust that no failure will dishearten me." [109]

He proved as good as his word, this earnest young follower of Henry Ward Beecher. Somewhat of a misfit in the rough and tumble of camp life, he made up in devotion what he lacked in camaraderie. Not once in his long service did he ask for a furlough, and on the field of battle he fought with reckless abandon. Gallantry in action brought promotions to captain, but he did not live to celebrate the victory he helped win. One week before Appomattox he died a hero's death at the head of his company.[110]

In marked contrast to those whose primary interest was in freeing the slaves stood a larger group who wanted no part in a war of emancipation. A soldier newspaper published at Williamsburg, Virginia, in 1862, which carried on its masthead the motto, "The Union Forever and Freedom to all," stated in the first issue: "In construing this part of our outside heading let it be distinctly understood that 'white folks' are meant. We do not wish it even insinuated that we have any sympathy with abolitionism." [111]

Some Yanks opposed making slavery an issue of the war because they thought the effect would be to prolong the conflict at an unjustifiable cost in money and lives. Others objected on the score of the slaves' ignorance and irresponsibility, while still others shrank from the thought of hordes of freedmen settling in the North to compete with white laborers and to mix with them on terms of equality. The opposition of many seemed to have no other basis than an unreasoning hatred of people with black skins.

The issuance of the Emancipation Proclamation aroused opponents of a "Negro War" to the highest level of bitterness. "Lincoln's proclamation . . . meets with denouncement among the men of the Army," wrote a soldier shortly after Antietam. "They do not wish to think that they are fighting for Negroes, but to put down the Rebellion. We must first conquer & then its time enough to talk about the *dam'd niggers.*" Early in 1863 this man remarked: "I . . . would like to see the North win, but as to any interest in freeing the Negroes or in supporting the Emancipation Proclamation I in common with every other officer & soldier in the Army wash my hands of it. . . . I came out to fight for the restoration of the Union and to keep slavery as it is without going into the territories & not to free the niggers." [112]

While many men registered their protest against the proclamation by threatening to desert, and officers to resign, few appear to have taken these extreme steps.

Opposition to emancipation sometimes manifested itself in vehement denunciation of abolitionists. A Massachusetts soldier who by the summer of 1862 had come to the conclusion that the war was caused by "old fusty abolishionists like Sumner and Wilson" thought that "they ought to be made to go into the ranks and be put in the front and have to work in the trenches." [113] A like-minded New Yorker wrote from McClellan's army in July 1862 that "the men are all exasperated against the Tribune and would hang Greeley if they had their way." Of abolitionists in general he added, "The army would hang them as quick as they would a spy." [114] An Ohioan, with more brevity and less delicacy, blurted: "If some of the niger lovers want to know what the most of the Solgers think of them they think about as much as they do a reble, they think they are Shit asses." [115]

In some instances those who entered the army to fight for freedom experienced a change of heart. A Massachusetts sergeant in July 1862 stated that he had "good reason to believe there are *thousands* of men who came out here as rabid abolitionists whose ideas are now *entirely* changed." [116] This estimate appears exaggerated, but there can be no doubt that many faltered in their opposition to slavery and a few were converted to its defense. Discovery that slavery was not so bad as represented had a softening effect on some. "The more I see of slavery the more I believe we have been deceived at the North," wrote a New Hampshire private after a brief residence in Virginia. "You had ought to have seen the darkes going to church," he added, "they were as happy as clams in high water." [117]

Others were influenced by finding Negroes less ready for the responsibilities of freedom than they had expected. Some, while holding to the desirability of emancipation, became doubtful that it was worth the blood being spilled for its accomplishment. A New York artilleryman wrote in July 1863: "I am not so friendly to the Negro race as when I first read 'Uncle Tom's Cabin.' Too many good men have been killed to Establish their freedom. . . . Nearly 100 of my Battery have lost their lives." [118]

A far greater number changed in the other direction. Abolitionists usually became more intense in their hatred of bondage; many mild opponents of the institution and some who had sat on the fence became ardent advocates of freedom. And some were converted from support to denunciation of slavery. One of the factors in the metamorphosis was the shock of slavery's inhumanity as evidenced by mulattoes, shackles, scarred bodies and ignorance. But a growing belief that emancipation was essential to victory appears to have been the most cogent influence.

A Minnesotan in March 1863 explained his change thus:

I have never been in favor of the abolition of slavery until since this war has detirmend me in the conviction that it is a greater sin than our Government is able to stand—and now I go in for a war of emancipation and I am ready and willing to do my share of the work. I am satesfied that slavery is . . . an institution that belonged to the dark ages—and that it ill becomes a nation of our standing to perpetuate the barbarous practice. It is opposed to the Spirit of the age—and in my opinion this Rebelion is but the death strugle of the overgrown monster.[119]

For every Yank whose primary goal was emancipation were to be found several whose chief goal was the Union and the system of government that it represented. The objective often was imperfectly expressed, but the ideal shines through in unmistakable clearness. Devotion to the Union was strong among immigrant groups such as the Germans who had seen the unhappy effects of division in their native land and who felt a special responsibility for preventing a similar fate from overtaking their adopted country. Then, too, the Union was associated with ideals and opportunities which had helped pull them across the sea and which they felt were now imperiled.

Native Americans associated the Union with the struggles of the Revolution and with the greatness achieved in the period of independence. Immigrants and natives alike deemed perpetuation of the Union important as a proof to the world of the soundness of the democratic experiment.

The rallying cry of some was "the Union and freedom" and this combination carried unusual appeal. But the men in blue, save for very brief periods of threatened invasion, had no cause so dynamic as that of the Confederates in defending their homes. "John Brown's Body" and "Hail Columbia" were stirring songs, but neither possessed the emotional tug of the Rebel favorite "The despot's heel is on thy shore, Maryland! My Maryland!"

CHAPTER II

FROM REVEILLE TO TAPS

Soldier life was an ordered life and the instruments of regimentation were the bugle and drum. Each activity in the day's routine had a distinctive "call" sounded by the buglers or tapped out by the drummer boys.[1] In an infantry camp daily calls normally aggregated about a dozen; in the artillery and cavalry, owing to additional signals for the care of horses, they sometimes ran to more than a score.[2] During a period of intensive refresher training in 1863, a cannoneer of Meade's army complained: "26 bugle calls to attend every day keeps us so [busy] we dont have much time to ourselves."[3]

The soldier's day began with the reveille, sounded usually about five o'clock in summer and an hour later in winter.[4] This was the signal for morning roll call, and as failure to answer meant extra duty or a stint in the guardhouse, Yanks were reasonably prompt in shaking off their blankets, donning shoes, blouses and hats (seasoned campaigners commonly slept in their trousers and shirts) and taking their allotted places on the color line in front of the camp. Of course almost every company had its quota of laggards who lingered in their bunks to the last minute and had to throw on their clothes as they rushed frantically to their posts.[5]

Some commanders required their men to turn out in full dress and equipment; others permitted them to appear in semiundress and without arms. The young correspondent George Townsend who late in 1861 witnessed soldiers of an Eastern regiment assembling at reveille reported: "Some wore one shoe and others appeared shivering in their linen. They stood ludicrously in rank, and a succession of short, dry coughs ran up and down the line."[6]

As the sleepy soldiers stood in their places the first sergeant of each company called the roll, after which the men usually were allowed to return briefly to their quarters to complete their toilet or perhaps to snatch a few extra minutes of sleep while the sergeant prepared the morning report. But some commanders, especially during the breaking-in

45

period, insisted on putting their men through a brisk drill immediately after morning roll call.

Approximately thirty minutes after reveille came the breakfast call, commonly known as "Peas on a Trencher," followed shortly by sick call for the ailing and fatigue call for the well.[7] When the sick call sounded, the first sergeant or one of the company's duty sergeants lined up all the ambulatory patients and marched them to the regimental surgeon for examination and prescription. Later in the morning bedridden patients were visited by the surgeon in their quarters or in the regimental hospital. Fatigue duty consisted in policing the company grounds and tidying up the quarters, digging drainage ditches, cutting wood and similar activities.[8]

About eight o'clock the musicians sounded the call for guard mounting, at which the first sergeant of each company turned out his detail for the next twenty-four hours' duty, inspected them carefully and marched them out to the regimental parade ground. While the regimental band or drum-and-fife corps provided appropriate music, the sergeant major formed the company details into line, after which the adjutant supervised their inspection and then sent them to their respective posts. Details were so arranged that each member stood guard only two hours out of every six.[9]

The next call was for drill which commonly lasted until the welcome notes of "roast beef," as the dinner call was usually termed, summoned the men to the noon meal. Then came another period of free time, followed by additional drilling. In the latter part of the afternoon companies were dismissed, and the quarters began to hum with activity as men brushed their uniforms, blacked their leather and polished their brass. This was in preparation for retreat exercises which consisted of roll call, inspection and dress parade. The last, held sometimes by regiment and sometimes by brigade and accompanied always by music, was the day's climactic and most impressive ceremony.[10]

A typical dress parade, as observed by an infantry regiment early in the war, was described thus by a soldier:

The troops are drawn up in line of battle and the order "Parade rest!" given by each Captain to his command. The band "beats off"; that is, marches down and back in front of the regiment, playing slowly down and a quick step back. The officers step four paces in front, the Major and Lieutenant-colonel in advance of the rest. The sergeants march to the centre of the column, and make their report to the Adjutant. He reports to the Colonel and steps behind him. There is then a brisk exercise in arms, and the order of "Parade rest!" is repeated. The officers sheath their swords, proceed to the centre, face the Colonel, and under the lead of the Adjutant march up to him touching their hats as they approach, and, encircling him, hear his remarks and orders. Returning to their posts, the regiment breaks up into companies, each of which marching to its quarters under the lead of the sergeants is disbanded.[11]

Dress parades were the occasion for reading orders, such as the findings of courts-martial, and other official communications. They were sometimes attended by civilian visitors and high-ranking officers. All in all they were colorful, dignified affairs conducted in a manner calculated to inspire in the soldiers a pride in the bearing of arms.

Supper call came shortly after retreat, followed not long after dark by tattoo, which brought another roll call and an ordering of the men to their quarters. The final call of the day was taps, at which signal "all lights must go out, all noises cease and every enlisted man be inside his quarters." [12]

This was the typical routine of an infantry regiment in camp during a period of relative quiet. As previously intimated, artillery and other branches followed a slightly different system. Among units of the same branch practices varied with the season and with the inclinations of individual commanders. Some colonels and brigadiers held dress parades both morning and afternoon and a few required their men to answer roll five times a day.[13] During periods of active campaigning the number of calls was reduced and life became considerably less formal. When on the move with battle in prospect, it was not uncommon for reveille to be sounded at two or three o'clock in the morning.

Sunday routine in all units was different from that of other days. The Sabbath was synonymous with inspection.[14] Hence, after breakfast Yanks busied themselves cleaning up the company streets, sweeping out their quarters, arranging their bunks and accouterments and putting a shine on all their leather and metal equipment. "Spit and polish" had literal meaning in the 1860s, for soldiers of that period, lacking such conveniences as blitz cloths, had to scrub their buttons and buckles with whatever they could improvise. Dust and chalk were commonly used abrasives, applied sometimes with brushes and again with corncobs or sticks.[15] Saliva was the most convenient solvent. Mess equipment was scoured with dirt—knives and forks by simply plunging them a few times into the ground.[16]

Following some two hours of preparation including preliminary inspections by first sergeants and captains, soldiers marched to the drill ground and formed by company—Company A on the right, B on the left, and the others in between—to await arrival of the visiting inspector who was usually the brigade commander or one of his staff. After scrutinizing field and staff officers and taking a summary view of the regiment by walking down the open column, the inspecting officer, beginning with Company A, minutely inspected the arms, equipment and dress of each soldier. Then, to appropriate orders of their captain, the men stacked arms, unslung and opened their knapsacks and laid them on the ground for examination. The inspector checked the contents of each knapsack by poking among them with the tip of his sword. If perchance he found a dirty sock or handkerchief concealed beneath the immaculate top layer of garments, he reprimanded the offender on the spot which, while embarrassing enough, was usually mild in comparison with the tongue-lashing administered by the captain after return to the company area. When the inspection of a company was completed, the men reslung knapsacks, recovered arms and marched back to quarters. Usually about an hour was required for examining the knapsacks of the ten companies, during which the unfortunate members of Company B had to stand in line. Few enjoyed "knapsack drill," as this phase of the Sunday morning exercise was called, and Company B least of all.[17]

After the last company had been examined, the inspecting officer made the rounds of the hospital, guardhouse, sutler's shop, kitchens and such other facilities as he chose to see. He then proceeded to the company quarters where, with the men standing in their allotted places, he examined floors, bunks and furnishings to see that everything was in the order prescribed by regulations. Completion of this, the final part of the inspection, usually consumed the remainder of the morning.[18]

Sunday afternoon, until retreat, was normally free time, though some commanders required that their men attend religious services.

Every other month soldiers were mustered for pay, usually by an inspector general or by an officer specially designated by the army commander.[19] Muster exercises commonly included a review and inspection, but the muster proper consisted of calling the names on the company roll by the visiting officer. When a soldier heard his name he replied "here," brought his gun snappily to the "carry" position, and then dropped the butt to the ground and held it in the position of "order arms." After the mustering officer had accounted for every man on the roster he forwarded a copy of the muster roll to The Adjutant General in Washington.[20] Soldiers were not paid at the time of the muster, but information was provided on which payments were based. The "here" which Billy Yank rendered at the muster was doubtless delivered with more than the usual enthusiasm because this act put him on record for pay and reminded him of the pleasant fact that a visit from the paymaster was forthcoming.

Pay was commonly tardy, sometimes more than six months, and in comparison with that of World War II it was lamentably low. Privates received only thirteen dollars a month during most of the war and a meager sixteen dollars a month after the final raise of May 1, 1864.[21] But dollars had more purchasing power in the 1860s than now, and Civil War soldiers, being unaccustomed to "the abundant life," probably did not consider themselves any less well paid than did their great-grandsons of World War II. Under a voluntary system of allotment initiated in 1861, many Yanks found it possible to send home a portion of their earnings.[22]

However tardy or paltry the pay, Yanks were glad to receive it. One of them irreverently opined that "a paymaster's arrival will produce more joy in camp than is said to have been produced in heaven over the one sinner that repenteth." [23]

Musters and pay were infrequent occurrences and full inspections rarely exceeded one a week. But during initial months of service and at times thereafter, as when preparing for active operations following a season of quiet, drill was a daily event.

In new units drill consisted mainly of exercise in the handling of arms, practicing various positions and facings and performing the simple maneuvers of squad or comparable unit as laid down in the manuals. These elementary exercises, grouped in the manuals under the heading "school of the soldier," taught the men such fundamentals as to stand erect; face left or right; salute; march forward, to the rear, by the flank and obliquely; shift arms to the various positions; load "in nine times," "in four times," or "at will"; fire in standing, kneeling and prone positions; and parry and thrust with the bayonet. As soon as recruits became reasonably proficient in individual and squad tactics they were introduced to company exercises. Then, as rapidly as their development allowed, they were launched into skirmish drill, school of the battalion and eventually, where circumstances permitted, into maneuvers by brigades or larger unit.[24]

This procedure applied specifically to the infantry, but other branches followed a comparable scheme of training.

Initiation of advanced training did not necessarily mean discontinuance of the more elementary types. Rather, the change was one of a gradually shifting emphasis from the simple to the complex.

In a unit that had been in service for two or three months, typical routine consisted of an hour or so of squad drill early in the morning, an equal stint of company drill just before noon and about an hour and a half of battalion drill in the late afternoon. More advanced units commonly omitted the squad drill, had an hour or two of company drill in the forenoon and of battalion drill after lunch. Following a few weeks of this routine, company drill might be dispensed with or held only on alternate days, and brigade drill introduced in the afternoon.

In the artillery the usual routine after the first few weeks of training was instruction of gun crews in the manual of the piece in the morning and drill by battery and battalion in the afternoon.

The training day for privates closed with retreat. But noncoms and officers of many units were required to go to night schools conducted by their superiors. Lessons, based on the manuals, usually emphasized subjects to be covered in the next day's training. A Massachusetts corporal noted in his diary in 1863 that the noncommissioned officers of his company "have lessons in tactics every night at the Captain's quarters to fit them to drill the privates in squads according to the book." [25] And an Ohio sergeant wrote his homefolk in December 1862: "Every night I recite with the other 1st Sergts and 2nd Lieutenants. We shall finish Hardee's Tactics and then study the 'Army Regulations.' Theory as well as practice are necessary to make the perfect soldier." [26]

Night sessions were usually conducted by captains, but colonels and even generals sometimes took an active part in them.[27]

Evening schools were sometimes supplemented by day rehearsals at which noncoms and officers, organized into skeleton units (pivot men holding strings or poles across the space normally occupied by privates), took turns in putting one another through various maneuvers of platoon, company or battalion. Commanders fortunate enough to have on their rosters men with prior military experience frequently called on the veterans to act as instructors in these exercises.[28]

Skirmish drill was sometimes enlivened by the firing of blank cartridges. Practice with live ammunition was a rarity, though diaries and letters now and then tell of men going out in small groups on their own, or with their officers, and trying out their muskets or carbines on fence posts, trees or small game. Perhaps one of the reasons for neglect of target practice early in the war was the notorious inaccuracy of the antiquated muskets with which many soldiers were armed at that time. Some Illinois soldiers who with smoothbore muskets fired 160 shots at a flour barrel 180 yards away registered only four hits.[29] These were not new troops but men who had been in uniform at least six months. The performance of their weapons can hardly be imagined as making these men eager for battle. If the captain afterward was no more than luke-warm about target practice, his attitude was to say the least understandable.

In at least one instance advanced training included drill in amphibious operations. Private M. L. Gordon, who participated in the exercises held on an island off the South Carolina coast in March 1863, wrote of the experience:

We had been thinking for some time that we had drilled in everything, but the past week we had "something new under the sun." We drill in getting on and off Transports. A Regt is taken on board & then put in small boats they are then formed in line and all strike for the shore —the moment the boats touch [land] the men spring out fix bayonets and make a charge. It is a good deal of fun, but we may see they day when it will not be quite so amusing.[30]

Some commanders supplemented training in the separate arms with combined exercises in which infantry, artillery and cavalry worked together in practice attacks, withdrawals and other battle maneuvers, or opposed one another in simulated combat. Such activities, when featured by the use of blank ammunition and accompanied by piercing yells, as was sometimes the case, were excitingly realistic and hence thoroughly enjoyed by both participants and spectators. A private in the Army of the Potomac who saw a brigade stage a sham fight in Virginia in December 1861 described it thus:

Infantry, cavalry and artillery were doing their best. The regiment of infantry were blazing away at each other when a squadron of cavalry dashed around a piece of woods and charged down on them with the wildest yells. Then the artillery commenced firing on them (the cavalry) and they gave it up, wheeled and retreated. . . . Quite a number of carriages were up from the city and I saw ladies watching the sport with a good deal of interest. They would start at the report of the cannons and give a nice little city scream, as ladies will. . . . I am getting some accustomed to the smell of powder.[31]

This soldier regarded the mock fight more as an amusement than a training exercise. His reference to getting accustomed to the smell of powder was an afterthought. But the opportunity to obtain an idea ahead of time of the atmosphere of battle—the noise, confusion, as well as the smell—and to carry out assigned duties under simulated combat conditions was the most valuable of training. It was especially beneficial to officers in that it taught them to maneuver and control their commands when orders could hardly be heard and when their men were keyed to a high pitch of emotion.[32]

Not the least of the returns from such exercises was the confidence that they gave to the men in their own effectiveness and in the co-operation of the other arms. A young soldier of a Western command, reporting in November 1862 on a recent series of exercises in which his regiment formed in hollow square to receive cavalry charges, stated: "When they charge us with wild yells (some of them get aufully excited, so do the horses) it takes some nerve to stand against them, although it is all a sham. But we have found out one thing—horses cannot be driven onto fixed bayonets and I dont believe we shall be as affraid of a real charge if we ever have to meet one in the future. We are learning a good deal, so are the Cavelry."[33]

A few weeks later a young infantryman stationed in Kentucky wrote his homefolk: "We had our first Brigade drill day before yesterday. There were in one field four Regts of Infantry, a Battery of Artillery, and a Squadron of Cavalry. . . . The Cavalry charged down on us and for the first time I saw something that looked like fighting. The artillery blazed away, and we had a regular sham battle. It was a beautiful sight, and our officers expressed themselves well satisfied with the drill." He then added significantly: "We began to think we can whip twice our weight in Rebels."[34]

Sometimes the sham fights were held in connection with grand reviews of several divisions. One of McClellan's men stated in November 1861: "One maneuver we pass through at these reviews . . . is this, we advance in line of battle and at a given signal, the men all lie down and the artillery come up and fire directly over our heads. This is done in order that if the enemy either Cavalry or infantry attempt to charge upon and take the cannon, we can rise up and protect them or charge upon the enemy if necessary."[35]

While the type of load used by the artillery in these particular exercises is not specified, the charges were unquestionably blanks. No instance was found of the firing of live ammunition over the heads of soldiers in Civil War training.

It would be misleading to leave the impression that combined or realistic exercises were commonplace. One gets a strong impression from letters and diaries of participants that training rarely was carried beyond the level of the regiment, and that few officers or men had the benefit of practicing the military art in joint exercises with members of other branches.

Some higher commanders realized the importance of large-unit training. Sherman, for example, wrote Thomas in April 1864, "to encourage drill by brigades and divisions and let the recruits practice at the target all the time." [36] But there is little ground for believing that brigade and division exercises in Sherman's or any other command often went beyond ceremonial parades and reviews.

One reason for this situation doubtless was the reluctance of brigade and division commanders to tackle the direction of large-unit maneuvers. Few of them had backgrounds commensurate with such responsibilities. Then, many must have felt, owing to such factors as lack of time and inexperience of regimental and lower commanders, that it was best to concentrate on more elementary matters.

Fundamental to the whole problem of training was the lack of high-level direction and co-ordination. As previously noted, the manuals prescribed certain basic principles and procedures, but lack of uniform training programs and a well-defined system of supervision naturally led to countless variations and numerous irregularities. To a large extent, especially in the crucial first year of the war, each colonel trained his regiment pretty much as he saw fit.

Hence, it is not surprising that in some units men were "burned out" by six or eight hours of drill a day, and in others they received not enough to harden their muscles; that some units had an overamount of company drill and insufficient practice in battalion maneuvers; and that some acquired proficiency with the bayonet while others had no more than a cursory knowledge of this form of training.

In all units drill was greatly curtailed during seasons of active campaigning. The same was generally true of the period when troops were holed up in winter quarters. One Yank wrote from Lookout Valley, Tennessee, in January 1864: "After breakfast there is little for the well men to do. . . . The forenoon is spent in poke, poke, poking around till the appetite says it is dinner time." [37]

Veteran units had considerably less drill than new ones, except when commanders ordered refresher exercises in anticipation of renewal of active operations or when large groups of filler replacements were being broken into the units. Replacement-training practices varied considerably. In some cases recruits before joining tactical units were drilled in fundamentals at a special camp of instruction, such as that set up near Annapolis in 1862 with a capacity of 50,000 men, "cavalry, artillery and infantry in due proportions." [38] In other instances new troops were sent directly from points of rendezvous to field commands for immediate assignment and training in the unit. The latter procedure was favored by Sherman who on August 7, 1864, wrote Grant: "Get the War Department to send us recruits daily as they are made, for we can teach them more war in our camps in one day than they can get at a rendezvous in a month." [39]

Replacements who came to their regiments with little or no prior instruction were usually placed under veteran noncommissioned officers for intensive segregated drilling in squad and company movements and then put in their regular places for training along with their seasoned comrades in battalion and higher exercises.[40]

Long hours on the drill field, the newness of soldiering, and the good-natured but brutal treatment by the veterans made the life of most recruits a hard one. An insight into the experience of one who joined a Massachusetts regiment in the late summer of 1862 is afforded by a letter which he wrote to his homefolk a short time afterward:

We recruits are getting kicked around pretty well now; we do all the duty in our company, and they call us d—d recruits. . . . I put up with things from minor officers . . . and even privates without a murmur, which I would have resented with a blow if I had been at home. . . . Our drill master (Sergeant William Salter), has gone to the hospital sick, and *common privates* grown old in sin and musty in discipline, are detailed to go through the movements with us. They are sick of soldiering and have no ambition to teach others.[41]

Drill to most Yanks, whether new or old in the service, was a dull, dreary chore and the more they had of it (except for the sham battles where realism relieved boredom) the less they liked it. A Pennsylvanian wrote after about six months' service: "The first thing in the morning is drill, then drill, then drill again. Then drill, drill, a little more drill. Then drill, and lastly drill. Between drills, we drill and sometimes stop to eat a little and have a roll-call." [42]

Combat veterans were especially unenthusiastic about tramping parade grounds under a crushing load of equipment; they had seen the elephant and were in no mood to "play soldier." An Ohioan of Hooker's army reflected a sentiment widely held among hardened campaigners when he wrote after an epidemic of refresher training in 1863: "Brigade drill and review today i dont know what will cum tomoror and dont cair one god dam sir." [43] But the discipline that was part of being a veteran caused the old-timers dutifully to take their places when the bugler's note rang out the unpleasant call to drill.[44]

An important aspect of the soldier's daily life was his shelter. The type of shelter varied considerably with time, season, location and other circumstances.

Except during periods of active campaigning, quarters were commonly arranged after a pattern specified in army regulations. In an infantry regiment, which at full strength approximated 1,000 men, tents or huts of privates were grouped by company with a street running between. Perpendicular to the company streets at the front of the camp was the color line, and at the rear in rows paralleling the color line were the quarters of the noncommissioned officers, then those of the company officers and finally those of the regimental commander and staff. Back of the officers' quarters were the baggage trains.[45]

Yanks who were stationed in permanent or semipermanent establishments such as Jefferson Barracks, in Missouri, had the privilege of living in frame buildings equipped with stoves and two-tier bunks.[46] But such installations were rarely to be found outside the North, and since they were used mainly as camps of rendezvous, sojourns in them usually were brief.

The normal home of a soldier in summer was a tent. During the early part of the war nearly all tents occupied by enlisted men were either the Sibley or the wedge type. The first of these was a bell-shaped structure supported by a center pole which rested on a tripod. It was equipped with a stove the pipe of which passed through an opening at the apex.[47]

The Sibley tent was designed for the accommodation of about a dozen men, but the emergency of war frequently resulted in the crowding in of a score. Inmates arranged themselves for sleeping in the manner of wheel spokes, with feet at the center and heads near the circumference.[48] In good weather the canvas was raised at the edges for ventilation, but when rain or cold required the capping of the apex and the closing of all other openings the air became stuffy and foul. One Yank stated in his reminiscences that "to enter one of them of a rainy morning . . . and encounter the night's accumulation of nauseating exhalations from the bodies of twelve men (differing widely in their habits of personal cleanliness) was an experience which no old soldier has ever been known to recall with any great enthusiasm." [49]

The wedge or "A" tent, which from the front looked like an inverted "V," was a piece of canvas stretched over a horizontal bar and staked to the ground on either side, with extensions for closing front and rear. The floor space, some seven feet square, was adequate for accommodation of four men; but when six were crowded in, as was frequently the case in the first months of war, soldiers had to sleep "spoon fashion" and when one Yank turned over all had to turn. Congestion brought greater discomfort in the daytime as there was no spot within where a tall man could stand erect, and the farther away from the ridge pole he moved the more he had to stoop. Furnishings, beyond an occasional box, were out of the question because of the space requirements of the six men and their "trappings." [50]

Wall tents, which were box-shaped structures with sloping roofs, were a common sight in most camps during the war's early years. But these were a luxury enjoyed only by the officers and Yanks sick enough to be sent to the hospital.[51]

After the first year of the conflict the standard field habitation of the rank and file was the shelter or dog tent. This was ordinarily a two-man dwelling made by buttoning together the half-shelters carried by the occupants as standard equipment and stretching them over a horizontal pole held in place by two upright sticks, or more commonly by muskets stuck into the ground with bayonets fixed. Ends were left open or draped with blankets or coats.[52]

In warm weather some Yanks elevated their shelter tents by tying the four corners to the upper ends of long stakes rather than fixing them flush with the ground. Others arranged the canvas in lean-to fashion or simply stretched it in a gentle slope over four uprights.[53] When they so desired, three or more soldiers could button their half-shelters together for a tent of larger size.

Occupants of shelters, and other type tents as well, sometimes built brush arbors either as porches or as separate structures, where in favorable weather they could lounge in greater comfort than that afforded by regular quarters.[54]

Many Yanks held the shelter tents in low esteem when first they were issued, one soldier writing in 1862 that he wished "the man who invented them had been hung before the invention was completed," as they reminded him "forceably of a hog pen." [55] The nickname "dog tent" reflected initial attitudes with a fair degree of accuracy. But disparagements declined in vehemence as the men became accustomed to their tiny dwellings, and in time references to them usually revealed more of affection than of disdain.

During the winter months inclemency of weather and the tendency toward a more settled mode of life combined to produce a great change in soldier dwellings. In areas where trees abounded and low temperatures were common, log huts built by the men were the vogue. Construction was commonly of the "pen" type, after the fashion of frontier cabins, with slanting roofs of board or thatch, but some Yanks preferred walls of stockade design.[56] In either case, cracks were filled with mud. If logs were not available, and sometimes when they were, Yanks might erect frame huts with materials obtained by wrecking abandoned Southern dwellings.[57]

Perhaps the most common type of winter quarters was a hybrid structure, part wood and part fabric, made by superimposing wedge or shelter tents on log bases. These "winterized," "stockaded" or "barricaded" tents, like the log huts, were usually designed for the accommodation of four men. Sometimes the occupants enhanced roominess and warmth, by digging out several feet of dirt. Roofs might be made more impervious by stretching rubber blankets or ponchos over the canvas.[58]

Both log cabins and winterized tents were commonly heated by fireplaces built of sticks and daubed with clay; but some Yanks preferred the "California" type of furnace which was made by digging a hole in the ground, covering it with a removable stone and tunneling the smoke to an outside flue.[59] Chimneys were usually of sticks and daubing topped by one or more barrels. The advantage of increased draft was offset to some extent by the tendency of the barrels to catch fire. A common occurrence in winter was the routing of soldiers from their quarters by the cry "Chimney afire!" The peril could usually be met by simply knocking the burning keg to the ground with a pole. Replacements were readily obtainable from the commissary, and the excitement produced by the conflagration afforded momentary relief from boredom.[60]

Floors were normally of boards or split logs laid with the flat side up. Some Yanks, however, simply covered the soil with straw or left it bare.

The average hut contained two bunks, one above the other, extending from wall to wall across the rear. The framework of the bunks was usually of boards or logs, while the bottoms were of barrel staves, slender poles or some other material flexible enough to give the effect of springs. Mattresses were improvised by adding a layer of pine needles, leaves or straw. Knapsacks were ordinarily kept at the head of the bunks, while other equipment and extra articles of clothing were hung from rails or pegs driven into logs along either side of the room.[61]

The lower bunk was used as a seat in daytime, though some soldiers objected to this practice on the ground that lice-laden callers might leave unwelcome reminders of their visits. Stools were made of pine slabs, boxes or upended logs, and tables of inverted hardtack cases mounted on legs. The customary candlestick was a bayonet with the candle fitted into the opening made for the gun barrel and the sharp end stuck into wall or floor. If candles were lacking, slush lamps might be made by filling a sardine container with grease and dropping a rag in one corner for a wick. Shelves were placed about the cabin as needed for pipes, books, papers, daguerreotypes and other possessions.[62]

These arrangements and furnishings sufficed for the general run of soldiers, but almost every camp had a few irrepressible "fixer-uppers" who insisted on papering their quarters, building fancy articles of furniture or adding other luxuries and adornments. One of these zealots wrote his homefolk: "We have our hut nearly finished. We have split little cedar for the floor they make a neat floor with their clean red and white, split them through the heart. Have been much reminded of Solomon's temple in the construction of this frail tenement, have used so much cedar." [63]

Decorative tendencies sometimes extended to the placarding of huts with high-sounding labels such as "The Astor House," fanciful designation of company streets, and even the erection of tremendous evergreen arches over thoroughfare entrances bordering the parade ground. The number of the regiment was frequently woven into the design and sometimes that of the brigade, division and corps, along with the names of the commanding officers.[64]

Whether their handiwork was pretentious or humble, Yanks usually regarded it with pride, and letters home were replete with details of construction and furnishing. "We want no better quarters than we now have," was written by a Massachusetts soldier shortly after completion of his hut in Virginia in the first year of the war, but the same statement might have been penned by almost any Yank during any winter of the conflict.[65]

Another basic item in the soldier's daily life was his clothing. Early in the war types of habiliment, as already noted, were so diverse as to make mockery of the term "uniform." But variation decreased with the passing of time and by 1863 a fair degree of standardization had been achieved.

In the infantry the uniform in its ultimate version consisted of a blue cap with black visor; a long single-breasted dress coat of dark blue with stand-up collar; a dark-blue jacket called a blouse; light-blue trousers; rough black shoes, known in soldier parlance as gunboats; wool flannel shirt; cotton flannel drawers; socks; and a long blue overcoat with cape. Artillery and cavalry regalia were the same as the infantry except that dress coats were shorter, boots were worn instead of shoes and trousers were reinforced in seat and legs.[66]

Black felt hats were an authorized item of issue and army regulations specified that they be worn for dress purposes. But many soldiers did not like them, one Yank writing to his homefolk, "My new hat looks as near like the pictures that you see of the pilgrim fathers landing on plymouth, tall, stiff, and turned up on one side with a feather on it. . . . I dont wear it any more than I am obliged to." [67] Another soldier described his hat as "rediculous." [68] Such attitudes were not universal and photographs, even of the late war period, reveal a number of hat wearers.[69] The most common headpiece for both formal and informal purposes, however, was the cap, worn with the crown sloping forward.

Another item prescribed in army regulations, but rarely used, was a cravat or stock made of stiff leather and fastened about the neck with a buckle. Soldiers called these uncomfortable articles "dog collars," and after the war one Yank stated that he never recalled seeing one worn "except as a joke." [70]

The short blouse was the favorite coat for field service, one veteran stating in his reminiscences that "Many regiments never drew a dress coat after leaving the state." [71] Overcoats also had only a limited use outside of camp owing to their cumbersomeness and weight. Drawers appear to have been regarded as superfluous by some. A young Hoosier, describing the initial issue of clothing to his unit, wrote: "Most of the boys had never worn drawers and some did not know what they were for and some of the old soldiers who are here told them that they were for an extra uniform to be worn on parade and they half believed it." [72]

Many Yanks commented on their poor luck in obtaining proper fits. The Indianian, quoted above, described his first experience with the quartermaster thus: "We had quite a time with our uniforms. . . . If they fit, all right; if not we had to trade around till we could get a fit as they are in different sizes. Being of medium size I got a fair fit but some of the very tall or short men were not so fortunate." [73] One Yank of low stature wrote after the war: "I . . . could never find in the quartermaster's department a blouse or a pair of trousers small enough, nor an overcoat cast on my lines. The regulation blue trousers I used to cut off at the bottoms and the regulation overcoat sleeves were always rolled up, which gave them the appearance of having military cuffs." [74]

In the latter part of the war some regiments were provided in the hot season with linen pants, light blouses and straw hats but, as a general rule, the present-day practice of issuing special summer uniforms appears not to have been followed in the Union Army.[75] Yanks adapted themselves to high temperatures by shedding all that commanders would allow, but even the most indulgent officers balked at the idea of letting their men go about in their underclothing. From June to September wool shirts and trousers were extremely uncomfortable in most parts of Dixie.

Uniforms were trimmed with cords or stripes in color and design appropriate to branch and rank. Infantry trimmings were blue; artillery, scarlet; and cavalry, yellow. Branch was also designated by brass insignia worn on the hats—a bugle for infantry, crossed sabers for cavalry and crossed cannon for artillery. After corps badges were introduced in 1863—for example, a sphere for the First Corps, cloverleaf for the Second, crescent for the Eleventh, star for the Twelfth, with a different color for each division—these were placed on top of the cap. Noncommissioned officers wore chevrons on their sleeves with ratings indicated by the same number of stripes as today. Insignia for the various commissioned ranks were also the same as today except that the bars of captains and first lieutenants were golden rather than silver and second lieutenants wore no bar, that rank being distinguished by the unadorned shoulder straps. Rank, rating and branch were distinguished also to some extent by design, arrangement and number of buttons, cut of coats and type of sash. Field-grade officers, for example, wore two rows of buttons on their dress coats, while captains, lieutenants and enlisted men had only a single row.[76]

During the early period of the war much of the clothing issued to the men in blue was of inferior quality. Unscrupulous contractors and corrupt officials frequently took advantage of the government's dire need and pawned off on the army at fantastic prices the most worthless of materials. The story of shoddy uniforms and imitation-leather shoes, some of which fell apart during the first heavy rain, has been fully told by Professor Fred A. Shannon and need not be repeated here.[77] Suffice to say, the contract situation was eventually cleaned up and after the first year or so of the conflict Billy Yank had relatively little ground for complaint as to the quality of clothing received from the quarter-master.

The same was generally true of quantity, though official reports and soldier accounts reveal numerous instances of raggedness and shortage. Deprivation was most common in periods of hard campaigning when rapid movement enhanced wear and made replenishment difficult. After Antietam, McClellan reported a serious deficiency of shoes and other articles of clothing in some of his corps;[78] and a soldier told of seeing "men with no coats, no underclothes, in rags, no shoes." [79] This Yank also stated that when Lincoln reviewed his regiment at this time "those who had overcoats were ordered to put them on, to hide the rags & make him believe that they had Jackets." [80]

During the Fredericksburg operations of December 1862, a New York surgeon reported that 200 of the men in his regiment were without shoes, and the next year while the Mine Run movement was in progress a sergeant of Meade's army wrote: "We had a light fall of snow last night. A great many of the troops are in want of clothes and shoes." [81]

The long marches of the Gettysburg campaign were exceedingly hard on clothing, one participant writing on July 8, 1863, that "the boys [are] almost wore out and a grate many shiewless," while another reported a little later: "I am awful ragged Imagine a modest, timid, & retiring young man like your son walking through the thickly populated land of Virginia . . . with a pair of pants on with a hole in the seat which like a broken window needs two old pots to stick through . . . to keep the cold out & the bottoms waving in rags between the knee and feet." [82]

The prolonged fighting in Virginia the next summer brought a recurrence of shortage, a New York *Tribune* correspondent reporting from Grant's headquarters on June 6, 1864, that "actual marching has worn out 50,000 pairs of shoes" and that "more than 100,000 have not changed a garment . . . [for] thirty days." [83]

Western soldiers suffered more from lack of clothing than did those of the East because of greater problems of distance and supply. In the Western armies, as in Eastern commands, deficiencies were most common during seasons of arduous campaigning. In May 1862, following a period of intensive operations in North Alabama, an Ohioan wrote a friend back home: "Our reg is purty naked they look moor like a reg of secesh than northern troops soom barfootted, soom with out coats soom with a citazens soot on. . . . I have ben barfooted evry sens we got back from brig porte." [84]

The long race through Kentucky after Bragg in the fall of 1862 was a severe strain on the wardrobes of Buell's men. The surgeon of an Ohio regiment wrote from Louisville in September that the hard stone pike had soon played havoc with leather and that some of his regiment had marched 200 miles without shoes.[85] The situation grew worse on the return, Rosecrans reporting to Halleck on December 4, 1862: "Many of our soldiers are to this day barefoot, without blankets, without tents." [86]

The strenuous operations about Vicksburg also produced instances of raggedness. One participant in the Port Hudson siege stated, "My shirt is more like a necklace than a shirt." [87] But the warmth of the climate prevented great discomfort save for those who had to march without shoes.

Sherman's long trek through Georgia and the Carolinas was marked by some raggedness and want of shoes.[88] The greatest hardship from lack of clothing on the Union side, however, seems to have occurred in the East Tennessee campaigns of November and December 1863.[89] Suffering was especially acute among members of the expedition to relieve Burnside, hundreds of soldiers marching entirely barefooted from Knoxville to Chattanooga over icy roads. A New Jersey sergeant wrote at the conclusion of this experience: "We reached our old camp [after] . . . 26 days march, without a blanket or shelter, barefooted and half pint of flour a day to live on. I wore raw cow skin shoes for ten days." [90]

Such experiences were exceptional and were due mainly to temporary failures of distribution rather than to shortages of stock. Some of the hardship was of the soldiers' own making, for Billy Yanks, like American soldiers of all time, were notoriously improvident of government issues.[91] They were especially resistant to lugging heavy loads for long distances; hence, a route of march during the winter season, particularly if the goal was a battlefield, was sure to be lined with an abundance of overcoats and blankets. Commanders railed against such profligate waste and recurrently made splurges of bringing offenders to justice, but their best efforts were no more than partially successful.

A number of items other than clothing figured prominently in the soldier's daily existence. The most important of these was his gun. As noted elsewhere the standard infantry arm, after a period of unhappy experience with antiquated American smoothbores and offcasts of European arsenals, was a Springfield or Enfield rifle musket.[92] The Springfield was of slightly larger caliber than the Enfield (.58 and .577 respectively) but was lighter and hence generally preferred by the soldiers. The difference in bore was not so great as to prevent use in both of the same bullet, which was an elongated, hollow-based cone commonly known as a Minié ball after the name of its French inventor. Both types of guns were muzzle-loaders. Breechloaders—and repeaters at that—were used by a few infantrymen in the latter part of the war and with great effectiveness, as for example by Wilder's brigade in the fighting about Chattanooga. But they were not an item of general issue to foot soldiers and their use was restricted largely to cavalrymen.[93]

The pride with which the few lucky possessors of the repeaters regarded their weapons was revealed by one of Sherman's soldiers who wrote in his journal on May 11, 1864: "I got a Henry rifle—a 16 shooter —yesterday. . . . I gave . . . 35 dollars—all the money I had for it. . . . I am glad I could get it. They are good shooters and I like to think I have so many shots in reserve." Ten months later he noted: "I think the Johnnys are getting rattled; they are afraid of our repeating rifles. They say we are not fair, that we have guns that we load up on Sunday and shoot all the rest of the week. This I know, I feel a good deal more confidence in myself with a 16 shooter in my hands than I used to with a single shot rifle." [94]

The muzzle-loading Springfields and Enfields were accurate guns, and most of the Yanks who carried them regarded them with affection and pride. A typical attitude was that of a New Hampshire private who wrote his parents in October 1861: "We have not got the enfield rifles but the spring field they are just as good and a good deel lighter. We went out the other day to try them We fired 600 yds and we put 360 balls into a mark the size of old Jeff, they will range 1500 yards with considerable certainty." [95]

Dependable as they undoubtedly were, these muzzle-loaders were far from being as good weapons as Billy Yank was entitled to expect. One of the major tragedies on the Union side was the failure of responsible authorities, with all the resources and talent which they had at their command, to provide the men in blue with more effective weapons.[96]

Artillerymen served a vast assortment of guns ranging from light fieldpieces loaded with canister, grape, shrapnel and solid balls, to enormous siege cannon hurling monstrous missiles over tremendous ranges.[97]

The cavalryman's gun was a pistol or carbine. Some of the early troopers carried cumbersome horse pistols, but these and similar types gradually were replaced by revolvers. The revolvers included products of Remington and Savage, but the prevailing model seems to have been the Colt six-shooter. Among carbines of the early war period were to be found the Gallagher, "Joslyn Patent" and Hall, but the Sharps apparently became the most widely used of the single-shot models. As already noted, repeating carbines had rather extensive use in the cavalry in the latter part of the conflict.[98] Favorite makes were the seven-shot Spencer and the sixteen-shot Henry. A young member of the Fourth Michigan Cavalry, who wrote home in March 1864 that his unit was about to swap its five-shot repeaters for a type that would shoot nine times, reported that a short time before some Confederates had given themselves up just to see the Yankee guns. "The rebs that we took while on a scout from Rossville said they dreaded to come across our brigade," he added, "for we kept shooting all of the time, when they see our guns they say 'no wonder *yourns* shoot so fast if *weuns* had such guns we'd fight longer.' "[99]

Billy Yank's other impedimenta consisted of a haversack or "bread bag"; cartridge box in which were carried his "forty dead men"; bayonet and scabbard; cap box; rubber and woolen blanket; canteen; and knapsack. The last-named article, called by some a "patent bureau," was packed with such items as underclothes, stationery, photographs, toothbrush, razor, soap, books, letters, and a mending kit known as a "housewife." Mess equipment, comprising a metal plate, knife, fork, spoon and cup—and sometimes a light skillet—was usually divided between knapsack and hooks attached to the belt. In winter an overcoat, tied above the knapsack while on the march, was an extra burden.[100]

The weight of all this equipment ranged in soldier estimates from forty to fifty pounds. A Yank who accepted the latter figure gave detailed estimates as follows: "40 rounds ammunition, belt &c . . . 4 lbs; canteen of water, 4 lbs; Haversack of rations, 6 lbs; Musket, 14 lbs; Knapsack at least 20 lbs, besides the clothes we have on our backs."[101] Another soldier, after a similar listing, noted: "In addition to the actual weight the five different straps which passed over every part of our bodies produced unpleasant touches of cramp now & then. I can appreciate the feelings of an animal in harness now."[102]

Most Yanks eventually found means of reducing the load. Indeed, the process of becoming a veteran was in large measure one of shedding.[103] Reference has already been made to the tendency to get rid of overcoats and dress coats. Another item which disappeared at a fairly early stage was the knapsack, its contents—considerably reduced—being rolled into the blanket. Many soldiers also dispensed with the canteen, carrying in its stead a small bottle of water, stored in pocket or haversack, and trusting to luck for quick refills from springs and branches

"DEAR FOLKS"
Drawing by Charles W. Reed

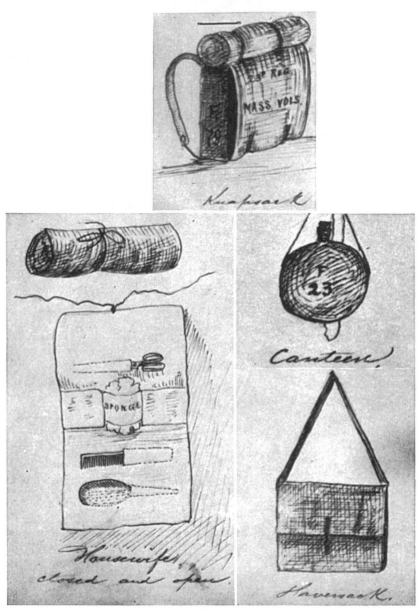

ITEMS OF SOLDIER EQUIPMENT
Drawings by Herbert E. Valentine, Company F, Twenty-third
Massachusetts Regiment

along the way. The tin cup or dipper did triple service as a coffee boiler, stewpot and drinking vessel, while a canteen could be blown apart with a small charge of powder to make a handy pair of combination plates and frying pans. Billy Yank model-1864, "in light marching order," was a lean, weather-beaten creature, topped by a battered cap and clad in a faded jacket, shaggy trousers—also considerably less blue than when first issued—and scuffed brogans.[104] Draped across his right shoulder with ends tied at hip level on the opposite side was a woolen blanket rolled in rubber within which was carried one or two extra garments and a minimum of small articles. On his right shoulder was his musket, and from his belt hung a sheathed bayonet, cartridge box, cap box, tin plate and cup. This with the haversack completed his load, except perchance there dangled from the musket barrel a portion of some yearling or shoat that had refused to take the oath or give the proper countersign.

CHAPTER III

THE SUPREME TEST

BATTLE is the ultimate of soldiering. All else in warfare is but incidental to the vital closing of opposing forces in conflict.

In recent times, owing to the tremendous increase in the range of weapons and introduction of such revolutionary instruments as radar, planes and rockets, "closing with the enemy" has lost much of its reality. Only a small portion of those who don uniforms ever draw a bead on an enemy or, for that matter, even have the field of combat as an objective. While the man with the rifle has proved less dispensable than was predicted before World War II, conflict has become increasingly mechanistic and impersonal.

In the Civil War, however, fighting was an intimate, elemental thing, with infantry bearing the brunt, and artillery and horse-mounted cavalry fighting, normally, in near support. The enemy could be seen with the naked eye by soldiers of all branches, and contests usually culminated in head-on clashes of yelling, shooting, striking masses. Closing with the enemy was more than a figure of speech.

Some Billy Yanks went into battle very soon after enlisting—a Federal brigadier after the Richmond, Kentucky, fight of August 30, 1862, reported that most of his command "had been less than a fortnight away from their homes." [1] Others waited many months for the fiery ordeal. One battle comprised the entire fighting experience of some, while many faced the jaws of death repeatedly. Regardless of when the test came or how many times, soldier reaction and experiences followed the same general pattern.

When circumstances permitted, certain preliminaries, more or less standard, were observed.[2] Among these was the issuance of three days' rations, sometimes more, with instructions to cook the meat immediately so that nourishment might be assured during the emergency. Benefits of this well-conceived measure often were lost, owing to the soldier's irrepressible bent for traveling light, eating when he was hungry and taking no thought of the morrow.

Next came the dispensing of ammunition. The usual allotment was

66

sixty rounds of the paper cartridges—with bullets at one end and a plug or twist at the other to contain the powder—used in the muzzle-loading Springfield and Enfield rifles, the standard shoulder arms of both Federals and Confederates. Forty rounds filled the leather cartridge boxes carried on the belt; the others had to be carried in pocket or knapsack. Percussion caps, issued in about the same quantity as the cartridges, were carried in a small leather container also fastened to the belt. If, when battle was imminent, guns contained charges inserted a long time before or if the weapons had been exposed to rain or mist, barrels were cleared by firing or by removing the damaged loads with special instruments designed for the purpose (carried as standard equipment by noncommissioned file closers), and new charges inserted. Soldiers took seriously the matter of readying their weapons, as they wanted no failures when the shooting started. On the eve of combat Yanks were considerably more provident of bullets than of biscuits.

Following these preparations, and assuming that the initiative lay with the men in blue, units were marched to their assigned positions on the field. Then followed, usually, a period of waiting while final dispositions were being made for the "opening of the ball."

Colonels, if they had not previously done so, took advantage of this lull to whip up the emotions of their men. Sometimes the prebattle exhortation consisted of the reading of a circular previously issued by a higher commander; in other instances the address was original and impromptu. Whatever the source, it usually included instructions and sentiments such as these: Men, the hour which you have so eagerly awaited has arrived. We are about to engage the enemy. Let every man do his duty. Be cool. Keep ranks. If any of your comrades fall, do not stop to help them; leave them to the care of the men who have been specially detailed for removal of the wounded. The best way to protect the wounded, and yourselves as well, is to press forward and drive the enemy from the field. Hold your fire until the Rebels are in easy range, then aim low, fire deliberately. Close steadily on the enemy, and when you get within charging distance, rush on him with the bayonet. If you do this, you are sure to win.[3]

When veterans were addressed, reference was almost sure to be made to their former exploits. And speeches tended to become shorter and more pointed with the passing of time. At Antietam a colonel, pacing up and down before his regiment and speaking in jerks, said: "Men you are about to engage in battle. You have never disgraced your State; I hope you won't this time. If any man runs I want the file closers to shoot him; if they don't, I shall myself. That's all I have to say." [4] When the signal came to advance at Fredericksburg, the colonel of another regiment took the flag out in front of his command and waving it said: "Now boys is the time to write your names. Let every man do his duty. Follow me!" And with that he led off in the assault.[5]

At Murfreesboro the commander of the Twelfth Ohio, who was a minister, had his address cut short and its character changed by a Rebel thrust. The colonel began quietly: "Now boys fight for your country and your God, and . . ." At this point the Confederates fired a volley and the colonel, instead of ending with an Amen! as his men expected, concluded by shouting "AIM LOW!" For weeks afterward, whenever he passed through the camp he was hailed from behind trees and tents with the cry "AIM LOW!" [6]

After the speeches by higher commanders, captains, if time permitted, walked about among the men of their companies advising and exhorting them. Now and then officers or chaplains led the men in prayer or other religious exercises.[7] Considerable praying was done by the men themselves, and supplication was by no means confined to the righteous. Prayers were usually offered in silence, though now and then some frightened individual would audibly beseech divine aid. At Fredericksburg a brigadier on coming up to tell a colonel to take his regiment forward noticed a soldier "half raised up from his laying position with his open bible in one hand in loud and earnest prayer." The general withheld the order to advance until the prayer was finished.[8]

Some of the waiting men would attempt to break the tension by laughing and joking, but their efforts, strained and hollow, would elicit small response. Silence—awful, impenetrable, lonely silence—was the prevailing mood.

What were the sensations of these Yanks as they lingered on the threshold of battle? Were they afraid? Yes—at least most of them were. "If you see anyone that says that they want any afraid, you may know that it want me," wrote a Maine soldier after his baptism of fire at Fredericksburg, "but I want so frightened but I obaid all the orders." [9]

Among soldiers untried in combat, the fear was often not so much of death or injury as of inability to stand up under the awful and unknown test that lay ahead. Better a thousand times to fall facing the enemy, they thought, than to play the coward and bring humiliation or shame to the folk back home.[10] But could their spirits compel their bodies to go forward into the hell of screeching missiles, thundering cannon, screaming wounded and bristling bayonets? That was the burning question.

"I have a mortal dread of the battle field," wrote Private Edward Edes to his father before his first entry into combat, "for I have never yet been nearer to one than to hear the cannon roar & have never seen a person die." He added: "I am afraid that the groans of the wounded & dying will make me shake, nevertheless I hope & trust that strength will be given me to stand up & do my duty." [11]

Veterans of prior conflicts were spared the novices' anxiety about standing the gaff, but their fear was no less. They knew what a battle was like, and their knowledge brought more of dread than of reassurance. Too, the matter of diminishing odds entered into their thinking. Did not each battle survived reduce the chance of living through another? How long, after all, could good luck last? Declining eagerness for the fray among the battle-wise was noted by Colonel Jacob Ammen at Shiloh. "The Twenty-fourth Ohio . . . has been under severe fire several times and behaved well," he wrote in his diary as troops of Buell's command approached the field of action, "but does not appear as anxious as the other regiments to get into a fight." After remarking on the anxiousness of new units to "see the elephant" he added: "The Twenty-fourth Ohio Volunteer Infantry had seen the elephant several times, and did not care about seeing him again unless necessary." [12]

The two most noticeable differences in the prebattle mood of veterans and nonveterans was a greater reticence of the old-timers when confronting danger and their ability to postpone acute concern about conflict much longer than their inexperienced comrades. Thus some of them could relax even to the point of drowsing, until the shells falling near proclaimed the actual beginning of hostilities.

Fear, whatever its basis and whenever it came, manifested itself in various ways. But the most obvious effects were dryness of the throat and lips; a sense of heaviness in the area of vital organs, as if a stone were weighing on the chest, making breathing difficult; and excessive perspiration. Some soldiers noted a sharpening of recollective powers with the result that many long-latent memories of home and childhood passed in rapid succession across the canvas of consciousness.

How did these men nerve themselves for the ordeal that lay ahead? Resort to Providence has already been noted, and of the bolstering effect of religion on sincere believers there can be no doubt. Others placed their hopes on chance, while still others found comfort in the fatalistic view that no harm could come to one until his allotted time was up.[13] A Maine soldier must have reflected a widespread sentiment when he wrote of his own attitude: "Death is the common lot of all and the diferance between dyeing to day and to morrow is not much but we all prefer to morrow." [14]

In the hour of crisis the thoughts of nearly all soldiers turned to loved ones at home, and the consciousness of their deep affection and concern gave heart to many. Still others found considerable strength in the conviction that they were doing their duty to family, friends, country and God.

Here and there among the impatient ranks might be found a soldier whose spirit was heavy with the conviction that he would not survive the fight. Thomas B. Barker must have felt thus as he stood in line on July 21, 1861, at Manassas, for at Centerville on the previous day he had written his younger brother: "We are to move on to attack them to-morrow. . . . Many will be slain . . . and I am as likely to fall as any one. But . . . I am content to take whatever is to come. Should I be slain you will then be the eldest left and I doubt not you will fill my place. On you will fall the delightful task of maintaining Father's and Aunt Charlotte's declining years. You will be kind to Walter & Abbey . . . forget my faults & forgive. . . . Good bye and God bless you. Tom." On the back of the letter Barker wrote: "If I am slain, whoever finds this will please to state the fact in this & forward it & confer a favor on the ashes of Thomas B. Barker." [15]

Many who entertained such sentiments lived to fight again, but not Barker. He died, and a Rebel surgeon who found his remains sent the farewell missive on its way. But before forwarding it he added this note: "This letter was found on the body of a man sacrificed by the Lincoln government in its unpatriotic, unholy, and hellish crusade against a people struggling for their rights under the Constitution. . . . A sad fate to fall in an unglorious cause." [16]

If the waiting troops were subjected to enemy fire as was sometimes the case, the suspense became almost intolerable. An Illinois sergeant, who experienced such a situation pending the deadly assault of May 22, 1863, at Vicksburg, wrote: "We lay there about eight minutes and yet it seemed an age to me, for showers of bullets and grape were passing over me . . . and not allowed to fire a single shot. . . . Oh how my heart palpitated! It seemed to thump the ground (I lay on my face) as hard as the enemy's bullets. The sweat from off my face run in a stream from the tip ends of my whiskers. . . . Twice I exclaimed aloud . . . *My God, why dont they order us to charge!*" [17]

Finally after a period ranging from a few minutes to several hours—but which in any case seemed interminable—came the order "fall in," followed by the command "forward, march." As the men moved out toward the Rebel position, officers kept shouting the words "center dress," "close up those gaps." Now that they were actually in motion the troops would feel better, though at first there would be considerable ducking and dodging as shells screeched close. Now and then a man would falter, but usually he responded readily to the officers' admonition to keep moving. If he did not, he would be helped into place by the spank of a sword and a resounding oath.[18]

At first the advancing men would not be allowed to fire. The inability to retaliate, especially after enemy shells began to cut down comrades, was a severe trial. When the whiz of bullets was added to the scream of shells, bringing an increase of casualties, the restraint became almost unbearable. In one engagement the suspense was so great that a calm corporal, about whose bravery there could be no doubt, was heard to exclaim, "Oh, dear! when shall *we* fire?" [19] And in others, the troops began to pop away without waiting for the command.

With the first shot would come a tremendous relief. "After the first round the fear left me," wrote a soldier to his mother after his initial battle, "& I was as cool as ever I was in my life. I think I have been a great deal more excited in attempting to speak a piece in school or to make remarks in an evening meeting." [20]

The sense of calm would be accompanied by an apparent indifference to the ghastly work in progress on every side, a circumstance which in reflection was both surprising and shocking. The day following Shiloh, Private Franklin Bailey wrote his parents: "I did not think any more of seeing a man shot down by my side than you would of seeing a dumb beast kiled. Strange as it may seam to you, but the more men I saw kiled the more reckless I became." [21]

The first shot would be followed by others, the soldiers dropping down after each round to reload, with many of them rolling over on their backs to ram the charge home and then rising to their feet to send the bullets on their way. Some fired from kneeling and prone positions, the latter gaining favor as the war progressed.

As the men tore open cartridge after cartridge with their teeth, black powder would spill out on their faces, forming dark circles around their mouths and giving their countenances a weird appearance befitting the fiendish task which now absorbed them.

The conduct of the men as they banged away at the Rebels was

such as to belie the calm which seemed to follow the first fire. The air
would be filled with profanity. Officers would urge their men on with
oaths. Soldiers would swear at one another and to themselves in sheer
excitement. The first indication of a missile finding its target was often
a profane exclamation from the man who was hit. Cursing was by no
means restricted to the habitually profane, for pious men from whose
lips no oath was ever heard in camp sometimes became surprisingly
eloquent swearers in battle.[22]

The continued firing would bring exhilaration to some, causing
them to punctuate their shots with cries of satisfaction and defiance.
At Opequon, for instance, after the fight got under way men praised a
comrade's act of gallantry by shouting as they next pulled their triggers,
"Here's one for Corporal Gray." Other volleys were accompanied by
the cries, "Here's one for Sheridan," "Here's one for Lincoln," and
"Here's one for Jeff Davis." [23] After Brandy Station a cavalryman wrote
his parents, "I never felt so gay in my life as I did when we charged with
the Sabre," and following Gettysburg an artilleryman remarked: "I
felt a joyous exaltation, a perfect indifference to circumstances through
the whole of that three days fight, and have seldom enjoyed three days
more in my life." [24]

For others the prevailing mood was anger. Sometimes anger sprang
from the failure of the attack or from the cowering of comrades. Of
his sensations at Fredericksburg when enemy fire and faltering associates slowed the advance, a Massachusetts soldier later wrote: "I went
so far ahead when I fired that I was ordered back by our major and
lieutenant. I was mad, yet calm; how I itched for a hand-to-hand struggle." [25] More commonly the anger was inspired by the sight of fellow
soldiers falling before the enemy fire. After Shiloh, Franklin Bailey recalled: "When George Gates who . . . stood next to me on my right
hand, was shot, I was so enraged, I could have tore the heart out of the
rebel could I have reached him." [26] And following Gaines's Mill,
O. W. Norton wrote:

My two tent mates were wounded, and after that . . . I acted like
a madman. . . . I was stronger than I had been before in a month and
a kind of desperation seized me. . . . I snatched a gun from the hands
of a man who was shot through the head, as he staggered and fell. At
other times I would have been horror-struck, and could not have moved,
but then I jumped over dead men with as little feeling as I would over
a log. The feeling that was uppermost in my mind was a desire to kill
as many rebels as I could. The loss of comrades maddened me.[27]

In the heat of fighting strange thoughts coursed through the minds of some. A Maine soldier who months before had received a letter from a girl back home urging him to gallantry had one of her phrases flash vividly in his mind in the advance at Brandy Station. "I heard her say as plain as day," he wrote his father after the fight, " 'I am confident that you will make a *brave and noble soldier.*' " [28] Others testified to recalling snatches of poetry, and interestingly enough the passages which raced through the minds of at least two Yanks, one at Fredericksburg and the other at Haines's Bluff, were the booming lines of Tennyson's "The Charge of the Light Brigade." [29]

The thoughts of many remained focused on religion. William O. Wettleson described his first engagement thus: "Strange feelings come over one when he is in battle and bullets are whizzing around one. . . . It is a wonderful place for one who believes he is a Christian to test his faith. I found my hope much weaker than I had thought, and I made good promises." [30]

As the men fired they would continue to move toward their objective. When a suitable position was reached officers would call a halt to re-form their lines, which in the course of the advance had become disorganized, and to prepare for the final dash on the Rebel works. During the lull, as the blood cooled, the spirit tended to weaken. A few, unable to steel themselves to a continuance of the ordeal, would take advantage of the interval to slip away to the rear. Some of the shirkers would use the excuse of assisting wounded comrades; others would claim the necessity of replacing damaged weapons or replenishing ammunition. Still others would take leave without any pretext. More would steal away were it not for the vigilance of officers and file closers.

But the majority would stay by their posts, however great their dread of the final assault. The force that compelled them, above all else, was the thought of family and friends and the unwillingness to be branded as cowards.

At this point, if not before, the men would receive the order to "fix bayonets," and steel would grate against steel as the sharp instruments were fitted over the ends of the rifle barrels. Then when all were ready would come the fateful command "charge," and the Yanks would spring forward with a cheer.

What sort of cheer? The battle cry of the men in blue was different from that of the Rebels. The standard Yankee version was a deeply intoned hurrah or huzza, while the Southern cry was a wild, piercing yell.[31] The contrast must have been a marked one, for it was the subject of considerable comment. A New York colonel testifying at the Fitz John Porter trial in 1862 remarked: "Our own men give three successive cheers, and in concert, but theirs is a cheering without any reference to regularity of form—a continual yelling." [32] An Ohio surgeon, commenting on an engagement near Chattanooga, stated: "I could hear the sharp, shrill *yells* of the rebs, so different from the *cheer* which our men use." [33] Another surgeon, who was at the Wilderness, was more specific: "I could easily tell whether our troops or the enemy were making a charge by the peculiar character of their outcry," he stated. "On our side it was a resounding, continuous hurrah," he added, "while the famous dread inspiring 'rebel yell' was a succession of yelps, staccato and shrill." [34] Junius Browne, correspondent of the New York *Herald*, noted at Vicksburg that the Rebel yell was "shrill, exultant, savage . . . different from the deep, manly, generous shout of the Union soldiers." [35]

But the Federal cheer, like the Rebel yell, had variations. Sometimes it was a "hi! hi!" Again it was an "Indian war whoop." [36] The commander of the Seventy-seventh Pennsylvania Regiment reported after Murfreesboro that his men had pitched into the Rebels "with a whoop and a yell," while an Indiana officer stated that in the same engagement: "We went forward toward a Rebel regiment . . . double quick, and uttering these unearthly Hoosier yells that have been heard so often on the Battlefields." [37]

Occasional reference in official reports to the men in blue charging with "furious yells" and "wild cheers" suggests that now and then the cry of the Federals bore some resemblance to that of the Rebels. However that may be, it is certain that the hurrahs and huzzas which distinguished the Yankee cry were sometimes shouted with savage abandon.[38]

Since the principal function of the battle cry was to relieve tension, it was usually spontaneous. But sometimes commanders specifically ordered their men to shout with the view of frightening the foe. At Antietam, Colonel Cross of the Fifth New Hampshire added another detail. "As the fight grew furious," according to one of his men, "the colonel cried out, 'Put on the war paint.' . . . Taking the cue . . . we rubbed the torn end of the cartridges over our faces, streaking them with powder like a pack of Indians, and the colonel to complete the similarity, cried out, 'Give 'em the war whoop!,' and all of us joined him in the Indian war whoop." In the ensuing fracas the whoopers were successful and the man who told the story was inclined to give some credit to the savage make-up and shouting.[39]

Whatever the nature or purpose of their shouting, the consuming impulse of the charging men was to reach the Rebel lines. This burning urge sprang in part from a hot-blooded desire to kill, and in part from a desperate eagerness to get beyond the flaming mouths of hostile guns, to strike danger at its source, to meet the worst that the battle had to offer and force a quick decision.

As the surging attackers closed on their objective, they would encounter an increasing flood of lead. At Lookout Mountain the fire was so intense that one charging Yank "thought it was raining bullets," and at Jackson, Mississippi, according to another, the balls "Sung Dixey around our years" while "the grape and Canister moed our Ranks Down like grass Before the Sithe." [40] Still another stated that at the Wilderness Confederate bullets rushed by in such swarms that it seemed "I could have caught a pot full of them if I had had a strong iron vessel rigged on a pole as a butterfly net." [41]

The fire might become so heavy that the men in blue would lean forward as they advanced, as if walking against a gale. At Fredericksburg a Yank found himself drawing his head down into his collar "the same as I would go through a storm of hail and wind." [42]

Minié balls, canister and grape would cut holes in the advancing lines. Officers would try to close up the gaps, but their efforts would have little effect. Eventually each man would fight on his own.[43]

The tempo of the assault would increase in the final stages and the last few yards be covered on a run. As the attackers threw themselves against the defending lines, shouting on both sides would rise to a tumultuous climax. Bayonets now came into play, though few of them actually pierced enemy flesh, and muskets were fired at such close range as to burn the faces of the contestants.[44] In the heated tussle men would pitch into one another with stones and fists, but most of the close-up fighting would be with the clubbed musket.[45]

At first the gray lines would bend back under the force of the assault. But if the defense was strong and the attack unsupported, the blue-clad survivors would fall back after a few minutes of desperate struggle and thus bring an end to this phase of the contest.

But before the battle was decided the Yanks might repeat the assault several times, as at Fredericksburg. Again they might have the defensive role as at Gettysburg. Or yet again, the contest might take the form of attack by one side and then the other as at Donelson and Shiloh.

The character of attacks varied greatly. Sometimes the only preliminaries were a hurried beating of the long roll, a quick forming of lines and a hasty dispensing of ammunition. Again, no distinct break occurred between advance to position and final charge. Many attacks were repulsed before reaching the assault stage, and some assaults were transformed into routs before hostile positions were ever reached. Some battles of course were more in the nature of piecemeal fire fights than of assaults and defenses. In almost any contest there was much more of waiting and maneuvering than there was of actual shooting.

Along with the variations, battles had a number of things in common. From the point of view of the man who carried the musket they were extremely exciting affairs. The mere rumor that a fight was in prospect would lift soldiers from the doldrums, and sustained firing on the picket line would affect a camp like an electric shock. Animation would redouble with the beating of the long roll and the rushing of men into line. And while the curve of emotions would show peaks and valleys as the drama was further unfolded, its general course would continue upward until clash with the foe brought thrill to a climax.

The thrill was the thing most remembered, but the sensational aspects were only the surface of the battle. The essence of fighting was hardship and discomfort. Owing to prior marching, soldiers were often tired when they entered combat. At Gettysburg and the Wilderness some units covered more than thirty miles in a stretch to reach the scene of action. Men advancing to battle commonly shed much of their equipment and clothing, as the littered approaches to almost any field would testify, and this practice, while affording some temporary relief, in the end frequently led to extreme discomfort. Soldiers at Donelson, for example, who had thrown away their overcoats as they marched in balmy weather from Fort Henry, suffered terribly when a cold snap overtook them on the eve of the battle. After the fort was taken a soldier wrote: "Wee had a hard time geting this place I beleave that we endured the most intence Sufering that ever an army did in the Same length of time. . . . We were bound to lay for fore days and knights without Sleeping and most of the time nothing to eat and raining and snowing a portion of the time with out any covering whatever was what I cald a bitter pill." [46]

But most fighting occurred in seasons other than winter, and heat rather than cold was the usual curse. Lying in the hot sun awaiting attack was enervating enough, but the yelling, rushing, shouting and excitement of the fighting itself caused the perspiration to run in streams and consumed one's energy at a fearful rate. Dust, kicked up by tramping feet and striking missiles, added to the discomfort, as did the thickening smoke that hung over the field like a cloud.[47] Exertion and tension brought enormous thirst which often could not be quenched because canteens had been discarded early in the battle. At First Manassas, when the Federal advance reached Sudley Ford, countless Yanks stopped to drink, dipping up the muddy water in their hands, their hats and their shoes.[48] A youngster who fought at Antietam wrote back to his father who had just joined the army: "If you ever go into battle, have your canteen full. I was so dry at one time I could have drank out of a mud puddle—without stopping to ask questions." [49]

Sometimes heavy rain beat down on the soldiers, increasing the weight of their clothing, making them uncomfortable by day and disturbing their rest at night. The constant seething of an army in motion soon converted the battlefield into a sea of mud which made marching difficult and clogged roads with stuck vehicles and swearing drivers.

Under any conditions fighting was extremely exhausting. A participant in First Manassas stated that before the Federal rout began he and the other members of his brigade "were so tired that we couldn't have left the field as fast as we had come to it." He added: "Men near me were plodding heavily and panting. Their faces were all sweat and grime, their eyes red from dust, their lips black with . . . powder. . . . They were dirty and weary and angry." [50] Another said of that engagement: "It was the hardest day's work I ever Expect to do." [51]

If the action extended over a considerable period, as in the Seven Days' and the Wilderness campaigns, weariness became so great that men plodded along numbly and without spirit, responding to orders like so many automatons.[52] A Vermonter wrote shortly after the Seven Days' battles that he was "so completely worn out that I can't tell how many days the has been in the last two weeks . . . five days . . . I went without sleeping or eating." [53]

A battle was also a chaotic event and especially so to the man in the ranks. As one soldier expressed it, "Nobody sees a battle." Regardless of how well-ordered the beginning or how thorough the over-all direction, most engagements seemed eventually to break up into innumerable small encounters, without shape or form, in which mixed units battled on their own against foes who could hardly be seen.

The confusion was disillusioning to some. Private William Brearley wrote after Antietam: "I have heard and seen pictures of battles—they would all be in line, all standing in a nice level field fighting, a number of ladies taking care of the wounded, &c &c. but it isent so . . . the rebels had Stone walls to get behind and the woods to fall back in." [54] Sergeant Matthew Marvin of the First Minnesota noted in his diary that at the conclusion of the Fredericksburg fight his regiment "was scattered from Hell to Breakfast." [55] Many soldiers commented on their inability to describe a battle, a circumstance which undoubtedly was due in no small part to the utter disorder which seemed to prevail.

Above all a fight was a noisy experience, and hardly any phase was the subject of so much comment as the sound of battle.[56] The blended fire of small arms was usually described as a rattle and that of artillery as a roll or a roar. The commingling of musket and cannon fire commonly suggested thunder; a New Yorker reported that the effect at Antietam was "not a noise, but a savage continual thunder that cannot compare to any sound I ever heard." [57]

The flight of bullets was variously described as a hum, whiz, whistle, whine and shriek, and some soldiers referred to the Minié balls as bumblebees, while others called them "swifts." Captain Oliver Wendell Holmes noted that at Seven Pines the Minié balls had "a most villainous greasy slide through the air." [58] Another Yank, telling of the fighting before Atlanta, stated: "We were sometimes amused by the music of musket balls.˙ One would come along with the 'meow' of a kitten, and the men would declare the rebels were throwing kittens at them. Another would come with an angry howl, as if seeking its Yankee victim. And we listened to others that had the wailing sound of a winter's wind. All these sounds were more musical than the 'zip' of the bullet at short range." [59] The sound of artillery missiles, to which soldiers gave such nicknames as "camp kettles," "cook stoves," "lamp posts," "iron foundries," "tubs" and "bootlegs," was most frequently referred to as a scream.[60] After Antietam a surgeon wrote: "You can have no idea of the horrible noise the shells make—when one passes over your head with its scream as if 50 Locomotive Whistles were blowing at once, no man can help dodging." [61]

The end of the battle brought various reactions. Perhaps the dominant feeling was one of relief at having come through the ordeal unharmed. But the satisfaction springing from personal safety was often marred by the wounding or death of beloved comrades. Indeed, one of the most trying aspects of combat was the moaning and screaming of the wounded that came in the wake of fighting; the situation was doubly grievous if, as was sometimes the case, one had to search among the casualties for a missing kinsman or friend.

Sadness over the loss of comrades combined with lingering weariness and the cooling of battle emotions to produce in some a sense of deep depression. Gloom was increased when the result of the fight was a humiliating defeat.

But as soldiers became accustomed to battle, the shock of both the fighting and the aftermath was considerably lessened. The degree of detachment attained by some was vividly revealed by a Yank who wrote after Antietam: "We dont mind the sight of dead men no more than if they was dead Hogs. . . . The rebels was laying over the field bloated up as big as a horse and as black as a negro and the boys run over them and serch their pockets as unconcerned. . . . I was going through a Cornfield and I run acros a big graback as black as the ase of spade it startled me a little at first but I stopt to see what he had but he had bin tended too so I past on my way rejoicing." [62]

The gathering of trophies, whether from dead bodies or the general litter of the fighting zone, was a standard feature of postbattle activity. A Yank who plundered a Rebel casualty in Virginia early in 1862 gave his homefolk the following report: "I give the slide 2 a division General, some of the butons 2 another general and the envelop 2 another general the slide I did not want 2 part with but I knew it wouldnt do 2 say no. . . . I will send some of the buttons in this letter and I may send the tooth brush in a paper if I dont conclude 2 use myself I also took one of his suspenders which was leather & I shall make a canteen strap of that a General tooke the other one." [63]

The souvenir mania was sometimes carried to ludicrous extremes. A New Yorker reported that at Fredericksburg some of his comrades came out of abandoned Rebel houses "with large doll babies & children's toys, whigs [wigs] on and white beavers & bonnets." [64]

For days after the fight, highlights of battle provided the theme of campfire discussions. Here hindsight tacticians told off the generals to their hearts' content. After Big Bethel a soldier reported, "Some who were in the Mexican and Crimean Wars say that we should not have made the attack without a good supply of artillery." [65]

Private Thomas N. Lewis must have echoed a sentiment often expressed over coffee cups by Shiloh survivors when he wrote on April 10, 1862: "Buell was the saving of Grant's army. . . . Grant is played out with me we wer strong enough to drive the rebells if we wer managed right, but no he would bring us up in a Single line when the rebells were 6 or 8 deep and any fool would know we could not stand then." [66]

Incidents of battle were the meat of these afteraction talks. Such dramatic episodes as Private Riley of the Ninth New York Heavy Artillery having his son slain by his side, and of a New Yorker who had joined the Confederate Army killing his youngest brother at Fredericksburg—and discovering the fact only when he turned his victim over to strip him—must have been often recounted.[67] But soldiers preferred to dwell on less tragic notes. Braggarts would sometimes wax eloquent on their exploits, though such claims were apt to be heavily discounted by the listeners. Lieutenant Henry Clune wrote after Shiloh that he had "been searching diligently during the past five days for the man who didnt kill Gen'l Johnston," adding: "He is the same individual who winged Genl Beauregard." [68]

Badger State soldiers never tired talking of the antics of "Old Abe," the eagle that accompanied the Eighth Wisconsin on its campaigns in the West. This mascot, the most famous of the war, usually behaved himself creditably on the march and in battle, but at Corinth, Mississippi, his courage suffered a lapse. When yelling Rebs charged the portion of the line where he was poised, wounding him slightly under the wing, "he hopped off his perch to the ground and ducked his head between his carrier's legs. He was thoroughly demoralized and the same feeling suddenly extended itself to the line and they broke and ran . . . the carrier of the Eagle picking him up and carrying him under his arm as fast as he could run." [69]

Mascots were not the only representatives of the bird and animal world that acted strangely on the battlefield. At Murfreesboro, according to a Union correspondent, flocks of sparrows from the cedar thickets "fluttered and circled above the field in a state of utter bewilderment, and scores of rabbits fled for protection to our men lying down in line on the left, nestling under their coats and creeping under their legs in a state of utter distraction. They hopped over the fields like toads, and as perfectly tamed by fright as household pets." [70] At the fighting about Spottsylvania Court House in May 1864 a flock of little chickens, according to Captain Oliver Wendell Holmes, came "peeping and cheeping" about his division's headquarters, completely ignoring the bullets whistling above their heads.[71]

Soldiers liked to recall the coolness and bravery with which their officers conducted themselves in battle. Members of the Fifteenth Iowa who gathered about campfires after Atlanta must have commented appreciatively on the feat in that engagement of their Colonel Belknap who, in the thick of fighting, took prisoner Colonel Lampley of the Forty-fifth Alabama by pulling him over the intervening works by his coat collar.[72] Hardly less amazing was the bold act of Colonel Isaac Suman of the Ninth Indiana at Chickamauga who, walking unexpectedly into a nest of Rebels and being called on by a gray-clad officer to surrender, coolly replied that he had surrendered some time before. The Rebel appeared satisfied at the moment and before he had time to discover the ruse Suman slipped away, organized some help and came back and drove his near captors away.[73]

But all officers were not brave, and soldiers probably had more fun talking about instances of their quaking than of their heroism. Private Frank Wilkeson got a hearty laugh from his comrades when he told them of catching an infantry colonel at Spottsylvania in a discreditable act. While walking to the rear on a water-hunting detail, Wilkeson espied the blond, bewhiskered wearer of eagles sitting behind a large oak tree "putting on his war paint." The officer "took a cartridge out of his vest pocket, tore the paper with his strong white teeth, spilled the powder into his right palm, spat on it, and then, first casting a quick glance around to see if he was observed, he rubbed the moistened powder on his face and hands and then dust-coated the war paint. Instantly he was transformed from a trembling coward who lurked behind a tree into an exhausted brave taking a little well-earned repose." [74]

Postbattle anecdotes had to do mainly with colorful incidents involving the rank and file. Ripples of laughter must have run through more than one campfire group when the story was told of the soldier who called on the file closer to unclog his rifle which he had inadvertently stuck in the mud, and the ensuing operation disclosed that the barrel contained very little mud but was full of unfired charges. In the excitement of fighting, this Yank had been loading and pulling trigger, but apparently had failed to put on new caps; and instead of mowing down the Rebels, as he thought, he had simply been stuffing his musket.[75]

Other soldiers made themselves vulnerable to teasing by pulling triggers before withdrawing ramrods and thus sending strange-looking missiles through the air. At the battle of Corinth a fast-firing Frenchman became so excited that he sent a bullet against the rifle of the man in front of him. The latter was so infuriated by this careless shooting that he laid down his gun and began to pommel the Frenchman, who returned the blows. After a brief duel of fists, while hostile bullets flew thick on all sides, honor was satisfied, the injured weapon was replaced by one picked up from the field and the two Yanks resumed their attack on the common foe.[76]

Private Dave Burns, an Irishman of the Fifth New York Regiment, afforded his comrades much amusement by a verbal exchange with a Rebel Irishman wounded and captured at Gaines's Mill. While the fight was still raging, Burns, noting that the prisoner had a revolver in his hand, asked him what he was doing with it. The Reb replied that the gun was for protection against Yankee bayonets. According to a comrade:

Burns waxed wroth at the idea of one of the Fifth doing anything so cowardly and berated him soundly; getting warmed up, he wished that the Confederate was a well man, and he would knock all the secesh blood out of him; that he was a disgrace to the Irish people for fighting against the flag, etc. Finally he took the revolver away from him and removed the caps, but the man begged so hard for it, as it was a present from one of his officers, he gave it back to him, and also a drink of water, and went at the fighting again, as if he had merely stopped work for a few moments to have an argument with a friend.[77]

Narrow escapes also figured prominently in the afteraction sessions. Soldiers must have chortled over such "mortal woundings" as that suffered by Iola Caleb of the Seventeenth Maine who at Chancellorsville lost part of his whiskers, though the ball doing the damage did "not bring more blud than many a barber." [78]

As soon after the fight as circumstances would permit, most Yanks took pen in hand to write their homefolk. The item of first priority, after the usual stereotyped opening, was the fate of the addressor: "I came out saft," or "I was slitely wounded in the rist." Then came an account of what befell soldier neighbors and relatives, followed in some cases by attempts to tell what the fight was like; the part played by the writer, how he reacted to the noise, the horror and the bloodshed; what unusual incidents he observed; the outcome of the encounter; and finally an expression of wonderment and thankfulness that the writer survived, and a hope that the war would soon come to an end.

Some soldiers told proudly, and no doubt with some exaggeration, how many shots they had fired. One Yank wrote of giving the Rebs forty rounds in a single advance at Mine Run, and another boasted that he shot eighty rounds "rite in frunt" before the repulse at Haines's Bluff.[79] "Sich firen a regment never dun," he added, "the ginerl Swore he never Saw a rigment lode and fier So faste." [80] After Gettysburg, Private

George Milledge of the Sixty-sixth Ohio Regiment reported to his wife: "i fired about two hundred rounds." [81] A number of Yanks stated that their guns became so hot from the rapid firing as to make them temporarily unusable. In any circumstances, much of the firing was wild and reckless and considerably more injurious to treetops than to Rebels.

Occasionally a Yank would keep tab of his marksmanship. Private W. O. Lyford informed his father after First Manassas that "I had the pleasure of shooting three rebels dead and wounding another." [82] But the man who could say with confidence after a fight that his bullets hit any foe, much less several, was an exception. Indeed, some, fearful of conscience, preferred not to know the results of their fire.[83]

Many Yanks passed on to their folk gruesome details of slaughter and horror—of screaming comrades, severed limbs, splashed brains, bodies blown to pieces by exploding shells, and the nauseous stench of the dead. After Seven Pines, Alfred Davenport wrote his father of seeing piles of slain Rebels with horrible expressions on their faces, "as if they had seen something that scared them to death," and Cyrus Stone, who went over the field after Antietam, informed his parents: "The rebel dead lay in winrows and both our men and the rebels lay in every direction. . . . We were glad to march over the field at night for we could not see the horrible sights so well. Oh what a smell some of the men vomit as they went along." [84]

One Yank recounted seeing Federal dead that had been overrun by wagons as the Rebels withdrew, "mangled and torn to pieces so that Even friends could not tell them." [85] But the soldier who merited the prize for gruesomeness was the one who wrote after Fredericksburg: "There was a Hospital with in thirty yards of us . . . about the building you could see the Hogs belonging to the Farm eating arms and other portions of the body." [86]

Little wonder that some manifested strong revulsion at the scenes forced upon them. Three days after Shiloh an Illinoisan wrote: "I wish it was over with I am tired of seeing dead and wounded men." [87] Later in the year an Eastern soldier commented: "The sight of Fredericksburg and the battlefield presented on the 14th inst. would have made even the old hell-hound Horace Greeley cry—peace!" [88] Others found in the profligate slaughter a shocking evidence of the cheapness of human life.[89]

Most Yanks who commented on their individual reactions and performances gave a favorable report. But some confessed flying lead made them terribly afraid. A Vermonter who was at Mine Run wrote shortly afterward to his wife: "I tell you Sally if I ever lay clost to the ground it was at this time." [90] And a New Jersey soldier, reporting to his homefolk on an engagement in North Georgia in May 1864, stated that he came near being taken prisoner and "if I hadent seen the fix I was in, and run like blazes I would have been a goner by this time." [91] Of his part in an engagement near Petersburg in September 1864, a Maine Yank wrote: "They came in on us in 5 lines of batel so sum of the boys say but I did not stop to count I limbered up for the rear as fast as legs cood cariery and that was prety fast." [92]

Soldier accounts of combat were as varied as the personalities and experiences of the men who wrote them. Typical of battle descriptions by more articulate Yanks was the following report of Antietam which sixteen-year-old William Brearley made to his father:

. . . the next morning we had our Second battle—it was rather Strange music to hear the balls Scream within an inch of my head. I had a bullett strike me on the top of the head just as I was going to fire and a piece of Shell struck my foot—a ball hit my finger and another hit my thumb I concluded they ment me. the rebels played the mischief with us by raising a U. S. flag. We were ordered not to fire and as soon as we went forward they opened an awful fire from their batteries on us we were ordered to fall back about ½ miles, I staid behind when our regiment retreated and a line of Skirmishers came up—I joined them and had a chance of firing about 10 times more— . . . Our Generals say they (the rebels) had as strong a position as could *possibly* be and we had to pick into them through an old chopping all grown up with bushes so thick that we couldent hardly get through—but we were so excited that the "old scratch" himself couldent have stopt us. We rushed onto them evry man for himself—all loading & firing as fast as he could see a rebel to Shoot at—at last the rebels began to get over the wall to the rear and run for the woods. the firing encreased tenfold then it sounded like the rolls of thunder—and all the time evry man shouting as loud as he could—I got rather more excited than I wish to again. I dident *think* of getting hit but it was almost a miricle that I wasent the rebels that we took prisoners said that they never before encountered a regiment that fought so like "Devils" (so they termed it) as we did—every one praised our regiment—one man in our company was Shot through the head no more than 4 feet from me he was killed instantly. after the Sunday battle I took care of the wounded until 11 P.M. I saw some of horidest sights I ever saw—one man had both eyes shot out—and they were wounded in all the different ways you could think of—the most I could do was to give them water—they were all very thirsty— . . . Our Colonel (Withington) was formerly a captain of the Mich 1st—he is just as cool as can be, he walked around amongst

us at the battle the bullets flying all around him—he kept Shouting to
us to fire low and give it to them——[93]

One important fact seems to have been only vaguely comprehended
by the soldiers in their home letters. This was the change which occurred
in the character of fighting. The last two years of the war witnessed a
decline of exposed, open conflict and an increase of protective procedures
and trench operations. In the shift the cannon and the rifle lost some
of their prestige and the mortar and the spade gained in importance.
Troops and officers who at Shiloh were disdainful of digging in had by
the opening of the Georgia campaign become eager and adept at throwing up hasty fortifications. Trench modes, introduced on a large scale at
Vicksburg in 1863, were transferred to the East the following summer,
where, with certain refinements in detail, they became the prevailing
pattern of subsequent operations about Richmond. Sapping, mining and
use of hand grenades were important features of the new order.

This metamorphosis and the soldiers' reaction to it was reflected in
the reports of officers. Captain Frederick E. Prime, commenting on operations at Vicksburg, noted the reluctance of work details from the line
to wield the pick and shovel and stated that their aversion to labor figured prominently in the decision to try to carry the works by assault.[94]
The engineer of the Thirteenth Corps reported the construction of
springboards, and the improvising of mortars from tree trunks, to lob
shells into the Rebel trenches.[95] Several officers in their accounts of
operations near Richmond in the summer of 1864 remarked on how
quickly soldiers dug in with whatever was at hand, including bayonets,
tin cups and plates.[96] On June 25, 1864, a brigadier of the Fifth Corps
wrote from before Petersburg to a friend: "We have never before used
the Spade as we have this summer. In any two days of the campaign
we have constructed more works than were thrown up by us two years
ago during the whole time we were in front of Richmond." [97] General
W. T. Sherman, in reporting a shift of positions before Atlanta, July
27-28, 1864, stated: "About 10 A.M. all the army was in position, and the
men were busy in throwing up the accustomed pile of rails and logs,
which after a while assumed the form of a parapet. The skill and rapidity
with which our men construct these is wonderful and is something new
in the art of war." [98]

Resort to trenches made warfare considerably less bloody, but danger
became more constant. As one of Sherman's generals, commenting on

the Atlanta campaign, put it: "No one could say any hour that he would be living the next. Men were killed in their camps, at their meals, and . . . in their sleep." He added: "So many men were daily struck in the camp and trenches that men became utterly reckless, passing about where balls were striking as though it was their normal life and making a joke of a narrow escape or a noisy, whistling ball." [99]

"In the Trenches before Petersburg" headed innumerable letters written during the last months of the war by Grant's soldiers. The contents told of watching the fiery trails of mortar shells on their arched flights through the air, the calling of shots, the scampering to bomb-proof shelters, the ever-present menace by day of the sharpshooters' bullets and the stifling heat of the trenches on summer nights. They also deplored the dullness of the dug-in existence and recounted the occasional exchange of taunts and pleasantries with Rebs across the way—Rebs whose lives were very much like their own, save for the Southerners' dearth of food and clothing and their ever-diminishing hope of victory.

Whatever the mode or period, the fighting of Billy Yanks was marked by varying degrees of proficiency. There was much of heroism and of cowardice and more of the solid, unsensational performance that lies between these two extremes.

In most engagements cowardice reared its ugly head before the shooting commenced. Some of the craven species resorted to self-mutilation in an effort to forestall exposure to enemy bullets. Shooting off toes and fingers became so flagrant in one division of the Army of the Potomac early in 1863 that the commanding general in May issued an order on the subject, requiring surgeons to make a complete report on such cases and threatening soldiers found guilty of the offense with severe punishment.[100] Another ruse frequently used for avoidance of battle was playing sick. A month before First Manassas an officer stationed near Washington noted in his diary: "Long Roll was beat about 11 oclock P.M. The Regt turned out to a man and were in line of Battle in 7 minutes, and ready for the enemy. Yet there was a number who were suddenly taken with a *pain in the stomach*' and felt like going back to their tents. The trouble evidently was cowardice." [101]

Some cowards invariably felt a pressing "call of nature" as lines formed for advance against the enemy, and then turned up after the fight with glib stories of getting lost, fighting in other regiments or being called to help out with the wounded. Others, as previously mentioned, used the excuse of damaged weapons—the unserviceability of which had escaped notice until the moment of attack—to abandon their posts. A lieutenant testifying at the trial of a soldier who had slipped off from his company at Chickamauga, after being refused permission to leave the ranks on the plea of a clogged gun, made the revealing statement: "It was expected of every man to ask leave to leave ranks under every circumstance." [102]

Cowards usually had a better opportunity to abandon their posts after the fighting got under way, because of the smoke and confusion, and in every major engagement large numbers sought the protection of trees, dived into ditches, cowered behind stumps or headed openly for the rear. Soldiers were quick to note that skulkers frequently included those who had been most vociferous in proclaiming their desire to meet the enemy.[103]

Many of those who showed the white feather apparently felt little shame. Others wanted to be brave but were hopelessly immobilized when confronting a maelstrom of fire and lead. Abner R. Small related the following incident from his own experience at Fredericksburg.

In the charge I saw one soldier falter repeatedly, bowing as if before a hurricane. He would gather himself together, gain his place in the ranks, and again drop behind. Once or twice he fell to his knees, and at last he sank to the ground, still gripping his musket and bowing his head. I lifted him to his feet and said "Coward!". . . His pale distorted face flamed. He flung at me, "You lie!" Yet he didn't move; he couldn't; his legs would not obey him. I left him there in the mud. Soon after the battle he came to me with tears in his eyes and said, "Adjutant, pardon me, I couldn't go on, but I'm not a coward." Pardon him! I asked his forgiveness.[104]

Some were pitiful in their fright; others were ludicrous. Thomas L. Livermore told of a soldier who after contriving successfully to avoid all prior fights finally was compelled to undergo the ordeal at Chancellorsville. "When the shells came screaming over and through our lines here," Livermore stated, this man "got an empty cracker box, the boards of which were not over half an inch thick, and setting it up in front of him crouched behind it to shelter himself from the shells. . . . Colonel Cross saw it and became so indignant that he strode up to —— and kicked him clear out of position . . . saying, 'You will disgrace my regiment.' " [105]

Soldiers who played the coward sometimes had to endure the jeers and taunts of their comrades. A Yank who slipped out of line at Corinth and came back after the fight with a story of being detailed to guard the water tank was mercilessly ridiculed by members of his company who afterward on the march would cry out "Who guarded the water tank at the battle of Corinth?" and then shout the offender's name.[106] When soldiers of a Pennsylvania regiment, whose conduct at Fredericksburg left much to be desired, boarded the train for home at the expiration of the unit's term of service, other Yanks impudently sent them on their way with the cry "Who run at Fredericksburg?" [107]

Defection in battle varied in character and extent from individual skulking and running on a small scale to wholesale straggling and mass panic. The stampede which took place at First Manassas is so well known that it need not be recounted here. The next notable instance of large-scale demoralization was at Shiloh. Grant's force did not stampede en masse as did McDowell's at Manassas, but running, individually and in groups, was commonplace and the total number who abandoned their posts in the course of the fight ran well up into the thousands. The report of a colonel told of an Ohio regiment breaking and running "in a manner that can only be stigmatized as disgraceful and cowardly . . . their officers . . . setting them an example of speed in flying from the enemy that even Floyd might envy." [108] General Stephen A. Hurlbut stated that on Sunday, April 6, 1862, "A single shot from the enemy's batteries struck in Myer's Thirteenth Ohio Battery, when officers and men, with a common impulse of disgraceful cowardice abandoned the entire battery, horses, caissons and guns and fled, and I saw them no more until Tuesday." [109] Other official reports gave similar examples. The cumulative results were vividly described by officers who came up at the end of the first day with advance units of Buell's command. General William Nelson reported: "I found cowering under the river bank when I crossed from 7,000 to 10,000 men frantic with fright and utterly demoralized, who received my gallant division with cries, 'We are whipped; cut to pieces.' They were insensible to shame or sarcasm." [110] Colonel Jacob Ammen told much the same story, though he estimated the number of skulkers at 10,000 to 15,000. "In crossing the river," Ammen stated, "some of my men called my attention to men with uniforms, even shoulder-straps making their way across the stream on logs and wished to shoot the cowards. Such looks of terror, such confusion, I never saw before, and do not wish to see again." [111]

At Seven Pines and again during the Seven Days considerable demoralization was reported in some units, but such instances were exceptional.[112] At Second Manassas panic occurred among Pope's troops, but it was not nearly so pervasive as that of the previous year and appears to have been due more to mismanagement and confusion of high command than to shortcomings of men in the ranks.[113] Running to the rear was relatively rare at Antietam, but straggling appears to have been woefully common in some parts of McClellan's army.[114] Fredericksburg, while demonstrating extremes of gallantry under the most trying conditions, was also marked by instances of shameful conduct. Lieutenant Henry Ropes wrote his father on December 16, 1862: "Hooker's men ran by us like Sheep. I saw a whole Brigade of Pennsylvania cowards (Tyler's Brigade) break and run in total disorder when they were brought up to our relief. Our men cursing them most heartily." [115] And Captain Henry Abbott reported to his brother: "The army generally didn't fight well. The new regiments behaved shamefully, as well as many of the old ones. The 15th Mass. was seized with a panic at nothing at all and broke like sheep. . . . Hooker's troops broke and ran." [116]

In the West in 1862 the story was very much the same as that in the East. While wholesale melting away such as occurred at Shiloh was not repeated, considerable demoralization occurred in every major engagement. Rosecrans charged the Seventeenth Iowa Regiment with disgraceful stampeding at Iuka,[117] and a signal officer who witnessed the Perryville fight wrote that when new troops under General Jackson encountered the Rebels "many of the Regts turned and fled at the first fire." [118] The officer reporting the incident placed the major blame on the officers, some of whom, from colonels on down, broke before their men and led them in disgraceful flight. The "wildest confusion" ensued, he stated, the panicky units completely overrunning the older ones behind them. "I saw one Regt. (a new one)," he added, "deliver its fire into another of our Regts and then turned and fled. . . . Men were flying in all directions from the field." [119]

At Murfreesboro a rout occurred in the right wing among troops commanded by McCook, and two days later panic seized Van Cleve's division on the opposite end of the line.[120] Colonel W. B. Hazen who was sent to support the portion of the line held by Van Cleve later reported: "It was difficult to say which was running away the more rapidly, the division of Van Cleve to the rear or the enemy in the opposite direction." [121]

The most notorious instance of mass demoralization in 1863 was at Chancellorsville, following Jackson's surprise attack on the Union right and rear. Details of the defeat, including the degree of panic, have been the subject of considerable controversy. But the fact remains that a panic did take place and that troops of the Eleventh Corps, while not universally guilty of arrant cowardice and not the only ones demoralized, had a prominent part in the rout.[122] At Gettysburg where the general circumstances of fighting were markedly different, the most notable case of demoralization occurred in Sickles' Corps when that unit bore the brunt of Longstreet's attack of July 2.[123]

The great battles fought in the West in 1863 also had their share of demoralization. Skulking and cowardice were much in evidence in Banks's assault of Port Hudson on May 27.[124] In the attack of May 22 at Vicksburg, where performance was generally gallant, an Ohio regiment "faltered and gave way" under a fire which was "far from being severe." [125] Chickamauga, like Fredericksburg, was marked by extremes of valor and demoralization, the superb performance of Thomas' men offering a distinct contrast to mass flight in some other commands. Reporting the effects of the Confederates' overpowering attack on the portion of the line held by Sheridan and Davis, Charles A. Dana wrote: "Before them our soldiers turned and fled. It was wholesale panic. Vain were all attempts to rally them." [126]

While large-scale demoralization was considerably less common during the last year and a half of the conflict and usually was in the nature of straggling and skulking rather than stampedes, panic continued to occur occasionally until the very end. One of the most frantic "skedaddles" of the whole war was that which took place among Banks's troops at Sabine Cross Roads, near Mansfield, Louisiana, when the vanguard of the Union force, estimated at 8,000 to 10,000 troops, fell back in "utter disorder and confusion" on the troops behind them, yelling "all is lost," and, according to Admiral David D. Porter, "such a scene ensued as was never seen before except at Bull Run." [127] Another panic took place at Brice's Cross Roads in North Mississippi in June 1864, when Forrest pounced upon Sturgis and sent his expedition flying back to Memphis.[128]

At Cedar Creek on October 19, 1864, near Winchester, Virginia— the fight made famous by Sheridan's anxious ride—two veteran divisions were demoralized by the surprise Confederate attack and "after a few minutes of fighting . . . fled in such dismay as to be of no further use that day except as a reserve late in the afternoon." [129] A lesser rout occurred in the Fourteenth Corps at Bentonville on March 19, 1865; and a Union general reporting the action of March 31, 1865, at White Oak Roads, Virginia, stated that when his troops reached the bank of Gravelly Run they met "the Third Division running to the rear in a most demoralized and disorganized condition." [130]

Demoralization, to be sure, was only one phase of Billy Yank's battle performance and, when the whole record is considered, a minor one at that. Individual acts of cowardice were paralleled by shining deeds of heroism and wholesale panics by brilliant displays of mass gallantry.

Of the countless feats of individual valor cited in official records, none was more remarkable than that of Private Samuel E. Eddy of the Thirty-seventh Massachusetts Regiment who voluntarily went beyond the Union line at Sailor's Creek, Virginia, in April 1865, to rescue his adjutant who had been wounded and was still being fired on by the Rebels. After killing one of the officer's assailants, Private Eddy was attacked by several Confederates, one of whom ran him through with a bayonet. While pinned to the ground Private Eddy shot and killed the man who bayoneted him. For his conspicuous gallantry he was awarded the Medal of Honor.[131]

At Spring River, Arkansas, on March 13, 1862, Sergeant Moody of the Sixth Missouri Cavalry saved a howitzer and wrote his name on the roll of heroes. After close pressure of the Confederates had driven the gun crew back, Sergeant Moody, lacking the rammer which had been carried away in the retreat, forced a canister down the barrel with his saber, touched off the charge and scattered the foe.[132]

In the fight at Hanover Court House, May 27, 1862, Private Leland of the Forty-fourth New York Regiment fired over twenty shots after losing a finger and receiving two head wounds. Another soldier of this regiment, mortally injured in the same engagement, called feebly to his colonel near the close of the battle. The officer approached the wounded man with the expectation of receiving a last message for a loved one, but instead was asked, "Colonel, is the day ours?" "Yes," responded the officer. "Then I am willing to die," was the soldier's reply.[133]

At Seven Pines, William Clemens, a bugler of whom no fighting was required, took the gun of the first casualty and gave a good account of himself on the firing line until killed near the close of the action.[134] Corporal Foreman and Private Samuel French, comrades of Clemens who were both shot in the leg in this engagement, continued to fight until they fainted from exhaustion and loss of blood; and Private Todd, after being mortally wounded, fought on till the close of the battle, then died on the field.[135]

Private Murray of the Fifty-second Illinois staged a one-man rally at the battle of Corinth. When the regiment fell back from the redan, Murray refused to withdraw, stating that the colonel's orders were to hold the fort to the last. A Rebel captain ordered Murray to surrender, but he refused and received a shot in the hand from the officer's revolver. But Murray killed the captain, took his revolver and then turned to meet another assailant whom also he quickly dispatched. His signal bravery was rewarded by a return of his comrades, and the Confederates were driven out of the redan.[136] This feat bears resemblance to one performed on the second day at Gettysburg by an unnamed artillery sergeant. When during the heat of fighting the infantry assigned to support his battery fell back and threatened to leave the field, the sergeant, who belonged to the Excelsior Brigade, "dashed along the line like an infuriated tiger, halted, and cried, 'Boys you said you'd stick to us. . . . There's the Guns . . . if you're men come on,' and with that he wheeled around, struck the spurs deep into his horse and dashed into the enemy's disorganized ranks, his sword flashing . . . as his brawny arm laid about with mad recklessness. With one impulse the whole line yelled 'Charge,' " dashed after the sergeant and saved the battery.[137] At Chickamauga, when a demoralized brigade came flying back through Captain Frank C. Smith's battery, one of the artillerymen, Private Savage, became so infuriated with one of the officers leading the rout that he struck him with his sponge "and damned him for running against his gun." [138]

Private John Kistler of the 132nd Pennsylvania established a record for coolness under duress. As his regiment moved into the attack at Fredericksburg, Kistler's arm was blown off at the elbow by a cannon ball. But instead of heading for the rear he had the stump tied up on the spot, and when the regiment returned after being repulsed he slipped up to the commander munching a cracker and said, "Colonel, I hope we shall whip them yet." [139]

When Sergeant George G. Sinclair of the Eighty-ninth Illinois fell with a serious chest wound in the advance at Liberty Gap, Tennessee, in June 1863, he refused to let his comrades take him from the line of fire, but urged them on with the shout "Let me alone, and hold that fence." In that same action, Corporal Philip Grub, mortally wounded, cried out to a dying comrade lying by his side, "Have I not always done my duty?" and then expired.[140]

At Lookout Mountain, Private Clark Thornton of the Ninety-ninth Ohio, under arrest for desertion, "voluntarily went with the regiment and engaged in the fight, acting with great coolness and bravery, always being in the front rank." [141] Deserters also distinguished themselves in several other engagements.[142]

Reference has been made to the gallantry of a bugler at Seven Pines. The valorous conduct of another at Chickamauga merits special notice. On September 19 when his unit, a brigade of regulars, was falling back, Private William J. Carson with a sword in one hand and his bugle in the other constantly sought to turn the tide by blowing the "halt," the "rally" and the "forward" calls. Then, noticing the colors of a near-by regiment, he rushed to them and sounded "to the color." This heroic performance was repeated on the following day, to the admiration of the entire brigade.[143]

Most conspicuous of all for heroism were those charged with bearing and guarding the colors. In numerous instances the color-bearers continued defiantly to wave their cherished emblem in front of the enemy after the cloth had been shot into shreds by enemy fire; and official reports cite repeated instances of mortally wounded standard-bearers trying desperately to hold the colors aloft and refusing to give them up except to another member of the guard or until death relaxed their stubborn hold. To one of these heroes the colonel of the Forty-second New York Regiment paid the following tribute in his official report of Gettysburg:

The color-bearer, Sergt. Michael Cuddy, who established his great and superior courage in the Fredericksburg battle on this occasion displayed the most heroic bravery. When he fell, mortally wounded, he rose by a convulsive effort and triumphantly waved in the face of the rebels, not 10 yards distant, that flag he loved so dearly of which he was so proud and for which his valuable life, without a murmur, was freely given up.[144]

The colors were an especial object of enemy fire, and casualties among the standard-bearers were unusually heavy. But one who seemed to live a charmed life was Sergeant Henry J. Grannis of the Twelfth Iowa who left Upper Iowa University to join the army when only twenty years old, carrying with him to camp a flag made by the girls of the college. He bore the regimental colors through many hot battles from Donelson to Nashville, being under fire for a period exceeding in the aggregate 100 days. Although the flag he carried was often riddled by Rebel fire he escaped without a scratch, though on the second day at Nashville he had a remarkably close call. While the regiment was charging across the field in that action a Confederate shell burst in the folds of the flag, tearing it to pieces and enveloping standard and bearer in a cloud of smoke. This seemed to be the end of Grannis, but even while his comrades were bemoaning his fate the noble Grannis emerged from the haze holding the tattered emblem proudly aloft.[145]

Repeatedly during the conflict individual exploits of men like Grannis were matched by heroic performances en masse. To recount all of these would be to tell again the story of the war. It must suffice here merely to note that every major engagement was marked by meritorious conduct of regiments, brigades and other large units.

In general, the battle performance of Billy Yank improved as the war progressed. Factors in his developing prowess were increasing experience, the weeding out of inferior officers, a growing confidence of the fighting men in one another and in their leaders, and—especially after Vicksburg and Gettysburg—an ever-deepening faith in the eventual triumph of the Union cause.

This progress in arms was observed and commented on by a number of participants. Colonel W. M. Stone in his report of Port Gibson remarked with pride on the improvement of his troops since Shiloh. "We fought the veteran troops of the Confederacy . . . hand to hand," he stated, "and demonstrated the fact beyond all dispute that the fiery valor of the South is no match for the cool and stubborn courage of the Western soldier." [146] And another brigadier, in his report of the desperate attack of May 22 on Pemberton's works, wrote: "This assault, though unsuccessful, demonstrated that the command possessed the most reliable characteristics of soldiers, implicit obedience to orders, undaunted courage, and great endurance. Not a gun was fired during the entire assault, although the most earnest appeals were made to the commanding general to do so, and when at length the command was ordered to retire, the men did so under the control and direction of their officers." This, indeed, was a high order of soldiering.[147]

Perhaps an even more convincing proof of the volunteer's developing effectiveness in combat was the ability evidenced at Gettysburg—and commented on by Captain Henry Abbott—to acquit himself well when the confusion of battle temporarily separated him from his fellows and forced him to fight on his own, and then quickly to join them again while the contest was still raging.[148]

After Chickamauga, Rosecrans remarked on the rapid improvement evidenced by the artillery, and an infantry colonel reported how completely his men had mastered the art of firing by volley.[149] Many officers commented with pride, following the November battles about Chattanooga, on the infrequency of straggling and the eagerness of their men to close with the enemy.

The general effectiveness—in supply, support, and co-operation of the various arms and services, as well as on the firing line—manifested in the spring and summer of 1864 by Western soldiers in Georgia and Eastern troops before Richmond was nothing short of superb. Indeed, soldierly performance on the Northern side seems to have reached its peak in these campaigns.[150] In the East, especially, several factors tended in the last year of the war to dull the army's sharp edge of combat efficiency. Outstanding among these were the dilution of experience owing to the discharge of many three-year veterans, the terrific slaughter of May and early June which took away many of the best officers and men, and finally the softening influence of long months in the trenches.

CHAPTER IV

IN DIXIE LAND

DURING the course of the war nearly two million Yanks crossed Mason and Dixon's line for sojourns varying from a few months to several years. Most of them approached the South with prejudices born of ignorance and nurtured by years of sectional controversy. Their opportunities for observation were restricted and their views were distorted by war psychology and the uncongeniality of army service. Even so, their comments as put down at the time in letters and diaries throw valuable light both on the observers and the observed.

The character of the Southern country was the subject of extensive comment on the part of the Northern soldiers, and the reaction of most was unfavorable. The thing that impressed the visitors most was the general backwardness of the South. "The country is behind the times 100 years," observed a New York soldier stationed near Richmond, while a New Hampshire man writing from Bladensburg, Maryland, remarked that "they dont have eny stoves here and half of them have no wagons but go horse back it is at least 150 years behind new england." [1]

A Norwegian boy serving in a Wisconsin regiment wrote from Dalton, Georgia, that "everything is a hundred years behind the times. . . . The land is very uneven and ugly. . . . I would not give one farm in Koshkonong for the whole South." [2] This Wisconsin-reared lad, in comparing the South with his own community, indulged in a practice that was widespread among the invading soldiers. And it goes without saying that the land of Dixie suffered considerably by the contrast. A Michigander serving in Northern Virginia found the land miserable and farming methods wasteful and antiquated. "A man is no farmer at all," he said, "unless he has fifteen hundred acors of land, 60 or 70 nigers and the same amount of Jack-asses. The man licks the nigers and nigers the jasacks, and in that way drive business. . . . It is like spring here all winter," he concluded, "but I would rather live in Mich or even at the Nort pole than here." [3]

A Minnesotan's appraisal was even more damning. "I dont like this country nor the people that live here at all," he wrote from Chattanooga,

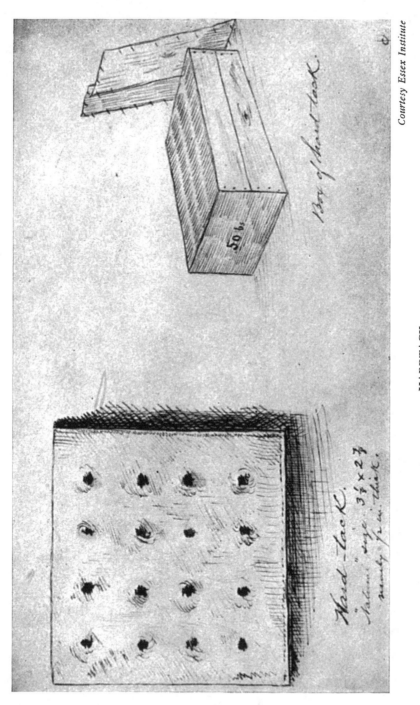

HARDTACK

Drawing by Herbert E. Valentine, Company F, Twenty-third Massachusetts Regiment

SOME SOLDIER TYPES
Drawings by A. R. Waud

"and wouldn't live here if they would give me the best farm in the State and the prettiest Girl in the State for a Wife throwd in. No not I. I had rather live in Minn. with no farm at all." [4]

The Midwesterners were hard enough on the South, but disdain reached its peak among the New Englanders. "You would laugh to see their wagons and harness tied up with leather strings," remarked one Massachusetts soldier, while another observed loftily that "it will probably be more than one generation before any of these slave-cursed states will rival New England in those elements which have made that little corner of the world of so much importance as affecting the human race." A third son of the Old Bay State hit the jack pot of disparagement; writing from near Opelousas, Louisiana, this man observed: "There is a good deal of this part of the world that the Lord has not finished yet. He meant the snakes & aligators to hold possession for a thousand or two years more before man [was allowed] to occupy it. The region from N.O. to Berricks bay is a part of this unfinished section. It is half land & half water." [5]

But from whatever part of the North they came, most of the soldiers who commented on the country conceded that it had tremendous potentialities. They found no deficiencies that could not be overcome by Northern energy and enterprise. As a Maine soldier writing from Virginia expressed it to his mother: "In the hands of New England people this country might be converted into a garden." [6]

The Southern climate inspired a considerable amount of growling. It is not at all surprising to find sarcastic allusion to the "Sunny South" in letters written by homesick Northerners shivering from the cold waves which in Civil War days, as now, occasionally gripped the upper South. An Illinois soldier, writing from a ragged tent in Memphis in December 1864, reported a thermometer reading of "full 250 miles below *Cairo*. . . . If this is a specimen [of Southern winter]," he added, "I want to winter at home next winter." But protestations of cold were mild in comparison to anathemas hurled at the heat. "The country about here reminds me more of New England than any place I have seen," wrote a New England sergeant from Fredericksburg in August 1862, "and the climate reminds me more of that infernal place down below that I have not seen but often heard of." And a Minnesotan, writing from Memphis in June 1864, remarked that he was "intirely cured of the old pashion for a warm Climate. . . . I had rather forego the fruit," he added, "and be where I can breath air that will not scorch my lungs when it goes down." [7]

Many complained of the enervating, depressing effects of the hot and humid atmosphere. A Massachusetts recruit recently come to Virginia wrote his homefolk in August 1862: "This climate is making me terribly lazy. I lose all my strength here, and feel dumpish continually; I want to lie down constantly; there seems to be something in the atmosphere that absorbs all my vitality." [8]

Expressions of opinion concerning Southern people were more frequent and in general more extensive than those about the country. In view of the emotion-charged atmosphere of the late fifties and early sixties in which Billy Yank's attitudes had been shaped, and considering the fact that during the war he was away from home, in a hostile country, and engaged in an unpleasant task, it is not surprising that most of his comment was unfavorable.

In considering Billy Yank's opinion of Southerners, however, it should be kept in mind that common soldiers had relatively little contact with the upper classes. The privileged groups constituted only a small part of the population; a goodly portion of them lived in isolated dwellings; and because of their way of life they were not generally as accessible to the man in the ranks as were people of lesser means and lower social standing. It was the common folk whom Billy Yank most frequently observed and hence who provided the basis of his estimates of the Southern people. But this is an advantage to one seeking information about the South's past, as the plain folk comprised the overwhelming majority of the population and less is known of them than of the upper classes.

No quality of the Southern inhabitants elicited more frequent or more disparaging comment than ignorance. Innumerable soldiers remarked on the dearth and poor quality of schools in Dixie. Further evidence of ignorance was found in the Southerner's rustic speech, his provincialism and his unawareness of time and distance. John P. Sheahan of the First Maine Cavalry reported that residents of Maryland "dont know anything atall, they dont know a mile from two miles, ask them how far it is to such a place they will at once say, 'well right smart distance I reckon,' and that is all that you can get out of them for that is all they know, and you can't get more out of anyone than what they know." Of Marylanders, also, another Yank remarked: "I dont believe the inhabitants even know the day of the week." [9]

A Connecticut soldier who on a short raid below Portsmouth, Virginia, in 1863, encountered people who ate their food with their hands and who never read newspapers was told by a comrade that the farther south he proceeded the less learning he would find. Pondering this suggestion, the New Englander concluded: "I cant form an Idea what they are in New Orleans if they continue 2 grow ignorant as they go South recollecting we onley went 26 miles from our Camp." [10]

When letters written by Southerners fell into Northern hands, great amusement was had in passing them about and making fun of their shortcomings in grammar and spelling. After such diversion a young Connecticut officer wrote his mother: "The ladies are so modest that they write of themselves with a little i. . . . Southern babies send their papas 'Howdy,' . . . a certain perfidious [stay-at-home] . . . is 'cortin the gall' of one of the brave palmetto soldiers." He concluded with the comment: "Above all penmanship, spelling and composition showed that the greatest need of the South is an army of Northern Schoolmasters." [11]

It is an interesting commentary on human nature that some of the most earnest critics of Southern culture were men who themselves were scarcely literate. Indeed, in the very act of disparaging they sometimes committed travesties that must have exceeded those of the ignoramuses whom they scorned. A striking example is afforded in the case of Private William B. Stanard of Michigan who wrote his sister from Bell's Tavern, Kentucky, in February 1862:

The Cuntry hear is the hardest plase that I ever Sea Wea Do Not Sea a Scool house near in one hundred Mills and you ask a man if they Go to Meaten they Say they Dont No What it is there aint one in 20 that Can tell one Leter from a Nother and every thing els in CordenCee with thear Lurnen.[12]

Another fault found with the Southern people was physical frailty which in some instances was attributed to the climate and in others seems to have been regarded as a congenital condition aggravated by bad habits. One soldier depicted men of the New Bern, North Carolina, area as being "all tall, lean, sallow, ugly-looking fellows," while another described Middle Tennesseans as "the poorest looking specimens phisically that I have ever seen—tall, thin, sickly looking mortals with hardly life enough to move." But the most expressive commentary on this trait was that of a Michigander serving near Little Rock who wrote that "the people look as though they have had the ague all their life." [13]

An impressive number of Yanks found Southerners to be lazy and indolent. An Ohioan whose comment is typical of many stated, after a tour of duty in Kentucky, Tennessee and Alabama: "The men are a very lazy trifling set; too lazy to work themselves but willing to sit around the store-doors whittling, smoking, and drinking. . . . The money comes from the labor of *women* of all ages from fifteen to fifty years and upwards, *in the field*, hoeing, plowing, and planting." This man found evidences of indolence among all classes. On one occasion he wrote of having viewed some splendid houses, but added:

With all the elegance and appearance of wealth, there is an air of "shiftlessness" around, hardly perceptible at first, but which never fails in forcing itself on you after looking closely. There is a paling out here, a window-blind hanging by one hinge there, a gate propped up with *both* hinges gone; and I have seen in some of the finest dwellings a sunbonnet, or *something* else with ruffles on it, stuck into the window where a pane of glass is broken.[14]

Southern women often were special targets of the Yankee disparagers. Some Yanks thought the "Secesh" women, as they usually referred to them, forward and immodest (one offered in evidence their overfondness for kissing games), while others condemned them as coarse and immoral. A considerable number attributed to the feminine portion of the population a sickly paleness which made them less appealing than the girls back home. For example, one soldier remarked: "They are void of the roseate hue of health and beauty which so much adorns our Northern belles." A youngster from Ohio carried the comparison farther. "The southern girls are quite different from the northern," he wrote; "they (the southern) are not as healthy and robust as the northern but are thin and pale, but are very sociable." [15]

Lack of shapeliness was also a fault cited by some. "They look more like polls than any thing else," observed one Yank, while another remarked disgustedly: "The women here generally are shaped like a lath, nasty, slab-sided, long haired specimens of humanity. I would as soon kiss a dried codfish as one of them." [16]

Other points cited in derogation of Southern womankind included their lack of accomplishment in household duties, the crudeness of their speech, their lack of education, or, if schooled, the superficiality of their learning and their poor taste in reading. Of a Virginia belle a New York soldier wrote: "She might have been a smart girl, but she has never done anything but read novels and she is a novel educated thing and all she knows is what she has learnt from reading novels. This is a specimen of Virginia Ladies." [17]

But more frequent than any of these was the charge of slovenliness in dress and lack of concern for cleanliness. An Indiana soldier wrote from near Vicksburg: "The women wear their dresses without any hoops & they only come about 3 inches below their knees & and they had peaks to their dresses about 7 inches & it is so slick with grease that it looks like an alligator's head. . . . their shoes look like bred trays & their tracks like sowbeds." [18]

Summarizing his impressions of the unattractiveness of women in a North Mississippi town, one dour Yank with a bent for exaggeration wrote: "[They are] sharp-nosed, tobacco-chewing, snuff-rubbing, flax-headed, hatchet-faced, yellow-eyed, sallow-skinned, cotton-dressed, flat-breasted, bare-headed, long-waisted, hump-shouldered, stoop-necked, big-footed, straddle-toed, sharp-shinned, thin-lipped, pale-faced, lantern-jawed, silly-looking damsels." [19]

An amazing number of soldiers commented on the prevalence of the tobacco habit among Southern women, especially the use of snuff. An Illinois captain wrote from Scottsboro, Alabama: "I went to the nearest house to camp today, to beg a little piece of tallow. . . . I sat down by a fire in company with three young women, all cleanly dressed, and powdered to death. Their ages were from 18 to 24. Each of them had a quid of tobacco in her cheek about the size of my stone inkstand, and if they didn't make the extract fly worse than I ever saw in any country grocery, shoot me. These women here have so disgusted me with the use of tobacco that I have determined to abandon it." The surgeon of an Illinois regiment wrote his wife from Western Tennessee: "As I walked the streets on Memphis I met a lady . . . quite finely dressed . . . [with] a little stick in her mouth. . . . As I approached her she removed it and spit upon the pavement a great stream of *Tobacco Juice.* She then returned the little stick which I saw had a little swab on the end of it. *She* was dipping." [20]

Even the children were said to be addicted to the habit. Corporal Edward Edes of Massachusetts wrote his sister from Lookout Valley, Tennessee: "The little girls in these parts about seven or eight years old chew tobacco like veterans and babies smoke before they are weaned." But it was the fondness of the "courting-age" females for tobacco that seemed to be most disturbing to the Yanks—especially the young ones. Wrote Private John Tallman from Vicksburg: "Thare are some nice looking girls, but they will chew tobaco, Sweet little things. Don't you think 'I' for instance would . . . *make* a nice show rideing along in a carrage with a young lady, me spiting tobacco juce out of one side of the carrage and she out the other . . . wall aint that nice, oh, cow!" [21]

A young Illinois officer stationed in North Mississippi informed his homefolk: "Snuff-dipping is an universal custom here, and there are only two women in all Iuka that do not practice it. . . . Sometimes girls ask their beaux to take a dip with them during a spark. I asked one if it didn't interfere with the old fashioned habit of kissing. She assured me that it did not in the least, and I marvelled." [22]

Soldier references to smoking, chewing, and especially to "dipping" among Southern women could be cited almost indefinitely, but further piling up of evidence on the subject seems pointless. Suffice to say that so much independent testimony is given in Union soldier letters and diaries of the use of tobacco in all parts of the country and among all classes that, even with due allowance for prejudice, revision of ideas as to the prevalence of the tobacco habit among the Old South's women is suggested.

Among traits of Southerners in general the penchant for military titles did not escape notice. "To give you an idea of Southern love for titles," wrote a Yank from near Scottsboro, Alabama, in April 1864, "I'll name part of the citizens who help to form our party next Wednesday. Colonel Cobb, Colonel Provinse, Colonel Young, and Majors Hall and Hust. Every man who owns as many as two negroes is at least a colonel. None of them rank as low as captains." [23]

Not a few invading soldiers found the South to be a land abounding with sin. From Baton Rouge, Louisiana, a Massachusetts sergeant wrote to fellow members of a temperance organization back home that "almost every one (I do not know of an exception) drink their wine or their beer. . . . Even the women drink in the bar-rooms here, it is of common occurrence, & they must do it to be fashionable & respected." Another soldier from the Bay State noted that many Southern women "can swear like troopers," and "the children swear and smoke precociously. . . . Children get blase at the age of 10." [24]

An animal quality in sexual relations was seen by some in the unusual fertility of the Southern race. An Illinoisan after citing an instance of a Georgia woman with eleven children, the eldest of whom was nine years old, remarked: "This is a great stock country." But the evidence most commonly offered of impure and unrestrained passion among Southerners was the multitude of mulattoes encountered throughout the country. An Illinois surgeon was "quite sure" that he could see white blood in half the Negro children about Pulaski, Tennessee, while a chaplain from Massachusetts reported that the streets of Thibodaux, Louisiana, "were full of its hybrid population." [25]

Instances of horrible treatment of slaves were cited by some to illustrate Southern brutality. These included the tying of a Negro to a tree by a Georgian, who first turned his dogs loose on the hapless slave, then lighted fires about him, and finally suspended him from a limb; a planter's wife who "kept her hand in practice by flogging some mulatto girls"; and an owner who punished his Negroes by nailing their ears to a tree, and by flogging them and leaving them tied naked to trees for the flies and mosquitoes to feed on their lacerated flesh.[26]

With such stories as these circulating in Union camps, it is not surprising to find a Massachusetts blue blood exclaiming: "Honestly, papa, I do not see how anyone can say that the Southern people are civilized." [27]

The Southern social system was the subject of occasional comment. The prevailing impression seems to have been the erroneous one held by many both North and South even to the present day that the white population consisted of two classes, one made up of wealthy, slave-owning aristocrats and the other of shiftless, down-at-the-heels, poor white trash, who were worse off than the slaves. The planters were represented as utterly despising those lower than themselves in the social scale and grinding the poor under their heels.

A Wisconsin Yank who marched with Grant's forces from Port Gibson to Jackson, Mississippi, noted that farmers who owned a few Negroes "scorn[ed] work themselves," made themselves ridiculous, and ran their property to waste "trying to ape the lordly owner of a hundred slaves." A young Massachusetts officer serving in South Carolina was even more strongly impressed by the force with which the idea of caste gripped the South. "I have grown immensely aristocratic since in South Carolina," he wrote his mother. "There is something in the air that's infectious. A few more weeks here, and I'll be able to stomach even a Bostonian." [28]

This man's attitude toward the South was softened by a sense of humor. But in many cases censure of the invaded land was accompanied by expressions of unmitigated hatred. As a Michigander put it: "Everything looks as if it is going to the devil & I know the citizens ought to, & I have faith they will." [29] Interesting for the light thrown on later Reconstruction policies was the satisfaction manifested by some of the soldiers at the destruction being wrought in Dixie, and the sentiment evidenced by them that the work should be continued until full penance had been done for the South's sins against the nation and against humanity. An Illinois soldier declared: "I think it perfectly right to take the hog and leave them none and then if they ain't Satisfied I am fore banishing ever Rebel and rebel simpathiser from the U. S. I . . . belive in giveing the rebels a lesson to be rememberd in after generations then we will never be troubled with Civil War again." [30] A Yankee diarist of rhyming bent stated his position thus:

> Emancipation without deportation
> Sequestration without Litigation
> Condemnation without mitigation
> Extermination without procrastination
> Confiscation without Botheration
> Damnation without reservation
> And no hesitation until
> there is a Speedy termination
> to this Southern Confederation.[31]

Certain Southern groups elicited more vengeful utterances than others. South Carolinians were singled out for special damnation because of the leading part borne by them in the secession movement. An Ohioan who had just entered South Carolina in February 1865 wrote his homefolk: "We will make her suffer wors than she did the time of the Revolutionary war we will let her know that it isened So Sweet to Secede as She thought it would be." And a Hoosier whose sister informed him that she had named her newborn son for him wrote in reply: "I fear you cannot get him into the service soon enough to help us in this war, but theare may be other wars hearafter be sure you teach him to despise South Carolinians & there is no danger of his ever fighting on the wrong side." [32]

Against the politicians who were deemed guilty of bringing on the war, and against Jefferson Davis in particular, many denunciations were hurled. A Michigan private, through the medium of his diary, vented his spleen against the Rebel President thus:

I pray God that I may be one of the men who will pull the rope to hang Jeff Davis and that the spirits of Washington, Jefferson and Jackson and Adams may look over the Batalments of Heaven down upon the Bleaching Carcuss as the flesh Drops from the Bones and Listen to the Winds Whistleing Hail Columbia and Yankee doodle through the Decaying ribs which once enclosed his corrupt and Traitirous heart—for causing this war and Still Caring on this Wicked and Cruell War and Keeping W. E. Limbarker from his Dear Wife and Daughter.[33]

While dislike of the South and its inhabitants was unquestionably the prevailing attitude among Union soldiers, a considerable number of them reacted favorably to the country and the people. Some even had kind words to say about the climate, though it is interesting to note that none of the complimentary references bear midwinter or midsummer dates. A Connecticut corporal was inspired by the charm of the country near Alexandria, Virginia, to exclaim: "This country is so beautiful I wish I had been born here." [34]

Certain areas elicited especially enthusiastic comment. The Florida coast and the country between Nashville and Chattanooga were rated as particularly attractive. Of Louisiana a Midwesterner said: "Louisiana is the Prettiest State that ever I Saw flowers of all kinds are out everything are green and nice." [35]

Occasionally Yanks reported evidences of refinement and culture in Southern homes. A Chicago artilleryman paid high tribute to the elegance and good taste in furnishings and grounds observed in the Lake St. Joseph area of Louisiana; and of planter dwellings in North Mississippi he remarked: "Everything about their places has a good old fashioned air of comfort, neatness and refinement; in the most unpretending houses we find generally a good library & piano, and a great deal of taste displayed inside and out of doors." [36]

While the majority of such comment was directed at the planter class, humbler groups were not entirely overlooked. Concerning homes observed in Thibodaux, Louisiana, a Massachusetts chaplain stated: "Each little cottage had its garden; . . . every window and pilaster buried in vines; every garden gilt-edged with ripe oranges along the borders." A New Yorker whose associations were with the middle and lower strata wrote from Florida in 1862: "I never met with a class of people who were more refined, friendly and hospitable." [37]

Indications of friendliness toward Southern civilians appear with impressive frequency in the letters and diaries of Billy Yank. For example, one file of manuscripts reveals a sergeant protesting vehemently the cruelty of a proposal of General Hunter to expel from his department all persons having husbands, sons or brothers in the Rebel Army; and another tells of a group taking up a collection for a poor Georgia woman reduced to the verge of starvation by the fortunes of war. A private's diary cites this instance in North Alabama: "Wensday we went up in to the mountains after a team it belonged to a widow woman it was all the team she had the lieutenant put it to vote whater [whether] we should take it or not we voted not to take it she came out and thanked us."

Another private, wounded at Brice's Cross Roads, lying in a hospital at Gunntown, Mississippi, reported: "Visited today by several Southern ladies with such delicacies for our wounded as they could raise. God bless them for their kindness." [38]

Revealing also is the instance of Northern soldiers pitching in to help a South Carolina woman put out the fire set to her cotton by less considerate comrades; of an Ohio farm boy turning aside from his military duties to help some Tennesseans plant potatoes; and a Massachusetts youngster trimming a grapevine for a "Secesh" woman of Maryland, "for which I got a pint of milk, which was a luxury for our coffee." [39]

Southern women, though more often maligned than praised, were not without admirers among wearers of the blue. Sometimes approval of Dixie's offerings in feminine charm was registered by such brief comments in letters or diaries as these: "Got some milk from a minister. . . . pretty lady." "Like Arkansas first-rate . . . good farms and orchards—pretty girls." "Thar is Som durnde good looking girls in the Soth." "Squads of 'em (some confounded good looking ones, too) were on dress parade." [40] But in other instances their estimates were couched in rapturous phrase. Private Isaac Taylor of the First Minnesota Regiment, while doing sentry duty on the Rappahannock River near Fredericksburg in March 1863, noted in his diary: "A pair of Secesh damsels promenade up & down the island opposite our post. . . . I call Sergt Wakefield down to the river bank & he goes into ecstacies at the sight of the fair ones, & sighs, 'oh this war.'" [41] And an Illinois captain on the eve of his departure from Savannah, Georgia, in January 1865 wrote his sister: "I found the sweetest girl here that ever man looked at. She is just your size & Form, with large very deep brown eyes, almost black that sparkle like Stars. I swear I was never so bewitched before." That the recipient considered this statement as heretical is suggested by the fact that when fifty years later she edited her brother's papers for publication the complimentary passage was deleted.[42]

Sometimes women encountered by Union soldiers insisted on making displays of their Rebel sentiments by singing Confederate songs or by cheering Southern leaders. But, if they were pretty enough, or if it had been an unduly long time since the Yanks gazed on a feminine form, such demonstrations would be overlooked; or they might even be regarded as commendable indications of spunk.

After a tour of duty in Paducah, an Illinois sergeant wrote his homefolk: "I fell in love with Paducah while I was there, and I think I will settle there when the war is over. I never saw so many pretty women in

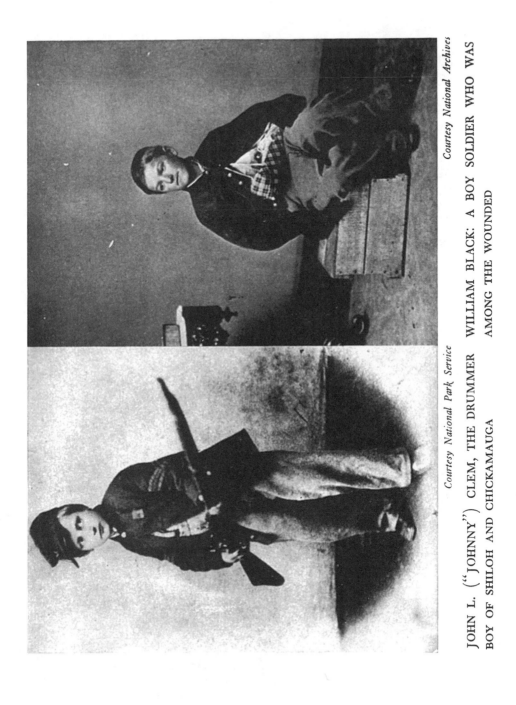

JOHN L. ("JOHNNY") CLEM, THE DRUMMER   WILLIAM BLACK: A BOY SOLDIER WHO WAS

BOY OF SHILOH AND CHICKAMAUGA   AMONG THE WOUNDED

THE COFFEE CALL

From Winslow Homer, *Campaign Sketches* (Copyright, L. Prang and Co., Boston, 1864)

my life. . . . They hollered 'Hurrah for Jeff' at us . . . but that's all right. I could write until tomorrow morning about Paducah." Other soldiers made similar statements about the girls of Murfreesboro, Franklin and Jackson, Tennessee; New Orleans; Winchester, Virginia; and Raleigh, North Carolina. The reaction of a captain to flauntings of disloyalty by some Tennessee girls is especially interesting. "Camped three miles from Somerville," he recorded in his diary, "on the farm of one Mitchell. His daughter gave us some chicken, coffee, mush & milk & 'Dixie' & the 'Bonnie Blue Flag' . . . but who cares. The music was good & the girls intelligent and kind hearted. Let the dear little rebels have their way in this respect." [43]

On many occasions the coming together of Federal soldiers and Southern women was marked by verbal jousts. These varied in intensity, but most of them seem to have had the character of good-natured banter. With Billy Yank performing the role of reporter of such contests, he usually emerged the victor, but occasionally he conceded himself the vanquished. A soldier named Dave Murphy, on meeting a sprightly young student of an Athens, Alabama, "female academy," took her to task for her Rebel sympathies. He told her of his hardships, of sleeping on the ground and marching over strange country, but said that these were freely endured for love of the cause and the old flag. She told him that she had brothers in the Confederate Army who likewise were suffering hardship. He said that he thought he loved his whole country as much as her brothers loved the half of it. To which she retorted half piqued, half defiantly: "Mr. Murphy, if you love your country as well as that, you're not a bit too good to sleep on it"—a reply that left Mr. Murphy speechless.[44]

The charm of Southern girls for Federal soldiers became so noticeable in some cases as to excite jealousy among the women of the North. In most instances the fears of lasting attachments being formed in Dixie did not materialize, but in a considerable number of cases, wartime acquaintances ripened into romances leading to marriage. And hundreds of Billy Yanks, some with Northern wives, settled permanently in Dixie after the war.

But wherever they took up their peacetime abode, and whatever their *post-bellum* attitudes, the men in blue left an enduring record of their wartime impressions in their letters and diaries. The South as portrayed in these documents, many of which are now fragile and faded, was in the main a land of extremes: the people were wealthy or poor, well-educated or illiterate, refined or crude, righteous or sinful. The country was one of light and darkness, with far more of the latter than the former. Intermediate shadings were only rarely discerned. This is not surprising, however, in view of the emotion-charged atmosphere of the period in which the impressions were formed and recorded. It is worthy of note that tolerance increased with continuing service in the occupied country, and soldiers who remained in Dixie for two years or more often were able to achieve a fair degree of objectivity and accuracy in their observations. Certainly their attitudes were more friendly than those of later years, when hatreds were aroused to unprecedented intensity by scheming politicians waving bloody shirts. On the whole the wartime reactions of Billy Yank compare favorably in interest and accuracy with those of other nineteenth-century visitors, and even with some of recent times.

CHAPTER V

ALONG FREEDOM ROAD

ONE WHO READS letters and diaries of Union soldiers encounters an enormous amount of antipathy toward Negroes. Expressions of unfriendliness range from blunt statements bespeaking intense hatred to belittling remarks concerning dress and demeanor.

"I dont think enough of the Niggar to go and fight for them. I would rather fight them," wrote an Ohioan shortly before enlisting, while a New Yorker after a few months' service remarked to his homefolk: "I think that the best way to settle the question of what to do with the darkies would be to shoot them."[1]

One of these men was middle-class and the other of humble station. But the meanest statement of all came from a young Boston blue blood who early in 1863 wrote his brother from New Orleans: "As I was going along this afternoon a little black baby that could just walk got under my feet and it look so much like a big worm that I wanted to step on it and crush it, the nasty, greasy little vermin was the best that could be said of it."[2]

Several factors contributed to anti-Negro feeling in the army. Many soldiers were deeply prejudiced before entering the service. This was especially true of those of border-state or Southern background and of Irishmen; it was apparently true of men belonging to lower educational and economic groups. Initial prejudices sometimes were softened by army experience, but usually the reverse was true.

A considerable amount of ill feeling sprang from the impression that military authorities were partial to Negroes. After a stint of shoveling mud a New Hampshire Yank observed disgustedly: "No matter, nothing but a soldier. Some of the Boys say that the Army Moto is First the Negro, then the mule, then the white man."[3] A Minnesota sergeant complained of the preferred status of a colored aide attached to General Howard's headquarters: "Their [are] 3 Dr. 3 chaplins & one of his Staff to look after the wants of the nigar. Their has been moore sympathy lavished on him than I ever saw on 20 white men. I guess the day is not distant when a white man will be as good as a Nigar."[4]

Similar sentiments were voiced by a Connecticut infantryman who wrote from Virginia, "A Negro here can ride a horse a private Soldier can walk"; and by a Maine cavalryman who complained, "Contrabands . . . have better places to sleep in and better grub than we do and that is the way all through the niggers . . . fare better than the soldiers do." Even more bitter was a New Yorker who growled: "Each one of them [officers] having a Nigger servant . . . whom they generally feed out of our Rations, it is a well known fact that they are treated better than we are, & in this very camp some of our men were turned out in the Rain from some Rebel Barracks . . . in order to accommodate the niggers." [5]

Many professed to dislike Negroes because they found them lazy and shiftless. "We have four nigger wench's to do our washing at no expense to us," wrote Private C. B. Thurston of Maine, "and as a general thing the clothes are not much dirtier when they come back from the wash than they were when we took them off. They are about as full of dust as an old carpet, from washing in Missippi river water." Another soldier remarked of the colored cook employed by his mess: "[He is] worth about as much as if he was blind for he hardly ever gets his eyes open." Still another Yank, after admitting that the freedmen had saved the soldiers much hard labor, had the following comment to make: "They are much more willing to work than I supposed, but a lasy white man will do more work in a day than half a dozen of the smartest specimens." [6]

Numerous Yanks, weighing laziness of Negroes against the cheapness of their labor, considered sending contrabands home for use as domestic servants and a number actually did so. A Hoosier captain who entertained the idea for a time, but who apparently decided against it, wrote his wife: "I dont know now but I may bring home a little contraband to nurse Aggy and tote up wood and help about the kitchen, but they are all so lazy I dont know about it . . . the niggers down here are not worth 3 cents . . . some of them [are] willing to work but you have to tell them every thing you want done. I have to tell the oldest monkey (about 6 years old) to keep the flies off the table every time I set down. They and their mother lays around on the ground like hogs and only gets up to Cook when told." [7]

A Michigan officer who appears to have entered the army without strong prejudice, after a few months' service in Kentucky noted in his diary:

Christmas. So the niggers all say, for it is a holiday with them in reality. From Christmas to New Years they are free to dance, make love, ride like mad, race horses and raise the devil generally——On the whole I think a system of servitude & serfdom better for both whites & blacks than immediate emancipation. It is true there are many of the blacks well qualified to take care of themselves, but the masses are lazy and shiftless & would become worthless vagabonds if free. They think to be free is to be free from labor. . . . A large portion of the blacks would very soon become intolerable nuisances. They have been for generations dependent & treated like children & mentally they are nothing else.[8]

Even among avowed emancipationists lapses of confidence in the Negro's sense of responsibility sometimes were evidenced. James T. Ayers, a somewhat erratic but usually intense friend of the freedmen, wrote while recruiting colored men in Alabama: "I feel now much inclined to go to Nashville and throw up my papers and Resign as I am hartily sick of Coaxing niggers to be Soaldiers Any more. They are so trifleing and mean the[y] dont Deserve to be free." [9]

Occasionally soldiers found fault with the Negroes on the score of lying and thieving, but more frequently their antipathy was based on what they regarded as insolence or sauciness. "I perfectly Detest the sight of them," wrote an Illinois private to his brother from Vicksburg in 1864. "You cant speak to them and have a civil answer. The smarter they are the worse they are." In like vein a Connecticut soldier wrote from New Bern, North Carolina, in 1862: "If a soldier goes down Town, ten to one he doesent get insulted by nigers! & he can't open his head because if he does, or insults a niger back, touches or strikes him . . . [he] is sentanced to Fort Macon for 6 months with a ball & chain to his leg to live on hard tac & water and Pay stoped. . . . I for one do not like niger society." [10]

The Negro's changing status aroused in some a fear of social equality enforced by Federal authority. A Massachusetts captain after observing a celebration honoring Negro soldiers of B. F. Butler's command on Christmas Day 1864 commented:

The "nigger" in this department is supreme and it is policy for those who desire to bask in the smiles of official favor to be its very devout worshippers. The darkeys make good soldiers enough, but the attempt to mix them up with white soldiers and people is productive of mischief, they are very arrogant and insolent, presuming altogether too much on their social position. Republican as I am, keep me clear of the darkey in any relation. My repugnance to them increases with the acquaintance, they have their place and their work, but the time is not yet, in my judgement, when they can strike hands with the whites.[11]

Social equality became even more of a bugaboo when associated with the thought of large-scale migration of freedmen to the North, as many predicted, to intermingle with the whites and compete for their jobs. A Hoosier private wrote from a hospital shortly after the Emancipation Proclamation: "As soon as I get my money . . . i am coming home let it be deserting or not, but if they dont quit freeing the niggers and putting them in the north i won't go back any more . . . it is very wrong to live with the niggers in freedom." [12]

The support given to colonization in the army sprang in part from a desire to prevent inundation of the North by equality-minded blacks. Some who strongly endorsed emancipation did so on the assumption that freedmen would be sent out of the country. Among soldiers having this view was J. R. Barney of Illinois who closed a letter praising the Emancipation Proclamation with the postscript: "I am not in favor of freeing the negroes and leaving them to run free and mingle among us nether is Sutch the intention of Old Abe but we will Send them off and colonize them. the government is already making preparations fore the Same and you may be assured it will be carried into Effect." [13]

The factor which probably contributed most to anti-Negro sentiment among the rank and file was the association of colored folk with the war itself. War was fun at first, but after a while it was grim and eventually it became for most a dull and wearisome chore. Bored by the routine, tired of the hardship, disgusted by mud, lice, mosquitoes, heat and hardtack, longing for home associations and unhappy at the prospect of continued peril, Yanks found it natural to seek out a pretext for their misery and heap on it their accumulated displeasure. The Negroes who flocked to the Union lines, identified as they were with the conflict, became scapegoats on whom the soldier could spill his hatred of the war.

Denunciations of the Negro were more frequent and more violent after long, hard and unsuccessful campaigns. The peaks of anti-Negro feeling in the Army of the Potomac seem to have been reached in the wake of McClellan's repulse before Richmond in the summer of 1862 and Burnside's bloody failure at Fredericksburg the following winter.

Manifestations of anti-Negro sentiment usually took the form of disparagement or denunciation. Occasionally a soldier made sly comments about physical peculiarities attributed to the colored folk. "If

I marry any one at all I believe I'll marry one of these nigger wenches down here," wrote a New Englander from Louisiana. "One that grease runs right off of one that shines and one that stinks so you can smell her a mile, and then you can have time to get out of the way." A barely literate Ohioan, writing home about "alegaters" in Southern swamps, observed with apparent seriousness: "Thay ar dangres thay will take a niger quicker than thay will a white man thay can smel them farther." [14]

It is plain that many Yanks regarded the colored folk as belonging to a lower physical order than the whites. A Massachusetts soldier remarked of a Negro child: "If her mouth had been two inches longer her head would have been an Island," while a Pennsylvanian reported his observations in South Carolina thus: "They are the genuine Negro here . . . as black as tar and their heels sticks out a feet behind and the young ones . . . butt each other like rams." Another soldier noted of freedmen near Washington: "Their physiognomy is a broad flat nose with thick lips and a very black complection." [15]

Prejudice and hostility frequently asserted themselves in abuse. Sometimes mistreatment was no more than a semi-good-natured playing on the freedmen's gullibility and ignorance. An Ohioan wrote his mother of an experience with a colored woman who came near his tent picking up cracker scraps:

> i got my hat foo [full] and giv her and tolde her to eat them and then die i ast her whie she wasent with her Master. . . . she sede that proclemation of Masey lincon sat us all free free the devil I told her affter the war was all over and the nigers was all free us Northern people lode [allowed] to make the men work for us and the wiman and children we lode to blinde fold them and drive them in to the river she rolde the white of her i up to me and sede mye god Masey i never go up dar i give her som mo crackers and then buted her of[f]. [16]

At Huntsville, Alabama, in May 1862, Union soldiers nabbed a sanctimonious-looking old Negro who came to their camp and compelled him to preach them a sermon. When early in his discourse, delivered from a stump, he stated that the Lord had been very kind to him and he could never repay Him for His goodness, the audience interrupted with "Never pay the Lord. . . . Oh, you wicked nigger! Just hear him! He says he is never going to pay the Lord!" The minister tried to explain, but the soldiers, ignoring him, chided: "Here is a nigger who will not pay the Lord. . . . Oh! Oh!" and vowed that they never before had seen such a wicked man. [17]

A Wisconsin Yank wrote from Columbus, Kentucky, of soldiers vulgarly taunting a mulatto girl who delivered laundry to their tents. Another Badger reported from near Vicksburg: "I have seen some of the soldiers of the so-called *gallant 28 Wis.* as well as others insult, by disrespectful & indecent language many, very many, blacks *men & women*. . . . On the contrary I have yet to see the first disorderly act & to hear the first insolent word from any of the many blacks which I have seen." [18]

Soldier ideas of fun were sometimes crude and the results brutal. A Connecticut soldier wrote from Virginia that his comrades had taken two "niger wenches . . . turned them upon their heads, & put tobacco, chips, sticks, lighted cigars & sand into their behinds." [19]

At Hampton, Virginia, in 1861, soldiers tied a rope around the neck of an officer's servant and hilariously drummed him about the camp with drawn bayonet, and at Paducah the next year, Midwestern troops pelted with stones colored fugitives who tried to enter their lines. In a few instances Negro camp followers were shot by Yanks whose hatred they had aroused to extreme heights.[20]

Court-martial proceedings and other records reveal occasional cases of assault and rape of Negro women. An Illinois chaplain told of a soldier who on a raid "stepped up to a colored lady who had come out of her cabin and grasping her round the waiste, forcibly marched off with her under his arm, while she struggled to get loose, and a hundred voices cheered." [21] One of the most shocking cases of maltreatment, occurring in connection with the invasion of the South Carolina coast in 1862, was described by a German soldier thus: "While on picket guard I witnessed misdeeds that made me ashamed of America. . . . For example about five miles from the fort about 8-10 soldiers from the New York 47th Regiment chased some Negro women but they escaped, so they took a Negro girl about 7-9 years old, and raped her." [22]

An Ohioan told of a comrade removing Negro babies from a cabin in Mississippi and riding off to camp with them, "gust taken them along for develment." [23]

More common forms of mistreatment were pillaging, theft and fraud. On Sherman's Carolina expedition both Generals O. O. Howard and A. S. Williams complained of the robbing of Negroes, Williams reporting that houses were "stripped of the necessary bedclothes and of family apparel." Soldiers in Louisiana in one instance sold unsuspecting Negroes worthless passes to or from the camp at one dollar each, and in another persuaded them to give up several hundred dollars in gold by telling them that "Massa Lincoln" wanted to borrow the money, issuing as guarantees of repayment soap-wrapper certificates.[24]

Considerable meanness and some outright fraud was practiced in connection with employment of Negroes as camp helpers and personal aides. A Massachusetts soldier writing from Louisiana summed up the situation thus: "Every private wants & Every officer has his colored servant whom he feeds scantily, clothes shabbily, works cruelly & curses soundly & in his curses includes the whole race." [25]

In view of the treatment accorded them by some who wore the blue, it is not surprising that Negroes occasionally became extremely dubious of freedom's blessings.

But the picture of soldier-Negro relations had its bright side. Many Yanks were favorably disposed toward the colored folk and dealt decently with them. Friendliness for the blacks in many instances had its springs in pity for a downtrodden people.

Stories heard in the North of suffering under slavery—sometimes confirmed by firsthand observations in the South—aroused the deep sympathy of humanitarians and promoted kindly relations with the freedmen. True, starry-eyed abolitionists were now and then "taken in" by the Negroes who, sensing the eagerness of their deliverers for horror stories of slavery, gave them an overflowing measure. But barbarism of masters, while undoubtedly not the rule, had been frequent enough to provide a bona-fide basis for earnest solicitude. One man in blue, not an extremist, gave his reaction to the sight which met his eyes when colored recruits were stripped for examination in Louisiana: "Some of them were scarred from head to foot where they had been whipped. One man's back was nearly all one scar, as if the skin had been chopped up and left to heal in ridges. Another had scars on the back of his neck, and from that all the way to his heels every little ways; but that was not such a sight as the one with the great solid mass of ridges from his shoulders to his hips. That beat all the antislavery sermons ever yet preached." [26]

Another Yank, who was hostile to slavery but who appears to be a credible witness, wrote of an experience near New Orleans: "Visited during the day several plantations and saw enough of the horrors of slavery to make one an Abolitionist forever. On each plantation . . . may be seen the stocks, gnout, thumb screw, ball and chain, rings and chain, by which victims are fastened flat to the floor; and others by which they are bound to perpendicular posts; iron yokes of different pattern, hand cuffs, whips and other instruments of torture, for the benefit of those who had been guilty of loving liberty more than life." On several occasions this man told in his diary of sawing heavy chains and weights from colored refugees. One entry stated: "Released another Negro from his iron yoke, and ball and chain, with which he had traveled 18 miles. His ear had been cut off, to mark him, and he had been well branded with the hot iron. His flesh was badly lacerated with the whip and torn by dogs, but he escaped and I have just dressed his wounds with sweet oil. There is little hope that he will live." It is not strange that this soldier professed a deepening hatred of slavery and gave himself to increased effort for ameliorating the condition of the freedmen with whom he came in contact.[27]

Further cause for kindly attitudes toward the Negroes was found in the good qualities manifested by many of those who came under Federal control. Many Yanks testified to their amiability, piety, intelligence, resourcefulness, eloquence and eagerness to learn. Evidence of these and other virtues tended to promote good will toward the colored folk and to stimulate confidence in their ability to pay their way in a free society.

Another influence working for a kindly disposition toward the Negroes was the support given by them to Union soldiers and their cause. All along the route of invasion, with some exceptions, slaves told what they knew about the strength and disposition of Rebel forces and revealed the location of valuables hidden by their owners.[28] The information was not always accurate, but the spirit of helpfulness which prompted the informers was nonetheless appreciated. Many an escaped prisoner owed his successful passage Northward to effective assistance given, sometimes at considerable risk, by colored bondsmen.[29]

Finally countless Yanks, hungry for hoecakes and for companionship, visited Negro cabins and were amply provided with both.[30] The welcome given by the Negroes was all the more appreciated because of the opposite treatment sometimes accorded by the whites.

Good will of soldiers toward the Negroes manifested itself in various ways. Many Yanks implemented their kindliness by teaching the freedmen to read and write. In some cases educational effort was in regular schools, but usually soldier instructors worked informally, sitting with one or more pupils under a tree, giving out words for spelling, setting copies on slates or shingles, or teaching the ABC's. The spelling and grammar used in home letters raise serious doubts as to the scholarly qualifications of some of the blue-clad dispensers of learning, but of their sincerity there can be no question.

Religiously inclined Yanks took delight in offering spiritual instruction to the Negroes and in sharing their church services. Laymen often taught Sunday schools, while ministers filled pulpits. Nearly all who worked among the freedmen were enthusiastic about their spiritual interest and progress. Some marveled at the eloquence and power of the colored exhorters and most were thrilled by the singing. A New York sergeant who went often to Negro churches wrote his parents after one visit: "I tell you they had a noisy time, but still there was apparently much of the spirit of the Master amoung them. I was very much surprised at the intelligence which they displayed in their remarks and exhortations. They show great knowledge of the Scriptures and in relating their experience use some beautiful illustrations." [31] A Massachusetts soldier who attended a Negro service in Virginia thought that the colored minister preached a much better sermon in fifteen minutes than the regimental chaplain could deliver in an hour.[32]

Interest in promoting the educational and spiritual progress of the colored folk was especially strong among soldiers of antislavery background. An Ohio company made up largely of Oberlin College boys sent one of the first fugitives who came under their control to Oberlin for education.[33]

Friendly relations between Yanks and Negroes sometimes took the form of intermingling at social functions such as parties and balls. A Pennsylvanian wrote of attending a Christmas Eve party in Fernandina, Florida, in 1864, where men in blue danced with colored women. The soldier historian of a New York artillery regiment told of a similar party in Danville, Virginia, in the spring of 1865, but the Virginia affair was allegedly brought to a premature end by colored friends of the Negro women visiting the dance hall and informing the Yanks "Dat de presence of de white gemmen was offensive to de ladies for dey couldn't stan' der odor." [34]

An indeterminable number of Yanks cohabited with colored women. A Pennsylvanian wrote his wife from Winchester, Tennessee: "I won't be unfaithful to you with a Negro wench . . . though it is the case with many soldiers. Yes, men who have wives at home get entangled with these black things." [35] Practices of this sort were by no means confined to the rank and file, for a number of instances were found of officers sharing their quarters with colored concubines.[36]

Usually such relations were without benefit of legal ceremony, but in a few instances marriage vows seem to have been exchanged by white soldiers and colored women. A Nashville newspaper in 1864 reported the trial of "Ellen and Sally, two Negroes," in the Recorder's Court for fighting. "Sally told her Union friend [Ellen] that she supposed she thought herself better than other niggers bekase she was the wife of a white soldier, but so far from any decent nigger thinking she had elevated herself thereby Sally thought her nothing but a ——." A fine of ten dollars was levied on each.[37]

Whether favorably or unfavorably disposed toward the colored folk, Yanks usually found them entertaining. When first they arrived in Dixie the invaders were exceedingly curious about the Negroes and would walk miles to get a close-up view of them. Eager for souvenirs, like American soldiers of all times, they would trade for articles of Negro clothing and other curiosities with the result that slave communities, sprinkled with Yankee blouses, trousers, hats and Zouave fezzes, sometimes acquired a military air. That the newcomers, despite their reputation for driving close bargains, occasionally met their matches among the colored folk is suggested by the fact that a venerable bondsman, claiming to be the original "Uncle Tom," sold a New Englander the lash with which he was so cruelly beaten.[38] Another instance of shrewdness, this time on the part of an urchin who sold milk at an exorbitant price, was reported by a Massachusetts soldier: "Some one asked him what made him sell so cheap! he said well gemmin, I tell you the truth. If I sell cheap one man he takes all I have for his ready money while the rest have to go without. So I charge twenty-five cents a quart so they all can have a little." This story must have made the rounds of the campfire with many an appreciative chortle.[39]

Yanks delighted in the quaint talk of the Negroes and many of them passed on to their homefolk choice samples of the slaves' vernacular. One of the reasons for the great popularity of Negro church meetings among the Yanks was the colorful phraseology heard there. A Hoosier sergeant was much impressed by this prayer: "O, Lo'd, Massa, come to dis e'th; an' when yo' do come, git on de fas'es' hoss yo' kin fin'; an' O, Lo'd, don' run ner gallop, but jest trot all roun' dis e'th, till des aw sinnehs is converted an' Massa Linkum's sojers whip all de secesh!" [40]

A Massachusetts soldier was amused by a prayer heard at a Negro revival in which the worshiper pleaded: "De good Lord take dese 'ere mourners & shake em over hell but dont lieff em go." This Yank also told of hearing one song with the lines:

> The devil's mad & I am glad—Glory Hallelujah!
> He's lost a soul he thought he had—Glory Hallelujah!

and another beginning:

Carrying a Log   Wearing a Placard

Bucking and Gagging

Drawings by Charles W. Reed from John D. Billings
Hard Tack and Coffee (Copyright, George M. Smith, Boston, 1888)

ARMY PUNISHMENT

A FRIENDLY GAME

Private J. H. Carpenter and comrades

Jesus said he'd come again
The devil's gone a howling.

In describing his reaction which, except for scoffers, must have been typical, he stated: "One of them would lead off and the rest join in the chorus at the top of their voices and though it made me laugh at first at the comical way they did it, yet I soon got over it and could join with them in spirit if not in words." [41]

A less reverent man from the Bay State gave his impression of another service: "We have been to the niger meeting tonight the Sprit mooved in one old lady and I guess it hurt her by . . . [the way] she hollered." [42]

Countless soldiers commented on the Negroes' accomplishments in music and dancing, and many an evening was enlivened by their impromptu performances about the campfire. An Illinois soldier wrote from Tennessee: "It would make you laugh yourself blind almost if you could see a lot of 'ebonics' congregated by moonlight or candlelight, one fiddling, another 'patting' (a mode of keeping time to music by patting with the hands & feet) and four or five dancing in their style." And a New Englander who apparently had paid to see minstrels at home reported from Virginia: "There were five negroes in our mess room last night, we got them to sing and dance! Great times. Negro concerts free of expense here . . . hope I shall not be obliged to leave." [43]

Even on the march soldiers were sometimes entertained by colored performers. After the campaign through Georgia a Minnesotan wrote his wife: "There were many comic occurrences on the Journey. At Shady Dale a large plantation about 35 miles West of Milledgeville there was 15 young Wenches came out and danced for every Regiment that passed the Brigade Band playing wile Each Brigade passed and the next one in turn taking its place. The way the[y] hoed down was caution and extremely ludicrous." He added: "We have a couple of little darkies with the Brigade that are called Tater Boys that can Beat anything in the Plan[t]ation dance I ever seen the[y] make their own music Singing the Melancholy Ya Ha all the time they are dancing." [44]

The attitude and demeanor of white Yanks toward the 200,000 Negroes who served in the Union Army deserves special mention. When enlistment of colored men first became an issue in Congress in the summer of 1862, the overwhelming majority of Union soldiers appear to have been against the proposal. The opposition of some was violent. A typical reaction was that registered by Sergeant Enoch T. Baker, a Pennsylvanian serving in Virginia, who in July 1862 wrote his wife:

Thair is a great controversy out hear about the nigger Question at present if they go to Sending them out hear to fight thay will get Enough of it for it Will raise a rebelion in the army that all the abolisionist this Side of hell Could not Stop the Southern Peopel are rebels to the government but they are White and God never intended a nigger to put white people Down if they would hang a few of the Speculators and leading politicians who are trying to make Presedents instead of good generals the War Wood Soon be over without the help of niggers.[45]

This Yank was averse to putting Negroes in uniform because he thought the measure unnecessary and especially because he saw in it a threat to white supremacy. His views were shared by countless Northerners in and out of the army. Others objected to arming the blacks because they thought them deficient in soldierly qualities. A Connecticut infantryman on hearing that colored regiments were being recruited wrote: "I think a drove of hogs would do better brought down here for we could eat them and the nigers we can't, the negroes are about as contrary as a hog since they have been free & as for fighting they wont be enclined that way I am afraid. I know they are all for getting out of the way when there is a battle afoot or any signs of it." [46]

Some were repelled by the prospect of having to serve in the same units with colored soldiers. This attitude was exemplified by some Kansas soldiers who, when an unusually dark-complexioned recruit joined their company in 1862, petitioned his transfer because "firstly we believe him to be a 'nigger'; secondly . . . he was . . . refused in several other companies." These men, while professing willingness to serve their country, declared that "to have one of the company . . . pointed out as a 'nigger' while on dress parade or guard is more than we like to be called upon to bear." [47]

Now and then a Yank talked of deserting when he heard that Negroes were coming into the army, but such threats rarely if ever were executed.

Opposition to colored soldiers subsided as recruiting progressed. One factor in this trend was the government's change in 1863 from hesitancy to aggressiveness in promoting Negro enlistments.[48] When white soldiers learned that high authorities were determined black men should be accepted and respected they tended to go along with the policy.

The fact that Negroes were used mainly for fatigue and garrison duties, thus relieving whites from these unpleasant chores, made many converts to Negro enlistment. Still others were won over by good reports of Negro performance under fire at Fort Wagner, Milliken's Bend and other engagements.

A considerable number of Yanks were moved to support the Negro soldier policy by the desire to secure commissions in colored units. Scores of enlisted men who never would have risen from the ranks in their own organizations found their way into the shoulder-strap fraternity through examination for commissions with the United States Colored Troops. By no means all who traveled this course were favorably disposed either toward the colored race or Negro soldiers, but a goodly portion were friendly to both.

Perhaps the most important influence of all in breaking down opposition to Negroes was the simple fact that Yanks grew accustomed to the sight of black men wearing the Federal uniform.

But it would be misleading to convey the impression that Negro soldiers won universal acceptance in the army. Many whites remained deeply antagonistic to the end of the war. An Ohio sergeant wrote from Beaufort, South Carolina, in January 1865: "The colored troops are very much disliked by our men & several affrays have taken place in town between them, in which the darkeys have always got the worst of it, two or three of them having been killed & several wounded." In New Orleans, colored soldiers occasionally were pounced on by white Yanks who stripped them of their clothing and forced them to return to their quarters naked. At Ship Island, Mississippi, white gunners on a boat (some of whose crew had recently been embroiled with the blacks), when ordered to support the advance of three colored companies, fired at the Negroes instead of the Rebels.[49]

Such instances of violence between white and black troops were matched, for the most part, by acts of genuine co-operation and friendship. Some Yanks, delighted by the government's decision to enlist the Negroes, sought earnestly to promote their well-being after they became a part of the armed forces. Among these was Rufus Kinsley of Vermont who, while serving in Louisiana in the early part of the war as a corporal in a white regiment, worked zealously for the improvement of the freedmen. In his spare time he taught scores of them the alphabet and on Sundays worked for their spiritual betterment. He also gave much attention to the care of the sick and needy. On one occasion he wrote: "In the education of the black is centered my hope for the redemption of the race and the salvation of my country."[50]

When the government began to organize Negro units Kinsley applied for a commission and was appointed lieutenant in the Second Regiment, Corps d'Afrique. In his new position he devoted himself unstintedly to making good soldiers and good citizens out of his men and to increasing his fitness to command them. On June 1, 1864, he wrote: "I have . . . [been] instructing as many of the soldiers as my time would allow, in the rudiments of an education. Have been very busy. Time has passed very pleasantly. No occasion to regret that I came here." [51]

Another consistent supporter of the colored folk, civilians as well as soldiers, was Henry Crydenwise of New York. His experience was similar to Kinsley's. After two years of enlisted service with white troops, marked by many acts of kindness toward the ex-slaves, he was in December 1863 commissioned captain of Company A, First Regiment, Corps d'Afrique (later the Seventy-third Regiment, United States Colored Troops). Shortly before receiving his captain's bars he wrote his parents:

I dont know what your feelings or prejudices may be in regard to colored troops. I am well aware that many are strongly prejudiced against colored soldiers and that with some I should loose caste by becoming an officer in a colored regiment. but I cannot think that the petty prejudices or even the frowns of others should deter us from persuing what we conceive to be a line of duty. The class of men who are engaged in this enterprise are certainly a superior class. Though there may be exceptions most of the officers of colored regiments are moral and intellectual men In organizing these regiments the Government is very careful to officer them with strictly moral men. and before one can get a position there he must pass a rigid examination and show testimonials of his good character. The association with such officers will be very pleasant. Then there is a system of instruction kept up in these regiments and the Government while it makes use of the negro in crushing out this rebellion also seeks to elevate and enlighten him that he may be prepared for the future which shall open before him Here then is a great field for Christian & philanthrophic labor. a field where great good may be accomplished. Then in a pecuniary view to one in humble circumstances like myself dependant upon my own hands for future support the prospect of permanent position at $120. or $130 per month is no small temtation By what I have written you will understand somewhat the motives which influence my choice. [52]

That the pecuniary motive was secondary in Crydenwise's case is attested both by his prior and subsequent conduct. He strove mightily to make his company a model of excellence, and had the satisfaction of twice having it commended for presenting the best appearance at regimental inspection. He never spoke disparagingly of his colored command. His culminating experience was the leading of his men in a charge at Blakely, Alabama, on the day of Lee's surrender. Of this engagement he wrote his homefolk:

O! My God how the rebs did sweep that line with those screeching, devilish shells & it seemed that nothing could live under such a fire. . . . The rebs still held that part of the works in our front & continued to fire upon us my boys wanted to go forward & capture it. But as my orders were to hold that line I told them to wait for orders. At that moment cheer after cheer went up from the line held by the colored troop & forward came the darkie boys. When my regt came up to where I was we all rushed togather for the rebel works & the old 73rd was the first to plant its flag upon that portion of the line captured by the colored troops. . . . I am proud Thankful & happy that my company did so well. Never have I known a company to do as well before under such circumstances.[53]

CHAPTER VI

THE DEPTHS OF SUFFERING

"I AM NOT very well and I do not think I ever will be again," wrote a New Yorker in December 1861, a few weeks after his arrival in Dixie. A year and a half later an Ohioan serving in Tennessee informed his parents: "Christopher Dimick was ded that makes 3 of the Dover boys that has died out of 42 and one killed. that is about the way there is more dies by sickness than gets killed." [1]

Statistics compiled by the Army Medical Department after the war confirm the observations of these soldiers as to the deadliness of disease.[2] In the Federal forces four persons died of sickness for every one killed in battle, and deaths from disease were twice those resulting from all other known causes.[3]

It is a sad fact of Civil War history that more men died of looseness of the bowels than fell on the field of combat. The best available figures show 57,265 deaths from diarrhea and dysentery as against 44,238 killed in battle.[4]

Disease was woefully prevalent. It was not uncommon for new regiments to have two thirds of their strength on the sick list, and among older units the ratio of one sick man to four or five well ones seems to have been fairly normal.

In the Union Army as a whole the heaviest incidence of disease came early in the war, and individual units suffered most during the first few months of their service. The sick rate for the year ending June 30, 1861, was 3,882 cases for each 1,000 soldiers and for the next annum 2,983. The trend thereafter was generally downward, the rate for the last year of the war being 2,273. The peak of sickness each year usually came during July and August. In 1862 two peaks were experienced, the second coming in October, owing to a large influx of new troops.[5]

Colored troops proved considerably more susceptible to disease than their white comrades. The average annual rate for whites was for each 1,000 of mean strength 2,435 cases of sickness and 53.4 deaths, while for Negroes the figures were respectively 3,299 and 143.4. To put it another way, each white soldier on the average was sick about 2½ times a year and each Negro about 3⅓ times; and the death rate from disease was nearly three times as great among Negro soldiers as among whites.[6]

Several factors contributed to the scourge of illness which bedeviled Federal camps. Basic among these was the failure to sift out unfit men at induction. This was especially true in the early part of the war. Of some 200 regiments investigated in the latter months of 1861 by the United States Sanitary Commission, 58 per cent were reported as having "had no pretence of a thorough inspection of recruits on enlistment," and in only 9 per cent "had there been a thorough inspection when or after they were mustered in." Not only did scores of weaklings enter the ranks under this loose system, but many men with hindering maladies, including hernia, varicose veins, tuberculosis and syphilis, donned uniforms and went hopefully to war.[7]

The associate secretary of the United States Sanitary Commission reported after an extensive visit to volunteer camps in the fall of 1861 that one tenth of the men in units observed by him "would be rejected on a thorough and rigid examination." Eventually most of these substandard specimens broke down and thus increased the burden of an already overloaded hospital system.[8]

Smallpox vaccination was known long before 1861, but the failure to make immunization a standard part of induction procedure led to many needless cases of this disease. Disregard of army regulations concerning both vaccination and physical examination was in large measure chargeable to the pre-eminent role of the states in the mobilization process. As a medical historian put it, "Regiments were raised by the various States and rushed to the front under the successive calls of the President for men without a thought of small pox or vaccination." A Sanitary Commission representative, who in late 1861 inspected thirteen Midwestern regiments stationed in Kentucky, found only one that had been "systematically vaccinated." About the same time the medical director of the Army of the Potomac reported some Eastern regiments with more than half of their men unprotected by vaccination.[9]

Ignorance of the cause of disease was, of course, a fundamental factor in epidemics and death. A veteran of the Union Medical Corps, contrasting in 1918 practices of the Civil War and World War I, stated: "In the Civil War we knew absolutely nothing of 'germs.' *Bacteriology*— the youngest and greatest science to aid in this conquest of death—*did not exist*. . . . Sanitation . . . was crude and unsatisfactory . . . research had not discovered any of the antitoxins nor the role of the insect world in spreading disease." [10]

Contaminated water sent thousands of men to the hospital. Troops in the vicinity of Cairo, a concentration point for Western forces, regularly drank the impure water of the Ohio and Mississippi rivers, and a like practice was followed throughout the army with rivers, creeks, ponds, springs and shallow wells constituting the principal sources.[11] Purification units were unknown. Medical authorities in some instances recommended that drinking water be boiled or filtered but the advice seems rarely to have been heeded.

The direful ignorance of water contamination even in supposedly informed circles was revealed by the following inspection report by the president of the United States Sanitary Commission:

The Mississippi water has a general reputation for wholesomeness. The Missouri mud, with which it is charged, in settling carries down whatever vegetable or animal substance may exist in the water and leaves it, though still colored, comparatively pure. The Ohio water, being more conveniently reached, is, however, chiefly used by the troops. They had all suffered diarrhoea from the use of this water, or from change. It took about a fortnight to accustom them to it. The surgeons were doubting the expediency of going into the use of the Mississippi water from fear that another change might produce another access of the same complaint.[12]

It is doubtful if the doctors received any help from their distinguished inspector in solving their problem.

Pitching of camps in swamps, poor provision for drainage and crowding together of tents occurred with shocking frequency. But far more injurious to health was the filth in which soldiers lived, especially in the early days of the conflict.[13] Latrines, or "sinks" as they were called in Civil War times, were standard camp fixtures, but often these were shallow trenches left uncovered for long periods of time and located so near the quarters as to subject the occupants to nauseous odors. Many Yanks from rural areas, accustomed at home to following the rule of convenience in answering nature's calls and shrinking from immodest exposure, declined using the sinks. Unfortunately the normal trend of camp life was in a back-to-nature direction; and some who at home had been fastidious in the observance of toilet practices, in the army became as indifferent as the most confirmed frontiersman.

An inspector of camps in the Washington vicinity in July 1861 reported: "In most cases the only sink is merely a straight trench some thirty feet long, unprovided with pole or rail; the edges are filthy, and the stench exceedingly offensive; the easy expedient of daily turning fresh earth into the trench being often neglected. . . . From the ammoniacal odor frequently perceptible in some camps it is obvious that men are allowed to void their urine, during the night, at least, wherever convenient." [14]

Garbage disposal left much to be desired. A survey of 200 regimental camps in the latter part of 1861 revealed that 26 per cent of them were "negligent and slovenly" in this respect, and 24 per cent "decidedly bad, filthy and dangerous." Among evils reported were: "Camp streets and spaces between the tents littered with refuse, food and other rubbish, sometimes in an offensive state of decomposition; slops deposited in pits within the camp limits or thrown out broadcast; heaps of manure and offal close to the camp." [15]

Neglect of personal cleanliness further darkened the picture. Army regulations prescribed daily washing of hands and faces, biweekly ablutions of the feet and complete baths once or twice a week. But few were the companies early in the war that complied fully with these provisions, and neglect was common in some units throughout the conflict. In 1861 men often went for weeks without bathing and without washing their clothing. For the latter, lack of a change of suits was sometimes given as an excuse.[16]

Inadequacy of clothing and shelter was also a factor in poor health. This was especially true of the first winter of the war, when production and supply lagged considerably behind the enormous needs resulting from rapid mobilization and when ruthless contractors so frequently defrauded the government with inferior materials. Inspectors during this period often noted a shortage of overcoats as well as insufficient shelter against cold and rain.

Exposure to the elements, while injurious enough, produced far less illness than did food. The ration specified in army regulations authorized both fresh and "desiccated" vegetables, and it was contemplated that regular allowances would be supplemented by purchases from company funds obtained by credits for unused portions of the issue.[17] But surpluses were commonly wasted instead of being applied to company funds, processed foods were spurned as unpalatable and fresh vegetables were hard to get. The net result was to confine camp fare largely to salt pork, bread and coffee. Yanks frequently supplemented commissary issues by purchases from sutlers and peddlers but since the standard items in stock were pies and cakes, or "pi-zan cakes" as the colored venders' cry was sometimes translated, the results were more harmful than helpful.[18] The widespread deficiency of vegetables and fruits not only helped swell the sick list but slowed down recovery from illness and wounds and increased mortality.

Despite persistent efforts by higher authorities to have food prepared in company quantity by experienced men detailed for the purpose, cooking was usually done by small groups or messes with each man taking his turn at the skillet. The results were deplorable, owing to ignorance, lack of sanitation and a propensity for frying everything in a sea of grease. Even the flour was commonly mixed with water and fried as flapjacks.[19] Culinary procedures improved with experience, but the general level of efficiency in food preparation remained lamentably low throughout the war.

As already implied, a basic factor underlying most unhealthful practices was incompetent leadership, especially on the regimental and company level. Discipline was especially poor during the early part of the war and to this circumstance, probably more than to any other, must be attributed the high tide of sickness which engulfed Federal camps in 1861 and 1862.

Volunteer officers, ignorant of their responsibilities and fearful of offending the men who elected them, were slow to lay down rules of sanitation and diet and even more reluctant to enforce them.[20]

The vital cog in the disciplinary system was the company commander. Initial concepts of this leader's role were based primarily on the militia system, in which the captain's duties were restricted largely to assembling his men on ceremonial occasions and leading them in parades. Hence, it was difficult for the captain in wartime to adjust to a situation which required him to become a father to his men—to live intimately with them, see that they bathed frequently, ate properly and reported to the surgeon when ill; and some captains, deeming such responsibilities and relationships unbecoming to their position, refused to accept them.[21] Only after much bearing down from above, considerable weeding out of incompetents and extensive instruction in the hard school of experience did the idea take hold that close attention to detail was not degrading and that a loose disciplinarian was an enemy rather than a friend of his men.

Eventually, and by a gradual process, a substantial portion of officers and men came to realize what the astute Frederick Law Olmsted had proclaimed in 1861: that there was "no disease so destructive to an army as laxity of discipline." [22] The decline in the sick rate which paralleled the rooting of this concept was no accident. It was regrettable for all concerned that the close correlation between discipline and health was

"WILD BLUE YONDER" BOYS OF THE 1860s
Cavalrymen of the Army of the Potomac

PORTRAIT OF A ZOUAVE
Drawing by Charles F. Johnson

not sooner understood and when at last comprehended not more generally followed by remedial action.

Listing of factors contributing to the prevalence of disease would be incomplete without reference to medical personnel and administration. The war was begun with a pitifully small staff, heavy at the top with old men who had attained their eminence solely by virtue of seniority. The system was based on peacetime conditions and was lamentably slow in gearing itself to the emergency needs of a great war, the greatest by far that the world had ever known.[23]

Deficiencies and delays were by no means the exclusive fault of the Medical Department. Congress held appropriations to miserly limits, and high army leaders sometimes displayed amazing unconcern and ignorance when reform measures were urged on them. But that the top leadership in the medical organization was notoriously weak during the war's first year is beyond question. Only after the death of one Surgeon General and the retirement of another was a man of real ability, William A. Hammond, placed at the head of the medical establishment; and his appointment, in April 1862, over the heads of less competent seniors, required the utmost exertion of the politically powerful United States Sanitary Commission. Even so, the pressure was not great enough to enable the new regime to function as it should. Hammond was defeated in his effort to appoint medical inspectors on a merit basis, and in less than a year and a half difficulties with Secretary of War Stanton drove him from his position.[24]

Hammond, though laboring under difficulty—some of which was caused by his own lack of tact—accomplished wonders, and by contrast brought into bold relief the weakness of his predecessors. Under his able administration, field surgeons and commanders for the first time received from the highest medical office effective advice and stimulating assistance. This, together with increases in personnel, selection of capable men for key positions—the most outstanding of whom was Jonathan Letterman, appointed Medical Director of the Army of the Potomac in June 1862—and important reforms in organization and procedure led to decided improvement in prevention and treatment of disease.[25]

Personnel weaknesses at the top of the medical organization in the early days were matched by deficiences even more grievous on the lowest level. In each regiment a surgeon and assistant surgeon were authorized and it was to these officers that the men looked immediately for medical care. The surgeons and their assistants, like other officers in volunteer organizations, were as a general rule commissioned by state governors.

Many appointments were based on political influence rather than on professional accomplishment and, while most of the regimental surgeons appear to have been well-meaning, a considerable number were utterly incompetent.[26] Data compiled by the United States Sanitary Commission on 200 regimental surgeons in 1861 indicated that 129 of them had discharged their duties with "competence, . . . creditable energy and earnestness" and 25 with "tolerable attentiveness," while 19 were reported as "negligent and inert."[27] In July 1861 an inspector reporting a visit to a volunteer regiment near Washington stated: "There is one surgeon and one assistant, father and son, who were appointed by the colonel and have not been examined by any medical board. . . . [I was told] that the former had been a barber . . . and an occasional cupper and leecher, and had no medical degree. The son's medical education was also doubted. . . . On examining the file of prescriptions at the hospital, I discovered that they were rudely written and . . . consisted chiefly of tartar emetic, ipecacuanha, and epsom salts, hardly favorable to the cure of the prevailing diarrhoea and dysenteries."[28]

Incompetence was even more prevalent among the contract physicians who were hired as occasion required to supplement the regularly commissioned medical staff.[29]

Surgeons who met desired professional standards were handicapped on first entering the service by ignorance of army procedure. Many regiments limped along with insufficient medical supplies through the peaks of illness which commonly followed induction simply because the doctors did not know what items were stocked by purveyors or how to make out the necessary requisitions.[30]

The life of a regimental surgeon was a trying one. This fact, coupled with easy access to liquor, caused some doctors to lean too heavily on the bottle. A division medical director reported after Fort Donelson that the senior medical officer of the Fifty-second Indiana Regiment, "an efficient and skillful surgeon when sober, was so much under the influence of liquor for twenty-four hours as to be incapable of discharging the responsible duties of his office." During the Atlanta campaign an assistant surgeon in the Army of the Tennessee was dismissed from the service "for habitual drunkenness while on duty and for leaving his command and abandoning the sick and wounded men of his regiment while on an active campaign and in the face of the enemy."[31]

An Ohio surgeon abandoned fifty-three sick men of his regiment in January 1862 and went North with his wife. The sick were left without a change of clothing and not "a particle of medicine, food, delicacies . . . & about half blankets enough." Before his departure the surgeon became so intoxicated that "he went staggering through the camp . . . with one man on each side of him." He was dismissed from the service ten months later, but in other instances drunkards of the Medical Corps were permitted to resign or had their offenses whitewashed.[32]

It is not meant to leave the impression that Union doctors in general were an incompetent, drunken lot. The majority were undoubtedly men of solid ability and character. It was inevitable that among the more than 5,000 surgeons and assistant surgeons who served in volunteer regiments some sorry specimens should be found, and, since misdeeds tend to attract more attention than everyday devotion to duty, care must be exercised in judging them and their work. Even in the war's first year many good doctors could be found for each worthless sot, and the passing of time brought steady improvement. Some incompetents resigned or were dismissed, while others by diligent application were converted into creditable practitioners.[33]

Heroism of the highest order was displayed by some of the surgeons. Indeed, the martial spirit was so strong in a few that in the heat of battle they swapped scalpel for musket and by so doing won official commendation.[34] Medical Corps casualties showed that 42 were killed in battle, 83 were wounded, 290 died of disease or accident and 4 died in Confederate prisons. Doctoring in the Union Army was dangerous business.[35]

Whatever their abilities, doctors were so frequently held in low esteem by officers and men as to lessen their usefulness in combating disease. Typical of the attitude of many officers was that registered by Captain E. G. Abbott of the Second Massachusetts Regiment in December 1862: "I pray the regiment may improve," he wrote his father, "but with our present surgeon I see no prospect of good medical attendance in case of sickness. He is a jackass—a fool—and an ignorant man—three quarters of the sickness could have been prevented by a good physician." [36]

Enlisted men were usually less restrained in their comment on surgeons, whom they variously nicknamed as "sawbones," "opium pills" and "quinine." [37] An Illinois soldier wrote disgustedly on June 7, 1861: "The Doctors are no acount the[y] cannot cure the Ague and be with the patient all the time." A comrade of the same regiment observed: "Our doctor knows about as much as a ten year old boy." Members of a New York regiment dubbed their doctor "Long John the Shoemaker" in tribute to the profession which they claimed he followed before joining their organization.[38]

An Ohioan, plagued by mud and mosquitoes near Vicksburg and alarmed by the tide of sickness, in March 1863 wrote in plaintive wrath: "The docters is no a conte . . . hell will bea filde with doters and offersey when this war is over." Another Ohioan in May 1864 reported a recent experience near Chattanooga: "The surgeon insisted on Sending me to the hospital for treatment. I insisted on takeing the field and prevailed—thinking that I had better die by rebel bullets than Union Quackery." [39]

The note stressed by all of these soldiers was inefficiency. Others based their objections on inhumanity. "Our Regimental doctor has no more respect for a sick soldier than I would have for a good dog," observed a Tennessee Unionist in his diary; "no not near so much, for if my dog was sick or wounded I would spend some little time in relieving him. Our doctor will not." A Massachusetts soldier reporting the death of a young comrade stated: "He never received humane treatment from the docters & I believe they thought no more of his death than they would of that of a sheep." [40]

Much of the complaint against doctors was nothing more than a manifestation of the soldiers' chronic bent for growling and was based on no deep antipathy. Moreover, some of the protest came from deadbeats whose shirking designs had been thwarted. But aversion to doctors, whether real or feigned, kept many men away from sick call who if promptly attended, even by less than perfect surgeons, might have avoided serious illness or dangerous complications. The all-too-prevalent attitude, "If a fellow has to [go to the] Hospital, you might as well say good bye," as expressed by one Yank, undoubtedly sent many soldiers prematurely to their graves.[41]

Disease began its onslaught soon after units were organized. Sometimes attacks approached epidemic proportions just as regiments moved to the seat of war, thus causing unusual suffering. In August 1861 an Indiana regiment arrived in Washington with thirty-six ill men isolated in a hot, dirty car, the toilet of which was "beyond use or endurance." These men had been deprived of medical treatment because the surgeon's chest was unavailable in the baggage car, and their only nourishment for twenty-four hours had been hard bread and water. Crowded conditions in the capital forced the men to remain in the car for the rest of the night while the surgeons went in search of medicine and quarters. Fortunately a Sanitary Commission agent, on a routine visit to the station, found the men early the next morning. He had the car cleaned up and distributed tea, bread and butter among the sick.[42]

In its initial attacks illness fell with unusual vehemence on rural units. Prior exposure to contagious disease and a more favorable attitude toward vaccination gave greater immunity to city-reared soldiers. Too, men of urban background were more adaptable psychologically to army life and, except for slum dwellers, were generally more sensitive to sanitary conditions. A Pennsylvania officer stationed near Washington observed in 1862:

Doctor Fulton today reported Bell's camp among others for bad sanitary arrangements. It is strange to see Bell's Company, 83 strong, rough back-woodsmen with 15 men sick, several cases serious, while Widdis' just along side, delicate, city bred men 85 strong have but 3 sick men, all light cases. The difference is no doubt mainly due to the great care Widdis forces his men to take in cleansing and airing their tents and blankets and ditching and policing his street, while the country officers almost entirely neglect all this.[43]

The disease which usually struck first in epidemic proportions was measles. Medical reports show that attacks usually came within a few months of a unit's organization and recurred after each large addition of recruits.[44] Among new regiments cases numbered from twenty to three hundred, the principal factor in the variation being the proportion of country troops. A private in a recently organized rural regiment wrote his parents in December 1861: "The measles went through our Reg. in such a manner that out of 560 men only some 250 are on duty." [45]

Measles showed a preference for the winter months. Ordinarily it ran its course in three or four weeks. Usually it was mild, but undue exposure and improper care frequently led to pneumonia and other serious complications. Private John McMeekin wrote his mother from near Vicksburg in February 1863: "We burred Simon Groves yestery he dide with the mesels that is what kilde the moste of our boys thay wod take the measels and haft to lay out in the rane and storm and thay wod only laste a bot 2 days." The disease was considerably more prevalent and more fatal among colored troops than among whites.[46]

"We are more afraid of ague here than the enemy," wrote an Illinois Yank from Cairo two weeks after Sumter's fall.[47] The observation was an apt one, for malaria, popularly known as ague or "the shakes," was distressingly common from the beginning to the end of the war. The malady's prevalence was due in no small part to ignorance of its cause, the accepted idea being that it resulted from poisonous vapors emanating at night from swamps. Some soldiers attempted to close their quarters to the miasma and incidentally they shut out the mosquitoes, but in so doing they made the atmosphere unhealthfully stuffy.

Mosquito bars were used by some, but the protection sought was against bites rather than the malaria that followed. In diary after diary the sad sequence was recorded of units arriving in low Southern areas, such as Baton Rouge, Ship Island and Key West, the appearance of clouds of mosquitoes and then in due time the outbreak of what the surgeons called "simple intermittent fever."

One out of every four cases of illness reported in the Union Army was malarial in character. The disease was so common, indeed, that a standard greeting in some camps was "Have you had the shakes?" If the vibrations of the more than one million cases of malaria that plagued the men in blue could have been synchronized the South might have been shaken into submission.[48]

The malarial graph prepared by the Army Medical Department shows peaks in the late summer or early fall and troughs in midwinter. Heaviest incidence of the disease came in August 1863.[49]

Less prevalent than malaria but far more deadly was typhoid. Owing to confusion in terminology, figures on this disease are not so reliable or meaningful as for most others. But "camp fevers" or "continued fevers," undoubtedly typhoid in the overwhelming majority of instances, comprised about one fortieth of total sickness and caused one fourth of all deaths from disease. Prevalency among white and colored troops was about the same, but the mortality rate for Negroes was 19.24 per thousand cases as against 13.27 for whites.[50]

Typhoid, like malaria, had its peak in summer or fall and its low in winter. The highest rate of prevalence during the war came in November 1861 following a rapid increase over the prior six months. It is noteworthy that during this period the troops on whom statistics were based increased from 16,000 to 300,000. No more striking commentary could be found on the poor state of discipline and sanitation among the first volunteers than is afforded by the sharp and lofty ascent of the typhoid frequency curve in the war's initial period.[51]

General trends become more appalling when viewed on the level of regiments and individuals. A colonel stationed in Kentucky reported to General George H. Thomas in December 1861: "Typhoid fever is striking our men a heavy blow; 233 of my regiment now down, and dying daily. My loss is greater here than during all the preceding service. Unless we are moved, the regiment will soon become greatly weakened. . . . We would rather die in battle than on a bed of fever." [52] From Louisiana in August 1863 the soldier-novelist John William De Forest wrote of companies appearing on dress parade with only fourteen men, and a little later his gifted pen spelled out the distressing details: "Two-thirds of the regiment are buried or in hospital. It is woful to see how nearly destitute of comforts and of attendance the sick are. They cannot be kept in their wretched bunks, but stagger about, jabbering and muttering insanities, till they lie down and die in their ragged, dirty uniforms. . . . We can distinctly hear the screams and howls of the patients in their crazy fits. It is woful to see a battalion of four hundred choice veterans thus ruined in a few weeks." Still later he reported: "Swamp fever has turned our fine regiment into a sickly, dispirited, undisciplined wreck. . . . Forty-two deaths in forty-two days; barely two hundred and twenty-five men left for duty; and most of those staggering skeletons covered with fever sores; if they were at home they would be in bed and asking the prayers of the congregation." [53] Little wonder that the well and the near-well turned to whisky for solace!

An Illinois private wrote from Camp Butler in November 1861: "Tiford fever is Rageing here verry much their has been several deaths of it . . . they hardley ever get over it." [54] Here, as in many other camps, alarm and depression were enhanced by the frequent carrying away of fever victims by burial details to the mournful cadence of muffled drums beating out the dead march.[55]

Yellow fever, while causing considerable apprehension from time to time, attained serious proportions in only three instances, the worst outbreak occurring at New Bern, North Carolina, in the fall of 1864 with 763 cases and 303 deaths. Of scarlet fever, only about 700 cases were reported for the entire war.[56]

Figures on certain other diseases of lesser prevalence during the period May 1, 1861—June 30, 1866, are tabulated below:

Disease	Cases			Deaths		
	White	Colored	Total	White	Colored	Total
Rheumatism	254,738	32,125	286,863	475	235	710
Pneumonia	61,202	16,133	77,335	14,738	5,233	19,971
Scurvy	30,714	16,217	46,931	383	388	771
Tuberculosis	13,499	1,331	14,830	5,286	1,211	6,497

This table shows that, except for pneumonia where the difference was not so striking, the diseases listed were far more fatal among colored than among white troops.[57]

Shortly after joining the army a Midwestern rustic informed his homefolk: "There is but one kind of Sickness here, and that is the diarhoea, and everybody has it." While some allowance usually has to be made for exaggeration when soldiers comment on their woes, it is entirely possible that this Yank was telling the truth. Certainly diarrhea or dysentery in one form or another made a complete run of some of the early camps, and the Yank who went through the war without a siege of flux —a term applied by doctors to bowel disorders in general—was indeed exceptional. Innumerable cases never came to the attention of surgeons because of widespread indulgence in self-treatment, but even so, more cases were reported of flux than of any other disease and no malady caused more deaths.[58]

No other ailment was so frequently mentioned in soldier letters and diaries. "My bowels trouble me a great deal," wrote a Massachusetts sergeant from Harrison's Landing, Virginia, in July 1862. A New Yorker in a diary comment of the previous year was more specific: "On as Corp. of the Guard . . . sick with diarhea. Sickest I ever was. My bowels moved 18 times in 3 hours." [59]

Various euphemisms were coined for the malady, the most popular of which was "the quickstep." Soldiers serving in the Old Dominion reported the "Virginia Quickstep"; those in the Volunteer State, the "Tennessee Quickstep"; and so on down through the list of states in which Union camps were found.[60]

Like most other diseases, diarrhea and dysentery struck most heavily during the early months of the conflict, the wartime high coming in midsummer 1861. The general pattern thereafter was a declining succession of summer peaks and winter lows, the one exception being a slightly higher rate in July 1864 than in the previous summer. This variation was no doubt attributable to the long, strenuous campaigns in Northern Virginia, before Atlanta, along Red River and in various other areas.[61]

Statistics compiled by the Medical Department show for the period May 1861—July 30, 1866, a total of 1,739,135 cases of diarrhea and dysentery with 57,265 deaths. These figures are obviously low, owing to the previously noted tendency of soldiers not to report bowel disorders and occasional crediting to other causes of death for which diarrhea and dysentery were responsible.[62]

Bowel diseases became increasingly deadly with the continuance of the war, owing to the cumulative tendency toward chronic conditions. The ratio of deaths to army strength during the last year of the war was more than five times that of the first.[63]

Diarrhea and dysentery were more prevalent among colored troops than among whites, and decidedly more fatal. During the year ending June 30, 1864—the first for which satisfactory figures on Negroes are available—the annual ratio of deaths per thousand of mean strength among colored soldiers was 43.54 and among whites only 15.78. For the next year the respective figures were 36.29 and 21.29.[64]

Medicine was in a relatively undeveloped state during the Civil War.[65] For this reason, treatment of illnesses in the Union Army often appears absurd to one accustomed to modern practice. Archaic concepts of the 1860s are strikingly illustrated by a statement of J. S. Newberry, one of the most eminent medical scholars of the period, following a visit to Western camps in 1861: "Bowel complaints . . . might still further be reduced," he reported, "by the general adoption of the habit of wearing flannel body bandages or stomach belts, of which there is a large number [on hand]." [66]

Diarrhea victims frequently had their bowels further irritated by heavy drafts of whisky and repeated doses of salts or calomel, though many doctors discountenanced such procedures and followed milder practices. Opium was widely used in combating dysentery and some chronic cases were treated with strychnine. Other medicaments for bowel disorders were turpentine, castor oil, camphor, ipecacuanha, laudanum and blue pills (blue mass) of mercury and chalk.[67]

Whisky and quinine was the standard treatment for malaria, but clinical records show use of a wide variety of other remedies, including iodide of potassium, sulphuric acid, syrup of wild cherry, blue pills, morphine, ammonia, iron, cod-liver oil, soda, sweet spirits of niter, cream of tartar and cinnamon.[68] Combinations in which these were used, as well as the effects, may be illustrated by a chills-and-fever case in the Twenty-ninth Michigan Regiment. Treatment began in quarters on October 10, 1864, with "eight grains of blue pill and a Seidlitz powder," which produced a bowel movement but caused nausea and vomiting. The next day the patient was taken to the hospital. Clinical records give his subsequent history as follows:

On admission he had fever, anorexia, great thirst, offensive breath, white furred tongue, constipated bowels and headache . . . pulse 120, respiration 30. Sweet spirits of nitre and extract of ipecacuanha, barley-water and cream of tartar were given, with a Dover's powder at bedtime;

next day quinine was administered. The fever, headache and constipation continued, and on the 14th the patient was delirious during the greater part of the day. Eight grains each of calomel and rhubarb were given, followed by a saline cathartic, which moved the bowels. Next day he was conscious, his pulse regular and slow. Tea, toast, soups and panada were given. After this he improved in condition; but on the 25th he had symptoms of cerebral congestion, which were relieved by cold to the head and mustard to the feet. These attacks recurred during the early part of November, but by avoiding excitement and errors of diet they ceased to trouble him. On October 31 Fowler's solution was given in fluid extract of cinchona and continued for three weeks.

Presumably the patient recovered and was returned to duty.[69]

For typhoid, one surgeon gave his remedy as "blue pill and quinine," while another reported: "Treatment is alterative, tonic and stimulating by blue mass, carbonate of ammonia, turpentine, quinine and brandy." [70] The methods of these two surgeons seem fairly representative. In coping with typhoid, as in treating diseases in general, army doctors relied heavily on stimulants and purges. Resort to calomel became so excessive in the opinion of Surgeon General Hammond that he issued a circular in May 1863 striking that medicine from the supply table of the army.[71]

Reactions of the men to army medical treatment, as might be expected, was predominantly unfavorable. One Yank who rose to the rank of major recorded his impressions after the war:

The regular prescriptions were numbered six, nine and eleven, which were blue pill, quinine, and vinum. We soon learned that "vinum" meant either wine or brandy. I have seen men count from right to left, "six, nine, eleven—six, nine, eleven—six, nine, eleven," and step into the line just where "eleven" would strike. It was a sure thing, since the surgeon gave in regular order, as the men filed past him, something as follows: "Well, what's the matter with you?" "I don't know, Doctor, I've got an awful pain in my bowels; guess I've got the chronic diarrhoea." "Let's see your tongue! Give him number six! Next, what's the matter with you?" "I was took with an awful griping pain in my bowels —guess I've got the chronic diarrhoea." "Give him number nine! Next, what ails you?" "I've g-g-got an almighty b-b-bellyache, g-g-guess I've got the chronic d-d-diarrhoea." "Run out your tongue! Give him number eleven!" [72]

Another soldier wrote while serving in Virginia: "A man might as well die as 2 go through the rounds for [he is] . . . stufed with all kinds of poison & then Sent 2 the Invalid Corps . . . & if he is not able 2 do duty there, he is stufed with Poison agen 2 months longer. . . . I had rather be here 10 years than 2 run the risk for I know what the medicine is they give, dont make [any] difference what ails you the same dose cures all blue Pills & other stufe as bad." [73]

"He prescribes 'salts' to everbody," complained a Pennsylvanian of his doctor, while a Connecticut Yank who had been on the sick list for three days wrote his sisters: "The first day Dr. gave me a powder that came very near turning my stomach inside out and today he gave me 20 drops of Aromatic Sulforic Acid 3 times a day; that goes better. . . . I will inclose one of my powders. It will cure any ails that flesh is heir to, from a sore toe to the brain fever." A third soldier noted in his diary: "Sick did nothing went to Dr he gave me a powder wonder it want a pill." [74]

Sometimes Yanks went to their captains for treatment rather than risk the doctor's cures. Members of Edward S. Redington's Company D, Twenty-eighth Wisconsin, received the benefit of an original remedy, hit upon by their captain in circumstances and with results stated thus by him:

Have a slight attack of Helena Quickstep, but feel much better tonight and think I shall be all right in the morning. I have been taking quinine, pain-killer, and whiskey and my head feels rather large and rings like a kettle. The way they all got mixed was in this way: a bottle of quinine and pain-killer got broken in my medicine chest; the quinine soaking up the pain-killer, so I put them in another bottle and filled up with whiskey. A more villianous compound to swallow never passed a man's lips. I have given several of the boys out of the same bottle and it has always cured them without fail. I think I shall apply for a patent on it as a cure for all the ills the flesh is heir to from colic to cholera.[75]

As previously noted, Yanks often chose to be their own doctors, and most who treated themselves claimed good results. One attributed robust health to keeping himself "dosed full of red pepper." Another cured his diarrhea with a patented product known as "Radways Ready Relief." The practice of one recuperating from "Yaller Janders," as he put it, is indicated by a plea to the homefolk to "Please send me some Flower and some salurates and Rusey save." [76]

While the confidence of soldiers in their own curative efforts was undoubtedly exaggerated, still it cannot be denied that owing to the backwardness of medical science, shortage of supplies and professional incompetence Yanks sometimes were as well off with home remedies as with the surgeon's services.

Deficient facilities combined with exigencies of the service to produce instances of unusual suffering among the sick. The period after Shiloh affords an example of extreme misery in the West. Medical supplies greatly depleted by battle requirements could not be immediately replenished because of confusion and lack of transportation. Disorganization ensuant to fighting, and exposure to the unfavorable weather which followed, led to an enormous swelling of the sick rolls. Despite this situation, Halleck in late April decided to move toward Corinth, and as a first step he ordered transfer of the sick to Hamburg, about six miles up the river from the Shiloh battleground. The sad consequences were described by Surgeon Charles McDougall who took over at this time as medical director: "Before the medical officers and attendants arrived at Hamburgh, the sick were pouring in from all quarters, and the hospital boats on the river were fast filling up. . . . For five days from morning until night, the unfortunate sick were thrown on the bank of the river in parties of from two to fifty, and in most instances, without any report in their cases, other than that they were sick." [77]

Suffering was enhanced by the shortage of doctors and attendants since regimental surgeons and their assistants had to join their units for the projected advance. Surgeon McDougall did the best he could with the three or four assistants available, but until receipt of additional help and supplies the woes of the sick were terrible.[78]

A similar circumstance marked McClellan's campaign of 1862 on the Virginia peninsula. When the forward movement was ordered after capture of Yorktown, regimental surgeons left their sick by the hundreds on the riverbank. Here the unfortunate men lay for days in poorly placed tents or completely exposed to sun and rain, without adequate attendance or food until boats came to remove them.[79]

Those who became ill during the subsequent campaign against Richmond suffered much from exposure to the frequent rain, shortage of food and medicine and lack of attention. When the army retired to Harrison's Landing after the Seven Days' battles, the plight of the ill, who increased greatly in number as a result of the hard campaign, became even worse.[80]

Other peaks of suffering were experienced during the Perryville campaign in 1862 when defective planning and rapid movement resulted in shameful neglect; the operations against Vicksburg early in 1863 when Grant's army was bedeviled by mud, mosquitoes and despondency; and the offensive efforts against Richmond of May and June 1864 when sustained fighting and enormous casualties created excessive burdens for medical authorities.[81] But, in general, care of the sick improved with the progress of the war.[82]

The same may be said of the care of the wounded, though battle casualties as a rule suffered more than the sick. In early engagements the wounded often had to get to hospitals under their own power or lie for long periods without succor. Commitment to medical care was by no means a guarantee of relief, for often during the war's first years hospitals were crowded, poorly run, ill equipped, dirty dens of butchery and horror.[83]

Several factors contributed to this sad situation. Basic among them were the lethargy and lack of vision which have already been noted as prevailing among responsible authorities, both in and out of the Medical Department. Realization was slow in dawning that a great war calling for swift and far-reaching adjustment was at hand. When the idea did begin to take hold, poor planning, competition for facilities and jealous clinging to prerogative often hamstrung efforts to meet the emergency.[84]

Much unnecessary suffering was caused by slowness in providing hospitals. At the outbreak of the war the only installations for treatment of the wounded were regimental hospitals consisting usually of one or more tents situated at the rear during combat and staffed by the regimental surgeon; the assistant surgeon normally followed the troops as they went into action.[85] When these facilities soon proved inadequate, general hospitals were established in cities and towns. The first general hospitals were improvised from schools, churches and other large buildings, expanded when necessary by erection of tents in the yards. To these makeshift affairs, manned by soldier details and volunteer nurses, came wounded from regimental hospitals or directly from the field of action. Provision for sanitation and comfort usually left much to be desired.[86]

Typical of early institutions was the Alexandria Hospital in which wounded from First Manassas were treated. Located in an old seminary this establishment was described thus in late July 1861:

It is an irregular structure, and badly adapted to hospital purposes. Its halls and stairways are narrow and abrupt, and many of its wards small and difficult of access. Its immediate precincts are damp . . . and the wood-work of its piazzas and sheds is rapidly decaying. Ventilation is even now very defective and an unhealthy odor pervades the building. The latter is due in a measure to the fact that troops recently quartered in the building, had been allowed to accumulate filth in some of the upper rooms and the cellar. . . . There being no in-door water-closets or baths, the same necessity for conveying close-stools through the house induces the risk that obtains in the Union Hotel and other Hospitals. . . . There is no dead-house. This Hospital now contains ninety-six patients.[87]

During McClellan's peninsula campaign, barracks in the vicinity of Washington and Baltimore, recently vacated by units moving to the front, were adapted for hospitalization of the flood of casualties pouring in from Virginia. These facilities were intended merely as makeshifts but many of them remained in use for the rest of the war.[88]

Importunities of wide-awake medical officers like Letterman and Hammond and pressure from the Sanitary Commission eventually caused the government to undertake erection of pavilion hospitals on the order of types developed in the Crimean War. The first hospitals of this model were completed in the spring of 1862 in Western Virginia and in Washington.[89]

These and similar hospitals built later in the year were not without structural defects, but improvements came with increasing experience. The basic type proved so satisfactory that it was followed in designing the famous Letterman General Hospital of Spanish-American War times and the "A" and "B" hospitals of World War I.[90]

Implementation of new developments, however, was generally slow. Not until July 1864 did the War Department get around to issuing comprehensive instructions embodying improved practices for guidance of the Quartermaster Department in building general hospitals. This was too late to be of much use.[91] All too many Yanks who went to general hospitals had to be treated in improvised and inadequately equipped facilities.

But the worst suffering was usually experienced before arrival at general hospitals. During the first year of the war, and to a considerable extent thereafter, wounded were collected on the battlefield by musicians, soldiers temporarily detailed from the line and self-appointed aides who frequently were shirkers. These men had little or no training for their duties and control over them was haphazard and ineffective.[92]

Wounded were removed by litter, crude ambulances or wagons to regimental hospitals where surgeons rendered first aid and operated on the most urgent cases—which usually meant amputation. The next step, early in the war, was evacuation to general hospitals by ambulance, wagon, train or boat. As the war progressed brigade and division hospitals were established, first informally and then by higher authority, as intermediate institutions.[93]

This system worked poorly. Transportation of the wounded was a quartermaster function and medical authorities often were unable to secure the needed ambulances, boats and other equipment.[94] Despite the vigorous protest of surgeons, ambulances often were used as personal conveyances for line and supply officers; and sometimes during evacuation crises quartermaster authorities peremptorily diverted to other service boats that had been fitted at great labor and expense for transportation of the wounded.[95]

Volunteer state agencies sometimes complicated the situation by appearing on the scene, as at Shiloh, with boats and medicines reserved for the use of soldiers from specific areas. These well-meaning efforts played into the hands of skulkers who, once aboard a locally sponsored transport and in the hands of friends, headed home for indefinite sojourns. The evil became so great in the West that Grant once issued an order forbidding removal of the wounded of his command beyond Memphis.[96]

The inadequacy of the system as it existed in the first part of the war may well be illustrated by some typical experiences. After First Manassas many men with bullet holes in their legs walked over twenty miles to Washington without prior treatment. A volunteer surgeon abandoned by his supposed helpers at Ball's Bluff had to force soldiers at the point of his revolver to aid in the removal of wounded; even so, many lives were lost for lack of evacuation facilities. At the battle of Belmont in November 1861, many wounded suffered prolonged exposure and neglect because the only transportation furnished the medical authorities by the quartermaster consisted of "two or three ordinary army wagons." [97]

After Shiloh, Grant's medical director, J. H. Brinton, told of "thousands of human beings . . . wounded and lacerated in every conceivable manner, on the ground, under a pelting rain, without shelter, without bedding, without straw to lay upon, and with but little food . . . the circumstances . . . were fearful, and the agonies of the wounded were beyond all description. They were, moreover, fearfully increased by the dearth of those nourishments and stimulants essential to relieve the shock of injury." [98]

Brinton attributed the unusual suffering mainly to lack of ambulances and medicine. The Army of the Ohio, coming by forced march from Nashville, had been compelled to leave most of their medical equipment behind, and in the Army of the Tennessee long-standing and oft-repeated requisitions remained unfilled because, as Brinton put it, "the medical department of the United States army had not yet freed itself from that system of blind routine," which, while adequate in peace, "failed utterly to meet the necessities of a gigantic war." [99]

During McClellan's peninsula campaign the story of Shiloh was in a measure repeated, though suffering was to some extent reduced owing to more ample supplies. At Seven Pines or Fair Oaks the need of a regularly constituted ambulance corps, trained ahead of time in its duties, was again brought into bold relief. According to an assistant surgeon who was there, "The bands of the various regiments proved utterly worthless in bringing off the wounded, behaving with the utmost cowardice, and required more persons to watch and see that they did their duty than their services were worth. As a natural consequence of this, whenever a man fell out of the ranks wounded four and sometimes six of his comrades would fall out for the purpose of carrying him away, thus seriously depleting the ranks and affording opportunity to the skulkers and cowards to sneak away." [100]

Eventually the wounded of Seven Pines arrived at the field hospitals, were treated and then carried to a depot a half mile to the rear for transfer by rail to points of embarkation. But for some reason the trains were slow in arriving, and suffering soldiers, their wounds teeming with maggots "as though a swarm of bees had settled" on them, "lay by the hundreds on either side of the railway track . . . exposed to a drenching rain . . . shivering from the cold, calling for water, food, and dressings . . . the most heart-rending spectacle. Many died from this exposure, and others prayed for death to relieve them from their anguish." [101]

Misery did not cease with removal, for on the peninsula as elsewhere during this period, wounded transported by rail "were placed in common burden cars, where, like so many sheep, jarred and jolted by every movement . . . without proper food, clothing or attention, they often passed hours and even days in indescribable agony." [102] Not until the autumn of 1862 were specially equipped hospital cars made available in anything like adequate numbers. [103]

After the Seven Days' battles, many wounded were forced to lie on the wharves for unduly long periods, owing to failure of the Quartermaster Department to provide needed boats. [104]

At Second Manassas confusion in arrangements, failure of the commanding general to inform medical authorities of his movements, and shameless behavior on the part of ambulance drivers led to deplorable neglect and suffering of the wounded, hundreds of whom lay on the battlefield for days without sufficient food and attention. Of the ambulance drivers the surgeon in charge of evacuation stated: "It was with the greatest difficulty that I could put a reasonable limit to their stealing from my commissary and hospital stores. . . . Very few would assist in placing the wounded in their ambulances; still fewer could be induced to assist in feeding them or giving them water. Some were drunk; many were insubordinate; others when detected with provisions or stores would not surrender them until compelled to by physical force." [105]

Once they got to Washington, where they flocked in the retreat, few of the drivers could be persuaded to return to the battlefield. As a last resort, five days after the battle a train consisting of "about one hundred hacks, forty omnibuses, wagons, and other vehicles" was dispatched from Washington to Centerville to bring in the wounded. The jolting and jarring of these crude conveyances must have brought indescribable agony to soldiers already miserable from nearly a week of torture and neglect.[106]

At Perryville terrible suffering was caused by Buell's refusal to permit surgeons to carry their ordinary stock of supplies and by the Quartermaster Department detaining for two weeks at Bardstown a shipment of medical stores sent out by the purveyor from Louisville.[107]

Unusual misery befell the wounded in a number of subsequent engagements, especially at Gettysburg where Union facilities already heavily strained were overtaxed by the responsibility of caring for several thousand Confederates left behind in Lee's retreat, and at Chattanooga where closing of supply lines caused a shortage of food and medicines.[108] But the fall of 1862 marked a turning point in the care of the wounded, and the person most responsible for the change was Jonathan Letterman who became Medical Director of the Army of the Potomac. In his reform efforts Letterman was strongly supported by Surgeon General William A. Hammond who shares with him the distinction of making the medical system of the Union Army a model of excellence. Letterman had already distinguished himself by taking the lead, while medical director for Western Virginia, in constructing general hospitals of the type later adopted throughout the army. Now, as chief medical officer of the Army of the Potomac, thirty-eight years of age, full of confidence, ability and enthusiasm, he at once ordered the setting up of an ambulance corps consisting of permanently detached men trained in their duties, commanded by line officers and all under the control of the Medical Department. He next worked out an effective supply plan which was put in operation in the East on October 9, 1862. The culminating step in his thoroughgoing reform was the institution of a field-hospital system centering in the division which provided a pooling of supplies and personnel at that level and permitted most effective utilization of available surgical skill.[109]

Letterman's new system required some time for implementation, but at Fredericksburg, where it received its first full trial, wonders were performed. Wounded were not only promptly collected and moved to tented field hospitals, but were quickly treated and well cared for until transferred to general hospitals.[110]

Surgeon General Hammond in August 1862 tried to get Halleck to adopt for all the Union forces an ambulance system similar to Letterman's but that officer, with a lack of vision too often found on high staff levels, turned it down on the amazing ground that the presence on the battlefield of noncombatants would encourage stampedes and panic! In March 1863, General Grant ordered establishment of an ambulance corps throughout the Army of the Tennessee. Finally in March 1864, by act of Congress and a War Department order, a uniform ambulance system, modeled after Letterman's plan as improved by experience, was prescribed throughout the Union Army.[111]

Medical service in the field, as ultimately perfected, comprised the following:

The personnel of the division hospital consisted of a Surgeon in charge, with an Assistant Surgeon as executive officer and a second Assistant Surgeon as recorder, an operating staff of three Surgeons aided by three Assistant Surgeons, and the requisite number of nurses and attendants.

The division ambulance train was commanded by a First Lieutenant of the line, assisted by a Second Lieutenant for each brigade. The enlisted men detailed for ambulance duty were a sergeant for each regiment, three privates for each ambulance, and one private for each wagon. The ambulance train consisted of from one to three ambulances for each regiment, squadron, or battery, a medicine wagon for each brigade, and two or more supply wagons. The hospital and ambulance train were under the control of the Surgeon-in-Chief of the Division. The division hospitals were usually located just out of range of artillery fire. Sometimes three or more division hospitals were consolidated under the orders of a Corps Medical Director, who was assisted by his Medical Inspector, Quartermaster, Commissary, and chief ambulance officer.

The medical officers not employed at field hospitals accompanied their regiments and established temporary depots as near as practicable to the line of battle.

As soon as possible after every engagement the wounded were transferred from the division or corps hospitals to the base or general hospitals.[112]

The system pioneered by Letterman and contributed to by many Civil War surgeons has no more eloquent testimonial than the fact of its remaining the basic structure of military medical care through World War II.[113]

Revision of general plans and procedures was paralleled by many improvements in detail. These included replacement of antiquated two-wheeled ambulances and rough wagons used for transporting wounded by smoother riding and more amply equipped vehicles, introduction of specially devised hospital cars on railroads and provision for more comfortable and better-staffed hospital boats. In general medical supplies became more plentiful and gross neglect less frequent.[114]

Surgical practice also improved as doctors gained experience and as the most competent were selected for wielding of the scalpel.[115] Another factor contributing to surgical progress was the periodic meeting of doctors in various commands to exchange experiences and to discuss new techniques.[116] Interest of medical men in enlarging the body of medical knowledge is attested by the careful and complete records which many kept of the wartime cases, and the specimens they sent in to the Army Medical Museum founded by Hammond in 1862.[117]

Despite earnest application and commendable progress, surgery in the Union Army was often painful and barbarous. Serious operations were sometimes performed by men sadly deficient in professional skill. Chloroform was widely used as an anesthetic and ether to a lesser extent, but sometimes neither was available and patients had to submit to the most painful operations without any deadening influence except such as could be obtained from a bottle of whisky.[118] When anesthesia was available some soldiers refused it for fear of never regaining consciousness, but medical records show relatively few cases of death from anesthesia alone.[119]

Army surgeons argued long and earnestly over the relative merits of amputation. Piles of severed arms and legs about field hospitals after any battle testified to a large membership in the school of the saw. But the frequency of gangrene, even in minor injuries, gave considerable support to advocates of radical surgery.[120]

Sometimes soldiers slated for loss of a member took things into their own control. An artillery corporal wounded in the knee at Hatcher's Run on being told that his leg must come off borrowed a pistol from his comrade and put it under his pillow. When the surgeon came to take him to the operating room the Yank drew the gun and exclaimed: "The man that puts a hand on me dies." The surgeon was momentarily taken aback, but recovering his poise he tried to convince the soldier that his only hope of survival lay in parting with the injured leg. The corporal adamantly held that if he died he wanted to take both limbs with him to the promised land. Finally the doctor, losing his patience, exclaimed: "Let the d— fool keep it and die." Since the story as here told was first related by the soldier himself, it goes without saying that he kept both his life and his leg.[121]

A close-up view of hospital experience near the middle of the war was related by a colonel who was wounded at Port Hudson and evacuated to Baton Rouge. On June 25, 1863, this officer wrote his wife:

I never wish to see another such time as the 27th of May. The surgeons used a large Cotton Press for the butchering room & when I was carried into the building and looked about I could not help comparing the surgeons to fiends. It was dark & the building lighted partially with candles: all around on the ground lay the wounded men; some of them were shrieking, some cursing & swearing & some praying; in the middle of the room was some 10 or 12 tables just large enough to lay a man on; these were used as dissecting tables & they were covered with blood; near & around the tables stood the surgeons with blood all over them & by the side of the tables was a heap of feet, legs & arms. On one of these tables I was laid & being known as a Col. the Chief Surgeon of the Department was called (Sanger) and he felt of my mouth and then wanted to give me cloriform: this I refused to take & he took a pair of scissors & cut out the pieces of bone in my mouth: then gave me a drink of whiskey & had me laid away.[122]

Ignorance was a prime factor in the deplorable conditions which prevailed in Union hospitals. A Federal surgeon, who lived through the revolution in medical science which came in the half century following Appomattox, in 1918 spoke thus of his Civil War experience:

We operated in old blood-stained and often pus-stained coats, the veterans of a hundred fights. . . . We used undisinfected instruments from undisinfected plush-lined cases, and still worse, used marine sponges which had been used in prior pus cases and had been only washed in tap water. If a sponge or an instrument fell on the floor it was washed and squeezed in a basin of tap water and used as if it were clean. Our silk to tie blood vessels was undisinfected. . . . The silk with which we sewed up all wounds was undisinfected. If there was any difficulty in threading the needle we moistened it with . . . bacteria-laden saliva, and rolled it between bacteria-infected fingers. We dressed the wounds with clean but undisinfected sheets, shirts, tablecloths, or other old soft linen rescued from the family ragbag. We had no sterilized gauze dressing, no gauze sponges. . . . We knew nothing about antiseptics and therefore used none.[123]

Little wonder that gangrene, tetanus and other complications were so frequent and that slight wounds often proved mortal.

Suffering of the sick and wounded would have been infinitely greater had it not been for the work of civilian agencies. True, voluntary effort occasionally was characterized by an overamount of state consciousness; and sometimes failure to take a realistic view of war and reluctance to work within the military framework caused more harm than good.[124]

It is also true that well-meaning exertions of individuals sometimes were carried to the point of absurdity—which fact did not escape the comment of soldiers. "There is lots of ladies comes here to the Hospital," wrote a New York private from Baltimore in 1862, "but they have not rubbed the skin off of any of the patients' faces yet." [125] A Missouri infantryman who was taken north during the Vicksburg campaign on a hospital boat noted that a slightly wounded patient received an embarrassing amount of attention from volunteer nurses and doctors. "Every one had eather a fan, and was fanning the poor man with such vivacity that had he not been a tolerable fat man [he] would have been blown off," he wrote, "or [was offering] a cup of tea, water, coffee or the devil Knows what all, and the doctors were discoursing wether the poor defender of his country ought to have his leg or arm . . . amputated or have some castor oil or some other damn stuff." [126]

An Indiana volunteer, describing the various classes of visitors who flooded Washington hospitals in 1864, wrote:

First, and least important, are the wordy sympathizers—of both sexes —the male portion of these "drones" are generally composed of broken-down, short-winded, long-faced, seedy preachers of all denominations. They walk solemnly up and down the wards, between the couches of patient sufferers; first casting their cadaverous looks and ghostly shadow upon all, and then, after a *whispered* consultation with the surgeon of the ward, offer to pray; do so, and retire, without having *smiled* on a single soldier or dropped a word of comfort or cheer. The females belonging to this (the "first class") go gawking through the wards, peeping into every curtained couch, seldom exchanging a word with the occupant, but (as they invariably "hunt in couples") giving vent to their pent up "pheelinks" in heart-rending(?) outbursts of "Oh, my Savior!" "Phoebe, do look here!" "Only see what a horrid wound!" "Goodness, gracious, how terrible war is!" "my! my!! my!!! Oh, let's go—I can't stand it any longer!" And as they near the door, perhaps these dear creatures will wind up with an audible—"Heavens! what a smell! Worse than fried onions!"

Class No. two is composed chiefly of flashy youths, got up in the latest style, and "perfectly regardless of expense," and every "har" in its proper place, kids, canes, and patent leathers, seal rings, and an odor of musk. Accompanying these are wasp-waisted, almond-eyed, cherry-lipped, finely-powdered damsels, carrying tiny baskets, containing an exquisitely embroided handkerchief, highly perfumed, and a vial or two of restoratives (to be used in case of sudden indisposition). This batch of "sight seers," do-nothings, idlers, time-killers, fops, and butterflies skip through the hospital, and like summer shadows, leave no trace behind.[127]

In the vast majority of instances, however, the assistance proffered the sick and wounded was well directed and helpful. In the field of nursing the Sisters of Charity and in the realm of general assistance the Sanitary and Christian Commissions were especially well organized and effective.[128] The United States Sanitary Commission was far and away the most outstanding of volunteer benevolent organizations. Ably directed by Henry W. Bellows as president, Frederick Law Olmsted as general secretary and J. S. Newberry as secretary of the western department—all of whom were advised and actively supported by some of the country's most distinguished doctors and philanthropists—it co-ordinated and turned into useful channels the activities of hundreds of small groups, raised millions of dollars, purchased and distributed vast amounts of food, clothing, medicines and supplies, provided scores of nurses and doctors at critical times, and equipped, staffed and put into operation hospital boats, trains and numerous other facilities. Its agents conducted innumerable inspections, collected valuable data and kept the country informed as to the needs and conditions of the sick and wounded. Its usefulness was enhanced by its studied policy of conforming to military practices and winning the good will and support of responsible commanders.[129]

Not the least of the contributions of the Sanitary Commission was the lead which it took in pointing up shortcomings and forcing corrective action. As already noted it was the moving spirit behind the house cleaning in high administrative circles in 1862 and the appointment of Hammond as Surgeon General. It also played a conspicuous part in modernizing the system of general hospitals and securing for the Medical Department adequate control over evacuation personnel, supply and transportation.[130]

Soldiers sometimes complained that Sanitary Commission representatives showed partiality to officers, and it may be that in efforts to promote good will in key places some of its representatives were overly sensitive to shoulder straps.[131] Its accomplishments far outweighed its shortcomings, however, and its efforts eased the suffering of countless wearers of the blue.

But all the zeal and competency marshaled for the great emergency— and the amount contributed of both was impressive—could not overcome the scientific lag of the age. The result was suffering on a scale without parallel in American military experience save in the Confederacy where equal ignorance and inferior resources led to even greater woe. In both armies the greatest heroes were not those who died at the cannon's mouth, but those who endured the lingering agonies of the sick and wounded.[132]

CHAPTER VII

GAY AND HAPPY STILL

A LONG MARCH might be hard work, but changing scenery and exciting prospects afforded relief from boredom. Battles, while nerve-racking and exhausting, were lively and absorbing, so much so that hours sometimes seemed to pass as rapidly as moments. But active campaigning, except in the last two years when entrenchments and sustained offensives gave a foretaste of future modes, comprised only a small part of Civil War operations. Warfare in the sixties consisted in the main of close engagements, each lasting only a short time, spaced by long static intervals devoted to recuperation, reorganization and waiting to see what the enemy was going to do.

Between November and April both sides usually suspended operations and holed up in winter quarters. Two major exceptions were Grant's Donelson campaign which after great suffering from exposure succeeded by the narrowest margin, and the Fredericksburg disaster following which Burnside became so hopelessly mired in Virginia clay that opposing Rebels tauntingly displayed placards reading: "Burnside's Army Stuck in the Mud." [1] After these discouraging experiences the seasons received their due respect.

What to do in the long periods between campaigns when dullness, homesickness and despondency hung like dark clouds over encampments, threatening to make life intolerable and to destroy the army's will to fight? In our day this question is a vital concern of command, and special staff sections devote full time to recreational functions. Civilian agencies join in with an impressive program featuring canteens, lounges, libraries and star-studded shows. As a result Yanks of World War II, whether in Fort Bragg or in Burma, could take their choice of a wide assortment of tedium-easers ranging from volleyball to variety shows, doughnuts to dominoes and colas to Crosby.

The situation was quite different in the 1860s—and the contrast is sharply reflected in the enormously higher desertion figures of that period. Command in Civil War times was literally a matter of discipline, drill and fight. Officers, if they gave a thought to recreation for their men, regarded the planning of such activities as extraneous if not down-right unbecoming to their positions.

The net result was to leave the soldiers largely to their own devices in seeking relaxation. And the men in blue, like their gray-clad opponents, displayed considerable ingenuity in meeting the problem. If their achievements seem meager in the light of present standards, let it be remembered that, because of a marked difference in taste and tempo, soldiers of the sixties were more easily satisfied than those of today.

Of the many diversions enjoyed by Billy Yank, reading was perhaps the most common. "Everybody has taken to reading," wrote one soldier, while another declared that he "longed more for something to read than for something to eat." [2] These men were undoubtedly stretching the truth, but an enormous craving for reading matter did exist. Readers were considerably more numerous in Union than in Confederate camps, owing to greater abundance of material and a higher degree of literacy.

Newspapers, rarely seen by Johnny Rebs, had a wide circulation among men in blue and headed the reading list of most. Local weeklies, sent by the homefolk, appear to have been the most popular. "The most satisfaction I have is in reading the news from home," wrote an Urbana, Ohio, Yank from Virginia. "I would like to have the Urbana paper sent me once in awhile I would sooner read it than any paper I can get hold of." Foreign-born soldiers found special delight in home papers printed in their native tongue. "As soon as 'Emigranten' arrives there are always many hands to grab for it," wrote a Norwegian from Maryland in 1861. "The condition imposed," he added, "is that he who gets it must read it aloud to his comrades." [3]

Metropolitan dailies such as the New York *Herald* and *Tribune*, the Boston *Transcript* and the Cincinnati *Commercial* also had many eager readers. Sometimes the city papers came by individual subscription, but more frequently they were distributed by sutlers or newsboys.

In June 1863 Hooker, in a competitive bidding, sold to John M. Lamb for $53.20 per day the exclusive privilege of supplying newspapers to the Army of the Potomac. Lamb agreed to provide all newspapers requested by the different commands at five cents a copy. [4]

Before the making of this contract New York papers had sold in Virginia for ten cents a copy. Soldiers earning only thirteen dollars a month could not afford to purchase many issues at this price. Newsboys did a thriving business immediately following payday, but after a short time sales fell off so sharply that they sometimes ceased making their rounds. [5]

One paper usually was made to serve many readers. Sometimes a group of soldiers would agree to share issues bought by each in turn. Again, a Yank with ready cash and good voice would read his paper aloud to a large audience of comrades. In any event, newspapers, like most other reading materials, were passed from one soldier to another until literally worn out.

The illustrated newspapers, especially *Frank Leslie's*, were eagerly sought by soldiers who were quick to discover errors in features about their own units.[6] Soldier letters leave the impression that journalistic art, especially that portraying combat operations, was notoriously inaccurate. But some allowance must be made for the exaggerated unit pride of Yanks who denounced artists for miscrediting feats of gallantry.[7]

Literary periodicals also had a wide following in Federal camps, though readers were confined largely to the cultural uppercrust. *Harper's* and the *Atlantic* are most frequently mentioned in letters and diaries, though considerable popularity seems to have been enjoyed by the *Continental Monthly*, *Littell's Living Age*, the *Eclectic Magazine* and the *North American Review*.

Religious periodicals and tracts, distributed by earnest individuals and by organizations such as the Christian Commission, were more widely read by soldiers than civilians. This was not because of a greater spiritual interest in camp, but was due rather to a greater dearth of other types of literature.

Books read by soldiers ranged from such classics as the *Divine Comedy*, *Macbeth* and *Paradise Lost* to trashy comics and cheap, yellowbacked thrillers. Extremes of taste may well be illustrated by some specific references in letters and diaries.

A Minnesota boy wrote his parents in March 1863 from Fredericksburg: "P H. & Fowler go down to the R. R. depot. They bring home 'Harper's Weekly,' 'Nix-Nax,' 'Budget of Fun,' 'Phunny Fellow' &c." About the same time a Massachusetts corporal who had come to the army by way of Harvard requested his parents to "send by the earliest opportunity Casey's Tactics & Mahan's Field Fortifications. I also want Hamlet & Macbeth. . . . I want something to read & know of nothing so condensed as Shakespeare." [8]

One youthful soldier who before the war had attended Washington and Jefferson College, revealed a varied appetite. On November 12, 1863, he wrote: "I read Jean Valjean through and think it splendid." A month later he reported: "I received the Dime Novel and will commence to read it as soon as I am done this letter. There is a good article in Littels Living Age about the *Millenium* you should read." In February

1864 he stated: "I received . . . the books. I have not forgotten my Horace yet but I need a lexicon very badly. I want to read all of Horace." Early in March he noted: "I have read a good part of Horace. . . . We have a splendid lot of novels, almost all of Sir Walter Scot's, and some of Cooper's." Later in the month he wrote: "I receive a Dime Novel occasionally and I find them very interesting. I have read all of Sir Walter Scott's novels within the last month, also a great many of Cooper's . . . [and] a novel called Earnest Linnwood by Mrs. Lee Hentz." An important factor in this soldier's volume of reading was his assignment to garrison duty where work was relatively light and permanency of station facilitated shipment of materials by his homefolk.[9]

Among readers of better taste, inclinations turned most commonly to history, drama and fiction, with Sparks, Parton, Shakespeare, Hugo, Dickens and Thackeray as favored authors. Foreign-born soldiers, while not nearly so well supplied with books and papers as their American comrades, took great delight in reading works of their homeland.[10] The Bible was a favorite among religiously inclined Yanks, and one soldier of college background found great satisfaction in reading his testament in the original Greek.[11] But devotees of good literature constituted only a small minority of soldier readers.

Yellow-covered, twenty-five-cent thrillers and Beadle's famous "Dime Novels," sold by sutlers, peddled by news venders or brought in by the soldiers themselves, fairly flooded some Yankee camps.[12] A Hoosier recalled after the war that in Middle Tennessee in 1863 "miserable worthless . . . novels . . . were sold by the thousand" and that men paid one dollar for "three worthless novelettes which contained a love story or some daring adventure by sea or land." Disapprovingly he added: "The minds of the men were so poisoned that they almost scorned the idea of reading a book or journal which contained matter that would benefit their minds. I can remember when the Atlantic and Continental Monthlies were considered dull reading, while the more enticing literary productions, such as Beadle's novels, novelettes and other detestable works were received with popular favor." [13]

Another soldier wrote that "high way stories and Beadle's dime novels with now and then a True Flag &c, form the principal part of reading." Unfortunately diarists and correspondents usually did not specify individual titles, though one revealed that he read Beadle's East and West and another the Gold Fiend, which he declared "the best Novelette story I ever saw." [14]

Chaplains and Christian Commission agents, fearing baneful effects of trashy writings on soldier morals, fought a hard but losing fight against them. But to one chaplain who scored a notable victory in Chattanooga we are indebted for an unusually revealing view of camp reading. This divine, meeting on a street a soldier loaded with twenty-five-cent novels —bought in the city at thirty cents each and to be sold in camp at forty— talked him into swapping the fiction for tracts and other "clean" literature. More than that, he obtained from the repentant Yank a pledge not to read or deal in novels again. The chaplain closed his account of the incident with the following inventory of confiscated books: "2 'Dick Turpin'; 2 'Pirates Son'; 4 'Flying Artillerist' and 1 each of 'Red Rover,' 'Iron Cross,' 'Red King' and 'Jacob Faithful.' " [15]

Reports of religious workers also indicate that "licentious books" and "obscene pictures" had some circulation among Yanks, but references are vague and give no information concerning authors, titles, publishers or content.[16]

War experience was not always degrading to reading habits. Some who at home would never have got around to good books were driven by the boredom of camp to read everything that came to hand including the works of the literary masters. In some cases first reactions to the classics were so favorable as to suggest a continuing interest in them.

One Yank predicted improvement of his own practices but on a negative basis. "I think by the time that the war is over," he wrote in February 1864, "I shall get so disgusted with light trash that I shall take to solid reading and hard study with much greater zeal than ever before." [17]

Various means were used to facilitate reading. The Christian Commission established in many hospitals loan libraries, each consisting of 125 volumes; publishers provided books at half price and the Adams Express Company transported them without charge. In 1864 the Christian Commission made a similar arrangement with publishers and shippers to furnish the Army of the Cumberland 25,000 magazines, mostly of the literary type.[18]

A number of regiments during winter months organized literary associations, the chief function of which was to maintain libraries or reading rooms. Often the chaplain was the moving spirit in such projects. A Chelsea, Massachusetts, soldier wrote from Maryland in February 1862: "I have joined the 'Fay Literary Institute' [named for the mayor of Chelsea], a sort of Lyceum. We have a library of about 500 or 600 volumes of good reading. . . . It is very pleasant all the boys in my section belong." [19] The next winter a Connecticut soldier reported from

Virginia: "We have a Library for the Regt. Maj. Lane elected president. Chaplain Welch elected librarian. . . . Books to be issued Tues & fri. Eve'gs of Each week." [20] Libraries were commonly housed in regimental chapels which ordinarily were tents or log structures.

Now and then a Yank would operate an informal library on his own.[21] Book collections of both individuals and organizations were occasionally supplemented by items confiscated from Rebels. One soldier wrote after the fall of Vicksburg that he had "plenty of papers and captured books to read," while another told of "picking up" numerous volumes in Florida. Corporal Samuel Storrow of Massachusetts, who on a raid in North Carolina appropriated a copy of the Rebel Pollard's *History of the First Year of the War*, stated of his prize: "The book pitches into Jeff Davis & his dictatorial power mercilessly & is really of a good deal of interest as a South Side view of the war. I intend to preserve it until we return home." [22]

Most reading was for entertainment but some was for self-improvement. A few soldiers wrote of studying such subjects as Greek, Latin and arithmetic. The most numerous and earnest pursuers of learning were the Negro soldiers recruited from the ex-slaves, and their emphasis was, of course, on elementary subjects.[23]

Ranking close to reading among camp diversions was music. On the march, sitting about the campfire, riding trains or transports, at home on furlough—wherever Yanks assembled—the strains of popular tunes were sure to be heard. The men who wore the blue, and the butternut Rebs who opposed them, more than American fighters of any period, deserve to be called singing soldiers.

Some Yanks on leaving home for the war took violins, guitars and other instruments along with them and entertained their comrades at informal camp sessions. These impromptu affairs were supplemented by band concerts featuring martial airs, patriotic selections and sentimental melodies. In the early part of the war each regiment was authorized a band, but in July 1862 a law was passed prohibiting bands below the brigade level; some regiments, however, found means of evading the act.[24] Since the best of the regimental musicians usually were transferred to the brigade bands, the effect was to improve the quality of the playing. When not on the march, brigade bands commonly gave twilight concerts which were greatly enjoyed by the soldiers. On holidays and other festive occasions the bands gave special programs. Now and then they serenaded high-ranking officers, much to the pleasure of the rank and file, after which the honorees commonly treated the

musicians to drinks. Not the least appreciated of the bands' performances were those given during the course of fatiguing marches.

Soldier appreciation of a good band is exemplified by the comment
of an unidentified member of the Twenty-fourth Massachusetts Regiment who wrote from the North Carolina coast in April 1862:

> I dont know what we should have done without our band. It is
> acknowledged by everyone to be the best in the division. Every night
> about sun down Gilmore gives us a splendid concert, playing selections
> from the operas and some very pretty marches, quicksteps, waltzes and
> the like, most of which are composed by himself or by Zohler, a member
> of his band. . . . Thus you see we get a great deal of *new* music, not-
> withstanding we are off here in the woods. Gilmore used to give some of
> the most fashionable concerts we had at home and we lack nothing but
> the stringed instruments now. In their place however we have five reed
> instruments, of which no other band can boast.[25]

This band was no doubt exceptional both in the nature of its selections and the quality of its performance.[26] More typical from the standpoint of pieces played was a concert reported while it was in progress in
1863 by an officer stationed at Folly Island, South Carolina: "The band
are just now playing 'Love Not.' It is a sweet air but the words are rather
heathenish. . . . They must be playing a medley of airs, for they have
just passed to 'Katy Darling' and are even now changing to 'Annie
Laurie.' . . . At this point they suddenly started off into 'Ain't you
glad to get out of the Wilderness.' . . . Here comes 'Pop Goes the
Weasel.' . . . They are winding up with the Lancers." [27]

In the peninsula campaign and at Shiloh, Cedar Mountain and
Chancellorsville men were urged to feats of valor by musicians playing
patriotic and martial airs.[28]

Soldiers transported on river steamers were sometimes treated to
calliope concerts. A member of a Tennessee River expedition to Shiloh
early in 1862 told of the calliopes playing "Starry Flag," "Red, White
and Blue," "The Old Folks at Home," "The Girl I Left Behind Me"
and "My Old Kentucky Home." [29]

The music enjoyed most was that made by the soldiers' own voices.
Yanks went to war with songs on their lips. They sang on the march, in
the trenches, on fatigue, in the guardhouse, on the battlefield and especially in bivouac. The urge to sing was so irrepressible that men on outpost duty sometimes had to be reprimanded for lifting their voices and
giving away their positions.[30]

Yanks sang individually as they puttered about the camp. They sang in duets, trios, quartets and glee clubs; and sometimes the country-side at night was made to reverberate with thousands of voices uniting in the strains of some cherished melody.[31]

Soldiers sang mostly for the sheer joy of making music. But they also sang to combat homesickness, to buoy drooping spirits, to relieve boredom and to forget weariness. The harder the going the more lustily they sang. After a rapid march into Murfreesboro early in 1863, one regiment struck up the song:

> Sometimes we have to double-quick;
> This Dixie mud is mighty slick.
> The soldier's fare is very rough,
> The bread is hard, and beef is tough,
> That's the way they put us through,
> I tell you what, it's hard to do.
> But we'll obey duty's call,
> To conquer Dixie, that is all! [32]

In response to the enormous demands of soldiers and the folk at home, publishers in New York, Philadelphia, Chicago and other cities ground out thousands of songs on broadsides, in folding cards much after the fashion of scenic sequences sold in modern tourist centers, in sheet folios and in pocket songbooks.[33] The name of Beadle adorned several of the songsters, in such titles as "Beadle's Dime Songs for the War," "Beadle's Dime Union Song Book" and "Beadle's Dime Military Song Book and Songs for the War." [34] Other booklets issued with the soldier market in view were "The Camp Fire Songster," "The Flag of Our Union Songster," "Tony Pastor's New Union Song Book," named for the famous singing showman of the period, "The Little Mac Songster," published during McClellan's heyday, "Nat Austin's New Comic and Sentimental Song Book," "Fred May's Comic Irish Songster," "The Frisky Irish Songster," "Shoddy Songster," "Stars and Stripes Songster," "Camp Fire Companion," "Dawley's Ten-Penny Song Book," "Union League Melodies," "Bugle Call," compiled by the famous composer George F. Root, "The American Union Songster," "War Songs for Freedom" and "The Yankee Doodle Songster." [35]

Only a few of the mass of songs hopefully launched by the publishers became popular in camp. A careful check of soldier references to music in all the letters, diaries and reminiscences used in this study indicates that the number-one song in Federal camps was "John Brown's Body." Yanks enjoyed especially the line beginning "We'll hang Jeff Davis," completing it with whatever tree came to mind but usually a sour apple or a palmetto.[36]

Parodies and variations were innumerable. One of the first to gain popularity was "Ellsworth's body lies a mouldering in the grave," sung in tribute to the famous Zouave leader killed in May 1861 while taking down the Rebel colors from a house in Alexandria, Virginia.[37] Another song sung to the John Brown tune by the soldiers was entitled "Song of the Volunteers," beginning "The bugle blasts are sounding, 'tis time to be away." [38]

Late in 1861 Julia Ward Howe wrote new words for this popular tune in order to provide a song of greater power and dignity. The resulting "Battle Hymn of the Republic," while a tribute to Mrs. Howe, never gained among soldiers anything like the popularity of the original "John Brown." [39]

Other martial songs which soldier accounts credit with a high degree of popularity were: "Happy Land of Canaan," "Yankee Doodle," "The Battle-Cry of Freedom," "The Star-Spangled Banner," "Weeping Sad and Lonely, or When This Cruel War Is Over," "The Girl I Left Behind Me," "Gay and Happy Still" and "Johnny Fill Up the Bowl." Of these one of the most stirring was "The Battle-Cry of Freedom," written by George F. Root, an outstanding composer of war songs, and popularized by the Lombard brothers and the Hutchinson family.[40] The soldiers usually referred to the piece by the opening words "We'll rally round the flag, boys." The appeal of the song was strikingly evidenced by an incident of the Wilderness fighting in Virginia in May 1864. At one point in the action a brigade of the Ninth Corps, after having broken the Rebel line, was thrown back in disorder by the threat of a flank attack. After the retreat the brigade re-formed and faced the enemy but apparently the prevailing mood was one of defeat. Just at this moment a soldier of one of the regiments—the Forty-fifth Pennsylvania—launched into the song:

> We'll rally round the flag,
> Boys, we'll rally once again,
> Shouting the battle-cry of Freedom.

The words were immediately picked up by the others, and soon the entire brigade was singing the defiant chorus:

> The Union forever,
> Hurray! boys, Hurrah!

A COCKFIGHT IN THE ARMY OF THE POTOMAC

UNION SOLDIERS PLAYING BASEBALL

Confederate Prison, Salisbury, N. C. Drawing by Major Otto Botticher

Down with the traitor, up with the star;
While we rally round the flag boys, rally once again,
Shouting the battle-cry of Freedom! [41]

"Weeping Sad and Lonely," which had a host of enthusiastic singers in both Union and Rebel camps, no doubt owed much of its popularity to the universality of the sentiment expressed in the doleful words:

Weeping, sad and lonely,
Hopes and fears how vain! . . .
When this cruel war is over,
Praying that we meet again.[42]

"Gay and Happy Still" appealed to soldiers because of its devil-may-care tone. A glimpse of its effect is afforded by the following reference of an Iowa soldier: "While passing through a deep ravine where clouds of dust rose in suffocating volumes to our faces, rendering breathing difficult, I began to doubt my ability to proceed, when suddenly the stillness of the scene was broken by Corporal N. B. Graham, of Company E, in a loud clear voice singing

Let the wide world wag as it will,
I'll be gay and happy still.

The sentiments of the song contrasted so strangely with our feelings and circumstances that we gained a momentary relief in a hearty laugh." [43]

An Indiana soldier, who after the war declared "Johnny Fill Up the Bowl" the "most popular of all the army songs," recalled that "While this was being sung, some would chime in with 'so ball, so ball.' Next time another would ring out, 'sow-belly! sow-belly!' . . . and so on, till every change was rung in on the refrain." [44]

Martial and patriotic hits of the period competed closely with sentimental, folk and religious favorites of the past for top rating.[45] The most popular of the old tunes was "Home, Sweet Home," but "Auld Lang Syne," "Annie Laurie," "Old Hundred," "I'm a Pilgrim," "There is a Happy Land," "Finnegan's Wake," "Bingen on the Rhine," "The Faded Flowers," "Go Tell Aunt Rhoda," "Pop Goes the Weasel" and "Come Where My Love Lies Dreaming" also had high standing among singers in blue.

Rating below songs of all types listed above, but still enjoying considerable popularity in Federal camps were: "Tenting on the Old Camp Ground," written by a draftee named Walter Kittredge; "When Johnny Comes Marching Home"; "Johnny Is Gone for a Soldier"; "Tramp, Tramp, Tramp" and "Just Before the Battle, Mother," both by the indefatigable George F. Root; "Grafted into the Army," and the Rebel-taunting "Kingdom Coming," by Henry Clay Work, another famous composer of the period; and "Who Will Care for Mother Now," by Charles Carroll Sawyer who also wrote the favorite "Weeping Sad and Lonely," and who shares with Root and Work highest honors as a producer of Civil War songs.[46]

Other selections rating as secondary favorites included: "Lilly Dale"; "Babylon Is Falling," which like "Kingdom Coming" was a thrust at slaveholders; the rollicking old army tune "Benny Havens, Oh!"; "Oft in the Stilly Night"; "Wait for the Wagon"; and "Poor Old Soldier." [47]

The Yanks, as if not content with their own tunes, appropriated a few songs from the Rebels. The "Homespun Dress" had appreciative singers among the men in blue, as did the "Bonnie Blue Flag," sung to the invaders by Southern girls in patriotic defiance, but in some cases liked so well by the Yankee listeners that they added it to their repertoire.[48] The "Bonnie Blue Flag," like some other tunes of the period, had both Northern and Southern versions.[49]

"Dixie" enjoyed considerable popularity in Northern camps, but since this song was of Northern origin, the men in blue cannot properly be charged with appropriating it.[50] Northern civilians were constrained by Rebel taint of the original to adopt a Yankee version, but soldiers seemed to prefer the original. Perhaps they regarded the taunting note which they injected as purifying enough to make it acceptable.[51] "Lorena," a song of Northern origin which became a favorite of Confederates, had many admirers among Federal troops.[52]

For "Dixie," as for many other songs, the soldiers improvised countless parodies. On the famous "mud march" after Fredericksburg, as men stumbled along in the mire with bodies weak and spirits depressed, an Illinois soldier heard some of his comrades up ahead singing:

> I wish I was in St Law County
> Two years up and I had my bounty,
> Away, Look away, Away, Away.

"The men kept stringing in yelling and hooting for miles back," he added, "and no trouble for those in the rear to know the way." [53]

An impressive proportion of war favorites had extremely doleful notes, but this does not necessarily mean that the ranks were filled with melancholy soldiers. Paradoxical as it may seem, carefree campaigners apparently derived satisfaction from dwelling on themes of suffering and death, enjoying their misery as it were, and emerging from excursions into gloom with hearts lighter than before.

But soldiers enjoyed many types other than lugubrious ballads, hymns and pure patriotics. The routine of camp life provided the theme for a number of lighter songs. Yanks readily found catchy words for the various bugle calls. A common accompaniment for reveille ran like this:

I can't wake 'em up, I can't wake 'em up, I can't wake 'em up in the morning,
I can't wake 'em up, I can't wake 'em up, I can't wake 'em up at all.
The corporal's worse than the private, the sergeant's worse than the corporal,
The lieutenant's worse than the sergeant and the captain's worst of all.
I can't wake 'em up, I can't wake 'em up, I can't wake 'em up in the morning,
I can't wake 'em up, I can't wake 'em up, I can't wake 'em up at all.[54]

Sick call would arouse a chorus:

> All ye sick men, all ye sick men,
> Get your calomel, get your calomel,
> Get your calomel, get your calomel.[55]

Still another sick-call accompaninent was:

> Are you all dead? are you all dead?
> No, thank the Lord, there's a few left yet,
> There's a few—left—yet! [56]

On the march, sounding of brigade call to fall in after a rest was sometimes greeted by the chant:

> Fall in, ye poor devils, as fast as ye can,
> And when ye get tired I'll rest you again.[57]

A popular adaptation to mess call was:

> Soupy, soupy, soupy, without any bean,
> Porky, porky, porky, without any lean,
> Coffee, coffee, coffee, without any cream.[58]

One of the most famous accompaniments of all was to a special brigade call used in Butterfield's command which ran:

> Dan, Dan, Dan Butterfield, Butterfield,
> Dan, Dan, Dan Butterfield, Butterfield.[59]

Army rations inspired a number of ditties. When the issue was reduced to a single cracker and when foraging "played out," an Illinois regiment sometimes struck up the refrain:

> Lord, what a wretched land is this,
> That yields us no supply! [60]

Hoosier soldiers, and others too, expressed their loathing of hardtack by parodying the song "Hard Times Come Again No More" in this fashion:

> 'Tis the song of the soldier, weary, hungry, and faint,
> Hardtack, hardtack, come again no more;
> Many days have I chewed you and uttered no complaint,
> O Greenbacks, come again once more.[61]

But it was to the old stand-by beans that most ration songs were inscribed. One of these, adapted to the religious air "The Sweet Bye-and-Bye," had these words:

> There's a spot that the soldiers all love,
> The mess-tent is the place that we mean,
> And the dish that we like to see there
> Is the old-fashioned, white Army bean.

Chorus:

> 'Tis the bean that we mean,
> And we'll eat as we ne'er ate before
> The Army bean, nice and clean;
> We will stick to our beans evermore.[62]

Favorite generals provided the theme for a few songs. While "Little Mac" was at the helm Eastern soldiers sang this piece with the chorus.

> For McClellan's our leader; he is gallant and strong.
> For God and our Country we are marching along.[63]

And after his removal a song came out with the title "Give Us Back Our Old Commander." [64] In the Western army admirers of Rosecrans, who were many in the period before Chickamauga, delighted in singing a tribute containing these words:

> Old Rosy is our man,
> Old Rosy is our man.
> He'll show his deeds, where'er he leads.
> Old Rosy is our man.[65]

In 1864 Grant was honored with a selection entitled "Ulysses Leads the Van." [66]

Some songs, such as "Chickamauga," had notable battles for their subjects, while others recounted in epic fashion high lights of a considerable portion of the conflict.[67] In the latter category falls E. W. Locke's "We're Marching Down to Dixie's Land." "Marching Through Georgia," written by Henry C. Work in honor of Sherman's famous expedition from Chattanooga to Savannah, also belongs in this group, but it was written too late to gain wide popularity before the end of the conflict.[68]

Various organizations had their special songs. "The Song of the Twentieth Corps" recounted the exploits of the famed unit that "wore a single star." [69] The "Song of the Michigan Second," set to the tune of "Drink Her Down," began with these lines:

> Of our regiment we will sing,
>   Bully boys!
> Join and make the chorus ring,
>   Bully boys!
> The "Michigan Second" is our name
> And we will sustain its fame,
> With our cool and deadly aim,
>   Bully boys!

Then followed a verse to each officer in the hierarchy of command, beginning with McClellan and coming on down through the regimental staff with a final verse paying tribute to company officers as a group.[70]

The First Arkansas, a colored unit, had a song written by one of its white captains to the tune of "John Brown's Body," the first verse of which ran:

Oh! we're de bully soldiers of de
　　"First of Arkansas";
We are fightin' for de Union, we are
　　fightin' for de law;
We can hit a rebel furder dan a
　　white man eber saw;
As we go marching on.[71]

Another group of songs lampooned unpopular aspects of army administration. Examples of this type are "Shoddy on the Brain," "Wanted a Substitute," "Our Brass Mounted Army" and "The Invalid Corps." [72] Foreigners in the service were good-naturedly caricatured in "I Goes to Fight Mit Siegel" and "Corporal Schnapps." [73] Confederate leaders came in for derision in a number of selections. An old English song, "Lord Lovel," was adapted to chide General Mansfield Lovell for his precipitate surrender of New Orleans.[74] General Bragg was satirized in several pieces, the most boisterous of which was "Bragg a Boo," the last verse and chorus of which were:

Dear General Bragg, here's to your health,
With Secesh script to swell your wealth;
Your coat of arms, when Fortune deals,
We trust will bear a pair of heels.

Chorus:

Then shout, boys, shout! The foe is put to rout,
And Bragg a Boo and Morgan, too,
Have started on for Dixie.
Hey, ho! we've laid them low,
Se-cessh are blue as in-di-go.[75]

The first citizen of Confederate Virginia was satirized in the lines of

Old Governor Wise
With his goggle eyes[76]

while Jeff Davis, in a song by that name set to "Nell Flaughtery's Drake," was the object of this thrust:

Bad luck to him early! Bad luck to him dearly!
May the devil admire him, where'er he may be!
May mosquitoes bite him, and rattlesnakes smite him,
The traitor that brought these hard times unto me.[77]

The South in general was taunted in a parody to "Dixie" which began:

> Away down South in the land of traitors,
> Rebel hearts and Union haters,
> Look away, look away, look away
> to the traitor's land.[78]

Yanks sang nonsense ditties, such as "Shoo Fly Shoo," and comic parodies galore.[79] They also delighted in giving roguish twists to old favorites. "Abraham's Daughter," not very reverent in its original form, was parodied by one group thus:

> I'm a raw recruit with a bran-new suit
> Nine hundred dollars bounty,
> And I've come down from Darbytown
> To fight for Oxford County.[80]

Even the sacrosanct patriotics did not escape the mischief-makers, as witness the following:

> Mary had a little lamb,
> Its fleece was white as snow,
> Shouting the Battle-Cry of Freedom!
> And everywhere that Mary went
> The lamb was sure to go,
> Shouting the Battle-Cry of Freedom! [81]

Hymns were occasionally used in a way that must have shocked the devout. Hardened soldiers of the West, when plodding wearily through rain and mud, sometimes would break out with "There is a land of pure delight," and their rendition must have been like that of World War II soldiers who in similar circumstances sang:

> I am Jesus' little lamb;
> Yes, by Jesus Christ, I am.
> I don't care if it rains or freezes,
> I am safe in the arms of Jesus.
> I am Jesus' little lamb;
> Yes, by Jesus Christ, I am.[82]

One night a group of Connecticut soldiers who had made a raid, apparently on a store reserved for officers, had trouble with the squawking of their quarry. The expedient to which they resorted, as recounted by one of them, was: "Of the first lot of hens, owls stole 7, brot them into tent & wrung their necks while others sang 'Come Holy Spirit Heavenly dove.' The job finished by roll call at 8." [83]

Yanks, like Rebs, had their off-color songs. Apparently they gave the famous ballad "Joe Bowers" a twist that jarred the chaplains. References to "vulgar songs" appear occasionally in letters and court-martial records, but unfortunately they do not give titles or words. Indeed, there is no more elusive phase of Civil War history than the seamy side of soldier life. In pursuing ribald music the researcher has to be content with such statements in letters as: "After the evening dress parade, some amuse themselves . . . in singing vulgar songs," and in official records: Captain James H. Slade, Thirty-eighth Massachusetts Volunteers, found guilty of entertaining two whores in his tent, serving them wine and having them sing "vulgar and secession songs." [84]

Music of national and racial groups deserves special notice. Colored aides or body servants of officers often entertained camp audiences with folk melodies and improvisations. A fourteen-year-old aide, who proudly bore the name Henry George General Washington, one evening near Memphis sang:

> Possum put on an overcoat,
> Raccoon put on gown,
> Rabit put on ruffled shirt,
> All buttoned up and down.
> Wait, Billy, wait, wait I say
> And I will marry you bime by.[85]

Nearly all Northern whites closely associated with colored soldiers commented appreciatively on their singing. An Amherst student, who worked among the wounded in Virginia in 1864, reported hearing several Negro casualties of the Crater fight singing in a field hospital:

> Times going away, why dont you pray,
> And end this cruel war in heaven,
> Oh my blessed Lord.
>
> I wish my Lord would come down
> And take us to wear the crown,
> Oh my blessed Lord.[86]

Lieutenant Colonel Charles B. Fox of the colored Sixty-sixth Massachusetts complimented the band of that regiment on a number of occasions for their rendition of such pieces as "Hail to the Chief," "Midnight Hour," "Gay and Happy Still," "Glory Hallelujah," and "Someone to Love." [87] He also told of the special enthusiasm with which Negro soldiers sang "Babylon Is Falling," and the beauty with which they rendered "All Hail" to the air "Greenland's Icy Mountains" at a festive meeting on Folly Island, South Carolina, in October 1864.[88]

Among foreign soldiers, the Germans were noted for their musical leaning and accomplishment. A New York private wrote "Friend Elvira" from Virginia in 1863: "I heard some splendid singing last night by the 20th N. Y. a German Regt. . . . They all belong to the society of Turners of which the celebrated Max Webber is leader. I went over to their camp and heard them and then they went over and Serenaded General Patrick." Another New Yorker, commander of an artillery unit, reported from Maryland: "We have pretty lively times in the evenings; the Germans of my company get together and sing very sweetly, and I try to join in with them. I send you a copy of one of their songs . . . it is simple but very sweet, I think, and shows a reflection and elevation of sentiment to be found only among the Germans." [89]

The favorite of the Germans seems to have been their stirring soldier song "Morgenroth," which they sang in their native tongue when on the march and about the campfire.[90] They also delighted in folk and national melodies of the homeland, and in patriotic and martial songs of their adopted America. Their bands were among the best in the army.[91]

Frenchmen, and their American-born comrades as well, sang the "Marseillaise" with gusto, especially when on the march.[92] The Irish had many native songs with which to entertain their fellow soldiers, and their broguish renditions were sure to bring smiles to all who listened.[93] The Scandinavians were accomplished in both secular and religious music. Colonel Hans C. Heg gave a glimpse of Norwegian proficiency in a letter from Louisville of September 1862, in which he stated: "My Regiment went through singing Norwegian Songs, and attracted more attention than any other regiment that passed." [94]

The Scots, the Italians and the many other nationalities represented in the Union Army had their special songs and music. Indeed, life in the Federal camps had no more enriching influence than the music contributed by the diverse and talented groups who wore the blue.

Sports and games were another very popular diversion. Foot races, wrestling, boxing, leapfrog, cricket, broad jumping and free-for-all scuffles helped Yanks while away many tedious hours. Football was occasionally mentioned in letters and diaries, but baseball, or "bass ball" as one Yank put it, appears to have been the most popular of all competitive sports. Baseball as played by Yanks differed considerably from that of today. A Vermont soldier gave this description: "The ball was soft, and a great bounder. To put a base runner out, he had to be hit by the ball, thrown by the pitcher." Another impressive difference was the score. A game between the Eighth and the 114th Vermont Regiments near Franklin, Louisiana, in February 1864 was won by the former 21 to 9. The "first team" of the Ninth New York Regiment beat the Fifty-first New Yorkers 31-34 at Yorktown, Virginia, in 1863. But a few days later the "second nine" of the two units played, with the Ninth Regiment triumphing by the fantastic score of 58-19! Soldier baseball must have been vigorous. One Yank noted after a contest in Tennessee, "We get lamed badly." [95]

In winter, snowballing was the order of the day. Sometimes units pitched into each other in regular battle fashion, led by their officers with bugles sounding and flags waving. A notable engagement was that between the Twenty-sixth New Jersey and a Vermont regiment near Fredericksburg early in 1863 when: "Both regiments formed a line of battle, each officered by its line and field officers, the latter mounted. At the signal the battle commenced; charges and counter-charges were made, prisoners were taken on either side, the air was filled with white missiles, and stentorian cheers went up as one or other party gained an advantage. At length victory rested with the Vermonters, and the Jersey boys surrendered the field defeated." [96] No mention was made of wounded casualties in this contest, but if Yanks battled with the same vehemence as Rebs—and there is no reason to believe that they did not— black eyes, bruised shins and gashed faces must have required the attention of first-aid men.[97]

Boating, fishing and hunting each had its followers among soldier sportsmen. Sometimes opossums, coons, squirrels and quail were the prizes sought by hunters, and less frequently deer, wild hogs, foxes and wild ducks. In coastal areas mammoth turtles and their eggs were objects of eager search. The usual weapon for small game was a gun, but now and then soldiers armed only with torches and sticks would bring in hundreds of birds knocked from their roosts in a thicket or canebrake. Next day camp fare would be varied by delectable servings of potpie.[98]

Rabbits abounded in most Southern areas, and it was to these fleet and savory animals that most seekers of game gave their attention. The sight of a cottontail in camp or on the march would almost invariably set off an epidemic of whooping and running, and if the terrain was favorable and the pursuers were numerous, the bewildered bunny would sometimes be surrounded and caught. Regardless of the outcome, the exciting chase was thoroughly enjoyed by all who participated.

In the long Southern summers every stream and lake of the invaded country was a swimming hole for men in blue, and sometimes Rebs and Yanks shared the same spot.[99] Bathing in some areas was not without its perils, as the diary of a private stationed in Louisiana pointedly disclosed: "Two men of the 8th Indiana killed by alligators. We saw the alligators and saw the boys go down, but never saw the bodies again. . . . There was great excitement for awhile as we were nearly all in the water." [100]

In the tent of an evening or any time on a stump or log, checkers, chess, dominoes or cards, the last usually for stakes but sometimes for fun, were the mode. When sedentary diversions lost their charm, a sham fight or a tug of war might be quickly arranged; or, better still, the sutler might be raided. One day a group of soldiers playing with an artillery rope, on a sudden impulse, headed for the brigade sutler's tent dragging the rope in a great loop between them. Soon, over went the tent and the vender's wagon with it, spilling out sutler, clerk, canned goods and knickknacks, all in a jumble. "All the boys ran to help pick up the scattered goods, but strange to say, no sooner were they picked up than they disappeared misteriously." The sutler stormed, and the colonel too. A detail was sent to search the quarters, but no rope or raider or lost delicacy was ever found.[101]

Billy Yank was an inveterate tease and prankster. A civilian who happened to come into camp wearing unusual attire or presenting any oddity of appearance was sure to be the victim of a chorus of derisive comments. One day near Atlanta a man riding a bony nag approached a large crowd of soldiers. The first Yank who noticed him let out a raucous "caw-caw-caw." Immediately others took up the cry and soon the whole camp joined in so that for several minutes it seemed that "10,000 crows were holding a jubilee." [102]

Recruits were of course a favorite target. A youngster who joined one unit, after drawing his clothing and equipment from the quartermaster, was asked by a veteran why he did not get his umbrella.

"Do they furnish an umbrella?" inquired the recruit naïvely.

"Why, certainly," replied the veteran. "It's just like that fraud of a quartermaster to jew a recruit out of a part of his outfit. . . . Go back and *demand* your umbrella."

Poor recruit! He returned only to find out how completely he had been taken in.[103]

First duty as sentry was an exceedingly shaky experience for new soldiers, as was attested by the number of cows and pigs that, mistaken for sneaking Rebels, became the targets of trigger-happy novitiates. The nervousness of new sentinels made them ready prey for pranksters who would dress themselves in awe-inspiring regalia, approach a post and when challenged with a palsied "Who goes there?" reply with some such nonsense as "The devil with the countersign" or "A flock of sheep." [104]

Fun seekers delighted in tying cans, baskets and other objects to the tails of stray animals and then helping the poor victim along its frenzied course by emitting loud whoops and setting off charges of powder. Men of one regiment adorned a mud turtle with a "Secesh" flag and laughed uproariously as they prodded him along the company street. Another group found great merriment in burning Jeff Davis in effigy while their band played "Yankee Doodle." [105]

The accent and unusual ways of foreigners often made them the victims of mischievous acts. Men of a New York artillery unit slipped a mouse into the little tin box which a German comrade used for carrying his fine plug tobacco—and then hid near his tent to hear the oaths that came when he reached for a chew.[106]

Negroes, as noted elsewhere, were favorite targets of pranksters. Civilian camp helpers, especially those who seemed inclined to take their freedom too literally, were commonly given the "blanket treatment," and the more aggravated the case the higher the toss. One victim, "elevated till the tossers themselves feared he would not come down," afterward "shook the dust of our camp from his feet, saying 'you tossed me too high entirely.' " [107]

As a rule Yanks confined their horseplay to civilians and fellow soldiers, but now and then they had fun at the expense of the "shoulder straps." Discomfiture of surgeons, owing to the low opinion which many soldiers had of them, afforded special pleasure. When an Illinois surgeon in full view of a marching regiment in North Alabama was pitched into a puddle by a stumbling mount "the boys," according to a captain who witnessed the incident, "consoled him with a clean 1,000 cheers, groans and sharp speeches." [108] But even a general might be considered fair game. When the new commander of a division in the West set out to curb the reckless firing of guns, for which the camps had become notorious, he found that he had taken a lion by the tail. His troubles were described by a soldier of the command:

The other night there were a number of loud explosions over in the Infantry camp. The boys take an empty canteen, put the powder from three or four catridges in it and cork it up tight, then throw it in the fire. It make considerable noise. The General (Harrow) called for the scouts and his horse. We started out. When we got to the Infantry camp all was quiet—men all asleep, Apparantly. Then it broke out over in the Artillery. Away we went, but could find no one there except the gaurd at the guns and he knew nothing about it. Could not leave his beat to find out. Then away over in the Cavelry—boom! boom! Another fast ride. No results—all quiet. My! but the General was hot. He left the scouts to look after things and went back to his Quarters.

The general eventually succeeded in catching two of the culprits and, by giving them a well-publicized ride on a wooden horse constructed especially for the occasion, brought the situation under control.[109]

Take-offs on army institutions and procedures relieved the tedium in a number of camps. In these burlesques, Yanks rarely passed up an opportunity to satirize the "brass." At a mock court-martial, staged with due regard for form as prescribed in regulations, soldiers of the Twenty-third Massachusetts tried one of their number on the following charges and specifications: "At supper, said Eben S. Perkins, with malice prepense and without provocation did throw into the face of one Alec Munroe a dipperful of hot tea, thereby burning him and stopping the growth (?) of a large pair of whiskers." After proceedings got under way, several officers joined the audience and immediately the trial took a new turn, featuring the quality of tea served to soldiers. One witness testified: "I saw the liquid thrown at Mr. M. Am not certain that it *was* tea, although it bore that name." Another stated that he "heard a sudden splash, and saw the hot water called tea." After further testimony along similar lines, the prisoner, who seems to have been so naïve as to think the trial a real one, was found guilty of a felonious assault with intent to kill. But leniency being recommended the sentence required only that the culprit ask pardon of his victim on bended knee and serve two weeks on the wood-and-water detail.[110]

The most common take-off was of dress parade. At these sham affairs, officers and noncommissioned officers were sometimes required to march in the ranks while privates with exaggerated shoulder straps, improvised from orange peelings and even canteens, gave the commands. Broomsticks and poles were substituted for muskets, and cannon were represented by logs borne on wagons or muskets laid across wheelbarrows. Knapsacks were dry-goods boxes, and haversacks sometimes were replaced by tiny bags labeled "ten days' rations." Nondescript clothing, blacked faces, "officers" riding broken-down horses or mules with saddles hind part before, shirttail flags, tin-pan drums, knee-length havelocks, candlesticks pinned on as medals and other ludicrous devices were introduced to add to the comic theme.[111]

Mock dress parades usually came on holidays as part of extensive programs featuring sports, horse races, competitive firing, feasting, drinking and other activities. Christmas, New Year's Day, Washington's Birthday, the Fourth of July and Thanksgiving were the most festively observed by Yanks in general, while the Irish made much of St. Patrick's Day and the other foreign groups celebrated occasions memorable in their respective national histories. Frequently at Christmastime and on St. Patrick's Day, regimental streets and quarters were elaborately decorated with evergreen wreaths, arches and other appropriate ornaments.[112]

In shooting matches, foot races, hurdles, sack races and wheelbarrow races, representatives of companies usually competed for cash prizes of one to five dollars. Chasing greased pigs or climbing slick poles at the top of which were nailed five-dollar bills were ordinarily free-for-all affairs, with the porker or money going to the first successful contestant. A special feature of some celebrations was a "scrape" in which "contrabands," with hands tied behind, rooted in tubs filled with meal or flour for pieces of money placed on the bottom.[113] Whisky flowed freely on these occasions, adding to the festivity and producing on the morrow a heavy crop of hang-overs. Sometimes intoxicants were contributed by officers.

Of a Christmas spree in 1864, Sergeant Onley Andrus of the Ninety-fifth Illinois Regiment wrote: "Col. Tom turned out 15 gal*ls* of Rotgut & several of the boys got Happy, and some got pugilistic, and as a consequence some had Eyes Red & some Black and all felt as though they had been poorly staid with at best." Another sergeant, of a New Jersey regiment, related a New Year's experience thus: "Last night I had plenty of Whiskey but to day I have none, we had five canteens full and we had a merry old Time. they broke all my furniture, tore my table cloth, and tore evry thing upside down, I thought I would fire a saulute, I got my musket and fired it, and I set my tent a fire, and by the time I got through, my tent was most burnt up. New Years dont come but once a year, & tents are cheap." [114]

In their efforts to make life more tolerable in ordinary seasons, soldiers resorted to some unusual expedients. One Yank told of a mock wedding of "J. Hamilton and V. Davy with B. Lee as chaplain," followed by music and dancing. Womanless nuptials seem to have been rare, but dances without benefit of ladies were common. Sometimes the women were simulated by Yanks who sent home for bonnets and hoop skirts or borrowed the finery of local Negroes; and when warmed by generous swigs of "tanglefoot" wheedled from the commissary participants seemed hardly aware of the pretense. Certainly, whether with or without resort to subterfuge and spirits, the dances were often lively affairs with cotillions, polkas and jigs constituting the usual forms. [115]

"From many of the [company] streets," wrote a Wisconsin officer from Milwaukee early in the war, "the sound of a violin in the last agonies of the 'Arkansaw traveler' or the 'Campbells are coming' greets the ear and following the sound one finds a ring formed and a merry sett 'going in' on a quadrille." [116] A few months later a New Yorker reported from a camp near Washington: "We have a ball almost every night. The ladies are personified by soldiers." [117] An Ohioan writing from Murfreesboro, Tennessee, in 1862 gave these details:

The boys are having a grand cotillion party on the green in front of my tent and appear to have entirely forgotten the privations, hardships, and dangers of soldiering. . . . The dance on the green is progressing with increased vigor. The music is excellent. At this moment the gentlemen are going to the right; now they promenade all; in a minute more the ladies will be in the center, and four hands round. That broth of an Irish boy, Conway, wears a rooster's feather in his cap and has for a partner a soldier twice as big as himself whom he calls Susan. As they swing, Conway yells at the top of his voice: 'Come round, old gal!' [118]

Billy Yank, like Johnny Reb, took considerable delight in exercising his dramatic talents. Sometimes the performances were staged in the open air on rough platforms and with meager properties. Again, when stationed for long periods in cities like Atlanta or Chattanooga facilities might be pretentious. Offerings of units, such as the Forty-fourth Massachusetts, composed largely of men from the Boston area who formed a regimental dramatic association, were varied and good. The "Second Dramatic and Musical Entertainment" given by this group consisted of songs by the Quartette Club, musical selections by the band, the trial scene from *The Merchant of Venice* by a cast from the regiment and a concluding number, " 'A Terrible Catastrophe on the North Atlantic R. R.' with Characters by the Company." [119]

The Forty-eighth New York Regiment, which also seems to have possessed unusual dramatic talent, gave a series of creditable productions at Fort Pulaski near Savannah, Georgia, in 1863. An officer of the regiment gave this account of the opening performance: "Address by Corporal Michaels. Singing by the members. Farce, 'Family Jars.' Song, 'The Flea,' by Owens, of Company H. Recitation by Hutchinson. Light balancing by Dr. Haven. Tragedy, 1st act of 'Richard III.' Song by Dickson. Concluding with the tableau, 'Washington's Grave.' The theatre was very pretty, and the performances excellent. The scene-painting was done by Harrison, who was by profession a scenic artist, and was very good." [120]

Minstrels and comedies seemed to be the most popular shows among both performers and audiences. Of a presentation by the Ninth New York Regiment's Zouave Dramatic Club, a soldier wrote: "Combastus De Zouasio, a burlesque performed well and after some very good comic songs and dancing the entertainment concluded with the farce 'Box & Cox'—the house was crowded to acces and the aristocracy of Roanoke was all there generally escorted by some members of our regiment. Gen. Hawkins atended and was receaved with enthusiastic cheers by the audience." [121]

Some of the most entertaining performances were those given about the campfire by talented individuals. Of one of these informal showmen, a comrade wrote: "Brown . . . is a perfect mimic, facile, quick, good looking . . . has a keen sense of the ridiculous & a good fellow for fun generally. Took off an old Orthodox nigger minister last night affected with bronchitis & applying his nostrils occasionally [to] his handkerchief in a professional way—got it all in—I haven't laughed so much since I came in the army." [122]

Occasionally, though rarely, soldiers in camp or hospital were treated to the offerings of itinerant entertainers. A nurse in the general hospital at Chester, Pennsylvania, told of visits to that institution by a Negro minstrel show from Philadelphia and by Antonio Blitz, the famous ventriloquist, bird imitator and sleight-of-hand artist.[123] Various singers gave camp performances, the most famous being the Hutchinson family troupe.[124] James Edward Murdoch, a notable tragedian of the time, entertained soldiers on a number of occasions, as did Thomas Buchanan Read, a famous poet, the two sometimes appearing together with Murdoch reading patriotic poems written by Read.[125] When Read himself attempted to perform, as he sometimes did, results were disappointing because his voice was weak and his material was over the heads of the listeners.[126]

Soldiers stationed near large cities now and then had the opportunity of attending the performances of leading actors and actresses of the period, but relatively few of them appear to have taken advantage of their privileged situation. When soldiers did attend good shows, they sometimes made things difficult for the artists by coarse and drunken conduct.[127] Farces, varieties and minstrel shows were far more attractive to soldier visitors to cities than were good plays.

A sample of dramatic offerings in Southern cities is afforded by the diaries of two soldiers. On August 21, 1863, an Ohioan noted at Vicksburg: "Went to the minstrels in town tonight . . . performances were good, it being the first night of the season. The female who performed the 'fancy dance' was very poorly formed, her limbs didnt amount to a cuss as far as beauty was concerned, but she handled them very gracefully, her face was pretty as she appeared on the stage. How it is naturally I can not say. The best thing of the evening was the map of the 'Southern Confederacy' with the nigger in the background. It was a soiled handkerchief all ragged held up before a darkey's face." [128] In addition to a tightrope walker and trapeze artists, seen at two different shows, an Illinois Yank reported the following from New Orleans:

Jan 4, 1865. Have been to the Varieties theater tonight. . . . The plays were Dot or the Cricket on the Hearth and Pocahontas. . . .

Jan 10, 1865. Went to the St. Charles Theatre in the Evening—Lucie De Arville & phenomenon in a Smock Frock . . .

Jan 24, 1865. Went to the morning Star Minstrels in the Evening. Damn poor show all of the performers drunk.[129]

Trips to towns and cities had attractions other than shows. Riding in the streetcars or rented hacks, gazing at the girls and gawking at the sights afforded diversion to many. Religiously inclined Yanks found pleasure in attending church and in mingling after the service with the members—especially the ladies. Seekers after more worldly pleasures commonly made a beeline for the barrooms, and some found their way to houses of prostitution. When money for drinks was exhausted before thirsts were quenched, saloons were sometimes raided in force. A jovial tippler from Chicago who frequented the gay spots of New Orleans wrote in his diary after one visit to the Crescent City: "Boys cleaned out a Bar up town, any amount of Whiskey, Rum, Gin, Brandy & Wine in camp. Most all got drunk as the Devil and had an awful time." [130]

Whether their excursions were to town or country, Yanks often managed to make the acquaintance of natives and to share their social activities. "You must not think you have all the fun at home," wrote a Philadelphian from a camp near Chambersburg, Pennsylvania, in 1864, "for I have been out several times and had a great deal of pleasure. I have been at a wedding and at Singing School and several places." [131]

Enterprising and attractive Yanks often gained entree to Southern homes. A young New Yorker confided to his diary while serving in Virginia: "At night after taps, run the Picets and went out in the cuntry to see the girls." [132] A Minnesotan, also youthful, wrote after a tour of guard duty on a planter's premises: "When not on post we sit in the house by the fire conversing with the old gentleman's daughters & enjoying ourselves hugely. It is a long time since I was in a private house and as the 'gals' are quite sociable I enjoy this treat 'right smart.' They amuse us with a warm dinner & 'Secesh songs.' . . . One of our special duties is to keep the boys from milking the old man's cow." [133]

Music was often the key which opened the door to acquaintance and provided the basis for continuing association. The talented and sociable Chicagoan, whose frequent trips to New Orleans have already been noted, wrote in his diary after one visit: "Dan and myself called on some of the town people who had a piano and amused ourselves for some time at music." Later he observed: "Called on Mrs. —— 4 Daughters . . . had quite a play on the Flute. Dyer played the Piano. . . . They have two splendid pianos. Old Lady very garrulous." Still later he reported: "Parker, Dyer, Robb & myself called on Miss Pfrang in the evening and had a sing." After moving to Franklin, Louisiana, in the autumn of 1863 he wrote: "Give Tracy 'Weeping Sad & Lonely' to give to a secesh wench that lives in town." [134]

Soldiers occasionally found diversion in calling on relatives or friends in other organizations, with eating, drinking and talk of home providing the principal activity. Once in a great while life might be brightened by visits from wives, fathers, ministers, politicians or other members of the home community. But in the main Yanks had to be content with such recreation as they themselves could provide in their own camps.

Debating afforded considerable fun in many organizations. Topics argued ranged from old favorites such as capital punishment and the relative pleasures of pursuit and possession to questions of the day such as "Resolved: That We Should Support the Constitution as It Is and the Union as It Was," and "Resolved: That the Present War Will Be More Productive of Good Than Evil." Members of the Twenty-fourth Iowa Regiment debated the proposition: "Which Has the Most Influence on Men, to-wit 'Money or Woman,'" and decided in favor of woman. They likewise found that the pen was mightier than the sword. The "Temperance Society" of the Sixteenth Connecticut Regiment weighed the relative influence on society of woman and man, but unfortunately no record was found of their conclusion. Other subjects discussed by this group were: "Resolved: That Public Speaking Is Not a Safe Rule of Action," and "Resolved: That Intemperance Is a Greater Evil Than War." With respect to the latter an hour and a half of serious argument resulted in the decision that Bacchus was more wicked than Mars.[135]

In some units debates, along with orations, recitations, spelling bees and other cultural exercises, were sponsored by "lyceums" and other imposingly named literary bodies. These organizations were usually much more active in winter than in summer because of the relatively stable conditions which prevailed during the cold season. A glimpse of one society's doings is given in a Hoosier sergeant's letter from Culpepper, Virginia, February 11, 1864: "We have built a hall that will hold about 125 men and organized . . . the 'Forest Lyceum'; order of Exercises—Declamations, Essays, Orations, Debate, Anonymous Communications &c. It is well attended and we have an excellent time. If you can find 'Poe's Raven,' a piece I used to declaim and copy it and Send it to me immediately I will be greatly obliged to you." [136]

Handicraft of various sorts, especially the carving of pipes and rings, was a favorite diversion in hospitals and prisons and was practiced to a considerable extent during periods of leisure in camp. For pipes, brier root was the usual medium and for rings and other ornaments, bone, sea shell or soft wood. Knitting had an occasional enthusiast among hospital patients, as did painting and drawing.

Nearly every regiment had one or more printers on its rolls and these, when circumstances permitted, delighted in teaming up with interested comrades to publish camp newspapers. Soldier papers ranged in character from elaborate dailies and weeklies extending over long periods of time to crude one-page affairs limited to a single issue. The strength of Billy Yank's urge to break into print is strikingly evidenced by the fact that soldiers established during the course of the war more than 100 different camp newspapers.[137] In addition to these, numerous papers were launched in Union hospitals and several by Yanks confined in Southern prisons. Moreover, soldiers had a part in publishing some of the official and semiofficial organs established in occupied areas for both military and civilian readers, such as the *New South* and the *Free South* issued in South Carolina and the *Union Appeal* in Memphis, Tennessee.[138]

The titles of the soldier papers throw some light on their character and are interesting in themselves. Three different organs, two published in camp and one in a New Orleans prison, bore the heading *Stars and Stripes*.[139] Several took their names from items of soldier equipment, as the *Buck and Ball, The Knapsack*, the *Union Guidon* and the *Camp Kettle*.[140] Some appropriated unit designations, as the *First Minnesota*, the *First Kansas*, the *Connecticut Fifth*, the *Pennsylvania Thirteenth*, the *Ohio Seventh*, the *New York Ninth*, the *Fifth Iowa Register*, the *Illinois Fifty-Second*, the *Dragoon*, the *Sixth Corps* and the *Letter H*.[141]

Patriotic themes provided the inspiration for a number of titles such as the *Whole Union*, the *War Eagle*, the *Union Volunteer*, the *Banner of Freedom* and the *American Patriot*.[142] Federal commanders were honored in three titles, namely, *Unconditional S. Grant, Grant's Petersburg Progress* and *Lauman's Own*.[143] Still other titles featured the names of camps, towns, states and rivers.

Hospital papers commonly had the same name as the institution in which they were issued, but interesting variations were found in such titles as the *Cripple*, the *Crutch* and the *Cartridge Box*.[144] One cannot but wonder whether the editors were trying to be witty or poetic when they issued to one group of patients a sheet headed the *Soldier's Casket*.[145]

A few organizations, such as the Thirteenth Pennsylvania Regiment, could boast of portable printing presses. In loyal areas local publishers sometimes made their facilities available without charge to soldier editors. But in the majority of cases camp papers were published on captured presses.[146]

When Federals occupied a Southern town soldier journalists usually made the newspaper office their primary objective, and as soon as other duties permitted they set up and published their own sheet. Sometimes, as in the case of the First Minnesota's occupation of Berryville, Virginia, in 1862, and the Twenty-fifth Ohio's entry into Manning, South Carolina, in 1865, the Yankee typographers, finding the local paper already in process of publication, simply let the Rebel portion stand and printed their own columns on the back or on additional sheets.[147]

When loyal soldiers of Missouri captured Boonville, Missouri, on June 18, 1861, and found one page of the "Secesh" paper, the *Boonville Patriot*, already in type they reset the title as *The American Patriot* and replaced four of the eight columns with Union material.[148] Occasionally the new editors chided their predecessor for urging his readers to defy the invaders to the last ditch and then taking inglorious flight before the men in blue came within gun range.

Most soldier editors aimed at a weekly schedule, though a number announced "semi-occasional" issues. The Corinth, Mississippi, *Chanticleer*, published by members of the Second Iowa Regiment, stated that it would appear "as often as possible," while editors of the *Union Advance Picket*, sponsored by the Third New York Cavalry at Washington, North Carolina, promised publication "whenever we have time." Ohio artillerymen who launched the *Battery Reveille* at Fayetteville, Tennessee, on June 7, 1862, informed their readers that issues would appear "as often as providence and the commanding general will permit." [149]

Whatever the announced intentions, most papers were issued irregularly and their life span was short. The *Badger Bulletin*, projected by a Wisconsin group, died with a single issue published at Iuka, Mississippi, on June 14, 1862. The editors explained the premature demise thus: Marching orders "nip our rising effort in the bud." [150] The same, no doubt, could have been said of scores of other papers.

Publication of the single issue, which comprises the career of many papers, sometimes was accomplished in the face of enormous difficulties. A case in point is the *Buck and Ball* printed by soldiers of the Eleventh Kansas Regiment at Cane Hill, Arkansas, in December 1862. This four-page paper bears the date of December 6 on the outside but an explanatory note inserted within indicates that printing begun on that date had to be suspended after setting up the first page, so that the staff could take part in the battle of Prairie Grove, December 7, 1862. The remaining portion, devoted largely to details of the fight, was not completed until December 15.[151]

Sometimes, when lack of facilities made printing impossible, determined Yanks wrote out their papers in longhand, passed the single copy about among their comrades and eventually sent it home for circulation.[152]

Content of the camp papers, whether printed or written, varied considerably. In some cases the columns were devoted almost exclusively to orders, reports of battles and other official matter. In others the publishers concentrated on editorials, essays, poems, jokes and stories and gave only scant attention to military items. In still other instances most of the space was devoted to lecturing local Rebels on the error of their ways and the blessings of Union.

Many papers carried advertisements. When these were genuine they consisted mainly of notices by sutlers, photographers and others attached to the military establishment who desired to do business with the soldiers. Illustrations were sparse, owing to limited facilities, and consisted largely of flags, mules, boots and other standard items which usually could be found in quantity in the morgue of confiscated journals. Sometimes considerable cleverness was demonstrated in adapting these stereotypes. Editors of the *Yazoo Daily Yankee* ran an elaborate cut of a cemetery scene, accompanied by these lines:

> Gentle stranger drop a tear
> The C.S.A. lies buried here;
> In youth it lived and flourished well
> But like Lucifer, it fell.
> Its body's here—its soul in . . . well,
> Even if I knew I would not tell.
> Rest from every care and strife,
> Your death were better than your life,
> And this one line shall grace your grave:
> Your death gave freedom to the slave.[153]

Poetic selections were standard features of many camp papers. Sometimes these were original pieces contributed by soldiers or their civilian friends, but more frequently they were borrowed from other sources. Popular songs such as "Weeping Sad and Lonely" were occasionally published, as were numerous parodies composed by the rank and file. One paper ran a parody on "Hard Times" under the title "Sow Belley." This song, as the title suggests, reflected the soldiers' disesteem of salt pork.[154]

Camp editors depended heavily on jokes, humorous stories and conundrums as fillers for their columns. Some of these were on the shady side. Readers of *Unconditional S. Grant* were treated to this tidbit: "If you wish to keep your oldest boy from walking in his sleep, let your servant girls be as old and ugly as possible." [155] The *Tri-Weekly Camp Journal*, under the heading "Insulting," carried the following:

"Have you a fellow feeling in your bosom for the poor women of Utah?" asked a speaker of the sister of Mrs. Parlington.

"Get out, you insulting rascal," said she. "I'll have you know I don't allow fellows to be feeling in my bosom. Oh, dear!" [156]

Editions varied in size from a few copies to thousands, and prices ranged from a penny to a quarter with a nickel being the usual rate. Of the first issue of the *Soldier's Letter* published at Harrodsburg, Kentucky, November 28, 1862, by the Ninety-sixth Illinois Regiment, 2,500 copies were printed at five cents a copy. Fourteen hundred copies of the *New York Ninth*, published at three cents in Warrenton, Virginia, on July 21, 1862, were exhausted so quickly that a second edition of 500 copies was run off. The *Sixth Corps*, published at Danville, Virginia, in the spring of 1865, had all the buyers it could accommodate at the high price of twenty-five cents a copy.[157]

Most soldier papers had as a partial aim the enlightenment and entertainment of the folk back home. At least two of them bore the title *Soldier's Letter*, and these along with many others were often used as substitutes or supplements for personal correspondence. Whether crude or elegant, these fugitive organs must have afforded keen pleasure to those who had a part in their preparation and must have had many interested readers both in camp and at home.[158]

Of far greater interest to the folk at home, however, were the personal letters of their soldier boys; and letter writing was one of the most pervasive of camp diversions. A civilian who visited many units in the autumn of 1861 reported that some regiments of 1,000 men had for weeks sent out an average of 600 letters a day.[159] This volume was probably not sustained, as soldiers usually carried on a more extensive correspondence during their first months of service. But outgoing mailbags were fat during any period of the war. One Yank with a penchant for record keeping reported the writing of 164 letters in 1863, 109 of which went to his homefolk and 55 "to other friends." In addition he wrote 37 letters "for other men" who presumably were illiterate comrades. Balanced against this impressive output was a total of 85 letters received.[160]

Letters were written under all sorts of conditions. In winter quarters, desks and other conveniences were usually available, but when life in the open was the vogue, as was the case most of the time, correspondents had to improvise much of their writing equipment. In 1861 Private Abraham Kendig began a letter to his homefolk: "By the light of a candle stuck in a pine stick, setting on the ground leaning against Bruce Wallace who is asleep . . . and two other fellows laying asleep in front of me I undertake to write you." Kendig was probably using his knapsack for a desk as this was a favorite makeshift, but he and other Yanks often rested their writing sheets on their knees, tin plates, books, cracker boxes or drumheads. The prone position was frequently employed, though not always with satisfactory results. "You must excuse bad writing," stated Bishop Crumrine to his brother on one occasion, "as I am almost dead lying on my belly." Another Yank who stretched himself out on the floor of his tent to write his wife had his effort brought to naught by the tramping feet of two scuffling comrades.[161]

Many Yanks interrupted their letters to take part in a skirmish or battle and some continued their scribbling even amid the confusion of screaming missiles. Most instances of writing under fire were during sieges or trench fights. "Not less than 50 balls have passed over me since I commenced writing," wrote a Yank from Vicksburg in 1863, and another, writing near Atlanta the next year, stated: "Sometimes a bullet comes a little to[o] near where I am writing and makes me spoil a letter; a man never gets so used to them but what he will dodge when they whistle past his ear." [162]

Stationery varied from fancy sheets adorned with patriotic emblems and verses (with envelopes to match) to ruled pages torn from army record books and rough paper taken from the Rebels. Ink was the preferred writing medium, but during periods of active campaigning pencils often had to be employed.

The form and content of letters varied greatly with the background and character of the writers. Some were models of literary excellence done in beautiful script, while others were so crudely written and so full of misspellings as almost to defy deciphering. The great majority of letters lay between these extremes, but since the typical private was of limited education the average was much nearer the lower than the higher end of the scale. It is not meant to imply that the polished missives were consistently superior to the roughhewn products in every respect, for sometimes the crudely scribbled and ungrammatical letters of semi-literate Yanks were absorbingly interesting, highly informative documents, rich in humor and replete with original and colorful phrase.

Often the letters of rustics told more of soldier life than did those of sophisticates, for the latter, assuming that their correspondents read the newspapers, touched certain subjects only lightly, while their less privileged comrades, unable to make such assumptions, would treat them extensively. Then, too, better-educated Yanks, because they had a more highly developed sense of delicacy, were more inclined to pass over the seamy side of camp life than were their less cultivated associates.

A characteristic letter of an average Yank would open with the words "Dear Wife [who sometimes was addressed as "Esteamed Friend"]: I seat myself and take pen in hand to drop you a few lines [or, I will take the present opertunity to drop you a few lines]. I am well at the present and hope you are injoyin a like blesson." Then would follow one or more pages of information about the writer and his comrades, interspersed with inquiries about home affairs. The writer would threaten recurrently to bring his note to a close, but other items of news coming to mind would set him going again. When finally he ran out of subject matter or writing space he would sign off with the words, "Your husband until deth [or, I remane yore afecshonet husban ontel deth do us part], John Jones to Elvira Jones." The correspondent might add a sentimental rhyme such as this: "When this you sea, remember me, though meny miles apart we bea." [163]

Favorite topics of soldier correspondents were battles, about which they wrote at great length; health; the weather; the land and people of Dixie, especially the Negroes who were a source of unusual curiosity; camp doings, particularly those involving residents of the writer's home community; rumors of future movements; food; and officers.

Sin was a subject on which both the ungodly and the righteous, especially the latter, liked to dwell. "George Farnum . . . has lost his Religion and Swars like a Salor," wrote one Yank, while another told what comrades had sired the crop of illegitimate babies recently born in the home community.[164] Others passed on information about fellow soldiers carrying on scandalously with Southern women. Young blades writing to male acquaintances of similar interests sometimes boasted of their own illicit doings, in phrases never intended for delicate readers.[165]

Tragedy was another favorite theme. Mortal illnesses and fatal accidents were recounted at length, and combat fatalities were reported in even greater detail. Executions, however, elicited the fullest descriptions, owing probably to the solemnly impressive manner in which they were staged.

Unpopular officers inspired some of the most expressive phrases of denunciation. One soldier wrote in disgust: "The Major is a hell of a man to go on a . . . [detail] with he dont no enough to learn a dog to bark." Another attributed the recent death of his general to an overdose of whisky and stated: "I did not see a tear shed but heard a great many speaches made about him such as he was in hell pumping thunder at 3 cents a clap." [166]

Writing came hard to most Yanks because of educational deficiencies, lack of experience and the seeming unimportance of camp routine. The tendency to regard as newsworthy only the unusual found frequent expression in the phrase, "I would have written before but I had nothing strange to tell you." Often those who maintained a considerable flow of correspondence, despite their handicaps, showed decided improvement in style during the course of their service.

As already noted and illustrated, letters of unsophisticated Yanks were replete with misspellings. Some of the most flagrant errors arose from efforts to tell about camp ailments. Pneumonia sometimes appeared as "nu mornia," again as "new mony," and one Yank put the word down as "new mornion." Diarrhea, a word formidable enough for educated Yanks, suffered all sorts of distortion at the hands of rustics; one victim of the disease wrote that he "had the camp Diary." Yellow jaundice was frequently "yaller ganders"; a Yank who served in General Landers' command wrote that "Landers has had the ganders." [167]

Among Northern soldiers as among their foes, "horsepittle" was standard spelling for hospital though occasionally variations were used. One Yank wrote that "James Swartz is some wares in the hose pittle." [168] Another reported that "they are deviding the Army up into corpses." [169] Typical misspellings included "stoode beanes" for stewed beans, "Hurey Can" for hurricane, "fortigg" for fatigue, "nea deap" and "axidently." "Haint" and "hant" had wide usage and the old English practice of prefixing a's to verbs, as in "agoing" (sometimes "agonter"), was common practice.

Difficulties of spelling and grammar did not prevent some Yanks from getting their ideas across with force, as witness the following outburst from an Ohioan to his sister:

Alf sed he heard that you and hardy was a runing to gether all the time and he thought he wod gust quit having any thing mor to doo with you for he thought it was no mor yuse. . . . i think you made a dam good chouis to turn of as nise a feler as Alf dyer and let that orney thefin, drunkerd, damed card playing Sun of a bich com to Sea you. the god damed theaf and lop yeard pigen tode helon, he is too orney for hel. . . . i will Shute him as shore a i Sea him.[170]

Some of the expressions used by soldier correspondents were original and vivid, while others were trite and colorless. Private Charles Babbott characterized a recently received letter as "Short and Sweet just like a rosted maget," while Henry Thompson, writing from "Camp Sh—t," informed his wife: "To tell the plain truth we are between a sh—t and a sweat out here." [171] An Ohioan stated that he had to answer roll call when it was "raining pitchforks," but, even so, he was "well, pot gugged and saucy." [172] Another Yank reported that he was "Hunkey Dora." [173]

An Ohio soldier wrote his wife that Rebel dwellings near Fredericksburg looked "like the latter end of original sin and hard times," and a Wisconsin Yank stationed in North Alabama informed a friend that "the folks [here] is pooer than skim piss." Private Michael Dresbach while convalescing in a Chattanooga hospital wrote his wife that he was so hungry that he "could eat a rider off his horse and snap at the stirrups." [171]

Other Yanks used the familiar phrases "snug as a bug in a rug," "chief cook and bottle washer," "sasia [sashay] around," "raise Ned," "raise the old hary," "let 'er rip," "midling peart," "i am well and a creking," "drunk as a fool," "scarce as hens' teeth" and "grab a root." Money was sometimes referred to as "rocks" and "spondulix."

Many slang terms which gained currency in the army also found their way into letters; included among these were "Who wouldn't be a soldier?" which meant, roughly, "Who cares?" and "Here's your mule," which was a nonsensical term used much in the same manner as soldiers of a later generation used the phrase "Kilroy was here."

A substantial portion of the letters written in camp were addressed to sweethearts who in camp parlance were known by such unflattering nicknames as "pigeon," "pig," "duck," "biddy," "jularky" and "hoosey dooksy." Correspondence between soldiers and the girls they left behind them was frequently formal and stilted, though now and then an established suitor would hazard the use of an endearing phrase. Despite the restrained tone dictated by usage of the time, a goodly number of Yanks were able, with the assistance of a timely furlough, subtle prodding by the girl and perchance a show of paternal opposition, to push their cases from a casual to a permanent basis.

Romantically inclined Yanks, like their opposites in gray, found poetry a convenient and effective agent in conveying the gentler sentiments, for poetry had the priceless quality of saying much or little, as the recipient chose; moreover, the ability to make verses was considered a mark of gallantry.

Francis S. Flint of the Second Minnesota Battery addressed these lines to his "Darling Jennie":

Oh I wish I was and I know whare
A sitt'ing in an old arm chair
And no boody thare but She & I
The door locked & the key laid by

Wouldnt we have a Gallant old
time Well we would perhaps
you'd like to know who she is well
the first letter of her name is
Jennie that's all I'll tell.[175]

From an unidentified Yank, Margaret McMeekin received the following verses which carried the bold heading "A Proposal to Maggie":

1 Do you darling do you Maggie
in my absence think of me
Think of him who loves you Maggie
And woud ever faithful be

2 Does your heart beat with emotion
Do the tear drops fill your eys
When I proffer my devotion
Do you find relief in Sighs

3 Tell me Maggie Darling tell me
Coud you trew and constant be
And whatever woses befell me
love me onely onely me

will you do hur Mag[176]

The most confirmed sentimental-verse addict encountered by the writer was Albert E. Trumble of the Fifteenth Illinois Regiment. Trumble's poetic flow, written in neat script and addressed to Amelia Boyce, began shortly after he joined the army and continued throughout his service. The first lines, sent as a postscript, were:

My pen is poor
My ink is pale
My love to you
As long as a rail.

As acquaintance ripened, Trumble waxed bolder in both his prose and poetry. From Bolivar, Tennessee, in August 1862 he penned the following:

Though waters may between us roll,
May friendship still unite our soul,
Though far distant may be our lot,
Dearest friend for get me not.

The next spring he wrote from Memphis:

When the waning moon beams sleep
At midnight on the lovely sea
And nature's pensive spirits weep
In all her dews remember me
     do it Amelia

And in August 1864, while campaigning in Georgia, he wrote as a postscript:

Way down here clear out of sight;
Three little words I wish to write
Forget me not

Trumble's capture a little later, followed by a long imprisonment, interrupted his poetic effusion. But after the war he renewed courtship of Amelia and apparently married her.[177]

Many Yanks advertised for feminine correspondents in the newspapers, but the tone of some of these notices is such as to suggest that they were inserted by pranksters.[178]

Regardless of whether or not they wrote to girls, nearly all unmarried soldiers wrote about "the dear little creeturs." A Missouri cavalryman directed his younger brother "to keep the Girls strate and wright to me and Let me now what Girl you are sparking," while a Kentucky Yank wrote his sister: "Give my love and respect to Miss Dumps Ritter tell her I feal mity like marying now. I would like to have a sweat buss from her rosy cheeks." Countless other Yanks enjoined friends at home to look after the girls for them until they returned to make up for lost time. "We have very good times here," wrote one soldier from deep in Dixie, "but i am agetting tired of dooing without girls. We dont have any women here in this wooden country." [179]

Far more diverting than the writing of letters was the reading of missives received from relatives and friends. The craving for correspondence was so great that Yanks would entreat, importune and even browbeat folk at home to write and to write fully and often. "FOR GOD-SAKE RITE" was a standard part of the letters of one soldier to his

parents and another wrote his sister: "I like to get big letters i want you
to fill up the whole Sheete." [180]

Sounding of the mail call—or as many Yanks put it the "male" call—
would produce a most enthusiastic response, causing soldiers to stop
any activity, even eating, and rush hopefully to the place of distribution.
"When the lieutenant came to the door and told ous that the male had
come Every one of the boys jumped up to heare his name called out,"
wrote Private John Herr to his sister; "it made the boys shout withe Joy
to heare from home once more." Another Yank wrote his parents that
he thought "more of a letter from home than I would a gold watch." [181]

The day following arrival of a long-delayed mail pouch in a North
Carolina camp, a Norwegian Yank wrote his parents: "I got my hands
on your letter . . . and one from my wife. . . . I can never remember
of having been so glad before. I cried with joy and thankfulness." [182]

Soldiers read and reread many times their letters from home. It was
not unusual for them literally to "wear out" the cherished missives; and
nothing did more to make camp life tolerable for most of them than a
regular flow of correspondence from loved ones.

When correspondence, journalism, music, reading, sports, horseplay
and other activities could not be enjoyed, soldiers might always turn to
conversation as a means of breaking the monotony. Chat sessions
about the campfire or in quarters were indeed a favorite mode of diversion. Topics were as varied as the soldiers' interests, but talk seemed
most frequently to turn to such subjects as home, women, religion,
battles, officers, food, politics, slackers, profiteering, freedmen and
Rebels. Discussion was frequently enlivened by rumors and the more
fantastic they were the more diverting. Humor also added sparkle,
especially when dispensed by masters of the storytelling art who were
to be found in almost any company.

One of the favorite stories that made the rounds of the campfires had
as its central character an awkward eccentric who was far better acquainted with the Bible than with tactics. In one version of the yarn,
the hero was Hackett and the details were as follows:

The guard-house was located just inside the Fort entrance and a
bridge spanned the moat to the entrance. Once, when Captain R was
officer of the day, it was his duty to inspect the guard at least once after
midnight. Hackett was at Post number one, near the gateway of the
Fort. It was a dark, rainy night, when Hackett heard Capt. R. Approach,
and called out, 'Who comes there?' Captain R. Being on one side of
the bridge, stumbled and fell headlong into the moat; as he fell he

exclaimed in a loud voice, 'J—s Ch—t.' Hackett faced about and called out promptly, 'turn out the Apostles. J—s Ch—t is coming.' Then the guard helped the Captain out of the moat.[183]

Another humorous item which must have produced hearty chortles was the famous saltpeter poem burlesquing Rebel expedients for making gunpowder.[184] Perhaps the favorite of all comic verses recited by the men in blue was a parody of the Lord's Prayer addressed to "Father Abraham," as the soldiers sometimes called Lincoln. As reported by a Connecticut soldier, the lines ran:

> Our Father who art in Washington,
> Uncle Abraham be they Name,
> Thy will be done at the South as at the North
> Give us this day our dailey rations,
> Of crackers salt horse and Pork,
> [For] Give us our short comeings,
> As we forgive our Quarter Master,
> For thine is the power,
> The soldiers and the Nigers,
> For the space of 2 Years,
>   AMEN [185]

The urge to have fun in one form or another was irrepressible. And despite the lack of organized efforts to promote recreation, wearers of the blue, like the men in gray, were able to make tolerable a life which to most was thoroughly unattractive.

CHAPTER VIII

TOEING THE MARK

A FEW WEEKS after Gettysburg one of Meade's veterans wrote to his wife: "We are bound up pretty tight here . . . the military law is quite diffrent from Common law we have to toe the mark." [1]

The military system of control which, rather than military law, was the subject of this Yank's comment was indeed different, as soldiers of all periods have readily attested. The disciplinary setup as it existed in the American Army at the time of the Civil War may be summarized briefly. [2]

Closest to the soldier in the scheme of control were the commanders of small units and their noncommissioned agents. These authorities habitually administered as "company punishments" minor penalties for trivial breaches of discipline, such as absence from roll call, violations of uniform regulations, neglect of equipment, loud talking after taps and petty altercations. But in certain circumstances commanding officers held supreme authority over their men, as in battle, in time of mutiny, or in any other emergency requiring extreme and immediate action for protection of the life of persons under their control. And in a few instances this power of life and death was exercised by unit commanders, with the approval of their superiors. A most amazing example was the shooting on August 30, 1863, of two soldiers by Lieutenant Colonel H. Robinson, commander of the First Louisiana Cavalry Regiment. When Robinson attempted to enforce an order issued by General Banks to absorb into his command some 200 soldiers of the disbanded Second Rhode Island Cavalry, the Easterners resisted, some of them saying: "We enlisted in the 2nd R. I. Cavalry, we will by God, serve in no other." After unsuccessful efforts to persuade the mutineers to comply, Robinson had the consolidation order reread to them and then threatened to shoot on the spot those who still refused to obey. Under force of this threat nearly all of the men took their places with the Louisiana regiment. From the very few still holding out Robinson selected two whom he adjudged the ringleaders and within half an hour, without resort to any sort of trial, had them executed. While the offenders were no doubt

WESTERN SOLDIERS ON PARADE

Company H, Forty-fourth Indiana Regiment

SOLDIERS OF COMPANY F, FOURTH VERMONT, IN CAMP

guilty of mutinous conduct, there is no indication that life was in danger or the case so urgent as to admit of no delay. Certainly Robinson had at his disposal a sufficient force to overpower the mutineers and hold them in restraint until a court could be assembled or the case referred to higher authority. A military commission, however, which on September 5-6 investigated the affair, not only exonerated Robinson but commended him for the "prompt and efficient manner" in which he suppressed the mutiny. General Banks, commander of the Department of the Gulf, in endorsing the court's findings, admitted that order could probably have been maintained without resort to capital punishment but declared that he was "unable, with his knowledge of the facts, to say that it was not justifiable in consideration of all the circumstances of the case." General in Chief Halleck and the Secretary of War, though obviously disturbed by a strong protest of Governor Smith of Rhode Island, apparently agreed with Banks. At least no record was found of disapproval of the execution by any military authority.[3] The incident may not have been startling to people of the sixties, but in the light of present concepts it is inconceivable that a regimental commander would presume on his own authority to shoot men except in extreme peril, or that if he did his action would go unreproved by higher authority.

While commanding officers in the Union Army seem usually to have respected the spirit of army regulations requiring them to dispose of only minor breaches of discipline and refer serious offenses to courts-martial, exceptions were by no means rare. John W. Geary and Stephen Weld were among those who assumed far-reaching authority. Geary, while still a colonel, took the responsibility of shaving a soldier's head and drumming him out of camp. After he became a general, he once knocked down and choked a soldier whom he caught straggling. Lieutenant Colonel Weld, after shooting an insubordinate private in the arm, wrote: "I meant to kill him, and was very sorry I did not succeed. . . . I called him up a few days after shooting him and told him that I meant to have killed him . . . but that if he would promise to let rum alone, I would release him from the guard-house. I might have had him tried by court-martial and shot, but I thought I would give him another chance." Another lieutenant colonel, commander of a Negro regiment, followed the interesting practice of giving serious offenders a choice between being punished by him or having their cases referred to courts-martial.[4]

Next above company punishment in the disciplinary scheme were the regimental and garrison courts-martial. These courts, convenable by order of commanders of posts, regiments and comparable organizations, consisted of three officers. Their jurisdiction was restricted to enlisted men and to noncapital cases. Since the articles of war prohibited regimental or garrison courts from inflicting fines exceeding one month's pay or imposing hard labor or prison sentences exceeding a month's duration, offenses tried by these bodies were usually of a minor character, such as petty theft, brief absences without leave, straggling, skulking and brawling.[5] Some of the punishments habitually meted out by regimental courts, such as tying up by the thumbs, carrying heavy weights, bucking and gagging, and riding wooden horses, while not specifically violating the maximum penalties authorized by the articles of war, actually exceeded them in severity.

The next higher organization in the disciplinary system was the general court-martial. At the outbreak of war, power to convene this type of court was restricted to commanders of armies or departments. But the unusual needs growing out of the war caused Congress in December 1861 to extend the convening authority to commanders of divisions and separate brigades.[6]

General courts-martial consisted of five to thirteen officers, and their jurisdiction extended to all ranks and comprehended all types of cases, including capital offenses. Army regulations specified the following legal punishments dispensable by courts-martial: death; imprisonment; confinement on bread and water; solitary confinement; hard labor; ball and chain; forfeiture of pay and allowances; discharge from the service; reprimand; and, in cases of noncommissioned officers, reduction in grade. Solitary confinement of a prisoner, or confinement on bread and water, was restricted to a total of eighty-four days out of a year, and in a lengthy sentence had to be broken every fourteen days with a two weeks' respite. Until its abolition in August 1861, flogging was a legal punishment for desertion.[7]

General courts-martial often prescribed a combination of legal punishments, and it was not unusual for them to impose penalties which violated the spirit if not the letter of the law, such as branding and head shaving.

Comparable in authority and procedure to the general court-martial was the military commission, a judicial body designed for enemy areas where civilian agencies were inoperative or for other localities under martial law. Jurisdiction of military commissions comprehended both military and civilian personnel, and soldiers were occasionally tried before these bodies, especially for offenses against civilians.[8]

Courts-martial and military commissions followed a well-defined procedure designed to assure a full hearing and a fair trial for the accused.[9] Persons on trial were allowed benefit of counsel, could challenge members of the court and had the right to question witnesses. An extensive record was kept of proceedings.[10] In a great number of cases sentences were set aside by higher authority, and prisoners found guilty of the most serious offenses were often relieved of punishment because of minor deviations from prescribed procedure.[11] For example, a private, sentenced to be shot for striking a superior officer and deserting, was ordered released and returned to duty by General Hooker because the record of proceedings did not explicitly state that the sentence had been concurred in by two thirds of the court.[12] In the case of another soldier convicted of desertion, proceedings stating that the court and the judge were "duly sworn" failed to include the phrase "in the presence of the accused" as required by army regulations. The Judge Advocate General of the Army called General Banks's attention to the flaw and suggested that the court be reassembled to correct it. General Banks replied that the court had been dissolved and stated he intended to have the soldier shot, in accordance with the court's sentence, as he deemed the irregularity a purely technical one. The Judge Advocate General commended Banks's desire to exercise a firm discipline but held that the defect was "fatal," and on his recommendation President Lincoln remitted the sentence.[13]

Beyond the court-martial and the military commission was a chain of higher commanders, the Judge Advocate General of the Army (which office was created in July 1862) and the President of the United States.[14] The commander who ordered a court reviewed its proceedings and, except when the sentence was death (or dismissal of an officer from the service), ordered it put into effect, mitigated or set aside. Dismissal of officers had to be approved by army or department commanders, and early in the war these commanders had the power to confirm and order execution of the death penalty. But in July 1862 Congress passed a law requiring referral of all sentences of death and imprisonment to the President. Subsequently this provision was modified to give army and department commanders final authority in death sentences for certain types of offenses, including spying, desertion, mutiny, arson, burglary and rape. When cases were referred to the President they were forwarded through command channels and the Judge Advocate General of the Army.[15]

The disciplinary system as it existed in 1861, while adequate in times of peace, failed to meet the unusual circumstances created by the war. Rapid mobilization of hordes of civilians unaccustomed to discipline led to a volume of offenses which swamped the courts-martial. Moreover, when active campaigning began, with straggling an inevitable concomitant, officers were too vitally needed in their units to permit the frequent holding of courts-martial. The result was the accumulation of enormous backlogs of prisoners whose diversion from soldierly duties, along with that of the force required to guard them, seriously impaired the armies' effectiveness. Then, too, the failure to bring offenders promptly to trial violated fundamental principles of justice and had an adverse effect on discipline.

The situation was further complicated by the dearth of officers skilled in court-martial procedure. As a general rule, only the Regular Army officers were thoroughly acquainted with the system and these officers were too few, too poorly distributed and too badly needed for other functions to be frequently available for courts-martial. Early in the war the regiment that could provide officers sufficiently informed to conduct any kind of court was a rarity, and throughout the conflict higher commanders seem to have had difficulty in finding personnel who could operate general courts-martial in complete accordance with regulations. On August 10, 1863, N. P. Banks, commanding general of the Department of the Gulf, wrote the Judge Advocate General of the Army: "With the utmost care in the selection of officers, I have found it impossible to assemble a court whose proceedings will not in some way violate the rules of military jurisprudence." [16]

Owing to these considerations, a law was passed in July 1862 providing that cases hitherto brought before regimental or garrison courts-martial should be tried by a field-grade officer specially detached for the purpose. The same law created the office of Judge Advocate General of the Army and authorized appointment in each field army of a judge advocate with rank of major whose function was to advise and assist in the administration of justice.[17] These changes expedited action and increased the general efficiency of judicial machinery.[18]

Even so, military justice was sometimes so ineffective that impatient and angry soldiers took punishment into their own hands. In July 1863 a New York regiment, while on the march from Harrisburg to New York City, became so infuriated with a chronic thief that they seized him, put him under guard, shaved his head, poured tar on him, wrote the word THIEF in large letters on his back and after parading him before the regiment drummed him from their ranks. While the main body of the regiment proceeded on its way, a few members followed the culprit, stoning and jeering him until he sank down in exhaustion, begging for his life; and thus they left him.[19] But instances of this sort were unusual.

Probably the most common of all offenses was absence without leave. In the overwhelming majority of cases absences were of short duration. Running the guard, or taking French leave as the soldiers commonly put it, was most frequent while units were encamped near large cities or in the vicinity of such irresistible attractions as chicken roosts, stock pens or orchards. The usual punishments for absence without leave and the concomitant evil of missing roll call or drill were: confinement in the guardhouse, which more often than not was a guarded tent; marching about the camp carrying a log, a bag of sand, a knapsack filled with rocks or some other weight; riding the wooden horse, which consisted of sitting astride a horizontal pole held aloft by upright supports; digging stumps; and doing extra duty.

Some commanders kept a black list made up of absentees from roll call and other minor offenders. From this list drafts were made when some particularly disagreeable task had to be performed, such as burying dead horses, digging latrines or cleaning up the camp.[20]

Punishments were adapted to the gravity of offenses by adjustments in time or quantity. For a brief overstaying of a pass or failure to answer roll by a soldier whose conduct generally was good, the guardhouse confinement might be limited to an hour or two; if the sentence was carrying a log, the weight might be light and the period brief; or if the penalty was grubbing stumps, their size might be small and the number few. But for serious or chronic offenders the dosage of punishment would be increased to considerable severity. In the Sixth Michigan Regiment, for example, breaking guard became so prevalent during a period of encampment near Baltimore that offenders were required to carry twenty-pound bags of sand for several days, walking in a ring for alternate hours from six o'clock in the morning until six at night.[21]

When unauthorized absence from camp extended over a period of several days or weeks, heavier penalties were applied, such as forfeiture of pay, wearing ball and chain and imprisonment for one or more months, sometimes with the stipulation that during part of the confinement rations be restricted to bread and water. A private of the Seventh Massachusetts Regiment received this sentence for absence without leave: "Stand on a barrel in front of Guard house with stick of wood on his shoulder from Reveille to Retreat for 2 days." [22]

Fighting and brawling, usually inspired by liquor, were also common offenses. "When they can't get Johnny Rebs to fight, some of the fellows do a good deal of fighting among themselves," wrote Private Edward L. Edes from East Tennessee in March 1864.[23] Brawls were more frequent during periods of inactivity and when encampment near large cities gave easier access to whisky. For minor altercations punishments were about the same as for running the guard, but when fighting was persistent or general, heavier penalties were imposed.

Drinking, per se, when not on duty and when held to moderation, was usually not regarded as a breach of discipline. But army regulations made corporal punishment mandatory for drunkenness on guard;[24] and habitual intemperance sometimes led to dishonorable discharge. Typical instances of punishment for drunkenness are afforded by comments of two soldiers on the subject. Richard L. Ashhurst of the 150th Pennsylvania Regiment wrote his homefolk on November 6, 1862: "Three men sentenced to walk in barrels for six days for continuous drunkenness." [25] Joseph D. Galloway of another Pennsylvania regiment noted in his diary July 5, 1861: "Desher being quite [drunk] as a punishment . . . was compelled to carry a musket and a carpet bag strapped to his [back] containing fifty pounds of stones. Gus Goodwin was put on guard over him to see that he kept moving." [26]

Promiscuous firing of guns was a common violation in many units. This practice, objectionable both on the score of wasting ammunition and of endangering life, frequently occurred in connection with unauthorized invasion of civilian premises for such delicacies as pork or poultry. The evil became so widespread in the Army of the Potomac in April 1862 as to elicit a prohibitory general order, and during Sherman's Georgia campaign the commander of the Seventeenth Corps found it necessary to charge foraging parties fifty cents for each missing cartridge that could not satisfactorily be accounted for.[27] In the army as a whole the customary penalty for this offense seems to have been confinement in the guardhouse.

Insubordination was shockingly prevalent during the early period of the war, owing to the civilian soldiers' aversion to discipline and the incompetency of officers. The low esteem in which many volunteers held their leaders was pungently expressed by Private Charles A. Barker, who seems to have been a Civil War version of Bill Mauldin. In 1862 Barker wrote: "The officers consider themselves as made of a different

material from the low fellows in the ranks"; and the next year he complained: "They get all the glory and most of the pay and don't earn ten
cents apiece on the average, the drunken rascals." Another private,
George Gray Hunter, hit the jackpot of disparagement. In response to
an inquiry as to his having a commission, Hunter exploded: "I am vary
glad to Be able to inform you that I have Not—and that ant all I would
have for a Dollar, for if thare is one thing that I hate more than anothe[r]
it is the Sight of a shoulder Strap, For I am well convinced in My own
Mind that had it not Been for officers this war would have Ended long
ago." [28]

In its most common form, insubordination consisted of the use of
contemptuous or disrespectful language toward superiors. A Michigan
private when ordered to extra duty for refusal to drill said to his captain:
"You are God damned trash. You think you can do just as you God
damn please because you are officers. I'll be God damned if I will [per-
form the duty]. . . . I'll see you in hell before I will." An Irish soldier
of a Pennsylvania regiment when ordered by his adjutant to keep
quiet while serving a sentence in the guardhouse replied: "I will not
keep quiet for you, you God damned low-lived son of a bitch, you
shit-house adjutant." An Ohio artilleryman when placed under arrest
by his lieutenant remarked: "You order me! You aint worth a pinch of
shit!," and another Yank chafing under reproof told a platoon leader,
"You kiss my arse, you God damned louse." Other officers who sought
to discipline refractory soldiers were dubbed with such uncomplimentary titles as "bugger," "dog," "green-horn," "whore-house pimp" and
"skunk." But by far the most frequently applied expletive was the time-
honored "son of a bitch." [29]

Occasionally soldiers flouted authority by refusing to obey orders or
perform required duty. In less frequent instances insubordination was
carried to the extreme of pushing, kicking, striking and even shooting
officers. An unpopular colonel awoke one morning to find that the tail
of his favorite horse had been shingled. Another officer narrowly escaped
serious injury when a grapeshot hurled by an aggrieved soldier came
flying through his tent at night, knocking over a candle. An Illinois
sergeant who killed a captain bent on punishing him remarked after the
fatal shooting: "I killed him. The company wanted him killed. . . . I
killed the son of a bitch and I was the only man in the company who
had the heart to do it." In numerous instances men stated their intention of shooting officers when they went into battle, but it is impossible
to establish instances of the threat being executed.[30]

Insubordination declined in frequency and gravity with the passing of time. But it remained a serious problem throughout the war. Penalties most frequently meted out to soldiers who became disorderly and disrespectful to their superiors were "tying up" and bucking and gagging. These punishments, imposed usually by order of unit commanders, were sometimes deemed sufficient in themselves. In other instances, especially when the resistance was unusually violent or the offenders were chronic troublemakers, the cases would be referred to courts-martial for trial and further punishment.

Tying up usually meant suspension by the thumbs from a limb or pole in such manner as to permit only the toes to touch the ground. When left in this position for an hour or more, as was not unusual, the victim suffered extreme pain. The severity was enhanced if the punishment took place outside during cold weather. Other forms of tying up were the strapping of offenders to trees, posts or other stationary objects in such a way as to immobilize them, or binding arms to the body and roping the feet so that the victims could only sit or lie on the ground.

Bucking consisted of setting the offender down, tying his wrists together, slipping them over his knees and then running a stick or musket barrel through the space beneath the knees and over the arms. Gagging was the tying of a bayonet or piece of wood in the mouth. A surgeon who witnessed this type of punishment wrote of the results: "The culprit was completely subdued . . . having been tied some 4 hours. He was sobbing and crying as though suffering greatly. When untied he was not able to walk. . . . He was *carried* to his quarters." [31] Sometimes brutality of this punishment was increased by forcing large gags into the mouth, thus causing excessive strain on the jaws or laceration of the mouth. One case is on record of a soldier dying from bucking and gagging. [32]

An unusually testy and cruel lieutenant became so infuriated at a soldier who talked back to him that he gagged him by tying a large rope tightly in his mouth and suspended him by the thumbs. The Yank placed as guard over this soldier wrote: "It was a cold day & the blood running down from his hands and arms & the tight cord cutting through the skin made the man groan so that I was strongly tempted to cut him down myself. . . . The Lieut. [ordered] . . . me if he Struggled to release himself to put my Bayonet through him. Once in a while the said Brute would come & visit him & seemed to enjoy his torture exceedingly." Fortunately for the victim, the colonel commanding the regiment came by and ordered the prisoner's release, but not until he had become so stiff and weak as to require assistance of two men in getting back to the guardhouse.[33]

When insubordination went beyond threats and nasty talk and involved physical violence against an officer, the offense assumed a graver character and led to more serious penalties. The ninth article of war, which can be traced directly to Prince Rupert's Code of 1672, stated that "any officer or soldier who shall strike his superior officer, or draw or lift up any weapon or offer any violence against him . . . shall suffer death, or such other punishment as shall . . . be inflicted upon him by the sentence of a court-martial." [34] But a sampling of courts-martial records indicates that death sentences for violent action against officers were rare; and executions were almost unheard of. An official list of executions published by the War Department, which appears fairly complete, shows only one instance of a soldier paying the extreme penalty for violation of the ninth article of war. This compares with twenty executions for mutiny.[35] The usual punishment for striking an officer was a long term of imprisonment at hard labor followed by dishonorable dismissal from the army.

Various types of insubordination and the punishments incurred may well be illustrated by a few specific cases. A Massachusetts private en route to the guardhouse for snapping his gun repeatedly on drill became so enraged at the sergeant escorting him that he called him a "God damned little piss-pot" and attempted to shoot him. The sentence imposed on this soldier by court-martial was forfeiture of ten dollars of each month's pay for one year and thirty days in the guardhouse. A Kansas cavalryman, when asked by his lieutenant why he gave whisky to some prisoners he was guarding, replied, "I thought I would give them a dram—You may shove it up . . ." This bit of impudence was adjudged "conduct prejudicial to good order and military discipline" and its perpetrator sentenced to confinement at hard labor and forfeiture of pay for three months. Even more rambunctious was an Irish sergeant of the Thirtieth Massachusetts Regiment who said to his first sergeant in the presence of other enlisted men of the company: "You are a God damned, white-livered, tallow-faced skunk, and if you say that again I will knock every tooth down your throat and kick your arse through the company streets if I lose the stripes by it." He did lose his stripes, ripped from his uniform in the presence of his regiment, and in addition paid a fine of twenty dollars.[36]

Private John Williams of the First New Jersey Cavalry, for striking his lieutenant and saying to him, "If I ever get liberated I will shoot you and all such sons of bitches," was sentenced to forfeiture of all pay, confinement in the penitentiary for the rest of his enlistment and dishonorable discharge from the service. A German private in the Twelfth Pennsylvania Cavalry became so insubordinate toward his major for tying up a comrade that the officer knocked him down. Afterward while the major was proceeding through the camp a shot was fired at him by a hidden assailant. The court had some difficulty establishing the insolence of the language since it was spoken in German and of definitely identifying the German as the person firing the shot, but the majority held him guilty and he was sentenced to five years in the penitentiary and dishonorable discharge.[37]

An Ohio artilleryman who cursed and twice struck in the face a lieutenant who was attempting to arrest him for disorderly conduct was sentenced to be shot. But President Lincoln, on recommendation of Army Commander George H. Thomas, commuted the sentence to forfeiture of all pay and imprisonment during the remainder of the offender's term of enlistment.[38]

Almost every regiment had a few rascals who were not above pilfering from their comrades. Punishments for this offense varied with the value of the articles stolen and with the reputation of the culprit, but dispensers of justice usually dealt more harshly with stealing (from soldiers) than with other noncapital crimes. Petty theft was often punished by unit commanders with such penalties as: marching about the camp in a "barrel shirt"—a commissary barrel slipped down over the offender's head—on which was painted THIEF; parading the drill ground or company streets with placards marked THIEF hanging front and back; standing on a barrel, a stump or other elevated place adorned with labels proclaiming their offense and displaying the stolen articles; and suspension by the thumbs. If the culprit was hailed before courts-martial, heavier penalties usually resulted. An Iowa soldier who stole nearly fifty dollars from two comrades forfeited all pay due him, had his head shaved, was placarded THIEF and drummed out of the service through the ranks of his regiment to the tune of the "Rogue's March." A Pennsylvania private who stole $260.00 from his fellow soldiers suffered similarly, with the added penalty of five years' imprisonment at hard labor. For appropriating five government blouses worth about ten dollars, an Illinois artilleryman forfeited a month's pay and worked for thirty days on the Vicksburg fortifications during which time there hung from his back a board two feet long and one foot wide inscribed with the word THIEF.[39]

Pillaging of civilians, particularly those of Rebel sympathies, was a common practice. While high commanders usually deplored the practice and issued repeated orders against it and while a few plunderers were shot, various factors prevented the punishment of more than a small percentage of those who looted Southern premises. In the first place, soldier sentiment, while by no means consistently condoning the practice, certainly was not so strongly opposed to stealing from Rebels as from one another; and many Yanks who at home had the most scrupulous regard for private property took the view that things were different now that they were down south. Lower-ranking officers often shared the views of their men that Rebels were rightful objects of plunder and hence were lax in compelling compliance with the injunctions of superiors.[40] Indeed, some lieutenants and captains were not above leading their men in raids upon Southern wardrobes and treasure troves.[41] At any rate the difficulty of distinguishing between authorized foragers and private plunderers worked against a close control over the invading forces. The net result, especially on rapid movements such as those of Grant in North Mississippi in 1862 and Sherman in Georgia and the Carolinas in 1864-1865, was to afford relative impunity to "bummers" and others determined to prey on civilians.

Sleeping on post occurred with notable frequency, especially during the early part of the war. While theoretically this was one of the most serious military offenses, punishable under articles of war by death, in practice it was treated with shocking leniency. In September 1861 a general court-martial of McClellan's command found six soldiers guilty of this offense. The severest sentence handed down was a month at hard labor and forfeiture of three months' pay. One of the men received no punishment at all on the ground that he had been on sentry duty two successive nights.[42] Courts of other commands, in the war's first year, viewed sleeping on sentry duty with similar nonchalance, imposing repeatedly such sentences as short confinement with ball and chain and light fines.[43]

The case of Private Joshua C. Ward affords one of the most amazing commentaries on the casualness with which sleeping on post was sometimes regarded. In February 1862 Ward was tried by a general court-martial of Banks's division, Army of the Potomac, and found not guilty. McClellan's review of the proceedings brought out the fact that Ward, after being duly posted as a sentinel, was found lying asleep on the ground and that when finally aroused after much shaking and shouting he "arose in great wrath against those who had waked him." The commissioned officer of Ward's company who turned him in, later remarked: "Had I known that he would have been reported to General Court-martial I would not have reported him because I had reason to believe others had been asleep on guard and not been reported." The court in returning a verdict of not guilty cited as extenuating circumstances: The post was not an important one as it was not in the face of the enemy and other guards were situated near by; the accused had marched seven miles and had been on guard duty the previous day; discipline was poor in the offender's regiment and instructions concerning guard duty were imperfect and erroneous; and acquittal of Ward would probably cause the army commander to issue a needed order for proper instruction of sentinels. Little wonder that this finding called forth a blistering rebuke from McClellan! But he did not order a new trial.[44]

As the war progressed a general trend toward severer punishment of those who slept at their posts was apparent, but as late as 1864 a court of the Army of the Potomac gave two sleeping guards a sentence of a thirty-dollar fine and carrying a twenty-pound log eight hours a day for thirty days.[45]

Throughout the war, courts occasionally issued the death sentence in cases of sleeping on post, but in most such instances army commanders, when they had authority to do so, would lighten the penalty and this despite their own prior protests against treating lightly the "sacredness" of a sentinel's duty. The few capital penalties for sleeping sentries which came to Lincoln's desk for final action were disapproved by him. One Yank thus saved by Presidential clemency was Private William Scott of the Third Vermont Regiment. His pardon was dramatically delivered at the last minute while he stood in the presence of his assembled division and awaited the fatal blast of the firing squad.[46] No record was found of any Union soldier dying for sleeping at his post.

Another serious offense was misbehavior before the enemy. Cowardice and skulking in battle, like most other delinquencies, were sometimes punished on authority of company or regimental commanders. For example, a Vermonter who showed the white feather in the fighting before Richmond in June 1862 was required by his colonel to walk a beat in front of regimental headquarters wearing a coffee barrel on which was inscribed in huge letters, FIRST MAN LOST AT SAVAGE STATION. But more frequently those who failed to do their duty in combat were called before courts-martial and given such sentences as: a fine of forty dollars and standing on a barrel every alternate hour for four days; a year at hard labor with forfeiture of all pay; and dishonorable discharge, which usually was attended by such tokens of disgrace as head shaving and drumming out in the presence of comrades. Sometimes branding the letter C with a red-hot iron on the culprit's hip or cheek was made a part of the penalty.[47]

Two Vermont soldiers who played the coward during the Seven Days' battles were sentenced to have half their heads and faces shaved, to have the buttons cut off their blouses and then to be drummed out of camp. A Yank who witnessed the punishment wrote: "[The] sentence was duly carried out, in the presence of the brigade, which formed in hollow square, the culprits under a Strong guard with fixed bayonets were marched around the inside of the square, in the following order, first, a file of our men with arms reversed, [then] a file on Each Side of the prisoners, followed by a file with bayonets at the charge; the whole preceded by the drum corps playing the Rogue's March, to which someone set these words: 'Poor old Soldier, poor old soldier, tarred and feathered, and drummed out of camp, because he was a deserter.' " [48]

While these measures fulfilled the terms of the court's sentence, more humiliation was yet to be endured by the unfortunate cowards. Other men of the regiment, smarting under the disgrace which their unit had suffered as a result of the craven act, now dressed the culprits in castoff slave clothing, spread molasses on the ground "and gave them a thorough rolling in the Stuff, and from thence to the red clay dust. When the operation was complete, they looked as though they had been [in] the hands of the Phillistines, and were allowed to go where they chose." [49]

Other serious offenses included treason, murder and rape, all of which were punishable by death, and which, more so than other capital offenses, actually led to the supreme penalty. The War Department's official list of 267 Union soldier executions records three deaths for spying, eighteen for rape, two for the double crime of murder and rape, one for rape and theft and seventy for murder. Two of the "spies" were bounty jumpers, caught deserting and giving important information to one whom they supposed a Rebel. General Sheridan had them summarily shot on his own authority.[50] Eleven of the rapists were Negro soldiers, five of whom were executed by order of drumhead courts-martial.[51] Of the murderers one was hanged by order of a regimental court-martial, in violation of army regulations which reserved capital sentences to general courts-martial.[52] Another of the executions for murder was done apparently on the sole authority of a lieutenant of cavalry.[53]

By far the most common of capital offenses was that of desertion. And probably for no other offense was such a wide variety of punishments imposed. Early in the war punishments were amazingly light, often not exceeding the forfeiture of one to three months' pay. As in other types of offenses, penalties became more severe after the first year or two of conflict, but even then deserters occasionally drew relatively trivial sentences. In the summer of 1863 a general court-martial of the Department of the Gulf let several deserters off with fines of thirty-nine dollars each, and another court which met in Arkansas in September 1864 required of four deserters only that they forfeit varying amounts of pay and make up the time lost from service.[54]

Except during the initial period of the war, the most frequently applied punishment for desertion was imprisonment for from one to five years, sometimes at hard labor, preceded or followed by dishonorable discharge from the service. As in the case of cowardice, branding (with the letter D) on shoulder, hip or cheek, shaving all or parts of the head and drumming out of camp were sometimes included in the sentence. During hard labor and prison periods, culprits in some cases were required to wear ball and chain.

The percentage of Union deserters apprehended and brought to trial is not known.[55] But some idea of the frequency of conviction and the meting out of the death sentence is afforded by a report prepared at Lincoln's request in November 1863. This document revealed that in the Army of the Potomac between July 1 and November 30, 1863, 592 men were tried for desertion, 291 were found guilty, 80 received capital sentences and 21 were eventually shot. During this same period about 2,000 deserters had been returned to their regiments.[56]

The War Department list of Union executions shows 141 deaths for desertion. This represents more than half of the total number executed for all offenses during the war.[57]

Executions for desertion, as for other crimes, were usually carried out in such manner as to inspire as much awe as possible. For the gruesome occasion the brigade or division to which the culprit belonged was formed around what was called a hollow square but which actually was a rectangle open at one end. After the troops had taken their places an escort marched the prisoner out. At the head of the procession was the provost marshal on horseback; next came the band playing the doleful strains of the "Dead March"; then followed a guard of twelve armed men which was deployed diagonally across the open end of the formation as protection against the prisoner's escape; next in order were four soldiers bearing the coffin, and after them came the condemned man accompanied by a chaplain and flanked on each side by a guard. Last in the solemn procession came the firing party composed usually of twelve men, one of whom bore a musket containing a blank charge; but as none knew which was the innocuous weapon each could hope that it was the one he carried. Sometimes a reserve firing squad was brought along to act in case the first group failed to accomplish its mission.

When the procession reached its destination the prisoner was seated on a coffin placed near the grave in the open end of the rectangle. Following the chaplain's final ministrations, the provost marshal came forward, blindfolded the culprit and read the official order of execution. He then directed the firing party to carry out the order and after a painful last moment, broken by the clicking of hammers, the fateful command "Fire!" brought a merciful end to the suspense.

Following the surgeon's pronouncement that life was extinct, all the soldiers comprising the formation were required to march by the corpse so that a close-up view might be had of a deserter's fate. The impression was tremendous, as letters of the spectators vividly attest.[58] Even so, there is no indication that desertion was greatly deterred by these gruesome dramas.

Executions sometimes were marked by unanticipated details which added to their horror. In one instance, two of a firing squad of six failed to discharge their muskets, a third missed the target, a fourth fired a blank cartridge and a fifth inflicted an unmortal wound. Fortunately the shot of the sixth was fatal. The two who disobeyed the order to fire were placed in irons and held for severe punishment.[59]

In other instances executions were woefully bungled. A surgeon recounts such an occasion in his diary thus: "Sgt Walker Co. A, 3rd S. C. Inf. [Union, colored] was shot by sentence of court martial at 10:00 A.M. . . . 5 balls entered the body, one the head. Two vollies were fired 12 paces off. At the first the culprit staggered back one pace & fell. I examined his wounds briefly and retired and the other volley was fired as he lay on the ground." A Pennsylvanian reported a case in which three attempts were required to dispatch a deserter. After the first fire the culprit remained sitting upright on his coffin. "Another platoon of the firing squad was hurried up and when they fired the poor fellow fell; his elbow struck the rough box; he recovered himself and sat up for the second time. The third squad was ordered up; they fired and he fell into his box dead." In still another case, where execution was by hanging, the rope broke when the trap was sprung and the hapless victim, crying pitifully "Shoot me! shoot me!" had to be lifted up and dropped a second time.[60]

From what has already been stated it is apparent that for offenses as a whole the most common penalties were confinement in the guardhouse, ball and chain, carrying logs or weighted knapsacks, wearing barrel shirts or placards, doing extra duty, standing on a barrel or other eminence, public reprimand by a superior, bread-and-water diet, stoppage of pay, tying up and bucking and gagging.

Commanders and courts supplemented these common penalties with an impressive array of unusual punishments, some of which were highly original and a few extremely brutal. Despite the Congressional interdiction of August 5, 1861, flogging was practiced to a limited extent throughout the war. In February 1863 General Jefferson C. Davis had four of his soldiers, who molested a Tennessee girl, tied to the wheel of a cannon, their heads shaved, their bare backs beaten with fifty lashes of a rawhide whip and then drummed out of camp. A fifth soldier escaped the flogging by turning informer, but he was compelled to wield the lash on his fellows. Of the culprits' reaction to the whipping, a soldier who witnessed the punishment wrote: "The first one yelled and screamed and prayed lustily—the 2d never uttered a groan. The 3d stood it better than the 1st but he whined considerably." [61]

An Ohio colonel had four stragglers of his command march for three hours with a rail, attached by rope to their necks, dangling in front of them, their guns hanging from the rail and their hands tied behind them.[62]

In the Fifty-first Indiana a minor offender sometimes was required to stand on one foot atop a cracker box while a comrade likewise guilty of some slight fault was stationed near by and instructed to prod the living statue with a bayonet should he lower the other foot. In case of the guard's failure to prod as ordered, he had to mount the pedestal himself and another comrade took over the role of guard for both. Soldiers of the Fifty-ninth Illinois Regiment were treated one day to the sight of a comrade parading through camp with both hands tied fast to a singletree which was hitched to a mule. Guards with fixed bayonets flanked the soldier while behind him came a fifer and drummer playing the "Rogue's March." [63]

Musicians, like other soldiers, sometimes were punished by doses of extra duty. A Massachusetts fifer, caught in some minor violation, was sentenced by regimental court-martial to play on his instrument for two hours before regimental headquarters. Instead of varying the tune, as was expected, the fifer devoted his talents exclusively to the doleful air "On the Road to Boston," with the result that the staff suffered almost as much punishment as the culprit.[64]

A Pennsylvania soldier named Spotswood, whose sentence was to dig a pit behind his colonel's tent, also gave an amusing twist to his punishment. As Spotswood dug he piled the dirt in such a manner as to resemble a parapet. When the excavation was completed holes were made in the parapet after the fashion of embrasures and black bottles pointed through them toward the tent, much to the merriment of the enlisted men.[65]

In the cavalry petty offenders were sometimes required to carry saddles about the camp, and artillerymen, for violations both serious and trivial, were tied spread-eagle fashion to the spare wheel which habitually rode at an angle on the rear of caissons; and in rare instances they were bound to the tailboard or the forage rack of battery wagons.[66] These latter punishments were uncomfortable under the best conditions, and when prolonged or when the vehicles were driven over rough roads they became excruciating. Of the brutality of the wheel penalty an artillery private wrote: "Feet and hands were firmly bound to the felloes of the wheel. If the soldier was to be punished moderately he was left bound in an upright position on the wheel for five or six hours. If the punishment was to be severe, the ponderous wheel was given a quarter turn . . . which changed the position of the man being punished from an upright to a horizontal one. . . . I have frequently seen men faint while undergoing this punishment. . . . To cry out, to beg for mercy, to protest ensured additional discomfort in the shape of a gag . . . being tied into the suffering man's mouth . . . no man wanted to be tied up but once." [67]

For the army as a whole, other unusual punishments included isolation of trivial offenders on elevated platforms, confinement in stocks and encasement in sweat boxes. The last-mentioned device was described by a soldier as "a box eighteen inches square, and of the full height of a man into which the culprit was placed to stand until released." One of the most original penalties was that inflicted by the colonel of the Thirty-fourth Indiana Regiment who, when a soldier was brought before him for stealing a shirt, ordered him to "go with the guard, and stick your head into each and every tent in the regiment beginning at Company A, and tell them you stole a shirt." Finally the thief was required to return the shirt to the owner and ask his forgiveness.[68]

What of the general quality of military justice in the Union Army? As previously intimated, undue leniency was common during the early part of the war, and while the trend was toward greater severity, grave offenses throughout the conflict occasionally were treated with shocking softness. The unwillingness of courts to "bear down" and issue sentences commensurate with the crimes was the subject of repeated complaint by higher commanders. Following the issuance of trivial penalties for the most serious offenses by a general court-martial in Hooker's command in September 1861, McClellan remarked: "It has seldom happened that military delinquencies so grave have been visited with punishments having so much the appearance of intending to sanction future violations of good order and discipline. . . . Military crimes to which the articles of war annex the heaviest penalties are treated as if they were the most venial misdemeanors." [69]

Early in 1862 McClellan rebuked even more severely a court-martial for letting off with a five-dollar fine a soldier who struck two of his sergeants and sentencing to only a ten-dollar fine another man who entered a private home, cursed the occupants and at the point of a gun forced them to feed him and his comrades. "Such offenses are punishable *capitally*," wrote McClellan in his review of the proceedings. "The paltry penalty exacted of the prisoners . . . is a burlesque upon military justice." But McClellan, notwithstanding his protests against undue leniency, proved squeamish when faced with the unpleasant task of approving death sentences. Of twenty-seven capital sentences meted out by eleven courts of the Army of the Potomac early in 1862, only five were confirmed by McClellan.[70]

The effect of unduly light punishment was to encourage misconduct. A typical reaction was that of a Norwegian in a Wisconsin regiment who reluctantly returned to his unit at the end of his furlough while some of his companions elected to stay at home another month. Writing later to his uncle about the delinquents, the Norwegian remarked: "They have had their trial and . . . were let off with the mere loss of a month's pay. I should have been happy to be at home a month longer than I was if I had been sure of getting off with such light punishment." [71]

Except during the early months of the war, however, punishments were overly harsh about as often as they were unduly mild. Captain John William De Forest, after sitting on a court near New Orleans in September 1862, wrote his wife: "The punishments are terribly severe. One poor blockhead, who had merely been absent without leave for five days, was allotted three years at hard labor on fortifications with loss of all pay and allowances except enough to cover his washing bill." A few months later Brigadier General J. J. Bartlett of the Army of the Potomac wrote another officer: "I am Pres. of a Court martial, principally trying deserters, poor fellows! & most all of them because their families were suffering at home for the Soldiers' pay. I could hate myself for being a soldier at times, for having to sit in judgement in such cases, hampered and restricted by the arbitrary rules of military law, which crushes heart and soul out of one's identity." [72]

Sometimes ignorant and even mentally defective soldiers, who failed at duties they were not competent to perform, were given the most serious sentences by courts that were unable or unwilling to temper the stark severity of the military code with mercy and common sense.

The disciplinary system sometimes acquired added harshness from failure to bring prisoners promptly to trial. The seventy-ninth article of war forbade confinement beyond eight days without trial except when circumstances prevented the prompt assembling of a court-martial. The exception allowed a latitude which tended to invalidate the rule, since under the conditions prevailing during periods of active campaigning it was easy to justify failure to convene courts. Postponement of trials was undoubtedly necessary in some cases, but in others the principal factor in delay was the unconcern of responsible authorities or their unwillingness to be inconvenienced. For example, inexcusable indifference seems to be the only explanation for allowing soldiers encamped near Baltimore to lie for several winter months "in irons in the Guard House." [73] A general order of the Department of the Gulf dated September 13, 1864, indicated that in New Orleans "many prisoners" were "confined in the various jails of the city used by the military authorities without any charges and in many cases without knowledge on the part of the keepers . . . or . . . the Provost Marshals of any offense having been committed by them." Possibly some of these prisoners were civilians, but the wording of the order leaves no doubt of soldiers being among those detained without charge or trial.[74]

Some of the most cruel and unreasonable penalties were those imposed by unit commanders without resort to courts. In some instances the excessive severity sprang from the fact of the punishment being summarily applied while the officer's anger was at high pitch. In others, the motivating factor was the desire to set an example that would deter future wrongdoing, or a determination to prove the officer's mastery by bearing down on the culprit. In still other cases cruelty derived from sheer highhandedness or bestiality.

Two specific cases will serve to illustrate the brutality which men suffered at the hands of sadistic officers. In 1861 a court-martial found a captain guilty "without just cause" of cursing a private, striking him with a saber on the neck and head, causing the blood to flow profusely, tying his hands and feet with a rope, roughly forcing an excessively large gag in his mouth, and then throwing him out on the cold, damp ground.[75] But this captain's action was mild in comparison with that of a lieutenant colonel of Negro troops who frequently beat and kicked his men for failure to polish their buttons and who, for the offense of pilfering roasting ears, removed the shoes and stockings of soldiers, tied them down on the ground with arms and legs outstretched, covered their faces, hands and feet with molasses and left them exposed all day to the sun, flies and ants.[76]

Whether applied by courts or officers, punishments in the Union Army were so uneven as to appear utterly capricious. A soldier might be sentenced to death for an offense for which a month earlier one of his comrades had had to pay only a token fine.

Still another characteristic of punishments, and of the disciplinary system in general, was a marked slanting in favor of officers. Not only did officers guilty of serious offenses such as cowardice, desertion and theft frequently escape punishment by resigning, but in instances where they were brought to trial they often got off much more lightly than enlisted men charged with the same breaches of discipline. Since the making of arrests and the preferring of charges were exclusive officer functions, commissioned personnel sometimes were inclined to consider themselves a mutual protective association and hence beyond the reach of the disciplinary code.

A major convicted in 1861 of participating in a public disturbance in Washington, refusing to submit to arrest and using contemptuous language toward the provost marshal, was let off with a mere reprimand. McClellan, characterizing the sentence as "a burlesque upon military punishments," ordered the case remanded but the court refused to modify its action.[77]

A sergeant told in his diary of an officer of the day being ordered to break up an after-taps gambling party and arrest all the participants; but when the officer found that a fellow "shoulder-strap" was involved in the game he turned away without making an arrest. In view of such inequities it is not surprising to find a soldier complaining: "If these had been poor privates nothing less than two or three months in the Guard house or hard labor on the forts would have been the sentence. When shall such a cursed state of affairs cease to exist?" [78]

Discriminatory treatment by courts-martial is well exemplified by an incident which took place in the Army of the Potomac early in 1862. A private soldier called as a witness by a court-martial in Baltimore was found to be intoxicated. The court sentenced him to wear a ball and chain for thirty days. Later, when an officer appeared before the court in the same condition, he was excused from testifying and given no punishment. An even more striking example of the slanting of the disciplinary system in favor of officers is to be found in the action of two courts-martial which met about the same time in 1864 in the Army of the Potomac. One sentenced to be shot a soldier who had abandoned his post in battle; the other on finding an officer guilty of the same offense deemed cashiering a sufficient penalty.[79]

In 1861 a lieutenant who left his unit while it was under fire at First Bull Run drew the amazingly light sentence of fifteen days' suspension of rank and pay.[80]

Inclination of courts-martial to tip the scales of justice to the advantage of fellow officers is also evidenced by an occasional juggling of charges to permit a lightening of the sentence. For example, a New York lieutenant early in 1862 appeared before a court charged with "conduct unbecoming an officer and a gentleman." This charge, if sustained, made dismissal from the service mandatory. The specification given in support of the charge was the lieutenant's remark to his captain in the presence of enlisted men: "If it were not for the difference in rank I would . . . knock shit out of you." The court found him guilty of the specification but held that the appropriate charge was "conduct subversive to good order and military discipline" which, under the articles of war, was punishable at the discretion of the court. Using the discretion thus assumed the court sentenced the lieutenant to reprimand by the colonel of his regiment in the presence of the noncommissioned officers only and a month's suspension from rank and pay. The court's action drew a rebuke from McClellan who held that the lieutenant should have been found guilty of conduct unbecoming an officer and a gentleman on the basis of the language that he unquestionably used.[81]

An even more flagrant case was that of an Illinois lieutenant tried in February 1863 on the charge of conduct unbecoming an officer and a gentleman on the basis of having a lewd Negro woman in his tent, fornicating with her there, and encouraging a private soldier to do the same in his presence. The court, while finding the lieutenant guilty of the specifications, chose to interpret the charge as "conduct prejudicial to good order and military discipline," and instead of sentencing him to dismissal from the service required only that he forfeit a month's pay and allowances! This amazing sentence, even though accompanied by an endorsement of the commander of the post where the accused was

stationed charging that he was "dangerously disloyal—flagitiously immoral—of evil example—health impaired by degrading vice—damaging
to discipline—useless to the service—" was approved all the way up
through the corps and army commanders (Hurlbut and Grant) only to
be set aside by the Judge Advocate General of the Army on the ground
that under established procedure a court-martial could not substitute
one charge for another.[82] The lieutenant apparently escaped punishment altogether because of this procedural fault. The Judge Advocate
General of the Army could have recommended dismissal to the President
(who could dismiss officers on his own authority) and his explanation of
the failure to do so is, to say the least, most interesting. "A recommendation for dismissal would be made," he wrote in an endorsement dated
October 29, 1863, "but for the long time that has elapsed . . . and a
doubt may be entertained whether meantime this officer may not have
retrieved his conduct." [83] Little wonder that soldiers sometimes complained of the army being an officers' world.

Some officers while under arrest were not above bringing pressure on
enlisted men likely to be called as witnesses. A captain was charged with
visiting a house of ill fame while on command of a picket detail and
telling the guards that they might all go to sleep just so they were awake
when he made the rounds about ten o'clock. He visited the witnesses a
few days before his trial and gave each of them a drink of whisky.[84] The
extent to which men were influenced by such overtures, and by hope of
favor or fear of reprisal, cannot be ascertained. But reading of courts-
martial proceedings discloses occasional instances of such poor memory
on the part of soldiers called as witnesses against their superiors that
doubt about the free flow of justice is inescapable.[85]

It is not meant to leave the impression that discipline was always
inequitable or oppressive, for such was not the case. Many officers were
humane and generous in dealings with their men and some carried leniency to harmful extremes. Moreover, Yanks, like all other soldiers, found
ways and means of evading restrictions. "The officers exercise all their
ingenuity to keep the men within the lines," wrote a New Yorker from
a camp near Baltimore in 1861, "but notwithstanding the strong guard
of 100 men on night & day, the men slip out with the connivance of the
sentries. I suppose there must be at least 30 or 40 go out and come in
every night in this way." An Iowa private made an even more illuminating comment on the effectiveness with which soldiers shielded themselves: "The boys stand up for one another in all scrapes that any member may get into," he wrote, "so that if some ones does something that

is against all rules such as knocking the lights out in a grocery and taking whatever is handy, or taking a milk pail from a pedlar wagon, any kind of stealing whatever is not reported." He added: "If any one gets drunk the orders are to report him so that he may be sent to the guard house. Instead of doing so we stow them away in some quiet place until sober." [86]

Sometimes men caught in the disciplinary net took their punishment with marked unconcern and even with levity. Such reactions were encouraged by the manner in which guardhouses occasionally were administered. Far from being dull and dreary, some of these institutions were lively places featured by card playing, laughing and singing. It must have been this sort of prison to which Private Wesley Armfield was sent for whistling after taps in the company streets, for when his colonel later offered him release on promise of good behavior Armfield replied: "I will not promise because the guard tent is more comfortable than my tent and I had rather stay here." [87]

Even the "Rip Raps," a prison near Norfolk which had an unenviable reputation, was so favorably regarded by one group confined there early in the war that they expressed regret at having to leave. But of the Dry Tortugas, a notorious prison situated off the coast of Florida, not one kindly comment was found. In general, guardhouses and other prisons were denounced by soldiers as filthy, loathsome places.[88]

The tendency of some soldiers to make a joke of their punishment is illustrated by the conduct of some New York soldiers sentenced to carry twenty-five-pound weights in front of the guardhouse. "They . . . have appointed a captain," wrote one of their comrades, "who with a stick to represent a sword, with the sole of an old shoe for a guard, is drilling in the most approved style. The man with the placard [marked 'Running Guard'] is in the middle to represent the color bearer. They seem to enjoy it." [89]

In some instances drumming out of the service, instead of being regarded as the shameful, humiliating ordeal contemplated in the articles of war, produced opposite reactions both on the part of the culprit and his comrades. A skulker who was drummed out of camp in March 1863 exclaimed at the conclusion of the exercises: "Who says I aint a citizen." Following the imposition of this penalty on two soldiers near Harrison's Landing, Virginia, a comrade wrote: "Instead of being looked on as a disgrace . . . by the majority of the men, they considered that they were better off and many almost envied them as they were free men as soon as outside of camp." [90]

The sympathy of soldiers for a comrade whom they thought unjustly ejected sometimes found tangible expression. A private in the Fifty-ninth Illinois Regiment who was drummed out of the service for insubordination received a considerable purse raised by his comrades to send him to parts unknown.[91]

Effectively registered group sentiment sometimes tended to restrain highhanded and brutal officers and to temper punishment. An extreme example was that of Kansas cavalrymen who, when one of their number was tied to a caisson and ordered whipped for some uncomplimentary references to the colonel, rushed out of their quarters shouting protests. The colonel and some of his officers drew their swords and dashed down the lines making threats and trying to quell the commotion. But the only response of the soldiers was to cry out, "Unloose the man or we'll blow you all to hell!" The man was released and the rioters were not punished.[92]

No discussion of factors mitigating the harshness of punishment would be complete without reference to the part played by Lincoln. Enlisted cases coming to his attention, as previously noted, consisted mainly of those involving long imprisonment or death sentences. Study of Presidential action in these cases reveals a rather well-defined pattern. In purely military offenses such as sleeping on post, insubordination and desertion where either a commanding general or the Judge Advocate General of the Army recommended clemency, Lincoln almost invariably accepted the recommendation. And in death sentences he frequently ordered mitigation or pardon on his own authority. In February 1864, by Lincoln's direction, the War Department issued a blanket order requiring mitigation of all pending sentences of death for desertion to imprisonment at the Dry Tortugas for the rest of the war. The order likewise empowered army and department commanders to restore to duty deserters under sentence when in their judgment the service would be benefited by the restoration. In pursuance of this order, sixty-two death sentences were commuted at one stroke in May 1864.[93]

Only in instances of crimes against civilians or those which civil courts treated as heinous was Lincoln consistently inclined to severity. When clear cases of rape, robbery, arson and the like came to him with the death penalty prescribed, the President usually approved them. But when all types of cases passed on by Lincoln are considered, it becomes readily apparent that his influence was a softening one.[94]

Sometimes Presidential clemency in capital sentences was initiated by the urgent request of a politically prominent person. A case in point is that of a private who deserted on August 26, 1863, from the Army of the Potomac. During the trial the accused testified that at the end of his tour of picket duty he chased a pig into a near-by wood. While he attempted to catch the pig, three Rebel cavalrymen approached, and to escape them he swam a river and concealed himself. When he came back later and inquired of the next picket detail as to the whereabouts of his unit he was arrested and charged with desertion. This was his story, but the court did not accept it and he was sentenced to die; the sentence was approved by the appropriate authorities and the execution ordered for the afternoon of September 25, 1863.[95]

On September 24 a Mr. Walsh, President of the Board of Aldermen of New York City, called at the White House bearing a note from the mayor asking Lincoln to look into the case. Walsh did not get to see the President personally, but left the mayor's note with one of his own which testified to the prisoner's good character, denied his intention to desert and requested a Presidential stay of the execution pending an investigation. Later in the day Lincoln telegraphed Meade to give him the facts in the case, which the general promptly did. That night Lincoln dispatched a telegram ordering suspension of the execution. But learning of a break in the telegraph line, he sent another message over another route, the delivery of which required transmission a part of the way by a colonel riding a special locomotive. The order reached its destination in due time and the shooting was stayed. Later the President commuted the sentence to six months' imprisonment at Albany. Thus was a soldier snatched from the jaws of death because prominent politicians actively interceded for him and the President, after investigation, deemed a lighter punishment appropriate, apparently on ground of doubt as to the man's intentions.[96]

In another instance Lincoln overruled himself and commuted a death sentence on application of a condemned soldier's counsel. The facts of this case, an especially interesting one because of the light it throws on the seriousness with which Lincoln regarded his control over the life of a fellow man (who in this case seems not to have had influence in high places), were briefly as follows: Private Blank, as he may be called since his real name is immaterial, in September 1863 deserted his original unit, a New York artillery regiment, and enlisted as a substitute in another organization. Almost immediately he deserted again and remained absent until apprehended about a year later. While imprisoned at Elmira, in a futile move to effect his escape he inveigled his guards into drinking some poisoned whisky which caused the death of one of them. In

December 1863 a general court-martial found him guilty of desertion and murder and sentenced him to be hanged.

When the papers in the case were referred to Lincoln on April 14, 1864, he indorsed them: "Sentence approved and execution fixed for Friday, April 22, 1864." But on application of Blank's counsel, who apparently entered a plea of mental defectiveness, Lincoln stayed the execution and on April 25 called on a Utica physician to inquire thoroughly into the prisoner's sanity. The physician heard a number of witnesses, among them Blank's father who testified that the prisoner had suffered a severe head injury when five years old and had afterward been erratic. To the question "Have any of your relatives been insane?" the father replied: "My father's sister was wild for years. Would run around the fields howling." [97]

The doctor reported to Lincoln on May 13, 1864, that Blank was a borderline case but was not insane; and that there was no doubt of his being lucid when he killed the guard on October 31, 1863, and when the physician interviewed him on April 29-30, 1864. After receipt of the physician's report Lincoln on January 25, 1865, commuted Blank's sentence to imprisonment at hard labor for ten years.

Now that offenses and punishments, the machinery of control and the character of military justice have been discussed, some comment on the state of discipline in the Union Army is in order. In general, discipline was weak early in the war, improving as the officer corps acquired experience and sloughed off incompetents, and as men became habituated to military life. Evidences of poor discipline during the first months of conflict could be cited almost indefinitely, but the general pattern may be indicated by a few specific testimonials. In November 1861 General Joseph Hooker, then a division commander, wrote the adjutant general of the Army of the Potomac: "In some regiments there appears to be a total absence of anything like authority. The officers are on the same footing with the men." And from the Department of Missouri in December 1861 General H. W. Halleck reported to General Winfield Scott: "This, General, is no army, but rather a military rabble. . . . I am almost destitute of regular officers, and those of the volunteers are, with some exceptions, entirely ignorant of their duties." A few weeks later, General D. C. Buell, commanding the Department of the Ohio, registered a similar complaint, citing as a source of special difficulty the interference of state authorities in disciplinary affairs.[98]

These comments of higher officers were borne out by inspectors who made the rounds of the camps during the war's first year. The following

notations, taken from the report of an inspection of the Department of
Missouri, are typical:

> 12th Iowa Infantry. . . . A fine body of men but entirely with-
> out discipline.
> Nebraska Cavalry. . . . Entirely without discipline.
> 23rd Indiana Infantry. . . . This regiment is entirely demoral-
> ized and discipline hopeless unless the colonel . . . is dis-
> missed.
> 2nd Missouri Infantry. . . . No discipline.
> Jeff. C. Davis Brigade (8th, 18th, 22nd, 25th Indiana Infantry;
> Hauser's Battery). . . . The whole appearance of the troops
> is unsoldierlike showing an almost total want of discipline.

Of the 159 units covered by this report only 4 were rated as *superior*
in discipline, while 34 were *good*, 39 *fair*, 25 *poor*; no comment was
made concerning the remaining 57. The colonel making the report attributed the low state of discipline primarily to the incompetence of
volunteer officers who seemed unaware of the importance of systematic
training, some even ridiculing drill as "playing soldier." [99]

Observations of commanders and inspectors were confirmed by informal comments contained in letters of the period. A lieutenant wrote
his homefolk from a training camp in Albany, New York, on May 7,
1861: "You can hardly realize in what sort of a constant turmoil we live
here now. There are some 1800 men in all sorts of command, in all stages
of civilization and in all states of content. Hardly a meal passes when
there is not some sort of a muss at the tables. Dishes are overturned,
victuals thrown, men refuse to eat, disobey orders. . . . We live in constant expectation of a general fight. . . . there has not been a day since
I have been here at the Barracks when we have not as officers taken our
pistols and gone out at some alarm to quell a riot." [100]

While the over-all trend was undoubtedly one of improvement, disciplinary lapses in specific units and areas were numerous and deterioration on an army-wide scale occasionally was apparent. Following the
retreat from Richmond in July 1862, the Army of the Potomac seems to
have experienced a disciplinary retrogression which persisted well into
1863, with lowest points occurring just before Antietam and just after
Fredericksburg. General orders of this period complain of infrequent inspections, neglect of drill, dirty clothing and equipment, omission of
officer schools, nonchalance in performance of guard duty and failure
to observe rules of military etiquette.

Soldier letters also noted a poor state of discipline. In September

1862 a Massachusetts private stationed near Falls Church, Virginia, wrote that "drill & saluting officers & guard duty is played out." About the same time a Michigander wrote from another Virginia camp that he had recently witnessed the passing of two divisions of the Army of the Potomac, and "it was almost impossible to tell which were the officers as they were all dressed alike, some of the privates had lost their muskets & had picked up swords on the Battlefield, and as most of the officers had lost their shoulder straps." A few days later this man reported: "I have never been told to salute an officer except when acting as a sentinel. I am just as free with those I am acquainted with as I would be at home." [101]

A similar deterioration of discipline appears to have occurred in Grant's army following the surrender of Vicksburg, though evidence is too sparse to permit a firm conclusion on the subject.

As a general rule, discipline was considerably worse among troops far removed from fighting areas and having little hope of combatant duty. Units held to service for long periods in Northern states, especially if stationed near the homes of the men, were frequently reported as sadly deficient in this respect. Colonel James Hardie of the Inspector General's Department in Washington wrote General Halleck in October 1864 that the Forty-third Indiana Regiment, on duty in its home state, was in a deplorable state of discipline. "They are little better than an armed mob. . . . New Enfield rifles issued to the men instead of making them clean their old arms. The officers are very negligent in the discharge of their duties. In my last month's report I had occasion to recommend them to be reprimanded—There is no improvement in them since last month's inspection." [102] Another inspector reported in January 1865 that Kentucky troops serving in their home state were "poorly officered . . . not at all instructed and destitute of discipline. . . . They are *a mere mob*. Less than half the aggregate reported are [present] for duty at any time of need; and this too when four fifths of the aggregate of troops from other states serving with them are [available] for duty." He added: "Their want of discipline and their serving at home are the causes conducing to such inefficiency." [103] Similar reports were found concerning locally recruited troops serving in Tennessee, Arkansas and Missouri.

Units assigned to garrison duty, especially in remote areas, were notably inclined to disciplinary deficiency. Of the Thirty-fifth Missouri Regiment stationed at Helena, Arkansas, Colonel D. B. Sackett of the Inspector General's Department in Washington reported in January

1865: "In service nearly 3 years . . . it is the poorest regiment in every respect I have ever seen since the commencement of the war. The Lt. Col. Commdg is wanting in nearly every quality that constitutes an officer. He has no force and is ignorant of the first principles of drill. The officers and men . . . have no energy or spirit in them; they move like drones . . . are not instructed in any kind of drill . . . arms and accoutrements . . . very dirty . . . clothing dirty and in many cases ragged . . . hair . . . very long." [104]

Reports of like tenor, dated for the most part in 1864, were found for garrison units in Minnesota, Western Virginia, Middle Tennessee, Mississippi, the Carolinas and the country along the Mississippi. Inspector William Sinclair in August 1864 found "two divisions of infantry . . . near Harper's Ferry . . . in a deplorable condition . . . commanding officers of regiments and companies generally ignorant of the condition of their commands . . . drills, parades and Sunday morning inspections . . . entirely neglected for months . . . orders not enforced . . . soldiers employed as servants and not mustered as such." Concerning his observations near Cumberland, Maryland, this officer reported a "large number of drunken ragged soldiers in the streets, and dirty officers about the hotels. . . . Many cases of officers and enlisted men wearing the grey pants of the rebel service . . . some enlisted men entirely dressed in rebel colors." [105]

Discipline became so lax among Nineteenth Corps troops stationed in the vicinity of Morganza, Louisiana, in the summer of 1864 that a general order had to be issued calling attention to the frequency with which men had been found playing cards while on picket and the failure to have "a man on duty either as a vidette in advance or on watch on the post." [106] Delinquency was hardly less flagrant at Fort Mitchell, South Carolina, where in August 1864 an inspector reported two large artillery pieces unserviceable from neglect and abuse. Rats and moths had been permitted to destroy the cartridges and spare powder bags. "The muzzles of the guns have not been kept depressed and the boxes have become rusted and covered with sand," he wrote. "In several pieces the elevating screws are broken. The guns have not been traversed and the traverse circles are so sunken as almost to make this impossible." [107]

Cavalry units as a rule were not so well disciplined as those of other branches, owing largely to the relative independence with which they operated and a certain jaunty, devil-may-care attitude which, while possibly adding to their effectiveness in combat, had the opposite tendency in other aspects of soldiering. It seems unquestionable that the poorest discipline in the entire Union Army was that of mounted units operating in remote areas on loosely defined missions. The following letter, written by an inspecting officer in September 1864 to the commander of the cavalry division stationed in Arkansas, speaks for itself:

> Gen'l . . . I visited the Stables of the 9th Kan. Cav. this morning . . . at least half an hour after reveille; and not one commissioned officer was present. . . . No stable call had been sounded. Most of the horses had been fed, many had not, and were restless and fretting for something to eat. Some of the horses were provided with feed boxes, the larger number had none. Upon inquiring of one of the men why all the horses had not been fed, his reply was that the men in charge of them had not got up, especially those under arrest. When I inquired of a private soldier present whether the officers were in the habit of attending stable calls, he laughed at the idea. . . . Horses unprovided with Boxes were obliged to eat their grain in the mud. . . . No provision is made for draining . . . the stables. . . .[108]

Even more damning to the cavalry was a report made by Colonel James Hardie in September 1864 concerning units of the Department of the Gulf. Of the Second New Hampshire Cavalry (dismounted) he stated: "Men in all kinds of rig on drill—officers and men surly. Discipline poor." The Eighteenth New York Cavalry had four field officers and one captain under arrest, and another field officer was absent, sick. Equipment was scant and in poor condition. "Most of the officers seemed careless and indifferent. . . . There seemed to be a total want of martial spirit and soldierly bearing such as springs from the heart of the true soldier. . . . The regiment can be of little service to the government in its present condition." But the Second Illinois Cavalry brought forth the most disparaging of all comments, which for emphasis was in part underscored by the inspecting officer: "*Nothing good can be said of them. Take officers and men, and they are the worst looking military organization I ever saw.* The only clean or respectable place I saw in camp was that occupied by their animals. . . . everything was uniformly in bad order." [109]

These examples, as previously noted, are from units which were assigned to outlying areas and performed for the most part noncombatant duties. But even when actively engaged in major operations, cavalry appear to have been inferior to infantry in discipline. It is worthy of note that in Sherman's campaign in Georgia and the Carolinas the command having the worst reputation for pillage was that of Kilpatrick.[110]

Some cavalry organizations, to be sure, were exceedingly well disciplined, for in the mounted service, as in any other branch, the state of discipline varied greatly from unit to unit and from time to time. Of the various factors influencing discipline such as character of duties, state of equipment, prospect of active service, background of the soldiers and quality of command, the last was far and away the most important. The nub of discipline was leadership, especially on the platoon and company levels. In fact, it hardly seems too much to say that a regiment was well disciplined if it had good lieutenants and captains and poorly disciplined if it did not. Good company officers could sometimes "carry" a weak regimental staff, but a good colonel, lieutenant colonel and major were of little avail if company officers were consistently weak.

In conclusion it should be stated that discipline was frequently not so bad as it seemed. Inspection reports as well as the informal comments of soldiers tended to stress deficiencies. A unit was expected to have good discipline; hence, failure to measure up to prescribed standards was more apt to attract attention and elicit remarks than was acceptable performance. This observation is likewise applicable to offenses and punishments. The unusual and the extreme tended more frequently to get into the record than the ordinary or the average. It is essential to consider all degrees and variations, but the mean must be ever kept in the forefront. Application of this formula to the present discussion requires the statement that while men were often intractable, officers incompetent, punishments unreasonable and discipline deficient, these facts are offset in large measure by opposite extremes of a positive character, and that the great bulk of instances lie in between. When the whole war, all the personnel and the complete system of control are considered, men were fairly orderly, officers generally creditable, punishments usually tolerable and discipline of most units passable. Otherwise the North would not have won the war. And despite the fact that a few Southerners have not yet "surrendered," the North *did* win.

CHAPTER IX

HARDTACK, SALT HORSE AND COFFEE

ABOUT the mid-point of the war a poetically inclined Yank sent to a Nashville editor a doggerel description of army life. The lines treating of food ran thus:

> The soldiers' fare is very rough,
> The bread is hard, the beef is tough;
> If they can stand it, it will be,
> Through love of God, a mystery.[1]

At the time this verse was published and throughout the war, except for the period before August 3, 1861, and after June 20, 1864, the daily allowance for each Union soldier was:

twelve ounces of pork or bacon, or, one pound and four ounces of salt or fresh beef; one pound and six ounces of soft bread or flour, or, one pound of hard bread, or, one pound and four ounces of corn meal; and to every one hundred rations, fifteen pounds of beans or peas, *and* ten pounds of rice or hominy; ten pounds of green coffee, or, eight pounds of roasted (or roasted and ground) coffee, or, one pound and eight ounces of tea; fifteen pounds of sugar; four quarts of vinegar; . . . three pounds and twelve ounces of salt; four ounces of pepper; thirty pounds of potatoes, when practicable, and one quart of molasses.[2]

In relative terms this was a generous allowance. It was about one fifth more than that of the British Army, almost twice that of the French, and compared even more favorably with that of the Prussians, Austrians and Russians.[3] It was also more liberal than the official diet of Confederates. The Southerners, after hopefully adopting the old army ration early in the conflict, were forced repeatedly to cut it, while the Federals in August 1861 effected a substantial increase. Surgeon General Hammond was on firm ground when he boasted after this augmentation that the men in blue had the most abundant food allowance of any soldiers in the world.[4]

224

CAMP OF SIXTEENTH VERMONT AT UNION MILLS, VIRGINIA

"CALIFORNIA JOE" OF BERDAN'S SHARPSHOOTERS WATCHING FOR REBS

Indeed, Union subsistence authorities were to conclude after long experience that the issue was overly generous to the point of encouraging waste. On their recommendation Congress in June 1864 revoked the increase, but a provision was retained which allowed substitution of fresh or processed vegetables for other items in the ration.[5]

Throughout the conflict, regulations permitted company commanders to sell back to the subsistence department any portion of the authorized ration not used by their men, the money thus obtained to become a part of the company fund. It was the intent of higher authorities that company commanders use the money accumulated for supplying their men with items not obtainable from commissaries and thus add variety to camp fare. But it seems that this wisely conceived aim rarely materialized in actual practice. Some captains did not know about the company fund; others did not want to be bothered with administering it; and still others appropriated it to their own use.[6] One Yank of unusual intelligence and broad experience wrote after the war: "I have yet to learn of the first company whose members ever received any revenue from such a source, although the name of *Company Fund* is a familiar one to every veteran." [7]

The specification of abundant fare by high authorities did not necessarily mean that the rank and file were consistently well fed. Far from it. Reports of officers and comments of soldiers reveal the greatest variation in the quantity of food actually made available to the men who did the shooting. As one lowly consumer aptly put it early in the war: "Some days we live first rate, and the next we dont have half enough." [8]

Almost every regiment suffered occasional periods of hunger, though usually these did not last more than a few days. But the course of the war was marked by a surprising number of what might be called major food crises, when deprivation extended over a considerable period and involved large numbers of men.

In the West in the early part of 1862 there were numerous instances of prolonged hunger. A member of the Fourth Iowa Regiment wrote after a period of arduous service in Missouri and Arkansas: "We have marched hundreds on hundreds of miles and on Short rations all the time and about one third of the time we had nothing but a little coffe indeed we have not had half rations since the 2nd of last January." [9] A Yank serving in Kentucky complained: "A man that Enlisted in the 18th Regt Is of but few days & with hard rasions to live on. . . . The last few weeks past we only get about ½ Enough to eat . . . for the last 10 days

. . . we have been living on Slap jacks . . . one the sice of my two hands every meal with Coffee & a chunk of meat. . . . We realy are about half starved." [10]

Rations were uncomfortably short among some of Buell's soldiers in the Kentucky campaign. An Illinois corporal wrote from Perryville on October 26, 1862: "The boys say that our *'grub'* is enough to make a *mule* desert, and a *hog* wish he had never been born. . . . Hard bread, bacon and coffee is all we draw." The Goldsboro expedition of December 1862 also was marked by subsistence failures. Some of the participants reported that they had nothing to eat for two days but three crackers. Others declared that they robbed horse troughs of hard corn to allay the gnawings of hunger.[11]

Similar conditions were experienced by troops serving in the Shenandoah Valley in the late spring of 1862. On June 12 Carl Schurz reported to Lincoln: "This morning I found General Fremont in a somewhat irritated state of mind, and I must confess I understand it. The Government has plenty of provisions and our soldiers die of hunger; plenty of shoes, and they go barefooted; plenty of horses, and we are hardly able to move." The hard fighting about Richmond during the Seven Days' campaign was also accompanied by some hunger, but the principal complaint there was lack of fresh vegetables and other specific items rather than empty haversacks. On the whole, the Army of the Potomac fared well as to quantity while McClellan was at the helm.[12]

Soldiers of that army experienced under Burnside their first general food shortage in the war's second winter. A Massachusetts Yank wrote his father from near Fredericksburg on November 28, 1862: "Yesterday was thanksgiving at home, but a dismal day for us. Never since I have been in the army have I seen supplies so short. Now we see soldiers going round begging hard bread." This Yank and others told of comrades haunting the slaughter pens picking up the heads, feet and tails of steers and other scraps to supplement their meager fare. A Connecticut corporal reported on December 1 that "there was a fellow got a bone with a little meat on it, he picked the meat off it and threw it away; another fellow found it and worked away on it awhile and threw it away; well, there were four men who picked that old bone." Early in January 1863 a private closed a letter to his sweetheart with the statement: "I must fall in for my beans or lose them We have two beans to a pint of water." [13]

Hooker's replacement of Burnside in January led to a revolution in the food situation. One of the first acts of the new commander was to order the erection of bakeries so that the men might have soft bread. He also attacked the whole problem of supply with a vigor that soon unchoked subsistence lines and brought to the hungry soldiers an unprecedented quantity and variety of food.[14] The results of his reforms are vividly revealed in the pages of a diary kept by a soldier detailed in one of the brigade commissaries. Following are some sample entries:

Feb 9, 1863. Dried apples and onions was issued to the brigade today.
Feb 15, 1863. Fresh bread was issued to the first and second regiments today from the ovens.
April 21, 1863. Supply train went to the landing and brought pork, bacon, sugar, hard bread and one day's issue of potatoes.
April 25, 1863. The supply train went to the landing and brought up sugar, coffee, candles, soap, carrots and turnips.
April 28, 1863. Supply trains went to the landing and brought hams and pork.
May 1, 1863. This morning went over the river with eight wagons and issued two days rations of pork, sugar, coffee, and one day's of soft bread.
May 6, 1863. Whiskey was issued twice today.[15]

Whatever they thought of Hooker's other qualities, soldiers highly approved his competency as a provider.[16]

Except for brief shortages during the Gettysburg campaign, the Army of the Potomac generally fared well through the summer and early fall of 1863, but the Mine Run campaign of November brought another "starvation time." [17] A New Yorker wrote his homefolk on November 18: "For six weeks past we have suffered a good deal from Fatigue and Hunger. . . . I *thought* I knew what hunger was before, but I did not." [18] Reopening of the railroad which had been cut by the Rebs and the return of more settled conditions brought an end to this emergency. And while the disorganization produced by the intensive operations of the next summer again caused some temporary hardship, soldiers in the East for the remainder of the war had little cause to complain about the quantity of their rations.

In the Western armies the story was different. Grant's soldiers in Tennessee and Mississippi were periodically hungry in late 1862 and early 1863, especially after Van Dorn's and Forrest's raids on their subsistence stores and supply lines. An Illinois Yank wrote his wife from Abbeville, Mississippi, on December 7, 1862: "I never thought I could relish a chunk of cold corn bread like I did last night; it was delicious sure. We have not been on full rations for several days." [19] After

Christmas another Illinois soldier stationed at Jackson, Tennessee, informed his father:

We got half rations of coffee and quarter rations of hardtack and bacon. What we call small rations, such as Yankee beans, rice and split peas are played out. . . . The hardtack is so precious now that the orderly sergeant no longer knocks a box open and lets every man help himself, but he stands right over the box and counts the number of tacks he gives to every man. . . . And that aint all. The boys will stand around until the box is emptied, and then they will pick up the fragments that have fallen to the ground . . . and scrape off the mud with their knives and eat the little pieces and glad to get them.[20]

A third participant in Grant's operations wrote that men of his unit confiscated a huge coffee mill in which they ground hard corn, using the meal thus obtained for making mush. "This served to fill up with," he added, "but with the majority it did not agree . . . giving them . . . the 'Miss. Quick Step.' After the first day the Surgeon could not begin to prescribe for his many patients." [21]

The "cracker line," as the Yanks called their subsistence channel, was clogged occasionally during the operations about Vicksburg, especially during the march from Bruinsburg to Edwards. Resulting deficiencies were frequently met—and more—by raids on civilians.[22]

Portions of Rosecrans' command suffered from hunger during the Tullahoma operations of June and July 1863, but the worst food crisis in the history of the Union Army came in connection with the ensuing Chattanooga and Knoxville campaigns. While the Army of the Cumberland was under siege in and about Chattanooga after Chickamauga, "starving soldiers would follow the wagon trains" that came in over the tortuous and uncertain route from Stevenson and Bridgeport, "hoping to pick up the few grains of corn that might fall in the road." Furthermore, "The feed troughs of the horses and mules had to be guarded to keep soldiers from taking the little allowance of grain that had to be given the animals to keep them going." [23]

A young Hoosier private wrote from Chattanooga on October 22, 1863, that since the Chickamauga fight he and his comrades were eating "but two meals per day, and one cracker for each meal." He added: "We generally draw five days' rations at one time and generally eat them up in three days and starve the other two. I was nearer starved here than ever, lived on parched corn. . . . You surely have heard the song entitled Hard Times, well we have seen 'em." [24]

The opening of the Tennessee River late in October to a point near Chattanooga removed the threat of starvation, but some units, at least, continued to feel the pinch of reduced rations for a long time afterward. An Ohioan stationed in Chattanooga complained on January 18, 1864: "When we came here we had about ½ rasion. . . . We were told that we would get more when the Boats came up the River. Then we got less & now as the Cars Comenced to run last Thursday we are still getting less. . . . If it keeps on like this we will starve to death Entirly." [25]

Actually this Yank should have considered himself fortunate. He doubtless fared much better than those soldiers who in December marched from Chattanooga to Knoxville and back with only three days' rations, supplemented as occasion would permit by contributions forced from farmers along the way.[26]

Some of Sherman's men complained of food shortages while pursuing Hood northward after the fall of Atlanta.[27] A Wisconsin soldier wrote from near Lafayette, Georgia, on October 18, 1864: "Some of the Boys got some corn along the Road and making their plates into graters they ground some corn and had some mush." [28] Short rations were even more common near the end of the march to the sea as foraging, in soldier parlance, "played out." Until the opening of water routes brought in a new stock of supplies shortly before Christmas, many veteran campaigners were reduced to a fare of coffee and rice.[29] The rice was issued unhulled, but the men soon devised means of meeting this situation. Some resorted to wooden pestles and mortars borrowed from slaves while others, according to an Ohio sergeant, hulled the kernels "by placing a handful in our haversacks which we lay on logs and pound with our bayonets. Then we pour the contents from hand to hand, blowing the while to separate the chaff from the grains." [30]

Even after the cracker line was opened, supplies were inadequate; as a result skimpy fare persisted until departure from Savannah brought better opportunity for foraging. But living off the country became difficult in North Carolina near the end of the march, and cries of short rations again became common. One Yank wrote from Fayetteville on March 12, 1865, that after crossing the South Carolina boundary he and his comrades had lived five days "on nigger Peas or Beans as the boys call them and were glad to get them." [31]

Several factors contributed to the food shortages experienced by the men in blue. Fare was often scant in the early part of the war because officers responsible for drawing and issuing rations were not fully acquainted with army procedure. Failure of supply agencies to have the necessary stocks at the right places at the right time also led to instances of want. This appears to have been the situation at Savannah during Sherman's sojourn in that city. An officer of the Inspector General's Department reported in February 1865: "There was an inexcusable neglect or delay in furnishing rations to the army. . . . Up to the time of leaving Savannah the QM & Commissary Depts failed most signally to supply this command with necessary subsistence. The men actually suffered." [32]

As previously intimated, shortages were most common during periods of rapid movement and active fighting. When intensive campaigns were in progress, or when the fortunes of war closed channels of supply, as at Chattanooga, reduced fare was unavoidable. But sometimes soldiers brought hunger upon themselves by the improvident practice of consuming several days' rations shortly after their issue.

Yanks frequently attributed their meager fare to corrupt officers, and unquestionably some of those involved in the procurement and distribution of food were dishonest.[33] It is improbable, however, that peculation was nearly so prevalent as the soldiers charged.

Two specific instances clearly demonstrate how selfishness, indifference and lethargy on the part of officers sometimes caused the enlisted men to receive less than their due allowance of food. In the second winter of the war a scurvy threat occurred in the Army of the Cumberland. Rosecrans was perplexed, since the commissary records indicated an issue of 100 barrels of vegetables daily in his command, and he had taken it for granted that this food was being consumed by the soldiers. But on investigation he was shocked to discover "that one fourth in amount of this issue went to the staff officers and their families at Head-Quarters, and that of the remaining three-fourths, the Commissaries of the various Corps, Divisions and Brigades obtained the larger portions, so that the Regimental Commissaries who supplied the wants of the private soldiers were left almost unprovided." Further inquiry by medical authorities "revealed the extraordinary fact that although this very liberal daily distribution was shown by the books . . . still the soldiers had not received on an average from the Government more than three rations of vegetables during the twelve months ending on the first of April, 1863." [34]

A similar instance occurred in the latter part of 1864 in the District of West Florida. There an investigation, inspired by appearance of scurvy, revealed that while officers were purchasing fresh vegetables and other choice items liberally for themselves they were not having comparable distribution made to the men. The table of returns for September showed that of 10,658 pounds of potatoes received by the Commissary Department the 250 officers received 1,850 pounds while only 165 pounds were issued to the 3,850 men; of 1,324 gallons of pickles, officers drew 190 gallons and the men 162 gallons; issues from a stock of 14,249 pounds of dried apples were 1,749 to officers and none to the men. The figures on whisky are especially interesting: From a store of 2,345 gallons the officers obtained 434 gallons and the men (who could not purchase commissary liquors as the officers but had to depend on commanders to order its issue as part of the ration) drew only 162 gallons; in other words, officers obtained on the average one and seven-tenths gallons of whisky each during the month, and the men forty-two one thousandths! [35]

The culpability of these officers was noted in Washington, a high-level staff member writing on a report forwarded from department headquarters: "The officers seem to have been most negligent of their men. . . . They seem to have appropriated the major portion of everything to their own use and let the men get along the best they could." Whether or not these or the officers involved in the Army of the Cumberland affair were disciplined is not known.[36]

The dietary deficiencies suffered by troops in West Florida in 1864 were due to failures of distribution. The same could be said of food shortages in general. Uncle Sam had at his command enough food to provide amply for all who wore the blue. The fact that soldiers were sometimes hungry was due to his inability always to make it available to them when they needed it.

Billy Yank was not solely dependent on Uncle Sam for his subsistence. His army rations were often supplemented by the homefolk. Soldier letters reveal a considerable flow of boxes, packed with all sorts of food, originating in every loyal state and extending to all areas where Federal troops were encamped. The most active channels of home-to-soldier supply were from Northeastern communities to the Army of the Potomac and from the Midwest to troops stationed along the Mississippi River and its tributaries. Rough handling along the way frequently jumbled contents of these shipments, but damaged boxes were better than none at all. Experience led to improvements in packing and recipients became experts at salvage.

"We have been living on the contence of those boxses you and George sent to us," wrote a New York soldier from near Fredericksburg, Virginia, March 8, 1863; "nothing was spoiled except that card of buiscuits . . . those wer molded some but we used over half of them this

morning in a soup we made of potatoes and onions and a little flour
to thicken it and then put the buiscuits in and it made a nice dish for a
soldier." [37] Contributions to the box from various neighbors was indicated by a request to "thank Mr. Burdicks a thousand times for me also
Mrs. Maxson for those pies . . . and those fride cakes and ginger snaps
are first rate and the dried berries they are nice . . . and the dried beef
. . . and aple sauce that was first rate." He added that the boxes had
been opened at headquarters to see if they contained any whisky, that
the investigators had sampled the apple sauce, "and a little of the juice
run out on my paper as you will see when you get this." [38]

The Sanitary Commission and other volunteer organizations also
distributed food from time to time. During the scurvy scare in Rosecrans' command early in 1863, the Sanitary Commission made available
a vast quantity of vegetables, and in February 1865 Rebecca Usher, representing the Maine State Agency at City Point, Virginia, reported receipt
of twenty-eight barrels of vegetables for Maine soldiers. "The soldiers
roasted potatoes all day in the ashes in the reading room," she wrote.
"The soldiers come in and ask for a potato as if it was an article of the
greatest luxury." She also told of giving out mince pies, apples, sauerkraut and other items that must have brought delight to the recipients.[39]

Sutlers also helped relieve the scantiness and monotony of camp fare,
but their cakes, pies, butter, cheese, apples and other delicacies were
offered at prices which frequently placed them beyond the reach of the
common soldier. Yanks often complained that sutlers were never around
except for brief intervals following payday.

The food venders most often patronized by the soldiers seem to have
been native peddlers who, as season, location and other circumstances
permitted, went through the camps selling pies, bread, butter, milk,
fruit, vegetables, watermelons and oysters. A Yank wrote from Savannah, Georgia, in January 1865: "The Negroes are selling all the oysters
they can get to our men. The soldier takes the tin cup and dips it into
the tub or bucket of oysters, fills it full and then drinks the oysters as
if he was drinking water." [40]

In one instance at least, enterprising Negroes set up a short-order
restaurant in camp. This institution, located near Louisville, Kentucky,
was described by a soldier thus:

Two Collered men . . . bring out a kettle of Buckwheat batter and
one corn batter and bake us cakes as we want them. I think them the
best I ever tasted they are always light and nice he gives us three large
cakes for 5 cts, Eggs in any style 3 for 5 cts, beef steak 10 cts he has for

dinner several kinds of pudding with sauce and apple dumplings baked (which I have a weakness for) large home made pies 5 cts &c &c, so we have a little something to fall back on if our rations prove a little indifferent.[41]

As noted elsewhere, Yanks occasionally supplemented their fare by eating at Southern tables.[42] Sometimes they were fed without charge and again they dined as paying guests. Negroes, in view of their friendlier attitude toward the invaders, played host far more frequently than whites. The meals served in Negroes' cabins were normally simple, consisting usually of such items as hoecake, corn bread, field peas, sweet potatoes and turnip greens, and now and then a piece of pork. Sometimes the visitors brought with them flour, sugar, meat and other ingredients not easily obtainable by civilians. Whatever the nature of the meal thus obtained, it afforded relief from camp offerings and was consumed with relish.

The statements of two soldiers will suffice to illustrate experiences and reactions of those who dined at Negroes' homes. From Key West, Florida, a New York sergeant wrote in 1862: "I was on guard down town the other day I went into an old negro woman's house and had a fine breakfast consisting of roast Beef fried onions a sweet Johny cake smoking hot boiled homony butter good tea &c &c all for two bits. Cheap enough." It seems not unlikely in view of the tendency of the colored folk to look on the Yanks as God-sent deliverers that this woman "put on a special spread" for her blue-clad guest.[43] In March 1863 another Yank wrote from Maryland: "We went up to old Pools and got old Diner to get us some bread and milk. It was good if the blacks did get it for us; after we ate our bread and milk we sat down and talked with the nigs awhile then went back to camp after dark." [44]

Some Yanks followed the practice of selling parts of their rations and using the money thus obtained to buy food from sutlers or natives. A Vermonter who followed this practice wrote from Louisiana to his brother: "I draw my rations in the morning, take what I want for the day & sell the rest. I keep my bread & potatoes sugar; sell all my meat . . . part of my soap & candles & the most of my Coffee & this I take to by milk, blackberrys cornbread Eggs fish &c &c so you see I live pretty well just now." [45]

The most common method of supplementing army fare was by foraging—which usually meant drawing on Rebel civilians, without measure and without price. If the despoiled owner denied being a Rebel, as he often did, then a receipt might be given and the responsibility of proving loyalty and obtaining compensation placed on the unwilling provider. As a rule, however, receipts were given only when provisions were taken by authorized foraging parties.

Much of the foraging was done by regularly appointed groups, led by officers and operating under authority conferred by higher commanders. This was the procedure ordered by Sherman on his famous march, and official records indicate a sincere effort by most of his corps and division commanders to enforce it.[46] But regardless of the directives and desires of the generals, Billy Yanks contrived to do a vast amount of food gathering on their own authority. Even the regularly organized foraging parties sometimes were under little control owing to the officers in charge of them—who usually were lieutenants or captains deeply imbued with the attitudes of the men—making no effort to enforce discipline.[47]

Appropriation of civilian edibles whether by authorized or irregular procedure sometimes gave Yanks a richness of fare that made them spurn the comparatively unsavory commissary issues. Living was more bounteous, of course, in prosperous areas not previously ravaged by either army.

The fertile country about Warrenton, Virginia, provided sumptuous food for the invaders during the first years of the war. A Connecticut corporal wrote his homefolk from this region in November 1862 that "on our way here . . . the boys took anything they wanted and some things they did not want. . . . They took Horses, killed cattle and brought in the quarters, Sheep, Hogs, Honey." He also reported that measures taken by the officers to protect civilians, such as calling the roll every hour and posting guards, were only partially effective in restraining the men. "The boys get lots of Geese, Ducks and Chickens in spite of the Guards," he stated.[48]

The coastal region of North Carolina also made rich contributions to soldier larders. From New Bern a Massachusetts Yank wrote his parents late in 1862: "Whenever we neared a town where we were to halt, our approach was marked by a spattering fussilade, amid which the last dying squeaks of the unfortunate pigs far and near were heard, and then we would see soldiers and sailors coming forth from the barnyards bearing their game impaled on a bayonet & dangling over their shoulders." He added: "When we first started the colonel tried to prevent our foraging but he quickly found out that all that was nonsense & before we got back we were as expert at it as any of the old hands." [49]

Middle Tennessee was another garden spot that yielded bountiful fare to its early occupants. Soldier letters frequently reported rich hauls of smoked hams, chickens, ducks, geese and other delicacies from premises about Nashville, Pulaski and Murfreesboro.[50]

The same was true of many other localities. Captain John William De Forest wrote appreciatively from a camp near Thibodaux, Louisiana, in November 1862: "When mealtime comes . . . I seat myself on a log, or a pumpkin, and devour the richness of the land. For we forage here; we go without hardtack and salt horse for the present; we live on roast pig, turkey, geese, chickens, beef and mutton; as for hoecake and sweet potatoes, they are nothing." [51]

From North Alabama a Wisconsin artilleryman wrote in November 1863: "Foraging done on a large scale by our boys sweet potatoes and chickens in plenty. . . . So soon as we came in sight of camp the Infantry went out in squads in search of meat the woods were full of hogs and it soon sounded like heavy skirmishing, General Smith riding in great fury back and forth endeavoring to punish the guilty parties and put a stop to it he tied up several men by their thumbs all night but the boys got their hogs." The next afternoon he wrote:

As we approached camp guns were heard in every direction more than last night several bullets flew directly over camp but fortunately no body was hurt Officers of the day and staff officers galloped in every direction endeavoring to stop it a camp guard was thrown around the Infantry with orders to keep all men from going in with meat or guns But Gen Smith had commenced to late to stop this division from foraging the guards sat down and always looked the wrong way and meat in plenty was brought.[52]

Yanks who campaigned in North Mississippi in the latter part of 1862 and about Vicksburg the next summer also had a picnic at the natives' expense.[53] There, and elsewhere, some of the soldiers made great sport of foraging, referring to their domestic prizes as wild game. Sergeant Onley Andrus stated that when his comrades "find a hog they down him & skin him & call it possum & it is very good eating for a hungry man." [54] In similar vein another Yank wrote from Western Tennessee: "There is not much game around here there is . . . however . . . *Bear, Swamp Oppossom, Turkey, Tame phesant,* & Squirles & so-fourth. All I have to say is that when any of the above see fit to come onto our table in the place of *spiled beef* or salty middling we dont grumble but try to eat them." [55] Even the officers sometimes made a joke of the plunder. In January 1863 a Wisconsin surgeon wrote his wife from Missouri: "Hogs run wild in the woods here. . . . Every hog seen is 'a wild hog' of course & in soldier parlance 'a slow deer' and very few escape alive. . . . Col. Harris & myself were standing together & the men aimed at the hogs . . . but did not hit them. The col. in a low tone said you shoot with your pistol and see if *you* can hit one. I did So & succeeded & the men in Soldier Style cried out 'bully!' " [56]

An Ohio soldier wrote his cousin that he could not help chasing Southern chickens, and added, "they are always sure to cackle at the Stars and Stripes and that would not do." [57]

A story that must have produced many a chuckle about the campfire told of an Irishman coming into camp with a hen and a goose hanging from his rifle. When reproached by an officer for robbing civilians the soldier glibly replied: "Oh! bedad S-r-r-r, this goose came out as I was wending my way along *pacably* and hissed at the American flag, and bejabez I shot him on the spot . . . and I found this hin laying eggs for the Ribil Army, and I hit her a whack that stopped that act *of treason* on the spot, too." [58] Other tall tales recounted attacks on unoffending men in blue by hens, geese and all sorts of edible creatures, ending of course in the aggressors' paying with their lives—and their savory flesh—for their unwonted conduct. Literal reading of soldier accounts would leave the impression that Southern poultry and livestock were even more disloyal and vicious than the Rebels who owned them.

The most notorious instances of foraging came in connection with Sheridan's valley campaign of 1864 and Sherman's march through Georgia and the Carolinas.[59] Soldier accounts and official reports indicate, however, that participants in these campaigns lived no better than those who first tapped the larders of other unusually productive areas. But they lived well enough—so well, indeed, that some professed to tire of the rich fare of chickens, turkeys, hams and honey and to long for the plainer offerings of the subsistence department. One of Sherman's sergeants reported from near Orangeburg, South Carolina, that the men "will not take the trouble to kill cattle, & if it is killed for them, they will not cook it." [60]

This sort of sumptuous living at the expense of Rebel civilians, while immensely gratifying and much discussed both during and after the conflict, was a relatively rare experience. Foraging in any area yielded diminishing returns and most Yanks did the majority of their soldiering in regions where opportunities for living off the country were scant. Procurement of food from sutlers, homefolk and other extraneous sources was also subject to many limitations. Hence, the men who wore the blue had to depend chiefly on army fare.

The staples of army diet were bread, meat and coffee. Bread was sometimes of the loaf variety, but more often it was a flour-and-water cracker or pilot biscuit, known commonly among soldiers as "hardtack."

A Yank who preserved some hardtack as mementos gave their dimensions as three and one eighth by two and seven eighths by one half inch. Commissary authorities usually considered ten or twelve crackers a full bread ration.[61]

Soldier accounts leave little doubt of the cracker being hard. Derisive references ranged from "teeth dullers" to "sheet-iron crackers." One Yank reported that the hardtack made his teeth so sore he could scarcely eat. Another thought that the crackers "would make good brest works," as they would surely stop a musket ball. A third told of carving a durable violin bridge from one of them. Others testified to the necessity of beating the crackers with their musket butts to make them edible.[62]

An Ohio soldier wrote a friend: "Without joking any thing about it I have eat crackers here that I could not take in my hands and break into without getting a pry on something." [63] And a Kansan reported this camp dialogue:

Sergeant: Boys I was eating a piece of hard tack this morning,
          and I bit on something soft; what do you think it was?
Private: A worm?
Sergeant: No by G—d, it was a ten penny nail.[64]

Another Yank recommended as a soldier's "Grace" before eating:

Oh! Lord of Love,
Look from above,
Upon we hungry sinners:
Of what we ask 'tis not in vain,
For what has been done can be
Done again, Please turn
Our water into wine, and bless
And *break* these *crackers*.[65]

Soldiers found various ways of softening the crackers and making them palatable. A favorite practice was to crumble them in coffee, soup or milk. Other methods were to toast the crackers over coals; fry them in bacon grease; or beat them into a powder, mix with boiled rice and serve as griddle cakes. Some Yanks made a dish they called "skillygalee" by soaking the hardtack in cold water and then browning them in pork fat and seasoning to taste. Others who varied this procedure by pulver-

izing the crackers before soaking them called the product "hell-fired
stew." [66]

Another improvisation was "hardtack pudding" which according to
one Yank:

was made by placing the biscuit in a stout canvas bag, and pounding
bag and contents with a club on a log until the biscuits were reduced
to a fine powder; then we added a little wheat flour, if we had it . . . and
made a stiff dough, which we next rolled out on a cracker-box lid, like
a pie-crust; then we covered this all over with a preparation of stewed,
dried, apples, dropping in here and there a raisin or two just for Auld
Lang Syne's sake, rolled and wrapped it in a cloth, boiled it for an hour
or so and ate it with wine sauce. The wine was usually omitted and
hunger inserted in its stead.[67]

When circumstances precluded preparation of any sort, as was often
the case, hungry Yanks ate the hardtack just as it came from the box,
or in a sandwich form with a slice of fat pork (spread with sugar if convenient) as filler.[68]

Aversion to hardtack sprang in part from the poor quality of the
product as issued in camp. Crackers often were stale from age or moldy
from storage in exposed or damp places. In many instances they were
infested with worms or weevils, a fact which gave rise to a flood of
irreverent comment. "All the fresh meat we had came in the hard bread
. . . and I preferring my game cooked, used to toast my biscuits," was
the remark of one disgusted campaigner. Another observed: "We found
32 worms, maggots, &c in one cracker day before yesterday. We do not
find much fault, however, but eat them without looking as a good way
to prevent troublesome ideas." Still another testified after the war: "It
was no uncommon occurrence for a man to find the surface of his pot
of coffee swimming with weevils after breaking up hardtack in it; . . .
but they were easily skimmed off and left no distinctive flavor behind."
In view of the frequency of animal occupation, it is not surprising that
some Yanks referred to their crackers as "worm castles," and that others
parodied "John Brown's Body" with these lines:

Worms eat hearty in the commissary stores
While we go starving on.[69]

Much of the criticism was, of course, embellished with fiction. And
however strong was the initial antipathy toward "Lincoln pies" or
"McClellan pies," as the government crackers were sometimes called,

many Yanks came eventually to like them. Hunger compelled soldiers to eat them and taste was acquired with use. One historian states: "In the Eighth Iowa Regiment the first issue of hard tack 'nearly created insurrection.' Later the men came to thank their stars they had even hard tack . . . to eat." Sometimes conversion came quickly. After only a few months of service a Pennsylvania soldier wrote: "I have got to like the army crackers very much. I eat them in the place of bread altogether now, though there is plenty of the latter." [70]

The meat portion of the army ration was normally pork or beef, though fish was issued occasionally in some commands. Pork now and then came in the form of cured bacon or ham, but, according to one veteran, the issue in either case "was usually black, rusty and strong and decidedly unpopular." [71] The meat served most frequently to Billy Yanks was salt pork.

When served in company quantities the salt pork was commonly boiled. But when the soldiers prepared rations individually or in messes, they fried it, broiled it on forked sticks, baked it with beans or used it as an ingredient of soup or stew. Soup seasoned with pork and thickened with hardtack made a dish known as lobscouse which, while associated traditionally with sailors, was relished nonetheless by Billy Yanks.

Seasoned campaigners, pressed for time or disinclined to cook, thought nothing of throwing their pork ration between hardtack and eating it raw.[72]

Men in blue, like their opponents, commonly referred to salt pork as "sowbelly"; one Yank with a penchant for detail added parenthetically "with the tits on." [73]

Beef was fresh or pickled. Fresh beef could be fried, broiled or cooked in soup or stew; but pickled beef, known almost universally among Yanks as "salt horse," presented special problems of preparation. Pickling as done for the army meant preserving the meat in a solution so briny that even the most hardened veterans would hardly presume to cook it without a thorough soaking in water. "It was not an unusual occurrence," according to one experienced Yank, "for troops encamped by a running brook to tie a piece of this beef to the end of a cord, and throw it into the brook at night, to remain freshening until the following morning." [74]

The soaking took away the natural juices along with the surplus salt, thus reducing taste as well as nutrition. Edibility was further impaired in many instances by poor preservation, and this despite the fact that the special pickling process was supposed to make the beef impervious to decay in any sort of climate for at least two years. Even with due allowance for soldier exaggeration, the conclusion is inescapable that "salt horse" dispensed in camp was commonly tainted and frequently, if not usually, tough enough to justify the soldier appellation of "old bull." [75]

Fresh beef was less than fresh at times and pork now and then was inhabited by worms. Hence, meat, like hardtack, came in for abundant reviling among consumers. "Fresh-killed beef . . . had to be eaten with the odor and warmth of blood still in it," wrote a soldier historian of his Louisiana experience, "under penalty of finding it fly-blown before the next meal." A Massachusetts Yank complained that the pickled beef "was ten times saltier than salt itself & almost blistered the tongue." A Pennsylvanian reported that smoked flitch which he received on one occasion "was so strong it could almost walk its self." [76]

"We drew meat last night that was so damd full of skippers that it could move alone," wrote an Ohioan, and a comrade reported: "Yesterday morning was the first time we had to carry our meat for the maggots always carried it till then. We had to have an extra gard to keep them from packing it clear off." An Illinois Yank stationed in Tennessee in 1862 found the so-called fresh beef so worthless "that one can throw a piece up against a tree and it will just stick there and quiver and twitch for all the world like one of those blue-bellied lizards at home will do when you knock him off a fence rail with a stick." [77]

Almost any camp contained wags who were ready to assert unequivocally that the stuff being issued as beef was not beef at all but mule. A camp newspaper in 1862 quoted a Connecticut soldier as stating "that the commissary at Annapolis has given the boys so much mule meat that the ears of the whole regiment have grown three and a half inches since their arrival at the Maryland capital." Sometimes Yanks who drew a particularly bad lot of meat would decide to lay it away with the honor due long service in the army. Hence, they would deposit the beef or pork in a hardtack box, surround it with scraps of harness for proper identity, bear it away with appropriate music and procession to a final resting place in the camp dump and fire the customary fusillade over the grave. Thus was hardship converted to merriment.[78]

Coffee was one of the most cherished items in the ration. Of this article the men in blue, in striking contrast with the experience of their opponents, usually had an ample supply. The effect on morale must have been considerable. And if it cannot be said that coffee helped Billy Yank win the war, it at least made his participation in the conflict more tolerable.

Soldiers who liked the beverage sweet commonly carried coffee and sugar ready mixed in a cloth bag.[79] At mealtimes, and often in between, they would bring water to a boil in pint dippers or tin cans rigged with wire bails and then dump in the mixture and let it boil until the desired hue was attained. As a general rule the longer a man served, the darker he liked his coffee.

The finished product was described by one of Sherman's veterans thus: "Black as the face of a plantation, 'strong enough to float an iron wedge,' and innocent of lacteal adulteration, it gave strength to the weary and heavy laden, and courage to the despondent and sick at heart." [80]

Now and then Yanks would lighten their coffee with milk "confiscated" from Rebel cows or with an evaporated product dispensed on rare occasions by commissaries; but usually army coffee was black.

Some soldiers consumed enormous quantities. "I can drink two and three quarts of coffee a day easily and want more," wrote a Pennsylvanian, "and I always was a fair coffee drinker." But his capacity was exceeded by an Ohioan who stated: "I have a large cup that holds nearly 2 qts. I now can manage that full 2 times a day and sometimes 3 of them a day." [81]

Yanks usually liked the coffee prepared in their individual pots much better than that brewed in large quantities by company cooks. An Irishman whose regiment followed the latter procedure wrote disgustedly: "The coffee is on the boarding house order. I find the greatest difficulty distinguishing between it and the soup. Therefore I . . . drink Adam's Ale instead." [82]

In the second year of the war the commissary department distributed to the field armies a product consisting of extract of coffee mixed with sugar and milk and known as "essence of coffee." This compound, according to a regimental adjutant, was packed in half-gallon tin cans and looked like axle grease. A teaspoonful mixed with a cup of hot water, he added, produced a beverage so villainous that the men would not drink it. This earlier version of "instant coffee" aroused similar reactions elsewhere; as a result it was shortly discontinued as an item of army issue.[83]

Essence of coffee was only one of several processed foods known to Billy Yank. The regulation ration in use at the outbreak of the war authorized desiccated potatoes as a substitute for beans; and revisions adopted during the conflict added desiccated vegetables and provided that either the potato or vegetable product might be substituted for beans, peas, rice, hominy or fresh potatoes. Late in the conflict a light ration, consisting in part of processed foods and known as "Dr. Horsford's Marching Ration," was approved, but this compound was not put into use until after the cessation of hostilities.[84]

Desiccated potatoes, which had been used by the British in the Crimea, were described by an Illinois veteran as "Irish potatoes cut up fine and thoroughly dried"; they "much resembled the modern preparation called 'grape nuts,'" he commented. Soldiers were hostile to this article at first but medical authorities, prompted by the erroneous belief that it would prevent scurvy, were so insistent on its use that many Yanks were forced to give it a trial. Some used it as an ingredient for soup while others converted it into small cakes. The cakes, when fried to a deep brown, came to be regarded by a few, at least, as "first rate." But the majority of soldiers seem never to have acquired a taste for desiccated potatoes in any form.[85]

The vegetable concentrate, specified in regulations as "desiccated compressed mixed vegetables" but commonly known by soldiers as "desecrated vegetables" or "baled hay," was made of an assortment of garden produce, including turnips, carrots, beets, onions and string beans. The compound was issued in hard, dry cakes. These when soaked would expand enormously, a circumstance which gave rise to the story of a Yank eating his ration raw, swelling up and almost dying.[86] About the only practical means of using the mixture was in soup.

The desiccated vegetables aroused even more consumer opposition than the potatoes. One factor working against them was their appearance; in solution they reminded an officer of "a dirty brook with all the dead leaves floating around promiscuously." Too, they were so heavily peppered (for antiseptic purposes), and so utterly insipid, as to repel most of "Uncle Sam's boarders." [87] But positive orders of commanders and periodic shortages of more palatable foods combined to compel a limited acceptance of the desiccated vegetables. Some of the reluctant consumers eventually found them tolerable—one even pronounced them "an excelent article." [88] But all were happier when sufficiency of regular rations made their issue unnecessary.

An often ridiculed but very important item of camp fare was the army bean. As a mainstay of diet it was outranked only by bread, meat and coffee.

New England soldiers, as might be expected, were especially fond of beans. When members of the Forty-fourth Massachusetts Regiment wrote an original comic opera for presentation before General Foster and other notables at New Bern, North Carolina, in March 1863, they included these lines:

Beans for breakfast—breakfast,
Beans for breakfast—breakfast,
Beans for breakfast
    Down on the Readville farm.[89]

The verse was repeated with substitution of dinner and supper for breakfast. The Readville farm represented the initial training camp, but beans accompanied the New Englanders on campaigns throughout Dixie and, while they rarely were dished out as often as three times a day, they were, indeed, a frequent item of issue.

Nor was their consumption limited to soldiers of the Northeast. Westerners and others adopted not only the beans but also the New Englander's favorite mode of preparing them. This method, as given by a young Minnesota private to his mother in 1863, was:

Take as many beans as you want for a mess and par boil or partly boil them then take a spade and dig a hole large aneugh for the pot you are going to cook the beans in and build a fire in it and get it as warm as you can, then take the pot of beans and put a peice of meat in the center of the pot then cover the pot over and put it in the hole covering the pot with the coals that are in the hole and shovel earth on top of them and in twenty four hours you have a soldiers dish of baked beans.[90]

Overnight, rather than twenty-four hours, seems to have been the usual baking period. That soldier was rare whose salivary glands did not begin an expectant flow when the beans were uncovered in the morning. "The best I ever eat," was the considered judgment of one who partook of this appetizing preparation.[91]

Beans were sometimes used in soup either as the principal ingredient or along with sundry other articles. Soup, in one form or another, was a common camp dish. To prepare it several soldiers usually pooled their rations, thus saving time and effort and securing maximum returns in savoriness and nourishment. Now and then a Yank would denounce the preparation as tasting more like dishwater than soup, but the majority judgment as recorded in letters and diaries was favorable.[92]

Shortage of rations and a bent for experimentation, common among amateur cooks, resulted in numerous variations and specialties. Hungry Yanks stationed in Louisiana, taking a cue from Seminole War experience, converted the tail of an alligator into soup. They pronounced it good, but the decision apparently was based more on necessity and pride than on taste; for, when after a brief interval the commissary dealt out a ration of bread and pork, the highly vaunted delicacy was quickly forsaken.[93]

Rattlesnakes also were killed and eaten in a few instances. But Sergeant Henry A. Buck apparently reflected prevailing opinion when he wrote: "The meat looked very nice and delicate, but I did not feel like trying it." Another dish of limited acceptance must have been the fried "jabird and a read headed wood pecker" which one Yank reported.[94]

Among miscellaneous delicacies receiving the favorable comment of soldier correspondents and diarists were hogs and chickens coated with clay and roasted in hot ashes; Indian pudding; doughnuts; and pies. Rebel apiaries were often raided to provide delicious sweetening; and Southern orchards and thickets yielded an abundance of apples, peaches, cherries, plums, blackberries and other fruits that were eaten as plucked or converted into pies or sauce. Typical of many soldier comments was that of Sergeant Onley Andrus written from the depths of Dixie in the spring of 1863: "I have been Blackberrying and Oh! I wish you was here to go with me. . . . I eat all the *black* ones & brot the red ones home to stew for *Sas!*" [95]

In the fall and early winter, Yanks frequently partook of the wild grapes and persimmons that grew in abundance in many parts of the South. Some even learned to relish the fruit of the lowly pawpaw tree.[96]

Culinary arrangements varied considerably from time to time and in different commands. But as a general rule the company plan, with cooking done for the whole group by a permanent or rotating detail, was followed during the period of initial training in home areas and in permanent camps and barracks. This system had the advantage of easier supervision and in theory, at least, conduced to more expert preparation.

When units moved to the field they usually went over to the mess or individual plan of cooking. Messes consisted normally of four to eight men, grouped on the basis of congeniality, each of whom took his turn in serving as cook—or "dogrobber" as some Yanks put it. The mess system worked well when troops were in a relatively settled state, as in winter quarters, but when on the march or in contact with the enemy they often found it more convenient to prepare their food individually.[97]

Sometimes members of a mess engaged the service of a Negro, obtainable from among the freedmen at nominal compensation, to relieve them of the drudgery of cooking and scrubbing. Frequently the blacks were better cooks than the soldiers, but a fault common to both was an overfondness for frying. It is only fair to add that commissary issues and field conditions were not such as to encourage artistry in cooking and that most camp chefs in time mastered essential principles.

Concern over the prevalence of disease in the army, which many civilians attributed to improper preparation of food under the mess plan, caused Congress in March 1863 to enact a law requiring cooking by companies and authorizing enlistment of Negroes to serve as assistants to soldier details.[98] But this legislation apparently had little effect outside the Northern states. Cooking in small groups or as individuals was the prevailing practice among seasoned troops in the field during any period of the war; and the tendency was toward the individual plan. A typical bivouac scene in the latter half of the conflict was a small party of Yanks hovering about a pile of burning rails or pine knots, each boiling his coffee in a dipper, broiling his sowbelly on a stick and, if hardtack happened not to be at hand, baking a flour-and-water dough ball on the end of a ramrod. Faces, already brown from exposure to wind, sun and dirt, grew darker as the veterans puttered about the fire, and "smoked Yanks" became something more than a catchy phrase.[99]

Many men were never able to adapt themselves with any degree of happiness to the rough fare of field and camp. Some, from much practice, achieved a high level of profane eloquence in denouncing it. One soldier wrote his brother: "We live so mean here the hard bread is all worms and the meat stinks like hell . . . and rice to or three times a week & worms as long as your finger. I liked rice once but god damn the stuff now." Another stated that "the butter we have had lately has been rather strong . . . if Samson had had a little to rub on his head after his hair was shaved off the Philistines never would have taken him prisoner." A third reported that owing to his inability to eat any of the beans, "rusty pork" or potatoes served in camp, he was forced "to live on faith and sour wheat bread." [100]

Numerous blasts were directed at the commissaries, whom the malcontents often envisioned as "damd old raskels" who cheated them out of their due allowances and fed them on condemned junk. In one instance about 300 soldiers gathered up the bread issued to them and "stormed the commissary with the sour loaves as ammunition." [101]

But outbreaks were rare and protests frequently reflected less of venom than a desire to keep alive a soldier's sacred right to grumble. The overwhelming majority of Yanks eventually learned to accept as a normal part of soldiering a fare considerably less attractive than that known at home. One factor working to this end was the natural tendency of human beings to adapt themselves to whatever they cannot avoid. Another was the stimulating effect of army life on appetite. Early in his camp career a Massachusetts man observed: "When I first came here I ate about one third of a ration but now neither coffee nor bread are long without a covering." After five months in service a Vermonter wrote his sister: "I'll bet when I get hom I Shall have an appetite to eat most anything . . . if a person wants to know how to apreciate the value of good vituals he had better enlist. . . . I have seen the time when I would have been glad to picked the crusts of bread that mother gives to the hogs." An Ohioan who had been through the strenuous Chickasaw Bayou and Fort Hindman campaigns informed his mother: "i often wish i hade to eate what ante poley doge gits and what you throe away." [102]

One of the most vivid glimpses of the impact of military life on appetite and eating practices was that given by a Pennsylvanian who wrote to his wife in 1864: "It goes perty greasey Some times but wee will have to be Satisfied. . . . When wee go to draw our Rashions it puts mee in mind as iff thare ware about Thirty hungray horgs In one pen and the trought onely Big a nough for about three to get in . . . that is the way it goes with us." [103]

In conclusion it may be said that as Billy Yank moved away from his civilian status he thought less and less about the quality of his rations and more and more about their quantity.

CHAPTER X

EVIL AND GOODNESS

"I will be a perfect Barbarian if I Should Stay hear 3 years," wrote a Vermonter from camp near Burlington in June 1861, while a Minnesotan who marched with Sibley against the Indians in 1863 noted in his diary a short time after the expedition got under way: "I must confess that I have seen but little of the wickedness and depravity of man until I Joined the Army." In similar vein, an Illinois soldier reported from Corinth, Mississippi, after Shiloh: "If there is any place on God's fair earth where wickedness 'stalketh abroad in daylight,' it is in the army. . . . Ninety-nine men out of every hundred are profane swearers . . . hundreds of young men . . . devote all their leisure time to [gambling]." [1]

Countless other Yanks serving in widely scattered commands testified to the prevalency of evil and the degenerating influences of army life. Alfred Davenport, a city-bred Easterner not overly pious or easily shocked, wrote his homefolk from near Baltimore in December 1861 that camp was "a hard school" and that scores in his regiment had been "ruined in morals and in health for they learn everything bad and nothing good." A year later he reported from Fredericksburg: "The more vulgar a man is, the better he is appreciated and as for morals . . . [the army] is a graveyard for them." Still later he observed: "If you think soldiering cures anyone of wild habits it is a great mistake, it is like Sending a Boy in the Navy to learn him good manners. We have Drummer Boys with us that when they came at first could hardly look you in the face for diffidence but now could stare the Devil out of contenance and cant be beat at cursing, swearing and gambling." [2]

In like tone Private Delos W. Lake of the Nineteenth Michigan wrote in 1864 from Middle Tennessee to a brother about to become a soldier: "The army is the worst place in the world to learn bad habbits of all kinds. there is several men in this Regt when they enlisted they were nice respectable men and belonged to the Church of God, but now where are they? they are ruined men." [3]

Observations of religious workers, records of the Medical Department and official reports of commanding officers confirm soldier impressions of the pervasiveness of evil in Union camps. It is not that bad men flocked to the colors while good ones stayed at home, or that the army was the devil's own instrument for making sinners out of the righteous. Men did not grow worse from the mere fact of becoming soldiers, for there is nothing contaminating about an army uniform. Unquestionably some men were as good when they came out of the service as when they enlisted, and a few were even better. But in general, among Yanks as among Rebs, evil flourished more than good. The degeneration came from the removal of accustomed restraints and associations, the urge to experiment with the forbidden, the desire to escape boredom and the utter inadequacy of religious and recreational facilities for soldiers of the sixties.

One of the most common evils of the camp was profanity. A New Englander serving on Staten Island in the fall of 1861 reported that "swearing is almost universal," while a Chicagoan stationed near Memphis observed: "The swearing especially is terrific, and even to a man accustomed to hear bad language, and with sensibilities not very easily shocked, it is really disgusting. The worst characters of the worst dens up North, I am afraid, would have to yield the palm for profanity to the gallant army of the Southwest." [4]

Articles of war forbade the use of profanity and, in the case of officers, prescribed a fine of one dollar for each offense.[5] But little attention was paid to the prohibition, and commissioned personnel, far from enjoining their men, seem rather to have set an unwholesome example in the use of oaths and execrations.

Occasionally a pious commander would publish an order against swearing and chaplains consistently made it one of their principal targets. Religiously inclined soldiers sometimes rebuked comrades for their blasphemy, but more often than not such endeavors were squelched by a flood of ridicule.

The drift toward swearing was so strong that it drew in many good men. A Hoosier boy of exemplary background found after a few months' service that it was remarkably easy for a soldier to be profane, and an Ohio surgeon noted in December 1861 that while at first little swearing had been heard in his regiment, "of late oaths and gross profanity are painfully on the increase." Even more to the point was the observation of a Connecticut captain who wrote from Louisiana in 1862: "It is wonderful how profane an army is. Officers who are members of the church, . . . who would not even play a game of cards, have learned to rip out oaths when the drill goes badly or when the discipline 'gets out of kilter.' " [6]

The type of profanity used in Federal camps is revealed in some detail by courts-martial proceedings, which specify *ad literam* objectionable phrases of soldiers charged with disrespectful conduct toward their superiors. These records indicate that the swearing of Billy Yank did not differ greatly from that of his descendants in World Wars I and II. "Hell" and "damn" were the most common expletives, but "God damn," "son of a bitch," "Jesus Christ," "kiss my arse," "go stick it up . . ." and the age-old array of smutty, four-letter words, used singly and in varying combinations, also had frequent usage.

Now and then a soldier made exuberant by drink would step out of his tent and yell "Hurrah for hell!" [7] If some nosy sergeant or despised officer should call him to task, he might become considerably more profane. Private Charles N. Heath when threatened with arrest by his sergeant replied: "If you arrest me, I will rip your God damned guts out and scatter them over the parade ground." And Private John Killeen when ordered to guard duty blurted: "By my living Jesus Christ I will have your life the first chance, you son of a bitch." Another soldier was so provoked by a sergeant's order to keep still while in formation as to exclaim "that he wished the whole God damned Army and Navy and every other God damned thing was in hell" and that "no God damn man could make him keep still." [8]

These were statements made in anger against offending superiors. But most of the profanity heard in camp was of the idle, uninspired sort, thrown in to keep up a flow of chatter or from sheer habit. As such, it was uttered without intent or consciousness of offense either to God or man.[9]

Gambling was hardly less prevalent than swearing. One Yank, while stationed near Petersburg in October 1864, noted in his diary that "so far as my observation goes, nine out of ten play cards for money," and another, writing after the war, recalled that after Fredericksburg he once sat for twenty-four hours in a poker game.[10]

The peak of gambling came on payday when clusters of soldiers might be seen on every hand, intently trying to multiply their greenbacks by resort to chance. As the money gradually shifted to the possession of Dame Fortune's chosen few, the crowds thinned out and chance took a holiday until the next return of the paymaster.

The gambling urge of some Yanks was so strong that they would indulge in it at the risk of their lives as well as their fortunes. One group of poker zealots who found themselves a special target of Rebel gunners completed the hand, though swearing incessantly at the enemy for disturbing them, and then leisurely shifted to the unexposed side of a large tree to continue their play.[11]

At the other extreme from those who brazenly shuffled and dealt to the accompaniment of whining bullets was a group so sensitive to the evil of gaming that they took no chances of being killed with the instruments of sin on their bodies. Several soldiers bore witness to the fact that the line of march leading to battle was strewn with playing cards, tossed aside by conscience-stricken gamblers fearful of their future. But if they survived, "these same fellows," according to one observer, "would immediately gather up the cards until they had a full deck." [12]

The principal gambling medium was cards and the favorite game was poker, commonly called "bluff," which was played in several variations. Other card games included twenty-one, euchre, faro and seven-up or "old sledge."

Crap shooting had some practitioners, but the most common dice game seems to have been chuck-a-luck, also called sweat, which was a banking contest played by rolling three dice on a board or cloth marked off into numbered squares. This game became so popular in Grant's army during the early months of 1863 that soldiers gave a water-surrounded retreat opposite Yazoo Pass the name of Chuck-a-luck Island.[13]

Raffling—of objects ranging from watches to horses—cockfighting and horse racing provided other means of gambling, though none of these had anything like the following of cards and dice. Contests between game roosters sometimes aroused unusual interest from the fact of the feathered gladiators representing organizations strongly imbued with unit pride. General John Beatty reported a fight between cocks sponsored respectively by Company G of the Third Ohio Regiment and Company G of the Tenth Ohio, with a side bet of fifteen dollars. "After numerous attacks, retreats, charges and countercharges, the Tenth rooster succumbed like a hero," wrote Beatty, "and the other was carried in triumph from the field." Just as enthusiasm ran highest General Ormsby Mitchel, the division commander, came riding by; thinking that the cheering was for him he "passed on, well pleased" with both the soldiers and himself.[14]

Whatever the form of gambling, the stakes were usually small; considering that the maximum pay of an infantry private was only sixteen dollars a month, they could not often be otherwise. But occasionally well-heeled and reckless individuals would push the betting to fantastic heights.[15]

Gambling sharks trained in metropolitan dens frequented some of the camps and on payday made heavy inroads on the meager resources of un-suspecting soldiers.[16] Now and then a Yank of pious background suc-ceeded by diligent application in becoming so expert at games of chance as to live sumptuously at the expense of his fellows. Such a one was C. W. Bardeen, a teen-aged fifer who was introduced to gambling when he joined the army and who became so proficient that many comrades would not risk sitting down with him in a friendly game. The following entries from his diary afford glimpses of his gambling experience:

> Aug. 22, 1863, Riker's Island, New York—We were paid off to-day. I made considerable playing Bluff. $27.00 at Draw Poker.
> Aug. 24—Played Bluff of course. Made pretty well.
> Aug. 25—Played Bluff as usual. Sent $50.00 home.
> Aug. 27—Made 20.00 at Bluff. . . . Sent $50.00 home.
> Aug. 28—Lost $5.00 at Sweat this morning but won it back again at Bluff. I seem to have uniform good success at Bluff this payday.
> Aug. 30—Sunday. . . . Lost $10.00 at Bluff & Sweat and set up a board winning more than I lost. Paid $25.00 to Hull for a watch.
> Sept. 1—Won $20.00 at Bluff in A.M. A full hand, two Flushes. I held the Full. In P.M. won twenty dollars at Sweat Got a $30.00 draft.

Bardeen's winnings in August and September 1863 aggregated several hundred dollars, permitting him to take a trip to the city, have his pic-ture taken, see the sights, attend the opera and subscribe to three news-papers. He resumed his gambling full blast at Brandy Station, Virginia, in October, adding raffling and "props" (played with four shells, two red and two white) to his repertoire. But in the latter part of the year his conscience began to bother him, as his diary entry of December 31, 1863, reveals:

> The year that has passed was passed by me in the Army. I bear wit-ness to its contaminating effects. Many an evil habit has sprung up in me since Jan. 1st 1863. God grant that the year in which we now have entered may not be so.

In February 1864, Bardeen, then sixteen years old, started attending reli-gious services, took the temperance pledge and shortly gave up gam-bling.[17]

In his case, abandonment of gambling resulted primarily from immi-nency of the fighting season and concern for the soul. Other soldiers were constrained to reform by the quick loss of badly needed wages.

Typical of those impelled to better ways by bad luck was Jacob E. Hyne-man of Grant's army who wrote in his diary on February 20, 1864, shortly after drawing four months' pay: "In camp. I must say that I feel down in the mouth, only paid a week ago and have not a cent now, having bluffed away all that I did not send home. I don't think I will play poker any more." [18]

Resolves to eschew chance, whatever the motivation, usually were ineffectual, and gambling, like swearing, was considerably more prevalent in 1865 than in 1861.

A frequent accompaniment of swearing and gambling was the drink-ing of intoxicating beverages. Whisky was the usual tipple, but gin, brandy, wine and—among German troops especially—beer were also con-sumed in large quantities. The cider stocked by sutlers sometimes had sufficient potency to make imbibers of a few glasses limber and joyful.

The prevalence of excessive drinking was such as to disturb moralists and greatly enhance the problem of discipline. After presiding over a court-martial session involving fifty men in July 1862, John William De Forest wrote that "every solitary case of misbehavior originated in whis-key. . . . It seems clear than an army of teetotalers would be one-fourth more reliable and effective than an army containing the usual proportion of hard drinkers." [19] And in reviewing a case of liquor-provoked insub-ordination in Hooker's division in February 1862, McClellan observed: "No one evil agent so much obstructs this army . . . as the degrading vice of drunkenness. It is the cause of by far the greater part of the dis-orders which are examined by courts-martial. It is impossible to estimate the benefits that would accrue to the service from the adoption of a resolution on the part of officers to set their men an example of total abstinence from intoxicating liquors. It would be worth 50,000 men to the armies of the United States." [20]

Drinking was more prevalent in some organizations than in others, owing to differences in the background of the men, the character of com-manders, the effectiveness of chaplains and various other factors. Regiments from large cities, especially those with a heavy Irish or Ger-man admixture, often were more inclined to strong drink than were those composed mainly of rural men. But organizations distinguished for sobriety might, under unusual temptation, go on a roaring spree. Such was the case with the Forty-eighth New York Regiment, known as Perry's Saints, whose colonel, James M. Perry, was a prominent minister. In June 1862 while this unit was stationed on Tybee Island, a storm blew ashore a large quantity of beer and wine and Perry's Saints proceeded to get gloriously drunk. The incident must have upset the reverend colonel greatly, for he was fatally stricken on the very next day while sitting at his desk.[21]

Excessive drinking was undoubtedly more common among Yanks than among Rebs. This does not mean that the Southerners were naturally more abstemious than their Northern counterparts but rather that they had less opportunity to partake of Bacchus' offerings. Intoxicants were more abundant in the North than in the Confederacy; Yanks had more money than Rebs; they were more frequently stationed near large cities; whisky was more often an item of government issue; and the Federals had a more effective system of supply.

Since drinking was largely a matter of opportunity, intemperance was most common during changes of station, especially those requiring passage through cities, on holidays and at paytime. Colonel Hans Heg of the Fifteenth Wisconsin wrote his wife after taking his command south by way of Chicago that he lost three men en route and many others "got awfull drunk." [22] The comment "pay day—most of the boys drunk," or "Christmas—nearly all tight" appears so often in soldier letters and diaries as to become monotonous.

The quality of liquor drunk by soldiers ranged from choice to vile, with the vile being far more common than the choice. Commissary whisky, denounced with about the same degree of enthusiasm as consumed, was analyzed by a soldier journalist as "bark juice, tar-water, turpentine, brown sugar, lamp-oil and alcohol." And a Yank who on Christmas Day 1864 imbibed so heavily of the government issue that he was not able to entertain his dinner guests wrote in his diary on December 26: "Got up this morning with severe bee hives in my head." Perhaps the most revealing commentaries on the varying quality of intoxicants were the nicknames applied to them in camp. These included "how come you so," "oil of gladness," "tanglefoot," "the ardent," "Oh, be joyful" and "Nockum stiff." [23]

Effects of drinking sprees varied with individuals and beverages. Many Yanks were aroused to extreme pugnacity, as the full guardhouses and numerous bruised heads after payday readily attested. Others became exceedingly gay, lifting their voices in laughter or song, while still others were reduced to misery and tears. A few sank unobtrusively into peaceful stupor and some ran the entire gamut of physical and emotional reaction.

Numerous and varied efforts were made to combat the tide of drinking which beset Union camps. Sutlers and peddlers caught selling liquor in camp forfeited their trading privileges and some were summarily punished. The sutler of a New York regiment who sold a large quantity of whisky to soldiers was drummed out of camp with a dozen liquor bottles dangling from his neck. A peddler who bootlegged "condensed corn" in another camp was forced to stand on a barrel, while his wife, likewise apprehended, was compelled to carry a log.[24]

Some commanders hated whisky so thoroughly that they spilled every drop found in possession of their men, though such extremes were greatly deplored by devotees of drink. When one officer emptied a demijohn found cached in a wagon during a march up the Shenandoah Valley, a thirsty Irishman, who looked ruefully on what seemed to him an unwarranted sacrifice, was heard to remark to a comrade: "Dennis if I'm kilt in the next battle, bring me back and bury me here." [25]

Sundry disciplinary expedients were invoked to restrain drinking. An engineer commander in Grant's army on one occasion sent the numerous drunks corraled on the night following payday to a riverbank where each was stripped, a rope was tied around his waist and he was pitched into the water.[26]

Efforts of officers, chaplains and civilian reformers to combat drinking in the army often were paralleled by temperance activities of the soldiers themselves. Sometimes these were quite informal, consisting simply of a few soldiers resolving to abstain from drink. In other instances entire companies entered into an agreement not to partake of any intoxicant.[27]

Many regiments had temperance associations which solicited abstinence pledges and worked generally to restrict the use of liquor. In the spring of 1864 a temperance movement originating in the Fifth Maine Regiment was said to have spread to numerous other organizations of the Army of the Potomac.[28] But these and all other attempts to curb drinking among the soldiers appear to have been of little avail.

Stealing from comrades, Northern civilians and especially from Southerners was another evil which had considerable prevalency among soldiers, though thievery was never so widespread as profanity, gambling and drinking.[29] A Wisconsin captain wrote from Waterford, Mississippi, November 6, 1862: "Until lately no pig, chicken, cow or sheep stood one chance in ten for its life, if within a mile of camp. . . . Stealing is the most common practice in the army. . . . It will be a great wonder, indeed, if the army does not turn out hundreds of men perfectly irresponsible and thievish, not to speak of uncontrollable licentiousness, who before the war were not bad men." [30] Because of greater opportunity, cavalrymen were worse plunderers than infantrymen. One trooper who accompanied Sherman wrote in his diary while at Lawrenceville, Georgia: "In Covington, Oxford, and indeed all the towns in Georgia, the conduct of our Division has been disgraceful—homes plundered, women insulted and every species of outrage committed." [31] From both cavalrymen and infantrymen South Carolinians, owing to a widespread tendency of Yanks to place first blame on them for bringing on the war, suffered the greatest outrages of all.[32] But even the hapless Indians, whose war guilt could hardly have been used as a pretext, suffered greatly when exposed to soldier villainy and greed. Long after the conflict a woman who had lived in Indian territory invaded by Federal troops told a historical researcher: "During the Civil War the Northern men were so mean to the Choctaw women, they would jerk their earrings from their ears and lock them in one stuffy room together, keeping them there for days." [33]

Vulgarity and obscenity, though not so pervasive as some other evils, were more common than one whose knowledge of soldier life is based on published works might suspect. Nineteenth-century Americans, while in most respects a robust, earthy folk, usually were restrained by an exaggerated sense of delicacy from putting the seamy side of life into print. Soldiers occasionally recorded off-color doings and sayings in their letters and diaries, but when in later years they or their descendants prepared these documents for publication false notions of propriety inclined them to delete items offensive to Victorian tastes.

Reticence concerning evil is not necessarily a proof of righteousness, and ample evidence joins with common sense to justify the conclusion that soldiers of the 1860s differed little from those of today in basic morality.

As previously noted one of the forms in which vulgarity manifested itself was the singing of ribald songs.[34] Occasional references point also to the popularity among campfire groups of racy stories and obscene jokes. Reports of religious workers indicate the circulation among Yanks of licentious books, though details as to character and quantity are not given. A Christian Commission representative told of finding obscene pictures in a tent of some of Grant's soldiers that he visited early in 1865, and the availability of charm-revealing pin-up girls is indicated in the following advertisement from a Chattanooga paper published primarily for Federal troops:

PHOTOGRAPHS, RICH, RARE & RACY

A very beautiful picture of the handsomest woman in the world; a peculiar rich-colored photograph in oil, taken from life; beautiful to behold. This is really a magnificent picture, a perfect gem. She is a bewitching beauty. Price fifty cents. Sent free by mail in a sealed circular envelope.[35]

Some off-color poetry also made the rounds of the campfires, though relatively little of this type of literature has been preserved. Thomas B. Wetmore's saltpeter verses, which originated in the Confederacy as a result of Captain Jonathan Haralson's advertisement for "chamber-lye," crossed over to the Federal lines soon after their composition.[36] No doubt many Yanks recited or sang the racy stanzas to appreciative comrades and some made copies for their homefolk.[37] Northern publishers ran off broadsides of the poetry for circulation among both soldiers and civilians. The version published by H. De Marsan of New York City carried an illustration which is so flagrant in its vulgarity as to prove conclusively that delicacy was not a universal trait in the 1860s.[38] Perhaps the salaciousness was rendered more acceptable to Northerners because of its being pointed at "Secesh" women.

In the correspondence of an Ohio Yank was found a poem, "Jeff Davis' Dream," which for gross obscenity would stand high in erotic literature of any period. But no information was given concerning the source or circulation of this item.[39]

In view of the roughness of camp ways, it is not surprising that Yanks threatened with visits from their womenfolk sometimes revealed signs of panic. John B. Cuzner of the Sixteenth Connecticut Regiment wrote his sweetheart from Portsmouth, Virginia, on August 28, 1863: "Mother wanted to come down and see me she wrote and asked me what I thought of it but the camp is no place for Women there is so much vulgar talk I thought I had got toughened to it, but last night one of the boys got tight and his swearing made my hair stand straight up." A Pennsylvania Yank in reply to his wife's proposal to come to see him in 1861 wrote: "As much as I wood like to See you i must Say this Place is not fit for you to come to. Nearly 600 men 3 miles from Eney town. Some of them . . . are not very particular What they Say if a Strange face Comes among them." Another Yank whose wife had registered hurt at her husband's apparent reluctance to have her visit him offered the following explanation: "You say I don't want you 2 come & see me, that

ARTILLERY PRACTICE, NEAR THE GAINES HOUSE

ON THE THRESHOLD OF FREEDOM

Family of Negroes at the Gaines House

is not so, I should be as glad 2 see you as anybody would 2 see their wife but . . . it is not a fit place for any woman, for there is all kinds of talk, songs and everything not good for them 2 hear." [40]

It is not at all unlikely that the desire of wives to visit camp sprang in part from concern over the constancy of soldier husbands. Well might the home ladies have been alarmed, for association with lewd women was one of the most notorious of soldier sins.

Prostitution was most rampant in the cities frequented by soldiers. The raising of the Northern armies was paralleled by informal mobilization for active service of a vast horde of loose women anxious to capitalize on the sexual longings of the men who donned the blue. In every Northern metropolis these unsavory characters set up shop and peddled their tawdry wares. A Cincinnati newspaper complained in January 1864 that *femmes du monde* had "nearly succeeded in elbowing all decent women from the public promenade" of that city, and in Chicago in 1864 and 1865 an estimated 2,000 lewd women thronged the streets and filled the bawdy houses. Boston was said to have swarmed with strumpets and in New York loose females doubling as waitresses in "concert saloons" became such a nuisance that a state law was passed in 1862 closing these dens of debauchery; but the dispensers of sin evaded the prohibition by simply dropping the concerts, and by 1864 houses in the Broadway area specializing in liquor and lewdness were more numerous and active than ever before.[41]

Washington, because of its prominence as a military center, became a mecca for whores. The local provost marshal in 1862 reported the existence in the capital of 450 houses of ill fame, and the next year the Washington *Star* estimated after a vice survey that prostitutes in the capital area numbered no less than 7,500. This figure did not include mistresses whom some of the better-situated soldiers and officers maintained in such circumstances as to prevent their being counted.

A war correspondent, resident in the capital during the early period of the conflict, stated that at the time of his departure in the fall of 1862 Washington probably "was the most pestiferous hole since the days of Sodom and Gomorrah. The majority of the women on the streets were openly disreputable . . . in fine, every possible form of human vice and crime, dregs, offscourings and scum had flowed into the capitol and made of it a national catch-basin of indescribable foulness." [42]

In a colorful portrayal of the seamy side of life in wartime Washington, Margaret Leech calls the roll of some of the leading prostitutes and bordellos. "Entire blocks on the South side of Pennsylvania Avenue were devoted to the business," she states, while Marble Alley between Pennsylvania and Missouri avenues, a section east and west of the White House, Lafayette Square and portions of Twelfth and Thirteenth streets were other areas noted as resorts for bad women. "One whole section," she adds, "was christened Hooker's Division." Soldiers knew some of the disreputable establishments as "the Ironclad," "Fort Sumter," "Head-quarters, U.S.A.," "the Devil's Own," "the Wolf's Den" (run by Mrs. Wolf), "the Haystack" (kept by Mrs. Hay) and "Madam Russell's Bake Oven." [43]

Yanks were almost as reticent as Johnny Rebs about their associations with loose women. But the comments of an exceptional few, mainly in letters to gay blades at home, afford glimpses of amorous adventures. A Massachusetts soldier stationed in Virginia wrote in April 1863 after a visit to Washington: "I had a gay old time I tell you. Lager Beer and a horse and Buggy [and] in the evening Horizontal Refreshments or in Plainer words Riding a Dutch gal—had a good time generally I tell you. I can take care of two correspondents for sometime. . . . I see . . . any quantity women around a Plenty whores. . . . [A] little toten Don't go Bad." [44]

In like vein an artilleryman reported a pleasure jaunt of the next year: "I have just returned from Baltimore where I have been on a short spree with one of our Wagon Masters; and you may guess that we had a good time, for you know it is a sporting place, and fast women are all the go now days. . . . We stoped in Washongton for two days and nights it is a hard place full of Officers, Soldiers and fast Women; we went into some hard places, but came out all right." [45]

Washington and the Northern cities held no monopoly on prostitu-tion, for in the wake of the invading forces moved an army of harlots, with the result that every occupied city became a haven of vice. Louisville, New Orleans, Portsmouth and Norfolk, all of which were teeming with Federal soldiers during most of the war, were notorious centers of prosti-tution. Of the two last-named towns, a Connecticut soldier in December 1863 wrote: "They call the places sodom and Gormorrow on account of the wickedness . . . both plases are full of bad wimmen, lots of them from Conn." Early in 1865 this same Yank remarked of New Bern, North Carolina, another town noted for military activity: "I have got back from town. I went after a broom, but did not get any for there was so many wimen looking around after men that I bought a pie & got out of the place as quick as I could. Where so many wimen came from

I dont know, this place is worse by double than any place we were in before." [46]

From City Point, Virginia, which in 1864 was an important Federal base, a New Hampshire soldier wrote with more frankness than refinement: "We cannot get any thing here but f—king and that is plenty." [47] And a Pennsylvanian assigned to sentry duty in Savannah, Georgia, wrote a few weeks after the Federal occupation of that city: "I'm on duty every other day; but the reason of it is because there are so many hore houses in town which must have a Sentinel at each door for to keep them Straight." [48]

Chattanooga also had its quota of soldier-frequented bawdy houses, but in scarlet doings it appears to have run a poor second to Nashville and Memphis. [49] The Tennessee capital, which passed into Federal hands before the war was a year old, soon became a favorite resort of fancy women. Its underworld districts of "Slabtown" and "Smoky Row" were scenes of nightly orgies involving convalescent, transient and occupying soldiers. But in Nashville, as elsewhere, the character of worldly women, euphemistically dubbed "Cyprians" by police reporters, ranged from filthy slatterns who served their customers for nominal fees in alleys to tastefully attired and sophisticated concubines kept in comparative luxury by prosperous and discriminating clients. In January 1865 a surgeon in the provost marshal's office reported that in the past six months 393 prostitutes had been registered in Nashville but that, as a result of departures, deaths and ten marriages, the number had been reduced to 236. In concluding the report he stated: "The prostitutes complain that they are not making much money now, because of the scarcity of troops around the city. These women are rapidly leaving in all directions; some profess to be going home, while others are looking out for situations where more money can be obtained where with to bedeck and bedizzen themselves." [50]

In 1863 prostitution became such a problem in Nashville that the post commander, on the score of military necessity, loaded approximately 150 "Cyprians" on a boat and shipped them north. But the authorities of Louisville and Cincinnati raised such a howl that the expulsion order was revoked and after a brief excursion the unwanted cargo was returned by government steamer. [51]

The experience of these travelers was far less exciting than that of two of their associates who shortly after the battle of Nashville took a carriage out to the site of the engagement. As bold in their sightseeing as they were loose in their morals, they ventured so far out as to fall into the hands of some Rebel cavalrymen who, suspecting them to be spies, took them to Franklin and placed them under guard in a hotel. Shortly afterward, when a change in the fortunes of war restored Franklin to Federal control, Yankee horsemen mounted the whores on a mule and brought them safely back to Nashville.[52]

In Memphis prostitution became so flagrant during the Federal occupation that newspapers complained repeatedly of whores—many of them escorted by men wearing the Federal uniform—usurping the streets and monopolizing amusement places; and citizens threatened to rise in wrath and drive them out of the city. In April 1863 the Memphis *Bulletin* complained: "Our city . . . is a perfect bee hive of women of ill fame. The public conveyances have become theirs by right of conquest." A few weeks later an Ohio captain stationed in the city wrote in his diary: "Memphis . . . can boast of being one of the first places of female prostitution on the continent. Virtue is scarcely known within the limits of the city." [53]

The *nymphs du pave* were the more objectionable because of being the scum of the Northern underworld. "Memphis is the great rendezvous for prostitutes and 'pimps,' " the *Bulletin* observed on May 1, 1863. "When a woman could 'ply her vocation' no longer in St. Louis, Chicago or Cincinnati, she was fitted up in her best attire and shipped to Memphis, and in more cases than one to prevent the 'package' from being miscarried, was accompanied by gentlemen (heaven save the mark) with the insignia of rank." [54]

The provost marshal of Memphis in April 1863 issued an order closing houses of ill fame, threatening prostitutes with expulsion and warning military personnel that any of them caught in bawdy establishments would be reported to their commanders.[55] About fifty lewd women were said to have departed for the North after issuance of this order and newspaper comments indicate a general slowing down of vice activities for a period of several months; but by the autumn of 1863 prostitutes again were swarming the streets, and houses of ill repute were operating full blast.[56]

The lewd creatures who accommodated wearers of the blue were not all imported from the North. In all Southern cities, and especially in those that had been frequented by Rebel soldiers, the invading forces were greeted by numerous harlots who quickly saw the error of their past associations or whose loyalty to the Union had been temporarily thwarted. It is only fair to this class of Southerners to state that some of them chose to follow the Rebel armies rather than bow to the conquerors, and that among those who nominally submitted to Federal authority were inveterate Rebels who would occasionally sing the "Bonnie Blue Flag" and let out a whoop for Jeff Davis.[57]

One of the consequences of soldier association with immoral women was a costly tide of venereal infection. Reported cases of venereal disease among white troops whose mean strength for the period covered (May 1, 1861—June 30, 1866) was 468,275 aggregated 182,779 of which 136 proved fatal; colored troops, for whom figures are available only during the period June 30, 1864—June 30, 1866, from a mean strength of 63,645 reported 14,257 venereal cases with 32 fatalities. The breakdown of diseases was as follows:

| | White | | Colored | |
	Cases	Deaths	Cases	Deaths
Syphilis	73,382	123	6,207	28
Gonorrhea	95,833	6	7,060	1
Orchitis	13,564	7	990	3 [58]

A statistician of the Union Medical Department found that during the first year of the war one Yank out of every twelve suffered from venereal disease, and that for the entire period of the conflict the annual venereal rate was 82 cases per 1,000 men.[59]

Prevalency of venereal disease varied with circumstances, the most important of which was the opportunity for lewd associations. Hence, the peaks of infection tended to come during encampments near cities and after furloughs, such as those given to units who signed up for additional terms of service. The incidence of disease was especially heavy among new units composed largely of rural men passing through metropolitan centers en route to the front. Freed of home restraints and facing an uncertain future, such men, inexperienced as they were in the ways of the world, often felt bound to taste the sweets of sin.[60]

Economics was another factor influencing venereal trends. Recruits on their way to war and veterans on re-enlistment furlough frequently had pockets full of bounty money which made them readier prey than usual for the fancy women who thronged metropolitan way stations.

While Confederate records are too scanty to permit a meaningful comparison of Northern and Southern experience, it seems reasonable to conclude that fornication and venereal infection were more common among Yanks than among Rebs. The men in blue were better paid, drew more generous bounties and had easier access to large cities than those

who wore the gray. If Rebs had the better record, it was not from superior goodness—for available venereal statistics on a few regiments transferred from the deep South to the vicinity of Richmond in the summer
of 1861 show a shocking fondness for the fleshpots—but rather the result
of a more limited opportunity for indulging lustful appetites.[61]

Army surgeons deplored the ravages of venereal disease and on their
suggestion controlled prostitution was instituted in at least two Southern
cities—Memphis and Nashville—with good results. In both cities prostitutes were required to register, submit to periodic examinations and have
certificates attesting freedom from infection. The Nashville project,
more elaborate than that of Memphis, included the setting up of a
hospital for treatment of diseased women. It was maintained from examining fees paid by registered prostitutes. Reports of the surgeon in
charge indicate greater concern about soldiers contaminating the women
than of the women infecting the men. Passage of the Eleventh and
Twelfth Corps through Nashville in November 1863 was said to have
caused cases treated in the hospital to jump from a daily average of
twelve to twenty-eight. As to ameliorative effects of the system on forces
garrisoned at Nashville, no figures are available on enlisted men; but a
final report on commissioned personnel shows a decline from "ten to
twenty officers at one time" before control was attempted, to no more
than one case a month during the last half year that it was in operation.[62]

While evil undoubtedly abounded among the men who wore the
blue, army life also had its better and brighter side. It is, of course, impossible to draw any firm conclusions as to the relative prevalency of
good and evil. Contemporaries tended to exaggerate the rampancy of sin
because wickedness made more of an impression than plain, everyday
goodness. On the other hand, postwar commentators, influenced by the
mellowing effects of time and anxious to enshrine the saviors of the
Union in sacred halls of memory, were inclined to take a far more chari-
table view of soldier morals than the facts warranted.

No matter how pervasive the forces of darkness, they were always
resisted and the usual medium of opposition was religion.

The religion of many Yanks was of the practical, unobtrusive sort,
marked by little if any conformity to conventional practices. Of the
Third Wisconsin Regiment, Private William F. Goodhue wrote in 1864:
"I know but two men in it who are realy Christians by creed, yet I know
a hundred . . . [who] like the good Samaritan will help a fellow being
when in trouble. . . . the Boys are a good, honest, intelligent sett of
men, some exceptions of course, full of fun & frolic; will share their last

biscuit yet there is the least religion among them than any Regt I know of." [63] Among individuals who fitted into the pattern described by Private Goodhue was Theodore Upson of the 100th Indiana Regiment. Upson told in his journal of earnestly seeking religion before he joined the army, but without success. After long anguish over his soul's salvation he finally concluded not to worry any more. "I think God knows all about me," he wrote shortly after donning the uniform, "and if he wanted me to feel a change he would have changed me and if I go along trying to do right . . . that is the best I can do and I shall just leave it to Him." Upson's day-by-day record indicates that he lived up to his resolution and that, while never claiming to be religious in the usual sense, throughout his service he was a moral man and an exemplary soldier.[64]

For the most part, however, religion in the army, as among civilians, was of the conventional kind, stressing recognized forms and services, depending heavily for inspiration and direction on a properly accredited ministry and following closely orthodox views of a loving but jealous God.

The Union Army, like the mid-nineteenth-century America from which it was drawn, was overwhelmingly Protestant, with a strong leaning toward evangelical denominations, especially Baptist, Methodist and Presbyterian. Catholics were also well represented, especially among soldiers of Irish, French and Italian extraction. Units from large cities contained a considerable sprinkling of Jews. Among Germans, especially the "Forty-eighters," were to be found a goodly number of "freethinkers" who openly scoffed at orthodox religion of any sort.[65]

Scoffing was not confined to the Germans, however. In almost any regiment there were individuals who laughed at the pious endeavor of their comrades and some even made mockery of worship. An Ohioan told of "Major Tracey and Alf Burnett" of the First Tennessee Cavalry going on a Sunday spree, forming the regiment in a hollow square and holding service, with Burnett doing the preaching. Burnett announced as his text, "And the Whangdoodle mourneth for its first born and fleeth to Mount Hepsidam," and launched into the famous take-off of a frontier sermon. But the listeners, many of whom were piously disposed, were so infuriated by the sacrilege that they booted both offenders out of camp and told them never to return.[66]

Religious activity centered about the chaplains, one of whom was authorized for each regiment, for specified army posts and, after May 1862, for general hospitals. In the volunteer regiments chaplains were selected by vote of the field officers and company commanders, approved by the state governor and officially appointed by the War Department. Hospital chaplains and those serving posts and Regular Army units were designated by the President. Initially, qualifications of chaplains were not specified, but a general order of May 4, 1861, required that each appointee be "a regularly ordained minister of some Christian denomination." When a Jewish chaplain was forced to resign under the terms of this order and the War Department refused appointment to a rabbi selected by a Jewish regiment, a wave of protest arose as a result of which regulations authorized as chaplain the properly certified representative of any "religious denomination." At the same time that it made this change, Congress added the requirement that chaplains must have the endorsement "of some authorized ecclesiastical body or not less than five accredited ministers belonging to said religious denomination." This change was the result of an indiscriminate commissioning early in the war of persons without ecclesiastical standing, many of whom had been attracted to the ministry by the prospects of collecting a chaplain's pay.[67]

Soldier comment on chaplains, while not always reliable, was derogatory far more often than otherwise. The most frequent complaint was neglect of primary duties in favor of lighter activities, especially those that entailed absence from camp. "Our chaplain is not very popular," wrote Private C. B. Thurston from Louisiana in 1863; "he hardly ever has any religious exercises and spends a great part of his time in New Orleans getting the mail, which generally takes longer than most of us think necessary." Private Edward Edes, writing from Fredericksburg in 1862, was even stronger in his denunciation. "I have lost all confidence in the chaplain," he stated; "he lied to me about carrying the mail & does nothing at all but hang around his tent & sort the mail. He never goes around any amongst the men & I think he is nothing but a confounded humbug & nuisance." Along the same lines was the statement of a Hoosier who wrote from Nashville the same year: "Our chaplain . . . started home this morning. A chaplain in the army is usualy of little force except to attend to the mail. I suppose the reason is that the most worthless prechers, those who can not make a good living at home, are the ones who strive to secure the position for the money." [68]

Common soldiers were quick to denounce chaplains who proved battle-shy. Furthermore, they had little use for those who from undue delicacy or a sense of superiority seemed unable to tolerate the hard facts of camp life. "Mr. Cummings is not liked here," wrote a Vermonter to his sister from Virginia in 1863; "he [is] to big fealing and an old maid. the regt does not like him." [69]

Occasionally a Yank would condemn chaplains on the score of their poor sermons. An Illinois private wrote his homefolk that "our minister is no account. he will get up and prais himself and tell the Lord what he must do." A youthful Minnesotan who complained he did not "hear any very good preaching" thought "the people at home have an idea that the soldiers cannot appreciate a good chaplain so that the scum is sent to the army." [70]

Unit commanders sometimes found chaplains less than realistic in disciplinary matters, one colonel deploring their constant interference with every prisoner put in the guardhouse whom they all desired to have released immediately for his supposed penitence.[71] But among officers, as among men, the prevailing complaint was their lack of attention to spiritual duties. A Maine captain who wrote from near New Orleans in 1862 that "our chaplain . . . drives a fast Horse [and] has never spoken of religion . . . since he has been in the army," reported the following conversation between the delinquent minister and General B. F. Butler:

Butler: When did you preach last?
Chaplain: I dont recollect.
Butler: How many funerals have you attended?
Chaplain: I dont know.
Butler: Well, G—d d—n you. You are a disgrace to your pro-
         fession.[72]

Another company commander, disgusted by the fact that "our chaplain in his usual romping style has been off at Martinsburg for the last ten days," was constrained to state: "Chaplains ought to be abolished in the Army, or else we ought to have a decent energetic one instead of the lazy fellow who pretends to officiate in that place now." [73]

Dislike of chaplains by the common soldier sometimes manifested itself in irreverent pranks. The sergeant major of an Illinois regiment on one occasion assembled the worst soldiers from each of the companies and ordered them to report to the chaplain for prayer. The colonel heard about the order but refused to countermand it, because he thought it an appropriate rebuke for a notorious neglect of duty that had aroused considerable resentment. The chaplain, much to the amusement of all, invited the "hard cases" into his tent and earnestly exhorted them to improve their ways. Even more impudent was an act credited to Bugler Buck Cole of the Seventh Kansas Cavalry. When the chaplain came to recover a book that the bugler had borrowed, Buck was carrying a rail in punishment for some minor breach of discipline. When approached about the book the soldier handed the chaplain his burden and asked him to hold it while he went to get the borrowed volume. But instead of returning he threw himself down on his bunk and went to sleep. On being rebuked by the captain, Buck roguishly answered that he thought the captain's idea was to have the rail carried and that he deemed the chaplain as capable of performing the chore as himself.[74]

Soldier disesteem of chaplains is also apparent in some of the nicknames which were applied to the spiritual counselors, though this was not necessarily true of "Holy Joe" and "Holy John." A Pennsylvania chaplain whose vociferous pledges to pray for the men, preach to them and even fight with them, were completely forgotten when the going became tough, was dubbed "the great thunderer." A New York chaplain who collected a penny for each letter that he carried for the soldiers was referred to as "One Cent by God," while a Massachusetts divine who confined his chaplain's activities almost exclusively to postal duties was hailed as "the postmaster." For reasons that are not ascertainable, but probably because of an undue dwelling on the uncertainty of life, a Maine chaplain was known by his charges as "Death on a Pale Horse." [75]

Antipathy of the soldiers, the dreariness and peril of camp life, homesickness and sundry other factors caused a heavy sloughing off of inferior chaplains after a brief period of service. This exodus together with the raising of standards for procurement led to an improvement in the quality of chaplains in the last two or three years of the war, though benefits were offset by inability of many regiments to keep spiritual counselors.

Many chaplaincies throughout the war were held by good men impelled by lofty motives and thoroughly devoted to the cause of righteousness. Such chaplains held services as regularly as military exigencies would permit, sought out the soldiers for individual counsel, shared fully the hardships and hazards of field service, were practical and discreet in their utterances, set a good example in their conduct and in general helped promote the physical and spiritual welfare of the organizations to which they were assigned.

The better chaplains, far from seeking shelter at the first sign of battle, went forward with their units, blessed the men as they prepared for the assault, nourished and comforted the wounded, performed last rites over the dead, wrote notes of condolence to the homefolk and collected and forwarded personal effects.

Billy Yanks were as quick to register approval of good chaplains as they were to condemn poor ones, and the qualities eliciting admiration were about the same in Civil War times as now. Not the least among these was proof of physical courage. "The new chaplain . . . is well liked by the boys," wrote Private Cyrus Stone shortly after Fredericksburg; "he kept long with the reg. all the time it was on the battle field." Another Yank, likewise stationed on the Virginia front, wrote in his diary on January 17, 1862: "The Rev. Dr. Strong has ben to See me this day and he wanted my Catrage Box and Belt and I gave them to him and I told him he aught to Shoot with Spiritual Balls in Sted of Lead but he says their [they] are not so good for Sesesh as lead ones. Buley for him." [76]

Unstinted devotion to duty, whatever the hazards or difficulties, was another quality highly appreciated by the men. Shortly after Chaplain John A. Brouse joined the 100th Indiana Regiment a private soldier wrote in warm approval of him: "Without a thought of his personal safty he was on the firing line assisting the wounded, praying with the dying, doing all that his great loving heart led him to do. No wonder our boys love our gallant Chaplain." Of another chaplain who faithfully attended his flock during the trying siege of Mobile late in the war, a New York lieutenant wrote: "I am particularly proud & thankful for him as some officers (nonprofessors) used to think & even say that a chaplain was a sort of fifth wheel . . . and even voted against having one, but now all are ready to admit that we could not get along without our Chaplain." [77]

Integrity, sympathy, goodness and a sincere interest in spiritual matters were also regarded as commendable if not essential traits. "He is truly a great and good man," wrote a sergeant of his chaplain in 1862, "an ornament to the cause of Christ and one in whose countenance is seen the radience of the inner light reflected through." Both men and officers, however, seemed to prefer chaplains whose righteousness was unostentatious and who could adapt religion to the realities of soldiering. A minister who deemed it not unbecoming to carry brandy along with the Bible when visiting the battlefield, if not acclaimed by all, was sure to win the hearty blessing of some. And the chaplain who was as zealous in helping the men with small problems of everyday living as he was in denouncing the sins of camp stood a good chance of being accorded a welcome place in the community of soldiers. If he could crown these virtues, as a chaplain of the Forty-fourth Massachusetts did, by the unselfish act of yielding his horse on a hard march to ailing privates while he himself plodded along with the rank and file, he was assured of an unassailable niche in the affections of his comrades.[78]

Of no less importance than the chaplains in influencing religious activities were the commanding officers, especially those of regiments, brigades and divisions. Spiritual efforts in many organizations were seriously hindered by the unco-operative attitude of tactical leaders who deemed religious exercises ineffectual if not a downright nuisance. Such officers were apt to make the chaplain's position an intolerable one by failing to allow time for services in the Sunday schedule and refusing to put at his disposal the necessary facilities for carrying out a constructive religious program.[79]

At the other extreme were officers who, because of pious inclination, belief in practical benefits or both, entered wholeheartedly into the religious activities of their commands. Such a leader was the Reverend Granville Moody, a distinguished minister who commanded the Seventy-fourth Ohio Regiment and who often preached to his own and other commands. An Illinois lieutenant who heard Colonel Moody preach to a soldier audience in Nashville in October 1862 stated: "It was one of the most eloquent sermons I ever heard, one which I shall always remember. I could have listened to him for hours without experiencing the least weariness." [80]

Preaching by commanders was usually limited to those of ministerial background, but laymen occasionally conducted prayer meetings and Bible-study sessions. Among higher commanders who frequently led divine service was General O. O. Howard. A Pennsylvania soldier who heard General Howard twice on the same Sunday said that he made "eloquent addresses and earnest exhortations, also a fervent prayer . . . thus showing to the world that though he ranked high among men, he humbled himself before God." [81] General William S. Rosecrans, a devout Catholic, aggressively promoted the spiritual interests of his men, and both Generals George B. McClellan and Ambrose Burnside, while commanding the Army of the Potomac, issued general orders stressing the importance of divine worship.[82]

Occasionally the religious activities of military personnel were supplemented by the ministrations of casual visitors and itinerant representatives of Northern churches and benevolent organizations. Among distinguished lecturers who toured the camps was Laura S. Haviland. Concerning her address at Ship Island, in 1864, a Vermont officer wrote: "I never listened to a more simple and at the same time more powerful sermon." [83]

Most of the civilian visitors who ministered to the spiritual needs of the soldiers in the latter part of the war were representatives of the Christian Commission. Some of these were full-time agents and others were ministers sponsored by the Commission for brief tours of duty in field and camp. Both types of representatives preached to the soldiers, visited them in their tents for individual conferences, distributed tracts, books, magazines and writing paper, dispensed hot drinks from "coffee wagons," acted as amanuenses and conducted elementary classes in reading and writing. They ministered also to the spiritual and physical needs of the wounded, maintained reading and writing rooms in cities and camps and dispatched soldier mail. Some of the representatives were of the opinion that the men whom they visited were interested only in the gifts distributed, but had they known the high esteem in which soldiers in general held the organization and its services they would have been reassured concerning the value of their work.[84]

Forms of worship varied with sects and circumstances, but the usual Sunday service, ordinarily held in the afternoon to avoid conflict with the weekly inspection in the morning, consisted of Scripture reading, songs and a sermon. Among Protestants, singing inclined to old favorites such as "All Hail the Power of Jesus' Name," "Blest Be the Tie That Binds," "Jesus Lover of My Soul," "Just As I Am without One Plea," "My Faith Looks Up to Thee," "On Jordan's Stormy Banks I Stand," "Rock of Ages," "Sweet Hour of Prayer" and "There Is a Fountain Filled with Blood." [85]

The heart of Sunday services was the sermon, delivered usually by the chaplain. Favorite texts were those stressing the homely virtues, warning against the evils of camp, proclaiming the transforming power of divine grace, calling attention to the precariousness of life and threatening sinners with eternal damnation. Some chaplains made a special point of identifying the Union cause with righteousness and hence bound to have God's blessing; when reverses were met they were interpreted as temporary setbacks resulting from sin, and the vicissitudes of the children of Israel in their epic struggles with ungodly foes were cited as examples.

Reaction of Yanks to camp sermons, as registered in their letters and diaries, ranged from enthusiastic approval to extreme derogation. "He done well" was a private's comment on a much-needed discourse about temperance heard by the Second Wisconsin Cavalry, and a lecture "on the use of tobacco and spirituous liquors" delivered to another group of Badgers was characterized by one of the audience as "real good." [86]

A Maine soldier noted appreciatively that "our chaplain is witty or rather he is brief and breavity is the soul of wit." These endorsements were much more restrained than those of a pious New Yorker who, after listening to sermons by chaplains in Sherman's command, entered in his diary such remarks as "felt much of influences of Spirits," "Received new strength from on high," "feel comforted," "a happy time," and "feel strengthened and blessed." [87]

In opposite vein, a lieutenant who served with Butler in Louisiana found almost intolerable the ill-adapted sermons which the chaplain of his regiment drew from prewar storage. On one occasion, according to the lieutenant, this minister "took an old piece of faded yellow manuscript and . . . discussed *infant baptism* and closed with an earnest appeal, touchingly eloquent, to *mothers*. . . . I'm sure there wasn't a mother in the regiment," added the officer sarcastically, "and not more than two or three infants." Of another chaplain's efforts, a Michigan colonel wrote protestingly to the governor: "He preaches doleful Sermons to the men about the hardships they will have to encounter, the Sickness & death and all the dificulties." [88]

Soldiers who found the chaplains' sermons uninspiring usually did not have to listen to them—a prerogative which most Yanks often chose to exercise—though some commanding officers made attendance of Sunday services compulsory. Members of the Third Pennsylvania Cavalry who indicated a desire to pass up the chaplain's ministrations on a December Sabbath in 1861 "were marched to the guard house where they had the articles of war read to them for punishment." Soldiers usually resented being mustered for church to the beat of drum and screech of fife, especially when the weather was foul and other duties onerous. A typical attitude toward mandatory worship was that expressed by M. P. Larry on a winter Sunday of 1863: "I scarcely write at all but what I expect to hear the bugle call for something and now I am waiting to hear the call to . . . a dry discourse from the chaplain. the sound will call fourth much profanity for it is a biter cold day and the Boys have just come in from inspection and have not had time to get diner or even to get warm." [89]

The religious zeal of a few commanders extended to the point of requiring the saying of prayers at daily dress parade which, according to a soldier, caused "some of the boys [to] sweare . . . cussing the minister the worst kind." [90]

Prayer meetings usually consisted of singing, Bible reading, supplication and testimonials of triumph over Satan. Sometimes these sessions were led by a chaplain or officer, but frequently the men themselves conducted the services. Most meetings were held at night and varied in frequency from one to several times a week.

Another type of worship was the informal singing of sacred songs. These sessions often had their origin in some lonely Yank lifting his voice as he sat at the campfire in the evening and the chiming in of a few comrades. Sometimes the tune was picked up by adjacent units and even by Rebs with the result that a whole countryside would reverberate with the strains of a majestic hymn. On such occasions the men "sang merely because they liked it, the tone was pleasing and the volume of sound was grand." [91]

In sad contrast to these spontaneous hymn fests were the services held in burying the dead. These were usually brief, consisting of the reading of prescribed ritual or simply the offering of a prayer. During large-scale campaigns, however, casualties were often so numerous and military exigencies so pressing as to prevent rites of any kind.

Places of worship varied with locale, season and other circumstances. In balmy weather outdoor meetings were common. Sometimes brush arbors were built for protection against rain and sun, and to afford privacy. In winter, soldier worshipers built log chapels and covered them with canvas or slabs. Late in the conflict the Christian Commission undertook to furnish canvas roofing to every brigade that would agree to erect chapel walls. As a result over 100 chapels were built in 1864 and supplied by the Commission with stoves, hymnbooks and other equipment.[92]

Sometimes Rebel churches were appropriated for soldier use. A private of the First Minnesota Regiment recorded in his diary on Sunday, March 9, 1862, that he went to services conducted by the chaplain in the Presbyterian church of Charlestown, Maryland. "The fine organ discoursed sweet music," he wrote. "The church is a fine brick building with gallery. . . . The Min. 1st run the whole institution, organ & all." An Ohioan recounted stumbling on a similar, though far less pretentious, service at the Cayuga Baptist Church in Mississippi during the Vicksburg siege. "I expect you would have laughed . . . at the oddity of the scene," he wrote his sister. "A house full of men in all styles of military dress almost, some with canteens hung around them and the most of them as dirty looking as they should be. The audience started up a hymn, but no go. Some too high and others too fast, and so they failed. But they succeeded at last. We had a very pleasant meeting notwithstanding." [93]

Religious activities were promoted by organizations among both chaplains and men. In the spring of 1863, thirty-nine chaplains assembled in Nashville and organized the "Council of Chaplains of the Army of the Cumberland" to discuss common problems and consider means of furthering the spiritual welfare of their respective organizations. Similar groups were formed in other commands. Among the soldiers the most common form of organization was the regimental Christian association. The constitution of "The Christian Association of the Thirteenth Regiment Pennsylvania Volunteers" specified that the object of the organization was the moral and religious improvement of its members and of their fellow soldiers of the regiment and required that members take a pledge to live according to the rule of the Bible. "The Christian Association of the Sixteenth Regiment of Connecticut Volunteers," among other activities, sponsored a series of debates on topics that included: "Resolved: that the present war will be more productive of good than evil" and "Resolved: that Intemperance is a greater evil than war." The negative came off victorious in the first of these arguments, but in the second, after an hour-and-a-half discussion, the affirmative was adjudged winner.[94]

The influence of the Christian associations cannot be definitely stated, but indications point to a limited effectiveness. The same soldier who on January 9, 1864, told of the organization of the Sixteenth Connecticut Association within two weeks reported two drunken sprees, one involving "most of Co. D" and the other resulting in the destruction of "a part of the cook house." [95]

An important aspect of promoting the spiritual welfare of soldiers was the publication and dissemination of religious literature. Religious periodicals circulated in the army aggregated scores of titles and included the *Sunday School Times, Episcopal Recorder, Presbyterian Standard, German Reformed Messenger, Christian Times, Congregationalist, Independent* and *Morning Star*.[96] *The American Messenger*, published and distributed gratuitously by the American Tract Society, was said to have had a circulation in 1864 among soldiers and sailors of 195,000.[97]

Hymnbooks, testaments and scriptural selections were also made available to Yanks in large quantities by the American Bible Society and various other organizations. But tracts were by far the most common form of religious literature dispensed to the soldiers. The American Tract Society was one of the most active organizations in circulating this type of publication, but the United States Christian Commission, the Young Men's Christian Association and various denominations and sects also participated in the work.

Tracts varied greatly in character and content. Some pointed up as pious examples the careers of great soldiers of former times, though distortion used in a pamphlet like *The Religious Character of Washington* must have been shocking to Yanks who knew history. Others, such as *The Gambler's Balance Sheet* and *The Temperance Letter* and *Satan's Baits*, warned against camp vices. Still others were devotional in nature while many were didactic essays on righteous living.[98]

Yanks showed a preference for tracts having a military slant, such as *Masked Batteries, A Greater Rebellion, Halt, The Grand Army, The Soldiers' Talisman, The Widow's Son Enlisting* and *A True Story of Lucknow*. They also liked hymns and poetry better than prose forms. Because of variety of content and greater convenience in handling, they favored bound volumes over leaflets; accordingly, tract publishers issued as little books with blue or red covers *Soldier's Pocket Book, Soldier's Text Book, Soldier's Prayer Book* and *The Soldier from Home*, all of which were well received, as was a bound collection of prize tracts issued by the American Tract Society.[99]

Some tracts were printed in several languages to meet the needs of foreign-nationality groups. German soldiers, who had a reputation for unusual diligence in reading as well as a preference for "stronger meat" than native Americans, found special pleasure in reading Hufacker's sermon entitled *Wie die Religion taeglich zu ueben sey* (How to Practice Religion in Daily Life).[100]

The stock of some tract dispensers included large quantities of *Uncle Tom's Cabin* and copies of this work apparently were made available to Yanks by the thousands in the latter part of the war. Records of the United States Christian Commission show that the Protestant Episcopal Book Society in August 1864 sent 47,000 copies of Mrs. Stowe's book to the central office of the commission at Philadelphia and that in August and September the central office forwarded 11,000 copies to its representatives in St. Louis, 5,000 to Nashville, 2,000 to Baltimore and 2,000 to Cincinnati.[101]

Distributing agents and some of the chaplains claimed that tracts were eagerly received, widely read and productive of distinct improvement in religion and morals. But soldier letters and diaries do not sustain these conclusions. Billy Yanks hardly ever mentioned religious literature of any kind, and their comment on the general tone of camp life leaves the impression that the combined influences of spiritual agencies operative in the Union Army were of little avail in combating the tide of evil.

This does not mean that religious endeavor was always defeated, for many organizations experienced periods of spiritual awakening. A "strong revival" was said to have occurred in the Fifth Maine Regiment during its encampment in Virginia in the second winter of the war, and a Hoosier sergeant stationed near Vicksburg noted in his diary August 8, 1863: "Have a protracted meeting in our Division. Very warm." [102]

Religious interest tended to quicken when large-scale fighting was in prospect. The imminence of an unprecedented spilling of blood was doubtless responsible in part for the unusual flurry of revivals that occurred in various parts of the army during the early months of 1864 and 1865. But these movements were local in character, usually restricted to regiments and brigades and rarely if ever overleaping the boundaries of divisions. They were also limited in duration and in harvest of converts. An Eastern soldier who in January 1865 wrote that "theaire is a great revival of religion here" added that eight or ten of his company had "got religion," and a Yank stationed in the Department of the Gulf, who about the same time reported "constant revival" in a camp comprising 6,000 soldiers, specified that "not less than 20 have received salvation." [103]

CHAPTER XI

THE SPIRITS EBB AND FLOW

BILLY YANKS, like Johnny Rebs, donned their uniforms in 1861 with tremendous enthusiasm. They rushed to arms in such numbers as to swamp state and Federal authorities who were trying desperately to provide equipment and to gear the nation for conflict. The Union volunteers, thinking that the Rebels would quickly be forced to submission, were extremely anxious to have a part in the first fight. For it was their strong opinion that the first battle also would be the last one, and hence to miss the initial encounter would be to have no sniff of powder.

This flood tide of enthusiasm was destined to be short-lived, and before many months had passed, the government, from rejecting clamors for service, was to be begging soldiers. In time conscription was to be invoked, but loopholes which allowed draftees to buy exemption from service for $300 or hire substitutes to go in their stead greatly impaired the effectiveness of this bungled first effort of the nation to press its citizens into uniform.

The morale of the army was nearly always better than that of the homefolk. But, even so, the spirit of the fighting forces drooped markedly after a few months of conflict and thereafter rose and fell periodically until the end of the war. Morale varied considerably among individuals and commands, but a general pattern existed, the tracing of which will be the first concern of this chapter.

Morale of some of the first volunteers began to sag before midsummer of 1861, owing to boredom of camp routine, discomfort of heat and pests and inability to engage the foe in the battle that would end the war and send the soldiers home in triumph. On July 14, 1861, a Pennsylvania private of a three-months regiment wrote:

The Erie Regiment is one grand fizzle out. We left home full of fight, earnestly desiring a chance to mingle with the hosts that fight under the Stars and Stripes. For two months we drilled steadily, patiently waiting the expected orders which never came but to be countermanded. We have now come to the conclusion that we will have no

275

chance, and we are waiting in sullen silence and impatience for the expiration of our time.[1]

First Manassas satisfied the volunteers' craving for action but disappointed their expectations of bringing the war to a victorious conclusion. The immediate effect of the defeat was dispiriting, but after the initial shock had passed, soldiers in both East and West seemed to be seized with a stubborn determination to recover lost prestige and to push the conflict with enhanced vigor. Gone was the illusion of a quick and easy triumph, and in its place there developed a deep earnestness to prove the North's superiority. This sentiment was reflected by a Western soldier who wrote not long after First Bull Run: "I shall See the thing played out, or die in the attempt; I am not generally very free to pitch in; but I am awful to hang on." [2]

In the East, McClellan's rigorous training program breathed life into the army and helped sustain morale at a relatively high level through the autumn of 1861. But as fall passed into winter without major commitment of the large force that had been so zealously prepared, discontent was manifest and spirits began to droop. Morale was further depressed as the troops, many of whom were inadequately clothed, began to experience for the first time the unpleasantness of wintering in the field. An Ohioan wrote his homefolk from camp in mid-December that "when we get up here in the morning we shiver like Belshazzier did when he seen the vishion on the wall." [3] Countless other Yanks stationed in the North and along the far-reaching Southern border had similar misery.

Spirits took an upward turn in the early part of 1862, owing to the bustle and stir of preparations for the Gulf and Yorktown expeditions and the heartening triumphs in the West and along the Eastern coast. Shortly after Grant's capture of Forts Henry and Donelson one Yank wrote from the Virginia front that "the news of the late brilliant victories . . . had aroused the fighting spirits of the whole army," while another gloated: "The Old Flag waves in triumph oe'r its foes. Co E. give 3 cheers & a 'tiger.' . . . Big grist of glorious news for *one* morning. The 'Anaconda' tightens well. Secession soon will go to— . . . We are growing fat on hard bread, victory & hope." A month later a participant in the Western exploits informed his wife that "we are driveing things right endways I think they [the Rebs] will have to give it up for a bad job it is gratifying to us solgers to hear of so many victories." [4]

Union triumphs at New Bern, North Carolina, Fort Pulaski, Georgia,

New Orleans, Shiloh and Memphis, and McClellan's initial successes on the Virginia peninsula helped sustain morale throughout the spring of 1862. But the stalemate and failure, sickness and suffering, toil and weariness that came with the summer months caused a recession. Many a Yank lost his enthusiasm, if not his patriotism, in the steaming lowlands near Richmond and New Orleans and the hot hills and valleys of the country about Corinth, Mississippi. The depression which overtook the army during this period was strikingly evidenced in the instance of Alfred Davenport, a soldier of McClellan's force. On May 23, 1862, Davenport wrote his homefolk from Cold Harbor: "We are all now in hopes that our trials will soon be at an end & that Richmond will be taken & we will be discharged, which is looked forward to as a shining light & alone keeps us up." On June 1, the day after Fair Oaks, he urged his mother not to let a brother enlist, stating that it would be better for him to be dead. "There are men who have been all over the world, in every station in life, with us," he added, but "[I] have not seen one that does not pine to get away, but honorably." The Seven Days' fighting and the failure to take Richmond plunged him into deeper gloom. On July 8, 1862, he stated: "Sometimes I think that I will try to get away as many have done, it is a horrible life, worse than State Prison, & there are few here but what would like to have some wound to get out of it." Four days later, as the army lay in misery at Harrison's Landing, he wrote despondingly: "The ringing laugh is now seldom heard, but men go dragging along with their long, sad & careworn faces, nothing to do but kill time and answer Roll Calls, with occasionally a little fatigue duty . . . each man doing as little as he can and stealing away if possible." [5]

Gloom abated somewhat in the autumn with the stopping of Lee's and Bragg's offensives in Maryland and Kentucky. But the respite was only an Indian summer, for in the winter of 1862-1863 soldier morale reached its nadir.

The extreme spiritual defection manifested itself in a flood of desertion and absence without leave. In February 1863 Hooker reported that twenty-five per cent of his army was absent and that desertions averaged several hundred a day. Around Union campfires everywhere criticism of the government was rife, and talk of quitting the service was common. During Burnside's brief command of the Eastern army, efforts of regimental officers to elicit cheers from their men as he made the round of camps sometimes produced open manifestations of disrespect.[6]

Morale may have been worse among Eastern commands than in

others but in this critical period it sank to a deplorably low level everywhere. In Grant's army members of one regiment when ordered to embark for the Vicksburg area stacked their arms and swore that they would not go.[7]

Dissatisfaction with army service became so great during this period that a rash of self-mutilation broke out among the soldiers. An Illinois Yank shot off the trigger finger of his right hand and a Vermont soldier got rid of three fingers while on picket by setting off his musket with a stick. A Massachusetts private, after failing in an effort to blow his toe off, succeeded a few days later in injuring his right forefinger to such an extent that it had to be amputated. The evil of self-injury became so widespread that authorities ceased granting discharges to those found guilty of the practice.[8]

This morale crisis of the war's second winter was the result of several influences. First was the accumulation of military reverses. In the East the failure to take Richmond had been followed by the disaster of Second Manassas, the escape of Lee and his army after an auspicious beginning at Antietam and then the futile and blundering effusion of blood at Fredericksburg with the humiliating sequel of Burnside's notorious "mud march." In Middle Tennessee Rosecrans' long-awaited advance bogged down at Murfreesboro after an enormous spilling of blood in the battle of Stone's River. Farther West, Grant's two-pronged thrust at Vicksburg was thwarted by Van Dorn's surprise attack on the Federal base at Holly Springs and Sherman's failure to penetrate the Confederate lines at Chickasaw Bayou. The capture of Arkansas Post on January 11, 1863, brightened the outlook, but the effects were soon lost as Grant's men floundered in the mud trying unsuccessfully to get at Vicksburg by canals and passes.

These reverses were the more depressing because of their costliness in lives, the absence of major successes to offset them and the discouraging outlook which they and the long train of prior setbacks gave to the future. Gloom was further enhanced by signs of defection on the home front, dwindling confidence in political leadership and repeated demonstrations of incompetency among military commanders. The effect of these combined influences was to produce in the minds of many Yanks a conviction that the prospect of Northern victory was too hopeless to justify further slaughter and that the South's independence should be conceded.

The extreme demoralization and the various factors contributing to it were vividly revealed in letters issuing from camp in the period December 1862—March 1863. Three days before Christmas, M. N. Collins, a Maine officer, wrote from camp opposite Fredericksburg:

The newspapers say that the army is eager for another fight; it is false; there is not a private in the army that would not rejoice to know that no more battles were to be fought. They are heartily sick of battles that produce no results.[9]

In like vein Edward Edes, a Massachusetts private, wrote a few days later:

It is my firm belief that the war will be settled in some way by compromise. That will be better than for any more lives to be thrown away so extravagantly by incompetent leaders & ambitious politicians. As far as I can judge from what I have heard, there is very little zeal or patriotism in the army now, the men have seen so much more of defeat than of victory & so much bloody slaughter that all patriotism is played out. Even in this regiment only out five months . . . I dont believe there are twenty men but are heartily sick of war & want to go home.[10]

Letters written by Grant's soldiers had the same tone. On February 1, 1863, Private John N. Moulton wrote his sister from near Vicksburg:

I am in moderate health . . . as to spirits I cannot Boast of their being very high. There is the most down cast looking set of men here that I ever saw in my life. the men are Beginning to talk opernly and to curse the officers and leaders and if the[y] go much farther I fear for the result. they are pretty well divided and nothing But fear keeps them under. . . . At Walnut hills . . . the whole thing was Badly managed by Sherman, and General Steel, my division commander, was drunk or he never would have ordered general Thayer to take us where he did. My regiment was within 70 yards of the Breast works at the Arkansas Post when the white flag was run up and we was preparing to make another charge. dam this charging I dont like it. More than that there was no kneed of it at the Post at all only to give certain men a Big name that was all.[11]

Six weeks later, after shivering through a long period of heavy rain which converted the low-lying country into a sea of mud, with disease rampant, rations short and recreational facilities severely circumscribed, this Yank lamented:

The cannal is a failure, the men all dying off pretty fast if you call 47 in two days anything out of one regiment. The 34th Iowa lost that amount. . . . I am lonesome and down hearted in Spite of my Self. I am tired of Blood Shed and have Saw Enough of it.[12]

Moulton's complaint was the more significant in that his morale during nearly two years of prior service had been consistently high.

That the gloom was not confined to Grant's and Burnside's armies is clearly indicated by the following letter, written from Nashville on February 3, 1863, by one of Rosecrans' soldiers:

The troops are becoming very much disheartened in consequence of recent disasters in the field and the bad management of the War Department. When we Enthusiastically rushed into the ranks at our Country's call, we all Expected to witness the last dying struggles of treason and Rebellion Ere this . . . But in these Expectations we have been disappointed. Over 200,000 of our noble soldiers sleep in the silent grave. Almost countless millions of treasure has been Expended in the Unsuccessful Effort of the Government to put down this Rebellion. But after all this sacrifice of valuable life and money we are no nearer the goal . . . than we were at the first booming of Sumter's guns. You can judge how we feel here in the 86th [Illinois] when I tell you that only 8 men in Co. K approve the policy and proclamation of Mr. Lincoln. Many are deserting 23 men from one Company in this brigade have deserted. . . . The unfortunate division at the North is the worst feature of the times. The army of traitors at the North is truly formidable. They ought to hang higher than Haman. Many of the boys here are in favor of a Compromise, some are of the opinion that the Southern Confederacy will soon be recognized by the U. S. Alas! for our beloved Republic! [13]

A recurring note in these and many other letters, written in the depths of gloom that marked the conflict's second winter, was loss of confidence in leadership, both political and military. Charges of incompetency, mismanagement and corruption were freely hurled at many incumbents in high position, though Lincoln usually was excepted from the roll of the damned. Two days before Christmas 1862 a Maine soldier stationed in Virginia wrote his sister:

I have nothing cheerfull to write. All though I am wel and able to do duty I am in a very unhapy state of mind. That delusive fantom of hope that has so long burnt dim has at last vanished and there is nothing to be seen in the distance but darkness and gloom. The great cause of liberty has been managed by Knaves and fools the whole show has ben corruption, the result disaster, shame and disgrace. . . . I am always ready to undergo the privations of a soldiers life if it is to do any good, but evry thing looks dark, not becaus the south are strong but becaus our leaders are incompitent and unprincipled. The whole thing is roton to the core.[14]

Admirers of McClellan—and no high-ranking general was so popular as he among the troops—saw in the removal of that leader an indication of evil influences in government.[15] Resentment of his final displacement was enhanced by the miserable failure of his successor and the general darkening of the military outlook. "I believe the wrong thing was done in the removal of McClellan," wrote Private Samuel Croft from Falmouth, Virginia, on December 21; " 'Little Mac' is the only man we have got who can match the Rebel Gen'l Lee. McClellan whipped the Rebs every time he fought them." On February 3, 1863, he added: "The North have kicked out the best and only man capable of copeing with Lee when they kicked out 'little Mac.' " In similar vein, Herman Chauncey Newhall wrote on December 28, 1862: "If we had the rebel generals to command this army more would be done. . . . They will have to give us McClellan before this army will be as efficient as it was before the last affair at Fredericksburg. . . . I am disgusted." [16]

Others regarded the Emancipation Proclamation and the calling of Negroes to arms as evidence that the radical element was corrupting the government and converting the war into an abolitionist crusade. The thought of fighting a "nigger war" was utterly abhorrent to some, and while the ultimate result of the policy of freeing and arming the blacks was helpful to morale, immediate effects, because of the state of mind which pervaded the country at the time, were probably more depressing than inspiriting. On February 22, 1863, a Pennsylvania private wrote that he was thoroughly tired of the war and that if he had known the issue was to be the freeing of the slaves, as he was inclined now to think it had become, he "would not have mingled with the dirty job." About the same time an Illinois soldier deplored the fact of the radicals having forced upon the administration the twin evils of emancipation and Negro recruiting. "I do not care how quick this war is brought to a close," he stated. "I have slept on the soft side of a board, in the mud & every other place that was lousy & dirty . . . drunk out of goose ponds, Horse tracks &c for the last 18 months, all for the poor nigger, and I have yet to see the first one that I think has been benefited by it." [17] The reactions of these soldiers to the change of policy toward the Negro, as previously stated, was mild in comparison with that of some of their comrades.

Further evidence of mismanagement was seen in the provisions of the conscription act which was going through the Congressional mill in the dark days of early 1863. Especially objectionable to soldiers, and extremely depressing to their morale, was the commutation clause which favored the rich over the poor. "I believe that a *poor* man's life is as dear as a rich man's," angrily wrote one Yank a short time after the law's enactment. "The blood of a poor man is as precious as that of the wealthy," he added, and the rich, having more at stake, "should sacrifice more in suppressing this infernal Rebellion and in restoring the Union and thereby save their property, homes and liberty." [18]

Though the cloud of gloom which engulfed the Union forces in the winter of 1862-1863 was larger, darker and more persistent than any that preceded or followed, it was finally dispelled, save for a thin mist and a few lingering thunderheads, by fresh breezes arising from the stubborn resolve, the reviving hope and the pure patriotism of the blundering but generally well-meaning devotees of the Union.

Several factors contributed to restoration of soldier morale. In the East, Hooker's dynamic leadership, which quickly manifested itself in such tangible matters as improvement of rations, replacement of worn-out clothing and equipment, renewal of ceremonies and drill and tightening of discipline, had a tremendous effect.[19] In the West the heartbreaking and ineffectual tussles with Ole Man River were finally abandoned in favor of a roundabout approach to Vicksburg by higher ground. Everywhere spring weather, increased activity and the prospect of aggressive campaigning helped Yanks to shake off their gloom and to get a new grip on life. Flurries of volunteering inspired by the draft act and the setting up of the Provost Marshal General's Bureau to implement conscription and apprehend deserters promised a strengthening of the armed forces.[20] Finally improvement of health which came with the passing of winter also helped mightily to restore drooping spirits.[21]

The brightening outlook was strikingly reflected in soldier letters. One of Burnside's New Jersey privates, who in January had despaired of victory, in April reported that "the blind acts of unqualified generals and statesmen" had not "chilled my patriotism in the least." A comrade from a Maine regiment, who in February had confessed that he and most of the other soldiers were in a deplorable state of morale, stated in April that "the Army is in as good if not better condition than I have ever before seen it." A third member of the Army of the Potomac whose spirit had sunk very low immediately after Fredericksburg wrote in the spring, "evry one seems ready to go into the fight with the note victory or death. this is fare different from the state of things before Hooker took command." [22]

Expressions of similar tone emanated from Western camps. For example, an Ohioan stationed at Milliken's Bend wrote on March 19,

1863: "A dark cloud has passed over and thank God the bright sky once more appears. You have no idea of the hard talk that I have heard come from the discouraged soldiers a short time since, but all that has passed. . . . You have never seen such a great change. . . . The men are in excellent spirits." [23]

The upward surge of spirit that came in the spring was so strong that it carried the Eastern army through the Chancellorsville disaster with flying colors. A typical reaction to this setback was that registered by a Minnesota participant who wrote in his diary on May 6, 1863: "It seems we have not *exactly* whipped the Secesh *this time*. The 11th Army Corps is said to have behaved badly. I suppose we will have to recruit up a little & 'try again.' " [24]

Two reasons for the failure of morale to sag in the East after Chancellorsville were the continuing activity and the shift of the battleground to the North, thus giving to Yanks the challenge of defending their homes against invasion. On July 1, 1863, a Federal surgeon wrote from near Gettysburg that "our men are three times as Enthusiastic as they have been in Virginia. The idea that Pennsylvania is invaded and that we are fighting on our own soil proper, influences them strongly. They are more determined than I have ever before seen them." [25] Still, as many Yanks realized, the thing most needed to buoy morale to a desirable level was success in the field.[26] That success came in overflowing measure at Gettysburg and Vicksburg.[27] The effects were tremendous. From Fort St. Philip, Louisiana, to cite only one of the many exultant expressions, a Maine Yank wrote:

Three times three for Grant and Banks! The Confederacy "played out!" Day before yesterday we received official news of the fall of Vicksburg, today we have news . . . that Hooker has whipped Lee. I wish you could have been here to see the boys when they got the news. Cheer after cheer for nearly an hour, one hundred guns from the two forts, everyone seemed as happy as they would be to hear of the death of a rich uncle making them his heirs.[28]

With these victories the lingering fear of Rebel invincibility that had bedeviled many Yanks was dispelled and in its place came a renewed faith in the triumph of Union arms. This confidence made hardships more tolerable and built up a spiritual reserve for the long pull ahead.

Morale receded considerably in the winter of 1863-1864, though it did not sink to nearly so low level as that following Fredericksburg. Factors in the decline were the failure of the Rebels to show the expected readiness to throw in the sponge, the setbacks at Chickamauga and Mine Run and the ensuant hardships experienced by many soldiers, especially those participating in the Chattanooga and Knoxville campaigns. Spirits rose with the coming of spring and the renewal of large-scale operations designed to break the back of Southern resistance.

But when these gigantic efforts of 1864 resulted in overt failure as in the Red River campaign, in blood-soaked stalemate as in Virginia and in only partial success as in Georgia, enthusiasm fell sharply and discontent again became rife in the army. The widespread defection on the home front did not help the situation. Especially dispiriting to the soldiers was the wholesale evasion of military duty by people of means who instead of taking their places in the ranks sent substitutes gathered from wharves and brothels or sorry specimens of humanity lured into the service by enormous bounties. Many of the recruits thus obtained were chronic "bounty jumpers" who had no interest in the war and who deserted soon after enlistment. Those who continued in the service were often despised as low characters and regarded more as liabilities than as assets. Frank Wilkeson after the war cited as the "potent cause of demoralization" in the last year of the conflict "the worthless character of the recruits who were supplied to the army" during that period. They were "the weak, the diseased, the feeble-minded," he added, "the scum of the slums of the great European and American cities . . . the rakings of rural almshouses and the never-do-wells of villages . . . the fainthearted and stupid. . . . Many were irreclaimable blackguards. . . . They were moral lepers. They were conscienceless, cowardly scoundrels, and the clean-minded American and Irish and German volunteers would not associate with them." [29]

The capture of Atlanta early in September, Sheridan's victories in the Shenandoah Valley a few weeks later and Lincoln's decisive triumph at the polls in November lifted ebbing spirits enormously. Some complaint was voiced in the camps about persistent shirking on the home front as evidenced in the continuing poor quality of recruits, but the general tone of soldier letters in the latter part of 1864 evidenced a growing conviction that despite evasion, disloyalty, mismanagement and all other handicaps the North was bound to win the war and that soon.

Sherman's march through Georgia and South Carolina raised the morale of his men to unprecedented heights, and this spectacular feat, together with Thomas' thumping victory over Hood at Nashville, gave heart to soldiers everywhere. Then Grant broke through the Confederate lines at Petersburg and a few days later forced Lee's surrender at Appomattox. Spirits soared to their highest peak and joy in Federal camps was without restraint.[30]

In tracing the general course of morale, it has been indicated that important factors influencing soldier spirit were the military situation, attitude toward the government's conduct of the war, degree of confidence in civilian patriotism, attitude toward military leadership, discipline, health, comfort and home conditions. Some of these factors require additional comment, especially as they affected individual soldiers, and others need to be added to the list.

Health had a tremendous bearing on morale. The presence in camp of large numbers of ailing soldiers was depressing to those who were well, for extra duties were often required of them to maintain the usual routine and assist in the care of the sick. Moreover, the ill were a constant reminder of the precariousness of one's own health; and heavy mortality among those stricken, evidenced by numerous processions to burial grounds to the doleful tunes of the dead march, gave emphasis to the tenuousness of life.[31] The prospect of dying far away from home, in a hostile country and among strangers, was far more terrifying than that of perishing on the field of battle, and even the strongest soldiers became jittery and despondent during an epidemic of measles or typhoid.

The sick were especially prone to defection of spirit. Even the most patriotic and uncomplaining of Yanks sometimes were converted by illness into creatures of the most abject gloom. William A. Harper of the Forty-seventh Indiana Regiment is a case in point. Harper entered the service in 1861 with strong belief in the rightness of the Union cause and firm confidence in its success. His spirit remained high through the first nine months of service. But after his transfer to Memphis, in the summer of 1862, his health wavered and he began to find fault with the conduct of the war. Early in 1863, while stationed at Helena, Arkansas, he became seriously afflicted and had to go to the hospital. That his spirit suffered no less than his body is suggested by the following letter which he wrote to his wife shortly after entering the hospital:

This is a world of trouble, sorow and afliction. We must look forward to a beter day although it seems that the whole human rase is lost in sin. Our country it seems is allmost gon to ruin it looks too me when I get too studieing over maters and the condition of maters that there certainly [is] a downfall of this nation.[32]

After Harper rejoined his unit his outlook began to improve rapidly and by the time he recovered his full physical strength he had regained his high morale also. Vicksburg and Gettysburg doubtless aided in both physical and spiritual restoration, but his morale continued good, despite subsequent fluctuations in the fortunes of war, throughout the remainder of the conflict. In Harper's instance, as in many others, health was of transcendent importance to morale.

Some Yanks were exceedingly sensitive to the attitude and conduct of civilians with reference to the war. They bitterly resented able-bodied males buying exemption from service and money-mad scoundrels pawning off on the government at exorbitant prices shoddy uniforms, worthless guns and rotten food which undermined the health and endangered the lives of soldiers fighting on token wages to protect those very swindlers. But even more damaging to morale was the specter of disloyalty which appeared on the horizon in the form of Copperheadism and other movements that had, or seemed to have, compromise with Rebels as their end. These movements were regarded by most Yanks as stabs in the back in that they gave aid and comfort to the enemy and prolonged the war. "If the mouths of the Northern traitor could only be shut," wrote one of Grant's sorely tried veterans in January 1863, "the rebellion would not last Sixty days longer. The hope of Rebellion in the free States is the only thing that keeps them up," he added, "and our friends at home are injuring the efficiency of the Army every day." Another Yank wrote indignantly from Georgia in April 1864: "Dont send me the Standard any more as It Is too much Secession for me to read while I am fighting in the front & they a talking in the rear of us men." [33]

Other soldiers were less restrained in their denunciation of the appeasers. "I think the rebels at home far meaner than the rebels of the South," wrote an Illinois Yank from Middle Tennessee in March 1863. "The latter has courage enough to meet me in open conflict while the former poor miserable sneaking hound, seeks to creep up in the dark and strike his dagger at my heart." [34]

Another Illinois soldier delivered himself thus: "You may tell evry man of Doubtful Loyalty for me up there in the north that he is meaner than any son of a bitch in hell. I would rather shoot one of them a great teal [more] than one living here. . . . there may be some excuse for the one but not for the other." [35]

Scorching comments about home "traitors" were not confined to Midwesterners. A New Yorker's reaction to the report of Lee's move into Pennsylvania was this:

I rejoice, & hope Lee will invade all the Copperhead territory of those border free states. I think a little smell of gun powder & a good taste of the bitter realities of war will have a salutary Effect upon their treason loving souls. I want no innocent women & children to suffer, but those God provoking, hell-deserving "Copperheads"—"Vallandighammers," I fain would see weltering in their own gore—The Devil ought to be ashamed of them.[36]

Another New Yorker, who on March 3, 1863, had expressed a desire "to send a couple of double charges of cannister in amongst . . . the Copperheads," wrote a friend in New York City after the draft riots of mid-July 1863:

Hang the leaders . . . hang them, damn them hang them. . . . I would show them no mercy. . . . What a pity there was not force enough to cut them down in heaps. How I would like to stand by a gun and mow them down.[37]

The soldiers, whose denunciatory statements have been cited, were so infuriated by the thought of disloyalty on the home front that their anger seemed to kindle their resolve to push the war to a successful conclusion and then give Northern traitors their due. But in other instances, particularly where spirits were already sagging from other causes, reports of compromise activities had an opposite effect. An Ohioan of Grant's army, immersed in the gloom that accompanied the canal-digging ventures, wrote from Young's Point, Louisiana, on February 11, 1863:

We got a lot of Cinnati papers the other day. thay dun us a hepe of goode to reade them. thay hade a hepe of nues in them a bote peas. the peopple in the north donte like the idy of freeing the nigers and be gode i donte eather. . . . Vallandigham tolde them thay code make peas rite now as well as in a year or 2 years for to whipe the Soth thay never can doo it in the worlde nor thay cante eather. this hole armey is afel dissadesfide and donte cear how the war goes. thay all Say thay ar going home this Spring if things donte look beter than thay doo now.[38]

In other letters this soldier wrote of his intention to desert and even told how he proposed to get away. A shell killed him on May 1, 1863, and thus brought an honorable end to his service. It seems not unlikely that he would have taken leave of the army early in the year had not his home-folk manifested concern over his plans. Certainly the Copperhead-inspired talk of peace and of the futility of continuing the war helped break down his will to fight and contributed to the desertion of many of his fellows-in-arms.[39]

Hardship was another factor which had an important bearing on morale. A short period of service sufficed to convince many Yanks that military life was far more onerous than they had imagined and some of them began to pine for their former status. "Soldiering does well for a few months," wrote one volunteer after a brief residence in camp, but "it dont ware like farming." Another, chafing under the deprivations and discomforts of a winter on the Virginia front, remarked: "I aint home Sick, i dont no what home Sick is, but i no the diferens between home and Soldieren." [40]

Others were more acerb in registering their disillusionment. "Uncal Sam has [not] as much care for his Nefews as he has for one of his mules or horses," wrote an Eastern soldier disgustedly after several stints of standing out in the rain waiting for "read tape" to unwind itself. A Westerner exposed to similar trials stated: "You can compare the Soldier to a mule he has to go when he is told to and never knows when he will stop untill his driver tells him, it makes no difference how the roads is or how hard it rains nor whether it is light or dark and he eats what is given him without the power to get any better." Soldiers in eating "are like a hog," he added, "as every one tries to get it all and worse than the Devil in evry other respect." [41]

A goodly portion of Yanks thus depressed by initial hardships eventually achieved a tolerable degree of equanimity. But a few, unable to make the adjustment, wallowed in gloom during each recurring period of unusual discomfort, comparing themselves to prisoners, slaves or friendless orphans.

Hardship was the more difficult to endure when it seemed to be the result of mismanagement or evil design. Much of the suffering to which the soldiers were subjected could have been avoided, of course, had supply services been better organized, logistics more refined or officers more competent. Some soldiers, of course, were so constituted that they attributed any forced march or diminution of rations, however unavoidable, as willful mistreatment by malicious superiors.

On the other hand, occasional instances were to be found, in the ranks, of rugged souls seemingly impervious to hardship. Among these was H. R. Leonard of Indiana who wrote from Maryland in November 1861:

RELIGIOUS SERVICE IN CAMP

Chaplain L. F. Drake preaching to Thirty-first Ohio Volunteers at Camp Dick Robinson, Kentucky, Nov. 10, 1861

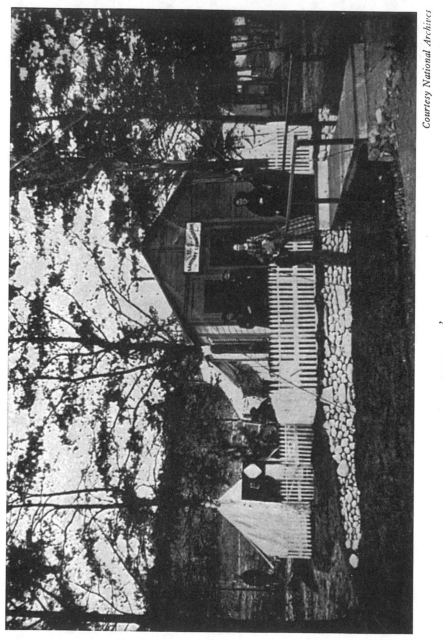

SOLDIERS' FRIENDS

U. S. Sanitary Commission Quarters, Brandy Station, Virginia

I have layed down in the rain and slep all night and got up in the morning driping wet cold and Hungry, but I would see my comrads in the same fix and think it no worse for me than for them. . . . We have all the chestnuts and persimmons we can Eate Every day. I have not been hungry cince we quit marching. We can live in the woods like hogs.[42]

Likewise of this stripe was C. B. Thurston of Maine who wrote his home-folk from Louisiana in 1863:

I expect that when my time is out I shall want to reenlist. I shan't feel at home out of the Army. I shall wake up in the morning and want to know if the drums have beaten and be asking for a pass when I want to go up town. . . . A greater part of the soldiers I have seen would leave the army if they possibly could. . . . I enlisted for three years and will stay my time out unless I am sick. I believe it to be the duty if not a pleasure . . . to help crush this rebellion.[43]

In this staunch group also was Vance Nelson of Ohio who remarked amid the discomforts of his first winter in camp:

We have some hard times but it is Nessary we should learn to indure hard ships in order that we may be good soldiers. We came out here to defend the best government that the sun ever shone on and this should stimulat any man to take misuseag if we have to eat hard crackers we must remembe that the union must be peserved the stars and stripes must Wave over the land of the free and the home of the brave. this is t[h]e sentiment union now and foreve one and inseparable.[44]

Home circumstances had an enormous influence on morale. A soldier who was confident that his loved ones were healthy, adequately provided with food, clothing and shelter, well treated by relatives and neighbors, constant in their affections and optimistic in their outlook was better satisfied with his lot than one whose family conditions were a source of anxiety. Letters bringing any sort of bad news from home were apt to be upsetting, and if they told of want, sickness, neglect or persecution by kinfolk, unfriendliness of neighbors, or indicated a weakening of marital bonds, they might lead to complete demoralization and desertion.

The wife of a Connecticut soldier undoubtedly was responsible for the chronically low state of her spouse's morale. The tone of her correspondence has to be inferred for the most part from her husband's replies, but there can be no question of its being generally plaintive. One of the few letters written by her that was preserved contains the statement:

> I have been to Williams . . . but he dont know anything about the war & cares less & that is the way withe the most of them hear. they have got you all into the scrape & that is all they care for. I dont think it will be half as much disgrace to you to have you come home as it will be to stay. . . . it is no worse for you than for thousands of others that is coming all the time. . . . dont stay for . . . a minute nor an hour if you see a chance . . . think not of the name in these times.[45]

Little wonder that the husband repeatedly reflected extreme dissatisfaction with his lot in the months following, though be it said to his credit that he served out his time.

Letters detailing home woes, while disturbing enough, were apparently not so demoralizing as no letters at all, especially if failure to receive them was interpreted as a token of marital infidelity, as was sometimes the case. A New Jersey Yank who failed to hear from his war bride for several weeks wrote angrily:

> I think it is damn mean. . . . Before we was married I heard from you every week and now we married I dont hear from you once a month. . . . it isnt Because you dont know where to write. . . . it seems as if you dont care the snap of your finger wether you write or not.

Ten days later he wrote again:

> I dont know what is the reason that I cant hear from the one that is nearest and dearest to me. it makes me feel down hearted and dull. . . . Mary I dont think you would deceive me so soon, if you have I am ashamed of you. I may be talking at random and I hope I am.

Failing still to get a letter, he wrote after the lapse of another week openly indicating his doubt of her faithfulness. When finally he heard from her he was reassured, but only for a little while, for in a subsequent note she made the mistake of asking permission to go out with male friends. This brought from the husband the blunt reply: "Go at your own risk. if I find out you go out with any one besides briggs or Jeff I will discard you for ever."

While being tortured by doubts of his wife's fidelity, this Yank was having other troubles, including reduced rations, disagreeable weather and uncongenial camp associations. All of these, coupled with what seems to have been a basic deficiency of spiritual stamina, caused him in October 1863 to send his wife the following remarkable message:

> I want to get out of this thing some way if I can, but I dont know how I will do it Hardley. there is no chance for deserting. I will have to work some plan to get my discharge. I have been stuffing medicine in myself since I been out here. I have been taking Pulsotil, Bryvina, Beladona, Acoute, Nuy Pom . . . Mucurins And Arsnic Poison when you write I wish you would send me some Arsnic or some other kind of stuff so as to make me look pale . . . find out at the druggist what will make you look pale and sickly . . . and send a small quantity in every letter. . . . If I aint Home . . . by next spring I dont care wether I ever get Home or not.

The recipient did not send the arsenic, but the husband contrived a visit home early in 1864, apparently by playing sick.

This case might be dismissed as that of a worthless character or hopeless psychopath were it not for the fact that he obviously had the respect of his associates, that he rose to the responsible position of orderly sergeant, and that, despite repeated talk of quitting the service and three unwarranted furloughs, he apparently acquitted himself creditably in combat and remained in the army until after Appomattox.[46]

Letters detailing home deprivations were especially depressing if the recipients' pay were in arrears, thus making it impossible for them to provide needed financial assistance. Failure to receive pay was the more disturbing in view of the uncertainty of aid from home-relief services which often were poorly administered. The worry experienced by unpaid soldiers over needy dependents was well illustrated in the instance of John N. Henry who in January 1863 wrote his wife:

> I have suffered more anxiety on account of my family for several weeks past than for the whole year. Six months pay behind & no knowledge of what the Forestville Committee were doing except the letter of Mrs. Pash to her [soldier] husband sometime ago that payment was refused her.[47]

Failure to draw wages when due was also hard on the morale of Yanks who had no hungry families looking to them for sustenance. In April 1864 an Ohio sergeant thus situated wrote in his diary near Chattanooga: "Weather cloudy and cold no news—Strapped for money, got the blues like a old maid." A year earlier a soldier correspondent wrote to a newspaper from the Virginia front: "The shameful neglect of the proper officials at Washington to pay our brave soldiers has been the principal means of causing the wholesale desertion in the army." [48]

Furloughs were hardly less important than pay as factors in morale. Policies governing leave, haphazard throughout the conflict, were especially unsatisfactory during the first half of the war. Apparent hopelessness of visiting home in the foreseeable future contributed much to the depression which pervaded camps in the winter of 1862-1863; and the frequency of furloughs resulting from the veteran re-enlistment program of the next winter helped sustain morale during that period.

Many soldiers completed three years of service without getting leave. A young Hoosier who requested and was refused a furlough in November 1863, after nearly two and a half years' absence from home, later wrote his sweetheart: "You ask when I am going to get my furlough. I 'holler' *never* and echo answers never—across Murphy Hollow [near Chattanooga]. I expect to get one in eight months." [49]

This soldier was able to laugh at his failure to get leave. The same was not true of most Yanks and especially of those with families. General Joseph Shields wrote General McDowell in June 1862 that volunteer troops "if not allowed to go home and see their families . . . droop and die. . . . I have watched this," he added. "The men who are denied this permission cease to be of any use." [50]

A Michigan soldier sick in body and spirit, the father of several children, wrote home from Alexandria, Virginia, in November 1862: "I sed that I shuld get a furlow and com home if I could. I have given up the Idea for it would cost me more figering & kiniving than it wold bea worth and I wold stand ten chances to bea struck with lightning whare I wold wone of getting a furlow." [51]

Still another consideration which greatly influenced morale was adjustment to unit, branch and associates. Some Yanks who were miserable as infantrymen became happy soldiers when transferred to the cavalry. Members of the mounted branch, on the other hand, sometimes were thoroughly demoralized by the mere prospect of being reduced to a walking state.

Enforced association with strangers, through transfer or by consolidation of units, also was apt to be demoralizing, especially during the period of adjustment following the change. But where initial assignments were uncongenial, transfers sometimes were the salvation of drooping spirits. An excellent case in point is that of W. O. Lyford who left college in the spring of 1861 to enlist in the Second New Hampshire Regiment. During the first few weeks he expressed contentment with his lot, but misconduct of some of his superiors at the First Battle of Bull Run undermined his confidence in them. A further source of discontent was the promotion over him of noncommissioned leaders whom he deemed less deserving than himself. In view of his changed attitude, it seems safe to assume that friction developed between him and those from whom he had to take orders. At any rate, from being a happy, eager soldier, he became a captious and dissatisfied one. On July 31, 1861, he complained about the excessive drinking of his officers and added, "I want my discharge right off, as soon as I can get it." A month later he wrote his parents: "I am satisfied that I cant live in the army. . . . I am tired and sick and hope it will be possible for me to come home and settle down."

In the autumn he transferred to the Fifth New Hampshire Regiment and was promoted from corporal to sergeant. The effect on his morale was revolutionary. In February 1862 he wrote his mother: "I have the care of the neatest and best boys in the company and I am contented as can be." The next month he devoted most of a letter to singing the praises of his captain whom he rated as by far the best in the regiment. "I would not be at home for anything," he stated, "for I am learning more about tactics than I ever knew." Shortly after the ordeal of Antietam he boasted to his father: "I am tough and rugged now and am willing to serve my country as long as I am able." [52]

Later in the year he received his lieutenant's bars. But illness overtook him soon afterward and he died before the end of the war.

In Lyford's instance the difference between poor morale and good morale was largely one of leadership. The same was true in countless other cases. Good leadership meant effective discipline, and effective discipline usually spelled high morale. Two regiments of the same brigade and even two companies of the same regiment might be poles apart in morale if one had superior officers and discipline while the other had ineffective leadership and loose discipline.

In August 1864 the close-observing John William De Forest, whose regiment had recently been transferred to Western Virginia from the Washington area, visited a near-by brigade of the Sixth Corps that had recently been through the hard fighting of Grant's "On to Richmond" campaign and had experienced an extreme deterioration of soldierly qualities. De Forest, coming from an organization where an opposite state prevailed, was shocked by the contrast. Irregular placing of tents, dirty guns, disregard of authority as manifested by a private telling a lieutenant "I'll slap your face if you say that again" and other conditions gave undeniable evidence that discipline had gone to pot and with it morale. Of the officers De Forest wrote: "Their talk about the war and our immediate military future had a tone of depression which astonished me."

"Don't you believe in Grant at all?" asked De Forest.

"Yes, we believe in Grant," a colonel answered, "but we believe a great deal more in Lee and in the Army of Virginia." [53]

And this was only eight months before Appomattox!

Yet another important factor in morale remains to be cited and this was age. Soldiers in their middle twenties and younger were of better spirit than older men; and men above forty had the lowest morale. Unmarried men, who for the most part were in the lower age groups, were less susceptible to depression than husbands and fathers. The youngsters pined less for home, endured privation more cheerfully, stood up better (if not so youthful as to be physically immature) under the wear and tear of strenuous campaigning, recovered more quickly from the shock of combat, manifested greater patience when sick or wounded and in general proved more adaptable than their elders.

One instance—that of Day Elmore—is cited elsewhere of a Yankee boy's unquenchable spirit.[54] Another shining example is found in Charles Ward, a Massachusetts lad who donned the uniform in his late teens and who, when offered a noncombatant post in regimental headquarters about the time of Antietam, turned it down with the comment: "I came to carry a gun and not to do the [clerical] work for others to fight." A little later, on the repeated urging of his officers, he accepted a clerkship, but he was troubled in conscience by not being in the ranks with his comrades at Fredericksburg. During the gloom of the war's second winter, while many wavered in spirit, his morale remained high. On one occasion, after marching fifty-five miles in three days, he boasted to his mother: "When we halted the first night I was the first man in the front rank and only 24 of us there. . . . They fell out one after the other, but I did not feel a bit tired."

At Chancellorsville he sneaked away from his desk and "fired one shot from a gun I picked up thrown away by one of our men who skedaddled." At Gettysburg, while performing the responsible duties of sergeant major of his regiment, he received a wound in the chest which caused his death on July 9, 1863. Two days before he died he wrote from his hospital bed this farewell message:

Dear Mother: I may not again see you but do not fear for your tired soldier boy. Death has no fears for me. My hope is still firm in Jesus. Meet

me and Father in heaven with all my *dear friends*. I have no special message to send you, but bid you all a happy farewell.

Your affect. and soldier Son[55]

A happy farewell was in keeping with his unwavering cheerfulness, his
noble character and his unsullied patriotism. To him and to the young
Minnesota farmer, Ira Butterfield, who in 1863 dismissed the suggestion
of a discharge with the statement, "I dont want a discharge by a long shot
for if I were at home I could not take any comfort as long as there was
men in the field doing Battle for me and my priveleges when I went in
I goes the whole hog and never take hold of the plow and look back" [56]
—to them and their kind for their dauntless spirit in fair weather or foul,
in victory or defeat, the Union will ever owe a debt of gratitude.

CHAPTER XII

THE MEN WHO WORE THE BLUE

THE MOST STRIKING thing about Union soldiers was their diversity. The visitor to a Federal camp at any period of the war would encounter persons of many nationalities, races, creeds and occupations and observe great variations in dress, habits, temperament, education, wealth and social status. Indeed, there was hardly a type or class of any conceivable kind that was not represented in the Northern ranks.

Yanks ranged in age from beardless boys to hoary old men. The youngest wearers of the blue were the drummer boys and cavalry buglers. Apparently no minimum age was specified for the juvenile musicians until March 3, 1864, when an act of Congress prohibited the enlistment of any person under sixteen.[1]

The principal duties of the drummer boys were to sound the daily calls on drum, fife or bugle and to assist the band in providing music for ceremonies and drill. In addition, they performed sundry chores about the camp. The diary of William C. Richardson, drummer boy of the 104th Ohio Regiment, shows that he supplemented his musical activities with barbering, carrying water for the soldiers, honing the surgeon's instruments, assisting in removal and care of the wounded, helping bury the dead and drawing maps. Another drummer boy sold cakes, nuts, watermelons and other delicacies to the soldiers at a profit which infuriated the men and which permitted him to send home in one lump the then fabulous sum of sixty-five dollars.[2]

In view of their associations, it is not surprising that some of the youthful musicians acquired bad habits. A famous Civil War photograph shows a uniformed stripling playing cards with a whiskered sergeant, while an even younger boy looks over his shoulder. An Ohio cavalryman reported seeing a fifteen-year-old win $120 in one gambling session.[3]

Private Harvey Reid in a remarkable letter to a very young brother gave the following delightful glimpse of little Johnnie Walker, twelve-year-old drummer in the Twenty-second Wisconsin Regiment:

Johnnie is drummer for the band, and when they play at dress parade every evening lots of gentlemen and ladies come from the city to hear them play and see the little drummer and when we are marching, and the ladies see the little soldier-boy they always give him apples, cakes or something. . . . When we are marching Johnnie always keeps up with the big men, and is always singing and laughing but when he gets tired the big Colonel or Lieutenant Colonel or Adjutant will let Johnnie have his horse to ride. Everybody in the regiment likes Johnnie because he is a good little boy, is always pleasant and polite and not saucy like a great many boys. His mother sent him a suit of clothes made exactly like officer's clothes, and Lieutenant Baumman says he will get him a pair of shoulder straps with silver drum sticks upon them. Johnnie used to live in Racine and he has a half brother who is corporal in our company (but he is a mean bad man, don't take care of Johnnie, who lives with the Captain of Company B).[4]

Martial exploits of drummer boys must be considered with caution, owing to the appeal which the subject has had for balladists and romancers. The "Drummer Boy of Shiloh," for example, who supposedly furnished the theme for Will S. Hays's song of that title, has been traditionally identified as Henry Burke of the Fifty-eighth Ohio Regiment. But a careful investigation by the historian of Shiloh National Park revealed that the only Henry Burke carried on the official lists of Ohio soldiers was a private in the 148th Regiment who enlisted on May 2, 1864, long after Shiloh; and examination of the Shiloh cemetery records indicates that the "Henry Burke" there listed was added to the burial roll after the Shiloh drummer boy became a celebrity.[5]

Shiloh had its real drummer boys, of course, though the deeds of none seem to accord fully with those of song and story. The most famous of the Shiloh drummers, and probably of the whole war, was John L. (Johnny) Clem who ran away from home to join the army in May 1861, though only nine years old. When he offered his services as drummer to a company commander of the Third Ohio Volunteer Regiment, the captain looked him over, laughed and, according to Clem, "said he wasn't enlisting infants." Johnny then tried to join the Twenty-second Michigan Regiment and was refused. But he "went along with the regiment just the same as a drummer boy, and though not on the muster roll, drew a soldier's pay of thirteen dollars a month," which was contributed by officers of the regiment.[6]

The smashing of Johnny's drum by a shell at Pittsburg Landing won for him the sobriquet of "Johnny Shiloh." Shortly afterward he was regularly enlisted as drummer. Subsequently he exchanged drum for musket because, as he put it, "I did not like to stand and be shot at without shooting back."

So at Chickamauga, Johnny, though still carried on the rolls as drummer, went into the fight riding an artillery caisson and carrying a musket cut down to size. When a Confederate colonel dashed up and demanded, "Surrender you damned little Yankee!" Johnny gave him a blast that knocked him from his horse. For this feat Clem, then twelve years old, was made a sergeant and became known as the drummer boy of Chickamauga. Some Chicago ladies who heard of his bravery and promotion sent him a new uniform. In typical soldier fashion the young hero donned the fancy regalia, armed himself with a musket and posed for the photographer.[7]

Johnny carried dispatches for General Thomas during the Atlanta campaign, had his pony killed under him and before the end of his service was twice wounded. After the war was over he sought admission to West Point, but was rejected on account of deficiency of his prior schooling. He then appealed to President Grant who appointed him second lieutenant in the Regular Army. Clem retired from the Army in 1916 as a major general.[8]

Other boy musicians had less spectacular careers than Clem, but many followed his example of swapping drums for guns in the heat of conflict. The colonel of the Fifty-second Ohio Regiment told of one such instance in his official report of Perryville where "Charley Common, a little drummer-boy, having lost his drum, took a musket and fought manfully in the line." [9]

One drummer boy, Orion P. Howe of the Fifty-fifth Illinois Regiment, for gallantry at Vicksburg was awarded the coveted Medal of Honor. His citation stated: "A drummer boy, 14 years of age and severely wounded and exposed to a heavy fire from the enemy, he persistently remained upon the field of battle until he had reported to Gen. W. T. Sherman the necessity of supplying cartridges for the use of troops under command of Colonel Malmborg." [10]

By no means all the youngsters who wore the blue were musicians. Despite issuance of War Department orders as early as August 1861 forbidding acceptance without parental consent of minors under eighteen and an unqualified barring of them the next year, thousands of boys seventeen years and younger found their way into the ranks.[11] Benjamin A. Gould, a United States Sanitary Commission actuary who compiled vital statistics for 1,012,273 Union volunteers, reported that 10,233 of

them were under eighteen at the time of their enlistment, with age group-
ings as follows:

Age	Number
13	127
14	330
15	773
16	2,758
17	6,425 [12]

Examination by the writer of the descriptive lists of 123 companies
containing 14,330 men and representing 96 regiments of infantry, 15 of
cavalry and 12 of artillery revealed 3 boys who were 12 years old when
mustered into service, 12 who were 13, 4 who were 14, 5 who were 15, 62
who were 16 and 160 who were 17. Boys under 18 comprised 1.02 per
cent of Gould's total and 1.6 of the writer's. While many of the youngsters in both groups were musicians, most of them apparently were full-
fledged soldiers. Some who started out as drummer boys graduated, while
still below the legal age, to positions in the ranks.[13]

The number of boys under eighteen was actually greater than that
shown in the surveys, for the figures were compiled from muster rolls and
many Yanks listed as eighteen and above in these records were in reality
below eighteen; they misrepresented their age in order to get into the
service.[14] Joseph T. Bushong of the Eighteenth Ohio Regiment, who
claimed to have completed a three-year enlistment before his eighteenth
birthday, declared that his false statement to the recruiting officer concerning his age was "the only lie I ever told in my life." [15] Chauncey H.
Cooke of the Twenty-fifth Wisconsin Regiment, whose letters home are
among the best of Civil War sources, wrote thus of his mustering-in
experience:

Every one he suspicioned of being under 18 he would ask his age. He
turned out a lot of them who were not quite 18. . . . Seeing how it was
working with the rest, I did not know what to do. . . . I saw our Chaplain and he told me to tell the truth, that I was a little past 16, and he
tho't when the mustering officer saw my whiskers he would not ask my
age. That is what the boys all told me but I was afraid. I had about made
up my mind to tell him I was going on 19 years, but thank heaven I did
not have a chance to lie. He did not ask my age. I am all right . . . but
the sweat was running down my legs into my boots when that fellow
came down the line and I was looking hard at the ground fifteen paces in
front.[16]

It is possible that boys even younger than twelve marched in the Union ranks, though the writer is not able to state this as a positive fact. The *Photographic History of the Civil War* contains the picture of William Black and describes him as the "youngest wounded soldier reported," but his age, unit and status are not given.[17] The Portland, Maine, *Transcript* of September 6, 1862, made a brief reference to the nine-year-old son of George H. Wilson who "went off without the knowledge of his parents with the 17th [Maine] Regiment and writes home that he 'likes the soldier's life' and is the pet of the regiment"; but this boy was undoubtedly a hanger-on rather than a soldier.[18] The claim to the distinction of being the "Youngest Yank" seems impossible of establishment.

Some of the boy soldiers deserted after a few months but most seem to have given a good account of themselves.[19] A Connecticut cavalryman who was at first skeptical of a group of recruits not big enough to "fill up the government breeches" that came to his unit in April 1864 wrote later of one of them: "He is about fourteen years of age . . . by occupation a shoemaker . . . a bright active boy full of enterprise & spirit. He had nearly or quite made his escape [when captured in a recent engagement] but went back to the rebel guard because his friend William Foley, also a young boy, who was to escape with him became exhausted on account of a wound. . . . I regard it as a remarkable instance of generosity & self sacrifice." [20]

On hard marches the ponies, as the boys were called, sometimes showed greater stamina than their mature comrades, a fact which afforded them much satisfaction. An Ohio lad wrote proudly to his parents after two days and a night of tramping through the rain in Virginia: "There was a grate many give out but i made the riffel some of the bigest men give out. . . . i told the boys that they ort to be ashamed of themselves for a boy like me to stand the march two days and not give out." [21]

The buoyancy and blitheness of the teen-agers often spread to their comrades and helped make soldiering more tolerable for all. The boys also carried their part of the load on the firing line. The colonel of the 102nd Pennsylvania Regiment reported after Seven Pines that "Privates W. C. Wall, Jr., and John Aiken, Jr., of Company M, two of the youngest soldiers bearing arms in the regiment . . . stood in a most exposed position . . . firing deliberately . . . and careful not to waste ammunition." Cited also for gallantry in action was Private David W. Camp who at Shiloh, "though a mere boy, only fourteen years old, served as No. 5 man at the left [artillery] piece with the skill and bravery of an old soldier," and Private Nathaniel Gwynne of the Thirteenth Ohio Cavalry who at Petersburg on April 2, 1865, was cautioned not to enter the action as he was only fifteen years old and had not been mustered; but Gwynne "indignantly protested," joined in the charge, lost an arm and was awarded the Medal of Honor.[22]

A substantial though indeterminable number of the boy soldiers paid the supreme price for their patriotism. Among the slain was W. W. Dutton of the Tenth Vermont Regiment who enlisted in December 1863 at seventeen, participated in the bloody battles of the Wilderness, Spottsylvania and Second Cold Harbor and was killed in July 1864 at Monocacy before attaining the age of eighteen.[23]

One of the most interesting things about the boy soldiers was the speed with which they matured under the stress and strain of army life. The quick metamorphosis was strikingly revealed in the letters of Charles Goddard who enlisted in the First Minnesota Regiment shortly before his sixteenth birthday. After only a brief period of service he wrote his widowed mother in paternal strain concerning a younger brother: "Tell him he must be a good boy and not trouble his mother as much as I did." Eight months later he replied to an indirect inquiry about correspondence with girls: "I have something els to do than to make love to the women"; at the same time he read his mother a lesson concerning her proposal to join his unit in the capacity of nurse: "I consider myself milatary General of our famly and I wont allow you to make such a rash move as that." Still a few weeks later he stated: "Tell brother that if any body abuses him to jest hint to them that he has a big brother in the army that may some day return when he will procede imediately to settle up all these little accounts." Following a wound at Gettysburg, though not far beyond the ripe age of seventeen, he wrote in old-soldier fashion: "My leg is a regular old weather clock for I can tell when it is going to be bad weather—it feels num and as if it had been froze and was not thourally thawed out yet." [24]

Goddard continued to grow in stature and wisdom, proving himself in every respect a worthy soldier of his country. His career in arms gave striking support to the observation that age is more a matter of experience than years. By the time of his return to civilian life in 1864 at the age of nineteen, he who had gone out three years before as a boy had unquestionably become a man.

Some of those who as boys donned the blue rose to high rank before the end of the war. Arthur MacArthur, father of General Douglas MacArthur, after being awarded at eighteen the Medal of Honor for carrying the colors of his regiment in the vanguard of a charge at Missionary Ridge was promoted to the command of the Twenty-fourth Wisconsin Regiment and led it through the bloody battles of Resaca and Nashville. After the conflict "the gallant boy colonel," as he was called by a superior during the war, rose to the grade of lieutenant general. Another brave soldier who commanded a Union regiment before his twenty-first birthday was Henry W. Lawton of Indiana. Still another boy colonel, James B. Forman of the Fifteenth Kentucky Regiment, was mortally wounded at twenty-one while leading his men in the thick of the fight at Stone's River.[25]

At the other extreme from the boys were the old men. Instructions issued by the War Department in September 1862 specifically forbade the mustering of persons above forty-five, but many men of middle age and beyond had already found their way into the ranks, and hundreds of others gained admittance after the prohibition by the simple expedient of putting up a bold front and lying.[26] Slightly more than one half of one per cent of the 1,012,273 Yanks surveyed by Gould were over forty-five when they entered the service and the writer's sample of 14,330 contained 85, or six tenths of one per cent, who were forty-six and older.[27] As previously suggested, the proportion of soldiers over forty-five was always greater than that shown on the muster rolls because older men, prompted by patriotism or bounty, sometimes overlooked one or more birthdays when they enrolled for service. The age distribution of the older men in the surveys of Gould and the writer was as follows:

	Gould's		The Writer's
Age	Number	Age	Number
46	967	46	21
47	712	47	11
48	699	48	12
49	469	49	7
50 and over	2,366 [28]	50	3
		51	4
		52	7
		53	3
		54	1
		55	2
		56	1
		57	3
		58	2
		59	2
		60	3
		62	2
		65	1 [29]

The sixty-five-year-old in the writer's survey was a musician in Company D, First Missouri Infantry.[30] Despite his advanced years he was by no means the eldest wearer of the blue. A chaplain encountered in an army hospital a septuagenarian who had been recruited "under a false representation of his age." [31] But the person who seems clearly entitled to the designation "oldest Yank"—and for that matter, "oldest Civil War soldier"—was Curtis King who was mustered into the Thirty-seventh Iowa Infantry on November 9, 1862, at the age of eighty and who was carried on the rolls until March 20, 1863, when he was discharged for disability.[32] The regiment to which King belonged was unique. Known as the Greybeards and organized for guard duty, this unit was composed mainly of men over forty-five. In its ranks were 145 men sixty years of age and older.[33]

The great mass of Yanks were neither very old nor very young but fell in the eighteen-to-forty-five group. Over 98 per cent of the million volunteers in Gould's survey were in this category and, despite some error resulting from false statements by those falling outside authorized limits, Gould's figures represent with reasonable accuracy the age pattern of the Union Army.[34]

On the basis of Gould's estimate it may be stated that in the first year of the conflict the largest single age group among the men who wore the blue was the eighteen-year-olds (even with due allowance for lying); that the next largest category was the twenty-one-year-olds, and that beyond twenty-one, as a general rule, age groups became progressively smaller.[35]

The average age of the men in blue increased slightly with the progress of the war. The age pattern of men coming into the service remained fairly constant, but as the old-timers matured they pushed the general age level upward. Gould estimates the average age of the army to have been 25.10 years in July 1862; 25.76 in July 1863; 26.06 in July 1864; and 26.32 in May 1865.[36]

The Union Army, then, was a youthful army.[37] At the mid-point of the conflict three out of every four Yanks were under thirty years of age and less than half of them had celebrated their twenty-fifth birthday.[38] This predominancy of youth was of incalculable moment both to the army and the nation. Youth gave a cheerful tone to camp life, made for generosity in human relations and provided a priceless core of ruggedness, optimism and resilience which a succession of defeats could not crush and which led eventually to victory, peace and Union.

Occupations and professions of the men in blue were considerably more varied than their ages. The writer's examination of 123 company rolls turned up more than 300 occupations and specialties. Alphabetically the vocations represented by the 14,000 Yanks considered extended from accountant to woodcutter and included such diversities as artists and barkeepers, brokers and brakemen, chemists and contractors, dancing masters and ditchers, grocers and glass blowers, hairdressers and heelers, Indian lecturers and ironworkers, landlords and locksmiths, miners and manufacturers, peddlers and pianists, surveyors and stonecutters, tinsmiths and teachers, varnishers and veterinarians and wheelwrights and waiters. Such well-known functionaries as the butcher, the baker and the candlestick maker stood side by side with oddities who classified themselves as gamblers, gentlemen and loafers. One Yank declared himself a "Jack of all traids." [39]

The most numerous groups were the farmers, who comprised nearly half the total, and common laborers, who accounted for more than a tenth. Other well-represented categories were carpenters who numbered 610; shoemakers, 374; clerks, 367; blacksmiths, 325; painters, 200; soldiers, 173; mechanics, 183; sailors, 178; machinists, 155; masons, 143; printers, 126; teamsters, 99; and teachers, 97. [40]

The varied accomplishment of the men in blue manifested itself in sundry and impressive ways. When the colonel of the First Michigan Regiment at dress parade called for printers to run off some official papers, eight men stepped forward to offer their services. [41] A Massachusetts colonel whose mobility was seriously impeded by Rebel destruction of transportation facilities in Maryland early in the war soon found that his men were equal to the emergency. Walking up to the debris of a dismantled locomotive one of the soldiers coolly remarked: "I made this engine and I can put it together again." Others of section-gang background soon had the rails relaid; and when an engineer was requested to start the train rolling, nineteen Yanks from this one regiment avowed themselves capable of taking over the throttle. [42] By these and countless other feats the citizen army mobilized by Lincoln demonstrated the genius and versatility of a people whose resourcefulness and energy carved a nation out of the wilderness, conquered its distances, harnessed its resources and ultimately made of it the arsenal of democracy in an epic struggle for individual freedom.

Educational backgrounds ranged from no schooling at all to the highest levels of specialized training, and intellectual qualities extended from imbecility to genius. Among the aristocrats of learning was Scotch-born Edward F. Reid of the Third Indiana Cavalry who began his soldier career as a private in 1861 and was commissioned second lieutenant in

January 1864. Reid's diary is sprinkled with quotations, some of them in Latin, Greek and German, from classical and contemporary literature. The first entry of his army service began:

> Came into camp—went home on furlough the same evg.
>   The Splendor falls on castle walls
>   And snowy summits old in story
>   The long light shakes across the lakes
> . . . .
>   Blow bugle blow. . . .
>   Blow bugle answer echoes dying, dying . . .

and concluded with a Greek quotation from the New Testament. On August 5, 1861, he wrote: "Eat, drank and drilled," and then transcribed extracts from Tennyson and other poets. On January 1, 1861, he summarized a *Harper's Monthly* article by Ruskin and two days later he copied excerpts from Seneca and Schiller.[43]

Another of the cultural upper crust was Samuel Storrow, a Harvard student who served as corporal in the Forty-fourth Massachusetts Regiment. Storrow's home letters indicate outstanding proficiency in Latin and Greek. They also show that familiarity with the classics tended to isolate the writer from the great mass of his comrades. "It has been one of the most unpleasant of my experiences as a private," he wrote in 1863, "to be unable to find any congenial companion and friend in my company, and to be obliged to associate with men whom nothing else could have forced me into such close intimacy with. . . . I do not regret having Entered . . . [the ranks], but I long ago found out that it was an uncongenial sphere, Even in the 44th, at least in Co. H." [44]

At the lower end of the educational and intellectual scale were the illiterates. Many of them were ignorant from lack of educational opportunity and some from native stupidity. In one notorious instance substitute brokers enticed an idiot from a New York asylum and palmed him off as a soldier.[45]

Among the illiterates were many Negroes recently redeemed from bondage and a considerable sprinkling of underprivileged whites from the large cities. A member of a Massachusetts company drawn largely from an industrial center stated that the only education found among his comrades was that which could be obtained "from a nail mill or rum shop," and a cavalryman from the New York City area reported that many of his company could neither read nor write. But such instances seem to have been exceptional. The average company in the Union Army had from one to a half-dozen illiterates. Many had none. A veteran corporal on encountering his first instance of a soldier requiring an amanuensis remarked: "There is not one in a thousand hardly but what can write." [46]

Schools were organized in many Negro regiments, and in some white ones, to teach the rudiments of learnir g on a voluntary basis. Both officers and men acted as instructors. A New York artillery captain described an educational enterprise in his own battery thus:

My school is in a flourishing condition; the boys built a table and desk, with forms out of split logs, and set it up under the shade of the trees, and every day at 2 P.M. the schoolmaster, an old corporal whom I detailed for the purpose, fetches the spelling-books and the writing materials, and sets his classes their lessons. You would be pleased to see the eagerness with which men from twenty to forty years of age seize upon this opportunity for repairing the defects of their early education, and the progress which they all make is most encouraging. [47]

While illiteracy was not so great a handicap to soldiers of the sixties as to those of today (since warfare is now far more technical), still it constituted a serious disadvantage and sometimes produced embarrassing and dangerous situations. Court-martial records tell of an illiterate Yank being assigned to guard a bridge leading into the nation's capital. When the soldier protested the order on grounds of his inability to read passes he was told by the sergeant, "Never mind, you only have to look at them." Instead of trying to conceal his ignorance the soldier left his post and got drunk, for which offense he was sentenced to two years of hard labor. [48]

Barely literate Yanks sometimes displayed an amusing sense of superiority over less polished comrades. An Ohio soldier, in a letter urging younger relatives to attend school, made the following statement:

i can see the good of what i have got now. there is lots of men here that cant wright and they have got to git somebody to wright there leters i wouldent take five hundered dolers for what learn i have got. [49]

The nativity of the Northern soldiers was an impressive conglomerate. Descriptive rolls show that every state in the Union and virtually every nation and province on the globe were represented in the Union ranks. [50]

The impression is strong and persistent that the Federal forces were made up largely of foreigners. Prevalence of this idea among Southerners is attributable in part to prejudice born of intersectional strife (the genuine Yankee had no love of fighting, suh, and if he had, he couldn't have whipped us; so in keeping with his scheming, cowardly nature, he took his filthy wealth, much of it ill-gotten from his less materialistic brothers in the South, and hired a horde of hungry foreigners to face the bullets for him, while he stayed at home and fattened his bank roll with war profits).[51] Another basis of the opinion is the ease with which foreign-born invaders could be distinguished by their speech and demeanor. A Southerner whose premises were visited by bluecoats was inclined to take more notice of one thick-brogued Irishman or guttural-speaking Teuton than a half-dozen smoothly articulating sons of America; and after the hostile forces passed on, he was apt to refer to them as horrible foreign scum.

Like many other stubborn traditions, the idea of foreigners constituting the bulk of the Northern Army is erroneous. The overwhelming majority of Yanks, probably more than three fourths of them, were native Americans. A sample of 14,330 cases taken from the descriptive books of 123 well-distributed regiments yielded 2,617 natives of New York, 1,808 of Pennsylvania, 1,751 of Ohio, 1,000 of Indiana, 474 of Illinois and lesser numbers born in other states. Every slaveholding state except Florida was represented in the list. Of the 14,330 men included in the sample, 814 were natives of the slaveholding states and 437 were born in the eleven states comprising the Southern Confederacy. Virginia, represented by 198 names, contributed more natives than any other Confederate state, Tennessee was next with 123 and North Carolina was third with 34. Louisiana led the Gulf states with 20 representatives, and Alabama was second with 17. A company raised in the Old Northwest or Middle West normally contained one or more sons of the Old Dominion in its ranks and frequently had representation from two or three other Confederate states.[52]

Germans were the most numerous of foreign-born Yanks. The Northern states in 1860 contained over a million persons of German birth, and the total number of German-born soldiers in the Union Army probably exceeded 200,000. Several divisions were made up largely of Germans, and the number of regiments comprised mainly of Teutons ran up into the scores. The State of New York raised ten regiments that were almost wholly German and many more that were predominantly so. Only a minority of the Germans, however, were grouped in foreign units. A majority, owing to the wide diffusion of the Teutons among the civilian population, were scattered throughout the entire army in quantities ranging from a dozen to several hundred per regiment. Indeed, it is hardly an exaggeration to state that the company which lacked a German-born member was a rarity among the Federal forces.[53]

Some of the Germans were less than admirable both as men and soldiers, but on the whole the contribution of this nationality to the Union cause was tremendous. Many Germans, and especially the Forty-eighters, were men of good education and refined tastes whose influence improved the cultural tone of the units to which they belonged. Their technical aptitude and skill helped meet specialist needs in artillery, engineer and signal units. The prior training of many of them in European organizations was utilized for instruction of vast levies of green recruits. Their neatness, precision and respect for authority was of infinite aid in molding a mob of individualists into an organized fighting force. What the Teutons lacked in quickness and glamour was more than offset by their patience and steadiness, not to mention the idealistic devotion of many of them to the cause of Union and freedom.[54]

Despite a reputation for cowardice, attributable largely to their alleged defection at Chancellorsville, the Germans were good fighters. Their effectiveness as artillerymen was well exemplified by Wiedrich's battery on the second day at Gettysburg. A Rebel officer who rushed up to this unit as its capture seemed assured crying "This battery is ours!" received the retort from a stubborn defender, "No, dis battery is *unser!*" and then was felled by a blow of this man's sponge staff.[55]

Second only to the Germans, among foreigners who fought for the Union, were the Irish. Native sons of Erin swelled the Northern ranks to the number of nearly 150,000. More than a score of regiments were pure Irish or nearly so when they donned the blue, and numerous others contained a heavy admixture of men born on the Emerald Isle. New York furnished more Irish than any other state. Among units raised in the Empire State was General Thomas F. Meagher's famous Irish Brigade, composed of the Ninth, Sixty-third and Eighty-eighth New York Regiments. This brigade covered itself with glory and blood in many battles and especially in the desperate assault on Marye's Heights at Fredericksburg. In New York also was recruited Corcoran's Irish Legion of five regiments whose original composition was predominantly Irish. Massachusetts, Pennsylvania, Indiana and Illinois each contributed two Irish regiments, and several other states each provided one. But the regiments tell only part of the story, as Irishmen in smaller units and individually flocked to the ranks from every part of the Union. Their motivation was less idealistic than that of the Germans and some of the other nationalities. It is quite possible that their predominant urge was the sheer love of combat.[56]

Certainly the sons of old Erin were among the most desperate and dependable of fighters. Their distinctive green flag, adorned with harp and sunburst, was usually to be found where the fire was hottest, giving assurance and inspiration to all who beheld it. Generals often called on them when the situation was most desperate, and comrades openly admired them for their reckless courage.[57] The reputation which they enjoyed is well illustrated by the statement of Corporal Charles Ward concerning the "Irish Ninth" of Massachusetts. "They fight like tigers," he wrote after Antietam, "& no regt. of Rebs can stand a charge from them. They have a name which our Regt. will never get." [58]

All Irishmen were not heroes, of course; nor were they faultless as soldiers. Some of them played the coward in combat and others carried recklessness to undesirable extremes. On the whole they were less effective in sustained defensive operations than in offensive spurts.[59]

Their pugnaciousness and the excessive fondness of many of them for strong drink sometimes made them difficult to discipline, but their troublesomeness was counterbalanced by their ready humor, sparkling repartee and matchless buoyancy.[60] Their joviality, aptitude for play and love of pageantry brightened camp life and made their festive days occasions which attracted hordes of visitors from far and wide. All in all their influence and example both in battle and in garrison was an immense asset to the Union cause.[61]

The same might be said of the other British peoples, from the mother isles and the various dependencies, who joined the Union ranks in large numbers. Their numbers and characteristics varied but their combined contribution was substantial. More than 50,000 Canadians wore the Federal uniform, along with 45,000 Englishmen and lesser numbers of Scotsmen, Welshmen and other natives of the empire.[62]

Germans, Irish, Canadians and British comprised about five sixths of the foreigners in the Union Army, but other nationalities were represented in impressive ratio to their part in the Northern population. Outstanding among the minor groups were the Scandinavians, who readily translated their ancient devotion to country and freedom into enthusiastic support of the Union cause. In numbers this group was small, but their hardihood and dependability as soldiers won for them a wholesome and far-reaching respect. The most famous Scandinavian unit was the Fifteenth Wisconsin, composed mainly of Norwegians with a sprinkling of Swedes and Danes and commanded by Colonel Hans C. Heg. The

Third Wisconsin Regiment contained one company known as the Dane Guards and another called the Scandinavian Guards. Several Illinois regiments had one or more companies made up largely of Scandinavians.[63]

The nativity of the Scandinavians was usually apparent from their names. One company of Colonel Heg's Fifteenth Wisconsin contained five Ole Olsens, another had three Ole Ericksons and still another included three Ole Andersons; in the whole regiment were at least 128 men who answered to the first name of Ole. Companies bore such designations as the St. Olaf Rifles, Oden's Rifles and the Norway Bear Hunters.[64]

Knute Nelson, a Norwegian youth, enlisted as a private in the Fourth Wisconsin in 1861, completed three years' service before his twenty-first birthday and after the war became governor of Minnesota and United States Senator. Nelson's war letters, some in English and others in Norwegian, reveal a deep love of Union, an abiding interest in emancipation and an earnestness about life in general that was far beyond his years. Sample glimpses of his attitudes and reactions may be had from two letters written while in Baton Rouge, Louisiana. In one of them, dated June 10, 1862, he said:

The careless reckless wild boy that left home a year ago will return home if Providence wills it, with more experience, and more thoughtful. He has at least learnt how to *associate* with his fellow beings. He has learnt that the world is not the school house nor the narrow limits of the litle farm. . . . I know that I caused you much grief in leaving you as I did; but my heart dictated it and I could not otherwise. Forgive me.

The other, written nearly two years later to a younger brother, lashes out at fellow immigrants who waited for rich bounties before entering the service:

You tell me that Lunner ag Björn Torsen have just enlisted and will receive 500 dolls Bonties each. Does it not look as though they inlisted for money rather than because they loved the Country? Why could not such big strapping fellows have gone to fight for their Country before now? [65]

Swiss, French, Italian, Mexican and Polish representation in the Union Army was indicated by such regimental designations as the Swiss Rifles (Fifteenth Missouri); Gardes Lafayette (Fifty-fifth New York), commanded by Regis de Trobriand; Garibaldi Guard (Thirty-ninth New York); Martinez' Militia (First New Mexico); and Polish Legion (Fifty-eighth New York). But, as in the case of other foreigners, most of the soldiers of these nationalities were scattered as individuals through units in which they were only a minority.

As a general rule regiments organized in the East had a heavier admixture of foreign-born members than did those formed in the West. The nationality profile of an Eastern unit may be illustrated by Company F, Forty-sixth Pennsylvania Regiment, which contained 78 natives of Pennsylvania, 33 of other American states, 11 Irishmen, 7 Welshmen, 4 Scotsmen, 2 Germans, 1 Frenchman and 1 Canadian; or Company B, Fifth New York Regiment, which had 67 New Yorkers, 8 other Americans, 35 Irishmen, 18 Germans, 14 Englishmen, 5 Canadians, 4 Scotsmen and 3 Frenchmen. The make-up of a Western regiment is exemplified by Company C, Second Illinois Cavalry, which had 30 natives of Illinois, 50 other Americans, 10 Germans, 6 Irishmen, 2 Englishmen, 1 Canadian, 1 Frenchman and 1 Swiss; or Company H, Eighth Michigan Infantry, which had 47 New Yorkers, 37 Michiganders, 26 other Americans, 7 Canadians, 5 Englishmen, 4 Germans, 2 Irishmen, 1 Scotsman, 1 Dutchman and 1 who gave his nativity as "the ocean." [66]

It seems probable that the portion of foreign-born in the army increased as the war progressed, because of the waning of the martial spirit among the domestic population and the greater susceptibility of immigrant groups to financial inducement and to the tricks and pressures of fraudulent recruiting agencies.[67]

The diverse national background of the Union soldiery manifested itself in many ways. One of the most noticeable of these was the babel of tongues that rose from the camps. The colonel of one regiment which included fifteen nationalities gave commands in seven different languages. In such an organization efforts of the various groups to hold conversation often led to ludicrous results. Americans derived much amusement from the speech gaucheries of foreign-born comrades wrestling with a strange language. The Yanks from distant lands also brought with them to camp peculiarities of dress which stubbornly resisted prescribed regulations; foods and beverages strange to the Federal commissariat; songs and music long cherished in the homeland; festivities and games better known to the Old World than to the New; and European practices in the arrangement of shelter and furnishings.[68]

These distinctive customs and traits gave color and variety to army life. They also aroused prejudice and friction. Taunts of "greenhorn" and the bandying of contemptuous epithets occasionally led to fisticuffs and riots. Some American-born officers complained of assignment to units composed largely of foreigners. A Yale-educated lieutenant who served in a battery of Germans and Irishmen wrote on one occasion: "What is most unpleasant to me of all, is, that I have to live with these men, to eat their onions and drink their lager and very rarely to hear a word of musical English from American lips as I am almost the sole specimen of a Yankee in the Company." Later he referred unhappily to "marching through much mud to this camp where the Teutonic element has its head-quarters, and revels in endless streams of lager, infinite plantations of sauerkraut, and strings of small but seductive sausages." Still later he noted: "This Division is called the German Division, and the officers at head-quarters have to do business in a polyglot fashion. I greatly outraged the assistant adjutant general by refusing to recognize a German order which was sent to me when I was in command." [69]

Even greater was the resentment manifested by some of the Americans in the ranks toward foreign-born officers. A tipsy Hoosier who was reprimanded by an Irishman recently elected lieutenant said: "I didnt vote for you and I . . . wouldn't vote for any damned Irish son of a bitch. I dont care a damn for you. . . . A damned Irishman always gets his ass up in about two days after he is promoted." And a German major who disciplined an unruly New York cavalryman was told to "Hold your barking and speak English, you damned Dutch son of a bitch." Another obstreperous citizen of the Empire State when placed in the custody of a detail of foreigners cried out in protest, "I am not going to be guarded by a lot of Dutch hounds." [70]

On June 23, 1861, Private Charles Wills of the Eighth Illinois Regiment wrote in his diary: "The Americans in our company think some of seceding, filling up from home with American boys, and letting the Dutch now in the company paddle their own canoe." [71] But this was early in the war, and the Americans instead of taking leave of the foreigners came to respect and like them and to take pride in the reputation which their soldierly qualities helped win for the unit. The experience of Private Wills's company was duplicated countless times throughout the army, and while prejudice existed as long as men of diverse nationalities remained in close association it was always accompanied by instances of camaraderie and mutual esteem. The most powerful influence in leveling barriers of nationality was the confidence and respect born of sharing hardship and danger. Courage in battle was the mark of a man, and the soldier who proved his bravery was not long disparaged for peculiarities of speech.

In sum, the ultimate standing of a foreigner, like that of an American, depended mainly on his character and habits. If he was shirking, filthy, dishonest or craven, he was held in low esteem and his deficiency associated with his foreignness. If he measured up well as a man and soldier, he stood a good chance of winning full acceptance by his comrades.

Whatever the reputation of foreign-born soldiers during the war, it can be unequivocally stated in the perspective of time that they compared favorably with their American associates in every respect and that their experience, talents and loyalty helped mightily in preserving the Union of their adopted country.

Racially the Northern Army was predominantly white. The largest non-Caucasian group were the Negroes, 186,017 of whom were carried on Federal muster rolls. Of these, 134,111 came from the slaveholding states and a substantial majority were bondsmen recently redeemed. Louisiana, with 24,052 Negro Yanks to her credit, headed the list of states whence Negroes were recruited, and Texas with 47 was at the bottom. Northern states contributing the most Negro soldiers were Pennsylvania (8,612), New York (4,125) and Massachusetts (3,966).[72]

Union authorities were slow in reaching the decision to arm the Negroes, but when policy finally crystallized early in 1863 recruiting was pushed with vigor and colored regiments were formed in the artillery, cavalry, infantry and engineer branches. Several divisions were composed in large part of Negro troops, and the Twenty-fifth Army Corps, organized in December 1864 and placed under the command of Major General Godfrey Weitzel, was predominantly Negro.[73]

A few of the Negro units were staffed initially with colored line officers—notably three regiments organized in Louisiana by General Benjamin F. Butler—but Federal policy was in general opposed to the commissioning of Negroes except as chaplains and surgeons; and most colored officers were eventually replaced by whites. An effort was made to fill noncommissioned positions in the colored units with Negroes, but educational deficiencies, especially among Southern recruits, worked against the realization of this goal. Some regiments of "United States Colored Troops," as all Negro soldiers except the Fifty-fourth and Fifty-fifth Massachusetts Regiments were ultimately designated, had only black noncommissioned officers, but this arrangement was by no means a satisfactory one. Colonel R. B. Marcy, who was favorably disposed toward the use of Negroes as soldiers, reported after an inspection of the Forty-ninth Regiment, United States Colored Troops: "All the noncommissioned officers were colored men, a few of which could read and write a little, but not sufficient to make out company papers, which gave the commissioned officers a great amount of office duty." Colonel Thomas Wentworth Higginson, prominent Massachusetts abolitionist and writer who commanded a regiment of Negroes recruited in South Carolina, stated: "I spend hours daily in doing what in white regts would be done by a secretary detailed from the ranks." Instruction in the three "R's" proved to be one of the major functions of officers assigned to colored units.[74]

Not all colored soldiers were at the bottom of the literacy scale. Some reared in the North or abroad had good educational background. A religious worker encountered in a Virginia camp a Negro soldier who as a merchant seaman had learned Spanish, Italian and Portuguese and another who could read Latin, Greek and Hebrew.[75]

Negro soldiers participated in several battles including Port Hudson, Milliken's Bend, Fort Wagner, Olustee, Fort Pillow, Brice's Cross Roads, the Crater and Nashville. The combat performance of the colored soldier is difficult to evaluate because of the prejudiced character of most of the evidence on the subject. Northerners who were unfriendly to Negroes or opposed to emancipation, and nearly all Southerners, tended to belittle the colored soldiers; while antislavery zealots and commanders of colored units were inclined to close their eyes to deficiencies of the Negro fighters and exaggerate their accomplishments. However, a careful sifting of available testimony indicates that some Negro soldiers conducted themselves heroically in battle while others skulked and ran; that leadership was a crucial factor in their combat performance; that units recruited in the North were more effective than those composed of recently freed slaves; that in offensive spurts the showing of Negroes compared favorably with that of whites of comparable background and training; and that the Civil War experience of colored troops was too limited to permit a meaningful conclusion concerning their ability to stand up against stubborn and sustained resistance.[76]

Because of its unusually calm tone the following statement about Fort Wagner, made by a young Massachusetts staff officer favorably disposed toward the colored race, is offered as a lone exhibit from a mass of conflicting evidence:

About the Negro troops, I find it hard to come to an opinion; no one says they behaved remarkably well. I think they did fairly, no better than the white troops and probably not so well, for they came back two hundred muskets short of the number of men, while the other regiments had a surplus. Tom Stephenson who has the 54th Massachusetts, [colored] in his brigade, spoke well of them but probably he would be slow to say anything in their disfavor. With long and careful discipline I suppose a regiment of negroes might do as well as a poor white regiment, but negro troops disciplined no better than many of our white regiments are would be useless.[77]

The principal use of colored soldiers was for garrison and labor purposes rather than for fighting. Their service in the lowlier capacities, while essential and valuable and while releasing thousands of whites for combat duty, was tedious, onerous and dispiriting. The lot of the Negro troops was made harder by an unbecoming discrimination on the part of the government in matters of equipment, clothing and pay. Not until 1864 did Congress get around to giving colored troops the same pay as whites.[78]

The Negroes, especially those from the North, protested discriminatory treatment, but in general they bore their lot with patience and good humor. Inspection reports and other comments testify to pride in their dress, aptitude and precision in drill, amenability to discipline, eagerness for the learning dispensed in unit schools, interest in religion and less addiction than white comrades to drinking, swearing, gambling and most other evils of camp.[79]

In addition to those who wore the Federal uniform, thousands of Negroes assisted the army in the capacity of personal servants, teamsters, laundresses and laborers. The servants, used for such purposes as foraging, cooking, cleaning and looking after horses, were usually the employees of officers, but occasionally the rank and file, individually or collectively, engaged a colored helper to lighten the drudgery of camp. A Connecticut cavalry sergeant wrote his sister from Virginia: "I have got a Slave boy about 16 years old who ran away from his master and offered to work for me for his rations and a small compensation a month. He takes care of my horse and Equipment and blacks my boots &c." Another Connecticut Yank, recently promoted from the ranks and of strong antislavery leanings, informed his brother: "I have a little nigger to wait on me and am growing quite respectably corpulent in my old age [he was 22]. How much easier it is to have a little nig to take your extra steps for you than it is to do it all yourself." [80]

Some of the blue-uniformed masters were no less harsh in their comments about colored servants than the most captious of slaveowners, but others praised highly their efficiency and devotion. A Massachusetts lieutenant who lost his colored aide and later discovered that he was dead wrote on locating the gravestone: "Poor Jack! if faithfulness has a reward in Heaven, Thou wilt surely find them." [81]

The aggregate of Negro helpers sometimes ran to considerable numbers. Captain John W. De Forest estimated that his regiment, while stationed in Louisiana in the summer of 1862, had fully sixty "contrabands" in its service.[82]

Ordinarily colored servants stayed in the rear during combat, but now and then they would succumb to the martial spirit, seek weapons and blaze away at the Rebels. De Forest stated that at the battle of Baton Rouge "the officers' waiters and other black camp followers picked up the rifles of the wounded and fought gallantly." [83] William Tecumseh Sherman, who in general was opposed to use of Negroes in combat, ordered the organization of plantation workers in Mississippi as "a kind of outlying picket." Concerning one such group, formed under their own leader, he wrote General John B. McPherson, half humorously, in September 1863:

There are about 100 negroes fit for service enrolled under the command of the venerable George Washington, who, mounted on a sprained horse, with his hat plumed with the ostrich feather, his full belly girt with a stout belt, from which hangs a terrible cleaver, and followed by his trusty orderly on foot, makes an army on your flank that ought to give every assurance of safety from that exposed quarter.[84]

Another racial group who wore the blue were the Indians. A brigade of red men was organized early in the war for service in the Indian country. This unit, commonly known as the Indian Home Guard, was composed of the First, Second and Third Indian Regiments. The First Regiment consisted mainly of Creeks, but had a sprinkling of Seminoles and other groups. The Second Regiment was comprised initially of Osages, Quapaws and "other broken fragments of tribes," but these Indians proved to be so unsatisfactory as soldiers that they were replaced by Cherokees, half-breeds and whites. The Third Regiment was a Cherokee organization whose ranks, like that of the Second, were filled largely with men won over from Confederate service. A Fourth and Fifth Indian Regiment were authorized at one time and their recruitment actually initiated, but the War Department reconsidered the action and assigned the recruits to other organizations.[85]

The Indian Brigade left a unique and interesting relic of its Civil War service in the form of muster rolls now preserved in the Oklahoma Historical Society. As one glances down the list of warriors he finds such distinctive names in the Second Indian Regiment as Captain Spring Frog and Private Arch Killer Clay and Bird Jones. In Company A, Third

Indian Regiment are listed Private Stephen Killer, John Bearmeat, Crying Bear, Little Dear, Alex Scarce Water, Spring Water, Wolfe, Poor Wolfe and Mixt Water. The file of Company B of the same regiment includes Big Mush Dirt Eater, Pot Falling, Oo-li-Skun-ee, Rabbit Jack, Soup, Swimmer Jack, Sharp and Warkiller Hogshooter.[86]

The Descriptive Book of Company F, Third Indian Regiment contains a tragic note concerning Sergeant Harrison Benge, a Georgia-born Cherokee listed as a farmer, who had joined the Union Army at Fort Gibson, Indian Territory, on May 1, 1863, at the age of thirty-two:

> Murdered on the 17th day of August, '64 by an assasin during his sleep in his tent. Sergt Benge deserves the praze of Evry true Patriot and good Soldiers for his fadelity honisty & Valor and the Co feels his loss the more that his plase cannot be filled for in F Co. his Equel do not Exist.

Possibly the hand that wrote the above tribute was that of the Indian orderly sergeant, Samuel Beinstick. Or it might have been one of the other red-skinned comrades whose names are listed on the same roll as Tyer Bigfeather, Flying Bird, Arch Bigfoot, Chickiller, Camp Chicken, Wade B. Fish, Edward Duck, George Hogtoter, James Sweetcaller, Himman Sweetkiller, Bone Eater and Do You Ne Se. Or the eulogy might even have been the work of Second Lieutenant Jumper Duck.[87]

Company M of the Fourteenth Kansas Cavalry was composed of Delawares and Shawnees, and various other organizations contained a sprinkling of red men. A Union captain told of receiving a detail of Indians from the Fifth Wisconsin Regiment to help him destroy Confederate stores in Jackson, Mississippi. "No sooner had they comprehended the nature of the work we had to do," he wrote, "than they 'put their war paint on,' and with demoniac yells and all sorts of leapings and wild motions began putting the torch to every house they came to." The fire engines were summoned to put out the flames which the savages had set to dwellings and churches, but the rampaging Indians blocked the firemen's efforts by jabbing their bayonets into the hoses. Finally the captain in desperation called out a company of white soldiers to run down the berserks and send them back to their quarters under guard, while paleface comrades less susceptible to frenzy took over the work of destruction.[88]

The Indian soldiers took part in a number of border engagements, including those at Newtonia, Missouri; Prairie Grove, Arkansas; and Honey Springs and Perryville in the Indian Territory.[89] At Honey Springs, as in some of their lesser battles, the Federal Indians were arrayed against red men bearing the Rebel standard. Indeed, the Honey Springs fight was primarily an Indian affair, though the Northern force included a colored regiment, the First Kansas Cavalry, and the Southern contained some white units from Texas. Official reports indicate that the Indians here, as elsewhere, raised the savage war whoop when the contest grew hot.

Confederate Indians were said to have mutilated the bodies of white foes killed in some engagements and it is probable that the Northern Indians did likewise.[90]

The Indian regiments initially were staffed with white field officers and Indian captains and lieutenants. Except in a few instances, however, the red men proved disappointing in command positions, not for lack of bravery but mainly because they were deficient in stability, administrative capacity and discipline. As a result, the War Department replaced most of the Indian officers with whites. The Third Indian Regiment, last to be organized from among the red men, had white first lieutenants and orderly sergeants specially selected for their character and leadership. This regiment also made the best record of any Indian unit on the Federal side.[91]

The Indians maintained a good reputation as fighters. In his official report of Prairie Grove the commander of the First Indian Regiment stated: "Of the Indian officers, Captain Jon-neh of the Uches, and Capt. Billy Bowlegs of the Seminoles and Captain Tus-te-nup-chup-ko of Company A (Creek), are deserving of the highest praise." He reported two killed and four wounded, but expressed doubt as to the accuracy of those figures since "the Indians entertain a prejudice against speaking of dangerous occurrences in battle and report no wounds but such as the necessities of the case demand." [92]

The conduct of Indians in other engagements also won praise from their officers. But the same cannot be said of their performance in noncombatant aspects of soldiering. Between battles the red men were often slovenly in dress, careless of equipment, neglectful of camp duties and indifferent to prescribed routine, especially that governing furloughs and passes. They also seemed inclined at times to support the side which appeared in strongest force among them. Colonel William A. Phillips, who knew the Indian soldier as well as any Federal officer, said of them in 1863: "The besetting sin of Indians is laziness. They are brave as death, active to fight but lazy." He also observed that absence without leave was a "chronic Indian weakness." General James G. Blunt, another officer with much experience in the command of Indian troops, remarked in August 1863 that the red men "are of little service to the Government compared with other soldiers." He stated further that the Cherokees were "far superior in every respect" to other Indians of his command, but that the Cherokees were effective only so long as they had in view the specific objective of occupying their own country. "I would not exchange one regiment of negro troops for ten regiments of Indians," he concluded.[93]

Indians who wore the blue sometimes received shabby treatment by the government. Reports of inspectors and commanding officers indicate that their arms were often obsolete, their pay frequently in arrears while their families suffered for food, and that in general they were more often dealt with as stepchildren of the Great White Father than as fighting sons supporting the cause of Union and freedom.[94]

Whatever their nationality or race Billy Yanks were distributed by assignment or detail among several branches.[95] The overwhelming majority were infantry, as the Civil War was primarily a musketman's conflict. Union infantrymen comprised the equivalent of 1,696 regiments, while cavalry aggregated 272 regiments and artillery 78.[96]

The nucleus of the Federal forces was the Regular Army which numbered approximately 13,000 in March 1861, and during the war added about 67,000 recruits. Other components of the army at various times were the state militia called to Federal service; conscripts whose net number was about 46,000; substitutes who usually were inducted in the stead of draftees and who aggregated about 118,000; and volunteers who made up the great bulk of the army.[97]

An infantry regiment of volunteers, whose authorized strength in 1863 was 39 officers and 986 men, was divided into ten companies each having 3 officers and 98 men. Each company was divided into two platoons and each platoon into two sections. Above the regimental level was the brigade, composed of four regiments; the division, consisting of three or four brigades; the corps (authorized by Congress on July 17, 1862), made up of two or more divisions; and the army, having one or more corps. Combination of arms began at the brigade level, with the bringing together of infantry and artillery, but on higher echelons other supporting branches were added.[98]

As previously noted the various branches were designated by distinctive trimmings and insignia, and units above the company level by their own standards.[99] In March 1863 corps badges were instituted and thereafter this symbol, worn usually on cap or hat, became a standard feature of the uniform. As a general rule the predominating color of first-division badges in each corps was red; second division, white; and third division, blue.[100]

In the volunteer force each regiment of cavalry was divided into twelve companies or troops and each regiment of artillery into twelve batteries. Organization of Regular Army units was different in that infantry regiments comprised two or more battalions of eight companies each; cavalry regiments had three battalions of two squadrons each, with two companies in a squadron; and artillery regiments consisted of eight or twelve batteries. Furthermore, Regular Army divisions were composed of two brigades.[101]

These were the arrangements specified in War Department orders; but in actual practice variations were common. After a brief period of service units were habitually below strength. Thomas L. Livermore gave as the average regimental strength in the Union Army during various engagements the following: Shiloh, 560; Fair Oaks, 650; Chancellorsville, 530; Gettysburg, 375; Chickamauga, 440; Wilderness, 440; and Sherman's battles of May 1864, 305.[102]

The regiment figured prominently in Billy Yank's loyalties. Regimental pride was especially strong in some of the older organizations which won fame in early engagements and became exceedingly jealous of their reputations. Typical of the fierce loyalty of members of such units was that manifested by Sergeant Matthew Marvin of the First Minnesota who wrote after Fredericksburg: "I would rather be a private in this reg[imen]t than captain in any that I know of"; and Private E. A. Johnson of the First Massachusetts who declared in April 1862: "I had rather be a private in the Mass. 1st regiment than to hold the highest commission in any of the others, and I have heard many say the same." [103]

Regimental consciousness occasionally reached such a high degree as to cause men of different units to pitch into each other with bricks, clubs and fists, but rivalry usually found an outlet in friendly banter.[104] Loyalty to regiment increased with the passing of time and in the latter part of the conflict became so strong that proposals of the War Department to consolidate depleted organizations aroused a howl of protest. "If we lose our name and number," wrote one Yank whose regiment was threatened by consolidation, "our record would soon be forgotten." [105]

Attachment to brigade and division usually was nominal while loyalty to corps was often strong. In some instances corps sensitiveness manifested itself in the exchange of abusive language by members of different organizations and even in free-for-all fighting. A captain of the Fifteenth Corps in Grant's old army wrote in March 1864, after corps' from

BILLY YANK POSES WITH THE BRASS
A Michigan Private and Lieutenant

IN THE DITCHES BEFORE ATLANTA

other commands had been brought in for the Chattanooga and Georgia campaigns: "Our corps dont get along well with these Cumberland and Potomac soldiers. To hear our men talk to them . . . you'd think the feeling between us and the Rebels could be no more bitter. We are well off by ourselves, but still we dont feel at home. We're too far from our old comrades, 13th, 16th, and 17th Corps. This feeling that grows up between regiments, brigades, divisions and corps is very strong and as strange." Soldiers of Burnside's Ninth Corps who served for a time with those of the Twenty-third in the West remarked of the latter that they were "the first to retreat and the last to advance . . . just what you might expect of the 23rd Corps." [106]

Many Yanks manifested outstanding pride in their army, but army consciousness was frequently so closely associated with sectional consciousness that the two were indistinguishable. Cleavage seems to have been primarily geographical, as between East and West, and secondarily organizational, as between the Army of the Potomac—which though heterogeneous in composition was regarded by outsiders as an Eastern group—and armies made up primarily of soldiers from other sections.

Eastern soldiers disparaged their Western comrades as crude, undisciplined and slovenly, while Yanks from Ohio, Michigan or Kansas denounced those of Massachusetts, New York or Pennsylvania as effete, liquor-soaked, money-mad dandies—"bandbox" troops, fit only for parade and garrison. Illustrative of Western attitudes (and the Westerners seem to have been the more outspoken of their prejudices) was that expressed by a Hoosier after attending a band concert by Maine troops at which the collection plate was passed: "D—n these 'Down East,' money-loving, Yankee band-box Provost Guard regiments," he stated. "Dressed out in full rig, with all the extra (brass) touches on, and polished boots, they take possession of the little towns along the line of march, *as fast as we run the rebels out—strut* about like turkey goblers with guns that have never fired a shot at secesh (nor never will)." [107] Even more pointed was the remark made after Antietam by one of Grant's Illinois soldiers: "Nobody in this country seems to care a cuss whether McClellan is removed or not," he disclosed. "General feeling is that the Potomac Army is only good to draw greenbacks and occupy winter quarters." [108]

The favorite theme of recrimination was relative fighting abilities. Soldiers of Western commands were convinced that they bore the brunt of the conflict while the Army of the Potomac was making no more than a halfhearted effort. An Indiana private of Rosecrans' army on hearing of Meade's victory at Gettysburg wrote: "Well it was a great wonder that the Army of the Potomac did not fall back, but it was time that they were doing something, this army . . . goes where it pleases . . . we have fought the most stubborn Battles of this war, but where has our praise gone to? why to the band box army on the Potomac, they needed it to keep up spirits, and we kept ours up by Victorious Battles . . . they have been in but one Confederate state while we have been through five." Repulse of the Eastern army in the Mine Run campaign provoked this soldier to state: "It is a most disgusting fact to again know that the *very grand army of the Potomac* have again been scared back to their old familiar haunts near Washington—the war would never end were it left to the fighting of the band box army in the east. Soon will be seen the Army of the Cumberland advancing upon Richmond from the Southwest leaving their many bloody battle fields, over which they have gained great victories, behind them." [109]

Western Yanks predicted that the assumption of command in the East by Grant, whom they esteemed as one of their own, would work a revolution in the Virginia theater, and when the offensive of 1864 bogged down they were not long in finding a scapegoat. "The final assault on Petersburg was rendered a failure by the gross cowardice of the Potomac Army which has ruined every Gen. before Grant," wrote an Illinois soldier in August 1864. But he confidently predicted that Grant would eventually "win the victory over all disaster" as "his grasp on the Rebel Capitol is like the hand of Fate." [110]

Some of the Westerners who marched triumphantly with Sherman through Georgia and the Carolinas became extremely cocky in their attitude. One of them, a Wisconsin private, went to Richmond and Petersburg just before the famous victory parade in Washington to look over the Rebel defenses that had thwarted the Easterners until the war was almost over. "I expected to see some big breastworks," he wrote, "but was disappointed. I have seen more works around Kennesaw Mountain than there are around both of these places." He concluded that "the Potomac Army has no doubt done some hard fighting, but it has been on a different scale than ours, and the most of it was done in the papers." [111]

When Eastern soldiers were transferred to Chattanooga and other Western points they were subjected to considerable abuse. A favorite form of insult was for the Westerners to greet the newcomers with such phrases as "Bull Run," "fall back on your straw and fresh butter," "advance on Washington," "Burnside crossing the Rappahannock," and "All Quiet on the Potomac." [112]

Such twitting and taunting often led to ill feeling and strife. "The 4th and 14th Corps Cumberland chaps, our men can endure," an Army of the Tennessee officer reported in March 1864, "[but] the 11th and 12th Corps Potomac men and ours never meet without some very hard talk." [113]

A Wisconsin private stationed in Louisiana noted in his diary in September 1863, shortly after some Nineteenth Corps troops from the East came to the Department of the Gulf: "They and the Western boys fight every time we meet. I think either side would rather shoot at each other than the Johnnies." [114]

Westerners had no monopoly on superiority complexes, for many Easterners were strong in the opinion that the "Potomac boys" were the bravest of the brave and that the battles fought in the hinterland were mere skirmishes compared to the bloody engagements of their own baili- wick. If perchance they conceded notable triumphs to the followers of Buell, Rosecrans or Sherman, they were apt to offer in explanation the comment that Western Rebs were far more docile than those led by Lee and Jackson. No less a personage than Grant was cited to support this claim by one Eastern veteran who wrote on June 12, 1864: "This last week Grant publicly acknowledged to our generals that he . . . *never knew what real hard fighting was until he came to the Army of the Potomac.* He says . . . that our Western army never had any *such men* to fight as we have, nor such able generals to contend against as Lee and his Lieuts. Ewell, Hill and Longstreet." This man added the observation that Grant's statement "but corroborates the opinion we have always had, and that was the Western rebels are nothing but an armed mob, and not anything near so hard to whip as Lee's well disciplined sol- diers." [115]

The Easterners were not above indulgence in name-calling and deri- sion. Ninth Corps troops sent to assist Grant's forces in the Mississippi campaign of 1863 chided their associates by asking, "Who had to come away out here to help you take a one-horse town like Vicksburg?" and "Who took Jackson for you?" [116]

It would be incorrect to assume, however, that troops from diverse organizations and areas were always hostile, for such was not the case. In many instances friendliness was predominant from the beginning of mixed associations. Much of the oral cross fire was idle chatter or good-natured banter. Even when relations were genuinely strained initially, tensions usually eased as the units intermingled; and if they became co-partners in battle antipathy frequently gave way to mutual admiration.

Moreover, rivalry and strife were by no means wholly reprehensible, for often they were but the obverse of a healthy pride and a high morale. The same Hoosier soldier who looked down his nose at the "band box army on the Potomac," wrote vauntingly: "I can (should I live to get home) be proud of being a soldier of Uncle Sam's a[nd] belonging to the best Army in the United States (not wishing to flatter any) but where has this Army of the Cumberland ever been defeated in all its travels from Kentucky, through Tennessee, Mississippi, Alabama and one corner of Georgia? Why no place, and that is not all we do not intend to be defeated with 'Rosie' in the lead." [117]

And who can say that this man was not a better soldier for his prejudice and pride?

State consciousness was strong in the Union Army though it was by no means so pronounced among the rank and file as among high-ranking officers. A Pennsylvania private observed in March 1862 that there was "no great love" between Keystone troops and those of certain New England states with whom they had the misfortune to be brigaded.[118] Similarly a Vermont lieutenant wrote in June 1861 that "We [of Vermont] are jealous of our honor and when Mass. cast any imputations upon us or our Col. they will be properly resented." The Massachusetts soldiers, he added, were offended that a Vermont colonel, and not their own, commanded the post, for to the Bay State men "Vermonters are bushwhackers." [119]

Actually there was no discernible difference in the fighting qualities of soldiers from the various sections. Nor were there any marked divergences in other basic characteristics. Eastern units, as already noted, normally had more foreigners than those recruited in the West, but this was due in large measure to the fact of the East having more large cities. A survey of 315,620 conscripts by the Provost Marshal General's Bureau indicated that Western Yanks were taller than those from the East, but the difference was negligible. Contrasts between city and country soldiers were greater than those between Easterners and Westerners. But the impressive diversity that existed among the Union privates was more a matter of individual differences than anything else.[120]

Another strong prejudice that existed in Federal camps, as in those of the Confederacy, was that of volunteers toward regulars. Here, again, the sentiment was not so marked among the men as among their leaders. Occasionally, however, the citizen soldiers would register resentment toward the professionals and the latter would look with contempt on the novitiates in arms. A Nashville newspaper in November 1864 reported a serious altercation in the bawdyhouse district of that city between regulars of the Thirteenth United States Infantry and volunteers of the Ninth Pennsylvania and Fourth Michigan Regiments. The point at issue was the respective fighting abilities of the two groups. The controversy moved swiftly from words to pistols and the regulars took refuge in a whorehouse. The volunteers soon drove their foes from this first line of defense to a second stronghold which also was a bawdyhouse, run by Dutch Lize. In the pitched battle that ensued before the provost guard intervened over a hundred shots were fired and some of the citizens were said to have concluded that "Hood with his whole army" was attacking the town. The fracas may have justified to each group its own martial superiority but outsiders were probably most impressed by the amazingly poor display of marksmanship, for the only casualty was one of the women who had part of her shoe cut away by a bullet.[121]

The volunteers' hostility toward the professionals was blended with admiration. "We're as good as the regulars," or, as some put it, "better," was deemed one of the highest tributes that the volunteers could pay themselves. One civilian soldier who visited a regiment of regulars in 1862 afterward wrote his homefolk: "Oh, father, how splendidly the regulars drill; it is perfectly sickening and disgusting to get back here and see our regiment and officers manoeuver, after seeing those West Pointers and those veterans of eighteen years' service go through guard mounting. . . . I am only glad I saw, for now I know I am a better soldier after seeing them perform." [122]

If this soldier was inspired thus by excellence in drill, how much greater must have been the admiration aroused in him, and in his comrades, by the performance of the regulars in combat! [123]

Some of the volunteers manifested strong bias against the conscripts. "Many of the boys sympathize with those who were drawn 'over the left,'" wrote a Michigander on hearing of the results of the draft in his home community, "and wish them all sorts of joy, such as long marches, heavy knapsacks, etc., saying it would have been much better to have volunteered and so got rid of the name of 'Conscript,' which they seem to dread more than the name of Convict in time of peace." Another Yank whose regiment was about to be replenished with draftees expressed great fear that "the 3d Wisconsin *volunteers* will be the 3d Regt. of *conscripts*," and added, "I pity the conscripts that come into our Regiment, the boys will annoy them to death." [124]

Of course if the conscripts proved themselves worthy men and good soldiers, as they frequently did, they were usually able to overcome prejudice and win full acceptance among their volunteer associates.

In the realm of interbranch relations, the favorite objects of abuse were the cavalrymen and the principal dispensers of invective were the infantrymen. The cavalry, whose status and demeanor in Civil War times bears striking resemblance to airmen of World War II, were themselves responsible for much of the derision heaped on them by the foot soldiers—though undoubtedly some of the ridicule was born of envy. Wearing spurs and fancy hats, dashing about on gaily caparisoned horses, forcing plodding infantrymen off the roads and perhaps showering them with mud, charging in and out of battle while other soldiers stayed on to wrestle with the foe, and afterward swaggering about as if theirs had been the crucial role in the conflict—all of which, and more, cavalrymen did or seemed to do—was not the sort of conduct to win friends in other branches. Few of the infantry considered the fact that cavalrymen were frequently scouting while other troops lay quietly in camp. The thing that stuck in the riflemen's minds was the exaggerated estimate of enemy strength which reconnoitering expeditions occasionally turned in.

A mule-mounted infantryman, who in 1864 was swept onto a Western column by a cavalry force which came rushing rearward with reports of Forrest and 10,000 troops ahead, was much put out by being mistaken for a member of the scorned branch. "I'm no lying cavalryman, boys," he hurriedly explained, "there ain't over 5,000 of them, but their [they're] coming right along." All except the cavalry had a good laugh when the source of panic proved to be a foraging party returning to the Federal lines.[125]

Infantrymen commonly regarded the cavalry as playboys who roamed the country at will leaving to foot soldiers the mud, misery and peril; and they took out their spite on the boot-and-saddle fraternity by whatever means they could. A mounted regiment from New Jersey, noted for the multicolored gaudiness of its irregular uniform, was dubbed the "Butterfly Cavalry" by their walking comrades and, until the garish regalia was exchanged for that prescribed in regulations, members of this unit were greeted with taunts and jeers wherever they went.[126]

Typical of infantry attitudes was that registered by one of Sherman's men while the Army of Tennessee was en route from Mississippi to

Chattanooga in 1863. "We have considerable cavalry with us," he noted in his diary, "but they are the laughing stock of the army and the boys poke all kinds of fun at them." He added: "I really have as yet to see or hear of their doing anything of much credit to them." [127]

It was said to have been a standing joke in Sherman's command late in the war that General John A. Logan had offered a reward for a dead cavalryman, blue or gray.[128]

The infantrymen's disesteem of the mounted branch was not so deep or real as to prevent his yearning to "jine the cavalry." Indeed, the urge proved so strong in some instances that infantry commanders had to take extraordinary measures, such as placing a double guard around the camp, to keep their men away from cavalry recruiting officers.[129]

Relations between infantry and artillery seem to have been consistently cordial, and friendliness seems generally to have existed between the musket-bearing soldiers and members of the other branches. Two exceptions were surgeons and regimental quartermasters whom common soldiers of all arms frequently reviled, but these functionaries were denounced partly for being officers. The attitude of the private toward quartermasters was aptly represented by an unidentified soldier when he wrote in his diary at Baton Rouge, January 27, 1863: "Prayer meeting in Chapel tent. Q. M. gets up and asks the forgiveness of the whole Regt for his misdeeds, professes to be under conviction. Glory Halleluiah!" [130]

Scattered through the army as a whole were a number of distinct types. Perhaps the most despised, and certainly the most maligned, was the deadbeat. Almost every company had a drone who shirked his duties and lived off his comrades. Such a man was a chronic borrower of money, tobacco, equipment and food; refused to carry a canteen, choosing rather to depend on the generosity of his fellows; avoided menial tasks such as gathering wood and pitching tents; dodged guard and fatigue details, or else contrived to throw most of the work on associates. Some were so lazy that they would not rise from their seats to receive what they borrowed, but instead requested the lender to "chuck it" to them. A favorite ruse of the deadbeat was to play sick, and some were capable of feigning the most distressing illness or deformity.[131] A goodly portion of the deadbeats were cowards who, by hook or crook, managed to find a place in the rear when fighting was imminent. But some entered wholeheartedly into combat.

Closely akin to the deadbeat was the blowhard, otherwise known as the puffer. This type of Yank was a leader in gabfests and lost no opportunity for self-glorification. He bragged of his family background, his achievements as a civilian, his prowess as a lover and his numerous triumphs in affairs of honor. In battle he was usually inconspicuous, if present at all, but this did not prevent him afterward from proclaiming himself a hero of the first magnitude. If comrades seemed unimpressed by his exploits, the blowhard sometimes sought a more distant audience, such as the family circle or the hometown editor. A Buckeye braggart, who was published in a Zanesville newspaper as the heroic killer of two Rebs at First Manassas, was shortly afterward called on by comrades bearing shovels who mischievously announced that they had come to bury the dead about whom they had read in the paper.[132]

The blowhards usually did not fade away in the postwar years, but rather waxed bolder in recounting their martial accomplishments. Defined aptly by Senator Benjamin Hill of Georgia as "invincible in peace and invisible in war," some of them rode by way of their fictitious achievements into public office.[133]

Another species encountered occasionally in Federal camps was the rogue. This type varied in character from the genial rake to the vicious scoundrel, and included thieves, cutthroats, pimps, murderers and other offscourings of humanity. Among the better class of rogues was a group who might be called the hell-raisers—mischievous men who would provoke a fight for pure devilment; or hurl derogatory epithets at an officer from some concealed spot and then laugh at his embarrassment; or get down on hands and knees and yelp like dogs when a spit-and-polish colonel ordered a more uniform pitching of pup tents.[134] At the lower end of the scale was the hardened knave who would pilfer the pockets of his comrades, ransack civilian premises, abuse defenseless women and take base advantage of gullible Negroes.

A roster of rascals in blue would include Joe Boner of a Minnesota unit who in 1862, along with a comrade, died in a jail to which they had set fire with a view to effecting their escape. Boner was so frequently in confinement that his associates called him "Guardhouse Joe." After his death a comrade wrote: "Boner was a fideler . . . he was about 30 years of age a very small man he was allways drunk when he could get a chance." [135]

Of similar ilk was an unnamed member of a New York regiment who in 1861 was bayoneted to death by camp guards whose restraining order he refused to heed. Concerning this soldier a comrade remarked: "[He] was the worst man I ever saw. He was always drunk, fighting and threatening the lives of the soldiers, he has been in the guard house times without number." [136]

Occasionally rogues revealed themselves as such in their correspondence. A Vermont scamp, who was well along in years and a snuff addict, boasted of feasting on chicken, cakes, pies and other delicacies stolen from the wagons of peddlers who thronged the camps. "We don't pay out any money for our liveing," he stated, "and we live better than uncle sam can a ford and it tase better than hard tacks salt beef and pork." [137]

Early in his service this man secured a detail as surgeon's assistant and then as a hospital worker. Though he was said to be healthy and tough, he does not appear to have done any fighting. He was quite active, however, in money-making projects of various sorts, including laundering the apparel of his associates at five cents a garment and selling at a handsome profit various articles of food and clothing sent at his request by the homefolk.[138] He even did a bit of bootlegging, as the following instructions which he sent from Virginia in 1864 to his son indicate:

I want yo to Send me 10 Galones of hye wines or Elcoll [alcohol] I want it to sell i can git fore dollars a pint for it yo can put it in tin canes [cans] And pack it in Saw dust have the canes made so you can cork them tight And put them in A good Stout Box fille the canes full so it wont ratle now Send it as Sun as yo git this leter And Send . . . me the coss of it canes And all . . . And when yo Send it Send me A letter the Same time. . . . bee cufule And pack it so it wont wratle for they are gitin very strick . . . if I can git it heare it will bring me good too hundred dolars the minet I git it if yo cant git hy wines git what yo can eny thing that is licker when yo Send it Direct it to Docter Sawin Just as yo have the rest.[139]

The box arrived in due time, but whether it contained "hy wines" or some other kind of "licker" is not known; nor is the recipient's profit from it a matter of record. But available correspondence indicates that this private's side earnings from various enterprises aggregated about fifty dollars a month. Indeed, financial gain seems to have been the principal concern of his military service. A comrade wrote the homefolk on one occasion that the old soldier was "making money like dirt" and an adult son who received this report, fearful that his father might become so enthralled by his profits as to prolong his army connection, wrote: "You said something about Enlisting over again. Dont for God's sake even menchion anything of that kind again. Money is entresing I know but it is better to Di poor than to fasten yourself for any longer time than what you are Fastened for." The parent evidently followed his son's advice about re-enlistment, but near the end of his original stint of service he fell from a hospital boat and drowned.[140]

Another type whose presence in the Union ranks was deplored by the overwhelming majority of Yanks was the sot. This species would drink any sort of intoxicant, however vile, and would stay tight (the word was current in Union camps) as long as liquor could be had by begging, buying or stealing. A New York soldier, whose attachment to drink won for him the nickname Whisky Bill, amazed his comrades by his never-failing ability to elude the camp guards, slip into near-by towns and get roaring drunk. Sots were usually worthless as soldiers and their departure from the service, whether by desertion, death or dishonorable discharge, caused little if any heartache among their associates. The low esteem in which they were held by conscientious comrades was pungently, if not delicately, illustrated by the comment of an Ohioan concerning some sots in his organization: "tom is the ornryist shit in the regamment. . . . tom and Pet drinks every think [thing] in the shape of Whiskey tom is perfectly orny." [141]

Still another type was the chronic forager, the soldier who spent a major portion of his time and energy supplementing the rations issued by the commissary. A good example of the archforager was Private Walter Kittredge of the Twenty-fourth Wisconsin Regiment. Kittredge rarely passed a day in which he did not enrich army fare by trading, begging or stealing—though for stealing he substituted the euphemisms "raising," "gobbling" and "drawing over the left"—edibles not obtainable from regular sources. So great was his resourcefulness, boldness and persistence that he was able to live sumptuously when comrades were bedeviled by the gnawings of hunger.[142]

Kittredge was as brave in combat as he was adept in foraging. He remained gallantly at his post at Stone's River while scores around him took to their heels, was seriously wounded and after a period in the hospital returned to civilian life a battle-scarred hero.[143]

The forager sometimes used the same techniques as the bummer, but the latter was a far more noxious type. The bummer was a scoundrel whose main interest was pillage and who had little concern for the war's basic objectives. His favorite arena was the periphery of the army where restraint was weakest and plunder richest. He greatly preferred raids on civilian Rebels to pitched battles against those bearing arms. As a group, bummers merit a place with the rogues whose character has already been delineated.[144]

One of the most distinctive types was the mournful one. This character saturated himself in gloom, wore a dejected mien and took a pessimistic view of the future. He never laughed, rarely smiled and seemed to be pained by the joviality of others. He liked to dwell on such themes as sickness, death and the depravity of man. His enjoyment, if any, derived from contemplation of woe—past, present and future.

The mournful one wrote gloomy letters home in which he spelled out the hardships of army life, expressed grave concern over the plight of his family and made dire predictions as to his own fate. One Yank of this species sprinkled missives to his wife with such doleful statements as these:

> I have Cum to the Conclusion that you hav fergot me intierly. . . .
> I want to get hom to see you all so bad I dont no what to do. . . . We live darnd hard.
>
> I am so fraid that our Dear little babes will get the flux I dont know what to do Mary you must Bee very Carful of them it seemes like all the old people is diing off their in ohio but that is the Way of the World the old must die and the young may die.[145]

The wife's letters in reply were not of the sort to alleviate melancholy. On one occasion she wrote: "i am very sorry to hear that you are a marching for i am a fraid that you are going in to a battel this is a world of troubel." [146]

Another prophet of gloom addressed these doleful sentiments to his spouse:

> Dear Sallie this is a hard place there is no pleasure here all is trouble and vexation this place lacks agreat deal of being at home with you and Willie. . . . god only knows when this war will be over or who will be the survivors of this war. I may have seen my home on earth with its many charms and its numerous friends the last time but dear sallie there is a home fare in the skies for you and I.[147]

This Yank was of religious bent and the same was true of some other doleful fellows. To this group, religion, instead of being a source of joy and hope, was essentially a spring of sorrow and of woe.

Some of the mournful ones were pathological cases whose chronic dejection was beyond control. No doubt some of the 278 recorded instances of suicide among wearers of the blue were of men sorely afflicted with depressive mental ailments.[148]

Closely related to the mournful one was the recluse—indeed the two were sometimes identical. Of recluses a Yank wrote after the war:

These men were irreproachable as soldiers . . . but they seemed shut up within an impenetrable shell, and would lie on their blankets silent while all others joined in the social round; or perhaps would get up and go out of the tent as if its lively social atmosphere was uncongenial. . . . Should you address them they would answer pleasantly but in monosyllables. . . . They could not be drawn out. They would cook by themselves, eat by themselves, camp by themselves . . . in fact keep by themselves at all times as much as possible.[149]

Sometimes the recluse was a snob. New England, and especially the intellectual circles of Boston, appears to have sent more soldiers of this type than other sections. A son of the Bay State wrote from Virginia early in 1863: "This company . . . is a sad place for a cultivated gentleman, no fit associates for a collegian & a poor company for me." A Yank who entered the service from Yale expressed similar sentiments, writing his mother while on detached duty: "I managed to get away from the Company [and come] . . . here in the woods where there would be less stealing whiskey, less swearing & less of Southwick's perpetual growl," (Southwick being his regular sergeant nicknamed "old rum blossom" from the redness of his nose).[150]

Now and then a dandy was to be found among the rank and file. John D. Billings, who served as an artilleryman in the Army of the Potomac and whose *Hard Tack and Coffee* is among the most delightful of published memoirs on the Union side, referred to this type as the "paper-collar young man" and pictured him as wearing "enamelled long-legged boots and custom made clothes," looking with disdain on regulation apparel and eating "in a most gingerly way of the stern, unpoetical government rations." He further described the dandy as an only son who had been "a dry-goods clerk in the city at home, where no reasonable want went ungratified." [151]

Another type was the maladroit one, known also as the Jonah. The Jonah was a constitutional blunderer, utterly devoid of the rhythm and co-ordination that are the essence of drill. He spilled his coffee down the necks of his comrades, kicked their shins on the march and prodded them with his bayonet while executing the manual of arms.[152] Concerning one of this type, who bore the nickname of "Molasses," Charles E. Davis of the Thirteenth Massachusetts Regiment wrote:

He was homely in appearance, unshapely in form, awkward in gait and as ignorant and dirty a slouch as could be found. His gait was like that of a man who, having spent his life in a ploughed field, could not divest his mind of the idea that he was still stepping over furrows. . . . He was generally absent when his services were needed. . . . Just before we went into the battle of Manassas . . . he stopped to tie his shoe and never returned to the regiment again. . . . We were glad he never came back.[153]

Held in even more contempt than the Jonah was the mamma's boy, the helpless one, who never quite cut the home ties and who had to be wet-nursed by his comrades. Of such a soldier, Private Alonzo Miller of the Twelfth Wisconsin Regiment wrote:

I . . . would have written more but I have had to take care of Jap. He is quite a baby. He does not know how to get along. . . . I cook for Jap and myself for he does not know how to do the very least thing. . . . He eats like sixty and does not have courage to stir to exercise it off. . . . He does not take care of himself as he ought. When he left me [to go to the hospital] he was lousy.[154]

In happy contrast to the long-faced kind was the bouncing optimist, or the I-love-life species. This type greeted reveille with a resounding whoop, mirthfully ogled sleep-heavy comrades, devoured the rough breakfast as if the fare were savory, tackled camp police details with a song, performed drill in the manner of one playing a pleasant game and repeated the colorless routine day after day without a show of boredom. During a hard march this type of Yank kept up a flow of quips and chatter and around the campfire at night was full of good humor. In any kind of gathering he was the life of the party. Even in sickness and suffering he was hard to down, the theme of his existence in darkness and in light being that of the popular camp song, "Gay and Happy Still." [155]

A blood relationship of the I-love-life type was the chronic prankster whose antics ranged all the way from laying dead snakes in soldier bunks to faking honeyed missives to love-smitten comrades. One Yank who was a victim of the latter trick wrote to the lady whose script had been forged:

Such people are low-minded and mean . . . they know you & know that I correspond with you and were impudent enough to write a letter while we were at Camp Morton imitating your hand writing & signing your name to it and directing it to me. . . . I feel thankful that all they can do or say cannot seperate me from my own sweet Maggie.[156]

The Union Army also had some soldiers of fortune. Yanks of this type were usually restless characters who had roamed the world and had many exciting experiences. Most of them delighted in regaling comrades with tales of their adventures, but some were extremely reticent. Of one of these nomads who served as a corporal in the Sixth New York Cavalry a comrade wrote:

His open countenance has something of the dash and "rough-&-ready" in it which you might expect to find in the runaway boy of sixteen, the whaler for three years (during which time he twice deserted), the merchantman, the backwoodsman, the cattle dealer, the speculator, the pedlar, the grocerman, the horse jockey, the butcher & the tinker. In each of these characters he has figured besides several others that might be mentioned. He has been in the Sandwich Islands & to the North Pole, in the South Seas & on the Spanish Main. He has picked up a good deal of information & can talk sensibly on most subjects.[157]

A character not so easily defined as some of the others, but none the less distinctive, was the sensitive type—the artist-in-arms; the man whose nature was attuned to beauty and light rather than sordidness and shadow, and whose inclination and genius were for creation rather than destruction. Few of these sensitive souls had ever fired a gun before joining the army. Some of them found soldiering intolerable while others— though sometimes at considerable pain—made the adjustment to warrior life with remarkable facility.

An excellent example of the latter group was George F. Newhall of the Eleventh Massachusetts Regiment who, with four brothers, enlisted early in the conflict and served in the Army of the Potomac. George came from a cultured home, had a good education, was of gentle disposition and refined tastes, manifested a profound interest in the world of nature and worked hard at soldiering. "I came out to see the country as well as to fight," he wrote his parents from Virginia in March 1862, "which I think can be done and still be a good soldier." [158]

At every opportunity Newhall roamed the lush Virginia countryside studying the flora and fauna, listening to the songs of birds and making sketches of leaves and blossoms. While his brothers passed on to the homefolk details of marches and battles, he preferred to describe the progress of the dogwood and the coloring of the azalea.

From a picket post near Yorktown in April 1862 Newhall wrote his father:

Perhaps Edd will keep you posted on war news while I branch off on other matters. The tree in blossom of which I wrote is the Mezeron and has been mistaken by a newspaper correspondent for the peach. . . . I find also the azalea with pink flowers, garlic in abundance. As we march along a bulbous rooted plant with deep blue flowers, bell shaped, attracts attention. Narcissus is found growing in the woods and candytuff with a prettier flower than the cultivated. . . . The trees are just beginning to leave out.[159]

He found it difficult, even as the rattle of musketry ahead urged the column onward, to keep from turning aside to explore the wonders of nature, as the following excerpts from letters written during the Peninsula campaign attest:

May 20, 1862 . . . We find the Callicanthey growing in the woods about Williamsburg, also lupins and azaleas and many other flowers I noticed while filing through the woods during the battle at that place.

June 21, 1862 . . . If you have seen the *red bud* or *Judas Tree* in bloom you can imagine the rare sight it was to see the forest full of them, even the trunks of some of them were clothed in bloom. Have fell into line of battle twice since I began to write this.[160]

By the cruel caprice of Mars, this devotee of beauty who fought gallantly through the Seven Days (but whose report of that campaign told not of hardship and slaughter, but rather of hills ripe with wheat, "bigonias all in bloom—fields full of passion flowers, some very handsome vetches or wild peas and other flowers") was listed among the missing at Second Manassas and apparently was not heard of again. His brother James informed the homefolk two months later: "I have talked with the boys of his company. The last seen of him he was rushing ahead." [161]

Perhaps he had his eye on a flower as he dashed forward in the charge. The place where he was last seen was heavily wooded. If he perished there, he must have died happy, for the forest was the joy of his life.

The roll of soldier types would not be complete without inclusion of one who may be aptly termed as ever faithful. Yanks of this species, except for sickness or some other disability, never missed a formation or battle; endured hardship without murmur; and, when fate required, uncomplainingly laid down their lives for country and cause.

To this exemplary group belonged Private Day Elmore, a country lad from near Aurora, Illinois. Elmore, after much persuading of his parents who objected on the score of his youth, enlisted in Company H, Thirty-sixth Illinois Infantry, in August 1861 when he was seventeen. He was mustered in as a drummer, but at the battle of Pea Ridge discarded his drum, took up the musket and henceforth was a full-fledged fighting man. He distinguished himself at Perryville and Murfreesboro and in November 1862 was promoted corporal. During the hard times of Buell's Kentucky campaign he wrote his homefolk: "If our Regt was Discharged tomorrow [and] . . . if this war was not at an End I would Enlist again." He added that the newspapers contained rumors of peace, but that he was opposed to compromise with the Rebels because "tha comenced it, and if they have not Enough we can give it to them to thare hearts content." [162]

At Chickamauga he was wounded in the chest, fell into Rebel hands and was sent to Belle Isle prison in Richmond. After a few months he was paroled and exchanged, but even before the exchange became official he joined his regiment and resumed his military duties. Long before his three-year term of enlistment expired he re-enlisted as a "Veteran Volunteer." Shortly after signing up as a veteran, Elmore wrote his father in explanation of his action: "I can not Express my self so I will only say that my whole soul is wrapt up in this our countrys caus I ought to be at school but I feel that I am only doeing my Duty to my self and you, Pa." [163]

On May 1, 1864, the young patriot was promoted sergeant, and in the ordeals of fire that marked the Georgia campaign he conducted himself with the same fidelity and gallantry that he had displayed throughout his prior career in arms. After the fall of Atlanta he went to Tennessee with General Thomas, the "Rock of Chickamauga," and at Franklin he received a wound which led shortly to his death. A local woman who found him in a hospital after the fight and took him to her home near by, holding him bleeding in her arms to protect him from the jolts of the buggy, wrote his parents a few days after his death: "His wound bled profusely but he thought all the time he would get well. . . . He suffered a great deal but did not complain, he was perfectly conscious to the last." [164]

So, calmly, without fear and without complaint, died this noble Yank, three months before his twenty-first birthday. Behind him lay more than three years of soldiering for the Union. Few of those who wore the blue endured more of suffering and peril than Day Elmore and probably none was purer in character, loftier in patriotism or more faithful in service. Throughout his army career he gloried in hardship and in his ability to endure it. After his fate was determined the captain of his company who had known him intimately since the time the regiment was formed wrote the bereaved parents: "Among all the brave men that I have seen march to battle I have never seen a braver, cooler man than my loved comrade Day Elmore." [165]

Not all who wore the blue were men. In addition to those employed as nurses, stewardesses and laundresses, or informally attached as vivandières, a large but indeterminable number of women actually served as soldiers. A few—such as "Major" Pauline Cushman, the famous spy of Rosecrans' command, Mary E. Walker and Sarah E. Clapp who served as assistant surgeons, and a Mrs. Reynolds who held a commission of major from the Governor of Illinois—gained official recognition without concealing their sex;[166] and Ella Hobart Gibson, while denied War Department approval as such, was elected chaplain of the First Wisconsin Regiment of Heavy Artillery in 1864 and for nine months actually performed the duties of that position.[167]

But since army policy of the period restricted membership in the military fraternity to males, the overwhelming majority of women who wore the Federal uniform had to pass muster as men. Some of the gentler sex who disguised themselves and swapped brooms for muskets were able to sustain the deception for amazingly long periods of time.

One of the most celebrated of the female Yanks was Sarah Seelye of Michigan who enlisted as Franklin Thompson in Company F of the Second Michigan Infantry in May 1861 at the age of twenty. Apparently she had little difficulty passing as a man. For nearly two years she performed the full duties of a soldier, including participation in the First Battle of Manassas and the Seven Days' campaign. Stricken with malaria while serving in Kentucky early in 1863, and being unwilling to go to the hospital, Sarah applied for a furlough. When this request was denied, she revealed her sex and became a nurse, to serve in that capacity until the end of the war. After the conflict Congress granted her a pension.[168]

Even more sensational was the career in arms of a woman who was listed in War Department records as Albert Cashier, but whose real name was Hodgers. She was born in Ireland but came to the United States as a child and settled in the Midwest where she worked as a farmer and shepherd, often wearing male attire and apparently posing on occasion as a boy. In August 1862, when nineteen, she enlisted as a private in Company G, Ninety-fifth Illinois Regiment. She served a three-year term of enlistment during which time she was regarded as unusually quiet and reclusive, but withal a good soldier. She was in the Vicksburg campaign, the Gunntown fight, the Meridian raid, the Red River expedition and the battle of Nashville. She was mustered out of the service in August 1865 and continued her masculine disguise in civilian life. In 1899 she applied for a pension and none of the three surgeons who examined her in connection with the filing of the claim indicated any suspicion of her not being a man, though one of them listed in his report some minor ailments which suggested an intimate examination.[169]

Not until about 1911, when an automobile accident compelled her hospitalization, was it revealed that Albert Cashier was a woman. After her sex was made public former comrades visited her; recognition was mutual, though the visitors were unanimous in stating that they had not suspected her femininity until they read newspaper accounts revealing her closely kept secret. One of the comrades, Harry G. Weaver, when called on by the Bureau of Pensions in 1914 for an affidavit stated:

When we were examined [at induction] we were not stripped. We were examined on the same day. All that we showed was our hands and feet. I never did see Cashier go to toilet nor did I ever see any part of his person exposed by which I could determine the sex. He was of very retiring disposition and did not take part in any of the games. He would sit around and watch, but would not take part. He had very small hands and feet. He was the smallest man in the company.

Another comrade deposed: "Cashier was very quiet in her manner and she was not easy to get acquainted with." [170]

Most of the other women known to have served as soldiers were less successful in concealing their sex than Privates Seelye and Cashier. Usually the fact of their being women was detected early and they were sent home, though in some cases not without emphatic protest.

Probably the majority of women who entered the ranks in male disguise were respectable characters, motivated by patriotism or the desire to be near husbands or sweethearts. But a few were persons of easy virtue who enrolled as soldiers to further their lewd enterprises.[171] The Memphis *Bulletin* of December 19, 1862, reported: "A woman formerly extensively known in this city as 'Canadian Lou,' was arrested in this city last night dressed in men's clothes. She was put in for inebriety. She was with a Missouri regiment in its recent march from this city to Holly Springs and back." [172]

Vivandières and other feminine camp followers sometimes became so imbued with martial ardor during battle that they joined in the fighting. Thomas L. Livermore told of a laundress attached to the Irish brigade who advanced with the unit at Antietam and in true Erin fashion stood with it in the fight, "swung her bonnet around and cheered on the men." [173]

Some of the Union amazons were casualties; at least one was fatally wounded, while another was killed outright.[174]

The attitude of male Yanks toward comrades disclosed as women was usually one of amused tolerance. A typical comment was that of a Hoosier cavalryman who wrote his wife in February 1863:

We discovered last week a soldier who turned out to be a girl. She had already been in service for 21 months and was twice wounded. Maybe she would have remained undiscovered for a long time if she hadn't fainted. She was given a warm bath which gave the secret away.[175]

Freaks and distinct types, however interesting, comprised only a minority of the rank and file. The overwhelming majority of Yanks were blended into a great mass of ordinary soldiers. But Billy Yanks en masse had some well-defined traits. In the first place they were ebullient. An Illinois officer observed of his own corps that "on the march they make it a point to abuse every man or thing they see. They always feel 'bully,' will certainly march further with less straggling and make more noise whooping than any other corps in the service." [176]

The soldier historian of an Indiana unit stated:

Our regiment yelled at everything they saw or heard. When another regiment passed, they yelled at them; they scared the darkies almost to death. . . . as they tumbled out to roll-call in the morning, they yelled . . . ; after a hard day's scouting they were never too tired to hail the end of their tasks with a joyous yell. . . . A yell would start in at one end of the division, and regiment after regiment and brigade after brigade would take it up and carry it along, then send it back to the other end; few knowing what it was about, or caring less.[177]

The appearance of a stray mule or dog along the route of march was certain to elicit a chorus of whoops that would put the poor animal to panicky flight; and discovery of a rabbit in camp would produce a pandemonium comparable to that of a surprise attack by the enemy.

Animals were not the only victims of soldier ebullience. If civilians came among the men in blue wearing strange apparel, asking foolish questions or otherwise appearing naïve or peculiar, they were sure to be swamped with a tidal wave of irreverent and impudent comment. When some Yank near the head of a marching column recognized a friend along the way and addressed him with a "How are you Jake?" the greeting would sometimes go all the way down the line, gaining volume as it went along.[178] Even officers were not immune to irreverent jibes.[179]

Billy Yank's high spirits sprang largely from his kindred trait of giving a comical twist to almost every aspect of soldier life. A company commander stated that "anything short of death is a capital joke," and a Pennsylvania private wrote: "*We laugh* at everything here. You wouldn't believe that anyone could make light of some of the scenes of which we are the witnesses. The roughest jokes I ever heard in my life were perpetrated under a heavy fire." This fun-loving quality manifested itself in many ways. Some found merriment in placarding their tents with such rakish inscriptions as "Pups for Sale," "Rat Terriers," "Bull Pups Here," "Doghole No. 1" and "Sons of Bitches Within." Others indulged their humor by applying grotesque nicknames to comrades. A ruddy-faced youth of a New England regiment was dubbed "Blossom," while a giant who marched by his side was called "Baby." In an Indiana company one soldier was known as "Billy Cat," and others as "Wolf," "Big Jig" and "Little Jig." A favorite sobriquet in many units was "Possum." [180]

Clannishness was a third trait common to most Yanks. Soon after donning the uniform soldiers of congenial character and habits gravitated to informal groups which usually became messes. These little families changed in composition with the caprices of fate and the fortunes of war, but rarely did they lose their close-knit quality. If a freak happened to be admitted to the sanctum through an error of judgment, he was usually frozen out in relatively short order. As already noted, a feeling of kinship also existed in company, regiment and larger units, but in no formal organization was loyalty as fierce as in the mess-size group of a man and his pals.

Those who wore the army uniform sometimes manifested a community consciousness as against those who did not. On visits to cities soldiers frequently helped shield spreeing comrades from the tentacles of the law, even when deploring their unseemly conduct. And Yanks were quick to gang up on any civilian who by word or deed appeared hostile to wearers of the blue.

Billy Yanks were also domestic creatures. Given even a slight prospect of an extended sojourn in a locality they would build huts, improvise furniture, decorate the walls with pictures, fashion shelves or pegs for their trappings and add to their surroundings sundry other touches of home. The Union soldiers were great fixer-uppers. Sketches of their premises show elaborately ornamented campsites and numerous improvisations for making their dwellings more attractive and comfortable. Decorative practices in some cases extended to affixing pin-up girls to the walls, but some of these, appareled after the fashion of *Godey's*, were in marked contrast to the scantily attired models favored by soldiers of later generations.[181]

Another trait manifested by Yanks en masse was wastefulness. This quality sprang in large measure from poor discipline. It was also attributable in part to American concepts of abundance, particularly as concerned the government's resources. Whatever the basis of the phenomenon, there can be no doubt that the average soldier was notoriously profligate of food, clothing, arms and other equipment issued by Uncle Sam. Lieutenant Samuel Fiske wrote after Antietam that "whole regiments threw away their overcoats and blankets and every thing that encumbered them." He added: "Just as it is said that out of the waste of an American kitchen, a French family would live comfortably, so it might almost be said, that out of the waste of an American war a European war might be carried on." [182]

Limitations of space preclude more than a brief mention of various special groups. Among these were the sharpshooters, two regiments of whom were formed among Regular Army units. The first was commanded by the famous Colonel Hiram Berdan, and numbered among its privates the fabulous character known as "California Joe." The sharpshooters were picked for their ruggedness and marksmanship and were armed with the best of rifles. They were used principally as skirmishers, but they proved very effective also in picking off Rebel artillerymen. They figured conspicuously in the Gettysburg, Mine Run and Wilderness campaigns.[183]

Another elite organization was the Pioneer Corps which served in the Army of the Cumberland. In the battle of Stone's River this unit, numbering 1,700 men detailed from infantry regiments and commanded by Captain James St. Clair Morton, Rosecrans' chief engineer, performed services comparable to that of combat engineers in World War II. In his report of Stone's River, Rosecrans paid high tribute to the Pioneer Corps, stating that "the efficiency and *esprit du corps* suddenly developed in this command, its gallant behavior in action, and the eminent services it is continually rendering the army entitle both officers and men to special public notice and thanks." [184]

"Mounted infantry" comprised another special type of troops. Soldiers of this category, as the name suggests, were doughboys on horses, though they enjoyed the luxury of riding for only a part of their service. The most famous troops of this class were those of Wilder's "Lightning Brigade" who, as already noted, were armed with repeating rifles and employed to excellent advantage in the battles about Chattanooga.[185]

Incapacitation of numerous soldiers for active service by disease, debility and wounds caused the setting up in April 1863 of the Invalid Corps. Members of this organization, the "limited service" personnel of the Civil War, were used for less strenuous duties in garrisons, prisons and hospitals, mainly as clerks, police, nurses, orderlies and cooks. In December 1863 the Invalid Corps numbered over 20,000 officers and men, organized as infantry into more than 200 companies.[186]

It naturally became a refuge for some able-bodied shirks, a circumstance which, along with its unfortunate name, made the organization the butt of many jibes. A song entitled "The Invalid Corps" which poked fun at the group was sung by a comic vocalist of the period and published as a broadside.[187]

In March 1864 the name of the organization was changed to the Veteran's Reserve Corps. Whatever others may have thought of them, the invalid veterans were rated high by the Secretary of War who credited them with a substantial contribution to the Union cause.[188]

A group who had no separate organization, but who enjoyed high standing among soldiers, were the Veteran Volunteers. These were the seasoned Yanks who in accordance with orders promulgated in June 1863 volunteered to extend their service for "three years or the war." As an inducement to this advance re-enlistment, the War Department offered veterans bounties of $400 and thirty-day furloughs. Back of this action was a deep concern for the future effectiveness of the army. A check made in the summer of 1863 revealed that the terms of service of more than half of the units then in the field would expire before the end of 1864. The prospective loss of all this man power and experience was viewed as a disaster that might prove overwhelming; hence, a determination to avert it.[189]

With the end of the season of active campaigning in 1863 authorities high and low applied tremendous pressure on the veterans to re-enlist. As a result of the combined influences of propaganda, patriotism, bounty and furloughs, an epidemic of re-enlistment passed through the armies during the following winter, with regiment after regiment going through the "veteranizing" process of signing up, returning north amid a fanfare of public receptions, visiting homefolk and then heading south for the all-out campaigns of 1864 and 1865.

The Veteran Volunteers received as distinctive emblems service chevrons of red and blue braid to wear on their left sleeves.[190] Comments in their letters and diaries indicate that the wearers of the veteran's badge took great pride in their status. And their satisfaction was eminently justified, for the 200,000 or more Yanks who were saved to continued service by the re-enlistment program were a tremendous influence in the ultimate triumph of the Northern armies.[191]

Retention of the veterans was especially vital in view of the woeful deterioration in the quality of men recruited from civilian life in the last two years of the war. The combined effects of war-weariness, the desire to profit from boom economic conditions created by the conflict and the notoriously defective system by which the ranks were replenished resulted in the offscourings of the world being dumped into the service in the latter stages of the war.

The miserable character of the substitutes, bounty jumpers and others who were hired to bear arms in the period following Gettysburg and Vicksburg is so well known as to require no elaboration here.[192] But examples may appropriately be cited to show effects in specific units. Charles E. Davis wrote of the replenishment of his own regiment, the Thirteenth Massachusetts in August 1863:

One hundred and eighty-six recruits arrived in camp to-day. Heretofore the men who came to us reflected credit on themselves, the regiment, and the State. This lot consisted of substitutes, bounty-jumpers, and one unfortunate conscript. Most of this number were thieves and roughs who were engaged in the draft riots, and were obliged to leave New York and Boston in self-defence. . . .

Strong men, particularly soldiers, are not easily moved to tears, yet the cheeks of a good many men were wet as they gazed on these ruffians drawn up in line for assignment to companies. The pride which we felt in the membership of the Thirteenth turned to bitterness at sight of these fellows.

As the roll was called we speculated as to which company they might be assigned, though there was little choice. More than half of them were under assumed names, and it frequently happened at subsequent roll-calls that some of them were unable to remember the names under which they enlisted. Among the nationalities represented there were Frenchmen, Italians, Germans, Spaniards, Portuguese, Costa Ricans, Greeks, Maltese, and Canadians; a deserter from the "Louisiana Tigers," one from a Georgia regiment, and one from an Alabama regiment. . . .

In the last batch that were told off there were six whom it was deemed unsafe to keep together, and they were separated by placing them in different companies. Three of the number assigned to Company K disappeared at once. During the first night after their arrival forty deserted.[193]

The story was very much the same in other organizations. In June 1864 the commanding officer of a regiment stationed in South Carolina wrote his wife:

If you could only see the miserable conscripts and substitutes bought up and sent out here to fill our regiments, the dregs of every nation, paupers and thieves, fools and knaves, not one in three who can be trusted on picket for fear they will desert to the enemy. You would not wonder at the indignation of the veterans, who enlisting at the outbreak of the war have fought thus far without bounty or reward, and are ready to fight to the end, if only they can be supported and strengthened. I honestly believe, that some regiments are weaker to-day for the recruits they have received, and though largely increased in numbers they would be of less service in action.[194]

Little wonder that officers charged with delivering recruits to regiments in the field sometimes found it necessary to treat them as prisoners from the time of their induction and to lock them up at every layover point along the way. Fortunately for the units receiving them, a goodly portion of the newcomers deserted within a short time of their arrival in combat areas.[195]

Of course some of the late-comers to the ranks were good men and, as previously stated, a substantial portion of them became creditable soldiers. But in general they fell far short of compensating for the volunteers of earlier periods who were lost to the service, as casualties or otherwise, in 1863 and 1864. The fighting quality of the army as a whole seems to have reached its zenith in the early months of 1863 and to have declined thereafter until the end of the war. The deterioration was less damaging than it might have been had the Confederate Army not undergone a similar experience—and in addition suffered a hopeless dwindling of numbers.

With due allowance for fluctuations in its combat effectiveness the fact remains that the Union Army during the whole of its war career was a good army. The men who wore the blue, whatever their peculiarities and shortcomings, proved themselves effective soldiers. Their faults were in essence those of the mid-century America of which they were a part; so likewise were their virtues.

The balance of weakness and strength was a citizen soldier who reflected credit on the young democracy which he represented and whose performance in battle, by the admission of professionals sent from European armies to observe him, compared favorably with that of soldiers anywhere.

CHAPTER XIII

BILLY YANK AND JOHNNY REB

THE ATTITUDE of the men in blue toward their opponents varied greatly with individuals and circumstances. Some Yanks professed a deep and abiding hatred for their foes. A Pennsylvanian who participated in the seesaw fighting of 1864 in the Shenandoah Valley wrote his wife: "I wish we could Ketch them Some place and Kill every Son of a Bitch [as] the[y] are nothing But Regular Raiders and Thiefs." [1] Three years earlier a New Englander had written from the Northern bank of the Potomac: "all i want to do now is to licke these Sons of B—chs across the river from us that is the height of my Ambition." [2]

But these declarations were mild in comparison to that of another Yank, T. R. Keenan of the Seventeenth Massachusetts Regiment, who wrote shortly after Lee's surrender:

I am sorry the war is ended. Pray do not think me murderous. No; but all the punishment we could inflict on the rebels would not atone for one drop of blood so cruelly spilled. I would exterminate them root and branch. They have often said they preferred it before subjugation, and, with the help of God, I would give it them. I am only saying what thousands say every day. [3]

Keenan was writing with the report of Lincoln's assassination fresh in mind but, even so, there can be no doubt of the genuineness of his hatred and that of many others who wore the blue.

Antipathy toward the Rebels sprang from sundry sources. Among these was the conviction that Southerners were a haughty, hot-tempered, overbearing, bloodthirsty people who in utter disregard of Northern concessions had turned their backs on the benefits of Union and thrust the nation into war.

Soldiers of the South, while not deemed as culpable as stay-at-home politicians in fomenting the rebellion, nevertheless were condemned as representatives of the war-guilty society. Furthermore, they were the obvious instruments of carrying on the war, with all its misery and woe; and

346

as the immediate agents of rebellion, bent on killing or being killed, they were a natural and convenient target for accumulated resentment.

In some instances hatred sprang from a belief that Confederates were semibarbarians who ignored usages of war recognized by civilized nations, tortured prisoners, mutilated the dead and engaged in various other inhuman practices. Atrocity stories began with the earliest skirmishes and were revived with almost every subsequent engagement. A Michigan soldier, in a letter dated June 21, 1861, and published in the Detroit *Free Press*, reported discovery near his tent in the District of Columbia of an infernal machine which in modern parlance would be called a booby trap. This gadget, planted presumably by the Rebels, was described as "consisting of two tin covers fitting together . . . [to resemble a] tobacco box . . . filled with percussion powder . . . [and] covered with iron caps . . . of so explosive a nature that a very slight pressure, as of a person stepping upon it, would cause an explosion . . . very destructive to a company of soldiers." This device, according to the correspondent, gave evidence that "we have to cope with an enemy who are bent upon our destruction by setting such traps and snares as these . . . without endangering their own lives. . . . They have all the craftiness and treachery of the Indian," he added, "with out any of his bravery. It is this which constitutes the boasted chivalry of the South." [4]

Other atrocities charged to Confederates at various times by their opponents included the use of poisoned bullets, the murdering of prisoners, the poisoning of cisterns and wells lying along the route of Federal advance, the maltreatment of the wounded and the desecration of the dead. After the First Battle of Bull Run a Connecticut soldier informed his sister that the "South Carolina Rebels are Barbarians and savages—the[y] yesterday bayoneted our wounded on the Battle field." Another Yank writing of the same engagement passed on as truth the report that the Rebels had set fire to a tent containing Yankee wounded and shot to death those occupants not destroyed by the flames. "Great God!" he added, "who [can] be merciful to such savages." [5]

A Massachusetts soldier reported to his homefolk in May 1862 that five skulls found in abandoned Rebel quarters near Centerville had been neatly polished and inscribed with words "Five Zouaves' Coconuts killed at Bull Run by Southern lead," while a Minnesotan told of rescuing from another Confederate campsite a cranium, supposedly of a Federal soldier, that had been "used by the Rebs for a soap dish." Still another Yank in all seriousness made the startling allegation that Confederates had used the skulls of slain Federals for soup bowls.[6]

Similar accusations were included in official reports of battles and published in the newspapers. A Northern authoress who was in Winchester, Virginia, in May 1862 when Jackson's troops captured that town was quoted by the press as stating that "the rebels . . . have no humanity. They kill our wounded soldiers and even our women nurses are said to be shot." [7]

Most of the atrocity reports were undoubtedly the products of imagination quickened by hysteria but, true or false, they had their influence in fanning the flame of hate already crackling from years of misunderstanding and controversy.

In November 1861 a chaplain of the Army of the Potomac made an address on the cruelty of Confederates to Federal wounded at Ball's Bluff, charging his listeners to remember the brutality when next they met the foe. After the service one of the audience wrote to a friend: "I believe the boys would have fought like the devil if they could have been lead into a fight after that address." [8]

During the Peninsula campaign of the next spring, some New Yorkers, infuriated by reports of Rebel atrocities on their comrades, swore that they would take no prisoners but would "bayonet every damned wounded rebel on the field." Afterward when one of their number was shot by a Confederate picket whose surrender they had demanded, they grabbed the offending sentry and, according to a soldier's report, "put a rope around his neck and hoisted him on a tree, made a target of his suspended body, then cut him down, bayoneted him in a dozen places, then dragged him to the road where they watched till long trains of wagons made a jelly of the remains." [9]

Other instances of a vengeful fury that would grant no quarter might be cited, but they were rare, as was the extreme hatred which inspired them.

While the number of Yanks who regarded the men in gray as little better than barbarians was relatively small, those who looked on their opponents as dirty and ignorant constituted a substantial portion of the Federal forces. Typical of many comments of the Union soldiers about the Rebels was that of a Wisconsin artilleryman who remarked of some Alabamians captured at Vicksburg: "I . . . found some of the greenest speciments of humanity, I think, in the universe, their ignorance being little less than the slave they despise, with as imperfect a dialect. 'They Recooned as how you'uns all would be a heap wus to we'uns all.' " [10]

A Minnesotan characterized the Confederates as "vagabonds," while a Kentucky Unionist was convinced by examining the faces of "thousands" of dead Rebels at Shiloh that a "very large majority" were "ruffians and desperadoes." [11]

Some Yanks professed to dislike the Southerners because of their fighting methods. In addition to attributing to their foes the use of hidden torpedoes and other trick killers, they condemned the Rebs for making sneak attacks in Yankee uniforms, donning cowbells and creeping through the sentry lines at night on hands and knees to reconnoiter Federal positions.[12]

Others denounced the Rebels as lacking in courage, but most of those who registered such sentiments had not been in a major battle. An Ohioan wrote his mother during Bragg's Kentucky invasion of 1862: "We will give the Rebels a dose that they wont like to take iff they wont Run they wont give us a fair fight they will Run every Chance they get . . . they have been Run all over they state." [13] About the same time another Yank boasted: "They won't fight us, they Know we can whip them with Mitens on." [14] The day before the capture of Jackson, Mississippi, a participant in the Vicksburg campaign observed to his wife: "Mary if Jackson is taken I dont think I will evry be in a battel for the rebes wont stand fight at all we have went for them three times but they ran evry time." [15]

Some who conceded a measure of courage to the Rebs in a shooting fight deemed them unable to withstand the near threat of cold steel. During McClellan's campaign for Richmond in June 1862 a New Yorker stated that the Confederates "will fight hard, but they will run at the sight of our bayonet." [16] In similar vein a Massachusetts soldier wrote from Virginia shortly after Chancellorsville: "They have shown they can fight but no better than our men. They cannot stand a charge—almost always break and run." [17]

Another Yank found the Southerners unduly cover-conscious. They "fight well when they can hide," he stated, "but when they have to come out into the open field, they dont come up to the scrach . . . they can stand bullets if they can skulk behind a tree, but when the bayonets come, they run." In this Yank's opinion the "rebles" were "as bad as the red skins of old." [18]

When disparagers of Southern bravery were confronted by a dashing performance which utterly contradicted their generalizations, they usually had a ready answer: The Rebels were crazy drunk on whisky and gunpowder. This claim, which interestingly enough was also used by Rebels to explain Yankee gallantry, was found in many soldier letters. An Ohioan of Sherman's command reported that prisoners taken in the battle of Atlanta "were too drunk to run back to their works," and quoted the Rebels as saying that they "were served with a pint & a half of whiskey before making the attack." A Massachusetts corporal informed his sister after Chancellorsville that he was discouraged from "fighting madmen or not men at all but whiskey & gunpowder put into a human frame." Still another Yank, a Regular who participated in the Georgia campaign, wrote of the battle of Resaca: "The rebs charged on our men 8 Different times but were repulsed every time with a Heavey loss. . . . [Their dead] lay like sheaves of wheat In a field, all very black from the Powter & Whiskey they drank to make them Brave & Bold." [19]

By no means did all those who wore the blue regard their foes with loathing or hatred. One does not have to hate to be effective in combat any more than a hunter has to despise the game he shoots on a sporting expedition. The eager expectancy, the thrill of the closing, the movement and noise and the nearness of danger get the participant's blood up and infuse him with a desire to bag his quarry. Hence, there were many instances where Yanks pitched into their foes in the spirit of adventure with little or no sense of hatred and derived immense exhilaration and even enjoyment from the experience. A young Boston blue blood wrote his father from Virginia in 1862 that skirmishing with the Rebels was very much like "hunting after some kind of animals instead of men. It may seem inhuman," he added, "but I must say that I never enjoyed anything better in my life than I do going on picket and getting a shot at the scamps." Another Yank, whose background was less cultured, put a similar reaction in earthier terms. "Went out a Skouting yesterday," he wrote his father from Western Virginia in September 1861. "We got To one House where there was Five Secessionest And they broke and Run and Arch . . . holoed out to Shoot the ornery Suns of Bitches . . . [and we] all let go . . . at them. . . . Thay may Say what they please but godamit pa It is Fun." [20]

In some instances where hatred was real and deep initially, it abated with the passing of time. Numerous factors contributed to this metamorphosis, but the most influential seems to have been the development after months of hardship of the conviction that the common soldiers of both sides were victims of political machinations. A New Yorker who early in his fighting career breathed the sentiment of "death to traitors," within a year was reporting friendly discussions with Rebel pickets. "We generally end [these sessions]," he stated, "by mutually wishing we had let those who made the quarrel be the very ones to fight. If the question was left to the two contending armies here, we would restore the Union tomorrow and hang both cabinets at our earliest convenience afterwards." [21]

One who reads extensively the literature of the war period, and especially the letters and diaries of soldiers, finds numerous indications of friendly sentiment among opposing participants. If the grim fact of the contestants actually meeting now and then in desperate battle could be overlooked, it might be inferred that good feeling outweighed hostility.

Several reasons may be found for amicable inclinations of Yanks toward Rebs. First was their admiration of the gallantry displayed by the men in gray, for more Yanks praised their opponents for bravery than condemned them for lack of it. An Illinois participant in the Vicksburg campaign who in the early days of his service had been quite contemptuous of his opponents was converted to open admiration of them by their gallantry at Haines's Bluff and Arkansas Post. After the latter engagement he wrote his wife: "The Rebles . . . are a motly looking crew but they fight like Devills . . . they held out [under the heaviest fire of infantry and gunboats] from half past one till half past 4. . . . I hope I did not hit any person [even] if they are Rebles. We shook hands after the fight. I was hungry and they gave me some meat and bread that was good sure." Several weeks later he stated: "We have no feelings of animosity toward a conquered foe; the Brave never has, as shown at the fight at the Post." [22]

At Malvern Hill, Gettysburg and other major battles featured by large-scale Confederate assaults, Yanks looked with respectful awe on the charging gray lines as they surged relentlessly onward against seemingly impenetrable walls of lead and fire. These displays of heroism had deep and lasting effect on the men in blue. In some cases the result was a gnawing doubt of the North's ability to conquer so brave a foe. After Chancellorsville one serious-minded Yank wrote: "The 'gentlemen' that used to [be] spoken of so contemptuously, the 'Southern gentlemen,' the fuming & tearing chivalry, outfight us, *outstand* us, out commonsense us, beat us in every battle. I admire the desperation, the patience too—the stern will of the South." [23]

Another factor leading to friendliness of Yanks toward their foes was the discovery among them of fine qualities of character. Generosity, honor, devotion to their cause, manliness in adversity—these were some of the virtues frequently attributed by the men in blue to opponents encountered during truces or as prisoners of war.

Sympathy also had a part in fomenting friendliness. As the Rebels captured at Port Hudson on July 9, 1863, stacked their arms in surrender one of the captors wrote: "For the first time I felt sorry for the brave fellows. If their cause is not just, they have been true to it and it must be like death itself for a brave fighter to lay his arms down before his enemy." He added: "In a twinkling we were together. The Rebs are mostly large, fine-looking men. They are about as hard up for clothes as we are. . . . They have treated the prisoners [captured during the prior siege] as well as they could, giving them the same sort of food they ate themselves." [24]

Many Yanks, especially after the tide turned against the South, registered sympathy for the deprivation and hardship suffered by the men in gray. "For a month they say they have been on half rations," wrote a Maine cavalryman from near Fredericksburg in 1863. "It does look pitiful to look across the river and see them . . . most of them are dreadful ragged so much so that they suffer a great deal with the cold." [25] Following a skirmish in Georgia in which the opposing force consisted in part of boys and old men, an Illinois captain wrote: "I hope we will never have to shoot at such men again. They knew nothing at all about fighting, and I think their officers knew as little." [26]

Good feeling of Yanks toward Rebs manifested itself in varied forms of fraternization. Whenever opposing forces came in holloing distance of each other confab was apt to become a principal activity. Often the conversation had a bantering tone, as witness the following exchange at Fredericksburg:

Reb: What makes your folks leave us so many good clothes and fine
      blankets?
Yank: We obey the injunction to clothe the naked and feed the
      hungry.[27]

or these dialogues at Vicksburg:

Reb: When is Grant going to march into Vicksburg?
Yank: When you get your last mule and dog eat up.

Yank: Havent you Rebs got a new general—General Starvation?
Reb: Have you Yanks all got nigger wives yet? [28]

or the pungent raillery at Mine Run:

Reb: Why the hell didnt you charge yesterday?
Yank: Go to hell, you Grayback S.O.B's, you're dammed glad we
      didnt.[29]

DISPENSERS OF ARMY JUSTICE
Court-Martial Group, Army of the Cumberland

ON THE ROAD TO RECOVERY

Wounded soldiers in convalescent hospital, Alexandria, Virginia

or the verbal jousts before Atlanta:

Yank: What is Confederate money worth?
Reb: What niggers command your brigade?
Yank: How much do you ask for your slaves?
Reb: Have the niggers improved the Yankee breed any? [30]

More frequently, however, gabfests were in the nature of friendly talk about such matters of common interest as rations, pay, the weather, lice, officers, home and peace.

During such discussions informal truces were observed. If for any reason resumption of firing became necessary, appropriate warnings would be issued and adequate time allowed for all to find cover.

Other forms of fraternization included joint swimming parties; musicals in which men of opposing camps sometimes took turns in rendering favorite selections; and gambling. On the Virginia front in 1863 a Yank and a Reb were competitors for a sheep that ventured between the lines. They finally agreed to compromise by dividing the prize, each taking half the carcass to his own camp.[31]

Sometimes pickets became so cordial that they took turns playing host at meals, and in rare instances Yanks and Rebs accepted invitations to spend the night as guests of their opponents, returning to their own quarters just before daybreak.[32]

On one occasion a Yankee lieutenant, considerately disguised by his hosts as a Southerner, was taken to a Virginia party by a group of Rebs with whom he had made a "hollering" acquaintance on the picket line.[33] The Chattanooga *Gazette* of February 17, 1864, reported a wedding at near-by Walden's Ridge in the following remarkable circumstances:

The party was composed of 1st Rebel and Union citizens; 2nd Rebel and Union soldiers; 3rd Rebel and Union deserters; 4th Rebel and Union spies; 5th Rebel and Union bushwhackers. Scarcely a harsh word was uttered during the whole night; all danced together as if nothing was wrong, and parted mutually the next morning, each party marching off separately.[34]

Strange war! But other incidents were hardly less fantastic. On several occasions soldiers of the two armies intermingled after battle to bury the dead, laying the Confederates in one big grave and the Federals in another close by, with "a chaplain of either army" administering the last rites. In one instance Rebs borrowed shovels from the Yankees to dig graves for their dead.[35]

At Chattanooga Private Ed Smith of a Pennsylvania regiment was disturbed several times one night by a Confederate picket posted near by calling for the corporal of the guard. The next morning when the Rebel officer of the guard came down the line Private Smith saluted him across the intervening creek and after the salute was returned said, "Lieutenant your Corporal on duty last night had a hard time of it. Cant you use your influence to get him to resign?" This bit of impudence produced a hearty laugh from both sides of the line.[36]

Near Fredericksburg during the second winter of the war opposing pickets on one occasion put each other through the manual of arms and then sang and danced together.[37] A few weeks later other Yanks on this front agreed while swimming with Confederates to make a temporary exchange of places. Without informing comrades on either side the Yanks then swam to the Southern bank and the Confederates to the Northern. As soon as they took their positions on the Northern shore, the Confederates, pretending to be Yankees, shouted to Southerners across the river, "How are you, pork and molasses? When are you going to pitch into us again?" After a brief period of such banter, the groups returned to their proper stations.[38]

One of the most common forms of fraternization was the bartering of small articles contributing to the comfort and convenience of soldier life. Innumerable trade sessions began with

> Hello, Yank!
> Hello, Johnny!
> Got any coffee?
> Yes.
> Got any tobacco?
> Yes, come and get it.
> Won't shoot?
> No.

The two soldiers, joined usually by a few others from either camp, would then lay down their guns, meet at a point about halfway between the lines, measure out and swap the coffee—scarce in the South—for tobacco —hard to obtain in the North—and then return to their respective positions.[39]

Another common item of barter was the newspaper. Beyond tobacco and news sheets, Confederates had little to offer in trade, but these were used extensively to obtain from Yanks such articles as canteens (more durable than those obtainable in the South), pocketknives, sugar, sardines, soap and whisky.

Many Yanks and Rebs carried on their trade by remote control. When rivers and lakes separated the lines tiny boats were loaded with commodities, fitted with sails and sent on their way. On reaching their destination the vessels were unloaded, filled with exchange cargoes as agreed on by shouting, signaling or other means of communication, and sent back to the opposite bank. On the Rappahannock early in 1863 some New Jersey soldiers received a shipment "by miniature boat six inches long" to which was attached the following note:

Gents U. S. Army
    We send you some tobacco by our Packet. Send us some coffee in return. Also a deck of cards if you have them, and we will send you more tobacco. Send us any late papers if you have them.
                                        Jas. O. Parker
                                        Co. H. 17th Regt. Miss. Vols.[40]

Dogs were also used to convey articles of trade. Alfred S. Roe who served in a New York artillery unit recalled that near Petersburg during the war's last winter "a certain canine of strictly impartial sentiments" was "taught to respond to a whistle from either side. Thus with a can of coffee suspended from his neck he would amble over to the Johnnies, and when they had replaced coffee with tobacco he would return in obedience to Union signals, intent only on the food reward both sides gave him." [41]

In the informal intermingling of the blue and the gray, whether for confab, trade, picking blackberries or burying the dead, friends of prewar days, and even close relatives separated by conflict, sometimes were brought together for brief periods of pleasant association.[42] Casual acquaintances thus initiated sometimes ripened into friendships when units were habitually opposed to each other. On June 20, 1863, a Norwegian Yank wrote from near Vicksburg:

I can inform you that we can converse with the enemy every evening. The other day when I was in the rifle pits we began to talk to them and asked them what their regiments were. Those we talked to belonged to . . . the 1st and the 3rd Missouri. They were the same regiments which were under Green in Missouri, and which we had fought at Monroe, Shelbina, and Blumelo; so you may be sure we knew them well. They inquired about Major Stone and many others whom they know. One day . . . a part of Co K and some of the enemy came together and stacked arms and talked for a long time. Our men cooked coffee and treated them and [afterward] . . . each one took up his position again and they began to fire at each other again, but not as hard as before.[43]

On the night after this episode nine Rebs deserted to the Yanks. In other instances get-togethers were followed by Yanks changing their allegiance to the Confederacy, though, owing largely to the better situation of the North with respect to food and clothing, desertion of Confederates to their foes was more common than otherwise. A more frequent consequence of fraternization than desertion was a momentary loss of enthusiasm for fighting. After a friendly meeting with opponents near Petersburg in 1865, a Yank noted in his diary: "It did not seem as though we were at war with them." [44] And in the wake of a similar occasion near Kennesaw Mountain in 1864 one of Sherman's young soldiers wrote his parents:

We made a bargain with them that we would not fire on them if they would not fire on us, and they were as good as their word. It seems too bad that we have to fight men that we like. Now these Southern soldiers seem just like our own boys. . . . They talk about . . . their mothers and fathers and their sweethearts just as we do. . . . Both sides did a lot of talking but there was no shooting until I came off duty in the morning.[45]

Officers usually discouraged fraternizing and many flatly forbade it, from considerations of intelligence and morale. Some soldiers likewise opposed friendly intercourse with their enemies, but they represented a decided minority. Among those who refused to "go the whole hog" was Sergeant Day Elmore who wrote from near Atlanta in July 1864: "The Boys have been to gather a number of times . . . traiding coffee for tobacco, but I do not love them so I could not take them by the hand as some of the Boys did." [46]

Friendliness of Yanks toward Rebs also found expression in numerous acts of kindness. Confederate prisoners often received food and water from their captors. Wounded Rebs lying between the lines were sometimes succored at considerable risk by sympathetic wearers of the blue. In field hospitals wounded of the opposing forces, lying sometimes side by side, received the same consideration from attendants and contributed as best they could to one another's comfort.[47] A Union captain who walked over the field after Gettysburg rendering aid to Confederate casualties wrote: "I was glad to do a little something for them. . . . Utterly as I detest a living active rebel, as soon as he becomes wounded and a prisoner, I dont perceive any differences in my feelings toward him and towards one of our wounded heroes." [48]

Sometimes acts of kindness were motivated by common membership in fraternal organizations, such as the Masonic Order. Again they were in reciprocation of good deeds done by the Rebels. In 1863 members of the Third Ohio Regiment en route to Richmond as prisoners of war were treated to a meal of bacon, bread and coffee by soldiers of the Fifty-fourth Virginia Regiment who happened to discover their lack of nourishment. Later the Ohioans were exchanged and sent back to duty near Chattanooga. At the battle of Missionary Ridge soldiers of the Fifty-fourth Virginia Regiment were captured and taken to Kelly's Ferry. Here their presence became known to some of the Third Ohio who rushed to their camp, gathered up all sorts of food and delicacies and gave them to their hungry benefactors of several months before.[49]

Kindly acts and friendly intercourse were, to be sure, not peculiar to the American Civil War. Every major conflict in history has been marked by fraternization of opposing troops. But owing to the fact of their speaking a common language, being of the same nationality and having a similar cultural background Yanks and Rebs fraternized more extensively than most warriors. Even so, the historian must treat the subject with care, since one incident of friendly commingling, because of the human interest and drama that it involved, was apt to receive more notice in the records than days of skirmishing and weeks of passive hostility. It must also be kept in mind that friendly get-togethers, despite concern of officers about the effect on morale, as a general rule had little if any effect on combat effectiveness. Amazing though it was to participants, and remarkable as it is to their descendants, Yanks and Rebs who met between the lines to swap coffee for tobacco, and who lingered to talk sympathetically over common problems, could in the space of a few minutes go after one another with demoniac yells and awful destructiveness. A brothers' war, this incredible war of the 1860s has been called, and instances are recorded of brother shooting brother; it has also been called a polite and a crazy war.[50] But, however incredible, polite or crazy, it *was* a war and the bloodiest one known to the world of that time.

In the light of the records and a calm and studied judgment of them nearly a century after the conflict, how does the common soldier of the Union compare with his opposite in gray? While admittedly numerous exceptions may be found, the following conclusions seem valid as broad generalizations.

First, Billy Yank was more literate than Johnny Reb. The Northern states made more adequate provision for elementary education and hence had fewer citizens who could not read and write. While it is true that the North had a considerably greater admixture of foreign-born among its population, many of the immigrants were literate. The better education of Yanks is plainly evident in their home letters. One who delves deeply into these sources encounters far fewer references to the use of amanuenses among wearers of the blue; and while spelling and grammar of the general run of correspondence on both sides left much to be desired, deficiencies of Southern soldiers were noticeably greater.

Then, one encounters among the Union ranks evidences of a healthier intellectual life. Owing to the North's better educational facilities, the more heterogeneous character of its population, the more varied pattern of its economy, the presence in its borders of more large cities, the greater prosperity of its citizens, the easier access to newspapers, books and periodicals, the greater freedom of thought and discussion and sundry other advantages, the Northern soldier manifested wider interests and greater curiosity about things past and present than his opposite in the Confederate Army. Common soldiers on either side who showed either a deep concern for philosophic aspects of the conflict or a grasp of their significance were rare, but the North appears to have had considerably more than its share of these exceptions.

Billy Yank revealed a far livelier interest in politics than Johnny Reb. On the national level this was due in large measure to the fact that on the one occasion when Rebs had an opportunity to vote for a President, Davis was without opposition, while in the North the campaign of 1864 was a real contest between aggressive candidates, with both parties making strong bids for the soldier vote. But this does not account fully for the difference. Rebs registered little concern for the outcome of Congressional and gubernatorial races, while their opponents often demonstrated an active interest in them.

The common soldier of the North was apparently less religious than his Southern counterpart. Certainly he was less emotional in his worship. Religious effusions appeared less frequently in his letters and he was considerably less susceptible to revivals. The Union Army experienced some evangelistic outbreaks, but they were small-scale phenomena rarely overleaping the boundaries of a brigade and were relatively subdued in character. The Confederate forces, on the other hand, were swept by tremendous revivals, army-wide in scope, in both the third and fourth winters of the war. These outbreaks were featured by enthusiastic praying, singing, shouting and other characteristics of rural protracted meetings.

The question naturally arises: Why this difference in armies of such similar composition and background? Several explanations may be suggested. In the first place, the Southern Army was considerably more rural in composition than the Northern, and American countryfolk historically have been more emotional in their religion than those of urban background. True, the Midwest was predominately rural, but Yanks from that area were frequently intermingled with those from Eastern cities. Then, the Southern forces probably had a heavier admixture of the frontier element than did those of the Union. In the third place, Confederates were more homogeneous than their foes, from standpoints of nativity, language and general culture; and evangelistic sects were stronger among them. A fourth basis of the difference may have been the greater emphasis which political and military leaders of the South placed on religion. Davis proclaimed more days of fasting and prayer than Lincoln did, and Lee and Jackson by example and precept did more to promote religious interest among their soldiers than Grant and Sherman. One does not find among high-ranking Northern leaders a match for Leonidas Polk, the bishop-general who habitually carried a prayer book into battle and who in the space of a few days baptized Generals Joseph E. Johnston and John B. Hood, the former an army commander at the time and the latter shortly to be elevated to that position.

Probably the most cogent factor in Johnny Reb's greater religiousness was the turn in his case of the tide of war from victory toward defeat. It is a noteworthy fact that the large-scale revivals did not occur until after Gettysburg and Vicksburg. Before these great reverses the men in gray had enjoyed a feeling of self-sufficiency. But from the summer of 1863 on, increasing doubt of their own strength caused them to look more and more to a higher power for sustenance and success. The trend among the men in blue was in the opposite direction.

Johnny Reb's greater emotionalism in religon accords with another and more basic difference between soldiers of the two armies; namely, that Billy Yank was of a more practical and prosaic bent of mind. This difference is less tangible than others, but it appears none the less real. The distinction was manifest in his greater concern with the material things of life. Northern soldiers more frequently engaged in side activities to supplement their army wages. Their letters contain far more references to financial matters—lending their earnings at interest, buying land, building up a store for the future—than those written by Confederates. It is true that Yanks had more money to write about, but the fact of better and more regular pay, important though it was, was not of sufficient moment wholly to account for the difference. :

Then, Billy Yank's letters were not so rich in humor and imagination as Johnny Reb's. When he took pen in hand he did not joke or break into poetry so often. He did not have so acute a sense of the ludicrous, the dramatic or the fanciful. His descriptions of battle were not so frequent, so full or so moving. In writing to his sweetheart or wife, he was not so playful, or so gallant, or so ready in the use of small talk; nor was he so prone to use endearing terms. Still another indication of the Northern soldier's more practical bent was his greater concern about rising in the military hierarchy; certainly his letters and diaries are more replete with comment about promotion.

Soldier attitudes as revealed in their letters and diaries leave the impression that Billy Yank was not so deeply concerned with the war as Johnny Reb. Financial considerations seem to have figured more conspicuously in his participation in the conflict, and he appears to have felt less of personal commitment and responsibility. This difference was due in part to the South's being the invaded land and Confederate soldiers thus being cast in the roles of defenders of family and fireside.

Other pertinent considerations were the Confederacy's smaller and more homogeneous population and the nature of its economy, for these circumstances caused the war to make a greater impact on Southerners than on Northerners. To a large extent the war was incidental to Northern life, while to Southerners it was of transcendent importance. Billy Yank was fighting to subdue a revolt against national authority and to free the slaves; Johnny Reb was fighting to establish an independent government, but he also was fighting for a peculiar way of life, for the defense of his home, and, as it often seemed to him, for life itself. Billy Yank could lose the war, go home and hope to resume living very much as before; but Johnny Reb was inclined to view defeat as a prelude to utter ruin.

What about the fighting qualities of the opposing participants? Johnny Rebs seem to have taken more readily to soldiering from their prior mode of life, the presence among them of a recognized leadership caste, and the strength in Southern society of the martial spirit. Moreover, the men who wore the gray fought with more dash, *élan* and enthusiasm, as witness the greater spontaneity and exuberance of their battle cheers. Their penchant for recounting the details of combat in home letters suggests that they derived a greater thrill from fighting. But

Billy Yanks often displayed more of tenacity, stubbornness en masse and machinelike efficiency.

Johnny Reb made a better showing on the battlefield during the first half of the war, but his superiority was attributable in the main to better leadership. There is no reason to believe, however, that he ever possessed more of determination, courage, pride, loyalty to fellows and other basic characteristics that go to make a good soldier. Such differences as existed in combat effectiveness had disappeared by the autumn of 1863, if not sooner, and on the basis of the whole war record it cannot be said that the common soldier of one side was any better or any worse fighter than the one who opposed him. Certainly the Confederates had no braver soldiers than those blue-clad heroes who responded to Grant's order to charge the works at Vicksburg on May 22, 1863, and at Second Cold Harbor on June 3, 1864. On the latter occasion Hancock's famous Second Corps lost over 3,000 men in about twenty minutes of fighting.[51] When informed that they were to make the assault these gallant soldiers, most of them veterans tried and true, calmly wrote their names and home addresses on slips of paper and pinned them to their uniforms so that their bodies might be identified and their homefolk informed promptly of their fate.[52]

In sum, it may be stated that the similarities of Billy Yank and Johnny Reb far outweighed their differences. They were both Americans, by birth or by adoption, and they both had the weaknesses and the virtues of the people of their nation and time. For the most part they were of humble origin, but their conduct in crisis compared favorably with that of more privileged groups and revealed undeveloped resources of strength and character that spelled hope for the country's future.

While it is indeed regrettable that people so similar and basically so well-meaning found it necessary to resort to arms in settling their differences, now that their doing so is a matter of history their descendants can point with justifiable pride to the part played in the struggle by both the Blue and the Gray.

NOTES, BIBLIOGRAPHY, AND INDEX

Chapter I

SOUTHWARD HO!

[1] For able discussions of Northern sentiment in the period preceding the war see Avery O. Craven, *The Coming of the Civil War* (New York, 1942) and Howard C. Perkins, editor, *Northern Editorials on Secession* (2 vols., New York, 1942).

[2] Detroit *Free Press*, April 19, 1861.

[3] Portland, Maine, *Transcript*, April 27, May 18, 1861.

[4] For examples see Detroit *Free Press*, April 15-30, 1861.

[5] *Ibid.*, April 18, 1861.

[6] Portland, Maine, *Transcript*, May 4, 1861; diary of Harvey Reid, April 22, 1861, manuscript, Univ. of Wis.

[7] Portland, Maine, *Transcript*, April 27, 1861.

[8] David P. Jackson, editor, *The Colonel's Diary* (Sharon, Pa., 1922), 39. The Detroit *Free Press* of June 4, 1861, reported: "On every corner squads of urchins armed with wooden guns and swords of tin make their mighty drill. . . . Every boy is the possessor and sole proprietor of a drum and many a home groans under its continued rub-a-dub . . . while many a head is caused to ache at the persevering efforts of sonny with his new fife."

[9] Portland, Maine, *Transcript*, May 25, 1861.

[10] *Ibid.*, April 27, 1861.

[11] Philip D. Jordan and Charles M. Thomas, editors, "Reminiscences of an Ohio Volunteer," *Ohio State Arch. and Historical Quarterly*, XLVIII (1939), 304-308. The Twentieth Ohio was an infantry regiment. Regiments mentioned throughout this study unless otherwise designated are infantry.

[12] Harvey Reid to his homefolk, April 20, 1861, and diary entry of April 24, 1861, manuscripts, Wis. Historical Society; Detroit *Free Press*, April 28, 1861.

[13] Robert S. Fletcher, *History of Oberlin College* (Oberlin, Ohio, 1943), II, 845, 881.

[14] Dewitt Mead to Aaron Mead, July 16, 1861, manuscript, Chicago Historical Society.

[15] H. C. Hawes, *Experiences of a Union Soldier* (Atlanta, Ill., 1928), 2; Col. H. Van Rensselaer, Report of Inspection, Dept. of the Missouri, dated Feb. 10, 1862, AGO Records, 1862, file 14-I, Nat'l Archives.

[16] *Dictionary of American Biography* (New York, 1928-1937), IX, 272. To be cited hereafter as *DAB*.

[17] Edward R. Perkins, "A Soldier's Memory of Abraham Lincoln," manuscript, Minn. Historical Society.

[18] *War of the Rebellion: A Compilation of the Official Records of the Union and Confederate Armies* (Washington, D. C., 1880-1901), series 3, I, 107, 140. To be cited hereafter as *O. R.*

[19] *Ibid.*, 101.

[20] *Ibid.*, II, 298-300.

[21] *Ibid.*, I, 824.

[22] For description of a typical recruiting meeting, see James S. Clark, *Life in the Middle West* (Chicago, 1916), 44-47.

[23] Oscar O. Winther, editor, *With Sherman to the Sea: The Journal of Theodore F. Upson* (Baton Rouge, 1943), 19. To be cited hereafter as *With Sherman to the Sea.*

[24] Capt. T. J. Wright, *History of the Eighth Kentucky Regiment Volunteer Infantry* (St. Joseph, Mo., 1880), 19.

[25] Cyril B. Upham, "Arms and Equipment for the Iowa Troops in the Civil War," *Iowa Journal of History and Politics*, XVI (1918), 35-36.

[26] Selden Connor, "The Boys of 1861," Military Order of the Loyal Legion of the United States, Maine Commandery, *War Papers*, I (Portland, Maine, 1898), 323-343; Fred A. Shannon, *Organization and Administration of the Union Army* (Cleveland, 1928), I, 90 ff.

[27] *O. R.*, series 1, II, 369-370; "The Fourteenth Indiana on Cheat Mountain," *Indiana Magazine of History*, XXIX (1933), 352.

[28] *O. R.*, series 1, III, 97.

[29] *Ibid.*, X, pt. 1, 84.

[30] Elizabeth Ring, "Reveille in Limington, 1861-1865," manuscript in possession of its author, to whom I am indebted for assistance in locating Maine materials; Charles E. Davis, *Three Years in the Army: The Story of the Thirteenth Massachusetts Volunteers* (Boston, 1894), xxviii, to be cited hereafter as *Three Years in the Army;* Shannon, *Organization and Administration of the Union Army*, I, 107 ff; Bell Irvin Wiley, *The Life of Johnny Reb: The Common Soldier of the Confederacy* (Indianapolis, 1943), 311.

[31] Herman C. Newhall to his brother, Aug. 4, 1861, manuscript, Boston Public Library.

[32] *O. R.*, series 1, V, 81; *Revised Regulations for the Army of the United States, 1861* (Philadelphia, 1861), paragraph 1261. To be cited hereafter as *Army Regulations.*

[33] Charles A. Barker to his parents, Nov. 10, 1861, manuscript, Essex Institute.

[34] Leander Stillwell, *The Story of a Common Soldier* (Erie, Kan., 1920), 15.

[35] See chapter XII.

[36] *O. R.*, series 3, II, 236.

[37] *Ibid.*, III, 136-140, 1071-1073; IV, 6 ff, 660 ff.

[38] For various nicknames of volunteer organizations see Richard C. Drum, *List of Synonyms of Organizations in the Volunteer Service of*

the United States during the Years 1861, '62, '63, '64, and '65 (Washington, D. C., 1885).

[39] C. Barney, *Recollections of Field Service with the Twentieth Iowa Infantry Volunteers* (Davenport, 1865), 33-35. A visitor to a regimental camp near Washington in July 1861 reported: "The colonel had his wife, one lieutenant his, many of the soldiers theirs. . . ." U. S. Sanitary Commission *Documents*, No. 17, "Report of a Preliminary Survey of the Camps of a Portion of the Volunteer Forces near Washington" (dated July 9, 1861), 18.

[40] Diary of Sgt. Henry A. Buck, Jan. 20, 1862, manuscript, Univ. of Mich.

[41] Eli R. Pickett to his wife, Sept. 6, 1862, manuscript, Minn. Historical Society; S. F. Fleharty, *Our Regiment: A History of the 102nd Illinois Infantry Volunteers* (Chicago, 1865), 8-9.

[42] A. Davenport to his homefolk, May 1, 1861, manuscript, N. Y. Historical Society

[43] O. R., series 3, II, 609 ff.

[44] Wirt A. Cate, editor, *Two Soldiers* (Chapel Hill, N. C., 1938), 222.

[45] A U. S. Sanitary Commission representative who inspected more than a score of regiments in the vicinity of Cairo in the latter part of 1861 commented on the "immense number" of photographs which the volunteers had made of themselves after drawing their uniforms. U. S. Sanitary Commission *Documents*, No. 36, 28.

[46] Detroit *Free Press*, June 20, Sept. 12, 1861.

[47] *Ibid.*, May 23, 1861; Winther, *With Sherman to the Sea*, 30-31. Accidental shooting was woefully prevalent among early volunteers. W. H. Russell reported after a visit to camps about Washington, D. C., in July 1861: "The number of accidents from the carelessness of the men is astonishing; in every day's paper there is an account of deaths and wounds caused by the discharge of firearms in the tents." *My Diary North and South* (Boston, 1863), 396.

[48] W. H. Darlington to his mother, July 25, Aug. 1, 1861, manuscript, Harvard.

[49] O. W. Norton, *Army Letters, 1861-1865* (Chicago, 1903), 16.

[50] Ellis Spear, "The Story of the Raising and Organization of a Regiment of Volunteers in 1862," Loyal Legion, District of Columbia Commandery, *War Papers*, No. 46 (Washington, D. C., 1903), 1 ff.

[51] Notation in back of diary of James P. Snell, manuscript, Illinois State Historical Library.

[52] Henry Crydenwise to his parents, Oct. 9, 1861, manuscript, Emory. In addition to the Crydenwise collection at Emory are a few letters at Duke. Charles W. Wills, *Army Life of an Illinois Soldier* (Washington, 1906), 14.

[53] Ruth A. Gallaher, editor, "Peter Wilson in the Civil War," *Iowa Journal of History and Politics*, XL (1942), 158, 163.

[54] Norton, *op. cit.*, 15-16.

⁵⁵ J. G. Fraser to his homefolk, April 25, 1864, manuscript, Indiana Historical Society.

⁵⁶ Detroit *Free Press*, June 23, 1861.

⁵⁷ *Ibid.*, Oct. 24, 1861.

⁵⁸ J. W. Rich, "The Color Bearer of the 12th Iowa," *Iowa Journal of History and Politics*, VI (1908), 95-99.

⁵⁹ Lt. F. M. Abbott to his brother, July 22, 1861, manuscript, Harvard.

⁶⁰ Diary of Harvey Reid, April 24, 1861.

⁶¹ Detroit *Free Press*, Aug. 31, 1861.

⁶² Everett W. Pattison, "Some Reminiscences of Army Life," Loyal Legion, Commandery of Missouri, *War Papers and Personal Reminiscences* (St. Louis, 1892), I, 248.

⁶³ Diary of Lt. T. Waldo Denny, April 17, 1861, manuscript, Veterans' Records, Nat'l Archives.

⁶⁴ Cyrus Stone to his mother, Oct. 22, 1861, manuscript, Minn. Historical Society.

⁶⁵ Urich N. Parmelee to his father, April 11, 1863, manuscript, Duke.

⁶⁶ Henry C. Hall to his brother, Nov. 6, 1861, manuscript, Duke.

⁶⁷ W. H. Darlington to his mother, July 23, 1861.

⁶⁸ William McCarter, "My Life in the American Army," I, 7-8, manuscript, N. Y. Public Library; Carl Wittke, "The Ninth Ohio Volunteers," *Ohio State Arch. and Historical Quarterly*, XXXV (1926), 402-417.

⁶⁹ For an example see William H. Bentley, *History of the 77th Illinois Volunteer Infantry* (Peoria, 1883), 16.

⁷⁰ This song's popularity among departing units is based on study of innumerable letters and diaries. A good example is afforded in a letter of Sgt. William T. Pippey, Jan. 15, 1862: "We had a jolly time in the cars singing 'John Brown.' " Manuscript, Duke.

⁷¹ Edward Louis Edes to his father, Oct. 1, 1863, manuscript, Mass. Historical Society.

⁷² C. A. Whittier, "Reminiscences of the War, 1861-1865," typescript, Boston Public Library.

⁷³ Journal of William E. Chase, Oct. 15, 1864, manuscript, Maine Historical Society.

⁷⁴ J. Bendernagel to William D. Murphy, April 29, 1861, manuscript, N. Y. Historical Society.

⁷⁵ J. H. Kendig to his brother, Dec. [no day], 1861, manuscript, Historical Society of Pa.

⁷⁶ C. B. Thurston to his parents, March 27, 1862 [misdated, 1861], manuscript, Emory.

⁷⁷ Capt. Charles A. Barnard to his wife, Feb. 13-19, 1862, manuscript, Maine Historical Society.

⁷⁸ Diary of Rufus Kinsley, March 12—April 5, 1862, manuscript, Vt. Historical Society.

⁷⁹ Lt. Roswell Farnham to his wife, May 2, 9, 10, 1861, typescript, Vt. Historical Society.

[80] Hercules Stanard to his sister, from Washington, D. C., June 13, 1861, manuscript, Univ. of Mich.

[81] Jasper Newton Searles to his homefolk, June 27, 1861, manuscript, Minn. Historical Society.

[82] "J.F.W.W.," "Our Hospital and the Men in Them," *Monthly Religious Magazine*, XXIX (1863), 241-242.

[83] Ransom E. Hawley to his sister, Sept. 21 [1863], manuscript, Ind. State Library.

[84] Franc B. Wilkie, *Pen and Powder* (Boston, 1888), 14-15.

[85] Joseph H. Diltz to B. F. Maden, Feb. 2, 1862, manuscript, Duke.

[86] "Letters of a Badger Boy in Blue," *Wis. Magazine of History*, IV (1920-21), 209.

[87] Henry Crydenwise to his parents, Oct. 20, 1861.

[88] Diary of William B. Gaskins, Sept. 20, 1861, manuscript, Duke.

[89] Wesley H. Day to Dudley Tillison, June 9 [1861], manuscript, Vt. Historical Society.

[90] Samuel C. Evans to his sister, Dec. 29, 1863, manuscript, Minn. Historical Society.

[91] Enoch T. Baker to his wife, Nov. 10, 1861, manuscript, Historical Society of Pa.

[92] William O. Wettleson to his parents, Oct. 12, 1861, manuscript, Luther College Library. I am indebted to Inga B. Norstog for translating and transcribing this and other Norwegian items in the Luther College collection.

[93] Arthur C. Cole, *The Era of the Civil War* (vol. 3, *Centennial History of Illinois*, Springfield, Ill., 1919), 278.

[94] Diary of W. H. Jackson, Aug. 18, 1862, manuscript, N. Y. Public Library.

[95] Detroit *Free Press*, April 19, 1861. W. H. Russell, the London *Times* correspondent, noted after a visit to an Illinois camp in June 1861: "During my short sojourn in this country I have never yet met any person who could show me where the sovereignty of the Union resides. General Prentiss, however, and his Illinois volunteers are quite ready to fight for it." *My Diary North and South*, 338.

[96] Diary of Philip Smith, July 22, 1861, bound series of articles from Peoria *Evening Star*, filed in Veterans' Records, Nat'l Archives.

[97] Samuel Storrow to his father, Oct. 12, 1862, manuscript, Mass. Historical Society.

[98] For an excellent discussion of motivations of World War II soldiers, see Samuel A. Stouffer and others, *The American Soldier* (New York, 1949), I, 430-485.

[99] John P. Moulton to his mother, Nov. 4, 1861, manuscript, Western Reserve Historical Society.

[100] For a further discussion of soldier attitudes toward slavery and the Negro, see chapter V.

[101] James Ford Rhodes, *History of the United States from the Compromise of 1850* (New York, 1892-1906), I, 278-285.

[102] "Letters of a Badger Boy in Blue," *Wis. Magazine of History*, IV (1920-1921), 90 ff.

[103] *Ibid.*

[104] *Ibid.*

[105] *Emigranten* (Norwegian newspaper published at Madison, Wis.), Oct. 7, 1861.

[106] Diary of Rufus Kinsley, Jan. 21, 1863.

[107] John P. Sheahan to his father, Oct. 14, 1862, manuscript, Maine Historical Society.

[108] Urich N. Parmelee to his mother, Sept. 8, 1862.

[109] *Ibid.*, March 29, 1863.

[110] This sketch is based on the Parmelee Papers.

[111] The *Cavalier*, published by the Fifth Pennsylvania Cavalry, June 25, 1862.

[112] A. Davenport to his homefolk, Sept. 26, 1862, Feb. 7, 1863.

[113] Henry L. Joslin to his mother, July 20, 1862, manuscript, American Antiquarian Society.

[114] A. Davenport to his homefolk, July 12, 1862.

[115] Charles D. Babbott to his father, Dec. 14, 1862, manuscript, Rutherford B. Hayes Memorial Library.

[116] William T. Pippey to "A.H. and B.Y.," July 31, 1862.

[117] Daniel E. Burbank to his parents, Aug. 11, 1861, manuscript, American Antiquarian Society.

[118] Samuel C. Evans to James Peet, July 27, 1863.

[119] Sgt. Eli R. Pickett to his wife, March 27, 1863.

Chapter II

FROM REVEILLE TO TAPS

[1] All the infantry calls are listed, with music for both drum and bugle, in Silas Casey, *Infantry Tactics* (N. Y., 1862), I, 227 ff. Those most frequently used, with music and accompanying remarks, are to be found also in the appendix of "Transcripts from the Letters and Diaries of Herbert E. Valentine, 1861-1864," manuscript, Essex Institute. To be cited hereafter as Valentine letters and diaries. Valentine was a musician in the 23rd Mass. Regt.

[2] For an excellent discussion of artillery routine and for camp life in general, see John D. Billings, *Hard Tack and Coffee* (Boston, 1888), 164 ff.

[3] David Leigh to "Mr. Drumgold," Aug. 1, 1863, manuscript, Dartmouth.

[4] Actually the signal which headed the official list of calls was a preliminary one known as the "assembly of buglers." But soldier narratives leave the impression that this was rarely used. The overwhelming ma-

jority of these accounts state that the notes of the reveille were the first heard by the men.

⁵ See the delightfully human illustration (by the soldier artist Charles W. Reed) in Billings, *op. cit.*, 167.

⁶ George A. Townsend, *Rustics in Rebellion* (Chapel Hill, 1950), 10.

⁷ Valentine letters and diaries, appendix.

⁸ Camp routine was outlined by innumerable diarists and letter writers, and the account here given of a typical day's activity, and the sections on training and equipment which follow, are drawn from so many different sources as to make it impractical to list them all. Important variations and details of special interest are cited at appropriate points in the narrative.

⁹ Charles Ward to his brother, Oct. 2, 1862, manuscript, American Antiquarian Society; Jesse A. Wilson to his father, Sept. 13, 1862, manuscript in possession of Mrs. Fred A. Johnson, Belfast, Maine.

¹⁰ Thomas L. Livermore, *Days and Events* (Boston, 1920), 35.

¹¹ G. Haven, "Camp Life at the Relay," *Harper's New Monthly Magazine*, XXIV (1861-1862), 631.

¹² Valentine letters and diaries, appendix.

¹³ See poetic description of camp life in Ruth A. Gallaher, editor, "Peter Wilson in the Civil War," *Iowa Journal of History and Politics*, XL (1942), 298.

¹⁴ For an unusually good description of Sunday inspection, see Livermore, *op. cit.*, 39.

¹⁵ Leander Stillwell, *The Story of a Common Soldier*, 90-91; Max H. Guyer, editor, "The Journal and Letters of William O. Gulick," *Iowa Journal of History and Politics*, XXVIII (1930), 215.

¹⁶ Billings, *op. cit.*, 77.

¹⁷ Haven, *op. cit.*, 632-633; Lawrence Van Alstyne, *Diary of an Enlisted Man* (New Haven, 1910), 56-57; Edward L. Edes to his father, July 13, 1862, manuscript, Mass. Historical Society; M. P. Larry to his sister, Jan. 31, 1863, manuscript, Maine Historical Society.

¹⁸ *Ibid.*

¹⁹ *Army Regulations, 1861*, article XXXI.

²⁰ *Ibid.*

²¹ At the outbreak of the war, pay of artillery and infantry privates was $11 per month and that of cavalry $12. Herbert E. Valentine letters and diaries, I, 8. On Aug. 6, 1861, Congress increased the rate to $13 per month for all arms, and on June 20, 1864, to $16 per month. War Department Adjutant General's Office *General Orders*, 1861, No. 54, and 1864, No. 216.

²² Assignment of pay to relatives was provided by Congress on July 22, 1861. See W.D.A.G.O. *General Orders*, 1861, No. 81. Cpl. Day Elmore wrote his father Sept. 30, 1862: "I signed . . . [the allotment roll] for sending you $16 evry 2 months." Manuscript in possession of Mrs. Hall Mosher, Memphis, Tenn. For an explanation of the allotment system see Billings, *op. cit.*, 97-98.

²³ Charles E. Davis, *Three Years in the Army*, 15.

[24] Details of training procedure on the various levels are given in Casey's, Hardee's and Scott's manuals of tactics; a convenient digest of all three is William Gilham, *Manual of Instruction for the Volunteers and Militia of the United States* (Philadelphia, 1861). The Civil War papers at Emory University of Capt. C. S. Wortley, 20th Michigan Regiment, contain in addition to Casey the following training guides: *Instructions for Officers and Non-Commissioned Officers on Outpost and Patrol Duty and Troops in Campaign* (Washington, 1863); *A System of Target Practice for the Use of Troops* (Washington, 1862); *Rules for the Management and Cleaning of the Rifle Musket, Model 1863* (Washington, 1863); and *Instructions to Mustering Officers and Others of Kindred Duties* (Washington, 1863).

[25] Diary of William Boston, Feb. 5, 1863, typescript, Univ. of Mich.

[26] George B. Turner to his father, Dec. 21, 1862, typescript, Ohio State Arch. and Historical Society.

[27] For example see John Beatty, *The Citizen Soldier; or, Memoirs of a Volunteer* (Cincinnati, 1879), 77.

[28] Gallaher, *op. cit.*, 174; diary of Cpl. Henry Clay Scott, Sept. 21, Oct. 21, 1861, manuscript, N. Y. Public Library.

[29] Fritz Haskell, editor, "Diary of Col. William Camm," Ill. State Historical Society *Journal*, XVIII (1926), 813.

[30] Donald Gordon, editor, *M. L. Gordon's Experiences in the Civil War* (Boston, 1922), 32.

[31] O. W. Norton, *Army Letters, 1861-1865*, 37-38.

[32] Lt. Col. Lucius Fairchild, acting commander of the 2nd Wis. Regt., and an unusually able officer, wrote to his sister, Dec. 20, 1861: "Day before yesterday Gen. McDowell had another of his division drills —& sham battle—It was a very fine affair, and a good drill for the soldiers . . . better still for the field officers . . . giving them practice in handling men for a definite purpose. I have been in command on all of our big division drill, & feel that I have learned a great deal—feel more confidence in being able to conduct a regt through battle—if I should ever be called on to do so." Manuscript, Wis. Historical Society. McDowell seems to have been one of the very few commanders who early in the war laid great stress on maneuvers by division. See O. R., series 1, XII, pt. 1, 91.

[33] Oscar O. Winther, editor, *With Sherman to the Sea*, 31.

[34] George W. Landrum to his sister, January [no day] 1862, typescript, Western Reserve Historical Society.

[35] Lt. Charles H. Salter to Mrs. Isabella G. Duffield [n.d., but 1861], manuscript among Duffield Papers, Detroit Public Library.

[36] O. R., series 1, XXXII, pt. 3, 323.

[37] Edward L. Edes to his father, Jan. 10, 1864.

[38] O. R., series 1, XII, pt. 3, 346. A camp of instruction, resembling the casual camp of World War II, was set up in Nashville, 1864. See *ibid.*, XXXII, pt. 3, 505. Early in the war a central signal camp of instruction was established at Georgetown, D. C., *ibid.*, V, 70. For reference to an artillery camp of instruction, which seems to have resembled a

World War II unit-training center, see Rhode Island Soldiers' and Sailors' Historical Society, *Personal Narratives*, 2nd Series, No. 11 (Providence, 1881), 36-37.

[39] *O. R.*, series 1, XXXVIII, pt. 5, 408.

[40] For example of a veteran first sergeant drilling a score of recruits that joined his company at Atlanta just before the beginning of Sherman's march to the sea, see diary of N. L. Parmater, Oct. 30, 31, Nov. 1, 5, 1864, typescript in possession of Dr. A. M. Giddings, Battle Creek, Mich. In the 16th N. Y. Regt., recruits received after Antietam seem to have been trained by themselves in the morning and with the old troops in the afternoon. See Cyrus R. Stone to his parents, Oct. 7, 1862, manuscript, Minn. Historical Society.

[41] R. G. Carter, *Four Brothers in Blue* (Washington, 1913), 315.

[42] Norton, *op. cit.*, 28.

[43] George Milledge to his brother, Joseph Diltz, June 9, 1863, manuscript, Duke.

[44] For example, on July 19, 1862, after participating in the Seven Days' campaign, James O. Newhall wrote his father from Harrison's Landing, Va.: "We have resumed drilling again. Some of the boys dislike it much, thinking they are well enough drilled already, but there is nothing like discipline, after all." Manuscript, Boston Public Library.

[45] *Army Regulations*, 1861, article XXXVI. Officer latrines were back of the baggage train. Enlisted men's latrines were at the opposite end of the camp.

[46] U. S. Sanitary Commission *Documents*, No. 26, 10.

[47] For illustrations of the various types of shelter, see Billings, *op. cit.*, 45 ff.

[48] A. C. Hawes, *The Experiences of a Union Soldier*, 10.

[49] Billings, *op. cit.*, 47.

[50] *Ibid.*, 48-50.

[51] *Ibid.*, 50-51.

[52] *Ibid.*, 52-53; Samuel Storrow to his parents, March 17, 23, 1863, manuscript, Mass. Historical Society.

[53] Billings, *op. cit.*, 54; Gilham, *op. cit.*, 643.

[54] Billings, *op. cit.*, 54; Lt. Roswell Farnham to his wife, May 25, 1861, manuscript, Vt. Historical Society.

[55] Asa Ward Brindle to "Frank and Flora," Oct. 25, 1862, manuscript (microfilm), Detroit Public Library.

[56] John P. M. Green, "Belated Diary of a Civil War Soldier in the First N. H. Light Battery," 2, 5, 6, typescript, N. H. Historical Society.

[57] Lt. Col. Roswell Farnham to his wife, Nov. 28, 1862.

[58] Frank M. Rood to his parents, Jan. 3, 1863, manuscript in possession of Frank M. Rood, Poultney, Vt.; Billings, *op. cit.*, 54-58, 66, 73-79.

[59] Mrs. Roswell Farnham to her brother, Dec. 24, 1862. Mrs. Farnham was visiting her husband in camp when she wrote the letter. For an excellent photograph showing many barrel-topped chimneys, see F. T. Miller, editor, *Photographic History of the Civil War*, (N. Y., 1911), VIII, 225.

[60] Billings, *op. cit.*, 56.

[61] *Ibid.*, 75-76.

[62] *Ibid.*, 77-80; diary of Ezra G. Huntley, Dec. 30, 1864, manuscript, Dartmouth.

[63] Urich N. Parmelee to his mother, Dec. 13, 1863, manuscript, Duke.

[64] Billings, *op. cit.*, 57; Edwin E. Newhall to his homefolk, Jan. 8, 1862; Miller, *Photographic History of the Civil War*, VIII, 258-259.

[65] Edwin E. Newhall to his parents, Jan. 8, 1862.

[66] Billings, *op. cit.*, 276-278, 316-320; *Revised U. S. Army Regulations*, 1861, article LI; W.D.A.G.O. *General Orders*, No. 108, Dec. 16, 1861, changed the color of trousers from dark blue to sky blue. Colored illustrations of various uniforms may be found in the *Atlas to Accompany the Official Records of the Union and Confederate Armies*, 1861-1865 (Washington, 1890-1895), plate 172. The illustrations are too artistic to be realistic, except in representing prescribed modes.

[67] Henry L. Joslin to his mother, Nov. 11, 1861, manuscript, American Antiquarian Society.

[68] Winther, *op. cit.*, 25.

[69] See Miller, *Photographic History of the Civil War*, especially volume VIII.

[70] O. B. Clark, editor, *Downing's Civil War Diary* (Des Moines, Iowa, 1916), 16; "Remarks by Capt. J. B. Molyneaux at a Dinner Given by the Cleveland Contingent, Ohio Commandery Military Order of the Loyal Legion . . . April 2, 1913," typescript, Duke.

[71] Billings, *op. cit.*, 316.

[72] Winther, *op. cit.*, 26.

[73] *Ibid.*

[74] John A. Cockerill, "What a Boy Did at Shiloh," in Portland, Maine, *Daily Express*, Jan. 21, 1890, supplement.

[75] O. R., series 1, XXXI, pt. 3, 392; G. W. Adams, "Health and Medicine in the Union Army, 1861-1865" (Ph.D. Dissertation, Harvard, 1946), II, 645.

[76] *Army Regulations*, 1861, article LI; O. R., series 1, XXV, pt. 2, 152, XLVI, pt. 3, 33, XLVII, pt. 2, 419. For colored illustrations of corps badges see *Atlas to Accompany O. R.*, plate 175. Insignia of rank and also buttons are shown in *ibid.*, plate 172.

[77] See Fred A. Shannon, *Organization and Administration of the Union Army*, I, 53 ff.

[78] O. R., series 1, XIX, pt. 1, 12.

[79] A. Davenport to his homefolk, April 19, 1863, manuscript, N. Y. Historical Society.

[80] *Ibid.*

[81] Asst. Surgeon Benj. S. Catlin to his parents, Dec. 9, 1862, manuscript, Conn. State Library; David Leigh to "Mr. Drumgold," Nov. 10, 1863.

[82] Diary of John H. Markley, manuscript, Historical Society of Pa.; Edward L. Edes to his father, July 26, 1863.

[83] N. Y. *Tribune*, June 6, 1864.

⁸⁴ Jacob E. Beltzer to William R. Keran, May 18, 1862, manuscript, Ohio State Arch. and Historical Society.

⁸⁵ Albert G. Hart to his wife, Sept. 26, 1862, manuscript, Western Reserve Historical Society.

⁸⁶ O. R., series 1, XX, pt. 2, 118.

⁸⁷ Van Alstyne, op. cit., 155.

⁸⁸ O. R., series 1, XLVII, pt. 1, 257.

⁸⁹ Ibid., XXXI, pt. 2, 262, 580-581, and pt. 3, 392.

⁹⁰ William H. Lloyd to his wife, Dec. 21, 1863, manuscript, Western Reserve Historical Society.

⁹¹ For example, see O. R., series 3, II, 804-805.

⁹² See chapter III.

⁹³ Shannon, op. cit., I, 113 ff; Comte de Paris, History of the Civil War in America (Philadelphia, 1875), I, 298-299; Bell Irvin Wiley, The Life of Johnny Reb, 291-292; DAB, XX, 209. For illustrations of the various types of guns, see Atlas to Accompany O. R., plate 173.

⁹⁴ Winther, op. cit., 107, 157-158.

⁹⁵ Daniel E. Burbank to his parents, Oct. 17, 1861, manuscript, American Antiquarian Society. Accuracy at 1500 yards by an average Yank seems an exaggeration.

⁹⁶ For an indication of the conservative attitude of the Chief of Ordnance late in the conflict, see O. R., series 3, IV, 802. Opposing viewpoints on culpability with reference to arms development are presented in Shannon, op. cit., I, 107-148 and Kenneth P. Williams, Lincoln Finds a General (N. Y., 1949), II, 784-785, 798-800.

⁹⁷ For drawings of various types of cannon, see Atlas to Accompany O. R., plate 173. The Comte de Paris discusses artillery pieces and projectiles at length in op. cit., I, 300-307.

⁹⁸ Several makes of carbines and pistols are illustrated in Atlas to Accompany O. R., plate 173. For references to types in the possession of soldiers, see Report of Col. H. Van Rensselaer, Inspector General's Office, Washington, D. C., on inspection of the Dept. of Mo., dated Feb. 12, 1862, manuscript, A.G.O. Records, file 14-I, Nat'l Archives; Flavius J. Bellamy, 3rd Ind. Cav., to his homefolk, Jan. 4, Aug. 12, 1862, Aug. 16, 1863, manuscript, Ind. State Library; William Blackburn to his brother, Feb. 11, 1862, manuscript, Historical Society of Pa.; Franklin H. Bailey to his father, Dec. 26, 1864, manuscript, Univ. of Mich.

⁹⁹ Franklin H. Bailey to his parents, March 16, 1864.

¹⁰⁰ Billings, op. cit., 76-79, 86, 126, 134, 272-278.

¹⁰¹ A. Davenport to his homefolk, April 18, 1862.

¹⁰² Samuel Storrow to his mother, Nov. 16, 1862. For other comment on individual equipment and its weight, see C. B. Thurston to his parents, July 20, 1862, manuscript, Duke; Clarence F. Cobb, The Maryland Campaign, 1862 (Washington, 1891), 15-16.

¹⁰³ Billings, op. cit., 343.

¹⁰⁴ Directives specified whether troops were to proceed "in heavy marching order"—i.e., carrying all their equipment—or "in light marching order," with only essentials. Henry S. Commager, The Blue and the

Gray (Indianapolis, 1950), I, 289, quoting Joel Cook, *The Siege of Richmond.*

Chapter III

THE SUPREME TEST

[1] O. R., series 1, XVI, pt. 1, 918.

[2] The account which begins here of preliminaries to battle and the action which followed is based on a mass of official and personal material. Specific citations are given only in the instance of direct quotations or where other considerations seem to make references desirable. The narrative is not of any particular engagement but all the incidents cited actually occurred in connection with some action.

[3] For examples of prebattle speeches and instructions see O. R., series 1, XX, pt. 1, 183, XXI, 241, XXXVIII, pt. 4, 41-42; Thomas W. Hyde, *Following the Greek Cross* (N. Y., 1894), 125-126; A. Davenport to his homefolk, June 4, 1862, manuscript, N. Y. Historical Society.

[4] Thomas L. Livermore, *Days and Events*, 133.

[5] A. H. Pickel to his father, Dec. 19, 1862, manuscript, Duke University.

[6] William D. Bickham, *Rosecrans' Campaign with the Fourteenth Army Corps* (Cincinnati, 1863), 362.

[7] Cyrus R. Stone to his parents, Dec. 20, 1862, manuscript, Minn. Historical Society; Harold A. Small, editor, *The Road to Richmond: The Civil War Memoirs of Major Abner R. Small* (Berkeley, Calif., 1939), 84-85; Chaplain Joseph H. Twichell to his father, June 2, 1862, manuscript, Yale.

[8] A. H. Pickel to his father, Dec. 19, 1862.

[9] M. P. Larry to his sister, Dec. 18, 1862, manuscript, Maine Historical Society.

[10] Ruth A. Gallaher, editor, "Peter Wilson in the Civil War," *Iowa Journal of History and Politics*, XL (1942), 298-299.

[11] Edward L. Edes to his father, April 14, 1863, manuscript, Mass. Historical Society.

[12] O. R., series 1, X, pt. 1, 332-333.

[13] One soldier recalled after the war that he thought of death when going into battle only as something that might befall "the other fellow." S. H. M. Byers, "How Men Feel in Battle," *Harper's Monthly Magazine*, CXII (1906), 931.

[14] M. P. Larry to his sister, Feb. 26, 1864.

[15] Thomas B. Barker to his brother, July 20, 1861, manuscript, Maine Historical Society.

[16] Undated note added to *ibid.*, signed: "A Surgeon C.S.A."

[17] Edgar L. Erickson, "With Grant at Vicksburg, From the Civil

War Diary of Capt. James F. Wilcox," Ill. State Historical Society *Journal*, XXX (1938), 479-480.

[18] James H. Croushore, editor, *A Volunteer's Adventures, A Union Captain's Record of the Civil War*, by John William De Forest (New Haven, 1946), 63. To be cited hereafter, De Forest, *A Volunteer's Adventures*; a lieutenant who went to the rear for ammunition at Winchester, Va., Sept. 19, 1864, told on his return to ranks of seeing file closers performing their work in dead earnest. "By Gad," he said, "I never saw such spanking and ferruling since I was at school." *Ibid.*, 186.

[19] *Ibid.*, 64.

[20] Herbert E. Valentine to his mother, Jan. 2, 1863, manuscript, Essex Institute.

[21] Franklin H. Bailey to his parents, April 8, 1862, typescript, Univ. of Mich.

[22] De Forest, *A Volunteer's Adventures*, 65, Small, *op. cit.*, 64, journal of Charles F. Johnson, Sept. 17, 1862, manuscript, Minn. Historical Society; Lt. W. Henry Clune to his wife, April 13, 1862, manuscript, Shiloh National Park.

[23] De Forest, *A Volunteer's Adventures*, 185-186.

[24] John P. Sheahan to his father, July 10, 1863, manuscript, Maine Historical Society; Mrs. J. D. Wheeler, compiler, *In Memoriam: Letters of William Wheeler of the Class of 1855, Y. C.* (Cambridge, Mass., 1875), 418.

[25] R. G. Carter, *Four Brothers in Blue*, 318.

[26] Franklin H. Bailey to his parents, April 8, 1862.

[27] O. W. Norton, *Army Letters, 1861-1865*, 93, 106-109.

[28] John P. Sheahan to his father, June 10, 1863.

[29] John N. Moulton to his sister, Jan. 29, 1863, manuscript, Western Reserve Historical Society; William Hamilton to his mother, Dec. 24, 1862, manuscript, Library of Congress.

[30] William O. Wettleson to his father, March 15, 1865, manuscript, Luther College Library. Translated from the Norwegian by Inga B. Norstog.

[31] For a discussion of the Rebel yell, see Bell Irvin Wiley, *The Life of Johnny Reb*, 71-72.

[32] O. R., series 1, XII, pt. 2, supplement, 1012.

[33] Albert G. Hart to his sons, Oct. 27, 1863, manuscript, Western Reserve Historical Society.

[34] Almon Clarke, "In the Immediate Rear: Experiences and Observations of a Field Surgeon," Mil. Order of the Loyal Legion, Wis. Commandery, *War Papers*, II (Milwaukee, 1896), 91.

[35] H. Allen Gosnell, *Guns on the Western Waters* (Baton Rouge, 1949), 228.

[36] O. R., series 1, XXXIV, pt. 3, 169; Livermore, *Days and Events*, 141; Cyrus R. Stone to his parents, Sept. 16, 1862.

[37] O. R., series 1, XX, pt. 1, 335; "G.S.G.," to William Wheatcraft, Jan. 11, 1863, manuscript, Misc. Civil War Letters, Ill. State Historical Library.

[38] For references to uninhibited yelling see Edgar L. Erickson, *op. cit.*, entry of May 1, 1863 and O. R., series 1, XII, pt. 2, 441, XVI, pt. 1, 804, XXX, pt. 1, 657, XXXVI, pt. 1, 668, XXXVIII, pt. 2, 371.

[39] Livermore, *Days and Events*, 141.

[40] Stephen A. Miller to his sister, Nov. 27, 1863, manuscript, Indiana Historical Society; Robert W. Rickard to his uncle, Aug. 14, 1863, manuscript. Ill. State Historical Library.

[41] Frank Wilkeson, *Recollections of a Private Soldier in the Army of the Potomac* (N. Y., 1887), 71-72.

[42] R. G. Carter, *Four Brothers in Blue*, 314.

[43] O. R., series 1, XXVII, pt. 1, 330-331, 446.

[44] Felix Brannigan to his sister May 15, 1862, typescript, Library of Congress; O. R., series 1, XXX, pt. 1, 60, 855.

[45] Small, *op. cit.*, 64 ff; O. R., series 1, XI, pt. 2, 391, XXVII, pt. 1, 234, XXXVI, pt. 1, 335-336, 358-359, 410, 704, XXXVIII, pt. 1, 710-711, pt. 3, 556-557; diary of Lt. Col. Allen L. Fahnestock, June 27, July 1, 1864, manuscript, Ill. State Historical Library.

[46] Unsigned letter, March 2, 1862 (erroneously dated March 2, 1861), manuscript in possession of Charles N. Owen, Chicago, who generously made available to me many rewarding letters.

[47] Gen. John Gibbon in his report of the second day's fighting at Gettysburg stated: "The smoke was at this time so dense that but little could be seen of the battle, and I directed some of the guns to cease firing fearing they might injure our own men." O. R., series 1, XXVII, pt. 1, 417. A soldier wrote after the Iuka, Miss., fight: "The smoke hung over the battlefield like a cloud, obscuring every object ten feet off." J. H. Greene, *Reminiscences of the War: Extracts from Letters Written Home from 1861 to 1865* (Medina, Ohio, 1886), 29.

[48] Small, *op. cit.*, 19-23.

[49] William H. Brearley to his father, Sept. 26, 1862, manuscript, Detroit Public Library.

[50] Small, *op. cit.*, 23.

[51] Edward L. Davis to "Friend Emma," July 27, 1861, manuscript, Wis. Historical Society.

[52] O. W. Norton wrote of his experiences at Malvern Hill: "We were so worn out by excitement, fatigue and want of sleep that there was not the spirit in the movement of the men that usually characterized them." *Army Letters*, 108.

[53] E. W. Robie to "Friend Lou," July 12, 1862, manuscript, Univ. of Vt.

[54] William H. Brearley to his father, Sept. 26, 1862.

[55] Diary of Matthew Marvin, Dec. 15, 1862, manuscript, Minn. Historical Society.

[56] An artillery private who was at Chancellorsville wrote: "We were all deaf for quite a while after the fight." Mrs. B. A. White, editor, *Richmond and Way Stations* (Milford, Mass., 1889), 43.

[57] Journal of Charles F. Johnson, Sept. 17, 1862.

[58] Mark De Wolfe Howe, editor, *Touched with Fire: Letters and*

Diary of Oliver Wendell Holmes, Jr. (Cambridge, Mass., 1946), 50-51.

[59] S. F. Fleharty, *Our Regiment: A History of the 102nd Ill. Inf. Vols.*, 83.

[60] Philip D. Jordan, editor, "Forty Days with the Christian Commission: A Diary of William Salter," *Iowa Journal of History and Politics*, XXXIII (1935), 147; unidentified officer of Grant's army to "Dear Henry," May, 28, 1863, manuscript in Lucian B. Case Papers, Chicago Historical Society; Herbert E. Valentine letters and diaries, June 22, July 2, Aug. 3, 1864.

[61] Edwin Hutchinson to his mother, Sept. 18, 1862, manuscript, La. State Univ.

[62] Joseph H. Diltz to his father, Oct. 10, 1862, manuscript, Duke.

[63] Henry J. H. Thompson to his wife, April 4, 1862, manuscript, Duke.

[64] A. Davenport to his homefolk, Dec. 17, 1862.

[65] *Ibid.*, June 11, 1861.

[66] Thomas N. Lewis to his uncle, April 10, 1862, manuscript among Moulton Letters, Western Reserve Historical Society.

[67] Alfred S. Roe, *The Ninth New York Heavy Artillery* (Worcester, Mass., 1899), 181; Nashville *Daily Union*, April 7, 1863.

[68] Lt. W. Henry Clune to his wife, April 13, 1862.

[69] Greene, *op. cit.*, 20; David McLain, who claimed that he carried Old Abe through the Corinth fight, while not specifically contradicting Greene's account, gives a much less spectacular version of the eagle's performance. See David McLain, "The Story of Old Abe," *Wis. Magazine of History*, VIII (1925), 410-411.

[70] Bickham, *op. cit.*, 363.

[71] Howe, *op. cit.*, 115.

[72] O. R., series 1, XXXVIII, pt. 3, 583.

[73] *Ibid.*, XXX, pt. 1, 769.

[74] Wilkeson, *op. cit.*, 95.

[75] R. G. Carter, *Four Brothers in Blue*, 253.

[76] Jasper Packard, *Four Years of Camp, March and Battle* (Washington, 1870), 5.

[77] Alfred Davenport, *Camp and Field Life of the Fifth New York Volunteer Infantry* (N. Y., 1879), 229.

[78] M. P. Larry to his sister, June 28, 1863.

[79] *Ibid.*, Dec. 8, 1863; John McMeekin to his mother, Jan. 15, 1863, manuscript, Western Reserve Historical Society.

[80] John McMeekin to his mother, Jan. 15, 1863.

[81] George Milledge to Mrs. J. H. Diltz, July 7, 1863, manuscript, Duke.

[82] W. O. Lyford to his father, July 22, 1861, manuscript in possession of Charles N. Owen, Chicago.

[83] For an example, see Lydia Minturn Post, editor, *Soldiers' Letters* (N. Y., 1865), 404-405.

[84] A. Davenport to his homefolk, June 1, 1862; Cyrus R. Stone to his parents, Sept. 23, 1862.

[85] John P. Sheahan to his father, Oct. [no day] 1863.

[86] William Hamilton to his mother, Dec. 24, 1862.

[87] Thomas N. Lewis to his uncle, April 10, 1862.

[88] *Indiana Magazine of History*, XXXIII (1937), 340.

[89] For example, see Lt. Henry W. Clune to his wife, April 16, 1862.

[90] Edwin Horton to his wife, Dec. 4, 1863, manuscript, Vt. Historical Society.

[91] William H. Lloyd to his wife, May 21, 1864, manuscript, Western Reserve Historical Society.

[92] Unidentified soldier (but apparently Sewell Welch) to Ansel Hawkes, Oct. 24, 1864, manuscript in possession of Delmont Hawkes, Sebago Lake, Maine, to whom I am indebted for its use.

[93] William H. Brearley to his father, Sept. 26, 1862.

[94] O. R., series 1, XXIV, pt. 2, 170-177.

[95] *Ibid.*, 186.

[96] For example, see *ibid.*, XXXVI, pt. 1, 366-367, 952.

[97] Brig. Gen. J. J. Bartlett to Col. Joseph Howland, June 25, 1864, manuscript, N. Y. Historical Society.

[98] O. R., series 1, XXXVIII, pt. 1, 77.

[99] *Ibid.*, 226.

[100] *Ibid.*, XXXVI, pt. 3, 240.

[101] Diary of S. E. Thomason, June 23, 1861, manuscript in possession of Charles N. Owen, Chicago.

[102] Judge Advocate General Records, MM1071, manuscript, Nat'l Archives.

[103] After Haines's Bluff a soldier wrote: "Lots of our best men run like thunder thar is som in our company run them big brags the cordley devils." John McMeekin to his mother, March 16, 1863.

[104] Small, *op. cit.*, 70.

[105] Livermore, *Days and Events*, 205.

[106] David P. Jackson, editor, *The Colonel's Diary*, 82.

[107] Hazel C. Wolf, editor, *Campaigning with the First Minnesota* (St. Paul, 1944), 349.

[108] O. R., series 1, X, pt. 1, 135.

[109] *Ibid.*, 203.

[110] *Ibid.*, 324.

[111] *Ibid.*, 333.

[112] *Ibid.*, XI, pt. 1, 843, 852, 878; pt. 2, 111.

[113] *Ibid.*, XII, pt. 2, 445, 482 and supplement, 1065.

[114] *Ibid.*, XIX, pt. 2, 348.

[115] Lt. Henry Ropes to his father, Dec. 16, 1862, manuscript (copy), Boston Public Library.

[116] Capt. Henry Abbott to his brother, Dec. 17, 1862, manuscript, Harvard.

[117] O. R., series 1, XVII, pt. 1, 76. The regiment redeemed itself at Corinth. See *ibid.*, 171.

[118] Lt. George W. Landrum to his sister, Oct. 12, 1862, typescript, Western Reserve Historical Society.

[119] *Ibid.*

[120] *Ibid.*, Dec. 31, 1862, and Jan. (no day) 1863; *O. R.*, series 1, XX, pt. 1, 289, 547-548; Albert G. Hart to his wife, Jan. 7, 9, 1863.

[121] *O. R.*, series 1, XX, pt. 1, 548.

[122] For examples of soldier comment on the Chancellorsville rout, see R. G. Carter, *Four Brothers in Blue*, 249, and David Leigh to "Mr. Drumgold," May 20, 1863, manuscript, Dartmouth. For a recent study of the Chancellorsville campaign, see K. P. Williams, *Lincoln Finds a General*, II, 589 ff.

[123] *O. R.*, series 1, XXVII, pt. 1, 380.

[124] Knute Nelson to his brother, May 22—June 3, 1863, manuscript, Minn. Historical Society; Henry Crydenwise to his parents, July 9, 1863, manuscript, Emory.

[125] *O. R.*, series 1, XXIV, pt. 2, 257-258.

[126] *Ibid.*, XXX, pt. 1, 192-193.

[127] *Ibid.*, XXXIV, pt. 1, 399, 416; pt. 3, 169-171.

[128] Diary of John Merrilies, June 10, 11, 1864; Robert S. Henry, *First with the Most Forrest* (Indianapolis, 1944), 293-298.

[129] De Forest, *A Volunteer's Adventures*, 210-211.

[130] *O. R.*, series 1, XLVI, pt. 1, 846 and XLVII, pt. 1, 435; diary of William C. Meffert, March 13 [19], 1865.

[131] *Medals of Honor Issued in the War Department up to and Including Oct. 31, 1897* (Washington, 1897), 43.

[132] *O. R.*, series 1, VIII, 339.

[133] *Ibid.*, XI, pt. 1, 732-733.

[134] *Ibid.*, 812.

[135] *Ibid.*

[136] *Ibid.*, XVII, pt. 1, 275-276.

[137] Felix Brannigan to his sister, n.d., but early 1863.

[138] *O. R.*, series 1, XXX, pt. 1, 431.

[139] *Ibid.*, XXI, 309.

[140] *Ibid.*, XXIII, pt. 1, 492, 497.

[141] *Ibid.*, XXXI, pt. 2, 169.

[142] For example, see *ibid.*, XI, pt. 2, 373.

[143] *Ibid.*, XXX, pt. 1, 317.

[144] *Ibid.*, XXVII, pt. 1, 451-452.

[145] J. W. Rich, "The Color Bearer of the Twelfth Iowa Volunteer Infantry," *Iowa Journal of History and Politics*, VI (1908), 96-102.

[146] *O. R.*, series 1, XXIV, pt. 1, 630-631.

[147] *Ibid.*, 720.

[148] *Ibid.*, XXVII, pt. 1, 446.

[149] *Ibid.*, XXX, pt. 1, 62, 695.

[150] Confederates noted the improvement in Billy Yank's fighting qualities. After Gettysburg Gen. A. P. Hill was said to have remarked that he "had never known the Federals to fight so well" as they did on the first day of the fight. *O. R.*, series 1, XXVII, pt. 1, 272. Long after the war a veteran, commenting on the repeated charges made by the Federals against heavy opposition at Fredericksburg, remarked to a young

relative: "Up until then, son, I felt we had them licked. After that I never was sure. They hadn't learned to fight by Fredericksburg, but they had learned to get killed and not to run. I knew they'd come back some other time." Ellis G. Arnall, *The Shore Dimly Seen* (N. Y., 1946), 125.

Chapter IV

IN DIXIE LAND

[1] J. W. Evans to James Peet and wife, May 25, 1862, Peet Papers, manuscript, Minn. Historical Society; Daniel E. Burbank to his parents, Aug. 11, 1861, manuscript, American Antiquarian Society.

[2] William O. Wettleson to his homefolk, Nov. 27, 1864, manuscript, Luther College Library, translated from the Norwegian by Inga B. Norstog.

[3] William F. Lerich to his father, Jan. 26, 1862, manuscript, Univ. of Mich.

[4] Francis S. Flint to Jennie Russell, Oct. 30, 1864, manuscript, Minn. Historical Society.

[5] Louis Westacott to B. F. Moulton, Jan. 18, 1862, manuscript, Western Reserve Historical Society; D. B. Bates to William P. Corthell, March 7 [1864], manuscript, American Antiquarian Society; J. F. Morris to Clarissa Butler, May 7, 1863, manuscript among Miscellaneous Civil War Letters, American Antiquarian Society.

[6] Jesse A. Wilson to his mother, June 23, 1863, manuscript in possession of Mrs. Fred A. Johnson, Belfast, Maine.

[7] L. Marion Moulton to his uncle and aunt, Dec. 10, 1864, Western Reserve Historical Society; Henry C. Hall to his sister, Aug. 10, 1862, manuscript, Duke; Eli R. Pickett to his wife, June 23, 1864, manuscript, Minn. Historical Society.

[8] R. G. Carter, *Four Brothers in Blue*, 260.

[9] John P. Sheahan to his father, Oct. 14, 1862, manuscript, Maine Historical Society; Frederick A. Dickinson to "Dear George," Aug. 14, 1861, manuscript, American Antiquarian Society.

[10] Henry J. H. Thompson to his wife, Oct. 17, 1863, manuscript, Duke.

[11] W. C. Lusk, editor, *War Letters of William Thompson Lusk* (N. Y., 1911), 66.

[12] William B. Stanard to his homefolk, Feb. 22, 1862, manuscript, Univ. of Mich.

[13] John H. B. Kent to George Baxter, Dec. 27, 1862, manuscript, Mass. Historical Society; James L. Sellers, editor, "The Richard H. Mockett Diary," *Miss. Valley Historical Review*, XXVI (1939), 240; C. Parrish to his brother, Sept. 23, 1864, manuscript among Stanard Papers, Univ. of Mich.

[14] Lt. George W. Landrum to his sister, March 28, April 23, April 28, 1862, typescript, Western Reserve Historical Society.

[15] George W. Driggs, *Opening of the Mississippi: or Two Years Campaigning in the Southwest* (Madison, Wis., 1864), 100-101; Willis D. Maier to Annie F. Howells, June 19, 1863, manuscript, Howells Letters, Hayes Memorial Library.

[16] Andrew K. Rose, Aug. 9, 1863, manuscript, Duke University; Henry S. Simmons to his wife, Nov. 16, 1862, manuscript, Lowdermilk's Bookstore, Washington, D. C. I am greatly indebted to P. P. Jones, manager of Lowdermilk's Bookstore, for permission to use this excellent source.

[17] Cyrus R. Stone to his parents, April 12, 1862, manuscript, Minn. Historical Society.

[18] D. H. Dodd to his father, Dec. 30, 1862, manuscript, Ind. Historical Society.

[19] William R. Hartpence, *History of the Fifty-first Indiana Veteran Volunteer Infantry* (Cincinnati, 1894), 49.

[20] Charles W. Wills, *Army Life of an Illinois Soldier*, 215; Surg. Humphrey H. Hood to his wife, Dec. 20, 1862, manuscript, Ill. State Historical Library.

[21] Edward L. Edes to his sister, March 6, 1864, manuscript, Mass. Historical Society; John Tallman to his sister, April 12, 1864, manuscript, Chicago Historical Society.

[22] Wills, *Army Life of an Illinois Soldier*, 99-101.

[23] *Ibid.*, 228.

[24] James E. Bates to "Brothers and Sisters of the Old Social," manuscript among William P. Corthell Letters, American Antiquarian Society; Frederick A. Dickinson to his father, Feb. 26, 1862.

[25] Diary of Charles W. Wills, June 14, 1864, manuscript, Ill. State Historical Library; *Diary of E. P. Burton* (Des Moines, 1939), 5; James K. Hosmer, *The Color-Guard* (Boston, 1864), 118.

[26] Capt. Hans Mattson to his wife, Jan. 1, 1862, manuscript, Minn. Historical Society; David P. Conyngham, *Sherman's March through the South* (N. Y., 1865), 149-152.

[27] Lt. F. M. Abbott to his father, March 12, 1862, manuscript, Harvard.

[28] J. H. Greene, *Reminiscences of the War*, 51-52; Lusk, *Letters of William Thompson Lusk, 1861-1863*, 110.

[29] Diary of Maj. Oliver L. Spaulding, June 22, 1863, manuscript, Univ. of Mich.

[30] J. R. Barney to his brother, Oct. 24, 1862, manuscript, Dinsmore Letters, Ill. State Historical Library.

[31] Diary of E. J. Sherlock, Aug. 25, 1863, manuscript, Ind. Historical Society.

[32] John Herr to his sister, Feb. 5, 1865, manuscript, Duke; D. H. Dodd to his sister, Dec. 24, 1862.

[33] Diary of William E. Limbarker, Jan. 16, 1862, manuscript, Univ. of Mich.

[34] Edward Whitaker to his sister, June 24, 1861, manuscript, Conn. State Library.

[35] Elitha House to "Dear Jennie," April 18, 1863, manuscript, Miscellaneous Civil War Letters, Western Reserve Historical Society.

[36] Diary of John Merrilies, Dec. 18, 1862, manuscript, Chicago Historical Society.

[37] Hosmer, *The Color-Guard*, 118-119; Henry Crydenwise to his parents, Jan. 22, 1862, manuscript, Emory.

[38] Henry Crydenwise to his parents, Feb. 25, 1862, March 10, April 6, 1863; Harold A. Small, editor, *The Road to Richmond*, 200-201; Robert J. Kerner, editor, "Diary of Edward W. Crippin, Private 27th Ill. Vols.," Ill. State Historical Society *Transactions*, 1909 (Springfield, Ill., 1910), 250; "Journal of Melvin Cox Robertson," *Ind. Magazine of History*, XXVIII (1932), 127.

[39] Diary of Capt. E. J. Sherlock, Feb. 2, 1865, typescript, Nat'l Archives. The manuscript of this diary is at the Ind. Historical Society. References to it from here on will be to the manuscript unless otherwise indicated. Clara A. Glenn, editor, *Letters of Robert Walker* (Viroqua, Wis., 1917), 22; George F. Newhall to "Dear Friends," March 14, 1862, manuscript, Boston Public Library.

[40] Frances A. Tenney, editor, *War Diary of Luman Harris Tenney, 1861-1865* (Cleveland, 1914), 34, 38; John McMeekin to his sister, Dec. 15, 1862, manuscript, Western Reserve Historical Society; "The Fourteenth Indiana in the Valley of Virginia," *Ind. Magazine of History*, XXX (1934), 294.

[41] Hazel C. Wolf, editor, *Campaigning with the First Minnesota*, 251.

[42] Diary of Charles W. Wills, Jan. 10, 1864 [1865]. At this time Wills was writing his diary in installments and sending them home as letters to his sister. For the printed version of this entry, see *Army Life of an Illinois Soldier*, 336.

[43] Wills, *Army Life of an Illinois Soldier*, 29; diary of Oliver L. Spaulding, Nov. 4, 1862.

[44] Diary of James P. Snell, July 26, 1862, manuscript, Ill. State Historical Library.

Chapter V

ALONG FREEDOM ROAD

[1] Artemas Cook to Curtis Babbott, Jan. 3, 1864, manuscript, Hayes Memorial Library; A. Davenport to his homefolk, June 19, 1861, manuscript, N. Y. Historical Society.

[2] Capt. F. M. Abbott to his brother, Feb. [no day or year, but 1863], manuscript, Harvard.

[3] Diary of Ezra G. Huntley, Dec. 29, 1864, manuscript (copy), Dartmouth.

[4] Diary of Sgt. Matthew Marvin, Jan. 12, 1863, manuscript, Minn. Historical Society.

[5] John B. Cuzner to Elsie Vandorn, Feb. 15, 1863, manuscript, Conn. Historical Society; John P. Sheahan to his homefolk, Sept. 22, 1862, manuscript, Maine Historical Society; A. Davenport to his homefolk, April 18, 1862.

[6] C. B. Thurston to his brother, Feb. 24, 1863, manuscript, Emory; Samuel W. Peter to his sister and brother, Oct. 27, 1862, manuscript, Ill. State Historical Library; Lt. Charles B. Stoddard to his aunt, Jan. 7, 1863, manuscript, Harvard.

[7] Capt. Gilmore Jordan to his homefolk, Aug. 17, 1862, manuscript, Ind. Historical Society.

[8] Diary of Capt. Oliver Lyman Spaulding, Dec. 25, 1862, manuscript, Univ. of Mich.

[9] John Hope Franklin, editor, The Diary of James T. Ayers (Springfield, Ill., 1947), 46.

[10] N. B. Bartlett to his brother, Aug. 2 [1864], manuscript, Chicago Historical Society; Henry J. H. Thompson to his wife, Sept. 7, 1864, manuscript, Duke.

[11] Capt. W. A. Walker to "Dear James," Jan. 16, 1864, manuscript, Princeton.

[12] Stephen A. Miller to his sister, Jan. 31, 1863, manuscript, Ind. Historical Society.

[13] J. R. Barney to his brother, Oct. 24, 1862, manuscript among Dinsmore Letters, Ill. State Historical Library.

[14] Samuel S. Hoyt to his brother, March 8, 1863, manuscript among Lucian B. Case Papers, Chicago Historical Society; John McMeekin to his mother, March 16, 1863, manuscript, Western Reserve Historical Society.

[15] Lt. Samuel Storrow to his mother, Dec. 24, 1864, manuscript, Mass. Historical Society; Abraham Kendig to his sister, May 16, 1862, manuscript, Historical Society of Pa.; George Newhall to his homefolk, Feb. 24, 1862, manuscript, Boston Public Library.

[16] John McMeekin to his mother, March [no day], 1863.

[17] John Beatty, The Citizen Soldier, 141-142.

[18] Chauncey H. Cooke to his homefolk, March 5, 1863, in "Letters of a Badger Boy in Blue," Wis. Magazine of History, IV (1920-1921), 324-327; James B. Loughney to Marie Brogan, Feb. 26, 1863, manuscript, Wis. Historical Society.

[19] Henry J. H. Thompson to his wife, June 20, 1863.

[20] A. Davenport to his homefolk, June 14, 1861; Thomas N. Lewis to his uncle, Nov. 14, 1862, manuscript among Moulton Letters, Western Reserve Historical Society; for an example of soldiers shooting Negroes, see diary of Matthew Marvin, Jan. 12, 1863.

[21] J. S. McCulloch, "Reminiscences of Life in the Army and as a Prisoner of War," manuscript (photoduplicate), Washington and Jef-

ferson College Library. I am indebted to C. M. Ewing of that college for locating this item and making it available to me.

22 John Bessemer to John Weissert, Nov. 17, 1861, manuscript, Univ. of Mich. This letter is in German script.

23 John McMeekin to his mother, Dec. 15, 1862.

24 O. R., series 1, XLVII, pt. 2, 33, 184; Bell Irvin Wiley, *Southern Negroes, 1861-1865* (New Haven, 1938), 235.

25 J. F. Morris to Clarissa Butler, May 7, 1863, manuscript among Miscellaneous Civil War Letters, American Antiquarian Society. An Indiana colonel wrote on one occasion that in Buell's army "some of the regiments seem to have as many servants as soldiers." A. T. Volwiler, editor, "Letters from a Civil War Officer," *Miss. Valley Historical Review*, XIV (1928), 509.

26 Lawrence Van Alstyne, *Diary of an Enlisted Man*, 213-214.

27 Diary of Rufus Kinsley, June 17, Aug. 26, 1862, manuscript, Vt. Historical Society.

28 Wiley, *Southern Negroes, 1861-1865*, 77.

29 For example, see *Diary of E. P. Burton*, 20.

30 Samuel Storrow wrote his homefolk, Feb. 4, 1863: "Oh many's the good meal I've had in an old 'nigger hut.' Their hoecakes are big things I tell you. The darkies are always very civil, obliging and ready to do anything in their power for one."

31 Henry Crydenwise to his parents, Feb. 5, 1862, manuscript, Emory.

32 Henry E. Simmons to his wife, June 6, 1863, manuscript, Lowdermilk's Bookstore, Washington, D. C.

33 Robert S. Fletcher, *History of Oberlin College*, II, 864.

34 Abraham Kendig to his brother, Jan. 4, 1864; Alfred S. Roe, *The Ninth New York Heavy Artillery*, 246-247.

35 Joseph F. Shelley to his wife, Nov. 6, 1863, in Fanny J. Anderson, editor, "The Shelley Papers," *Indiana Magazine of History*, XLIV (1948), 197.

36 Most of the instances were noted in manuscript court-martial proceedings, Nat'l Archives. An example of apparent concubinage is recorded in *The Soldier's Friend* of Aug. 8, 1868.

37 Nashville *Dispatch*, June 17, 1864. An instance of what appears to be marriage of a Negro woman to a white soldier was found in a provost marshal's report dated Newport News, Va., June 6, 1861, filed with the Roswell Farnham Letters, typescript, Vt. Historical Society.

38 Edward E. Newhall to his homefolk, Dec. 19, 1861, and Henry A. Newhall to his homefolk, Feb. 2, 1862, manuscripts, Boston Public Library.

39 Edward E. Newhall to his homefolk, June 22, 1862.

40 William R. Hartpence, *History of the Fifty-first Indiana Veteran Volunteer Infantry*, 72. Chaplain Arnold T. Needham on March 6, 1864, gave his wife the following version of an Alabama Negro preacher's account of the crucifixion: "Dey put him up on de cross, dey drove de ten-penny nails troo his hands, and dey stick de spear in his

side, and de blood run down on de ground, until as de Scripture saith it roared like a bull in de pen." Manuscript, Chicago Historical Society.

[41] Henry E. Simmons to his wife, Nov. 23, 1862, and June 6, 1863.

[42] G. F. Jourdan to his wife, May 3, 1863, manuscript among Miscellaneous Civil War Letters, American Antiquarian Society.

[43] James W. Smith to Mattie C. Howard, Nov. 4, 1862, manuscript, Ill. State Historical Library; Henry Warren Howe to his homefolk, June 19, 1861, in Henry Warren Howe, *Passages from the Life of Henry Warren Howe* (Lowell, Mass., 1899), 93.

[44] Michael R. Dresbach to his wife, Dec. 14, 1864, manuscript, Minn. Historical Society.

[45] Enoch T. Baker to his wife, July 27, 1862, manuscript, Historical Society of Pa.

[46] Henry J. H. Thompson to his wife, March 6, 1863.

[47] Wiley, *Southern Negroes, 1861-1865*, 325.

[48] *Ibid.*, 305.

[49] Diary of Sgt. William D. Evans, Jan. 11, 1865, manuscript, Western Reserve Historical Society; Wiley, *Southern Negroes, 1861-1865*, 324-325.

[50] Diary of Rufus Kinsley, Sept. 21, 1862.

[51] *Ibid.*, June 1, 1864.

[52] Henry Crydenwise to his parents, Nov. 28, 1863.

[53] *Ibid.*, April 10, 1865.

Chapter VI

THE DEPTHS OF SUFFERING

[1] Benjamin F. Green to William D. Murphy, Dec. 15, 1861, manuscript, N. Y. Public Library; Andrew K. Rose to his parents [July 1863], manuscript, Duke.

[2] After this chapter was drafted the writer had the privilege of reading G. W. Adams' "Health and Medicine in the Union Army, 1861-1865" (Ph.D. Dissertation, Harvard, 1946). This study by a competent historian of Civil War medicine is by far the best work on the subject. It is scheduled for publication in revised form by Henry Schuman of New York under the title *Doctors in Blue: An Account of Health and Medicine in the Union Army, 1861-1865*. Several references to the dissertation, particularly in instances where Mr. Adams' treatment is much fuller than that permitted here, were added to the notes of this chapter.

[3] Surgeon General of the U. S. Army, *Medical and Surgical History of the War of the Rebellion* (Washington, D. C., 1870-1888), Medical Volume, pt. 1, xxxvii, xliii, pt. 2, 3, and pt. 3, 3 ff. Hereafter this source will be cited as *Med. and Surg. Hist.*

[4] *Ibid.*, pt. 1, xxxvii and pt. 2, 3.

[5] *Ibid.*, pt. 3, 18 and diagram opposite p. 24. The figures cited in this paragraph are for white troops.

[6] *Ibid.*, 6.

[7] U. S. Sanitary Commission *Documents*, No. 40, 9, No. 43, 2.

[8] *Ibid.*, No. 36, 32; O. R., series 1, V, 81, XXXVI, pt. 1, 213.

[9] *Med. and Surg. Hist.*, Medical Vol., pt. 3, 626; U. S. Sanitary Comm. *Documents*, No. 36, 19; O. R., series 1, V, 85; vaccination was required by paragraph 1261, *Army Regulations*, 1861.

[10] W. W. Keen, "Military Surgery in 1861 and 1918," *Annals of the American Academy of Political and Social Science*, LXXX (1918), 12, 18.

[11] U. S. Sanitary Comm. *Documents*, No. 26, 5, 6, 11.

[12] *Ibid.*, 5.

[13] For example see *ibid.*, No. 17, 5; No. 26, 5; and No. 36, 28. W. H. Russell in a tour of the Army of the Potomac shortly before First Manassas found "the camps . . . dirty to excess." *My Diary North and South*, 403.

[14] U. S. Sanitary Comm. *Documents*, No. 17, 4.

[15] *Ibid.*, No. 40, 16.

[16] *Army Regulations*, 1861, paragraphs 100-101; U. S. Sanitary Comm. *Documents*, No. 17, 4-5; No. 40, 18-20.

[17] "Desiccated," or processed, foods are discussed in chapter IX.

[18] *Army Regulations*, 1861, paragraph 1191; U. S. Sanitary Comm. *Documents*, No. 17, 8-13; No. 26, 7; No. 40, 21-24; Capt. Edward S. Redington to his wife, March 28, 1863, manuscript, Wis. Historical Society; C. Barney, *Recollections of Field Service with the Twentieth Iowa Infantry Volunteers*, 27-28.

[19] U. S. Sanitary Comm. *Documents*, No. 36, 20.

[20] *Ibid.*, No. 24, 3; No. 26, 2; No. 36, 30-31; W. H. Russell, *My Diary North and South*, 404.

[21] *Ibid.*

[22] U. S. Sanitary Comm. *Documents*, No. 24, 2.

[23] P. M. Ashburn, *A History of the Medical Department of the United States Army* (Boston, 1929), 72 ff; Francis R. Packard, *History of Medicine in the United States* (N. Y., 1931), 639 ff; G. W. Adams has an excellent discussion of medical administration at the beginning of the war and its subsequent reform in *op. cit.*, chaps. 1-2.

[24] Charles J. Stille, *History of the U. S. Sanitary Commission* (Philadelphia, 1886), 124-137; Ashburn, *op. cit.*, 72-73; Packard, *op. cit.*, 641.

[25] Ashburn, *op. cit.*, 74-75, 85-86; Evelyn S. Drayton, "William Alexander Hamond 1828-1900," *Military Surgeon*, CIX (1951), 559-565.

[26] U. S. Sanitary Comm. *Documents*, No. 36, 32; No. 40, 53; O. R., series 1, XI, pt. 1, 192.

[27] U. S. Sanitary Comm. *Documents*, No. 40, 33.

[28] *Ibid.*, No. 17, 17.

[29] O. R., series 1, XI, pt. 1, 189. Known as acting assistant surgeons,

contract surgeons employed during the war aggregated 5,532. *Ibid.*, series 3, V, 150.

[30] U. S. Sanitary Comm. *Documents*, No. 26, 12; No. 38, 7.

[31] O. R., series 1, VII, 242-243; Hq. Army Dept. and Army of the Tenn. G. O. No. 8, June 11, 1864.

[32] Surgeon Henry P. Strong to his wife, Jan. 19, 24, 1862, typescript, Wis. Historical Society; Adjutant Richard L. Ashhurst to his homefolk, March 21, 1863, typescript, Historical Society of Pa.; J.A.G. Records MM-756, manuscript, Nat'l Archives.

[33] O. R., series 1, XXXVIII, pt. 3, 57; series 3, V, 150. If contract physicians, hospital surgeons and all other classes are included, the number of doctors serving in the army by April 1865 exceeded 12,000. For an extensive discussion of army doctors and their practice, see Adams, *op. cit.*, especially chap. 3.

[34] For two examples see O. R., series 1, III, 70 and X, pt. 1, 361.

[35] Harvey E. Brown, *History of the Medical Department of the United States Army* (Washington, 1875), 254.

[36] Capt. Edward G. Abbott to his father, Dec. 13, 1861, manuscript, Harvard.

[37] Alfred Davenport, *Camp and Field Life of the Fifth New York Volunteer Infantry*, 134; David Lathrop, *History of the 59th Regiment Illinois Volunteers* (Indianapolis, 1865), 169; John D. Billings, *Hard Tack and Coffee*, 310-311.

[38] Thomas N. Lewis to his uncle, June 7, 1861, manuscript among Moulton Letters, Western Reserve Historical Society; Thomas M. Moulton to his brother, May 22, 1865; A. Davenport to his homefolk, June 17, 1862, manuscript, N. Y. Historical Society.

[39] John McMeekin to his mother, March [no day], 1863, manuscript, Western Reserve Historical Society; diary of M. F. Roberts, May 3, 1864, manuscript, Western Reserve Historical Society.

[40] William N. Price, *One Year in the War* (n.d., n.p.), 42; Edward L. Edes to his father, Aug. 12, 1863, manuscript, Mass. Historical Society.

[41] Jacob Weidensall to his brother, March 1, 1862; Ill. Historical Records Survey, *Calendar of the Robert Weidensall Correspondence, 1861-1865 at George Williams College, Chicago, Illinois* (Chicago, 1940), 2.

[42] U. S. Sanitary Comm. *Documents*, No. 35, 5.

[43] Richard L. Ashhurst to his homefolk, Sept. 18, 1862.

[44] Joseph J. Woodward, *Outlines of the Camp Diseases of the United States Armies* (Philadelphia, 1863), 268. To be cited hereafter as Woodward, *Camp Diseases. Med. and Surg. Hist.*, Medical Vol., pt. 3, 649 ff. Figures given in *Med. and Surg. Hist.* for measles and all other diseases must be regarded as only approximate. See introductory statement, Medical Volume, pt. 1, i-xliii.

[45] Ruth A. Gallaher, editor, "Peter Wilson in the Civil War," *Iowa Journal of History and Politics*, XL (1942), 180-181.

[46] *Med. and Surg. Hist.*, Medical Vol., pt. 3, 650; John McMeekin to his mother, Feb. 5, 1863.

[47] Charles W. Wills, *Army Life of an Illinois Soldier*, 8.

[48] *Med. and Surg. Hist.*, Medical Vol., pt. 3, 77; Woodward, *Camp Diseases*, 28 ff; C. B. Thurston to his father, Nov. 23, 1863, manuscript, Emory.

[49] *Med. and Surg. Hist.*, Medical Vol., pt. 3, diagram opposite p. 90.

[50] *Ibid.*, 11, 192, 196.

[51] *Ibid.*, 199, and diagram opposite p. 199.

[52] *O. R.*, series 1, VII, 513.

[53] John W. De Forest, *A Volunteer's Adventures*, 152-154.

[54] Elias R. Goad to a friend, Nov. 7 [1861], manuscript in possession of Charles N. Owen, Chicago.

[55] Lucius F. Hubbard, "Minnesota in the Battle of Corinth," Minn. Historical Society *Collections*, XII (1905-08), 533. Theodore Upson wrote in his journal July 27, 1863: "It is fearfully hot and there is a great amount of sickness . . . so many are in the hospitals that we are not allowed to fire volleys over the graves for fear it will discourage the sick ones." Oscar O. Winther, editor, *With Sherman to the Sea*, 65-66.

[56] *Med. and Surg. Hist.*, Medical Vol., pt. 3, 662, 675-679; O. R., series 3, V, 151.

[57] *Med. and Surg. Hist.*, Medical Vol., pt. 1, 636-641, 710-711. Figures for Negro troops are for the period June 30, 1864—June 30, 1866.

[58] J. J. Moulton to his homefolk [n.d., but May or June 1861]. Diarrhea and dysentery, owing possibly to poorer discipline, were considerably greater among Western troops than among Eastern. *Med. and Surg. Hist.*, Medical Vol., pt. 2 (which is devoted to the "fluxes"), 9.

[59] William T. Pippen to "A. H. and B. G.," July 11, 1862, manuscript, Duke; diary of Henry Clay Scott, July 18, 1861, manuscript, N. Y. Public Library.

[60] Henry J. H. Thompson wrote his homefolk March 6, 1863: "I am alive and moveing & lively to[o] last Night for I had the Virginia Quickstep I had to ease myself 2 times." Manuscript, Duke.

[61] *Med. and Surg. Hist.*, Medical Volume, pt. 2, diagram opposite p. 22.

[62] *Ibid.*, 2-3.

[63] *Ibid.*, 6.

[64] *Ibid.*, 6-7.

[65] Ashburn, *op. cit.*, 82 states: "Unhappily, not much progress had been made in the prevention of disease, which is fully explained by the fact that bacteriology and its twin, modern hygiene, were yet unborn."

[66] U. S. Sanitary Comm. *Documents*, No. 27, 5.

[67] *Med. and Surg. Hist.*, Medical Vol., pt. 2, 661 ff, 718, 808, 818.

[68] *Ibid.*, pt. 3, 112 ff.

[69] *Ibid.*, 115.

[70] *Ibid.*, 369, 371. For numerous clinical records, many of which specify treatment in detail, see *ibid.*, 216-267.

[71] *Ibid.*, pt. 2, 718-722.

[72] Harold A. Small, editor, *The Road to Richmond*, 188.

[73] Henry J. H. Thompson to his wife, Aug. 15, 1863.

[74] Daniel Beidelman to his mother, Sept. 18, 1862, manuscript, Duke; Leland O. Barlow to his sister, Jan. 26, 1863, manuscript, Conn. State Library; diary of Stillman H. Budlong, Oct. 31, 1861, manuscript, Westerly, R. I., Public Library.

[75] Capt. Edward S. Redington to his wife, June 16, 1863.

[76] Henry J. H. Thompson to his wife, April 5, 1863; Edward L. Edes to his mother, Sept. 25, 1862; Benjamin E. Sweetland to his wife, Nov. 15 [1862], manuscript, Boston Public Library.

[77] *Med. and Surg. Hist.*, Medical Vol., pt. 1, appendix, 40.

[78] *Ibid.*

[79] Stille, *op. cit.*, 153 ff; [Frederick Law Olmsted] *Hospital Transports, A Memoir of the Embarkation of the Sick and Wounded from the Peninsula of Virginia in the Summer of 1862* (Boston, 1863), 18 ff; to be cited hereafter as Olmsted, *Hospital Transports*; George T. Stevens, *Three Years in the Sixth Corps* (N. Y., 1870), 44, 46. Stevens was surgeon of the 77th N. Y. Regt.

[80] *Med. and Surg. Hist.*, Medical Vol., pt. 1, appendix, 92; Stevens, *op. cit.*, 114.

[81] *Med. and Surg. Hist.*, Medical Vol., pt. 1, appendix, 148 ff, 253, 255; U. S. Sanitary Comm. *Documents*, No. 75, 3; Stille, *op. cit.*, 277, 393-400; U. S. Sanitary Comm. *Bulletin*, I (1864), 424.

[82] This statement is based primarily on a study of medical reports in *Med. and Surg. Hist.*, pt. 1, appendix, and U. S. Sanitary Commission *Documents*. All materials used point to general improvement, especially after 1862 when the reforms of Hammond and Letterman began to bear fruit.

[83] U. S. Sanitary Comm. *Documents*, No. 23, 1 ff, No. 36, 5 ff and No. 41, 3 ff; *Med. and Surg. Hist.*, Medical Vol., pt. 3, 896 ff.

[84] Stille, *op. cit.*, 153.

[85] Ashburn, *op. cit.*, 70; *Med. and Surg. Hist.*, Medical Vol., pt. 3, 896-909. James A. Tobey, *The Medical Department of the Army: Its History, Activities and Organizations* (Baltimore, 1927), 15-17.

[86] *Ibid.*

[87] U. S. Sanitary Comm. *Documents*, No. 23, 3.

[88] *Med. and Surg. Hist.*, Medical Vol., pt. 3, 908-909.

[89] *Ibid.*; Ashburn, *op. cit.*, 79-80.

[90] *Ibid.*

[91] *Med. and Surg. Hist.*, Medical Vol., pt. 3, 943-945.

[92] *Ibid.*, Surgical Vol., pt. 3, 923-935; Medical Vol., pt. 1, appendix, 78; U. S. Sanitary Comm. *Bulletin*, I (1864), 520.

[93] *Med. and Surg. Hist.*, Surgical Vol., pt. 3, 923-935; Medical Vol., pt. 1, appendix, 78.

[94] U. S. Sanitary Comm. *Documents*, No. 48, 12-13; *Med. and Surg. Hist.*, Surgical Vol., pt. 3, 931-935; J. S. Newberry, *The U. S. Sanitary Commission in the Valley of the Mississippi* (Cleveland, O., 1871), 66. This is U. S. Sanitary Comm. *Documents*, No. 96.

[95] *Med. and Surg. Hist.*, Medical Vol., pt. 1, appendix, 49; Stille, *op. cit.*, 157-158.

[96] Stille, *op. cit.*, 150-153; *Med. and Surg. Hist.*, Medical Vol., pt. 1, appendix, 30.

[97] U. S. Sanitary Comm. *Documents*, No. 23, 5; No. 40, 79; O. R., series 1, III, 274-275; *Med. and Surg. Hist.*, Medical Vol., pt. 1, appendix, 19.

[98] *Med. and Surg. Hist.*, Medical Vol., pt. 1, appendix, 31.

[99] *Ibid.*

[100] *Ibid.*, 70, 78.

[101] *Ibid.*, 88; Mrs. E. N. Harris to Mrs. Joel Jones, June 5, 1862, in "Anecdotes of our Wounded and Dying Soldiers in the Rebellion," manuscript, Historical Society of Pa.

[102] Stille, *op. cit.*, 161.

[103] *Ibid.*, 161-164; *Med. and Surg. Hist.*, Surgical Vol., pt. 3, 958 ff.

[104] *Med. and Surg. Hist.*, Medical Vol., pt. 1, appendix, 88, 93; Olmsted, *Hospital Transports*, 98-110, 166.

[105] *Med. and Surg. Hist.*, Medical Vol., pt. 1, appendix, 117, 125-127, 129.

[106] *Ibid.*, 127; a U. S. Sanitary Commission representative reported on May 8, 1864, concerning removal of the wounded from the Wilderness: "The sufferings of these men cannot in any degree be realized. The road —an old plank road—was in a wretched condition, and the groans and shrieks of the sufferers were truly heart-rending." U. S. Sanitary Comm.

[107] Newberry, *op. cit.*, 63 ff; *Med. and Surg. Hist.*, Medical Vol., pt. 1, *Bulletin*, I (1864), 425. appendix, 253.

[108] *Med. and Surg. Hist.*, Medical Vol., pt. 1, appendix, 140 ff; 268, 283 ff.

[109] Ashburn, *op. cit.*, 73 ff; Packard, *op. cit.*, 641-655; *Time* magazine, Nov. 24, 1947; *Med. and Surg. Hist.*, Surgical Vol., pt. 3, 933 ff.

[110] *Ibid.*; U. S. Sanitary Comm. *Documents*, No. 57, 5-10, 23-24. The ambulance and field-hospital systems are treated in detail in Adams, *op. cit.*, chapters 6 and 7.

[111] *Med. and Surg. Hist.*, Surgical Vol., pt. 3, 933-934, 938, 941-943. Letterman had issued an order on Aug. 24, 1863, improving the ambulance system. See U. S. Sanitary Comm. *Bulletin*, I (1864), 151-152.

[112] *Med. and Surg. Hist.*, Surgical Vol., pt. 3, 902.

[113] Ashburn, *op. cit.*, 80; *Time* magazine, Nov. 24, 1947.

[114] Stille, *op. cit.*, 161 ff; *Med. and Surg. Hist.*, Medical Vol., pt. 1, appendix, 1 ff; Surgical Vol., pt. 3, 916 ff.

[115] This was provided by Letterman's reorganization circular of Oct. 30, 1862. Copy in U. S. Sanitary Comm. *Documents*, No. 57, 6-8.

[116] For an example, see O. R., series 1, XXXVIII, pt. 2, 526-527.

[117] Many of these specimens were reproduced, some in color, in the surgical volumes of the *Med. and Surg. Hist.*

[118] *Med. and Surg. Hist.*, Medical Vol., pt. 1, appendix, 70 and Surgical Vol., pt. 3, 887-898; U. S. Sanitary Comm. *Documents*, No. 40, 53-54; O. R., series 1, XI, pt. 1, 192, XXV, pt. 1, 400; Adams, *op. cit.*, chaps. 8-9.

[119] Col. T. D. Kingsley to H. D. Rallion, June 25, 1863, manuscript in possession of Towner K. Webster, Chicago, photostat obtained through kindness of Monroe F. Cockrell.

[120] O. R., series 1, XXXVIII, pt. 2, 526-527. For statistics and other information on amputations see Med. and Surg. Hist., Surgical Vol., pt. 3, 869-886. Gangrene is discussed in ibid., 824-851. For a gory illustration of gangrene effects, see colored picture, ibid., 850.

[121] Billings, Hard Tack and Coffee, 310-311.

[122] Col. T. D. Kingsley to H. D. Rallion, June 25, 1863.

[123] Keen, "Military Surgery in 1861 and 1918," Annals of the American Academy of Political and Social Science, LXXX (1918), 14, 15.

[124] For criticisms of civilian agencies by medical authorities, see O. R., series 1, X, pt. 2, 62, XI, pt. 1, 177-178, XXXVIII, pt. 5, 7.

[125] B. B. Brown to his sister, Oct. 28, 1862, "Civil War Letters," North Dakota Historical Quarterly, I (1927), 66.

[126] Diary of Lt. Henry A. Kircher, June 8, 1863, manuscript, Ill. State Historical Library.

[127] "Prock's Letters from Camp, Battlefield and Hospital," Indiana Magazine of History, XXXIV (1938), 96.

[128] Commendation of the Sisters of Charity was found in a number of soldier letters and no criticism was found. Adams, op. cit., II, 562, notes that soldiers referred to several nun groups as "Sisters of Charity." Work of the Christian and Sanitary Commissions also elicited a considerable amount of favorable comment, though the U. S. Sanitary Commission was condemned by some on the score of partiality to officers. The Christian Commission differed from the Sanitary Commission in that its primary function was the spiritual care of the soldiers, though it did distribute delicacies and reading materials to the sick and wounded. For a commendatory statement by a soldier concerning the Christian and the U. S. Sanitary Commissions see [David Lane], A Soldier's Diary (n.d., n.p., but 1905), 150-151.

[129] The work of the Christian Commission is related in the published Annual Reports of that organization, and in manuscript reports of its agents filed in the National Archives. The United States Sanitary Commission issued a series of ninety-six Documents (N. Y., 1866-1871), a Bulletin (3 vols., N. Y., 1864-1866), and various other publications. Charles J. Stille wrote a contemporary account of its work, and the Western phase was treated by J. S. Newberry in U. S. Sanitary Comm. Documents, No. 96. Recent studies include Marjorie B. Greenbie, Lincoln's Daughters of Mercy (N. Y., 1944) and an unpublished Ph.D. dissertation at Columbia University by William Maxwell. The Western Sanitary Commission, a separate organization, is treated in J. G. Forman, The Western Sanitary Commission. A Sketch of Its Origin, History, Labors for the Sick and Wounded......with Incidents of Hospital Life (St. Louis, 1864). The work of all civilian defense agencies is ably discussed by Adams, op. cit., chap. 5.

[130] See Stille, op. cit., Newberry, op. cit., and U. S. Sanitary Comm. Documents.

[181] E. A. Peterson wrote his homefolk from Chattanooga June 21, 1864: "The blamed Sanitary & Christian [Commissions] will not help a fellow unless he has shoulder straps." Manuscript, Duke; C. B. Thurston wrote his father July 1, 1863, from Fort St. Phillip, La.: "The Sanitary Commission in this department . . . has been a humbug."

[182] Bell Irvin Wiley, *The Life of Johnny Reb*, 244-269.

Chapter VII

GAY AND HAPPY STILL

[1] A. Davenport to his homefolk, Jan. 26, 1863, manuscript, N. Y. Public Library; Edmund English to his mother, Jan. 27, 1863, microfilm of manuscript, Huntington Library.

[2] A. Davenport to his homefolk, March 27, 1863; L. Marion Moulton to his homefolk, Dec. 13, 1864, manuscript, Western Reserve Historical Society.

[3] John Milledge to Mrs. Joseph H. Diltz, May 20, 1863, manuscript, Duke; Lt. Widwey to "Dear Friend," Sept. 8, 1861, in *Emigranten* (a Norwegian newspaper published at Madison, Wis.), Oct. 7, 1861. Translation by Inga B. Norstog.

[4] *O. R.*, series 1, XXIX, pt. 2, 26.

[5] Cyrus R. Stone to his parents, June 24, July 15, 1862, manuscripts, Minn. Historical Society.

[6] Frank Leslie published both *Frank Leslie's Illustrated Newspaper* and *Frank Leslie's Monthly*.

[7] For an example of a severe soldier criticism of Frank Leslie's battle artists, see Sgt. Henry C. Hall to his sister, Oct. 5 [1862], manuscript, Duke.

[8] Hazel C. Wolf, editor, *Campaigning with the First Minnesota*, 250; Samuel Storrow to his parents, Feb. 15, 1863, manuscript, Mass. Historical Society.

[9] Bishop Crumrine to his brother, Nov. 12, Dec. 17, 1863; Feb. 12, March 6, March 24, 1864, manuscripts, Washington and Jefferson Library. Copies furnished by the courtesy of Charles M. Ewing. The Mrs. Hentz referred to was Caroline Lee Whiting Hentz (1800-1856) and the book, *Ernest Linwood*. See DAB, VIII, 565-566.

[10] U. S. Christian Commission, Daily Record Book for 9th Corps, 1864, manuscript, Nat'l Archives. Knute Nelson, "Civil War Notes and Memoranda," manuscript, Minn. Historical Society.

[11] Urich N. Parmelee to his mother, Oct. 26, 1863, manuscript, Duke.

[12] For an extensive discussion and full cataloguing of Beadle publications, see Albert Johannsen, *The House of Beadle and Adams* (2 vols., Norman, Okla., 1950). Johannsen discusses the popularity of Beadle books in the Union Army on p. 39 of vol. 1.

[13] Asbury L. Kerwood, *Annals of the Fifty-Seventh Regiment Indiana Volunteers* (Dayton, Ohio, 1868), 188-189.

[14] Edward L. Edes to his mother, Feb. 5, 1864, manuscript, Mass. Historical Society; C. W. Bardeen, *A Little Fifer's War Diary* (Syracuse, 1910), 291; diary of Florison D. Pitts, Sept. 29, 1863, manuscript, Chicago Historical Society; the author of *East and West* was Mrs. Frances F. Barritt, Johannsen, *op. cit.*, II, 29-30. *The Gold Fiend* was not a Beadle publication.

[15] U. S. Christian Commission, *Third Annual Report* (Philadelphia, 1865), 50-51.

[16] For examples, see U. S. Christian Commission, Daily Record Book, 5th Corps, entries of Dec. 30, 1864, by Samuel Hopley and Feb. 8, 1865, by W. M. Lisle, manuscript, Nat'l Archives.

[17] Edward L. Edes to his mother, Feb. 5, 1864

[18] U. S. Christian Commission, *Third Annual Report*, 47-50.

[19] E. A. Johnson, editor, *The Hero of Medfield. The Journals and Letters of Allen Alonzo Kingsburg* (Boston, 1862), 62.

[20] Diary of Horton P. Rugg, March 12, 1863, manuscript (hand copy), Conn. State Library.

[21] For example, see Edward L. Edes to his mother, March 29, 1863.

[22] Jenkin Lloyd Jones, *An Artilleryman's Diary* (Madison, Wis., 1914), 85; C. B. Thurston to his brother, October 21, 1862, manuscript, Emory; Samuel Storrow to his parents, Dec. 26, 1862.

[23] U. S. Christian Commission, Daily Record Book, 9th Corps, entry of Sept. 20, 1864, by A. J. Wilcox and Sept. 25, 1864, by a Mr. Petty.

[24] Hq. Army of the Potomac, G. O. No. 151, Aug. 4, 1862. A number of references were found in soldier accounts to regiments having bands after their discontinuance was ordered. See for example, James K. Hosmer, *The Color-Guard*, 37.

[25] "John" to Fannie L. Partridge, April 19, 1862, manuscript, Chicago Historical Society. The band leader referred to was Patrick Sarsfield Gilmore, famous Irish-born bandmaster and composer of the period 1850-1890. After directing the 24th Mass. band, 1861-1863, he was put in charge of all army bands in the Department of the Gulf, where, at Governor Hahn's inauguration in 1864, he inaugurated a type of mammoth concert for which he later became nationally famous. While in New Orleans, Gilmore composed, under the pseudonym Louis Lambert, the popular war song "When Johnny Comes Marching Home." *DAB*, VII, 312.

[26] *DAB*, VII, 312.

[27] Journal of Maj. Charles B. Fox, Nov. 7, 1863, Mass. Historical Society.

[28] Col. John A. Cockerill, "What a Boy Did at Shiloh," Portland, Maine, *Daily Express*, Jan. 21, 1890, supplement; *O. R.*, series 1, XI, pt. 1, 458-459; Charles Ward to his brother, May 11, 1863, manuscript, American Antiquarian Society; Leander Stillwell, *The Story of a Common Soldier*, 62; E. T. Baker to his wife, Sept. 9, 1862, manuscript, Historical Society of Pa.

²⁹ J. M. Roberts, *The Experience of a Private in the Civil War* (privately printed, 1924), 10.

³⁰ Lt. Col. Charles B. Fox to his wife, Jan. 10, 1864, manuscript, Mass. Historical Society.

³¹ Bell Irvin Wiley, *The Life of Johnny Reb*, 318.

³² Capt. T. J. Wright, *History of the Eighth Regiment Kentucky Volunteer Infantry*, 146.

³³ The New York Public Library, the Library of Congress, the Historical Society of Pennsylvania, Brown University and the American Antiquarian Society have especially good collections of Civil War Songs and Music.

³⁴ The three Beadle titles cited are in the New York Public Library Music Division Collection. For other Beadle songbooks, see Johannsen, *op. cit.*, I, 41, 43, 48, 49.

³⁵ The first seven songsters listed in this sentence were found in the New York Public Library. The others used were in the Historical Society of Pennsylvania, except "The Yankee Doodle Songster" which was seen in the Burton Collection of the Detroit Public Library.

³⁶ For a palmetto tree version, see copy of the song in George B. Sprague Papers, Wis. Historical Society. Leland O. Barlow in a letter to his sister, July 24, 1863, mentions a crab-apple tree version. Manuscript, Conn. State Library. The origin of "John Brown's Body" has been the subject of considerable discussion. Katherine Little Bakeless in *Glory Hallelujah: The Story of the Battle Hymn of the Republic* (Philadelphia, 1944), accepts the claim of T. Brigham Bishop, minstrelman and composer, that he wrote the words and music in 1858. Most earlier writers incline to the view that the tune was based on a plantation or camp-meeting melody and that the words originated among members of a Boston militia organization which became a part of the 12th Mass. Regt. The regiment was said to have sung the song as it marched down Broadway in New York en route to Virginia in the summer of 1861. See Nicholas Smith, "The Battle Hymns of Nations," Military Order of the Loyal Legion of the United States, Wisconsin Commandery, *War Papers*, III (Milwaukee, 1903), 471 ff; Brander Matthews, "Songs of the War," *Century Magazine*, XXXIV (August 1887), 619-629; *Our War Songs North and South* (Cleveland, 1887), 7-9; and Philip D. Jordan, *Singin' Yankees* (Minneapolis, 1946), 229-230.

³⁷ "Civil War Diary of William C. Benson," *Indiana Magazine of History*, XXIII (1927), 360; *DAB*, VI, 110.

³⁸ A copy of this parody was found in the front of the diary of Sgt. William H. Tyner, 38th Ill. Regt. This manuscript is in possession of Mrs. Richard Alison of Jackson, Tennessee, to whom I am indebted for its use.

³⁹ Colonial Dames of America, *American War Songs* (Philadelphia, 1925), 70-72. For a full account of the song's origin, see Bakeless, *op. cit.*

⁴⁰ Nicholas Smith, *op. cit.*, 484-486.

⁴¹ *Ibid.*

⁴² It is interesting to note that a German soldier, Franz Eder of the

119th N. Y. Regt., who kept his diary in his native tongue copied this song in the back in neatly written English. Manuscript, N. Y. Public Library. The words of this song, along with many other war lyrics, may be found in F. T. Miller, editor, *Photographic History of the Civil War,* IX, 342-352.

[43] Capt. C. Barney, *Recollections of Field Service with the Twentieth Iowa Infantry,* 38. For the complete lyrics of "Gay and Happy Still," see Miller, *op. cit.,* IX, 349.

[44] William R. Hartpence, *History of the Fifty-first Indiana Veteran Volunteer Infantry,* 251-252.

[45] For a discussion of folk songs of the era, see Alfred M. Williams, "Folk Songs of the Civil War," *Journal of American Folklore,* V (1892), 265-283.

[46] Most of the war songs listed here may be found, along with sketches of the principal composers, in *Our War Songs North and South,* published by S. Brainards' Sons. Good collections of folk and sentimental songs have been published by Carl Sandburg, *The American Songbag* (N. Y., 1927), John A. and Alan Lomax, *American Ballads and Folk Songs* (N. Y., 1934), and Philip D. Jordan and Lillian Kessler, *Songs of Yesterday* (Garden City, 1941). But one interested in lyrics used in Civil War times should consult original sheet music of the period which is obtainable in most major libraries. The Library of Congress and the New York Public Library collections are especially good. Sigmund Spaeth's *A History of Popular Music in America* (N. Y., 1948), 153-161, contains a brief but able discussion of Northern songs and composers of the war period.

[47] For comment on the popularity of "Wait for the Wagon," see "Songs of the Long Ago" in Chicago *Tribune,* Nov. 26, 1887. Lloyd D. Harris in "Army Music," Military Order of the Loyal Legion, Commandery of Missouri, *War Papers and Personal Reminiscences,* I (St. Louis, 1892), 291, stated: "Every officer in our regiment who sang the solo of 'Benny Havens, O!' was killed in battle."

[48] Stephen A. Miller to his sister, Oct. 16, 1863, manuscript, Ind. Historical Society; Harvey Reid to his homefolk, June 3, 1863, manuscript, Wis. Historical Society; William Bircher, *Diary of a Drummer Boy* (St. Paul, Minn., 1889), 161; diary of Oliver L. Spaulding, Nov. 4, 1862, manuscript, Univ. of Mich.; J. H. Greene, *Reminiscences of the War,* 41. A copy of the "Homespun Dress" made by a soldier, and apparently sent to his homefolk, is in the Ezra Rickett Collection, manuscripts, Ohio State Arch. and Historical Society.

[49] Spaeth, *op. cit.,* 154; Wiley, *The Life of Johnny Reb,* 318. The best study of Southern songs of the war years is Richard B. Harwell, *Confederate Music* (Chapel Hill, 1950). The same author has also compiled a handsome book of facsimiles of Confederate sheet music under the title *Songs of the Confederacy* (N. Y., 1951).

[50] For a splendid discussion of the origin and history of "Dixie," see Hans Nathan, "Dixie," *The Musical Quarterly,* XXXV (1949), 60-84.

[51] George T. Stevens in *Three Years in the Sixth Corps,* 268, states

that as the Sixth Corps, returning south from the Gettysburg campaign, crossed the Potomac the bands played "Oh, Carry Me Back to Ole Virginia," thus bearing out the claim that while Bland's song of that title was not published until 1878, an earlier version was in circulation during Civil War times. See letter to the editor by Henry S. Commager in New York *Herald-Tribune* Book Review section, Jan. 22, 1950, 13.

[52] Richard B. Harwell, "Confederate Carrousel: Southern Songs of the Sixties," *Emory University Quarterly*, VI (1950), 90-91; S. J. Adair Fitz-Gerald, *Stories of Famous Songs* (Philadelphia and London, 1906), I, 131.

[53] Cyrus R. Stone to his wife, Jan. 12, 1863. Members of the 138th New York Regiment, many of whom were from Wayne County, N. Y., while digging ditches near Washington in 1862, sang it thus:

> I wish I was in Old Wayne County,
> My three years up, and I had my bounty,
> Look away, look away . . .

Alfred S. Roe, *History of the Ninth New York Heavy Artillery*, 39. For a parody called the Jay Hawker's Dixie, sung by the Seventh Kansas Regiment, see Theodore C. Blegen, editor, *Civil War Letters of Colonel Hans C. Heg* (Northfield, Minn., 1936), 94-97.

[54] O. W. Norton, *Army Letters, 1861-1865*, 324. For a slightly different version, see Roe, *op. cit.*, 68 and John D. Billings, *Hard Tack and Coffee*, 168-169.

[55] Norton, *op. cit.*, 324. For other versions. see Billings, *op. cit.*, 172 and Roe, *op. cit.*, 68.

[56] Roe, *op. cit.*, 69.

[57] Norton, *op. cit.*, 325.

[58] Roe, *op. cit.*, 68.

[59] Norton, *op. cit.*, 325.

[60] William H. Bentley, *History of the 77th Illinois Volunteer Infantry*, 138.

[61] Billings, *op. cit.*, 118.

[62] *The Good Old Songs We Used to Sing '61 to '65* (Washington, D. C., 1902), 11.

[63] Charles E. Davis, *Three Years in the Army*, 156.

[64] Broadside among Civil War Lyrics, Emory.

[65] Journal of David H. Haines, Oct. 20, 1863, manuscript, Detroit Public Library.

[66] Broadside among Civil War Songs, Maine Historical Society.

[67] Reference to "Chickamauga" was found in a letter of William H. Lloyd to his wife, Sept. 13, 1864, manuscript, Western Reserve Historical Society, and a hand copy of this and of "An Epick" on Murfreesboro and on Chattanooga are in the Ezra E. Rickett Collection. A song glorifying the exploits of the 2nd Division, 20th Corps, in the battles about Chattanooga of November 23-25, 1863, was sent home by William H. Lloyd on Aug. 23, 1861.

[68] See *Our War Songs North and South*, 42-44, 310-311. "We Are Marching Down to Dixie" was copied by Sgt. Will H. Tyner, 38th Ill. Regt. and preserved with his papers.

[69] Hand copy in Ezra E. Rickett Collection.

[70] "Extracts from the War Diary of John V. Ruehle," manuscript, Detroit Public Library.

[71] Broadside in Ill. State Historical Library.

[72] The 69th New York Regiment provided the theme for a number of ballads. Alfred M. Williams, "Folk Songs of the Civil War," *Journal of American Folklore*, V (1892), 268.

[73] *Our War Songs North and South*, 179-185.

[74] A hand copy of "A New Ballad of Lord Lovel" was found in the Ezra E. Rickett Collection. For a discussion of the original ballad and various adaptations, including two of the Civil War period, see H. M. Belden, editor, "Ballads and Songs Collected by the Missouri Folk Lore Society," University of Missouri *Studies*, XV (1940), 52-54.

[75] Copy from front of diary of Sgt. William B. Tyner. A note by Tyner credits the song to E. W. Locke. The ballad "Chattanooga," adapted to the air "Nelly Bly," began:

> General Bragg, how do you like
> The looks of General Grant?

Copy in Ezra E. Rickett Collection.

[76] John Beatty, *The Citizen Soldier*, 64.

[77] Broadside, Emory. "The Yankee Doodle Songster" contains "Jefferson D" by H. S. Cornwall and "O! Jeff Davis" by H. Angelo.

[78] *Ibid.*

[79] Vance Randolph, in *Ozark Folk Songs* (Columbia, Mo., 1948), II, 352, says that "Shoo, Fly, Shoo" was "one of the most popular nonsense songs of the Civil War period."

[80] Billings, *op. cit.*, 215. For the original version of "Abraham's Daughter," see *Our War Songs North and South*, 461-463.

[81] *Our War Songs North and South*, 10.

[82] John Beatty, *op. cit.*, 119. "I Am Jesus' Little Lamb" was heard by the writer in a World War II training center.

[83] Diary of an unidentified soldier of the 24th Conn. Regt., Jan. 17, 1863, manuscript, Conn. State Library.

[84] Lloyd D. Harris, *op. cit.*, I, 289-291; Henry M. McIntire to his parents, Sept. 8, 1861, manuscript, Mass. Historical Society; Hq. Dept. of the Gulf, G. O. No. 19, Feb. 26, 1863.

[85] Asst. Surg. Humphrey H. Hood to his wife, Dec. 6, 1862, manuscript, Ill. State Historical Library.

[86] Diary of Charles E. Bolton, Aug. 1, 1864, manuscript, Mass. Historical Society.

[87] See especially letters of Fox to his wife, Jan. 13, Sept. 5, and Nov. 1, 1864.

[88] *Ibid.*, Oct. 16, 1864.

[89] Frank M. Rood to "Friend Elvira," Aug. 31, 1863, manuscript in possession of Harry Rood, Poultney, Vt.; Mrs. J. D. Wheeler, compiler, *In Memoriam: Letters of William Wheeler of the Class of 1855 Y. C.,* 30.

[90] Carl Wittke, "The Ninth Ohio Volunteers," *Ohio State Archaeological and Historical Quarterly,* XXXV (1926), 415; Walter Koempel, editor, *Phil Koempel's Diary* (n.p., n.d.), 41. The diarist, a member of Co. B, 1st Conn. Cav., quotes a portion of the song.

[91] Lt. Col. Charles B. Fox to his mother, Feb. 6, 1864; Adam Muenzenberger to his homefolk, April 20, 1863, manuscript (typescript translation), Wis. Historical Society.

[92] Regis de Trobriand, *Four Years with the Army of the Potomac* (Boston, 1889), 95.

[93] See for example, Beatty, *op. cit.,* 64; Lloyd D. Harris, *op. cit.,* 289-291.

[94] Blegen, editor, *Civil War Letters of Colonel Hans C. Heg,* 140.

[95] Diary of James F. Williams, Feb. 20, 1864, manuscript, N. Y. Public Library; Josiah S. Chandler, "What a Private Saw Thought and Did during the War of the Rebellion," 120-121, manuscript, Western Reserve Historical Society; diary of James F. Williams, Feb. 6, 1864; diary of Charles F. Johnson, March 4, 8, 1863, manuscript, Minn. Historical Society; Edward L. Edes to his father, April 3, 1864.

[96] Stevens, *Three Years in the Sixth Corps,* 183.

[97] A Vermonter who recorded a rough-and-tumble affair in his unit reported that the "Conal broak one Lieutenant's nose." Albert Harris to his brother, March 1, 1863, manuscript, Vt. Historical Society.

[98] David Lathrop, *History of the 59th Regt. Illinois Vols.,* 184-185.

[99] Wiley, *The Life of Johnny Reb,* 319.

[100] Henry P. Whipple, *The Diary of a Private Soldier* (Waterloo, Wis., 1906), 12.

[101] Oscar O. Winther, editor, *With Sherman to the Sea,* 47.

[102] Diary of Charles W. Wills, Oct. 7, 1864, manuscript, Ill. State Historical Library.

[103] Billings, *op. cit.,* 204.

[104] Norton, *op. cit.,* 32-33.

[105] *Ibid.,* 18; Capt. Lucius Fairchild to his mother, May 25, 1861, manuscript, Wis. Historical Society.

[106] Roe, *op. cit.,* 74.

[107] *Ibid.,* 258-259.

[108] Diary of Charles W. Wills, May 2, 1864.

[109] Winther, *op. cit.,* 93-94.

[110] Herbert E. Valentine to his homefolk, Dec. 10, 1861.

[111] C. B. Thurston to his brother, March 29, 1863; journal of Charles F. Johnson, July 4, 1862; Edward E. Newhall to his homefolk, Nov. 21, 1861, manuscript (typescript), Boston Public Library; diary of Philip H. Smith, Dec. 26, 1861, bound series of articles from Peoria *Evening Star,* 1917, in Veterans' Records, Nat'l Archives; George Monteith to his mother, Jan. 2, 1862, manuscript, Univ. of Mich.

[112] Lt. John R. Wintherbotham to his homefolk, March 21 and Dec. 28, 1863, manuscripts, Chicago Historical Society; Wesley A. Brown to his wife, Dec. 25, 1861, manuscript in possession of Alice L. Pendleton, Isleboro, Maine, to whom I am indebted for the use of a number of excellent letters.

[113] Abraham Kendig to his father, Dec. 23, 1862, manuscript, Historical Society of Pa.; diary of an unidentified Union sergeant, Jan. 1, 1863, quoted in Charleston, S. C., *Daily Courier*, July 18, 1863; Lt. Charles B. Stoddard to his parents (n.d., but Dec., 1862), manuscript, Harvard University.

[114] Fred A. Shannon, editor, *Civil War Letters of Sgt. Onley Andrus* (Urbana, Ill., 1947), 72; William H. Lloyd to his wife, Jan. 1, 1865.

[115] Diary of John N. Williams, June 5, 1863; John J. Wyeth, *Leaves from a Diary* (Boston, 1878), 33; Bardeen, *A Little Fifer's War Diary*, 295; Hazel C. Wolf, *op. cit.*, 236; George T. Stevens, *op. cit.*, 183.

[116] Charles Fairchild to his mother, May 27, 1861.

[117] Felix Brannigan to his homefolk, Oct. 29, 1861, typescript, Library of Congress.

[118] John Beatty, *op. cit.*, 121-122.

[119] Wyeth, *Leaves from a Diary*, 31.

[120] James M. Nichols, *Perry's Saints, or the Fighting Parson's Regiment in the War of the Rebellion* (Boston, 1886), 147.

[121] Journal of Charles F. Johnson, June 30, 1862.

[122] Urich N. Parmelee to his brother, Aug. 6, 1863.

[123] Rebecca R. Usher to her sister, Nov. 23, 1862, and an undated letter apparently written in Jan. 1863, typescripts, Maine Historical Society.

[124] Jordan, *op. cit.*, 230-244; Carol Brink, *Harps in the Wind: The Story of the Singing Hutchinsons* (N. Y., 1927), 204-219; the Hutchinsons (John's group) were barred by McClellan from the Army of the Potomac early in 1862, because a program which they gave soon after receiving a pass from Cameron to sing in Union camps provoked a minor disturbance among those hostile to abolitionism.

[125] E. W. Locke, *Three Years in Camp and Hospital* (Boston, 1870), 33; DAB, XIII, 341 and XV, 431-432.

[126] Beatty, *op. cit.*, 225-226.

[127] *Ibid.*, 85-86.

[128] Diary of James E. Graham, April 21, 1863, manuscript, Ohio State Arch. and Historical Society.

[129] Diary of Florison D. Pitts.

[130] *Ibid.*, Oct. 4, 1863.

[131] Jacob H. Kendig to his parents, May 9, 1864.

[132] Diary of O. B. Hinckley, May 5, 1865, manuscript, Duke University.

[133] Hazel C. Wolf, *op. cit.*, 230.

[134] Diary of Florison D. Pitts, Sept. 16, 17, 25, and Oct. 20, 1863.

[135] *Iowa Historical Record*, XVI (Iowa City, 1900), 138; diary of George N. Champlin, Jan. 4, 11, 18, and March 1, 1864, typescript, Conn. State Library.

[136] Flavius J. Bellamy to his homefolk, Feb. 11, 1864, manuscript, Ind. State Library.

[137] The writer is planning a special study of soldier newspapers of the Civil War. To this end he has collected photographic reproductions of well over 100 titles of camp newspapers located in public depositories and in private possession.

[138] The Historical Society of Pennsylvania and Duke University have runs of the *New South* and the *Free South*. An excellent file of the *Union Appeal* is in the Cossitt Library in Memphis.

[139] The prison paper is reproduced in *Stars and Stripes in Rebeldom* (Boston, 1862). Two issues of *Stars and Stripes* published at Thibodaux, La., are in the American Antiquarian Society; another paper of that name, published in Missouri, is in the William L. Clements Library.

[140] Issues of these papers are, in the order listed, in the Kansas State Historical Society, the G.A.R. Memorial Hall, Scranton, Pa., the New York Historical Society and the Library of Congress. The Massachusetts Historical Society and the Chicago Historical Society also have some issues of the *Camp Kettle*.

[141] Copies of the *First Minnesota* may be found in several libraries, including the Minnesota Historical Society, the Confederate Museum, the American Antiquarian Society and Western Reserve Historical Society. Other items in this sentence, in the order listed, may be found at the Kansas State Historical Society, the Connecticut State Library, the Huntington Library, Western Reserve Historical Society, the American Antiquarian Society, the Wisconsin Historical Society, the Illinois State Historical Library, private collection of Foreman Lebold, Chicago (to whom I am indebted for a photographic copy), the Chicago Historical Society and the Western Reserve Historical Society.

[142] Issues of these papers, in the order listed, are in the American Antiquarian Society, the Wisconsin Historical Society, the Chicago Historical Society, the Minnesota Historical Society and the Missouri Historical Society of St. Louis.

[143] Issues of *Unconditional S. Grant* are in the Chicago Historical Society and the Massachusetts Historical Society; *Grant's Petersburg Progress* in the Minnesota Historical Society; and *Lauman's Own* in the Chicago Historical Society.

[144] Best file of the *Cripple* is in the Connecticut State Library. The *Crutch* and the *Cartridge Box* are in the Library of Congress.

[145] This item is in the Library of Congress.

[146] A. M. Stewart, *Camp, March and Battlefield* (Philadelphia, 1865), 102.

[147] Charles E. Goddard to his mother, March 18, 1862, manuscript, Minn. Historical Society; Edward C. Culp, *The 25th Ohio Veteran Volunteer Infantry in the War for the Union* (Topeka, Kan., 1885), 122-126.

[148] *The American Patriot*, June 18, 1861, Mo. Historical Society.

[149] Corinth *Chanticleer*, July 31, 1863, Minn. Historical Society; *Union Advance Picket*, May 15, 1862, Western Reserve Historical So-

ciety; *Battery Reveille*, June 7, 1861, Western Reserve Historical Society.

[150] This item is in the Wisconsin Historical Society.

[151] This paper is in the Kansas State Historical Society.

[152] For an example, see "The Veteran Banner," April, 1865, in the Ohio State Archaeological and Historical Society.

[153] *Yazoo Daily Yankee*, July 20, 1863, Ohio State Arch. and Historical Society.

[154] *The Volunteer*, Nov. 7, 1863, Washington County Indiana Historical Society. I am indebted to Prof. Chase Mooney, Univ. of Ind., for a photostatic copy of this item.

[155] Issue of Oct. 21, 1863, New Iberia, La.

[156] Issue of Jan. 22, 1862, Somerset, Ky., in Wis. Historical Society.

[157] Charles A. Partridge, *History of the 96th Illinois Regiment Volunteer Infantry* (Chicago, 1887), 71; William Todd, editor, *History of the 9th Regiment New York State Militia* (N. Y., 1889), 148-152; Hyde, *op. cit.*, 267.

[158] The Kansas State Historical Society has a good file of the *Soldier's Letter* of the 2nd Colorado Cavalry. The *Soldier's Letter* published in the 96th Illinois Regiment is in the Illinois State Historical Library.

[159] U. S. Sanitary Comm. *Documents*, No. 40, 29.

[160] Simon B. Hulbert, Monthly Record for 1863, manuscript, N. Y. Historical Society.

[161] Abraham Kendig to his homefolk, Nov. 28, 1861; Bishop Crumrine to his brother, Aug. 23, 1862; Edwin Horton to his wife, March 30, 1864, manuscript, Vt. Historical Society.

[162] Richard Puffer to his sister, May 28, 1863, manuscript, Chicago Historical Society; John N. Moulton to his mother, Aug. 7, 1864.

[163] This sample is a composite based on many letters; all of the phrases are authentic.

[164] H. R. Leonard to Elizabeth Davis, Oct. 5 [1861], manuscript among Miscellaneous Civil War Letters, Western Reserve Historical Society; William A. Harper to his wife, Jan. 13, 1865, manuscript, Ind. Historical Society.

[165] For examples of uninhibited comments on amorous activities, see Patrick Heffron to "Dear Friend John," Dec. 4, 1862, and "Jake" to "Friend Page," Aug. 11, 1863, manuscripts in possession of Beverly DuBose, Jr., Atlanta; Isaac Mertz to Jefferson Hartman, March 8, 1865, manuscript, Duke; Frank R. Lyman to Royale E. Cook, Oct. 9, 1864, manuscript, Dartmouth.

[166] "Jake" to "Friend Page," Aug. 11, 1863; W. H. Campbell to his sweetheart, March 4, 1862, manuscript in private possession.

[167] D. H. Dodd to his homefolk, Jan. 8, 1863, manuscript, Ind. Historical Society.

[168] John C. Arnold to his wife, May 28, 1864, typescript, Nat'l War College.

[169] Calvin B. Crandall to his parents, Feb. 9, 1863, typescript of original manuscript, Neb. Historical Society.

[170] John McMeekin to his sister, Nov. 13, 1862, manuscript, Western Reserve Historical Society.

[171] Charles Babbott to his father, Jan. 1, 1863, manuscript, Hayes Memorial Library; Henry J. H. Thompson to his wife, n.d., but summer of 1861, manuscript, Duke.

[172] Robert M. Atkinson to his homefolk, Dec. 16, 1863, manuscript, Ohio State Arch. and Historical Society.

[173] Henry Warren Howe, *Passages from the Life of Henry Warren Howe*, 174.

[174] James Rich to his wife, n.d., but spring of 1863, typescript in possession of Dr. A. M. Giddings, Battle Creek, Mich.; Thomas Wall to Andrew Weld, March 21, 1864 [1865], manuscript, Wis. Historical Society; Michael R. Dresbach to his wife, Aug. 22, 1864, manuscript, Minn. Historical Society.

[175] Francis S. Flint to "Darling Jennie," Aug. 24, 1863, manuscript, Minn. Historical Society.

[176] Unidentified soldier to Margaret McMeekin, letter not dated.

[177] Albert E. Trumble to Amelia Boyce, Dec. 17, 1861, Aug. 19, 1862, May 25, 1863, and Aug. 5, 1864, manuscripts in possession of Faith Wirsching Lemmer, San Francisco.

[178] For examples of an advertisement for correspondents, see New York *Herald*, Jan. 16, 1864, section headed "Matrimonial," and Chattanooga *Daily Gazette*, March 6, 1864.

[179] F. F. Dean to Will Robinson, Jan. 2, 1861, manuscript, Ind. State Library; William H. Crawford to his homefolk, n.d., but 1861, typescript, Univ. of Missouri; Bailey Sutherland to his sister, June 22, 1862, manuscript, Univ. of Ky.; Charles C. Garrett to his cousin, Jan. 29, 1862, manuscript, Ohio State Arch. and Historical Society.

[180] William Worthington to his homefolk, various dates, manuscripts in private possession; John Herr to his sister, Nov. 6, 1863, manuscript, Duke.

[181] John Herr to his sister, Nov. 6, 1862; Franklin H. Bailey to his parents, Dec. 14, 1861, manuscript, Univ. of Mich.

[182] William O. Wettleson to his parents, March 13, 1865, manuscript, Luther College. Translated from the Norwegian by Inga B. Norstog.

[183] Charles M. Anson, "Reminiscences of an Enlisted Man," Military Order of the Loyal Legion, *Wis. Commandery*, IV (Milwaukee, 1914), 279-290.

[184] For a discussion of the origin and circulation of the poem, see chapter X and Wiley, *The Life of Johnny Reb*, 305.

[185] This version is from an undated note of Henry J. H. Thompson to his wife. It differs from most others in that the last line usually was "For the space of three years."

Chapter VIII

TOEING THE MARK

[1] Amory K. Allen to his wife, Sept. 20, 1863. "Letters of Amory K. Allen," *Indiana Magazine of History*, XXXI (1935), 374.

[2] For basic provisions concerning courts-martial, see *Army Regulations* for the war years (to be cited from here on as A. R.), especially Article XXXVIII and "The Articles of War" (to be cited hereafter as A. W.) in the appendix. A useful commentary on the articles of war and the system of military discipline is George W. Davis, *A Treatise on the Military Law of the United States* (N. Y., 1901).

[3] For a full report of this affair, see O. R., series 1, XXVI, pt. 1, 262-272.

[4] J. Albert Monroe, "Reminiscences of the War of the Rebellion," Soldiers and Sailors Historical Society of Rhode Island, *Personal Narratives*, 2nd series, No. 11 (Providence, 1881), 11-12; diary of George W. Little, entry of Dec. 17, 1862, manuscript, Chicago Historical Society; Stephen M. Weld to his father, March 25, 1864, *War Diary and Letters of Stephen M. Weld 1861-1865* (Cambridge, Mass., 1912), 266-268; Lt. Col. Charles B. Fox to his wife, Sept. 16, 1864, manuscript, Mass. Historical Society.

[5] 66 and 67 A. W.

[6] Hq. Dept. of the Gulf, Office of J.A.G., circular dated Oct. 12, 1863.

[7] 64, 65 A. W.; A. R., 1861, Article 38; George B. Davis, *op. cit.*, 524.

[8] For a discussion of the character and jurisdiction of military commissions, see Davis, *op. cit.*, 309-311.

[9] For details of court-martial procedure, see A. R., 1861, Article 38.

[10] Manuscript copies of proceedings of cases referred to the Judge Advocate General are filed in the J.A.G. Records Division of the Nat'l Archives. These will be cited hereafter as J.A.G. Records. Findings and sentences of courts-martial were published in appropriate general orders, cited as G. O.

[11] For examples of wholesale invalidation of court-martial actions in 1863 for procedural defects, see War Dept. Adjutant General's Office (cited hereafter as W.D.A.G.O.) G. O. 292, Aug. 22, 1863, and 297, Sept. 3, 1863.

[12] Hq. Army of Potomac, G. O. 38, April 2, 1863.

[13] J.A.G. Records MM 752.

[14] A. R., 1863 (Washington, 1863), 538.

[15] *Ibid.*; Hq. Dept. of the Gulf, office of J.A.G., circular dated Oct. 12, 1863.

[16] J.A.G. Records MM 752.

[17] A. R., 1863, 538.

[18] Lt. Col. Charles B. Fox, commanding officer of the 66th Mass. Inf.

Regt., wrote to his father, Aug. 18, 1864, that a field officer's court could decide on cases "in the same day that the crime is committed and the sentence goes at once into effect."

19 Diary of A. W. Tower, entry of July 16, 1863, manuscript, N. Y. Public Library.

20 John D. Billings, *Hard Tack and Coffee*, 145.

21 William H. White to his mother, Oct. 9, 1861, manuscript, Hager Family Papers, Univ. of Mich.

22 Clothing, Order, Descriptive and Morning Report Book, Company B, 7th Mass. Inf. Regt., manuscript, Nat'l Archives.

23 Edward L. Edes to "Robert," March 1, 1864, manuscript, Mass. Historical Society.

24 45 A. W.

25 Richard L. Ashhurst to his homefolk, Nov. 6, 1862, typescript, Historical Society of Pa.

26 Manuscript, N. Y. Public Library.

27 O. R., series 1, XI, pt. 3, 83-84 and XLIV, 596.

28 Charles A. Barker to his homefolk, March 30, 1862, Aug. 17, 1863, manuscripts, Essex Institute; George Gray Hunter to his brother, Feb. 20, 1864, manuscript in possession of Wm. A. Hunter, Harrisburg, Pa.

29 Hq. Dept. of the Gulf, G. O. 11, April 14, 1862; Hq. Army of the Potomac, G. O. 58 and 87, Feb. 18, March 4, 1862; J.A.G. Records MM 219, manuscript, Nat'l Archives.

30 Surgeon Albert G. Hart to his wife (n.d., n.p., but apparently Louisville, Ky., Sept., 1862), manuscript, Western Reserve Historical Society; J.A.G. Records MM 512, 989, manuscripts, Nat'l Archives. For an instance of a colonel having his skull crushed after return to civilian life by a soldier who bore a lingering grudge, see Barbara Burr, editor, "Letters from Two Wars," Ill. State Historical Society *Journal*, XXX (1937-1938), 157.

31 Humphrey H. Hood to his wife, Oct. 8, 1864, manuscript, Ill. State Historical Library.

32 John P. Moulton to his sister, Nov. 15, 1861, manuscript, Western Reserve Historical Society.

33 A. Davenport to his homefolk, Jan. 17, 1863, manuscript, N. Y. Historical Society.

34 9 A. W.; George B. Davis, *op. cit.*, 378.

35 *List of the U. S. Soldiers Executed by United States Military Authorities during the Late War* (n.p., n.d.), pamphlet in War Records Division, Nat'l Archives. Fourteen of the soldiers executed for mutiny were Negroes.

36 Hq. Army of the Potomac, G. O. 12, Jan. 17, 1862; Hq. Dept. of Kansas, G. O. 15, April 5, 1864; Hq. Dept. of the Gulf, G. O. 11, April 14, 1862.

37 Hq. Army of the Potomac, G. O. 33, Jan. 29, 1862; J.A.G. Records NN 3798.

38 *Ibid.*, MM 1137.

³⁹ Hq. 17th Corps, G. O. 26, Sept. 15, 1863 and G. O. 37, Oct. 29, 1863; J.A.G. Records MM 923.

⁴⁰ Billings, *Hard Tack and Coffee*, 155.

⁴¹ For example see Susan R. Jervey and Charlotte St. J. Ravenel, *Two Diaries* (n.p., 1921), 13, 21.

⁴² Hq. Army of the Potomac, G. O. 15, Sept. 20, 1861.

⁴³ For example, see Hq. Dept. of the Gulf, G. O. 85, Oct. 25, 1862.

⁴⁴ Hq. Army of the Potomac, G. O. 74, Feb. 26, 1862.

⁴⁵ J.A.G. Records NN 2158.

⁴⁶ Hq. Army of the Potomac, G. O. 6, Sept. 4, 1861, and G. O. 8, Sept. 8, 1861; George T. Stevens, *Three Years in the Sixth Corps*, 42-43.

⁴⁷ Josiah S. Chandler, "What a Private Saw, Thought and Did during the War of the Rebellion," 196, manuscript, Western Reserve Historical Society; Cyrus R. Stone to his parents, Jan. 4, 1863, manuscript, Minn. Historical Society; Hazel C. Wolf, editor, *Campaigning with the First Minnesota*, 233; Billings, *Hard Tack and Coffee*, 155-156; Joseph T. Embree to his homefolk, Dec. 25, 1862, manuscript, Ind. State Library.

⁴⁸ Josiah S. Chandler, "What a Private Saw, Thought and Did during the War of the Rebellion," 158-159.

⁴⁹ *Ibid.*

⁵⁰ *List of U. S. Soldiers Executed by United States Military Authorities during the Late War; O. R.*, series 1, XLVI, pt. 2, 56.

⁵¹ The only other instance of execution by a drumhead court-martial recorded in the War Department list is that of a white soldier convicted of desertion.

⁵² The soldier was a private of the 18th Ill. Inf., executed on Oct. 2, 1861.

⁵³ The culprit was a private of the 2nd Colorado Cav., hanged on Nov. 10, 1864.

⁵⁴ Hq. Dept. of the Gulf, G. O. 46, June 2, 1863; J.A.G. Records NN 3900.

⁵⁵ Ella Lonn, best authority on the subject, estimates total Union desertions at 200,000. *Desertion during the Civil War* (N. Y., 1928), 154.

⁵⁶ Gen. George G. Meade, "Report of the Number of Men in the Army of the Potomac tried for desertion from July 1 to date, number guilty and shot," dated Nov. 30, 1863. Manuscript among Robert T. Lincoln Papers, Library of Congress. I am indebted to Helen Bullock of the National Council for Historic Sites and Buildings for calling this item to my attention.

⁵⁷ *List of U. S. Soldiers Executed by the United States Military Authorities during the Late War.* Helen Bullock, from a study of cases referred to Lincoln, found for all offenses four executions not included in the W.D. list. Helen Bullock to the writer, March 7, 1950.

⁵⁸ For typical comment on execution, see letters of Thomas Clark to his sister from Fernandina, Fla., Feb. 29, 1864, manuscript, Historical Society of Pa.; Henry J. H. Thompson to his wife from New Bern, N. C.,

Aug. 13, 1864, manuscript, Duke; Calvin B. Crandall to his parents, Aug. 29, 1863, manuscript, Neb. Historical Society.

[59] W. C. Ford, editor, *War Letters, 1862-1865 of John C. Gray and John C. Ropes* (Boston, 1927), 165-166.

[60] Diary of John M. Hawkes, entry of Feb. 29, 1864, manuscript, Boston Public Library; M. S. Schroyer, "Company G. History," *Snyder County Historical Society Bulletin*, II (1939), 97; diary of Sgt. James F. Williams, entry of Dec. 2, 1864, manuscript, N. Y. Public Library.

[61] Diary of Wm. H. Tyner, entry of Feb. 11, 1863, manuscript in possession of Mrs. Richard Alison, Jackson, Tenn. The fourth soldier was shot and so badly wounded by the father of the girl that he was spared the flogging. For an instance of a colonel having three colored soldiers tied to stakes and flogged with horsewhips in March 1864, see W.D. A.G.O. *General Court Martial Orders*, No. 265, Aug. 30, 1864.

[62] J.A.G. Records NN 2156.

[63] William R. Hartpence, *History of the Fifty-first Indiana Veteran Volunteer Infantry*, 86; David Lathrop, *History of the 59th Regiment Illinois Volunteers*, 187.

[64] Edwin C. Bennett, *Music, Musket and Sword, or the Camp, March and Firing Line in the Army of the Potomac* (Boston, 1900), 13.

[65] "Captain Samuel A. Craig's Memoirs of the Civil War and Reconstruction," *West Pennsylvania Historical Magazine*, XIII (1930), 231.

[66] Diary of Isaac Walker, entry of July 24, 1862, typescript, Dartmouth; Billings, *Hard Tack and Coffee*, 148-149; Frank Wilkeson, *Recollections of a Private Soldier in the Army of the Potomac*, 32-35.

[67] Frank Wilkeson, *op. cit.*, 32-33.

[68] Billings, *Hard Tack and Coffee*, 148; E. R. Hutchins, compiler, *The War of the 'Sixties* (N. Y., 1912), 327-328.

[69] Hq. Army of the Potomac, G. O. 36, Oct. 31, 1861.

[70] *Ibid.*, G. O. 40, Feb. 4, 1862, and G. O. 87, March 4, 1862.

[71] G. A. Hanson to "Dear Uncle," March 4, 1863, manuscript, Luther College Library. Translation from the Norwegian by Inga B. Norstog.

[72] John W. De Forest, *A Volunteer's Adventures*, 45; Gen. J. J. Bartlett to Col. Joseph Howland, Feb. 12, 1863, manuscript among Howland Letters, N. Y. Historical Society.

[73] A. Davenport to his homefolk, March 9, 1862.

[74] Hq. Dept. of the Gulf, G. O. 129, Sept. 13, 1864.

[75] Hq. Army of the Potomac, G. O. 34, Jan. 30, 1862.

[76] O. R., series 1, XXVI, pt. 1, 456-479.

[77] Hq. Army of the Potomac, G. O. 29, Jan. 28, 1862.

[78] Diary of George O. Hand, entry of Sept. 16, 1862, manuscript (photostat), Library of Congress; diary of Private Johnson, entry of March 21, 1863, manuscript, Historical Society of Pa.

[79] Hq. Army of the Potomac, G. O. 57, Feb. 17, 1862, and G. O. 18, May, 1864.

[80] *Ibid.*, G. O. 11, Sept. 14, 1861.

[81] Hq. Army of the Potomac, G. O. 73, Feb. 26, 1862; 83 A. W.

[82] J.A.G. Records MM 189.

[83] *Ibid.*

[84] J.A.G. Records MM 672.

[85] For a specific example of a witness' forgetfulness, see J.A.G. Records MM 189.

[86] A. Davenport to his homefolk, Aug. 12, 1861; Peter Wilson to his brother, Jan. 28, 1863. Ruth A. Gallaher, editor, "Peter Wilson in the Civil War," *Iowa Journal of History and Politics*, XL (1942), 346-347.

[87] Thomas H. Parker, *History of the 51st Regiment Pennsylvania Vols.* (Philadelphia, 1869), 172-173; Hq. Army of the Potomac, G. O. 58, Feb. 18, 1862.

[88] Diary of Joseph Isaacs, entry of Aug. 23, 1861, manuscript, N. Y. Public Library; a New Yorker confined in Elmira wrote his colonel Oct. 21, 1863: "This Guard House is a horrible, filthy, dirty hole, and full of lice and is a place that I can leave with pleasure." J.A.G. Records LL 1431. For unfavorable comments on guardhouses by inspecting officers, see report by Col. H. Van Rensselaer of inspection of the Dept. of Missouri, dated Feb. 10, 1862, in A.G.O. Records, 1862, file 14-I, and report by Col. D. B. Sackett, of inspection of Dept. of the Cumberland, dated Aug. 10, 1864, in I.G.O. Letters Received, Box 5, manuscripts, Nat'l Archives.

[89] A. Davenport to his homefolk, Jan. 3, 1862.

[90] Hq. Army of the Potomac, G. O. 58, Feb. 18, 1862; C. W. Bardeen, *A Little Fifer's War Diary*, 169; A. Davenport to his homefolk, July 21, 1862.

[91] David Lathrop, *op. cit.*, 88-89.

[92] "Reminiscences of John Culbertson," 69-71, typescript in possession of Gladys Culbertson, Detroit.

[93] Bell Irvin Wiley, "Billy Yank and Abraham Lincoln," *Abraham Lincoln Quarterly*, VI (1950), 106; O. R., series 3, IV, 418; W.D.A.G.O. *General Court Martial Order* No. 89, May 9, 1864 (copy filed in J.A.G. Records MM 950).

[94] These statements are based on an interview, March 30, 1949, with Helen Bullock who has made an intensive study of courts-martial cases referred to the President, and on the writer's own research in the manuscript courts-martial proceedings in the Nat'l Archives.

[95] J.A.G. Records MM 922.

[96] *Ibid.*

[97] J.A.G. Records LL 1431.

[98] O. R., series 1, V, 637; VII, 511-512; VIII, 409.

[99] Col. H. Van Rensselaer, Report of Inspection, Dept. of the Missouri, dated Feb. 10, 1862, A.G.O. Records, 14-I, manuscripts, Nat'l Archives.

[100] Willoughby M. Babcock, editor, *Selections from the Letters and Diaries of Brevet Brigadier General of the 75th N. Y. Volunteers* (n.p., 1922), 87. W. H. Russell, London *Times* correspondent who observed many soldiers in camp and in Washington in the summer of 1861, made frequent reference to poor discipline and incompetent officers. For ex-

amples, see *My Diary North and South*, 340, 482, 561, 586. Russell leaves the impression that saluting, even of top-ranking generals, was exceptional and that volunteer officers knew little about their duties and had little control over their men.

[101] Charles Ward to his folk, n.d., n.p., but apparently from near Falls Church, Va., Sept. 1862, manuscript, American Antiquarian Society; Asa Ward Brindle to his aunt, Sept. 7, 18, 1862, manuscripts (microfilm), Detroit Public Library.

[102] Col. James A. Hardie to Halleck, Oct. 27, 1864, Hq. of the Army Records, Document File, Inspections, Box 131, manuscripts, Nat'l Archives.

[103] Maj. E. H. Ludington to Secretary E. M. Stanton, Jan., 1865, item L-4, 1865, Box 8, Letters Received, I.G.O. Papers, manuscripts, Nat'l Archives.

[104] Report dated Jan. 13, 1865, item S-17, 1865, Box 10, Letters Received, I.G.O. Papers.

[105] Report dated Sept. 19, 1864, Box 5, Letters Received, I.G.O. Papers.

[106] Hq. 3rd Div., 19th Corps, Dept. of Gulf, G. O. 3, Aug. 29, 1864, 19th Army Corps Records, Misc. Papers and Reports, manuscripts, Nat'l Archives.

[107] Col. James A. Hardie to Halleck, April 23, 1864, submitting extracts from inspection reports, Dept. of the South. Hq. of the Army Records, Document File, Inspections, Box 130.

[108] Maj. M. Hazen White, A.A.I.A. to Brig. Gen. J. R. West, Sept. 29, 1864, manuscript, Hq. of the Army Records, Document File, Inspections, Box 131.

[109] Hardie to Halleck, Sept. 2, 1864, submitting extracts from inspection reports, Dept. of Arkansas and Dept. of the Gulf, Hq. of the Army Records, Document File, Inspections, Box 131.

[110] J. F. Rhodes, *History of the United States Since the Compromise of 1850*, V, 89.

Chapter IX

HARDTACK, SALT HORSE AND COFFEE

[1] Nashville *Daily Union*, April 16, 1863.

[2] A. R., 1863, article 43, paragraph 1190.

[3] G. W. Adams, "Health and Medicine in the Union Army" (Ph.D. dissertation, Harvard, 1946), II, 619. For a comparison of the Federal ration with that of other nations, see Austin Flint, editor, *Contributions Relating to the Causation and Prevention of Disease* (N. Y., 1867), 73 ff. This book was published under the auspices of the U. S. Sanitary Commission as a part of its "Sanitary Memoirs."

[4] Bell Irvin Wiley, *The Life of Johnny Reb*, 91; *O. R.*, series 3, I, 399; Adams, "Health and Medicine in the Union Army," II, 619.

[5] Col. A. B. Eaton, Report to the Secretary of War on Inspection of Disbursing Branches of the Department of the South, dated June 2, 1864. I.G.O. Letters Received, Box 2, manuscripts, Nat'l Archives; *O. R.*, series 1, XI, pt. 1, 175-176; *ibid.*, series 3, IV, 481-482; *Med. and Surg. Hist.*, Medical Volume, pt. 3, 711.

[6] U. S. Sanitary Comm. *Documents*, No. 40, 21. In reviewing a court-martial case in 1862, McClellan stated: "It has been made painfully apparent during the last few months that under the name of *Company Savings* large quantities of stores belonging to the U. S. have been embezzled by dishonest men entrusted with their keeping." Hq. Army of the Potomac, G. O. 89, March 5, 1862.

[7] John D. Billings, *Hard Tack and Coffee*, 112.

[8] E. A. Johnson, editor, *The Hero of Medfield*, 33.

[9] John N. Moulton to his homefolk, July 16, 1862, manuscript, Western Reserve Historical Society.

[10] Charles K. Bailer to his parents, Feb. 8, 1862, typescript, Western Reserve Historical Society.

[11] Levi A. Ross to his father, Oct. 26, 1862, manuscript, Ill. State Historical Library; George W. Kimball to his wife, Dec. 28, 1862, manuscript in possession of Stetson Conn, Washington, D. C.

[12] *O. R.*, series 1, XI, pt. 1, 207-209, 214; XII, pt. 3, 379-381.

[13] Herman C. Newhall to his father, Nov. 28, 1862, manuscript, Boston Public Library; Leland O. Barlow to his sister, Dec. 1, 1862, manuscript, Mass. Historical Society; John B. Cuzner to Ellen Vandorn, Jan. 8, 1863, manuscript, Conn. Historical Society.

[14] For one soldier's reaction to the changed order, see A. Davenport to his parents, Jan. 30, Feb. 15, March 27, 1863, manuscript, N. Y. Historical Society.

[15] Diary of Stephen W. Gordon, typescript in possession of Fred L. Williams, Atlanta, to whom I am indebted for its use. The original is in the headquarters of the National Military Park, Fredericksburg, Va.

[16] For example, see A. Davenport to his parents, March 27, 1863.

[17] Adams, "Health and Medicine in the Union Army," II, 620.

[18] Frank M. Rood to "Friend Elvira," Nov. 18, 1863, manuscript in possession of Harry Rood, Poultney, Vt.

[19] Henry C. Bear to his wife, Dec. 7, 1862, manuscript in possession of Mrs. Stanley B. Hadden, Urbana, Ill.

[20] Leander Stillwell, *The Story of a Common Soldier*, 124.

[21] Diary of David J. Brothers, Dec. 10, 1862, manuscript, Wis. Historical Society.

[22] On June 19, 1863, an unidentified Norwegian soldier wrote Magnus Anderson Linnevolden from near Vicksburg: "We got to the Black River on the 17th. . . . We had long been on half rations and on the last days we had had only one cracker a day." Manuscript, Luther College Library, translation by Inga B. Norstog. For evidence of excessive

foraging and plundering during the Vicksburg campaign, see diary of John Merrilies, May 6, 9, 15, 1863, manuscript, Chicago Historical Society.

[23] O. R., series 1, XXIII, pt. 1, 461, 478; XXX, pt. 3, 247; Flint, *Contributions Relating to the Causation and Prevention of Disease*, 60-62. Robert S. Henry, *The Story of the Confederacy* (Indianapolis, 1931), 316.

[24] Willis D. Maier to Annie F. Howells, Oct. 22, 1863, manuscript, Hayes Memorial Library.

[25] Charles K. Bailer to his sister, Jan. 18, 1864.

[26] O. R., series 1, XXXI, pt. 2, 262, 580-581, pt. 3, 392; *Med. and Surg. Hist.*, Medical Vol., pt. 1, appendix, 286. Only a part of the troops made the return trip to Chattanooga.

[27] For example, see Michael R. Dresbach to his wife, Oct. 16, 1864, manuscript, Minn. Historical Society.

[28] Diary of Reuben Sweet, entry of Oct. 18, 1864. This diary was published in the Antigo, Wis., *Daily Journal*, March 9—May 25, 1939; clippings of the articles are in a scrapbook in the library of the Wis. Historical Society.

[29] For example, see George Sharland, *Knapsack Notes* (Springfield, Ill., 1865), 49-53.

[30] O. B. Clark, editor, *Downing's Civil War Diary*, 237.

[31] Col. James A. Hardie to Gen. H. W. Halleck, Feb. 24, 1865, Hq. of the Army Records, Documents File, Inspections, Box 131, manuscripts, Nat'l Archives; Michael R. Dresbach to his wife, March 12, 1865.

[32] U. S. Sanitary Comm. *Documents*, No. 40, 21; Col. James A. Hardie to Gen. H. W. Halleck, Feb. 9, 24, 1865.

[33] Hq. Army of the Potomac, G. O. 85, March 5, 1862.

[34] Charles J. Stille, *History of the U. S. Sanitary Commission*, 326. Officers were following authorized procedure in purchasing provisions from commissary stocks; their offense was in taking nearly all the vegetables before the enlisted men had a chance to draw them.

[35] Lt. Col. E. G. Beckwith to Gen. A. B. Eaton, No. 5, 1864, and accompanying paper, I.G.O. Letters Received, Box 2, manuscripts, Nat'l Archives.

[36] *Ibid.*

[37] Calvin B. Crandall to his parents, Oct. 21, 1862, typescript of original in Neb. Historical Society.

[38] *Ibid.*

[39] Stille, *op. cit.*, 327; Rebecca Usher to her sister, Feb. 8, 1865, manuscript, Maine Historical Society.

[40] Diary of Capt. E. J. Sherlock, entry of Jan. 7, 1865, typescript, Nat'l Archives.

[41] William Blackburn to his brother, Feb. 26, 1862, manuscript, Historical Society of Pa.

[42] See chapters IV and V.

[43] Henry Crydenwise to his parents, May 19, 1862, manuscript, Emory.

[44] Diary of Lorenzo S. Leavitt, entry of March 17, 1863, manuscript in possession of Harry C. Leavitt, Turner, Maine.

[45] Franklin J. Hubbard to his brother, June 18, 1862, manuscript, Univ. of Vt.

[46] This statement is based on a study of correspondence and reports in O. R., series 1, XXXVIII, XXXIX, XLIV and XLVII.

[47] For examples of officers actively participating in pillage, see: Proceedings and Report of Court of Inquiry on Sale of Cotton and Produce, held at St. Louis in March, 1863, Gen. Irvin McDowell, President, manuscripts, I.G.O. Papers, Nat'l Archives; Susan R. Jervey and Charlotte St. J. Ravenel, *Two Diaries*, 10, 20.

[48] Leland O. Barlow to his sisters, Nov. 1, 1862.

[49] Samuel Storrow to his parents, Nov. 19, 1862, manuscript, Mass. Historical Society.

[50] For example, see letters of Andrew K. Rose, 1862-1863, manuscripts, Duke.

[51] John W. De Forest, *A Volunteer's Adventures*, 74.

[52] Diary of Jenkins Lloyd Jones, entry of Nov. 3, 4, 1863, manuscript, Wis. Historical Society.

[53] For examples, see diaries of Florison D. Pitts and John Merrilies, both in the Chicago Mercantile Battery, for the period of these campaigns, manuscripts, Chicago Historical Society.

[54] Fred A. Shannon, editor, *Civil War Letters of Sgt. Onley Andrus*, 42.

[55] William Henry Peter to his brother, Dec. 3, 1862, manuscript, Ill. State Historical Library.

[56] Surgeon Henry P. Strong to his wife, Jan. 22, 1863, typescript, Wis. Historical Society.

[57] Willie H. Barnes to Annie F. Howells, May 3, 1863, manuscript, Hayes Memorial Library.

[58] R. G. Carter, *Four Brothers in Blue*, 411.

[59] Alfred S. Roe, *The Ninth New York Heavy Artillery*, 164-166; O. R., series 1, XLIV, 726-727, 792-793.

[60] Diary of William D. Evans, Feb. 13, 1865, manuscript, Western Reserve Historical Society.

[61] Billings, *Hard Tack and Coffee*, 113; Daniel Beidelman, Jr., to his father, Nov. 12, 1862, manuscript, Duke.

[62] John C. Arnold to his wife, June 12, 1864, typescript, National War College (Arnold's spelling made it "teeth dollers"); J. W. Danford to Amanda Wright, Oct. 24, 1861, manuscript among Miscellaneous Civil War Letters, Western Reserve Historical Society; George B. Sprague to his mother, Oct. 7, 1862, typescript of original furnished through courtesy of Hazel Wolf, Peoria, Ill.; Charles Babbott to his father, Dec. 16, 1862, manuscript, Hayes Memorial Library; extracts from the war diary of John V. Ruehle, Jr., Dec. 13, 1862, manuscript, Detroit Public Library; William B. Stanard to his sister, Jan. 12, 1862, manuscript, Univ. of Mich.

[63] J. W. Danford to Amanda Wright, Dec. 21, 1861.

[64] S. M. Fox, "Story of the Seventh Kansas," Kansas State Historical Society *Transactions*, VIII (1903-1904), 46.

[65] William F. Goodhue to his parents, Jan. 10, 1863, manuscript, Ill. State Historical Library.

[66] Billings, *Hard Tack and Coffee*, 117; William Bircher, A *Drummer Boy's Diary*, 125-127.

[67] Bircher, A *Drummer Boy's Diary*, 125-127. Bircher's description of hardtack pudding is almost word for word the same as that given by Henry M. Kieffer in *The Recollections of a Drummer Boy* (6th edition, Boston, 1889), 223-225, but I do not know which one of the authors deserves credit for the original account.

[68] Bircher, A *Drummer Boy's Diary*, 125.

[69] Samuel Storrow to his parents, Nov. 26, 1862; Charles A. Barker to his mother, Aug. 2, 1863, manuscript, Essex Institute; Billings, *Hard Tack and Coffee*, 116; Harold A. Small, editor, *The Road to Richmond*, 51.

[70] Reminiscences of Daniel H. Rowe, 34, manuscript, Ind. Historical Society; Cyril B. Upham, "Arms and Equipment for the Iowa Troops in the Civil War," *Iowa Journal of History and Politics*, XVI (1918), 47; W. H. Darlington to his mother, Sept. 6, 1861, manuscript, Harvard.

[71] Billings, *Hard Tack and Coffee*, 136.

[72] *Ibid.*, 135; Bircher, A *Drummer Boy's Diary*, 126.

[73] Shannon, *Civil War Letters of Sgt. Onley Andrus*, 95.

[74] Billings, *Hard Tack and Coffee*, 135.

[75] G. W. Adams, "Health and Medicine in the Union Army," II, 622; N. B. Bartlett to his mother, April 3 [1864], manuscript, Chicago Historical Society.

[76] Richard B. Irwin, *History of the Nineteenth Army Corps* (N. Y., 1893), 127; Samuel Storrow to his parents, Dec. 2, 1862; diary of John H. Markley, entry of July 10, 1863, manuscript, Historical Society of Pa.

[77] Joseph H. Diltz to B. F. Maden, Feb. 2, 1862, manuscript, Duke; Charles Anderson to his sister, Aug. 26, 1861, manuscript among Miscellaneous Civil War Letters, Western Reserve Historical Society; Stillwell, *The Story of a Common Soldier*, 124.

[78] *Tri-Weekly Camp Journal* (Somerset, Ky.), Jan. 22, 1862; Billings, *Hard Tack and Coffee*, 135; Johnson, *The Hero of Medfield*, 26.

[79] Billings, *Hard Tack and Coffee*, 124.

[80] F. Y. Hedley, *Marching through Georgia* (Chicago, 1890), 82.

[81] William Hamilton to his mother, Nov. 15, 1862, manuscript, Library of Congress; Isaac Jackson to his brother, Oct. 21, 1862, typescript, in possession of J. O. Jackson, Highland Park, Mich.

[82] Felix Brannigan to an unidentified correspondent, June 18, 1861, typescript, Library of Congress.

[83] Hedley, *Marching through Georgia*, 82-83; O. R. series 1, XI, pt. 1, 175.

[84] O. R., series 3, IV, 481; *Med. and Surg. Hist.*, Medical Volume, pt. 3, 711; *Med. and Surg. Hist.*, Medical Volume, pt. 2, 627.

[85] Stillwell, *The Story of a Common Soldier*, 266; G. W. Adams, "Health and Medicine in the Union Army," II, 638.

[86] Stillwell, *The Story of a Common Soldier*, 266; C. W. Bardeen, *A Little Fifer's War Diary*, 198-199; M. S. Schroyer, "Company 'G' History," Snyder County Pennsylvania Historical Society *Bulletin*, II (1939), 74.

[87] Small, *The Road to Richmond*, 197; G. W. Adams, "Health and Medicine in the Union Army," II, 638.

[88] William Henry Peter to his sister, March 18, 1863.

[89] *Il Recruito: A Comic Opera* (n.d., n.p.), 6. This rare item is at Emory.

[90] Charles Goddard to his mother, Jan. 24, 1864, manuscript among Orrin F. Smith Papers, Minn. Historical Society.

[91] Lt. Col. Roswell Farnham to his sister, Oct. 3, 1862, typescript, Vt. Historical Society.

[92] Diary of Joseph Isaacs, entry of July 13, 1861, manuscript, N. Y. Public Library; Charles Ward Newton to his brother, Oct. 2, 1862, manuscript, American Antiquarian Society; Abraham Kendig to his sister, Dec. 4, 1864, manuscript, Historical Society of Pa.

[93] De Forest, *A Volunteer's Adventures*, 155.

[94] Henry A. Buck to his homefolk, July 29, 1863, manuscript, Univ. of Mich.; Jasper N. Barritt to his brother, Jan. 18, 1864, manuscript, Library of Congress.

[95] Shannon, *Civil War Letters of Sgt. Onley Andrus*, 54.

[96] Charles W. Wills, *Army Life of an Illinois Soldier*, 34. The writer in his boyhood knew a Union veteran, G. W. Bunker, in West Tennessee, who ate pawpaw apples, much to the amazement of the natives. Bunker said that he acquired a taste for the fruit while serving in the army.

[97] Lt. J. S. Pierson to Emma Harris, Aug. 23, 1864, manuscript, Ohio State Archaeological and Historical Society; Billings, *Hard Tack and Coffee*, 131.

[98] O. R., series 3, III, 94.

[99] Lt. Col. Roswell Farnham to his sister, June 19, 1863; S. H. M. Byers, "How Men Feel in Battle," *Harpers Monthly Magazine*, CXII (1906), 933; diary of Capt. E. J. Sherlock, Jan. 1, 1865.

[100] H. Holden to his brother, Aug. 30, 1862, manuscript among Miscellaneous Civil War Letters, American Antiquarian Society; C. B. Thurston to his brother, March 30, 1863, manuscript, Emory; Henry J. H. Thompson to his wife, Sept. 29, 1864, manuscript, Duke.

[101] Joseph H. Diltz to B. F. Maden, Feb. 2, 1862; "Letters of a Badger Boy in Blue," *Wisconsin Magazine of History*, IV (1920-1921), 216.

[102] Edward L. Edes to his uncle, July 1, 1862, manuscript, Mass. Historical Society; Albert Harris to his sister, Jan. 18, 1863, manuscript, Vt. Historical Society; John McMeekin to his mother, Jan. 15, 1863, manuscript, Western Reserve Historical Society.

[103] John C. Arnold to his wife, March 10, 1864.

Chapter X

EVIL AND GOODNESS

[1] J. E. Hart to his wife, June 16, 1861, manuscript, Vt. Historical Society; "On the March with Sibley in 1863: The Diary of Private Henry J. Hagadorn," *North Dakota Historical Quarterly*, V (1930), 125; David Lathrop, *History of the Fifty-ninth Regiment Illinois Volunteers*, 126-127.

[2] A. Davenport to his homefolk, Dec. 13, 1861, manuscript, N. Y. Historical Society; *ibid.*, Dec. 6, 1862, March 9, 1863.

[3] Delos W. Lake to Calvin Lake, Feb. 12, 1864, microfilm of manuscript, Huntington Library.

[4] Urich N. Parmelee to his brother, Oct. 22, 1861, manuscript, Duke; diary of John Merrilies, general entry covering period Sept. 3—Nov. 26, 1862, manuscript, Chicago Historical Society.

[5] 3 A. W.

[6] Oscar O. Winther, *With Sherman to the Sea*, 38; Albert G. Hart to his wife, Dec. 15, 1861, manuscript, Western Reserve Historical Society; John W. De Forest, *A Volunteer's Adventures*, 43.

[7] Diary of Capt. Van S. Bennett, entry of Jan. 6, 1864, manuscript, Wis. Historical Society; John Hope Franklin, editor, *The Diary of James T. Ayers*, 16.

[8] W.D.A.G.O. G. O. 225, July 22, 1863; Hq. Army of Potomac, G. O. 91, March 6, 1862.

[9] For a soldier's comment on the nature of profanity used in camp, see Winther, *With Sherman to the Sea*, 103-104.

[10] [David Lane], *A Soldier's Diary*, 217; Thomas L. Livermore, *Days and Events*, 182.

[11] A. S. Roe, *The Ninth New York Heavy Artillery*, 102.

[12] Reminiscences of John Newton Culbertson, 78, typescript in possession of Gladys Culbertson, Detroit Public Library; Winther, *With Sherman to the Sea*, 123; M. S. Schroyer, "Company 'G' History," Snyder County Historical Society *Bulletin*, II (1939), 97.

[13] C. W. Bardeen, *A Little Fifer's War Diary*, 263; diary of John Merrilies, March 21, 1863.

[14] John Beatty, *The Citizen Soldier*, 150. For another instance of a unit-sponsored cockfight, see diary of Stephen Gordon, March 16, 1864, typescript in possession of Fred L. Williams, Atlanta.

[15] Michael R. Dresbach to his wife, Jan. 7, 1865, manuscript, Minn. Historical Society; diary of William D. Evans, entry of Dec. 3, 1864, manuscript, Western Reserve Historical Society.

[16] John P. M. Green, "Belated Diary of a Civil War Soldier in the First N. H. Light Battery," 2, typescript, N. H. Historical Society; [Thomas W. Fanning], *The Adventures of a Volunteer* (Cincinnati, 1863), 27-28.

¹⁷ Bardeen, A *Little Fifer's War Diary*, 181-182, 262-275, 290-299.

¹⁸ Diary of Jacob E. Hyneman, Feb. 20, 1864, typescript in possession of Charles N. Owen, Chicago.

¹⁹ De Forest, A *Volunteer's Adventures*, 30.

²⁰ Hq. Army of Potomac, G. O. 40, Feb. 4, 1862.

²¹ James M. Nichols, *Perry's Saints*, 113.

²² Theodore C. Blegen, editor, *Civil War Letters of Colonel Hans C. Heg*, 60.

²³ "Prock's Letters from Camp, Battle-field and Hospital," *Indiana Magazine of History*, XXXIV (1938), 87; diary of Jacob E. Hyneman, Dec. 26, 1864; diary of Jacob H. Mechling, Feb. 26, 1863; D. J. Miller to Fielding Beeler, March 27, 1864; manuscript, Ind. State Library; diary of N. L. Parmater, Oct. 10, 1861, typescript in possession of Dr. A. M. Giddings, Battle Creek, Mich.

²⁴ Charles E. Goddard to his mother, Dec. 2, 1861, manuscript among Orrin F. Smith Papers, Minn. Historical Society; Edward E. Newhall to his homefolk, Nov. 21, 1861, manuscript, Boston Public Library.

²⁵ Abner Doubleday, "Some Experiences of Wit, Humor and Repartee in Army and Navy Life," manuscript, N. Y. Historical Society.

²⁶ James G. Nash to his homefolk [undated fragment, but 1864]. This manuscript is among the John P. Bannon Papers, N. Y. Historical Society.

²⁷ William Blackburn, to his brother, Feb. 26, 1862, manuscript, Historical Society of Pa.

²⁸ Portland, Maine *Transcript*, April 23, 1864.

²⁹ Leonard E. Wilder of the 7th Ohio Regt. wrote his homefolk Nov. 27, 1861: "The *Glorious Army* is an awful place to keep anything. You must freeze to it or it will be gone." Manuscript among Franklin J. Hubbard Letters, Univ. of Vt.; Cyrus R. Stone of the 16th N. Y. Regt. wrote his parents Sept. 27, 1862: "Anyone have got to take care of his things if he do not want them stole. There are those in the army who would steal at home and there are those who steal here who would not at home. I would hate to have an army in the vicinity where I live." Manuscript, Minn. Historical Society.

³⁰ J. H. Greene, *Reminiscences of the War*, 35. For a detailed discussion of plunder by Union forces, see E. M. Coulter, *The Confederate States of America, 1861-1865* (Baton Rouge, 1950), 363-370.

³¹ Diary of Capt. Heber S. Thompson, entry of July 23, 1864, manuscript in possession of Dr. A. M. Giddings, Battle Creek, Mich.

³² For a vivid description of pillage in South Carolina, see Susan R. Jervey and Charlotte St. J. Ravenel, *Two Diaries*, 8 *et passim*.

³³ Works Progress Administration, "Indian Pioneer History," XIV, 12 (interview of Christian Bates by Lula Austin, March 27, 1937), bound transcript, Foreman Collection, Okla. Historical Society.

³⁴ See chapter VII.

³⁵ Chattanooga *Daily Gazette*, Sept. 1, 1864.

³⁶ A broadside copy of the advertisement and accompanying verses

is in the Alabama Department of Archives and History, Montgomery, Ala.

[37] A copy of the advertisement and verses in the handwriting of Florison D. Pitts, bugler in the Chicago Mercantile Battery, was found among the Civil War letters of Florison D. Pitts; at the bottom of the page containing the poetry, Pitts wrote for the information of his homefolk: "The above was found on the person of a rebel prisoner taken near Chattanooga in Jan. 1864." Manuscript, Chicago Historical Society.

[38] E. L. Rudolph, *Confederate Broadside Verse* (New Braunfels, Texas, 1950), 15.

[39] Manuscript, dated Nov. 23, 1863, among Keran Collection, Ohio State Arch. and Historical Society.

[40] John B. Cuzner to Ellen Vandorn, Aug. 28, 1863, manuscript, Conn. Historical Society; Enoch T. Baker to his wife, Nov. 10, 1861, manuscript, Historical Society of Pa.; Henry J. H. Thompson to his wife, June 20, 1863, manuscript, Duke.

[41] Cincinnati *Enquirer*, Jan. 2, 1864, quoted in A. C. Cole, *The Irrepressible Conflict* (N. Y., 1934), 366-367; Annual Report of N. Y. Police Commissioner for 1863 in New York *Herald*, Jan. 5, 1864.

[42] Margaret Leech, *Reveille in Washington, 1860-1865* (N. Y., 1941), 261 ff; Franc B. Wilkie, *Pen and Powder*, 198-199.

[43] Leech, *Reveille in Washington*, 262-264.

[44] Eli Veazie to Jeremiah Norris, April 20, 1863, manuscript among George E. Norris Letters, Duke.

[45] J. L. Bassett to "Friend George," Feb. 22 [1864], manuscript among Miscellaneous Civil War Letters and Documents, Essex Institute. For a thinly disguised account of a homebound Yank's three-day spree with a *nymph du monde* of Memphis, see diary of John B. Fletcher, Dec. 18-20, 1863, manuscript, Ill. State Historical Library.

[46] Henry J. H. Thompson to his wife, Dec. 4, 1863 and Jan. 16, 1865.

[47] Frank R. Lyman to Royal E. Cook, Oct. 9 [1864], manuscript among uncataloged Civil War Personal Narratives, Dartmouth.

[48] Samuel Jarrett to Jefferson Hartman, Jan. 15, 1865, manuscript, Duke.

[49] For vice conditions in the cities named, see local and police news columns for the occupation period of the Chattanooga *Daily Gazette*, Nashville *Dispatch*, Memphis *Bulletin* and Memphis *Union Appeal*.

[50] Surgeon W. M. Chambers, "Sanitary Report of the Condition of the Prostitutes of Nashville, Tenn.," Jan. 31, 1865, manuscript, Western Reserve Historical Society, file P-188.

[51] *Ibid.*; Nashville *Dispatch*, July 8, 10, 26 and 28, 1863.

[52] Nashville *Dispatch*, Dec. 22, 1864.

[53] Memphis *Bulletin*, April 30, 1863; David P. Jackson, editor, *The Colonel's Diary*, 98-99.

[54] Memphis *Bulletin*, May 1, 1863.

[55] *Ibid.*

[56] *Ibid.*, May 3, 1863, and various subsequent issues, especially that of Aug. 12, 1863.

[57] Leech, *Reveille in Washington*, 265.

[58] *Med. and Surg. Hist.*, Medical Volume, pt. 1, 636-637, 710-711; pt. 3, 891-896.

[59] *Ibid.*, pt. 3, 891; J. J. Woodward, *Outlines of Camp Diseases of the U. S. Army*, 21-22; for a graph showing the venereal trend July 1861 —June 1866, see *Med. and Surg. Hist.*, Medical Volume, pt. 3, plate opposite p. 890.

[60] A sampling of regiments in the Army of the Potomac for the period July—October 1861 showed 308 cases of gonorrhea as against 224 cases of measles. U. S. Sanitary Comm. *Documents* No. 40, 41.

[61] For a discussion of venereal disease in the Confederate Army, see Bell Irvin Wiley, *The Life of Johnny Reb*, 55-57.

[62] *Med. and Surg. Hist.*, Medical Volume, pt. 3, 893-896; W. M. Chambers, "Sanitary Report of the Condition of the Prostitutes of Nashville, Tenn."

[63] William F. Goodhue to his parents, Oct. 1, 1864, manuscript, Ill. State Historical Library.

[64] Winther, *With Sherman to the Sea*, 20 *et passim*.

[65] Ella Lonn, "The Forty-Eighters in the Civil War," in A. E. Zucker, editor, *The Forty-Eighters: Political Refugees of the German Revolution of 1848* (N. Y., 1950), 215-216.

[66] George W. Landrum to his sister, May 15, 1863, typescript, Western Reserve Historical Society.

[67] *United States Statutes at Large*, chap. IX, sec. 9; William R. Eastman, "The Army Chaplain of 1863," Military Order of the Loyal Legion of the U. S., N. Y. Commandery, *Personal Recollections of the Rebellion*, IV (N. Y., 1912), 339-340; *O. R.*, series 3, I, 154, 157, II, 223, III, 175-176; Bertram W. Korn, "Jewish Chaplains during the Civil War," *American Jewish Archives*, I (Cincinnati, 1948), 8-12; Edwin C. Bennett, *Musket and Sword, on the Camp, March and Firing Line in the Army of the Potomac*, 178-179. The pay of Chaplains was $100 per month plus allowances that brought annual compensation to about $1400.

[68] C. B. Thurston to his parents, March 7, 1863, manuscript, Emory; Edward L. Edes to his father, Dec. 19, 1862, manuscript, Mass. Historical Society; J. D. Barnhart, editor, "A Hoosier Invades the Confederacy," *Indiana Magazine of History*, XXXIX (1943), 151.

[69] Albert Harris to his sister, Feb. 14, 1863, manuscript, Vt. Historical Society.

[70] Thomas N. Lewis to his uncle, June 7, 1861, manuscript among Moulton Letters, Western Reserve Historical Society; Charles E. Goddard to his mother, Jan. 12, 1864.

[71] Doubleday, "Some Experiences of Wit, Humor, and Repartee in Army and Navy Life."

[72] Charles Barnard to his wife, Dec. 8, 1862, manuscript, Maine Historical Society.

[73] Edward Gardner Abbott to his father, June 10, 1862, manuscript, Harvard.

[74] Fritz Haskell, editor, "Diary of Col. William Camm," Ill. State Historical Society *Journal*, XVIII (1926), 825; S. M. Fox, "Story of the 7th Kansas," Kansas Historical Society *Transactions*, VIII (1903-1904), 47.

[75] H. Clay Trumbull, *War Memories of an Army Chaplain* (N. Y., 1898), 8; Bardeen, *A Little Fifer's War Diary*, 294; O. W. Norton, *Army Letters*, 100; W. C. Ford, editor, *War Letters, 1862-1865, of John C. Gray and John C. Ropes*, 217; Herbert E. Valentine to his mother, Sept. 7, 1862, manuscript, Essex Institute; Charles W. Oleson to C. B. Thurston, April 15 [1863].

[76] Cyrus R. Stone to his parents, Dec. 20, 1862; diary of William E. Limbarker, Jan. 17, 1862, manuscript, Univ. of Mich.

[77] Winther, *With Sherman to the Sea*, 87; Henry Crydenwise to his parents, April 13, 1865, manuscript, Emory.

[78] Henry Crydenwise to his parents, March 13, 1862; Harold A. Small, editor, *The Road to Richmond*, 32, 142; Samuel Storrow to his parents, Dec. 6, 1862, manuscript, Mass. Historical Society; Chaplain Joseph Hopkins Twichell to his father, Aug. 4, 7, 1861, and Aug. 28, 1862, manuscript, Yale.

[79] For difficulties encountered by chaplains, see Ethel Lowerre Phelps, editor, "Diary of Winthrop Henry Phelps," May 24, 1862, and subsequent entries, typescript, Minn. Historical Society; "A Chaplain's Experience in the Army," *Monthly Religious Magazine*, XXIX (1863), 223-232.

[80] Henry A. Buck to his sister, letter-journal covering period Oct. 4—Nov. 12, 1862, manuscript, Detroit Public Library; see also Lathrop, *History of the 59th Regt. Ill. Vols.*, 205-206.

[81] Diary of Uriah McCracken, May 31, 1863, manuscript in possession of George McCracken, Davenport, Iowa.

[82] O. R., series 1, XX, pt. 2, 203; Hq. Army of the Potomac, G. O., 7, Sept. 6, 1861; John D. Gaylord to his homefolk, Nov. 10, 1862, manuscript, Duke.

[83] Diary of Rufus Kinsley, April 10, 1864, manuscript, Vt. Historical Society.

[84] For details on activities of Christian Commission, see the published annual reports of the organization and the Daily Record Books of its representatives, manuscripts, Nat'l Archives. For typical reactions of soldiers to the Commission and its agents, see Diary of George Rolfe, Jan. 19, 1865, typescript, Saratoga National Military Park; Edmund Newsome, *Experience in the War of the Great Rebellion* (Carbondale, Ill., 1880), 136-137; Day Elmore to his mother, May 2, 1864, manuscript in possession of Mrs. Hall Mosher, Memphis, Tenn.

[85] Most of these hymns, and many others, were included in *The Soldier's Hymn Book*, published by the Chicago Y.M.C.A. in 1864, a copy of which is in the Chicago Historical Society. I am indebted to Betty Baughman of the Chicago Historical Society for calling this item to my attention and providing a table of contents.

[86] Diary of George Rolfe, Jan. 24, 1864—April 16, 1865; diary of

Rodney Seaver, June 15, 1864, manuscript, Western Reserve Historical Society; Alonzo Miller to his homefolk, Feb. 14, 1864, typescript, Kennesaw Mountain National Park.

[87] M. P. Larry to his sister, Jan. 31, 1863, manuscript, Maine Historical Society; diary of George Rolfe, March 27, April 24, May 22, June 12, July 2, July 3, 1864.

[88] "Capt. Samuel Craig's Memoirs of Civil War and Reconstruction," *Western Pa. History Magazine*, XIII (1930), 233; Col. F. Quinn to Gov. Austin Blair, April 26, 1862, manuscript, Detroit Public Library.

[89] Diary of Joseph D. Galloway, Dec. 15, 1861, manuscript, N. Y. Public Library; M. P. Larry to his sister, Dec. 20, 1863.

[90] Delos W. Lake to his homefolk, Nov. 9, 1862.

[91] Diary of Jenkins Lloyd Jones, Feb. 1, 1863, manuscript, Wis. Historical Society; Small, *Road to Richmond*, 145.

[92] U. S. Christian Commission, *Third Annual Report* (Philadelphia, 1865), 28. For a description of large-scale outdoor meetings in North Carolina late in the war, see Delos W. Lake to his mother, April 7, 1865.

[93] Hazel C. Wolf, editor, *Campaigning with the First Minnesota*, 32-33; Isaac Jackson to his sister Sallie, May 27, 1863, typescript in possession of J. O. Jackson, Highland Park, Mich.

[94] Nashville *Daily Union*, April 7, 15, 1863; A. M. Stewart, *Camp, March and Battlefield*, 98; diary of George N. Champlin, Jan. 4, 11, 1864, typescript, Conn. State Library.

[95] Diary of George N. Champlin, Jan. 18, 20, 1864.

[96] For detailed information on religious periodicals distributed in the army, see "Religious Newspapers ordered for 1865," manuscript, among U. S. Christian Commission Papers, Nat'l Archives.

[97] Ethel Lowerre Phelps, "Diary of Winthrop Henry Phelps," Jan. 1, 1865 (citing *Thirty Ninth Annual Report of American Tract Society*, 1864).

[98] *Second Report of the Maryland Committee, U. S. Christian Commission* (Baltimore, 1863), 45, 72; *A Memorial Record of the U. S. Christian Commission* (N. Y., 1866), 54; A. M. Stewart, *Camp, March and Battlefield*, 60.

[99] *Second Report of the Maryland Committee, U. S. Christian Commission*, 72.

[100] *Ibid.*

[101] "Publications Received, 1864-1865," ledgers 1 and 3.

[102] Emily Adams Bancroft, compiler, *Memorial and Letters of Rev. John R. Adams* (Cambridge, Mass., 1890), 87-88; diary of E. J. Sherlock, Aug. 8, 1863, manuscript, Ind. Historical Society.

[103] John W. Clark to his sister, Jan. 29, 1861, manuscript in possession of the writer; *A Memorial Record of the New York Branch of the U. S. Christian Commission*, 52-53.

Chapter XI

THE SPIRITS EBB AND FLOW

[1] O. W. Norton, *Army Letters, 1861-1865*, 23.

[2] J. J. Moulton to his homefolk, n.d., but summer of 1861, manuscript, Western Reserve Historical Society.

[3] Vance Nelson to Amanda Wright, Dec. 12, 1861, manuscript among Miscellaneous Civil War Letters, Western Reserve Historical Society.

[4] Edward Whitaker to his homefolk, Feb. 24, 1862, manuscript, Conn. State Library; Hazel C. Wolf, editor, *Campaigning with the First Minnesota*, 28; William A. Harper to his wife, March 26, 1862, manuscript, Ind. Historical Society.

[5] A. Davenport to his homefolk, May 23, June 1, July 8, July 12, 1862, manuscripts, N. Y. Historical Society.

[6] Ella Lonn, *Desertion during the Civil War*, 145; Herman Chauncey Newhall to his homefolk, Dec. 18, 1862, manuscript, Boston Public Library; Henry S. Abbott to his brother, Dec. 17, 1862, manuscript, Harvard.

[7] Surgeon Humphrey H. Hood to his wife, March 26, 1863, manuscript, Ill. State Historical Library; Hq. Dept. of Tenn., G. O. 12, Feb. 1, 1863.

[8] John N. Tallman to his brother, March 3, 1863, manuscript, Chicago Historical Society; diary of John H. Williams, Dec. 9, 1862, typescript translation from the Welsh, Vt. Historical Society; Samuel Storrow to his parents, Dec. 23, 1862, manuscript, Mass. Historical Society; C. W. Bardeen, *A Little Fifer's War Diary*, 169.

[9] M. N. Collins to C. H. Bell, Dec. 22, 1862, manuscript, Dartmouth.

[10] Edward L. Edes to "Charlotte," Dec. 28, 1862, manuscript, Mass. Historical Society.

[11] John N. Moulton to his homefolk, Feb. 1, 1863.

[12] *Ibid.*, March 16, March 19, 1863.

[13] Levi Ross to his father, Feb. 3, 1863, manuscript, Ill. State Historical Library.

[14] M. P. Larry to his sister, Dec. 23, 1862, manuscript, Maine Historical Society.

[15] Bell Irvin Wiley, "Billy Yank and the Brass," Ill. State Historical Society *Journal*, XLIII (1950), 250.

[16] Samuel W. Croft to his sister, Dec. 21, 1862, and Feb. 3, 1863, manuscripts, Washington and Jefferson College. I am indebted to C. M. Ewing for calling these manuscripts to my attention and lending me copies of them. Herman Chauncey Newhall to his father, Dec. 28, 1862.

[17] A. H. Pickel to his father, Feb. 22, 1863, manuscript, Duke;

Richard Puffer to his sister, Feb. 12, 1863, manuscript, Chicago Historical Society.

[18] Levi Ross to his father, March 25, 1863.

[19] A. Davenport to his homefolk, March 27, 1863; diary of Stephen
W. Gordon, Feb. 7—May 6, 1863, typescript in possession of Fred L.
Williams, Atlanta; Edmund English of the 2nd N. J. Regiment wrote,
after the war, of the period following Burnside's removal: "I did not
think it possible that such a change could have taken place for the
better as has been effected in the short space of two months. From a
dissatisfied and almost mutinous mob, we have become a good and well-
disciplined army second to none." "Memoirs of Campaign Life," manuscript among the Edmund English Papers. I am indebted to the Huntington Library for lending me a microfilm copy of these papers.

[20] The Provost Marshal General's Bureau was created on March
3, 1863. National Archives *Guide* (Washington, 1948), 395.

[21] For one soldier's comment on the effect of improving health on
morale, see Isaac Jackson to his brother, March 23, 1863, typescript in
possession of J. O. Jackson, Highland Park, Mich.

[22] Edmund English to his mother, Jan. 27, April 12, 1863; Jesse A.
Wilson to his parents, Feb. 10, April 12, 1863, manuscripts in possession
of Mrs. Fred A. Johnson, Belfast, Maine; M. P. Larry to his sister, April
12, 1863.

[23] Isaac Jackson to his brother, March 19, 1863.

[24] Wolf, *Campaigning with the First Minnesota*, 347.

[25] Surgeon Edwin Hutchinson to his mother, July 1, 1863, manuscript, La. State Univ.

[26] On Dec. 28, 1862, one soldier wrote from Falmouth, Virginia: "I
want just one *good show*, one hack at them, where I can reach them;
when our army can be victorious; and that's what we want—a victory!"
R. G. Carter, *Four Brothers in Blue*, 324.

[27] Of Gettysburg one Yank later wrote: "I hesitate to say how much
it meant to our army, but as I am telling everything else I may as well tell
this, that if the battle had gone against us, I should have made straight
for Fitchburg [his home] and I should have had lots of company. We
had lost battle after battle, by blunder after blunder, of commander after
commander, and we had lost all confidence. It was common talk in the
ranks, 'We'll do our level best here, but if we cant lick the rebs on Yankee
soil, that's the end of it for us.'" Bardeen, *A Little Fifer's War Diary*,
214.

[28] C. B. Thurston to his father, July 10, 1863, manuscript, Emory.

[29] Frank Wilkeson, *Recollections of a Private*, 185-187.

[30] Private E. W. Chase of Sherman's army wrote in his journal on
April 12, 1865: "News reached us that Lee had surrendered his army.
The tumult of joy was indescribable." Manuscript, Maine Historical
Society.

[31] In one instance, at least, the burial routine was given a lightening
touch. In relating the death and interment of a comrade who died
on a march from Kentucky to Tennessee in 1863, a Michigan soldier

stated: "A prayer over the grave and three volleys completed the ceremony. The band played the death march while going towards the grave and Yankee doodle comming back." William H. Brearley to his sister, Oct. 17, 1863, manuscript, Detroit Public Library.

32 William A. Harper to his wife, Feb. 16, 1863, manuscript, Ind. Historical Society.

33 J. J. Moulton to his homefolk, Jan. 25, 1863; Charles K. Bailer to his sister, April 25, 1864, manuscript, Western Reserve Historical Society.

34 David Williams to John R. Corrie, March 9, 1863, manuscript in possession of Mrs. Lester L. Corrie, Urbana, Illinois.

35 H. C. Bear to his wife, Dec. 7-14, 1862, manuscript in possession of Mrs. Stanley B. Hadden, Urbana, Illinois.

36 Levi Ross to his parents, June 26, 1863.

37 David Leigh to "Mr. Drumgold," March 3, Aug. 1, 1863, manuscript, Dartmouth.

38 John McMeekin to his mother, from near Young's Point, La., Feb. 11, 1863, manuscript, Western Reserve Historical Society.

39 *Ibid.*, Jan. 15, March 16, 1863; Lonn, *Desertion during the Civil War*, 204-205; Wood Gray, *The Hidden Civil War* (N. Y., 1942), 132-135, 154-155.

40 Anson W. Bristol to Lucian B. Case, May 17, 1863, manuscript, Chicago Historical Society; Seth H. Cook to Curtis Babbott, Dec. 10, 1862, manuscript, Hayes Memorial Library.

41 John W. Clark to his sister, April 3, 1864, manuscript in possession of the writer; Thomas N. Lewis to his aunt, Jan. 24, 1862, manuscript, Western Reserve Historical Society.

42 H. R. Leonard to Jennie Davis, Nov. 23 [1861], manuscript among Miscellaneous Civil War Letters, Western Reserve Historical Society.

43 C. B. Thurston to his brother, March 30, 1863, and to his father, June 3, 1863.

44 Vance Nelson to Amanda Wright, Dec. 12, 1861.

45 Lucretia E. Thompson to Henry J. H. Thompson, Jan. 14, 1863, manuscript, Duke. She headed this letter appropriately, "Camp Lonely."

46 William H. Lloyd to his wife, various dates, 1863-1865, manuscripts, Western Reserve Historical Society. The letters quoted are those of Sept. 24, Oct. 3, Oct. 10, Dec. 21, Dec. 23, 1863.

47 John N. Henry to his wife, Jan. 2, 1863, manuscript, Minn. Historical Society.

48 Diary of M. F. Roberts, April 12, 1864, manuscript, Western Reserve Historical Society; Portland, Maine, *Transcript*, May 2, 1863.

49 Willis D. Maier to Annie F. Howells, Nov. 21, 1863, Jan. 6, 1864, manuscripts, Hayes Memorial Library. His three-year term was to expire in eight months.

50 O. R., series 1, XII, pt. 3, 410.

51 Hercules Stanard to his father, Nov. 17, 1862, manuscript, Univ. of Mich.

52 W. O. Lyford to his homefolk, July 31, Aug. 31, 1861; Feb. 14,

March 8, Oct. 8, 1862, manuscripts in possession of Charles N. Owen, Chicago.

[53] John W. De Forest, *A Volunteer's Adventures*, 165. For the superior discipline of De Forest's regiment and the triumph of good morale over hardship, see *ibid.*, 151.

[54] See chapter XII.

[55] Charles Ward to his homefolk, Sept. 14, Sept. 22, Nov. 14, 1862; May 7, July 7, 1863, manuscripts, American Antiquarian Society.

[56] "Correspondence of Ira Butterfield," *North Dakota Historical Quarterly*, III (Jan., 1929), 130.

Chapter XII

THE MEN WHO WORE THE BLUE

[1] *O. R.*, series 3, V, 130.

[2] Diary of William C. Richardson, 1862-1865, 4 vols., *passim*, manuscript, Western Reserve Historical Society; J. H. Kendig to his brother, Aug. 10, 1863, manuscript, Historical Society of Pa.

[3] F. T. Miller, editor, *Photographic History of the Civil War*, VIII, 195; Frances A. Tenney, editor, *War Diary of Luman Harris Tenney, 1861-1865*, 65.

[4] Harvey Reid to his brother Charles [n.d., but 1862], manuscript, Wis. Historical Society.

[5] Ray H. Mattison, "The Drummer Boy of Shiloh," manuscript, Shiloh National Park. Mattison was historian of the Shiloh Park at the time he made this study. I am indebted to Superintendent James Holland of the Shiloh Park for making it available to me and for furnishing additional information; also to E. J. Pratt, his assistant, for showing me the "doctored" cemetery roll. The collection at Shiloh contains a copy of the Hays song, "The Drummer Boy of Shiloh" (Louisville and Chicago, 1862), and a play, "The Drummer Boy: Or the Battle-field of Shiloh, a New Military Allegory in Six Acts" (Pittsburgh, 1870) by Comrade Samuel J. Muscroft. Neither Hays nor Muscroft mention a drummer boy by name. Various depositories other than Shiloh have files on the drummer boy of Shiloh.

[6] This account of Clem's service, except as otherwise indicated, is based on John L. Clem, "From Nursery to Battlefield," *Outlook* magazine, CVII (1914), 546-547. At one place in the article Clem states that it was to the 23rd Michigan Regiment that he attached himself as drummer, but this is obviously an error.

[7] Prints of this photograph are at the Chickamauga-Chattanooga National Military Park and Shiloh National Military Park.

[8] For details of Clem's career, other than those contained in his own article cited above, see Miller, *Photographic History of the Civil*

War, VIII, 192; *Who's Who in America*, 1912-1913 (Chicago, 1912), 400; Indianapolis *Star*, May 24, 1936 and May 15, 1937; A. S. Roe, *The Youth in the Rebellion* (Worcester, Mass., 1883), 10-11. I am indebted to Caroline Dunn of the William Henry Smith Memorial Library, Indiana Historical Society, for finding important information about Clem and other drummer boys.

[9] O. R., series 1, XVI, pt. 1, 1086.

[10] *Medals of Honor Issued by the War Department up to and Including October 31, 1897*, 66. See also O. R., series 1, XXXVIII, pt. 3, 192. Samuel Scoville in *Brave Deeds of Union Soldiers* (Philadelphia, 1910), 54, 63, tells of heroic deeds by Johnny McLaughlin and Eddie Lee at Shiloh and Wilson's Creek, respectively. But the tone of the account is not such as to create confidence in its reliability. A check of the records of Indiana and Iowa, states from which these boys were supposed to have entered the army, failed to reveal any trace of them or their careers. Moreover, the units to which they were said to have belonged did not take part in the actions with which their heroism allegedly was connected. For ten interesting letters by a young musician, see Don Russell, "Letters of a Drummer Boy," *Indiana Magazine of History*, XXXIV (1938), 324-339.

[11] O. R., series 3, I, 454 and II, 236, 612.

[12] Benjamin A. Gould, *Investigations in the Military and Anthropological Statistics of American Soldiers* (N. Y., 1869), 38. This volume, to be cited hereafter as Gould, *Anthropological Statistics*, was published by the United States Sanitary Commission in the series, "Sanitary Memoirs of the War of the Rebellion."

[13] The lists examined by the writer are in the manuscript Regimental Descriptive Books, Nat'l Archives. Selection was made in such a way as to obtain a sample representative of the three principal branches (infantry, cavalry and artillery), the various states, and organizations formed at different stages of the war. The lists include both original enlistees and recruits added throughout the war. This tabulation will be cited hereafter as Regimental Descriptive Lists. For an example of drummer boys graduating to the fighting ranks, other than that of Clem, see Charles E. Davis, *Three Years in the Army*, 110-111.

[14] G. L. Kilmer, "Boys in the Union Army," *Century Magazine*, LXX (1905), 269.

[15] Martha N. McLeod, editor, *Brother Warriors, The Reminiscences of Union and Confederate Veterans* (Washington, 1940), 47.

[16] Chauncey H. Cooke, *A Soldier Boy's Letters to his Father and Mother* (n.d., n.p., but 1912), 2. These letters were also published serially in the *Wisconsin Magazine of History*, IV (1920-1921), 75-100, 208-217, 322-344, 431-456, and V (1921-1922), 63-98.

[17] Miller, *Photographic History of the Civil War*, IX, 67.

[18] Portland, Maine, *Transcript*, Sept. 6, 1862.

[19] For a court-martial case involving desertion of a soldier who was younger than eighteen, see Hq. Army of the Potomac, G. O. 71, Feb. 21,

1861. McClellan approved discharge of the youth and issued a rebuke to recruiting officers who enlisted minors. *Ibid.*

[20] Urich N. Parmelee to his brother, April 4, 1864, and to his mother, Dec. 11, 1864, manuscripts, Duke.

[21] O. R., series 1, XI, pt. 1, 896; Francis M. Field to his parents, Jan. 28, 1863, manuscript, Ohio State Arch. and Historical Society.

[22] Roe, *The Youth in the Rebellion*, 10-11; O. R., series 1, X, pt. 1, 376 and XI, pt. 1, 896; *Medals of Honor Awarded by the War Department up to and Including October 31, 1897*, 56.

[23] Kilmer, "Boys in the Union Army," 271.

[24] Charles E. Goddard to his mother, especially letters of Dec. 2, 1861, Aug. 7, 1862, Sept. 28, 1862, and Dec. 4, 1863, manuscripts, Minn. Historical Society.

[25] Robert U. Johnson and Clarence C. Buel, editors, *Battles and Leaders of the Civil War* (N. Y., 1888), III, 624; Kilmer, "Boys in the Union Army," 275.

[26] O. R., series 3, II, 236, 612; W.D.A.G.O. G. O. 104, Dec. 2, 1861.

[27] Gould, *Anthropological Statistics*, 34-35.

[28] *Ibid.*, 34.

[29] Regimental Descriptive Lists.

[30] Descriptive Book, 1st Mo. Inf. Regt., manuscript, Nat'l Archives.

[31] A *Memorial Record of the New York Branch of the U. S. Christian Commission* (N. Y., 1866), 56.

[32] Office of the Iowa Adjutant General, *Roster and Record of Iowa Soldiers* (Des Moines, 1911), V, 786, 788. I am indebted to Mildred Throne of the State Historical Society of Iowa for providing data concerning King. The oldest Confederate known to the writer was E. Pollard who enlisted in the 5th North Carolina Infantry at 73. See Bell Irvin Wiley, *The Life of Johnny Reb*, 332.

[33] W. W. Gist, "The Ages of Soldiers in the Civil War," *Iowa Journal of History and Politics*, XVI (1918), 396.

[34] Gould, *Anthropological Statistics*, 34; G. D. Kilmer, "Boys in the Union Army," *Century Magazine*, XII (1905), 269.

[35] Gould, *Anthropoligcal Statistics*, 34.

[36] *Ibid.*, 86-88.

[37] The degree of youthfulness has been grossly exaggerated on the basis of false statistics circulated in the early 1900s. As late as 1918 a religious periodical stated that the average age of Civil War soldiers at the end of the conflict was 19, and a G. A. R. speaker declared that the armies of the sixties contained a million soldiers who were under 16! W. W. Gist, "The Ages of Soldiers in the Civil War," *Iowa Journal of History and Politics*, XVI (1918), 387.

[38] Gould, *Anthropological Statistics*, 88.

[39] Regimental Descriptive Lists; Descriptive Book, 15th Ohio Infantry Regt. (Company A), manuscript, Nat'l Archives.

[40] Regimental Descriptive Lists.

[41] Detroit *Free Press*, May 31, 1861.

[42] Frank Moore, editor, *The Rebellion Record,* I (N. Y., 1861), 148-154, quoted in Henry S. Commager, editor, *The Blue and the Gray,* I, 86-87.

[43] Reid's manuscript diary is in the Ill. State Historical Library. The first quotation is from the entry of July 30, 1861.

[44] Samuel Storrow to his parents, May 12, 1863, manuscript, Mass. Historical Society.

[45] Thomas L. Livermore, *Days and Events,* 400-401.

[46] Edward L. Edes to his father, Feb. 20, 1863, manuscript, Mass. Historical Society; Urich N. Parmelee to his brother, Aug. 4, 1862; Leland O. Barlow to his sister, Sept. 4, 1863, manuscript, Conn. State Library.

[47] Mrs. J. D. Wheeler, compiler, *In Memoriam: Letters of William Wheeler of the Class of 1855 Y.C.,* 423.

[48] When after six months the case came to Lincoln's attention the sentence was remitted and the soldier restored to duty. J.A.G. Records NN 1844, manuscript, Nat'l Archives.

[49] Francis M. Field to his homefolk, Dec. 23, 1862.

[50] Regimental Descriptive Lists.

[51] As recently as a year ago an author whose history has a decided Southern slant asserted very positively in a meeting attended by the writer that "the majority of Yankee soldiers were foreign hirelings."

[52] Regimental Descriptive Books.

[53] Ella Lonn, *Foreigners in the Union Army and Navy* (Baton Rouge, 1951), 90-110, 146, 578, 663-672; Regimental Descriptive Books.

[54] Lonn, *Foreigners in the Union Army and Navy,* 44-56, 485-545, 648-651; letters of Adam Muenzenberger to his wife, typescript translation from the German, Wis. Historical Society; Rebecca R. Usher to her sister Ellen, March 31, 1865, typescript, Maine Historical Society; diary of Calvin Fletcher, Sept. 5, 1861, manuscript, Ind. Historical Society; Urich N. Parmelee to his mother, Jan. 26, 1863.

[55] *The Reminiscences of Carl Schurz* (N. Y., 1908), I, 25.

[56] Lonn, *Foreigners in the Union Army and Navy,* 116-126, 510-512, 578, 672-674.

[57] *Ibid.,* 645-648.

[58] Charles Ward to his brother, Oct. 2, 1862, manuscript, American Antiquarian Society.

[59] For a penetrating discussion of Irish fighting characteristics, see Lonn, *Foreigners in the Union Army and Navy,* 645-648.

[60] Thomas L. Livermore relates an amusing incident of an Irishman who, feeling the need of a spree, requested permission of his commanding officer to get drunk. *Days and Events,* 215.

[61] Lonn, *Foreigners in the Union Army and Navy,* 383 ff.

[62] Gould, *Anthropological Statistics,* 27; Lonn, *Foreigners in the Union Army and Navy,* 578-579.

[63] Gould, *op. cit.,* 27; Theodore C. Blegen, editor, *Civil War Letters of Colonel Hans C. Heg,* 21 *et passim;* Lonn, *Foreigners in the Union Army and Navy,* 131-132, 576-580, 674.

[64] Blegen, *op. cit.*, 25-26.

[65] The Knute Nelson manuscripts are in the Minn. Historical Society. The letters quoted are dated June 10, 1862, and Feb. 3, 1864. Revealing also as to Scandinavian characteristics and experience are the Hans Mattson letters in the Minn. Historical Society and a Miscellaneous Scandinavian Collection at Luther College, soldier items of which were translated for the writer by Inga B. Norstog.

[66] Regimental Descriptive Lists; Lonn, *Foreigners in the Union Army and Navy*, 674-675.

[67] Lonn, *Foreigners in the Union Army and Navy*, 155, 436-478.

[68] *Ibid.*, 162, 347-405.

[69] Wheeler, *In Memoriam: Letters of William Wheeler*, 305, 313, 316.

[70] Hq. Army of the Potomac, G. O. 38, 41, Feb. 1, 6, 1862; J.A.G. Records MM 672, manuscript, Nat'l Archives.

[71] Charles W. Wills, *Army Life of an Illinois Soldier*, 20.

[72] O. R., series 3, V, 662. Some of the Negroes credited to the Northern states actually were recruited in the South. *Ibid.*

[73] *Ibid.*, 660-661; Joseph T. Wilson, *The Black Phalanx* (Hartford, Conn., 1891), 464-480. The artillery brigade of the 25th Corps was white.

[74] O. R., series 1, XXVI, pt. 1, 689; Wilson, *Black Phalanx*, 195; R. B. Marcy, Report of an Inspection of the Dept. of Miss. and the Gulf, March—June, 1865. Item M-63, I.G.O. Letters Received, manuscripts, Nat'l Archives; Thomas W. Higginson to his wife, May 9, 1863, manuscript, Harvard.

[75] U. S. Christian Commission, Daily Record Book, entry by A. B. Peffers, Wild's Station, March 29, 1865, manuscript, Nat'l Archives.

[76] This summary of the Negroes' combat performance is based mainly on Bell Irvin Wiley, *Southern Negroes, 1861-1865*, 295-344 and on battle reports in the *Official Records*.

[77] W. C. Ford, editor, *War Letters, 1861-1865 of John C. Gray and John C. Ropes*, 184.

[78] Wiley, *Southern Negroes*, 313 ff.

[79] The inspection reports, filed in the I.G.O. Records, Nat'l Archives, of R. B. Marcy, D. B. Sackett and James A. Hardie, are especially valuable. Comments of officers that are particularly revealing, in addition to Higginson's, are those of Charles B. Fox (manuscripts, Mass. Historical Society), Henry Crydenwise (manuscripts, Duke and Emory), and Rufus Kinsley (manuscripts, Vt. Historical Society).

[80] Wiley, *Southern Negroes, 1861-1865*, 313 ff; Edward Whitaker to his sister, June 26, 1862, manuscript, Conn. State Library; Urich N. Parmelee to his brother, May 22, 1864.

[81] Diary of Lt. H. S. Adams, Sept. 16, 1863, manuscript, N. Y. Public Library.

[82] John W. De Forest, A *Volunteer's Adventures*, 26.

[83] *Ibid.*, 40.

[84] O. R., series 1, XXX, pt. 3, 336.

[85] *Ibid.*, XXII, pt. 2, 56-58; R. B. Marcy, Report of an Inspection of the Dept. of Arkansas made in June and July 1864, I.G.O. Letters Received, Item M-69, manuscript, Nat'l Archives. For extensive accounts of the role of the red man in the Union Army, see Annie Heloise Abel, *The American Indian as Participant in the Civil War* (Cleveland, 1919), and Wiley Britton, *The Union Indian Brigade in the Civil War* (Kansas City, 1922).

[86] Muster-out Rolls, Co. C, Second Indian Regt. and Co. B, Third Indian Regt., manuscripts (photostats), Okla. Historical Society. Originals of these rolls are in the Nat'l Archives; Record Book of Co. A (clothing account), Third Indian Regiment, manuscript, Okla. Historical Society.

[87] Descriptive Book, Co. F, Third Indian Regt., manuscript, Okla. Historical Society.

[88] Capt. J. H. Greene, *Reminiscences of the War*, 54.

[89] Wiley Britton, "Union and Confederate Indians in the Civil War," in *Battles and Leaders of the Civil War* I, 335.

[90] O. R., series 1, XIII, 894 and XXII, pt. 1, 447-462; Wiley, *The Life of Johnny Reb*, 326. An Arkansas pioneer in 1937 told of seeing Union Cherokee soldiers scalp Rebel opponents after a Civil War engagement in the Indian country. W.P.A. "Indian Pioneer History," XII, 390, interview of James Robert Barnes, bound typescript, Foreman Collection, Okla. Historical Society.

[91] O. R., series 1, XXII, pt. 2, 56-58 and XXXIV, pt. 2, 754-755. James Hardie, Extracts from Inspection Reports, District of the Frontier, for June 1864, Department of the Army Records, Document File, manuscript, Nat'l Archives.

[92] O. R., series 1, XXII, pt. 1, 94.

[93] *Ibid.*, 314-315, 337-338, 378-382, 447-456; pt. 2, 56-58, 371, 465; XXXIV, pt. 2, 754-755; R. B. Marcy, Report of an Inspection of the Dept. of Arkansas Made in June and July, 1864.

[94] O. R., series 1, XXII, pt. 2, 283-284; James Hardie, Extracts from Inspection Reports, District of the Frontier for June, 1864; R. B. Marcy, Report, Aug. 15, 1864, of a Special Inspection of the Dept. of Arkansas, I.G.O. Letters Received, item M-64, manuscript, Nat'l Archives. For a dramatic account of Cherokee participation and suffering in the Civil War, and of pillage of loyal Indians by Union soldiers, see T. W. Wright, Attorney for Cherokees, to Col. Garrett, Commanding Officer, Fort Gibson [July 31, 1865], manuscript, Indian Archives, Okla. Historical Society.

[95] Branches represented in the Union Army included infantry, cavalry, artillery, engineers, signal corps, adjutant general's department, medical service, ordnance, quartermaster, subsistence and finance; M. J. O'Brien, translator, *The American Army in the War of Secession*, by General DeChanal (Leavenworth, Kan., 1894), 5.

[96] Frederick Phisterer, *Statistical Record of the Armies of the United States* (Supplementary Volume, *Campaigns of the Civil War*, N. Y., 1883), 22-23.

[97] *Ibid.*, 11; James G. Randall, *Civil War and Reconstruction* (N. Y., 1937), 266, 411. For a full discussion of substitution see Fred A. Shannon, *Organization and Administration of the Union Army*, II, 49-99.

[98] W.D.A.G.O. G. O. 110, April 29, 1863; O. R., series 3, I, 153 and II, 518-520; Silas Casey, *Infantry Tactics*, I, 11; Phisterer, *Statistical Record*, 55.

[99] See chapter II.

[100] O. R., series 1, XXV, pt. 2, 152; for colored illustrations of corps badges, see *Atlas to Accompany O. R.*, plate 175, and Billings, *Hard Tack and Coffee*, 250-268.

[101] O. R., series 3, II, 518-520; W.D.A.G.O. G. O. 110, April 29, 1863.

[102] Thomas L. Livermore, *Numbers and Losses during the Civil War* (Boston, 1900), 68.

[103] Matthew Marvin to his brother, Dec. 24, 1862, manuscript, Minn. Historical Society; E. A. Johnson, editor, *The Hero of Medfield*, 72.

[104] For examples of interregimental brawls, see Enoch T. Baker to his wife, Nov. 18, 1861, manuscript, Historical Society of Pa.; Lawrence Van Alstyne, *Diary of an Enlisted Man*, 85; Leland O. Barlow to his sister, Feb. 1, 1863.

[105] Van Alstyne, *Diary of an Enlisted Man*, 169.

[106] Wills, *Army Life of an Illinois Soldier*, 218; Frank E. Lansing to his mother, Feb. 13, 1864, manuscript, Detroit Public Library.

[107] "The Fourteenth Indiana in the Valley of Virginia," *Indiana Magazine of History*, XXX (1934), 293.

[108] Wills, *Army Life of an Illinois Soldier*, 144.

[109] Willis D. Maier to Annie F. Howells, July 20, 1863 and Dec. 15, 1863, manuscript, Hayes Memorial Library.

[110] Ransom Bedell to his cousin, Aug. 24, 1864, manuscript, Ill. State Historical Library.

[111] Alonzo Miller to his sister, May 21, 1865, typescript, Kennesaw Mountain National Park.

[112] William Benjamin Johnson, *Union to the Hub and Twice Around the Tire: Reminiscences of William Benjamin Johnson* (n.d., n.p., but privately printed, 1950), 108; excerpts from the diary of Osborn H. Oldroyd, June 13, 1863, typescript, Vicksburg National Park; diary of Charles W. Wills, May 1, 1864, manuscript, Illinois State Historical Library.

[113] Wills, *Army Life of an Illinois Soldier*, 218. Wills stated that the Westerners were usually the aggressors in the oral jousts.

[114] Henry P. Whipple, *The Diary of a Private Soldier*, 27.

[115] Capt. Charles H. Salter to Mrs. I. G. Duffield, June 12, 1864, manuscript, Detroit Public Library.

[116] Thomas H. Parker, *History of the 51st Regiment Pennsylvania Vols.*, 362.

[117] Willis D. Maier to Annie F. Howells, June 19, 1863.

[118] Abraham Kendig to his homefolk, March 29, 1862.

[119] Lt. Roswell Farnham to "Friend Harding," June 3, 1861, typescript, Vt. Historical Society.

[120] *Statistics, Medical and Anthropological of the Provost Marshal General's Bureau* (Washington, 1875), I, 29.

[121] Nashville *Dispatch*, Nov. 27, 1864.

[122] R. G. Carter, *Four Brothers in Blue.*

[123] For one of many tributes to the Regulars' combat performance, see O. R., series 3, III, 1110.

[124] Frank E. Lansing to his mother, Nov. 13, 1863; William F. Goodhue to his parents, March 13, 1863, manuscript, Ill. State Historical Library.

[125] Diary of John Merrilies, May 8, 1864, manuscript, Chicago Historical Society.

[126] Davis, *Three Years in the Army*, 191-192.

[127] Diary of Philip Smith, Oct. 22, 1863, bound volume of articles from Peoria *Evening Star*, 1917, in the Veterans' Records Division of the Nat'l Archives.

[128] Diary of Charles W. Wills, Feb. 1, 1865.

[129] Hazel C. Wolf, editor, *Campaigning with the First Minnesota*, 229-230.

[130] Diary of an unidentified soldier of Co. B, 24th Conn. Regt., Jan. 27, 1863, manuscript, Conn. State Library.

[131] Davis, *Three Years in the Army*, 183-184; Charles Ward to his parents, n.d., n.p., but near Falmouth, Va., April, 1863; Capt. Charles Barnard to his wife, Sept. 25, 1862, manuscript, Maine Historical Society; John D. Billings, *Hard Tack and Coffee*, 95 ff.

[132] John Beatty, *The Citizen Soldier*, 40.

[133] Billings, *Hard Tack and Coffee*, 101.

[134] Lt. Henry A. Buck to his sister, April 1, 1863, manuscript, Detroit Public Library.

[135] Eli R. Pickett to his wife, Dec. 29, 1862, manuscript, Minn. Historical Society.

[136] Henry M. Crydenwise to his parents, Dec. 18, 1861, manuscript, Duke.

[137] Charles Tillison to his homefolk, Oct. 22, 1862, manuscript, Vt. Historical Society.

[138] *Ibid.*, various home letters in the winter of 1862-1863; T. J. Tillison to Dudley Tillison, May 15, 1863.

[139] Charles Tillison to Dudley Tillison, Feb. 21, 24, 1864.

[140] W. J. Jackson to Dudley Tillison, June 4, 1863; Dudley Tillison to Charles Tillison, Dec. 25, 1863; Vermont Adjutant General's Office, *Revised Roster of Vermont Volunteers* (Montpelier, 1892), 49.

[141] A. S. Roe, *The Ninth New York Heavy Artillery*, 274; Joseph H. Diltz to his wife, Nov. 24, 1862, manuscript, Duke.

[142] Diary of Walter F. Kittredge for 1862, especially entries of Oct. 29, 31, Nov. 2, 8, 14, 19, 20, 27, Dec. 3, 12, manuscript in possession of Robert B. Holtman, La. State Univ.

[143] *Ibid.*, entries for Jan. and Feb. 1863.

[144] For a full description of the bummer type, see George Sharland, *Knapsack Notes*, 46-47.

[145] Joseph H. Diltz to his wife, Jan. 24, 1862 and Aug. 10, 1863.

[146] Mary Diltz to Joseph Diltz, May 3, 1863.

[147] Thomas L. Pankey to his wife, July 18, 1863, manuscript, Ill. State Historical Library.

[148] *Med. and Surg. Hist.*, Surgical Volume, pt. 3, 641.

[149] Billings, *Hard Tack and Coffee*, 67.

[150] Edward L. Edes to his uncle, Feb. 10, 1863; Urich N. Parmelee to his mother, June 25, 1862.

[151] Billings, *Hard Tack and Coffee*, 105.

[152] *Ibid.*, 91-95.

[153] Davis, *Three Years in the Army*, 177-178.

[154] Alonzo Miller to his homefolk, April 22, April 27, July 9, 1864.

[155] O. W. Norton, *Army Letters, 1861-1865*, 75-76.

[156] "Letters of Privates Cook and Ball," *Indiana Magazine of History*, XXVII (1931), 256.

[157] Urich N. Parmelee to his mother, Nov. 20, 1862. For a brief history of another interesting soldier of fortune, killed at Antietam, see diary of Thomas Francis Galwey, Sept. 17, 1862, typescript in possession of Col. Geoffrey Galwey, Washington, D. C.

[158] George F. Newhall to his father, March 28, 1862, manuscript, Boston Public Library.

[159] *Ibid.*, April 22, 1862.

[160] *Ibid.*, May 20, June 21, 1862.

[161] *Ibid.*, July 4, 1862; James D. Newhall to his parents, Nov. 5, 1862, manuscript, Boston Public Library.

[162] Day Elmore to his parents, Sept. 29, 1862, manuscript in possession of Mrs. Hall Mosher, Memphis, to whom grateful acknowledgment is made for the use of these letters. In preparing this sketch of Elmore's war service, I have drawn on an unidentifiable newspaper obituary and several official documents filed with the letters.

[163] *Ibid.*, Feb. 3, 1864.

[164] Mrs. William Hume Harris, Franklin, Tenn., to Daniel Elmore, Dec. 14, 1862, manuscript among Day Elmore letters.

[165] Capt. Horace Hittenden to Daniel Elmore, Dec. 8, 1864, manuscript among Day Elmore letters.

[166] Miller, *Photographic History of the Civil War*, VIII, 273; file no. 184934Y-1, "Women Who Served in Wars of the United States," Record and Pension Branch, A.G.O. Records, Nat'l Archives; file 132D, A.G.O. Records, "Remarkable Cases and Names," Nat'l Archives; Adjutant General, U. S. Army to John Hix, June 27, 1932, A.G.O. file AG291.9 (6-17-32) ORD; George W. Driggs, *Opening of the Mississippi*, 95.

[167] File W3370, 1864, Record and Pension Branch, A.G.O., Nat'l Archives.

[168] "Women Who Served in Wars of the United States"; Office of Adjutant General of Michigan, *Record of Service of Michigan Volunteers in the Civil War, 1861-1865* (Kalamazoo, 1902), II, 170; diary of William Boston, April 22, 1863, typescript, Univ. of Mich.

[169] Pension file of Albert D. J. Cashier (certificate no. 1,001,132), manuscripts, Veterans Administration's Records, Nat'l Archives.

[170] *Ibid.*

[171] For example see Nashville *Dispatch,* Aug. 29, 1862, and Henry C. Bear to his wife, Dec. 7-14, 1862, manuscript in possession of Mrs. Stanley B. Hadden, Urbana, Illinois.

[172] Memphis *Bulletin,* Dec. 19, 1862.

[173] Livermore, *Days and Events,* 146.

[174] New York *Tribune,* Feb. 20, 1864, quoting Detroit *Advertiser;* William F. Fox, *Regimental Losses in the Civil War* (Albany, N. Y., 1889), 60.

[175] Fanny J. Anderson, editor, "The Shelley Papers," *Indiana Magazine of History,* XLIV (1948), 186.

[176] Wills, *Army Life of an Illinois Soldier,* 218.

[177] William R. Hartpence, *History of the Fifty-first Indiana Veteran Volunteer Infantry,* 68-69.

[178] "The Fourteenth Indiana in the Valley of Virginia," *Indiana Magazine of History,* XXX (1934), 293.

[179] Wills, *Army Life of an Illinois Soldier,* 233.

[180] *Ibid.;* Donald Gordon, editor, *M. L. Gordon's Experiences in the Civil War,* 34; Beatty, *op. cit.,* 231-232; Thomas L. Livermore, "The Northern Volunteers," *Granite Monthly,* X (1887), 247; Hartpence, *History of the Fifty-first Indiana Veteran Volunteer Infantry,* 208; see Oscar O. Winther, editor, *With Sherman to the Sea,* 115.

[181] For a sketch of the interior of a soldier's hut, showing pin-up girls on wall, see diary of Thomas Francis Galwey.

[182] [Samuel Fiske], *Mr. Dunn Brown's Experiences in the Army* (Boston, 1866), 50-51.

[183] C. A. Stevens, *Berdan's United States Sharpshooters in the Army of the Potomac, 1861-1865* (St. Paul, Minn., 1892), *passim;* Fox, *Regimental Losses in the Civil War,* 418-419; Wesley Bradshaw (pseud. for Charles W. Alexander), *The Volunteer's Roll of Honor* (Philadelphia, 1863), 40-42.

[184] O. R., series 1, XX, pt. 1, 197-198.

[185] See chapter II; Fox, *Regimental Losses in the Civil War,* 503, 507.

[186] O. R., series 3, III, 999, 1002, 1052, 1131-1132.

[187] A broadside copy of the song is in the Ezra E. Rickett Collection, Ohio State Arch. and Historical Society. The composer was Matt Gebler and the printer J. H. Johnson of Philadelphia.

[188] O. R., series 3, III, 1132, IV, 188.

[189] *Ibid.,* III, 414-416, 997-999, V, 650.

[190] Hartpence, *History of the Fifty-first Indiana Veteran Volunteer Infantry,* 201.

[191] O. R., series 3, IV, 930, 1214, V, 651; Livermore, *Numbers and Losses in the Civil War in America,* 1.

[192] For a discussion of substitutes, bounty jumpers and other evils attendant on raising and maintaining the Union forces, see Fred A.

Shannon, *Organization and Administration of the Union Army,* especially II, 54 ff.

[193] Davis, *Three Years in the Army,* 263-264.

[194] Lt. Col. Charles B. Fox to his wife, June 25, 1864.

[195] Maj. George Blagden, Report of a Special Inspection of the Recruiting Service at Pottsville, Pa., May 9, 1864, I.G.O. Letters Received, manuscripts, Nat'l Archives.

Chapter XIII

BILLY YANK AND JOHNNY REB

[1] John C. Arnold to his wife, Aug. 7, 1864, typescript, National War College.

[2] Henry Wilson to Jeremiah Norris, Dec. 29, 1861, manuscript, Duke.

[3] Lydia Minturn Post, editor, *Soldiers' Letters,* 468-469.

[4] Detroit *Free Press,* June 28, 1861.

[5] Edward Whitaker to his sister, July 19, 1861, manuscript, Conn. State Library; Samuel W. Croft to his sister, July 26, 1861, typescript, Washington and Jefferson College.

[6] Edward E. Newhall to his homefolk, March 12, 1862, manuscript, Boston Public Library; Charles E. Goddard to his mother, Nov. 13, 1863, manuscript, Minn. Historical Society; Charles W. Wills, *Army Life of an Illinois Soldier,* 60-61.

[7] Portland, Maine, *Transcript,* June 7, 1862.

[8] Frederick C. Dickinson to "Dear George," Nov. 2, 1861, manuscript, American Antiquarian Society.

[9] Felix Brannigan to his sister, June 17, 1862, typescript, Library of Congress.

[10] Diary of Jenkins Lloyd Jones, July 8, 1863, manuscript, Wis. Historical Society.

[11] Lt. L. Muller to his cousin, Oct. 14, 1861, typescript translation from the German original, Minn. Historical Society; Maj. B. F. Buckner to Helen Martin, April 18, 1862, manuscript, Univ. of Ky.

[12] Diary of Jacob E. Hyneman, Oct. 31, 1864, typescript in possession of Charles N. Owen, Chicago; Cyrus R. Stone to his homefolk, Dec. 11, 1861, manuscript, Minn. Historical Society.

[13] John Herr to his mother, Oct. 5, 1862, manuscript, Duke.

[14] Unidentified Indiana soldier to his sister, Sept. 26, 1862, manuscript, Ransom T. Young Papers, Ind. State Library.

[15] Joseph H. Diltz to his wife, March 13, 1862, manuscript, Duke.

[16] Cyrus R. Stone to his parents, June 7, 1862.

[17] Charles Ward to his sister, May 23, 1863, manuscript, American Antiquarian Society.

[18] Daniel E. Burbank to his brother [July 21], 1861, manuscript, American Antiquarian Society.

[19] Diary of William D. Evans, July 29, 1864, manuscript, Western Reserve Historical Society; Edward L. Edes to his sister, May 10, 1863, manuscript, Mass. Historical Society; Charles K. Bailer to his sister, May 20, 1864, typescript, Western Reserve Historical Society.

[20] F. M. Abbott to his father, April 10, 1862, manuscript, Harvard; Felix William Worthington to his father, Sept. 11, 1861, manuscript in private possession.

[21] Felix Brannigan to his sister, undated fragment, but written shortly after Gettysburg.

[22] Henry C. Bear to his wife, Dec. 14, 1862, Jan. 4, Jan. 13, April 14, 1863, manuscripts in possession of Mrs. Stanley B. Hadden, Urbana, Ill.

[23] Urich N. Parmelee to his brother, May 21, 1863, manuscript, Duke.

[24] Lawrence Van Alstyne, *Diary of an Enlisted Man*, 146-147.

[25] John P. Sheahan to his father, April 8, 1863, manuscript, Maine Historical Society.

[26] Diary of Charles W. Wills, Nov. 22, 1864, manuscript, Ill. State Historical Library.

[27] Martin Haynes, *History of the Second Regiment New Hampshire Volunteers* (Manchester, N. H., 1865), 124.

[28] M. Ebenezer Wescott, *Civil War Letters* (n. p., 1909), 14; diary of Maurice K. Simons, May 25, 1863, manuscript, Univ. of Texas.

[29] Diary of Francis Galwey, Dec. 1, 1863, typescript in possession of Col. Geoffrey Galwey, Washington, D. C.

[30] A. S. Neal to his father, May 15, 1864, typescript, Ga. Archives.

[31] Charles E. Davis, *Three Years in the Army*, 289.

[32] John P. Sheahan to his parents, Feb. 18, 1863; Bell Irvin Wiley, *The Life of Johnny Reb*, 321.

[33] Wiley, *The Life of Johnny Reb*, 321.

[34] Chattanooga *Daily Gazette*, March 6, 1864.

[35] Oscar O. Winther, editor, *With Sherman to the Sea*, 116-117; Wiley, *The Life of Johnny Reb*, 317.

[36] M. S. Schroyer, "Company 'G' History," Snyder County Historical Society *Bulletin*, II (1939), 107.

[37] Hazel C. Wolf, editor, *Campaigning with the First Minnesota*, 251.

[38] Portland, Maine, *Transcript*, June 13, 1863.

[39] Diary of Capt. James Biddle, Aug. 13, 1864, typescript, Detroit Public Library.

[40] Benjamin Borton, *A While with the Blue: Memories of War Days* (Passaic, N. J., 1898), 76-77.

[41] A. S. Roe, *The Ninth New York Heavy Artillery*, 216.

[42] For examples, see Richard Puffer to his sister, May 28, 1863, and diary of John Merrilies, May 25, 1863, manuscripts, Chicago Historical Society; *Publications of the Mississippi Historical Society*, Centenary Edition, V (Jackson, Miss., 1925), 273.

[43] H. A. Nelson to "Good Friend Harway," June 20, 1863, manuscript, Luther College Library. I am indebted to Inga B. Norstog for translating this item from the Norwegian.

[44] Diary of Ezra G. Huntley, March 20, 1865, manuscript, Dartmouth.

[45] "Letters of a Badger Boy in Blue," *Wisconsin Magazine of History*, V, 81-82.

[46] Day Elmore to his parents, July 2, 1864, manuscript in possession of Mrs. Hall Mosher, Memphis.

[47] George G. Agassiz, editor, *Meade's Headquarters, 1863-1865: Letters of Colonel Theodore Lyman from the Wilderness to Appomattox* (Boston, 1922), 106.

[48] Mrs. J. D. Wheeler, compiler, *In Memoriam: Letters of William Wheeler of the Class of 1855, Y.C.*, 414.

[49] Portland, Maine, *Transcript*, Jan. 23, 1864.

[50] Frank E. Smith, "The Polite War," *Coronet*, III (1937), 44-46. For an instance of a Confederate killing a Yankee brother at Fredericksburg and his shock on discovering the identity of the man he had slain, see Nashville *Daily Union*, April 7, 1863. *Grant's Petersburg Progress*, April 7, 1865, reported the case of a Yankee lieutenant capturing his Rebel father in one of the final actions near Petersburg.

[51] O. R., series 1, XXXVI, pt. 1, 345, 366-367; James Ford Rhodes, *History of the United States from the Compromise of 1850*, IV, 446. The entire action lasted about an hour, but the assault phase in which most of the casualties were suffered was completed in about twenty minutes.

[52] *Century Magazine*, LIII (1897), 720. Yanks ordered to make a desperate assault at Mine Run in November 1863 were also said to have pinned their names on their uniforms to facilitate identification. See G. Albert Monroe, "Reminiscences of the War of the Rebellion," Rhode Island Soldiers and Sailors Historical Society *Personal Narratives*, 2nd Series, No. 11 (Providence, 1881), 42-43.

BIBLIOGRAPHICAL NOTES

The quantity of material on soldier life in the Union Army is so enormous as to make impractical a listing of all the items used in the preparation of this work. The following brief note is intended as a general guide to the principal types of sources, with emphasis on relevancy to soldier life. Full information on specific references will be found in the footnotes; for the convenience of the reader location of each manuscript is given the first time it is cited in every chapter.

MANUSCRIPTS

The most revealing and interesting of the manuscripts are the letters of the rank and file. Extant letters of Union soldiers greatly outnumber those on the Confederate side, owing to the larger size of the Federal army, the North's higher rate of literacy and the greater effectiveness of Billy Yanks and their descendants in collecting and preserving war correspondence. The most extensive letter collections are those at Duke University, the Western Reserve Historical Society, the University of Michigan, the Wisconsin Historical Society, the Minnesota Historical Society, the Illinois State Historical Library and the Indiana State Library and Historical Society. Smaller, but still highly rewarding, are the holdings of the Maine Historical Society, the Vermont Historical Society, the Baker Library of Dartmouth College, the Boston Public Library, the Essex Institute, the American Antiquarian Society, the Connecticut Historical Society, the Connecticut State Library, the New York Historical Society, the New York Public Library, the Historical Society of Pennsylvania, the Burton Collection of the Detroit Public Library, the Hayes Memorial Library, the Ohio State Archaeological and Historical Society, the Chicago Historical Society and the Library of Congress.

Some valuable nuggets were found in the Massachusetts Historical Society, but soldier materials at this depository could not be fully exploited because of the name system of filing and the lack of a descriptive guide. A number of the National Military Parks have acquired respectable collections of manuscripts and these were generously made available to the writer by the National Park Service.

Several hundred unpublished diaries were read, but since many diarists wrote with one eye on posterity, these sources are generally not so revealing as letters composed in the spirit of the moment with little or no thought of their being read by anyone except the recipients. A few diaries are so exceptional in their tone and content, however, as to merit special mention. Those of Florison D. Pitts and John Merrilies in the Chicago Historical Society are frank, sprightly accounts of service in Western commands of two gay young artillerymen from Chicago. That of Charles W. Wills, in the Illinois State Library, is an excellent source.

438

This account was printed, along with other journals, in *Reminiscences of the Civil War from Diaries of Members of the 103rd Illinois Infantry* (Chicago, 1904) and again, with letters added, as a separate volume under the title *Army Life of an Illinois Soldier* (Washington, 1906); but the sister of Wills who prepared the work for publication in its latter form deleted some of the most revealing passages. Sergeant Matthew Marvin's diary, in the Minnesota Historical Society, throws valuable light on many phases of soldier life in the Army of the Potomac. The diary in the Western Reserve Historical Society of another sergeant, M. F. Roberts, records interesting details of Sherman's march through Georgia and the Carolinas. The journal of Stephen Gordon, the original of which is in the Fredericksburg National Military Park, and a copy of which was generously placed at my disposal by Fred L. Williams, Jr., of Atlanta, is of outstanding value for the detailed information it gives about food and commissary operations on the Virginia front. In the main library of the University of Michigan is a diary which startles by its very appearance, for this journal, kept by Henry A. Buck, was completely penetrated by a bullet on December 31, 1862, at Stone's River. A note by Buck bearing the date of January 1, 1863, states: "The faithful record saved my life."

Other manuscript records used in large quantity included regimental descriptive books, courts-martial proceedings, inspection reports, and United States Christian Commission papers. By far the richest collections of these materials are those in the National Archives. The courts-martial proceedings, which exist in formidable quantity, proved to be especially valuable social documents.

PRINTED CORRESPONDENCE AND DIARIES: BOOKS

Officers are better represented in this category of sources than are the men of the ranks, but even so a considerable quantity of soldier letters and diaries has been published in book form. One of the most interesting is *A Little Fifer's War Diary* by C. W. Bardeen (Syracuse, 1910) which, contrary to many works of this type, records the evil as well as the good of camp life. Excellent also is Robert Goldthwaite Carter, compiler, *Four Brothers in Blue, or Sunshine and Shadows of the War of the Rebellion* (Washington, 1913) which consists largely of the home letters of four Massachusetts soldiers who served in the Army of the Potomac. *The Civil War Diary of James T. Ayers* edited by John Hope Franklin (Springfield, Ill., 1947) is a pungent, forthright and extremely readable account of an unpolished Yank who recruited Negroes in Alabama. *The Hero of Medfield: Containing the Journals and Letters of Allen Alonzo Kingsbury* edited by E. A. Johnson (Boston, 1862), while covering a relatively brief period, is an interesting, informative, undoctored account of a bugler's service in Virginia during the early part of the conflict. One of the very best of all the published journals is Jenkins Lloyd Jones, *An Artilleryman's Diary* (Madison, Wis., 1914). O. W. Norton's *Army Letters, 1861-1865* (Chicago, 1903), while bearing the earmarks of prepublication polishing, is a superior record of one who served as a private in the Army of the Potomac until November 1863, when he became a lieutenant of colored troops. More readable than Norton's letters and excellent in every respect are the *Civil War Letters of Sgt. Onley Andrus*, edited by Fred Albert Shannon (Urbana, 1947). Most of Andrus' service was in Tennessee, Mississippi and Louisiana. Lawrence Van Alstyne's *Diary of an Enlisted Man* (New Haven, 1910) gets off to a slow start but the author's style, like that of some other diarists, improves with practice and the end product of his efforts is an absorbing book. The account is a memoir rather than a diary for the period after June 15, 1864. Mrs. J. D. Wheeler, compiler, *In Memoriam: Letters of William Wheeler of the Class of 1865, Y[ale] C[ollege]* (Cambridge, Mass., 1875) is an unusually fine collection of letters written by a graduate of Yale who served three months as an infantry private in 1861, then became an artillery officer and died from a sharpshooter's bullet before Atlanta in June 1864. Another Yank killed during the conflict (at Gettysburg) who left a full and frank record of his service was Isaac Lyman Taylor whose diary, edited by Hazel C. Wolf, was printed first as a series of articles in *Minnesota History*, volume 25, and then in book form under the title *Campaigning with the First Minnesota* (St. Paul, 1944). Perhaps the most readable of all the common-soldier journals is that of the young Hoosier Theodore F. Upson, edited by Oscar O. Winther under the title *With Sherman to the Sea* (Baton Rouge, 1943). This work, however, is not strictly a journal, but rather a postwar adaptation by Upson of letters and diaries written during the conflict.

Some of the published papers of officers give exceedingly valuable information about the life of the men. Especially outstanding in this respect, and thoroughly fascinating in general, are the letters and journal of John William De Forest, edited by James H. Croushore under the title *A Volunteer's Adventures, A Union Captain's Record of the Civil War* (New Haven, 1946). Other outstanding letter or diary accounts of officers issued in book form include: Willoughby M. Babcock, Jr., *Selections from the Letters and Diaries of Brevet-Brigadier General Willoughby Babcock of the Seventy-fifth New York Volunteers: A Study of Camp Life in the Union Armies during the Civil War* (Albany, 1922); Theodore C. Blegen, editor, *The Civil War Letters of Colonel Hans Christian Heg* (Northfield, Minn., 1936); W. C. Ford, editor, *War Letters, 1862-1865 of John Chipman Gray and John Codman Ropes* (Boston, 1927); J. H. Greene, *Reminiscences of the War. Bivouacs, Marches, Skirmishes, and Battles. Extracts from Letters Written Home from 1861 to 1865* (Medina, Ohio, 1886); Mark De Wolfe Howe, editor, *Touched with Fire, Civil War Letters and Diary of Oliver Wendell Holmes, Jr., 1861-1864*; and W. C. Lusk, editor, *War Letters of William Thompson Lusk* (New York, 1911).

PRINTED CORRESPONDENCE AND DIARIES: PERIODICALS

Some excellent letter and diary accounts by common soldiers have appeared in the journals and occasional publications of state historical societies. The files of the *Indiana Magazine of History* are especially rich in this type of material. John D. Barnhart, editor, "A Hoosier Invades the Confederacy: Letters and Diaries of Leroy S. Mayfield," *Indiana Magazine of History*, XXXIX (1943), 144-191, traces the career of a young Hoosier who served both as a private and a junior officer under Sherman. "The Shelley Letters," edited by Fanny J. Anderson, *Indiana Magazine of History*, XLIV (1948), 181-198, relate the experiences of a German native who went to war as a substitute and who was stationed in Tennessee during most of his service. Max Hedrick Guyer, editor, "Journal and Letters of Corporal William O. Gulick" and Ruth A. Gallaher, editor, "Peter Wilson in the Civil War," in the *Iowa Journal of History and Politics*, XXVIII (1930), 194-268, 390-456, 534-604 and XL (1942), 153-204, 261-321, 339-415, are full and interesting reports of Iowa soldiers, one a cavalryman and the other a foot soldier, who fought in Western commands. Unusual, though disappointingly few, are the "Edgar Dinsmore Letters" written by a Negro soldier of the Fifty-fourth Massachusetts Regiment and edited by Richard B. Harwell for the *Journal of Negro History*, XXV (1940), 363-371. The best collection of soldier correspondence published in any of the historical journals is "A Badger Boy in Blue: The Letters of Chauncey H. Cooke" in the *Wisconsin Magazine of History*, IV (1920-1921) and V (1921-1922). Cooke was a Wisconsin farm boy who served first against the Indians in Minnesota and then with Grant and Sherman in Mississippi, Tennessee and Georgia. Before their appearance in the *Wisconsin Magazine of History* these letters were published in a newspaper and then in book form under the title *Soldier Boy's Letters to his Father and Mother* (Independence, Wis., 1915).

Among the better officer collections appearing in historical society publications are: "The Civil War Letters of Major James Zearing, M.D. 1861-1865" and "Major Connolly's Diary and Letters to his Wife, 1862-1865" in the Illinois State Historical Society *Transactions* for 1921 and 1928 respectively (Springfield, 1922 and 1928); Fritz Haskell, editor, "Diary of Colonel William Camm in the *Journal* of the Illinois State Historical Society, XVIII (1926), 793-980; and Willie D. Halsell, editor, "The Sixteenth Indiana Regiment in the Last Vicksburg Campaign," *Indiana Magazine of History*, XLIII (1947), 67-82. The letters of "Prock" (William Landon) published in volumes 29, 30, 33 and 34 of the *Indiana Magazine of History* are interesting communications of a Hoosier who served as an enlisted man and an officer in the Army of the Potomac.

PRINTED MEMOIRS

In the years following Appomattox hundreds of Yanks wrote memoirs of their war experiences and hopefully issued them as books or pamphlets. The total output fills several shelves of the Library of Congress. The quality of these accounts varies greatly and all have to be used with care. In this work, as in *The Life of Johnny Reb*, I have followed the policy of accepting only those reminiscent items which accorded with records of a more substantial character. In my judgment the best memoir by an enlisted participant on either side is Leander Stillwell's *The Story of a Common Soldier of Army Life in the Civil War, 1861-1865* (second edition, Erie, Kansas, 1920). The author, an Illinoisan of humble background, enlisted in January 1862 at eighteen and served for nearly four years, mainly in Mississippi and Tennessee. This account, based largely on wartime diaries and letters, was begun with a view of informing young Jeremiah Stillwell of his father's soldier experience. As the writing progressed a larger audience was envisioned, but the narrative retained the simple, straightforward quality of a story told by a parent of "what I saw and did during the war." Another superb memoir is *Hard Tack and Coffee, or the Unwritten Story of Army Life* by John D. Billings (Boston, 1888). Billings' work is in essence a depiction of soldier life in the Army of the Potomac built around his personal experience and observations as an artilleryman. It is rich in humor, franker than most reminiscences and has the flavor of authenticity. Its value is greatly enhanced by more than 200 realistic illustrations from the gifted pen of Charles W. Reed, many of which were sketched during the artist's service with the Ninth Massachusetts Battery. Frank Wilkeson's *Recollections of a Private Soldier in the Army of the Potomac* (New York, 1887) is the account of another artilleryman who served in the East, but he did not enter the army until the third winter of the war and most of his service was as an officer. The narrative is readable but the author seems a bit reckless in the use of quotation and anecdote. Certainly the book is not in the same class with that of Stillwell or Billings. Warren Lee Goss's *Recollections of a Private: A Story of the Army of the Potomac* (New York, 1890) is apparently more a secondary account than of Goss's own experiences. The author, like some other professional writers who reported the conflict, is overly free with the use of the first person and seems more interested in telling a good story than an authentic one.

A better than average memoir, though restricted in scope, is John A. Cockerill, "A Boy at Shiloh," published by the Ohio Commandery of the Military Order of the Loyal Legion of the United States in its *Sketches of the War*, VI (1908), 14-34. In general the publications of the various components of the Loyal Legion were less rewarding for my purposes than were *Personal Narratives of the Rhode Island Soldiers' and Sailors' Historical Society* (six series in six volumes, Providence, 1878-1905). Both were disappointing but the same may be said of memoir literature in general. Striking exceptions to the general rule, in addition to the narratives of Stillwell and Billings, are three officer accounts of outstanding merit. Thomas L. Livermore, *Days and Events, 1860-1866* (Boston, 1920) is a fascinating memoir written soon after the conflict by an interesting participant who enlisted as a private at seventeen but whose ability pushed him upward so rapidly that he was a colonel before his twenty-second birthday. He wrote frankly, accurately and attractively of many phases of his experience in the Army of the Potomac. John Beatty's *The Citizen Soldier; or Memoirs of a Volunteer*, (Cincinnati, 1879) is an equally admirable record of service in Kentucky and Tennessee of an Ohio banker who rose to the command of a brigade before leaving the service early in 1864. Beatty's narrative is honest and realistic and tells far more about the common soldiers than most writings of general officers. Even better in some respects than Beatty's and Livermore's books is Harold A. Small, editor, *The Road to Richmond; The Civil War Memoirs of Abner R. Small of the Sixteenth Maine Volunteers: Together with the Diary Which He Kept When He Was a Prisoner of War* (Berkeley, Calif., 1939). Small's narrative, which apparently follows closely notes jotted down during the war, is a thoroughly delightful commentary by a close observer and talented writer. His service included most of the major campaigns in Virginia.

Of journalistic accounts of the war, the one richest in information about soldier life is George Alfred Townsend, *Campaigns of a Non-Combatant* (New York, 1866), which has been recently reproduced with an introduction by Lida Mayo under the title *Rustics in Rebellion* (Chapel Hill, 1950).

UNIT HISTORIES

Histories of Federal units exist in large quantity, with those of regiments being most numerous. These works, like those on the Confederate side, vary greatly in character and scope. Charles E. Davis, *Three Years in the Army: The Story of the Thirteenth Massachusetts Volunteers from July 16, 1861 to August 1, 1864* (Boston, 1894) is one of the best regimental histories. Based in large part on diaries of five members of the organization, it is unusually rich in details of camp life and in descriptions of the Southern country and people. A valuable feature is a descriptive roll of the whole regiment for the entire period of the war. Another unit history of rare excellence is Alfred Seelye Roe, *The Ninth New York Heavy Artillery* (Worcester, Mass., 1899). In preparing this history the author, who was a member of Company A, drew heavily on letters and diaries of comrades and his own experience. A felicitous style, an abundance of human-interest detail and an appealing format make this an attractive volume. *Camp and Field Life of the Fifth New York Volunteer Infantry (Duryee Zouaves)*, by Alfred Davenport, draws heavily on the author's fascinating home letters written while a member of the unit. Manuscript copies of these letters are in the New York Historical Society. In writing up the Peninsula campaign of 1862, Davenport also borrowed freely from Samuel Tiebout's diary. The generous use of this excellent source material and the fact of the account being drafted soon after the war combine with Davenport's gifts as a reporter to make this a readable and valuable work. Other organizational histories of exceptional merit are: Richard B. Irwin, *History of the Nineteenth Army Corps* (New York, 1893); James Dugan, *History of Hurlbut's Fighting Fourth Division* (Cincinnati, 1863); Stephen F. Fleharty, *Our Regiment: A History of the 102nd Illinois Infantry Volunteers* (Chicago, 1865); William R. Hartpence, *History of the Fifty-first Indiana Veteran Volunteer Infantry* (Harrison, Ohio, 1894); David Lathrop, *History of the Fifty-ninth Regiment Illinois Volunteers* (Indianapolis, 1865);

Thomas H. Parker, *History of the Fifty-first Pennsylvania Volunteers and Veteran Volunteers* (Philadelphia, 1869); and Thomas J. Wright, *History of the Eighth Regiment Kentucky Volunteer Infantry* (St. Joseph, Mo., 1880). In a class by itself is Sergeant M. S. Schroyer, "Company 'G' History" in the Snyder County Historical Society *Bulletin*, II (1939), 64-156. This work abounds with human-interest detail and colorful anecdote, but the tone is such as to make one wonder if the author did not at times confuse recollection with imagination.

A useful though old list of unit histories and personal narratives is contained in *Bibliography of State Participation in the Civil War, 1861-1866* (Washington, 1913). Much extremely valuable information about this type of literature is given by E. Merton Coulter in *Travels in the Confederate States* (Norman, Okla., 1948). Henry S. Commager's *The Blue and the Gray* (2 vols., Indianapolis, 1950) is a mine of bibliographical data for both sides.

PERIODICALS AND NEWSPAPERS

The richest periodical sources, as previously noted, are the publications of the state historical societies. Some valuable material is also to be found in the *American Historical Review* and organs of regional societies such as the *Mississippi Valley Historical Review*. The *Century Magazine, Scribner's, Atlantic Monthly, Harper's* and similar periodicals printed many articles about the Civil War, but most of these have an officer slant and are concerned mainly with general operations. One article that deserves special mention for the valuable light which it throws on the common soldier is Thomas L. Livermore, "The Northern Volunteers," *Granite Monthly*, X (1887), 239-247, 257-266. Also valuable, for its analysis of soldier reaction to combat, is S. H. M. Byers, "How Men Feel in Battle," *Harper's*, CXII (1906), 931-936. Interesting sidelights on religious life are given in "A Chaplain's Experience in the Army," *Monthly Religious Magazine*, XXIX (1863), 223-232, 343-352. C. King's meaty article, "The Volunteer Soldier of 1861," which appeared in *Review of Reviews*, XLIII (1911), 709-720, was also published in Francis Trevelyan Miller, editor, *Photographic History of the Civil War* (New York, 1911), VIII, 58-104.

A sampling of newspapers confirmed prior experience that, while not without value, these sources for study of soldier life are so far inferior to unpublished letters and diaries as to justify only a limited use of them. Newspaper files surveyed in this study included those of Portland, Maine, New York City, Detroit and, for the period of Federal occupation, those of Memphis, Nashville, Chattanooga and New Orleans. In addition, many regimental newspapers printed by and for soldiers, usually on captured presses, were consulted.

GOVERNMENT AND INSTITUTIONAL DOCUMENTS

By far the richest source among government publications is the monumental *War of the Rebellion: Official Records of the Union and Confederate Armies* (Washington, 1880-1910) which, owing to limitations of the index, has to be leaved for a study of this sort. Useful also are the various editions of *Army Regulations* which as a rule contain the articles of war; some of the later editions also include in appendices important legislation affecting the army. The *General Orders* both of the War Department Adjutant General's Office and of lower commands contain a wealth of information bearing on soldier life. Orders convening courts-martial and announcing their findings are usually included in the regular series of general orders, but beginning in 1864 the Adjutant General's Office at Washington began publishing *General Court-Martial Orders* as a separate series. The best collection of general orders known to the writer is that in the National Archives. A vast amount of information on health and medical treatment is contained in the *Medical and Surgical History of the War of the Rebellion* issued by the Surgeon General's office in six large books (Washington, 1870-1888). Of institutional publications the most useful in this study were the *Documents* of the United States Sanitary Commission (2 vols., New York, 1866) and the *Annual Reports* of the United States Christian Commission (Philadelphia, 1863-1865).

SPECIAL STUDIES AND OTHER SECONDARY WORKS

Fred Albert Shannon's *Organization and Administration of the Union Army, 1861-1865* (2 vols., Cleveland, 1928) was enormously helpful in the planning of this study and provided indispensable information about high-level policy and its bearing on the fighting forces.

Ella Lonn's recent *Foreigners in the Union Army and Navy* (Baton Rouge, 1951) is a remarkably thorough and penetrating study by the author of *Foreigners in the Confederacy* (Chapel Hill, 1940). The medical aspect of army life is definitively treated in George W. Adams' *Doctors in Blue: Health and Medicine in the Union Army, 1861-1865* (New York, 1952) which the author very generously permitted me to read in manuscript.

PICTURES

The National Archives and the Library of Congress have immense collections of Civil War photographs taken for the most part by Matthew B. Brady and assistants. Several thousand pictures in the National Archives file were examined. Some of the state historical societies also have good picture collections, as does the American Antiquarian Society, many of which were taken by local "daguerrean artists." In the Prints and Photographs Division of the Library of Congress are drawings of a number of Civil War artists, including A. R. Waud, Edwin Forbes and Winslow Homer.

Filed with the personal papers of Charles W. Reed in the Manuscripts Division of the Library of Congress are many sketches by that talented soldier-artist who, as previously noted, was the illustrator for John D. Billings' *Hard Tack and Coffee*. Some of the most authentic sketches of soldier equipment and surroundings found by the writer are those with which Herbert E. Valentine, a Massachusetts soldier, illustrated his manuscript letters and diary; this interesting item is in the library of the Essex Institute. Published collections of war pictures usually do not feature the common soldier, but a number of soldier likenesses and camp scenes are to be found in Miller's *Photographic History of the Civil War* (10 vols., New York, 1911); *Battles and Leaders of the Civil War* (4 vols., New York, 1887-1888), Roy Meredith, *Mr. Lincoln's Camera Man* (New York, 1946); and Edwin Forbes, *Life Studies of the Great Army* (New York, 1876). *Frank Leslie's Illustrated Newspaper* contains many camp scenes, but these, like many reproduced in popular periodicals of the time, often give distorted impressions of the subjects depicted.

The most delightful of published drawings are those of the talented Winslow Homer, an army artist for *Harper's*. In 1864 L. Prang of Boston issued a group of Winslow Homer sketches under the title *Life in Camp*. This firm also issued a series of separate lithographs made from Homer drawings (Boston, n.d.). Homer's pictures are exceptional for their emphasis on the common soldier and their authentic representation of soldier life.

INDEX

Abbott, Captain E. G., 131
Abbott, Captain Henry, 89, 94
Absence without leave, 197-198, 277
Adams Express Company, 156
Adrian, Michigan, 28 f.
Age, 296, 298-303
Aiken, Private John, Jr., 300
Alexandria Hospital, 141
Ambulance system, 146-147
American Bible Society, 272
American Tract Society, 272
Ammen, Colonel Jacob, 69, 88
Ammunition, 66-67, 78-79
Amphibious training, 51
Andrus, Sergeant Onley, 174, 235 f., 244
Antietam, battle of, 27, 61, 74, 89
Arkansas, troops of, 22; First Regiment, 165
Armfield, Private Wesley, 215
Arms, 22-23, 50-51, 62-64, 94
Army Medical Department, 124, 134, 136
Army Medical Museum, 147
Army of the Cumberland, 156, 231, 272
Army of the Ohio, 143
Army of the Potomac, 206, 219, 220, 226-227, 254, 321-322
Army of the Tennessee, 143, 146
Artillery, training, 51, 52; progress, 94; punishments, 209; numbers, 319; organization, 319, 320; interbranch rivalry, 327
Ashhurst, Richard L., 198
Atlantic Monthly, 154
Atrocity stories, 347-348
Ayers, James T., 111

Babbott, Private Charles, 186

Bailey, Private Franklin, 71, 72
Baltimore, Maryland, 35
Bangor, Maine, 17
Banks, General N. P., 193, 195, 196
Bardeen, C. W., 251
Barker, Private Charles, 23, 198
Barker, Thomas B., 70
Barney, J. R., 112
Bartlett, General J. J., 210
Baseball, 170
Bath, Maine, 18
Battle conduct, 66-95
Battle cry, 73-75
Beatty, General John, 250
Beinstick, Samuel, 317
Belfast, Maine, 18
Belknap, Colonel, 81
Bellows, Henry W., 150
Bellows Falls, Vermont, 34
Belmont, battle of, 143
Benge, Sergeant Harrison, 317
Bentonville, Virginia, 90
Berdan, Colonel Hiram, 341
Billings, John D., 332
Billy Yank, origin of expression, 13; volunteers, 17-24; training, 24-29; transportation, 30-36; reception of, 34-36; camp life, 45-58; clothing, 58-62; arms, 62-64; impedimenta, 64-65; conduct in battle, 66-95; opinion of South and Southerners, 96-108; attitude toward Negroes, 109-123; health, 124-151; recreation, 152-191; military justice and discipline, 192-223; food, 224-246; morals, 247-274; morale, 275-295; age, 296-303; occupations, 303-304; education, 304-306; nationality, 306-313; race, 313-319;

447